Handbook of Operant Behavior

Handbook of Operant Behavior

Edited by

WERNER K. HONIG
Dalhousie University

J. E. R. STADDON
Duke University

Prentice-Hall, Inc., Englewood Cliffs, New Jersey

Library of Congress Cataloging in Publication Data
Main entry under title:

HANDBOOK OF OPERANT BEHAVIOR.

(The Prentice-Hall century psychology series)

Includes bibliographies and index.
1. Operant behavior. I. Honig, Werner K. II. Staddon, J. E. R.
BF319.5.06H36   152.3'224   76-26034
ISBN 0-13-380535-2

THE PRENTICE-HALL

CENTURY PSYCHOLOGY SERIES

© 1977 BY PRENTICE-HALL, INC., ENGLEWOOD CLIFFS, NEW JERSEY

*All rights reserved. No part of this book
may be reproduced in any form
or by any means without permission
in writing from the publisher.*

Printed in the United States of America

10 9 8 7 6 5 4 3 2 1

Prentice-Hall International, Inc., *London*
Prentice-Hall of Austria Pty. Limited, *Sydney*
Prentice-Hall of Canada, Ltd., *Toronto*
Prentice-Hall of India Private Limited, *New Delhi*
Prentice-Hall of Japan, Inc., *Tokyo*
Prentice-Hall of Southeast Asia Pte. Ltd., *Singapore*
Whitehall Books Limited, *Wellington, New Zealand*

Contents

ACKNOWLEDGEMENTS, ix

CONTRIBUTORS, xi

INTRODUCTION, 1

WERNER K. HONIG AND J. E. R. STADDON

    References, 6

1

LEVELS OF INTEGRATION OF THE OPERANT, 7

PHILIP TEITELBAUM

    Introduction, 7
    Historical Background, 8
    The Operant as a Criterion for Motivation, 12
    Puzzling Operants, 13
    Similar Puzzles in Motivated Behavior, 14
    Recovery from Lateral Hypothalamic Lesions, 16
    Parallel Between Recovery and Development in the Lateral Hypothalamic Syndrome, 17
    Stages of Recovery and Development of the Human Grasp, 19
    Transformation of Sensory Control over an Approach Response, 19
    Stages of Recovery and Development of Learned Behavior, 20
    Stages of Encephalization of the Operant, 20
    Summary and Conclusions: Levels of Operant Behavior, 23
    References, 24

2

THE OPERANT REVISITED, 28

GEORGE COLLIER, EDWARD HIRSCH, AND ROBIN KANAREK

    Introduction, 28
    Free Feeding, 34
    Availability, 36
    Caloric Regulation and Choice of Dietary Items, 43
    Other Environmental Constraints, 44
    Response Strength, 44
    Food Economy, 46
    Conclusions, 49
    References, 50

3

PAVLOVIAN CONTROL OF OPERANT BEHAVIOR, 53

BARRY SCHWARTZ AND ELKAN GAMZU

    Introduction, 53
    Autoshaping and Automaintenance, 54
    The Role of Stimulus-Reinforcer Relations in the Control of Behavior Maintained by Response-Reinforcer Relations, 71
    Conclusion, 91
    References, 92

4

THE NATURE OF REINFORCING STIMULI, 98

Philip Dunham

    A Historical Perspective, *98*
    Premack's Reinforcement Theory, *101*
    Biological Constraints on Reinforcement, *112*
    Concluding Comments, *122*
    References, *123*

5

SCHEDULE-INDUCED BEHAVIOR, 125

J. E. R. Staddon

    Introduction, *125*
    Behavior Induced by Periodic Food, *126*
    Temporal and Sequential Structure of Induced Activities, *140*
    Concluding Comments, *148*
    References, *148*

6

THERMOREGULATORY BEHAVIOR, 153

Evelyn Satinoff and Robert Hendersen

    Introduction, *153*
    Separation of Operant and Respondent Temperature Regulation, *154*
    Using Behavior to Assess Regulation, *156*
    Thermoregulation and the Concept of Set Point, *160*
    Thermal Preference, *162*
    Operant Contingencies in Thermal Homeostasis, *164*
    The Operant as a Measure of Set Point After Drug Administration, *165*
    References, *169*

7

DETERMINANTS OF REINFORCEMENT AND PUNISHMENT, 174

W. H. Morse and R. T. Kelleher

    Reproducible Behavioral Processes, *174*
    The Continuity of Behavior in Time (Shaping), *177*
    Disparate Effects of Consequent Events, *178*
    Ongoing Behavior, *180*
    Characteristics of Responses, *183*
    Adventitious Reinforcement and Punishment: Importance of History, *184*
    Criteria for Comparing Consequent Events, *186*
    Comparisons of the Effects of Drugs on Performances Maintained by Different Consequences, *188*
    Drug Injections as Consequent Events Maintaining Behavior, *192*
    Response-Produced Electric Shocks as Consequent Events Maintaining Behavior, *193*
    Conclusions, *197*
    References, *198*

8

SCHEDULES OF REINFORCEMENT: THE CONTROLLING VARIABLES, 201

Michael Zeiler

    Introduction, *201*
    Types of Schedules, *202*
    Types of Controlling Relations: Variables and Effects, *203*
    Variables Determining Response Frequency, *206*
    Response Patterning: The Temporal Organization of Behavior, *213*
    Sequences and Units, *221*
    Summary and Concluding Remarks, *228*
    References, *230*

9

CHOICE IN CONCURRENT SCHEDULES AND A QUANTITATIVE FORMULATION OF THE LAW OF EFFECT, 233

Peter de Villiers

    Introduction, *233*
    Concurrent Schedules, *234*
    The Matching Relation in Concurrent VI Schedules— Reinforcement Frequency, *235*
    Maximizing or Matching, *245*
    Time Matching as the Fundamental Matching Process, *246*
    The Generality of the Matching Relation, *248*
    Absolute Rates of Responding and a Quantitative Law of Effect, *257*
    Alternative Theories of Response Strength, *263*
    Application of Herrnstein's Equations to Other Schedules, *265*
    An Alternative Theory of Matching and Behavioral Contrast, *272*
    Discussion, *275*
    Conclusion, *278*
    Appendix A, *278*
    Appendix B, *279*
    Appendix C, *279*
    Appendix D, *281*
    Appendix E, *281*
    Appendix F, *282*
    References, *282*

10

CONDITIONED REINFORCEMENT: SCHEDULE EFFECTS, 288

LEWIS GOLLUB

Introduction, 288
Chained Schedules of Reinforcement, 289
Schedules of Brief Stimulus Presentation, 299
Concluding Remarks, 308
References, 309

11

CONDITIONED REINFORCEMENT: CHOICE AND INFORMATION, 313

EDMUND FANTINO

Introduction, 313
Observing Responses and Conditioned Reinforcement, 318
Choice and Conditioned Reinforcement, 326
Conclusions, 336
References, 337

12

CONDITIONED SUPPRESSION AND THE EFFECTS OF CLASSICAL CONDITIONING ON OPERANT BEHAVIOR, 340

DEREK BLACKMAN

Introduction, 340
The Estes-Skinner Procedure and the Measurement of its Effects, 341
Investigations of Classical Conditioning Parameters, 342
Investigations of Operant Conditioning Parameters, 344
Measurement of Conditioned Suppression, 348
Some Interpretations of Conditioned Suppression, 351
A Brief Review of Some Other Classical-Operant Interactions, 358
Conclusion, 360
References, 361

13

NEGATIVE REINFORCEMENT AND AVOIDANCE, 364

PHILIP N. HINELINE

Introduction, 364
Two Illustrative Experiments, 365
Negative Reinforcement Without Added Cues, 367
Negative Reinforcement With Added Cues, 381
Considerations Regarding Initial Acquisition, 406
References, 410

14

BY-PRODUCTS OF AVERSIVE CONTROL, 415

R. R. HUTCHINSON

Introduction, 415
Methods, 416
Behavior Caused by Aversive Stimulation, 418
Behavior Caused by Aversive Stimuli in Escape Paradigms, 425
Behavior Caused by Aversive Stimuli in Punishment Paradigms, 427
References, 430

15

STIMULUS CONTROL AND INHIBITORY PROCESSES, 432

MARK RILLING

Overview, 432
The Definition and Measurement of Stimulus Control, 433
Some Determinants of Generalization Gradients, 436
Influence of Discrimination Training on the Generalization Gradient, 439
Determinants of the Peak Shift and Inhibitory Stimulus Control, 453
Errorless Learning Reconsidered, 464
Summary, 475
References, 476

16

STIMULUS CONTROL: ATTENTIONAL FACTORS, 481

N. J. MACKINTOSH

Introduction, 481
Conditions Affecting the Establishment of Stimulus Control, 483
Experimental Procedures: Nondifferential Reinforcement and Discrimination Training, 488
Discussion, 505
References, 510

17

ANIMAL PSYCHOPHYSICS, 514

DONALD BLOUGH AND PATRICIA BLOUGH

Introduction, 514
Measuring Sensory Thresholds, 515
Supraliminal Stimuli, 525
Signal Detection Theory in Animal Psychophysics, 532
References, 537

18

OPERANT BEHAVIORAL PHARMACOLOGY, 540

TRAVIS THOMPSON AND JOHN J. BOREN

> Introduction, 540
> Principles of Drug Action, 543
> Analyzing Behavioral Mechanisms of Drug Action, 551
> Traditional Problems Formulated Within an Operant Framework, 560
> Future of Behavioral Pharmacology, 562
> References, 566

19

CENTRAL REINFORCEMENT: A BRIDGE BETWEEN BRAIN FUNCTION AND BEHAVIOR, 570

GORDON MOGENSON AND JAN CIOÉ

> Introduction, 570
> Methodological Considerations, 572
> Central Reinforcement Compared to Conventional Reinforcement, 574
> Some Implications of Comparing Central and Conventional Reinforcers, 580
> The Nature of Central Reinforcement, 581
> Summary, 588
> Appendix A, 589
> References, 590

20

THE EXPERIMENTAL PRODUCTION OF ALTERED PHYSIOLOGICAL STATES: CONCURRENT AND CONTINGENT BEHAVIORAL MODELS, 596

JOSEPH BRADY AND ALAN HARRIS

> Introduction, 596
> Concurrent Models, 596
> Recent Developments, 598
> Contingent Models, 606
> References, 611

21

PROCEDURES FOR THE ACQUISITION OF SYNTAX, 619

GEORGE ROBINSON

> References, 627

22

TOWARD A COHERENT PSYCHOLOGY OF LANGUAGE, 628

EVALYN SEGAL

> Toward a Coherent Psychology of Language, 628
> Competence:Performance::Structure: Function, 628
> Chomsky's Standard Theory of Transformational-Generative Grammar, 629
> The Psychological Reality of Transformational-Generative Grammar, 632
> Skinner's Functional Theory of Verbal Behavior, 633
> Comments on Skinner's Functional Theory, 635
> Functionalism vs. Mentalism, 640
> The Complementarity of Functional and Cognitive Theory, 642
> Paraphrase, the Problematic Listener, and Mentalese, 649
> More on the Complementarity of Functional and Cognitive Theories, 651
> References, 652

AUTHOR INDEX, 655

SUBJECT INDEX, 663

Acknowledgements

The authors who have contributed to this book deserve most of the credit for its content, and as editors we want to express our gratitude to them. All of them have worked hard, and cooperated with us. Some have had to await the publication of manuscripts that they completed all too long ago; others were called upon to prepare chapters late in the game, and had to work under pressure of time. It is to their credit that we have had little cause for argument or complaint in preparation of these pages.

The authors have themselves received help and support from colleagues and granting agencies. These persons and sources are mentioned in their individual chapters.

As editors, we have also been encouraged by our colleagues, students, and wives in our work on this project. They have been tolerant while we turned our attention to the many detailed considerations that go into the preparation of a book of this size. In particular, we want to acknowledge the support of Kenneth MacCorquodale, the consulting editor who worked with us, encouraged us, and reviewed each chapter. Both of us have benefitted from the support of research grants that have provided the sort of research staff that made our own time available for editorial work. Thanks are due to the National Research Council of Canada for grant APT-102 to WKH, and to the U.S. National Science Foundation for grant BMS71-01402 to JERS, who gratefully acknowledges support from both NSF and Duke University for a sabbatical year at Oxford University when some of the work that went into this book was done.

Much of the tedious labor has been done by the following people: Janet Lord handled an enormous amount of correspondence, typed up many pages of comments, and organized the complex procedure of obtaining permissions. Edna Bissette coped with ill-typed manuscripts mailed from overseas, as well as mumbled audio tapes of editorial comment. Janice Frank is responsible for the monumental effort that went into the subject index, and also helped with editorial work. Catherine Moore prepared the author index with its many hundreds of entries. This book could not have been published without the unstinting contribution of their time and effort.

Many journals, societies, and authors have granted permission for the use of illustrations in this book. These are acknowledged in the captions of the figures.

W.K.H.
J.E.R.S.

Contributors

DEREK E. BLACKMAN (Chapter 12), Ph.D. The Queen's University of Belfast, is Professor and Head of Department of Psychology at University College, Cardiff, Wales. He is the author of *Operant Conditioning: An Experimental Analysis of Behaviour* (1974), and he organized the Experimental Analysis of Behavior Group in the U.K. for five years. Dr. Blackman has published many research papers in British and American journals. His current interests center on the effects of drugs on operant behavior, and he is editing a book with Dr. D. J. Sanger on behavioral pharmacology.

DONALD S. BLOUGH (Chapter 17), Ph.D. Harvard University, is Professor of Psychology at Brown University. He is interested in the methodology of animal psychophysics and animal information processing, and more generally in operant conditioning and stimulus control; he has published extensively in these areas.

PATRICIA M. BLOUGH (Chapter 17), M. S. Tufts University, is Research Associate in Psychology at Brown University. Her combined interests in the areas of vision and animal psychophysics have led to a number of publications concerning the electrophysiology and psychophysics of pigeon vision. She is also interested in general comparative problems and in problems of stimulus control in animals.

JOHN J. BOREN (Chapter 18), Ph.D. Columbia University, is Professor of Psychology at The American University. He has researched and published on a number of issues in the experimental analysis of behavior, behavioral pharmacology, and applications of behavioral principles to human affairs. He has been the president of the Behavioral Pharmacology Society, the editor of the *Journal of the Experimental Analysis of Behavior,* and the president of the Division of Psychopharmacology of the American Psychological Association. His current interests include the variables that determine behavior, the repeated acquisition of behavior, the effects of acute and chronic administration of cocaine and other stimulant drugs, and the applications of behavioral principles to clinical problems.

JOSEPH V. BRADY (Chapter 20), Ph.D. University of Chicago, is Professor of Behavioral Biology at The Johns Hopkins University School of Medicine. He has published extensively in the areas of behavioral physiology and behavioral pharmacology, and served on the editorial boards of several professional journals including the *Journal of the Experimental Analysis of Behavior,* the *Journal of Comparative and Physiological Psychology,* and *Behavior Research Methods and Instrumentation.* Professor Brady's principal scientific contributions have been in the area of somatic and physiological affects of behavioral stress.

JAN D. D. CIOÉ (Chapter 19), M.A. University of Western Ontario, is at present a Lecturer in Psychology at the College of New Caledonia, Prince George, British Columbia, Canada. He was a winner of a number of academic awards and prizes in his undergraduate and graduate years and his proposed Ph.D. thesis is concerned with brain self-stimulation and ingestive behaviors.

GEORGE COLLIER (Chapter 2), Ph.D. Indiana University, is a Professor of Psychology at Rutgers University. His research interest is the evolutionary origin of feeding behavior. He is testing ecological models in laboratory simulations of ecological niches.

PETER A. DE VILLIERS (Chapter 9), Ph.D. Harvard University, is Assistant Professor of Psychology at Harvard University. He has published several research papers in the areas of operant conditioning, language acquisition, and psycholinguistics. He is joint author, with his wife Jill, of *Early Language* (forthcoming), an introduction to first language acquisition. His current research includes quantitative approaches to the law of effect with special reference to aversive conditioning, and early grammatical and semantic development in children.

PHILIP J. DUNHAM (Chapter 4), Ph.D. University of Missouri, is Associate Professor of Psychology at Dalhousie University in Halifax, Nova Scotia. In addition to journal articles and reviews, he is author of the textbook *Experimental Psychology: A process approach* (Harper and Row, in press). His main research interests are in the areas of animal learning and motivation.

EDMUND FANTINO (Chapter 11), Ph.D. Harvard University, is Professor of Psychology and a member of the Neurosciences Group at the University of California, San Diego. He is author of *Introduction to Contemporary Psychology* (with George S. Reynolds, 1975) and of articles appearing in professional journals. He has served as Associate Editor of the *Journal of the Experimental Analysis of Behavior* (1971–1974), is on the Board of Directors of the Society for the Experimental Analysis of Behavior (1972–1980) and has been visiting professor at the Primate Research Institute, Kyoto University (1974). His principal research interests are choice, conditioned reinforcement, and self-control. He is currently writing a text on learning and motivation, with an emphasis on comparative psychology (with Cheryl Logan).

ELKAN GAMZU (Chapter 3), Ph.D. University of Pennsylvania, is presently a senior scientist at Hoffmann-LaRoche Inc. His research interests include psychopharmacology, taste aversion learning, autoshaping, and biological constraints on learning.

LEWIS R. GOLLUB (Chapter 10), Ph.D. Harvard University, is Professor of Psychology at the University of Maryland. He has published numerous papers in behavioral and pharmacological journals, and has served on the board of editors of the *Journal of the Experimental Analysis of Behavior.* His main interests have been in the experimental analysis of conditioned reinforcement, behavioral pharmacology, and effective teaching.

ALAN H. HARRIS (Chapter 20), Ph.D. Columbia University, is an Associate Professor in the Department of Psychiatry and Behavioral Sciences at The Johns Hopkins University School of Medicine, and the Assistant Director of the Division of Behavioral Biology. His major research interests are in the areas of conditioning and learning, and he is currently a principal investigator for the National Heart and Lung Institute studying the circulatory effects of operant cardiovascular conditioning in primates.

ROBERT W. HENDERSEN (Chapter 6), Ph.D. University of Pennsylvania, is an Assistant Professor in the Psychology Department of the University of Illinois at Champaign-Urbana. His major research interests are aversive learning and acquired motivation.

PHILIP N. HINELINE (Chapter 13), Ph.D. Harvard University, is Associate Professor of Psychology at Temple University. His research has dealt mainly with the aversive control of behavior, attempting to isolate the several meanings of avoidance, and to break the constraints of traditional avoidance procedures. Additional work has been concentrated on an analysis of "nuisance phenomena" of transience in aversively conditioned behavior. In addition, he maintains an active interest in experimental approaches to teaching the psychology of music.

Contributors

EDWARD HIRSCH (Chapter 2), Ph.D. Rutgers University, is an Assistant Professor at Mount Holyoke College. His research interests are the nutritional, physiological, and environmental bases of obesity.

WERNER K. HONIG (co-editor of the book, co-author of the Introduction), Ph.D. Duke University, is Professor of Psychology at Dalhousie University. He has published a number of articles and chapters on stimulus control in animals, and has participated in several conferences. He spent a year working on the relations between behavior in natural settings and instrumental learning as a Guggenheim Fellow at Madingley, England (1970–71). His principal edited book is the 1966 version of *Operant Behavior,* published by Appleton-Century-Crofts. He has also co-edited smaller books on associative learning and on animal memory. His current interests are in cognitive aspects of animal learning, particularly "working memory" in animals, and the associative significance of stimuli controlling behavior.

RONALD R. HUTCHINSON (Chapter 14), Ph.D. Yale University, is President and Director of Research at the Foundation for Behavioral Research. Dr. Hutchinson's major research interests include the effects of aversive stimulation, environmental causes of aggression in man and animals, and effects of drugs on emotional behavior.

ROBIN BETH KANAREK (Chapter 2), Ph.D. Rutgers University, is a Research Fellow at the Harvard School of Public Health. Her research interests are the nutritional, physiological, and environmental bases of feeding behavior.

R. T. KELLEHER (Chapter 7), Ph.D. New York University, is Professor of Psychobiology at the New England Regional Primate Research Center, Department of Psychiatry, Harvard Medical School. His principal work has been in the field of behavioral pharmacology.

N. J. MACKINTOSH (Chapter 16), is Professor of Psychology at the University of Sussex. He is the author of *The Psychology of Animal Learning* (1974) and (with N. S. Sutherland) of *Mechanisms of Animal Discrimination Learning.* His research interests include the study of discrimination learning and stimulus control, selective association in conditioning, and comparative psychology.

GORDON J. MOGENSON (Chapter 19), Ph.D. McGill University, is Professor of Physiology and Psychology at the University of Western Ontario, London, Canada. He has published over 100 research papers and review articles and was Editor of the *Canadian Journal of Psychology* from 1969–1974. He is presently a Regional Editor of *Physiology and Behavior* and the *Canadian Journal of Psychology.* Professor Mogenson's research is concerned with the role of the nervous and endocrine systems in the control of motivated and emotional behavior.

W. H. MORSE (Chapter 7), Ph.D. Harvard University, is Associate Professor of Psychobiology in the Department of Psychiatry at Harvard Medical School. His principal work has been in the field of behavioral pharmacology.

MARK RILLING (Chapter 15), Ph.D. University of Texas, is Professor of Psychology at Michigan State University. His published research papers have appeared in the *Journal of the Experimental Analysis of Behavior, Learning and Motivation, Animal Learning and Behavior,* and *Science.* His main research interests are stimulus control and inhibition.

GEORGE M. ROBINSON (Chapter 21), Ph.D. University of Chicago, is Assistant Professor of Psychology at Duke University. His research efforts and publications are in the areas of cognitive psychology and psycholinguistics. He is coauthor of *The Organization of Language* (with J. M. Moulton, forthcoming).

EVELYN SATINOFF (Chapter 6), Ph.D. University of Pennsylvania, is Professor of Psychology and Physiology at the University of Illinois at Urbana-Champaign. Her major research interests are in the fields of motivation and biological regulation, and she has published numerous experimental articles and several chapters in these areas. Her current concern is with the neuroanatomical and pharmacological bases of thermoregulation.

EVALYN F. SEGAL (Chapter 22), Ph.D. University of Minnesota, is Professor of Psychology at San Diego State University. She is an Associate Editor of *Learning and Motivation* and serves on the editorial boards of the *Journal of the Experimental Analysis of Behavior, Behaviorism,* and *Contemporary Psychology.* Her research publications include a chapter on induction and the provenance of operants and experimental reports on schedule-induced polydipsia, timing behavior, and conditioned reinforcement. She was for a time Director of the Institute for Child and

Family Development at the University of North Carolina at Greensboro. She recently completed a textbook on the principles of operant behavior and the operant analysis of language, which are also her current research interests.

J. E. R. Staddon (Chapter 5), Ph.D. Harvard University, is Professor of Psychology at Duke University. He has also taught at the University of Toronto and recently spent a sabbatical year with the Animal Behavior Research Group at Oxford University. He has done research on learning and adaptive behavior in animals, philosophical aspects of psychology, and neurobiology. He is interested in the relations between learning mechanisms and evolutionary biology.

Barry Schwartz (Chapter 3), Ph.D. University of Pennsylvania, is Associate Professor of Psychology at Swarthmore College. His major research interests are in the area of biological constraints on learning, particularly the phenomena of autoshaping and behavioral contrast. He has just completed a text on learning titled *The Control of Behavior*.

Philip Teitelbaum (Chapter 1), Ph.D. The Johns Hopkins University, is Professor of Psychology at the University of Illinois at Champaign-Urbana. He is the author of *Physiological Psychology: Fundamental Principles*. His numerous articles have been concerned mainly with the aberrations in food and water intake produced by damage to the hypothalamaus. His current major research interest is in the stages of recovery of motivated eating and drinking and their implications for normal behavior.

T. Thompson (Chapter 18), Ph.D. University of Minnesota, is Professor of Psychiatry and Psychology at the University of Minnesota in Minneapolis. He has published many original research articles, is coeditor of *Advances in Behavioral Pharmacology* and is a Regional Editor for *Pharmacology, Biochemistry and Behavior*. Among his books are *Behavioral Pharmacology* and *Reinforcement Schedules and Multioperant Analysis*. His main research interests are in behavioral pharmacology and interactions among environmental and pharmacological variables in treatment of retarded and psychotic patients.

Michael D. Zeiler (Chapter 8), Ph.D. New School for Social Research, is Professor of Psychology at Emory University. He has published a number of research papers in professional journals and authored several chapters. He is presently the Editor of the *Journal of the Experimental Analysis of Behavior*. His major research interest is in the experimental and theoretical analysis of schedules of reinforcement.

Introduction

Werner K. Honig
and
J. E. R. Staddon

Ten years and more have passed since the publication of *Operant Behavior*, which was the first effort to provide a reasonably comprehensive account of those areas of thought and research in psychology which were influenced substantially by operant methods. The time has come for a reassessment of several of those areas, for a description of other topics involving operant methods or bearing upon them, and for a conceptual examination of the fundamental principles of the Experimental Analysis of Behavior and its relationship to other parts of experimental psychology. The present Handbook cannot pretend to accomplish all of these aims, or even to do justice to any, but it provides much relevant empirical material, and many discussions which are both incisive and enlightening.

Certain aspects of operant behavior were deliberately excluded from the outset. The enormous increase in the use of operant methods for both fundamental and applied research makes it impossible to cover these major areas in one volume. This book is devoted entirely to topics in experimental psychology. We have welcomed the planning and publication of two companion books: One is the *Handbook of Applied Operant Behavior*, edited by Harold Leitenberg, and in press with Prentice-Hall. The other is entitled *Social and Instrumental Processes: Foundations and Applications of Behavioral Analysis*. It is edited by T. A. Brigham and A. C. Catania, and will be published by Irvington.

Our own book provides a mixture of experimental and theoretical material which reflects the current status of operant behavior. No chapter is "strictly experimental" in the sense that it fails to raise conceptual and theoretical issues, or concentrates entirely upon methodology. Only a few chapters—those on language—are largely theoretical, although empirical studies do, of course, provide some of the material for discussion. Perhaps we would be wisest to let the chapters follow without further comment, but after giving them many hours of scrutiny, we succumb to the temptation of providing the reader with a few general impressions.

First, it is becoming quite clear that operant methods and principles are becoming increasingly integrated in general experimental psychology. At first, the operant movement (if such it should be called) was quite isolated, largely due to negative reactions from its critics and enemies, who were put off by Skinner's radical behaviorism, by the artificial and restricted environment of the "Skinner box", by the lack of concern with theoretical issues, or by the apparent threat to traditional freedoms and values posed by the prospective control of human behavior through operant methods. Furthermore, operant methods facilitated new research strategies with little regard for traditional principles of experimental design. The intensive study of individual subjects across a variety of treatments was indeed promoted as a kind of model of experimental method (Sidman, 1960). But the isolation felt by workers in the area of operant behavior was partly self-imposed. One does not gain a sense of compromise from Skinner's writings. The impression conveyed is that the study of operant behavior should not be contaminated by attention to traditional problems, methods, and theoretical issues. The movement was named The Experimental Analysis of Behavior, suggesting that the operant method provides the only valid and constructive approach to the systematic study of behavior.

But the interest in operant behavior has not declined, and the use of operant methods is certainly no longer restricted to Skinner's students and associates. The advantages of these methods, reviewed in the preface to the previous volume (Honig, 1966), are so clear that many psychologists used them to study problems outside the original purview of the Experimental Analysis of Behavior. As interest in the construction of and debate over grand theoretical systems declined, experimental psychologists concentrated on the explanation of more limited aspects of behavior, and these could be studied systematically through operant methods in a tractable experimental setting that provided greater flexibility than its reputation had suggested. Younger psychologists, no longer absorbed by debates among "schools" of psychology, felt less inclined to exclude operant behavior from their scope of interest, or, conversely, to restrict their attention to the limited range of problems addressed by Skinner. While the "passing of the pressing of the bar" never did come about, Skinner's methods and principles have not dominated experimental methodology, nor have they supplanted all other means by which orderly data can be obtained. The operant is still a very viable unit, as demonstrated in the many pages of this text, but it can no longer be so clearly separated from other modes of behavior. The relation of operants to the latter has come under close examination over the last ten years. Some of the conclusions are worth reviewing.

Operant behavior is studied by arranging for the animal to affect its environment in some way—by pressing a lever, pecking a lighted key, or breaking a photobeam. This effect, which can be accomplished in any way the animal chooses, is termed the response. If it changes the environment in a way that has motivating consequences, giving access to food or water, or escaping electric shock, the animal will generally learn to make the response more frequently. This change defines the consequence as a reinforcer. The prescribed relation between responding and reinforcement is a response-reinforcer contingency. The frequency of the response will be strongly affected by stimuli that signal availability or unavailability of the reinforcer (discriminative stimuli).

The rule or rules prescribing the relations among stimuli, responses, and reinforcers is a reinforcement schedule. Schedules are of interest both in their own right, and as useful "contrivances", in Jenkins' phrase, that can be used to tease apart the mechanisms that underlie learned behavior. Much of this book has as its experimental basis the very extensive work on schedules that has taken place in the past fifteen years. One approach is to treat reinforcement schedules as an opportunity for a sort of experimental ecology, as a way to set up a novel set of relations between an animal's behavior and its consequences, and then to observe how the subject copes with this new situation. By studying a range of situations a taxonomy may be derived and general principles induced in Baconian fashion. Although much data of this sort has been gathered and is reviewed by Zeiler in this book, Skinner's strictures against theorizing and "botanizing" have discouraged both systematic exploration of non-schedule variables, such as species differences and type of reinforcer, and persistent attempts to make theoretical inferences. Zeiler describes schedule control based on the delivery of primary reinforcers in Chapter 8, while Gollub reviews the parallel role of conditioned reinforcers in Chapter 10. These writers analyse in detail the controlling variables, involving both response-contingent and non-contingent delivery of stimuli; their treatments verge on theoretical accounts of the temporal patterning of behavior.

Schedules in the broader sense are also used as analytic devices. A particular set of relations between responding, stimuli, and the reinforcer is used for the study of particular empirical or theoretical questions. The elegant demonstrations of autoshaping (Brown and Jenkins, 1968; Williams and Williams, 1969) demonstrated that key-pecking in the pigeon can be generated and maintained through "classical" contingencies. Likewise, Reynolds' (1961) experiments on behavioral contrast are among many other examples of the power of operant techniques to reveal properties of learned behavior that are indirectly determined by effective schedules. Chapter 3 by Schwartz and Gamzu brings together these lines of work. When it is shown that schedules controlling instrumental behavior generate and maintain classically conditioned responses, the whole relationship between these two classes of behavior needs to be reexamined. Teitelbaum undertakes this task in Chapter 1; he shows how physiological techniques are used to identify the motivational substrates that underlie instrumental behavior in the intact animal.

While the use of operant techniques continues to prosper, the conceptual framework that has grown up around them has begun to show signs of strain in recent years. The terms "response", "reinforcer", and "stimulus" imply classes of events that are similar in their essential properties and can be combined in arbitrary ways. One reinforcer is, if not the same as another, at least not qualitatively different. All responses (at least all operant, as opposed to respondent, responses) are more or less equally reinforcible by all reinforcers and can with equal facility come under the control of any stimulus. This story is a familiar one and recent discussions of "constraints on learning" (Hinde and Stevenson-Hinde, 1973) have made its imperfections well known. The important point with respect to constraints is that the selection of one particular stimulus, response, or reinforcer may well limit the selection of others that will be effective in conjunction with it. Some stimuli may control behavior more readily in avoidance paradigms than in conjunction with positive reinforcement, and the converse can also be demonstrated. This sort of constraint need not invalidate, although it may extend, principles obtained with the use of the most appropriate experimental elements. In most situations the functional elements "stimulus", "response", and "reinforcer" can be identified and the relations among them are more or less what we have learned to expect from studies of bar pressing or key pecking. So while the "arbitrary response" is no longer with us, the concept of reinforcement contingency has, if anything, gained in scope.

Instrumental responses are closely related to the species-specific consummatory behavior which is contingent upon them, and this relationship underlies some of the constraints just mentioned. In Chapter 4, Dunham reviews some of the "misbehaviors of organisms." These observations have provided us with a general principle, namely that instrumental responses often approximate consummatory behaviors, and may be easiest to teach when they do so. Furthermore, it is likely that if instrumental behavior is separated from species-specific patterns, greater flexibility may be observed. Responses which, let us say, control the duration of stimuli differentially correlated with reward, may be more tractable, and thus can be more "arbitrary" than those that procure the reward itself. When consummatory behavior is preceded (and "predicted") by a signal it often emerges as a classically conditioned, or "autoshaped", response to that signal.

The significance of autoshaping for the area of operant behavior is threefold. First, the status of the arbitrary operant was reduced when it was discovered that such cherished instrumental behaviors as the pigeon's key peck could readily be conditioned through classical means. Second, it suggested that both the form and the quantity of operant behavior could be influenced through classical (stimulus) contingencies, as a current analysis of contrast effects suggests. Schwartz and Gamzu trace this relationship in their chapter. Third, the "instinctive drift" which underlies the misbehavior of organisms can be explained through the operation of classical conditioning principles: An instrumental response reliably precedes the consummatory behavior occasioned by the presentation of the reinforcer. Thus, depending on the schedule, the instrumental response is a more or less reliable predictor of the consummatory response. In accordance with classical conditioning principles the instrumental response may therefore come to act as a conditioned stimulus, eliciting components of the unconditioned response. To the extent that instrumental and unconditioned responses are incompatible, interference may result and instrumental responding may be suppressed, as the Brelands found. On the other hand, if the instrumental response is judiciously chosen to be compatible with the consummatory response, facilitation will be the rule. However, the classically conditioned nature of the response can be revealed by special scheduling arrangements such as the Williams's omission procedure. The chapters by Schwartz and Gamzu, Dunham, and Staddon deal with these matters.

A less direct, but equally fruitful, approach to the relationship between instrumental and consummatory responses is provided by the presentation of "free" reinforcers on a temporally defined schedule. Work of this nature indicates that *terminal behaviors* approximating the consummatory response occur shortly before the presentation of the reinforcer, while other *interim behaviors* occur when the likelihood of reinforcement is low. This method is but one example of a significant change in operant experiments, namely the simultaneous observation and recording of various responses in addition to the instrumental behavior.

Such observation, facilitated by closed-circuit television, is, of course, a change from the traditional emphasis upon a single "externalized" response, but it has enormously enriched and broadened the analysis of behavior in a controlled environment. It also provides a bridge to the ethological study of animal behavior, a field whose avowed interests sometimes appear very different from those of operant psychology (although the reality of the difference is often arguable), but whose methods are quite similar. Thus, while the pressing of the bar has not passed, it has been supplemented by other concurrent observations. Staddon reviews this work in Chapter 5, and Hutchinson in Chapter 14 describes related experimental results in situations involving electric shock.

Just as the concept of the response has undergone a searching analysis which is reflected in this book, the process of reinforcement has also been re-evaluated, and in several very different ways. Premack's theory (Premack, 1965), which was being developed while *Operant Behavior* was being written, has left its mark. The Experimental Analysis of Behavior is well suited to the notion that reinforcers have no absolute qualities, but are functionally defined, and situationally determined. The development of these ideas is traced by Dunham in Chapter 4. Morse and Kelleher, in Chapter 7, take a yet more radical view, suggesting that reinforcement and punishment are often the outcome of particular scheduling contingencies, and their functional analysis is not necessarily bound up with the presumed noxious or appetitive qualities. Their careful argument and analysis cannot be summarized in a few words, but one of their contributions should be pointed out: Once and for all, they separate the presumed appetitive or aversive qualities of response-contingent stimuli from the identification of such stimuli as reinforcers or punishers in terms of their effects in maintaining patterns of instrumental responding.

The process of reinforcement is analyzed in this book in two other, quite different ways. In Chapter 6, Satinoff and Hendersen describe the maintenance of an internal state, namely temperature, via instrumental behavior. This leads quite naturally into feedback theory. Here reinforcing effects are best regarded not in terms of some presumed strengthening effect but as adjustments to deviations from an internal "set point". Operant behavior is but one of several mechanisms, physiological as well as behavioral, that help maintain the stability of the *milieu interne*. It is interesting that behavioral thermoregulatory mechanisms appear to be phylogenetically older than the physiological regulatory processes that supplement behavior in so-called warm-blooded animals.

This approach is presented in an even more radical form in Chapter 2 by Collier, Hirsch, and Kanarek, who describe a situation where animals live in the experimental setting and can gain all of their required food (or water) in the form of unrestricted meals. When the meal, rather than the pellet, becomes the unit of reward, it supports a very large amount of behavior, in spite of the absence of the deprivation condition commonly thought necessary for the performance of an instrumental repertoire. These findings may pose some real problems for reinforcement theory, while at the same time they support the "relevance" of the Experimental Analysis of Behavior to human affairs, since the environment that Collier *et al.* are working with is rather naturalistic, and provides an apt parallel for much of the human condition. Aside from its contributions toward the theoretical analysis of reinforcement, this research broadens our concept of instrumental behavior as an activity rather than a response. It can occur in "bouts", as do the consummatory behaviors contingent upon it. Such a view permits a conceptual re-evaluation of instrumental behavior as an activity that is chosen, from among others, for a proportion of the available time.

The theoretical analysis of reinforcement has in this book also been extended far beyond the parallel efforts in 1966, especially with respect to quantification. Where behavior is related in an orderly fashion to other, controlled aspects of the environment, mathematical analysis becomes fruitful. De Villiers devotes Chapter 9 to an examination of quantitative versions of the Law of Effect, largely through a review of experiments on choice. His approach resembles Premack's and, in a related field, Helson's adaptation-level theory, in being relativistic. While debate continues on the best form of theory, the notion that levels of instrumental responding are determined by the context of reinforcement, by relative rather than absolute reinforcement rates, is clearly here to stay. De Villiers well illustrates the trend towards integration of operant with general experimental psychology because he re-analyzes results from standard discrete-trial situations in accordance with his quantitative formulations. To this end, he considers running in an alley (for example), as an extended quantifiable response, which can be represented in such a way to make it amenable to an analysis originally based on concurrent operants. Conditioned reinforcement is also subjected to a mathematical treatment in Chapter 11 by Fantino, as another illustration of the quantitative trend in the theory of operant behavior.

Not only do we find new and very different treatments of the concepts of response and reinforcement, but the role played by theoretical analysis itself seems quite to have changed in the last ten years, no doubt due in part to the reanalysis of the basic terms and concepts. The chapters on stimulus control and aversive control, in addition to those cited here already, attest to this. Concepts such as inhibition and attention no longer require justification or defense, but rather a searching analysis of their determining characteristics, as Rilling and Mackintosh show in Chapters 15 and 16 respectively. In his careful review of the role of errors in the attainment of discriminations, Rilling concludes that the correlation between discriminative stimuli and rewards, rather than the emission of unreinforced responses, determines the inhibitory properties of a stimulus. Again, a relationship between stimuli, rather than between a response and a stimulus, seems to govern processes that in turn control instrumental performance. Mackintosh uses the slope of the generalization gradient as an index of attention to an extent that could hardly have been anticipated a decade ago. His theoretical discussion takes into account the role of repeated instrumental responses as stimuli which in their own right may share stimulus control with other events explicitly programmed by the experimenter. While Blough and Blough, in Chapter 17, are less concerned with theoretical questions in the study of animal psychophysics, they give an account of signal detection theory as one method for the analysis of instrumental behaviors used to assess the perception of, and the discrimination between, stimuli.

Other theoretical treatments, particularly in the area of aversive control, reflect a more purely behavioristic orientation. In Chapter 12 Blackman provides a much needed analysis of the importance of the operant baseline in its interaction with other fundamental processes when conditioned suppression is obtained. This topic was not included in the predecessor of this volume. Hineline elaborates on avoidance in Chapter 13; he continues an analytic orientation toward free-operant avoidance that was already in progress a decade ago. It is interesting how this area has changed from an emphasis on the methods which will produce free-operant avoidance to experiments that analyze the variables and processes that maintain such behavior. The current theoretical context emphasizes the organism's evaluation, as it were, of the correlations between responding and the absence of aversive events.

Operant methods have also become ubiquitous in the study of electrical, chemical, and physiological determinants of behavior. Aside from some general discussion in Teitelbaum's chapter, three other chapters are specifically concerned with these problems. In these areas we see that again, a given treatment or a given behavioral effect may play more than one functional role in the ultimate patterning of responses. Thus, electrical brain stimulation can act as a powerful reinforcer, as Mogenson and Cioé show in Chapter 19, but it can also elicit patterns of behavior closely related to the reinforcing effect. Furthermore, a functional analysis of the reinforcing process involved with such stimuli reveals that they do not act very differently from "standard" reinforcers, once parameters such as immediacy of delivery are controlled for. With the behavioral effects of drugs we see a converse set of relationships. Drugs are not limited to their traditional actions as depressants, stimulants, and the like. They also can act as powerful reinforcers (or punishers), as those who are concerned with applied problems can well testify. Thompson and Boren treat behavioral pharmacology in Chapter 18. The effects of stress on biochemical and other physiological processes are reviewed by Brady and Harris in Chapter 20, and here again we have evidence of the dual role of such "internal effects". They may reflect external treatments which control behavior, but if they can be made accessible to the subject by being "externalized" as feedback stimuli, they can participate in the control of behavior as discriminative and reinforcing stimuli.

An analysis of language derived from the study of operant behavior in animals was proposed by Skinner in his 1957 *tour de force*, *Verbal Behavior*. This work has excited much subsequent controversy but little by way of empirical test. Noam Chomsky (1959) in a famous critique roundly condemned the work as empirically ill-founded, quantitatively implausible, and little more than a restatement of the familiar in neologistic terms. Chapter 21 by Robinson deals with one aspect of this debate. He shows how a purely associationistic model can lead to the development of a language structure. Hence the existence of structure in language does not require either that its basis is innate or that people learn "rules" in the conventional sense. It is perhaps helpful to be reminded that learning by association implies only that things become joined to other things through experience, a "mental chemistry" in Mill's phrase, and not that the conjoined entities are of necessity stimuli and overt responses. In Chapter 22, Segal provides a clear and concise summary of the meat of *Verbal Behavior*, a book often cited but, we suspect, less often read. She stresses the parallels between Skinner's views on language and contemporary structural approaches. She provides a framework for the conciliation of a conflict originally generated by these approaches, a conflict which was for a long time viewed as typical of the separation of operant analysis from more traditional forms of theorizing. Her achievement is perhaps symbolic of a more general *rapprochement* that will, in our opinion, gain strength over at least the next few years.

In many ways, then, research based on operant behavior is becoming more closely integrated into general experimental psychology. Theoretical questions are asked of the manner in which different forms of operant behavior are generated and maintained. Yet this behavior is itself used in turn to obtain answers to theoretical questions of all kinds. Our brief overview of this book has stressed conceptual and theoretical developments relevant to operant behavior over the last ten years. We have said little about operant methodology itself, which has changed but little. Operant methods continue to be used widely as tools; in many ways the parallel between the operant chamber in psychology and the microscope in biology is justified. The advantages of operant methods were recounted a decade ago in the introduction that corresponds to this article. These advantages have not diminished. We hope that this handbook reaffirms the value of operant methods as well as the vitality of the empirical questions to which they continue to be applied.

REFERENCES

Brown, P. L., & Jenkins, H. M. Auto-shaping of the pigeon's key-peck. *Journal of the Experimental Analysis of Behavior,* 1968, *11,* 1–8.

Chomsky, N. *Review of Verbal Behavior.* By B. F. Skinner. *Language,* 1959, *35,* 26–58.

Hinde, R. A., & Stevenson-Hinde, J. (Eds.), *Constraints on learning.* New York: Academic Press, 1973.

Honig, W. K. Introductory remarks. In W. K. Honig (Ed.), *Operant behavior: Areas of research and application.* New York: Appleton-Century-Crofts, 1966. Pp. 1–11.

Premack, D. Reinforcement theory. In D. Levine (Ed.), *Nebraska symposium on motivation,* 1965. Nebraska: University of Nebraska Press, 1965. Pp. 123–180.

Reynolds, G. S. Behavioral contrast. *Journal of the Experimental Analysis of Behavior,* 1961, *4,* 57–71.

Sidman, M. *Tactics of scientific research.* New York: Basic Books, 1960.

Skinner, B. F. *Verbal Behavior.* New York: Appleton-Century-Crofts, 1957.

Williams, D. R., & Williams, H. Auto-maintenance in the pigeon: Sustained pecking despite contingent nonreinforcement. *Journal of the Experimental Analysis of Behavior,* 1969, *12,* 511–520.

1
Levels of Integration of the Operant*

Philip Teitelbaum

INTRODUCTION

As a practical approach to the control of behavior, B. F. Skinner's operant psychology is clearly a success. His approach has been embodied in distinctive attitudes toward the study of learned motivated behavior, which in turn have generated a specialized terminology and have led to the design of automated and computerized equipment for detecting an individual's behavior, for reinforcing it according to particular schedules, and for recording the way the behavior is shaped by the process (Ferster & Skinner, 1957). In psychopharmacology, these techniques have been used to generate stable base lines to assess the behavioral effects of drugs. Physiological psychologists use them to interpret the effects of localized brain damage (Honig, 1966). In human education, teaching machines and programmed texts are being developed to individualize and enhance the learning of conceptual material in a variety of fields (Anderson, 1967; Skinner, 1961). In mental hospitals, therapists apply the principles of reinforcement by using token economies to shape up socially acceptable behavior patterns (Kazdin & Bootzin, 1972). In the therapist's office, impulsive behavior is brought under control (Halmi, Powers, & Cunningham, 1975; Stunkard, 1974; for possible perils, however, see Bruch, 1974). Experimental communities, presaged in *Walden Two* (Skinner, 1948a), are being explored as ways of solving the problems of social living. New journals, both theoretical and applied, are devoted to the operant approach, and the number of adherents continues to grow.

However, some aspects of the concept of the operant have come under attack. Laboratory learning phenomena such as autoshaping (Brown & Jenkins, 1968) look like operants but seem not to fit the principles of operant conditioning, and there are other examples of the "misbehavior of organisms" (Breland & Breland, 1961, 1966). Ethologically oriented workers encounter biological constraints on learning, in which specialized evolutionary adaptations, either in nontraditional physiological systems (taste-aversion learning) or in nonmammalian species, suggest to some that the search for general laws of learning may be

* This paper was written with the support of funds from NIH Grant #R01 NS 11671. The author wishes especially to thank Evelyn Satinoff for incisive editorial revision and conceptual sharpening. Helpful criticisms were also received from Donald Davidson, Robert Hendersen, Werner K. Honig, Howard Rachlin, B. F. Skinner, John E. R. Staddon and Herbert S. Terrace.

premature or even unwarranted (Garcia, Hankins, & Rusiniak, 1974; Hinde & Stevenson-Hinde, 1973; Rozin & Kalat, 1971; Shettleworth, 1972, 1975).

Such scientific paradoxes indicate that our present thinking may need re-evaluation (Teitelbaum, 1974). We must go back to the history of our ideas to discover how to revise them. In this chapter, I shall therefore discuss how the operant came to be, and then some of the phenomena that seem to pose difficulties for it. These difficulties are related to similar problems in our thinking about all motivated behavior. Finally, I will summarize new evidence from the physiological study of brain-damaged animals and people that suggests that it may be fruitful to look at the operant in terms of levels of integration.

The operant philosophy has structured, not only our thinking about behavior, but also our ideas about how to study it. Implicit in it has been the rejection of alternative approaches, particularly physiological analysis. I will try to characterize the various forms of analysis and synthesis used in the experimental approach to understanding behavior in order to see why operant analysis went one way, while physiological analysis took another. Then I will point out that there are new physiological approaches that can meet the objections raised by Skinner and are compatible with his thought and work. The time may be ripe to merge the operant and physiological methodologies in a concerted intellectual and experimental attack upon the levels of integration of the operant. Through behavioral analysis of developing infants and of adults recovering from brain damage, we may extend our understanding of the operant. The result can be a basic behavioral approach that preserves the values of the operant while linking it, by a set of physiological principles, to the fields of neurology, physiological psychology, developmental psychology and ethology. In short, we must bridge the gap between Sherrington and Skinner.

HISTORICAL BACKGROUND

All psychologists assert a common goal—the attempt to understand human behavior. However, apart from differences in topics of interest, they adopt different fundamental beliefs about the best way of reaching this goal. Such beliefs, which are characteristic of all the academic subdivisions of our field, have created different "schools," many of which have become so insular that they hardly communicate with one another any more. For example, it is commonly felt that the "operant" approach is incompatible with a physiological analysis of behavior.

As Descartes (1637) pointed out, the experimental approach to understanding involves two intellectual or experimental processes: (1) breaking down a phenomenon into simpler elements (analysis) and (2) recombining those parts to make sure that they are sufficient to reconstitute the original phenomenon (synthesis). It is in the choice of simpler elements, and in the methods of using them to account for behavior, that the various "schools" differ. For instance, physiological psychologists have long tried to simplify behavior by chopping the nervous system into smaller chunks. This is the classic levels-of-function approach to the nervous system used by Flourens (1824), Sherrington (1906), and many others. Such experimental analysis in animals yields direct evidence for simple subcomponents of behavior, such as spinal reflexes, and for their more complicated integration as postural and movement patterns, like those described by Magnus (1926) in decerebrate animals. Comparative psychologists, like their European counterparts, the ethologists, use the simpler nervous system of insects, birds, and fish to study reflexes and the more complex hormonally controlled instinctive patterns such as feeding, fighting, and mating. In general, they all agree with Descartes that to understand, one must simplify.

However, these surgically or phylogenetically simplified preparations yield phenomena (reflexes, instinctive patterns) and theoretical constructs based on them that do not seem to help much in understanding the phenomena of language, thought, neurosis, and psychopathology that fascinate us in human behavior. We still do not know how to use our knowledge of these simple phenomena synthetically to predict or control very much that is significant in everyday human life (Skinner, 1957).

We all face this dilemma very early in our study of behavior, and it is at this point that we split up. Some of us (the physiological types) go toward the molecular. We say that behavior reflects the action of the nervous system, so we must understand the latter before anything else. Although we keep human behavior in mind to return to eventually, we work on animals and concentrate on understanding molecular phenomena such as synaptic transmission (with possible relevance to mechanisms of learning and memory), and sensory physiology (how does the nervous system transform a stimulus into a sensation?). Some use electrical and chemical stimulation and ablation to study brain mechanisms of motivation and reinforcement. Others try to identify areas of the brain concerned with learning and memory. Because function must depend on structure, many spend a great deal of time mapping functional systems neuroanatomically.

All physiological experimenters share the belief that the most fruitful experimental analysis is real, not hypothetical. By a real analysis, I mean using experimental techniques to isolate physically a fraction of a more complex system, yielding a system for study that has fewer variables acting on it, yet which still preserves the essential phenomena that are of interest; hence the emphasis on developing finer electrodes to measure the activity of fewer cells, or even one cell at a time, and on finding ever simpler nervous systems (e.g., the horseshoe crab *Limulus* or the sea hare *Aplysia*). Because human behavior is so complicated, most feel they cannot now make much progress with it, and they study molecular phenomena, firm in their belief that such knowledge is fundamental to human behavior and will eventually pay off. As a consequence, they deemphasize the synthetic application of their understanding. Many do not even try to extrapolate their findings to people, feeling that there is too great a gap between their observations on animals and analogous phenomena in humans, in whom cultural and social factors loom so large.

When faced with this dilemma—dealing with subcomponents of behavior that are real but too simple to use in controlling or predicting the interesting aspects of human behavior—many psychologists reject the physiological approach entirely. They pick important aspects of human behavior—phenomena of language, modes of problem solving, associative thought processes, social attitudes toward others, etc. They bring them or their analogs into the laboratory and try to figure out the environmental and constitutional variables that determine them. From each particular approach they deduce hypothetical variables for use in explanatory and predictive theories. For example, people have thought in terms of frequency and recency of associations, perceptual dispositions or "sets," stimulus-response (S–R) bonds in habit strength, tendencies to increase or decrease "cognitive dissonance," ego, id, or superego, etc. All are highly abstract, and even though they may be useful in trying to deal with real human problems, to a physiological psychologist they do not seem very tangible or relevant to known phenomena in the nervous system. So we drift further apart.

In his book *The Behavior of Organisms* B. F. Skinner (1938) grappled with the same dilemma. He very carefully considered the value of simplifying behavior by neurosurgery, as in the work of Sherrington (1906) on spinal reflexes. He realized that when such a simplification was achieved, the main scientific value for behavior was that for each reflex the adequate stimulus could be identified, and because of its close, virtually invariable association with the motor act, the laws governing the S–R correlation could be worked out. The variables governing any reflex can be classified into two types: (1) environmental (the strength, number, and duration of stimuli and their spatial and temporal interaction) and (2) organismic (the central states—such as hunger, fatigue, and hormonal conditions). In spinal reflexes, the organismic states do not seem to affect the S–R correlation very much and for most purposes are largely ignored. Because such reflexes seem relatively uninfluenced by learning or the central "motivational" states that affect learning, the phenomena most germane to human behavior do not appear to have any obvious similarities to reflexes.

When Pavlov (1927) discovered conditioned reflexes, many psychologists believed that they had a simple system that could reveal the laws of animal and human learning. If an unconditioned reflex such as salivation at the sight or taste of food could come to be elicited by any arbitrary stimulus, such as a flash of light or the sound of a buzzer, and if this association could be remembered for long periods of time, then perhaps the laws of learning could be quickly worked out. Many still have faith in this paradigm (e.g., Moore, 1973). To Skinner, however, it seemed clear that much of the behavior of animals and people was not based on autonomic responses, evoked automatically by stimuli. Most of their behavior seems to be emitted as an act that modifies an environment in which no eliciting stimulus is readily identifiable, rather than automatically evoked as a respondent like salivation at the sight of a stimulus paired with food. Furthermore, attempts to synthesize an understanding of complex behavior from the concepts of the reflex, conditioned or unconditioned, led to fruitless "physiologizing" (a tendency to push explanation back to the level of neural phenomena, without any proof that such hypotheses are valid), or to a great deal of speculation about theoretical constructs involved in learned behavior. In the extreme, the latter can be compared to the uselessness of medieval scholasticism—i.e., how many S–R bonds can dance on the head of a pin? To Skinner (1950, 1972a, 1972b), both forms of hypothetical synthesis led away from direct contact with real phenomena and therefore did more harm than good.

In order to evaluate Skinner's solution to the problem of the analysis and synthesis of behavior, we should first briefly review the common experimental methods of scientific synthesis. After an analysis, real or theoretical, that has broken a phenomenon down into simpler parts, how do we put them back together? As far as I have been able to determine, there are five methods, four of which I have described earlier (Teitelbaum, 1967). In what seems an increasing order of abstraction (with, therefore, an increasing possibility of error in their application), they are as follows:

1. DIRECT SYNTHESIS

This method is often used in chemistry. When a chemist wishes to determine the nature of an unknown substance, he breaks it down into its components. If his analysis is correct, he should be able to synthesize the original substance by taking the individual components from completely different sources and putting them together under the appropriate environmental conditions. A classic example of this in physiology was carried out by the Nobel Prize winner George Wald in collaboration with Ruth Hubbard (Hubbard & Wald, 1951). After years of working out the experimental analysis of rhodopsin, they took the individual subcomponents from completely different sources and put them all together. Purified opsin from the retinas of cattle, crystalline alcohol dehydrogenase derived from horse liver, vitamin A from fish liver oil, and cozymase (now called DPN) from yeast when brought together in solution formed a compound with all the properties of natural rhodopsin. This is a beautiful example of the proof of an analysis by direct synthesis.

2. COUNTEREXPERIMENT: SYNTHESIS AFTER FRACTIONATION

This was the favorite method of Claude Bernard (1865), the great French physiologist. In essence, the principle is: when a change occurs after you remove something, put back a fraction of what you have removed. If you restore the original state, the fraction contains the essential ingredient. (If it is the only sufficient ingredient, the remainder will not restore the original state.) For instance, in a famous example of Bernard's application of this method, after removal of the pancreas, rabbits waste away and die. If a different pancreas is transplanted anywhere into the body of such a pancreatectomized rabbit, it lives relatively normally. Therefore, the transplanted pancreas, even without its normal nervous connections, can maintain life. If an extract of pancreas is injected daily into a pancreatectomized rabbit, it too will live normally. Therefore, something in the extract is vital. Continue this process of analysis and synthesis, and eventually, as is now well known, you will discover that the hormone insulin, manufactured by the islets of Langerhans in the pancreas, counteracts the otherwise fatal disease of diabetes mellitus.

3. SYNTHESIS BY MODEL

We can test our understanding of a phenomenon by constructing a model. We build into the model the elements we think are important and also our conception of the way these elements interact to produce the phenomenon. Such models can be purely theoretical, as in mathematical models of learning behavior, in which after a theoretical analysis we postulate the essential elements and processes involved in such a way that they can be described quantitatively. Then, in situations which are simple enough to handle mathematically, we attempt to predict in an equation how the behavior will change as the variables are manipulated. We can also construct physical analogies, as an engineer does when he tries to simulate human behavior by building a computerized robot. All such models are attempts to synthesize a behavioral phenomenon through a model which embodies its essential elements.

4. SYNTHESIS BY PREDICTION

If we have correctly analyzed the elements of a given form of behavior, we should be able to predict which variables will control them and the way the behavior will change as these variables are manipulated experimentally. This is the most common test of an analysis by synthesis. It lends itself very easily to theoretical analysis and in formal versions much akin to mathematical models has played a prominent role in learning theory (e.g., Clark Hull's [1943] hypothetico-deductive approach to laws of learning).

5. SYNTHESIS BY PARALLEL

So far, none of the above methods has been very successful in enabling us to reconstitute complex animal and human behavior from the real, simpler subcomponents of behavior isolated so far (reflex, instinct). We may not be able to do so until we know a great deal more about how reflexes and instincts work. However, there is another method of synthesis, rather little exploited, which can supplement the previous ones. It allows immediate useful application to complex behavior of any knowledge we have obtained about simpler, experimentally isolated behavior systems. It is "synthesis by parallel," which in essence says that something new is like something else that is already familiar. A parallel is a similarity, and the more detailed it is the more confidence we have that the similarity is not mere coincidence. One uses this method from the conviction that nature is parsimonious: if a given phenomenon works in a particular fashion, it is likely that the same method is used to produce other phenomena which up to now we have not recognized as being the same. Therefore, look for a parallel. After evaluating Skinner's use of analysis and synthesis, I shall illustrate the use of parallels as a possible way of increasing our understanding of operant behavior.

What was B. F. Skinner's solution to the problem of how to apply analysis and synthesis to the understanding of learned motivated behavior? Following firmly in the footsteps of Descartes, Sherrington, and Pavlov, Skinner opted for a real simplification of behavior. However, the physiological method of transecting the nervous system yielded preparations whose behavior was too simple—spinal or decerebrate reflexes and postural changes seemed unsuitable to reveal the laws of learning because these preparations could no longer learn. Moreover, trying to build theories of behavior from these overly simple preparations proved in most instances to be a waste of time. Therefore, instead of transecting the nervous system to purify the S–R correlation between environment and behavior, Skinner chose to simplify the environment. He put the organism into an isolated environment—an opaque, sound-insulated chamber where one or more stimuli could be introduced whenever the experimenter desired (Skinner, 1956). In this, Skinner followed Pavlov, whose work on conditioned reflexes had demonstrated that in order to reveal lawful correlations between stimuli and conditioned reflexes it was absolutely essential to eliminate extraneous stimuli. Respondent autonomic responses do not act on the world; therefore, Skinner chose an arbitrary act (but only one), like pressing a bar or pecking a key, and rewarded the hungry or thirsty animal with a tiny amount of food or water each time it performed the desired act. In a simplified world of one stimulus and one response, it immediately becomes apparent that the presentation of a reinforcing stimulus to an appropriately motivated animal powerfully shapes its behavior. As will be discussed more fully below, since the response and the reinforcement appear to be completely arbitrary, we have thus achieved a simplified prototype of adaptive high-level motivated behavior—a unit of behavior whose laws we can now study.

Skinner then devised a "microscope" to study the newly isolated "operant"—the cumulative record. Using the most advanced telephone relay circuitry then available, he was able to detect the correct response (a bar press or a key peck sufficient to close a microswitch) automatically, to deliver the reinforcement instantaneously, and to record each response and reinforcement as they occurred. By recording such responses cumulatively, one could almost see the developing shape of an animal's expectations—for instance, on a fixed-interval schedule (where a reinforcement only occurs after a fixed time has elapsed since the previous one), the animal uniformly pauses in its responding immediately after reinforcement, then gradually accelerates its responding as the probability of a reinforcement increases with time.

Skinner used the cumulative record to insure the purity of his simplified preparation. When he got smooth curves he believed he had pure operant behavior under the control of the reinforcement contingencies. In a way, this is like the electrophysiologist who, when dissecting a nerve bundle to isolate one fiber, watches the oscilloscope and dissects until the preparation responds with impulses all of the same amplitude. The all-or-none law (that a single neuron always fires with impulses of the same amplitude) thus assures the purity of the dissected nerve preparation. In a similar fashion, a smooth cumulative record is taken to mean that we have only one kind of behavior being recorded—each response follows the next so regularly (here uniform frequency rather than amplitude is used) that they add up smoothly rather than discontinuously. (If the curve is irregular, as is often true early in training, it frequently indicates that we have more than one act being used to press the bar. However, see below for further discussion of the adequacy of this method.)

Having experimentally isolated and purified the operant, Skinner then faced the problem of using it to understand the laws of learned motivated behavior. In his early work (1938) he used prediction as a method of synthesis. He formulated concepts such as the reflex reserve to embody the idea of a reservoir of responses that is affected both by central organismic states and past experience with reinforcement. The level of the reflex reserve determined the probability of an animal's behavior in particular instances. Similar hydraulic models of instinctive behavior have been used in psychoanalysis (Freud, 1912) and in ethology (Lorenz, 1952).

But Skinner soon came to feel that such attempts at theoretical prediction possessed the same drawbacks of fruitless speculation and lack of contact with the real phenomena of behavior that were met with in at-

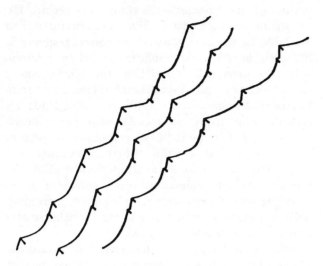

Fig 1. Tracings of three curves which report behavior in response to a multiple fixed-interval fixed-ratio schedule. One of them was made by a pigeon, one by a rat, and one by a monkey. (From Skinner, © 1956 by the American Psychological Association. Reprinted by permission.)

tempting to reconstruct complex behavior from physiological or hypothetical simplifications. "A purely descriptive science is never popular. For the man whose curiosity about nature is not equal to his interest in the accuracy of his guesses, the hypothesis is the very life-blood of science" (Skinner, 1938, p. 426). He therefore broke with traditional forms of theory (Skinner, 1950). The operant was simple—but not too simple. It was of sufficient complexity to embody the interesting phenomena of learning and motivation. Environmental analysis assured sufficient simplicity to reveal reliable S–R relationships that could form the framework of a scientific description of behavior. Instead of using a mathematical model or prediction for synthesis, Skinner used the successful control of behavior as his validation criterion. The phenomenon we are interested in (learned motivated behavior) is clearly evident in the simplified world of the Skinner box, so all we have to do is describe the way the response varies as stimuli and internal states are varied. The fact that they do control the probability of response guarantees their validity. I call this "synthesis by success." As shown in Figure 1, a given fixed-interval type of schedule (this is actually a multiple schedule: fixed intervals combined with fixed ratios) produces virtually identically shaped smooth curves in several species; therefore, the laws being formulated have great generality. The procedure is a variant of "synthesis by model"—our simplified laboratory model, derived from animals, works when applied to humans in the real world. Skinner's method thus applies Francis Bacon's (1620) dictum that we should engage in "experiments of fruit" as well as "experiments of light"—making useful working application of the scientific laws we are formulating.

Bacon also suggested that we draw up "tables of discovery" describing the relationships we have worked out. By classifying these relationships, similar within category and different between categories, fundamental generalities governing each category should leap to the eye and mind, and valuable data will be gathered in the process. This nonspeculative form of data gathering is an empirical approach to experiment—it is concrete, not abstract; therefore, no one can dispute the facts generated by it. Such "botanizing" of behavior has great value when applied simultaneously over many species of animals, as in comparative physiology or taxonomic ethology. However, because taxonomy has not been explicit in the operant approach (but see Skinner, 1966), some behaviorally oriented workers become impatient with it and suspect its practitioners of application of the operant method in trivial instances. Because it is still in its early stages, the separate categories of operant analysis of behavior are not yet clearly apparent, so many do not see its theoretical value. Also, because operant terminology is not widely used, many psychologists do not see how the operant "school" adds more than simple technology for providing stable behavioral base lines. But operant methods work, so their application becomes more widespread.

THE OPERANT AS A CRITERION FOR MOTIVATION

In an earlier discussion of this subject (Teitelbaum, 1966), I pointed out:

> When we speak of purposive acts in humans, we mean behavior that is directed toward a goal and is accompanied by a corresponding motivation to obtain that goal. The essential quality is the motivational state—the physiological state of events that corresponds to the urge to perform a particular act, to obtain a certain object, or to produce a desired outcome. If we could be sure that such a state exists in animals during a given act, we could justifiably call that act motivated behavior.
>
> Clearly, if the response is a completely automatic consequence of the stimulus, we cannot speak of motivation. As long as a fixed built-in relation exists between a stimulus and a response, we have no justification for inferring the

additional existence of a motivational state underlying that response to the stimulus. Such a state may exist, but we can have no positive proof of it. (p. 566)

By definition, therefore, a reflex excludes motivation. It is unconscious, unlearned, and involuntary (Skinner, 1931). To infer motivation we must break the fixed reflex connection between stimulus and response. By its very nature, the operant appears to do so.

In effect, in any operant situation, the stimulus, the response and the reinforcement are completely arbitrary and interchangeable. No one of them bears any biologically built-in fixed connection to the others. We arrange the experimental situation so that the response produces the reward and the animal learns the connection between them. Once having learned this relationship, the animal reveals its motivation by the fact that it works to obtain the reinforcement. This is what all operant conditioning situations have in common: the animal's motivation to obtain the reinforcement . . . If an operant occurs, motivation exists. (p. 567)

Thus by using learning to break the fixed reflex connection between stimulus and response, Skinner created an emergent unit of behavior—the operant—which could be experimentally isolated, whose laws could be studied in their own right, and which could serve as the prototype of all learned motivated behavior. Because the degree of environmental control over the operant in the Skinner box is so great, the close S–R correlation is preserved and, with it, the scientific power of the laws describing it. Indeed, to avoid the pitfalls of speculation and to eliminate the "idols of the marketplace" described by Francis Bacon (1620) (the tendency to use words with surplus meanings to describe simpler phenomena), Skinner preferred to eliminate entirely such constructs as motivation and awareness. The operant embodies them in clear-cut S–R relations, and a categorization of those relationships should form an adequate scientific basis for the control of operant behavior.

PUZZLING OPERANTS

As described above, the laws of the operant are remarkably well suited for application to humans (Millenson, 1967) and have been highly successful when applied to human learning and motivation. However, both in the laboratory, and in applied situations, work on animals has continued apace, and, with increasing frequency, seemingly paradoxical phenomena are being demonstrated. Early reports of the "misbehavior of organisms" came from Breland and Breland (1961, 1966), students of Skinner who applied operant methods to the training of a wide variety of animals in situations designed to entertain the public. Chickens were taught to swing a bat to hit a ball out onto a "playing field," raccoons or pigs to "save" wooden coins or dollar bills in piggy banks, whales or porpoises to play with rubber balls, and so on. However, particularly as such animals became better and better trained, their performance very often deteriorated. Chickens would run out onto the "playing field" to chase the baseball they had just hit with a bat; raccoons would "wash" their coins instead of dropping them in the box, and pigs would root and toss their dollars rather than depositing them in the piggy bank. In all these instances, the interfering behavior delayed the reinforcement, sometimes to the point where the animals underwent serious weight loss, since the conditioned acts were their sole means of obtaining food.

Hineline and Rachlin (1969) pointed out that in many circumstances there is great difficulty involved in training a pigeon to peck a key to avoid electric shock, though it could readily learn to do so for food. Pigeon key pecking seemed still more perplexing when Brown and Jenkins (1968) demonstrated that contingent reinforcement with food was not necessary to train a pigeon to peck an illuminated key—merely using the key to signal the opportunity to eat food at brief intervals was sufficient to induce them to peck the key light, independent of the reinforcement, at very high rates. One might conceive of such "autoshaping" as an example of "superstitious" responding (Skinner, 1948b), but the work of Williams and Williams (1969) on "negative autoshaping" (where a pigeon will learn and continue such key pecking even when each response actually prevents the reinforcement) makes this less tenable. (However, for evidence of operant control of autoshaped behavior, see Barrera, 1974.) These behaviors seem to fit in the operant category but can be extremely difficult to shape, occur without reinforcement, despite reinforcement, or deteriorate rather than improve with training.

Puzzling phenomena are being found in other types of learning situations. When a rat feels sick after poisoning or exposure to X-rays, it will develop an aversion for a novel taste (such as saccharin) but does not link the illness to other stimuli such as lights or sounds, which were equally available for association

(Garcia & Koelling, 1966). However, in the identical situation, if the negative reinforcement is the pain of electric shock, the light or sound becomes the danger signal, whereas the novel taste is ignored. So taste for a rat seems physiologically tied to the nausea and malaise of poisoning and X-ray exposure, but lights, sound, and locations seem linked to the peripheral pain caused by electric shock. More visual species, such as birds, link the sickness of poisoning to the color of a nutrient solution rather than to its taste (Wilcoxon, Dragoin, & Kral, 1971).

Taste aversion learning is special in other ways as well. It seems far more powerful than the instrumental learning which has served as the paradigm of conditioning for so many years. In traditional conditioning experiments, an association between an arbitrary stimulus and the sight of food can be formed only if they occur virtually simultaneously. If there is more than a few seconds' delay, it is very difficult to produce a learned linkage between them. Rats, however, can associate sickness with a novel taste, even if the taste occurred as much as 12 hours earlier (Smith & Roll, 1967). (Histamine secreted by the body in reaction to X-ray exposure seems to be involved in such learning and may be related to these powerful effects—Levy, Carroll, Smith, & Hofer, 1974.)

To ethologically oriented workers, such phenomena indicate that it may be premature to seek general laws of learning, including those of the operant. They suggest that a deceptive generality may result when work is limited to too few species (Beach, 1950; Bolles, 1970; Rozin & Kalat, 1971; Seligman & Hager, 1972; Shettleworth, 1972; Tinbergen, 1951). For some species the innate connections between certain stimuli and responses may be too reflexive to serve in operant behavior. They involve stimulus-bound, nonarbitrary, and noninhibitable acts. Yet in an operant paradigm the probability of their occurrence can often be manipulated by reinforcement contingencies. Are they operants? If so, what is wrong with our concept of operants? If not, what are they, and why do many of them often seem to obey the laws of reinforcement?

SIMILAR PUZZLES IN MOTIVATED BEHAVIOR

As described above, an operant act is proof of the existence of motivation—if a completely arbitrary operant occurs, motivation exists. If we are running into difficulties with our conception of the operant, the same must be true of our concept of motivation. By examining motivation, we may gain greater insight into operant behavior.

Since the fundamental work of W. R. Hess (1932, 1954), it has been known that electrical stimulation of the brain of an unanesthetized animal can elicit instinctive behavior patterns such as mating, feeding, drinking, or fighting. A sated rat stimulated through implanted electrodes in the lateral hypothalamus will eat large quantities of food (Hoebel, 1971). If this is done every day, the rat will overeat and even become obese (Steinbaum & Miller, 1965). Such an animal will learn a new operant or perform a previously learned one (e.g., running a maze or pressing a bar to get food) during stimulation, thus supporting the idea that this is truly motivated behavior, not merely some kind of motor automatism (such as chewing), where the ingestion of food is an accidental by-product of the behavior, rather than a desired outcome (Coons, Levak, & Miller, 1965; Mendelson & Chorover, 1965; Miller, 1971). The same is true of thirst (Andersson & Wyrwicka, 1957) and other species-typical behaviors (Roberts, 1970).

However, a fundamental problem in our conception of motivated behavior has been identified in the work of John Flynn and his colleagues (e.g., Flynn, 1973). They implanted electrodes in the lateral hypothalamus of cats. Many normal cats do not ordinarily kill rats. However, when stimulated in the lateral hypothalamus, such cats chase and strike or bite a rat, usually killing it if the current is left on. Two forms of such attack were seen. One was accompanied by a display of rage (retraction of the lips, exposure of the canine teeth, piloerection and arching of the back, hissing, growling, pupillodilation—the typical "Halloween cat"). In the other form, which Flynn and co-workers called the "quiet biting attack," the cat moved swiftly about the cage with its nose low to the ground, back somewhat arched, and hair slightly on end, and usually went directly to the rat and bit it viciously. In the absence of an attack object, neither form of directed attack would occur. Therefore, stimuli provided by the rat are necessary before electrical stimulation can evoke attack behavior. What are these stimuli?

In their early studies, Flynn and his colleagues took a Sherringtonian approach to this problem. The final component in the attack sequence is the killing bite. Which stimuli elicit it? They restrained the intact cat so that the animal could lunge, or turn its head and bite, but could not otherwise walk around. Without hypothalamic stimulation, touch around the mouth and on the lips evoked no response. However, during electrical stimulation, touch around the

Fig. 2. (Left) The cat's muzzle. (Center) Maximum extent of the maxillary sensory field for head-orienting responses during relatively intense hypothalamic stimulation. A similar mandibular field has not yet been mapped in detail. (Right) Maximum extent of the sensory field for the jaw-opening response during relatively intense stimulation. (From MacDonnell & Flynn, 1966a. © 1966 by the American Association for the Advancement of Science.)

mouth, on the side contralateral to the stimulation, evoked head turning toward the stimulus (see Figure 2). When the lips contacted the stimulus, mouth opening and biting occurred. Increasing the strength of hypothalamic stimulation increased the extent of the sensory field around the mouth and on the lips from which the response could be evoked (MacDonnell & Flynn, 1966a). Conversely, if these sensory fields were denervated by section of the appropriate branches of the trigeminal nerve, touch stimuli were no longer effective in evoking head turning, mouth opening, and biting, but electrical lateral hypothalamic stimulation could still evoke attack: the cat pounced on the rat and lowered its head for the killing bite—but then did not open its mouth when it contacted the rat—"kissing" rather than biting. The cat could open its mouth (it did so normally when eating food spontaneously), but not when stimulated to attack and kill (MacDonnell & Flynn, 1966b).

Implicit in this finding is a paradox with potentially important implications for our thinking about motivated behavior. On the one hand, if the operant is a learned arbitrary act, its occurrence depends upon (1) the memory of past response-reinforcement contingencies, (2) the central motivated state which makes that outcome reinforcing, and (3) the expectation that the operant will continue to produce the reinforcing stimulus. A cat is motivated to kill a rat if the cat will press a lever or run a maze to be presented with a rat which it then kills (Roberts & Kiess, 1964).

On the other hand, we can take an ethological view of a cat's rat killing. We can assume that there are specific fixed action patterns built into the cat's nervous system. They are selectively potentiated by hormonal or other internal states and released by particular, somewhat complex stimuli, called sign stimuli. Each S–R fixed action pattern forms a segment in a chain of behavior which we call the *instinctive act*. To account for rat killing by a cat, we assume that (1) the sight of the rat (its color, small size, and movement) and its smell activates stalking behavior; (2) when close to the rat, the cat is stimulated to pounce, to swipe at the rat with its paws, and to lower its head for the killing bite; (3) when the cat's whiskers or muzzle contact the rat's fur or skin, its head turns and brings the lips into contact; (4) touch on the lips elicits mouth opening; and (5) touch and taste stimulation of the mouth and tongue evoke biting and swallowing.

This description dovetails very well with the findings of Flynn and co-workers described above and their additional work on the releasing effects of visual and other stimuli on the components of electrically evoked attack (Bandler & Flynn, 1972; Flynn, Edwards, & Bandler, 1971). The ethological view is strongly supported in studies of birds and fish in which removal of a stimulus in the S–R chain aborts the instinctive behavior pattern (Tinbergen, 1951).

But this view implies that the instinctive act is not outcome-dependent. The eliciting stimulus, not the reinforcement, determines the response. How can we reconcile this with our view that rat killing by a cat *is* outcome-dependent?

Perhaps electrically evoked attack is not controlled by all the variables controlling rat killing in a normal cat. Electrically evoked eating in rats seems more stimulus-bound and more stereotyped than normal hunger (Valenstein, 1973; Valenstein, Cox, & Kakolewski, 1968). If this is correct and if normal rat killing is determined by the reinforcement rather than the sign stimulus, then an unstimulated cat killing spontaneously, even with denervated mouth and lips, should open its mouth, bite, and kill a rat when hungry or when provoked to rage by pain. This experiment is theoretically very important and should be carried out.

Suppose that, in the trigeminal-sectioned cat killing a rat spontaneously, the killing kiss rather than a bite occurs. Does this mean that killing is not motivated—i.e., not outcome-dependent? Not necessarily—our view of the reinforcement may have been incorrect. Perhaps each sign stimulus in the ethological chain may be reinforcing. Part of its releasing action, particularly in the experienced animal, may be due to the memory of the reinforcement provided by that stimulus in the past. This means that such an animal should press a lever to gain the opportunity to swipe at a rat, to pounce on it, or merely to see and chase it. In fish, for instance, sign stimuli can be reinforcers. A Siamese fighting fish will learn to press a lever for the mere sight of another fighting fish (Thompson, 1963). In their mating dance, a male stickleback will perform an operant for the opportunity to see a receptive female whom he then courts (Sevenster, 1973). There is still another way of reconciling sign stimuli with reinforcement, but it must wait till we consider the evidence on motivation as revealed during recovery from brain damage.

RECOVERY FROM LATERAL HYPOTHALAMIC LESIONS

As we have seen from the work of MacDonnell and Flynn (1966a), electrical stimulation in the lateral hypothalamus opens peripheral sensory fields around the mouth whose stimulation then yields head orientation and biting, reflexive components of the cat's instinctive attack pattern. Increasing the intensity of the stimulation expands the fields. Does lateral hypothalamic damage shrink such fields and prevent normally effective stimuli from acting on them? The lateral hypothalamus is involved not only in attack, but also in eating. Does the lateral hypothalamic syndrome of aphagia and adipsia depend, in part, on loss of responsiveness to sensory stimuli?

In order to answer these questions, Marshall, Turner, and Teitelbaum (1971) applied a series of simple neurological tests to normal rats. A normal rat investigates a stimulus by orienting its head toward it. This natural response was used to determine the responsivity of rats before and after lateral hypothalamic damage. For example, to test vision on each side of the body, a 2-in. square (5 × 5 cm) piece of white or yellow cardboard was moved in front of each eye. Normal rats typically turn their heads toward this visual stimulus. To test olfaction, they looked for head orientation to a ¼-in. cube of chocolate held in forceps or to a cotton swab soaked in Mennen shaving lotion (both of which elicited approach) or to an ammonia-soaked swab (which elicited approach followed by turning the head away).

In an exact converse of the results of MacDonnell and Flynn (1966a), damaging the lateral hypothalamus on one side profoundly impaired the rat's ability to orient to stimuli on the side contralateral to that of the lesion (see Figure 3). Rats with unilateral lesions initially showed no orientation to contralateral visual, olfactory, whisker-touch, or somatosensory stimulation, whereas they responded promptly to the same stimuli presented ipsilaterally. Rats with bilateral lesions showed impaired responsivity to sensory stimuli on either side.

Although the precise nature of such sensory neglect

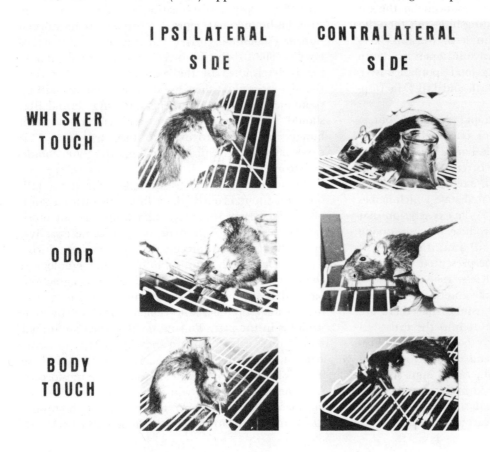

Fig. 3. A rat with unilateral (right) lateral hypothalamic damage shows precise head orientation and biting to various kinds of stimuli (whisker touch, odor, body touch) on the ipsilateral side (pictures at left) while neglecting the same stimuli presented contralaterally (pictures at right). (From Marshall, Turner, & Teitelbaum, 1971. © 1971 by the American Association for the Advancement of Science.)

needs further behavioral analysis (see Turner, 1973), several observations suggest that the orientation impairment is neither a total motor paralysis nor an inability to sense the stimuli. In normal grooming, a rat usually starts by grooming its face and head, turns and grooms one side and flank, and terminates the sequence by grooming the opposite side and flank. Thus during normal grooming the rat's head is turned and oriented to one or the other side side just as it is during normal orientation to tactile stimuli from that side. After unilateral lateral hypothalamic damage, the rat grooms first the ipsilateral, then the contralateral side of the body. However, even seconds after grooming the side contralateral to the lesion, the rat ignores tactile stimuli to that side and fails to turn toward them. Such failure to respond to stimuli, even though the animal can perform the necessary head movements, suggests that the deficit is more sensory than motor. However, the deficit does not resemble deafferentation, because autonomic (respiratory changes) and skeletal reflex (eye closure, tooth chattering) behaviors often occurred when a stimulus was presented on the contralateral side. The deficit seems to be more of an inability on the rat's part to integrate the sensory information with the adaptive motor patterns involved in orienting to a stimulus (Marshall & Teitelbaum, 1974; Turner, 1973).

Such sensory neglect can drastically affect the instinctive behavior patterns involved in eating, drinking, and attack. Bilateral lateral hypothalamic lesions produced total aphagia and adipsia lasting as long as 9 days, followed by the usual stages of recovery. Analysis of the recovery of orientation to sensory stimuli showed that the transition from Stage I (complete aphagia) to Stage II (accepting only highly palatable foods) occurred on the same day or shortly after direct head orientation to olfactory stimuli and whisker touch first appeared. Rats with unilateral lesions that were tested for side preference in feeding generally took more food from the container located in the ipsilateral field, though preoperatively no such preference had existed. Similarly, after unilateral lateral hypothalamic lesions, rats that normally killed mice ignored the mouse when it was in the contralateral field. However, as soon as the mouse moved across the midline into the ipsilateral field, the rats showed oriented biting attack.

In summary, the evidence from electrical stimulation or ablation strongly suggests that the role of the lateral hypothalamus in the control of motivated behavior is at least in part due to its ability to potentiate the action of peripheral stimuli in eliciting the fixed instinctive action patterns involved in eating, drink-

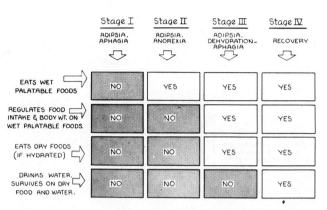

Fig. 4. Stages of recovery seen in the lateral hypothalamic syndrome. (The critical behavioral events which define the stages are listed on the left.) (From Teitelbaum & Epstein, 1962.)

ing, or attack. But where does the operant fit into this picture?

PARALLEL BETWEEN RECOVERY AND DEVELOPMENT IN THE LATERAL HYPOTHALAMIC SYNDROME

Some insight into the role of the operant comes from the analysis of the stages of recovery from the aphagia and adipsia that result from bilateral lateral hypothalamic damage. The pattern of behavioral recovery is summarized diagrammatically in Figure 4. (For a detailed analysis of the homeostatic mechanisms in the lateral hypothalamic syndrome, see Epstein, 1971.) The striking fact about this syndrome is that every lateral hypothalamic animal shows the same sequence of recovery. Depending on the lesion size and accuracy of placement, animals recover more or less rapidly. Also, although they may start their recovery at any point in the sequence, the progression from that point follows an invariable pattern. Therefore, the pattern of recovery could indicate a basic process of neural reorganization.

A newborn suckling rat ingests milk but refuses water. At weaning, although they eat dry food and drink water, infants still do not respond fully to dehydration (Adolph, 1957; Heller, 1947, 1951; Krček & Krčeková, 1957). This resembles some of the symptoms seen during the various stages of recovery of food and water regulation in the adult rat after lateral hypothalamic damage (Teitelbaum & Epstein, 1962). In a sense the lateral hypothalamic rat during part of its recovery is like an infant rat.

If a parallel exists between adult recovery and infant development, each stage in recovery from the

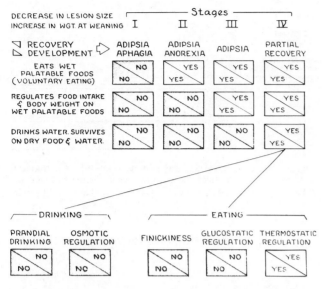

Fig. 5. Comparison of the development of eating and drinking in rats' infancy and their recovery after hypothalamic lesion in adult. (The upper right half of each block represents the recovering lateral hypothalamic rat, and the lower left half the growing thyroidectomized or starvation-stunted rats. Uniform coloring in each full block indicates similar responses in recovery and development.) (From Teitelbaum, Cheng, & Rozin, 1969a.)

lateral hypothalamic syndrome should be reflected in proper sequence during development in infancy. To study this in detail, we slowed down the course of normal development by thyroidectomizing infant rats at birth or shortly thereafter and studied their regulatory capacity at the normal weaning age of 21 days (Teitelbaum, Cheng, & Rozin, 1969a, 1969b).

At that age, thyroidectomized weanling rats displayed every stage of the lateral hypothalamic syndrome. If greatly retarded in development (as reflected in their body weights at weaning), some were completely aphagic and adipsic when offered wet palatable foods or ordinary food and water. Others, more fully developed at weaning, accepted wet palatable foods but did not eat enough to maintain their weight. If this stage lasted too long, they died. Other weanlings, even less retarded, gained weight and regulated their caloric intake of a liquid diet (they at least doubled their volume intake when the caloric density was one-third as great), but were still adipsic and would have died (some did die) when offered only dry food and water. Finally, the least retarded weanlings accepted dry food and water, but drank only when they ate; like recovered adult rats, they were prandial drinkers and did not drink in response to body dehydration.

They were finicky, and although they ate more in the cold they did not eat more in response to glucoprivation. As shown in Figure 5, depending on the degree of retardation, every stage of the adult lateral hypothalamic syndrome was seen in thyroidectomized rats at weaning.

In a separate experiment (Cheng, Rozin, & Teitelbaum, 1971), we severely starved neonatal rats throughout the suckling period by limiting their access to the mother. Control litters with unlimited access to their mother developed normally. The starvation-retarded runts, when tested at weaning (21 days of age), showed every stage of the lateral hypothalamic syndrome. Like the thyroidectomized infants, if they survived they progressed through the various stages as they developed.

One may immediately object to drawing a parallel between recovery from lateral hypothalamic damage and stages of development of the regulation of food and water intake in infancy. After all, lateral hypothalamic animals die of starvation and thirst, whereas infants do not. But we do not ask newborn infants to eat like adults—they nurse at the breast until they can be weaned. It follows that adult lateral hypothalamic animals should nurse like infants, and, without any other maintenance, should be able to keep themselves alive until they recover additional regulatory capacities. Figure 6 shows such an experiment. Merely by offering repeated access to a substitute mother (a milk bottle with a modified drinking spout, provided at frequent intervals day and night), Dr. Cheng (un-

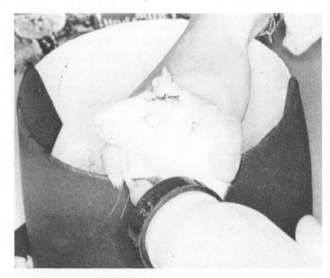

Fig. 6. A lateral hypothalamic adult rat, otherwise totally aphagic for nine days, nurses reflexively at a milk-containing baby bottle (with modified nipple). Frequent feedings allowed it to ingest sufficient quantities to stay alive and recover to the anorexic stage.

published results) showed that an otherwise completely aphagic and adipsic adult lateral hypothalamic rat in Stage I was able to ingest sufficient quantities to keep itself alive for 9 days. Then it progressed to Stage II; i.e., it ate wet palatable baby foods from a dish. Thus otherwise aphagic adult animals, like infants, can ingest sufficient food to stay alive by nursing reflexively.

STAGES OF RECOVERY AND DEVELOPMENT OF THE HUMAN GRASP

If the parallel between adult recovery and infant development emerged from the study of another brain system, independent of feeding and drinking, one could be more sure of its validity. From work on a different species and on a different brain system, a very similar parallel has independently been demonstrated. T. E. Twitchell studied the recovery of movement following cerebral hemiplegia in human patients. His work stemmed from the earlier observation of Seyffarth and Denny-Brown (1948), who pointed out that several types of reflexive movements could be elicited from a paralyzed limb although the limb could not be used for voluntary movement. In the hand, for instance, they identified three types of reflexive grasping—the traction response, the true grasp, and the instinctive grasp reaction. In studying the recovery of stroke patients, Twitchell (1951) discovered that these grasping automatisms could always be identified and that they represented distinct sequential stages in the recovery of voluntary control of movement.

In subsequent studies, Twitchell (1965, 1969, 1970) found that very similar stages to those seen in recovery from hemiplegia in adults can be demonstrated in the normal development of voluntary control of grasping in newborn infants (Figure 7). In a human system as well as in the rat, adult recovery recapitulates infantile ontogeny.

TRANSFORMATION OF SENSORY CONTROL OVER AN APPROACH RESPONSE

The concept of stages of sensory control over a response is implicit in the parallel between recovery and development. During recovery of the grasp, spinal proprioceptive mechanisms in the form of tendon jerks and increased stretch reflexes (spasticity) occur first. These are modified by tonic neck and vestibular body-righting reflexes into the traction response. The recovery process then proceeds to the next stage, in which flexion of the fingers can be obtained reflexively by a distally moving tactile stimulus to the medial palm. This is the true grasp reflex. In a sense, as Twitchell (1951) points out, the tactile grasp reflex facilitates the proprioceptive grasp (the traction response). Eventually, the sight of a stimulus is enough to cause the hand to reach out and grasp it (Twitchell, 1970). Presumably, with sufficient recovery, true "operant" use of the hand returns.

The sequence of development and recovery of sensory controls over an approach reaction may be more general than is now suspected. For instance, a similar sequence seems to govern the gaping response of the newborn thrush. Immediately after hatching, the stimulus modalities that appear to elicit the gape are proprioceptive and vestibular; the chicks gape when the parent bird alights on the nest, which shakes the head and body of each chick. The gape is directed vertically upward (vestibular control), inde-

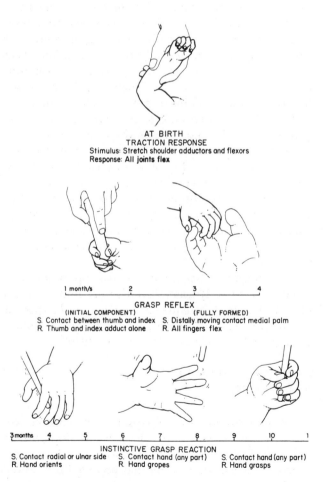

Fig. 7. Evolution of the automatic grasping responses of infants. (Twitchell, 1965.)

Fig. 8. Nestling thrushes gaping upward in response to visual stimulus but not directed by it. (From Tinbergen, 1951. By permission of Oxford University Press.)

pendent of the position of the parent bird. Touching the side of the face near the mouth also elicits the gape, which is still directed upward. Later, the sight of the parent bird (or the approaching hand of the experimenter—see Figure 8) elicits gaping, but it is still directed upward. Finally, the gape is directed toward the visual stimulus (visual control now not only triggers the response but also guides its orientation—Tinbergen & Kuenen, 1939). Although Tinbergen and Kuenen did not investigate it, it is possible that, still later, operant gaping as an emitted response would develop in such birds. If so, then, as in recovering hemiplegic humans and developing normal infant rats, the end result of such a sequential transformation of control of a reaction pattern would be voluntary or self-initiated action—an operant response. If there is generality in the sequence of sensory transformation of a reaction pattern, we may have a beginning insight into a mechanism of transformation of reflexes into operants during infant development or adult recovery of function.

STAGES OF RECOVERY AND DEVELOPMENT OF LEARNED BEHAVIOR

If these concepts apply to the study of operant behavior, we should be able to demonstrate stages of integration of learned responses during recovery from brain damage and in early infantile development. For instance, Glavcheva, Rozkowska, and Fonberg (1970) studied the lateral hypothalamic syndrome in dogs. As in other animals, such lesions produce aphagia and adipsia with eventual recovery. Operant responding for food after such lesions also disappears and eventually recovers (Rodgers, Epstein, & Teitelbaum, 1965). When a normal dog swallows food, gastric contractions are inhibited and the stomach relaxes. This is its action as an unconditional stimulus. After training sessions presenting the sound of a metronome for 50–60 sec preceding the presentation of food, the sound of the metronome alone can produce stomach relaxation and inhibition of motility. After bilateral lateral hypothalamic damage, Glavcheva et al., showed that such conditioning is completely abolished. Stages of recovery of conditioning can then be demonstrated. At first, there is stomach atonia—a complete loss of tonus and spontaneous hunger contractions. This stage generally corresponded to complete aphagia or anorexia with adipsia. Then a stage of rhythmic automatic gastric contractions appears, but the stomach still seemed completely cut off from influence by the rest of the nervous system—the unconditioned relaxation effect of food in the stomach and the conditioned effect of the sound were both absent. In the next stage of recovery of control of gastric motility, the unconditioned relaxation effect of food reappeared, but the conditioned stimulus (sound) was still ineffective. Finally, in the last stage, the conditioned stimulus regained its effectiveness.

It would be interesting to investigate, both in recovering lateral hypothalamic dogs and in newborn puppies, whether there may be a similar sequence of stages of conditionability of sensory control over gastric motility (kinesthetic, vestibular, touch, and vision). Since salivary conditioning is also impaired after lateral hypothalamic damage (Rozkowska & Fonberg, 1972), the sequence of recovery and development of its conditioned sensory control should be investigated as well.

It is suggestive (see Table 1), as support for such a sequence, that Russian investigators find a rather similar, immutable sequence of sense modalities in the development of the capacity for Pavlovian conditioning in human infants (Kasatkin, 1960).

STAGES OF ENCEPHALIZATION OF THE OPERANT

To understand any behavioral phenomenon, we must view it as we would a stage of development or recovery. These only make sense as a transformation from the stage of integration that preceded it (a lower level of encephalization) toward a higher level of integration. Like the nervous system whose action it re-

Philip Teitelbaum

Table 1 Developmental Sequence of Conditionability as a Function of Type of Conditional Stimulus

SENSORY ANALYZERS

SIMPLE CONDITIONED RESPONSE	Vestibular	Auditory	Tactile	Olfactory	Taste	Visual
	(e.g., change of body position)	(e.g., complex 65-db tone)	(e.g., tickle, sole of foot)	(e.g., oil of roses or lavender)	(e.g., 5% sugar solution)	(e.g., colored light)
First appearance	8d	15d to 24d	28d	28d	35d	40d
Semistable response	15d	40d	45d	45d	45d	2m
100% stable response	20–24d to 1m	35d to 2 m	2m	2m	2.5m	3m
SIMPLE DISCRIMINATION						
	(e.g., up–down from sideways)	(e.g., 1 octave higher or lower from CS+)	(e.g., right from left foot)	(e.g., roses from lavender)	(e.g., 1% from 5% solutions)	(e.g., red from green or blue)
First appearance	1m	2m	2m	2m	2.5m	3m
Semistable response	1.5m	2.5m	2.5m	2.5m	3m	3.5m
100% stable response	2m	3m	3m	3m	3m	3.5m

NOTE: *Ages appear as days (d) or months (m) (Kasatkin, 1960).*
Reprinted with permission of Macmillan Publishing Co., Inc. from *Infancy and Early Childhood*, Y. Brackbill (ed.). © 1967 by the Free Press, a Division of the Macmillan Company.

flects, behavior is a hierarchically organized structure.

This point of view may help resolve some of the apparent paradoxes in behavior which now exist. A striking example of such a resolution comes from the study of sexual behavior (Beach, 1966). Adult female rodents in estrus show lordosis when stroked around the flank or genital region. This has long been used as a criterion of adult sexual receptivity. It was therefore extremely surprising to discover that newborn guinea pigs (male or female) displayed such lordosis in the first few hours, or even for some days, after birth. Was this due to the surge of female estrual hormones in the mother that occurs at parturition? No—pups born of mothers ovariectomized midway through their pregnancy showed the same lordosis when stroked (Boling, Blandau, Wilson, & Young, 1939). Careful behavioral analysis revealed that in infant guinea pigs, lordosis is the basic posture assumed reflexly during urination evoked by the mother's licking of the infant's genital region as it stands and nurses underneath her. Indeed, such tactile stimulation is necessary for survival in infancy (Beach, 1966), because, as in spinal adult animals shortly after surgery, bladder distension does not produce relaxation of the urinary sphincter. With recovery from spinal shock in the adult, such control by distension returns. Apparently, in the newborn infant the tactile lordosis reflex promotes urination. Later in development, this reflex disappears and bladder distension becomes sufficient to produce urination. In the adult female, estrus hormones reinstate the lordosis reflex. Just as hypothalamic stimulation involved in killing opens and expands tactile sensory fields around the mouth (MacDonnell & Flynn, 1966a), estrual hormones elicit lordosis through tactile sensory fields around the genitals (Komisaruk, Adler, & Hutchison, 1972). Therefore, the reappearance of infantile reflexes can occur not only in brain damage, but also in the normal action of hormones which produce instinctive behavior.

Other instinctive behavior patterns go through successive levels of ontogenetic transformation of nervous control. Each stage of transformation in the hierarchy allows new controls to modify the action of the lower stage of integration. For instance, as McGinty (1971) has pointed out (see Figure 9), the various stages of sleep may be conceived of as separate stages of encephalization of the sleep system. It is well known that

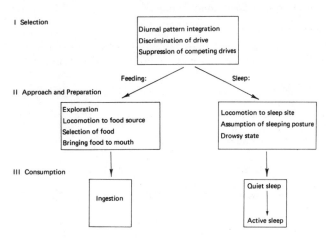

Fig. 9. Appetitive behavior chain in the adult. (From McGinty, 1971.)

newborn infants are capable mainly of rapid eye movement (REM) sleep. This seems a relatively reflexive, obligatory form of sleep: the infant has little control over it (it cannot inhibit sleep) and lapses readily into it when its stomach is full and it is not cold or wet. When its nervous system matures, slow-wave sleep emerges as a separate stage with consequent inhibition of the amount of REM sleep. (In the adult decorticate animal, REM represents about 40 percent of total sleep, versus about 20 percent for a normal cat—Jouvet, 1962; and personal communication.) It is as though each higher stage of encephalization limits access to the less encephalized stage preceding it in ontogeny. This may be adaptive: the more reflexive form of sleep (REM) is suppressed and partially replaced by slow-wave sleep which in turn can be more readily inhibited, thus allowing more opportunity for adaptive waking behavior.

When the normal adult animal goes to sleep, it goes through a fixed sequence of stages—it must enter slow-wave sleep before it can proceed to the stage of REM sleep. Perhaps, therefore, not only can slow-wave sleep inhibit REM, but also during each normal bout of adult sleep, slow-wave sleep may serve as a selective facilitating mechanism in the transition from waking to REM sleep. This resembles the way the true grasp allows touch to act as a facilitator in the release of the more infantile proprioceptive grasp—the traction response (Twitchell, 1951, 1970).

The above example of sleep behavior is important because it suggests that in adult behavior, the normal act of going to sleep involves a rapid, reversible deencephalization of function: sleep, as an instinctive behavior pattern proceeds from the appetitive behavior patterns involved in searching for an appropriate

place, circling and curling up, lowering the head, closing the eyes, etc., and progresses through successive stages to the consummatory act—the achievement of REM sleep. Like food and water intake, the amount of REM appears to be regulated homeostatically; e.g., after deprivation of REM, more of it occurs (is consumed?) when free access is once again possible (Dement, Henry, Cohen, & Ferguson, 1967).

Perhaps every adult motivated behavior pattern proceeds in a similar sequence from operant and Pavlovian approach behavior to the reflex consummatory act. In the study of instinctive behavior, ethologists have roughly distinguished such levels of nervous control by referring to appetitive versus consummatory behavior (Tinbergen, 1951). Similarly, in man, the appetitive act of reaching for food is more operant in its character (less stereotyped, more subject to willed inhibition) than is a later act in the chain—reflexive chewing—and much more so than swallowing, which is completely reflexive once the food has reached a point far enough back in the mouth. Each behavioral event is followed by the next more automatic one until the final molecule-to-molecule match is achieved (Breland & Breland, 1966).

Operant behavior may have a similar hierarchical structure, built up by successive levels of transformation in development. The adult operant may be viewed as the initial, most arbitrary (learned) part of an approach sequence toward a fixed consummatory act. During that sequence, the behavior becomes progressively deencephalized (more stimulus-bound, less subject to willed inhibition), culminating in reflexive consummatory behavior.

Of what use is it to think this way if the sequence reels itself off so quickly in an operant act that we cannot isolate its parts? In a way, this is like the problem faced by George Wald in isolating the transition states in the transformation of rhodopsin to vitamin A (Wald, 1968). Lumi-rhodopsin and meta-rhodopsin were isolated by literally freezing the reaction—at a temperature below $-40°$C, the reaction only proceeded to lumi-rhodopsin. Gradual warming allowed it to proceed to meta-rhodopsin and eventually to reach its final transformation state—vitamin A plus opsin. In like manner, stages of encephalization of behavior can be "frozen" in recovery after brain damage or in normal development in infancy. Starvation or thyroidectomy in infancy can slow the development process still further.

Is it possible to reveal such stages during normal motivated acts, where, if they exist, they are so fleeting and evanescent that we cannot now isolate them? Perhaps the apparent errors in operant behavior can help to reveal the stages of transformation. In the ethological study of instinct, "mistakes" in apparently purposive acts are useful diagnostic indicators. For instance, when rolling its egg back into the nest, the greylag goose must complete the head-withdrawal pattern even if the egg slips out from under its beak during the act (Tinbergen, 1951). To the ethologist this proves that egg rolling is a fixed, built-in, instinctive action pattern rather than an outcome-determined operant. Likewise, the fixed response of a fish or a bird to a dummy model defines the existence of a sign stimulus and proves that the act it releases is an instinctive, rather than learned, pattern. As we have seen, such "errors" in adult mammalian behavior (called abnormalities) are often diagnostic of damage to the central nervous system. In a similar way, what seem today like paradoxes in learned behavior may turn out to be diagnostic indicators of the level of encephalization of that behavior.

SUMMARY AND CONCLUSIONS: LEVELS OF OPERANT BEHAVIOR

As discussed earlier, several phenomena in operant behavior (the "misbehavior" of organisms, negative automaintenance, etc.) may seem puzzling because we assume the operant to be an indivisible, emergent unit, with laws different from those governing the simpler subcomponents of behavior (reflex, instinctive fixed action pattern). In its idealized form, perhaps best expressed in human behavior, it is the very antithesis of a reflex. A reflex is an unconscious, unlearned, involuntary, built-in fixed response to a particular kind of stimulus. As idealized, the operant is a conscious arbitrary act which, through learning, has become associated with an arbitrary stimulus and whose frequency is maintained by an arbitrary reinforcement. In principle, all stimuli, all operants, and all reinforcements are interchangeable because no one of them bears any biologically built-in connection to the others.

In the laboratory, or in real life, when reinforcement is used to shape behavior, paradoxes may appear when one or more of these idealized assumptions is violated. As Skinner (1938) pointed out, one source of error may arise in the act chosen as the operant. Perhaps, especially in lower animals like pigeons and rats, the operants usually used to study the laws of reinforcement are not as arbitrary as we have thought. In autoshaping, orienting toward the key is more readily influenced by food reinforcement than is the act of pecking it (Wessells, 1974). Pecking for food reward may be very closely tied physiologically to the act of eating and may not be very arbitrary at all (Moore, 1973). Pressing a bar for a rat may be an act borrowed from some other instinctive pattern, but by the power of reinforcement or through Pavlovian conditioning may be shaped up to act as the initial approach segment of the chain leading to the consumption of food or water. A lighted key that signals food or water may become a sign stimulus releasing the consummatory act of pecking in a pigeon, thus yielding some of the phenomena of autoshaping (Jenkins & Moore, 1973).

Even if a given act satisfies the criteria of interchangeability that assure its arbitrariness at the beginning of training (in other words, if the act is so highly encephalized that it bears little resemblance to a reflex), it may become rapidly deencephalized under many circumstances: as the consummatory act is approached; with routinization in overtraining (the "misbehavior" of organisms); or with the fatigue, frustration, conflict, and thwarting (lack of reinforcement) that are the inevitable accompaniments of any reinforcement schedule. If we assume that fatigue or conflict can inactivate the higher-level neural controls characterizing the appetitive components of an instinctive behavior chain, then the very same act may become less encephalized (more stimulus-bound, stereotyped, synergistic, and exaggerated in its intensity) as the behavior is constantly repeated. These are all attributes of release phenomena usually seen most clearly after brain damage. Displacement phenomena in instinctive behavior might be viewed as manifestations of deencephalization. Indeed, components of instinctive patterns that are normally considered inappropriate (i.e., that are normally suppressed during the behavior in question) may be released as displacement activities. As Falk (1971) has pointed out, many of the adjunctive behaviors seen in operant situations (psychogenic polydipsia, pica, etc.) resemble displacement activities. Similarly, during the frustration induced by thwarting on a food-reinforcement schedule, a pigeon or squirrel monkey may display release of attack normally elicited by painful external stimuli (Azrin, Hutchinson, & Hake, 1966; Hutchinson, Azrin, & Hunt, 1968).

Many of these paradoxes that seem so perplexing arise from our view of the operant as an indivisible emergent unit whose laws differ from the simpler subcomponents of behavior revealed by physiological and ethological analysis. It is possible that the operant undergoes many transformations, and we must devise methods to isolate its transition forms. We must increase the magnifying power of our behavioral microscopes. The smooth curves in our cumulative records may no longer appear smooth if we speed up the motor of the recorder. As Schwartz and Williams (1972) have demonstrated, an autoshaped peck has a different duration from a peck that obeys the reinforcement contingencies. Slow-motion photography in the operant setting may reveal further changes in the topography of the key peck during thwarting. We should use evolutionary taxonomy as a microscope to reveal differences in the character of operants that will eventually fit into Baconian tables of similarities and differences. In my opinion, these will correspond to developmental and phylogenetic levels of encephalization.

Our search for general laws of learning is indeed premature, but not unwarranted. Taste-aversion learning now seems bizarre and difficult to encompass in our previous conceptions of learning. However, it may illustrate that learned associations between stimuli and physiological states undergo transformations and become less arbitrary as they are tied to sensory and motor systems which develop earlier in ontogeny or recover differentially after brain damage. Perhaps, as in the grasp reflex, such sensory controls develop in a characteristic sequence.

We have a long way to go in our study of motivation, learning, and operant behavior. We must use all the techniques of real simplification: physiological (the study of brain damage), developmental (the study of maturing infants), and ethological (the taxonomic study of the similarities and differences seen in operants). It is not yet possible to use direct synthesis to assemble the real, simpler subcomponents of behavior to prove that our analysis is valid. However, the study of the parallel transformations in behavior during recovery and development can provide a real synthesis. The behavioral description of S–R correlations at each level of encephalization are as much in accord with the approach of Sherrington as they are with Skinner. They fit Skinner's criteria for a scientific approach to behavior, yet enable us to perfect our understanding of the levels of integration of the operant.

REFERENCES

Adolph, E. F. Ontogeny of physiological regulations in the rat. *Quarterly Review of Biology*, 1957, *32*, 89–137.

Anderson, R. C. Educational psychology. *Annual Review of Psychology*, 1967, *18*, 129–164.

Andersson, B., & Wyrwicka, W. The elicitation of a drinking motor conditioned reaction by electrical stimulation of the hypothalamic "drinking area" in the goat. *Acta Physiologica Scandinavica*, 1957, *41*, 194–198.

Azrin, N. H., Hutchinson, R. R., & Hake, D. F. Extinction-induced aggression. *Journal of the Experimental Analysis of Behavior*, 1966, *9*, 191–204.

Bacon, F. *The new organon* (ed. and trans. J. Spedding, R. L. Ellis, & D. D. Heath) in Works, Vol. 8. Boston: Taggard and Thompson, 1963. (Reprinted, F. H. Anderson, Ed., Indianapolis: Bobbs-Merrill, 1960.) (Originally published, 1620.)

Bandler, R. J., & Flynn, J. P. Control of somatosensory fields for striking during hypothalamically elicited attack. *Brain Research*, 1972, *38*, 197–201.

Barrera, F. J. Centrifugal selection of signal-directed pecking. *Journal of the Experimental Analysis of Behavior*, 1974, *22*, 341–355.

Beach, F. A. The snark was a boojum. *American Psychologist*, 1950, *5*, 115–124.

Beach, F. A. Ontogeny of "coitus-related" reflexes in the female guinea pig. *Proceedings of the National Academy of Sciences*, 1966, *56*, 526–533.

Bernard, C. *Introduction to the study of experimental medicine* (trans. H. C. Greene, 1926). Republished, New York: Dover Press, 1957. (Originally published, 1865.)

Boling, J. L., Blandau, R. J., Wilson, J. G., & Young, W. C. Post-parturitional heat responses of newborn and adult guinea pigs: Data on parturition. *Proceedings of the Society for Experimental Biology and Medicine*, 1939, *42*, 128–132.

Bolles, R. C. Species-specific defense reactions and avoidance learning. *Psychological Review*, 1970, *77*, 32–48.

Breland, K., & Breland, M. The misbehavior of organisms. *American Psychologist*, 1961, *16*, 681–684.

Breland, K., & Breland, M. *Animal behavior*. New York: Macmillian, 1966.

Brown, P. L., & Jenkins, H. M. Auto-shaping of the pigeon's key-peck. *Journal of the Experimental Analysis of Behavior*, 1968, *11*, 1–8.

Bruch, H. Perils of behavior modification in treatment of anorexia nervosa. *Journal of the American Medical Association*, 1974, *230*, 1419–1422.

Cheng, M. F., Rozin, P., & Teitelbaum, P. Semi-starvation retards the development of food and water regulations in infant rats. *Journal of Comparative and Physiological Psychology*, 1971, *76*, 206–218.

Coons, E. E., Levak, M., & Miller, N. E. Lateral hypothalamus: Learning of food-seeking response motivated by electrical stimulation. *Science*, 1965, *150*, 1320–1321.

Dement, W. C., Henry, P., Cohen, H., & Ferguson, J. Studies on the effect of REM deprivation in humans and animals. In S. S. Kety, E. V. Evarts, & H. L. Williams (Eds.), *Sleep and altered states of consciousness*. Baltimore: Williams and Wilkins, 1967.

Descartes, R. *Discourse on method* (2nd ed.) (trans. L. J. Lafleur). New York: Liberal Arts Press, 1956. (Originally published, 1637.)

Epstein, A. N. The lateral hypothalamic syndrome: Its implications for the physiological psychology of hunger and thirst. In E. Stellar & J. M. Sprague (Eds.), *Progress in physiological psychology* (Vol. 4). New York: Academic Press, 1971.

Falk, J. L. The nature and determinants of adjunctive behavior. *Physiology and Behavior*, 1971, *6*, 577–588.

Ferster, C. B., & Skinner, B. F. *Schedules of reinforcement*. Englewood Cliffs, N.J.: Prentice-Hall, Inc., 1957.

Flourens, M. J. P. *Recherches expérimentales sur les*

propriétés et les fonctions du systeme nerveux, dans les animaux vertébrés. Paris: Crevot, 1824.

FLYNN, J. P. Patterning mechanisms, patterned reflexes, and attack behavior in cats. In J. K. Cole & D. D. Jensen (Eds.), *Nebraska Symposium on Motivation* (Vol. 20). Lincoln: University of Nebraska Press, 1973.

FLYNN, J. P., EDWARDS, S. B., & BANDLER, R. J. Changes in sensory and motor systems during centrally elicited attack. *Behavioral Science,* 1971, *16,* 1–19.

FREUD, S. Types of neurotic nosogenesis. In J. Rickman (Ed.), *A general selection from the works of Sigmund Freud.* Garden City, N.Y.: Doubleday, 1957. (Originally published, 1912.)

GARCIA, J., HANKINS, W. G., & RUSINIAK, K. W. Behavioral regulation of the milieu interne in man and rat. *Science,* 1974, *185,* 824–831.

GARCIA, J., & KOELLING, R. A. Relation of cue to consequence in avoidance learning. *Psychonomic Science,* 1966, *4,* 123–124.

GLAVCHEVA, L., ROZKOWSKA, E., & FONBERG, E. The effect of lateral hypothalamic lesions on gastric motility in dogs. *Acta Neurobiologiae Experimentalis,* 1970, *30,* 279–293.

HALMI, K. A., POWERS, P., & CUNNINGHAM, S. Treatment of anorexia nervosa with behavior modification. *Archives of General Psychiatry,* 1975, *32,* 93–96.

HELLER, H. The response of newborn rats to administration of water by stomach. *Journal of Physiology,* 1947, *106,* 245–255.

HELLER, H. The water metabolism of newborn infants and animals. *Archives of Disease in Childhood,* 1951, *26,* 195–204.

HESS, W. R. *Die Methodik der lokalisierten Reizung und Ausschaltung subkortikaler Hirnabschnitte.* Leipzig: G. Thieme, 1932.

HESS, W. R. *Diencephalon: Autonomic and extrapyramidal functions.* New York: Grune and Stratton, 1954.

HINDE, R. A., & STEVENSON-HINDE, J. (Eds.). *Constraints on learning.* New York: Academic Press, 1973.

HINELINE, P. H., & RACHLIN, H. Escape and avoidance of shock by pigeons pecking a key. *Journal of the Experimental Analysis of Behavior,* 1969, *12,* 533–538.

HOEBEL, B. G. Feeding: Neural control of intake. *Annual Review of Physiology,* 1971, *33,* 533–538.

HONIG, W. K. (Ed.). *Operant behavior: Areas of research and application.* Englewood Cliffs, N.J.: Prentice-Hall, Inc., 1966.

HUBBARD, R., & WALD, G. The mechanism of rhodopsin synthesis. *Proceedings of the National Academy of Sciences,* 1951, *37,* 69–79.

HULL, C. L. *Principles of behavior.* New York: Appleton-Century-Crofts, 1943.

HUTCHINSON, R. R., AZRIN, N. H., & HUNT, G. M. Attack produced by intermittent reinforcement of a concurrent operant response. *Journal of the Experimental Analysis of Behavior,* 1968, *11,* 489–495.

JENKINS, H. M., & MOORE, B. R. The form of the autoshaped response with food or water reinforcers. *Journal of the Experimental Analysis of Behavior,* 1973, *20,* 163–181.

JOUVET, M. Recherches sur les structures nerveuses et les mecanismes responsables des differentes phases du sommeil physiologique. *Archives of Italian Biology,* 1962, *100,* 125–206.

KASATKIN, N. I. 1960, as cited in Y. Brackbill & M. M. Koltsova, Conditioning and learning. In Y. Brackbill (Ed.), *Infancy and early childhood.* New York: Free Press, 1967.

KAZDIN, A. E., & BOOTZIN, R. R. The token economy: An evaluative review. *Journal of Applied Behavior Analysis,* 1972, *5,* 343–372.

KOMISARUK, B. R., ADLER, N. T., & HUTCHISON, J. Genital sensory field: Enlargement by estrogen treatment in female rats. *Science,* 1972, *178,* 1295–1298.

KŘEČEK, J., & KŘEČEKOVÁ, J. The development of the regulation of water metabolism, III: The relation between water and milk intake in infant rats. *Physiologia Bohemoslovenica,* 1957, *6,* 26–33.

LEVY, C., CARROLL, M. E., SMITH, J. C., & HOFER, K. G. Antihistamines block radiation-induced taste aversions. *Science,* 1974, *186,* 1044–1046.

LORENZ, K. The past twelve years in the comparative study of behavior. In C. H. Schiller (Ed. and Trans.), *Instinctive behavior.* New York: International Universities Press, 1957. (Reprinted from the Report of the Zoological Convention, Freiburg, 1952.)

MACDONNELL, M. F., & FLYNN, J. P. Control of sensory fields by stimulation of hypothalamus. *Science,* 1966, *152,* 1406–1408. (a)

MACDONNELL, M. F., & FLYNN, J. P. Sensory control of hypothalamic attack. *Animal Behaviour,* 1966, *14,* 399–406. (b)

McGINTY, D. J. Encephalization and the neural control of sleep. In M. B. Sterman, D. J. McGinty, & A. M. Adinolfi (Eds.), *Brain development and behavior.* New York: Academic Press, 1971.

MAGNUS, R. Some results of studies in the physiology of posture. *The Lancet,* 1926, *211,* 531–536; 585–588.

MARSHALL, J. F., & TEITELBAUM, P. Further analysis of sensory inattention following lateral hypothalamic damage in rats. *Journal of Comparative and Physiological Psychology,* 1974, *86,* 375–395.

MARSHALL, J. F., TURNER, B. H., & TEITELBAUM, P. Sensory neglect produced by lateral hypothalamic damage. *Science,* 1971, *174,* 523–525.

MENDELSON, J., & CHOROVER, S. L. Lateral hypothalamic stimulation in satiated rats: T-maze learning for food. *Science,* 1965, *149,* 559–561.

MILLENSON, J. *Principles of behavioral analysis.* New York: Macmillian, 1967.

MILLER, N. E. *Neal E. Miller: Selected papers.* Chicago: Aldine-Atherton, 1971.

MOORE, B. R. The role of directed Pavlovian reactions in simple instrumental learning in the pigeon. In R. A. Hinde & J. Stevenson-Hinde (Eds.), *Constraints on learning.* New York: Academic Press, 1973.

PAVLOV, I. P. *Conditioned reflexes: An investigation of the physiological activity of the cerebral cortex* (ed. and trans. G. V. Anrep). Oxford: Oxford University Press, 1927. (Republished, New York: Dover Press, 1960.)

ROBERTS, W. W. Hypothalamic mechanisms for motivational and species-typical behavior. In R. E. Whalen (Ed.), *The neural control of behavior.* New York: Academic Press, 1970.

ROBERTS, W. W., & KIESS, H. O. Motivational properties of hypothalamic aggression in cats. *Journal of Comparative and Physiological Psychology,* 1964, *58,* 187–193.

RODGERS, W. L., EPSTEIN, A. N., & TEITELBAUM, P. Lateral hypothalamic aphagia: Motor failure or motivational deficit? *American Journal of Physiology*, 1965, *208*, 334–342.

Rozin, P., & Kalat, J. Adaptive specializations in learning and memory. *Psychological Review*, 1971, *78*, 459–486.

Rozkowska, E., & Fonberg, E. Impairment of salivary reflexes after lateral hypothalamic lesions in dogs. *Acta Neurobiologia Experimentalis*, 1972, *32*, 711–720.

Schwartz, B., & Williams, D. R. Two different kinds of key peck in the pigeon: Some properties of responses maintained by negative and positive response-reinforcer contingencies. *Journal of the Experimental Analysis of Behavior*, 1972, *18*, 201–216.

Seligman, M. E. P., & Hager, J. L. *Biological boundaries of learning*. New York: Meredith, 1972.

Sevenster, P. Incompatibility of response and reward. In R. A. Hinde & J. Stevenson-Hinde (Eds.), *Constraints on learning*. New York: Academic Press, 1973.

Seyffarth, H., & Denny-Brown, D. The grasp reflex and the instinctive grasp reaction. *Brain*, 1948, *71*, 109–183.

Sherrington, C. S. *The integrative action of the nervous system*. Forge Village, Mass.: Murray Printing Co., 1906. (Republished, New Haven: Yale University Press paperback, 1961).

Shettleworth, S. J. Constraints on learning. In D. S. Lehrman, R. A. Hinde, & E. Shaw (Eds.), *Advances in the study of behavior* (Vol. 4). New York: Academic Press, 1972.

Shettleworth, S. J. Reinforcement and the organization of behavior in golden hamsters: Hunger, environment, and food reinforcement. *Journal of Experimental Psychology: Animal Behavior Processes*, 1975, *104*, 56–87.

Skinner, B. F. The concept of the reflex in the description of behavior. *Journal of General Psychology*, 1931, *5*, 427–458.

Skinner, B. F. *The behavior of organisms: An experimental analysis*. New York: Appleton-Century, 1938.

Skinner, B. F. *Walden Two*. New York: MacMillan, 1948. (a)

Skinner, B. F. Superstition in the pigeon. *Journal of Experimental Psychology*, 1948, *38*, 168–172. (b)

Skinner, B. F. Are theories of learning necessary? *Psychological Review*, 1950, *57*, 193–216.

Skinner, B. F. A case history in scientific method. *American Psychologist*, 1956, *11*, 221–233.

Skinner, B. F. The experimental analysis of behavior. *American Scientist*, 1957, *45*, 343–371.

Skinner, B. F. Why we need teaching machines. *Harvard Educational Review*, 1961, *31*, 377–398.

Skinner, B. F. The phylogeny and ontogeny of behavior. *Science*, 1966, *153*, 1205–1213.

Skinner, B. F. *Cumulative record* (3rd ed.). Englewood Cliffs, N.J.: Prentice-Hall, Inc., 1972. (a)

Skinner, B. F. The flight from the laboratory. In B. F. Skinner, *Cumulative record*. Englewood Cliffs, N.J.: Prentice-Hall, Inc., 1972. (b)

Smith, J. C., & Roll, D. L. Trace conditioning with x-rays as an aversive stimulus. *Psychonomic Science*, 1967, *9*, 11–12.

Steinbaum, E. A., & Miller, N. E. Obesity from eating elicited by daily stimulation of hypothalamus. *American Journal of Physiology*, 1965, *208*, 1–5.

Stunkard, A. J. New treatments for obesity: Behavior modification. In G. A. Bray & J. E. Bethune (Eds.), *Treatment and management of obesity*. New York: Harper & Row, 1974.

Teitelbaum, P. The use of operant methods in the assessment and control of motivational states. In W. K. Honig (Ed.), *Operant behavior: Areas of research and application*. Englewood Cliffs, N.J.: Prentice-Hall, Inc., 1966.

Teitelbaum, P. *Physiological psychology: Fundamental principles*. Englewood Cliffs, N.J.: Prentice-Hall, 1967.

Teitelbaum, P. The encephalization of hunger. In E. Stellar & J. M. Sprague (Eds.), *Progress in physiological psychology* (Vol. 4). New York: Academic Press, 1971.

Teitelbaum, P. Discussion: On the use of electrical stimulation to study hypothalamic structure and function. In A. N. Epstein, H. R. Kissileff, & E. Stellar (Eds.), *The neuropsychology of thirst*. New York: V. H. Winston, 1974.

Teitelbaum, P., Cheng, M. F., & Rozin P. Stages of recovery and development of lateral hypothalamic control of food and water intake. *Annals of the New York Academy of Science*, 1969, *157*, 849–860. (a)

Teitelbaum, P., Cheng, M. F., & Rozin, P. Development of feeding parallels its recovery after hypothalamic damage. *Journal of Comparative and Physiological Psychology*, 1969, *67*, 430–441. (b)

Teitelbaum, P., & Epstein, A. N. The lateral hypothalamic syndrome: Recovery of feeding and drinking after lateral hypothalamic lesions. *Psychological Review*, 1962, *69*, 74–90.

Thompson, T. I. Visual reinforcement in Siamese fighting fish. *Science*, 1963, *141*, 55–57.

Tinbergen, N. *The study of instinct*. London: Oxford University Press, 1951. [Reissued in 1969.]

Tinbergen, N., & Kuenen, D. J. Über die Auslosenden und die richtunggebenden Reizsituationen der Sperrbewegung von jungen Drosseln (Turdus m. merula L. und T. e. ericetorum Turton). *Zeitschrift für Tierpsychologie*, 1939, *3*, 37–60. (Trans. and reprinted in C. H. Schiller [Ed.], *Instinctive behavior*. New York: International Universities Press, 1957.)

Turner, B. N. A sensorimotor syndrome produced by lesions of the amygdala and lateral hypothalamus. *Journal of Comparative and Physiological Psychology*, 1973, *82*, 37–47.

Twitchell, T. E. The restoration of motor function following hemiplegia in man. *Brain*, 1951, *74*, 443–480.

Twitchell, T. E. The automatic grasping responses of infants. *Neuropsychologia*, 1965, *3*, 247–259.

Twitchell, T. E. Early development of avoiding and grasping reactions. In S. Locke (Ed.), *Modern neurology*. Boston: Little, Brown, 1969.

Twitchell, T. E. Reflex mechanisms and the development of prehension. In K. J. Connolly (Ed.), *Mechanisms of motor skill development*. New York: Academic Press, 1970.

Valenstein, E. S. Invited comment: Electrical stimulation and hypothalamic function: Historical perspective. In A. N. Epstein, H. R. Kissileff, & E. Stellar (Eds.), *The neuropsychology of thirst*. Washington, D.C.: V. H. Winston, 1973.

Valenstein, E. S., Cox, V. C., & Kakolewski, J. W. The motivation underlying eating elicited by lateral hypothalamic stimulation. *Physiology and Behavior*, 1968, *159*, 1119-1121.

WALD, G. Molecular basis of visual excitation. *Science*, 1968, *162*, 230-239.

WESSELLS, M. G. The effects of reinforcement upon the pre-pecking behaviors of pigeons in the autoshaping experiment. *Journal of the Experimental Analysis of Behavior*, 1974, *21*, 125-144.

WILCOXON, H. C., DRAGOIN, W. B., & KRAL, P. A. Illness-induced aversions in rat and quail: Relative salience of visual and gustatory cues. *Science*, 1971, *171*, 826-828.

WILLIAMS, D. R., & WILLIAMS, H. Auto-maintenance in the pigeon: Sustained pecking despite contingent non-reinforcement. *Journal of the Experimental Analysis of Behavior*, 1969, *12*, 511-520.

2

The Operant Revisited*

George Collier,
Edward Hirsch, and Robin Kanarek

INTRODUCTION

Operant psychology started with a meal. Using eating as a means of studying reflexes and reflex chaining, Skinner developed the apparatus, the conceptual framework, and the methodology of operant analysis (Skinner, 1930, 1931, 1932a, 1932b, 1935).

The focus on eating stemmed from the search for a recurrent, lawful behavior for analysis. The "orderly periodicity in . . . eating activity" reported in Richter's 1927 study of meal taking by the rat provided Skinner with such a phenomenon. Skinner sought to account "for the appearance or nonappearance of a given set of behavior at a given time." Richter's "simple observation of whether a rat eats" was, "after all, only an all-or-none measure" (Skinner, 1930, 1932a). His analysis focused on meal frequency and duration in a freely feeding animal. In consequence, therefore, Skinner devised a measure of the strength of feeding behavior based upon the rate of eating *within a meal* (Skinner, 1932a). The assumption underlying this strategy was that knowledge of the strength of the chain of reflexes *within* a meal would make it possible to predict both the onset and termination of a meal and thus the pattern of meals. Skinner's interest in the strength of the feeding reflexes within a meal led to a shift from this continuous sampling of a nondeprived animal's behavior to a sample gained in a short, constrained experimental session in a food-deprived animal. With his parsimonious, Baconian devotion to the observable, Skinner sought the laws of eating solely in the relations between reflex probabilities and such operations as fasting and feeding which changed these probabilities (Skinner, 1931, 1932a). He eschewed any dependence upon hypothetical, neurological, or physiological structures or states. The behavior laws were considered to be self-sufficient. There was no need to reduce them to or explain them by phenomena from some other domain. Today, this tradition, further refined, is continued by such investigators as Herrnstein (1970), Morse and Kelleher (1970), Pre-

* This research was supported by Research Grants HD-00941 and HD-03279 from the National Institutes of Health, Bethesda, Maryland, and the Rutgers University Research Council. The authors are indebted to Nicholas Mrosovsky and Sarah Shettleworth at the University of Toronto and Robert Bolles at the University of Washington (Seattle) for their critical reading of the early manuscript and to Carolyn K. Rovee of Douglass College, Rutgers University, for both her intensive editing and her critical commentary.

mack (1959), and Timberlake and Allison (1974).

To study feeding behavior an *eatometer* was devised! This apparatus consisted of a door which the rat had to push open in order to seize a single pellet from a food magazine. Following a period of time without food, the rats were placed within the apparatus and allowed to consume food until eating ceased. Each door opening was recorded on a *cumulative recorder* which produced a record of the rate of eating. Rate, then, was considered to be the measure of reflex strength (Skinner, 1932a).

The behavior was so orderly that Skinner succumbed to temptation and fitted a curve to the data [$N = Kt^n$; where N is the amount (number of pellets) eaten, t the time in session, and n and K curve-fitting constants].

At this juncture Skinner, still under the influence of the Sherringtonian definition of the reflex, was interested in analyzing the rate of occurrence of the various members of the reflex chain. In particular, he was concerned with the influence of eating time (chewing and swallowing) on the refractory phase of the initial reflex in the chain (seizing) and sought to discover if "the law expressed in the equation $N = Kt^n$ is independent of the particular reflex that initiates the eating behavior" (Skinner, 1932b). To deal with this question, Skinner introduced an *"arbitrary initial member"* to the reflex chain, the lever press.

> The food tray is accordingly replaced by a repeating "problem box" which delivers a pellet of food into an open trough each time a horizontal lever is pressed downward.

Thus the *Skinner box* was born. The results obtained from the Skinner box showed that "the rate of change of the rate of eating is independent of the nature of the particular reflex with which eating behavior begins." The delight in this conclusion, however, was soon surpassed by the excitement generated by new discoveries concerning the *arbitrary initial member* and the subsequent interest in elaborating the concept of the operant. This diversion left the original problems unexplored.

In this chapter we wish to focus on three points in Skinner's original analysis of feeding. First, we shall consider whether Skinner's use of the reflex as the unit of analysis was a felicitous choice. Second, we shall examine the "orderly periodicity" of eating reported by Richter which stimulated Skinner's analysis. And third, we shall explore whether operations other than fasting and feeding control the pattern of meal taking.

Eating as a Reflex

The basic assumption of the operant analysis of behavior is that current consequences control future performance. An important, interesting, and very difficult question concerns the specification of the units of behavior on which these consequences act. The characterization of these units can vary from simple muscular movements devoid of meaning (Guthrie, 1935) to complex patterns of responses whose dynamic interaction is intrinsic and is shaped by their consequences (Kohler, 1929). As the first step in his analysis of this problem, Skinner chose the reflex as the functional unit.

The reflex as a unit of analysis has a long history (Fearing, 1930; Skinner, 1931). In 1662, an era when physical science was in the first flush of its initial successes in devising mechanical models of the physical universe, Descartes introduced the concept of the reflex as an attempt to explain *animate motion* with a mechanical model (Jaynes, 1970). He derived his inspiration from the hydraulically actuated dolls in the gardens of St. Germain which executed intricate patterns of movement when "stimulated" by someone treading upon a concealed pedal (Fearing, 1930; Jaynes, 1970; Skinner, 1931). In Descartes's view, animals were automatons. Only the voluntary activity of humans was excepted from this categorization. Behavior could be exhaustively duplicated by sufficiently complex machines obeying only physical principles.

The *reflex* has been accepted by physiologists and psychologists of all persuasions as an accurate characterization of at least some aspects of behavior. There are at least three major reasons for this attraction:

1. Once Pavlov (1927) had demonstrated the conditionability of reflexes, it was relatively easy to conceive of reflexes as the building blocks for complex sequences of behavior (Guthrie, 1935; Hull, 1937; Skinner, 1938). These sequences could be assembled by an organism's phylogenetic or ontogenetic interaction with its environment (Skinner, 1966). In this view, order in behavior only reflects order in the environment, not structure in the organism.

2. Mentalistic or nonphysical language can be avoided in the analysis of behavior by defining the stimulus component of the reflex as any arbitrary change in the environment and the response component as any arbitrary movement of the organism without reference to intention, purpose, or function. This stratagem precludes any biological or psychological terms at the level of the data language. The psychological meaning of a behavior sequence derives from such criteria as establishing "smooth curves for dynamic laws" (Skinner, 1938). Skinner cau-

tioned against the use of vernacular, biological, neurological, or mentalistic concepts for other than heuristic purposes in the search for useful classes of variables (Skinner, 1938).

3. Finally, acceptance of the reflex requires little or no theoretical commitment to mental or physiological processes as behavioral substrates. In this search for functional laws devoid of causal explanations, Skinner followed Mach and Bridgman (Skinner, 1931).

Historically, the major disadvantage of a reflex analysis is that description of behavior has, in fact, become circumstantial and complex. It has become necessary to elaborate complex concepts such as the "observing response" (Wyckoff, 1952) or "pure stimulus acts" (Hull, 1930) to deal with phenomena such as *attention* or *intention*.

Reflex-based descriptions of behavior are also plagued by the ultimately difficult problem of the infinite number of movements and stimuli which might occur at any given cross section in time and place. Skinner's concept of the generic nature of the stimulus and response allowed him to circumvent the tedious problem of botanizing stimuli and responses (Skinner, 1935). The stimulus class was defined by the experimental context, and the response class by its effect on the environment rather than by its detailed topography. In fact, Skinner advocated watching the recorder rather than the animal. Conceptual utility was determined by the extent to which a given set of environmental variables resulted in "simple" laws when a given category of behavior was used (Skinner, 1938).

Skinner's generic characterization of a response was a historically important step away from his original analysis of the "strengths" of the specific reflexes (seizing, chewing, swallowing) involved with the ingestion of food (Skinner, 1932a). His finding that the "rate of change of the rate of eating is independent of the nature of the particular reflex with which eating begins" (Skinner, 1932b) made possible his use as an *arbitrary initial member,* a specific *environmental* event—that is, a bar press—to represent the whole chain of behavior.

Richter (1927) had shown that a freely feeding rat exhibited periodic episodes of eating, defined as meals, which excluded other activities. His rats were not deprived in the usual sense, and the initiation or termination of a particular bout of eating was not predictable from the variables he analyzed. Rather, he was only able to characterize the number, duration, and distribution of these episodes of behavior. Skinner approached the problem of determining such an episode of eating by introducing the *operation* of fasting, which *insured* initiation of eating. That is, it placed *initiation* under the experimenter's control and made the description of within-meal behavior the locus of analysis. The basic data of the within-meal analysis was the initial rate of ingestion and the rate of change of rate of ingestion within a session as functions of such operations as fasting and feeding. Since only a single episode of eating, defined by the experimental session, was observed, no data on the frequency, duration, and distribution of meals in time was obtained.

Even after interest in eating per se had shifted to the effects of *schedules* on behavior, the same experimental paradigm was maintained: Animals were deprived of food, and their behavior was measured during an experimental session. The analysis still focused on "reflex strength" as Skinner originally defined it (Skinner, 1935). Complex behavior was *constructed* from the simplest reflex components. The laws of combination are derived from the laws of reflex strength. Thus since in this experimental paradigm only a single meal, initiated and terminated by the experimenter, was observed, the analysis of the results obtained was of within-meal behavior. The question raised by employing this tactic is whether the same variables which predict within-meal behavior also predict between-meal behavior, and if so, are the functions the same? We shall attempt to demonstrate that this analysis does not predict the pattern of feeding in the freely feeding, nondeprived animal and has led to the neglect of several important variables in the study of animal learning and motivation.

Skinner followed in the footsteps of the early physicists in developing his research strategy. Having borrowed a mechanical model (i.e., the reflex) from physics for the study of behavior, it was also natural to borrow a methodology in the form of the refinement experiment. Early physics was hampered by poor tools and materials and a lack of coherent theory for identification of variables. Relations established between variables were subject to large amounts of error, and the program was one of successive refinement of the experiment to reduce input from "extraneous" sources in order to eliminate error and discover the "true" law. The best experiment was one in which the effects produced by the variable(s) being studied were large relative to all other effects. Operant analysis has not strayed from this path (Sidman, 1960). To study an automaton, one needed to reduce extraneous stimuli and restrict the response possibilities so that one could find the law hidden in the variety of activities observed. Hence a highly inbred, docile animal, limited in historical inputs (naïve), was chosen as the object of experimentation. He was placed in a box isolated from the sight, sounds, and smells of his neighbors, where the only question was "to press or not to press." It was a study of performance in solitary confinement. Different animals and different situations were not required to discover basic laws (Skinner, 1938). The conviction was that laws derived using the reflex as the unit of analysis are universal. That is, such laws are invariant across species, response classes, and reinforcers (see Skinner, 1966, for a qualification of this thesis). It should be emphasized that the experimenter exerts close control over the behavior that is exhibited within this paradigm. The animal is (purposely) restrained from exhibiting its full repertoire of behavior. Although these procedures reduce "extraneous" sources of variation and limit the behavior displayed, they offer little opportunity for observing the kinds of "solutions" the animal might make to a similar problem occurring in his "natural," noisy, and (to the experimenter) confusing environment. Rather, it is assumed that knowledge of an animal's evolutionary history, his classification, his current situation, his ecological niche, and his present habitat does not contribute in any fundamental way to the understanding of the principles of behavior acquisition and maintenance.

It will be the argument of the present chapter that the meal, as originally defined by Richter (1927), is a better unit of analysis than the reflex for the study of hunger, because, in the original sense of Skinner (1938), it "gives smooth curves for dynamic laws." This unit will best reveal its utility in an environment in which the animal himself schedules the initiation and termination of behavior. It seems possible that the discovery of the important variables in such an environment is most likely to solve Skinner's original problem of accounting "for the appearance of a given act of behavior at a given time" (Skinner, 1930, 1932a—see above).

Feeding and Fasting

One of the great conceptual difficulties with a mechanical model of animate behavior is the provision of a motive force and direction for the organism. The solution to this problem for the early mechanists was homeostasis (cf. Pavlov, 1927). The theory of homeostasis derived from the concept of equibrium systems developed in thermodynamics. It was originally used to describe the dynamic constancy of the fluid matrix of the cells (Cannon, 1932). Its meaning has since been extended to include any steady state in which some parameter is regulated around a privileged value. Regulation of energy balance is inferred when average energy expenditure and intake are matched. This condition must be met by any organism maintaining a constant size or fixed pattern of growth or senescence. In addition, regulation can be the result of many different mechanisms, both behavioral and physiological (Yamamoto & Brobeck, 1965). In the strict sense, homeostasis implies negative feedback, specialized receptors, and moment-to-moment monitoring of energy balance. In the case of feeding, the process is assumed to consist of successive depletion and repletion phases (DeRuiter, 1967). Depletion occurs as a result of metabolism. When energy stores are depleted below a threshold or critical value, feeding behavior (search, seizure, ingestion) preempts other ongoing activities. Ingestion leads to repletion, and, when an upper threshold of the energy stores or some surrogate of these stores is exceeded, ingestive behavior ceases. This depletion-repletion cycle differs from the more usual homeostatic systems since the item being controlled (e.g., food or water) is discontinuously present in most environments in contrast to an item such as oxygen which is continuously present (cf. Cannon, 1932). Thus feeding can only occur in episodes rather than continuously. It is important to note that in this model, feeding is initiated in response to a substantive deficit. The character of this deficit is still unspecified and is the locus of most speculation and current research activity in feeding. The depletion-repletion model has been invoked to explain a variety of motivated behaviors, including those for which there is no obvious biological substrate (e.g., curiosity). In fact, the view of *necessity* as the *driving force* of behavior is an important part of the conventional wisdom of Western civilization. Western laws and customs are based on the notion that a person or animal will only perform some act if some essential requirement is taken from him (deprivation) and given back (reinforcement) in small units contingent upon the individual performing the required act. This historical fact may account for past failure to consider alternative models in analyzing motivation.

The depletion-repletion model of motivated behavior has generated two main problems yet to be resolved: (1) What is the nature of the signals which are correlated with depletion and repletion? and (2) What mechanisms detect and interpret these signals? A variety of physiological processes have been proposed to serve as the signals, from stomach contractions or dry mouths (Cannon, 1932) to circulating metabolites and/or electrolytes (cf. Fitzsimons, 1971;

Hoebel, 1971; LeMagnen, 1971; Mayer, 1955). The most popular "interpreter" of these hypothetical signals has been the hypothalamus, with the two processes, depletion and repletion, being represented in the lateral and ventromedial nuclei, respectively (cf. Hoebel, 1971). This simple, elegant, two-stage model has generated most of the research on feeding and most theories of food-based motivation, with the result that there has been little systematic research on feeding outside this framework or on animals other than rats.

The pattern of this research has been to test the implications of various versions of the homeostatic-hypothalamic model. This pattern of research exemplifies explanation in terms of a conceptual nervous system decried by Skinner (1931). For example, homeostatic models dominated research in the area of feeding long before any of the requisite physiological and neurological measurements were possible (e.g., Hull, 1943). Only recently have strong reservations about the underlying assumptions of this model been expressed (e.g., Collier, Hirsch, & Hamlin, 1972; Falk, 1971; Fitzsimons, 1971; Kissileff, 1973; Oatley, 1970).

The Skinnerian analysis of *hunger* avoided these problems of homeostatic theorizing and can best be summarized in a quotation from *The Behavior of Organisms* (1938, pp. 342 f; see also Skinner, 1932a, 1932b):

> In dealing with the kind of behavior that gives rise to the concept of hunger we are concerned with the strength of a certain class of reflexes and the two principal operations that affect it—feeding and fasting.

This proposition asserts the primacy of behavioral analysis. It is possible that history may show that more progress in the study of hunger would have been made had the laws of feeding behavior been investigated within the positivistic framework advocated by Skinner rather than within those of the ever-changing models of the central nervous system (see also Adolph, 1947; Brody, 1945; Kleiber, 1961; Richter, 1927; Young, 1936).

Meals

Richter's early observations showed that rats distributed their feeding in episodes which can be regarded as discrete meals. Over a 24-hr period of free feeding, he observed 8–10 meals (Richter, 1927). The definition of the term *free* in these studies does not imply cost, quantity, or availability, but rather that the animal determines the initiation and termination of a meal. This becomes clear when the six parameters which exhaustively described meals are considered: frequency, duration, amount, rate, intermeal interval, and choice of items. The meal as a unit of analysis satisfies the criteria of *reliability*. When a minimum amount of ingestive activity (e.g., 10 sec in the feeder or 3 pellets consumed) is used to define *meal initiation*, and a period of time without ingestive activity (e.g., 10 min of no eating) defines *meal termination*, meals prove to be discrete events which are relatively insensitive to changes in the criteria (e.g., Baker, 1953; Hirsch, 1973; Kissileff, 1970; Levitsky, 1970; Panksepp, 1973; Richter, 1927; Thomas & Mayer, 1968; Wiepkema, 1968). It is clear that meals can be consistently measured. The question of interest is whether systematic laws can be found using meals as the units of analysis.

The current revival of interest in meals stems from the hypothesis that meals reflect the *momentary* physiological state of the organism (cf. LeMagnen, 1971; Teitelbaum & Campbell, 1958; Thomas & Mayer, 1968). An animal is presumed to initiate a meal following a period of time without eating when the level of circulating metabolites, hormones, or reserves reflects a critical level of depletion. Similarly, the meal is terminated when ingestion effects some critical change in physiological condition. A logical implication of the depletion-repletion model is the existence of significant correlations between size of meals and intermeal intervals. There are two possible correlations. The first is between the intermeal interval preceding a meal and the size of the meal. The second is between the size of the meal and the following intermeal interval. In the first case, if the amount eaten in a meal is a function of the degree of depletion, it should reflect time since the last meal. That is, the meal following a long period of no eating should be larger than one following a short intermeal interval. If, however, the time lapse between meals is too short for the depletion threshold to be exceeded, some other mechanism must instigate meals. Similarly in the second case, following a large meal, the intermeal interval should be longer than that following a small meal, reflecting the influence of a "satiety" mechanism.

A significant correlation between meal size and the premeal interval has not been demonstrated under free-feeding conditions (Baker, 1953; Balagura & Coscina, 1968; Booth, 1972; Hirsch, 1973; LeMagnen & Devos, 1970; LeMagnen & Tallon, 1966; Levitsky, 1970; Levitsky & Collier, 1968; Snowden, 1969; Thomas & Mayer, 1968; Wiepkema, 1968; Zeigler, Green, &

Lehrer, 1971). It is important to note that this finding is in marked contrast to the results obtained when an animal undergoes *substantial* deprivation preceding a meal (Adolph, 1947; Bolles, 1967; Stellar & Hill, 1952). Whenever weight loss exceeds 7–10% of ad lib weight, there is a linear relation between body weight loss and many different measures of performance (cf. Collier, 1969). The fact that meal size is a function of the deprivation interval when depletion exceeds a certain critical size reflected in body weight but not for the minor weight loss occurring between meals in freely feeding animals suggests that different processes may be involved in initiating eating in these two cases. Studies of stomach and intestinal contents in freely feeding rats and guinea pigs which have average intermeal intervals of 2–4 hrs indicate that there is a continuous and relatively constant intestinal load, even though the stomach load fluctuates with meals. Thus any fluctuations in the input across the intestinal lumen would be endogenous in origin (Collier, Hirsch, & Hamlin, 1972). It would seem that in environments in which the commodity whose intake (e.g., food or water) is being controlled is discontinuously present, animals have met the problem of maintaining a constant *milieu interne* by establishing a constant *milieu externe* in the gut. The gut acts as a reservoir which buffers the episodic pattern of intake. This is most obvious in the large ruminants. An adult dairy cow, for example, usually has approximately 60 gallons of fluid in the rumen. The existence of these continuous intestinal loads suggests that meals in freely feeding animals might not be initiated by depletion, but rather by some endogenous process. The null hypothesis in this case would be that there is a base rate of meal initiation in the freely feeding animal generating a random sequence of meals which, on the average, result in an adequate intake. Individual meals occur independently of the state of the organism (Premack & Kintsch, 1970). Only the parameters of this distribution, not the individual events, would reflect regulatory control.

On the other hand, a significant correlation between meal size and the interval following a meal has been reported by LeMagnen (LeMagnen, 1971; LeMagnen & Devos, 1970; LeMagnen & Tallon, 1966) and a number of other investigators (e.g., Balagura & Coscina, 1968; Booth, 1972; Levitsky, 1974; Snowden, 1969; Thomas & Mayer, 1968). Recent papers have raised statistical, methodological, and theoretical objections to the validity of this correlation (Collier, Hirsch, & Hamlin, 1972; Hirsch & Collier, 1974a, 1974b; Panksepp, 1973). For example, the pooling of subjects (LeMagnen, 1971) can produce a significant correlation simply as a result of intersubject differences in meal frequency and duration. Panksepp (1973), in an elaborate analysis, has shown other statistical artifacts in computation of the correlation. There is, further, the suggestion that both diet composition (Levitsky, 1974) and texture (Thomas & Mayer, 1968) may affect the size of the correlation. The failure to find either correlation consistently, the continuity of intestinal load, and the small weight loss in the intermeal interval all suggest that the operations of *fasting* and *feeding* (Skinner, 1932a, 1938) are not the sole determinants of the appearance or nonappearance of eating in *freely feeding animals*. A new class of variables must be sought in order to discover lawful relations.

Richter (1927) found that the daily pattern of meals was sensitive to a variety of environmental variables. The availability of alternative activities such as climbing on towers, running in wheels, and nesting in boxes substantially affected meal frequency and duration. Another such effect is the duirnal rhythm in eating. That is, a rat is most likely to be found eating in the dark phase of the light-dark cycle, irrespective of the time between meals or the size of the previous meal (Baker, 1953). These observations, buttressed by recent laboratory results (Collier, Hirsch, & Hamlin, 1972; Hirsch, 1973; Hirsch & Collier, 1974a, 1974b; Kanarek, in press; Levin & Levine, 1974; Marwine, 1974) and field studies (Bell, 1971; Estes, 1967a, 1967b; Kruuk, 1972; Schaller, 1967, 1972), suggest that an analysis of the relations between the parameters of meals and environmental variables may be fruitful.

One can speculate that species have evolved feeding patterns through the course of evolution that reflect their niche (Schoener, 1971). Animals have specialized in the exploitation of specific food sources, which vary in (1) availability, (2) nutritional quality, and (3) caloric density. If the energy budgeted for the procurement and ingestion of food represents an important portion of the total energy budget, it seems improbable that animals could afford the risk of substantial depletion before instigating feeding behavior. This might create a condition of insufficient energy for successful feeding activity. Further, it is a striking observation that animals living in undisturbed ecological systems appear to match their numbers to resources. Since resource matching implies that the behavior of animals must "anticipate" their needs rather than respond to them, variables other than immediate physiological state must mediate the initiation and termination of feeding. Hungry or at least starving animals are very seldom observed in the wild except for reasons of illness, age, or social status (Wynne-

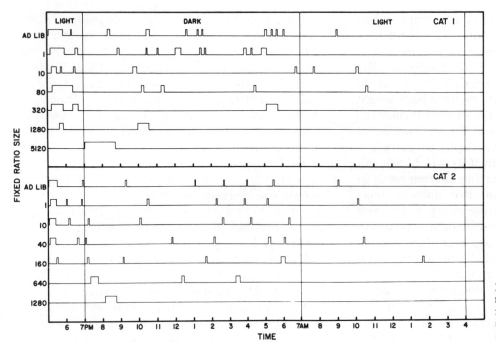

Fig. 1. Temporal sequence of the meals of two cats at several ratio requirements. The width of pip shows the duration of the meal. (From Kanarek, 1975.)

Edwards, 1962). This fact suggests that animals in undisturbed habitats have developed behavior, both social and nonsocial, which insures an adequate intake of food. For example, when the available food is insufficient, the dominance hierarchy in a flock of chickens insures that the dominant birds consume their usual rations, while the subdominants receive the remainder. The subdominants will starve to death in the presence of food rather than challenge the dominant birds. There is no direct competition for food, only for status (Wynne-Edwards, 1962). Similarly, when food is seasonally abundant, both birth rate and consumption are constrained in such a fashion that the population density matches the period of least availability of food (Wynne-Edwards, 1962). A final example can be drawn from ruminants. These animals have a large storage capacity in the rumen and a long transit time from ingestion to absorption. A consistent intake must be maintained to provide the raw materials for fermentation. The end product only gradually becomes available for regulatory information. It seems unlikely that intake can directly track the momentary metabolic state under these circumstances.

The considerations discussed above suggest that it may be useful to return to Richter's original methodology and study animals in environments in which they can exhibit the behavior which they have evolved to solve both the economics as well as the physiology of feeding. This would require a return to the situation in which the animal initiates and terminates feeding and in which the meal is the useful unit of analysis. Such an analysis may well reveal new classes of variables and relationships controlling feeding.

FREE FEEDING

The environments in which free feeding has been studied have varied widely. One which has been extensively used provides a caged laboratory animal with nutritionally complete food (as the experimenter perceives it) and water. Both commodities are continuously available. The ad lib lines in Figure 1 show sample 24-hr records of such feeding behavior in two house cats (Kanarek, 1975). The food was Purina Cat Chow available in a hopper attached to a large cage. The feeding episodes were distributed as discrete meals of varying size. The majority of the meals were consumed in the dark. Approximately 9–10 meals per 24 hr were taken. There were no consistently significant meal-intermeal correlations. The largest meals typically preceded and followed the intervention of the experimenter for purposes of weighing and daily maintenance. This can be clearly seen in Figure 1, where management occurred at 5 P.M. Similar effects of experimenter intervention on meal size have also been seen in rats and guinea pigs (Hirsch, 1973; Levitsky, 1970; Marwine, 1974).

Although the characteristic number of meals taken within a 24-hr period varies widely among species and may be species-typical, the same general *pattern* of meal-taking behavior has been described in animals

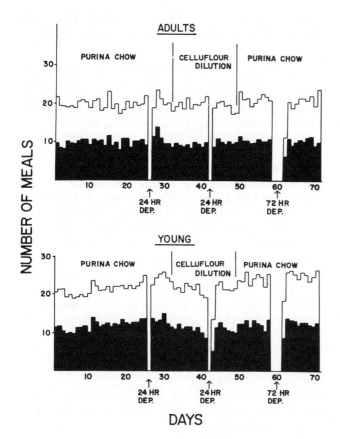

Fig. 2. Mean daily number of meals for young and adult guinea pigs. The darkened portion of the histogram shows the number of meals taken at night, and the unfilled portion shows the number of meals taken during the day. (From Hirsch, 1973.)

as diverse as rats (e.g., Richter, 1927), mice (Wiepkema, 1968), guinea pigs (Hirsch, 1973), gerbils (Kanarek, unpublished observations), pigeons (Ziegler, Green, & Lehrer, 1971), chickens (Duncan, Duncan, Hughes, & Wood-Gush, 1970), cats (Kanarek, 1975), dogs (Robinson & Adolph, 1943), and cockroaches (Faber, 1975).

When food and water are readily available, meal frequency is the parameter of free feeding that remains invariant under a variety of experimental conditions. This constancy is seen clearly in a developmental study of free-feeding behavior in the guinea pig (Hirsch, 1973). Figure 2 shows meal frequency for two groups of five guinea pigs each. The young animals were 10 days of age at the start of the experiment, and the adults were 100 days old. Meal frequency did not change from 10 days to almost 6 months of age. Growth-related changes in food intake were accomplished entirely by increases in meal size. The day-night (shown respectively by the unfilled and filled portions of the histogram) distribution of meals

also remained constant over this time period, with as many meals taken in the light as in the dark.

The relative insensitivity of meal frequency to experimental modification is also illustrated by the fact that water restriction did not influence the daily number of meals. Adolph (1947) first pointed out the strong interrelation between food intake and water intake. There is a voluntary reduction in food intake when water is given in a limited ration, resulting in a linear relation between the size of the water ration and food intake (Collier & Knarr, 1966; Collier & Levitsky, 1967). For our present purposes, the surprising observation is that both rats (Levitsky, 1970; Marwine, 1974) and guinea pigs (Hirsch, 1973) initiate as many meals during periods of water restriction as they do when water is freely available. The reduction in food intake occurs because smaller meals are taken. These results are obtained when the water is given in a limited ration (Levitsky, 1970), for a limited amount of time (Hirsch, 1973), or if a reduction in intake occurs when animals are required to lever-press for their daily water allotment over the 24-hr period (Hirsch & Collier, 1974b; Marwine, 1974). These findings are surprising in light of the close temporal relation between feeding and drinking in animals fed and watered ad lib.

Another example of the insensitivity of meal frequency to manipulation is seen following lesions that destroy the ventromedial region of the hypothalamus. The overeating that results from these lesions is due entirely to changes in meal size (Teitelbaum & Campbell, 1958; Thomas & Mayer, 1968). These observations indicate that, under a variety of conditions, animals with free access to food modulate intake by adjustments in meal size rather than frequency.

The preceding description is not meant to suggest that regulatory changes in feeding behavior cannot be mediated by adjustments in feeding frequency. Changes in meal frequency occur following olfactory bulbectomy (LaRue & LeMagnen, 1971) and lateral hypothalamic lesions (Kissileff, 1970), during chronic diabetes (Booth, 1972; Panksepp, 1973), and during intragastric nutrient infusion (Thomas & Mayer, 1968). Further, those species which make compensatory changes in food intake in response to manipulations of caloric density of diet appear to accomplish these primarily by changes in meal frequency (Kanarek, 1974; LeMagnen, 1971; Thomas & Mayer, 1968). For our present purposes, we simply wish to emphasize that (1) a wide range of intact animals with food and water readily available distribute their feeding behavior into distinct episodes which can be classified as meals; and (2) the daily frequency of the meals is relatively insensitive to a number of experimental manipulations which produce large changes in daily food intake, the latter changes being accomplished solely by changes in rate and duration of feeding.

Drinking can be analyzed in the same fashion as eating, but there is much less information available regarding the pattern of drinking that occurs under conditions of unlimited access to water. Siegel and Stuckey (1947) were the first to quantify Richter's (1927) observation of a diurnal pattern in rats. They found that rats consume approximately 75% of their water at night. This diurnal drinking pattern has been found to persist during food deprivation (Fitzsimons & LeMagnen, 1969; Oatley, 1971), following bilateral nephrectomy when water intake is sharply reduced (Fitzsimons, 1969), and even when the animal's fluid requirements have been met by continuous intragastric water infusion (Fitzsimons, 1957). In the rat (Fitzsimons & LeMagnen, 1969; Kissileff, 1969; Marwine, 1974), dog (Robinson & Adolph, 1943), guinea pig (Hirsch, 1973; Hirsch & Collier, 1974b), and cat (Kanarek, 1975), drinking occurs in discrete bouts with a strong temporal association between feeding and drinking. In a carefully detailed analysis, Kissileff (1969) has shown that in the rat, bouts of drinking are small, with 78% of them being between .5 and 2.5 ml. Approximately 75% of these bouts occur either 10 min prior to a meal, during the meal itself, or 10 min after the meal (see also Marwine, 1974).

AVAILABILITY

Another possible environment is one in which food and water are not readily available and considerable time or effort is associated with obtaining food and water. One obvious example of this situation in the natural environment is the feeding pattern exhibited by carnivores which must pursue and capture reluctant prey varying in distribution and numbers (Schaller, 1972). A second example is provided by those herbivores which exploit vegetation dispersed widely over their pasturage (Bell, 1971; Westoby, 1974). A final example is visits to the water hole. Animals which must make periodic pilgrimages of varying distances to a water hole are, as a result, subject to varying degrees of predation and competition. The timing of the trip may be determined more by the factors of predation, competition, and effort than by water and electrolyte needs (MacFarlane & Howard, 1972).

When environments of varying availability are simulated in the laboratory by the use of operant techniques, several important theoretical questions arise:

1. Will nondeprived animals tolerate demanding instrumental response requirements to obtain their daily allotment of food or water in the free-feeding paradigm? That is, when food is delivered on schedules requiring large numbers of responses and long periods of time in which to execute them, must animals undergo "substantial" deprivation in order to initiate a meal?
2. Is it necessary for the initial training of the response to take place under deprivation? This question speaks to the old controversy concerning the relation between habit and drive (Hull, 1943) and/or the conditions for reinforcement (Skinner, 1938).
3. Do animals undergo substantial weight loss between meals when large response requirements are imposed?
4. Will schedules and parameters of reinforcement exert typical effects given the modifications of the experimental environment conditions?
5. What seem to be the most appropriate units of analysis for assessing these conditions?

A number of experiments were carried out in an attempt to answer these questions. The resulting data will be considered below.

Meal Frequency as a Function of Ratio Size

In the first experiment that explored an environment resembling natural feeding conditions, rats were continuously housed in the experimental chamber (Collier, Hirsch, & Hamlin, 1972). Both food and water were always available during the first stage of the experiment, and the pattern of feeding and drinking was monitored. After a stable base line of feeding and drinking was established, a lever was introduced and access to food was made contingent on completing a fixed-ratio (FR) schedule of reinforcement. Food remained available after a reinforced lever press for as long as the animal was eating and until 10 additional consecutive minutes after feeding had terminated. This criterion for a meal is similar to that which is commonly used in other research of feeding (e.g., Kissileff, 1970; LeMagnen, 1971; Thomas & Mayer, 1968). This reinforcement paradigm differs from the classical one in which a fixed amount of food or a fixed time of access is made contingent upon the *required* behavior. In the present situation, the animal *both initiated* and *terminated* the meal. The following ascending series of FR requirements were

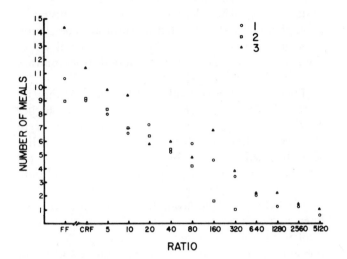

Fig. 3. Frequency of meals for three rats as a function of ratio size. (From Collier, Hirsch, & Hamlin, 1972.)

used: 1, 5, 10, 20, 40, 80, 160, 320, 640, 1,280, 2,560, and 5,120. Each schedule remained in effect for 10 days. No special shaping or training procedures were necessary. The animals were not deprived by any experimenter-controlled procedure, and at no time did their body weights deviate by more than 5–6% from their initial body weight. The data presented here were taken from the last five days under each condition.

This set of requirements produced orderly changes in both instrumental and consummatory behavior. Figure 3 shows that these requirements led to a reduction in meal frequency that was linearly related to log FR size. Under free-feeding conditions these animals had been eating 9–14 meals per day. This value decreased to 1 meal per day at FR 5,120. The performance of subject 2 began to deteriorate at FR 320, and his ratio was not increased over 640. The reductions in meal frequency were associated with compensatory increases in meal size. The latter resulted from an increase in the amount eaten during a meal rather than from changes in rate of eating (see Figure 4). Figure 5 shows that insignificant amounts of weight were lost under these conditions, even though there were small declines in daily food intake. The animals were run subsequently on a random sequence of these ratios, and the function was exactly recovered. There were no discernible practice or order effects.

Several noteworthy features of instrumental performance were apparent when free feeding was constrained in this manner. First, all animals acquired the lever-pressing response without shaping within hours after the contingency was imposed. At FR 1 all

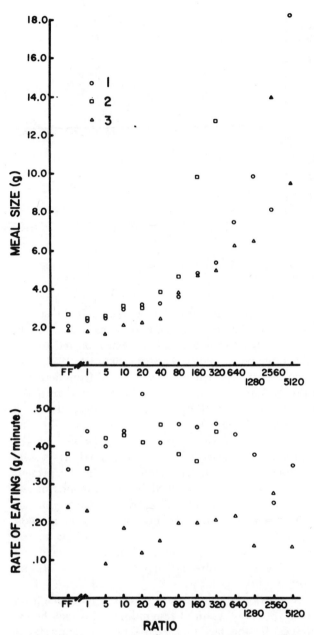

Fig. 4. Meal size and rate of eating for three rats as a function of ratio size. (From Collier, Hirsch, & Hamlin, 1972.)

bar-pressed in excess of the schedule requirement; by FR 5, however, the number of reinforcements was an accurate reflection of the number of meals consumed. The rate of responding was not systematically related to FR size. One animal showed ratio strain at FR 320 with long pauses between bursts of responding. At FR 5,120 a second animal began to show signs of ratio strain. The third animal never showed evidence of ratio strain. At the higher ratios the animals tended to respond at steady rates for periods of up to 2–3 hr.

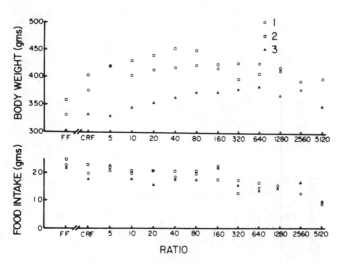

Fig. 5. Body weight and food intake for three rats as a function of ratio size. (From Collier, Hirsch, & Hamlin, 1972.)

The most striking feature of these data is the size of the ratios tolerated by these nondeprived animals. Ratios of this size have seldom been reported to sustain stable performance (Ferster & Skinner, 1957), and when they have, the data were obtained from deprived animals with conditioned reinforcers built into the schedule (Findley, 1962; Findley & Brady, 1965). It should also be noted that in the Findley situation the reinforcement was of a fixed size determined by the experimenter rather than by the animal. It is conceivable that the limits on ratio size in the present situation are not determined by the demands of the schedule of reinforcement, but by the inability of rats to process large volumes of food in short time periods. When food availability is restricted to an hour or less a day, rats do not maintain ad lib levels of intake and lose weight (Ehrenfreund, 1959; Lawrence & Mason, 1955).

As previously stated, there was little tendency for a rat to interrupt a run of responding. This may be explained by the fact that each schedule requirement has associated with it a certain number of initiations per day. For example, at FR 80, the rats typically ate six meals per day. Thus it would appear that the effect of a long pause in a run of responses would be similar to requiring another *initiation* of responding and at any given ratio reduce the actual number of meals the animal would obtain. This consequence of pausing would tend to enforce uninterrupted runs of responses to the completion of the requirement.

The reduced frequency of meals resulting from increased ratio requirements is associated with a compensatory increase in the size of the meals. Thus it appears that both meal initiation and termination are under strong schedule control. This conclusion is strengthened by the fact that a significant correlation between meal size and the intermeal interval under these conditions has not been found (for contrary data, see Levitsky, 1974).

There are large individual differences in the size of the ratio tolerated. It is possible that much higher ratios could be sustained if the meal definition were changed to allow pauses greater than 10 min. Such a procedure would allow the animal to extend a meal and slow ingestion rate without facing *reinitiation*. However, this variable remains to be explored.

The effect of food availability (FR size) on frequency and duration of meals is not unique to rats. Adolescent cats (Kanarek, 1975) and young, growing guinea pigs (Hirsch & Collier, 1974a), who not only must maintain intake at the base line level but also must increase intake in order for growth to progress in a normal manner, respond to the regulatory problems posed by constraints on food availability in remarkably similar ways. Figure 6 shows the growth curves of six male guinea pigs tested under these conditions. Each successive FR represents a block of four days. It is apparent that normal rates of growth, established by a control group of six animals maintained concurrently on noncontingent feeding, were maintained in all animals until at least FR 1,280. The guinea pig adopts a somewhat different strategy than the rat for conserving normal levels of food intake. His increase in meal size results from increases in both meal duration and eating rate (see Figure 7).

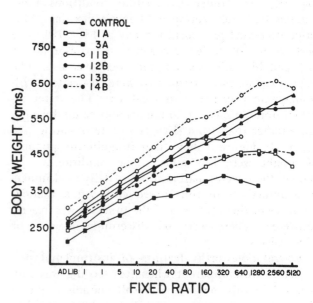

Fig. 6. Body weight of six guinea pigs at successive ratios. Each ratio was in effect for four days. (From Hirsch & Collier, 1974a.)

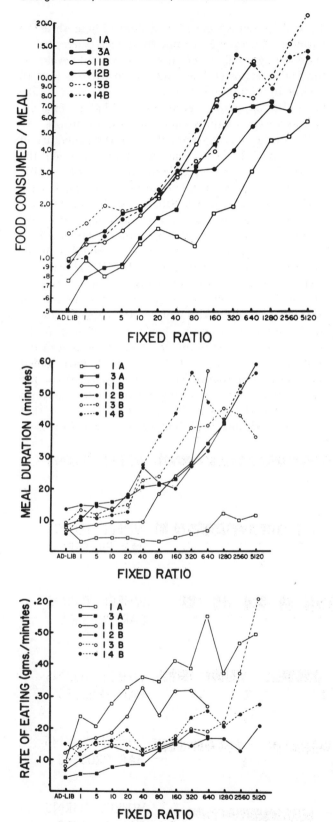

Fig. 7. Food consumed per meal, meal duration, and rate of eating for six guinea pigs as a function of ratio size. (From Hirsch & Collier, 1974a.)

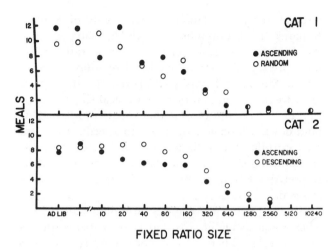

Fig. 8. Frequency of meals for two cats as a function of ratio size. (From Kanarek, 1975.)

The strategy of the cat is more similar to that of the rat: increases in meal size are accomplished solely by changes in meal duration rather than in rate of ingestion. Particularly notable was the fact that one cat was able to sustain stable performance at FR 10,240. Both the reduction in meal frequency (Figure 8) and the increase in meal size (Figure 9) as a function of the ratio requirement were completely recoverable during a random sequence of FR values for one cat and during a descending sequence for the other.

In these three species, the relationships between food availability (FR size), the parameters of feeding behavior, and instrumental performance are also observed when the nature of the operant is varied. In an

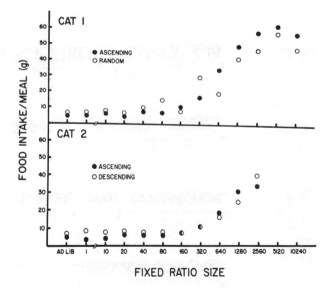

Fig. 9. Food intake per meal for two cats as a function of ratio size. (From Kanarek, 1975.)

attempt to manipulate the energy cost of a meal, Kanarek (1973, unpublished research) made access to the feeder contingent on wheel turns rather than lever presses. The same functional relations were obtained. Similarly, Levitsky (1974) found a decrease in meal frequency and an increase in meal size as a function of the amount of time that rats were required to hold down a lever to gain access to a feeder when the rat controlled the initiation and the size of the meal. It should be noted that his data are reported and interpreted solely in terms of meal size and intermeal interval.

Almost identical relations are observed in rats when water availability is restricted by increasing FR requirements. There is a monotonic decreasing relationship between FR size and the number of bouts of drinking that occur over a 24-hr period (Marwine, 1974). The paradigm used to study drinking is equivalent in all major respects to that previously described for the feeding environment. Following the completion of the FR requirement, a drinking tube is inserted into the cage. The tube remains available for as long as the animal is licking plus 5 min. There is a regular decrease in bout frequency and an increase in bout size as a function of the ratio requirement. Both functions are completely recoverable during a descending sequence of FR values. These shifts in patterns of drinking are not completely successful in maintaining total water intake at control levels. At the higher ratios (FR 80 and above) there is a small decline in total intake, but this does not reduce intake below the obligatory requirement. That is, food intake and weight gain do not differ from controls.

Two other observations illustrate the generality of the behavioral effects that are observed when the availability of a reinforcer is constrained. Rats readily learn to lever press on FR schedules (Collier & Hirsch, 1971) or to lick (Premack, Schaffer, & Hundt, 1964) for access to a running wheel. They will also lever-press to start a voluntary treadmill (Collier & Hirsh, 1971). When the duration of the running episodes is under the animal's control, increases in the FR size lead to a decrease in the number of bouts of running (Figure 10), but a compensatory *increase* in the amount of running per bout. Although these changes conserve total amount of running, they are insufficient at the highest ratios to maintain the level of running of the controls. Also, Adair and Wright (1973) have shown that behavioral thermoregulation is sensitive to the effort involved in controlling environmental temperature. When the force required to pull a chain that changes environmental temperature was increased,

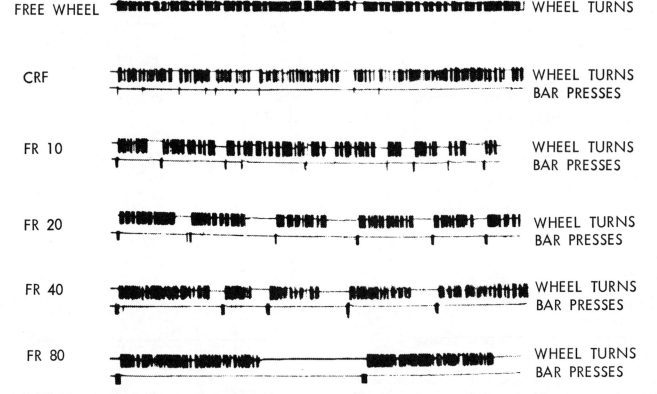

Fig. 10. Wheel turns for one rat as a function of ratio size. (From Collier & Hirsch, 1971. © 1971 by the American Psychological Association. Reprinted by permission.)

squirrel monkeys tolerated greater extremes in the amplitude of the air temperature. Not only did they allow a cold environment to become much colder at high force requirements, but also they tolerated a much warmer temperature before chain pulling was initiated.

Rate of Ingestion

Another version of a free-feeding environment is one in which the meal consists of discrete units—for example, nuts, berries, or pellets. The laboratory version is accomplished via the pellet dispenser in which the rate of delivery of pellets is usually under the animal's control (Balagura & Coscino, 1968; Kissileff, 1970; Teitelbaum & Campbell, 1958). Under these circumstances, meals consist of a number of pellets. This is similar in some respects to the classic reinforcement paradigm in which a deprived subject is provided small units of the appropriate commodity contingent upon a specified response sequence. The size of the unit (weight, volume, concentration, access time) is fixed. The rate at which the item is delivered to the subject is dependent upon rate or pattern of responding on some schedule (e.g., ratio) and is independent of response rate on others (e.g., interval). In our major departure from this traditional procedure, the animals live in the experimental space and obtain all their food or water over the 24-hr period by satisfying the schedule requirements. On this 24-hr regimen the animal can initiate the required response sequence at any time and by successive repetitions of this sequence can control the amount consumed. As stated before, a meal consists of a series of discrete pellets, each obtained on an FR schedule. The end of a meal was defined by the passage of 10 min without the initiation of a ratio run. The rate of ingestion is constrained by both the size of the reinforcer and the schedule on which it is delivered.

Adult rats and growing guinea pigs were tested on an ascending series of FR schedules with reinforcement consisting of single 45-mg pellets (Collier, Hirsch, & Hamlin, 1972; Hirsch & Collier, 1974b). The sequence of FR sizes used was 1, 5, 10, 20 followed by increments of 20 up to FR 240. Each schedule remained in effect for 10 days. Figure 11 shows the changes in instrumental performance for two rats tested under these conditions. Rate of responding increased sharply as a function of FR size. The changes in momentary rate were actually larger than the figure indicates because the rate measure included the post-reinforcement pause, which also increased substantially with FR size. Although not measured directly,

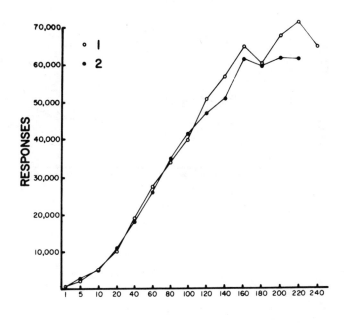
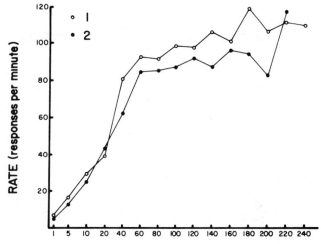
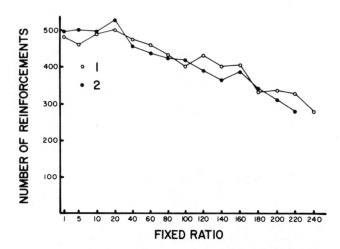

Fig. 11. Number of responses, rate of responding, and number of reinforcements for two rats as a function of ratio size. (From Collier, Hirsch, & Hamlin, 1972.)

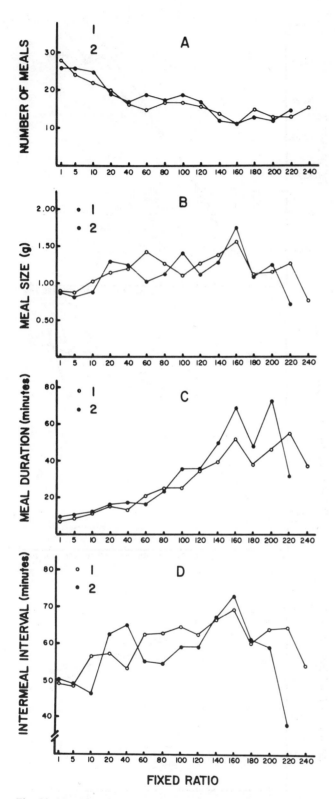

Fig. 12. Number of meals, meal size, meal duration and intermeal intervals for two rats as a function of ratio size. (From Collier, Hirsch, & Hamlin, 1972.)

the increase in the postreinforcement pause was visually evident in the cumulative records (see Collier, Hirsch, & Hamlin, 1972). Response output, which stabilized between 60,000 and 70,000 responses per day at FR 160, was a monotonic increasing function of FR size. At asymptote, animals lever-pressed for almost 14 hr per day. Despite the large increases in response output and rate of responding, the daily number of reinforcements was a decreasing function of FR size.

Figure 12 shows concomitant changes in the parameters of feeding behavior under the same conditions. At low ratios, meal frequency was somewhat higher than that normally observed when powdered chow is fed. Both animals showed a gradual reduction in feeding frequency from FR 1 to FR 160. That is, the increasing number of responses required to obtain a pellet extended the time required to obtain a fixed number of pellets but did not affect the number of pellets consumed per meal. The increase in meal size may be an artifact of meal duration, in that successive meals necessarily began to overlap since so much time was spent obtaining meals as the length of the meals increased. Meal duration was an increasing function of the ratio size, which reached asymptote at 60 min at FR 160. Meal size showed a small increase to FR 160 and then decreased. The function relating the length of the intermeal interval to FR size was less regular but tended to increase up to FR 160 and then to decrease. The changes in the parameters of free feeding were small and in many ways were secondary relative to changes in the level and rate of responding in conserving the animal's rate of ingestion, pattern of feeding, and level of intake. Figure 13 shows that food intake and body weight were maintained at a constant level until FR 80 under these conditions. The control animals were maintained in the same housing as the experimental group, but two had noncontingent access to a dish of pellets and four were fed powdered Purina Chow.

Growing guinea pigs tested under very similar conditions showed the same general pattern of feeding and changes in instrumental performance (Hirsch & Collier, 1974). However, performance tended to deteriorate at somewhat lower ratio requirements.

When small amounts of water rather than food were used as the reinforcer in the paradigm requiring animals to complete an FR requirement for a fixed-size reinforcer, rats (Marwine, 1974) and guinea pigs (Hirsch & Collier, 1974b) showed a similar profile of adjustment and maintained intake at the control levels until approximately FR 50. Under the latter condition, the daily number of drinking bouts stayed relatively constant, and there was a small reduction in

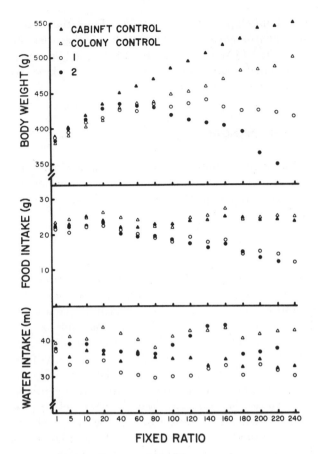

Fig. 13. Body weight and food intake for two rats as a function of ratio size. (From Collier, Hirsch, & Hamlin, 1972.)

the size of these bouts at the higher ratios when total intake declined. The temporal association between feeding and drinking (Kissileff, 1969) was largely unaffected by this constraint on drinking behavior. In the free-feeding paradigm, when the rate of ingestion was constrained there were several noteworthy features of instrumental performance. Again, it was observed that nondeprived animals required no shaping. Also, nondeprived animals defended their total intake by meals of large response outputs at very high rates of responding, over very long (14-hr) periods of time.

CALORIC REGULATION AND CHOICE OF DIETARY ITEMS

Species differ widely in their ability to control caloric intake and to select a nutritionally adequate diet. These differences reflect both their ecological niche and position in the food chain.

Regulation

Regulation of energy balance implies a matching of caloric intake to caloric expenditure. One common test of regulation is to present animals with diets of varying caloric density. Regulation is inferred when the animal adjusts volume intake in such a fashion that total caloric intake remains constant across diets. When the availability of the source of calories is concurrently varied such that meal frequency and size both vary, the test becomes more powerful. Using both availability and caloric concentrations as variables, Kanarek (1974) tested the ability of rats and cats to maintain body weight by adjusting volume food intake. Availability was manipulated by the use of ratio schedule, and the reinforcer consisted of unlimited access to a tunnel feeder. In the rat, low- and high-caloric-density food increased and decreased, respectively, the frequency of feeding in such a fashion that caloric intake remained constant. These relations were obtained at each level of availability and were additive rather than interactive.

On the other hand, cats faced with the same problem did not control total intake appropriately at any level of availability; rather, they appeared to eat solely for bulk. Guinea pigs similarly tested also tended to hold bulk intake constant. However, they surpassed the cats in their ability to vary the efficiency of food utilization, and their weight did not fluctuate as widely when their caloric intake varied to the same degree (Hirsch, unpublished observation; Kanarek, 1974). The above results show that the nutritive properties of the reinforcer are important in determining both the pattern of feeding and the ancillary instrumental behavior. These species differences have important implications for an analysis of reinforcement which will be considered subsequently.

Self-Selection

Faced with a variety of dietary items, some animals are able to select a nutritionally adequate diet. Rats are well known for this ability (Lát, 1967). An experimental paradigm that permits study of the strength of the tendency of an animal to balance its diet has been developed by Hirsch (unpublished data). In this procedure, one component of the diet (e.g., a carbohydrate source such as sucrose) is presented freely while a second component (e.g., a protein source such as Purina Chow) is presented contingent upon an operant. The effort requirement can be varied and its effect on the intake of the two items explored. In a first experiment, rats pressing for Noyes pellets (approximately 23% protein) and offered "free" sucrose made as many as 50,000 responses per day maintaining at least a minimal (6%) protein intake at the highest ratio. Similarly, when the protein-containing component of the diet was free and the rat worked for carbohydrate (sucrose), a large number of responses were expended to maintain the protein/carbohydrate ratio (Collier, unpublished data). Thus under free-feeding conditions, some species will expend a large number of responses to maintain their dietary balance.

OTHER ENVIRONMENTAL CONSTRAINTS

In the two preceding sections, we have shown that constraints on two parameters of meals, frequency and rate of ingestion, lead to compensatory changes in other parameters such that total intake is conserved. Constraints on the distribution of meals have similar effects. For example, many animals show diurnal cycles of feeding. These cycles have been the inspiration for the study of a wide variety of biological rhythms (Richter, 1927). Most recently, feeding cycles have been hypothesized to reflect changes in the basic metabolic processes involved in the control of food intake. For example, LeMagnen and co-workers (LeMagnen, Devos, Gaudilliere, Louis-Sylvestre, & Tallon, 1973) have argued that rats eat in excess of their requirements in the dark and store energy (i.e., are lipogenic), whereas in the light they eat less than their requirements and consume energy (i.e., are lipolytic). Levin and Levine (1974) placed rats on a free-feeding regime pressing a lever for pellets and found that constraining the rate of ingestion by introducing a ratio requirement profoundly affected the temporal distribution of free-feeding behavior. Under conditions in which the ratio requirement was the same in both parts of the 12-hr light-dark cycle, the rats ingested approximately 70% of their food in the dark phase, the commonly reported value. However, this pattern of eating could be completely reversed by programming food to be available on a multiple schedule with continuous reinforcement during the 12-hr light period and various FR sizes during the dark. The larger the FR, the greater the shift of eating to the light component. It appears that, given a choice, rats prefer to obtain food in the most "efficient" manner available, even if this requires altering their customary diurnal patterns. Boice (1972) had previously reported similar data for water intake. Finally, increasing the palatability of the diet in the light phase also effected a shift in the diurnal distribution of intake (Panksepp, 1973; Panksepp and Krost, 1975). Thus the underlying physiological substrate such as that demonstrated by LeMagnen et al. (1973) can be easily disassociated from the pattern of meal taking by environmental constraints.

RESPONSE STRENGTH

One of the assumptions of Skinner's original analysis was that rate of responding is *the* measure of the strength of the response components in the consummatory chain.

Response Rate

One interesting finding of the present studies is the differential sensitivity of both average and local rates of responding to the two experimental paradigms. With unrestricted access to the food magazine, no increase in the average rate of responding during a ratio run was observed in cats or rats, and only a small increase was seen in the guinea pig. This finding contrasts with the dramatic increase in response in the more typical "within-meal" (i.e., between-pellet) procedure in which each ratio run is followed by a single pellet or a small drop of water. The differential effects of FR size on rate of responding can be understood if one considers the *utility* of rate increases in the two cases. An increase in the rate of responding when the duration of access to food is not constrained has no effect on food availability or rate of ingestion. The only contingency between rate and the parameters of meal taking is that increases in rate will shorten the time from the initiation of a ratio run to the delivery of food. This contingency appears to exert some control on the guinea pig which eats faster when access is constrained (cf. Hirsch & Collier, 1974a, 1974b). On the other hand, in the pellet or drop paradigm when only single pellets of food or drops of water are available, a long FR chain between pellets or drops decreases the rate of ingestion. In this instance, increases in the rate of responding serve to counteract the constraint on rate of ingestion. This contingency exerts strong control in the two species tested. Thus we have two different situations. In one, changes in ratio size do not affect rate of instrumental responding; in the other, they do. These appear to result from the effect of the schedule on the rate of ingestion. This difference might be dramatized if the two paradigms were combined in such a fashion that the subject would be required to complete a ratio to gain access to a meal. The meal would consist of pellets delivered on a second ratio requirement which would remain in effect until 10 min of no responding had passed. In this situation, each ratio would be expected to have different effects on the meal parameters. The size of the first ratio would influence the frequency of initiating meals and the size of the meals and would *not* affect the rate of responding between pellets.

Preliminary results confirmed these expectations. Thus there appears to be a direct relationship between the rate of responding and the utility of a given rate in the food economy. This suggests that the classical notion of rate as a measure of response strength only obtains under carefully circumscribed conditions.

Magnitude of Reinforcement

The rate analysis can be explored further by considering "magnitude of reinforcement." In the conventional account, increasing the concentration, quality, amount, or time of access to reinforcement increases the rate (e.g., Collier, 1962; Collier & Siskel, 1959; Collier & Willis, 1961; Guttman, 1953) or reciprocal latency (e.g., Bolles, 1967) of responding. In the 24-hr procedure in which the rat earns his total intake by bar-pressing for pellets and in which there are no constraints on the initiation and termination of meals, the prediction is exactly the opposite. For example, an adult rat will eat about 500 45-mg standard Noyes pellets per day. A ratio requirement of 200 bar presses per pellet would require an output of 100,000 presses per day to maintain this intake. Neither the rat nor the guinea pig defends its intake completely, but each comes close: the rat makes on the order of 70,000 presses per day at this ratio, the guinea pig somewhat less. If the pellet size is increased to 90 mg, it would require one-half the responses to maintain intake, and if it were reduced to 22 mg, it would require double the number of responses. It is not surprising that this actually occurs. It is surprising, however, that the average between-pellet rate of responding (including the postreinforcement pause) is higher for small pellets and lower for large pellets. This is contrary to usual magnitude-of-reinforcement predictions. Although the local rate in this situation has not been analyzed in detail, preliminary evidence suggests that even local rate is higher for the smaller pellet and lower for the larger. This negative relation between pellet size and rate appears to be the case only for *nondeprived* animals whose total intake is gained in the experimental situation. When the animal is depleted (i.e., greater than 7–10% body weight loss), there is a positive relation between the parameters of reinforcement (e.g., volume, concentration, duration) and rate of responding (Collier & Meyers, 1961; Collier & Willis, 1961). Here again we see an important difference between the freely feeding animal and the depleted one.

Ratio Tolerance

In the situation in which access to the feeder is unrestricted until the meal is completed, it can be asked whether the tolerance of very large ratios is simply a matter of the size of the reinforcement taken following the response chain, or whether this tolerance embodies other principles. The most attractive conjecture is that the subject's *termination* of the meal (running burst, etc.) is the critical event. That is, consider a meal to be not simply a collection of reflexes waxing and waning in strength, but rather a dynamic unit, the initiation and termination of which reflect central processes under the control of the animal's total economy. From this perspective, then, the *completion of the meal* may control response strength, rather than the summation of strengths of the individual response units which make up the meal. It is quite clear, for example, that those features of the environment which cause an animal to eat fewer meals also cause him to eat longer meals. Total intake is conserved. Thus at the same body weight, eating the same food item, meal length covaries with frequency of initiation. How does the animal measure the amount consumed? It is unlikely, particularly when frequency has only been partially reduced, that the stomach will be emptied or the reserves depleted to such a degree that they can act as signals for extending a meal. The likelihood of immediate feedback in the free-feeding situation seems low enough to encourage speculation about a guidance system which anticipates rather than responds to needs (cf. Oatley, 1970).

Unit of Analysis

One last argument that can be made with respect to response strength derives from the question of the appropriate unit of analysis in feeding behavior. From studies in which the "effort" to obtain a meal is varied, it is clear the relations between frequency, duration, amount, and rate of eating covary in such a fashion that total intake over a given 24-hr period is conserved. The implication of these facts is that Skinner's focus on the dynamics of the within-meal reflex chain as the way in which to study total intake may have been misdirected. He argued that all-or-none events such as meals were most appropriately analyzed in terms of the within-meal strength of the reflex chain involved in ingestion. The frequency of occurrence and size of meals should be predictable from a knowledge of the "strength" of the components. However, it would appear from the present data that total intake over the feeding cycle is the important boundary condition. Feeding behavior is path-independent in the sense that the final state, total intake, does *not* depend on the particular responses and their rate of occurrence within a meal. Thus one would not expect correlations among the more typical measures of response strength such as rate, extinction, or ratio tolerance except under particular circumstances. The path-independence argument is similar to Skinner's (1935) argument for the generic nature of the reflex in which the class is defined by its effect rather than by the order and topography of its members. If we accept the path-independence argument, we must concur with Richter's (1927) original conjecture that the meal is the appropriate unit of analysis of feeding behavior.

FOOD ECONOMY

Psychologists have long paid lip service to the theory of evolution, but they have seldom paid attention to its consequences for psychological theory except in the most global terms. Most have accepted the notion that the morphology of a species reflects its adaptation to a particular ecological niche, but until recently few have accepted the notion that particular patterns of behavior similarly represent such adaptations (Barash, 1974).

Historically, the most important variables in the study of feeding related to depletion and repletion of some nutritional item. One had only to find the substrate which the hypothalamus was monitoring and one could predict the onset and offset of feeding behavior from knowing its current state. Aside from slight differences in equipment, all species would behave similarly—that is, obey the same laws. Behavior successful in meeting nutritional needs was thereby strengthened; unsuccessful behavior was thereby weakened.

Our suspicion that animals were economists as well as physiologists led to the research discussed in this chapter. It is obvious that feeding patterns (i.e., item choice and the frequency, duration, rate, and distribution of meals) differ widely from species to species. Of greater interest and import, however, are the questions of how these different patterns relate to the ecological niche in which the animal naturally operates and of how they are reflected in general problems of behavior. One approach to these problems is taken by the ecologists. For example, quoting from Schoener (1971, p. 369):

> Natural history is replete with observations on feeding, yet only recently have investigators begun to treat feeding as a device whose performance—as measured by net energy yield/feeding time or some other units assumed commensurate with fitness—may be maximized by natural selection. . . . The primary task of a theory of feeding strategies is to specify for a given animal that complex of behavior and morphology best suited to gather food energy in a given environment.

Schoener views the problem as one of optimization which can be further "trisected" into tasks of: (1) choosing a currency, (2) choosing the appropriate cost-benefit function, and (3) solving for the optimum. For our present discussion, the most important idea in this view is that an animal does not approach the problem of feeding naïvely; rather, he brings a *strategy* to the problem—a strategy which psychologists typically do not see because of the restrictions of their experimental situations. The usual laboratory setting is specifically arranged to minimize or prevent the display of any pattern of behavior other than that which the experimenter is measuring.

In an animal's natural environment, both the initiation and termination of feeding are under the control of the animal. "When," "how often," and "the size and type of item" are the basic parameters of any feeding strategy which have to be adjusted to the density (i.e., probability of encounter) of the item, its caloric and nutritional content, and energy or time cost of obtaining the item. The basic problem for the animal is to partition his time and energy between the many different activities which insure his reproductive success. An animal which did not consider the density, cost, and character of the item to be procured but waited to initiate feeding when it was "hungry" in the physiological sense would simply be unlikely to survive in any but the most permissive environment. It seems more likely that animals must, in some sense, feed in anticipation of, rather than in response to, their needs. Obvious examples of such anticipating behavior are premigration hyperphagia (Odum, 1960) and hibernation (Mrosovsky, 1971). To investigate these speculations, it is necessary to introduce ecological variables into the laboratory—that is, to construct analogues of niches in laboratory situations. We view the present research as such an attempt.

Some insight into the role of these biological variables can be gained by examining a class of phenomena not typically considered by psychologists. From the work of ecologists, it is clear that there are many environmentally defined events which control feeding. If one examines the feeding pyramid, there is a chain of exploitation of resources. Animals can be grouped into three major categories: herbivores, carnivores, and omnivores. Herbivores harvest the readily available plant energy, but they pay for this in terms of low nutritional quality and low caloric density of their food. Their foods require intensive mechanical degradation (e.g., rumination) and chemical conversion (fermentation) before digestion to produce a nutritionally adequate diet. Because the varied ingestants of the generalized herbivore (Westoby, 1974) are modified by fermenting into a nutritionally adequate diet, it is unnecessary for him, except in the case of certain minerals, to eat a highly selected diet. At the other extreme, the carnivores exploit a niche in which the food is of the highest quality and caloric density but is not readily available. The carnivore's problem is one of procurement. Bulk intake alone can accurately regulate both calories and nutritional quality. Finally, omnivores, by being opportunists, can occupy a wide variety of habitats. This poses quite different problems for these animals. The variability in both caloric density and nutritional quality of the omnivore diet requires the omnivore to adjust his intake to his needs by choice of item and amount consumed on a day-to-day basis (Schoener, 1971; Westoby, 1974).

The extensive use of the rat in the study of feeding and nutrition has blinded many researchers to this variety of feeding patterns and strategies. As a result, the physiological models on feeding based on the behavior of the rat are limited to the omnivore model and a very restricted experimental procedure.

In addition to considerations of the environmental niche, it is clear that social, seasonal, and climatic factors have important impacts on feeding schedules (Westoby, 1974). Feeding strategies are intensively conditioned by environmental considerations (cf. Schoener, 1971). Operant psychologists, by their implicit acceptance of the rat feeding model, have failed to consider such ecological variables in their analyses of behavior. Attention must be paid to the structure of the environment and its interaction with response patterns. These factors may specify the units of behavior upon which reinforcement operates.

Considering only the variables arising from an animal's niche, we can make a very preliminary analysis of their role in feeding patterns. The FR constraint on meal frequency can be viewed as a laboratory analogue of a niche in which food varies in availability. The usual situation of the carnivore exemplifies this niche (Estes, 1967a, 1967b; Kruuk, 1972; Schaller, 1967, 1972). The most typical circumstance is one of low availability of prey. Carnivores typically, but not always, have a pattern of infrequent large meals. Since it appears, however, that the carnivorous mode of feeding is in the repertoire of many species (Collier, Hirsch, & Hamlin, 1972; Hirsch & Collier, 1974a, 1974b; Kanarek, in press; Westoby, 1974), an important generalization might be made regarding the effect of food availability on ingestive behavior.

Law of Availability

As commodities (e.g., food, exercise, heat) become less readily obtainable, the frequency of initiating behavior which procures them decreases, but the amount taken per occasion increases in such a fashion that the total amount consumed is conserved. Thus the *law of availability* appears to relate to the animal's efficiency of allocation of resources. For example, as food becomes less readily available, the amount of time, effort, and/or energy expended to obtain it increases. As a result, it becomes more efficient to expend this amount of time, effort, or energy less often and to take larger amounts on any given occasion. On the other hand, when the commodity is readily available, frequency of initiation increases. This suggests that there is a "tradeoff" between the cost of procurement and the cost of use, the cost of use being related, for example, to such variables as the cost of ingestion or absorption and their effect on the efficiency of utilization. The feeding behavior of large carnivores, such as the lion, provides a classic example. These animals must expend considerable effort and undergo high risks of injury in procuring their usual game. As a result they live on a "feast-or-famine" regime (Schaller, 1972) which fluctuates with the density and size of prey. Large and/or scarce prey lead to infrequent large meals, whereas small and/or numerous prey lead to frequent small meals (Schaller, 1972). It would seem that the processing cost of large infrequent meals is higher than the cost of small frequent meals (cf. Morrison, 1968), such that animals revert to small frequent meals when possible.

The law of availability is parallel to Schoener's (1971) principle that the ratio of energy yield/time expended is maximized. Both principles raise, again, the difficult question of the appropriate dimensions for their terms. For example, what is the measure of the cost of "search time"? Is it the time, or the energy expended per unit of time, or the amount of other behavior excluded during the search, or all of these? Similarly, what are the dimensions of availability (cf. Westoby, 1974)? Are they dispersion, density, difficulty, effort required, or danger?

In any case, it is clear that this law cannot be observed in the usual experimental situation, since both initiation and termination of meals are constrained. In fact, the usual situation in which a deprived animal works for reinforcers of fixed size on a schedule for a fixed session length amounts to a single meal. What is being studied is the effect of various experimental variables on the course of a single meal. This is Skinner's original paradigm. The failure of this paradigm to generate the laws which govern an animal's usual pattern of feeding has led to a questioning of the assumptions on which it is based. In the more "natural" situation, irrespective of the scarcity or abundance of resources and the circumstances of their availability, the animal initiates and terminates meals and controls the amount of the commodity consumed. It is the circumstances of *availability* which appear to be crucial.

Schedules

At the present time a set of unrelated principles and laws specifies what is known about schedules of reinforcement. Attempts to organize these principles into a coherent whole and reduce them to the deductive consequences of a few axioms have mainly been directed toward probabilistic relations defining reinforcement density (Schoenfeld, 1970). However, schedules of reinforcement may also have biological significance, and examination of schedules in light of biological variables may yield the organization investigators have been seeking. For example, one aspect of the carnivore's feeding which a schedule in the laboratory may possibly simulate is *stalking*. Characteristic of some hunting patterns are long periods of waiting. Schaller (1972) documented this point in a description of hunting lionesses:

> What impressed me most was the patience and incredible fussiness they displayed. On a number of occasions I have sat for more than an hour watching a lioness or a young lion waiting for a herd of gnus or zebras, already close, to come closer. Once, two lionesses let a file of gnus and zebras trek within fifty yards of where they crouched, in plain sight but unnoticed. Several times one or the other tensed for a spring when a member of the file came slightly closer than the rest. But still they waited, until a zebra spotted them and snorted an alarm.

Schaller did not label this as a contingency differential reinforcement, at low rates of responding (DRL), but it is difficult not to. If the lioness were to move too soon or be seen, the entire behavior sequence would have to be reinitiated. This aspect of carnivore behavior could be simulated in the laboratory by imposing a DRL contingency and allowing the animal to control the size of the meal that became available when the DRL contingency was satisfied. The DRL contingency would functionally reduce itself to continuous reinforcement (CRF) if the interval requirement did not exceed the animal's typical intermeal interval length. For the rat, this time requirement would be approximately 90–120 min. Based on DRL performance in short test sessions, one would be forced to predict that this contingency exceeds the rat's capacity for temporal discrimination. However, behavior of this type is observed routinely on the part of carnivores that rely on stealth and short bursts of speed to capture prey. Such an experiment (DRL 2 hr or more) has not yet been conducted, but we would predict this type of performance to be in the repertoire of some animals. If so, increases in DRL length should lead to compensatory increases in meal size. Thus an analysis of the function of schedules in an animal's economics may provide some order to schedule effects. These accounts may not be unique, as the two different effects of FR in the meal and pellet paradigms reported above show, and may be best understood from the perspective of the niche in which the schedules are employed. Thus two schedules identical in terms of temporal and numerical structure may be functionally different depending upon the environment in which they occur.

Dietary Selection and Regulation

Niche variables can also be used to predict "nutritive" behavior. As a result of their particular diet and their mechanics and chemistry of digestion, herbivores must consume large quantities of food at relatively low rates. Thus one would predict not only a high meal frequency, as previously pointed out, but also a relative insensitivity to the nutritional quality or caloric density of their food. Studies using guinea pigs, a monogastric herbivore, have supported these conjectures (cf. Hirsch, 1973). Studies on the ability of herbivores to self-select a balanced diet are not known to the authors.

Cats likewise appear to be bulk eaters and relatively insensitive to the caloric content of the diet (Hirsch, unpublished data; Kanarek, 1974). Their ability to select a nutritionally adequate diet also remains unexplored. Like their wild counterparts, domestic cats can go for long periods without food and then consume an amount sufficient to maintain growth or adult body weight. Rats, on the other hand, are well known for their ability to regulate caloric intake and select an adequate diet.

Thus it seems that exogenous variables play a dominant role both in feeding and in determining the effect of schedules on response patterns. Further, it appears possible to translate the parameters of feeding in the wild into operant laboratory procedures.

CONCLUSIONS

At the outset of this chapter, we considered two questions raised by Skinner's original formulation of an analysis of feeding behavior. The first concerned the definition of a unit of analysis: Is the reflex, an arbitrary unit which acquires its behavioral meaning by its appearance in "simple" laws, the most appropriate unit with which to study feeding behavior, or would larger units such as the meal or the feeding cycle lead to a more general principle which might be translatable within a natural context? Data presented in this chapter showed that, using the meal as the basic unit of analysis, such laws can be stated, and suggested exploration of a different class of variables which reflect the structure of the animal's environment.

The second question concerned the model of motivation (reinforcement) which would be most useful in studying feeding behavior. The classic model of feeding is one in which behavior is generated, shaped, and maintained in response to physiological needs (deficits). This model has led to the search for underlying physiological perturbations as the occasion for all behavior, whether it be to meet other environmental demands (e.g., temperature regulation) or social behavior (e.g., courtship or maternal care). Recent descriptions by ethologists have emphasized the elicitation of such behavior by particular concatenations of events in the environments rather than by the push of physiological needs. In the present analysis, we have suggested that, except in cases of emergency, the ethological model which describes social behavior is also appropriate for feeding behavior. That is, animals possess a repertoire of feeding strategies which are appropriate to the niche they occupy and which vary with varying habitats within the niche. It is obvious that for many species these strategies are in whole or in part constructed and/or modified by interaction with the environment.

Returning to the problem of the unit of analysis and the question of the units upon which the consequences of behavior act, let us examine the question of reinforcement. The classic view is that complex behavior is assembled from reflexes and that consequences operate directly on the individual reflex units. Another possibility, however, is that behavior is preassembled into dynamic units and that the changes induced by the outcome of a behavior sequence affect not only the occurrence of the larger unit, but also the interrelations of members within the unit. For example, hyenas hunt in packs. When the available game hunted is small and the hunt results in a few well-fed and several frustrated and quarreling members of the pack, the pack will break into smaller units suitable to the game size. If the available game again becomes numerous, the pack will reassemble (Kruuk, 1972). This example illustrates how the consequences, insufficient food in a single meal, can affect a complex social structure. We would conjecture that a common principle underlies feeding patterns of individual animals as well. That is, the feeding strategies of all animals are matched to the niches in which they operate. Further, these feeding strategies are adjusted as a unit when the parameters of the niche change in such a fashion that the ratio of calories gained per meal to the time and/or effort procuring the meal is maximized. Where do learning and motivation enter into this process? We think that "learning" in this situation is the process by which the animal modifies the parameters of his habitat, and motivation is basically the maximization function. We have shown that animals behave in such a fashion as to maximize their ration and to reduce the effects of constraints placed on their normal feeding patterns. We assume that modifications of feeding patterns which increase the probability of finding suitable food in a given habitat will also occur, thus improving the niche. Consider, for example, the problem of a sit-and-wait predator whose food consists of two sizes of prey. When large prey predominates, the optimal strategy is to concentrate on the large prey; but as the ratio of large to small prey decreases, the frequency of attack on small prey should increase (Schoener, 1971). A second strategy, different from optimization, also is possible. The predator can move to a part of his environment in which the ratio of large to small prey is more favorable. Thus the animal can either maximize within a given habitat or he can improve the habitat by modifying its parameters. It is the latter skill which is so characteristic of the human animal. It is our conjecture that the essence of reinforcement lies in "controlling" the environment, where control is evaluated in terms of its effect on the total economy of the animal.

Although the present theoretical speculations are crude, we think that a fruitful research strategy is one which attempts to study variables derived from ecological descriptions in a controlled laboratory situation using operant analogues. This approach may yield a more generalized understanding of the mechanisms underlying learning and motivation than otherwise has previously been possible.

REFERENCES

ADAIR, E., & WRIGHT, B. Behavioral thermoregulation: Task difficulty as a measure of motivational strength. Paper presented at the 14th Annual Meeting of the Psychonomic Society, St. Louis, 1973.

ADOLPH, E. F. Urges to eat and drink in rats. *American Journal of Physiology*, 1947, *151*, 110–125.

BAKER, R. A. A periodic feeding behavior in the albino rat. *Journal of Comparative and Physiological Psychology*, 1953, *46*, 422–426.

BALAGURA, S., & COSCINA, D. V. Periodicity of food intake in the rat as measured by an operant response. *Physiology and Behavior*, 1968, *3*, 641–643.

BARASH, D. P. The evolution of marmot societies: A general theory. *Science*, 1974, *185*, 415–421.

BELL, R. H. V. A grazing ecosystem in the Serengeti. *Scientific American*, 1971, *224*, 86–93.

BOICE, B. Some behavioral tests of domestication in the Norway rat. *Behaviour*, 1972, *42*, 198–231.

BOLLES, R. C. *Theory of motivation*. New York: Harper & Row, 1967.

BOOTH, D. A. Caloric compensation in rats with continuous or intermittent access to food. *Physiology and Behavior*, 1972, *8*, 891–899.

BRODY, S. *Bioenergetics and growth*. New York: Reinhold, 1945.

CANNON, W. B. *The wisdom of the body*. New York: Norton, 1932.

COLLIER, G. Consummatory and instrumental responding as functions of deprivation. *Journal of Experimental Psychology*, 1962, *64*, 410–414.

COLLIER, G. Body weight loss as a measure of motivation in hunger and thirst. *Annals of the New York Academy of Science*, 1969, *157*, 594–609.

COLLIER, G., & HIRSCH, E. Reinforcing properties of spontaneous activity in the rat. *Journal of Comparative and Physiological Psychology*, 1971, *7*, 155–160.

COLLIER, G., HIRSCH, E., & HAMLIN, P. The ecological determinants of reinforcement in the rat. *Physiology and Behavior*, 1972, *9*, 705–716.

COLLIER, G., & KNARR, F. Defense of water balance in the rat. *Journal of Comparative and Physiological Psychology*, 1966, *61*, 5–10.

COLLIER, G., & LEVITSKY, D. Defense of water balance in rats: Behavioral and physiological responses to depletion. *Journal of Comparative and Physiological Psychology*, 1967, *64*, 59–67.

COLLIER, G., & MYERS, L. The loci of reinforcement. *Journal of Experimental Psychology*, 1961, *61*, 57–66.

COLLIER, G., & SISKEL, M., JR. Performance as a joint function of amount of reinforcement and inter-reinforcement interval. *Journal of Experimental Psychology*, 1959 *57*, 115–120.

COLLIER, G., & WILLIS, F. N. Deprivation and reinforcement. *Journal of Experimental Psychology*, 1961, *62*, 377–384.

DERUITER, L. Feeding behavior of vertebrates in the natural environment. In Code & Heidel (Eds.), *Handbook of physiology* (Vol. 1). Washington, D.C.: American Physiological Society, 1967.

DUNCAN, I. H. H., DUNCAN, A. R., HUGHES, B. O., & WOOD-GUSH, D. G. M. The patterns of food intake in female brown leghorn fowls as recorded in a Skinner box. *Animal Behavior*, 1970, *18*, 245–255.

EHRENFREUND, D. The relationship between weight loss during deprivation and food consumption. *Journal of Comparative and Physiological Psychology*, 1959, *52*, 123–124.

ESTES, R. D. Predators and scavengers, I. *Natural History*, 1967, *76*, 20–29 (a)

ESTES, R. D. Predators and scavengers, II. *Natural History*, 1967, *76*, 38–47. (b)

FABER, B. *The effects of several environmental factors on feeding behavior in the American cockroach*, Periplaneta americana (L). Unpublished dissertation, Rutgers University, 1975.

FALK, J. L. The nature and determinants of adjunctive behavior. *Physiology and Behavior*, 1971, *6*, 577–588.

FEARING, F. *Reflex action: A study in the history of physiological psychology*. Baltimore: Williams & Wilkins, 1930.

FERSTER, C. B., & SKINNER, B. F. *Schedules of reinforcement*. Englewood Cliffs, N.J.: Prentice-Hall, Inc., 1957.

FINDLEY, J. An experimental outline for building and exploring multioperant behavior repertoires. *Journal of the Experimental Analysis of Behavior*, 1962, *5*, 113–166.

FINDLEY, J. D., & BRADY, J. V. Facilitation of large ratio performances by use of conditioned reinforcement. *Journal of the Experimental Analysis of Behavior*, 1965, *8*, 125–129.

FITZSIMONS, J. T. Normal drinking in rats. *Journal of Physiology* (London), 1957, *138*, 39P.

FITZSIMONS, J. T. Effect of nephrectomy on the additivity of certain stimuli of drinking in the rat. *Journal of Comparative and Physiological Psychology*, 1969, *68*, 308–314.

FITZSIMONS, J. T. The physiology of thirst: Extraneural aspects of the mechanisms of drinking. In E. Stellar & J. M. Sprague (Eds.), *Progress in physiological psychology* (Vol. 4). New York: Academic Press, 1971.

FITZSIMONS, J. T., & LEMAGNEN, J. Eating as a regulatory control of drinking in the rat. *Journal of Comparative and Physiological Psychology*, 1969, *67*, 273–283.

GUTHRIE, E. R. *The psychology of learning*. New York: Harper, 1935.

GUTTMAN, N. Operant conditioning extinction, and periodic reinforcement in relation to concentration of sucrose used as a reinforcing agent. *Journal of Experimental Psychology*, 1953, *46*, 213–224.

HERRNSTEIN, R. J. On the law of effect. *Journal of the Experimental Analysis of Behavior,* 1970, *13,* 243–266.

HIRSCH, E. Some determinants of intake and patterns of feeding in the guinea pig. *Physiology and Behavior,* 1973, *11,* 687–704.

HIRSCH, E., & COLLIER, G. The ecological determinants of reinforcement in the guinea pig. *Physiology and Behavior,* 1974, *12,* 239–249. (a)

HIRSCH, E., & COLLIER, G. Effort as determinant of intake and patterns of drinking in the guinea pig. *Physiology and Behavior,* 1974, *12,* 647–655. (b)

HOEBEL, B. Feeding: Neural control of intake. *Annual Review of Psychology,* 1971, *33,* 533–568.

HULL, C. L. Knowledge and purpose as habit mechanisms. *Psychological Review,* 1930, *37,* 511–525.

HULL, C. L. Mind, mechanism, and adaptive behavior. *Psychological Review,* 1937, *44,* 1–32.

HULL, C. L. *Principles of behavior.* New York: Appleton-Century-Crofts, 1943.

JAYNES, J. The problem of animate motion in the seventeenth century. *History of Ideas,* 1970, *31,* 219–234.

KANAREK, R. B. *The energetics of meal patterns.* Unpublished dissertation, Rutgers University, 1974.

KANAREK, R. B. Availability and caloric density of the diet as determinants of meal patterns in cats. *Physiology and Behavior,* 1975, *15,* 611–618.

KISSILEFF, H. R. Food-associated drinking in the rat. *Journal of Comparative and Physiological Psychology,* 1969, *67,* 284–300.

KISSILEFF, H. R. Free feeding in normal and "recovered lateral" rats monitored by a pellet detecting eatometer. *Physiology and Behavior,* 1970, *5,* 162–173.

KISSILEFF, H. R. Nonhomeostatic controls of drinking. In Epstein et al. (Eds.), *Neuropsychology of thirst.* Washington, D.C.: V. H. Winston, 1973.

KLEIBER, M. *The fire of life.* New York: Wiley, 1961.

KÖHLER, W. *Gestalt psychology.* New York: Horace Liveright, 1929.

KRUUK, H. *The spotted hyena: A study of predation and social behavior.* Chicago: University of Chicago Press, 1972.

LARUE, C. G., & LEMAGNEN, J. The olfactory control of meal patterns in rats. *Physiology and Behavior,* 1971, *9,* 817–821.

LÁT, J. Self-selection of dietary components. In Code & Heidel (Eds.), *Handbook of physiology* (Vol. 1). Washington, D.C.: American Physiological Society, 1967.

LAWRENCE, D. H., & MASON, W. A. Food intake in the rat as a function of deprivation intervals and feeding rhythms. *Journal of Comparative and Physiological Psychology,* 1955, *48,* 267–271.

LEMAGNEN, J. Advances in studies on the physiological control and regulation of food intake. In E. Stellar & J. M. Sprague (Eds.), *Progress in physiological psychology* (Vol. 4). New York: Academic Press, 1971.

LEMAGNEN, J., & DEVOS, M. Metabolic correlates of meal onset in the free food intake of rats. *Physiology and Behavior,* 1970, *5,* 805–814.

LEMAGNEN, J., DEVOS, M., GAUDILLIERE, J.-P., LOUIS-SYLVESTRE, J. & TALLON, S. Role of a lipostatic mechanism in regulation by feeding of energy balance in rats. *Journal of Comparative and Physiological Psychology,* 1973, *84,* 1–23.

LEMAGNEN, J., & TALLON, S. La Periodicité spontanée de la prise d'aliments ad libitum du rat blanc. *Journal of Physiology* (Paris), 1966, *58,* 323–349.

LEVIN, R., & LEVINE, S. Ecological determinants of circadian rhythms in rats. Paper presented at the meeting of the Eastern Psychological Association, Philadelphia, 1974.

LEVITSKY, D. Feeding patterns of rats in response to fasts and changes in environmental conditions. *Physiology and Behavior,* 1970, *5,* 291–300.

LEVITSKY, D. Feeding conditions and intermeal relationships. *Physiology and Behavior,* 1974, *12,* 779–787.

LEVITSKY, D., & COLLIER, G. Effects of diet and deprivation on meal eating behavior in rats. *Physiology and Behavior,* 1968, *5,* 291–300.

MACFARLANE, W. V., & HOWARD, B. Comparative water and energy economy of wild and domestic mammals. *Symposium of the Zoological Society of London,* 1972, *31,* 261–296.

MARWINE, A. G. *Patterns of intake in the rat as a function of the effort required to obtain water.* Unpublished doctoral dissertation, Rutgers University, 1974.

MAYER, J. Regulation of energy intake and the body weight: The glucostatic theory and the lipostatic hypothesis. *Annals of the New York Academy of Science,* 1955, *63,* 15–42.

MORRISON, S. D. Regulation of water intake by rats deprived of food. *Physiology and Behavior,* 1968, *5,* 75–81.

MORSE, W. H., & KELLEHER, R. T. Schedules as fundamental determinants of behavior. In W. Schoenfeld (Ed.), *The theory of reinforcement schedules.* Englewood Cliffs, N.J.: Prentice-Hall, Inc., 1970.

MROSOVSKY, N. *Hibernation and the hypothalamus.* Englewood Cliffs, N.J.: Prentice-Hall, Inc., 1971.

OATLEY, K. Brain mechanisms and motivation. *Nature,* 1970, *225,* 797–801.

OATLEY, K. Dissociation of the circadian drinking pattern from eating. *Nature,* 1971, *229,* 494–496.

ODUM, E. P. Premigratory hyperphagia in birds. *American Journal of Clinical Nutrition,* 1960, *8,* 621–629.

PANKSEPP, J. Reanalysis of feeding patterns in the rat. *Journal of Comparative and Physiological Psychology,* 1973, *82,* 78–94.

PANKSEPP, J., & KROST, K. Modification of diurnal feeding patterns by palatability. In *Physiology and Behavior,* 1975, *15,* 673–677.

PAVLOV, I. P. *Conditioned reflexes.* Oxford University Press, 1927.

PREMACK, D. Toward empirical behavior laws, I: Positive reinforcement. *Psychological Review,* 1959, *66,* 219–233.

PREMACK, D., & KINTSCH, W. A. Description of free responding in the rat. *Learning and Motivation,* 1970, *1,* 321–336.

PREMACK, D., SCHAEFFER, R. W., & HUNDT, A. Reinforcement for drinking by running: Effect of fixed ratio and reinforcement time. *Journal of the Experimental Analysis of Behavior,* 1964, *7,* 91–96.

RICHTER, C. P. Animal behavior and internal drives. *Quarterly Review of Biology,* 1927, *2,* 307–343.

ROBINSON, E. A., & ADOLPH, E. F. Pattern of normal water drinking in dogs. *American Journal of Physiology,* 1943, *139,* 39–44.

SCHALLER, G. B. *The deer and the tiger: A study of wildlife in India.* Chicago: University of Chicago Press, 1967.

SCHALLER, G. B. *The Serengeti lion: A study of predatory-prey relations.* Chicago: University of Chicago Press, 1972.

SCHOENER, T. W. Theory of feeding strategies. *Annual Review of Ecology and Systematics,* 1971, *2,* 369–404.

SCHOENFELD, W. N. *Theory of reinforcement schedules.* Englewood Cliffs, N.J.: Prentice-Hall, Inc., 1970.

SIDMAN, M. *Tactics of scientific research.* New York: Basic Books, 1960.

SIEGEL, P. S., & STUCKEY, H. L. The diurnal course of water and food intake in the normal mature rat. *Journal of Comparative and Physiological Psychology,* 1947, *40,* 365–370.

SKINNER, B. F. On the conditions of elicitation of certain eating reflexes. *Proceedings of National Academy of Science,* 1930, *16,* 433–438.

SKINNER, B. F. The concept of the reflex in the description of behavior. *Journal of General Psychology,* 1931, *5,* 427–458.

SKINNER, B. F. Drive and reflex strength. *Journal of General Psychology,* 1932, *6,* 22–37. (a)

SKINNER, B. F. Drive and reflex strength, II. *Journal of General Psychology,* 1932, *6,* 38–48. (b)

SKINNER, B. F. The generic nature of the concepts of stimulus and response. *Journal of General Psychology,* 1935, *12,* 40–65.

SKINNER, B. F. *The behavior of organisms.* New York: Appleton-Century-Crofts, 1938.

SKINNER, B. F. The phylogeny and ontogeny of behavior. *Science,* 1966, *153,* 1205–1213.

SNOWDEN, C. T. Motivation, regulation, and the control of meal parameters with oral and intragastric feeding. *Journal of Comparative and Physiological Psychology,* 1969, *69,* 91–100.

STELLAR, E., & HILL, J. H. The rat's rate of drinking as a function of water deprivation. *Journal of Comparative and Physiological Psychology,* 1952, *45,* 96–102.

TEITELBAUM, P., & CAMPBELL, B. A. Ingestion patterns in hyperphagic and normal rats. *Journal of Comparative and Physiological Psychology,* 1958, *51,* 135–141.

THOMAS, D. W., & MAYER, J. Meal taking and regulation of food intake by normal and hyperphagic rats. *Journal of Comparative and Physiological Psychology,* 1968, *66,* 642–653.

TIMBERLAKE, W., & ALLISON, J. Response deprivation: An empirical approach to instrumental performance. *Psychological Review,* 1974, *81,* 146–164.

WESTOBY, M. An analysis of diet selection by large generalist herbivores. *American Nature,* 1974, *108,* 290–304.

WIEPKEMA, P. R. Behavior changes in CBA mice as a result of one goldthioglucose injection. *Behavior,* 1968, *32,* 179–210.

WYCKOFF, L. B., JR. The role of observing responses in discrimination learning, I. *Psychological Review,* 1952, *59,* 431–442.

WYNNE-EDWARDS, V. C. *Animal dispersion in relation to social behavior.* London: Oliver and Boyd, 1962.

YAMAMATO, W. S., & BROBECK, J. R. (Eds.). *Physiological controls and regulations.* Philadelphia: W. B. Saunders, 1965.

YOUNG, P. T. *Motivation of behavior.* London: Wiley, 1936.

ZEIGLER, H. P., GREEN, H. L., & LEHRER, R. Patterns of feeding behavior in the pigeon. *Journal of Comparative and Physiological Psychology,* 1971, *76,* 468–477.

3

Pavlovian Control of Operant Behavior

an analysis of autoshaping and its implications for operant conditioning*

Barry Schwartz
and
Elkan Gamzu

INTRODUCTION

In the beginning, there was the reflex. Pavlov employed the reflex arc as a model in establishing the laws of classical conditioning. Under a variety of conditions, stimuli which had previously had no relation to particular reflexes could be made to trigger or elicit them. This process of classical (or respondent or Pavlovian) conditioning was taken by Pavlov as the basic constituent of all learning—of all adaptive modification of behavior.

From the outset, however, it was clear that Pavlov's phenomenon could not explain all he hoped. The problem lay in the reflex arc model itself. Some, indeed most, behaviors in which complex organisms en-

gaged did not appear to be elicited at all. While it was easy to specify the stimulus which produced salivation or flexion of a hind limb, it was difficult indeed to find the stimulus which triggered walking, or writing, or playing the piano. These behaviors appeared voluntary and decidedly unelicited. They could not be captured by the reflex arc concept or by the principles of Pavlovian conditioning. A new learning principle was required to explain their development and continued occurrence. This principle was Thorndike's law of effect.

The rest, of course, is history. It remained for Skinner to highlight the distinction between the two kinds of learning, to emphasize the particular importance of the law of effect in learning—operant or instrumental conditioning—and to develop a brilliant set of methods for the study of operant conditioning. The research which is the fruit of Skinner's pioneering work is prodigious. The study of animal learning currently, at least in the United States, is heavily focused on operant conditioning. This volume and its predecessor (Honig, 1966) are testimony to the rather rapid development of sophisticated analyses of the principles which govern operant behavior.

---

* The authors wish to thank Robert Boakes, Len Cook, Francis Irwin, Barry Polsky, Daniel Reisberg, Elias Schwam, Myrna Schwartz, Sara Shettleworth, Alan Silberberg, Herb Terrace, Teresa Vollmecke, and Edward Wasserman for providing critical insight at various points in the preparation of this chapter. We wish to thank Herb Jenkins, J. A. Nevin, Howard Rachlin, Herb Terrace, and David Williams for providing prints of figures which appeared in their journal articles. Most especially, though, we wish to thank David Williams, whose contribution to our thinking over the years has been profound and, we hope, obvious in these pages. Preparation of the chapter was facilitated by NSF grant BMS 73-01403 to the first author.

Meanwhile, the study of Pavlovian conditioning has also progressed, although more slowly. Most of Pavlov's initial findings are reproducible, and the domain over which Pavlovian conditioning extends has been enlarged. In addition, there have been occasional new ideas about Pavlovian conditioning which have changed our understanding of its basic nature (e.g., Kamin, 1969; Rescorla, 1967).

In the midst of this atmosphere of progress, there is one problem which has consistently resisted solution: the problem of the relation between Pavlovian and operant conditioning. How are the two types of learning to be defined? What are the processes which underly them? Are they mutually exclusive, or can they operate simultaneously on the same class of behavior? Are there any empirical findings which unequivocally allow one to distinguish between them? These questions do not have secure answers. The history of the problem has seen attempts to reduce one type of learning to the other. The characteristics of the two types of learning have been exhaustively specified in an effort to highlight their differences (Kimble, 1961). What emerged from this analysis, however, was their remarkable similarity. More recent efforts to distinguish between the two types of learning (Rescorla & Solomon, 1967) have been similarly frustrated. Defining the two types of learning in terms of the procedures used to produce them is the best our current understanding allows.

Consider an example. The prototypic experimental context for the study of operant conditioning currently is the study of the pigeon pecking at a response key. The key peck is presumably a voluntary behavior, governed by the law of effect. Yet in 1968 Brown and Jenkins showed that Pavlovian conditioning procedures could also generate and sustain pecking.

Does this mean that pecking is both voluntary and reflexive? Does it mean that pecking is sometimes voluntary and sometimes reflexive? The best one can do at present is suggest that pecking which is produced by a Pavlovian procedure is reflexive while pecking which is produced by an operant procedure is voluntary. The experimental procedure defines the learning process. Unfortunately, this is demonstrably false. Pecking which is produced by a Pavlovian procedure is also governed by the law of effect. It is just these interactions between Pavlovian and operant conditioning variables in the control of key pecking in the pigeon which is the concern of this chapter. Rather than endeavor to classify instances of learning on the basis of the two procedures, we shall try to assess the joint influence of each on the occurrence of a single class of behavior. We hope to demonstrate that Pavlovian and operant principles represent good analytic tools though they are problematic as classificatory categories.

In the first part of the chapter we shall review the evidence that Pavlovian procedures are sufficient to produce and maintain pecking in the pigeon. Most of this evidence centers on the study of autoshaping and automaintenance. In the second part of the chapter we shall show that the Pavlovian control of key pecking revealed by autoshaping studies enters significantly into many standard operant conditioning procedures. The bulk of this section will be a discussion of multiple schedules of reinforcement. It will be a kind of case study, designed to illustrate the pervasive influence of Pavlovian conditioning on the control of operant behavior. The chapter will not provide an exhaustive discussion of either autoshaping or multiple-schedule performance. Very thorough recent reviews have been provided by Hearst and Jenkins (1974) of the former and by Mackintosh (1974) or the latter.

AUTOSHAPING AND AUTOMAINTENANCE

Autoshaping: Necessary and Sufficient Conditions

In 1968 Brown and Jenkins reported the following experiment. Deprived, magazine-trained, but otherwise naïve pigeons were placed in a dimly illuminated chamber. Once every 60 sec, on the average, a response key was illuminated for 8 sec and followed by the delivery of grain. The surprising result of this procedure was that even though food delivery was independent of the pigeons' behavior, all 36 subjects began pecking at the illuminated key after between 6 and 119 key-food pairings. Once pecking occurred, each peck at the illuminated key extinguished the key light and produced immediate food delivery. Brown and Jenkins called this procedure *autoshaping* (because it was *automatic,* the pigeon *shaped itself*). As such, it represented an important technical advance over the previously used "method of successive approximations" (e.g., Ferster & Skinner, 1957), which was as inexact as it was artful.

However, autoshaping has represented considerably more than technological improvement. The phenomenon has raised theoretical issues which go to the heart of the experimental analysis of behavior. The reason is that key pecking in the pigeon has been considered a prototypic operant—an arbitrarily defined class of skeletal behavior which is sensitive to and controlled by its consequences. Indeed, most of our present understanding of the control of behavior by its consequences has come from the study of key pecking. Yet the autoshaping paradigm is Pavlovian: An arbitrary conditional stimulus or CS (key light) precedes an unconditional stimulus or US (grain). As in other Pavlovian procedures, the sequence of events is completely unaffected by the organism's behavior, a characteristic which does not fit well with our definition of operants. Moreover, Pavlovian procedures are usually said to influence reflexive, nonskeletal, non-operant activities. Thus autoshaping seems to represent Pavlovian conditioning of a prototypic operant response (Gamzu & Williams, 1971; Hearst & Jenkins, 1974; Jenkins, 1973; Jenkins & Moore, 1973; Moore, 1973). How can the same response be both operant and reflexive? How secure is the distinction between operant and Pavlovian conditioning? Is susceptibility to Pavlovian influence unique to key pecking, or do all operants share this property? Are there other phenomena which demonstrate Pavlovian control of key pecking which have been overlooked or misinterpreted in the past? These and other questions will be addressed in the sections which follow. The first order of business, however, is an assessment of whether autoshaping is unequivocally the product of a Pavlovian, stimulus-reinforcer association. In this section we shall consider the conditions which are necessary and sufficient for the *acquisition* of key pecking in autoshaping procedures.

Just as in standard studies of Pavlovian conditioning, a variety of control procedures are required to ascertain whether an *association* of CS (key light) and US (food) is what produces autoshaping. Many of these control procedures were included in Brown and Jenkins's demonstration of autoshaping. The results and procedures are shown in Figure 1. Brown and Jenkins reported only the trial on which the first key peck occurred. The reason for this is that in all but the last of their procedures, a key peck immediately produced food. Thus once the first peck occurred, the response-reinforcer relation would exert control over pecking and increase its likelihood. In most later studies of autoshaping, food delivery has always been independent of responding. This makes the study of pecks after the first one of interest. The first panel shows the basic procedure already described. The second panel shows that when key and food were paired in reverse order (backward conditioning) only 2 of 12 pigeons pecked the key. When the key was illuminated without food (CS only—third panel), no pigeons pecked the key. When the key was continually illuminated and food was presented periodically (US

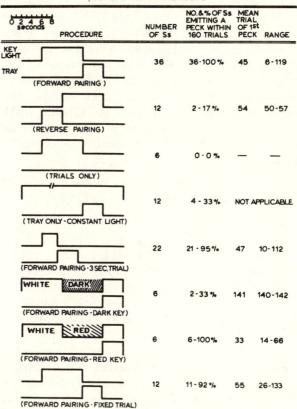

Fig. 1. Schematic representation of the procedures used by Brown and Jenkins and summary acquisition results. The top procedure is the standard autoshaping paradigm. (From Brown & Jenkins, 1968. © 1968 by the Society for the Experimental Analysis of Behavior, Inc.)

only), 4 of 12 pigeons pecked the key (fourth panel). When the key light was illuminated for 3 rather than 8 sec, 21 of 22 pigeons pecked the key (fifth panel). When a dark key was paired with food, only 2 of 6 pigeons pecked the key, while when a red key (which was otherwise white) was paired with food, all 6 pigeons pecked the key (sixth and seventh panel). These control conditions appear to demonstrate that pairing is necessary and sufficient (except when a dark key is the CS) to produce autoshaping.

However, in the province of standard Pavlovian conditioning, Rescorla (1967) has persuasively argued that none of the control procedures employed by Brown and Jenkins are sufficient to allow an unequivocal conclusion that autoshaping is the result of CS–US relation. What is needed is a procedure in which CS and US are neither paired nor unpaired, but independent of one another. This, of course, is the truly random control procedure. In such a procedure, pairings of CS and US occasionally occur, but the occurrence of the CS provides no information about the likelihood of occurrence of the US; i.e., the probability of the US given the CS equals the probability of the US given no CS $[P(\text{US}/\text{CS}) = P(\text{US}/\overline{\text{CS}})]$. Peterson (1972), Bilbrey and Winokur (1973), and Wasserman, Franklin, and Hearst (1974) have employed this procedure and have shown that it does not result in autoshaping. The procedure has been studied most extensively, however, by Gamzu and Williams (1971, 1973), and it is to their work we now turn in discussing the importance of the informativeness of the CS for autoshaping.

Informativeness of the CS

CONTINGENCY VS. PAIRING

Gamzu and Williams (1971, 1973) studied a variant of the autoshaping procedure similar to that used in recent studies of Pavlovian aversive conditioning (Rescorla, 1968). A response key was periodically illuminated for 8.6-sec trials, with a variable intertrial interval (ITI) with a mean of 30 sec. Once every second during the trial a random probability generator was sampled, and an output occurred with a probability of .03 ($p = .03$). Each output operated the feeder for 4 sec. Thus food was delivered once every 33 sec or once every fourth trial, on the average. This *differential* procedure is depicted in the second panel of Figure 2. It differs from standard autoshaping in two respects: first, food is not delivered in every trial; second, food can be delivered at any moment during the trial, not just at the end. Key pecking was acquired and maintained at high rates in all pigeons tested. The procedure was then modified so that the probability generator was sampled (and food delivered) at the same rate during intertrial intervals as during trials: the key was *nondifferentially* related to food, i.e., food was as likely in its absence as in its presence. This procedure is equivalent to the truly random control procedure (Rescorla, 1967) and is depicted in the third panel of Figure 2. Pigeons exposed to this procedure did not peck the key. The two other control procedures depicted in Figure 2 were also run. In one (*differential-absence*) food was presented only in the ITI, and in the other (*no-reinforcement*) food was never presented. Neither procedure generated consistent key pecking. The birds on these three procedures were then exposed to the differential procedure, and pecking was obtained in all of them. Thus key pecking was reliably obtained only when the illuminated key was differentially associated with food. These data led Gamzu and Williams to conclude that the acquisition (and indeed, as we shall see later, the maintenance) of

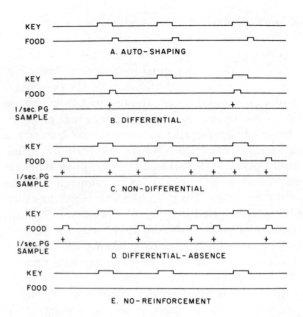

Fig. 2. Schematic representation of (a) the basic autoshaping paradigm and (b–e) procedures in which food presentation was determined by sampling a probability generator (PG): (b) The *differential* procedure, in which food was presented randomly in time, but only during illuminated key trials. (c) The *nondifferential* procedure, in which food was presented randomly in time during trial and intertrial intervals. (d) The *differential-absence* procedure, in which food was presented only in the intertrial interval. (e) The *nonreinforcement* procedure, in which food was never presented. (From Gamzu & Williams, 1973. © 1973 by the Society for the Experimental Analysis of Behavior, Inc.)

autoshaped key pecking depended on the information the CS conveyed about the US, rather than a mere pairing of the two. These conclusions parallel those drawn by Rescorla (1972) about the crucial relationships in Pavlovian conditioning.

REDUNDANCY

Egger and Miller (1962, 1963) suggested that the informativeness of a stimulus with respect to reinforcement determines its power as a secondary reinforcer. They pointed out that just because a stimulus always precedes reinforcement does not guarantee that it is informative. For example, if a series of pairings always consists only of tone followed by food, then the tone is informative. If, however, the tone is always preceded by a light, then the tone is now redundant because the light reliably predicts reinforcement, and that "information" is available before the tone is sounded. However, if the light is sometimes followed by tone and food and sometimes not, then the mere presentation of the light does not "guarantee" reinforcement, while the tone does. Thus, the tone is once again informative. Egger and Miller substantiated this argument by showing that the relative efficacy of two stimuli as secondary reinforcers depended on whether they were informative or redundant in the sense outlined.

Allaway (1971) tested the Egger and Miller conceptualization of informativeness in autoshaping. Three groups of pigeons were exposed to a basic fixed-trial autoshaping procedure in which 6-sec key illuminations were always followed by access to food. For one group (key-only) no additional manipulations were involved. For the second group, 2 sec before each illuminated key trial a tone was sounded for 8 sec after which food was delivered. For this group the illuminated key was redundant (key-redundant). The third group had the same conditions as the key-redundant group, but in addition an equal number of 8-sec tone trials that were associated with neither key nor food (tone-irrelevant). Throughout the experiment, reinforcement was delivered response-independently. In general, key pecking was far less frequent when the key was redundant than in either of the other two procedures. Indeed, some naïve birds failed to autoshape when the lit key was always preceded by a tone. Allaway's data confirm the fact that the important feature of the CS–US relationship in autoshaping is the informativeness of CS with respect to the US and not merely the pairing of the two. Wasserman and his co-workers have obtained data consistent with Allaway's with a variety of similar procedures (Wasserman, 1972, 1973b, 1974; Wasserman & Anderson, 1974; Wasserman & McCracken, 1974).

Trial and ITI Duration Effects

Another aspect of informativeness which is not captured by measures of conditional probability is the importance of relative trial and intertrial interval (ITI) durations. To understand the informativeness of these events, consider the following analogy. Imagine waiting at a train station, through which five differently numbered trains continually pass. Only one number will take you to your destination. If the trains arrive once every minute, you can afford to read your copy of this volume and only look up occasionally. However, if the trains come in once every 10 minutes, you will certainly pay more attention to the train arrivals (trials). Consider now the difference between waiting at the terminal and waiting at a through station. At the terminal the trains roll in and wait for, say, a minute, so that once you notice that a train is in, you can go over and inspect the number. However, at the through station the train only stops for 20 seconds, so that it is necessary to be constantly alert in order to determine whether the incoming train is the one you want to board. As the waiting time (trial duration) gets shorter until the train stops only on demand, the vigilance required increases. The relevance of this analogy to autoshaping is as follows: we would expect that with ITI held constant, shorter trials will convey greater information, and will thus engender more pecking. Similarly, with trial duration constant, longer ITIs will generate more pecking during a trial.

In their very first experiments, Brown and Jenkins (1968) compared an 8-sec trial with a 3-sec trial but did not find much difference in rate of acquisition. Ricci (1973), however, reported that with a constant mean ITI of 4 min, autoshaping was much more rapid when the trial duration was 30 sec than when it was 120 sec.

An extensive study of trial duration has been made by Baldock (1974). When ITI duration was held constant, the rate of acquisition of autoshaping was inversely related to trial duration; that is, autoshaping was most rapid when the CS was brief (4 sec) and was gradually less rapid as the trial duration increased (up to 32 sec).

Terrace, Gibbon, Farrell, and Baldock (1975) in-

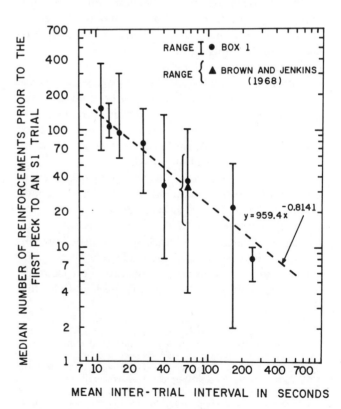

Fig. 3. Median number of reinforcements prior to first trial on which a peck occurred as a function of the mean intertrial interval. Trial durations were always 10 sec. (From Terrace et al, 1975.)

vestigated the other side of this coin. They used a constant 10-sec trial and varied the mean ITI from 5 to 400 sec. The rate of acquisition was a direct monotonic function of the ITI. Some of the data are presented in Figure 3. Thus both intuitions about the role of trial and ITI durations are confirmed. The next logical step was to combine them. Baldock (1974) showed that the important dimension in determining the rate of acquisition of pecking is the ratio of trial to ITI time. Over a wide range of trials (4 to 32 sec) and mean ITIs (8 to 78 sec), acquisition was always more rapid when the ratio of trial to ITI was smaller.

We can summarize briefly what is presently known about the necessary CS–US relationships for autoshaping to occur: specific pairings are neither necessary nor sufficient. Rather, the CS must provide information (broadly construed) about the occurrence of the US. The more informative the CS is, the more rapid acquisition is.[1]

Types of US and the Relation Between the US and Response

The apparent similarity between the conditions necessary to produce autoshaping and the necessary conditions for more standard demonstrations of Pavlovian conditioning leads one to look for further evidence that autoshaping is an instance of Pavlovian conditioning. One obvious thing to investigate is the relation between the US or reinforcer and the conditioned response. Pavlovian conditioned responses typically are some component of the unconditioned response to the US. In this section we review evidence that the same is true of autoshaping.

In the most common autoshaping situation, with pigeons as subjects and food as the US, the conditioned response is key pecking. Pecking is of course the major component of the pigeon's feeding repertoire (e.g., Craig, 1912). Other species also show this similarity between the response elicited by the reinforcer and the autoshaped response. For example, bobwhite quail peck to feed and peck a light that signals food (Gardner, 1969). Squier (1969) in a discussion of autoshaping in different species of fish, stated that "the topography of key responses varied, each type closely resembling the consummatory response" (p. 178). Smith and Smith (1971) demonstrated autoshaping in the dog, and S. G. Smith (personal communication) remarked that licking the response key was observed. Rats lick and gnaw at laboratory food, and indeed Peterson, Ackil, Frommer, and Hearst (1972) reported that rats react in the same way to a response lever when it is the signal for food in an autoshaping paradigm. Stiers and Silberberg (1974) have made similar observations. The two exceptions to this general trend were reported by Sidman and Fletcher (1968), who autoshaped rhesus monkeys for food, and Gamzu and Schwam (1974), who studied squirrel monkeys. Sidman and Fletcher noted that "although the monkey used its fingers both to press the key and to pick up the pellet, the topography of these two behaviors is quite different" (p. 308). Gamzu and Schwam found similar results and reported that some monkeys eventually made nose-pressing responses. They suggested that these response-topography differences resulted from the fact that the consummatory behavior of the monkey is quite variable in comparison to that of the pigeon. It is possible that in species with varied feeding behaviors, the particular behavior one observes will be governed primarily by the manipulandum. For example, Moore (1973) reported that monkeys grasped and bit a protruding key "as if it were food" (p. 187).

Food Versus Water

Jenkins and Moore (1973), Moore (1973), Morrison (1974), and Woodruff (1974) have all autoshaped pigeons using water rather than food as the reinforcer. All found that the autoshaped response resembled drinking movements. Perhaps the most elegant demonstration of the relationship between US and autoshaped response can be found in Jenkins and Moore's (1973) study. First they made high-speed films and videotapes of the unconditional behaviors to food and water. Using these as prototypes, judges were then asked to evaluate the response form of birds autoshaped for food or water. The judges who were presented with videotapes of the learned response only (but not with the whole sequence, which would have allowed them to see the reinforcer itself) correctly identified the approach and contact movements as grain-related or water-related on 87% of the trials. The response was either like grain pecking or like drinking. Sample photographs of the two types of key pecking are presented in Figure 4.

---

[1] Throughout this discussion we have finessed the problem that the concept "informativeness" cannot at present be defined to include all the senses in which we have used it here. There have been a few attempts to provide such a definition (Bloomfield, 1972; Gibbon, Berryman, & Thompson, 1974; Rescorla, 1972), but none have been complete. Most recently, Gibbon et al. (1974) have proposed a metric for evaluating contingencies in classical and instrumental conditioning. Their model can incorporate the conditional probability studies and trial and ITI duration studies described above. It cannot account for the redundancy effects. It is, however, the most thorough and complete account to date.

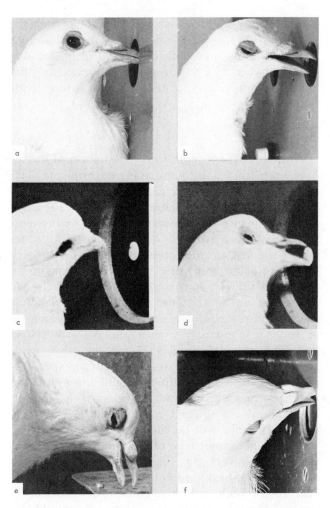

Fig. 4. Photographs of pigeons pecking at response keys. Pictures (a) and (b) show the consummatory topographies obtained when key responses are autoshaped with water (a) and food (b) reinforcement; (c) and (d) show a food-reinforced instrumental response. The spot of light is a discriminative stimulus. Part (e) shows the consummatory reaction which often arises even when lever pressing rather than key pecking is reinforced. When presses are reinforced only in the presence of some positive cue, the cue itself may elicit consummatory reactions, as shown in (f). (From Moore, 1973.) (photo by Roy DeCarava)

In their second and third experiments, Jenkins and Moore showed that the determinant of the response form was the reinforcer itself and not the deprivational state. As long as the key predicted food and not water the response form was foodlike, even if the dominant deprivational state was changed to thirst. Finally, in a most convincing experiment, Jenkins and Moore exposed food- and water-deprived pigeons to a procedure in which two different colored key illuminations were used, one to signal food and the other to signal water. In most pigeons the response to the stimulus predicting water reinforcement was a drinkinglike movement, while the response to the signals for food was appropriately like a grain peck. Because the stimuli were presented randomly and equally often and because both deprivation states were induced, these data represent the clearest evidence for the dependence of the autoshaped response on the actual consummatory response.

Other USs

Farris (1967) conditioned the courting behavior of three male Japanese quail. On four separate occasions each day a buzzer was sounded for 10 sec at the end of which a female quail was introduced to the cage and was left there until copulation occurred or 1 min had passed. The CS overlapped the presence of the female by 5 sec. Within as few as 5 pairings, part of the male display began to occur in the presence of the buzzer. After 32 pairings all components of the characteristic male display were reliably elicited by the CS in all three birds. In a similar experiment, Rackham (1971, cited in Moore, 1973) exposed pigeons to repeated pairings of a stimulus light and a sexual reinforcer. He, too, found that the behavior to the signal (and in this case it was directed to the visual signal) strongly resembled the unconditioned response that would be elicited by the forthcoming reinforcement.

Similar findings have been reported for Pavlovian conditioning of aggressive display in Siamese fighting fish (Adler & Hogan, 1963; Murray, 1974; Thompson & Sturm, 1965). Thompson and Sturm, for example, paired a red stimulus light with a mirror presentation and found gradual acquisition of conditioned behavior that was identical to the unconditioned aggressive display. A study by Rachlin (1969) could also be interpreted as an instance of autoshaped aggressive behavior. Rachlin exposed pigeons to an autoshaping-like procedure with shock as the US. A response on the key, which was fitted with a transparent hemispheric extension, turned off the shock. Rachlin found that key responding could be conditioned, but that some birds pecked the key while others struck it with their wings. Moore (1973) has suggested that since wing flapping and pecking are both parts of the pigeon's normal aggressive behavior pattern, and since shock elicits aggression, Rachlin's data are another instance of reinforcer-appropriate conditioned behavior.

Wasserman (1973a) recently reported that 3-day-old chicks would peck at a key, the illumination of which always preceded the illumination of an overhead heat lamp. In order to insure the reinforcing quality of heat, the experiments were conducted in a cold chamber (5–15°C). Appropriate control groups were run, and the subjects in those groups seldom pecked the key. In the group exposed to the pairings of key illumination and heat, seven of eight chicks pecked the CS within the first 20 trials, although on some trials they contacted the key with a "snuggling" response. The unconditioned response to the heat lamp was described as a reduction of activity accompanied by an extension of the wings and the emission of twittering sounds. Other aspects of the response were less uniform. Both Hearst and Jenkins (1974) and Wasserman (1973a) regard this experiment as showing autoshaping of a response that is different in topography from the response to the US. Hogan (1974) has pointed out that pecking and snuggling are part of the normal heat-seeking repertoire of chicks, however.

Peterson, Ackil, Frommer, and Hearst (1972) implanted electrodes in the lateral hypothalamus of rats. After it was determined that the sites were positively reinforcing, the rats were exposed to autoshaping. One illuminated retractable lever (CS+) was inserted for 15-sec periods after which a train of rewarding stimulation was presented. A second lever (CS−) was presented equally often but was never paired with reinforcement. Each rat soon began to approach the CS+ and "sniff" it, making contact with the lever with its whiskers. The CS− was generally ignored. Peterson et al. reported that the exploratory behavior in the vicinity of the signal for brain stimulation was quite constant for a given rat, but varied among rats. However, "there seemed to be a definite relation between the behaviors directed at the CS+ and those elicited by the brain stimulation: if an animal sniffed or displayed certain postural adjustments during US presentation, we often noticed fragments of the same general pattern during presentation of the CS+" (p. 1011). In experiments with a design similar to the Jenkins and Moore (1973) experiment, Peterson (1972) confirmed and extended these findings. Rats that were both hungry and had electrode implants showed directed responses to a CS+ lever that were classified either as licking-gnawing or sniffing-exploring. These were perfectly correlated with the type of reinforcer and corresponded to the topography of the response to the US.

Finally, Woodruff (1974) employed an ingenious technique to study the importance of localizability of the US. A small hole was made in the upper mandible of pigeons and a chronic cannula implanted. Through this cannula small amounts of water were delivered as the USs in an autoshaping procedure. When water was placed directly in the beak, the pigeons drank it, usually without any peckinglike behavior. Nonetheless, key pecking was autoshaped, and, not surprisingly, the topography of the peck was "drinking"-like and altogether indistinguishable from key pecks autoshaped with water presented in the standard fashion. Thus it appears that neither the sight of the US nor the occurrence of US-appropriate consummatory behavior is a necessary feature of autoshaping with water.

SUMMARY

A wide variety of reinforcers in a number of species have been studied in autoshaping experiments. The overwhelming impression derived from these data is that the autoshaped response usually bears a remarkable resemblance to the response elicited by the reinforcer. There are two types of exceptions to this statement. The first are the counterexamples, particularly in the primates (but also Wasserman's experiment with heat as the US in chicks). Moore (1973) feels that the use of an appropriate stimulus/manipulandum would convert the primate work into positive examples of response similarity. Gamzu and Schwam (1974) and Schwam and Gamzu (1975), on the other hand, have argued that in primates one ought to expect dissimilarities between conditioned and unconditioned responses, because the latter are so variable. Indeed, it is difficult in squirrel monkeys to specify what skeletal behavior will be elicited by the presentation of food. The second type of exception is less severe. Certain reinforcers (e.g., brain stimulation and water directly in the beak) are not localizable in the chamber. Yet in both cases the autoshaped behavior is clearly directed toward the signal. It should be pointed out that it is only the directed aspect of these behaviors that is problematic. In both cases the autoshaped response is clearly similar to the unconditioned behavior.

Discussion and Conclusion: Autoshaping as Pavlovian Conditioning

Brown and Jenkins (1968) in their discussion of the autoshaping phenomenon posed the possibility that key pecking might have emerged as a result of Pavlovian conditioning, although it seemed unlikely to them at that time. Since then, autoshaping has been interpreted as an instance of Pavlovian conditioning with varying degrees of reservation (cf. Gamzu, 1971; Peterson et al., 1972). Perhaps the most wholehearted adoption of the Pavlovian conditioning account of autoshaping can be found in Moore (1973), who brings together a great deal of evidence in support of this approach. The data that have been presented here overwhelmingly suggest that autoshaping is Pavlovian. First of all, in all cases of autoshaping that have been extensively studied the crucial variable has always been the signaling relationship between the CS and US. Autoshaping occurs if and only if the CS reliably predicts a period of relatively higher density of reinforcement than otherwise obtains. Control procedures such as the truly random control, CS-alone, US-alone, and backward-pairing all fail to generate the autoshaped behavior. Indeed, when a CS⁻ is paired with the absence of food, pigeons tend to move away from it (Jenkins & Boakes, 1973; Wasserman et al., 1974) and one can independently demonstrate that such CS⁻s have the inhibitory properties (Wessells, 1973) that are predicted from Pavlovian theory. Secondly, the responses that are autoshaped are far from being arbitrary. On the contrary, they tend to be very constrained within a given species and are demonstrably similar to the responses that are unconditionally elicited by the particular reinforcer being used.

Given the quality and quantity of the data, it is surprising that there is still considerable reluctance to accept the notion that autoshaping is Pavlovian (cf. Herrnstein & Loveland, 1972; Hursh, Navarick & Fantino, 1974). Other than dogma, there appear to be three reasons for this reluctance: the directedness of the response, the absence of a deleterious effect of partial reinforcement, and a continuing dispute about the process presumed to underlie Pavlovian conditioning.

Among the many aspects of autoshaping that make it an interesting phenomenon is the directedness of the response. Indeed, this may be the only way of distinguishing autoshaping phenomena from more familiar instances of Pavlovian conditioning. Traditionally, salivation, galvanic skin response (GSR), heart rate, and eye blinking have been the behaviors studied in Pavlovian conditioning experiments. None of these behaviors could be called directed. However, when other components of behavior are noted, directed behavior is often observed. For example, Pavlov noted that dogs licked an electric bulb that was a CS for food (Pavlov, 1955); indeed, if the stimulus was within reach, the dog usually tried to touch it with its mouth (Pavlov, 1941). Similar findings were reported by Zener (1937). Thus directedness of behavior has been observed in Pavlovian conditioning experiments but simply was not the focus of the research. As a result, it has been more or less ignored. Autoshaping redresses that wrong and provides a vehicle for the study of Pavlovian control of directed skeletal behavior.

The reader will have already noted that partial reinforcement does not seem to have a deleterious effect on autoshaping (e.g., Farrell, 1974; Gamzu & Williams, 1971, 1973; Gonzales, 1973, 1974; Schwartz & Williams, 1972a), although it is claimed severely to retard acquisition of classically conditioned responses. Indeed, Spence (1966) suggested that this effect of partial reinforcement be used to distinguish between Pavlovian and operant conditioning. However, Gormezano and Moore (1969) summarized the literature as being equivocal. Grant and Schipper (1952) found conditioning to be unimpaired by partial reinforcement. More representative are findings that Pavlovian conditioning (of eye blink reflex on the whole) will occur at partial reinforcement (even as low as 25%), but that the magnitude of the effect is smaller than in 100% control groups (e.g., Ross, 1959). Another effect of partial reinforcement is to increase resistance to extinction. This phenomenon is well documented in operant learning (cf. Lewis, 1960) but it is not always seen in Pavlovian conditioning in infrahuman subjects (e.g., Thomas and Wagner, 1964). However, the original report of this partial reinforcement effect (PRE) by Humphreys (1939) was based on classical conditioning. Recently Hilton (1969) has shown a clear-cut PRE using a conditioned emotional response (CER) paradigm which is most commonly interpreted as resulting from Pavlovian conditioning (cf. Rescorla & Solomon, 1967). Indeed, although Hilton provides no details of acquisition, he does indicate that all the groups (consistent and partial reinforcement) showed equally effective complete suppression to the CS. This very cursory review should be sufficient to indicate that the effects of partial reinforcement in Pavlovian conditioning are sufficiently equivocal that they cannot possibly be used to distinguish it from operant conditioning or to define a phenomenon as an instance of Pavlovian conditioning. Thus it seems illogical to refute a Pavlovian conditioning approach to autoshaping on these grounds.

Finally we come to the mechanism presumed to underlie Pavlovian conditioning. If there were one or more clear-cut mechanisms that were unequivocally acceptable as an explanation of Pavlovian conditioning, then it would indeed be fair to ask that all the autoshaping data be encompassed by one or more of these mechanisms. Unfortunately, this is not the case, and thus we are left with an important theoretical problem for behavioral psychology.

Stimulus substitution is the most commonly cited mechanism and is often the only mechanism considered (cf. Terrace, 1973). It refers to the view that the CS in a Pavlovian conditioning experiment comes to substitute for the US and generate responses identical to those produced by the US. The lack of well-established alternatives is surprising, since it is quite clear that a literal interpretation of stimulus substitution is inadequate to explain even the most unequivocal examples of Pavlovian conditioning. Typically one observes CRs which (a) omit portions of the unconditioned response (UR) and (b) include components which are absent from the UR. Because of the documented similarity of autoshaped and consummatory responses, stimulus substitution has been the suggested mechanism for autoshaping. The shortcomings of explanations of autoshaping that are based on Pavlovian conditioning are often related to the weakness of the stimulus-substitution concept. It seems unreasonable to expect conceptualizations of autoshaping to be more precise than the theory on which they are based.

A more reasonable approach is to use autoshaping phenomena as a tool for better understanding the mechanisms of Pavlovian conditioning. To some extent this has already happened. For one thing, alternatives to stimulus substitution have begun to be articulated. Hearst and Jenkins (1974) have pointed out that Pavlov himself probably thought of the CS as a *surrogate* rather than as a substitute for the US. Indeed, Gamzu (1971) preferred the term *stimulus surrogation* as capturing the essence of the idea without the limitations of *stimulus substitution*. Bindra (1972) considered the US an unconditional incentive stimulus and the CS a conditional incentive stimulus. This apparently eliminates some of the problems posed by the stimulus-substitution concept (cf. Hearst & Jenkins, 1974; Moore, 1973), but still leaves the CS as surrogate for the US. Hearst and Jenkins (1974) have coined the term *object substitution* as capturing Bindra's approach. The most recent attempt to specify the mechanism arises from the work of Woodruff and Williams on autoshaping with water injected directly into the beak. Williams (1974) and Woodruff (1974) have referred to this experiment as demonstrating that the key in autoshaping is a "learned releaser." Williams points out that food on the tongue and not the sight of food is the important feature of Pavlovian salivary conditioning. Likewise, grain in the mandibles and not the sight of grain is the US in autoshaping. Via Pavlovian conditioning the sight of grain (paired with grain in the mandibles as the US) releases pecks at grain. Similarly, by Pavlovian conditioning the response key (paired with the sight of grain) releases pecking.

Most of these approaches to the mechanism of autoshaping can be transposed to other approaches with appropriate assumptions. Which is the most acceptable approach or whether they clearly differ from one another are matters for further exploration. Nonetheless, this debate clearly revolves around facts that indicate that Pavlovian conditioning—whatever its underlying mechanisms may turn out to be—is the major learning process in the *acquisition* of autoshaping. The next section will indicate that this is also true in the *maintenance* of autoshaped behavior, where operant relations also exert a powerful role—sometimes in opposition to Pavlovian relations.

Automaintenance: Interaction of Pavlovian and Operant Contingencies

The phenomenon of autoshaping seems like such a straightforward example of Pavlovian conditioning that one wonders why it has generated so much interest and research activity. While it is true that key pecking has not traditionally been viewed as a member of the class of behaviors which is susceptible to Pavlovian procedures, there has been virtually no systematic investigation of key peck acquisition in the past, and the discovery of a method other than shaping by successive approximation for instituting key pecking might well have been viewed as just another fact and a methodological convenience. In relating autoshaping to the operant conditioning literature, one might reasonably adopt this model: Pavlovian conditioning procedures may be used to produce the first key peck. This peck is followed by food, and the law of effect then takes over. Thus autoshaping and the control of behavior by its consequences reflect independent processes. This, indeed, is not unlike the initial tentative explanation of autoshaping put forth by Brown and Jenkins (1968). However, such an account is dramatically inadequate.

The experiment which demonstrated that the processes which underlie autoshaping extend beyond the *acquisition* of key pecking, and which is probably responsible for the enormous research interest in the phenomenon, was conducted by Williams and Williams (1969). Naïve pigeons were exposed to trials in which the brief illumination of a key light was followed by food. Until the first peck occurred, the procedure was almost identical to the Brown and Jenkins procedure. The crucial difference was this: if the pigeon pecked the key, the trial was terminated and food was omitted. What might one expect the results of such an experiment to be? The Pavlovian contingency would generate the initial key peck (autoshaping). However, key pecks would not be followed by food. Indeed, they would prevent food delivery, while any other behavior that the pigeon engaged in would be followed by food. The expectation is clear: the negative contingency between pecking and food would quickly eliminate pecking. The result, however, was that key pecking was maintained at substantial frequency over many hundreds of trials in virtually all pigeons. As Williams and Williams (1969) noted, this phenomenon is virtually identical to what Sheffield (1965) observed in studying the effects of a similar procedure on salivation in dogs. Sheffield labeled the phenomenon *omission training*. Williams and Williams labeled their finding *automaintenance*. It has since been referred to in the literature as *negative automaintenance* to highlight the negative response-reinforcer contingency. This, however, is a rather cumbersome term, and so we shall hereafter refer to it as *omission training* or the omission effect (cf. Hearst & Jenkins, 1974).

The Williams and Williams study made it clear that the Pavlovian pairing of key and food contributed to the *maintenance* of responding, and not just to its acquisition. It demonstrated a clear violation of the law of effect. The phenomenon has since been demonstrated in numerous experiments (e.g., Herrnstein & Loveland, 1972; Schwartz, 1972, 1973b; Schwartz & Williams, 1972a, 1972b), though occasional investigations have failed to obtain it reliably (e.g., Hursh et al., 1974). Jenkins (see Hearst & Jenkins, 1974) has also reported a variant of the effect. In a study described as the "long box" experiment, pigeons were exposed to autoshaping trials in an unusually long chamber. Response keys, which signaled food, were located at the ends of the chamber, and the feeder was located in the center of the chamber. Key pecking was acquired and maintained under these conditions despite the fact that when the pigeons pecked the key, it took them so much time to move from the key to the feeder that food presentation usually terminated before they arrived. Thus, in this procedure, key pecking did not prevent food presentation, but it effectively prevented food consumption.

What is one to make of the omission effect? The maintenance of key pecking in the face of a negative response-reinforcer contingency strongly supports the view that stimulus-reinforcer relations dominate response-reinforcer relations in controlling key pecking in autoshaping-type procedures, and even suggests that response-reinforcer relations might exert no control at all. We shall evaluate these possibilities in the following sections, focusing first on the role of stimulus-reinforcer relations in automaintenance, and second on the role of response-reinforcer relations.

STIMULUS-REINFORCER RELATIONS IN AUTOMAINTENANCE AND OMISSION

Many of the studies already discussed in connection with the Pavlovian control of acquisition of responding are also relevant to the question of maintenance. The simplest demonstration of automaintenance is a study by Schwartz and Williams (1972b). Pigeons were exposed to 6-sec trials which terminated with food. Responses had no programmed consequence. Key pecking was nevertheless maintained at rates between 8 and 15 responses per trial over many sessions in all pigeons. While this simple demonstration of automaintenance seems to suggest Pavlovian control of pecking, there is, of course, an alternative explanation. We can presume that the control over initial responding is Pavlovian. However, once these responses occur, they are followed in time by food. There is thus an adventitious response-reinforcer relation which may contribute substantially to the maintenance of responding once initiated (Herrnstein, 1966; Skinner, 1948). A series of studies by Gamzu and Schwartz (1973), Gamzu and Williams (1971, 1973), and Schwartz (1973a) strongly suggest that such an account is inadequate. Let us suppose that responding during trials was being maintained by an adventitious response-reinforcer relation. What influence would the delivery of food during the intertrial interval have on this putative relation? It seems clear that these extra reinforcements might be expected to increase pecking, or perhaps not influence it. Certainly, they would not be expected to decrease pecking. On the other hand, from the Pavlovian point of view, food deliveries during the ITI would decrease the differential predictiveness of the trial stimulus and, as a result, decrease Pavlovian control over pecking. The Pavlovian view makes the paradoxical prediction that increasing the rate of food delivery will decrease responding. This indeed is what occurs. In the Gamzu and Williams studies, in which trials were 8.6 sec long and ITIs averaged 40 sec, food delivery during the ITI at the same rate as during the trial virtually eliminated responding. In the Gamzu and Schwartz (1973) study, which involved the regular alternation of two key colors for 27-sec periods, when food was presented in only one key color substantial responding was maintained to that color. When food was then presented in both colors with equal frequency, responding was substantially decreased, though not eliminated. The Schwartz (1973a) study was similar to that of Gamzu and Schwartz except that decreases in responding were even more dramatic. It should be noted that these studies cannot logically rule out the possibility that adventitious response-reinforcer relations contribute to the maintenance of responding on autoshaping procedures. Only procedures employing a negative response-reinforcer dependency can do that. However, they do make it clear that such relations are not sufficient.

The Response-Reinforcer Relation

The mere demonstration of the omission effect suggests that autoshaped pecking is insensitive to its consequences. However, while responding on automaintenance procedures is maintained at levels of 80–120 pecks per min, responding on the omission procedure is maintained at substantially lower levels, often only 15–30 responses per min (Schwartz & Williams, 1972a, 1972b). This discrepancy suggests that the response-reinforcer dependency does exert control over responding, though it is secondary to the control exerted by the stimulus-reinforcer dependency. Williams and Williams (1969) examined this possibility. A response key was illuminated for 6-sec trials and followed by food unless a key peck occurred (omission). A second response key was illuminated whenever the first one was. Pecks on this key had no programmed consequences. Pigeons quickly learned to peck exclusively at this second key, and thus obtain nearly all of the scheduled reinforcement. From this result, Williams and Williams argued that the key pecking which occurred on the omission procedure was sensitive to its consequences. Unfortunately, the design of the Williams and Williams experiment permits an alternative interpretation. Let us assume that on each trial, the pigeon looks at only one key, and that the pigeon is likely to peck at the key it looks at. With this assumption, one can explain the Williams and Williams results in purely Pavlovian terms. Despite the fact that both keys are simultaneously illuminated, if the pigeon only looks at one key per trial, it is experiencing automaintenance trials and omission trials separately. Automaintenance trials always terminate with food. Omission trials terminate with food only if the pigeon does not peck the key. Since the pigeon does peck the key, there are fewer omission key-food pairings than automaintenance key-food pairings. Moreover, the omission key-food pairings are effectively on a partial reinforcement schedule, which often weakens Pavlovian conditioning. There might thus be stimulus-reinforcer relations of different strengths between each of the keys and food, and this might account for the observed difference in levels of responding.

To test this account of the Williams and Williams study, Schwartz and Williams (1972a) did an experiment in which the frequency of automaintenance key-food pairings and omission key-food pairings was kept

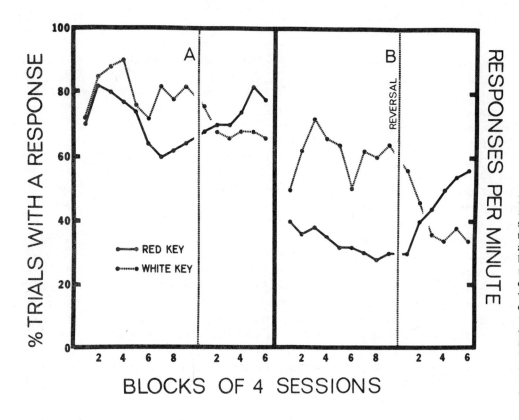

Fig. 5. Percentage of trials with at least one response and responses per minute throughout the experiment, averaged across all eight subjects in four-session blocks and separated according to key color. To the left of the dotted vertical lines, the red key was associated with the omission condition, the white key with the yoked control. To the right of the dotted vertical lines, the significance of the key colors was reversed. (From Schwartz & Williams, 1972a. © 1972 by the Society for the Experimental Analysis of Behavior.)

equal. The two types of pairings occurred on separate trials indicated by different key colors. If an omission trial terminated with food, a subsequent, yoked, automaintenance trial also terminated with food. If the pigeon pecked the key during the omission trial and prevented food, food was not delivered at the end of the yoked automaintenance trial. In this way, the two types of trials differed only in the relation between key pecks and food. Under these conditions pigeons pecked the automaintenance key on many more trials and at twice as high a rate as they pecked the omission key. The data are presented in Figure 5. From this, Schwartz and Williams concluded that autoshaped responding was to some degree sensitive to its consequences.

Some more recent research on the omission effect has examined in more detail the behaviors which are actually conditioned by the contingency relation between the key light and food. Wessells (1974) observed that what was conditioned in addition to pecking was orientation toward and approach to the response key. When a negative contingency was established between any approach to the key and food, Wessells observed the gradual elimination of approach behavior. The response elimination required a good deal of experience. After about 10 sessions, the subjects were still approaching the key on 30–40% of the trials. Nevertheless, what is of prime interest in this context is that approach *was* eliminated by the negative response-reinforcer contingency. It should be noted, in addition, that orientation toward the key continued at high frequency even after approach had been eliminated. A similar study by Browne and Peden (see Hearst & Jenkins, 1974) produced somewhat different results. Imposition of a negative contingency between approach and food never completely eliminated approach behavior. After 35 sessions, subjects were still responding on 12–60% of the trials. In another study, Barrera (1974) observed that key pecking occurred at a lower rate under a negative contingency than under standard automaintenance conditions. However, he observed that pecking per se was occurring at as high a rate as ever. The effect of the negative contingency was to displace pecking off the key. Interestingly, Dunham, Mariner, and Adams (1969) observed the same phenomenon when key pecks were punished with electric shock.

There is more evidence that responses which occur in the face of a negative response-reinforcer contingency are nevertheless sensitive to their consequences. Morrison (1974) studied automaintenance in the pigeon with water as a reinforcer. In conducting the research, he noticed that in addition to pecking the response key, pigeons also "bowed" and "rooted" when the signal was present. Morrison then systematically examined the effects of a negative response-reinforcer contingency on each of these behaviors. The general result was that a negative contingency suppressed, but did not eliminate, the target behavior, with the result that each of the other behaviors increased in frequency. When a negative contingency was established simultaneously between each of the behaviors and food, the pigeons emitted all of the behaviors rather than suppressing them all. Murray (1974) recently observed the same sort of effects in a study of Siamese fighting fish (*Betta splendens*). The reinforcer was presentation of a mirror, which reliably produces display in the fish. Murray observed four distinct behaviors conditioned to the signal. When a negative contingency was imposed between any of the behaviors and the mirror, that behavior was suppressed, while the others continued to occur. Like Morrison's observations, Murray observed that while the negative contingency reduced the behavior, in all cases it failed to eliminate the behavior.

The study by Murray is the first one we have discussed which examined the omission procedure in a species other than the pigeon. Actually, the omission procedure has also been studied with rats, chicks, and squirrel monkeys, and not always yielded the same results. Wasserman (1973a) studied chicks with heat as the reinforcer. Pecking and nuzzling the response key were maintained despite the negative contingency. Stiers and Silberberg (1974) observed maintenance of responding in rats in the face of a negative contingency. The signal for food was the insertion in the chamber of a retractable lever. The response was not lever pressing, but lever contact, typically with the mouth or vibrissae. Interestingly, Stiers and Silberberg observed licking, pawing, and biting in an automaintenance procedure, but nose contact of the lever on the omission procedure. Finally, Schwam and Gamzu (1975) studied the omission procedure with squirrel monkeys as subjects. Across different index responses, the uniform result was that responding was not maintained in the face of the negative contingency. Schwam and Gamzu explained the discrepancy between the squirrel monkey and the pigeon on omission procedures by arguing that the omission effect occurs only in species for which there is a relatively rigid pattern of reinforcer-appropriate consummatory activity. In these cases the stimulus-reinforcer association determines the response which will occur. On the other hand, in species which have a large repertoire of consummatory activities (e.g., in the squirrel monkey, biting, mouthing, pawing, licking, etc.) there is no inflexible link between any one of these activities and food, so that any of them can be eliminated by the negative response-reinforcer relation.

Stimulus-Reinforcer and Response-Reinforcer Interaction

In the preceding discussion, we have shown that both stimulus-reinforcer and response-reinforcer relations exert control over behavior in automaintenance and omission studies. In automaintenance the two types of relation may be mutually facilitative. The stimulus-reinforcer relation generates pecking, which may then be adventitiously reinforced with food. While adventitious reinforcement is not itself sufficient to maintain responding, it may make a substantial contribution to the high rates at which pecking occurs. In omission training, the stimulus-reinforcer and response-reinforcer relations are antagonistic. While the stimulus-reinforcer relation generates pecking, the response-reinforcer relation works, with only partial success, to eliminate pecking. Indeed, it is the lack of success of the negative response-reinforcer contingency which has generated such interest in the phenomenon. It is a tribute to the remarkable power of the stimulus-reinforcer relation that it can compete effectively with a response-reinforcer contingency for control of a behavior which is ordinarily quite sensitive to its consequences. We would like to be able to specify the variables which determine the relative contributions of these two types of contingency to the outcome of omission training and automaintenance studies. Unfortunately, there is little evidence on this point. One systematic investigation of the problem is a study by Williams (1974). The study involved four groups of pigeons. One group was exposed to a variant of the omission procedure. The response key was illuminated periodically, and if the pigeon did not peck the key for 6 sec, the key light was extinguished and food was presented. Each time the pigeon pecked the key, the trial was restarted. Thus a trial did not terminate until 6 sec without a peck had elapsed, and every trial terminated with food. Conditions for a second group were determined by conditions obtained by the first group. Trials were identical in length. In this group, however, there was no programmed relation between responding and trial duration or food. We shall call this group the "yoked omission" group. A third group was exposed to a discrete trials DRL (differential reinforcement of low rate) procedure. When the key was illuminated, the pigeons had to peck the key after 6 sec elapsed to obtain food. Premature pecks reset the DRL timer and prolonged the trial. Each trial terminated with food. Finally, the fourth group was yoked to this DRL group. Responses had no programmed consequences, and trial duration was determined by obtained trial duration in the DRL group. Each of the pigeons in the nonyoked groups was exposed to both DRL and omission procedures, in counterbalanced order. Each of the pigeons in the yoked groups was exposed to both yoked procedures, in counterbalanced order. Each group contained eight pigeons.

What prediction might one make about the levels of responding maintained in the four groups? Let us consider first the response-reinforcer contingency. The DRL group is exposed to a positive contingency, the omission group to a negative contingency, and the two yoked control groups to no contingency (except perhaps an adventitious one). On this basis alone, we would expect responding to be strongest in the DRL group and weakest in the omission group, with the other two groups somewhere in between.

Now let us consider the stimulus-reinforcer relation. As we have already mentioned above, increases in the trial/ITI ratio (i.e., increases in trial length with ITI constant) reduce the level of responding maintained on autoshaping procedures (Baldock, 1974). We would therefore expect that responding controlled by the stimulus-reinforcer relation in these groups will be inversely related to the trial duration obtained. Since the DRL should maintain more responding than the omission procedure, DRL trials should be longer than omission trials. Hence stimulus-reinforcer control should be weaker in the DRL and DRL-yoked groups than in the other two groups. Since trial durations are equal in experimental groups and their yoked partners, we would expect no difference in stimulus-reinforcer control between each experimental group and its yoked partner.

The results of the experiment, in asymptotic responses per minute, were as follows: DRL—14.0; omission—4.0; DRL-yoked—6.2; omission-yoked—25.0. Thus all predictions were confirmed. Omission-yoked pigeons responded more than DRL-yoked pigeons (equal response-reinforcer contingencies but longer trials for the DRL-yoked group); DRL pigeons responded more than omission pigeons (difference in the response-reinforcer dependency); DRL pigeons responded more than their yoked partners, and omission pigeons responded less than their yoked partners (in both cases as a result of equal trial durations but different response-reinforcer dependencies). The data provide clear evidence that stimulus-reinforcer and response-reinforcer relations are both importantly involved in the control of responding by these procedures.

Are the Behaviors Influenced by Stimulus-Reinforcer/Response-Reinforcer Relations Different?

Throughout the discussion thus far we have been assuming that the pecking which is influenced by stimulus-reinforcer relations and occurs on automaintenance and omission procedures belongs to the same class as the pecking which is maintained by response-reinforcer relations and occurs in standard free operant procedures. It is possible, however, that the two types of contingency control two different types of peck which are as independent of one another as salivation and panel pushing in the dog. Schwartz and Williams (1972b) conducted a series of experiments designed to explore this possibility. The property of key pecks they measured was their duration, since Wolin (1968) had previously observed that key peck duration was influenced by the nature of the reinforcer, either food or water. Schwartz and Williams found that key pecks maintained on the omission procedure were of almost uniformly short duration—less than 20 msec. Distributions of response duration on standard fixed-interval and fixed-ratio schedules also included short duration pecks, but the majority of pecks were long in duration—greater than 40 msec. This suggested that there might indeed be two different classes of key peck, one of which (short-duration) was reflexive, controlled by stimulus-reinforcer contingencies and representing the dominant response on omission procedures, while the other (long duration) was nonreflexive, sensitive to response-reinforcer contingencies and representing the dominant response on free operant reinforcement schedules. To test this possibility, Schwartz and Williams tried to differentially reinforce both short- and long-duration responses. The rationale behind the study was this: short-duration pecks, if insensitive to their consequences, would not increase in frequency when differentially reinforced, while long-duration pecks, if sensitive to their consequences, would increase in frequency if differentially reinforced. The results obtained by Schwartz and Williams supported this hypothesis. However, other investigations (cf. Moore, 1973) have failed to find duration differences across different procedures and have offered alternative interpretations for the data observed by Schwartz and Williams. Thus the argument for two kinds of key peck must be taken as tentative.

If there are two different kinds of key peck, each sensitive to different variables, how is one to explain the apparent interaction of response-reinforcer and stimulus-reinforcer contingencies which the research reviewed above suggests? There are two possibilities. One is that the apparent interaction is not an interaction at all. Instead, stimulus-reinforcer relations control short-duration pecks and response-reinforcer relations control long-duration pecks, and the "interaction" simply results from the fact that in most studies both kinds of key peck are lumped together as instances of switch closure. A second and more intriguing possibility is that the two kinds of peck do interact, but only indirectly. This possibility has been discussed by Gamzu (1971) and by Schwartz and Williams (1972b). We might call it the "minimal-unit" hypothesis. Briefly, the argument is this: short-duration pecks are generated and controlled by stimulus-reinforcer relations. Moreover, they comprise the basic biological units out of which long-duration, operant pecks develop. Furthermore, the long-duration pecks continue to depend for their occurrence upon the simultaneous occurrence of short-duration pecks. Thus the operant key peck may be viewed as an "anaclitic operant" (Kimble and Perlmutter, 1970), since it is built from, and depends upon, the members of a different response class. From this account, the interaction between stimulus-reinforcer and response-reinforcer relations reflects the dependence of reflexive pecks on the former, the dependence of operant pecks on reflexive pecks, and, finally, the sensitivity of operant pecks to their consequences. It should be noted that this account is almost entirely unsupported, and at present it raises more questions than it answers. How, for example, do operant pecks develop out of reflexive pecks? This question is merely a specific restatement of a question which has haunted experimental psychology since its inception: how does voluntary behavior emerge out of the collection of infantile reflexes? Also, one might wonder whether enough experience with operant contingencies eventually frees the operant peck from its reflexive origins. These and other questions require empirical investigation. For the present, let us discuss one finding which offers some support for the minimal-unit hypothesis.

We discussed above, in the section which addressed the conditions necessary for the acquisition of pecking in autoshaping procedures, a series of studies by Gamzu and Williams (1971, 1973). The reader will recall that when food presentation was as likely during the intertrial interval as during the trial, key pecking either did not develop or, if already developed, was eliminated. Gamzu and Williams observed that pigeons initially exposed to a differential procedure (food presented only during the trial) would peck the key at least 60 times per min. However, they also observed the curious phenomenon that if the pigeons were initially exposed to a nondifferential procedure (food equally likely during trial and ITI) during which they did not peck the key and were subsequently exposed to a differential procedure, key pecking developed at a normal rate but reached a much lower asymptotic level. This effect persisted seemingly indefinitely. The explanation offered by Gamzu (1971) was that during the nondifferential procedure a feeding-related behavior other than key pecking occurs and is maintained (Staddon and Simmelhag, 1971). When the differential procedure is introduced and key pecking develops, the other behavior continues to occur and to be reinforced. Thus the development of operant pecks is essentially blocked by the occurrence of these adventitiously reinforced other behaviors, and the pecking one does observe is strictly under the control of the stimulus-reinforcer relation. The implication of this account is that the duration of key pecks which occur under these conditions should be almost exclusively short. In an unpublished portion of his doctoral dissertation Gamzu (1971) measured response durations. In Figure 6 durations are presented for a pigeon exposed to the differential procedure after the nondifferential procedure. It can be seen that both early and late in training, response durations are exclusively short. Contrast this with the data in Figure 7 for a pigeon exposed to the differential procedure from the outset. Here response durations are short early in training, but by later sessions there are substantial numbers of long-duration responses. These data support the views that (a) there are two different kinds of key peck, identifiable on the basis of duration; (b) the two types of peck are controlled by different variables; and (c) short-duration pecks seem to occur initially while long-duration pecks only develop with experience. Moreover, the fact that a procedural shift from differential to nondifferential conditions eliminates pecking entirely, despite the fact that only the stimulus-reinforcer relation is changed, suggests that instrumental responses are indirectly controlled by stimulus-reinforcer contingencies.

Autoshaping and Automaintenance: Theoretical Analysis

In the sections above we have suggested that autoshaping is best described as Pavlovian conditioning and that automaintenance entails the joint action of Pavlovian and operant contingencies. There have been two attempts to capture the autoshaping literature theoretically, one by Hearst and Jenkins (1974) and one by Williams (1974).

Hearst and Jenkins treat autoshaping and auto-

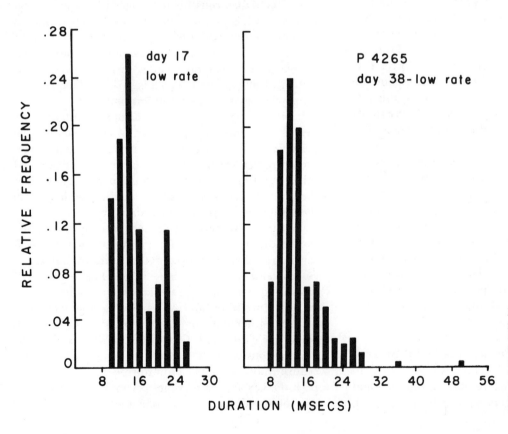

Fig. 6. Relative-frequency histogram of response durations of a single pigeon during two sessions of the differential procedure. Prior to the introduction of this procedure the pigeon was exposed to the nondifferential procedure for 14 days. (From Gamzu, 1971.)

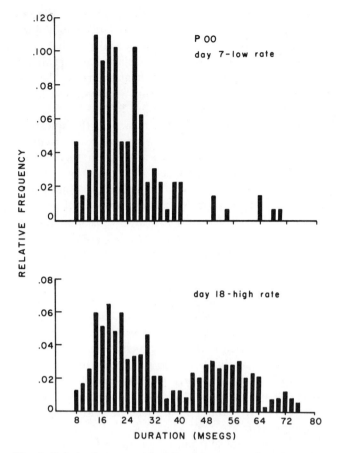

Fig. 7. Relative-frequency histogram of response durations of a single pigeon during two sessions of the differential procedure, which was the first procedure to which the bird was exposed. (From Gamzu, 1971.)

maintenance as an instance of *sign tracking*, which is defined as "behavior that is directed toward or away from a stimulus as a result of the relation between that stimulus and the reinforcer or between that stimulus and the absence of the reinforcer" (p. 4). They suggest that sign tracking is a general phenomenon and may contribute substantially to many observations in the study of discrimination learning. Our primary concern here, however, is with sign tracking as an account of autoshaping.

In Hearst and Jenkins's view, as long as a stimulus can be localized, so that behavior can be directed toward or away from it, such behavior will develop as a function of the relation between that stimulus and a reinforcer (US). The importance of localizability of the CS has been indicated by Wasserman (1973b). One group of pigeons was exposed to an autoshaping procedure with the houselight illuminated. A second group was exposed to the same procedure but with the houselight off. Only the first group acquired key pecking. Wasserman's explanation is that in a dark chamber the key light provides general illumination which can be seen anywhere, i.e., it is a nonlocalized CS. On the other hand, when the chamber is lit, the pigeon must look at the key to see the stimulus change, i.e., the CS is localized.

Thus the sign-tracking view places most of its emphasis on the stimulus side of the phenomenon. It does not explain why pigeons *peck* the key rather than engage in some other directed behavior. Hearst and Jenkins (1974) acknowledge the fact that in almost all autoshaping studies the conditioned response is a component of the unconditioned response to the reinforcer. However, the implication of their account is that if the signaling stimulus were somehow inappropriate for directed consummatory activity, some other activity (e.g., approach) would nevertheless be directed at it. In the standard pigeon autoshaping experiment, there is no way to test this view. The CS is typically response key illumination, and thus is in many ways an ideal stimulus for pecking (Cruze, 1935; Fantz, 1957; Hunt & Smith, 1967; Padilla, 1935). There are some autoshaping studies, however, in which tones rather than lights were used as signals. Gamzu (1968) and Schwartz (1973a) both failed to observe pecking at the tone source in such experiments. More significantly, the pigeons in these studies also failed to reliably approach the tone. After a brief period of orientation to the tone early in the experiments (owing, presumably, to its novelty), orientation ceased, and in later tone presentations pigeons simply moved to the feeder. Jenkins (in Hearst & Jenkins, 1974) did manage to condition approach to a tone source and even conditioned pecking, when the tone was localized behind a continuously illuminated perforated hemisphere. Thus the efficacy of a tone as a signal is still debatable. What is clear is that a tone is far less effective than a key light.

In our view, the sign-tracking account of autoshaped key pecking places too much emphasis on the key and not enough emphasis on pecking. The autoshaping phenomenon raises two questions: Why does the pigeon peck, and why does the pigeon peck the key? Hearst and Jenkins may have provided a satisfactory answer to the latter question. However, the answer to the former question is different. Pecking is conditioned because it is the central component of the feeding pattern of the pigeon. As Staddon and Simmelhag (1971) have shown, pecking is observed in pigeons when food is presented at regular intervals with no signal. Thus it is the mere presentation of food which engenders pecking. The key light in the autoshaping procedure directs pecks but does not gen-

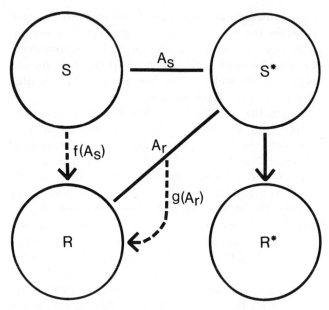

Fig. 8. Schematic outline of the critical events underlying biconditional behavior. See text for details. (From Williams, 1974.)

erate them. Moreover, the nature of the reinforcer (US) in an experiment determines not only what behavior will occur, but also which conditional stimuli will be maximally effective. Both Shettleworth (1972b) with chicks and Foree and LoLordo (1973) with pigeons have shown that visual CSs dominate auditory ones only when food rather than electric shock is the US.

A second and somewhat more comprehensive account of autoshaping and automaintenance has been provided by Williams (1974). Autoshaped pecking, to Williams, is an instance of "biconditional behavior." This term refers to the fact that both stimulus-reinforcer and response-reinforcer contingencies play significant roles in controlling key pecking. Williams' conceptual scheme is presented in Figure 8, where S designates a stimulus, S* the reinforcing event, R* the consummatory response, and R the conditioned behavior; A_s refers to the associative link between S and S*. As we discussed above, the formation of an association seems to require a differential predictive relation between S and S*, and in this respect autoshaping does not differ from standard Pavlovian conditioning. Precise specification of the conditions necessary for the formation of an association is a problem Williams refers to as the "psychophysics of association." It is a general problem of definition and specification of contingency spaces and has already been discussed above. The main point, again, is that autoshaping is in no sense unique in terms of the nature of the S–S* association.

It is just the S–S* relation which generates the behavior R, and this process is labeled $f(A_s)$ in Figure 8. Williams argues that the form which a behavior takes as a function of the S–S* relation is a problem which is quite distinct from characterizing the association itself. He refers to this problem, which involves the relation between R and R*, as the "biology of association." In general, the answer to this question will be specific to the species, reward, and situation under investigation. Williams argues, in the case of autoshaping, that the R set is a collection of unlearned consummatory behaviors. The learning which occurs in autoshaping is the development of control over response R by a new stimulus, S, such that S becomes capable of releasing the behavior R. Thus Williams identifies his account as a "learned release" hypothesis. Whether all Pavlovian conditioning experiments should be viewed as learned release experiments or whether autoshaping is unique in this regard is discussed in detail by Williams. As we suggested above, the question of what is actually conditioned in Pavlovian conditioning experiments has been more evaded than analyzed in the past. Whether stimulus substitution, stimulus surrogation, learned release, or some other label aptly characterizes most or all conditioning results cannot at present be addressed with any confidence.

The feature of Williams's account which is unique to the autoshaping literature is the relation between the R set and the S* event, labeled A_r and $g(A_r)$ in Figure 8. This of course reflects an operant contingency between response and reinforcer. Williams's account incorporates the fact that once behavior is generated by an S–S* association, it is subsequently further enhanced by an R–S* relation. Both $f(A_s)$ and $g(A_r)$ feed into the R set and increase the probability of R. Williams's model is thus an explicit effort to account for the joint action of the two types of contingency in the determination of a particular class of behavior. The function $g(A_r)$ is a positive feedback loop which, once the behavior has occurred, will insure its continued occurrence. This feature of Williams's model is specific to autoshaping, as we have said. This, however, is more historical accident than logical necessity. The fact that key pecking has for so long been studied in operant situations and has so clearly been shown to be sensitive to its consequences demands that an account of Pavlovian control of pecking also include a vehicle for control by response-contingent reinforcement. It is entirely possible that other behaviors which have been traditionally studied in Pavlovian contexts are also sensitive to R–S* links which are built into experimental procedures. This possibility has simply not been systematically explored.

THE ROLE OF STIMULUS-REINFORCER RELATIONS IN THE CONTROL OF BEHAVIOR MAINTAINED BY RESPONSE-REINFORCER RELATIONS

Having reviewed above the phenomena of autoshaping, automaintenance, and omission, and having suggested that key pecking in these Pavlovianlike procedures is influenced by both stimulus-reinforcer and response-reinforcer relations, it seems appropriate to ask now whether the same kind of interaction can be demonstrated in operant procedures which bear no obvious formal relationship to Pavlovian ones. An understanding of the influence of autoshapinglike phenomena in standard operant situations is essential before the full significance of autoshaping for the experimental analysis of behavior can be evaluated. In the remainder of the chapter we shall explore the possibility that in situations in which control of behavior by response-reinforcer contingencies is dramatic and unequivocal, stimulus-reinforcer contingencies nevertheless play a vital role. Most of the phenomena we shall discuss come from the literature on multiple schedules of reinforcement. We shall first review the phenomena observed on multiple schedules and the standard accounts of these phenomena. We shall then apply some of the principles which have developed out of the study of autoshaping and automaintenance to these phenomena. We shall argue that no account of multiple-schedule phenomena will be accurate unless it includes an analysis of autoshaping-like stimulus-reinforcer relations and that, indeed, the most dramatic findings in studies of multiple schedules result from the influence of these relations.

That a prototypic operant, key pecking, *can* be influenced by Pavlovian operations does not mean that it *must* be so influenced. It is possible that, in standard operant situations, the control of behavior by response-reinforcer relations simply dwarfs the influence of stimulus-reinforcer relations, even though certain operant conditioning procedures have Pavlovian stimulus-reinforcer contingencies built into them. The remainder of this chapter will be concerned with assessing the influence of these Pavlovian contingencies on behavior which is already controlled by operant contingencies. This issue will be discussed mainly in the context of the control of behavior by multiple schedules of reinforcement. A *multiple schedule* is one "in which two or more component schedules operate in alternation, each in the presence of a different stimulus" (Catania, 1968, p. 339).

Multiple-schedule procedures are instances of what has traditionally been called successive discrimination. Conditions of reinforcement in the presence of one stimulus typically differ from conditions of reinforcement in the presence of a second stimulus. Of major interest is the extent to which the two stimuli control behavior appropriate to their correlated reinforcement conditions and the extent to which the component schedules interact. The emphasis in the study of multiple schedules is on maintenance of intermittently reinforced behavior rather than its acquisition. These characteristics set the study of multiple schedules apart from most other successive discrimination studies.

Interactions in Multiple Schedules

The feature of the control of behavior by multiple schedules which has attracted the greatest research interest is the interaction of the component schedules. Suppose, for example, a pigeon is pecking a response key illuminated by a red light for reinforcements programmed on a variable-interval 2-min (VI 2-min) schedule. When the pigeon's behavior is stable, the procedure is changed so that 3-min periods of red key illumination alternate with 3-min periods of green key illumination. The same VI 2-min schedule is in effect in the presence of both key colors. This procedure is defined as a multiple VI 2-min VI 2-min schedule (*mult* VI 2-min VI 2-min). It differs from the preceding only in that there are two alternating stimuli instead of one. Suppose responding to the red key in the *mult* differs in some way from responding in the previous procedure when the key was always red. This difference would be presumed to result from an interaction between the two component schedules. Indeed, there is evidence that responding is maintained at a higher rate by a simple VI schedule than by a *mult* VI VI, in which the value of the VI schedules is the same as in the simple VI (Bloomfield, 1967).

Now suppose the behavior of our pigeon in the *mult* VI 2-min VI 2-min schedule has stabilized. The procedure is then changed to *mult* VI 2-min extinction (EXT). When the key is red, the same VI 2-min schedule is in effect as before, but when the key is green, no reinforcement is scheduled. The effects of this procedural change are twofold. First, responding on the green key decreases. This effect is not considered the product of an interaction, since the schedule on the green key has changed from VI to EXT. Second, responding on the red key increases. This increase must be attributed to an interaction between the two components of the multiple schedule, since the reinforcement schedule in the presence of the red stimulus has not been altered. This particular type of interaction is called *positive behavioral contrast* (Reynolds, 1961a), and it will command most of our attention in the remainder of this chapter. Before actually reviewing research on interactions in multiple schedules, however, we shall discuss some general issues regarding the terminology and measurement of interactions.

Interactions between components of a multiple schedule can never be directly assessed. If one is interested in the effects of component B of a multiple schedule on responding in component A, then one alters conditions in component B, keeps conditions in component A constant, and looks for changes in responding in component A.

If responding in component A changes when component B conditions are changed, then one might infer that B has been influencing A all along. Thus assessments of interaction in multiple schedules typically require within-subject, across-procedure comparison. Usually one component schedule remains constant from one procedure to the next while the other component changes. While interactions probably occur on all multiple-schedule procedures, *an interaction can only be unequivocally demonstrated and categorized in a multiple-schedule component which is unchanged*. While the strategy for demonstrating interactions seems straightforward, there are some complexities. Suppose pigeons are exposed first to a *mult* VI 1-min VI 1-min schedule, and then to a *mult* VI 1-min EXT schedule. Responding in the unchanged VI component increases (positive contrast). Is this a clear indication of schedule interaction? It certainly seems to be, since the VI component has not changed while the behavior in that component has changed. However, what has also changed is the amount of exposure to the procedure. It is possible that responding changes merely as a function of sessions of exposure to a procedure. Thus in order clearly to identify the effect as an interaction, it must be shown that if the pigeons are returned to the *mult* VI 1-min VI 1-min procedure, responding in the unchanged component will decrease and return to its initial levels. In short, in order to demonstrate component interaction in a multiple schedule, the interaction effect must be reversible, i.e., *the base line against which interactions are assessed must be recoverable*. Many studies which have purported to demonstrate schedule interaction have failed to satisfy this baseline recovery criterion (cf. Gonzalez & Champlin, 1974).

To summarize, the ideal procedure for demonstrating multiple-schedule interactions contains three stages: first, exposure to a *mult* with equal components until behavior is stabilized; second, alteration of one component schedule; and third, return to the first procedure to recover the baseline.

Types of Interaction

There are four possible types of schedule interaction: positive and negative contrast and positive and negative induction. Part A of Figure 9 presents schematic diagrams of positive contrast and negative in-

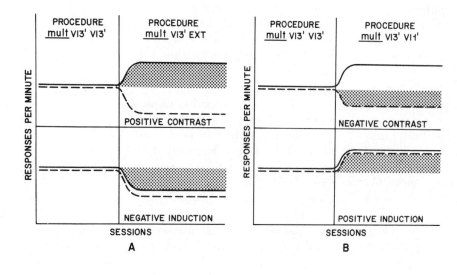

Fig. 9. Schematic diagrams of the four types of behavioral interaction. In A, after behavior has stabilized on a *mult* VI 3-min VI 3-min, the schedule associated with the second component is changed to EXT and response rate decreases (dashed line). The upper portion of the figure demonstrates positive contrast (shaded area). The lower portion of A demonstrates negative induction (shaded area). In B, after stabilization on *mult* VI 3-min VI 3-min, the schedule in the second component is changed to VI 1-min, i.e., more reinforcements are available per unit time (solid line). The shaded area in the upper portion of B is an example of negative contrast, while the shaded area in the lower portion of B is an instance of positive induction. Note that in all four cases the schedule in the first component does not change, nor does reinforcement density. Thus these changes are the result of interactions with the adjacent schedule.

duction. *Positive contrast* is defined as *an increase in responding in an unchanged component of a multiple schedule with decreases in responding in the other component.* *Negative induction* is defined as *a decrease in responding in an unchanged component of a multiple schedule with decreases in responding in the other component.* Positive induction and negative contrast are diagrammed in part B of Figure 9. *Positive induction* is *an increase in responding in an unchanged component of a multiple schedule with increases in the other component,* while *negative contrast* is *a decrease in responding in an unchanged component of a multiple schedule with increases in the other component.* These four types of interaction are not independent. In any particular experimental manipulation only two types of interaction are possible. Decreases in responding in the changed component of a multiple schedule can produce either increases (positive contrast) or decreases (negative induction) in the other component. Similarly, increases in responding in the changed component can produce either decreases (negative contrast) or increases (positive induction) in the unchanged component. It should be noted that all four types of interaction are defined in terms of response rate rather than some other feature of the experiment. This is meant only to be descriptive. It does not imply that response rate changes in one component *cause* rate changes in the other component. We shall see below that while some investigators have argued this position, the matter is still quite controversial. The definitions given here are not meant to imply support for any particular causal account of schedule interaction.

In the sections to follow we first describe reported instances of the different types of schedule interaction. The remainder of the chapter will focus almost exclusively on behavioral contrast. We discuss the different accounts in the literature offered to explain behavioral contrast. We next review some of the temporal properties of contrast. Next the relation between schedule interactions in multiple and concurrent schedules is discussed. Finally, a new account of contrast, based upon the phenomena of autoshaping and automaintenance, is presented and evaluated.

Positive Behavioral Contrast

The classic demonstration of positive behavioral contrast was Reynolds's (1961a) experiment in which pigeons were exposed to a series of multiple schedules with two alternating components. Each component was in effect for 3 min during which the key was illuminated by a specific color. At the end of the 3 min the color of the key changed and the second component was in effect. This cycle was repeated 30 times each session. During the first component the schedule of reinforcement for pecking was VI 3-min. Several different schedules were used in the second component, but we shall focus on the transition from VI 3-min to EXT and back to VI 3-min.

Figure 10 shows what happens to rate of responding in the unchanged component of these different schedules. (The data are approximations from Reynolds's figures and are plotted for only three of the pigeons, since the rate of responding for the fourth pigeon did not appear to be stable.) The introduction of the EXT component resulted in a large increase in responding (positive contrast) in the unchanged VI 3-min component. Reintroduction of the VI 3-min schedule in the second component reversed this effect and restored the original response rate.

Many of the features of Reynolds' experiment have become standard parts of investigations of positive contrast. First, the reinforcement schedule in the unchanged component is typically a VI, though occasionally fixed schedules (Reynolds 1961b, 1961c), fixed-interval schedules (Reynolds & Catania, 1961; Staddon, 1969) and DRL schedules (Reynolds, 1961b) have been used. Second, the reinforcement schedule in the changed component is typically also VI, and the change is to EXT. However, many other procedures have been used (Brethower & Reynolds, 1962; Terrace, 1968), and one of the uncertainties in the contrast literature centers on what procedure changes are necessary to produce contrast. Third, usually the same response is required and the same reinforcer delivered in both components of the multiple schedule. An exception is a study by Scull and Westbrook (1973) in which key pecking was required in one component and bar pressing in the other. This experiment failed to result in positive contrast.

Finally, the use of pigeons as subjects is a crucial feature of the basic demonstration of positive contrast. Species differences are evident in contrast experiments, and indeed the theory of contrast that we shall propose predicts that this should be so. When rats are subjects, the results are equivocal. These studies of contrast with rats fall into three categories according to the experimental results, which occasionally give evidence of contrast in rats, more often are equivocal, and sometimes clearly fail to find contrast in this species.

The first, small, category includes studies that provide positive evidence for contrast. Coates (1972) exposed rats to a *mult* VI 30-sec VI 30-sec until response rates had stabilized. Then the procedure was changed

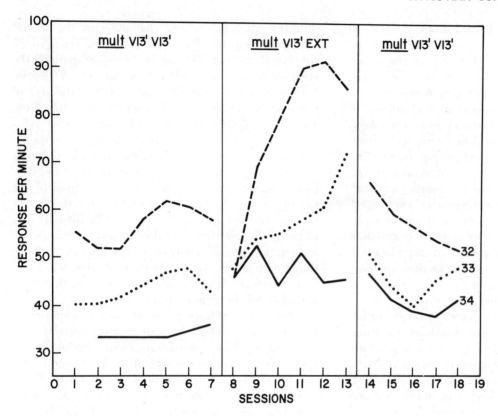

Fig. 10. Individual response rates in the unchanged VI 3-min component of a series of multiple schedules for three pigeons. (Estimated from Reynolds, 1961a.)

to a *mult* PUN+EXT, VI 30-sec, EXT, VI 30-sec, in the first component of which not only was bar pressing not reinforced but each response resulted in shock. Response rates in the VI components increased, with rate in the VI following PUN+EXT slightly higher than in the VI following regular EXT. Wilkie (1972) exposed four rats to a *mult* VI 30-sec VI 30-sec and then changed the second component to EXT. In all four subjects response rates in the VI component increased. Henke, Allen, and Davison (1972) studied four rats on a *mult* VI 1-min EXT after a *mult* VI 1-min VI 1-min, and again all four subjects showed positive contrast in the unchanged component. Thus positive contrast can be observed in rats.

More characteristic of the outcome of contrast studies using rats is the second category, in which equivocal results are obtained. Pear and Wilkie (1970) exposed two rats to six sessions of VI 30-sec, followed by a number of sessions on *MIX* VI 30-sec EXT. (A mixed schedule is just like a multiple schedule, except that components are not signaled.) After 10 sessions one rat showed positive contrast, but the other showed negative induction to the extent that the VI 30-sec had to be changed to a VI 20-sec to maintain responding. In a second experiment (Pear & Wilkie, 1971) eight rats were exposed to the following sequence of schedules: VI; *mult* VI EXT; *mult* VI VI. The VI schedule was always VI 30-sec. In the transition from simple VI to *mult* VI EXT, five of eight rats showed positive behavioral contrast. However, two of the other three rats showed negative induction. A final complicating factor is that the elevated VI rate in *mult* VI EXT shown by two rats did not return to base line in stage III, when both components were equal VIs.

Other mixed results come from a set of experiments employing shock. In these studies rats are first exposed to a *mult* VI 30-sec fixed ratio (FR) 10. Subsequently shock is introduced to the second component, so that each tenth response results in both a food pellet and a shock (Cook & Davidson, 1973; Cook & Sepinwall, 1974; Davidson & Cook, 1969; Sepinwall, 1973). The initial effect of introducing shock is negative induction (Cook & Davidson, 1973; Davidson & Cook, 1969), but after a few sessions there is often evidence of positive contrast (Sepinwall, personal communication).

The third class of rat studies either failed to find positive contrast or found negative induction. The procedures used have varied from *mult* VI EXT after simple VI (Freeman, 1971a; Jaffe, 1973; Weiss, 1971) or after *mult* VI VI (Dickinson, 1973) to *mult* VI VT (a VT or variable-time schedule is one in which reinforcements are delivered at irregular intervals independent of responding) after either simple VI or *mult* VI VI (Freeman, 1971a; Lattal & Maxey, 1971).

DEMONSTRATIONS OF
NEGATIVE CONTRAST

There are certain logical problems in evaluating negative contrast. Rachlin (1973) has suggested that positive and negative contrast are the same phenomenon, but that they occur at different points in an experimental sequence. Consider the top of part A in Figure 9, which depicts positive contrast schematically. Suppose a third procedure, the return to VI VI after VI EXT, to recover base line, were added there and the base line recovered. Base line recovery means that responding in the unchanged component decreases as responding in the changed component increases. But this defines negative contrast. Thus an unambiguous demonstration of positive contrast entails a later demonstration of negative contrast, and there is a logical argument for treating them as instances of the same phenomenon. Investigators in the past have failed to notice this interdependence between the two types of contrast because they have explicitly designed experiments to look for one or the other type.

Terrace (1968) exposed three pigeons to a *mult* VI 5-min VI 5-min and then to a *mult* VI 1-min VI 5-min. Only one pigeon showed negative contrast (decreases in responding in the unchanged VI 5-min component). Nevin (1968) observed negative contrast in a *mult* with a VI 3-min schedule in the constant component and different DRO (differential reinforcement of other behavior) schedules in the changing component. There are a number of demonstrations of local negative contrast (contrast with temporal characteristics) which will be taken up in detail in a later section (e.g., Bernheim & Williams, 1967; Nevin & Shettleworth, 1966; Williams, 1965). The only clear demonstration of large negative contrast effects in multiple schedules was obtained by Schwartz (1974a, 1975). Pigeons were shifted from *mult* 3-min VI 3-min to *mult* VI 3-min VI 72-sec. Responding in the unchanged component is shown in Figure 11. Data points below the dashed horizontal line indicate negative contrast.

Explanations of Multiple-Schedule Interactions

Contrast has received far more theoretical attention than induction in the literature. The reason for this asymmetry is probably historical. Induction effects follow from classical Hull-Spence discrimination theory (Spence, 1936), while contrast explicitly contradicts it (Allen, Capehart, & Hebert, 1969). In that context induction is the normal, expected effect and contrast is the surprise (cf. Bloomfield, 1969).

From the outset, explanations of contrast have included some notion of inhibition (Pavlov, 1927—though he labeled what is now called contrast "induction"). Almost all of the major current alternative explanations of contrast on multiple schedules include an inhibition component (Bloomfield, 1969; Catania, 1969; Malone & Staddon, 1973; Staddon, 1969; Terrace, 1966a, 1966b, 1968, 1972). The point of contention among the different accounts is the source of inhibition, not its existence. In this section we shall outline the different accounts of contrast and review the evidence which makes a distinction among them possible. Our treatment will roughly parallel recent reviews of the problem (Freeman, 1971b; Terrace, 1972).

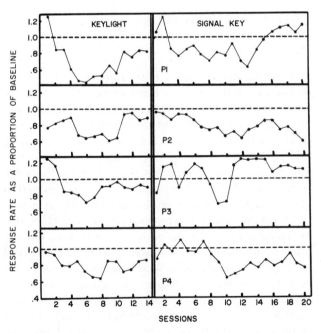

Fig. 11. Response rate to the operant key in the unchanged (VI 3-min) component of a *mult* VI 3-min VI 72-sec as a proportion of response rate in the same component in a prior *mult* VI 3-min VI 3-min. Points below the dashed line are indicative of negative contrast; points above the dashed line are indicative of positive induction. The data in the left-hand panel are from a series of conventional multiple schedules and show clear negative contrast. In the right-hand panel both components were signaled on a separate key. Responses to the second key were recorded but had no experimental consequences. (From Schwartz, 1974a.)

The Reinforcement Frequency Account

Reynolds's pioneering research on contrast (1961a, 1961b, 1961c, 1961d) suggested that the variable responsible for contrast in the unaltered component of a multiple schedule was a change in reinforcement frequency in the other component. *Contrast* was a change in response rate in one component in the opposite direction from a change in reinforcement frequency in the other component. Thus increases in reinforcement in component B of a multiple schedule result in negative contrast in component A, decreases in reinforcement in component B result in positive contrast in A, and changes in B which do not influence reinforcement frequency will not result in changes in responding in A. The role of inhibition in this account of contrast has been most explicitly and generally stated by Catania (1969). Reinforcement of one class of behavior is argued to have an inhibitory effect on all other classes of behavior. Thus reinforcement in one component of a multiple schedule will inhibit responding in the other component, and the procedural change from *mult* VI VI to *mult* VI EXT results in an increase in VI responding because it is released from previous inhibition by reinforcement in the other component.

The Response Suppression Account

Terrace (1963a, 1963b, 1966, 1972) observed that when a discrimination is learned without errors—i.e., when a simple VI schedule is gradually transformed into a *mult* VI EXT in such a way that virtually no responses are made to the EXT stimulus—positive contrast is not observed in the VI component. This observation led Terrace to propose that response rate reduction, not reinforcement frequency reduction, is responsible for contrast. Note that in the errorless procedure, response rate reduction does not occur, since errors are never made. Note also that in the most common contrast-inducing procedure, shift from *mult* VI VI to *mult* VI EXT, response rate reduction and reinforcement rate reduction are perfectly confounded, and the two explanations are not separable. In more recent accounts Terrace has refined his view of contrast. Response reduction is necessary but not sufficient to produce contrast. Responding must be actively suppressed, i.e., it must be inhibited. It is the inhibition of responding in one component which produces contrast in the other component. This view is much like Amsel's account of contrastlike effects in very different experimental situations (1962). The inhibition of responding produces an emotional by-product, which in turn energizes responding in neighboring situations. Thus in Terrace's view any manipulation which suppresses responding and is demonstrably aversive will result in contrast in the adjacent component of a multiple schedule. The response suppression procedure may, but need not, involve reinforcement reduction. Similarly, reinforcement reduction may not involve response suppression. Thus reinforcement reduction is neither necessary nor sufficient to produce contrast.

A related account has been proposed by Bloomfield (1969). He argued that any procedure change which "worsens" conditions will result in contrast, and that any procedure which does not worsen conditions will not result in contrast. The major difference between Bloomfield's view and Terrace's is that Bloomfield looks to the antecedent conditions which produce response suppression rather than to the suppression itself to explain contrast. This has the logical advantage of substituting a causal relation for Terrace's correlational one. However, in terms of specific application, the two accounts are not very different.

Experimental Separation of Reinforcement Reduction and Response Reduction

Experimental attempts to separate the two theories of contrast fall into two main classes. One class involves the reduction of reinforcement frequency without concomitant reduction in responding. It includes Terrace's research on errorless discrimination learning (1963a, 1963b, 1966a, 1966b, 1972). Terrace demonstrated that contrast does not occur after errorless discrimination training. Since errorless discrimination involves a reduction in reinforcement without a concomitant reduction in responding, Terrace takes this as strong support for his account of contrast. On the other hand, Halliday and Boakes (1974) have observed contrast in procedures in which response rate was not reduced (see Rilling chapter 15 in this volume for additional contradictory evidence). The second and more diverse class of studies attempts to reduce rate of responding without reducing rate of reinforcement. In these procedures Terrace would predict contrast while Reynolds would not. The results of these studies are mixed and open to methodological criticism (Freeman, 1971b).

One class of studies which manipulates response rate without changing reinforcement rate involves switching from *mult* VI VI to *mult* VI VT (e.g., Halliday & Boakes, 1972). Such procedures fail to produce contrast, which seems to support the reinforcement reduction account. However, Terrace's recent (1972) view is that response suppression, produced by nonreinforcement or by some aversive stimulation contingent on responding, and not merely response reduction is the necessary condition for contrast. Response-independent reinforcement, while it reduces responding, presumably does not suppress it. Hence this class of studies is not decisive.

Another class of studies reduces responding with punishment by electric shock. The punishment parameters are chosen so as to substantially reduce responding, but nevertheless to maintain it at a high enough rate so that reinforcement frequency is unaffected. Change from *mult* VI VI to *mult* VI VI+ punishment results in positive behavioral contrast (Brethower & Reynolds, 1962; Terrace, 1968), offering clear support for Terrace's view.

There is finally a class of studies which reduces response rate by manipulating the schedule in effect during one of the multiple-schedule components. *Mult* VI VI is switched to *mult* VI DRL (differential reinforcement of low rates) or *mult* VI DRO (differential reinforcement of other behavior). Terrace (1968) and Weisman (1969) have shown that as response rate is reduced in DRL, contrast occurs in the other component. More recently, however, Boakes, Halliday, and Mole (1974) failed to observe contrast in a similar experiment. The Boakes et al. study controlled very carefully for differences in local patterns of reinforcement between the VI and DRL components, which Terrace's study did not. In the *mult* VI DRO procedures, as response rate is reduced in DRO, contrast is usually not observed (Boakes, Halliday & Mole, 1974; Nevin, 1968; Nevin & Shettleworth, 1966; Reynolds, 1961a; but see Weisman, 1970, for a demonstration of contrast under these conditions). Thus the data from these studies are not decisively in support of one or the other account of contrast.

In summary, we have discussed the major views of behavioral contrast in this section and have seen that experimental tests yield contradictory results. We shall see below that none of these accounts is sufficient.

Temporal Properties of Contrast

Our definitions and examples of contrast so far have dealt with session-to-session changes in rate of responding in the constant component. These comparisons are typically made in terms of overall rate responding (total number of responses in a component divided by the total session time in which they may be emitted). There is, however, substantial evidence that the pattern of responding *within* a multiple-schedule component is not constant. Response rate changes are often most dramatic at the beginning of a component. These changes, which are restricted to only a portion of a component, will be referred to as *local contrast* (Malone & Staddon, 1973). They have also been referred to in the literature as *transient contrast* (Nevin & Shettleworth, 1966). However, we wish to reserve the latter term to describe a different phenomenon, i.e., that sometimes contrast dissipates with extended exposure to a procedure.

To be consistent with the definition of *contrast* that we have already given, *local contrast* must be defined relative to the adjacent schedule. Indeed, without reference to the prior component, any time an FI (fixed-interval) or FR schedule is used one would have to call the resulting behavior an example of local contrast, since the pattern of responding maintained on those schedules is not constant. Consequently, an initial elevation followed by a lower constant response rate in a given component (A) will be defined as local positive contrast if the overall response rate in an immediately prior component (B) is lower than the overall response rate in component A. If the overall response rate in component B is greater than the overall response rate in component A, then the local effect is defined as local positive induction. Conversely, an initial depression in response rate at the beginning of a component is defined as either local negative contrast or local negative induction, depending on the response rate in the prior component.

Boneau and Axelrod (1962) studied pigeons on a VI 1-min schedule for six days and then changed the procedure to a *mult* VI 1-min EXT. Each component lasted 60 sec. As might be expected, overall contrast was found. Responding in the presence of the VI stimulus more than doubled after the introduction of an extinction component. Local positive contrast was found in the next stage, in which instead of alternating between VI and EXT components, Boneau and Axelrod introduced either the EXT stimulus or a time-out (TO) only every ninth component. Thus the VI component lasted 8 min. Response rate in the first minute was substantially higher than in subsequent 1-min blocks and showed a gradual decrease until the block immediately preceding the EXT or TO. However, after four sessions of this procedure, these local contrast effects were no longer evident. Thus Boneau and Axelrod had reported the first instance of transient local contrast. It should also be noted that while the overall rates of responding in the VI component showed a slight decrease during the four days of testing, the basic overall contrast effect remained even

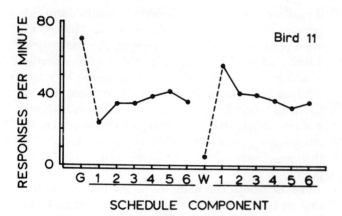

Fig. 12. Performance of one bird on a 3-ply multiple schedule in which a VI 8-min component alternated with either a VI 2-min or an EXT schedule. Response rate in the VI 8-min (red) is broken down into six successive 20-sec periods and is averaged over three sessions (10–12). The depression and elevation in the first 20 sec of VI 8-min are examples of negative and positive local contrast effects respectively. (Adapted from Nevin & Shettleworth, 1966. © 1966 by the Society for the Experimental Analysis of Behavior, Inc.)

though the local effect had disappeared. Catania and Gill (1964) observed local positive contrast on a *mult* FI EXT schedule. However, unlike the Boneau and Axelrod data, these effects persisted for 52 successive daily sessions. Similarly, Arnett (1973) reported local contrast effects in a *mult* VI 3-min EXT schedule for up to 65 sessions.

Nevin and Shettleworth (1966) studied a procedure in which 2-min components of VI 8-min reinforcement in red were preceded by either a VI 2-min component (green) or an EXT component (white). Figure 12 presents response rates in successive 20-sec segments of the VI 8-min component. Local negative contrast was observed when this component followed VI 2-min, and local positive contrast was observed when this component followed EXT.

There has not been a great deal of research on local contrast. It is, therefore, difficult to enumerate with confidence the conditions necessary to produce it. Some generalizations can be stated briefly, however. First, there is good evidence that local contrast effects increase with increases in the duration of the changed component (Staddon, 1969; Wilton & Clements, 1971). These effects parallel the results of studies of trial and ITI duration in autoshaping procedures (e.g., Baldock, 1974; see p. 77, above), if the unchanged component is viewed as a "trial" against the background of the changed component. These studies found that the rate of responding on autoshaping procedures increased with increases in the ITI. Second, there is evidence that pigeons and rats differ in showing local contrast—at least local positive con-

trast. In pigeons both positive and negative local contrast are reliably observed. In rats positive local contrast is typically not observed, though negative local contrast is (Bernheim & Williams, 1967; Williams, 1965). Third, the necessary prerequisite for local contrast appears to be a difference in reinforcement frequency, not response frequency, in adjacent components (Freeman, 1971a; Nevin & Shettleworth, 1966; Williams, 1965). Finally, although the conditions from which local contrast arises are often identical to the conditions which produce overall contrast, it is clear that the latter is not made up merely of the former. Overall positive contrast has been observed after local contrast has ceased (Boneau & Axelrod, 1962), and local contrast has been observed in a situation which produced overall induction (Freeman, 1971a).

Interactions in Concurrent Schedules: Relations Between Multiple and Concurrent Schedules

Concurrent schedules are two or more schedules which are simultaneously in effect, each associated with a different response. The prototypic concurrent procedure has involved the study of pigeons pecking one of two simultaneously illuminated response keys, with pecks on each key associated with a different schedule (e.g., Catania, 1966). An alternative procedure involves two keys. Pecks on the operant key produce reinforcement, while pecks on the changeover key change the schedule (and the correlated stimulus) on the operant key (Findley, 1958). A great deal of research, especially on the quantitative aspects of schedule control, has been done with concurrent schedules, and is discussed in detail by de Villiers (Chapter 9 of this volume), Catania (1966), and Herrnstein (1970). Moreover, Herrnstein (1970) has drawn attention to the parallels between phenomena observed on multiple and concurrent schedules and suggested that performance on both types of schedules reduces to a common explanatory principle. It seems appropriate, therefore, to discuss the relations between these schedules briefly.

The findings obtained in studies of concurrent schedules can be summarized by the word *matching*. Relative rate of responding in component A (rate of responding in component A/rate in component A plus rate in component B) matches relative rate of reinforcement in that component (Catania, 1966; Herrnstein, 1970). This is the epitome of schedule interaction. Responding in one component varies inversely with reinforcement frequency in the other component.

If a concurrent VI VI (*conc* VI VI) procedure is shifted to a *conc* VI EXT, an increase in responding in the unchanged VI component occurs (Catania, 1969). Similarly, if a *conc* VI EXT procedure is switched to *conc* VI VI, a decrease in responding in the unchanged VI component occurs (Catania, 1969). These outcomes are analogous to demonstrations of positive and negative behavioral contrast in multiple schedules. Indeed, the matching law is a general statement about schedule interactions which subsumes positive and negative contrast.

The foregoing is not meant to suggest, however, that multiple and concurrent schedules always yield identical results. First, matching does not usually occur on multiple schedules. Rather than allocating responses in the two components in direct proportion to reinforcements in the two components, organisms tend to undermatch (Reynolds, 1961b). The equation relating relative response rate to relative reinforcement rate has a slope less than 1.0 and a positive intercept.

In a recent quantitative analysis, Herrnstein (1970) attempted to capture both the similarities and differences between multiple and concurrent schedules. The quantitative relation he proposed was

$$P_A = \frac{Kr_A}{r_A + mr_B + r_0}$$

where P_A = rate of responding in component A; r_A = rate of reinforcement in component A; r_B = rate of reinforcement in component B; r_0 = rate of reinforcement for responses other than A and B (e.g., grooming); and m = a constant representing the degree of interaction between components. In concurrent procedures, $m = 1$; i.e., interaction is maximal. Matching is reflected by the following equation, with $m = 1$:

$$\frac{P_A}{P_A + P_B} = \frac{r_A}{r_A + r_B}$$

In multiple schedules, m approaches 1.0 as component duration decreases.

As is apparent from Equation 1, any alternative reinforcement for responses other than P_A will decrease P_A (contrast). Also apparent is the prediction that as component duration in multiple schedules is shortened, approximations to matching should get closer and closer, since m grows larger and larger. There is substantial empirical support for this prediction. Shimp and Wheatley (1971) and Todorov (1972) have shown that with extremely short (i.e., about 10-sec) component durations, matching is obtained on multiple schedules. Indeed, one could view a concurrent procedure as a special case of a multiple procedure, where the subject rather than the experimenter controls component duration. On concurrent procedures, subjects tend to produce short component durations (i.e., change keys at a high rate). Hence one observes matching with concurrent procedures. Killeen (1972) examined the possibility that multiple and concurrent procedures are intimately related by exposing pigeons to a concurrent procedure and arranging for switches from one component to the other to produce component changes for other pigeons that were responding on multiple schedules identical in reinforcement frequency to the concurrent schedules. This enabled Killeen to compare the control over responding exerted by concurrent schedules and multiple schedules which were identical in both reinforcement frequency and component duration. Killeen found that *mult* and *conc* pigeons allocated their responses to the different components identically, thus strengthening the view that multiple and concurrent schedules are not fundamentally different. However, the generality of Killeen's findings has recently been questioned in an experiment by Silberberg and Schrot (1974). They pointed out that in Killeen's study, since the concurrent-schedule pigeons switched frequently between components, the resulting multiple schedule had short component durations. Both Herrnstein's theoretical account and the data obtained by Shimp and Wheatley (1971) and Todorov (1972) suggest that multiple schedules and concurrent schedules have similar effects only when the multiple schedules are short. Thus Silberberg and Schrot asked whether the similarity between *mult* and *conc* performances on a Killeen-type procedure would persist even when the *conc* pigeons created long *mult* components. They accomplished this by introducing long *changeover delays* (CODs). A COD is a contingency which prevents reinforcement of a response on one key until some amount of time has elapsed since the last response on the other key. Long CODs have been shown to decrease the likelihood of switching between components in concurrent procedures (Shull & Pliskoff, 1971). Thus they should result in lengthened components for the pigeons on *mult* procedures. Silberberg and Schrot found that as COD increased, thus increasing component duration in both *conc* and *mult* procedures, differences in response allocation between *conc* and *mult* subjects increased. Thus they argued that since matching on concurrent procedures is independent of component duration, while matching on multiple procedures depends upon component duration, there are fundamental differences in the control over behavior exerted by the two types of procedure.

There are other reasons for believing this to be the case. Despite the gross similarity between responding maintained by multiple and concurrent schedules, molecular analysis of how matching occurs on concurrent schedules makes it clear that matching on concurrent and multiple schedules is different. Rachlin (1973) has discussed this in detail. On concurrent schedules, animals distribute the time spent responding in the two components in proportion to the relative reinforcement rate in those components (Baum & Rachlin, 1969). For example, if reinforcements in component A are twice as frequent as reinforcements in component B, animals will spend twice as much time responding in component A and make twice as many responses. What this means, however, is that local response rate (responses divided by the time available in which to make them) will be equal in the two components. This cannot be true of multiple schedules. Since component duration in multiple schedules is fixed, increases in responding in component A as a function of decreases in reinforcement in component B must result from increases in local response rate and not from increases in time allocation.

What might be the source of this increase in local response rate which occurs in multiple schedules? We shall now describe a new theory of behavioral contrast which attributes these extra responses to autoshaping-like stimulus-reinforcer relations which are sometimes present in multiple schedules.

An Additivity Theory of Contrast

The phenomena of autoshaping and automaintenance have been thoroughly discussed above. The available evidence clearly indicates that autoshaping reflects the control of key pecking by Pavlovian, stimulus-reinforcer contingencies. One series of experiments, by Gamzu and Williams (1971, 1973), makes the parallel between autoshaping and Pavlovian conditioning particularly clear and is especially relevant to the theory of contrast we shall propose. Pavlovian conditioning depends upon the existence of an informative or differential relation between the CS and the US. Pairing is neither necessary nor sufficient (Rescorla, 1967). Gamzu and Williams applied this analysis to autoshaping by showing that unless the response key was a differential predictor of food $[P(\text{food}/\text{key}) > P(\text{food}/\overline{\text{key}})]$, autoshaping would not occur and already established key pecking would cease. The question of primary relevance to the phenomenon of contrast raised by the Gamzu and Williams experiments and other studies of autoshaping and automaintenance is this: given that stimulus-reinforcer relations control key pecking in the absence of response-reinforcer relations, what is their effect when response-reinforcer dependencies are also present? To examine this question, let us return to the standard sequence of multiple schedules employed to demonstrate behavioral contrast. One begins typically with *mult* VI-VI. In this procedure response-reinforcer dependencies exist in both components. However, there is no *differential* stimulus-reinforcer relation. Food is equally likely in both components of the multiple schedule. When the procedure is changed to *mult* VI EXT, the response-reinforcer dependency continues in the VI component. Now, however, a differential stimulus-reinforcer relation is also introduced. The VI-correlated stimulus predicts food while the EXT-correlated stimulus does not. This state of affairs is what generated and maintained pecking in the Gamzu and Williams experiments. Thus we might expect two sources of control of pecking to be operative in the VI component of a *mult* VI EXT schedule (both stimulus-reinforcer and response-reinforcer relations), while only one was operative in the preceding *mult* VI VI schedule. By assuming, for simplicity, that the two sources of control interact additively, one would expect pecking to increase in the VI component of a *mult* VI EXT schedule relative to its rate of occurrence on a *mult* VI VI. This, of course, defines positive contrast. Thus the additivity theory of contrast is simple: contrast occurs because a differential stimulus-reinforcer dependency is imposed upon an already existing response-reinforcer dependency, and the two sources of control combine to increase the rate of key pecking. A number of investigators arrived at roughly this conclusion simultaneously (Boakes, 1973; Gamzu & Schwartz, 1973; Hemmes, 1973; Rachlin, 1973; Staddon, 1972). The theory was first articulated in its present form by Gamzu and Schwartz (1973) on the basis of an experiment which extended the findings of Gamzu and Williams (1971, 1973) to procedures employing parameters akin to those employed on standard multiple schedules. Pigeons were exposed to a multiple schedule with regularly alternating components signaled by key color. The components were 27 sec long, and reinforcements were always delivered independently of responses. The procedures were either differential (*mult* VT 33-sec EXT) or nondifferential (*mult* VT 33-sec VT 33-sec). As Gamzu and Williams found with a discrete-trials procedure, pecking was generated and maintained on the differential procedure and essentially eliminated

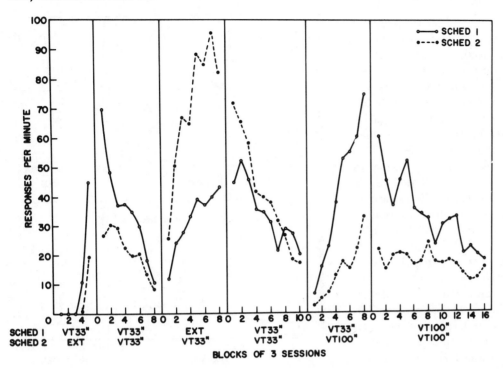

Fig. 13. Responses per minute in each component of a series of multiple schedules for Pigeon 85, averaged across blocks of three sessions. Component schedules are identified on the abscissa. (From Gamzu & Schwartz, 1973. © 1973 by the Society for the Experimental Analysis of Behavior, Inc.)

on the nondifferential procedure. These data are summarized in Figure 13. Gamzu and Schwartz argued that it was these responses which summed with those maintained by response-reinforcer dependencies in standard multiple schedules to produce contrast.

PREDICTIONS BASED UPON THE
ADDITIVITY THEORY OF CONTRAST
AND THEIR CONFIRMATION

The central component of the additivity theory, stated generally, is that whenever a differential stimulus-reinforcer relation exists, that stimulus will exert control over some class of behavior. The obvious problem which arises is the specification of the class of behavior which will be controlled. There are at least two views on this matter. One view suggests that the class of behavior which will be controlled by stimulus-reinforcer relations is just that class which is appropriate to the reinforcer—i.e., a class of consummatory responses—and that these responses will be directed at the signaling stimulus. This view is in keeping with our traditional understanding of Pavlovian conditioning, which is that a conditional stimulus comes to elicit some component(s) of the unconditional response to the US. The evidence in support of this view of autoshaping is good, as discussed earlier (cf. Moore, 1973). In the pigeon, pecking is a consummatory response (Jenkins & Moore, 1973; Staddon & Simmelhag, 1971), and the form of autoshaped re-

sponding is appropriate to the reinforcer—food or water pecks with food or water reinforcers (Jenkins & Moore, 1973). When rats are autoshaped to contact rather than to press a lever, they contact the lever by chewing it (Peterson, Ackil, Frommer, & Hearst, 1972; Stiers & Silberberg, 1974). A second view, which has been labeled "sign tracking" (Hearst and Jenkins, 1974) includes the directedness of the previous view, but suggests that within limits, organisms will direct whatever skeletal activity is possible toward a stimulus which signals food. The form of the response need not, though it might, bear any clear resemblance to the unconditional response to food. It is not clear which of these views is correct, but they make the same predictions about contrast in standard pigeon and rat experiments. In the standard multiple-schedule procedure employed with pigeons, pecking is the measured response (consummatory), and the discriminative stimuli are located on the response key (sign tracking). Thus either view of autoshaping would predict that stimulus-reinforcer and response-reinforcer relations will both influence the same behavior—key pecking. (The difference between the two views is in whether one underlines "key" or "pecking" in "key pecking.")

Now consider the standard multiple-schedule procedure employed with rats. Rats press a lever (nonconsummatory) for food. The discriminative stimuli are located away from the lever (no sign tracking). Thus either view would predict that when rats are exposed to *mult* VI EXT after *mult* VI VI (i.e., when a differential stimulus-reinforcer relation is introduced), bar pressing will not be enhanced. Indeed, to the extent that the stimulus-reinforcer relation is effective, it will generate some other consummatory behavior, directed at the signal, which may compete with bar pressing. This competition would result in negative induction of bar pressing (reduction in VI rate when the second component is changed from VI to EXT) rather than contrast. Thus the additivity theory of contrast would predict that contrast will not be obtained with bar-pressing rats as subjects. There are no features of other theories of contrast already discussed which would lead one to this prediction. The literature suggests that, indeed, with bar-pressing rats, induction rather than contrast is the rule (e.g., Freeman, 1971b). To summarize, contrast is not expected simply because response-reinforcer and stimulus-reinforcer relations do not influence the same class of behavior. If the discriminative stimuli were located on the lever, then contrast might occur. The stimulus-reinforcer contingency would generate some form of lever contact, perhaps biting, which would sum with the lever presses already being maintained by the response-reinforcer dependency.

The implication of this theory of contrast is that the bulk of demonstrations of positive contrast are the result of a fortuitous procedural convention which (a) measures as operants consummatory responses and (b) localizes discriminative stimuli on the response key. The theory predicts that if either of these procedural features is altered, contrast will not appear. Again, other theories make no such prediction. A number of experiments have recently been conducted which put this aspect of the theory to empirical test. Westbrook (1973) and Hemmes (1973) exposed pigeons to standard multiple schedules except that the required operant was treadle hopping in Hemmes' experiment and bar pressing in Westbrook's. Under these conditions, we would expect the pigeons to behave like rats. The differential stimulus-reinforcer relation established during *mult* VI EXT would not enhance treadle hopping or bar pressing, but some other behavior directed at the signaling stimulus. Thus probably negative induction, but certainly not positive contrast, should occur. Both studies failed to find contrast, and Westbrook's study demonstrated large negative induction effects. Some data from Westbrook's study are presented in Figure 14. An especially interesting feature of the Westbrook study is that generalization tests around the stimulus associated with EXT were performed, and inhibitory generalization gradients were obtained. Thus Westbrook's study

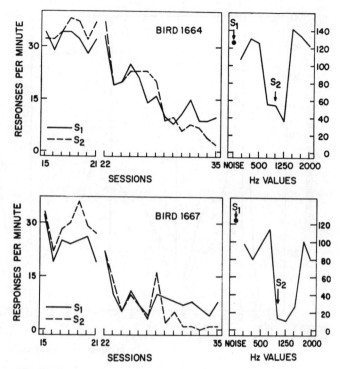

Fig. 14. Bar presses per minute for two pigeons over the last 7 sessions of *mult* VI 1-min VI 1-min and 14 sessions of *mult* VI 1-min EXT (lefthand panels) with results of a generalization test around the stimulus associated with EXT (S2) in the right-hand panels. Both negative induction and inhibitory control are demonstrated (From Westbrook, 1973. © 1973 by the Society for the Experimental Analysis of Behavior, Inc.)

shows that inhibitory control can be established in such an experimental situation, but that it is not sufficient to produce behavioral contrast.

A second class of relevant studies employs key pecking as the operant but removes the discriminative stimuli from the response key. Again, the additivity theory would predict that the differential stimulus-reinforcer contingency would control behavior, but that since the stimulus was off the key the behavior would not sum with operant pecks, and hence no contrast would result. Experiments by Redford and Perkins (1974) and Schwartz (1974a, 1974c, 1975) confirm this expectation. In Schwartz's experiments, pigeons were exposed to a series of multiple schedules, both *mult* VI VI and *mult* VI EXT. What varied from one set of schedules to the next was the location and/or modality of the discriminative stimuli. Figure 15 presents, for a representative pigeon, rates of responding in both components of the series of multiple schedules. Each exposure to the *mult* VI EXT schedule was characterized by a different set of discriminative stimuli, identified in the figure. Contrast was only observed when the signals for the multiple-schedule components were on the response key. The data pre-

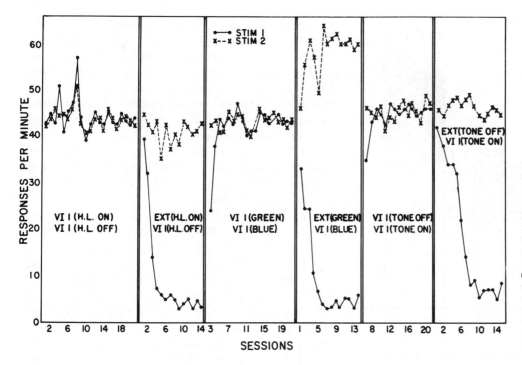

Fig. 15. Responses per minute for one pigeon exposed to a repeated cycle of *mult* VI VI (panels 1, 3, and 5) followed by *mult* VI EXT (panels 2, 4, and 6). The location and modality of the discriminative stimuli were varied as indicated in each panel. Contrast was only observed when the discriminative stimuli were on the key. (From Schwartz, 1974a.)

sented in the figure were characteristic of all subjects, except that some pigeons evidenced a small contrast effect with tone off as S+. This latter effect has also been reported by Hemmes (1973) and Westbrook (1973) and may require additional explanatory concepts.

We shall conclude this section by describing a study by Keller (1974) which is a most elegant support for the additivity theory of contrast. Keller exposed pigeons to a standard sequence of multiple schedules and obtained positive contrast. He then spatially separated response-reinforcer and stimulus-reinforcer relations. The old response key was always illuminated by the same stimulus, and reinforcement depended upon pecks on this key (operant key). The stimuli which signaled components of the multiple schedule were now alternated on a second key (signal key). During *mult* VI VI, responding was maintained as normal on the operant key, and there was no responding on the signal key. During *mult* VI EXT, response rate on the operant key did not change substantially during VI. However, most of the pigeons now started pecking at the VI stimulus on the signal key. Responding on the two keys together, if summed, showed behavioral contrast.

A second study produced more impressive results. Pigeons were exposed to three-component multiple schedules of reinforcement. Pecks on the operant key were required for reinforcement, while the multiple-schedule components were signaled on a second key.

Initially, the component schedules were VI, VI, and EXT. Under these conditions, pigeons pecked at both of the VI stimuli on the signal key. When the procedure was changed to *mult* VI EXT EXT, Keller observed the following: (1) pecks on the signal key at the EXT stimulus which was previously correlated with VI were substantially reduced; (2) pecks on the signal key at the VI stimulus were substantially increased; (3) pecks at the operant key during VI were substantially reduced, i.e., negative induction was observed; (4) despite induction on the operant key, if operant key pecks and VI signal pecks were summed, the uniform result was behavioral contrast. Some of these data are presented in Figure 16.

Relations Between an Additivity Theory of Contrast and Existing Theories

In the preceding section we outlined a new account of behavioral contrast. We shall now consider the possible relation between this theory and other theories of contrast, which focus on the concept of inhibition. Logically, the two accounts are not incompatible. It is entirely possible that inhibition produced in some way is a necessary condition for contrast. The autoshaping theory simply asserts that inhibition is not sufficient. As the experiment by Westbrook (1973), discussed in the last section, clearly demonstrates, one can obtain inhibitory stimulus con-

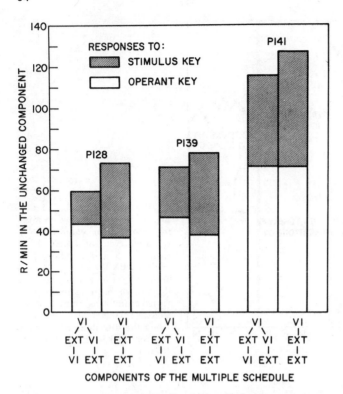

Fig. 16. Responses per minute during the unchanged component of a series of three-component multiple schedules. Response rates are segmented into responses to the operant key and responses to the signal key (shaded). The multiple schedules are divided into those with two VI components (regardless of order of presentation) and those with two EXT components. The data are averages of data presented in Keller (1974, Table 2). In all cases the overall contrast effect can be completely attributed to increased responding to the signal key.

trol without obtaining contrast. Contrast requires more than inhibition, i.e., it requires the appropriate choice of response and discriminative stimulus by the experimenter. Thus the question of whether inhibition is sufficient for contrast has already been answered negatively. The unresolved question is whether inhibition is necessary. Current controversies regarding inhibitory theories of contrast focus upon the response-reinforcer relation. Inhibition produced by nonreinforced responding results in a rebound increase in the rate of reinforced responses on one view (Terrace, 1972). Inhibition of responding in one component of a multitude schedule by reinforcement of responding in the other component is eliminated in a shift from *mult* VI VI to *mult* VI EXT, thus increasing unchanged VI response rate on the other view (Catania, 1969; Reynolds, 1961a). The additivity theory of contrast suggests a different approach to inhibition—one which focuses on stimulus-reinforcer relations. It is an excitatory stimulus-reinforcer relation which produces contrast according to the theory.

However, on a *mult* VI EXT procedure, the EXT stimulus resembles procedurally a Pavlovian conditioned inhibitor (Rescorla, 1969b). Thus the standard procedural progression from *mult* VI VI to *mult* VI EXT inevitably introduces both excitatory and inhibitory Pavlovian contingencies.[2] The obtained contrast effect could ostensibly result from either or both of these contingencies. The *mult* VI VI procedure is the operant analog to the Pavlovian truly random control (Rescorla, 1967). Neither stimulus is a differential predictor of food, and there should be no Pavlovian conditioning.

Support for the possibility that the extinction stimulus may be a Pavlovian conditioned inhibitor comes from a study by Jenkins and Boakes (1973). Pigeons were exposed to three different stimuli on response keys. One stimulus reliably signaled food. One stimulus reliably signaled no food. Food delivery was random with respect to the third stimulus. Autoshaped pecking occurred only to the stimulus which signaled food. Of interest to the present topic, however, is that measured by their position in the chamber relative to the stimuli, pigeons preferred the random stimulus to the stimulus which signaled no food. If the relative aversion to the no-food stimulus in the Jenkins and Boakes study is taken as an indication of Pavlovian conditioned inhibition, and if the no-food stimulus is considered the analog of an extinction stimulus in a multiple schedule, then the Jenkins and Boakes study supports the view that the EXT signal in a multiple schedule functions as a Pavlovian conditioned inhibitor.

Having suggested that contrast may depend upon the joint action of Pavlovian excitation and inhibition of the same response, let us consider the following experiment. Pigeons are exposed to a *mult* VI 1-min VI 1-min schedule, then shifted to a *mult* VI 1-min VI 5-min (Guttman, 1959; Terrace, 1968). Such a procedure results in positive behavioral contrast. While it is not unreasonable to suggest that such a procedure shift introduces an excitatory stimulus-rein-

---

[2] It should be noted that this feature of multiple schedules is an inherent feature of all Pavlovian conditioning experiments. If a differential positive contingency exists between a CS and a US, then a differential negative contingency must exist between the absence of the CS and the US. That this relation may sometimes be crucial is discussed in Seligman's (1969) criticism of Rescorla's truly random control procedure. This fact is a consequence of the modern view of Pavlovian conditioning as being dependent on more than the mere pairing of stimuli (Rescorla, 1967). Indeed, Pavlov (1927) expected that in standard experimental procedures background stimuli would become weak conditioned excitatory stimuli by virtue of being sometimes paired with a US. On the modern view, background stimuli would not be expected to be excitatory, and might even be inhibitory.

forcer relation in the unchanged VI 1-min component, can one argue that the change from VI 1-min to VI 5-min in the other component results in an inhibitory stimulus-reinforcer relation? Neither of the two recent reviews of research on conditioned inhibition (Hearst, Besley, & Farthing, 1970; Rescorla, 1969b) present any relevant data from the Pavlovian conditioning literature. One piece of experimental evidence which is available suggests that inhibition is not produced by such a procedure. In the Gamzu and Schwartz (1973) experiment discussed above, one sequence of procedures involved a shift from *mult* VT 33-sec VT 33-sec to *mult* VT 33-sec VT 100-sec. Response rate increased dramatically in the unchanged VT 33-sec component—presumably due to excitatory Pavlovian conditioning. However, response rate also increased dramatically in the VT 100-sec component relative to prior rate when the schedule in that component was VT 33-sec. This increase in rate is incompatible with the idea that such changes in procedure might produce inhibition. On the other hand, a study by Weisman (1969) suggests that the stimulus signaling reduced reinforcement may be inhibitory. Weisman shifted pigeons from *mult* VI 1-min VI 1-min to *mult* VI 1-min VI 5-min and observed positive behavioral contrast in the unchanged VI component. Concurrently, he observed gradients of inhibition about the stimulus correlated with the VI 5-min schedule. Also, a study by Rilling, Askew, Ahlskog, and Kramer (1969) has shown that pigeons will peck a key to escape from the stimulus correlated with VI 5-min on a *mult* VI 30-sec VI 5-min procedure. Thus at present the question of whether Pavlovian inhibition is *necessary* for contrast to occur must be left unresolved.[3]

---

[3] We have been using the term *inhibition* somewhat loosely in this section, and we shall not attempt a rigorous definition of the term. Reviews by Rescorla (1969) and Hearst, Besley, and Farthing (1970) have dealt extensively with the problem of establishing defining criteria for the presence of inhibition. We have cited evidence from Jenkins and Boakes (1973) that pigeons withdraw from an S−, and from Rilling et al. (1969) that pigeons peck a key to escape from a stimulus correlated with a relatively low density of reinforcement as instances of inhibitory control. Technically, they are not. Rather, they are demonstrations of the relative aversiveness of these stimuli. The relation between these indications of aversiveness and inhibition is an open question. For the present purposes, however, the concepts of inhibition and aversion are functionally equivalent: they both imply a reduction in responding. There is still a problem, however. How can an S− reduce responding which is already at zero, which is the level of Pavlovian responses we would expect to be present in a *mult* VI VI with equal-density components? A possible solution to this problem may arise from an evaluation of the stimulus-reinforcer relations which exist in the chamber from a broader perspective. While it is true that neither *mult* stimulus is a better predictor of food than the other, it is also true that both stimuli are differential predictors of food in contrast with the stimuli present outside the chamber. If this

There is one final issue to be discussed with regard to the additivity theory of contrast. How does such a theory account for negative contrast? As mentioned above, *negative contrast* refers to a decrease in response rate as response rate in the other component increases. In studies of multiple schedules, negative contrast is not obtained as reliably, or in as great a magnitude, as positive contrast. For example, Terrace (1968) shifted pigeons from *mult* VI 5-min VI 5-min to *mult* VI 1-min VI 5-min and obtained little negative contrast, a finding which he interpreted as support for his view that contrast results from the frustration of nonrewarded responses, or, as Bloomfield has described it, from a worsening of conditions. There are, however, demonstrations of local negative contrast in both rats (Bernheim & Williams, 1967) and pigeons (Nevin & Shettleworth, 1966). An additivity theory of negative contrast encounters the same problem discussed above with regard to conditioned inhibition. Multiple VI 5-min VI 5-min schedules presumably result in no Pavlovian conditioning. The shift to *mult* VI 5-min VI 1-min must make the VI 5-min stimulus a conditioned inhibitor in order to account for negative contrast. As we have seen, such an argument is problematic. An alternative possibility is that negative and positive contrast are causally unrelated—that despite their symmetrical appearance, they are produced by different variables. Bernheim and Williams (1967) demonstrated that positive and negative contrast are dissociable: they appear to occur independently of one another. Some rats in their study showed one type and some the other, and the same rats showed each effect at different points in the experiment. One way to investigate this possibility more systematically is to assess whether manipulation of the variables which influence positive contrast (e.g., location of discriminative stimuli or required response) have similar effects on negative contrast. Schwartz (1975) has recently done such an experiment. Pigeons were exposed to a *mult* VI 3-min VI 3-min schedule with the components signaled by green and white key color and then shifted to a *mult* VI 3-min VI 72-sec schedule. Absolute rates of responding in both components are presented for one pigeon in Figure 17. It can be seen from the second panel that negative contrast occurred. The pigeons were then returned to the *mult* VI 3-min VI 3-min schedule. Now, however, the operant key was always blue. A second key, the signal key, alternated between green and white. Recall that with pro-

---

logical truth is also a psychological one, we would expect both *mult* stimuli to be slightly excitatory, in which case an inhibitory operation *could* be expected to reduce responding.

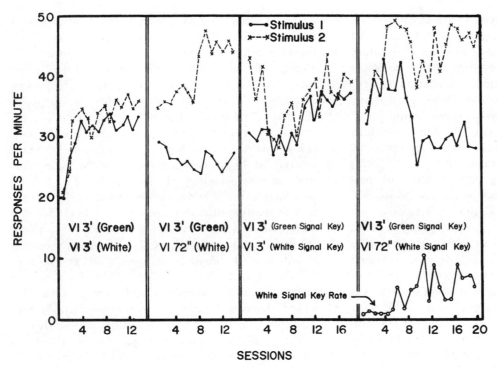

Fig. 17. Responses per minute for one pigeon exposed to a series of *mult* VI 3-min VI 3-min schedules alternating with *mult* VI 3-min VI 72-sec schedules. In panels 1 and 2 the discriminative stimuli were displayed successively on the same key. In panels 3 and 4 two keys were used. One key was constantly illuminated blue and pecks at it could be reinforced by the prevailing VI schedule, the value of which was signaled by either green or white illumination of a second key. Pecking at the second key was recorded but had no experimental effect. Responses per minute to the white signal key are shown at the bottom of the last panel. (From Schwartz, 1975. © 1975 by the Society for the Experimental Analysis of Behavior, Inc.)

cedures designed for assessing positive contrast, no contrast effect appears on the operant key (Keller, 1974). Rather, pecks are directed at the signal key. The fourth panel of Figure 17 indicates that negative contrast does in fact appear on the operant key with this procedure. Incidentally, substantial signal-key pecking occurred during the changed component (VI 72-sec). This is represented at the bottom of the fourth panel of Figure 17. Data from all pigeons in this experiment have already been presented earlier (see Figure 11).

Thus both logic and preliminary evidence suggest that the additivity theory of contrast may not be applicable to negative contrast. This conclusion is similar to the one suggested by studies of contrast in very different experimental contexts. Studies of rats in runways and mazes, typically involving variations in reward magnitude rather than frequency, have occasionally provided evidence for both positive and negative contrast (Crespi, 1944). However, the most common finding in such studies is clear negative contrast but no positive contrast (e.g., Bower, 1961; Glass & Ison, 1966; Spear & Hill, 1965; see Dunham, 1968, for a review of this literature). Both the lack of positive contrast and the presence of negative contrast in these studies is consistent with the additivity theory, since it suggests that (a) positive contrast is unlikely in most of the traditional situations to which rats are exposed and (b) positive and negative contrast may be fundamentally different phenomena.

ADDITIVITY THEORY AND LOCAL CONTRAST

A prominent feature of demonstrations of contrast is its time dependence or local character. Much of this literature has already been reviewed above. Let us simply summarize by asserting that the magnitude of contrast decreases with time after the preceding component ends and increases as a function of its duration.

It is possible that the distinction between local and overall contrast effects may help reconcile those contrast phenomena which are consistent with the additivity theory with those which are not (see de Villiers, Chapter 9 of this volume). The consistent phenomena have already been discussed in detail. Some of the inconsistencies are (1) occasional demonstrations of contrast with discriminative stimuli located off the key (Hemmes, 1973; Schwartz, 1974a, 1974c; Westbrook, 1973); (2) occasional demonstrations of contrast in bar-pressing rats (Gutman & Sutterer, 1974; Pear & Wilkie, 1971); (3) demonstration of contrast in rats with procedures employing only aversive stimuli (de Villiers, 1972, 1974); and (4) lack of contrast in some errorless discrimination procedures (Terrace, 1966). Rachlin has provided evidence which suggests that the contribution of a stimulus-reinforcer contingency to contrast may be largely restricted to periods just after a change in multiple-schedule components—i.e., that the stimulus-reinforcer effect may be local. Pigeons were exposed to *mult* VI 2-min VI

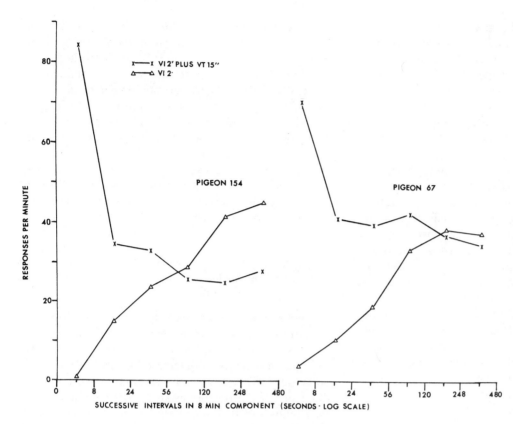

Fig. 18. Rates of responding of two pigeons in successive intervals of 8-min components of a *mult* VI 2-min VI 2-min plus VT 15-sec. The duration of each interval increases logarithmically along the abscissa. For instance, the first points on the abscissa show rates of responding during the first 8 seconds; the last 8 points show rates during the 248th to 480th seconds of the component. (From Rachlin, 1973.)

2-min schedules. In one of the components additional reinforcements were delivered independent of responding on a variable time (VT) 15-sec schedule. Let us consider the expected effect of these free rewards from the additivity theory of contrast. The free reinforcements would create a differential stimulus-reinforcer contingency, which would generate additional pecks in that component. Thus response rate should be higher when free rewards are presented than when they are not presented. Rachlin observed that when the components were 8 sec long, response rate was higher in the component which included free reinforcements. However, when the components were 8 min long, this was no longer true.

Figure 18 presents response rates in successive subcomponents of the 8-min multiple procedure. Early in each component containing free reinforcement responding was higher than in the other component. Later in each component containing free reinforcement responding was lower. Rachlin's study suggests that the main effect of the stimulus-reinforcer contingency may be confined to the part of a multiple-schedule component which borders the other component, i.e., the stimulus-reinforcer relation may be responsible primarily for local contrast. If components are very long, the local effect will be averaged across the entire component and represent only a small increase in overall response rate (no contrast). The shorter the component, the larger the contribution made by the local contrast effect to overall rate. Boakes, Halliday, and Poli (1975) have supported Rachlin's findings. They studied a procedure very similar to Rachlin's, but with 2-min component durations. They found increases in responding when free reinforcements were added to a component of a multiple schedule under these conditions.

Another study which suggests that the stimulus-reinforcer relation contributes mainly to local contrast was done by Schwartz, Hamilton, and Silberberg (1975). Schwartz et al. exposed pigeons to a sequence of multiple schedules in which the signal for the components was located on a second key (see Keller, 1974). In addition, they recorded the duration of key pecks on both the operant key and the signal key. The reader will recall that Schwartz and Williams (1972b) and Gamzu (1971) have obtained evidence which suggests that pecks controlled by the response-reinforcer relation are long-duration pecks, while pecks controlled by the stimulus-reinforcer relation are short-duration pecks. If the Keller procedure spatially separates behavior controlled by the two different contingencies, one would expect response durations on the signal key to be substantially shorter than response durations on the operant key. On the *mult* VI EXT procedure, Schwartz et al. obtained evidence that this was the case. Median response durations on the operant key were about 50 msec, while median durations on the signal key were about 20 msec. Of greater relevance to the present discussion, however, was the finding that most signal-key responses occurred during the first 10 sec of each 120-sec VI component. The four pigeons emitted 14, 32, 59, and 77% of their signal-key responses during the first 10 sec of the VI component. If there were no local effect, 8.5% of responses would have occurred in the first 10 sec. These data support both the view that the stimulus-reinforcer contingency exerts its main effect on local contrast and the view that there are two distinct classes of pecks which may be separated on the basis of duration (Schwartz & Williams, 1972b). If the additivity theory of contrast offered here accounts mainly for local contrast, then one might expect to see contrast (though of lesser magnitude) in some situations to which the additivity theory does not apply, since not all contrast is local. Unfortunately, since only a small proportion of the studies which demonstrate behavioral contrast provide the evidence necessary for assessing local contrast, it is not possible to say anything very definitive on this matter. For example, in studies which offer clear support for the additivity theory (e.g., Keller, 1974; Schwartz, 1975) there are no data available on whether the observed contrast effects were local. As we mentioned above, local positive contrast is almost never reported with rats as subjects, although overall contrast occasionally is. This one bit of confirming evidence is a slender reed on which to support a theory, however, and until more experimental analysis has been carried out the resolution of this matter will have to wait.

ADDITIVITY THEORY OF
CONTRAST: CONCLUSIONS

We have presented a theory of contrast which relates it to autoshaping and automaintenance and have discussed the findings which lend support to the theory. Much of the evidence one would like in order to evaluate the theory is not presently available. However, there is enough confirming evidence to indicate that stimulus-reinforcer relations play a significant role in the phenomenon of behavioral contrast. This being the case, it becomes clear that the phenomenon of behavioral contrast has been improperly labeled a "schedule interaction" (Reynolds, 1961b). Behavioral contrast reflects not so much schedule interaction as it does process interaction. The two processes which interact are Pavlovian and operant conditioning processes. Thus it is appropriate to examine some of the research explicitly designed to assess such process interactions in order to shed more light on what have been termed schedule interactions. Some of these studies are reviewed in the next section. In concluding our discussion of multiple-schedule interactions, it is important to emphasize that we view behavioral contrast merely as an example of how Pavlovian relations may control operant behavior. We have devoted a great deal of space to this example, but we expect that once investigators start looking for other examples the interactions discussed here will turn out to be pervasive.

Interactions Between Pavlovian and
Operant Conditioning and the
Additivity Theory of Contrast

The interaction between Pavlovian and operant conditioning processes has been a traditional concern in the study of animal learning, especially with regard to avoidance learning (Herrnstein, 1969; Rescorla & Solomon, 1967). Most of the research which has been done on this problem has been done in avoidance paradigms and is thus not the proper concern of this discussion. The research of interest here involves the superimposition of free food reinforcement (either signaled or unsignaled) on a base line of operant responding which is itself maintained by food reinforcement.

POSITIVE CONDITIONED SUPPRESSION

What might one expect to be the effects of a signal for food delivery on operant responding? The literature on Pavlovian-operant interactions suggests that Pavlovian excitation will result in an increase in response rate (Rescorla & Solomon, 1967), a phenomenon we shall call *conditioned enhancement*. It is the Pavlovian alimentary analog of conditioned suppression (Estes & Skinner, 1941). What might one expect on the basis of the additivity theory of contrast outlined in this chapter? Its predictions are more equivocal. A stimulus-reinforcer contingency will result in excitation, but whether this excitation is reflected in an increase in operant responding will depend upon (a) the spatial relation between the stimulus and the target for operant responses; (b) the nature of the operant; and (c) the relation between the Pavlovian US and the operant reinforcement. If, for example, the operant is key pecking and the CS is located on the key, we would expect to observe conditioned enhancement. If, on the other hand, the operant is treadle hopping and the signal is an illuminated response key, we would expect to observe decreases in treadle hopping (called hereafter *positive conditioned suppression* to distinguish it from the more familiar demonstration of suppression by a CS which signals electric shock). It is interesting that the existing literature has precisely the equivocal character which the present account would predict. For example, one recent experiment examined the two hypothetical situations just described, and indeed found conditioned enhancement of key pecking and conditioned suppression of treadle hopping (LoLordo, McMillan, & Riley, 1974). This study is described in detail below. In brief, the present theory of contrast would predict conditioned enhancement of responding by a Pavlovian contingency under just those conditions which would also yield positive contrast with the appropriate experimental manipulations. Those situations which yield negative induction would be expected to result in positive conditioned suppression when Pavlovian contingencies are applied to operant base lines. This formulation is much like one advanced by Staddon (1972) in somewhat less detail.

The available evidence tends to support these predictions. Azrin and Hake (1969) studied the effects of Pavlovian contingencies on bar pressing in rats. Pressing was maintained by either food or water, and the Pavlovian CS (either a 6-per-sec relay click or a 10-per-sec blinking light) signaled either food, water, or intercranial stimulation (ICS). In cases where food and water were USs, they were five times as large as the food and water operant rewards. In all there were five groups of rats: three groups bar-pressed for food and received either food, water, or ICS as a Pavlovian US; two groups bar-pressed for water and received either food or water as a Pavlovian US. All groups but one showed substantial suppression of bar pressing in the presence of the CS. The water-water group displayed conditioned enhancement. With the exception of this group, Azrin and Hake's results confirm expectations from the additivity theory of contrast. However, the authors made a point of noting that no behaviors were observed during the CS which might have competed with bar pressing. This observation presents something of a problem, since we might expect orientation toward and perhaps contact of the CS to occur and to mediate the suppression effect. Van Dyne (1971) observed similar suppression effects in a study of bar pressing in rats much like the Azrin and Hake study. Both Azrin and Hake and Van Dyne offered interpretations of their results which were similar to the present account. The Pavlovian contingency results in the conditioning of a respondent which is incompatible with the operant. Neither study, however, attempted to measure the putative respondent. A more recent study by Kelly (1973) did attempt to measure respondent behavior. The lever pressing of monkeys was maintained on a VI schedule, and occasional pairings of tone and food were superimposed on the operant procedure. Conditioned suppression of bar pressing by the tone rapidly developed and was sustained over 275 sessions. Concurrent measurement of heart rate and blood pressure gave no indication that either of these autonomic systems was influenced by the Pavlovian contingency. Thus just as Azrin and Hake failed to observe skeletal behaviors which might compete with lever pressing, Kelley failed to observe potentially competing autonomic behaviors.

There are a number of demonstrations that the duration of the CS influences its effects. Henton and Brady (1970), Meltzer and Brahlek (1970), and Miczek and Grossman (1971) studied the effects of CS duration on the positive conditioned suppression effect. Henton and Brady superimposed Pavlovian conditioning trials on responding maintained on a DRL 30-sec schedule in squirrel monkeys. At CS durations of 20 and 40 sec they observed no effect. At CS durations of 80 sec they observed conditioned enhancement, with most of the responding occurring early in the CS. Meltzer and Brahlek exposed rats whose bar pressing was maintained on a VI 2-min schedule of reinforcement (Noyes pellets) to pairings of a CS followed by access to a sucrose solution. When the CS was either 12 or 40 sec long they observed conditioned suppression. However, when the CS was 120 sec long they observed about a 5% enhancement of bar pressing. Finally, Miczek and Grossman exposed squirrel monkeys to a similar procedure, in which the Pavlovian and operant rewards differed. With a 30-sec CS they observed large suppression effects. With 1-, 2-, or 3-min CSs, suppression still occurred, but substantially less. How do these effects of CS duration—i.e., the longer the CS, the less the suppression—relate to the additivity theory of contrast? According to the additivity theory, positive conditioned suppression results from Pavlovian conditioning of a response which competes with the operant. Thus the less the suppression, the weaker the competing response. Seen in this light, the CS duration effects merely reflect weaker Pavlovian conditioning with longer CSs. If the Pavlovian conditioned response were compatible with the operant (e.g., key pecking in pigeons), one would expect increases in CS duration to produce exactly the opposite effects. At long CS durations Pavlovian conditioning would be weakened and little or no increase in pecking would occur. A recent study by Smith (1974) provides direct support for this argument. A 5-sec CS on the key enhanced responding, while 30- and 60-second CSs either had no effect or reduced responding. There is also indirect evidence which supports this view. First, it has been demonstrated that in auto-shaping situations, increases in trial duration result in decreases in responding (Ricci, 1973). Second, Rachlin's (1973) study of the effects of component duration on multiple-schedule performance makes a similar point. Recall that in Rachlin's study free reinforcements were delivered in one component of a multiple schedule, both components of which were correlated with identical VI schedules of response-dependent reinforcement. Rachlin found that when the component duration was short (8 sec) free reinforcement increased overall response rate, while when component duration was long (8 min) free reinforcement decreased overall response rate. If one views the stimuli correlated with the components of the multiple schedule as being Pavlovian CSs as well (as the additivity theory of contrast suggests), then Rachlin's study can be interpreted as showing facilitation of pecking with a short CS, but not with a long CS.

Conditioned Enhancement

LoLordo (1971) exposed pigeons to a VI 2-min schedule with 4-sec access to grain as the reinforcer. Superimposed on this were presentations of 20-sec CSs. The CS+ was terminated in food delivery, with the duration of reinforcement varied from 2 to 8 sec. The second CS, the CS−, was correlated with no food. Clear enhancement of pecking developed to the CS+ as a direct function of reinforcement duration. No clear evidence of suppression of pecking developed to the CS−. What makes this study different from the ones described in the preceding section is that the Pavlovian contingency and the operant contingency both influenced the same class of behavior—key pecking. These are just the conditions under which contrast is expected by the additivity theory, and LoLordo's data offer strong support for that theory.

In a second, larger study, LoLordo, McMillan, and Riley (1974) provided more complete support for the additivity theory. Pigeons whose key pecking was maintained on a DRL schedule were exposed to pairings of CSs and food. For some pigeons the CSs were located on the response key; for other pigeons the CSs were tones. Only the first group showed conditioned enhancement of pecking. The second group showed no clear effects. This study is exactly analogous to the studies by Redford and Perkins (1974) and Schwartz (1974a, 1974c, 1975), which showed that behavioral contrast in multiple schedules only occurred when the discriminative stimuli were on the response key. LoLordo et al. also exposed two other groups of pigeons to the same procedures, except that these pigeons were treadle-hopping for food rather than key-pecking. In this case, the response-key CS suppressed the treadle hopping and autoshaped key pecking! This study is of course analogous to the demonstrations by Hemmes (1973) and Westbrook (1973) that induction rather than contrast occurs with pigeons on multiple schedules if treadle hopping is the required operant. Further supportive evidence comes from the study by Boakes, Halliday, and Poli (1975) described earlier. Pigeons were exposed to a *mult* VI 2-min VI 2-min schedule. When free reinforcement was delivered on a VT 30-sec schedule in one component only, responding increased in that component. When it was delivered in both components, there was no consistent effect on responding. When bar-pressing rats were exposed to virtually identical procedures, suppression resulted from the differential presentation of free food. One other study consistent with those just described was conducted by Schwartz (1976). Pigeons were exposed to a VI 2-min schedule of reinforcement for key pecking. Periodically, the response key changed color for 12 sec after which response-independent food was delivered. Rate of pecking in the presence of this stimulus was almost twice that in its absence. In another procedure the response-independent food was signaled on a second key while the VI key remained illuminated. Under these conditions, VI responding in the presence of the food signal was almost completely suppressed. Meanwhile, substantial responding was maintained on the food signal key. The results from these two procedures illustrate the difference between conditioned enhancement studies with pigeons and rats. In rat studies, where the signal is located away from the bar, suppression is observed. Schwartz similarly observed suppression in the pigeon when the signal was off the key. On the other hand, when the signal is on the key, enhancement is observed. No exactly comparable procedures have been studied with the rat. An approximation is provided by one final recent study which offers support for the additivity theory of contrast. Christoph, Peterson, Karpicke, and Hearst (1973) studied rats as subjects and imposed Pavlovian conditioning trials on an operant base line and varied the location of the CS relative to the bar. When the CS was near the bar, they observed almost no suppression. When the CS was far from the bar, substantial suppression of bar pressing developed, accompanied by approach and contact of the CS.

CONCLUSION

The research discussed in this chapter suggests the following conclusions:

1. Autoshaping of the pigeon's key peck is the result of Pavlovian stimulus-reinforcer contingencies.
2. The maintenance of responding in autoshaping procedures is partly determined by operant response-reinforcer contingencies.
3. In standard operant procedures, stimulus-reinforcer contingencies, when present, will exert an influence on behavior which is consistent with Pavlovian theory.
4. In multiple-schedule procedures, analysis of the interaction between Pavlovian and operant contingencies allows one to predict which species in which situation will show behavioral contrast. The substantial differences in the literature between rats and pigeons are consistent with this analysis.
5. In procedures in which Pavlovian contingencies are explicitly superimposed on operant contingencies, the present account rationalizes a literature which has been marked by inconsistent experimental outcomes as a function of the species and the situation under investigation.

In addition, the ideas put forth in this chapter speak to two broader issues. The first is the distinction between Pavlovian and operant conditioning. This issue has been discussed in various parts of the chapter. We have no solution to offer to the problem of classifying learning phenomena as one or the other type of conditioning. Rather, the analysis presented in this chapter represents a somewhat different approach. The approach is to choose a particular class of behavior, and rather than classify it as Pavlovian or operant, analyze the extent to which both types of contingency contribute to its occurrence. With regard to the class of behavior under scrutiny here—key pecking—this approach has proven fruitful. Moreover, the analysis can easily be extended to the behavior of other species in other situations.

The second major issue addressed by this chapter is the biological boundaries or constraints on learning. A number of major recent contributions to the field (Bolles, 1970; Hinde & Hinde, 1973; Rozin & Kalat, 1971; Schwartz, 1974b; Seligman, 1970; Seligman & Hager, 1972; Shettleworth, 1972a; Staddon & Simmelhag, 1971) have challenged the sometimes tacit and sometimes explicit assumption that general laws of learning exist and that they can be discovered by exploring the control of behavior in arbitrary experimental situations. Seligman (1970) has referred to this as the "equipotentiality premise." A better label for it might be the "assumption of interchangeability." Whatever its label, what it conveys is the view that if the world of a particular species is partitioned into three sets—stimuli, behaviors, and rewards—then any member of a set can be substituted for any other member without materially altering the relations one observes among sets. This view is now demonstrably false. There is substantial evidence that some associations are more rapidly acquired than others—that some members of the stimulus set, the behavior set, and the reward set "belong" together (Bolles, 1970; Garcia & Koelling, 1966; cf. Seligman & Hager, 1972; Schwartz, 1974b). Indeed, a good deal of the research discussed in this chapter violates the assumption of interchangeability. It seems undeniable that there are significant biological constraints on what organisms can learn, as the ethologists have always argued (Lorenz, 1965). The problem which now confronts the study of learning is the determination of what modifications in both method and theory are demanded by these biological constraints on learning. One possibility is that the search for general laws must be abandoned and a "botanizing" strategy adopted. It was Skinner's explicit rejection of this approach (1938) which led to the development of current experimental methods. A second possibility is that one should search for different types of laws which take account of biological constraints on learning (Seligman, 1970). The research discussed in this chapter suggests that at least in some cases neither botanizing nor the development of new laws is necessary. The autoshaping literature is unequivocal evidence that the key peck is a special, biologically relevant behavior. In many areas, the study of key pecking in pigeons, bar pressing in pigeons, and bar pressing in rats yield different results. Nevertheless these differences can be interpreted and understood in terms of learning principles which are already well established. They require no new formulation—only new combinations of old formulations. Whether similar analyses will provide sufficient explanations of other biologically constrained phenomena is an open question. For the present, it would be ill advised to give up the "general principles" which guide our investigations without a struggle. They may be far more general than anyone could reasonably have suspected.

REFERENCES

Adler, N., & Hogan, J. A. Classical conditioning and punishment of an instinctive response in *Betta splendens*. *Animal Behavior*, 1963, *11*, 351–354.

Allaway, T. A. *Attention, information and auto-shaping*. Unpublished doctoral dissertation, University of Pennsylvania, 1971.

Allen, D., Capehart, S., & Herbert, S. Spence's theory of discrimination: A reevaluation. *Psychological Record*, 1969, *19*, 443–456.

Amsel, A. Frustrative nonreward in partial reinforcement and discrimination learning. *Psychological Review*, 1962, *69*, 306–328.

Arnett, F. B. A local-rate-of-response and interresponse-time analysis of behavioral contrast. *Journal of the Experimental Analysis of Behavior*, 1973, *20*, 489–498.

Azrin, N. H., & Hake, D. F. Positive conditioned suppression: Conditioned suppression using positive reinforcers as the unconditioned stimuli. *Journal of the Experimental Analysis of Behavior*, 1969, *12*, 167–173.

Baldock, M. D. Trial and intertrial interval durations in the acquisition of autoshaped key pecking. Paper presented at the meetings of the Eastern Psychological Association, Philadelphia, 1974.

Barrera, F. J. Centrifugal selection of signal directed pecking. *Journal of the Experimental Analysis of Behavior*, 1974, *22*, 341–355.

Baum, W. M., & Rachlin, H. C. Choice as time allocation. *Journal of the Experimental Analysis of Behavior*, 1969, *12*, 861–874.

Bernheim, J. W., & Williams, D. R. Time-dependent contrast effects in a multiple schedule of food reinforcement. *Journal of the Experimental Analysis of Behavior*, 1967, *10*, 243–249.

Bilbrey, J., & Winokur, S. Controls for the constraints on auto-shaping. *Journal of the Experimental Analysis of Behavior*, 1973, *20*, 323–332.

Bindra, D. A unified account of classical conditioning and operant training. In A. H. Black & W. F. Prokasy (Eds.), *Classical conditioning II: Current theory and research*. Englewood Cliffs, N.J.: Prentice-Hall, Inc., 1972.

Bloomfield, T. M. Behavioral contrast and relative reinforcement frequency in two multiple schedules. *Journal of the Experimental Analysis of Behavior*, 1967, *10*, 151–158.

Bloomfield, T. M. Behavioral contrast and the peak shift. In R. M. Gilbert & N. S. Sutherland (Eds.), *Animal discrimination learning*. New York: Academic Press, 1969.

Bloomfield, T. M. Reinforcement schedules: Contingency or contiguity? In R. M. Gilbert & J. R. Millenson (Eds.), *Reinforcement: Behavioral analyses*. New York: Academic Press, 1972.

Boakes, R. A. Response decrements produced by extinction and by response-independent reinforcement. *Journal of the Experimental Analysis of Behavior*, 1973, *19*, 293–302.

Boakes, R. A., Halliday, M. S., & Mole, J. S. Successive discrimination training with equated reinforcement frequencies: Failure to obtain behavioral contrast. Submitted for publication, 1974.

Boakes, R. A., Halliday, M. S., & Poli, M. Response additivity: Effects of superimposing free reinforcement on a variable-interval baseline. *Journal of the Experimental Analysis of Behavior*, 1975, *23*, 177–191.

Bolles, R. C. Species-specific defense reactions and avoidance learning. *Psychological Review*, 1970, *77*, 32–48.

Boneau, A., & Axelrod, S. Work decrement and reminiscence in pigeon operant responding. *Journal of Experimental Psychology*, 1962, *64*, 352–354.

Bower, G. H. A contrast effect in differential conditioning. *Journal of Experimental Psychology*, 1961, *62*, 196–199.

Breland, K., & Breland, M. The misbehavior of organisms. *American Psychologist*, 1961, *16*, 681–684.

Brethower, D. M., & Reynolds, G. S. A facilitative effect of punishment on unpunished behavior. *Journal of the Experimental Analysis of Behavior*, 1962, *5*, 191–199.

Brown, P. L., & Jenkins, H. M. Auto-shaping of the pigeon's key-peck. *Journal of the Experimental Analysis of Behavior*, 1968, *11*, 1–8.

Catania, A. C. Concurrent operants. In W. K. Honig (Ed.), *Operant behavior: Areas of research and application*. Englewood Cliffs, N.J.: Prentice-Hall, Inc., 1966.

Catania, A. C. (Ed.). *Contemporary research in operant behavior*. Glenview, Ill.: Scott, Foresman, 1968.

Catania, A. C. Concurrent performances: Inhibition of one response by reinforcement of another. *Journal of the Experimental Analysis of Behavior*, 1969, *12*, 731–744.

Catania, A. C., & Gill, C. A. Inhibition and behavioral contrast. *Psychonomic Science*, 1964, *1*, 257–258.

Christoph, G., Peterson, G., Karpicke, J., & Hearst, E. Positive conditioned suppression as a function of CS location. Paper presented at the meetings of the Psychonomic Society, St. Louis, 1973.

Coates, J. The differential effects of punishment and extinction on behavioral contrast. *Psychonomic Science*, 1972, *27*, 146–148.

Cook, L., & Davidson, A. B. Effects of behaviorally active drugs in a conflict-punishment procedure in rats. In S. Garrattina, E. Mussini, & L. O. Randall (Eds.), *The benzodiazepines*. New York: Raven Press, 1973.

Cook, L., & Sepinwall, J. Parameters of Emotion: Psychopharmacological parameters and methods. In L. Levi (Ed.), *Emotions: The parameters and measurement*. New York: Raven Press, 1974.

Craig, W. Observations on doves learning to drink. *Journal of Animal Behavior*, 1912, *2*, 273–279.

Crespi, L. P. Amount of reinforcement and level of performance. *Psychological Review*, 1944, *51*, 344–358.

Cruze, W. W. Maturation and learning in chicks. *Journal of Comparative Psychology*, 1935, *19*, 371–409.

Davidson, A. B., & Cook, L. Effects of combined treatment with tri-fluoperazine-HCl and amobarbital on punished behavior in rats. *Psychopharmacologia* (Berlin), 1969, *15*, 159–168.

de Villiers, P. A. Reinforcement and response rate interaction in multiple random-interval avoidance schedules. *Journal of the Experimental Analysis of Behavior*, 1972, *18*, 499–507.

de Villiers, P. A. The law of effect and avoidance: A quantitative relationship between response rate and shock-frequency reduction. *Journal of the Experimental Analysis of Behavior*, 1974, *21*, 223–235.

Dickinson, A. Septal lesions in rats and the acquisition of free-operant successive discriminations. *Physiology and Behavior*, 1973, *10*, 305–313.

Dunham, P. J. Contrasted conditions of reinforcement: A

selective critique. *Psychological Bulletin,* 1968, *69,* 295–315.

DUNHAM, P. J., MARINER, A., & ADAMS, H. Enhancement of off-key pecking by on-key punishment. *Journal of the Experimental Analysis of Behavior,* 1969, *12,* 789–797.

EGGER, M. D., & MILLER, N. E. Secondary reinforcement in rats as a function of information value and reliability of the stimulus. *Journal of Experimental Psychology,* 1962, *64,* 97–104.

EGGER, M. D., & MILLER, N. E. When is reward reinforcing? An experimental study of the information hypothesis. *Journal of Comparative and Physiological Psychology,* 1963, *56,* 132–137.

ESTES, W. K., & SKINNER, B. F. Some quantitative properties of anxiety. *Journal of Experimental Psychology,* 1941, *29,* 390–400.

FANTZ, R. C. Form preference in newly hatched chicks. *Journal of Comparative and Physiological Psychology,* 1957, *50,* 422–430.

FARRELL, L. The role of partial reinforcement in the acquisition of an autoshaped response. Paper presented at the meetings of the Eastern Psychological Association, Philadelphia, 1974.

FARRIS, H. F. Classical conditioning of courting behavior in the Japanese quail, *Coturnix coturnix japonica. Journal of the Experimental Analysis of Behavior,* 1967, *10,* 213–217.

FERSTER, C. B., & SKINNER, B. F. *Schedules of reinforcement.* Englewood Cliffs, N.J.: Prentice-Hall, Inc., 1957.

FINDLEY, J. D. Preference and switching under concurrent scheduling. *Journal of the Experimental Analysis of Behavior,* 1958, *1,* 123–144.

FOREE, D. D., & LOLORDO, V. M. Signalled and unsignalled free-operant avoidance in the pigeon. *Journal of the Experimental Analysis of Behavior,* 1973, *13,* 283–290.

FREEMAN, B. J. The role of response-independent reinforcement in producing behavioral contrast effects in the rat. *Learning and Motivation,* 1971, *2,* 138–147. (a)

FREEMAN, B. J. Behavioral contrast: Reinforcement frequency or response suppression? *Psychological Bulletin,* 1971, *75,* 347–356. (b)

GAMZU, E. *The classical conditioning paradigm in the "autoshaping" of the pigeon's key peck.* Unpublished master's thesis, University of Pennsylvania, 1968.

GAMZU, E. *Associative and instrumental factors underlying the performance of a complex skeletal response.* Unpublished doctoral dissertation, University of Pennsylvania, 1971.

GAMZU, E., & SCHWAM, E. Autoshaping and automaintenance of a key-press response in squirrel monkeys. *Journal of the Experimental Analysis of Behavior,* 1974, *21,* 361–371.

GAMZU, E., & SCHWARTZ, B. The maintenance of key pecking by stimulus-contingent and response-independent food presentation. *Journal of the Experimental Analysis of Behavior,* 1973, *19,* 65–72.

GAMZU, E., & WILLIAMS, D. R. Classical conditioning of a complex skeletal act. *Science,* 1971, *171,* 923–925.

GAMZU, E. R., & WILLIAMS, D. R. Associative factors underlying the pigeon's key pecking in autoshaping procedures. *Journal of the Experimental Analysis of Behavior,* 1973, *19,* 225–232.

GARCIA, J., & KOELLING, R. Relations of cue to consequence in avoidance learning. *Psychonomic Science,* 1966, *4,* 123–124.

GARDNER, W. M. Autoshaping in bobwhite quail. *Journal of the Experimental Analysis of Behavior,* 1969, *12,* 279–281.

GIBBON, J., BERRYMAN, R., & THOMPSON, R. L. Contingency spaces and measures in classical and instrumental conditioning. *Journal of the Experimental Analysis of Behavior,* 1974, *21,* 585–605.

GLASS, D. H., & ISON, J. R. The effects of incentive shifts following differential conditioning. Paper presented at the meetings of the Psychonomic Society, St. Louis, October 1966.

GONZALEZ, F. A. Effects of partial reinforcement (25%) in an autoshaping procedure. *Bulletin of the Psychonomic Society,* 1973, *2,* 299–301.

GONZALEZ, F. A. Effects of varying the percentage of key illuminations paired with food in a positive automaintenance procedure. *Journal of the Experimental Analysis of Behavior,* 1974, *22,* 483–490.

GONZALEZ, R. C., & CHAMPLIN, G. Positive behavioral contrast, negative simultaneous contrast, and their relation to frustration in pigeons. *Journal of Comparative and Physiological Psychology,* 1974, *87,* 173–187.

GORMEZANO, L., & MOORE, J. W. Classical conditioning. In M. H. Marx (Ed.), *Learning: Processes.* London: Macmillan, 1969.

GRANT, D. A., & SCHIPPER, L. M. The acquisition and extinction of conditioned eyelid responses as a function of the percentage of fixed-ratio reinforcement. *Journal of Experimental Psychology,* 1952, *43,* 313–320.

GUTMAN, A., & SUTTERER, J. R. Positive behavioral contrast in rats. Paper presented at the meetings of the Eastern Psychological Association, Philadelphia, 1974.

GUTTMAN, N. Generalization gradients around stimuli associated with different reinforcement schedules. *Journal of Experimental Psychology,* 1959, *58,* 335–340.

HALLIDAY, M. S., & BOAKES, R. A. Discrimination involving response-independent reinforcement: Implications for behavioral contrast. In R. A. Boakes & M. S. Halliday (Eds.), *Inhibition and Learning.* London: Academic Press, 1972.

HALLIDAY, M. S., & BOAKES, R. A. Behavioral contrast without response rate reduction. *Journal of the Experimental Analysis of Behavior,* 1974, *22,* 453–462.

HEARST, E., BESLEY, S., & FARTHING, G. W. Inhibition and the stimulus control of operant behavior. *Journal of the Experimental Analysis of Behavior.* 1970, *14,* 373–409.

HEARST, E., & JENKINS, H. M. *Sign tracking: The stimulus-reinforcer relation and directed action.* Monograph of the Psychonomic Society: Austin, Texas, 1974.

HEMMES, N. S. Behavioral contrast in pigeons depends upon the operant. *Journal of Comparative and Physiological Psychology,* 1973, *85,* 171–178.

HENKE, P. G., ALLEN, J. D., & DAVIDSON, C. Effects of lesions in the amygdala on behavioral contrast. *Physiology and Behavior,* 1972, *8,* 173–176.

HENTON, W. W., & BRADY, J. V. Operant acceleration during a pre-reward stimulus. *Journal of the Experimental Analysis of Behavior,* 1970, *13,* 205–209.

HERRNSTEIN, R. J. Superstition: A corollary of the principles of operant conditioning. In W. K. Honig (Ed.), *Operant behavior: Areas of research and application.* Englewood Cliffs, N.J.: Prentice-Hall, Inc., 1966.

HERRNSTEIN, R. J. Method and theory in the study of avoidance. *Psychological Review*, 1969, 76, 49–70.

HERRNSTEIN, R. J. On the law of effect. *Journal of the Experimental Analysis of Behavior*, 1970, 13, 243–266.

HERRNSTEIN, R. J., & LOVELAND, D. H. Food avoidance in hungry pigeons and other perplexities. *Journal of the Experimental Analysis of Behavior*, 1972, 18, 369–383.

HILTON, A. Partial reinforcement of a conditioned emotional response in rats. *Journal of Comparative and Physiological Psychology*, 1969, 69, 253–260.

HINDE, R. A., & HINDE, J. S. (Eds.). *Constraints on Learning*. London: Academic Press, 1973.

HOGAN, J. A. Responses in Pavlovian conditioning studies. *Science*, 1974, 186, 156–157.

HONIG, W. K. (Ed.). *Operant behavior: Areas of research and application*. Englewood Cliffs, N.J.: Prentice-Hall, Inc., 1966.

HUMPHREYS, L. G. The effect of random alternation of reinforcement on the acquisition and extinction of conditioned eyelid reactions. *Journal of Experimental Psychology*, 1939, 25, 141–158.

HUNT, G. L., & SMITH, W. S. Pecking and initial drinking responses in young domestic fowl. *Journal of Comparative and Physiological Psychology*, 1967, 64, 230–236.

HURSH, S. R., NAVARICK, D. J., & FANTINO, E. "Automaintenance": The role of reinforcement. *Journal of the Experimental Analysis of Behavior*, 1974, 21, 112–124.

JAFFEE, M. L. The effects of lesions in the ventromedial nucleus of the hypothalamus on behavioral contrast in rats. *Physiological Psychology*, 1973, 1, 191–198.

JENKINS, H. M. Effects of the stimulus-reinforcer relation on selected and unselected responses. In R. A. Hinde & J. Stevenson-Hinde (Eds.), *Constraints on learning*. New York: Academic Press, 1973.

JENKINS, H. M., & BOAKES, R. A. Observing stimulus sources that signal food or no food. *Journal of the Experimental Analysis of Behavior*, 1973, 20, 197–207.

JENKINS, H. M., & MOORE, B. R. The form of the auto-shaped response with food or water reinforcers. *Journal of the Experimental Analysis of Behavior*, 1973, 20, 163–181.

KAMIN, L. J. Predictability, surprise, attention, and conditioning. In B. A. Campbell & R. M. Church (Eds.), *Punishment and aversive behavior*. Englewood Cliffs, N.J.: Prentice-Hall, Inc., 1969.

KELLER, K. The role of elicited responding in behavioral contrast. *Journal of the Experimental Analysis of Behavior*, 1974, 21, 249–257.

KELLY, D. D. Long-term prereward suppression in monkeys unaccompanied by cardiovascular conditioning. *Journal of the Experimental Analysis of Behavior*, 1973, 20, 93–104.

KILLEEN, P. A yoked-chamber comparison of concurrent and multiple schedules. *Journal of the Experimental Analysis of Behavior*, 1972, 18, 13–22.

KIMBLE, G. A. *Hilgard and Marquis' conditioning and learning*. Englewood Cliffs, N.J.: Prentice-Hall, Inc., 1961.

KIMBLE, G. A., & PERLMUTTER, L. C. The problem of volition. *Psychological Review*, 1970, 77, 361–384.

LATTAL, K. A., & MAXEY, G. C. Some effects of response-independent reinforcers in multiple schedules. *Journal of the Experimental Analysis of Behavior*, 1971, 16, 225–231.

LOLORDO, V. M. Facilitation of food-reinforced responding by a signal for response-independent food. *Journal of the Experimental Analysis of Behavior*, 1971, 15, 49–55.

LOLORDO, V. M., MCMILLAN, J. C., & RILEY, A. L. The effects upon food-reinforced pecking and treadle-pressing of auditory and visual signals for response-independent food. *Learning and Motivation*, 1974, 5, 24–41.

LORENZ, K. *Evolution and the modification of behavior*. Chicago: University of Chicago Press, 1965.

MACKINTOSH, N. J. *The Psychology of Animal Learning*. London: Academic Press, 1974.

MALONE, J. C., & STADDON, J. E. R. Contrast effects in maintained generalization gradients. *Journal of the Experimental Analysis of Behavior*, 1973, 19, 167–179.

MELTZER, D., & BRAHLEK, J. A. Conditioned suppression and conditioned enhancement with the same positive UCS: An effect of CS duration. *Journal of the Experimental Analysis of Behavior*, 1970, 13, 67–73.

MICZEK, K. A., & GROSSMAN, S. P. Positive conditioned suppression: Effects of CS duration. *Journal of the Experimental Analysis of Behavior*, 1971, 15, 243–247.

MOORE, B. R. The role of directed Pavlovian reactions in simple instrumental learning in the pigeon. In R. A. Hinde & J. Stevenson-Hinde (Eds.), *Constraints on learning*. New York: Academic Press, 1973.

MORRISON, R. R. The effects of a negative reinforcement contingency on auto-shaped key pecking and other water-associated behaviors. Paper presented at the meetings of the Eastern Psychological Association, Philadelphia, 1974.

MURRAY, C. S. Conditioning in *Betta splendens*. Paper presented at the meetings of the Eastern Psychological Association, Philadelphia, April 1974.

NEVIN, J. A. Differential reinforcement and stimulus control of not responding. *Journal of the Experimental Analysis of Behavior*, 1968, 11, 715–726.

NEVIN, J. A., & SHETTLEWORTH, S. J. An analysis of contrast effects in multiple schedules. *Journal of the Experimental Analysis of Behavior*, 1966, 9, 305–315.

PADILLA, S. G. Further studies of the delayed pecking of chicks. *Journal of Comparative Psychology*, 1935, 20, 413–443.

PAVLOV, I. P. *Conditioned reflexes*. London: Oxford University Press, 1927.

PAVLOV, I. P. *Lectures on conditioned reflexes, Vol. 2: Conditioned reflexes and psychiatry* (trans. W. H. Gantt). New York: International, 1941.

PAVLOV, I. P. *Selected Works* (trans. S. Belsky). Moscow: Foreign Languages Printing House, 1955.

PEAR, J. J., & WILKIE, D. M. Behavioral contrast in mixed schedules of reinforcement. *Psychonomic Science*, 1970, 20, 167–168.

PEAR, J. J., & WILKIE, D. M. Contrast and induction in rats on multiple schedules. *Journal of the Experimental Analysis of Behavior*, 1971, 15, 289–296.

PETERSON, G. B. *Auto-shaping in the rat: Conditioned approach and contact behavior toward signals of food or brain-stimulation reinforcement*. Unpublished doctoral dissertation, University of Indiana, 1972.

PETERSON, G. B., ACKIL, J. E., FROMMER, G. P., & HEARST, E. S. Conditioned approach and contact behavior toward signals for food or brain-stimulation reinforcement. *Science*, 1972, 177, 1009–1011.

RACHLIN, H. Autoshaping of key pecking in pigeons with

negative reinforcement. *Journal of the Experimental Analysis of Behavior,* 1969, *12,* 521–531.

RACHLIN, H. Contrast and matching. *Psychological Review,* 1973, *80,* 217–234.

RACKHAM, D. *Conditioning of the pigeon's courtship and aggressive behavior.* Unpublished Master's thesis, Dalhousie University, 1971.

REDFORD, M., & PERKINS, C. C. The role of auto pecking in behavioral contrast. *Journal of the Experimental Analysis of Behavior,* 1974, *21,* 145–150.

RESCORLA, R. A. Pavlovian conditioning and its proper control procedures. *Psychological Review,* 1967, *74,* 71–80.

RESCORLA, R. A. Probability of shock in the presence and absence of the CS in fear conditioning. *Journal of Comparative and Physiological Psychology,* 1968, *66,* 1–5.

RESCORLA, R. A. Conditioned inhibition of fear. In W. K. Honig & N. J. Mackintosh (Eds.), *Fundamental issues in associative learning.* Halifax: Dalhousie University Press, 1969. (a)

RESCORLA, R. A. Pavlovian conditioned inhibition. *Psychological Bulletin,* 1969, *72,* 77–94. (b)

RESCORLA, R. A. Informational variables in Pavlovian conditioning. In G. H. Bower (Ed.), *The psychology of learning and motivation* (Vol. 6). New York: Academic Press, 1972.

RESCORLA, R. A., & SOLOMON, R. S. Two-process learning theory: Relationships between Pavlovian conditioning and instrumental learning. *Psychological Review,* 1967, *74,* 151–182.

REYNOLDS, G. S. Behavioral contrast. *Journal of the Experimental Analysis of Behavior,* 1961, *4,* 57–71. (a)

REYNOLDS, G. S. An analysis of interactions in a multiple schedule. *Journal of the Experimental Analysis of Behavior,* 1961, *4,* 107–117. (b)

REYNOLDS, G. S. Relativity of response rate and reinforcement frequency in a multiple schedule. *Journal of the Experimental Analysis of Behavior,* 1961, *4,* 179–184. (c)

REYNOLDS, G. S. Contrast, generalization, and the process of discrimination. *Journal of the Experimental Analysis of Behavior,* 1961, *4,* 289–294. (d)

REYNOLDS, G. S., & CATANIA, A. C. Behavioral contrast with fixed-interval and low-rate reinforcement. *Journal of the Experimental Analysis of Behavior,* 1961, *4,* 387–391.

RICCI, J. A. Keypecking under response-independent food presentation after long simple and compound stimuli. *Journal of the Experimental Analysis of Behavior,* 1973, *19,* 509–516.

RILLING, M., ASKEW, H. R., AHLSKOG, J. E., & KRAMER, T. J. Aversive properties of the negative stimulus in a successive discrimination. *Journal of the Experimental Analysis of Behavior,* 1969, *12,* 917–932.

ROSS, L. E. The decremental effects of partial reinforcement during acquisition of the conditioned eyelid response. *Journal of Experimental Psychology,* 1959, *57,* 74–82.

ROZIN, P., & KALAT, J. W. Specific hungers and poison avoidance as adaptive specializations of learning. *Psychological Review,* 1971, *78,* 459–487.

SCHWAM, E., & GAMZU, E. Constraints on autoshaping in the squirrel monkey: Stimulus dimension and response topography. *Bulletin of the Psychonomic Society,* 1975, *5,* 369–372.

SCHWARTZ, B. The role of positive conditioned reinforcement in the maintenance of key pecking which prevents delivery of primary reinforcement. *Psychonomic Science,* 1972, *28,* 277–278.

SCHWARTZ, B. Maintenance of key pecking by response-independent food presentation: The role of the modality of the signal for food. *Journal of the Experimental Analysis of Behavior,* 1973, *20,* 17–22. (a)

SCHWARTZ, B. Maintenance of key pecking in pigeons by a food avoidance but not by a shock avoidance contingency. *Animal Learning and Behavior,* 1973, *1,* 164–166. (b)

SCHWARTZ, B. Autoshaping and behavioral contrast: The key to contrast is on the key. Paper presented at the meetings of the Eastern Psychological Association, Philadelphia, April 1974. (a)

SCHWARTZ, B. On going back to nature: A review of Seligman and Hager's *Biological Boundaries of Learning. Journal of the Experimental Analysis of Behavior,* 1974, *21,* 183–198. (b)

SCHWARTZ, B. Behavioral contrast in the pigeon depends upon the location of the stimulus. *Bulletin of the Psychonomic Society,* 1974, *3,* 365–368. (c)

SCHWARTZ, B. Discriminative stimulus location as a determinant of positive and negative behavioral contrast in the pigeon. *Journal of the Experimental Analysis of Behavior,* 1975, *23,* 167–176.

SCHWARTZ, B. Positive and negative conditioned suppression in the pigeon: Effects of the locus and modality of the CS. *Learning and Motivation,* 1976, *7,* 86–100.

SCHWARTZ, B., HAMILTON, B., & SILBERBERG, A. Behavioral contrast in the pigeon: A study of the duration of key pecking maintained on multiple schedules of reinforcement. *Journal of the Experimental Analysis of Behavior,* 1975, *24,* 199–206.

SCHWARTZ, B., & WILLIAMS, D. R. The role of the response-reinforcer contingency in negative auto-maintenance. *Journal of the Experimental Analysis of Behavior,* 1972, *71,* 351–357. (a)

SCHWARTZ, B., & WILLIAMS, D. R. Two different kinds of key peck in the pigeon: Some properties of responses maintained by negative and positive response-reinforcer contingencies. *Journal of the Experimental Analysis of Behavior,* 1972, *18,* 201–216. (b).

SCULL, J., & WESTBROOK, R. F. Interaction in multiple schedules with different responses in each of the components. *Journal of the Experimental Analysis of Behavior,* 1973, *20,* 511–519.

SELIGMAN, M. E. P. Control group and conditioning: A comment on operationism. *Psychological Review,* 1969, *76,* 474–491.

SELIGMAN, M. E. P. On the generality of laws of learning. *Psychological Review,* 1970, *77,* 406–418.

SELIGMAN, M. E. P., & HAGER, J. L. (Eds.). *Biological boundaries of learning.* Englewood Cliffs, N.J.: Prentice-Hall, Inc., 1972.

SEPINWALL, J. Some pharmacological aspects of benzodiazepines. *Folha Medica,* 1973, *67,* 727–735.

SHEFFIELD, F. D. Relation between classical conditioning and instrumental learning. In W. F. Prokasy (Ed.), *Classical conditioning.* Englewood Cliffs, N.J.: Prentice-Hall, Inc., 1965.

SHETTLEWORTH, S. Constraints on learning. In D. S. Lehrman, R. A. Hinde, & E. Shaw (Eds.), *Advances in the study of behavior* (Vol. 4). New York: Academic Press, 1972. (a)

SHETTLEWORTH, S. Stimulus relevance in the control of drinking and conditioned fear responses in domestic chicks (*Gallus gallus*). *Journal of Comparative and Physiological Psychology*, 1972, *80*, 175-198. (b)

SHIMP, C. P. & WHEATLEY, W. L. Matching to relative reinforcement frequency in multiple schedules with short component duration. *Journal of the Experimental Analysis of Behavior*, 1971, *15*, 205-210.

SHULL, R. L., & PLISKOFF, S. S. Changeover behavior under pairs of fixed-ratio and variable-ratio schedules of reinforcement. *Journal of the Experimental Analysis of Behavior*, 1971, *16*, 75-79.

SIDMAN, M., & FLETCHER, F. G. A demonstration of autoshaping with monkeys. *Journal of the Experimental Analysis of Behavior*, 1968, *11*, 307-309.

SILBERBERG, A., & SCHROT, B. A yoked-chamber comparison of concurrent and multiple schedules: The relationship between component duration and responding. *Journal of the Experimental Analysis of Behavior*, 1974, *22*, 21-30.

SKINNER, B. F. *The behavior of organisms*. New York: Appleton-Century-Crofts, 1938.

SKINNER, B. F. "Superstition" in the pigeon. *Journal of Experimental Psychology*, 1948, *38*, 168-172.

SMITH, J. B. Effects of response rate, reinforcement frequency, and the duration of a stimulus preceding response-independent food. *Journal of the Experimental Analysis of Behavior*, 1974, *21*, 215-221.

SMITH, S. G., & SMITH, W. M., JR. A demonstration of autoshaping with dogs. *Psychological Record*, 1971, *21*, 377-379.

SPEAR, N. E., & HILL, W. F. Adjustment to new reward: Simultaneous and successive contrast effects. *Journal of Experimental Psychology*, 1965, *70*, 510-519.

SPENCE, K. W. The nature of discrimination learning in animals. *Psychological Review*, 1936, *43*, 427-449.

SPENCE, K. W. Cognitive and drive factors in the extinction of the conditioned eye blink in human subjects. *Psychological Review*, 1966, *73*, 445-458.

SQUIER, L. H. Auto-shaping key responses in fish. *Psychonomic Science*, 1969, *17*, 177-178.

STADDON, J. E. R. Multiple fixed-interval schedules: Transient contrast and temporal inhibition. *Journal of the Experimental Analysis of Behavior*, 1969, *12*, 583-590.

STADDON, J. E. R. Temporal control and the theory of reinforcement schedules. In R. M. Gilbert & J. R. Millenson (Eds.), *Reinforcement: Behavioral analysis*. New York: Academic Press, 1972.

STADDON, J. E. R., & SIMMELHAG, B. The superstition experiment: A reexamination of its implications for the principles of adaptive behavior. *Psychological Review*, 1971, *78*, 3-43.

STIERS, M., & SILBERBERG, A. Autoshaping and automaintenance of lever-contact responses in rats. *Journal of the Experimental Analysis of Behavior*, 1974, *22*, 497-506.

TERRACE, H. S. Discrimination learning with and without "errors." *Journal of the Experimental Analysis of Behavior*, 1963, *6*, 1-27. (a)

TERRACE, H. S. Errorless transfer of discrimination across two continua. *Journal of the Experimental Analysis of Behavior*, 1963, *6*, 223-232. (b)

TERRACE, H. S. Behavioral contrast and the peak shift: Effects of extended discrimination training. *Journal of the Experimental Analysis of Behavior*, 1966, *9*, 613-617. (a)

TERRACE, H. S. Stimulus Control. In W. K. Honig (Ed.), *Operant behavior areas of research and application*. Englewood Cliffs, N.J.: Prentice-Hall, Inc., 1966. (b)

TERRACE, H. S. Discrimination learning, the peak shift, and behavioral contrast. *Journal of the Experimental Analysis of Behavior*, 1968, *11*, 724-741.

TERRACE, H. S. By-products of discrimination learning. In G. H. Bower (Ed.), *The psychology of learning and motivation* (Vol. 5). New York: Academic Press, 1972.

TERRACE, H. S. Classical conditioning. In J. A. Nevin (Ed.), *The study of behavior*. New York: Scott, Foresman, 1973.

TERRACE, H. S., GIBBON, J., FARRELL, L., & BALDOCK, M. D. Temporal factors influencing the acquisition of an autoshaped key peck. *Animal Learning and Behavior*, 1975, *3*, 53-62.

THOMAS, E., & WAGNER, A. R. Partial reinforcement of the classically conditioned eyelid response in the rabbit. *Journal of Comparative and Physiological Psychology*, 1964, *58*, 157-158.

THOMPSON, T., & STURM, T. Classical conditioning of aggressive display in Siamese fighting fish. *Journal of the Experimental Analysis of Behavior*, 1965, *8*, 397-403.

TODOROV, J. C. Component duration and relative response rates in multiple schedules. *Journal of the Experimental Analysis of Behavior*, 1972, *17*, 45-50.

VAN DYNE, G. C. Conditioned suppression with a positive US in the rat. *Journal of Comparative and Physiological Psychology*, 1971, *77*, 131-135.

WASSERMAN, E. A. *Auto-shaping: The selection and direction of behavior by predictive stimuli*. Unpublished doctoral dissertation, University of Indiana, 1972.

WASSERMAN, E. A. Pavlovian conditioning with heat reinforcement produces stimulus-directed pecking in chicks. *Science*, 1973, *181*, 875-877. (a)

WASSERMAN, E. A. The effect of redundant contextual stimuli and autoshaping the pigeon's keypeck. *Animal Learning and Behavior*, 1973, *1*, 198-206. (b)

WASSERMAN, E. A. Stimulus-reinforcer predictiveness and selective discrimination learning in pigeons. *Journal of the Experimental Analysis of Behavior*, 1974, *103*, 284-297.

WASSERMAN, E. A., & ANDERSON, P. A. Differential autoshaping to common and distinctive elements of positive and negative discriminative stimuli. *Journal of the Experimental Analysis of Behavior*, 1974, *22*, 491-496.

WASSERMAN, E., FRANKLIN, S., & HEARST, E. Pavlovian appetitive contingencies and approach vs. withdrawal to conditioned stimuli in pigeons. *Journal of Comparative and Physiological Psychology*, 1974, *86*, 616-627.

WASSERMAN, E. A., & MCCRACKEN, S. B. The disruption of autoshaped key pecking in the pigeon by food-tray illumination. *Journal of the Experimental Analysis of Behavior*, 1974, *22*, 39-45.

WEISMAN, R. G. Some determinants of inhibitory stimulus control. *Journal of the Experimental Analysis of Behavior*, 1969, *12*, 443-450.

WEISMAN, R. G. Factors influencing inhibitory stimulus control: Differential reinforcement of other behavior during discrimination training. *Journal of the Experimental Analysis of Behavior*, 1970, *14*, 87-91.

Weiss, S. J. Discrimination training and stimulus compounding: Consideration of non-reinforcement and response differentiation consequences of S^Δ. *Journal of the Experimental Analysis of Behavior*, 1971, *15*, 387–402.

Wessells, M. G. Errorless discrimination, autoshaping, and conditioned inhibition. *Science*, 1973, *182*, 941–943.

Wessells, M. G. The effects of reinforcement upon the pre-pecking behaviors of pigeons in the autoshaping experiment. *Journal of the Experimental Analysis of Behavior*, 1974, *21*, 125–144.

Westbrook, R. G. Failure to obtain positive contrast when pigeons press a bar. *Journal of the Experimental Analysis of Behavior*, 1973, *20*, 499–510.

Wilkie, D. M. Variable-time reinforcement in multiple and concurrent schedules. *Journal of the Experimental Analysis of Behavior*, 1972, *17*, 59–66.

Williams, D. R. Negative induction in behavior reinforced by central stimulation. *Psychonomic Science*, 1965, *2*, 341–342.

Williams, D. R. *Biconditional Behavior: Conditioning without constraint*. Unpublished manuscript, University of Pennsylvania, 1974.

Williams, D. R., & Williams, H. Automaintenance in the pigeon: Sustained pecking despite contingent non-reinforcement. *Journal of the Experimental Analysis of Behavior*, 1969, *12*, 511–520.

Wilton, R. N., & Clements, R. O. The role of information in the emission of observing responses: A test of two hypotheses. *Journal of the Experimental Analysis of Behavior*, 1971, *16*, 161–166.

Wolin, B. R. Difference in manner of pecking a key between pigeons reinforced with food and water. In A. C. Catania (Ed.), *Contemporary research in operant behavior*. Glenview, Ill.: Scott, Foresman, 1968.

Woodruff, G. Autoshaping: A "learned release" hypothesis. Paper presented at the meetings of the Eastern Psychological Association, Philadelphia, April 1974.

Zener, K. The significance of behavior accompanying conditioned salivary secretion for theories of the conditioned response. *American Journal of Psychology*, 1937, *50*, 384–403.

4

The Nature of Reinforcing Stimuli*

Philip Dunham

Consider for a moment an instrumental environment which is equipped with several items of interest to the small rodent known as the Mongolian gerbil (*Meriones unquiculates*). The chamber contains a small box of sand, some sunflower seeds, a drinking tube, an activity wheel, and some bristol board which the animal enjoys shredding. This environment, or variations on it, will be referred to on several occasions in the discussion which follows. Given unconstrained access to this environment for one hour each day, the gerbil will distribute much of the available time among the various items of interest in the chamber. Once stable behavior patterns emerge, a small amount of engineering permits us to arrange any one of 20 possible instrumental contingencies in the gerbil's world. We can require the animal to eat in order to run, run in order to eat, drink in order to shred paper, etc. Imposing a contingency can cause an increase, a decrease, or no change in the probability of the instrumental behavior. If a particular contingency produces a change in the probability of instrumental responding, most psychologists would agree that some hypothetical process has operated (although not all would agree that we should pursue the matter). The term *reinforcement* is typically used to refer to this process with the label *reward* reserved for increases in instrumental responding and *punishment* for decreases in instrumental responding. The general purpose of this chapter will be to consider the current status of our attempts to predict the outcome of instrumental contingencies like those which we might wish to arrange for the gerbil.

A HISTORICAL PERSPECTIVE

If we ignore some of the fine grain of the historical record, I would suggest that history has provided the contemporary experimental psychologist with one of three points of departure if one is interested in an analysis of the reinforcement process.

---

* Research presented in this manuscript was supported by Grant APA-194 from the National Research Council of Canada. The manuscript was prepared during the author's tenure on a leave fellowship granted by the Canada Council. I am most grateful to Carol Anderson, Sue Cohen, Pat Kelly, Sue Marmaroff, Robyn Pascoe, and Pat Thomas for assistance in the various tasks of data collection, analysis, and manuscript preparation.

Traditional Reinforcement Theory

In its initial form, the reinforcement process served one simple explanatory function. It functioned as the "glue" which cemented together the ubiquitous Ss and Rs of early associationism—or conversely, as the "solvent" which dissolved S–R connections already formed. Thorndike's (1914) statement of his symmetrical *law of effect* is a classic example of this tradition:

> *The Law of Effect*—to the situation, a modifiable connection being made by him between an S and an R and being accompanied or followed by a satisfying state of affairs, man responds, other things being equal by an increase in the strength of that connection. To a connection similar, save than an annoying state of affairs goes with or follows it, man responds, other things being equal, by a decrease of the connection. (p. 71)

Starting from this assumption, the basic task which confronted the reinforcement theorist was to provide an indexing system which would tell us the category into which any particular contingent event might fall—"satisfier," "annoyer," or "neutral." With an adequate set of rules, we should be able, for example, to predict the outcome of any one of the 20 contingencies possible in our gerbil environment.

As Premack (1969) has suggested, this traditional view of reinforcement asserts that there are three mutually exclusive categories of contingent event to be found in nature and assumes, implicitly or explicitly, that particular contingent events are incontrovertible members of a particular category. From this fundamental assumption, the search was initiated to find the property or properties which would permit us to know the particular category into which a particular event might fall. It is in this context that such prominent notions as drive reduction, drive induction, arousal, optimal level, and other major concepts were developed. The conceptual and empirical deficiencies of the major theoretical schemes in this tradition have been extensively reviewed and criticized in a number of articles (cf. Miller, 1963; Wilcoxon, 1969) and need not be repeated here. Although one might take exception to some of the particulars, the general consensus of contemporary critics is that concepts such as drive reduction have serious shortcomings as a basis for predicting when a particular contingent event might function as a reward.

The search for the nature of negative or aversive events took a curious twist when Thorndike (1932) rejected the negative side of his classic law of effect. All subsequent attempts to account for the observation that some events will produce a decrease in the probability of instrumental responding adopted some variation on what has been called the *alternative response assumption* (cf. Dunham, 1971). In its weakest form, this assumption suggests that the decrease in instrumental responding produced by some contingent events is the indirect result of an increase in some alternative behavior. The alternative behavior is assumed to be developed and maintained by the positive side of the law of effect (i.e., an escape from aversive stimulation mediated by either a two-process or single-process conditioning model).

Parallel with the decline in popularity of concepts such as drive reduction, there is also a contemporary disenchantment with the various forms of the alternative response assumption as explanations of the effects which aversive events are observed to have upon behavior. Rachlin and Herrnstein (1969) and Dunham (1971) have discussed both data and conceptual arguments against the alternative response assumption as an explanation of the effects which negative contingent events have upon instrumental behavior.

To summarize, the fundamental task posed by traditional reinforcement theorists was to predict the effect a particular contingent event might have—positive, negative, or neutral. Although the notions generated by this task appear to be in some disfavor at present, it remains as one possible point of departure for the contemporary student of reinforcement.

The "Incentive" Function of Reinforcement

As Walker (1969) has suggested, the general trend in the development of theoretical views of reinforcement has been to expand the explanatory powers of the concept. This expansion provides us with a second point of departure for studying reinforcement.

As stated earlier, the process was initially a "glue" in the chemistry of associationism. Primarily under the direction of Hull, the concept started to mutate into a much more powerful explanatory mechanism. Concerned with such problems as the rate at which performance changed with changes in magnitude of reward, Hull decided that the process not only cemented the habit structure together, but pulled the organism down the runway via K (incentive) and its machinery, the r_g mechanism. Hence by the 1950s the reinforcement process was busy with such additional tasks as moving the animal out of the start box and mediating changes in performances which accompanied changes in the magnitude of reward. The addition of incentive motivation to the function served by the reinforcement process added a large and persisting area of research and theorizing to the reinforcement literature. It permitted us to deal with the tangled problems raised by the incentive concept without being distracted by the questions raised by Thorndike and the early associationists. For example, given the observation that a hungry rat will run down a runway for food pellets, it is possible to proceed with an extensive empirical analysis of the effects which a shift in the number of food pellets might have upon the rat's performance without ever worrying about the more fundamental question of why the rats ran for the food in the first place. Any thirst for theoretical analysis can be quenched quite readily by considering the rather complicated manner in which the incentive mechanism has been suggested to mediate changes in performance produced by a shift in the number of food pellets (cf. Dunham, 1968).

The "Weak Law of Effect"

Yet a third point of departure in the analysis of reinforcement starts from the assumption which has been called the *weak law of effect*. Although the weak law of effect has been given a number of different labels and definitions, all versions imply that we can conduct an empirical analysis of various contingency operations until, for example, we find that food is an effective contingent event for training a hungry rat to press a lever. We can then proceed with an analysis of variations on this contingency (e.g., schedules of reward), assuming that we have found at least one of several possible cases in which the reinforcement process is operating. As discussed by Meehl (1950), one way in which the weak law of effect can escape circularity is by assuming that food is also an effective contingent event for a variety of instrumental responses (i.e., the reward event is transituational). The same arguments can be used, for example, if electric shock is used as a contingent event which will effectively suppress a number of different behaviors.

The contents of this volume provide ample evidence for the popularity of the weak law of effect as a point of departure in the analysis of reinforcement. The adoption of the empirical approach to reinforcement represented by the weak law of effect and the transituational assumption also permits one to ignore the traditional questions about reinforcement posed by Thorndike and his successors.

Current Status of the Reinforcement Concept

In my opinion, contemporary psychologists working in the context of reinforcement phenomena have opted almost exclusively to approach the problem using the weak law of effect as a justification for an extensive analysis of scheduling effects or to investigate the incentive function of the contingent event (be it fear or the r_g mechanism). Attempts to develop a theory of reinforcement which is capable of predicting the effects of a particular contingent event prior to arranging the contingency are sparse. Perhaps most of us have accepted the statement made by Meehl (1950) concerning the problems which would confront such an effort:

> Finally, it would be very nice if in some magical way we could know before studying a given species exactly what stimulus changes would have the reinforcing property; but I have tried to indicate that this is essentially an irrational demand. (p. 74)

In support of using the weak law of effect as an approach to reinforcement, Meehl promised us some 20 years ago that such an inductive empirical examination would lead to some potent predictive rules (even for visiting Martians). I would suggest that the track record for the past few decades is not as impressive as Meehl hoped, and it is perhaps time for a more concerted emphasis upon some of the fundamental questions posed by traditional reinforcement theory. First, the data base generated by the inductive analysis is dangerously circumscribed. It is difficult to find much more than the various combinations of lever press, key peck, food, water, and electric shock upon which to base generalizations. Unlike Meehl's Martian, I find little information upon which to base an inductive leap into the multiple-response world of the gerbil described earlier. Perhaps the problem has been less with the inductive process than with the convenience of the manufactured operant chamber. Second, and related, is that the critical assumption that rewards (or punishments) are transituational has not been subjected to extensive, rigorous testing, again perhaps because of the compatibility of key pecks and impulse counters.

In view of these problems, it would appear that there is some justification for returning to the question of how we might predict the outcome of an instrumental contingency *before* it has been arranged. Hence, the remainder of the chapter will be devoted to a discussion of two contemporary trends in the literature which run counter to the weak law of effect as an approach to reinforcement and which have generated data which question the validity of the assumption that rewards are transituational. The first trend, an attempt to return to a symmetrical law of effect, is represented by the work of Premack (1959. 1965, 1971) and his students. The second is recent research concerned with the biological constraints which operate when an organism is exposed to particular instrumental contingencies. The result of this exercise will be to demonstrate that the transituational assumption is not valid and that a symmetrical law of effect based upon preference notions represents a more fruitful approach to reinforcement theory.

PREMACK'S REINFORCEMENT THEORY

The essential features of Premack's reinforcement theory are contained in three major papers (Premack, 1959, 1965, 1971). He suggests that the organism places the events in its world on a unitary dimension of value or preference. The relative value of a particular event can be measured in terms of the amount of time the organism spends engaging in that event. If we use time as an indicator of value, it is possible, according to Premack, to predict the outcome of any particular instrumental contingency. If we arrange a contingency in which value of the contingent event is higher than the value of the instrumental event, Premack predicts that we will observe an increase in the probability of the instrumental response. If we arrange a contingency in which the value of the contingent event is lower than the value of the instrumental event, Premack predicts that we will observe a decrease in the probability of the instrumental response. It should be noted that the value of a particular event is measured in terms of the amount of time the organism spends indulging in that event *when permitted unconstrained access to it*. These rules are simple and testable. They suggest that the organism will increase the probability of a behavior which moves it from a less to a more preferred state, but that it will not engage in a behavior which moves it from a more to a less preferred state.

Historical Context of Premack's Position

Before looking at the evidence for these assumptions it may be helpful to see where Premack fits into the three approaches to reinforcement discussed earlier. Essentially, Premack is concerned with the problem that Meehl finds "irrational." It is Thorndike's problem and the question central to traditional reinforcement theory: How can we predict the outcome of an instrumental contingency? There is a fundamental difference in approach, however. Thorndike's analysis implies that there are three different types of event in nature which have absolute properties termed satisfying, annoying, and neutral. Hence Thorndike and those who followed in his tradition attempted to find the absolute properties which permitted certain events to be assigned to fixed categories (i.e., satisfiers and annoyers). Premack makes the fundamentally different presupposition that the property of being rewarding or punishing is relative. Food, for example, can be either a reward or a punishment depending upon the relative value of the instrumental response. If an instrumental running response is less probable than eating, the food will function as a rewarding event. If the running response is more probable than eating, the food will function as a punishing event. The recognition of the relativistic nature of reward and punishment represents a significant departure from traditional thought about the reinforcement process.

The relativistic position necessarily contradicts the assumption that rewards are transituational. The direct and testable implication of Premack's rules is that a given contingent response like eating can function as a reward in one context and as a punishment in another context. If food is demonstrated to reward running in one instrumental contingency and punish running in another instrumental contingency, food, by definition, is not a transituational reward.

Finally, Premack's position can be viewed, in a curious sense, as having continued the trend described by Walker (1969) of increasing the explanatory powers of the reinforcement concept. As a miniature model, typical of contemporary psychological theory, it omits reference to such concepts as habit, incentive, the r_g mechanism, or the "glue" which were so prominent in the heyday of multiconcept theories such as Hull's (1943, 1952). A consequence of these omissions is that Premack's reinforcement concept is a single motivational construct which is assumed to account for all changes in performance observed when an instrumental contingency is instituted. Although I have yet to learn the Angerthas, I suspect that Walker has accused Professor Premack of having found the "one ring."

Evidence for Premack's Assumptions

Prior to 1971 most of the evidence in support of Premack's position was restricted to the positive side of the symmetrical rules which he proposes. Most experiments were designed to test the assumption that the contingent response must be more probable than the instrumental response for there to be an increase in the probability of instrumental behavior. The basic design used in all experiments, with minor variations, is a three-stage (ABA) procedure. During the first stage the independent probabilities of the responses which are to be used in the instrumental contingency are measured. The organism is permitted unconstrained access to the appropriate manipulanda (e.g., a drinking tube and a running wheel), and the amount of time spent engaging in each of these behaviors is measured. During the second stage a contingency is arranged in which the organism is required to engage in a specified amount of instrumental behavior in order to gain access to a specified amount of contingent responding. Any increase (or decrease) in instrumental responding above (or below) the previously measured base line probability indicates that the reinforcement process has operated. A third stage is often included in which the animal is permitted to return to the unconstrained base line condition.

Using this basic procedure, the evidence which supports the positive side of Premack's differential probability rules extends over a wide range of species and responses. Using Cebus monkeys which were given unconstrained access to one of four manipulanda during base line sessions (a door, a plunger, a vertical lever, and a horizontal lever), Premack (1963) arranged instrumental contingencies in a manner which required the monkeys to respond on a less probable manipulandum in order to gain access to a more probable manipulandum (low to high), or in which the animals were required to respond to a more probable manipulandum in order to gain access to a less probable manipulandum (high to low). In all cases, the low-to-high contingency increased the probability of the instrumental response and no such increase was observed when the contingent response was less probable.

In a similar series of experiments in which rats were used as subjects and running and drinking were the members of the instrumental contingency, the reinforcement relation was demonstrated to be reversible, as the differential probability rules predict. Using a low-to-high contingency in which drinking was more probable than running, drinking was observed to increase the probability of running—a rather typical observation. Less often observed, however, was the reverse case in which the running response was made contingent upon drinking. With appropriate manipulation of the deprivation parameters, the relative probability of the two responses was reversed, and running was demonstrated to be an effective contingent event for increasing the probability of instrumental drinking (cf. Premack, 1962; Schaeffer, 1965).

The generality of these findings has been extended to include contingencies between intracranial stimulation (ICS) and drinking (Holstein & Hundt, 1965) and between running and lever pressing (Hundt & Premack, 1963). The experiments have also included both children (Premack, 1971) and college students (Schaeffer, Hanna, & Russo, 1966) as subjects.

It was not until 1971 that the punishment side of Premack's formulation was presented in any detail (Premack, 1971). Although the punishment rule is the simple converse of the reward rule, testing it poses some problems. Consider, for example, a thirsty rat which is given free access to a running wheel and a drinking tube. With appropriate deprivation parameters, drinking can be made more probable than running. If a contingency is now arranged in which the animal is required to drink in order to run (high to low), the animal will very likely continue to drink until satiated because drinking is the preferred state. To demonstrate that the less probable response is an aversive event, the animal must be forced to run; and it must be demonstrated that the forcing operation per se is not the effective punishment event.

The initial work on this problem was presented in a paper by Weisman and Premack at the meetings of the Psychonomic Society in 1966 and discussed subsequently by Premack (1971). Weisman and Premack permitted rats free access to a drinking tube and a motorized running wheel for daily 15-min sessions. Two rats were maintained on a 23-hr water deprivation schedule, which made drinking more probable than running, and two rats were maintained ad lib, which made running more probable than drinking. After base line probabilities of responding were established for all four animals, contingency sessions were initiated in which 15 laps on the drinking tube produced 5 sec of motorized running in the wheel. For the two deprived animals the lick-to-run contingency (high to low) suppressed the amount of drinking, as predicted. For the ad lib animals the lick-to-run contingency (low to high) increased the amount of drinking, as predicted. The results in the latter condition also indicate that the forcing operation per se was not aversive. Subsequent recovery of the base line probabilities was followed by a reversal of deprivation conditions for each subject. A crossover design revealed results identical to those obtained in the first phase of the study.

The results of a subsequent, similar study by Terhune and Premack (1970) also indicate that forced running is an aversive event when it is less probable than instrumental drinking. In addition, Terhune and Premack reported that the amount of suppression produced by forced running was a linear function of the probability that the animal would not be in the state of running at any fixed time after running had been initiated.

Problems with Premack's Formulation

As is obvious from the preceding discussion, a substantial amount of data has accumulated to support Premack's differential probability rules (particularly the reward side). There are, however, several basic problems with the supporting data which suggest that some additional experimentation and a reformulation of the position might be in order.

An examination of the data in support of both the reward and the punishment assumption reveals two basic confoundings:

1. With respect to the reward assumption, in every procedure in which it has been demonstrated that a more probable response will reinforce a less probable response, the subject was required to increase the probability of the less probable instrumental response in order to maintain the contingent response at the independently measured free performance level.
2. With respect to the punishment assumption, every procedure in which it was demonstrated that a less probable contingent response would punish a more probable instrumental response, the subject was required to increase the probability of the contingent response above the independently measured free performance level in order to maintain the instrumental response at its free performance level.

In view of these two basic confoundings, the possibility remains that:

1. A less probable contingent response can be demonstrated to reinforce a more probable instrumental response if the contingency requirements are such that the subject must increase the probability of the instrumental response above its free performance level in order to maintain the free performance level of the contingent response.
2. A more probable response can be demonstrated to punish a less probable instrumental response if the contingency arrangements are such that the subject must increase the probability of the contingent response above its free performance level in order to maintain the instrumental response at its free performance level.

Evidence for a Response Deprivation Hypothesis

There are three independent lines of experimentation available at the present time which have been generated by the preceding rationale. The results of all three efforts indicate that, contrary to Premack's assumptions, under certain conditions a less probable response can serve as a reward for a more probable instrumental response.

Eisenberger, Karpman, and Trattner (1967) were the first to examine the problem. They reported a series of experiments in which college students were given access to two different manipulanda: a wheel which could be hand-cranked and a lever which could be pressed. In the critical experiment in the series, each subject was run in a 5-min base line session in which both wheel and lever were freely available. This was followed by a 5-min contingency session in which the subject was required to crank the wheel 10 revolutions in order to press the lever once. The results of the base line session revealed that most subjects preferred cranking the wheel to lever pressing. During the subsequent contingency session, if the lever-press response was suppressed by the contingency requirement, an *increase* in instrumental wheel cranking was observed—even if the contingent lever-press response was *less* probable than the instrumental response.

Eisenberger et al. interpreted their results in terms of a response suppression hypothesis which stated that the necessary condition for an increase in instrumental responding is the suppression of the contingent response, independent of the relative probability of instrumental and contingent responses. As they stated:

> The present set of experiments suggests the necessary and sufficient condition for reinforcement in the contingency situation is the animal's necessity to increase instrumental responding if it is to maintain contingent responding at the free performance level. (p. 350)

The second line of experimentation designed to examine this problem consists of two experiments performed in our laboratory using subjects, procedure, and apparatus which more closely approximate Premack's early experimentation.

The first experiment was a master's thesis conducted by Susan Marmaroff (1971) which employed albino rats as subjects and running and drinking as the members of the instrumental contingency. The apparatus, identical to that described in a paper by Dunham (1972), consisted of a single modified activity wheel housed in a dark, ventilated, sound-attenuating chamber located in a room adjacent to the control apparatus. A motor-cam mechanism permitted us to insert or retract a drinking tube to which the animal had access through a small hole in the stationary wall of the wheel.

The rats were on 23-hr water deprivation, and daily sessions 60 min in length were conducted 7 days per week. The experimental procedure was divided into four phases. During Phase 1 the animals were permitted free access to the running wheel with the drinking tube retracted for 15 consecutive sessions. Animals were permitted access to water for 1 hr in the home cage immediately after the session.

During Phase 2 the running wheel was mechanically locked so that no running could occur. The drinking tube was inserted, and a base line level of free operant drinking was observed. Phase 2 continued for 15 sessions.

During Phase 3 the subjects were permitted free access to both the drinking tube and running wheel. In all phases of the experiment, drinking was defined as a single lap on the tube and running as a 90-deg revolution of the wheel. Electronic circuitry divided the entire session into 2-sec intervals, and each interval was scanned for an instance of either drink or run. The data were converted to a probability measure by dividing the number of intervals in which a response occurred by the total number possible in the session (cf. Premack, 1965).

During Phase 4, a run-to-drink contingency was arranged for all animals. To commence each session, the wheel was available for free-access running (brake released) and the drinking tube was retracted. A fixed-ratio schedule was selected for each animal in which a fixed number of 90-deg revolutions in the wheel (instrumental response) produced the drinking tube for a fixed number of licks (contingent response), after which the tube was retracted. The instrumental and contingent requirements were arranged such that each animal had to increase the base line amount of running (as measured in Phase 3) by approximately 50% in order to maintain the contingent response at its base line level. As indicated in Table 1, the base line level of responding in Phase 3 shows that run was consistently more probable than drink for subjects 3, 5, and 6; that drink was more probable than run for subject 1; and that no consistent preference was observed for subjects 2 and 4. A subject was judged inconsistent if it reversed its preference more than once during the six sessions immediately prior to the contingency training. The running wheel remained in the free-access state throughout the session; thus running was possible during both states of the drinking tube, inserted or retracted. Phase 4 lasted for 15 sessions and was followed by a final phase in which the contingency was eliminated and free access to the wheel and tube was reinstated.

Table 1 Instrumental and contingent response requirements for each subject during contingency training, Phase 3

SUBJECT	INSTRUMENT (No. of 90-deg revolutions)	CONTINGENT (No. of licks)	CONTINGENCY
1	5	30	low to high
2	8	35	no preference
3	10	20	high to low
4	8	35	no preference
5	10	30	high to low
6	9	30	high to low

The results of the five phases of the experiment for each of the subjects are presented in Figure 1. As is evident from the base line data, the deprivation parameters produced low-to-high, high-to-low, and nondifferential probability cases. The major result was that the contingency produced an increase in the instrumental performance of all subjects. Reinforcement was thus observed in low-to-high, high-to-low, and nondifferential probability cases. A *t*-test for correlated observations indicated that the increase in

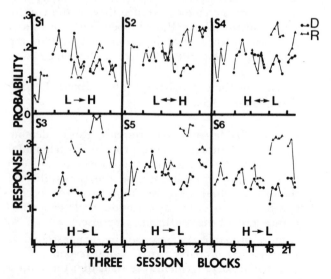

Fig. 1. Probability of running and drinking for each subject during each of the five phases of the first experiment.

the probability of instrumental running reliably exceeded *both* the single-response base line (Phase 1) and the two-response base line (Phase 3) (single-response base line comparison: $t = 6.662$, $p < .005$; two-response base line comparison: $t = 8.50$, $p < .005$).

The contingency also suppressed the contingent drinking response. The amount of suppression was not great, and drinking tended to recover over the course of training. A correlation between the amount of suppression of contingent drinking and the amount of increase in instrumental responding was reasonably high, but not reliable ($r = .48$; $df\ 5$; $p > .05$). The presence of some degree of positive correlation supports the suggestion of Eisenberger et al. that suppression of contingent responding is an important factor in obtaining the reinforcement effect (see also Premack, 1965, p. 172), although the sample size is not large enough to argue persuasively either way.

During the nine sessions of Phase 4, the subjects returned, in general, to the base line probability of responding.

In summary, the data from Marmaroff's thesis also question the validity of Premack's reward rule. A knowledge of the independent probability of instrumental and contingent responses is apparently not an adequate basis for predicting reward (and by implication punishment) effects in a run-to-drink contingency.

A second experiment has since been completed, using a drink-to-run contingency instead of the previously employed run-to-drink contingency. In the first experiment, the run-to-drink contingency reduced the total amount of water intake during the early sessions of training. It is possible that such a change in water intake was responsible for the increase in instrumental running as a general activity phenomenon (cf. Campbell & Lynch, 1968). By reversing the contingency and establishing drinking as the instrumental event, the confounded change in water deprivation is eliminated. In addition, the generality of the argument against Premack's assumptions is increased to include the drink-to-run situation.

The second experiment followed the same procedure used in the first. It was divided into three phases: a two-response base line phase; a contingency training phase; and a two-response base line recovery phase. The single-response base line phases used in the first experiment were not included as control conditions, largely because the reinforcement effects obtained in the first experiment were observed to exceed both the single- and the two-response base line.

During Phase 1 the animals were permitted free access to the running wheel and drinking tube each daily session. This phase continued for 15 days, and the base line probability of each response was measured with the same method as employed in the first experiment.

During Phase 2 a drink-to-run contingency was established for all subjects. The contingency required the subjects to complete 50 laps on the drinking tube in order to obtain five 90-deg revolutions of the wheel. This contingency, as in the first experiment, required each subject to increase the amount of instrumental responding above its base line level if contingent responding was to be maintained at the base line level. Unlike the first experiment, however, the use of the same contingency requirement for each subject meant that each subject had to increase instrumental responding by different amounts in order to maintain contingent responding at base line level. Phase 2 continued for 10 sessions and was followed by 2 sessions of recovery with free access to both wheel and tube.

The results of this experiment are presented in Figure 2. In Phase 1 of the experiment subjects 1 and 5 showed consistent preferences for running over the last six sessions of the two-response base line. Subject 3 revealed a consistent preference for drinking, and subjects 2, 4, and 6 failed to reveal any consistent preference.

The introduction of the drink-to-run contingency in Phase 2 provided three types of probability relation. Subjects 1 and 5 participated in a low-to-high contingency; subject 3 participated in a high-to-low

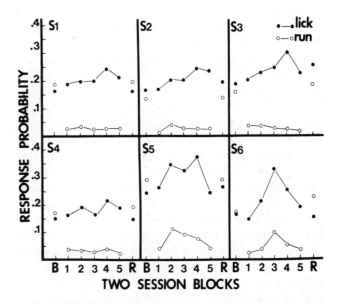

Fig. 2. Probability of running and drinking during the last six sessions of base line (B), contingency (C), and recovery (R) phases of the second experiment.

contingency; and subjects 2, 4, and 6 represented the indifferent case. As seen in Figure 2, all subjects increased the probability of drinking to levels which exceeded the base line probability. A t-test for correlated observations revealed this increase to be reliable ($t = 6.50$, $p < .05$). The contingency also suppressed contingent running, and again the correlation between the amount of suppression and the amount of increase in instrumental responding was substantial but not reliable with the same sample ($r = .74$, df 5; $p > .05$). During the two sessions of base line recovery in Phase 3, the responses tended to return to their original base line levels.

Along with the results reported by Eisenberger et al. (1967), the data from these two experiments directly question the validity of Premack's reward and punishment assumptions. A contingent response was demonstrated to reinforce an instrumental response whether the contingent event was higher or lower in probability than the instrumental response.

More recently a third series of experiments based upon the same rationale has been reported by Allison and Timberlake (1974). Their first experiment was designed to demonstrate that a less probable response would reward a more probable instrumental response if the contingency was arranged so that the animal had to increase the probability of the instrumental response in order to obtain the base line (free-access) amount of contingent responding. In the first phase of the experiment, albino rats were given daily 10-min base line sessions in which they had simultaneous access to two drinking tubes. One tube contained a .4% saccharine solution, the other a .3% solution. The rats consistently preferred the .4% solution during this base line exposure. Following base line sessions, contingency sessions were conducted in which the rats were required to lick the .4% solution for 80 sec in order to gain access to the .3% solution for 10 sec. This contingency arrangement required that the rats increase the amount of .4% instrumental licking if they were to obtain their usual base line amount of .3% contingent licking.

Contrary to Premack's reward rule, this high-to-low contingency increased the amount of instrumental .4% licking to levels which exceeded the base line. The amount of contingent licking was suppressed by the contingency, and, curiously, the rats licked the contingent .3% solution for only a small percentage of the time that it was made available during the contingency sessions. A second experiment using .4% and .1% saccharin solutions, as instrumental and contingent events respectively, corroborated the results obtained in the first study.

The final experiment in the Allison and Timberlake series followed the same procedure as the first two, except that the contingency arranged did not require an increase in the amount of .4% licking in order to receive the base line amount of .1% contingent licking. This procedure failed to increase the .4% instrumental licking.

The results reported by Allison and Timberlake add further support to the data which question Premack's differential probability rules. To account for their findings, Allison and Timberlake (1974) and Timberlake and Allison (1974) have outlined a position called the *response deprivation* hypothesis. For a particular contingency arrangement, response deprivation is identified "if the animal, by performing its baseline amount of instrumental response, is unable to obtain access to its baseline amount of the contingent response" (Timberlake & Allison, 1974, p. 152). They suggest that the necessary and sufficient condition for an increase in instrumental responding is that the instrumental contingency employed produce the response deprivation state. The response deprivation hypothesis, as outlined by Timberlake and Allison, does not differ in any essential manner from the response suppression hypothesis offered earlier by Eisenberger et al. (1967). In future discussion these two positions will be treated as identical and referred to as the response deprivation hypothesis.

Taken together, the evidence obtained in the three independent lines of experimentation which have been discussed in this section permit two conclusions: (a) all of the experiments described directly question the validity of Premack's differential probability rules; and (b) the data consistently suggest that the instrumental contingency must force the amount of contingent responding below its base line operant level in order to observe an increase in instrumental responding—i.e., the response deprivation hypothesis.

Some Control Considerations

THE YOKED CONTROL PROCEDURE

Before the evidence leading to the two above-mentioned conclusions can be completely accepted, a number of control questions need to be considered. First and perhaps most important, it is obvious that the introduction of most instrumental contingencies will drastically change the manner in which the organism normally distributes the contingent response in time when compared to the base line performance. It is possible that many of the changes observed with the use of Premack's typical experimental procedure can be produced by simply changing the manner in which the organism is permitted access to the contingent event in time *without arranging an instrumental contingency*. In order to examine this possibility, the most appropriate control procedure would be to include a group of animals in each experiment which were yoked to the instrumental contingency group and received the reward in the same temporal pattern without any contingency in effect. With the yoked control group, one should be able to judge the effects which the change in the temporal distribution, as well as the amount of contingent responding per se, had upon the designated instrumental behavior. Premack (1965, pp. 166–172) recognized this problem and suggested that the reduction in the amount of contingent responding usually produced by an instrumental contingency may, along with the low-to-high probability differential, be necessary for an increase in the probability of instrumental behavior.

Various approximations to the yoked control procedure described above can be found in some of the experimentation concerned with Premack's theoretical position. Most of them attempt to control for the reduced amount of contingent responding and do not consider changes in the temporal distribution of the contingent response produced by the contingency. The results of these efforts have been inconsistent. Eisenberger et al. (1967) recognized the possibility that simple suppression of the contingent response by the instrumental response requirement might produce an increase in the instrumental behavior. They conducted a control experiment (Experiment III of their series) in which they removed access to the lever-press response (nominally their contingent response) and measured the effects of such removal upon the wheel-turning response (nominally their instrumental response). Although the complete removal of access to the contingent response is not as informative as the yoked control described earlier, it does control for the effects of simply reducing the amount of contingent responding produced by the contingency. The results revealed that removal of access to the lever-press response reduced, rather than increased, the amount of wheel-turning behavior. Hence they concluded that the instrumental requirement was a necessary aspect of their procedure and that contingent response reduction alone was not sufficient to increase the probability of the instrumental response.

A more recent experiment suggests that the results obtained in the control experiment reported by Eisenberger et al. may have limited generality. While working with a different context, I conducted an experiment in which rats were given free access to a drinking tube and a running wheel during daily half-hour sessions (Dunham, 1972). Subsequent removal of access to either one of these responses by braking the wheel or removing the tube during the session produced an increase in the amount of the alternative behavior observed during the session. Contrary to the observations made by Eisenberger et al., it would appear that removal of a response from the animal's repertoire will, in some cases, produce an increase in an available alternative. In our case, the two responses measured were topographically quite different.

Bernstein (1973) has also recently reported data relevant to this control question. He used a fascinating procedure in which human subjects were placed in a controlled experimental environment containing various items of interest (e.g., sewing materials, reading, art work). The subjects lived continuously in this environment for periods as long as 34 consecutive days. The amount of time which each subject spent indulging in a number of selected activities was measured on a 24-hr basis. Following the measurement of base line durations, Bernstein arranged various contingencies in which the subjects were required to engage in a fixed amount of a less probable behavior in order to gain access to a fixed amount of a more probable behavior (e.g., read fiction in order to sew). All of the contingencies studied, with one exception, increased the amount of instrumental behavior observed and suppressed the amount of contingent behavior below base line levels. In the case where no increase in instrumental behavior was observed, it is interesting to note that the contingent response was not suppressed by the contingency requirement.

More important in the present context is Bernstein's use of a matched control procedure in which the same subjects were subsequently exposed to sessions in which the previously designated contingent response was simply restricted in the same manner in which the previous contingency had restricted the response, without any instrumental response requirement. This procedure comes very close to the yoked control procedure described earlier. In two of the five instrumental-contingent response pairs which were observed, Bernstein found that simply restricting the amount of contingent activity (with no instrumental response required) was sufficient to produce increases in the response which had previously been designated as the instrumental response. Again we see that restricting the contingent response in the absence of an instrumental response requirement has inconsistent effects. In some instances an increase in the nominal instrumental behavior is observed, in other cases no changes occur.

Allison and Timberlake (1974) also attempted to assess the effects of a restriction in the contingent response in the absence of an instrumental response requirement. In Experiment 3 of their series they observed that the amount of unconstrained .4% saccharin drinking (the nominal instrumental response) was the same in both the presence and the absence of the .1% solution (the nominal contingent response). In this case, completely suppressing the contingent response appears to have no effect upon instrumental behavior in the absence of the contingency—and it might be noted that the topography of the instrumental and contingent response was identical: licking a drinking tube.

The results produced by these approximations to the yoked control procedure suggested in earlier discussion are inconsistent. Simple removal of the contingent response from the unconstrained repertoire has been observed to produce increases, decreases, and no change in an alternative response designated as the instrumental behavior. If we are going to properly assess the relative merits of Premack's differential probability rules and the response deprivation hypothesis, it behooves us first to determine whether the increases in instrumental behavior observed in these experiments are the product of the reinforcement operation (i.e., the response requirement) or whether the increase reflects an interaction between unconstrained responses which would have occurred in the absence of any instrumental contingency. As I have noted in another context (Dunham, 1971), the question of what changes will occur in an unconstrained multiple-response repertoire when we restrict (or increase) one or more members has received very little experimental attention. At present we have little more than our intuition upon which to base our predictions about such changes (cf. Bernstein, 1973).

Premack's Control Requirements

In addition to the yoked control question discussed above, Premack (1971) has outlined a number of procedural problems which he suggests will invalidate tests of the differential probability rules. We shall now briefly consider each of these problems as they relate to the negative evidence which has accumulated concerning Premack's position.

All three of the procedural problems discussed by Premack revolve around a loosely defined concept of "momentary response probability." Specifically, he suggests that there are three conditions under which the total-duration measure of responding obtained during base line sessions is likely to be a distorted estimate of "momentary response probability" and consequently of the reward (or punishment) value of a response. The first case described is a situation in which the two responses to be used in the contingency have a different rate of decay (habituation or satiation) within a session. If, for example, drinking is more probable than running during the first 10 min of a 1-hr session, but substantially less probable during the last 50 min of the session, a total-duration measure would indicate in some cases that running was the more probable of the two. Hence in subsequent contingency sessions a run-to-drink contingency would be considered to be a high-to-low contingency based upon total-duration measures, but actually should be considered a low-to-high contingency for the first 10 min of the session and a high-to-low contingency during the last 50 min. At first glance, it does seem reasonable to stipulate that a fair test of the probability differential rules require that these within-session duration-time curves not intersect. In fact, in the running and drinking experiments discussed earlier we have measured changes in the probability of drinking and running in consecutive 20-min segments of the session, and in four subjects so observed both responses decline over the 1-hr session but the curves do not cross over. Eisenberger et al. (1967) also failed to observe within-session crossovers of response probability in their experiments. Presumably, then, these data would meet the criterion specified by Premack, and total duration is a good estimate of "momentary response probabilities."

A more basic problem arises, however, when one considers how "momentary" a momentary probability estimate should be. If, for example, one divided an entire session of running and drinking into successive 5-min segments, a number of reversals in response probability would be observed over the course of the session. Using this latter time scale on the abscissa, our experiments would not be considered a proper test of Premack's position. As suggested earlier, the concept "momentary probability" needs to be defined more precisely if it is to be anything other than a post hoc analysis of obstreperous results.

A second stipulation, if we are to obtain good estimates of "momentary probability," is that the parameter values used during the contingency sessions be the same as those used to measure the independent probability of responding during base line sessions. Premack (1971) suggests:

For example, if the reinforcement session is to use a [variable-interval] 60 second schedule with a contingent [response] time of 5 seconds, then

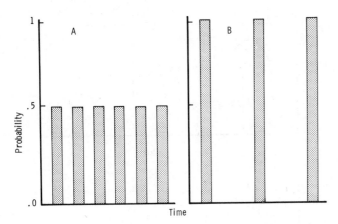

Fig. 3. See text for explanation. (From Premack, 1969, p. 132.)

exactly those parameters should be used in the measurement of response probabilities. (p. 130)

Unless this requirement is met, it is suggested that the total duration measure will be a distorted estimate of "momentary response probability." Again, however, this requirement poses some problems for the experimenter who wishes to meet the conditions specified. Unless the experimenter exercises complete control over the onset and offset of both instrumental and contingent responses (a condition which would eliminate the response requirement), it is the case that any instrumental contingency which we arrange will produce some changes in the manner in which the organism distributes its behavior in time when compared to base line performance. Consequently, it is impossible strictly to meet the requirement imposed by Premack. The best one can do is keep the base line and contingency situations as similar as possible and depend upon the yoked control discussed earlier to detect any changes in instrumental response probability produced by the temporal constraints placed upon contingent behavior.

The third procedural problem discussed by Premack (1971) can best be explained by reference to Figure 3. Referring to this figure, he says:

Response A depicted in the curve on the right attains an extremely high probability at relatively long intervals, whereas response B shown on the left attains half that probability but at half the interval. The average probability of the two responses are thus equal; however, their momentary reinforcement values will not be equal. (p. 131)

The spirit of this suggestion is that certain responses like copulation (Response A) do not occur very frequently, but when they do occur they should be considered to be at the top of the preference structure. With all due respect to the data of introspection, this stipulation reduces in operational terms to the suggestion that the duration of some responses is not a proper estimate of their relative position in the preference structure. Again, an experimenter who wishes to comply with this stipulation must have some criterion for knowing when he is dealing with a response like Response A in Figure 3. The unique property of Response A appears to be that it has a relatively long interval which separates successive instances of the behavior and a high position in the preference structure when an instance of the behavior is observed. The unique property of Response B is that it has a relatively short interval which separates successive instances of the behavior and a relatively low position in the preference structure when an instance of the behavior is observed. Obviously all responses have these two properties in differing degrees. Unless it is specified how long an interresponse interval, for a given session length, is required for membership in the class of Response A, of how short an interval is required for membership in the class of Response B, we cannot know if we have underestimated or overestimated the "momentary probability" of these responses by measuring their total duration. With reference to our running and drinking experiments, we typically observe longer interresponse intervals for running than we do for drinking during the 1-hr session, but one cannot determine whether running deserves membership in the special class of response A from the information provided in Figure 3.

To summarize briefly, it appears to be difficult, if not impossible, to meet the requirements specified by Premack for a valid test of the differential probability rules. In the experiments cited as evidence against the differential probability rules, it is possible to suggest that the total-duration measures are, indeed, a distorted estimate of the "momentary probability" of the contingent responses employed. I would argue that such an interpretation is necessarily an ad hoc analysis until such time as the concept "momentary probability" and its relationship to the total duration measure are more precisely defined.

An Optimal-Duration Model as an Alternative Interpretation

If we assume that subsequent research continues to question Premack's position and to support the response deprivation hypothesis, we are placed in a curiously counterintuitive position. The evidence cited thus far suggests that the organism will, under certain conditions, increase the probability of a response which is instrumental in placing it in a less preferred state—when preference is measured in terms of the total duration of responding during base line sessions. For example, most people, given the choice, would prefer eating in a nice restaurant to visiting the dentist. Taken literally, the response deprivation hypothesis suggests that it is possible to increase my patronage of local restaurants by arranging a contingency in which I must go to a restaurant in order to visit my dentist, and that this contingency will work only if it reduces the amount of time I spend at the dentist below my base line, unconstrained level of dental care.

Rather than accept such a counterintuitive notion, it would seem more judicious at present to suggest that the total-duration measure is a distorted measure of preference. It may still be possible to develop an alternative measure which will permit us to maintain Premack's fundamental, commonsense assumptions about a symmetrical reward-punishment mechanism that depends upon the organism's preference structure.

For the remainder of the discussion in this section of the chapter, I shall outline, in rudimentary form, a reinforcement model which maintains many of the features of Premack's analysis but suggests a basic change in the manner in which we measure the organism's preference structure. It is designed to detect the momentary changes in preference that are necessarily obscured by the total-duration measure.

The most convenient way to describe the essential features of the model is to make reference to the multiple-response repertoire of our gerbil again. Assume for the moment that our observations of the gerbil for a 20-min period each day revealed that the gerbil spent most of its time shredding paper. Given a definition for the onset and offset of the paper-shredding behavior, two properties of the behavior are considered important. The first property, called the *burst duration,* refers to the amount of time spent paper shredding once the animal enters the state. Second, *the interburst interval,* refers to the amount of time observed between successive bursts of paper shredding. Assume that we have made these tedious observations of the gerbil's paper-shredding behavior over a period of several unconstrained base line sessions and the results are those observed in Figure 4. Looking first at the frequency distribution for burst durations (solid-line curve), the most frequently observed duration represented as point A on the curve

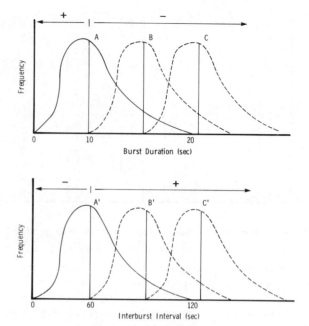

Fig. 4. Hypothetical frequency distributions for burst durations and interburst intervals of paper shredding in the gerbil. As the burst-duration distribution is displaced to the left, the paper-shredding behavior is a preferred event; as it is displaced right, paper shredding acquires negative properties. As the interburst interval distribution is displaced to the left, the paper shredding acquires negative properties; as it is displaced to the right, it is a preferred event.

is 10 sec, and all instances observed during base line sessions fall between a minimum duration of 1 sec and a maximum duration of 20 sec. Looking now at the frequency distribution of interburst intervals, the most frequently observed interval between successive bursts of paper shredding is 60 sec (point A' on the solid curve) with a minimum interval of 1 sec and a maximum interval of 120 sec.

I suggest that a knowledge of these two distributions, and of the variables which alter them, is essential for predicting whether a particular contingent event will function as a reward or as a punishment in an instrumental contingency. If we consider, for example, paper shredding as a contingent event for instrumental running behavior, the base line observations we have made of paper shredding tell us how the animal *prefers* to expose itself to paper shredding over the time permitted in the session. These base line observations should, of course, be made with running also available, since the presence of the running response per se will very likely be one of the variables which would alter the burst duration and interburst interval distributions of paper shredding. Assume that we can regulate the exact amount of paper shredding which the gerbil is permitted for each completion of the instrumental response requirement—specifically, that we can either give the gerbil access to the paper for durations shorter than its preferred (average) base line duration or force the gerbil to shred paper for durations longer than its preferred (average) base line burst duration.

To the extent that the contingency which we arrange between running and paper shredding shortens the intervals between successive bursts of paper shredding and/or lengthens the duration of a burst (relative to base line durations), I would suggest that paper shredding will function as an aversive event.

To the extent that the contingency we arrange lengthens the interval between successive bursts of paper shredding and/or shortens the bursts of paper shredding (relative to base line durations), I would suggest that paper shredding will function as a positive event. Finally, if the contingency we arrange simply feeds paper shredding back to the gerbil in a way that does not alter his record of self-exposure (as manifested in the two distributions), we should observe neutral motivational properties as evidenced by no change in the probability of instrumental behavior.

These general predictions made by the model can be made more specific by reference to Figure 4. Using these hypothetical data for paper shredding, it is suggested that *given no change in the distribution of interburst intervals,* paper shredding will function as a reward as long as the contingency we arrange displaces the distribution of burst durations in the direction of durations less than the *optimal duration* of 10 sec as observed during base line sessions. Conversely, assuming that we can force the behavior, paper shredding will function as an aversive event as long as the contingency we arrange displaces the distribution of burst durations in the direction of durations greater than the optimal duration of 10 secs (see the broken-line curves).

Given no change in the distribution of burst durations, paper shredding will function as a reward as long as the contingency we arrange displaces the distribution of interburst intervals in the direction of intervals greater than the optimal interburst interval of 60 sec, as observed in base line sessions. Conversely, assuming that we can force the behavior, paper shredding will function as an aversive event as long as the contingency we arrange displaces the distribution of interburst intervals in the direction of intervals shorter than the optimal interburst interval of 60 sec.

To digress briefly, it might be noted that the yoked control procedure, discussed earlier with reference to the experimental tests of Premack's differential probability rules and the response deprivation hypothesis, should also be considered in the context of the present model. It would be interesting, for example, to observe the effects upon other unconstrained responses in the gerbil's repertoire of placing various temporal constraints upon paper shredding (changing the burst duration and interburst interval distributions with or without changes in total durations). It is possible that there would be systematic changes in other responses similar to those produced by arranging an instrumental contingency. These operations make some contact with the recent suggestions made by Baum (1973) concerning a correlation-based law of effect.

Since the predictions made by this conceptual scheme are made with reference to the optimal durations observed during base line sessions, the model will be called an *optimal-duration model* in future discussion.

To conclude the discussion of the optimal-duration model, it is instructive to describe one additional hypothetical procedure which would pit the predictions made by this model against both Premack's differential probability rules and the more recent response deprivation hypothesis. Because some of the predictions to be discussed require us to "force" the contingent response for durations which exceed the optimal duration, we shall consider a modification of the gerbil environment described earlier in which the animal now has access to only two sources of enjoyment. Assume that the gerbil is placed in a motorized activity wheel which can be activated by simply rotating the wheel 10 deg in either direction. In addition, simply rearing up on the hind legs is sufficient to produce an intracranial stimulus (ICS) in the lateral hypothalamic area using shock parameters within the "positive" range. Dropping back on all four feet terminates the ICS.

Assume also that half-hour unconstrained access to each of these events reveals that the gerbil spends a total of 10 min per session running in the wheel and a total of 5 min receiving the ICS. Consider the predictions of the three models when we arrange some possible instrumental contingencies between these two responses.

The predictions made by Premack's differential probability rules are quite clear. Running is the more probable contingent event; hence a self-stimulate–to–run contingency (low-to-high probability) should produce an increase in the amount of self-stimulation the animal will take. Conversely, a run–to–self-stimulate contingency (high-to-low) should produce a decrease in running.

The predictions made by the response deprivation

hypothesis are very different. According to this position, either a self-stimulate–to–run or a run–to–self-stimulate contingency will produce increases in instrumental responding if the contingency arranged reduces the amount of the contingent event below the base line level. Hence, contrary to Premack's rules, the run–to–self-stimulate contingency will, under response deprivation conditions, increase the probability of running.

According to the optimal-duration model, either of the above contingencies (run–to–self-stimulate or self-stimulate–to–run) can be demonstrated to produce either the reward or the punishment outcome or no change depending upon how we distribute the contingent event in time. Consider, for example, a high-to-low contingency in which the animal is required to run in order to self-stimulate. Assume, also, for the moment that our base line observations indicated that the optimal duration for self-stimulation was 5 sec with an optimal-duration interburst interval of 30 sec between successive stimuli. If we now arrange the contingency in which each ICS is 5 sec in duration, the ICS will increase the probability of running as long as the interburst interval distribution is displaced in a direction of intervals greater than the optimal-duration interburst interval (60 sec). Conversely, if the interburst interval produced by the contingency is shorter than the 60-sec optimal duration, a 5-sec ICS will be aversive. On the other hand, if the contingency we arrange does not alter the interburst interval distribution, we can make the ICS aversive by displacing the distribution of burst durations in a direction greater than the optimal duration of 5 sec, or we can make it positive by displacing the distribution of burst durations in a direction less than the 5-sec optimal duration.

Finally, if one feeds back the ICS as a tape recording of the pattern revealed by the animal during the base line observations, it is predicted that the event will be motivationally neutral as indicated by no change in the probability of the instrumental response.

These predictions differ from those made by Premack in specifying that there are certain conditions in which a high-to-low probability contingency (as defined by total duration of base line responding) will produce an increase in the probability of the instrumental response. The predictions also differ from those made by the response deprivation hypothesis. The optimal-duration model does not require that the amount of contingent responding permitted during a session be suppressed below the base line *total duration* of that response. It requires instead that (a) each instance of the contingent response be shorter than the optimal duration of base line bursts; and/or (b) the intervals between instances of contingent responding be longer than the base line optimal duration of interburst intervals. The total duration of contingent responding can remain the same as it was during base line sessions, and it is predicted that either of the above constraints on the contingent behavior will be sufficient to produce an increase in instrumental responding.

Although we do not yet have appropriate data to support the optimal-duration model, I would argue that it provides a viable alternative interpretation to the response deprivation hypothesis and has the advantage of specifying the conditions under which we should observe increases, decreases, and no change in instrumental behavior. As stated earlier, the optimal-duration model is, in some sense, an attempt to translate Premack's notion of "momentary probability" into operational terms. Basically, the two distributions described are assumed to provide a better basis than does the total duration of responding for predicting when a contingent event will be more or less probable than an instrumental event. In more recent work, Premack and his students appear to recognize the possible importance of the organism's more momentary tendencies to turn a response off or on. In the punishment study by Terhune and Premack (1970) mentioned earlier the amount of suppression produced by a less probable running response was demonstrated to be a linear function of the probability that the animal would turn off the running response at fixed times after its initiation. Obviously, the probability that the organism will turn off a particular response some fixed time after its initiation is readily derived from the burst duration distribution, which is one component of the optimal-duration model. Hence the results reported by Terhune and Premack can be subsumed by both the optimal-duration model and Premack's differential probability rules.

BIOLOGICAL CONSTRAINTS ON REINFORCEMENT

With the possible exception of autonomically innervated responses (cf. Miller, 1969), we have typically assumed that all responses in an organism's repertoire are equally eligible for modification using an instrumental learning procedure. Premack's differential probability rules, the response deprivation hypothesis, and the optimal-duration model described in the first part of this chapter all reflect this assumption. These positions specify the necessary and sufficient conditions for the observation of changes in instrumental behavior and assume that these conditions will hold, in general, for any pair of responses in any particular species.

Recently, however, evidence has been accumulating which suggests that certain responses may not be susceptible to such modification while others are highly susceptible. The general explanation which has emerged to account for such evidence is the notion that the organism brings certain "biological predispositions" into the instrumental learning situation which can either facilitate or inhibit the effectiveness of certain response-reinforcer combinations (cf. Seligman, 1970).

An example of the type of evidence which has provided the basis for speculation about such biological constraints is Shettleworth's (1973) recent work. She has demonstrated that food is an effective reinforcement for a number of responses emitted by the hamster, *Mesocricetus auratus,* but will not function as a reward for various grooming responses such as face washing. Data such as these have at least two major implications in the context of the present discussion. First, they directly question the assumption that reinforcers are transitational. If food is an effective reward for rearing responses made by hamsters, it should be an effective reward for face-washing responses in the same species. Hence, along with Premack's model, the response deprivation hypothesis, and the optimal-duration model discussed earlier, the research concerned with biological constraints on instrumental learning runs counter (for very different reasons) to the contemporary tendency to accept the weak law of effect as a point of departure in our analysis of reinforcement. Second, an adequate theory of reinforcement will have to take account of any evidence that there are certain response-reinforcer combinations which are not effective (or vice versa) and will have to describe the conditions under which we can expect to observe such constraints.

Consider, for example, Premack's notion that a low-to-high probability contingency will produce an increase in the probability of instrumental responding. This assumption is directly questioned by Shettleworth's hamster data. Eating was more probable than either rearing or face washing. Nevertheless, eating would reinforce rearing but not face washing. Premack's position seems at the very least to require an additional assumption to subsume these discrepant cases.

In the discussion which follows I shall critically examine some of the theory and data concerned with the role of biological constraints in instrumental learning situations. I have attempted to restrict the discussion to the most recent data and to arguments specifically concerned with constraints upon instrumental *response-reinforcer* combinations. For a more extensive discussion of earlier work and a broader perspective, the reader is urged to consult a number of different reviews already available in the literature (cf., Bolles, 1970; Garcia, McGowan, & Green, 1972; Moore, 1971, 1973; Seligman, 1970; Shettleworth, 1972, 1973; Staddon & Simmelhag, 1971).

The various attempts to explain why particular response-reinforcer combinations are effective while others are not are, in my opinion, all variations on a common theme. The general theme is that an organism has certain species-typical behavior patterns which it exhibits under certain conditions in its natural habitat. To the extent that a particular response-reinforcer combination requires behavior which is consistent with the organism's natural behavior, the reinforcer will be very effective in controlling responding; to the extent that the combination is inconsistent with the organism's natural behavior, the reinforcer will be ineffective. I shall consider several variations on this theme which are to varying degrees successful in translating this idea into a testable proposition.

The "Functional Relevance" Hypothesis

The basic notion is that certain responses are functionally relevant in the context of certain reinforcers but not in the context of other reinforcers. For example, in hamsters, digging responses are usually observed as a part of procuring food, but not seen in situations involving sexual behaviors. The functional relevance hypothesis suggests that a sexually receptive female would not be particularly effective as a reinforcer for digging, since digging is not particularly relevant in the organism's species-typical reactions to sexual stimuli.

Three representative versions of the "functional relevance" hypothesis have emerged in the context of: (1) Shettleworth's work with instrumental reward procedures; (2) work by Walters and Glazer (1971) and Melvin and Ervey (1973) with instrumental punishment procedures; and (3) Bolles's (1970) work with avoidance learning procedures.

Shettleworth (1973) observed golden hamsters in a chamber similar to an open field apparatus which had a sand floor, a magazine for delivering food pellets, and a typical response lever. A number of species-typical behavior patterns were measured: (1) face washing, (2) digging, (3) open rearing, (4) "scrabbling" (which is a type of digging movement with the forelegs on the side walls), and (5) bar pressing (shaping was necessary). After reducing the animals to 80% of their ad lib weights, different groups were exposed to five possible instrumental contingencies with food as the contingent event (e.g., scrabble to eat, face-wash to eat, etc.). Contingent upon performing the appropriate instrumental response for a period of .5 sec, the food pellets were delivered on a variable-interval (VI) 20-sec schedule (following initial sessions of continuous reinforcement). The results demonstrated convincingly that the hamsters increased the probability of four of the five instrumental responses. Face washing was the only instrumental response which could not be brought under the control of the reinforcement contingency, even under extended training conditions with continuous reinforcement.

To account for these results, Shettleworth suggested that face washing was perhaps the only response of the five selected which was not a part of the animal's natural behavioral sequence in obtaining food. There are, however, a number of alternative explanations. First, as Shettleworth recognizes, the hamster needs a supply of saliva in order to lick its paws for face washing. It is possible that the use of the dry food pellets acts to decrease the amount of face washing by using up excess saliva for food mastication. Or the rate of saliva production per se may simply be inadequate for the maintenance of high rates of face washing; i.e., this may be a trivial instance of requiring an animal to perform a response which is beyond its physical capability (like training a rat to fly). As Shettleworth suggests, it would be interesting to repeat these experiments with water as the reinforcer for thirsty hamsters, thus eliminating the problem of a "dry mouth."

There is another explanation for these data that is of particular interest because it has general implications for research of the type reported by Shettleworth. One of the several effects of arranging an instrumental contingency is that the contingent event adds a response to the organism's repertoire in the experimental situation. The food used in Shettleworth's experiments produced a certain amount of eating behavior. The introduction of this response to the organism's repertoire can, in and of itself, facilitate or inhibit other instrumental responding. An extreme case of this can be seen in Figure 5, which presents the results of a simple experiment conducted in our laboratory.

Subject A was a hungry gerbil given free access to three items in an experimental chamber for 1 hr each day. The items were a running wheel, a box of sunflower seeds, and a strip of bristol board for shredding.

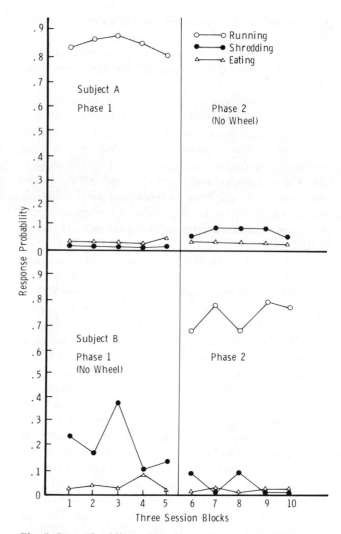

Fig. 5. Paper-shredding and eating response probability as a function of the presence and absence of a running wheel in the environment.

The animal spent 80% of the session running in the wheel, a small amount of time eating seeds, and no time at all shredding the bristol board. In Phase 2 gerbil A was denied access to the running wheel, and the gerbil added paper shredding to the response repertoire and increased the amount of time spent eating. Subject B was exposed to the same conditions in reverse order. During Phase 1 the wheel was not available, and paper shredding was the most probable response in the response repertoire. In Phase 2 the addition of the wheel to the chamber reduced and eventually eliminated paper shredding, and the animal spent 70–80% of the session running.

Thus the addition of running to the response repertoire of the gerbil eliminates paper shredding. The results in general suggest that the simple addition or deletion of a response from the repertoire can have profound effects upon the probability of other existing responses. Although the simple experiment has yet to be completed, it would not be surprising to find that running is not a terribly effective reward for paper shredding, since the former has direct inhibitory effects upon the latter when the two are observed together in the complete absence of the instrumental contingency operation.

It is possible that the basis for predicting the effectiveness of particular response-reinforcer combinations is an understanding of the conditions under which interactions occur between responses in the absence of the contingency. The implication of these observations is that a control condition should always be employed in research of the type reported by Shettleworth in which we measure the probability of the instrumental response in the simple presence and absence of the contingent response prior to arranging any contingency between the two. The reader might note that the rationale for this control is identical to the rationale proposed for the use of a yoked control procedure in the context of Premack's position (p. 106).

Shettleworth gives some attention to this problem of direct inhibitory effects in preliminary work which assessed the effects of both food deprivation and pellet delivery upon the various behaviors measured in the experimental situation. Her observations suggest that such inhibitory interactions among responses might account for the results. For example, she notes that food deprivation (which presumably increased the probability of eating) appeared to inhibit face-washing activity, with little effect upon the other responses. It was not clear from her results if the simple addition of the food pellets per se had any effects upon the alternative responses.

The counterpart to Shettleworth's work with "appetitive" response-reinforcer combinations is some recent work concerned with the possible biological constraints upon "aversive" response-reinforcer combinations. Walters and Glazer (1971), for example, suggest that the organism's species-typical responses to aversive stimulation may not be susceptible to the usual suppressive effects of response-contingent punishment. They observed the behavior of Mongolian gerbils in a large chamber with a sand floor. Two responses, alert posturing and digging in the sand, were selected for study from the gerbil's repertoire. The rationale for selecting these two behaviors was as follows:

> Given the different biological functions of these behaviors, it was felt that they would be differentially affected by punishment. Specifically, we expected digging to be relatively easily suppressed by punishment, while alert posturing, since it itself is a reaction to sudden or aversive stimuli, was expected to show little suppressive effect. (p. 332)

Following their base line observations of digging and alert posturing, and a series of habituation sessions during which a tone was made contingent upon either alert posturing (eight gerbils) or digging (eight gerbils), the gerbils were split into four groups. Two groups received daily classical conditioning sessions in which a tone was paired with a relatively strong shock (2 mA, 1 sec). These conditioning sessions were conducted inside a plexiglass chamber with a grid floor which was placed inside the larger sand chamber. Two control groups received identical treatment without the shock being administered. Following each daily conditioning session, the gerbils were placed back in the experimental chamber with the sand floor and the tone was made contingent upon the digging response (8 gerbils) or upon posturing responses (eight gerbils). When compared to control subjects which had not received the tone-shock pairings, digging was suppressed by the presentation of the conditioned punisher (tone) contingent upon digging. However, alert posturing was facilitated by presentation of the conditioned punisher. Walters and Glazer conclude that the differential effect of the conditioned punisher can best be understood in terms of the differential biological functions served by these two responses in the gerbil's natural environment. Digging is presumably associated with nest building and food gathering, and alert-posturing with the animal's defensive reactions.

There is, however, a plausible alternative explanation for these results. We have observed, informally, that these desert rodents appear to reduce the aversiveness of grid shocks by rocking back on the insulating fur of their hind legs into a position which very much resembles alert posturing as described by Walters and Glazer. Hence, it seems possible that the animals exposed to the classical conditioning procedure might have learned this type of alert-posturing response as a preparatory response to the tone in anticipation of the impending shock. During subsequent punishment training, the gerbil's reaction to the tone would then be the conditioned "posturing" response. This would also account for their observation that animals punished for digging also increased the amount of alert posturing during suppression of the digging response.

Presumably, if digging could have served as a preparatory response during classical conditioning sessions, results exactly opposite to those reported by

Walters and Glazer could have been obtained. Any reference to the presumed biological function of the response in the animal's natural habitat would be unjustified.

Until appropriate controls are added to determine if such preparatory behaviors were acquired during the classical conditioning phase of the study, one cannot accept the interpretation offered by Walters and Glazer.

A second, more recent experiment, which claims to have demonstrated that the organism's species-typical reactions to danger or threat are not susceptible to the usual suppressive effects of punishment, was reported by Melvin and Ervey (1973). These authors punished the gill-extension response which is part of the aggressive display of Siamese fighting fish (*Betta splendens*) in response to the presence of a conspecific (or mirror image). In this experiment each fish was exposed to its mirror image for 60 consecutive trials, each 2 min in duration, with an intertrial interval of 40–60 sec. Using this basic procedure the fish were randomly assigned to one of five different treatment conditions. Group HC was a habituation control to monitor the decline in responding which is typically observed over trials with this procedure; two groups, 7E and 7L, received a 7-V electric shock as the punishing stimulus either early in training (trials 16–30), or late in training (trials 45–60). Similarly, two groups, 13E and 13L, received a 13-V electric shock either early or late in training. The results indicated that the intense 13-V shock suppressed gill extension whether presented during early or late trials. The 7-V mild shock, however, did not suppress the gill extension when presented during early trials and *facilitated* gill extension responses when presented during the late trials. Suppression or facilitation was always measured relative to the performance of the habituation controls, which revealed a steady decline over the course of training.

Melvin and Ervey suggest that the facilitation of gill extension in the 7L group indicates that species-typical aggressive behaviors are perhaps not susceptible to the usual suppressive effects of mild punishment. Again, however, a number of problems with the experiment suggest that the conclusion is premature.

First, a control is required in which a referent response (with the same operant rate) is used that does not have the unique biological function. It is possible that Melvin and Ervey would have observed the same results using sexual or feeding behavior, indicating that the results were not unique to the presumed function of the response.

Second, it seems possible that the same results might be obtained by simply presenting a novel stimulus to the 7L group instead of the mild electric shock which was assumed to be aversive. Brimer (1970) has demonstrated that the effects of a novel stimulus upon an ongoing response are dependent upon the operant level of that response. For a given response, the presentation of a novel stimulus will reduce the rate of responding if that rate is very high or increase (disinhibit) the rate of responding if the base line response is very low. Since gill extension had habituated to about half its original probability when the 7L group received the mild shock, it is possible that the increase was an instance of disinhibition similar to that described by Brimer. A novel stimulus control group would presumably answer this question.

In view of the problems with the preceding experiments and with a number of other experiments in the literature which suggest that elicited defensive or aggressive reactions can be suppressed by response-contingent punishment (cf. Azrin, 1970; Baenninger & Grossman, 1969), the view that the animal's defensive response repertoire is refractory to the effects of punishment contingencies seems questionable at this point.

Having considered the recent evidence which argues for important biological constraints in the context of reward and punishment contingencies, we can now turn to the third variation on the basic theme which occurs in the context of avoidance learning. Bolles (1970) has been most explicit in developing the notion of biological constraints on avoidance learning. His hypothesis, which is referred to as the *species-specific defense reaction* (SSDR) *hypothesis*, states:

> For an [avoidance response] to be rapidly learned in a given situation, the response must be an effective SSDR in that situation and when rapid learning does occur, it is primarily due to the suppression of ineffective SSDR's. (p. 35)

Bolles uses this argument effectively to explain why certain responses such as lever pressing are not readily acquired as avoidance responses (cf. Meyer, Cho, & Wesemann, 1960) and why, when such responses are readily trained, they are observed to be modified forms of defensive reactions such as freezing (cf. Bolles & McGillis, 1968).

The primary evidence cited in support of Bolles's hypothesis was an experiment in which rats were placed in a running wheel and required to make one of three different responses in order to avoid a signaled shock (Bolles, 1969). The responses were rearing on the hind legs, a 180-deg about-face, or a 90-deg revolution of the wheel. The results clearly indicate that the running response was more rapidly acquired than the turning response, and that rearing was not increased at all by the avoidance contingency. This conclusion held true whether running was also required as the escape response or whether some alternative behavior was required as the escape response. Bolles concludes from these results that the speed of learning an avoidance response can be related to the animal's species-specific defense reactions, and that running, as a part of the animal's natural reactions to aversive stimuli, will be rapidly acquired relative to responses like turning and rearing which are not primarily defensive reactions.

More recent experiments reported by Grossen and Kelley (1972) lead to a similar conclusion. These authors observed that rats placed in a large chamber tend to spend more time in contact with the walls of the chamber (thigmotaxis) and more time in a "freezing" posture when exposed to intermittent electric shock from a grid floor than they do under appetitively motivated conditions. They suggested that this thigmotactic behavior is one of the rat's species-specific defense reactions and should, according to Bolles, be acquired very rapidly as an avoidance response. In a subsequent procedure using the same large chamber, two platforms were placed in the chamber; one around the perimeter of the chamber and one in the center of the chamber. Three groups of rats were assigned to one of three avoidance learning conditions: Group C only had access to the center platform as a place to avoid or escape the shock; Group P had access to the perimeter platform; and Group PC had access to both. In 30 subsequent acquisition trials in which the animals were placed in the chamber and had to jump on one of the platforms to escape or avoid shock, Group P made 77% avoidance responses, Group C 57%, and Group PC 72% with 92% of the responses going to the perimeter platform. In a similar control experiment, three groups of rats were required to climb either the center or perimeter platforms to obtain food pellets or given a choice of platforms. No differences in acquisition performance were observed, and no systematic preference between platforms was observed.

Although the results are suggested to support Bolles's SSDR hypothesis, there is an equally obvious alternative which Grossen and Kelly recognize. If one simply assumes that shock increases the operant rate (probability of contact) with the perimeter platform, the different rates of acquisition can be considered to reflect differences in the initial operant rate of the two responses. It would be of some interest to replicate the experiment reported by Grossen and Kelley and use a forced-choice procedure in the early acquisition trials to make sure operant rates to each platform were equated, then give the animals a choice of the center vs. the perimeter to see which is preferred.

There are at least two general criticisms of Bolles's (1970) position which should be noted. Consider a hypothetical case of an animal with a repertoire of two responses: A and B. If an aversive stimulus is now introduced, typically a third response (or group of responses) will begin to occur which Bolles would call the animal's species-specific defense reaction(s). According to Bolles, the SSDR will be acquired more rapidly as an avoidance response than either response A or response B. I would suggest that this might often be observed to be the case, but only because the SSDR has a unique advantage over responses A and B. The SSDR is sequentially dependent upon the aversive stimulus and as such predicts the absence of that aversive stimulus for a longer period of time than any other response in the animal's repertoire. This implicit avoidance contingency provides an alternative explanation for the observation that shock-elicited behaviors are often observed to develop rapidly as avoidance responses—an alternative, that is, to the notion that these responses enjoy a special status as members of the category known as the animal's natural defense reactions. A more extensive analysis of this implicit contingency and its implications for avoidance learning has already been considered elsewhere and need not be repeated here (cf. Dunham, 1971).

A second and perhaps more important criticism of Bolles's position can also be directed at the other variations on the "functional relevance hypothesis" which I have considered on the preceding pages. As stated at present, most versions of the functional relevance hypothesis are very much ad hoc propositions. There is no clearly defined criterion for determining, independent of the rate of learning, whether a particular response is or is not "functionally relevant." It is not unusual to find various proponents of the notion elaborating at length about how a particular operant might be considered a short-term mutation of behavior in the wild. For example, in discussing the differential rates at which rats acquire an avoidance response in the shuttlebox and in an activity wheel, Bolles (1970) states:

> It cannot be argued that running in the wheel constitutes an effective SSDR while running in the shuttlebox is marginally effective merely

because the former is more rapidly acquired than the latter. From the viewpoint of the SSDR hypothesis, both situations are ambiguous in that they permit only limited or compensated flight. The running wheel has been recognized as a peculiar piece of apparatus by many investigators who have used it in general activity studies, however, and perhaps it does permit the rat to get away in some meaningful sense. (p. 38)

Until less arbitrary, independent criteria for determining membership in various response categories is proposed, it will not be possible to conduct critical tests of the suggestion that certain response-reinforcer combinations are constrained because the response is not "functionally relevant" in the context of the reinforcer.

As stated earlier, the same problem is characteristic of the other versions of the functional relevance hypothesis which have been considered. For example, Shettleworth suggests that face washing is not a functionally relevant response in the context of food gathering, but that rearing, digging, scrabbling, and lever pressing are. To argue, alternatively, that rearing could be considered a part of the animal's defense reactions and that bar pressing is not particularly concerned with food gathering would simply beg the question. What is needed if the "functional relevance" hypothesis is going to be testable is an independent criterion for defining "functional relevance."

There are, in my opinion, two recent developments in this area of research which escape, to some extent, this problem of ad hoc reference to the biological significance of the response and provide us with some independent criteria for predicting whether or not a particular response-reinforcer combination will be effective. Black and Young (1972) working with rats and avoidance responding have suggested what might be called a *systems constraint hypothesis*. Moore (1971, 1973) working with pigeons and an autoshaping procedure, and Sevenster (1973) working with sticklebacks, have both proposed what might be called a *Pavlovian hypothesis*. In the remaining discussion I shall briefly consider each of these two hypotheses and the associated data.

The "Systems Constraint" Hypothesis

Black and Young (1972) recently reported an interesting experiment in which one group of thirsty rats was trained to bar-press for food during presentation of one discriminative stimulus (S^D) and to lick a drinking tube to avoid shocks during a second S^D. The animals learned the appropriate responses in order to obtain food and avoid the shocks. Following the period of initial training, the rats were satiated with water prior to some training sessions. On these days, the licking avoidance behavior dropped out and the animal took a substantial number of shocks, while lever pressing for food was maintained at its previous level. Black and Young interpret these results in terms of *system constraints*. Specifically, they suggest that the normal causal factors of a response (e.g., the water regulatory system) may place constraints on the extent to which that response can be brought under the control of a different set of factors (e.g., the avoidance contingency). If the normal causal factors for drinking are present (e.g., deprivation), the animal will learn to drink to avoid shocks; if the normal causal factors are not there, drinking will not be controlled by the avoidance contingency. Bar pressing is assumed not to be under any such system constraints. To quote Black and Young:

> It would seem, then, that one dimension along which responses might be classified is the degree to which they are constrained from being changed by operant reinforcement by the properties of the regulatory systems of which they are a part. The criterion for classifying responses is not so much the conditionability of the response or its ease of conditioning under optimal circumstances, but rather the limitations on such conditioning. In this sense, bar pressing might be described as a better operant than drinking because it is less constrained by the regulatory control system of which it is a part then is drinking. (p. 44)

Stated as such, the proposition suggested by Black and Young is as ad hoc as some of those discussed earlier and differs very little from the functional relevance hypothesis. There is no criterion specified which would permit us to know, a priori, whether or not the regulatory system of a response will place constraints upon its use as an operant. Consider, for example, trying to predict whether a gerbil's running behavior or paper-shredding behavior would be subject to serious "system constraints" of the sort observed when drinking was used as an avoidance behavior. It is not possible, from the preceding comments, to determine if these responses are subject to such constraints independent of the situation in which the constraints are observed to operate.

Black and Young do, however, recognize the problem and offer a partial escape from it by making use of Vanderwolf's (1969) observation that some phasic skeletal movements are accompanied by dorsal hippocampal theta waves while others are not. Responses typically labeled "instinctive" or "consummatory" (eating, drinking, etc.) are not accompanied by theta activity. Black and Young suggest that responses which are not accompanied by theta waves from the dorsal hippocampus *will be constrained* as operants by their normal regulatory system; responses which are accompanied by theta activity *will not be constrained*.

Hence we are now in a position to make some testable predictions and, hopefully, accept or reject the "system constraints" hypothesis. For example, if theta waves do not accompany paper-shredding behavior in the gerbil, its use as an avoidance operant should be constrained in Black and Young's study. Specifically, if paper shredding is established as a Sidman avoidance response, satiation of the paper-shredding behavior should reduce avoidance responding. If it does not, we can reject the theta wave criterion and the system constraints hypothesis, unless someone wants to argue about the "normal" causal factors for paper shredding in gerbils. To my knowledge, such an experimental test has not been conducted.

The Pavlovian Hypothesis

Another formulation which generates a number of testable predictions is the *Pavlovian hypothesis*. Moore (1971, 1973), working primarily in the context of the "autoshaping phenomenon" reported by Brown and Jenkins (1968), suggests that most instrumental learning situations also contain the necessary ingredients for the emergence of classically conditioned responses and that such implicit conditioning can either facilitate or inhibit the effectiveness of certain response-reinforcer combinations.

The manner in which this Pavlovian conditioning mechanism is suggested to operate is best explained by direct reference to some of the data which argue, quite convincingly, for its existence. Brown and Jenkins (1968) reported that repeated pairings of an illuminated response key and the presentation of grain were sufficient to cause pigeons to peck the key when it was illuminated. As Moore (1973) suggests, this phenomenon, called *autoshaping,* is potentially important because it indicates that a standard Pavlovian conditioning procedure "could generate the key-pecking response so often used in operant conditioning research" (p. 160). Moore presents a varied array of data which argue collectively that the instrumental key peck is primarily the product of a Pavlovian process. It will be possible to consider only the most direct arguments in the present discussion. A series of well-controlled experiments done in collaboration with Jenkins (cf. Jenkins & Moore, 1973) are perhaps most convincing. These authors demonstrated that birds concurrently autoshaped with grain and water reinforcement "pecked" the key stimulus associated with grain and "drank" the key stimulus associated with water reinforcement. These results, which were observed when birds were both hungry and thirsty, indicate that an organism develops a conditioned response to the manipulandum which is similar in topography to the response elicited by the reinforcer.

David Rackham, a graduate student in Moore's laboratory, conducted similar experiments (Rackham, 1971) in which a light stimulus was paired with access to a sexually receptive female pigeon. Although the controls for nonassociative effects were less extensive than in the food and water experiments, the results indicated that the topography of the response to the light was similar to the topography of the response to the female. Specifically, the male bird tended to "court" the visual stimulus.

In the context of the autoshaping procedure, perhaps the most direct rationale for determining if the instrumental response emerges from a Pavlovian process, as opposed to adventitious reinforcement of arbitrary, emitted operants, is to use an omission training procedure in which any pecks made during the presentation of the conditioned stimulus actually cancel the presentation of grain on that trial. If the pecking actually develops from the Pavlovian contingency, the animal should persist in pecking the conditioned stimulus at rates appropriate to a partial-reinforcement schedule. If the pecking develops from the adventitious reinforcement of emitted skeletal movements, the omission training contingency prevents such reinforcement, and pecking should not develop. Results of an omission training experiment conducted by Audrey Kirby (1968), another of Moore's students, and by Williams and Williams (1969) indicate that the omission procedure does not stop the development of pecking in the autoshaping procedure, hence supporting the Pavlovian mechanism.

Of several implications of Moore's work, the one which is most directly relevant in the context of the present discussion is that such Pavlovian conditioning would be expected to make certain response-reinforcer combinations very effective, while others would not work very well at all. Specifically, if the instrumental response which we require of the organism is compatible with the species-typical reaction (unconditioned response) elicited by the reinforcer, the reinforcer should very rapidly gain control over the instrumental behavior. If, alternatively, the instrumental response we require is not compatible with the species-typical reaction elicited by the reinforcer, the reinforcer should not be very effective in gaining control over the instrumental behavior. Hence if we can specify what the unconditioned response to a particular reinforcer will be and determine if that response is incompatible with the instrumental response, it is possible to predict whether a particular response-reinforcer combination will be effective or not. Moore (1971, 1973) describes a number of examples of effective and ineffective response-reinforcer combinations from both the ethology literature and the operant conditioning literature which support his contention. Pigeons, for example, can easily be trained to peck a key for food, since the unconditioned response to grain (pecking) is perfectly compatible with the instrumental response (pecking). Alternatively, a number of examples indicate that it is very difficult to train a bird to peck a key in order to avoid shock (cf. Hoffman & Fleshler, 1969). When key pecking is developed with any impressive reliability as an avoidance response, either elaborate shaping (see Perrari, Todoroff, & Graeff, 1973) or an extensive history of food reinforced pecking (see Foree & LoLordo, 1974) appears to be necessary. In defense of the Pavlovian hypothesis, Moore (1973, p. 172) has argued persuasively that many instances of key-pecking avoidance might be interpreted as elicited aggressive reactions to the aversive stimuli.

Bolles's SSDR hypothesis, considered earlier, is similar in spirit to Moore's Pavlovian mechanism when the latter is considered in the context of avoidance learning. Bolles's SSDRs are, in effect, unconditioned responses to aversive stimuli. The essential difference between the two positions with reference to avoidance learning is that Moore's Pavlovian mechanism is more precisely specified and testable, and vulnerable for that reason. To the extent that it becomes difficult to specify, a priori, in a given situation what the unconditioned response and the relevant conditioned stimuli are, Moore's Pavlovian mechanism could also become an ad hoc proposition which is difficult to disprove.

In addition to the various evidence reviewed by Moore in support of the Pavlovian analysis, several more recent experiments have appeared which are directly relevant to the suggestion that this mechanism can facilitate or inhibit the effectiveness of certain response-reinforcer combinations.

Peterson, Ackil, Frommer, and Hearst (1972) paired a 15-sec presentation of a retractable lever with either food reinforcement or intracranial stimulation (ICS) in two different groups of rats. A second retractable lever in the same chamber was presented randomly without any relationship to the other events in the chamber. A measure of the number of contacts with the lever indicated that the rats, like the pigeons in Brown and Jenkins's (1968) experiment, learned to contact the lever if it signaled food or ICS and paid little attention to the random lever. Of more interest, videotaped records of the rats' behavior revealed qualitative differences in the response made to the lever by subjects receiving food and the response made to the lever by subjects receiving ICS. According to Peterson et al., in the group receiving the food reward "visual observations and the videotaped records revealed that contacts of CS+ were almost exclusively oral and consisted mainly of licking responses and gnawing behavior" (p. 1010). Alternatively, in the group receiving the ICS reward the rats typically showed sniffing and exploratory behavior of the same type as *elicited by the ICS alone*. These results directly support the main implication of Moore's Pavlovian analysis—that the unconditioned response to the reinforcer determines the topography of the response to stimuli paired with that reinforcer.

A second, more recent experiment reported by Wasserman (1973) appears, however, to pose some problems for Moore's Pavlovian mechanism. Wasserman used 3-day-old chicks as subjects and an autoshaping procedure which consisted of 50 daily pairings of an 8-sec green key light with the 4-sec activation of a heat lamp located in the ceiling of a small chamber. The chicks, which were placed in the cold chamber, pecked the green response key on 80% of the trials, as compared to a group presented with the stimuli using Rescorla's (1967) random control procedure. When the experimental group was subsequently switched to the random control condition, the pecking slowly extinguished. When the random group was switched to paired stimulus conditions, they started to peck and reached an asymptote of pecking on 40% of the trials.

In order to determine if the emergence of key pecking in this situation was the result of Pavlovian as compared to instrumental contingencies, chicks were trained using an omission procedure in which pecks on the key would cancel the forthcoming heat lamp. The results, similar to those reported by Kirby (1968) and described earlier, indicated that all chicks did peck the key at reduced rates under the omission training contingency. The omission training results provide strong support for Moore's suggestion that autoshaping phenomena are under Pavlovian rather than instrumental control. A problem arises, however, with the implication of Moore's analysis, which requires that the unconditioned response to the reinforcer will determine the topography of the response to the operant manipulandum. In Wasserman's procedure, the response to the heat lamp was suggested to be a species-typical wing-extension response, yet the initial autoshaped response was to *peck* the light. Wasserman notes that the pecking response was observed during early trials and eventually gave way to a response which he described as "snuggling up to the response key." It would appear then that Wasserman is dealing with a Pavlovian phenomenon, but one in which the conditioned and unconditioned responses are completely different in topography.

Some recent work appears to reconcile Wasserman's results with Moore's Pavlovian analysis. Hogan (1974) observed that chicks placed in a cold environment often peck at their mother, causing the adult bird to move closer, providing a source of heat. Hence pecking at warm objects is one of a number of unconditioned responses to the cold environment employed by Wasserman which might be expected to emerge from the autoshaping procedure.

Although there is a substantial amount of support for Moore's suggestion, a potential problem with his analysis is hinted at by the difficulty encountered trying to interpret Wasserman's data. When a bug enters the visual field of a hungry frog, the unconditioned response (UR) seems to be the result of some precise and hard-wired circuitry between visual input and tongue. Hence there is no basis for confusion when attempting to specify the UR a priori, or in recognizing what responses are compatible or incompatible with that tongue flip. Higher up the phylogenetic scale, however, that "hard wiring" appears to disappear in a good many cases with the net result that the UR to a given stimulus is much less predictable. Hence a strict application of Moore's analysis in the case of higher organisms would require, as he has indicated, a more extensive analysis of what factors determine which of several possible URs will emerge in a given situation.

The final position to be considered was proposed by Sevenster (1973) and is very similar to Moore's Pavlovian mechanism. In initial experimentation Sevenster observed that a male stickleback (*Gasterosteus aculeatus*) would readily learn to swim through a ring or bite the top of a rod in order to be able to attack another male stickleback displayed at the end of an aquarium. Both of these instrumental responses were performed at very high rates with short interresponse intervals. When a sexually ripe female was used as the reinforcer, however, a male stickleback again learned how to swim through a ring at high stable rates, but revealed very slow and variable rod-biting performance. It appeared from these data that some type of constraint was operating which prevented rod-biting behavior from developing when courting a female was the reinforcer.

In subsequent experiments, Sevenster analyzed interresponse times when the courtship reinforcer was presented on a variable-ratio schedule for rod biting. The results indicated that the interval between rod-biting responses got shorter as the interval of time since the last reward got longer. The longest interresponse interval was observed to be immediately after the opportunity to court. Taken together, the results indicate that some property of courtship behavior actually inhibits (temporarily) the ability of the animal to perform the biting response.

In order to determine if the actual pairing of the rod biting with the courtship response was necessary for such inhibition to be observed, Sevenster conducted yet another experiment in which a male fish was trained to bite the rod in order to attack another male. As in earlier experiments, the response was rapidly acquired and performed at a high rate. Once the fish was biting the rod at high rates, a sexually ripe female was introduced into the tank for brief periods of courtship, with care taken not to associate the rod with the courtship response. A comparison of the latency between the opportunity to court and the next biting response and the opportunity to fight and the next biting response indicated that the opportunity to court had little effect upon the latency to the next bite. The results of this experiment (which used only one subject and should be extended) indicate that the inhibitory effect which courtship has upon biting behavior depends upon the prior temporal pairings of the operant manipulandum with the sexually ripe female.

Of equal interest are Sevenster's anecdotal observations of what the fish were actually doing during the long interresponse intervals following presentation of the sexually ripe female. He observed:

> The fish would approach the rod and start circling around it with zig-zag like jumps and often with open mouth, sometimes making snapping movements at the tip or softly touching it. (p. 277)

In other words, the fish was treating the rod tip like a "dummy female," and the behavior during the long interresponse intervals was the species-typical courtship ritual.

Sevenster's interpretation of these results is identical, in some respects, to Moore's suggested Pavlovian process. With reference to the courtship experiments, Sevenster suggests that the fish are conditioned to react to the biting rod as a "dummy female" and respond to it with courtship behaviors which are incompatible with the biting behavior required. Alternatively, swimming through the ring is suggested to be compatible with the elicited approach responses associated with courtship and aggression; hence this response is performed at relatively high rates. It would, however, be interesting to know if the swimming response did reveal the topography appropriate to the reinforcement. Presumably, the way a fish swims through a ring would differ depending upon his intentions to fight or to copulate.

Up to this point, the results of Sevenster's experiments and his analysis are completely compatible with Moore's analysis and results which were developed in the context of autoshaping. In addition to the Pavlovian mechanism, Sevenster suggests that there may be a mutually inhibitory interaction between the motivational system which controls courtship and the motivational system which controls aggressive behavior. Without entering the semantic jungle which attempts to distinguish between associative and non-associative effects, it is suggested that the data considered thus far do not seem to justify the introduction of hypothetical competing "motivational states." It should be difficult enough to determine if two observable responses are "compatible" or "incompatible" using the relatively parsimonious Pavlovian mechanism outlined by Moore.

In summary, there is a growing amount of evidence to indicate that not all response-reinforcer combinations are equally effective in developing control over instrumental behavior. I have attempted to isolate and criticize several variations on the general theme that the organism brings certain "biological predispositions" into the instrumental learning situation which either facilitate or inhibit the development of instrumental responding. Of these variations, I would suggest that Black and Young's system constraints hypothesis and Moore and Sevenster's Pavlovian hypothesis have the advantage of being vulnerable to relatively precise testing and have generated the most convincing data.

CONCLUDING COMMENTS

We started the discussion with the relatively concrete problem of predicting the outcome of any one of 20 possible instrumental contingencies which might be arranged in the hypothetical world of our gerbil. We considered a number of different contemporary positions, all of which reject the "weak law of effect" as a point of departure for the analysis of reinforcement phenomena. The six positions considered were: (a) Premack's differential probability position; (b) the response deprivation hypothesis; (c) the optimal-duration model; (d) the functional relevance hypothesis; (e) the system constraints hypothesis; and (f) the Pavlovian hypothesis. The last three positions emphasize the importance of the biological predispositions of particular species in attempting to predict the effectiveness of particular response-reinforcer combinations. The first three positions have, in general, ignored such biological constraints and concentrated upon developing a set of predictive rules which are implicitly assumed to hold for all species and response-reinforcer combinations.

Each of the above approaches offers a viable alternative to the weak law of effect as a point of departure in our analysis of the reinforcement process. They are not, however, without their problems. The major problem with Premack's differential probability position and with the response deprivation hypothesis is that much of the research surrounding these positions has failed to include control conditions to determine if the changes in instrumental behavior can be produced by changing the distribution and/or amount of contingent responding without a contingency in effect. It is possible that many of the increases in instrumental responding that have been interpreted as evidence for a reinforcement process in the context of the Premackian methodology would have occurred in the absence of the reinforcement operation, i.e., an instrumental response requirement.

As a viable alternative to both the response deprivation hypothesis and Premack's differential probability rules the optimal-duration model also remains to be investigated before either of the former positions can be unequivocally accepted or rejected.

The three positions which have emphasized the role of biological constraints which operate upon particular response-reinforcer combinations also suffer some serious problems. A number of specific criticisms were offered with reference to specific experimentation in this area in the preceding discussion. These criticisms are, however, overshadowed by the general lack of precise definitions and testability which is characteristic of many theoretical notions in this area. Before one can test predictions made by the functional relevance hypothesis, for example, it is necessary to have a precise definition of the term *functional relevance* which can be translated in experimental operations. There is no doubt that the three positions which have emphasized the importance of biological constraints directly question the generality of alternative theoretical accounts of reinforcement such as Premack's differential probability rules and the response deprivation hypothesis. They imply, for example, that the response deprivation rule will not apply to particular cases. In some instances substantial reductions in the amount of contingent responding will not increase instrumental responding, while in others an increase in instrumental responding might be observed without a reduction in contingent responding. In order, however, to pit the response deprivation hypothesis against such positions as the functional relevance hypothesis, it will be necessary to have some method of determining if particular response-reinforcer combinations are "functionally relevant" prior to conducting the experiment.

It seems, at present, reasonable to assume that theoretical schemes such as Premack's probability rules, the response deprivation hypothesis, and the optimal-duration model will have to be modified to account for the biological predispositions which are being discussed by theorists such as Shettleworth, Moore, and Sevenster. It will be helpful, when these two contemporary approaches to reinforcement are merged in a theoretical scheme, if both approaches are precisely enough formulated to produce testable hypotheses.

REFERENCES

Allison, J., & Timberlake, W. Instrumental and contingent saccharin licking in rats: Response deprivation and reinforcement. *Learning and Motivation*, 1974, *5*, 231–247.

Azrin, N. H. Punishment of elicited aggression. *Journal of the Experimental Analysis of Behavior*, 1970, *14*, 7–10.

Baenninger, R., & Grossman, J. C. Some effects of punishment on pain elicited aggression. *Journal of the Experimental Analysis of Behavior*, 1969, *12*, 1017–1022.

Baum, W. H. The correlation based law of effect. *Journal of the Experimental Analysis of Behavior*, 1973, *20*, 137–153.

Bernstein, D. J. *Structure and function in response repertoires of humans.* Unpublished doctoral dissertation, University of California at San Diego, 1973.

Black, A. H., & Young, G. A. Constraints on the operant conditioning of drinking. In R. M. Gilbert & J. R. Millenson (Eds.), *Reinforcement: Behavioral analyses.* New York: Academic Press, 1972.

Bolles, R. C. Avoidance and escape learning: Simultaneous acquisition of different responses. *Journal of Comparative and Physiological Psychology*, 1969, *68*, 355–358.

Bolles, R. C. Species-specific defense reactions and avoidance learning. *Psychological Review*, 1970, *77*, 32–48.

Bolles, R. C., & McGillis, D. B. The non-operant nature of the barpress escape response. *Psychonomic Science*, 1968, *11*, 261–262.

Brimer, C. J. Disinhibition of an operant response. *Learning and Motivation*, 1970, *1*, 346–371.

Brown, P. L., & Jenkins, H. M. Auto-shaping of the pigeon's key-peck. *Journal of the Experimental Analysis of Behavior*, 1968, *11*, 1–8.

Campbell, B., & Lynch, G. S. Influence of hunger and thirst on the relationship between spontaneous activity and body temperature. *Journal of Comparative and Physiological Psychology*, 1968, *65*, 492–498.

Dunham, P. J. Contrasted conditions of reinforcement: A selective critique. *Psychological Bulletin*, 1968, *69*, 295–315.

Dunham, P. J. Punishment: Method and theory. *Psychological Review*, 1971, *78*, 58–70.

Dunham, P. J. Some effects of punishment upon unpunished responding. *Journal of the Experimental Analysis of Behavior*, 1972, *17*, 443–450.

Eisenberger, R., Karpman, M., & Trattner, J. What is the necessary and sufficient condition for reinforcement in the contingency situation? *Journal of Experimental Psychology*, 1967, *74*, 342–350.

Ferrari, E. A., Todorov, J. C., & Graeff, F. G. Nondiscriminated avoidance of shock by pigeons pecking a key. *Journal of the Experimental Analysis of Behavior*, 1973, *19*, 211–218.

Foree, D. D., & LoLordo, V. M. Transfer of the pigeon's key peck from food reinforcement to avoidance of shock. *Journal of the Experimental Analysis of Behavior*, 1974, *22*, 251–259.

Garcia, J., McGowan, B. K., & Green, K. F. Sensory quality and integration: Constraints on conditioning. In A. H. Black & W. F. Prokasy (Eds.), *Classical conditioning.* Englewood Cliffs, N.J.: Prentice-Hall, Inc., 1972.

Grossen, N. E. & Kelley, M. J. Species-specific avoidance behavior in rats. *Journal of Comparative and Physiological Psychology*, 1972, *81*, 307–310.

Hoffman, H. S., & Fleshler, M. Aversive control with the pigeon. *Journal of the Experimental Analysis of Behavior*, 1959, *2*, 213–218.

Hogan, J. Respondents in Pavlovian conditioning. *Science*, 1974, *186*, 156–157.

Holstein, S. B., & Hundt, A. G. Reinforcement of intracranial self-stimulation by licking. *Psychonomic Science*, 1965, *3*, 17–18.

Hull, C. L. *Principles of behavior: An introduction to behavior theory.* New York: Appleton-Century, 1943.

Hull, C. L. *A behavior system.* New Haven: Yale University Press, 1952.

Hundt, A. G., & Premack, D. Running as both a positive and negative reinforcer. *Science*, 1963, *142*, 1087–1088.

Jenkins, H., & Moore, B. R. The form of the auto-shaped response with food or water reinforcers. *Journal of the Experimental Analysis of Behavior*, 1973, *20*, 163–182.

Kirby, A. J. *Explorations of the Brown-Jenkins auto-shaping phenomenon.* Unpublished masters thesis, Dalhousie University, 1968.

Marmaroff, S. *Reinforcement: A test of Premack's differential probability rules.* Unpublished master's thesis, Dalhousie University, 1971.

Meehl, P. E. On the circularity of the law of effect. *Psychological Bulletin,* 1950, *47,* 52–75.

Melvin, K. B., & Ervey, D. H. Facilitative and suppressive effects of punishment of species-typical aggressive display in *Betta splendens. Journal of Comparative and Physiological Psychology,* 1973, *83,* 451–457.

Meyer, D. R., Cho, C., & Wesemann, A. F. On problems of conditioning discriminated lever press avoidance responses. *Psychological Review,* 1960, *67,* 224–228.

Miller, N. E. Some reflections on the law of effect produce a new alternative to drive reduction. In M. R. Jones (Ed.), *Nebraska Symposium on Motivation.* Lincoln: University of Nebraska Press, 1963.

Miller, N. E. Learning of visceral and glandular responses. *Science,* 1969, *163,* 434–445.

Moore, B. R. On directed respondents. Doctoral dissertation, Stanford University, 1971. Ann Arbor, Michigan: University Microfilms No. 72–11, 623.

Moore, B. R. The role of directed Pavlovian reactions in simple instrumental learning in the pigeon. In R. Hinde & J. Hinde (Eds.), *Constraints on learning.* New York: Academic Press, 1973.

Peterson, G. B., Ackil, J. E., Frommer, G. P., & Hearst, E. L. Conditioned approach and contact behavior toward signals for food and brain stimulation reinforcement. *Science,* 1972, *177,* 1009–1011.

Premack, D. Toward empirical behavior laws, I: Positive reinforcement. *Psychological Review,* 1959, *66,* 219–233.

Premack, D. Reversibility of the reinforcement relation. *Science,* 1962, *136,* 255–257.

Premack, D. Rate-differential reinforcement in monkey manipulation. *Journal of the Experimental Analysis of Behavior,* 1963, *6,* 81–89.

Premack, D. Reinforcement theory. In D. Levine (Ed.), *Nebraska Symposium on Motivation.* Lincoln: University of Nebraska Press, 1965.

Premack, D. Catching up on common sense, or two sides of a generalization: Reinforcement and punishment. In R. Glaser (Ed.), *On the nature of reinforcement.* New York: Academic Press, 1971.

Rachlin, H., & Herrnstein, R. J. Hedonism revisited: On the negative law of effect. In B. A. Campbell & R. M. Church (Eds.), *Punishment and aversive behavior.* Englewood Cliffs, N.J.: Prentice-Hall, Inc., 1969.

Rackham, D. W. *Conditioning of the pigeon's courtship aggressive behavior.* Unpublished masters thesis, Dalhousie University, 1971.

Rescorla, R. A. Pavlovian conditioning in its proper control procedures. *Psychological Review,* 1967, *74,* 71–80.

Schaeffer, R. W. The reinforcement relation as a function of the instrumental response base rate. *Journal of Experimental Psychology,* 1965, *69* 419–425.

Schaeffer, R. W., Hanna, B., & Russo, P. Positive reinforcement: A test of the Premack theory. *Psychonomic Science,* 1966, *4,* 7–8.

Seligman, M. E. P. On the generality of the laws of learning. *Psychological Review,* 1970, *77,* 406–418.

Sevenster, P. Incompatibility of response and reward. In R. Hinde & J. Hinde (Eds.), *Constraints on learning.* New York: Academic Press, 1973.

Shettleworth, S. J. Constraints on learning. In D. S. Lehrman, R. A. Hinde, & E. Shaw (Eds.), *Advances in the Study of Behavior* (Vol. 4). New York: Academic Press, 1972.

Shettleworth, S. J. Food reinforcement and the organization of behavior in golden hamsters. In R. Hinde & J. Hinde (Eds.), *Constraints on learning.* New York: Academic Press, 1973.

Staddon, J. E. R., & Simmelhag, V. L. The "superstition" experiment: A re-examination of its implications for the principles of adaptive behavior. *Psychological Review,* 1971, *78,* 3–43.

Terhune, J. G. & Premack, D. On the proportionality between the probability of not running and the punishment effect of being forced to run. *Learning and Motivation,* 1970, *1,* 141–149.

Thorndike, E. L. *Educational psychology: Briefer course.* New York: Columbia University, 1914.

Thorndike, E. L. *The fundamentals of learning.* New York: Columbia University, 1932.

Timberlake, W., & Allison, J. Response deprivation: An empirical approach to instrumental performance. *Psychological Review,* 1974, *81,* 146–164.

Vanderwolf, C. H. Hippocampal electrical activity and voluntary movement in the rat. *Electroencephalography and Clinical Neurophysiology,* 1969, *26,* 407–418.

Walker, E. L. Reinforcement: The "one ring." In J. T. Tapp (Ed.), *Reinforcement and behavior.* New York: Academic Press, 1969.

Walters, G. C., & Glazer, R. D. Punishment of instinctive behavior in the Mongolian gerbil. *Journal of Comparative and Physiological Psychology,* 1971, *75,* 331–340.

Wasserman, E. A. Pavlovian conditioning with heat reinforcement produces stimulus directed pecking in chicks. *Science,* 1973, *181,* 875–877.

Weisman, R. G., & Premack, D. Reinforcement and punishment produced by the same contingent event. Paper presented at the meetings of the Psychonomic Society, St. Louis, 1966.

Wilcoxon, H. C. Historical introduction to the problem of reinforcement. In J. T. Tapp (Ed.), *Reinforcement and behavior.* New York: Academic Press, 1969.

Williams, D. R., & Williams, H. Auto-maintenance in the pigeon: Sustained pecking despite contingent non-reinforcement. *Journal of the Experimental Analysis of Behavior,* 1969, *12,* 511–520.

5

Schedule-Induced Behavior*

J. E. R. Staddon

INTRODUCTION

In most operant conditioning experiments, a single aspect of behavior such as a key peck or a lever press is selected as the instrumental response. Although a reinforcer will not ordinarily follow every instance of the response, it follows some, usually immediately, and does not occur other times. There are departures from this rule (such as delay of reward procedures, mixed classical and operant procedures, and some conjunctive schedules), but it is so common, and seems so close to the "natural" contingencies of the animal's wild environment that it has become the norm. Yet it embodies a number of arbitrary features: the single instrumental response, the fixed short delay between response and reinforcer, and the absence of reinforcement in the absence of the response. The term "response-contingent reinforcement" usually embraces all three of these features.

Because of the apparent naturalness of the response-contingent procedure, it has held the limelight over the years. A mass of experimental literature has developed describing results that are in many cases difficult to interpret. The ubiquitous feedback loop between behavior and its consequences makes it very hard to discern the behavioral mechanisms that allow the combined animal-schedule system to settle down into the classical "schedule performances." In any response-contingent procedure, the pattern of responding necessarily influences not only the correlation between responding and reinforcement, but also the correlation between reinforcement, and temporal and stimulus variables. For example, if an animal on a fixed-interval schedule responds only sporadically, the reinforcements may occur at variable rather than fixed intervals. Yet it is these temporal correlations (termed by Zeiler "indirect" variables, see Chapter 8) that are most important in determining the final pattern of performance. If the way they act is to be understood, the response contingency is an unnecessary complication. Consequently this chapter is devoted primarily

* Research supported by grants from the National Science Foundation and the National Institute of Mental Health, USPHS, to Duke University. I thank the Department of Experimental Psychology, Oxford University, for facilities during preparation of the chapter. Several colleagues were kind enough to comment on earlier versions. I am especially grateful to Dalbir Bindra, Janice Frank, Werner Honig, Nancy Innis, Peter Killeen, Jock Millenson, Evelyn Segal, and Michael Zeiler.

to behavior induced by response-independent (classical conditioning) procedures, and to those aspects of response-contingent schedules that are not directly dependent on the response contingency.

The term *schedule-induced* does not yet have a widely accepted definition. However, it is clear that when an animal is exposed to a schedule of periodic food or electric shock, some activities are facilitated and others are reduced by this operation. Only those activities that are *facilitated* by the schedule (by comparison with a pre- and post-schedule baseline when no food or shock is delivered) will be termed *induced behaviors*. The term *facultative behavior* has been coined to refer to activities that occur on schedules but do not appear to be directly affected by schedule factors (p. 135).

Schwartz and Gamzu, in Chapter 3 of this volume, discuss the problem of *terminal responses,* i.e., induced behavior that emerges in the presence of, or is directed toward, stimuli that are highly predictive of food or some other positive reinforcer; and Hutchinson in Chapter 14 deals with behavior induced by schedules of aversive events. This chapter is mainly concerned with *interim activities* on schedules of positive reinforcement; that is, induced behaviors which occur at times when a reinforcer is unlikely to be delivered. Terminal responses are discussed only as much as is necessary to present a comprehensive picture of the ways in which induced and facultative behaviors interact under the influence of schedule factors.

The first part of the chapter will be concerned with the factors that determine *what* induced activities will occur, *where* (in relation to time and stimuli) they occur, and *how much* (with what 'strength') they occur. The second part deals with the temporal and sequential constraints that underlie induced behavior sequences.

BEHAVIOR INDUCED BY PERIODIC FOOD

The simplest case to consider is the periodic presentation of "free" food to a hungry rat or pigeon (FT: fixed-time reinforcement). At first, the animal is likely to spend much of its time between food deliveries exploring around the food site. However, within a few sessions this behavior drops out and is replaced by a regular sequence of activities within each interval. Each activity becomes increasingly well defined and the sequence as a whole becomes increasingly stereotyped as training proceeds. Figure 1 shows the patterns of behavior developed by a pigeon and a rat under broadly similar conditions of periodic food delivery. Both animals were hungry. The pigeon was in a bare enclosure and received 3-sec access to food every 12 sec. The rat was in a hexagonal enclosure that allowed drinking and running in a wheel, as well as other activities, and received a food pellet every 30 sec. Despite these differences the general features of the behavior are similar. Activities occur in sequence, with some (interim activities) typically occurring early in the interval (facing the window wall and wing flapping for the pigeon; drinking and running for the rat). A single terminal response (pecking for the

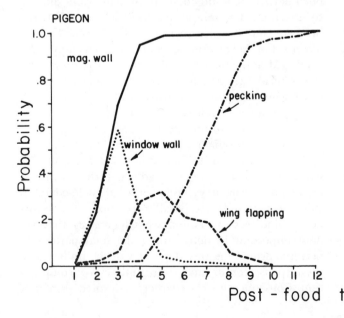
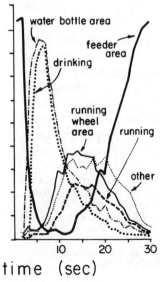

Fig. 1. The relative frequency of various activities as a function of post-food time for a rat (right panel) and a pigeon (left panel) on periodic food schedules. The pigeon data are taken from Staddon and Simmelhag (1971); the bird was on a fixed-time 12 sec schedule. The rat data are from Staddon and Ayres (1975); the rat was on a fixed-time 30 sec schedule in a hexagonal enclosure that permitted drinking, wheel running and other activities in addition to eating.

pigeon; "food anticipation" for the rat) increases in frequency up until the end of the interval. First, I discuss the types of behavior that have been observed under conditions of periodic food delivery. In later sections I consider the sequential properties of induced behavior and the possible mechanisms of interaction that these imply.

Terminal Responses

In the above examples, time is the variable that signals the imminence of food. This is not necessary. Indeed the most popular procedure for studying induced terminal responses (autoshaping: Brown & Jenkins, 1968) follows the standard classical-conditioning paradigm: food is intermittently presented, usually at variable intervals, each delivery being signalled by a brief (5–10 sec) stimulus. The conclusions of this work can be summarized quite briefly (see Ch. 3 for additional references and a fuller account). (1) Some behavior will be induced in the presence of the stimulus that signals food. (2) It seems to be necessary that the stimulus predict food, i.e., precede food more reliably than any other stimulus precedes food. Simple pairing is not enough by itself (Bilbrey & Winokur, 1973; Gamzu & Williams, 1971, 1973; Rescorla, 1967). (3) The type of induced behavior depends on a number of factors. (a) The type and strength of the signalled reinforcer (food, water, shock, sex, etc., cf. Jenkins & Moore, 1973). Often the behavior resembles the consummatory response usually made to the reinforcer. (b) The nature of the signal stimulus, e.g., whether or not it can be manipulated, its location in relation to the reinforcer site, whether it can be sensed without the animal orienting towards it, its intensity, and its biological "relevance" for the signaled reinforcer. (c) Past history, e.g., food-related responses acquired in an instrumental situation may reappear in an autoshaping situation. (d) How good a predictor the signal stimulus is. For example, induced pecking is more likely to develop and is stronger if the signal stimulus is short than if it is long (Innis & Keehn, personal communication; Ricci, 1973) or if the inter-stimulus (inter-trial) interval is long rather than short (Groves & Brownstein, 1973; Terrace, Gibbon, Farrell, & Baldock, 1975; see also Wilton & Clements, 1971). The induced behavior is more likely to resemble the consummatory response, and to be more vigorous, the better the relative proximity of the signal stimulus to the signalled reinforcer (Jenkins, 1970; Hearst & Jenkins, 1974; Staddon & Simmelhag, 1971).

As the chapter by Schwartz and Gamzu in this volume attests, there is still considerable controversy about the correct explanation for the terminal responses which develop on response-independent schedules. A confusing factor is the misleading opposition between "Pavlovian" and "operant" views, as if these two classes were mutually exclusive. Historically this opposition is in part traceable to Skinner's (1948) particular operant account. His "adventitious reinforcement" hypothesis is that a terminal response occurs first for unspecified reasons, is accidentally contiguous with food delivery, is strengthened thereby, and is thus more likely to occur again. This cycle repeats and the result is persistent, stereotyped "superstitious" behavior. This view owes nothing to Pavlovian processes and rests on a contiguity view of the action of reinforcers for which the evidence is weak. Moreover, its lack of any quantitative content robs it of predictive power: How often must a given response be contiguous with reinforcement to become fully conditioned? How contiguous must it be? Are all responses the same in these respects? Without good answers to these questions, the hypothesis is essentially untestable since a response which is increasing in frequency, for whatever reason, is more likely to occur in close proximity to reinforcement and thus to fulfill Skinner's condition for its further increase.

There are several versions of the Pavlovian view of terminal responses. Perhaps the simplest is that any situation which predicts food is likely to induce food-related behavior (cf. Moore, 1973). Hearst and Jenkins have developed a refinement of this view to deal with the directed nature of much induced activity (*sign tracking*: Hearst & Jenkins, 1974). Yet another view points to the effect of *contingency strength* (predictiveness) on the range of behavioral variation (Staddon, 1976): Stimuli that are good predictors of food, for example, reliably produce stereotyped behavior. This restriction of variability is taken as the fundamental property of strong contingencies.

ADVENTITIOUS REINFORCEMENT

Induced behavior is a phenomenon worthy of independent study. It cannot convincingly be dismissed as a curious illustration of learning principles better studied directly in other ways. The latter position is most strongly represented by Skinner's adventitious reinforcement hypothesis. The arguments against this view have been elaborated elsewhere (e.g., Gamzu & Schwartz, 1973; Rachlin & Baum, 1972; Staddon, 1972b, 1976; Staddon & Simmelhag, 1971) and need only be summarized here: (a) During the development of induced terminal responses a response such as the animal's putting its head into the food aperture may predominate for a while, only to be supplanted by another response, such as pecking, despite consistent initial pairing of the first response with food. Adventitious reinforcement cannot account either for the decline in the first activity or the appearance of the second. (b) Terminal responses such as pecking in a food situation are quite resistant to response contingencies that make food delivery less likely if the response occurs (negative automaintenance or omission training: Williams & Williams, 1969). A response that occurs in spite of a negative contingency is unlikely to require a positive one for its maintenance. (c) Negative contingencies do have some suppressive effect on a response such as pecking. However, much of the effect is attributable to effects of the contingency on the frequency and pattern of food delivery, i.e., on temporal and stimulus (not response) contingencies. (d) There is a logical problem in attributing the maintenance of a response to accidental conjunctions between it and food delivery. This problem is not overcome by demonstrating that the imposition of a negative contingency reduces the level of the behavior, even if the reduction is below the level that would be maintained by yoked response-independent food delivery. Showing that a response is sensitive to a real negative contingency does not force the conclusion that its prior occurrence was owing to an accidental positive one. (e) Occasional response-independent food deliveries, superimposed on a baseline of responding maintained by response-dependent food delivery, often result in suppression of the instrumental response, even though the absolute number of response-food conjunctions is increased by this operation (Rachlin & Baum, 1972). The addition of "free" reinforcements makes the instrumental response less *predictive* of the reinforcer. Hence these results support the conclusion from experiments on response-independent procedures that a schedule is effective in modifying behavior only to the extent that it arranges a predictive relation (i.e., a real contingency) between an event (a stimulus or a response) and the occurrence of a reinforcer (Rescorla, 1967; Rescorla & Wagner, 1972).

"Prediction" of reinforcer A by response B means, in this context, that $p(A|B)$ is greater than $p(A|\bar{B})$ or, in temporal terms, that B precedes A more closely than A is preceded by any other response (see Gibbon, Berryman, & Thompson, 1974, for a careful discussion of quantitative measurement of contingency strength). The adventitious reinforcement hypothesis, of course, attends only to positive pairings, i.e., to $p(A|B)$. Moreover, if, in the ideal case, $p(\bar{B})$ approaches zero (the animal does nothing but B), B cannot really be said to predict A, since one of the terms of the relation that defines predictiveness, $p(A|\bar{B})$, has vanished. Thus this hypothesis implies a more primitive view of the concept of contingency than can be justified by recent experimental work.

The adventitious reinforcement hypothesis arose from a tacit assumption that the effects of response-dependent reinforcement are somehow more fundamental than those of response-independent reinforcement. Skinner explained the response-independent case by means of an account derived from experiments on response-dependent reinforcement. Even if he is right in believing that the two cases share common mechanisms, the proper translation may be in the opposite direction. Perhaps mechanisms derived from a study of response-independent procedures can be applied to explain the effects of response-dependent reinforcement. This is not a new idea. However, the failure of the adventitious reinforcement notion, and recent advances in our understanding of the concept of contingency, make it once again a viable one (cf. Schwartz & Gamzu, Chapter 3 in this volume; Staddon, 1976).

Interim Activities

On periodic food schedules a variety of activities occur at times when food delivery cannot occur, for example, early in the interval on fixed-time schedules. Some are directed at objects in the environment (e.g., pecking in birds, chewing, drinking, or pawing by rats), others have no obvious referent (e.g., head bobbing, beak movement, pacing). Directed activities come under the control of their own "incentive stimuli" (Bindra, 1972). All induced activities appear to depend on motivational variables. Two kinds of motivational variable are important: variables related to the scheduled reinforcer (e.g., things that affect hunger, if food is scheduled); and variables related to the particular activity (e.g., to thirst, for induced drinking).

Induced behaviors are not all affected in the same way by schedule variables. Hence there is much need for a "natural history" of induced behaviors. More purely descriptive work needs to be done to map out the sequences of behavior that occur with a variety of combinations of species, schedule, reinforcer, and supporting environment. In the absence of the information such studies could give, generalizations about underlying mechanisms must be tentative. Only one interim activity, schedule-induced drinking, has been studied in anything like the necessary depth (Falk,

1969, 1971). Running (Levitsky & Collier, 1968; Segal, 1969), and schedule-induced aggression (Azrin, Hutchison, & Hake, 1966; Flory, 1969; Richards & Rilling, 1972) have also received some attention. Most of this work has been done with rats. The following discussion, therefore, rests more heavily on these behaviors, and particularly on studies of induced drinking, than is perhaps desirable.

Induced Drinking

Falk (1961) was the first to draw attention to the curious fact that hungry rats responding on a schedule of intermittent food reinforcement will ingest large quantities of water (polydipsia). This occurs even though the rats are not deprived of water, so that their total intake may be several times that necessary to maintain water balance. Since Falk's original paper, he and others have demonstrated induced drinking in numerous species (squirrel monkeys, chimpanzees, pigeons and doves to some degree), and on a variety of intermittent food schedules (see Falk, 1969 and 1971, for reviews).

Falk's original emphasis was on the excessive (polydipsic) aspect of schedule-induced drinking. Hence much of the initial research was an attempt to reconcile the behavior with known regulatory mechanisms. As is by now well known, none of these attempts was wholly successful. Neither central effects, in the form of an altered water balance caused by intermittent food, nor peripheral regulatory mechanisms (the "dry mouth" theory) seem adequate to explain schedule-induced drinking. It would be rash to dismiss this line of work as unprofitable. More recent efforts of this sort (for example, explorations of the link between temperature and water regulation systems, e.g., Carlisle, 1973) may yet uncover a regulatory basis for the effect. However, the relative lack of progress along physiological lines revives interest in the behavioral determinants of the phenomenon. These are the focus of the present account.

The most striking thing about schedule-induced polydipsia is that the total amount of water drunk each day is so much greater than normal. This accounts for Falk's original emphasis on *total intake,* as a function of various schedule variables. However, in most studies of operant behavior the total amount of the behavior is of much less interest than the *rate* at which it occurs, or the *percentage of time* that it takes up (see de Villiers, Chapter 9 and Dunham, Chapter 4 in this volume). Moreover, the obvious adaptiveness of operant behavior in general has long stood in sharp contrast to its maladaptiveness in particular situations. Some years ago, for example, Skinner (1961) pointed out that on certain schedules the energy expended by the animal in responding exceeds that received from the food reinforcement obtained. Despite these failures of energy regulation, response and reinforcement rates usually follow some simple functional relation. Hence total intake may not be the most useful measure of induced drinking. How then should induced behavior be measured?

Measurement of Induced Activities

The most important factor that determines choice of a particular dependent measure is the experimenter's belief about its probable cause. So long as induced drinking was thought to derive from an altered state of water balance, total amount drunk (over the 24 hours) was an appropriate measure. It now seems that this may not be the best way to look at it. Induced drinking may somehow be related to schedule variables and to the mechanisms through which they affect operant behavior. From this point of view appropriate measures might be ingestion rate (ml/min), drinking rate (licks/min), or the fraction of time engaged in drinking.

However, the schedule-induced nature of this effect introduces three complications (Flory, 1971; Staddon & Simmelhag, 1971). The first concerns the *stimulus control* of induced drinking. On fixed- and variable-interval schedules, drinking typically occurs just after food delivery, and it can easily be shown that once behavior has stabilized, drinking is directly under the control of each eating bout: each bout of eating produces a bout of drinking. Since we are interested in the relation between frequency and amount of food delivery and the animal's tendency to drink, this controlling relation introduces a confounding factor. First, suppose that all the induced drinking is simply post-prandial with each "meal" producing a fixed amount of drinking (Lotter, Woods, & Vasselli, 1973; Stein, 1964). While the rate of food delivery determines the rate of drinking in such a situation, it would be a mistake to conclude that this variable has a direct effect on the tendency to drink. (Similarly, the rate at which conditioning trials occur tells us nothing about the animal's tendency to make the conditioned response.)

A second confounding factor is the *opportunity* for drinking. If, to continue with the post-prandial example, the drinking bout produced by each food delivery is of a fixed duration, scheduling food deliveries too frequently could reduce the time available for drinking and thus actually reduce the amount drunk

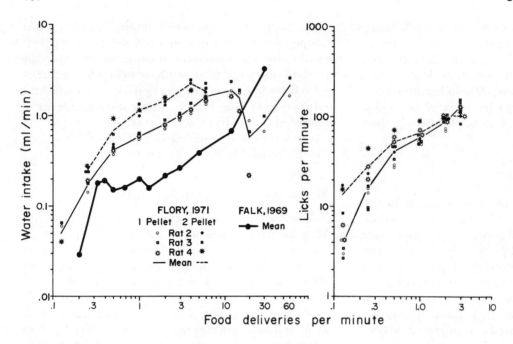

Fig. 2. Data replotted from Flory (1971), and Falk (1969) relating measures of drinking (licks/min, ml. drunk/min) to food rate (pellet deliveries/min).

per food delivery. This would artificially limit the function relating food and drink rates.

A third complication is the limit on the total amount of food that food-deprived animals can be permitted to ingest each day. This usually forces a reduction in the total number of daily food deliveries if the size of each delivery is increased. Consequently, the total amount of water drunk might appear to decrease as food portion size is increased, even though the rate of drinking is directly related to portion size (Falk, 1967; Flory, 1971; Hawkins, Schrot, Githens, & Everett, 1972; Staddon & Simmelhag, 1971). These problems make a number of experimental results difficult to interpret.

EFFECT OF FOOD RATE

The two panels of Fig. 2 show data relating rate of drinking (ml/min, left panel; licks/min, right panel) to frequency of food delivery (opportunities to eat/min, here referred to as food rate), replotted from studies by Flory (1971) and Falk (1969). These response rate *vs* food rate functions will be referred to as *response functions*. Food was delivered on fixed-interval schedules of different values, and the data represent stable performance. Similar results have been found by Hawkins et al. (1972) with fixed and variable-time food schedules, and by Segal, Oden, and Deadwyler (1965) and Staddon and Ayres (unpublished) with fixed-time schedules. As others have shown, the presence or absence of a response contingency makes little difference to the amount and temporal placement of schedule-induced drinking (Burks, 1970; Segal et al., 1965; Wayner & Greenberg, 1973).

Three aspects of these data are important for future discussion: (a) The functions are all monotonically increasing, with higher food rates associated with higher rates of drinking, until food deliveries are spaced very close together indeed. The functions for amount drunk in the left hand panel turn down only when food deliveries occur once every four seconds or oftener. (b) The functions for lick rate and rate of ingestion are generally similar in form, implying that an approximately fixed amount of water is ingested with each lick (see Figure 3). (c) Flory's data show that at a given food rate, two pellets per food delivery induce more drinking than one pellet per delivery. Moreover, this difference in terms of lick rate is greater when food delivery is infrequent. Since the ordinate is logarithmic, this means that the proportionate (but not the absolute) increase in lick rate is greater at low food rates.

HYPOTHESES TO EXPLAIN
SCHEDULE-INDUCED DRINKING

Four simple behavioral hypotheses have been proposed, explicitly or implicitly, as explanations for schedule-induced drinking. These are: (a) the postprandial hypothesis, (b) the opportunity hypothesis, (c) the adventitious reinforcement hypothesis, and (d) the motivation hypothesis. These are discussed next, followed by an account of running during food schedules and a summary of the relations between running and drinking.

Post-Prandial Hypothesis. The simplest hypothesis is that the drinking is simply normal post-prandial drinking, so that the more "meals" or "bites" the rat takes, the more he drinks (Kissileff, 1969; Lotter et al., 1973; Stein, 1964). This idea implies simple proportionality between the rate of drinking and the rate of food delivery up to a maximum when the animal drinks all the time except when he is eating. Formally it implies a relation of the form $D = K_1R + K_2$, where D is the rate of licking (licks/min; or water ingestion, ml/min), R is the frequency of opportunities to eat (food rate), K_1 is a constant representing the size of each post-prandial drinking bout, and K_2 is the rate of drinking in the absence of the food schedule.

The empirical functions in Figure 2 are not compatible with this equation because they all show considerable negative acceleration (in linear coordinates as well as the log-log ones of Figure 2) over much of their range. The post-prandial hypothesis can nevertheless be applied to these functions if they are approximated by two line segments, one with a steep slope starting at the origin ($K_2 = 0$) followed by a shallower segment after a break point in the vicinity of a food rate of one pellet every two min. However, these two segments suggest two contradictory interpretations. The steep segment from the origin is perfectly consistent with the post-prandial view with drinking rate proportional to food rate. However, the shallow segment then represents some kind of suppression of drinking at high food rates, perhaps due to restricted opportunity to drink. On the other hand, if the shallow segment is considered to represent the post-prandial view, the y-intercept, K_2, is much greater than the rate of drinking in the absence of the food schedule (which will usually be close to zero since the animals have unlimited access to water in their home cages). Hence K_2 must be interpreted as some kind of "inducing" effect of the food schedule.

In addition to its incompatibility with the functions in Figure 2, there are three other difficulties with the post-prandial hypothesis. (1) Schedule-induced drinking usually takes a few sessions to develop (Hawkins et al., 1972; Reynierse & Spanier, 1968; Staddon & Ayres, 1975). Yet post-prandial drinking is presumably well developed in normal adult rats. If drinking on schedules of food delivery is simply post-prandial drinking, there seems to be no reason why it should not occur from the start. (2) Drinking on periodic food schedules is not always restricted to the period just after food delivery. Its location within the interfood interval depends on interval length—the longer the interval, the later the onset of drinking (Segal et al., 1965)—and if, after the rat has learned to drink in the post-food period, access to the water bottle is restricted to a time late in the interval, drinking eventually recovers to essentially full strength (Flory & O'Boyle, 1972; Gilbert, 1974). (3) Drinking and eating in rats with free access to food and water are linked, but not in the way required by the post-prandial hypothesis. In a careful series of studies, Kissileff (1969) showed that drinking occurs both just after and *just before* eating bouts.

Lotter et al. (1973) have recently revived the post-prandial hypothesis in an attempt to explain schedule-related drinking as an "artifact" of the small "meal" size imposed by intermittent schedules. Much of their argument rests on demonstrations that increasing reward size reduced overall rate of drinking during single test sessions. These tests are not valid because the *increased* drinking that is associated with increases in amount of food takes time to develop, as the animals must have time to learn that the reward size (incentive value) in the situation has increased (e.g., Hawkins et al., 1972). It is known that induced drinking, once developed, is controlled by each meal, as a discriminative stimulus (e.g., Staddon & Ayres, 1975). Hence a reduction in meal rate, such as might occur following an increase in meal size, would automatically yield a reduction in rate of drinking, at least at first. It seems likely that a reduction in meal rate did occur, since although Lotter et al. do not report the actual (as opposed to the scheduled) intermeal interval in their one hour test sessions, the total number of pellets consumed during tests was disproportionately small. For example, in their third experiment reward size was increased from one to 12 pellets. Yet the number of pellets consumed per hour increased from 70.5 to only 218.5. Hence the number of meals must have dropped. A reduction in rate of drinking under these conditions says something about the stimulus control of drinking once it has developed, but nothing about the reasons for its development.

On periodic schedules, the "post-reinforcement pause" is controlled by food delivery as a discriminative stimulus. Since the pause is generally taken up with interim activities, their duration must be similarly controlled by food. When the duration or amount of food delivery is increased (as occurred during test sessions in the Lotter et al. experiment), post-reinforcement pause generally increases, although the increase may be transient (Jensen & Fallon, 1973; Staddon, 1970, 1974). Thus the first effect of increasing "meal" size should be an increase in the amount of drinking per meal. In a careful reanalysis of the test session data of Lotter et al., Millenson (1975) has recently shown this to be the case. Thus, their data are consistent with what is known about schedule-induced drinking and temporal control on periodic schedules but not, unfortunately, with their conclusion.

Opportunity Hypothesis. Falk (1969) originally suggested that schedule-induced drinking is related to the intermittency of food delivery. In its simplest form this view suggests that the rate of drinking is more or less constant with the animal drinking for a fixed fraction of the time available between pellets. It implies that the function relating amount drunk per interval to size of interval should be monotonically increasing; whereas this function is actually bitonic (Flory, 1971). Hence this view is not acceptable.

Adventitious Reinforcement Hypothesis. This hardy perennial has been applied to interim drinking as well as to terminal "superstitious" responses (e.g., Clark, 1962; Moran, 1974; Segal, 1965). All the objections to it raised earlier (p. 127) also apply here. In addition, induced drinking rarely occurs contiguously with food delivery (Segal, 1969 is an exception), and is little affected by lick-contingent delays of food delivery unless these are so extreme as substantially to reduce food rate. As Figure 2 shows, over most of the range a reduction in food rate results in a decrease in drinking rate. Unless food rate is controlled, therefore, suppressive effects of a negative contingency cannot be interpreted as acting directly on the tendency to drink. Induced drinking develops relatively slowly, in step with the development of temporal discrimination on periodic schedules (Staddon & Ayres, 1975). Hence activities other than drinking are at first contiguous with food delivery. The adventitious reinforcement view neither explains why these drop out, nor why drinking (rather than some other activity) supplants them in almost every individual rat. When the water bottle is made available for only a brief period during the inter-food interval (Flory & O'Boyle, 1972), drinking still develops, even though lick-food contiguities are specifically excluded and the water bottle itself is a stimulus signaling the absence of food (S^Δ).

Motivation Hypothesis. The steep fall-off in the functions of Figure 2 at low food rates, the greater drinking with 2-pellet versus 1-pellet food deliveries, the progressive development of schedule-induced drinking, in step with food-anticipation (Reynierse & Spanier, 1968; Staddon & Ayres, 1975), and the inverse relation between schedule-induced drinking and body weight (Bowen, 1972; Falk, 1969), all point to an effect of food motivation, hunger, and incentive, on induced drinking. The more motivated the animal (hunger: deprivation, body weight) and the more motivating the situation (incentive: frequency, amount, and type of food) the greater the tendency to drink. The incentive motivation factor seems to follow the principles now being codified as the quantitative law of effect (see de Villiers, Chapter 9). Thus drinking rate appears to be directly related to amount of food (Figure 2), palatability of food (Falk, 1971), and frequency of food (Figure 2). Jacquet (1972) has studied the interactions between two components of a multiple VI VI schedule in terms of the relative and absolute rates of both bar pressing and induced drinking in rats. She found that as the relative rate of food reinforcement in one component increased (owing to a decrease in the rate of reinforcement in the other component), the absolute rate of drinking tended to increase. This is *positive behavioral contrast*, an effect often found with food-reinforced behaviors and generally attributed to a change in stimulus contingencies (see Chapter 3).

Thus, the evidence appears to support the view that induced drinking is related to food motivation, which is, in turn, affected both by internal factors (deprivation) and external factors (incentive). In a later section I discuss possible mechanisms of interaction between the motivational states of hunger and thirst that might underlie the empirical relation between induced drinking and food motivation.

INDUCTION: TERMINAL AND INTERIM ACTIVITIES

Since both interim activities and the terminal response tend to increase with food rate, and since neither can increase without limit, it seems likely that these two classes of activity are in competition. This section presents the evidence for such competition and looks at some of its effects.

Functions relating food-reinforcement rate to rate of pecking or lever pressing (response functions) have for some years been a standard way of representing the effects of schedules on behavior. The typical schedule has been variable-, rather than fixed-interval, and the response an instrumental rather than an induced one. However, there is every reason to suppose that terminal responses on both response-contingent and response-independent schedules are related in similar ways to reinforcement and motivational variables. Manipulations such as a shift in relative reinforcement frequency produce similar contrast effects in both (e.g., Gamzu & Schwartz, 1973; Redford & Perkins, 1974), and the response contingency seems to act more to select one terminal response over others than to affect the "strength" of the response once selected (Staddon & Simmelhag, 1971). This is not to say that all terminal responses have similar properties —there is by now ample evidence that they do not (e.g., Hinde & Stevenson-Hinde, 1973)—just that there seems to be no strong effect of response contingency *per se* on the properties of a given terminal behavior once it is established.

An analysis in terms of terminal and interim periods associated with different regions of post-food time does not seem as applicable to variable-interval as to fixed-interval schedules. Food does not seem to have the same kind of discriminative-stimulus status on variable-interval schedules as it does on fixed-interval. Nevertheless it can be argued that on VI, as on FI, time is segmented into interim and terminal periods, although these are not as simply related to post-reinforcement time (Rachlin, 1973). (The factors accounting for this difference, and for the temporal location of activities within the inter-food interval, will be taken up in the third section.) Thus it seems reasonable to assume that the rate of a terminal response such as pecking, once it is established, depends much more on variables such as food rate, palatability of food, size of food portion, and hunger than on temporal relations between the response and food delivery. We have just seen that these are the variables that determine the level of induced drinking. In a sense, therefore, (instrumental) terminal as well as interim responses can be regarded as schedule-induced behavior.

If each terminal or interim response (e.g., lick, peck, bar press) is assumed to require an approximately constant time, then any increase in rate of responding with food rate implies that the responding will take up an increasing fraction of the interfood interval as interval length decreases.[1] As we have already seen, the rates of both induced drinking and instrumental responding increase with food rate. Hence it is reasonable to postulate the eventual development of *competition* between drinking and the terminal response at high food rates. Moreover, there is some evidence that induced drinking (at least) tends to grow with food rate rather faster than terminal responding. For example, the 1-pellet lick rate function in Figure 2 has an initial slope greater than one. Yet instrumental (terminal) responding, which is often well described by Herrnstein's equation, $P = kR_1/(R_1 + R_2)$, grows linearly at first, since when R_1 is small the equation reduces to $P = kR_1/R_2$, i.e., a slope of one in the log-log coordinates of Figure 2. This implies that the fraction of the interval taken up by an interim activity such as drinking should increase with food rate. The eventual flattening out of the response functions for both interim and terminal activities can be taken as one outcome of the competition between them.

Running. Figure 3 illustrates another effect of competition between terminal and interim activities. The figure shows rates of wheel running and drinking (in licks/min and ml/min) of five female rats exposed to five different fixed-time schedules in a hexagonal apparatus that afforded access to a variety of activities (Staddon & Ayres, 1975 and unpublished). Drinking rate increases with food rate, as in Figure 2, and the function form for licks/min and ml/min is the same. However, the rate of wheel running decreases as food rate increases, suggesting suppression by competition from drinking and the terminal response (which in this case was waiting in the feeder area accompanied by pawing and chewing at the feeder opening: "food anticipation"). Thus, it appears as if running is not schedule induced, but rather "fits in" at times when the tendency to engage in the two dominant classes of activity is weak. This view is in agreement with the temporal distribution of the three classes of activity, with drinking occurring first in the interval, followed by running and then food anticipation (cf. Figure 1). It is also consistent with the finding of Staddon and Ayres (1975) that during acquisition, the temporal pattern of food anticipation and drinking developed to essentially its final form before much running had occurred.

Other evidence suggesting that running is not schedule induced is that when food delivery is discontinued (extinction), running rate and the fraction of total time the animal spends in the running wheel area increases (Staddon & Ayres, 1975, and unpublished). Even if running is required for the production of food, its overall frequency may not be in-

---

[1] This can easily be shown algebraically. For an interim activity A, where each response takes up a fixed time t_A, then if A takes up a fixed fraction, k_1, of the interfood interval, T: $N_A t_A = k_1 T$, where N_A is the average number of occurrences of A per interval. The response function for A is then given by $N_A/T = k_1/t_A$, which is a constant. Hence any growth in the rate of A with food rate means that A takes up an increasing fraction of the interval as food rate increases. If the rate of A is proportional to food rate, $N_A/T = k_2/T$, then the fraction of the interval taken up by A is equal to $t_A k_2/T$, i.e., also proportional to food rate. Similar calculations can be carried out for the terminal response, B, and it is clear that when $t_A k_2 + t_B k_3 = T$ (where k_2 and k_3 are the constants of proportionality) the entire interval is taken up.

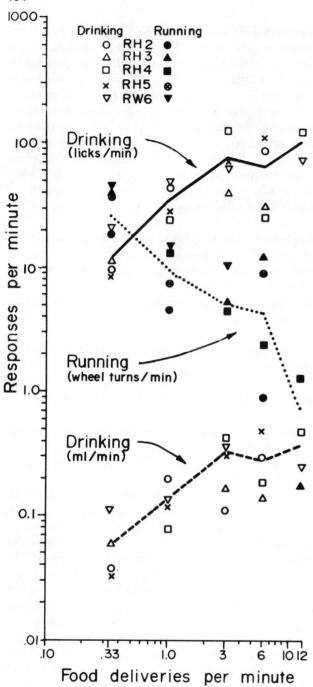

Fig. 3. Drinking rate (licks/min and ml/min) and running rate (turns of a 27cm dia running wheel/min) vs. food rate on various fixed time food schedules for four female rats (Staddon and Ayres, unpublished data.) Points show individual rats, lines are means. Each rat was exposed to four of the five food rates; hence each point is the average of four animals.

creased, although its temporal distribution adapts to the schedule (Skinner & Morse, 1958).

Levitsky and Collier (1968) have reported an increase in running under schedule conditions as opposed to extinction. However, the rat was entirely enclosed in a running wheel in their apparatus, so that running may have been confounded with general activity, which, as Killeen (1975) has shown, increases with food rate. Similarly, Staddon and Ayres (1975) report a decrease in overall activity, measured as area changes per min, in extinction, but wheel running in their apparatus increased in extinction. Smith and Clark (1974), using an apparatus similar to that of Levitsky and Collier and a multiple spaced-responding schedule, obtained mixed results: one rat showed less running at low food rates, two others showed a bitonic relation. Thus, apart from exceptions that may reflect peculiarities of some kinds of running-wheel apparatus, it appears that running is suppressed by a food schedule.

The picture that emerges from this account is summarized in Figure 4. The figure shows the inter-food interval divided into three periods: an interim[2] period, devoted to drinking (if water is available) and perhaps other activities, such as aggression (see below); a terminal period, devoted to food anticipation or the instrumental response; and a third period,

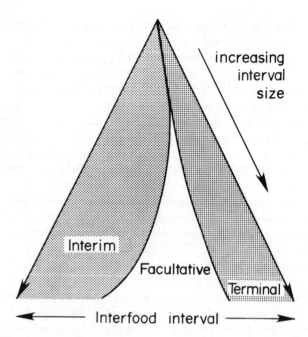

Fig. 4. Schematic representation of the relation between interfood interval and the proportion of the interval taken up by interim, "facultative," and terminal behaviors.

---

[2] Until this point the term "interim" has been applied to all those activities which precede the terminal response within the interfood interval. In Figure 4, however, only activities induced by the schedule, such as drinking, are so labelled; "neutral" activities, such as running, fall into the "facultative" category. There seems to be no reason to settle on either usage as definitive, providing that whenever the term is used it is clear which is intended.

when activities not induced by the schedule, *facultative activities,* can occur. Running appears to be a facultative activity in this sense. Other possibilities are comfort activities, such as preening and grooming. The diagram has two critical features: (a) that the percentage of time devoted to both terminal and interim activities increases as interval size decreases, and (b) that this progressive increase is limited at short intervals, when the entire interval is taken up by the two classes of induced activities.

The diagram reveals several uncertainties. First, the exact form of the area boundaries is not known. In particular, it is necessary to know the function relating overall rate of an activity such as licking or key pecking to the percentage of time taken up. The simple proportionality assumed for illustrative purposes in footnote 1 may not hold generally. Such functions are not available at present. It is also likely that the boundaries of the interim and terminal areas are not fixed, but depend on the strength of behavior in the "other" category. For example, in the experiment by Staddon and Ayres (1975), one rat showed anomalous behavior traceable to a very strong tendency to run. It failed to show the usual temporal distribution of activities within the inter-pellet interval until either running was prevented, or more time was made available for it by preventing drinking (see p. 147). The diagram is also restricted to periodic food schedules in which opportunities for all activities are continuously available; it does not deal with either variable schedules or limited-availability schedules. Finally, the possible mechanisms underlying the distribution of activities remain to be considered.

Interim Activities and S^Δ Periods

Drinking and other schedule-induced interim activities always seem to occur (in the steady state) at times, or in the presence of stimuli, that signal the absence of food (S^Δ or interim periods). On fixed-interval schedules, food is not available early in the interval. Hence the occurrence of schedule-induced drinking or attack at those times is explainable. However, food can occur at any time on variable interval schedules: food delivery is as likely just after food as it is at other times. Yet even on variable schedules, induced drinking still tends to be restricted to the period just after food delivery. How can this be explained?

Under free conditions, rats tend to drink just before and just after meals (e.g., Kissileff, 1969). It seems likely that post-prandial drinking, at least, is maintained when animals are exposed to intermittent food.

Hence even on a variable schedule, if water is available it is possible that food will not be eaten in the period just after a previous food delivery. This period therefore qualifies as an interim period in terms of the obtained, if not the scheduled, distribution of food deliveries. The temporal locus of induced drinking on variable schedules may thus be traced to the way in which the animal's initial behavior interacts with the properties of the schedule; by drinking after eating, the animal can produce an obtained distribution of intereating times that is quite different from the programmed distribution. The obtained distribution then maintains the behavior that led to it. This kind of "self-fulfilling" schedule-behavior interaction is not an uncommon occurrence in situations that allow for the expression of induced behavior (see Staddon & Ayres, 1975, for other examples). Any irregularity in the function relating probability of food to post-food time (i.e., any deviation from a constant probability) should accentuate this "self-fulfilling" tendency, especially if the probability is relatively lower (not necessarily zero) in the immediate post-food period. Millenson (personal communication) has data in support of this inference, since he finds that schedule-induced drinking is less reliably obtained on a random-interval (i.e., constant probability) schedule than on a variable-interval schedule with an arithmetic progression of intervals (in which the probability of food increases with post-food time).

This interpretation recognizes a link between eating and subsequent drinking, although such a link need not be either strong or unmodifiable. For example, Flory and O'Boyle (1972) have shown that if drinking is prevented in the period just following food delivery, but is permitted later in the interfood interval, the rat drinks almost as much as when water is continuously available. Gilbert (1974) has reported a similar result. Drinking occurs after each response on spaced-responding schedules (Segal & Holloway, 1963) and has been reported to occur after brief stimuli on second-order schedules (Porter & Kenshalo, 1974; Rosenblith, 1970) although there are some conflicting results (Allen, Porter & Arazie, 1975; Porter, Arazie, Holbrook, Cheek & Allen, 1975). These results all suggest that although the link between eating and subsequent drinking is a factor in the temporal location of drinking in the interfood interval, it is not essential to its induction.

In limited-availability procedures, presentation of the water bottle signals a period when food will not be delivered. The fact that rats drink with undiminished vigor during these periods conforms to the general conclusion that induced drinking is characteristic of interim (S^Δ) periods (Falk, 1969, 1971; Staddon & Simmelhag, 1971). It also indicates that such periods need not be defined temporally (cf. Wüttke & Innis, 1972). If interim activities have something to do with the animal's ability to "time," i.e., to refrain from making the terminal (food-related) response at times when food is not available, one might expect them to be reduced in strength when an external cue is available. Unfortunately the effect of stimuli on the strength and locus of interim activities has not been systematically assessed.

SCHEDULE-INDUCED ATTACK

Rats show strong induced drinking on periodic food schedules, but pigeons and doves show weaker effects (Shanab & Peterson, 1969). However, several experiments have shown that these birds on food schedules will attack another bird, a stuffed model, a mirror, or even a color slide of a pigeon (e.g., Azrin, Hutchinson, & Hake, 1966; Cohen & Looney, 1973; Flory & Ellis, 1973). Squirrel monkeys show schedule-induced biting attack on a rubber hose (Hutchinson, Azrin, & Hunt, 1968) and rats on schedules of food or water reward will attack another animal (Gentry & Schaeffer, 1969; Thompson & Bloom, 1966).

Figure 5 shows data replotted (in log-log coordinates) from three experiments that have studied schedule-induced attack in pigeons as a function of food rate (Cherek, Thompson, & Heistad, 1973; Cohen & Looney, 1973; Flory, 1969). Cherek et al. measured the rate at which pigeons pecked against the front of a transparent box containing a live target bird, on a response-initiated fixed-interval schedule. Flory used a stuffed target pigeon and a fixed-time food schedule; and Cohen and Looney used a mirror as the target and a multiple fixed-ratio 25 fixed-ratio N (N varied from 25 to 150) schedule. Cherek et al. and Flory both used a "delay" contingency which prevented food delivery within 15 sec of an attack response—a common protection against "adventitious" reinforcement of attack by food delivery. The target bird was available on a fixed-ratio 2 schedule for 15 sec at a time in the Cherek et al. study, but continuously available in the others. Despite these differences of target, schedule, and target availability, the attack rate data in Figure 5 show considerable overall agreement. Rate of aggressive pecking peaks at a food rate between .30 and 1.0 per min and declines sharply at lower and higher rates. In linear coordinates the falloff at high food rates is more gradual than the falloff at low rates. The absolute rate of target pecking in the Cohen and Looney study was higher than in the others because they report "local" rate (i.e., rate in the post-food pause) rather than overall rate. The decline in responding at higher food rates in their study was more gradual (in linear coordinates), but it is not clear whether this was because of the ratio food schedule, the mirror-image target, or other features of their situation.

The general agreement among the functions in Figure 5 suggests that food rate (deliveries/min) is the determining factor in all these experiments and that the way in which this food rate comes about, whether via an interval or a ratio schedule, is much less important. Certainly periodic food is essential to the attack responding, since attack declines to a negligible level in extinction (Cherek et al., 1973). In an explicit ABAB comparison of response-dependent and response-independent interval schedules of food delivery, Cherek et al. found little consistent effect of the response contingency on rate of attack. There are as yet no data on yoked-control comparison of time versus ratio procedures, so factors in addition to food rate cannot be entirely excluded.

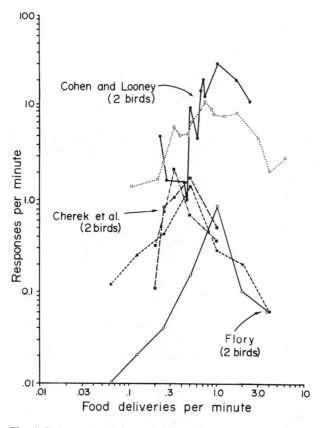

Fig. 5. Data replotted from Cohen and Looney (1973), Cherek et al. (1973) and Flory (1969) relating measures of attack rate to food rate on various intermittent schedules (see text for details).

Drinking and Attack

Comparison of the attack rate data in Figure 5 with the drinking rate data in Figure 2 shows that although both types of behavior fall off drastically at food rates less than about 0.5 per min, attack responding also shows a decline at higher food rates. Induced drinking only shows such a falloff at very high food rates (in excess of about one per 4 sec, Flory, 1971). Staddon and Ayres (unpublished) find that this decline in the average function occurs because some individuals fail to drink at all when food is delivered very frequently. When pellets were delivered every 5 sec perhaps half the rats in the Staddon and Ayres study failed to drink in most intervals (cf. Segal et al., 1965). The most obvious explanation for this is that the time available between food pellets is simply insufficient, although since some rats continued to drink the limitation seems not to be the purely mechanical one of getting to the water bottle and back again before the next pellet delivery—especially as rats on some variable schedules will drink so much that they postpone food delivery or fail to pick up the pellet when it is delivered (Clark, 1962; Falk, 1961). The decline in the attack rate function occurs at relatively low food rates and cannot be explained by any kind of mechanical limitation.

Induced attack, like induced drinking, is an interim activity and occurs in the period just after food delivery on fixed-interval and fixed-ratio schedules (Richards & Rilling, 1972). Like induced drinking, it occurs after each response on spaced-responding (DRL) schedules (Knutson & Kleinknecht, 1970). However, data are lacking on its temporal position relative to other induced activities, such as drinking, preening, etc., when opportunities for several are available. Comparison is made more difficult because most attack studies have been done with pigeons, most studies of induced drinking with rats. It would also be useful to find a facultative activity analogous to running in rats, that could be used in similar fashion to help clarify the interactions among induced activities in pigeons.

The early falloff in attack rate as food rate increases beyond one delivery per 2 min suggests a difference in the time courses of drinking and attack. Perhaps there is a limit to the speed with which a tendency to post-eating attack can build up, no matter how strong the inducing factors, i.e., the hunger and incentive motivation associated with the food schedule. Data on the effects of hunger and of food type and amount on attack rate would help to sort this out. For example, a direct relation between hunger and attack rate on FI 2 min would suggest that the decline in attack rate at higher food rates reflects a time-course limitation, rather than a non-monotonic relation between food motivation and tendency to attack.

Other Interim Activities

Data on interim activities other than drinking, running, and attack are sparse (see Falk, 1971, for a review). Pica (eating of non-food objects) has been observed in rats and monkeys (e.g., Villareal, 1967); and pigeons, humans, and sometimes rats, show a variety of stereotyped motor patterns, such as pacing, neck stretching, wing flapping and preening or grooming (Kachanoff, Leveille, McLelland & Wagner, 1973; Keehn, 1972; Staddon & Simmelhag, 1971). In unpublished observations I have noticed that schedule-induced wing flapping in pigeons is a strikingly autonomous behavior. Although all the necessary tests have not been carried out (see pp. 145 et seq.), it appears as if each bout is internally timed (see pp. 145) so that wing flapping persists even if food is made available during a bout. Pigeons will sometimes repeatedly miss food deliveries in this way. Gilbertson (personal communication) has obtained reliable induced preening by attaching a piece of solder wire to the pigeon's wing as a minor irritant. There is also one report in which pigeons, trained to key peck for food on a fixed-ratio schedule, pecked a bolt head as an interim activity (Miller & Gollub, 1974).

There are also few data on schedules using positive reinforcers other than food or water. Gilbertson (personal communication) has trained male pigeons to peck on a ratio schedule for the sight of a female. These birds show courtship behavior, bow-cooing and wing flapping, as interim activities, as an after-effect of the sight of the female (see also Nelson, 1965; Sevenster, 1973).

Induced States

The regions of post-food time identified in Figure 4 as "interim," "facultative," and "terminal," and their associated behaviors are more properly considered as *states* or "moods" of the behaving animal (rather than simply as "behaviors"). This is because they represent different kinds of behavioral *potential*. The same stimulus, water for example, has different effects during the interim period from those it has during the terminal period. The rat drinks in the one but not in the other; hence his state must have changed, and this change can be traced to the different temporal cues effective during these two periods. Similarly, brief test presentations of food during the interim period may fail to elicit eating (Konorski, 1967; Staddon, unpublished observations), at least the first couple of times. Eventually the animal will eat, but by then the duration of the interim period (which is defined by the animal's history of exposure to food opportunities) will have changed to allow for eating earlier in the interval, as it does when an animal is shifted from a fixed–to a variable-interval schedule (e.g., Innis & Staddon, 1971; Rachlin, 1973).

The states that fill up the interfood interval differ in their motivational properties. Not only does the rat drink during the interim period, but its state resembles thirst, just as the terminal state resembles hunger. For example, rats and monkeys will learn to press a lever to obtain access to water during the interim period (Falk, 1971). Whether "thirst" in this sense is identical to "thirst" that follows water deprivation is hard to say. They certainly share many properties, as will become clear in a moment.

Perhaps because of a preoccupation with stimulus-response notions of behavioral causality, the properties even of terminal states have been little explored until recently. Pavlov (1927) induced such states by means of stimulus-reinforcer contingencies, but studied only a fraction of the animal's potential behavior: the "conditioned response" of salivation. Occasional anecdotes filtered out of his laboratory suggesting that the conditioning operations produced much more extensive changes than this. For example, Liddell (recounted in Lorenz, 1969) noticed that a dog released from its harness would approach and jump upon the metronome CS. Zener (1937) in a classic paper described a variety of other behaviors in the presence of the conditioned stimulus, suggesting that animals develop "expectations" about the imminence of food. Bolles (1972) has recently defended a revival of this position. Recent work on auto shaping (e.g., Browne, 1973) lends it some support.

Labelling induced states with terms such as "hunger" or "food expectancy" is convenient, and reminds us of moods familiar from introspection. Unfortunately a feeling of familiarity is not the same thing as exact knowledge, and may even hinder the search for it. Induced states can be explored in two main ways: (a) By looking at the effect of various test *stimuli,* when the animal is in the state, as compared to when it is not; (b) by looking at the effectiveness of various *reinforcers* when it is in the state as compared to when it is not. The first is equivalent to the method of transfer tests, used to discover "what is learned" in a learning situation. It is concerned with what might be termed the cognitive and perceptual properties of the induced state. For example, one could see whether a rat on a periodic food schedule will respond in the interim period to stimuli that in its past have been associated with access to water. The second method is concerned with the motivational properties of the state, with for example, the reinforcing effectiveness of water during a food schedule as compared with its effectiveness in the absence of the schedule.

The cognitive properties of induced interim states have not been adequately explored; much more has been done on their motivational properties. I first consider the similarities between induced drinking and thirst, and then the properties of interim states generally.

Induced Drinking and Thirst

Falk (1969, 1971) has identified several factors that point to a similarity between thirst and the rat's state when induced drinking is observed: (a) The acquisition of induced drinking is impaired by pre-loading with water; (b) rats and squirrel monkeys will learn to press a lever during the interim period to obtain access to water; (c) rats drink less if the terminal food reinforcer contains water; (d) rate of induced drinking is directly related to the palatability of the available liquid. To these can be added the finding that water-deprived rats will lick a stream of air (e.g., Mendelson, Zielke, Slangen & Weijnen, 1972; Werner & Freed, 1973), and this activity can be induced by food schedules in the same way as drinking. On the other hand, some physiological studies report differences between schedule-induced and "normal" drinking (e.g., Carlisle, 1971, 1973).

Water acts as a reinforcer for water-satiated rats on periodic food schedules, as shown by its effectiveness in maintaining lever pressing. Along the same lines, a study by Allen and Porter (personal communication) using a multiple FI 1 min FI 1 min food schedule, showed positive contrast effects with a water-reinforced response. Water was at first available in both components of the multiple schedule on a FI 0.75 sec schedule. Later, response rate on the water lever was recorded in one component as a function of whether or not water was available in the other. When water was removed in one component, response rate on the water lever in the other component increased (positive contrast). Thus, the tendency to drink on periodic food schedules is determined both by food rate variables and by variables related to water availability. Since the effectiveness of water as a reinforcer is presumably also related to food rate, these effects point to quite complex interactions between food rate (the fundamental instigating variable), the tendency to drink, and the capacity of water to act as a reinforcer.

These data on the effects of water motivation on induced drinking support the earlier generalization that the strength of schedule-induced drinking is jointly determined by both food and water motivation. Its sensitivity to water-motivation factors underlines both its "state" character and its similarity to normal thirst. The evidence is not sufficient to assert that deprivation-induced and schedule-induced "thirst" are identical, however, and it would be surprising if they were in view of the different temporal properties of the two.

TERMINAL-INTERIM INTERACTION

Several lines of evidence suggest that for many species the interim period on periodic food schedules is aversive: (a) Many of the interim activities developed by pigeons on fixed-time schedules are suggestive of flight: neck-stretching, hopping, wing flapping, and even brief hopping flights (Staddon & Simmelhag, 1971; unpublished observations). Many of their movements resemble the intention movements made by wild pigeons just before they take flight (e.g., Davis, 1973). (b) Pigeons will learn to peck a key during the interim period on FI to produce a timeout (houselights off and different stimuli on the response keys), and their tendency to do so is bitonically related to interval value, although the peak is at about FI 4 rather than FI 2, the value for maximum attack (Brown & Flory, 1972). Numerous other studies have shown that both rats and pigeons find interim periods aversive (e.g., Appel, 1963; Azrin, 1961; Thompson, 1964). (c) As we have already seen, pigeons, rats, and monkeys will attack other animals, objects, or representations during the interim period, and pigeons will peck a key for the opportunity to do so (Cherek et al., 1973).

Staddon and Simmelhag (1971) tentatively proposed that there is a reciprocal interaction between the terminal and interim states on periodic schedules; and that this mechanism serves the adaptive function of removing animals from food situations at times when food delivery is unlikely. There is some evidence that enforced proximity to the food site enhances schedule-induced drinking. Clark (1962) found less drinking when the water bottle was moved away from the food tray, and Staddon and Ayres found much less drinking in their hexagonal apparatus (in which food and water sites were separated) than that reported by Flory (1971) and others (compare Figures 2 and 3). Induced drinking and the food-related terminal response are related to food motivation in a similar way; hence the "hungrier" the animal during the terminal period, the "thirstier" he is during the interim period. These data, together with physiological links between hypothalamic structures involved in eating and drinking (Åkerman, Andersson, Fabricius, & Svensson, 1960; Wayner, 1970), and at least one demonstration, with doves, of adjunctive eating on a water schedule (McFarland, 1965), make the idea of a reciprocal interaction between these two motivational states a plausible one. There are difficulties in testing the idea of complete reciprocality, however, because severely water-deprived animals will not eat. This may underlie the failure of Carlisle, Shanab, and Simpson (1972) to induce eating in thirsty rats by means of a periodic water schedule.

The notion that during the interim period on a food schedule animals are motivated in ways antagonistic to food motivation explains the apparent aversiveness of the interim period. A thirsty animal might well try to escape from a food situation. Indeed, Pliskoff and Tolliver (1960) have shown that hungry rats maintained on a fixed-ratio food schedule will respond more on a second lever that removes them from the food schedule (by producing a 5-min timeout) when deprived of water for three days than when not water-deprived. There are several uncertainties, however. For example, even in large enclosures pigeons do not stray far from the response key during the interim period (Staddon, unpublished observations), although careful studies of the effects of schedule variables on spatial position have not been carried out. Hence the induced aversiveness of the food site (or response key—the data do not distinguish between the two) must decline faster with distance than its attractiveness. What determines the form of such gradients and how might they be measured? Another difficulty is that most of the data on the aversiveness of the interim period come from pigeons, most data on induced drinking from rats. How legitimate is generalization from one species to another?

Schedule-induced aggression poses a related problem. Is it induced by the schedule in the same way as drinking? The falloff in the response function at high food rates suggests not, but there may be other explanations for this. Or is aggression one outcome of the conflict between the tendencies to approach and retreat from the food site? This kind of explanation—disinhibition of activity A owing to conflict between strongly excited incompatible activities B and C—has been proposed for the displacement activities studied by ethologists (cf. Hinde, 1970). However, the hypothesis has not been presented in a quantitative way that allows for a convincing test.

It is also clear that the division into terminal and interim periods is an oversimplification. At interfood intervals greater than 20 or 30 sec the middle of the interval seems to be a period when non-induced (facultative) activities, such as running, can occur. The growth of this period with interval duration parallels the shift from "break and run" to "scallop" on fixed-interval schedules as interval value increases (Schneider, 1969). The "scallop" period, when the cumulative record shows a gradual transition to a high, steady rate, may correspond to the "facultative" period in Figure 4. Possibly activities such as preening and grooming, which are not sensitive to food reinforcement contingencies (Shettleworth, 1973) and do not compete with other activities ("disinhibited" activities; McFarland, 1970), can occur at this time.

There are other puzzling facts that emphasize how little we understand the mechanisms underlying induced behavior. For example, pigeons trained to peck for food on a fixed-interval schedule will continue to do so if periodic food delivery is maintained independently of responding. However, if the interfood interval is relatively long, pecking often becomes confined to the middle of the interval (Shull, 1970; Staddon & Frank, 1975a). Is this pecking different from food-related pecking, such as that induced in auto shaping situations, which tends to occur with highest probability close to food delivery? Or is it simply induced by the food situation in a similar way to induced drinking, where, at low food rates, each food delivery seems to produce a more or less constant amount of drinking? A final problem is the role of stimulus control and "conditioning." A behavior induced originally for one reason may be maintained for another. Thus an interim activity that develops in the post-food period because this period signals the absence of food may subsequently come under partial control by features of the environment (as drinking comes under the control of the water-bottle, for example). Consequently, a change in the animal's environment may affect terminal and interim behaviors differently. This differential effect may explain the effects of restraint on "temporal discrimination" described below.

TEMPORAL AND SEQUENTIAL STRUCTURE OF INDUCED ACTIVITIES

All the species commonly used in operant conditioning experiments, rats, pigeons, monkeys, and people, adapt the temporal pattern of their behavior to the temporal pattern of reinforcer delivery. Indeed, the temporal pattern of the instrumental response was the aspect of reinforcement-schedule performance that first attracted attention (Ferster & Skinner, 1957), and it continues to provide a topic for dozens of research reports each year. This temporal regularity raises two obvious questions: (a) What determines the temporal locus of the various activities? (b) What is the nature of the "clock" that times these activities? I take up these two questions first. The third section deals more generally with types of sequential interaction.

Factors Affecting the Temporal Locus of Terminal and Interim Periods

Most studies of the relation between the temporal sequence of reinforcers and the temporal sequence of behaviors have been concerned only with the pattern of the instrumental response. As we have already seen, periodic reinforcement generally produces a corresponding periodicity in behavior, with the instrumental response occupying the last third or so of the inter-reinforcement interval. There are some exceptions, in situations with weak reinforcers or labile responses (e.g., Weiner, 1969), and many species (fish, octopus) apparently fail to show this kind of temporal adaptation. However, it is sufficiently common that the search for rules to describe it seems justified.

The rule seems to be that the local rate of responding (i.e., rate over some short time interval) is directly related to the relative proximity to reinforcement or, on aperiodic schedules, the relative density (i.e., rate over some brief time interval) of reinforcement (Catania & Reynolds, 1968; Jenkins, 1970; Staddon, 1972b; Zeiler, Chapter 8 in this volume). In short, pigeons peck more at times when food is more likely. No one has yet succeeded in reducing this rather common-sensical principle to a mathematical form that is universally satisfactory (see de Villiers, Chapter 9 in this volume, on the quantitative law of effect), but the details are not important for present purposes.

This relative proximity rule should not be thought of as a causal law about the effect of independent reinforcement variables on dependent behavioral ones. It is an *equilibrium principle,* that describes the steady-state relation between reinforcement and behavior, once behavior has settled down. On response-contingent schedules reinforcement rate is affected by behavior (as well as vice versa) and often many equilibria are possible. For example, a pigeon on a high-ratio schedule may cease to respond because its initial response rate is too low to produce sufficient reinforcement to sustain pecking. This outcome, with zero reinforcement supporting zero responding, is just as consistent with the law of effect as an equilibrium in which a high response rate is maintained by a high reinforcement rate. By itself the law of effect does not predict which will occur. Other factors, involving the historical development of the final equilibrium, and including factors that may facilitate or inhibit induced behavior, must be understood for a full account.

We have already seen that even when no instrumental response is required, behavior can usually be subdivided into terminal and interim classes, with the (induced) terminal response apparently following the same set of rules as if it were an instrumental response. As in other cases discussed in this chapter, most of the evidence comes from the study of a few behaviors in a few species. Pecking in pigeons seems to follow the density of food delivery in the same way on non-contingent as on response-contingent schedules, at least under the restricted conditions studied by Staddon and Simmelhag (1971). However, under other conditions, particularly when (free) food delivery is relatively infrequent (less than one per 2 min or so), this relation breaks down. Instead of occurring in anticipation of food delivery, pecking may occur in a burst in the middle of each interval (Shull, 1970; Staddon & Frank, 1975a). Unfortunately the observational work necessary to decide whether or not there is another response, other than pecking, that anticipates food in these cases (i.e., a terminal response) has not been done, although it is clear that pecking is not induced on long fixed-time schedules as it is on short (Simmelhag, unpublished observations).

Interim activities occur at times when the terminal response is not occurring. There seem to be two conditions under which a terminal response fails to occur (or occurs at a reduced rate): (a) When relative reinforcement rate is low, but there is the *opportunity* for reinforcement at any time (e.g., variable-interval schedules); (b) when there is *no* reinforcement opportunity (overall reinforcement rate may be high or low; the period immediately following food on fixed-interval schedules, and following a response on spaced-responding schedules, are examples). In case (b), the terminal response does not occur at all during S^Δ periods, which are the occasion for observable interim activities. However, in case (a), if interim periods can be said to exist at all they must be brief and interspersed between occurrences of the terminal response: variations in rate then correspond to variations in the percentages of time taken up by the terminal and interim periods (see footnote 4, p. 144, and Rachlin, 1973). Because interim periods must be short under these conditions, there is no opportunity for full-blown interim activities, and thus no easy verification of the hypothesis.

With the exception of a number of experiments on quantitative aspects such as duration (Schwartz & Williams, 1972) and force (Chung, 1965; Cole, 1965), study of the topographic details of pecking on various schedules has not been extensive. In informal observations I have noticed that on variable-interval schedules pigeons generally turn away from the key between pecks, whereas pecking on ratio schedules, or during the terminal "run" on fixed-interval, is much more single-minded, with little turning away. It does not seem far-fetched to interpret this turning away (and thus the gap between pecks associated with it) as an interim period, with properties similar to interim periods on periodic schedules.

Timing of Induced Sequences

The reliable association between induced interim activities and periodicity of the terminal, generally instrumental response, has led to a number of attempts to find a causal link between the two (e.g., Glazer & Singh, 1971; Hodos, Ross, & Brady, 1962; Nevin & Berryman, 1963; see Harzem, 1969, and Kramer & Rilling, 1970, for reviews). Is the periodicity of the terminal response on, say, a fixed-interval schedule caused in some way by the regular sequence of interim activities that typically precedes it? This question cannot be answered until the mechanism by which interim activities might serve to "time" the terminal response is made more explicit. Suggestions in previous published work are of two general kinds: chaining explanations, and "behavioral clock" explanations.

CHAINING

Chaining is the simplest possibility. The model is the "domino theory," according to which each behavior in the temporal sequence A-B-C-D- etc. directly produces the next: the offset of activity A produces the onset of B, the offset of B the onset of C, and so on. In the usual form of this explanation, each individual activity is assumed to take a characteristic time, i.e., the distribution of bout durations will show a mode at a "preferred" duration (see McGill, 1963, for a review of stochastic processes and "temporal discrimination"). This is not necessary, however. If the number of links in the chain is fixed, the time from the beginning of the chain to the onset of a given later member will not be random (i.e., exponentially distributed) even if each link has a random duration. This follows directly from the central limit theorem, since the time of onset of chain link M is equal to the sum of the durations of links 1 through M-1. The more intervening links, the more sharply peaked will be the distribution of times of onset of an activity late in the chain. Thus, whether or not each activity is intrinsically timed, the chaining mechanism can nevertheless result in "temporal discrimination," defined as a peaked, nonrandom distribution of starting times, for an activity late in the chain.

Unfortunately, chaining explanations do not fit the facts for behavior sequences induced by periodic schedules. There are three kinds of evidence that pose problems:

(a) Interim activities such as drinking are often repetitive. Thus the kind of chain actually observed is closer to A–A–A– . . . –Q (a homogeneous chain) than to the A–B–C– . . . –Q (heterogeneous chain) of the model. What determines run length in the homogeneous chain? No merely probabilistic process will suffice to make the length of the chain other than random (i.e., independent of time); some kind of counting mechanism is required. Yet there is no evidence that animals can count better than they can time, so that an explanation of timing in terms of counting is unsupported.

(b) In a simple chain, the necessary and sufficient cause of activity N is the occurrence of activity N-1. Hence prevention of activity N-1 should eliminate activity N. This is not what happens in temporal behavior sequences. For example, elimination of the water bottle normally present during a fixed-time food schedule usually causes rats to make the terminal response *earlier* in the interval (Staddon & Ayres, 1975). Many experiments, using both spaced-responding and periodic schedules, have shown that prevention of interim activities disrupts temporal discrimination by causing the instrumental response to occur too soon (e.g., Frank & Staddon, 1974; Glazer & Singh, 1971; Laties, Weiss, Clark, & Reynolds, 1965; Laties, Weiss, & Weiss, 1969).[3] Since the terminal response is usually preceded by interim activities such as drinking, and elimination of these activities if anything facilitates the terminal response, they cannot be links in a chain that ends with that response.

---

[3] This discussion considers spaced-responding (DRL) schedules on the same basis as interval schedules. In the spaced-responding case, the terminal response is timed from the previous terminal response, whereas in interval schedules it is timed from reinforcement, but performance on both schedules seems to be similarly affected by (for example) prevention of interim activities.

It is perhaps worth noting that most attempts to explain wholly endogenous behavior sequences by means of behavior or reflex chains have been unsuccessful. For example, insect flight and walking patterns, once thought to depend on chain reflexes, have been shown to involve central programming (e.g., Wilson, 1961, 1966). However, chain accounts have been quite successful in explaining behavior sequences incorporating extrinsic stimuli, such as the "lock and key" courtship sequences described by Tinbergen (1951), and the hunting behavior of the wasp *Philanthus triangulum* and many other invertebrate predators (see Hinde, 1970, for a review). In the context of operant behavior, the chaining concept arose in connection with chained schedules. These parallel the ethological examples just mentioned, in that responses produce *external* stimuli that in turn produce other responses. It seems prudent to reserve chaining accounts specifically for situations in which the successive stimuli are provided by the environment, with only the response elements of the chain being contributed by the animal.

(c) Induced sequences show both *variability of succession* (A is not always followed by B) and *temporal variability* (B does not always occur at, or for, the same time). Both these features are incompatible with simple chaining, but might be modeled by a Markov process (Cane, 1959, 1961; Staddon, 1972a). However, analyses of behavior sequences in both pigeons (Staddon, 1972a) and rats (Staddon & Ayres, 1975) show that even a Markov account is not adequate, at least in a simple form. The essential property of a Markov process is that each state (activity) is dependent only on the preceding one. Therefore there should be no dependence of the onset (or offset) of an activity on time, other than the time elapsed since the preceding activity (or since the beginning of the activity). Yet on fixed-time schedules both pigeons and rats show such dependencies. The time between two successive activities tends to be shorter the later the first activity ends within the interval; and the duration of a given activity tends to be shorter the later it begins.

Davey, Harzem, and Lowe (personal communication) report that "running" rate on fixed-interval schedules (i.e., rate of lever pressing following the first press in each interval) is directly related to pause (time to the first lever press): the later the rats begin to press, the faster they go. Pigeons showed no effect of pause on overall running rate. In subsequent experiments Staddon and Frank (1975b) have found that the rate at which many pigeons *accelerate* to their fixed terminal rate depends on pause: the longer the pause, the more rapidly they accelerate. The low rate at which they start, and the high rate that they finish up with, is more or less constant, but the time they take to get from one to the other decreases as the time available for responding before food delivery decreases.

All these observations underline the dependence of induced activities on the time elapsed since the beginning of the fixed interval. Chaining cannot easily account for this dependency.

Behavioral Clocks

"Behavioral clock" interpretations are less explicit than the chaining account. They are based on the frequent observation that prevention of interim ("collateral") activities disrupts "temporal discrimination" (i.e., pausing) on fixed-interval and spaced-responding (DRL) schedules. The idea that the animal "uses" the interim activities to suppress the terminal response for a time is little more than a restatement of this observation. One refinement is to attribute to the collateral activities an intrinsic periodicity, so that they serve the function of a behavioral clock. In this form the hypothesis resembles chaining. The difference is that the stimuli ("causal factors") for the terminal response are assumed to be present all the time; the response fails to occur early in the interval only because it is suppressed by the "collateral" behaviors that constitute the clock. When they have run their course, the terminal response occurs. The mechanism in this case is a type of *disinhibition,* whereas in chaining the terminal response is directly produced (elicited, controlled) by the penultimate behavior in the chain. However, the arguments against chaining apply also to this form of behavioral clock. In particular, the negative correlation between the offset of the last interim activity and the onset of the terminal response shows that the terminal response is directly affected by post-food time. Although evidence from prevention experiments shows that interim activities do exert some suppressive effect on the terminal response (since their elimination causes the terminal response to occur earlier), the correlation data show that this disinhibiting effect is not the sole determiner of the temporal locus of the terminal response; some kind of "internal clock" is also involved.

Although inhibition due to interim activities is not the only factor affecting the timing of the terminal response, it may be *a* factor. A further refinement of the behavioral clock view is to suppose that some measure of temporal discrimination is a function of some property of the interim activities—vigor, rate, etc. This relation can be looked at either within or across individuals. Within individuals it is plausible: suppression of interim activities disrupts a developed temporal discrimination (Frank & Staddon, 1974; Schwartz & Williams, 1971), and interim activities such as drinking tend to develop in step with a terminal response such as food anticipation during training (e.g., Pouthas & Cavé, 1972; Staddon & Ayres, 1975). There is less evidence for a correlation across individuals. For example, Smith and Clark (1974) found no correlation between rates of running or induced licking and efficiency of performance on spaced-responding schedules. However, Glazer & Singh (1971) found that temporal discrimination was inversely related to degree of restraint in three groups of rats that were either unrestrained, partially restrained, or severely restrained. In informal observations we have noticed that pigeons trained in small Skinner boxes sometimes fail to show the typical fixed-interval "scallop" and respond more or less continuously; animals trained in the usual large boxes rarely show this pattern. These various experiments cannot be rigorously compared, because of species differences and because amount of training obviously interacts with these differences. Nevertheless, taken together there is much evidence that temporal discrimination is favored by an environment that affords animals opportunities for interim activities.

Although there is evidence for some relation between temporal discrimination and interim activities, no *particular* interim activity is necessary for appropriate timing. While many authors report vigorous "collateral" behaviors on temporal schedules (e.g., Hendry & Dillow, 1966; Laties et al., 1965; Zuriff, 1969), others report none (e.g., Anger, 1956; Kelleher, Fry, & Cook, 1959; Reynolds & Catania, 1962). And although pigeons trained under unrestrained conditions show the expected disruption when shifted to conditions of bodily restraint, the disruption is transient and after protracted training there is little steady-state difference (Frank & Staddon, 1974). Presumably the transient disruption occurs because interim activities possible under free conditions are prevented when the pigeon is restrained. Evidently other interim activities soon develop, however, since behavior recovers to almost the same level as before the shift. Frank and Staddon also found a disruption when birds trained under restrained conditions were shifted to free conditions. This disruption is harder to explain in terms of prevention of previously available interim activities. However, it can be understood in terms of a wider scheme for classifying sequential interactions, to which I now turn.

Types of Sequential Interaction

It has not yet proved possible to explain in detail the mechanisms underlying induced, or indeed any other, behavior sequences. Short of such a complete explanation, terms such as *inhibition, disinhibition, elicitation,* and *causal factors* have become current in the animal behavior literature as a way of classifying types of sequential interaction. These terms can be employed in several ways. The present section develops an approach that is consistent with the facts already discussed and suggests questions that can be answered empirically. This approach is closely related to the more formal state-space approach recently elaborated by McFarland (McFarland, 1974; McFarland & Sibly, 1975; Sibly & McFarland, 1974) and to the theoretical system of Atkinson & Birch (1970).

DEFINITIONS

Behavioral State. Evidence already discussed shows that the overt activity that is actually observed (performance) is only one aspect of an underlying behavioral *state*. Terms that convey aspects of the term state, in the sense used here, are "mood," "expectation," "motivational state," and even "operant," in the sense that an operant is a class of behaviors with common controlling factors. Bindra's (1969) "central motive state" is also close to the present meaning. States are mutually incompatible; they are the basic interacting elements in this scheme.

Activity. This is an observed class of motor patterns; it has both stimulus and response components. These motor patterns (e.g., pecking, drinking, pacing in a particular place, etc.) are necessarily defined subjectively, but little practical difficulty is usually encountered in settling on reliable categories. A state exists independently of any particular activity, but the performance of an activity may act back on the strength of a state (i.e., on the level of its causal factors), either increasing it ("momentum" effects; positive feedback) or decreasing it (self-inhibition: negative feedback). Providing the environment is constant, activities are assumed to be generally reliable (one-to-one) indicators of their associated states, and the terms activity and state are treated as equivalent in the following discussion.

Causal Factors. These are environmental factors affecting the strength of states. Causal factors are assumed always to be facilitatory, so that suppression of a given activity by a stimulus is assumed to be due to a decrease in its causal factors and/or an increase in the causal factors for an incompatible activity. The idea that *inhibition* is due to the activation of an incompatible activity follows directly from the hypothesis that interim and terminal states are incompatible and has gained some currency in studies of conditioned inhibition in Pavlovian situations (e.g., Anokhin, 1974; Konorsky, 1967). The "strength" of a state (activity) is equivalent to the strength of its causal factors. Examples of causal factors are discriminative and eliciting stimuli, time, and antecedent activities (as in chaining).

COMPETITION ASSUMPTION

For simplicity, I assume that the animal can be in only one state at a time. Thus, states *compete* for access to what might be termed the behavioral final common path.[4] In the following discussion it is assumed that this competition is all at one level, every state (activity) competing directly with all the others that are possible in the situation. However, the scheme can easily be generalized to allow for hierarchical or other multilevel interactions, with a given state competing directly only with states at its own level.

This scheme suggests a taxonomy of simple behavioral interactions. I first develop such a taxonomy, and then apply it to some of the data and concepts discussed earlier in the chapter.

SIMPLE SEQUENTIAL INTERACTIONS

This view allows for two kinds of simple interaction between successive behaviors. It is assumed that the shift from one behavior to another is owing to a change in only one causal factor, which either increases (inhibition, elicitation) or decreases (disinhibition, subduction) with time. These two types of interaction define four terms, as follows:

Inhibition. This occurs when activity A ceases to occur because of an increase in the causal factors

[4] Quantitative variations in response rate can be handled within this scheme by assuming that repetitive activities occur at a more or less fixed, maximum rate, so long as the animal is in the appropriate state, and that variations in rate occur because of switching between states. There is evidence for this kind of fixity in the case of drinking: licks occur at a more or less fixed rate within each bout (e.g., Marowitz & Halpern, 1973). Variations in overall lick rate are therefore associated with a proportional increase in the percentage of time spent in the licking state. There is some evidence that even "operant" behaviors such as pecking are similarly constrained, although perhaps not to the same degree (Blough, 1963; Gilbert, 1958). The notion is hard to test unless typical bout lengths are considerably longer than the modal interbehavior interval. The problem of defining the length of an activity bout, discussed by ethologists (e.g., Isaac & Marler, 1963; Nelson, 1973), confronts essentially the same issue.

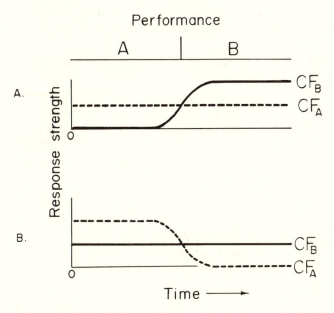

Fig. 6. Simple dyadic interactions.

(CFs) for some other activity, B (the next-in-priority activity). When $CF_B > CF_A$, A is displaced by B. Inhibition is illustrated in Figure 6A. The top line shows the observed sequence of behaviors: A followed by B. The curves below show the changes in stimulus factors (CFs) hypothesized to underlie this change. They show that the level of CFs for A remains constant, but that A is supplanted by B when the CFs for B increase beyond the level of those for A.

Disinhibition. This is simply the reverse of inhibition: activity B occurs (and activity A ceases to occur) because the CFs for antagonistic activity A decrease below the level of those for B. This is illustrated in Figure 6B.

Elicitation. The causation of behavior B in Figure 6A illustrates elicitation: B occurs because its CFs increase, all other CFs remaining constant.

Subduction. This is a neologism to describe the opposite of elicitation: a behavior ceases because its CFs decrease in strength, all other CFs remaining constant. It is illustrated by the offset of behavior A in Figure 6B.

It is clear that the two kinds of interaction illustrated in Figure 6 are simply extreme cases on a continuum of dyadic interactions between successive behaviors. For two such behaviors, A and B, the CFs for A can either decrease, increase, or remain constant with time, and similarly for B. If A is occurring initially, a shift to B will occur only if the maintained rate of change in CF_B is greater than that for CF_A

(and this differential persists for a sufficient time): $\frac{dA}{dt} > \frac{dB}{dt}$, where $\frac{dA}{dt} = \frac{d}{dt}(CF_A)$. It is assumed that the CF functions are continuous.

Experimental Analysis. In the examples illustrated in Figure 6 all that is actually observed is a switch from one activity to another. The diagrams showing changes in CF strength with time constitute hypotheses about the underlying causation and must be tested by manipulating the putative causal factors. In each example, only one CF changes with time; if it is under direct experimental control, verification of the causal hypothesis is a trivial matter. However, in the cases discussed in this chapter, the changing CF is usually an inferred "internal clock" that is only under indirect experimental control. For example, suppose (for the sake of illustration) that behavior A is an interim activity such as drinking, and B a terminal response such as lever pressing, with the switch from A to B timed from food delivery. Then the changing CF (CF_B in Figure 6A, CF_A in Figure 6B) must also be assumed to be timed from food delivery, so that the absolute time of the origin of the curves in Figure 6 can be controlled, but not their form.

How might the two cases in Figure 6 be distinguished experimentally? The answer to this question depends critically on quantitative issues: the absolute values of the strengths of the CFs for the two activities. With the values shown in Figure 6 it is apparent that complete elimination of activity A (e.g., by removing a constant CF not shown in the diagrams: the water bottle) will cause activity B to occur earlier in the interval under case B than under case A. Similarly, removal of a constant CF for activity B (the lever) should cause activity A to occur throughout the interval, under case A, but prolong A only slightly under case B. In this simple case, therefore, it is relatively easy to distinguish between these two hypotheses. However, if the CFs for *both* activities change with time, or if neither CF ever decreases to zero, discrimination is much more difficult. One possible technique in that case is to introduce a third competing activity, such as running, whose CFs can be assumed to be constant during the test period. By manipulating its strength, an estimate of the relative strengths of A and B, as a function of time, might be arrived at.

Internal Feedback. The diagrams in Figure 6 imply that the CFs for a given activity do not depend on whether or not that activity is actually occurring. Yet this kind of independence is unlikely to be general. Once begun, an activity may have a certain momentum and resist competition from other activities that might have been sufficient to prevent its initial occurrence. Conversely, even in the absence of competition, most activities cease to occur after a time, presumably because of some kind of self-inhibition (Hull's, 1943, "reactive inhibition"; the "consummatory force" of Atkinson & Birch, 1970). The circumstantial evidence for these kinds of internal feedback interaction is strong. Unfortunately, they are hard to measure directly just because the loops are internal ones.

For example, self-inhibition cannot immediately be distinguished from the hypothesis of an internal clock. When first exposed to a running wheel, a rat may tend to run for a more or less fixed time; is this because of a fixed internal clock that times the run bout, or because of negative feedback from the response? The second possibility can be evaluated by surgical intervention (e.g., deafferentation), or by varying the resistance of the running wheel. If these operations change the duration of running, some role for feedback is demonstrated. In any particular case, tests of this sort can usually be devised. However, the possibility of self-feedback greatly complicates the task of experimental analysis.

This general problem is a familiar one to students of the major homeostatic systems such as food and water regulation (see Satinoff & Henderson, Chapter 6). However, much more is known about the internal feedbacks that affect the duration of an eating bout, for example, than about the comparable factors affecting running, preening or lever pressing. The fact that the mechanisms underlying such responses are unlikely to be fixed, but may depend on the situation in which the response occurs (e.g., whether the response is schedule-induced, or occurs under free conditions), is a further complication.

Variability. Although schedule-induced behavior is characteristically highly stereotyped, there is nevertheless variation in its form and, particularly, its temporal pattern from one interfood interval to the next. Temporal variability (variation in the temporal location of an activity as a function of post-food time) is always found, but variability of succession (variation in the order of activities) is less common. Thus, the function relating the strength of causal factors to post-food time must be assumed to vary from interval to interval. The simplest form of variation is a stochastic process with zero mean superimposed on the average CF functions (e.g., the curves in Figure 6). Since it is assumed that the CF functions change at a finite rate (i.e., there are no step-functions other than

those due to the onset of extrinsic stimuli), variation in relative levels will cause variation in the time of switching from one behavior to another and, if the added random variation is large, may even cause reversals of order.

APPLICATIONS

Variability, internal feedback, and the possibility of competition at several levels, can obviously combine to produce sequences of behavior that defy analysis by means of simple experimental tests. Bearing these complex possibilities in mind, it may nevertheless be useful to see to what extent relatively simple interactions, such as those illustrated in Figure 6, can explain the experimental results discussed earlier. Three cases will be considered: interactions between running and drinking, the effect of interfood interval, and an anomalous experimental result owing to the persistence of running.

Running/Drinking Interactions. Figure 7A shows the postulated time course of CFs for eating (E), drinking (D), running (R), and food anticipation (FA), underlying the maintained temporal distribution of these activities shown in Figure 1B, which shows data from a rat on a fixed-time 30 sec schedule. The vertical lines marked "P" in Figure 7 show the times of pellet delivery. The CFs for running are assumed to be essentially constant, so that running constitutes a disinhibited activity which occurs only when the strengths of drinking and food anticipation are low. One prediction from this hypothesis is that the elimination of drinking (e.g., by removing the water bottle) should cause running to occur earlier in the interval, but should have little effect on the time of onset of food anticipation. Elimination of running (by removing the running wheel) should cause food anticipation to begin earlier and drinking to persist later in the interval. Elimination of drinking and running should

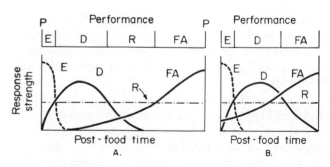

Fig. 7. Hypothesis for interactions among behaviors induced by periodic food. A: Low to intermediate food rate. B: High food rate.

cause food anticipation to begin sooner than elimination of running alone. These predictions assume that the pattern of CFs illustrated in Figure 7 remains more or less constant during the test period, i.e., they are predictions about *transfer* effects.

In general these predictions are borne out. Elimination of running does appear to cause drinking to persist longer and food anticipation to begin earlier in the interval, and elimination of drinking does seem to have more effect on running than on food anticipation (Segal, 1969; Staddon & Ayres, 1975). However, the Staddon and Ayres data come from steady-state adjustments to the manipulations rather than transfer (first-day) measures, the Segal data do not show temporal location of activities, and exact data do not seem to be available elsewhere. Hence these predictions cannot yet be precisely evaluated.

Effects of Interfood Interval. Figure 7B shows the postulated interactions on a short (5-15 sec) fixed-time food schedule. The CFs for running are the same as in Figure 7A, but the CFs for food anticipation rise to their asymptote more quickly, because of the shorter interval. Consequently, the crossover of the curves for drinking and food anticipation occurs at a level higher than the level of the CFs for running, which cannot therefore occur, apart from the effects of random variation. Thus the decrease in the frequency of running with interfood interval shown in Figure 3 is explained by assuming that the CFs for drinking and food anticipation reach the same asymptote in short intervals as in long ones, and therefore cross over at a level that is inversely related to interval length: the shorter the interval, the higher the crossover point.

Frank and Staddon (1974) found that pigeons trained on a periodic schedule under conditions of bodily restraint showed disrupted temporal discrimination (i.e., the terminal response, key pecking, occurred earlier in the interval) when shifted to unrestrained conditions. Figure 7B sheds some light on this result if it is assumed that the shift had more effect on the CFs (controlling stimuli) for whatever interim activity was occurring under restrained conditions (analogous to drinking in Figure 7B) than on the terminal response. This assumption seems reasonable since the main CF for pecking was the response key, which was not affected by the shift. Figure 7B makes it clear that any reduction in the CFs for the interim activity, relative to those for the terminal response, will cause the terminal response to occur earlier in the interval, as Frank and Staddon found.

Persistence of Running. Figure 8 shows the frac-

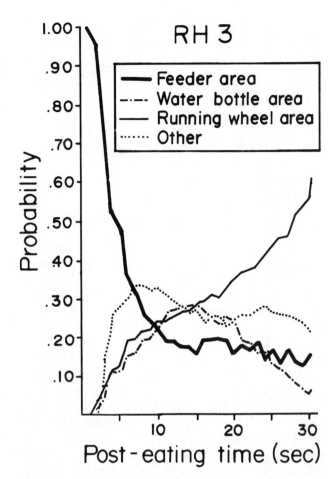

Fig. 8. An unusual pattern of behavior induced in a female rat by a 30-sec periodic food schedule.

tion of time spent in various activities (activity areas) by a female rat in a hexagonal apparatus in which it received a food pellet every 30 sec (Staddon & Ayres, 1975). The behavior of this animal was anomalous, as can be seen by comparing Figure 8 with Figure 1B. The rat in Figure 8 showed running as an apparent terminal response, since the activity increased in frequency up until the time of the next food delivery. A naive reinforcement theory interpretation might conclude that running in this case was adventitiously reinforced by food delivery—with which it was almost invariably contiguous. However, this interpretation is contradicted by the results of extinction tests, in which the first effect of food omission was an increase in food anticipation, followed later by an increase in running above the level observed under the food schedule.

Figure 9 shows what may be a more accurate representation. The curves are identified as in Figures 6 and 7. However, the abscissa is post-eating (rather

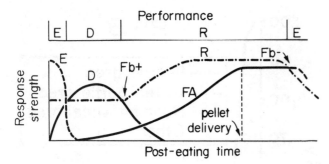

Fig. 9. Hypothesis for interactions underlying behavior shown in Figure 8.

than post-pellet-delivery) time, since this animal did not always eat the pellet as soon as it was delivered. The main difference between Figure 9 and Figure 7A is in the postulated CF function for running, which shows positive acceleration once the response is expressed (a positive feedback, Fb+, "momentum" effect), and declines with the continued occurrence of running (a negative feedback, Fb−, "self-inhibition" effect). A consequence of the momentum effect is that when the food pellet is delivered, the CFs for running are above those for eating. The pellet is not eaten until the CFs for running decrease (self-inhibition) below those for food anticipation, the animal enters the feeder area, sees the food, and eats.

The model predicts the initial perseveration of food anticipation in extinction as well as the eventual dominance of running. It also predicts that the temporal pattern of food anticipation will approach that shown by the other rats (e.g., the animal in Figure 1B) if drinking is eliminated (allowing running to cease earlier in the interval), and should be essentially the same as the pattern shown by the others if running is eliminated. The data support both these predictions. Other features of the model for this animal have not been tested in detail (for example, the proper tests to distinguish response-produced feedbacks from response-produced clocks were not carried out). However, the basic hypothesis that the anomalous behavior of this individual is largely, perhaps entirely, attributable to its tendency to run seems quite well supported.

Once the mechanisms underlying behavioral sequences are fully understood, the representations in Figures 6, 7, and 9 will undoubtedly appear cumbersome and redundant. However, these diagrams force one to be precise about often loosely applied terms such as inhibition. They also suggest clear experimental tests. Without such a framework it is often difficult to ask good experimental questions about temporal sequences, or to interpret the results of experimental manipulations.

CONCLUDING COMMENTS

The experimental literature on schedule-induced behavior, though extensive, is too unsystematic to point clearly to any particular theoretical integration. This chapter is an attempt to provide an organizing framework to guide both experimentation and interpretation.

The traditional emphasis on a single, instrumental response is misplaced. The work reviewed here shows that the temporal pattern of any activity depends on its interactions with other activities that are induced by the situation. These induced behaviors must be considered on the same footing as the instrumental response. They are often just as vigorous (sometimes even more vigorous), are as reliably produced, and share some of the same causal factors. The "laws" of operant behavior are not a property of isolated reflexes, but emergent properties of a set of interactions among induced states and their associated behaviors. Each behavior has its own controlling (causal) factors, both stimuli and time. Any environmental change affects the instrumental response both directly, and indirectly through its effects on other causally related activities. The effects of such changes cannot be fully understood until these interactions have been teased out.

REFERENCES

Åkerman, B., Andersson, E., Fabricius, E., & Svensson, L. Observations on central regulation of body temperature and of food and water intake in the pigeon (*Columba livia*). *Acta Physiologica Scandanavica*, 1960, *50*, 328–336.

Allen, J. D., Porter, J. H., & Arazie, R. Schedule-induced drinking as a function of percentage reinforcement. *Journal of the Experimental Analysis of Behavior*, 1975, *23*, 223–232.

Anger, D. The dependence of interresponse times upon the relative reinforcement of different interresponse times. *Journal of Experimental Psychology*, 1956, *52*, 145–161.

Anokhin, P. K. *Biology and neurophysiology of the conditioned reflex and its role in adaptive behavior.* S. S. Corson. Trans. New York: Pergamon, 1974.

Appel, J. B. Aversive aspects of a schedule of positive reinforcement. *Journal of the Experimental Analysis of Behavior*, 1963, *6*, 423–428.

Atkinson, J. W., & Birch, D. *The dynamics of action.* New York: Wiley, 1970.

Azrin, N. H. Time-out from positive reinforcement. *Science*, 1961, *133*, 382–383.

Azrin, N. H., Hutchinson, R. R., & Hake, D. F. Extinction-induced aggression. *Journal of the Experimental Analysis of Behavior*, 1966, *9*, 191–204.

Bilbrey, J., & Winokur, S. Controls for and constraints on auto-shaping. *Journal of the Experimental Analysis of Behavior*, 1973, *20*, 323–332.

Bindra, D. A unified interpretation of emotion and motivation. *Annals of the New York Academy of Sciences*, 1969, *159*, 1071–1083.

Bindra, D. A unified account of classical conditioning and operant training. In A. H. Black and W. F. Prokasy (Eds.), *Classical conditioning II: Current research and theory*. Englewood Cliffs, N.J.: Prentice-Hall, Inc., 1972.

Blough, D. S. Interresponse time as a function of continuous variables: A new method and some data. *Journal of the Experimental Analysis of Behavior*, 1963, *6*, 237–246.

Bolles, R. C. Reinforcement, expectancy, and learning. *Psychological Review*, 1972, *79*, 394–409.

Bowen, C. *The how, when and where of polydipsia*. Unpublished M. A. thesis, Duke University, 1972.

Brown, P. L., & Jenkins, H. M. Auto-shaping of the pigeon's keypeck. *Journal of the Experimental Analysis of Behavior*, 1968, *11*, 1–8.

Brown, T. G., & Flory, R. K. Schedule-induced escape from fixed-interval reinforcement. *Journal of the Experimental Analysis of Behavior*, 1972, *17*, 395–403.

Browne, M. *Latent learning revisited: The role of reward and overt behavior changes in the acquisition of stimulus relations*. Unpublished doctoral dissertation, Indiana University, 1973.

Burks, C. D. Schedule-induced polydipsia: Are response-dependent schedules a limiting condition? *Journal of the Experimental Analysis of Behavior*, 1970, *13*, 351–358.

Cane, V. Behaviour sequences as semi-Markov chains. *Journal of the Royal Statistical Society*, B, 1959, *21*, 36–58.

Cane, V. Some ways of describing behaviour. In W. H. Thorpe and O. L. Zangwill (Eds.), *Current problems in animal behaviour*. London: Cambridge University Press, 1961.

Carlisle, H. J. Fixed-ratio polydipsia: Thermal effects of drinking, pausing, and responding. *Journal of Comparative and Physiological Psychology*, 1971, *75*, 10–22.

Carlisle, H. J. Schedule-induced polydipsia: Blockade by intrahypothalamic atropine. *Physiology and Behavior*, 1973, *11*, 139–143.

Carlisle, H. J., Shanab, M. E., & Simpson, C. W. Schedule-induced behaviors: Effect of intermittent water reinforcement on food intake and body temperature. *Psychonomic Science*, 1972, *26*, 35–36.

Catania, A. C., & Reynolds, G. S. A quantitative analysis of the responding maintained by interval schedules of reinforcement. *Journal of the Experimental Analysis of Behavior*, 1968, *11*, 327–383.

Cherek, D. R., Thompson, T., & Heistad, G. T. Responding maintained by the opportunity to attack during an interval food reinforcement schedule. *Journal of the Experimental Analysis of Behavior*, 1973, *19*, 113–123.

Chung, Shin-Ho. Effects of effort on response rate. *Journal of the Experimental Analysis of Behavior*, 1965, *8*, 1–7.

Clark, F. C. Some observations on the adventitious reinforcement of drinking under food reinforcement. *Journal of the Experimental Analysis of Behavior*, 1962, *5*, 61–63.

Cohen, P. S., & Looney, T. A. Schedule-induced mirror responding in the pigeon. *Journal of the Experimental Analysis of Behavior*, 1973, *19*, 395–408.

Cole, J. L. Force gradients in stimulus generalization. *Journal of the Experimental Analysis of Behavior*, 1965, *8*, 231–241.

Davis, J. M. *Socially-induced flight reactions in pigeons*. Unpublished doctoral dissertation, Duke University, 1973.

Falk, J. L. Production of polydipsia in normal rats by an intermittent food schedule. *Science*, 1961, *133*, 195–196.

Falk, J. L. Control of schedule-induced polydipsia: Type, size, and spacing of meals. *Journal of the Experimental Analysis of Behavior*, 1967, *10*, 199–206.

Falk, J. L. Conditions producing psychogenic polydipsia in animals. *Annals of the New York Academy of Sciences*, 1969, *157*, 569–593.

Falk, J. L. The nature and determinants of adjunctive behavior. *Physiology and Behavior*, 1971, *6*, 577–588.

Ferster, C. B., & Skinner, B. F. *Schedules of reinforcement*. New York: Appleton-Century-Crofts, 1957.

Flory, R. K. Attack behavior as a function of minimum inter-food interval. *Journal of the Experimental Analysis of Behavior*, 1969, *12*, 825–828.

Flory, R. K. The control of schedule-induced polydipsia: Frequency and magnitude of reinforcement. *Learning and Motivation*, 1971, *2*, 215–227.

Flory, R. K., & Ellis, B. B. Schedule-induced aggression against a slide-image target. *Bulletin of the Psychonomic Society*, 1973, *2*, 287–290.

Flory, R. K., & O'Boyle, M. K. The effect of limited water availability on schedule-induced polydipsia. *Physiology and Behavior*, 1972, *8*, 147–149.

Frank, J., & Staddon, J. E. R. Effects of restraint on temporal discrimination behavior. *Psychological Record*, 1974, *24*, 123–130.

Gamzu, E., & Schwartz, B. The maintenance of key pecking by stimulus-contingent and response-independent food presentation. *Journal of the Experimental Analysis of Behavior*, 1973, *19*, 65–72.

Gamzu, E., & Williams, D. R. Classical conditioning of a complex skeletal response. *Science*, 1971, *171*, 923–925.

Gamzu, E. R., & Williams, D. R. Associative factors underlying the pigeon's key pecking in auto-shaping procedures. *Journal of the Experimental Analysis of Behavior*, 1973, *19*, 225–232.

Gentry, W. D., & Schaeffer, R. W. The effect of FR response requirement on aggressive behavior in rats. *Psychonomic Science*, 1969, *14*, 236–238.

Gibbon, J., Berryman, R., & Thompson, R. L. Contingency spaces and measures in classical and instrumental conditioning. *Journal of the Experimental Analysis of Behavior*, 1974, *21*, 585–605.

Gilbert, R. M. Ubiquity of schedule-induced polydipsia. *Journal of the Experimental Analysis of Behavior*, 1974, *21*, 277–284.

Gilbert, T. F. Fundamental dimensional properties of the operant. *Psychological Review*, 1958, *65*, 272–282.

Glazer, H., & Singh, D. Role of collateral behavior in temporal discrimination performance and learning in rats. *Journal of Experimental Psychology*, 1971, *91*, 78–84.

GROVES, L. C., & BROWNSTEIN, A. J. Effects of trial and cycle duration on automaintenance. Paper presented at South Eastern Psychological Association Meeting, New Orleans, 1973.

HARZEM, P. Temporal discrimination. In R. M. Gilbert & N. S. Sutherland (Eds.), *Animal discrimination learning.* New York: Academic Press, 1969.

HAWKINS, T. D., SCHROT, S. H., GITHENS, S. H., & EVERETT, P. B. Schedule-induced polydipsia: An analysis of water and alcohol ingestion. In R. M. Gilbert & J. D. Keehn (Eds.), *Schedule effects: Drugs, drinking and aggression.* Toronto: University of Toronto Press, 1972.

HEARST, E., & JENKINS, H. M. Sign-tracking: The stimulus-reinforcer relation and directed action. *Psychonomic Society Monograph,* 1974.

HENDRY, D. P., & DILLOW, P. V. Observing behavior during interval schedules. *Journal of the Experimental Analysis of Behavior,* 1966, 9, 337–349.

HINDE, R. A. *Animal behaviour: A synthesis of ethology and comparative psychology.* Second edition. New York: McGraw-Hill, 1970.

HINDE, R., & STEVENSON-HINDE, J. (Eds.) *Constraints on learning.* London: Academic Press, 1973.

HODOS, W., ROSS, G. S., & BRADY, J. Complex response patterns during temporally spaced responding. *Journal of the Experimental Analysis of Behavior,* 1962, 5, 473–479.

HUTCHINSON, R. R., AZRIN, N. H., & HUNT, G. M. Attack produced by intermittent reinforcement of a concurrent operant response. *Journal of the Experimental Analysis of Behavior,* 1968, 11, 489–495.

HULL, C. L. *Principles of Behavior.* New York: Appleton-Century, 1943.

ISAAC, D., & MARLER, P. Ordering of sequences of singing behaviour in Mistle Thrushes in relationship to timing. *Animal Behaviour,* 1963, 11, 179–188.

INNIS, N. K., & STADDON, J. E. R. Temporal tracking on cyclic-interval reinforcement schedules. *Journal of the Experimental Analysis of Behavior,* 1971, 16, 411–423.

JACQUET, Y. F. Schedule-induced licking during multiple schedules. *Journal of the Experimental Analysis of Behavior,* 1972, 17, 413–423.

JENKINS, H. M. Sequential organization in schedules of reinforcement. In W. N. Schoenfeld (Ed.), *The theory of reinforcement schedules.* Englewood Cliffs, N.J.: Prentice-Hall, Inc., 1970.

JENKINS, H. M., & MOORE, B. R. The form of the auto-shaped response with food or water reinforcers. *Journal of the Experimental Analysis of Behavior,* 1973, 20, 163–181.

JENSEN, C., & FALLON, D. Behavioral aftereffects of reinforcement and its omission as a function of reinforcement magnitude. *Journal of the Experimental Analysis of Behavior,* 1973, 19, 459–468.

KACHANOFF, R., LEVEILLE, R., MCLELLAND, J. P., & WAGNER, M. J. Schedule-induced behavior in humans. *Physiology and Behavior,* 1973, 11, 395–398.

KEEHN, J. D. Schedule-dependence, schedule-induction, and the Law of Effect. In R. M. Gilbert & J. D. Keehn (Eds.), *Schedule effects: Drugs, drinking, and aggression.* Toronto: University of Toronto Press, 1972, Pp. 65–94.

KELLEHER, R. T., FRY, W., & COOK, L. Interresponse time distribution as a function of differential reinforcement of temporally spaced responses. *Journal of the Experimental Analysis of Behavior,* 1959, 2, 91–106.

KILLEEN, P. On the temporal control of behavior. *Psychological Review,* 1975, 82, 89–115.

KISSILEFF, H. R. Food-associated drinking in the rat. *Journal of Comparative and Physiological Psychology,* 1969, 67, 284–300.

KNUTSON, J. F., & KLEINKNECHT, R. A. Attack during differential reinforcement of low rate of responding. *Psychonomic Science,* 1970, 19, 289–290.

KONORSKI, J. *Integrative activity of the brain.* Chicago: University of Chicago Press, 1967.

KRAMER, T. J., & RILLING, M. Differential reinforcement of low rates: A selective critique. *Psychological Bulletin,* 1970, 74, 225–254.

LATIES, V. G., WEISS, B., CLARK, R. L., & REYNOLDS, M. D. Overt "mediating" behavior during temporally spaced responding. *Journal of the Experimental Analysis of Behavior,* 1965, 8, 107–116.

LATIES, V. G., WEISS, B., & WEISS, A. B. Further observations on overt "mediating" behavior and the discrimination of time. *Journal of the Experimental Analysis of Behavior,* 1969, 12, 43–57.

LEVITSKY, D., & COLLIER, G. Schedule-induced wheel running. *Physiology and Behavior,* 1968, 3, 571–573.

LORENZ, K. Z. Innate bases of learning. In K. H. Pribram (Ed.), *On the biology of learning.* New York: Harcourt, Brace and World, 1969.

LOTTER, E. C., WOODS, S. C., & VASSELLI, J. R. Schedule-induced polydipsia: An artifact. *Journal of Comparative and Physiological Psychology,* 1973, 83, 478–484.

MAROWITZ, L. A., & HALPERN, B. P. The effects of environmental constraints on licking patterns. *Physiology and Behavior,* 1973, 11, 259–267.

MCFARLAND, D. J. Hunger, thirst and displacement pecking in the barbary dove. *Animal Behaviour,* 1965, 13, 293–300.

MCFARLAND, D. J. Adjunctive behaviour in feeding and drinking situations. *Revue du Comportement Animal,* 1970, 4, 64–73.

MCFARLAND, D. J. Time-sharing as a behavioural phenomenon. In D. Lehrman, R. Hinde, & E. Shaw (Eds.), *Advances in the study of behavior.* Vol. 5., New York: Academic Press, 1974.

MCFARLAND, D. J., & SIBLY, R. The behavioural final common path. *Philosophical Transactions of the Royal Society of London,* Series B, 1975, 270, 265–293.

MCGILL, W. J. Stochastic latency mechanisms. In R. D. Luce, R. R. Bush, & E. Galanter (Eds.), *Handbook of mathematical psychology.* Vol. I. New York: Wiley, 1963.

MENDELSON, J., ZIELKE, S., WERNER, J. S., & FREED, L. M. Effects of airstream accessibility on airlicking in the rat. *Physiology and Behavior,* 1973, 11, 125–130.

MILLENSON, J. R. The facts of schedule-induced polydipsia. *Behavior Research Methods and Instrumentation,* 1975, 7, 257–259.

MILLER, J. S., & GOLLUB, L. R. Adjunctive and operant bolt pecking in the pigeon. *Psychological Record,* 1974, 24, 203–208.

MOORE, B. The role of directed Pavlovian reactions in simple instrumental learning in the pigeon. In R. Hinde & J. Stevenson-Hinde (Eds.), *Constraints on learning.* London: Academic Press, 1973.

MORAN, G. The effects of lick-contingent delays of reinforcement on the development of schedule-induced polydipsia. M.A. Thesis, Dalhousie University, 1974.

NELSON, K. After-effects of courtship in the male three spined stickleback. *Zietschrift für vergleichende Physiologie*, 1965, *50*, 569–597.

NELSON, K. Does the holistic study of behavior have a future? In P. P. G. Bateson & P. H. Klopfer (Eds.), *Perspectives in ethology*. New York: Plenum Press, 1973.

NEVIN, J. A., & BERRYMAN, R. A note on chaining and temporal discrimination. *Journal of the Experimental Analysis of Behavior*, 1963, *6*, 109–113.

PAVLOV, I. P. *Conditioned reflexes*. Trans. G. V. Anrep. London: Oxford University Press, 1927.

PLISKOFF, S., & TOLLIVER, G. Water-deprivation-produced sign reversal of a conditioned reinforcer based upon dry food. *Journal of the Experimental Analysis of Behavior*, 1960, *3*, 323–329.

PORTER, J. H., & KENSHALO, D. R. Schedule-induced drinking following omission of reinforcement in the Rhesus monkey. *Physiology and Behavior*, 1974, *12*, 1075–1077.

PORTER, J. H., ARAZIE, R., HOLBROOK, J. W., CHEEK, M. S., & ALLEN, J. D. Effects of variable and fixed second-order schedules on schedule-induced polydipsia in the rat. *Physiology and Behavior*, 1975, *14*, 143–149.

POUTHAS, V., & CAVÉ, C. Evolution de deux conduites collatérales au cours d'un conditionnement au temps chez le rat. *L'Année Psychologique*, 1972, *72*, 17–24.

RACHLIN, H. Contrast and matching. *Psychological Review*, 1973, *80*, 217–234.

RACHLIN, H., & BAUM, W. M. Effects of alternative reinforcement: Does the source matter? *Journal of the Experimental Analysis of Behavior*, 1972, *18*, 231–241.

REDFORD, M. E., & PERKINS, C. C., JR. The role of autopecking in behavioral contrast. *Journal of the Experimental Analysis of Behavior*, 1974, *21*, 145–150.

RESCORLA, R. A. Pavlovian conditioning and its proper control procedures. *Psychological Review*, 1967, *74*, 71–80.

RESCORLA, R. A., & WAGNER, A. R. A theory of Pavlovian conditioning: Variations in the effectiveness of reinforcement and nonreinforcement. In A. Black & W. F. Prokasy (Eds.), *Classical Conditioning II*. Englewood Cliffs, N.J.: Prentice-Hall, Inc., 1972.

REYNIERSE, J. H., & SPANIER, D. Excessive drinking in rats' adaptation to the schedule of feeding. *Psychonomic Science*, 1968, *10*, 95–96.

REYNOLDS, G. S., & CATANIA, A. C. Temporal discrimination in pigeons. *Science*, 1962, *135*, 314–315.

RICCI, J. A. Key pecking under response-independent food presentation after long simple and compound stimuli. *Journal of the Experimental Analysis of Behavior*, 1973, *19*, 509–516.

RICHARDS, R. W., & RILLING, M. Aversive aspects of a fixed-interval schedule of food reinforcement. *Journal of the Experimental Analysis of Behavior*, 1972, *17*, 405–411.

ROSENBLITH, J. Z. Polydipsia induced in the rat by a second-order schedule. *Journal of the Experimental Analysis of Behavior*, 1970, *14*, 139–144.

SCHNEIDER, B. A. A two-state analysis of fixed-interval responding in the pigeon. *Journal of the Experimental Analysis of Behavior*, 1969, *12*, 677–687.

SCHWARTZ, B., & WILLIAMS, D. R. Discrete-trials spaced responding in the pigeon: The dependence of efficient performance on the availability of a stimulus for collateral pecking. *Journal of the Experimental Analysis of Behavior*, 1971, *16*, 155–160.

SCHWARTZ, B., & WILLIAMS, D. R. The role of the response-reinforcer contingency in negative automaintenance. *Journal of the Experimental Analysis of Behavior*, 1972, *17*, 351–357.

SEGAL, E. F. The development of water drinking on a dry-food free-reinforcement schedule. *Psychonomic Science*, 1965, *2*, 29–30.

SEGAL, E. F. The interaction of psychogenic polydipsia with wheel running in rats. *Psychonomic Science*, 1969, *14*, 141–144.

SEGAL, E., & HOLLOWAY, S. M. Timing behavior in rats with water drinking as a mediator. *Science*, 1963, *140*, 888–889.

SEGAL, E. F., ODEN, D. L., & DEADWYLER, S. A. Determinants of polydipsia: IV. Free-reinforcement schedules. *Psychonomic Science*, 1965, *3*, 11–12.

SEVENSTER, P. Incompatibility of response and reward. In R. Hinde & J. Stevenson-Hinde (Eds.), *Constraints on learning*. London: Academic Press, 1973.

SHANAB, M. E., & PETERSON, J. L. Polydipsia in the pigeon. *Psychonomic Science*, 1969, *15*, 51–52.

SHETTLEWORTH, S. J. Food reinforcement and the organization of behavior in Golden Hamsters. In R. Hinde & J. Stevenson-Hinde (Eds.), *Constraints on learning*. London: Academic Press, 1973.

SHULL, R. L. The response-reinforcement dependency in fixed-interval schedules of reinforcement. *Journal of the Experimental Analysis of Behavior*, 1970, *14*, 55–60.

SIBLY, R., & MCFARLAND, D. J. A state-space approach to motivation. In D. J. McFarland (Ed.), *Motivational control systems*. London: Academic Press, 1974.

SKINNER, B. F. "Superstition" in the pigeon. *Journal of Experimental Psychology*, 1948, *38*, 168–172.

SKINNER, B. F. *Cumulative record*. Englewood Cliffs, N.J.: Prentice-Hall, Inc., 1961.

SKINNER, B. F., & MORSE, C. W. Fixed-interval reinforcement of running in a wheel. *Journal of the Experimental Analysis of Behavior*, 1958, *1*, 371–379.

SLANGEN, J. L., & WEIJNEN, J. A. The reinforcing effect of electrical stimulation of the tongue in thirsty rats. *Physiology and Behavior*, 1972, *8*, 565–568.

SMITH, J. B., & CLARK, F. C. Intercurrent and reinforced behavior under multiple spaced-responding schedules. *Journal of the Experimental Analysis of Behavior*, 1974, *21*, 445–454.

STADDON, J. E. R. Effect of reinforcement duration on fixed-interval responding. *Journal of the Experimental Analysis of Behavior*, 1970, *13*, 9–11.

STADDON, J. E. R. A note on the analysis of behavioral sequences in *Columba Livia*. *Animal Behaviour*, 1972, *20*, 284–292. (a)

STADDON, J. E. R. Temporal control and the theory of reinforcement schedules. In R. M. Gilbert & J. R. Millenson (Eds.), *Reinforcement: Behavioral analyses*. New York: Academic Press, 1972. (b)

STADDON, J. E. R. Temporal control, attention, and memory. *Psychological Review*, 1974, *81*, 375–391.

STADDON, J. E. R. Learning as adaptation. In W. K. Estes (Ed.), *Handbook of learning and cognitive processes*. Vol. II. New York: Erlbaum Associates, 1976.

STADDON, J. E. R., & AYRES, S. L. Sequential and temporal

properties of behavior induced by a schedule of periodic food delivery. *Behaviour,* 1975, *54,* 26–49.

Staddon, J. E. R., & Frank, J. The role of the peck-food contingency on fixed-interval schedules. *Journal of the Experimental Analysis of Behavior,* 1975, *23,* 17–23. (a)

Staddon, J. E. R., & Frank, J. A. Temporal control on periodic schedules: Fine structure. *Bulletin of the Psychonomic Society,* 1975, *6,* 536–538. (b)

Staddon, J. E. R., & Simmelhag, V. L. The "superstition" experiment: A re-examination of its implications for the principles of adaptive behavior. *Psychological Review,* 1971, *78,* 3–43.

Stein, L. S. Excessive drinking in the rat: superstition or thirst? *Journal of Comparative and Physiological Psychology,* 1964, *58,* 237–242.

Terrace, H. S., Gibbon, J., Farrell, L., & Baldock, M. D. Temporal factors influencing the acquisition and maintenance of an autoshaped keypeck. *Animal Learning and Behavior,* 1975, *3,* 53–62.

Thompson, D. M. Escape from S^D associated with fixed-ratio reinforcement. *Journal of the Experimental Analysis of Behavior,* 1964, *7,* 1–8.

Thompson, T., & Bloom, W. Aggressive behavior and extinction-induced response rate increase. *Psychonomic Science,* 1966, *5,* 335–336.

Tinbergen, N. *A study of instinct.* London: Oxford University Press, 1951.

Villareal, J. *Schedule-induced pica.* Paper read at Eastern Psychological Association Meeting, Boston, 1967.

Wayner, M. J. Motor control function of the lateral hypothalamus and adjunctive behavior. *Physiology and Behavior,* 1970, *5,* 1319–1325.

Wayner, M. J., & Greenberg, I. Schedule dependence of schedule-induced polydipsia and lever pressing. *Physiology and Behavior,* 1973, *10,* 965–966.

Weiner, H. Controlling human fixed-interval performance. *Journal of the Experimental Analysis of Behavior,* 1969, *12,* 349–373.

Williams, D. R., & Williams, H. Auto-maintenance in the pigeon: Sustained pecking despite contingent non-reinforcement. *Journal of the Experimental Analysis of Behavior,* 1969, *12,* 511–520.

Wilson, D. M. The central nervous control of flight in a locust. *Journal of Experimental Biology,* 1961, *38,* 471–490.

Wilson, D. M. Insect walking. *Annual Review of Entomology,* 1966, *11,* 103–122.

Wilton, R. N., & Clements, R. O. Behavioral contrast as a function of the duration of an immediately preceding period of extinction. *Journal of the Experimental Analysis of Behavior,* 1971, *16,* 425–428.

Wüttke, W., & Innis, N. K. Drug effects upon behaviour induced by second-order schedules of reinforcement: The relevance of ethological analyses. In R. M. Gilbert & J. D. Keehn (Eds.), *Schedule effects: Drugs, drinking, and aggression.* Toronto: University of Toronto Press, 1972.

Zener, K. The significance of behavior accompanying conditioned salivary secretion for theories of the conditioned response. *American Journal of Psychology,* 1937, *50,* 384–403.

Zuriff, G. E. Collateral responding during differential reinforcement of low rates. *Journal of the Experimental Analysis of Behavior,* 1969, *12,* 971–976.

6

Thermoregulatory Behavior*

Evelyn Satinoff
and
Robert Hendersen

INTRODUCTION

Temperature regulation is a homeostatic process which is mainly behavioral, but for many years behavior was largely ignored in its analysis. There are two probable reasons for this omission. First, no convenient method for quantifying thermoregulatory behavior was available until 1957. In that year, Carlton and Marx in one study and Weiss in another demonstrated that operant behavior was precisely attuned to regulating body temperature. They showed that rats in the cold would press a bar that turned a heat lamp on, thereby preventing a fall in internal temperature.[1]

* The preparation of this chapter and some of the unpublished research described in it was supported by Research Grant #NS 12033 from the National Institute of Neurological Diseases and Stroke and Grant #CRR Psychology from the University of Illinois Research Board to the first author. We thank Drs. R. D. Luce, H. Rachlin, B. Schwartz, and especially W. Honig and J. Staddon for their helpful comments on previous versions of this manuscript.

[1] The effectiveness of thermal reinforcement has been demonstrated in various species, including baboons (Gale, Mathews, & Young, 1970), macaques (Carlisle, 1970), squirrel monkeys (Adair, 1970; Carlisle, 1966), dogs (Cabanac, Duclaux, & Gillet, 1970), cats (Clark & Lipton, 1974; Weiss, Laties, & Weiss, 1967), pigs (Baldwin & Ingram, 1967), rats (Epstein & Milestone, 1968;

Second, it was assumed that when sufficient information about the neural control of reflexive thermoregulatory responses was obtained, it would account for operant behavior as well. The first purpose of this chapter is to show that the neural controls of thermoregulatory reflexes and operants are functionally and neuroanatomically separate and that we can never fully understand thermal homeostasis without understanding its operant aspects.

Operant behavior provides an elegant means of tapping important features of thermoregulation. A second purpose of this chapter is to demonstrate the utility of behavior in interpreting the effects of various drugs on body temperature, in analyzing thermal preferences, and in studying phylogenetic and ontogenetic differences in thermoregulatory functioning.

Thermoregulation, because it is an exemplary negative feedback system, is usually discussed within the framework of control theory. One of the most impor-

Lipton, 1968; Matthews, 1969; Weiss & Laties, 1961), mice (Baldwin, 1968; Revusky, 1966), Barbary doves (Budgell, 1971), chicks (Zolman, 1968), lizards (Hammel, Caldwell, & Abrams, 1967), alligators (Davidson, 1966), and goldfish (Rozin & Mayer, 1961).

tant concepts in control theory is the *set point*—that value of the input at which the output is zero. This chapter will show how behavior is an invaluable tool in determining, when body temperature changes, whether the change is due to a shift in set point.

SEPARATION OF OPERANT AND RESPONDENT TEMPERATURE REGULATION

For many years integrated control of body temperature was thought to depend on the integrity of two areas of the brain, the preoptic/anterior hypothalamic area (for brevity, we shall call this the *preoptic area*) and the posterior hypothalamus. Damage to the preoptic area produced animals that could not reflexively maintain their body temperatures within normal limits when placed in hot environments (Teague & Ranson, 1936); after posterior hypothalamic lesions animals were able to regulate normally in the heat, but became hypothermic in the cold (Keller, 1963; Pachomov, 1962). This concept of two equal and opposing centers, one in the posterior hypothalamus controlling heat production and the other in the preoptic area controlling heat loss, gradually gave way to a theory in which the preoptic area was preeminent in temperature regulation. The change occurred for a number of reasons:

1. Thermally sensitive units (that is, neurons whose firing rates are greatly influenced by their temperature) were found in much greater abundance in the preoptic area than in the posterior hypothalamus (Edinger & Eisenman, 1970; Eisenman & Jackson, 1967).
2. Heating the preoptic area caused sweating, panting, vasodilation, and all other autonomic correlates of heat loss with a concomitant fall in body temperature (Magoun, Harrison, Brobeck, & Ranson, 1938; Proppe & Gale, 1970). This would be expected from a heat loss center. But cooling the preoptic region caused the heat-producing responses of shivering and increased metabolic rate, the heat loss response of vasoconstriction, and a rise in body temperature (Hammel, Hardy, & Fusco, 1960; Morishima & Gale, 1972; also see Satinoff, 1974, for review). This would *not* be expected. Heating or cooling the posterior hypothalamus did not elicit any of these responses (Adair & Hardy, 1971; Freeman & Davis, 1959).
3. After lesions in the preoptic area, animals were unable to regulate their body temperatures reflexively in either warm or cool environments (Carlisle, 1969; Satinoff, 1974; Satinoff & Rutstein, 1970; Squires & Jacobson, 1968).

These facts imply that the preoptic area is important for maintaining body temperature by activating reflexive responses. In most of the experiments leading to this conclusion, the animals had no opportunity for operant control of their temperature. Except for occasional observations on postural changes, such as huddling or sprawling (Freeman & Davis, 1959; Hellstrom & Hammel, 1967), measurements were made only of body temperature and of such reflexes as shivering, panting, and changes in vasomotor tone.

In 1964, Satinoff combined the neurophysiological technique of cooling the brain with the operant measure of bar pressing for radiant heat. She found that cooling the preoptic region of rats elicited not only shivering and an increase in body temperature, but operant responding for heat as well. As with reflexes, skin and brain temperatures interact in controlling operant responding. Brain cooling increases the rate of working for heat much more in cold than in neutral environments. Conversely, when their hypothalamus was warmed, rats decreased responding for external heat in the cold (Carlisle, 1966; Corbit, 1970; Murgatroyd & Hardy, 1970).

Because preoptic thermal stimulation produces both reflexive and operant responding, it is reasonable to expect that damage in that area would eliminate both types of controls. Although such damage impairs reflexive responses, it does not impair thermally motivated instrumental responding. Lipton (1968) demonstrated that rats with preoptic lesions would, when placed in a hot environment, turn a heat lamp off and a cooling fan on, thereby avoiding death from overheating. Carlisle (1969) later showed that such lesioned rats pressed at a much higher than normal rate for heat reinforcement in the cold and were able to prevent severe hypothermia. Satinoff and Rutstein (1970) tested rats with preoptic lesions in a 5°C chamber twice a week. In one of the weekly sessions no bar was available; body temperatures fell an average of 2.4°C in a 1-hr session for at least two months postoperatively. In the other session, which lasted for 2 hr, holding a bar down kept a heat lamp on, and the rats depressed the bar 32% of the time, maintaining their temperatures within .7°C of normal. Controls kept the bar depressed only .05% of the time (Figure 1).

These experiments demonstrate that operant behavior can compensate for reflexive deficits. In the examples cited above, the reflexive deficits were produced by hypothalamic lesions. In other experiments, reflexive deficits were caused by thyroidectomy (Laties & Weiss, 1959), vitamin deficiency (Weiss, 1957; Yeh & Weiss, 1963), or various drug treatments (see page

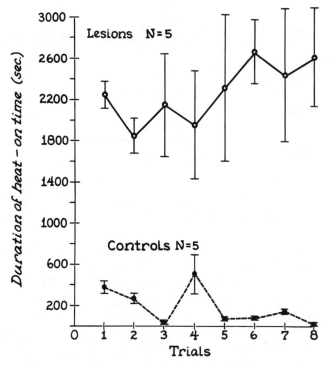

Fig. 1. Duration of heat-on time for the first eight trials in the cold of rats with preoptic lesions and of normal rats maintained at 80% normal body weight. (From Satinoff & Rutstein, 1970. © 1970 by the American Psychological Association. Reprinted by permission.)

167), and rats also learned to compensate through instrumental behavior.

It further appears that the neural networks controlling reflexive and operant thermoregulatory responses are to a large degree independent of one another. Operant responses are not integrated solely in the preoptic area because they continue to appear when that region is largely destroyed. Additional evidence for this independence is that lateral hypothalamic lesions can disrupt thermoregulatory operants without affecting reflexive regulation (Satinoff & Shan, 1971). Well-trained rats that had pressed a lever that turned on a heat lamp in the cold no longer did so after lateral hypothalamic lesions. Most of the animals were nonetheless able to maintain their body temperature reflexively. The operant deficit was not always accompanied by impairments in feeding or drinking. When it was, the behaviors recovered at different rates. For instance, in Figure 2, rat SY18 regained its preoperative body weight in 10 days, yet it did not bar-press for heat at preoperative levels until over 40 days had elapsed.

Of course, there are several ways in which a treatment may result in a loss of (or decrement in) responding. These include general debilitation, forgetting, impairments in arousal, motor, or sensory processes,

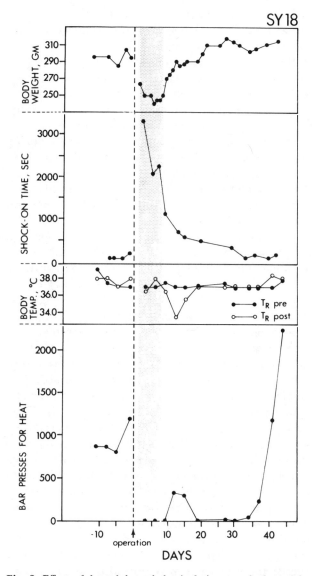

Fig. 2. Effect of lateral hypothalamic lesions on body weight, core temperature, responding for heat, and shock avoidance. Shaded area indicates period of tube feeding; T_R pre—rectal temperature immediately before the 1-hr test; T_R post—rectal temperature at the end of the test. (From Satinoff & Shan, 1971. © 1971 by the American Psychological Association. Reprinted by permission.)

or any of these in combination. In this case, we can rule out debilitation, forgetting, and motor problems. On some tests in the cold, rats were injected with quinine HCl, a drug that lowered their internal temperature by interfering with shivering (Satinoff, unpublished research). On those tests the rats responded at preoperative levels, whereas their response rates returned to near zero on nondrug days. This demonstrates that the rats were able to make the response and had not forgotten how. Sensory deficits possibly contributed to the loss of responding. Rats with lateral hypothalamic lesions may not be as sensitive as normals to skin temperature changes (or skin temperature pathways may be damaged by the lesion so the signal is inaccurate), and it may require the addition of a fall in internal temperature to get them working for heat. There may well also have been a deficit in arousal, and the lesions may have elevated the threshold for operant behavior. However, since thermoregulatory reflex adjustments are made during sleep, arousal level presumably would not have affected those components. Thus it appears that thermally motivated operant behavior depends on a distinct neural system passing through the lateral hypothalamus.

Operant and reflexive thermoregulation appear to be uncoupled in the posterior as well as the lateral hypothalamus. Although local heating or cooling in that area does not elicit reflexive thermoregulatory responses (Adair, 1974; Freeman & Davis, 1959), these treatments do alter operant thermoregulation. When squirrel monkeys were given control over their ambient temperature, they selected higher air temperatures when the posterior hypothalamus was cooled and lower air temperatures when it was warmed. This operant regulation was just as precise as when the preoptic region was heated or cooled (Adair, 1974). These results are compatible with the decreased operant responding after lateral hypothalamic lesions reported above. The lateral and posterior hypothalamus appear to be part of the same pathway, which is involved in the control of thermoregulatory operants. Lesions in the posterior hypothalamus generally lead to more drastic deficits, including somnolence and complete and possibly permanent adipsia and aphagia (McGinty, 1969). Lateral hypothalamic lesions cause less severe effects: the rats are drowsy instead of totally somnolent (Wampler, 1970), and later their adipsia and aphagia recover through stages to relatively normal eating and drinking (Teitelbaum & Epstein, 1962). The medial forebrain bundle, possibly part of a mechanism which facilitates operant behavior (Stein, 1964), includes both the lateral and posterior hypothalamus, so it is reasonable that lesions in those areas should eliminate and stimulation excite the same sorts of behavior.

Even though the preoptic area appears to be involved primarily in respondent thermoregulation, preoptic thermodetectors also affect the operant system. In fact, both systems can be conceptualized as in Figure 3, which admittedly is a tremendous oversimplification with respect to reflexive controls and probably with respect to operant controls as well. Nevertheless, it adequately accounts for four impor-

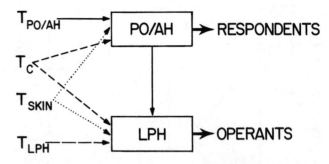

Fig. 3. Diagramatic representation of the mechanisms for operant and respondent temperature regulation. T = temperature; C = core; LPH = lateral posterior hypothalamus; PO/AH = preoptic anterior hypothalamus.

tant facts: (1) Preoptic thermal stimulation leads to coordinated operant and reflexive responses. This is because the temperature of the preoptic area affects neural activity in both preoptic tissue and the lateral posterior hypothalamus. (2) Preoptic lesions lead to a loss of thermoregulatory respondents while leaving operants intact. It is assumed here that operant thermoregulation after such lesions depends mainly on extrapreoptic temperature receptors. (3) Posterior hypothalamic thermal stimulation leads to operant responses, but not to reflexive ones. (4) Lateral hypothalamic lesions eliminate operant responding only.

In thermoregulation, then, reflexive and operant responses to thermal stresses are functionally and anatomically separate, and animals can compensate for deficits in one system through the mechanisms of the other system.

USING BEHAVIOR TO ASSESS REGULATION

The separation of reflexive and nonreflexive thermoregulation appears phylogenetically. Fish, amphibians, and reptiles have highly sophisticated nonreflexive means of regulating their body temperature, whereas automatic mechanisms are either nonexistent or few and inefficient (see Templeton, 1970, for a review). For this reason, ectotherms[2] are excellent preparations for studying homeostasis. One need not damage the brain to isolate its systems. Instead, we can

[2] The familiar terms for "cold-blooded" and "warm-blooded" animals are *poikilotherm* (from the Greek *poikilos*, "varied, changing," and *therme*, "heat") and *homeotherm* (Greek *homoios*, "like"). Since all of these animals thermoregulate, more appropriate words describe them on the basis of whether the heat source is external or internal. Hence we are using the more precise terms *ectotherm* (Greek *ektos*, "outside") and *endotherm* (Greek *endon*, "within") (Cowles, 1962).

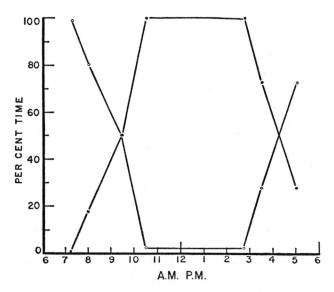

Fig. 4. The percentage of time spent in the sun (open circles) and the shade (solid circles) by a horned lizard, *Phrynosoma coronatum*, during August. The values given are midpoints for 1-hr intervals. (From Heath, 1965. Reprinted by permission of the University of California Press.)

study organisms with a simpler thermoregulatory organization (Rozin, 1968).

Thermoregulation in Ectotherms

For many years it was assumed that vertebrates other than mammals and birds could not control their body temperatures at all. When lizards, for example, were trapped and put into a cage in the laboratory, their temperatures fluctuated with that of the surrounding medium. However, in their natural environments these reptiles regulate with a variety of behavioral mechanisms (Cowles & Bogert, 1944).[3] Figure 4 illustrates one common behavior—shuttling back and forth between sun and shade. This enables the animal to maintain its body temperature within a fairly narrow range, generally no more than 3 or 4°C (Figure 5; Heath, 1965). Once within this range it can attend to business other than thermoregulating. If the regulated range were narrower, the lizard would have to spend all of its time shuttling back and forth. As Heath (1970) points out, such an animal would be a very good thermoregulator but a very inefficient lizard.

[3] This may not be characteristic of all vertebrates, however. Bogert (1959) noted that when several green iguanas, the largest lizards on the American continent, were exposed to direct sunlight in the desert in summer, they did not seek shade but sat in the sun until they died. One specimen at the San Diego zoo never went indoors on cool evenings and had to be taken inside. One night it was inadvertently overlooked by its keeper and was found the next morning in a state of cold narcosis.

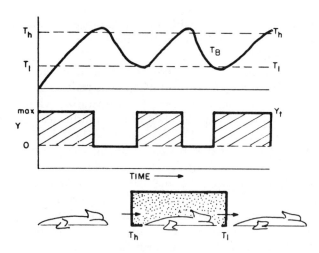

Fig. 5. A lizard moves from direct sun (left) into shade (middle) at body temperature T_h, and it moves from shade to sunlight at body temperature T_1. The difference in temperature, $T_h - T_1$, is a refractory range in which the lizard can operate without resorting to thermoregulatory activities. The effector output Y is here equated with the availability of sun. Y = 0 in the shade and Y = maximum in direct sunlight. (From Heath, 1970.)

Because shuttling is a common thermoregulatory behavior of lizards in their natural environment, it is relatively easy to study in the laboratory. Hammel, Caldwell, and Abrams (1967) demonstrated that blue-tongued lizards regulated their internal temperature between 30 and 37°C by shuttling between 15 and 45°C chambers. In a different situation, the lizards were placed in a hot compartment and allowed to escape to a cooler one. Increasing the temperature of the hot compartment caused the animals to escape at lower colonic temperatures (Myhre & Hammel, 1969). Lizards also learned to go to a platform which, when depressed by the weight of the animal, turned on an overhead heat lamp. Response frequencies increased and response duration decreased with increasing intensity of the heat reinforcer. As the intensity of the heat changed, the lizards compensated behaviorally, receiving a roughly constant amount of heat per hour (Garrick, 1973).

Frogs and fish also clearly show a thermoregulatory component in their behavior. Frogs selected temperatures from 25–28°C in a thermocline (a long, thermally graded alley) ranging from 0–40°C (Cabanac & Jeddi, 1971). Different species of fish aggregated at different points in a thermal gradient (Fry & Hochachka, 1970). Six species of fish were trained to regulate the temperature in their tanks by their spatial movements (Neill, Magnuson, & Chipman, 1972). Swimming into warmer water caused the entire tank to heat up, whereas swimming into cooler water caused a drop in tank temperature. The fish all kept the tank temperature within a 4–7°C range, the mean varying for different species, although a range of 22°C was available.

Such experiments do not guarantee that the behavior is under the control of operant contingencies. The behavior may not even be temperature-related, but may instead depend upon other stimulus features of the environment. For example, if a heat lamp is used to generate the thermal gradient, the resulting behavior may be controlled by the light, rather than the heat, produced by the lamp. To demonstrate preference, behavior must shift appropriately when the relationship between the thermal stimuli and other environmental cues is reversed. Furthermore, the behavior may be a form of kinesis or taxis (Fraenkel & Gunn, 1961). What appears to be choice among thermal stimuli may instead be behavior elicited by them. In a thermal gradient these stimulus functions are confounded. Nevertheless, there are a few experiments which unambiguously demonstrate operant regulation. Iguanas learned to press a disc to escape from heat. The responses were independent of substrate temperature or heating rate, and appeared to depend solely on internal temperature (Kemp, 1969). Goldfish can press levers and keep the temperatures of their aquariums between 33.5 and 36.5°C. In a thermal titration situation they pressed the lever both to decrease water temperature when it was too high and to prevent its rising above the desired levels (Rozin & Mayer, 1961).

What Controls the Regulation?

Thermoregulatory behavior in ectotherms is controlled by a combination of brain and other body temperatures, just as it is in mammals and birds. When the brainstem was heated to 41°C, lizards exited from the hot side of a shuttle box at colonic temperatures 1 to 2°C lower than normal. When the brain was cooled to 25°C, the lizards exited at colonic temperatures 1 to 2°C higher than normal (Hammel, Caldwell, & Abrams, 1967). Arctic sculpins were placed in warm water from which they could escape by swimming back to water at 5°C to which they had been adapted. Heating the forebrain lessened the time spent in warm water, while cooling the brain sometimes suppressed the escape response (Hammel, Stromme, & Myhre, 1969). These results have been repeated in several species of fish, from both warm and cool waters, and in every case altering brainstem temperature affected the tank temperature the fish selected (Crawshaw & Hammel, 1971, 1973, 1974). In frogs, abdominal (Cabanac & Jeddi, 1971) or spinal cord (Duclaux, Fantino, & Cabanac, 1973) heating caused the animals to move toward colder water, indicating that amphibians also are responsive to changes in both internal and skin temperature.[4]

If fish, amphibians, and reptiles prefer some temperatures to others, and these preferences can be altered by thermally stimulating the brain, there must be temperature-sensitive neurons in the brain. Both cold- and warm-sensitive cells have been found in the diencephalon of Australian lizards (Cabanac, Hammel, & Hardy, 1967) and brook trout (Greer & Gardner, 1970).

In summary, ectothermic temperature regulation is determined by a combination of skin, brain, and other body temperatures, just as it is in mammals and birds. These conclusions could only have been drawn on the basis of behavioral experiments, because nonreflexive behavior is the sole or predominant means of thermoregulation in these organisms.

Thermoregulation in Infants

Many newborn mammals and birds have great difficulty maintaining their body temperatures in the cold. Because they are so small, they have a large surface-to-volume ratio and they lose heat very rapidly. Under natural conditions there are a variety of solutions to this problem—staying in a nest, bassinet, or marsupial pouch, clinging to the mother, or huddling with siblings (Dawes, 1968). However, if such a newborn is unfortunate enough to stray from the mother or nest, it will die at air temperatures that would not bother an adult. Is there a regulated body temperature even in newborns, and is their problem simply that they do not have the mechanisms to maintain it? Or is a temperature control system lacking at birth, developing only later in life? We can answer this question by providing behavioral opportunities for temperature selection.

Piglets less than 1 day old chose thermal environments that allowed them to maintain their body temperatures within .03°C of what it was when they were

[4] In these experiments, large deviations from normal brain temperature (at least 5°C) produced relatively small change in the deep body temperature threshold at which behavioral responses appeared (only 1–2°C). Similar effects have been seen in mammals. Corbit (1970) reported a number of experiments on rats in which he examined the effects of changes in hypothalamic temperature on lever pressing for convective cooling. The hypothalamic temperature threshold for the behavioral heat loss response was very high (40.3–43°C). However, reflexive heat loss responses (which lizards lack) were activated at the much lower brain temperatures of 38°C. It may simply be that the thresholds for activating behavioral and reflexive thermoregulatory responses are very different, although see Corbit (1970) for alternative explanations.

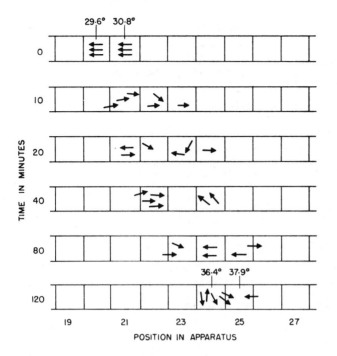

Fig. 6. Response of 1-day-old laboratory mice taken from the mother and placed together at a moderately warm position in the temperature gradient. All animals initially faced down the gradient. (From Ogilvie & Stinson, 1966. Reprinted by permission of the National Research Council of Canada.)

with the sow (Mount, 1963). This indicates a very good behavioral thermoregulatory system. Neonatal hamster pups were also very sensitive to thermal gradients and moved quickly away from cooler areas toward a heat source, where they became quiescent. However, if they were placed directly under the heat source, they did not move away and died from overheating (Leonard, 1974). Similarly, 1-day-old mice moved from a cooler to a warmer environment. Figure 6 shows the behavior of six newborn mice placed in a thermocline. Within 2 hr they were all in positions at substrate temperatures at least 5°C higher than at their initial positions (Ogilvie & Stinson, 1966).

Neonatal puppies and rabbits also show thermoregulatory behavior. Puppies aged 12 hr to 10 days were placed in the presence of two artificial mothers constructed of metal coils, one of which was covered with fur. In a warm environment (30°C) the puppies preferred the furred coil (Figure 7a). However, when the metallic surrogate was warmed and the fur mother cooled, the puppies spent almost 100% of the time with the metallic mother (Figure 7b; Jeddi, 1970). Rabbits oriented toward a furred artificial mother in a cold environment but not in a warm one. This behavior was very efficient in regaining normal body temperature, which had dropped precipitously before

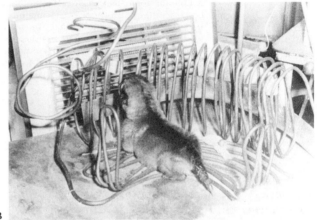

Fig. 7. A: In a neutral environment puppies prefer the fur mother and avoid the metallic one. B: The fur mother has been cooled to 14°C and the metallic mother warmed to 33°C. The puppy was fed before the beginning of the test. (From Jeddi, 1970.)

contact was established (Jeddi, 1971). Thus the search for contact comfort in very young animals may have a thermoregulatory component. In fact, Harlow (1971, p. 70) reports that infant macaques given a choice between warm wire surrogate mothers and cool cloth surrogates showed a preference for the warm surrogate during the first 20 days of life.

Generally, young mammals select temperatures higher than those chosen by adults. As physiological and hormonal capabilities develop and physical characteristics change (fur appears and surface-to-mass ratio declines), selected temperatures become lower.

Young birds also thermoregulate behaviorally. Hogan (1974) observed that when the hen did not initiate brooding (which warms the chicks), 3- to 8-day-old chicks became cool and stimulated the hen to sit by rubbing against her and pecking her feathers. In an experimental situation, two breeds of 1- and 2-day-old chicks quickly learned to peck a key when that

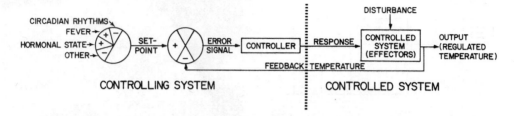

Fig. 8. Control diagram of the relation between set point (or reference input), actual body temperature, and a reflexive response. The comparators (circles) are mixing points. Whenever the combination of pluses and minuses do not cancel one another, an error signal is generated. When this occurs (that is, whenever there is a disturbance such that heat gain and heat loss mechanisms are not at minimum levels), a response is activated which alters the regulated body temperature. Information from temperature receptors is then fed back to the comparator and the error signal is adjusted. Several points must be clarified: (1) There is no single regulated body temperature. That term is a convenient fiction for some mathematical combination of all the temperatures that contribute to effector output (Brown & Brengelmann, 1970). (2) The reference input variables leading into the set point indicate that the set point is not constant but fluctuates because of the influence of a variety of nonthermal inputs. (3) This diagram is not sufficient to describe the control of operant responses. For that, additional loops feeding back to the response controller are required for both response effectiveness and response cost (Van Sommers, 1972).

response was reinforced with heat and light (Zolman, 1968).

Is the thermoregulatory behavior of neonatal mammals and birds under the control of operant contingencies? The interpretation of existing behavioral experiments remains ambiguous. Of the experiments discussed above, only the behavior of the young chicks that pecked a key for heat is clearly under the control of an operant contingency, and even this may have a large respondent component (Wasserman, 1973).

In summary, many neonatal animals that do not possess reflexive mechanisms sufficient for maintaining body temperatures nevertheless demonstrate thermoregulatory capabilities when provided with behavioral opportunities to do so. In this respect, young mammals and birds are much like ectotherms.

THERMOREGULATION AND THE CONCEPT OF SET POINT

So far we have been describing how animals lacking reflex mechanisms are nonetheless able to thermoregulate behaviorally. Normally, of course, in mammals and birds, both reflexes and operants maintain a constant body temperature. Control theory provides a useful framework for describing this thermal integration. A control system maintains its output (actual body temperature) at or near some reference value (thermal set point). If there is a discrepancy (error signal) between the set point and the achieved output, corrective measures (effector responses) which reduce the error are activated. If the system is working optimally, temperature is maintained as closely as possible to the set point (Figure 8; see Milsum, 1966, for a comprehensive discussion of biological control systems). Set point is the value of the input of a control system at which the output is zero. It is neither a theory nor an explanation; it is merely a descriptive device which is useful in describing the operation of homeostatic systems. Clearly, there would be no set point without a nervous system, but for our purposes it does not matter where or how the set point is achieved. It is irrelevant whether the reference temperature is a function of the difference in firing rates between temperature-independent and temperature-sensitive neurons, or whether it is the point at which warm- and cool-sensitive neurons are minimally active (to enumerate just two of the ways it could be represented). This does not imply that the same set point will be adequate for describing characteristics of the system at more fine-grained levels of analysis. Thermoregulatory functioning may be described in terms of one, two, or many set points. The formulation we choose depends on the aspect of the system being studied. For example, for a physician concerned about a feverish patient, the deviation of the patient's body temperature from normal is all he needs to know in order to decide whether or not to institute corrective measures. The physician can operate as if there is a single set point, as illustrated in Figure 9a. We have already seen that although reflexive and operant

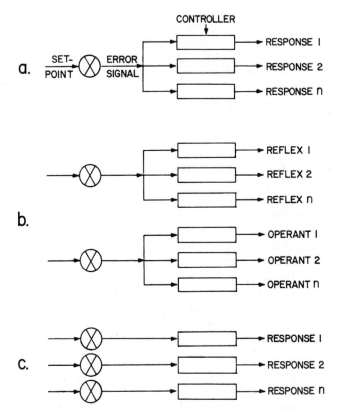

Fig. 9. Schematization of three possible controlling systems for thermoregulation. For clarity, feedback loops are not shown. The controller equation relating error signal and response determines both the threshold and the size of the response. Note that models (b) and (c) are equivalent to model (a) if we assume that the thresholds for elicitation of the various responses need not be identical. (a) One central thermostat whose output activates all available operant and reflexive thermoregulatory responses. (b) Two central thermostats, one controlling all reflexive, the other all operant responses. (c) Each thermoregulatory response is independent of any other.

mechanisms normally work in concert, they are in fact functionally distinct. Therefore, the behavioral scientist must use a more detailed level of analysis. He can operate within the framework of Figure 9b. For the physiologist interested in a particular thermoregulatory response, such as vasomotor tone, the level of analysis must be finer still, allowing a detailed, quantitative analysis of the vasomotor controller. He might use the control diagram outlined in Figure 9c. For most purposes in this chapter, a single set point notion is sufficient to characterize general features of thermoregulation.

The thermoregulatory set point is affected by a variety of internal and environmental variables and fluctuates from time to time. Because ectotherms have only nonreflexive regulatory mechanisms, we can see many of the determinants of the set point more clearly in them than in mammals.

Circadian Rhythms

One might assume that diurnal reptiles become cold at night because they have no choice; they derive their heat primarily from the sun, so they necessarily cool down and become inactive when the sun sets. However, the decrease in body temperature which occurs at night is more than the passive result of cooler surroundings. Four species of lizards living in a thermocline for several days maintained a high body temperature when the lights were on, whether they were active or not, but they selected the cooler part of the gradient during the lights-off part of the cycle (Regal, 1967). Thus the lizards moved into ambient temperatures at which they became sluggish and uncoordinated.

Because lizards cool down at night, they have problems in the morning. If they were to remain underground until their burrows warmed up sufficiently to allow them to begin daily activity, they would lose a lot of valuable activity time. Fortunately for them, a warm burrow is not necessary for activity. In the laboratory, horned lizards emerged from their burrows before sunrise at body temperatures about 15°C below their normal activity levels. Two groups of lizards were kept at constant conditions of 18 to 27°C, except for 8 hr a day when they had access to heat lamps. Both groups emerged from the sand at about the same time prior to the onset of the heat lamps, although, of course, each group's internal temperature was close to that of its environment (Heath, 1962). Thus reptiles appear to show a circadian variation in their thermal set points.

Mammals also show circadian fluctuations in body temperature. If we extrapolated from reptiles, we would say that these diurnal oscillations are rhythmic shifts in set point. However, peaks in body temperature normally coincide with periods of activity. Are animals active because their temperatures are high, or are their temperatures high because they are active? One way of answering this question would be to measure all reflexive thermoregulatory responses (metabolic rate, vasomotion, etc.). If different body temperatures are observed, and yet the reflexive thermoregulatory responses do not vary so as to change them, then one could assume a shift in set point (Hensel, 1974). Another, less cumbersome way would be to use operant behavior to determine thermal preferences. If there are rhythmic shifts in set point, preferred temperature should reflect them.

Hormonal State

Regulated temperature varies with reproductive

condition. Pregnant blue spiny lizards regulated at lower temperatures than did males or postparturient females. They tolerated lower minimum internal temperatures and stopped basking at lower maximums (Garrick, 1974). Plasma progesterone levels were twice as high in pregnant lizards of this species as in postparturients (Callard, Chan, & Potts, 1972), which suggests that this hormone may be involved in the change in behavior. When Garrick injected progesterone into postparturient lizards, it lowered the temperature around which the lizards regulated.

Progesterone caused hyperthermia in female rats (Freeman, Crissman, Louw, Butcher, & Inskeep, 1970) and in humans (Gordon, 1972). This appears to be an upward shift in set point, because human females preferred warmer stimuli during the luteal phase of the menstrual cycle, when progesterone levels are high, than during the follicular phase, when levels are low (Cunningham & Cabanac, 1971). Of course, thermoregulatory changes during the menstrual cycle may not be caused by progesterone per se. Levels of other gonadal hormones, particularly estrogen, wax and wane simultaneously, and nongonadal hormones affect temperature as well. Regardless of which hormones are involved, however, it is clear that the set point changes with reproductive condition in lizards and mammals, although in opposite directions.

Thermoregulatory effector mechanisms serve nonthermoregulatory functions as well. Interpreting behavior changes is difficult, because nonthermal factors may produce such changes. For example, McLean and Coleman (1971) noted that female rats housed in large cages showed less of a drop in body temperature during estrus than did restricted rats. They concluded that the increased activity commonly seen in estrual rats was a response to a lower body temperature. This conclusion is not warranted. Increased activity may be a sign of sexual agitation, and sexual responses may take precedence over thermoregulatory responses during estrus. If the activity were truly a response to a lower body temperature, one would expect to see increases in other heat-producing and heat-conserving behaviors at the same time, but food intake and nest building actually decrease during estrus (Wade, 1972).

Food Intake

Digestion is another activity which affects thermoregulation. Regal (1966) noted that certain reptiles, active at low temperatures, moved toward the warmer parts of their terraria after they had eaten. He measured the body temperature of a boa constrictor by sewing a thermocouple into one of the mice that the snake ate. The snake moved so as to keep warm that part of the body containing the bolus. As soon as the snake defecated, basking abruptly ended. Thus in cool-active reptiles, digestive requirements determine thermoregulatory activity.

Reptiles need more heat after eating so that they can digest their meals. Mammals need less external heat after eating because of increased metabolic heat production. Rats bar-pressed more for heat when they were fed immediately after a 1-hr test session in the cold than when they were fed before the session (Hamilton & Sheriff, 1959). Internal temperatures were elevated after feeding and did not return to prefeeding base lines for an average of 2 hr (Grossman & Rechtschaffen, 1967). Decreased rates of pressing for heat following a meal thus help maintain a constant thermal balance. Varying the quality of the diet also affects response rate for heat. Rats fed a high-fat or high-carbohydrate diet gained weight, and worked less for heat than they did when they were fed a high-protein or powdered chow diet (Hamilton, 1963). Conversely, rats fed a high-fat diet or made hyperphagic by hypothalamic lesions worked more than did controls to escape heat (Lipton, 1969). The increases in responding were related to higher body weight. These changes in response rate for both heat escape and heat reinforcement can be interpreted as behavioral compensation for the lessened ability to lose heat reflexively (fat animals have more insulation). There does not appear to be any shift in thermal set point.

THERMAL PREFERENCE

Control theory is a way of systematically describing how preferences for thermal stimuli vary under different conditions. Stimuli that decrease the deviation from set point are desired, whereas those that increase the error signal are aversive. Factors such as fever, circadian rhythms, and hormonal changes which shift the set point do not change the basic relationship between error signal and stimulus preference. Thus the same thermal stimulus may be positively reinforcing in one condition and aversive in another. The value of a given stimulus is determined by the context within which it is applied.

Preference and Subjective Pleasure

Preferences for thermal stimuli are related to reports of subjective comfort. Just as people can judge brightness, loudness, and warmth, so can they judge the pleasure a particular stimulus provides. Pleasure judgments are assessments of affective quality, whereas preference is a description of choice behavior. Nothing in their respective definitions demands that the two measures be associated. Nevertheless, it is probably reasonable to assume that stimuli judged as pleasant would also be desirable in preference tests, while those judged as unpleasant would be aversive.

Cabanac (1971) has beautifully demonstrated how judgments of pleasure depend on context. Each of his subjects was immersed up to his chin in a tub of water whose temperature was controlled by the experimenter. With heat loss controlled this way, the subject's core temperature could be maintained above or below his set point. (Note that this procedure does not change the set point, but instead increases the error signal by altering the regulated variable—actual body temperature.) While sitting in the bath, each subject dipped his left hand for 30 sec into a container filled with water at a particular temperature and judged the pleasure provided by this thermal stimulus. Then the subject put his hand back into the bath until the sensation disappeared, then dipped his hand once more into the container, which was now filled with water of yet a different temperature, and judged it. A series of such ratings is shown in Figure 10a. The subjects perceived stimuli at the extreme ends of the scale as pleasant or unpleasant depending upon whether they were hypothermic or hyperthermic. Thus when they were hypothermic (internal temperature below 37°C) they reported that warm or hot stimuli to the hand were pleasant. When they were hyperthermic (internal temperature above 37°C) they perceived cool or cold hand stimuli as pleasant. The change in hand temperature was not sufficient to change deep body temperature. However, in every case, the pleasant stimulus was one that, had it been extended over the entire body, would have decreased the difference between the set point and the actual body temperature.

Similar results were obtained in an experiment in which the dependent variable was a measure of preference (Cabanac, Massonnet, & Belaiche, 1972). Subjects sitting in a water bath had to manipulate a valve to change the temperature of another bath in which an arm was immersed. Results paralleled those from the experiments using judgments of thermal pleasure. Thermal preference systematically changed when the temperature of the bath in which the subjects sat was varied.

In the experiments discussed above, the set point remained constant while body temperature was al-

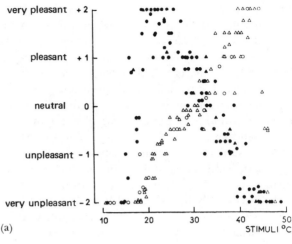

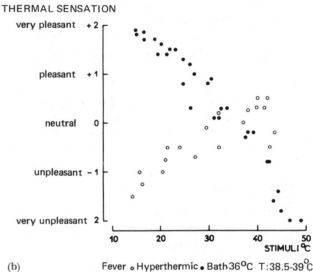

Fig. 10. (a) Judgments of thermal pleasure given by a single subject when hypothermic (open symbols) and hyperthermic (closed symbols). (b) Similar judgments made when the subject was feverish (open circles) or hyperthermic (closed circles). The bath temperature was 36°C. The subject's internal temperature was 38.5–39.0°C. (From Cabanac, 1969.)

tered. The error signal can also be manipulated by changing the set point while maintaining a constant body temperature. Fever can be described as an upward shift in set point (see page 166). Cabanac (1969) tested a subject when he had a fever (because of influenza) and when he was well. The temperature of the water bath, and hence the subject's internal temperature, was identical in both series of tests. Judgments of pleasure, however, were very different (Figure 10b). The subject liked warmer stimuli when he had a fever and cooler stimuli when he was well but hyperthermic. These experiments were later repeated in four other subjects (Cabanac & Massonnet, 1974), and the results strongly support the theory that reported pleasure is determined by deviations from set point. They further imply that when body temperature is abnormal, preference measures can determine whether or not the abnormal level is caused by a change in set point. We shall develop this idea more fully when we discuss drug administration.

Cabanac's experiments demonstrate that the same peripheral stimulus is perceived as pleasant or noxious depending upon the person's internal state. Placing a subject in a temperature-controlled bath affects peripheral, core, and brain temperatures. Information from all three normally covaries. Are these signals functionally interchangeable, or can organisms distinguish among them? When Corbit and Ernits (1974) warmed the hypothalamus, rats pressed a bar that cooled their hypothalamus rather than a bar that lowered the air temperature. When the skin was warmed, the opposite preference appeared. When the animal has no choice (e.g., when its hypothalamus is being warmed and all it has available to it is a bar that cools the air), it will use any opportunity which is available to decrease the error signal. However, the animal can detect the site of the disturbance and, given the choice, will direct its behavior toward changing the temperature at that site.

Nonthermal Determinants of Thermal Choice

Operant selection of thermal reinforcers depends upon what other sorts of reinforcers are concurrently available. One may forego the opportunity to thermoregulate efficiently in order to engage in a more highly preferred activity, as when an avid football fan sits shivering in the cold to watch an exciting game.

Carlisle and Snyder (1970) demonstrated this effect very dramatically. Rats bar-pressed for heat and maintained their body temperatures very well in the cold. However, when a lever press which produced electrical stimulation in the posterior hypothalamus was concurrently available, the rats worked for the brain stimulation exclusively, allowing their body temperatures to fall to the point of death. In another experiment (Weiss & Laties, 1963), injections of d-amphetamine increased the rate of heat-reinforced bar pressing of rats in the cold. The opposite result, a decrease in rate, was produced when a food-reinforced fixed-ratio schedule was concurrently available (Laties, 1971). Thus effects of thermal reinforcement (or any type of reinforcement, for that matter) must be considered in a broad context which includes other available reinforcers.

Thermoregulatory behavior also depends on the amount of effort involved in making a response. Monkeys pulled a chain that warmed their chamber. When the force requirement was increased, the monkeys tolerated wider air temperature fluctuations and their interresponse times lengthened. Eventually they stopped working completely and just sat and shivered (Adair & Wright, 1976). Response cost also determines behavioral thermoregulation in the tropical lizard *Anolis cristellus* (Huey, 1974). In an open park, where basking sites were readily available, the lizards kept their body temperatures within fairly narrow limits. In an adjacent forest where shuttling from shade to sun required much more movement, the animals tolerated lower and more variable body temperatures.

OPERANT CONTINGENCIES IN THERMAL HOMEOSTASIS

Thermoregulation differs in important ways from other regulatory systems. It should come as no surprise, then, that there are substantial differences between the effects of thermal reinforcers and the effects of more traditional reinforcers such as food and water. For instance, one feature of thermally reinforced behavior that may seem curious is that response rate varies inversely with magnitude and duration of heat reinforcement (Carlisle, 1966; Weiss & Laties, 1961). This would be expected if we consider how the reinforcement is tied to thermal homeostasis. The animals do not respond so as to produce a *maximal* amount of heat; rather, they produce an *optimal* amount. In most experiments with heat reinforcement, the animal can reach "satiation" (i.e., set point) within a single session or even within a fraction of a session. Because the animal stops responding whenever set point is reached, an inverse relation between reinforcement rate and response rate is to be expected under these conditions.

Although animals perform very well under intermittent schedules with ingestive reinforcers, this is not the case with thermal reinforcers. Carlisle (1969) had difficulty obtaining stable fixed-ratio (FR) responding in rats with schedules as low as FR 5 or FR 10. However, when bar pressing was reinforced intermittently by access to heat on a continuous reinforcement (CRF) schedule with a second bar (an FR-CRF chained schedule), good performance was obtained with schedules as high as FR 128 (Carlisle, 1970). Pliskoff, Wright, and Hawkins (1965) obtained similar results with rewarding brain stimulation, another case in which performance on intermittent schedules is often quite poor. Thus thermal reinforcers resemble brain stimulation more than they resemble ingestive reinforcers. This is not surprising considering the similarities between the two. Both are direct and prompt, no consummatory response is made, and neither can be stored the way food and water can.

Avoidance of Thermal Change

People anticipate temperature changes. Someone who goes outside on a bitterly cold day equips himself with coat, hat, and gloves before leaving the warmth of a heated building, or, knowing that it is very hot outside, chooses not to leave his air-conditioned home. Can animals similarly anticipate and avoid thermal change?

Rats can avoid heat. Matthews, Morin, and Church (1971) placed animals in a temperature-controlled chamber and programmed a version of a Sidman (1953) avoidance schedule. A 5-sec exposure to heat occurred every 5 sec if a bar was not pressed. Each response delayed the onset of the next heat exposure for 15 sec. When ambient temperature was manipulated, behavior which avoided very hot air occurred at different rates. Response rates were higher in the hotter environments. Thermal avoidance thus depends on the relationship between the ambient temperature and the thermal effects of responding rather than on the absolute values of the stimuli. This is similar to the context dependencies we noted previously in Cabanac's work.

Analyses of avoidance learning that emphasize species-specific defense reactions (Bolles, 1970) have been based almost entirely on data collected with electric shock as the aversive stimulus. By using heat as an aversive stimulus, one can study avoidance learning in a situation where reactions other than those characteristically produced by shock may be prepotent. Overheated rats are initially active, but later spread out and sprawl (Roberts, Mooney, & Martin, 1974). That rats learn to bar-press to avoid and to escape heat suggests they can learn responses which are quite different from their unconditioned reactions to the aversive stimulus.

THE OPERANT AS A MEASURE OF SET POINT AFTER DRUG ADMINISTRATION

Operant methods are extremely useful in analyzing drug effects on body temperature. If all we know about a drug is that it changes body temperature, we cannot assign it any particular role in thermoregulation. This problem arises because there are a number of ways in which drugs alter body temperature. For instance, many general anesthetics depress central nervous system function, including most thermoregulatory reflexes (Lomax, 1970), and body temperature then varies with ambient temperature.[5] Drugs like amphetamine generally stimulate behavior, making an animal active and emotional, and body temperature may passively rise. Other drugs act directly on effector mechanisms involved in thermoregulation. For example, cholinesterase inhibitors cause profuse sweating and salivation (Koelle, 1970) and so lower body temperature. Adrenergic blocking agents may produce the same outcome by causing peripheral vasodilation (Nickerson, 1970). Some compounds shift the set point. Pyrogens, for example, displace it upward. This phenomenon is called fever.

What we want to know about any drug that affects body temperature is whether it changes the set point or merely alters effector activity. One of the easiest ways to determine whether a body temperature change represents a change in set point is to measure the thermally reinforced responses that accompany it. Operant behavior reflects the error signal—the difference between the set point and the achieved temperature. Because of this we can make the following two assertions:

1. If an animal's body temperature changes to a new level, and if the animal selectively performs operants which defend the new level against deviations in either direction, then the temperature change represents a set point displacement.

2. If an animal's body temperature changes to a new level, and if the animal selectively performs operants which counteract the change, then the temperature change represents something other than a shift in set point.

To illustrate these points, let us consider the effects of raising the body temperature in two different ways in a situation in which an animal has the opportunity to alter its thermal environment:

1. Make the animal febrile by injecting a pyrogen. If pyrogens raise the set point, the animal will respond for warmth, but not for cooling, until its body temperature approaches the new, elevated set point. A commonplace example of this is that people in the first stages of a fever report feeling cold and try to warm themselves.

---

[5] In the days before air conditioning a serious problem with surgery on hot summer days was keeping the patient's temperature down. Now, with operating rooms maintained at about 24°C, the problem is to keep it up at normal levels.

2. Make the animal hyperthermic by placing it in a hot environment. In this case, body temperature rises not because the set point is elevated, but because reflexive heat loss mechanisms are inadequate to the task of removing excess body heat. The animal should work to cool itself, whereas it should not work for warmth.

Compounds That Alter Set Point

Pyrogens cause fever. The current concept of fever is that injection or natural entry of bacterial pyrogens into the body causes the release of an endogenous pyrogenic substance from blood leucocytes. This leucocytic pyrogen then travels to the brain and acts on thermosensitive cells, raising the set point. This leads to increased heat production and decreased heat loss until body temperature rises to the new set level. Fever was accompanied by heat-producing instrumental responding in baboons (Gale, Mathews, & Young, 1970), cats (Weiss, Laties, & Weiss, 1967), and dogs (Cabanac, Duclaux, & Gillet, 1970). Febrile dogs, for example, worked more for heat in the cold and less for cool air in hot environments than did normal animals (Figure 11).

The height of a fever is determined to some extent by the ambient temperature; it is lower in the cold (Fekety, 1963; Weiss et al., 1967). Does this imply that fever represents an alteration in the sensitivity of peripheral cold receptors? Operant measures suggest a different interpretation. In the Weiss et al. experiments, the cats were also tested in a chamber which had a heat-producing lever. When the operant was available, the fever of cats in the cold was substantially higher than when it was not available, and in fact was very close to the levels attained in a neutral environment. It thus appears that reflexive mechanisms are simply inadequate to accomplish the full rise in temperature when the environment is cold.

Can reptiles develop fevers? Despite an almost complete lack of reflexive thermoregulatory mechanisms, ectotherms, as we have seen, do indeed regulate their temperatures when they have the behavioral opportunity to do so.

In an ingenious experiment, Bernheim, Vaughn, and Kluger (1974) allowed iguanas to adjust their body temperatures by shuttling between cold and warm chambers. Then they injected the iguanas with a pyrogen (one that caused fever in rabbits). Following the injection the iguanas spent more time in the warmer side of the chamber and developed an average fever of 2°C. Another group of lizards were given the same dose of pyrogen but kept in a constant ambient temperature (below the febrile level). There was no change in body temperature, indicating that the fever was produced solely behaviorally.

Other sorts of data can be combined with operant measures to assess changes in set point. Clark and Coldwell (1973) reported that after intraventricular injection of tetrodotoxin—the puffer fish poison—cats had lowered body temperatures even though regulatory mechanisms appeared to be intact. While the animals were recovering but still hypothermic, they were exposed to infrared heat lamps, which raised their temperature sharply. When the lamps were turned off, their body temperature returned to where it would have been had the heat load not been imposed. The cats did not shiver while they were recovering from the hypothermia caused by the poison, but when body temperature was further lowered with ice packs, they did shiver. This is good evidence that tetrodotoxin lowers the thermoregulatory set point. Clark and Lipton (1974) then showed that patterns of instrumental responding for thermal reinforcement were compatible with this interpretation. After tetrodotoxin, while body temperature was falling rapidly, the cats increased lever pressing to escape heat in a warm environment and decreased pressing for heat in the cold. Declines in body temperature were very similar whether the cats were in the cold without a bar, or whether they were responding for heat reinforcement or escaping from heat. The lowered body temperature represents a downward shift in set point.

Many drugs lower body temperature, but their mechanisms of action may be dissimilar. Behavior differentiates among them. To illustrate this, we shall

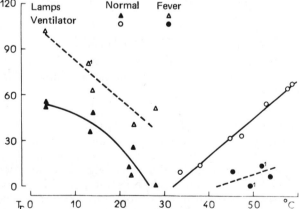

Fig. 11. Operant responding for infrared heat and for cool air in a dog with and without a fever. Responding varies systematically with ambient temperature. When feverish, the dog responds more for heat and less for cool air than when not feverish. (From Cabanac et al., 1970.)

consider three compounds, all of which, when injected systemically, lower body temperature in rats, but which have very different effects on operant responding: chlorpromazine, quinine, and sodium salicylate. Chlorpromazine depresses operant behavior in a dose-related manner regardless of whether the response produces heat in the cold (Weiss & Laties, 1963) or reduces heat in a warm environment (Polk & Lipton, 1975). Thus the hypothermic effect of chlorpromazine is probably not due to its specific action on temperature pathways, but rather is a side effect of the general central depressant properties of this drug. Quinine, on the other hand, increases lever pressing for heat in the cold (Satinoff, unpublished research). This is not a general excitation but rather a specific thermoregulatory effect; in food-deprived rats, responding for food decreases after quinine injection (Figure 12). Behavior compensated for the fall in body temperature, suggesting that quinine was simply acting on one or several effector mechanisms. In fact, when we measured the physiological responses of quinine-treated rats in the cold, we found that all reflexive responses were normal except shivering, which was greatly reduced. Sodium salicylate has a quite different effect—the rats increased responding to escape heat even while their body temperature was dropping (Polk & Lipton, 1975). Thus there was a coordinated change in body temperature and instrumental behavior.

In summary, all of these compounds lower body temperature, but chlorpromazine depresses operant behavior regardless of whether it is heat-producing or heat-reducing, quinine causes a compensatory change in behavior, and sodium salicylate elicits parallel behavioral and physiological responses.

Of these, the results with sodium salicylate are potentially the most interesting from our point of view. They imply that this drug is shifting the thermoregulatory set point downward. One must be extremely cautious in making this interpretation because the increase in responding may represent a general activation. If salicylate is in fact lowering the set point, not only should responding to escape heat increase, but responding for heat should decrease.

Neurochemical Basis of Thermoregulation

In recent years one of the major efforts in the study of temperature regulation has been to identify the neurotransmitters released at the synapses of neurons in thermoregulatory pathways. The protocol in many of these studies is simple: inject the transmitter and measure pre- and postinjection body temperatures. From these sorts of data pharmacological models of heat loss and heat production are constructed.

Not surprisingly, pharmacological models abound. The data on which they are based vary with the species tested, the dose of drug used, and the route of injection. We shall first list some of the conflicting results in this field to give an idea of the magnitude of the problem, and then we shall demonstrate why operant measures can provide the right sorts of data on which to build a pharmacological model.

In the first experiments studying neurotransmitters and body temperature, Feldberg and Myers (1963) reported that intraventricular injections of norepinephrine (NE) abolished shivering and lowered pyrogen-induced fever in cats. Serotonin (5-HT), on the other hand, caused shivering and a rise in rectal temperature in afebrile cats. When smaller doses were injected into the preoptic/anterior hypothalamus, the results were similar. Injections into other areas of the brain did not affect body temperature. On the basis of these results, Feldberg and Myers suggested that NE activates heat loss effectors (sweating, panting, vasodilation) and 5-HT activates heat-production pathways (shivering).

This was the first neurochemical model of temperature regulation. Similar results with dogs (Feldberg, Hellon, & Lotti, 1967) and monkeys (Myers & Yaksh, 1969) led to the hope that this model might be applicable to all mammalian species. However, different results soon appeared in other species. With intraventricular administration, rabbits became hyperthermic after NE and hypothermic after 5-HT (Cooper, Cranston, & Honour, 1965; Jacob & Peindaries, 1973). Mice responded to both of these amines with a drop in body temperature (Brittain & Handley, 1967; Handley & Spencer, 1972). Rats became hypothermic after 5-HT (Feldberg & Lotti, 1967; Myers & Yaksh, 1968), but it was found that NE can lead to either a fall in temperature (Bruinvels, 1970, 1973; Satinoff & Cantor, 1975), a rise (Myers & Yaksh, 1963), or a fall

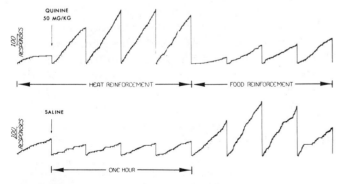

Fig. 12. Cumulative record showing response rate for heat and food of one rat before and after injection of quinine HCl (50 mg/kg) and saline. The pen resets to base line every 15 min.

followed by a rise (Feldberg & Lotti, 1967). To compound the problem, intrahypothalamic and intraventricular injections sometimes lead to opposite effects. Furthermore, acetylcholine (ACh) has potent thermoactive properties which vary with the species (Brimblecombe, 1973). Histamine also affects body temperature (Brezenoff & Lomax, 1970), as does dopamine (Hansen & Whishaw, 1973; Yehuda & Wurtman, 1972). As things stand now, no one can predict how a particular transmitter will affect thermoregulation in an untested species.

Most of the experiments on transmitter substances, temperature regulation, and instrumental behavior have been done with rats. We shall use this work to illustrate how operant measures can clear up confusion about pharmacological mechanisms. Our analysis rests on the assertions made on page 165: when set point is displaced, animals will work to bring actual body temperature as close as possible to the new level; when body temperature is altered without a set point change, behavior will be compensatory.

Norepinephrine

In a neutral environment (25°C) preoptic injection of low doses of NE (.05–.15 μg) raised hypothalamic temperature. The same effect occurred in the cold, and the rats increased lever pressing for heat. Both of these effects were monotonic functions of the concentration of NE (Beckman, 1970). The operant augmented the rise in internal temperature, which suggests that the set point had been raised. (However, before this conclusion can be reached it must be shown that the increased responding for heat is a specific thermoregulatory effect and not just a general increase in activity.) If low doses of NE in the preoptic area shift the thermoregulatory set point upward, then we would expect that *all* reflexive responses would be integrated so as to increase heat production and decrease heat loss. In fact, this is exactly what happens. The rise in temperature is caused by increased shivering, increased metabolic rate, and vasoconstriction (Satinoff & Hackett, 1975).

Avery (1971; see also Avery & Penn, 1973) has reported quite different results. In room air (23°C), preoptic injection of high doses of NE (25 μg) lowered body temperature. Heat escape was the behavioral measure: as long as the bar was held down, the heat lamp was off and a cooling fan on. The rats held the bar down *less* postinjection; that is, they allowed the chamber to stay hot. The body temperature change and the operant behavior moved in opposite directions: body temperature dropped, yet the rats decreased responding to escape heat. In this case behavior compensated for the lowering of internal temperature. The drug effect is therefore not a change in the set point.[6] We would not expect the fall in body temperature to be the result of an integrated thermoregulatory process. Although there were no measures of reflexive responses in these experiments, Satinoff and Cantor (1975) reported similar results after intraventricular injections of NE: body temperature fell and the rats compensated in the cold by increasing lever pressing for radiant heat. This was not a general activating effect of the NE, because when it was injected in a warm environment and body temperature fell, the rats did *not* increase responding to escape heat. When these authors later examined how the fall was brought about, they found that at normal room temperature it was caused by an immediate and intense peripheral vasodilation. Metabolic rate actually increased quickly thereafter as if to compensate for the fall (Cantor & Satinoff, 1976). Wherever intraventricular NE is acting, it is not shifting the set point.

We can tentatively conclude that, in rats, NE injected in the preoptic area shifts the set point upward by activating both operant and reflexive mechanisms leading to augmented heat production and decreased heat loss. Any hypothermic effects of NE, either after intraventricular injection or after injection of agents such as 6-hydroxydopamine, which causes release of endogenous NE (Breese, Moore, & Howard, 1972; Hansen & Whishaw, 1973; Nakamura & Thoenen, 1971; Simmonds & Uretsky, 1970), are apparently caused by action either on a controller that activates effector pathways or on the effector pathways themselves. We predict that the hypothermia seen after 6-hydroxydopamine injections will be accompanied by increases in heat-reinforced behavior.

Acetylcholine

The same reasoning can be applied in interpreting the effects of other transmitter substances implicated in thermoregulation. ACh and other cholinomimetic agents lowered body temperature in rats when injected intrahypothalamically (Beckman & Carlisle, 1969; Crawshaw, 1973; Kirkpatrick & Lomax, 1970).

---

[6] Similar considerations apply to the analysis of the effects of brain stimulation on body temperature. Electrical stimulation of the preoptic area while the rats were working for heat in the cold produced changes in body temperature but did not cause appropriate shifts in operant behavior (Crawshaw & Carlisle, 1974). Thus although electrical stimulation produced changes in body temperature, it did not affect motivational aspects of thermoregulation, and therefore such changes in body temperature need not be interpreted as changes in thermal set point.

ACh (50 μg) caused both a fall in brain temperature and a decrease in rate of working for heat in the cold (Beckman & Carlisle, 1969). Here the behavior and the physiological responses are complementary, and if it has no general depressant effect on operant responding, we can assume that ACh lowers the set point.

On the other hand, carbachol (a cholinomimetic drug) (8 μg) increased body temperature and also increased bar holding to escape heat (Avery & Penn, 1973). In this case the behavior compensated for the change in body temperature, and therefore this dose of carbachol did not change the set point. Like high doses of NE, it might have acted directly on effector pathways (in this case to promote heat loss) or blocked the appropriate synapses linking the central controller to those pathways. This latter possibility is likely because atropine, a cholinergic blocking agent, led to a rise in body temperature in rats when injected into the preoptic area (Kirkpatrick & Lomax, 1967).

Serotonin

This indoleamine lowered body temperature in rats when injected intraventricularly (Bruinvels, 1970; Feldberg & Lotti, 1967; Myers & Yaksh, 1968). As with NE, intrahypothalamic injections of 5-HT had the opposite effect, but produced little change in the rate of bar pressing for heat in the cold (Crawshaw, 1972). Crawshaw concluded that 5-HT does not act in the preoptic area to shift the set point, but rather that its effect on body temperature is unspecific. Bruinvels (1970), on the basis of pharmacological data, also concluded that 5-HT does not act on thermosensitive receptors, but instead its hypothermic effect is caused by some unspecific action.

From all of these experiments we can tentatively conclude that in rats, NE raises the set point, ACh lowers it, and 5-HT does not affect it. The number of experiments investigating the action of transmitter substances on both body temperature and operant behavior is still small, and even when such experiments become more numerous everything will not magically fall into place. Some of the species differences may indeed be real. However, many of the conflicting results about the action of transmitter substances on body temperature could be cleared up if operant measures were used more often to specify whether the set point was being altered. It is fruitless to build neurochemical models of thermoregulation without knowing if a compound is really changing the set point. This can best be done by a careful analysis not only of physiological responses, but of operant responding as well.

REFERENCES

Adair, E. Control of thermoregulatory behavior by brief displacements of hypothalamic temperature. *Psychonomic Science*, 1970, *20*, 11–13.

Adair, E. Hypothalamic control of thermoregulatory behavior: Preoptic-posterior hypothalamic interaction. In *Recent studies of hypothalamic function* (international symposium in Calgary, Alberta.) Basel: Karger, 1974.

Adair, E. R., & Hardy, J. D. Posterior hypothalamic thermal stimulation can alter behavioral, but not physiological, temperature regulation. Paper presented at International Congress of Physiology, Munich, 1971.

Adair, E. R., & Wright, B. A. Behavioral thermoregulation in the squirrel monkey when response effort is varied. *Journal of Comparative and Physiological Psychology*, 1976, *90*, 179–184.

Avery, D. D. Intrahypothalamic adrenergic and cholinergic injection effects on temperature and ingestive behavior in the rat. *Neuropharmacology*, 1971, *10*, 753–763.

Avery, D. D., & Penn, P. E. Effects of intrahypothalamic injections of adrenergic and cholinergic substances on behavioral thermoregulation and associated skin temperature levels in rats. *Pharmacology, Biochemistry, and Behavior*, 1973, *1*, 159–165.

Baldwin, B. A. Behavioural thermoregulation in mice. *Physiology and Behavior*, 1968, *3*, 401–407.

Baldwin, B. A., & Ingram, D. L. The effect of heating and cooling the hypothalamus on behavioural thermoregulation in the pig. *Journal of Physiology* (London), 1967, *191*, 375–392.

Beckman, A. L. Effect of intrahypothalamic norepinephrine on thermoregulatory responses in the rat. *American Journal of Physiology*, 1970, *218*, 1596–1604.

Beckman, A. L., & Carlisle, H. Effect of intrahypothalamic infusion of acetylcholine on behavioral and physiological thermoregulation in the rat. *Nature*, 1969, *221*, 561–562.

Bernheim, H. A., Vaughn, L. K., & Kluger, M. J. Induction of fever in lizards in response to gram-negative bacteria. *Federation Proceedings*, 1974, *33*, 457.

Bogert, C. M. How reptiles regulate their body temperature. *Scientific American*, 1959, *200*, 105–120.

Bolles, R. C. Species-specific defense reactions and avoidance learning. *Psychological Review*, 1970, *77*, 32–48.

Breese, G. R., Moore, R. A., & Howard, J. L. Central actions of 6-hydroxydopamine and other phenylethylamine derivatives on body temperature in the rat. *Journal of Pharmacology and Experimental Therapeutics*, 1972, *180*, 591–602.

Brezenoff, H. E., & Lomax, P. Temperature changes following microinjection of histamine into the thermoregulatory centers of the rat. *Experientia*, 1970, *26*, 51–52.

Brimblecombe, R. W. Effects of cholinomimetic and cholinolytic drugs on body temperature. In E. Schonbaum & P. Lomax (Eds.), *The pharmacology of thermoregulation*. Basil: Karger, 1973.

Brittain, R. T., & Handley, S. L. Temperature changes produced by the injection of catecholamines and 5-hydroxytryptamine into the cerebral ventricles of the conscious mouse. *Journal of Physiology* (London), 1967, *192*, 805–813.

BROWN, A. C., & BRENGELMANN, G. L. The interaction of peripheral and central inputs in the temperature regulation system. In J. D. Hardy, A. P. Gagge, & J. A. J. Stolwijk (Eds.), *Physiological and behavioral temperature regulation.* Springfield, Ill.: C. C. Thomas, 1970.

BRUINVELS, J. Effect of noradrenaline, dopamine, and 5-hydroxytryptamine on body temperature in the rat after intracisternal administration. Neuropharmacology, 1970, *9,* 277–282.

BRUINVELS, J. Effects of intracisternal administration of metaraminol and noradrenaline on body temperature in the rat. In E. Schonbaum & P. Lomax (Eds.), *The Pharmacology of thermoregulation.* Basil: Karger, 1973.

BUDGELL, P. Behaviour thermoregulation in the Barbary dove (*Streptopelia risoria*). Animal Behaviour, 1971, *19,* 524–531.

CABANAC, M. Plaisir ou déplaisir de la sensation thermique et homéothermie. *Physiology and Behavior,* 1969, *4,* 359–364.

CABANAC, M. Physiological role of pleasure. Science, 1971, *173,* 1103–1107.

CABANAC, M., DUCLAUX, R., & GILLET, A. Thermorégulation comportementale chez le chien: Effets de la fièvre et de la thyroxine. *Physiology and Behavior,* 1970, *5,* 697–704.

CABANAC, M., HAMMEL, H. T., & HARDY, J. D. *Tiliqua scincoides:* Temperature-sensitive units in lizard brain. Science, 1967, *158,* 1050–1051.

CABANAC, M., & JEDDI, E. Thermopreferendum et thermorégulation comportementale chez trois poïkilothermes. *Physiology and Behavior,* 1971, *7,* 375–380.

CABANAC, M., & MASSONNET, B. Temperature regulation during fever: Change of set point or change of gain? A tentative answer from a behavioural study in man. *Journal of Physiology* (London), 1974, *238,* 561–568.

CABANAC, M., MASSONNET, B., & BELAICHE, R. Preferred skin temperature as a function of internal and mean skin temperature. Journal of Applied Physiology, 1972, *33,* 699–703.

CALLARD, I. P., CHAN, S. W. C., & POTTS, M. A. The control of the reptilian gonad. *American Zoologist,* 1972, *12,* 273–287.

CANTOR, A., & SATINOFF, E. Thermoregulatory responses to intraventricular norepinephrine in normal and hypothalamic rats. Brain Research, April 1976, Vol. 106.

CARLISLE, H. J. Behavioural significance of hypothalamic temperature-sensitive cells. Nature, 1966, *209,* 1324–1325.

CARLISLE, H. J. The effects of preoptic and anterior hypothalamic lesions on behavioral thermoregulation in the cold. Journal of Comparative and Physiological Psychology, 1969, *69,* 391–402.

CARLISLE, H. J. Thermal reinforcement and temperature regulation. In W. C. Stebbins (Ed.), *Animal psychophysics: The design and conduct of sensory experiments.* Englewood Cliffs, N. J.: Prentice-Hall, Inc., 1970.

CARLISLE, H. J., & SNYDER, E. The interaction of hypothalamic self-stimulation and temperature regulation. Experientia, 1970, *26,* 1092–1093.

CARLTON, P. L., & MARX, R. A. *Heat as a reinforcement for operant behavior.* United States Army Medical Research Laboratory Technical Report No. 229. Fort Knox, 1957.

CLARK, W. G., & COLDWELL, B. A. The hypothermic effect of tetrodotoxin in the unanaesthetized cat. *Journal of Physiology* (London), 1973, *230,* 477–492.

CLARK, W. G., & LIPTON, J. M. Complementary lowering of the behavioural and physiological thermoregulatory set-points by tetrodotoxin and saxitoxin in the cat. *Journal of Physiology* (London), 1974, *238,* 181–191.

COOPER, K. E., CRANSTON, W. I., & HONOUR, A. J. Effects of intraventricular and intrahypothalamic injection of noradrenaline and 5-hydroxytryptamine on body temperature in conscious rabbits. *Journal of Physiology* (London), 1965, *181,* 852–864.

CORBIT, J. D. Behavioral regulation of body temperature. In J. D. Hardy, A. P. Gagge, & J. A. J. Stolwijk (Eds.), *Physiological and behavioral temperature regulation.* Springfield, Ill.: C. C. Thomas, 1970.

CORBIT, J. D., & ERNITS, T. Specific preference for hypothalamic cooling. Journal of Comparative and Physiological Psychology, 1974, *86,* 24–27.

COWLES, R. B. Semantics in biothermal studies. Science, 1962, *135,* 670.

COWLES, R. B., & BOGERT, C. M. A preliminary study of the thermal requirements of desert reptiles. *Bulletin of the American Museum of Natural History,* 1944, *83,* 265–296.

CRAWSHAW, L. I. Effects of intracerebral 5-hydroxytryptamine injection on thermoregulation in the rat. *Physiology and Behavior,* 1972, *9,* 133–140.

CRAWSHAW, L. I. Effect of intracranial acetylcholine injection on thermoregulatory responses in the rat. Journal of Comparative and Physiological Psychology, 1973, *83,* 32–35.

CRAWSHAW, L. I., & CARLISLE, H. J. Thermoregulatory effects of electrical brain stimulation. Journal of Comparative and Physiological Psychology, 1974, *87,* 440–448.

CRAWSHAW, L. I., & HAMMEL, H. T. Behavioral thermoregulation in two species of antarctic fish. Life Sciences, 1971, *10,* 1009–1020.

CRAWSHAW, L. I., & HAMMEL, H. T. Behavioral temperature regulation in the California horn shark, *Heterodontus francisci.* Brain, Behavior, and Evolution, 1973, *7,* 447–452.

CRAWSHAW, L. I., & HAMMEL, H. T. Behavioral regulation of internal temperature in the brown bullhead, *Ictalurus nebulosus.* Comparative Biochemistry and Physiology, 1974, *47A,* 51–60.

CUNNINGHAM, D. J., & CABANAC, M. Evidence from behavioral thermoregulatory responses of a shift in set-point temperature related to the menstrual cycle. *Journal of Physiology* (Paris), 1971, *63,* 236–238.

DAVIDSON, R. S. Operant stimulus control applied to maze behavior: Heat escape conditioning and discrimination reversal in *Alligator mississippiensis. Journal of the Experimental Analysis of Behavior,* 1966, *9,* 671–676.

DAWES, G. S. *Foetal and neonatal physiology.* Chicago: Year Book Medical Publishers, 1968.

DUCLAUX, R., FANTINO, M., & CABANAC, M. Comportement thermorégulateur chez *Rana esculenta. Pflüger's Archives,* 1973, *342,* 347–358.

EDINGER, H. M., & EISENMAN, J. S. Thermosensitive neurons in tuberal and posterior hypothalamus of cats. *American Journal of Physiology,* 1970, *219,* 1098–1103.

EISENMAN, J. S., & JACKSON, D. C. Thermal response patterns of septal and preoptic neurons in cats. *Experimental Neurology,* 1967, *19,* 33–45.

EPSTEIN, A. N., & MILESTONE, R. Showering as a coolant for rats exposed to heat. Science, 1968, *160,* 895–896.

FEKETY, F. R., JR. Heat balance and reactivity to endotoxin. *American Journal of Physiology*, 1963, *204*, 719–722.

FELDBERG, W., HELLON, R. F., & LOTTI, V. J. Temperature effects produced in dogs and monkeys by injection of monoamines and related substances into the third ventricle. *Journal of Physiology* (London), 1967, *191*, 501–515.

FELDBERG, W., & LOTTI, V. J. Temperature responses to monoamines and an inhibitor of MAO injected into the cerebral ventricles of rats. *British Journal of Pharmacology and Chemotherapy*, 1967, *31*, 152–161.

FELDBERG, W., & MYERS, R. D. A new concept of temperature regulation by amines in the hypothalamus. *Nature*, 1963, *200*, 1325.

FRAENKEL, G. S., & GUNN, D. L. *The orientation of animals.* New York: Dover, 1961.

FREEMAN, M. E., CRISSMAN, J. K., LOUW, G. N., BUTCHER, R. L., & INSKEEP, E. K. Thermogenic action of progesterone in the rat. *Endocrinology*, 1970, *86*, 717–720.

FREEMAN, W. J., & DAVIS, D. D. Effects on cats of conductive hypothalamic cooling. *American Journal of Physiology*, 1959, *197*, 145–148.

FRY, F. E. J., & HOCHACHKA, P. W. Fish. In G. C. Whittow (Ed.), *Comparative physiology of thermoregulation*, Vol. 1: *Invertebrates and nonmammalian vertebrates*. New York: Academic Press, 1970.

GALE, C. C., MATHEWS, M., & YOUNG, J. Behavioral thermoregulatory responses to hypothalamic cooling and warming in baboons. *Physiology and Behavior*, 1970, *5*, 1–6.

GARRICK, L. D. *Internal and external environmental influences on thermoregulation in two lizard species.* Unpublished doctoral dissertation, Rutgers University, 1973.

GARRICK, L. D. Reproductive influences on behavioral thermoregulation in the lizard, *Sceloporus cyanogenys*. *Physiology and Behavior*, 1974, *12*, 85–91.

GORDON, M. S. *Animal physiology: Principles and adaptations* (2nd ed.). New York: Macmillan, 1972.

GREER, G. L., & GARDNER, D. R. Temperature-sensitive neurons in the brain of brook trout. *Science*, 1970, *169*, 1220–1222.

GROSSMAN, S. P., & RECHTSCHAFFEN, A. Variations in brain temperature in relation to food intake. *Physiology and Behavior*, 1967, *2*, 379–383.

HAMILTON, C. L. Interactions of food intake and temperature regulation in the rat. *Journal of Comparative and Physiological Psychology*, 1963, *56*, 476–488.

HAMILTON, C. L., & SHERIFF, W., JR. Thermal behavior of the rat before and after feeding. *Proceedings of the Society of Experimental Biology and Medicine*, 1959, *102*, 746–748.

HAMMEL, H. T., CALDWELL, F. T., JR., & ABRAMS, R. M. Regulation of body temperature in the blue-tongued lizard. *Science*, 1967, *156*, 1260–1262.

HAMMEL, H. T., HARDY, J. D., & FUSCO, M. M. Thermoregulatory responses to hypothalamic cooling in unanesthetized dogs. *American Journal of Physiology*, 1960, *198*, 481–486.

HAMMEL, H. T., STROMME, S. B., & MYHRE, K. Forebrain temperature activates behavioral thermoregulatory responses in arctic sculpins. *Science*, 1969, *165*, 83–85.

HANDLEY, S. L., & SPENCER, P. S. J. Thermoregulatory effects of intraventricular injection of noradrenaline in the mouse and the influence of ambient temperature. *Journal of Physiology* (London), 1972, *223*, 619–631.

HANSEN, M. G., & WHISHAW, I. Q. The effects of 6-hydroxydopamine, dopamine, and *dl*-norepinephrine on food intake and water consumption, self-stimulation, temperature, and electroencephalographic activity in the rat. *Psychopharmacology*, 1973, *29*, 33–44.

HARLOW, H. *Learning to love.* San Francisco: Albion, 1971.

HEATH, J. E. Temperature-independent morning emergence in lizards of the genus *Phrynosoma*. *Science*, 1962, *138*, 891–892.

HEATH, J. E. Temperature regulation and diurnal activity in horned lizards. *University of California Publications in Zoology*, *64*, No. 3, 97–136. Published in 1965 by The Regents of the University of California.

HEATH, J. E. Behavioral regulation of body temperature in poikilotherms. *Physiologist*, 1970, *13*, 399–410.

HELLSTROM, B., & HAMMEL, H. T. Some characteristics of temperature regulation in the unanesthetized dog. *American Journal of Physiology*, 1967, *213*, 547–556.

HENSEL, H. Neural processes in thermoregulation. *Physiological Review*, 1974, *53*, 948–1017.

HOGAN, J. A. Responses in Pavlovian conditioning studies. *Science*, 1974, *186*, 156–157.

HUEY, R. B. Behavioral thermoregulation in lizards: Importance of associated costs. *Science*, 1974, *184*, 1001–1003.

JACOB, J., & PEINDARIES, R. Central effects of monoamines on the temperature of the conscious rabbit. In E. Schonbaum & P. Lomax (Eds.), *The pharmacology of thermoregulation*. Basel: Karger, 1973.

JEDDI, E. Confort du contact et thermoregulation comportementale. *Physiology and Behavior*, 1970, *5*, 1487–1493.

JEDDI, E. Thermoregulatory efficiency of neonatal rabbit search for fur comfort contact. *International Journal of Biometeorology*, 1971, *15*, 337–341.

KELLER, A. D. Temperature regulation disturbances in dogs following hypothalamic ablations. In J. D. Hardy (Ed.), *Temperature: Its measurement and control in science and industry* (Vol. 3). New York: Reinhold, 1963.

KEMP, F. D. Thermoregulatory operant behavior in the lizard *Dipsosaurus dorsalis* as a function of body temperature, substrate temperature, and heating rate. *Journal of Biological Psychology*, 1969, *11*, 36–39.

KIRKPATRICK, W. E., & LOMAX, P. The effect of atropine on the body temperature of the rat following systemic and intracerebral injection. *Life Sciences*, 1967, *6*, 2273–2278.

KIRKPATRICK, W. E., & LOMAX, P. Temperature changes following iontophoretic injection of acetylcholine into the rostral hypothalamus of the rat. *Neuropharmacology*, 1970, *9*, 195–202.

KOELLE, G. B. Anticholinesterase agents. In L. S. Goodman & A. Gilman (Eds.), *The Pharmacological basis of therapeutics.* New York: Macmillan, 1970.

LATIES, V. G. Effects of *d*-amphetamine on concurrent schedules of heat and food reinforcement. *Journal of Physiology* (Paris), 1971, *63*, 315–318.

LATIES, V. G., & WEISS, B. Thyroid state and working for heat in the cold. *American Journal of Physiology*, 1959, *197*, 1028–1034.

LEONARD, C. M. Thermotaxis in golden hamster pups. *Journal of Comparative and Physiological Psychology*, 1974, *86*, 458–469.

LIPTON, J. M. Effects of preoptic lesions on heat-escape responding and colonic temperature in the rat. *Physiology and Behavior*, 1968, *3*, 165–169.

Lipton, J. M. Effects of high-fat diets on caloric intake, body weight, and heat-escape responses in normal and hyperphagic rats. *Journal of Comparative and Physiological Psychology*, 1969, *68*, 507–515.

Lomax, P. Drugs and body temperature. *International Review of Neurobiology*, 1970, *12*, 1–43.

Magoun, H. W., Harrison, F., Brobeck, J. R., & Ranson, S. W. Activation of heat loss mechanisms by local heating of the brain. *Journal of Neurophysiology*, 1938, *1*, 101–114.

Matthews, T. J. A convective thermal controller for behavioral experiments. *Behavioral Research and Methodological Instrumentation*, 1969, *1*, 126–128.

Matthews, T. J., Morin, L. P., & Church, R. M. Avoidance of thermal stimuli in the rat. *Psychonomic Science*, 1971, *22*, 59–60.

McGinty, D. J. Somnolence, recovery, and hyposomnia following ventro-medial diencephalic lesions in the rat. *Electroencephalography and Clinical Neurophysiology*, 1969, *26*, 70–79.

McLean, J. H., & Coleman, W. P. Temperature variation during the estrous cycle: Active vs. restricted rats. *Psychonomic Science*, 1971, *22*, 179–180.

Milsum, J. H. *Biological control systems analysis.* New York: McGraw-Hill, 1966.

Morishima, M. S., & Gale, C. C. Relationship of blood pressure and heart rate to body temperature in baboons. *American Journal of Physiology*, 1972, *223*, 387–395.

Mount, L. E. Environmental temperature preferred by the young pig. *Nature*, 1963, *199*, 1212–1213.

Murgatroyd, D., & Hardy, J. D. Central and peripheral temperatures in behavioral thermoregulation of the rat. In J. D. Hardy, A. P. Gagge, & J. A. J. Stolwijk (Eds.), *Physiological and behavioral temperature regulation.* Springfield, Ill.: C. C. Thomas, 1970.

Myers, R. D., & Yaksh, T. L. Feeding and temperature responses in the unrestrained rat after injections of cholinergic and aminergic substances into the cerebral ventricles. *Physiology and Behavior*, 1968, *3*, 917–928.

Myers, R. D., & Yaksh, T. L. Control of body temperature in the unanesthetized monkey by cholinergic and aminergic systems in the hypothalamus. *Journal of Physiology* (London), 1969, *202*, 483–500.

Myhre, K., & Hammel, H. T. Behavioral regulation of internal temperature in the lizard *Tiliqua scincoides*. *American Journal of Physiology*, 1969, *217*, 1490–1495.

Nakamura, K., & Thoenen, H. Hypothermia induced by intraventricular administration of 6-hydroxydopamine in rats. *European Journal of Pharmacology*, 1971, *16*, 46–54.

Neill, W. H., Magnuson, J. J., & Chipman, G. D. Behavioral thermoregulation by fishes: A new experimental approach. *Science*, 1972, *176*, 1443–1445.

Nickerson, M. Drugs inhibiting adrenergic nerves and structures innervated by them. In L. S. Goodman & A. Gilman (Eds.), *The pharmacological basis of therapeutics.* New York: Macmillan, 1970.

Ogilvie, D. M., & Stinson, R. H. The effect of age on temperature selection by laboratory mice (*Mus musculus*). *Canadian Journal of Zoology*, 1966, *44*, 511–517.

Pachomov, N. The effects of posterior and anterior hypothalamic lesions on the maintenance of body temperature in the rat. *Journal of Neuropathology and Experimental Neurology*, 1962, *21*, 450–460.

Pliskoff, S. S., Wright, J. E., & Hawkins, T. D. Brain stimulation as a reinforcer: Intermittent schedules. *Journal of the Experimental Analysis of Behavior*, 1965, *8*, 75–88.

Polk, D. L., & Lipton, J. M. Effects of sodium salicylate, aminopyrine, and chlorpromazine on behavioral temperature regulation. *Pharmacology, Biochemistry, and Behavior*, 1975, *3*, 167–172.

Proppe, D. W., & Gale, C. C. Endocrine thermoregulatory responses to local hypothalamic warming in unanesthetized baboons. *American Journal of Physiology*, 1970, *219*, 202–207.

Regal, P. J. Thermophilic response following feeding in certain reptiles. *Copeia*, 1966, *3*, 588–590.

Regal, P. J. Voluntary hypothermia in reptiles. *Science*, 1967, *155*, 1551–1553.

Revusky, S. H. Cold acclimatization in hairless mice measured by behavioral thermoregulation. *Psychonomic Science*, 1966, *6*, 209–210.

Roberts, W. W., Mooney, R. D. & Martin, J. R. Thermoregulatory behaviors of laboratory rodents. *Journal of Comparative and Physiological Psychology*, 1974, *84*, 693–699.

Rozin, P. The use of poikilothermy in the analysis of behavior. In D. Ingle (Ed.), *The central nervous system and fish behavior.* Chicago: University of Chicago Press, 1968.

Rozin, P., & Mayer, J. Thermal reinforcement and thermoregulatory behavior in the goldfish, *Carassius auratus*. *Science*, 1961, *134*, 942–943.

Satinoff, E. Behavioral thermoregulation in response to local cooling of the rat brain. *American Journal of Physiology*, 1964, *206*, 1389–1394.

Satinoff, E. Neural integration of thermoregulatory responses. In L. V. DiCara (Ed.), *Limbic and autonomic nervous system: Advances in research.* New York: Plenum Press, 1974.

Satinoff, E., & Cantor, A. Intraventricular norepinephrine and thermoregulation in rats. In P. Lomax, E. Schonbaum, & J. Jacob (Eds.), *Temperature regulation and drug action.* Basil: Karger, 1975.

Satinoff, E., & Hackett, E. R. Reflexive thermoregulatory responses after intrahypothalamic injection of norepinephrine in rats. *Neuroscience Abstracts*, 1975, *1*, 416.

Satinoff, E., & Rutstein, J. Behavioral thermoregulation in rats with anterior hypothalamic lesions. *Journal of Comparative and Physiological Pyschology*, 1970, *71*, 77–82.

Satinoff, E., & Shan, S. Y. Y. Loss of behavioral thermoregulation after lateral hypothalamic lesions in rats. *Journal of Comparative and Physiological Psychology*, 1971, *77*, 302–312.

Sidman, M. Avoidance conditioning with brief shock and no exteroceptive warning signal. *Science*, 1953, *118*, 157–158.

Simmonds, M. A., & Uretsky, N. J. Central effects of 6-hydroxydopamine on the body temperature of the rat. *British Journal of Pharmacology*, 1970, *40*, 630–638.

Squires, R. D., & Jacobson, F. H. Chronic deficits of temperature regulation produced in cats by preoptic lesions. *American Journal of Physiology*, 1968, *214*, 549–560.

Stein, L. Reciprocal action of reward and punishment mechanisms. In R. B. Heath (Ed.), *The role of pleasure in behavior.* New York: Harper & Row, 1964.

Teague, R. S., & Ranson, S. W. The role of the anterior hypothalamus in temperature regulation. *American Journal of Physiology*, 1936, *117*, 562–570.

Teitelbaum, P., & Epstein, A. N. The lateral hypothalamic syndrome: Recovery of feeding and drinking after lateral hypothalamic lesions. *Psychological Review*, 1962, *69*, 74–90.

Templeton, J. R. Reptiles. In G. C. Whittow (Ed.), *Comparative physiology of thermoregulation*, Vol. 1: *Invertebrates and nonmammalian vertebrates*. New York: Academic Press, 1970.

Van Sommers, P. *The biology of behaviour.* New York: Wiley, 1972.

Wade, G. N. Gonadal hormones and behavioral regulation of body weight. *Physiology and Behavior*, 1972, *8*, 523–534.

Wampler, R. S. *Changes in sleep and arousal accompanying the lateral hypothalamic syndrome in rats.* Unpublished doctoral dissertation, University of Pennsylvania, 1970.

Wasserman, E. A. Pavlovian conditioning with heat reinforcement produces stimulus-directed pecking in chicks. *Science*, 1973, *181*, 875–877.

Weiss, B. Thermal behavior of the subnourished and pantothenic acid-deprived rat. *Journal of Comparative and Physiological Psychology*, 1957, *50*, 481–485.

Weiss, B., & Laties, V. G. Behavioral thermoregulation. *Science*, 1961, *133*, 1338–1344.

Weiss, B., & Laties, V. G. Effects of amphetamine, chlorpromazine, and pentobarbital on behavioral thermoregulation. *Journal of Pharmacology and Experimental Therapeutics*, 1963, *140*, 1–7.

Weiss, B., Laties, V. G., & Weiss, A. B. Behavioral thermoregulation by cats with pyrogen-induced fever. *Archives of International Pharmacodynamics*, 1967, *165*, 467–475.

Yeh, S. D. J., & Weiss, B. Behavioral thermoregulation during vitamin B_6 deficiency. *American Journal of Physiology*, 1963, *205*, 857–862.

Yehuda, S., & Wurtman, R. J. The effects of *d*-amphetamine and related drugs on colonic temperatures of rats kept at various ambient temperatures. *Life Sciences*, 1972, *11*, 851–859.

Zolman, J. F. Discrimination learning in the young chick with heat reinforcement. *Psychological Record*, 1968, *18*, 303–309.

7

Determinants of Reinforcement and Punishment*

W. H. Morse
and
R. T. Kelleher

REPRODUCIBLE BEHAVIORAL PROCESSES

The scientific study of behavior poses many difficulties. One difficulty results, paradoxically, from our familiarity with numerous isolated facts about the behavior of ourselves, other people, and animals. The interpretations customarily given to these facts lead to preconceived opinions, which frequently interfere with the unbiased study of behavior. Moreover, behavior is essentially dynamic in the sense that behavioral processes reflect changes in the interactions between an individual and his environment which take place *in time*. Even the simplest relationships may not be readily apparent to casual observations at any moment. Finally, a pattern of behavior is the result of many interrelated factors, including environmental circumstances that have long since ceased to exist, thus posing special problems for identification and study.

*The preparation of this chapter was supported by U.S. Public Health Service Grants MH 07658, MH 02094, DA 00499, and RR 00168 and by Research Career Program Award 1-K5-MH22589 (RTK). We thank Mrs. Patricia Lavin for help in preparation of the manuscript and Drs. P. B. Dews, J. W. McKearney, and J. B. Smith for helpful comments about the manuscript.

In the early 1930s B. F. Skinner developed techniques for the experimental study of behavior. An essential feature in his approach to behavior was the emphasis on the rate of occurrence of some identifiable "response" as a significant property of behavior. Techniques for studying reflexly elicited behavior had already been developed, but it is not possible to identify an eliciting stimulus for much of the behavior of an individual that can be predicted and controlled. To say that behavior occurs in the absence of an identifiable eliciting stimulus does not imply that the behavior is not determined, but simply that it does not have the functional properties of reflexly elicited behavior. For example, a food-deprived rat given access to a supply of small food pellets will eat for a period of time and then cease. If the rate of ingesting pellets is recorded, a simple and reproducible curve of eating is obtained that describes the ingestion of food under these conditions (Skinner, 1930, 1938). Although the rate of eating following food deprivation is a reproducible temporal process, it is not possible to analyze this behavior simply in terms of momentary eliciting stimuli. Because the presentation of food is often immediately followed by ingestion, it may seem that the ingestion of food is elicited by the presence of food itself (presumably its sight and smell). But the rate of eating declines in time; the presence of food does not continue to have the same preemptiveness. Thus it is necessary to invoke some other factors, such as habituation, fatigue, adaptation, or deprivation, operating in conjunction with the sight and smell of food. The deprivation of food critically determines rate of eating and also changes other classes of responses in a reproducible way, but it is not an eliciting stimulus in the sense in which the term is used in reflex physiology.

The occurrence of emitted behavior generally bears a temporal relation to the deprivation and presentation of particular environmental conditions, whether or not the deprivation produces any conspicuous physiological change. For example, if a rat is confined in a small space and then given access to a revolving wheel, it will run for some time and then gradually cease. As in the example of the rat eating, a record in time of the running behavior will reveal that the running has a characteristic temporal pattern. After the rat is deprived of access to the wheel, the availability of the wheel is closely followed by running, yet it is not useful to regard the wheel as an eliciting stimulus for running. In studying the occurrence of such behavior in time, it is clearly desirable that particular instances be easily identified, reproducible, and functionally significant. The criterion for specifying functionally significant emitted responses as operants will be taken up later in this section.

Behavioral phenomena that have an identifiable temporal pattern under specified conditions and which are reproducible in different individuals may be described as *reproducible behavioral processes* (Zimmerman, 1963). An understanding of such reproducible behavioral processes is to be found in the exact characterization of the temporal relations among the events comprising such processes and in the specification of the conditions under which they occur. The present chapter will discuss reinforcement and punishment in the context of reproducible behavioral processes. In many respects, reinforcement and punishment are analogous if not equivalent processes; therefore, considerations pertaining to the one will usually apply to the other.

Future behavior is mainly determined by the consequences of past behavior. How behavior is changed by experience can be demonstrated as a reproducible behavioral process with a food-deprived rat in an apparatus containing a food dispenser and a lever projecting from the wall. Any response of the rat that depresses the lever will be followed by the presentation and ingestion of food. Under such circumstances, the likelihood that a similar response will occur again after the food is eaten is increased, and further responses will occur with a characteristic temporal patterning. If behavior is so altered by the presentation of food, the conditions under which food presentation occurs—in this example, the depression of the lever—define the property with respect to which responses are called similar. Skinner (1937; 1938; 1953, p. 66) uses the term *operant* to describe this functionally identifiable class and calls the change in the frequency of the operant the process of *operant conditioning*. Because subsequent behavior is altered under these conditions, the food is said to be a *reinforcer* and presenting food in a specified relation to an operant is *reinforcement*.[1]

If only depressions of the lever exceeding a certain force are followed by food presentation (differential reinforcement), weaker responses diminish and stronger responses become more frequent. Even stronger responses can be selected through further progressive differential reinforcement. It should be noted that merely specifying relations between responses and consequent stimuli may not specify a functional class of responses that could be called operant. "No property is a valid defining property of a class until its experimental reality has been demonstrated, and this rule excludes a great many terms commonly brought into the description of behavior" (Skinner, 1938, p. 41; 1969). Yet it is important to recognize that these broad principles do apply beyond experimental situations that can be precisely described. In his recent writings, Skinner has used the term *contingencies of reinforcement* to refer to the interrelations between antecedent behavior and consequent events that define operants (Skinner, 1969, pp. 7, 127).

The examples above are important because basic concepts applicable to the formulation of behavior as a scientific system were developed in this situation. It is clear from Skinner's experimental reports that the basic data in the example of "conditioning" and in the earlier one of "changes in hunger" (food deprivation) were the orderly changes in rate of responding.

> "Conditioning" . . . and "a change in hunger" differ as processes only with respect to the conditions under which they are observed. The *thing changing* (the observed aspect of behavior) is the same in both. (Skinner, 1932, p. 276)

[1] Skinner uses *reinforcement* to refer to the specifiable conditions in the environment that give rise to *operant conditioning*. In this chapter the single term *reinforcement* will be used to refer to both the orderly change in behavior and its environmental determinants.

The change in behavior under the specified conditions that identifies the food as a reinforcer and identifies lever pressing as an operant is a reproducible behavioral process.

A distinction has been made between *operations* as experimental procedures that are imposed by the environment and *processes* as the behavioral effects of these procedures (Catania, 1973, p. 33; Ferster & Skinner, 1957, p. 730). Although reinforcement is often described as a relation or operation (the presentation of a reinforcer in a specified temporal relation to an operant), it is clear that the operation of reinforcement (or punishment) has a behavioral effect implicit in its meaning. Behavioral processes are best viewed as orderly changes in time and need not imply intervening mechanistic principles. The terms *reinforcement* and *punishment* are used here to refer to the reproducible changes in behavior resulting from the experience of the individual under certain specified conditions. The connotations of these terms include both a temporal sequence of behavior and the conditions under which this behavior occurs.

Since the time of the first reports by Skinner, many orderly changes in rates of responding under other specified conditions have been described (see especially Ferster & Skinner, 1957; Skinner, 1938). Among the most important specifications are the schedules describing the arrangements for initiating and terminating stimuli in time and in relation to specified responses. Such schedules engender changes in behavior with characteristic temporal properties and rates of responding that are consistent in different individuals. Hence it is appropriate to view schedule-controlled performances as reproducible behavioral processes.[2] This conception differs from the usual approach of analyzing schedule performances as special consequences of reinforcement (or punishment). While the latter approach has the advantage of limiting the number of basic behavioral processes to two fundamental cases, some schedule-controlled patterns are more sensitive dependent variables in revealing how behavior is modified by environmental conditions than the changes in level of responding that are usually used to define reinforcement or punishment. In particular, the effects of consequent stimuli can be greatly changed, depending upon how they are scheduled (see this chapter's sections on disparate effects of consequent events and response-produced shocks as consequent events maintaining behavior). Thus the status of consequent events defined as "reinforcers" or "punishers" in one context may be changed when they are scheduled differently. This raises important questions about the fundamental concepts applicable to a scientific formulation of behavior and about the generality of the concepts of "reinforcers" and "punishers." The defining characteristics of reinforcers and punishers do not encompass all the effects of such stimuli on behavior. How consequent events modify behavior is to be understood in both the development and the maintenance of subsequent behavior.

The description of reinforcement and punishment as reproducible behavioral processes differs from the usual description of these terms as operations (see especially Catania, 1968, 1969). A discussion of the differences is instructive in clarifying the precise usage of terms. In common usage the terms *reinforcer* and *punisher* are emphasized as basic terms, while *reinforcement* and *punishment* are defined as the presentation of a reinforcer or punisher in a specified temporal relation to an operant. The increased occurrence of responses similar to one that immediately preceded some event identifies that event as a reinforcer. A punisher is defined in an analogous way: the decreased occurrence of responses similar to one that immediately preceded some event identifies that event as a punisher. Reinforcers and punishers, as environmental "things," appear to have a greater reality than orderly temporal changes in ongoing behavior. Such a view is deceptive. There is no concept that predicts reliably when events will be reinforcers or punishers; the defining characteristics of reinforcers and punishers are how they change behavior. Events that increase or decrease the subsequent occurrence of one response may not modify other responses in the same way. The modification of behavior by a reinforcer or by a punisher depends not only upon the occurrence of a certain kind of consequent environmental event but also upon the qualitative and quantitative properties of the ongoing behavior preceding the event and upon the schedule under which the event is presented.

In characterizing reinforcement as the presentation of a reinforcer contingent upon a response, the tendency is to emphasize the event and to ignore the importance of both the contingent relations and the antecedent and subsequent behavior. It is how they change behavior that defines the terms *reinforcer* and *punisher;* thus it is the orderly change in behavior that is the key to these definitions. It is not appro-

---

[2] The characterization of different schedule performances as behavioral processes and the specifications of the conditions under which these performances occur are beyond the scope of this chapter (see Ferster & Skinner, 1957; Morse, 1966; Skinner, 1966; Zeiler, chapter 8 in this volume). The present chapter emphasizes the importance of basing behavioral concepts on orderly reproducible changes in behavior.

priate to presume that particular environmental events such as the presentation of food or electric shock are reinforcers or punishers until a change in rate of responding has occurred when the event is scheduled in relation to specified responses. There is little value in naming only one of the conditions necessary for the change. Identifying an event as a reinforcer or punisher independently of the conditions of use has limited predictive utility. On the other hand, prior identification of the suitable conditions that will result in the same behavioral process does provide generality. The purpose of the present chapter is to give perspective to basic concepts used in the experimental study of behavior by discussing some of the determinants of reinforcement and punishment.

THE CONTINUITY OF BEHAVIOR IN TIME (SHAPING)

Because reinforcement and punishment are behavioral processes occurring in time, they can only be understood in the temporal context of sequential interactions of behavior with the environment.[3] Emphasizing "reinforcers" and "punishers" as primary events neglects the importance of both antecedent and subsequent behavior. Operant behavior is determined mainly by the consequences of past behavior—not so much the particular consequences, but their sequence in time and in relation to the individual's behavior. The scheduling of events is critically important. The outstanding characteristic of operant behavior is that it can be differentiated in form and in temporal patterning by consequent events. Conditioned operant behavior emerges from existing behavior through successive approximations to new and more complex forms of behavior by the process of successive differential reinforcement (shaping). Behavior that has become highly differentiated can be understood and accounted for only in terms of the history under which the behavior was shaped by different consequences. This schedule gives the exact historical specification of the temporal and sequential relations between environmental events and behavior.

One purpose of this chapter is to emphasize how present and future behavior depends upon the sequential ordering of behavior. Because it is generally understood that behavior can be shaped by successive differential reinforcement, it is useful to consider the shaping of responses commonly studied in experimental situations. Knowing the appropriate conditions for using a reinforcer, one can give a general specification for shaping operant behavior with it: select a response with vector properties, follow the occurrence of a particular magnitude of this response one or more times with the reinforcer, then withhold it until the response magnitude exceeds the value previously reinforced, and reinforce this greater magnitude. Thus by making the presentation of reinforcers intermittent and dependent upon some progressively changing property of behavior, one can shape behavior toward some ultimate specification through successive approximations. By the shaping of behavior, one can develop new forms of behavior that could not exist without an explicit history of differential reinforcement. Nevertheless, important aspects of the shaping process are still unknown. Different responses vary in stereotypy, rate of occurrence, discreteness of identification, and the extent to which they are changed by consequent events. A consequent event can be more easily used to increase the frequency of occurrence of an operant with a low initial frequency than one with a high initial frequency. Because the presentation of a reinforcer tends to enhance behavior, it is easier to shape a response involving some discrete activity than a response involving sustained immobility. In fact, it may be difficult to shape an operant involving little or no movement, such as "holding" or "standing still" (Blough, 1958). Yet operants come under the *schedule control* of consequent events even when their average rate is refractory to change (Skinner & Morse, 1958).

The importance of the shaping sequence is recognized in cases where the final form of behavior did not occur initially, which is the situation usually described to illustrate the principle of shaping. Under such circumstances it is clear that transitional behavior is essential in developing the final behavior. It is less often recognized that an individual's past experience—how his behavior has been shaped—is usually a determinant of his subsequent behavior. Even in dealing with repetitive responses such as a rat pressing a lever or a pigeon pecking at a disc, the quantitative effect of presenting a particular event after an instance of such a response depends on the subject's history. For example, when food is presented after every 100 responses under a fixed-ratio schedule, responding may be well maintained in a subject with a history of responding under this or other schedules but not in a subject without an appropriate history. The effectiveness of an event in maintaining a sequential pattern

---

[3] Perhaps shaping the suppression of behavior with punishment is not exactly analogous to shaping with reinforcement; little is known about the former. The work of Azrin (1960) clearly indicates that punishment depends upon sequential relations between behavior and the environment.

of responding depends on the ongoing pattern of responding itself, which in turn depends on the subject's experimental history. These topics will be taken up in following sections.

DISPARATE EFFECTS OF CONSEQUENT EVENTS

A remarkable diversity exists in the physical characteristics of events that can reinforce behavior. Included among these events are: food, water, sex, electric shock, and intracranial stimulation; changes in lights, sounds, temperature, and gravity; opportunity to explore, run, groom, lick a stream of air, play, or fight; and the injection of various drugs. It has been assumed wrongly that the reinforcing or punishing effect of an event is a consistent property of the event itself; the presentation of food after a response has been considered an inherently positive event that will enhance subsequent responding, while the presentation of electric shock after a response has been considered an inherently negative event that will suppress subsequent responding. That food presentation may not affect responding in an animal that has not been deprived of food is usually considered a quantitative variation in the effect of food presentation rather than evidence against food presentation having inherent properties as a reinforcer. But the effects of reinforcing events are not invariant. Even under a given degree of deprivation, the presentation of food to an individual may not have a consistent reinforcing quality. One may have an aversion to a particular food as a child, be indifferent to it as an adolescent, and eat it readily as an adult. It is less widely recognized that under appropriate conditions the suppressive effects of electric shock presentation can be reduced or even converted to an enhancing effect. Such disparate effects of consequent events are most likely to occur when there is a history of schedule-controlled responding and when there are multiple determinants of behavior.

In common practice experimenters normally use consequent events that do reliably modify the response classes that are being studied and do have generality from individual to individual. In most experiments in which food is used as the reinforcing consequence, the subject is initially deprived severely (65 to 80% of free-feeding body weight) and its response to the presentation of food preempts other activity. The presentation of food is made contingent upon a simple response, such as pressing a key for a rat or monkey, that occurs infrequently before it is followed by food presentation. Under these conditions the subject's behavior changes in a predictable way. The development of standardized equipment and the use of standardized procedures has increased the likelihood that any experimenter can reproduce such results. Unfortunately, this success in engendering behavior under what are actually special conditions has led to uncritical beliefs about reinforcers and punishers.

Of particular significance are instances in which the same event can under different conditions reliably produce opposite effects on behavior. With events, such as presentation of food or water, that characteristically lead to further behavior on the part of the individual, such changes in the direction of effect are easily missed. If an individual fails to consume food or water presented under the usual conditions, for example, the possibly suppressing effects of these events may not be apparent. Disparate effects of the same event are most likely to be observed when the presentation of the event directly affects the individual. Such changes in the reinforcing (or punishing) effectiveness of intracranial stimulation, electric shock, and drug injections will be discussed below.

Opposite effects of intracranial stimulation on lever-pressing responses in the rat have been shown by Steiner, Beer, and Shaffer (1969). In the initial phase of their study, each lever-pressing response on one of two levers (lever S) resulted in electrical stimulation of an area of the hypothalamus; at appropriate stimulus parameters, rapid and reliable responding was engendered and maintained on lever S. The patterns of responding and intracranial stimulation were tape-recorded. In subsequent phases of the study, intracranial stimulations of the same intensity were presented to each rat according to the pattern previously recorded for that rat. Responses on lever S were recorded but had no programmed consequences, whereas responses on lever E postponed the scheduling of further intracranial stimulations for 20 sec. Under these conditions, the rates of responding on lever S decreased to near zero, while rates of responding on lever E increased and were stably maintained in subsequent sessions. These results show that depending upon the circumstances, responding could be maintained by either the presentation or the postponement of the same intracranial stimulation.

Opposite effects of presenting electric shock under different schedules have been studied by Kelleher and Morse (1968a). Squirrel monkeys were trained initially under a variable-interval (VI) schedule of food presentation that maintained a steady rate of responding. Then a 10-min fixed-interval (FI) schedule of electric

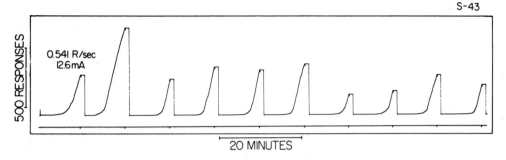

Fig. 1. Alternate periods of maintenance and suppression of responding by different schedules of electric shock presentation in a squirrel monkey. Ordinate—cumulative number of responses; abscissa—time. Electric shock presentations (12.6 mA) are marked by short diagonal strokes on the cumulative record and the event record. The recording pen reset to the base line at the end of each 11-min cycle. The paper did not move during the 1-min time-out period at the end of each cycle. During the first 10 min of each cycle, positively accelerated responding, characteristic of performance under fixed-interval (FI) schedules, was maintained; during the last min of each cycle, in which each response produced an electric shock, responding was suppressed. (From Morse & Kelleher, 1970.)

shock presentation was superimposed upon the schedule of food presentation. When the schedule of food presentation was eliminated, responding characteristic of FI schedules could be maintained by the schedule of electric shock alone. In one experiment, when an electric shock was produced by each response during the last minute of an 11-min cycle ending with a time-out period, responding was positively accelerated during the first 10 min (FI schedule) but suppressed during the last minute of each cycle (Figure 1). Thus electric shocks of the same intensity that maintained responding under the FI schedule suppressed responding during the part of the cycle in which each response produced electric shock.

Another study suggests that intravenous injections of nalorphine, a drug that antagonizes the actions of morphine, can function in seemingly opposite ways in rhesus monkeys (Goldberg, Hoffmeister, Schlichting, & Wuttke, 1971). The administration of nalorphine to a morphine-dependent monkey precipitates an immediate and severe withdrawal syndrome. In one phase of the study, morphine-dependent monkeys were trained under a schedule in which key pressing produced intravenous injections of morphine. After stable performance had developed, injections of either saline or nalorphine were substituted for morphine. Although response-produced nalorphine injections did precipitate a severe withdrawal syndrome, response rates were higher than those maintained by morphine or saline. In a subsequent phase of this study with morphine-dependent monkeys, intravenous injections of nalorphine were automatically delivered in the presence of a stimulus; responding terminated the stimulus and the associated injections. Under this schedule of stimulus-injection termination, responding was well maintained with nalorphine injections but not with saline injections. These results with intravenous injections of nalorphine, like those obtained with intracranial stimulation and with electric shocks, indicate that factors such as the controlling schedule can determine the effect of an event on behavior. Interestingly, the experiments on electric shock are more puzzling to many people than those on intracranial stimulation or drug injections. This undoubtedly occurs because the latter two situations are relatively unfamiliar, suggesting that tacit commonsense notions pervade scientific thinking more than is usually realized.

With quantitative variations in the magnitudes of consequent events, the possibilities of varied effects are increased. Simply altering some parameter of a consequent event can completely change the subsequent frequency of occurrence of responses which produce the event.[4] Responses that produce intracranial stimulation, for example, will usually increase in frequency as the intensity or duration of stimulation is increased over some range of values; however, at higher values responding will decrease and eventually cease. When responding is maintained by response-

[4] When suppression of responding occurs only at certain parameter values of a consequent event, the suppression may be lasting or transitory. In most instances in which responding is suppressed by intense electric shock, the effect has been shown to be lasting and is appropriately described as operant punishment. Responding will also be suppressed just after it has resulted in the presentation of a large amount of food or the injection of a high dose of drug. Yet under certain circumstances, it may be possible to show that rate of responding generally increases as the amount of food or dose of drug increases even if responding just after the event is suppressed temporarily. (For example, see the description below of the experiment by Hawkins & Pliskoff, 1964.)

produced electric shocks, similar increases and decreases in rate of responding would be expected with increases in intensity or duration of electric shock. In some circumstances, responding is not initiated even under conditions in which it has previously been well maintained by an event. With intracranial stimulation, for example, responding may not occur unless each daily session begins with an automatically presented stimulation. A similar phenomenon is described in the section headed "Characteristics of Responses" under conditions in which electric shock both elicits and modulates responding. Such results further indicate the varied effects of environmental events in controlling responding.

When an event that occurs after a response increases the subsequent frequency of occurrence of that response, the presentation of the same event after a different response or according to a different schedule may not affect behavior in the same way. The conditions required for the suitability of various events in modifying behavior can differ markedly, but under suitable conditions even different events can function similarly. Thus it is imperative to study factors in addition to the events themselves which are involved in the processes of operant reinforcement and punishment.

ONGOING BEHAVIOR

Both the qualitative and quantitative properties of ongoing behavior are important aspects of reinforcement and punishment. Emphasizing the sequential patterning of behavior as a determinant of subsequent behavior shifts the focus of the interaction between behavior and environmental events toward behavior itself. Historically the situation has always been just the opposite. A stimulus paired with a reinforcer is said to have become a conditioned reinforcer, but actually it is the behaving subject that has changed, not the stimulus. Similarly, the physical properties of a discriminative stimulus are the same before and after it controls behavior; it is the subject that has become discriminative, not the stimulus. It is, of course, useful shorthand to speak of conditioned reinforcers or discriminative stimuli, just as it is convenient to speak about a reinforcer rather than speaking about an event that has followed an instance of a specific response and resulted in a subsequent increase in the occurrence of similar responses. The latter may be cumbersome, but it has the advantage of empirical referents. Because many different responses can be shaped by consequent events, and because a given consequent event is often effective in modifying the behavior of different individuals, it becomes common practice to refer to reinforcers without specifying the behavior that is being modified. These common practices have unfortunate consequences. They lead to the erroneous views that responses are arbitrary and that the reinforcing or punishing effect of an event is a specific property of the event itself.

The commonly used contingency table describing relations between the presentation and withdrawal of stimuli and their behavioral effects (Skinner, 1953, pp. 73, 185; Rachlin, 1970, p. 79) provides an example of the tendency to categorize stimuli in terms of inherent properties. When the borders of the table are designated in terms of stimulus classes (positive-negative; pleasant-noxious) and experimental operations (stimulus presentation–stimulus withdrawal), the cells of the table are, by definition, varieties of reinforcement and punishment. One problem is that the processes indicated in the cells have already been assumed in categorizing stimuli as positive or negative; a second is that there is a tacit assumption that the presentation or withdrawal of a particular stimulus will have an invariant effect. These relations are clearer if empirical operations are used to designate the border conditions, as shown in Table 1. In this case the cells of the table are unambiguously related to the designated conditions; the top row indicates the process of reinforcement and the bottom row the process of punishment. If the presentation of a particular stimulus increases behavior under one condition and decreases behavior under another condition, there is no need for a category of paradoxical reinforcement or punishment. In trying to understand why the same stimulus event can have different effects on behavior it is no help to consider reinforcement or punishment as paradoxical. The characterization of behavioral processes depends upon empirical observations. The same stimulus event, under different conditions, may increase behavior or decrease behavior. In the former case the process is called *reinforcement* and in the latter the process is called *punishment*.

The work of Premack (1959, 1965, 1971) has emphasized that reinforcers and punishers are not discrete

Table 1

	Present Stimulus	*Withdraw Stimulus*
Increase Behavior	Reinforcement	Reinforcement
Decrease Behavior	Punishment	Punishment

fixed classes of events. He has made the intriguing proposal that reinforcement and punishment are based on the probabilities of responses associated with different events. He suggests that when an event associated with a high response probability follows an event associated with a low response probability, reinforcement will occur; however, when an event associated with a low response probability follows an event associated with a high response probability, punishment will occur. As noted previously, the process of reinforcement can be demonstrated in the situation in which the lever-pressing responses of a food-deprived rat result in the delivery of food pellets. Under the conditions of this demonstration, the initial probability that the rat will press the lever is low, whereas the initial probability that it will eat the food pellets is high; thus reinforcement is easily demonstrated.

A notable aspect of Premack's formulation is its recognition of the relativity of events as reinforcers or punishers. This relativity has been demonstrated under conditions in which the access of rats to a drinking tube or an activity wheel could be controlled experimentally (Premack, 1971). Licking on the drinking tube was sensed automatically by means of an electronic circuit and recorded on a counter (drinkometer). The activity wheel revolved at a preset rate for 5 sec whenever the rat pressed a retractable lever. The initial relative probabilities of drinking and running responses were assessed in daily 15-min control sessions. The rats spent more time drinking than running when they were water-deprived, but spent more time running than drinking when they were not water-deprived. In subsequent experimental sessions, the activity wheel was operated only after the rat made a specified number of licks on the drinking tube; that is, drinking resulted in brief periods of forced running. Drinking responses were increased above control levels (reinforcement) by operation of the activity wheel in rats which were not water-deprived but were decreased below control levels (punishment) by operation of the activity wheel in rats which were water-deprived. Moreover, the degree of suppression was inversely related to the probability of operating the activity wheel in the control sessions. Thus operation of the activity wheel could be either a reinforcer or a punisher depending on whether the initial relative probability of running was high or low.

The results of some experiments with two-component chained schedules seem inconsistent with the notion that the reinforcing effectiveness of an event is directly related to the response probability associated with it; that is, responding in the first component can be well maintained by the presentation of the second component despite a low rate of responding in the second component (see Gollub, Chapter 10 of this volume). For example, relations between rates of responding controlled by various intensities of intracranial stimulation and the effectiveness of such stimulation in controlling behavior have been studied by Hawkins and Pliskoff (1964). Each response on one of two response keys resulted in electrical stimulation of an area of the hypothalamus; this response key (key B) was retracted from the apparatus after every fifth response. Responses on the other response key (key A) were maintained under a VI schedule by the reintroduction of key B. As the intensity of the intracranial stimulation was increased over a range of parameter values, the rate of responding on key B (computed from the latency of the first of five responses) increased and then decreased (or simply decreased). Over the same range of intensities, however, the rates of responding on key A increased. Thus under this two-component chained schedule, the effectiveness of the second component in maintaining responding in the first component was directly related to the intensity of intracranial stimulation but was not related in any simple way to rate of responding in the second component. This type of experiment, like those described in the preceding section, indicates the importance of the schedule of presentation of any event in determining how it affects behavior.

Premack's promising theoretical account of the conditions under which an event will function as a reinforcer or as a punisher is being refined and extended, but it is still difficult to apply in some situations. One problem is how to assign an initial probability of response to certain types of events—for example, events such as intracranial stimulation or intravenous drug injection that are delivered directly to the animal. Premack notes that it should be possible to develop indirect ways of assessing the initial response probabilities of such events. It seems likely, however, that this indirect approach would entail the same difficulties as the discriminative stimulus hypothesis of conditioned reinforcement (see Gollub, Chapter 10 of this volume). Although the point of view in the present chapter is similar to that of Premack in stressing the relativity of events as reinforcers and punishers, our emphasis is on the ongoing rate of responding at the time an event occurs and on the way in which the event is scheduled. The role of schedules will be considered in more detail at the end of this chapter.

It is clear that the effect of a given consequent event on rate of responding is likely to be different when it follows responding occurring at different frequencies. Depending on the frequency of ongoing responding, behavior may be modulated more than changed in absolute level. For example, Skinner and Morse (1958) studied rats running in an activity wheel under conditions in which running resulted in the presentation of a food pellet under a 5-min FI schedule. The rats characteristically paused for a relatively long period of time after each food presentation and then ran until food was presented again. Whether or not the overall rate of running was increased or decreased from the level of running that prevailed when the schedule was not in effect, the pattern of running became orderly with respect to the schedule of food presentation.

Reinforcement depends upon the quantitative properties of behavior, so that different responses are modified differently. It is usually easier to increase the frequency of an operant that is occurring infrequently than that of an operant that is occurring frequently. Although interactions between the levels of ongoing behavior and consequent events have tended to be ignored in studies on reinforcement, these considerations have become increasingly important with the development of techniques for engendering strong, reproducible patterns of behavior.

Much information is available on the importance of ongoing maintenance conditions in determining the effects of consequent noxious stimuli. As noted previously, the defining operation of a punisher is a subsequent decrease in the frequency of responses similar to one that immediately preceded the punisher. There is no fundamental logical difference between the punishment and reinforcement situations; in both there is an assumption that the level of behavior before the presentation of the event is measurable and sufficiently reproducible to permit identification of changes in its rate. In dealing with reinforcement, the level is usually low or is developed through shaping, and experimenters may easily conduct experiments without forcing themselves to ponder the determinants of behavior in the absence of reinforcement (cf. Segal, 1972). In dealing with punishment, the practical situation is entirely different. Measurable levels of some behavior are required both before and after the introduction of the punishing event; in practice this is usually accomplished by using some schedule of reinforcement to engender a sustained rate of responding. Here the experimenter is forced to use some explicit condition, and therefore evidence has accumulated on the effects of using noxious stimuli as consequent events under different maintenance conditions (Azrin & Holz, 1966; Fantino, 1973). For example, when a brief electric shock follows each response under FR (fixed-ratio) and FI schedules of food presentation in the pigeon, a pattern of suppression develops that is different under the two schedules (Azrin, 1959; Holz & Azrin, 1962). Under a single type of schedule, the effects of response-contingent electric shocks may be different when they are introduced in different temporal relations to the consequent event (Holz & Azrin, 1962). Besides the type of maintenance schedule, other parameters are also important in determining the effects of noxious stimuli as consequent events. When behavior is maintained under VI or FR schedules of food presentation, the suppressive effect of response-produced electric shocks is critically dependent upon the degree of food deprivation (Azrin, 1960; Azrin, Holz, & Hake, 1963). For example, the suppression produced by an intense shock delivered every 100 responses became progressively greater as the maintenance body weight of the subject was increased from 60 to 85% (Azrin et al., 1963). This finding shows clearly that the effect of a response-produced electric shock depends on the prevailing conditions. In this case, whether the same intense electric shock suppressed behavior or not depended on the degree of food deprivation.

Because the suppressive effects of response-produced electric shocks do depend upon the exact maintenance conditions, experiments on the effects of introducing response-produced electric shocks have often yielded different results. At one time such differences were interpreted as indicating that punishment was a less reliable behavioral process than was reinforcement. Such differences are due entirely to a lack of comparability in other features of the situation being studied; when the maintenance conditions of experiments are comparable, the effects of response-produced electric shocks are comparable and reproducible from experiment to experiment.

The process of reinforcement is as dependent upon variations in environmental conditions as is the process of punishment. The historical difference between reinforcement and punishment is that a greater range of maintenance conditions has been studied with punishment, which explains why punishment may have appeared to be variable. In actual fact, studies on reinforcement have dealt mostly with restrictive, idealized cases, which may have given the false impression that the effects of known reinforcers are not critically dependent upon conditions under which they operate. The important point is not that punishment is a variable process, but that both punishment and reinforcement depend upon the quantitative conditions of the environment. When one considers the potential range of environmental conditions under which behavior can be studied, perhaps more is known about punishment than about reinforcement.

CHARACTERISTICS OF RESPONSES

Although the range of behaviors that can be controlled by operant conditioning is vast, the type of response selected for measurement can be critical. Responses of the classes most commonly used have the following characteristics: they are easily identifiable so that repeated instances can be reliably counted; they are easily recorded with automatic equipment; they have short durations; and they are readily repeatable. Some operants are easily established and "well behaved." In contrast, certain types of species-specific responses, especially elicited responses, are difficult to control directly by reinforcement or punishment.

Responses elicited by electric shock in the squirrel monkey are of interest because their temporal patterning can be modulated by consequent events. These stereotyped patterns of behavior include attacks on other members of the same species or on certain other nearby objects (Azrin, Hutchinson, & Hake, 1967; Hake & Campbell, 1972; Hutchinson, Azrin, & Hake, 1966; Hutchinson, Azrin, & Renfrew, 1968; Hutchinson, Renfrew, & Young, 1971). If the monkey is partially restrained in a chair, for example, electric shocks to the monkey's tail will cause it to pull and bite a leash attached to its collar. In one study, electric shock was used both to elicit and to modulate leash-pulling responses (Morse, Mead, & Kelleher, 1967). The leash was fastened to a lever so that biting and pulling on the leash repeatedly closed a switch attached to a lever. Two of the three monkeys were studied initially under an FT (fixed-time) schedule in which an electric shock was delivered automatically every 60 sec. Each electric shock elicited pulling and biting the leash, which caused a burst of switch closures temporally related to the biting and pulling. The burst of switch closures just after shock usually ceased abruptly after a few seconds; however, a few more switch closures often occurred just before the next electric shock was delivered. As the session proceeded, the number of switch closures just after shock tended to decrease, while the number occurring just before shock tended to increase (Figure 2A).

Subsequently, the schedule was changed so that the first closure of the switch 30 sec after an electric shock produced the next shock; if no switch closure occurred between 30 and 60 sec, the shock was delivered automatically at 60 sec after the previous shock. Under this FI 30-sec schedule, the switch closure was considered a response, defined by its relation to the shock. Initially, this response occurred predominantly after an electric shock; however, most shocks were produced by a response occurring between 30 and 60 sec after the preceding shock (left of Figure 2B). With further

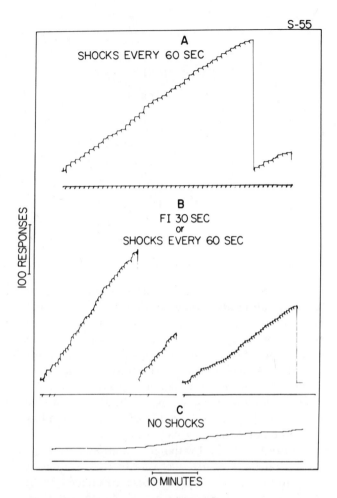

Fig. 2. Different patterns of responding (switch closures related to pulling and biting a leash) in a squirrel monkey under fixed-time (FT) (A) and FI (B) schedules of electric shock presentation, and rapid cessation of responding when shocks were not presented (C). Ordinate—cumulative number of responses; abscissa—time. Electric shock presentations (7 mA) are indicated by short diagonal strokes on the cumulative record; strokes on the event record indicate shocks delivered under the FT 60-sec schedule. The recording pen reset to the base line whenever 250 responses accumulated and at end of session. A—Session 18, FT 60-sec schedule; B—Sessions 5, 9, and 99, shocks scheduled under a FI 30-sec schedule; C—Session 104, no shocks scheduled. In part A responding occurred predominantly after shocks, producing a pattern of deceleration. With continued exposure to the FI schedule (B), responding occurred predominantly before the shock, producing a pattern of acceleration. When shocks were omitted (C), few responses occurred. (From Morse & Kelleher, 1970.)

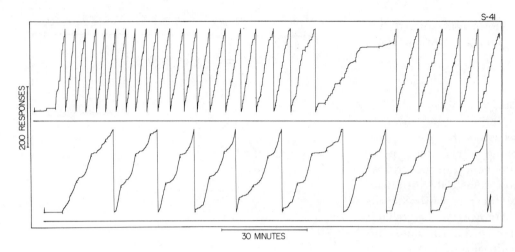

Fig. 3. Development of positively accelerated responding (switch closures related to pulling and biting leash) in a squirrel monkey under a 5-min FI schedule of electric shock presentation (7 mA). Recording as in Figure 2. Top—Session 117, initial performance under 5-min FI schedule after 30-sec FI schedule; bottom—Session 153. (From Morse & Kelleher, 1970.)

exposure to the FI 30-sec schedule (right of Figure 2B), responding declined soon after an electric shock was delivered and then increased until the first response after 30 sec produced the next shock. Only the first electric shock in most sessions was delivered automatically. When electric shocks were not delivered (Figure 2C), this monkey seldom responded.

The rapid loss of responding in the absence of electric shocks distinguishes this FI pattern of responding from other FI patterns of key pressing engendered in the squirrel monkey by the presentation of electric shock (Kelleher & Morse, 1968a) or by the termination of a stimulus-shock complex (Morse & Kelleher, 1966). Although the performances were developed and maintained by the shock, two of the monkeys usually began responding only after a shock occurred. In another monkey, responding was maintained under only the FI 30-sec schedule (no shocks delivered automatically) and then under a FI 5-min schedule of electric shock presentation (Figure 3). A positively accelerated responding characteristic of FI schedules subsequently developed, most responding occurring before the response-produced electric shock. The leash pulling and biting controlled by the electric shock appear to have characteristics of both elicited and operant behavior (see also the section on response-produced electric shocks near the end of the chapter).

ADVENTITIOUS REINFORCEMENT AND PUNISHMENT: IMPORTANCE OF HISTORY

Adventitious relations between behavior and the occurrence of some event are especially useful in understanding reinforcement and punishment. In this case, the event is presented in time independently of any particular behavior. For example, if a food pellet is delivered to a rat according to an FT schedule under suitable conditions (appropriate type of food, degree of deprivation, and temporal parameter of the schedule), some identifiable sequence of behavior will develop. There is no correct response or problem solution in this situation, but the rat's behavior is changed. The delivery of the pellets inevitably follows some operant feature of the rat's behavior. This feature then becomes more prominent and more likely to be followed by a subsequent pellet delivery and thus becomes a maintained response. A positively accelerated pattern of responding can be developed and maintained under such an FT schedule of food presentation (Skinner, 1948).

Adventitious punishment differs from adventitious reinforcement only in the direction of the effect (cf. Fantino, 1973), but in this case it is necessary to study some prominent feature of behavior that can be decreased in frequency. For example, Azrin (1956) maintained key pecking in pigeons under a VI schedule of food presentation and then presented an intense electric shock according to an FT schedule. A negatively accelerated pattern of responding was engendered and maintained under this FT schedule.

In determining the effects of events presented independently of responding, the quantitative properties of ongoing behavior are especially important. These properties, in turn, depend on such factors as the history of the individual and the tendency of the event to elicit responding. It has become accepted that an event is more likely to change ensuing behavior when it coincides with certain features of behavior than when it coincides with other features. Thus different behaviors vary in their frequency of occurrence and in their susceptibility to modification by response-independent environmental events (Staddon & Simmelhag, 1971; also see Schwartz & Gamzu, Chapter 3 of this volume). In pigeons with a long history of responding under schedules of response-dependent food presentation, the presentation of food under FT schedules can maintain responding indefinitely. Although the rates of responding under such FT schedules are characteristically lower than those under comparable FI schedules, similar patterns of responding can be maintained (Zeiler, 1968). In pigeons which have had only three response-dependent food presentations, however, FT schedules maintain low rates and erratic patterns of responding (Neuringer, 1970). It is frequently asserted that FI responding maintained by response-produced electric shocks is basically different from other instances of FI responding; however, phenomena involved in studies of electric shock are analogous to those involved in studies of food presentation. As noted in the preceding section, electric shocks do elicit various responses, but similar phenomena are reported in studies of autoshaping with food. Moreover, studies comparing FT and FI schedules of electric shock presentation have produced results similar to those obtained with schedules of food presentation; that is, under the FT schedules, rates of responding were relatively lower and responding was not always positively accelerated (Kelleher, Riddle, & Cook, 1963; McKearney, 1974; Morse & Kelleher, 1970).

Experimental history can be critical in determining whether an event occurring independently of responding will result in adventitious punishment or adventitious reinforcement. For example, responding maintained under a schedule of food presentation is suppressed under many conditions in which response-independent electric shocks are delivered intermittently (Azrin, 1956; Estes & Skinner, 1941). When responding in the rhesus monkey was maintained under a schedule of electric shock postponement, however, it was found that superimposing an FT schedule of electric shock delivery markedly increased responding (Sidman, Herrnstein, & Conrad, 1957). Moreover, when electric shocks were no longer scheduled under the avoidance procedure, responding not only persisted under the FT schedule but became positively accelerated as "the animal lever-pressed right 'into' the shock" (Sidman, Herrnstein, & Conrad, 1957, p. 53). Many subsequent studies have shown that the delivery of electric shocks independently of responding can enhance responding in animals that have responded under schedules of electric shock postponement (for example, Kelleher, Riddle, & Cook, 1963; Waller & Waller, 1963). After avoidance responding had been

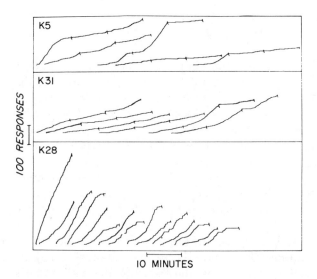

Fig. 4. Patterns of responding under a 10-min FT schedule of electric shock presentation (3 mA) in squirrel monkeys with a history of responding under schedules of electric shock postponement. Ordinate—cumulative number of responses; abscissa—time. Short diagonal strokes on the cumulative record indicate shock presentations. The records of monkeys K5 and K31 have been broken into 30-min segments and displaced along the abscissa; those of monkey K28 have been broken into 10-min segments. Note that the pattern of responding in many of the individual segments were S-shaped because responding decreased near the end. (From Kelleher, Riddle, & Cook, 1963. © 1963 by the Society for the Experimental Analysis of Behavior, Inc.)

well established and then extinguished in squirrel monkeys, for example, responding recovered when electric shocks were presented independently of responses, but ceased again when no shocks were delivered. When electric shocks were delivered under a 10-min FT schedule, substantial levels of responding were maintained, as shown in Figure 4. The patterns of responding were comparable to those that have been described under FT schedules of food presentation.

Circumstances in which adventitious punishment could be changed to adventitious reinforcement were first described by Herrnstein and Sidman (1958). Initially, responding of rhesus monkeys under a schedule of food presentation was suppressed in the presence of a clicking sound by intermittent electric shocks delivered under an FT schedule. Then the monkeys were trained to respond under a schedule in which responses postponed electric shocks. Finally, the schedule of food presentation was reinstated, but when the clicking sound associated with the FT schedule was presented, responding was enhanced rather than suppressed. Whether response-independent electric shocks suppressed or enhanced responding depended on the experimental history of the monkey.

CRITERIA FOR COMPARING CONSEQUENT EVENTS

The fundamental importance of orderly changes in rate of responding to the study of behavior was discussed in the first section of this chapter. *Operants* were defined as functionally identifiable, reproducible classes of responses. The behavioral changes associated with increases in responding were considered *reinforcement*, and those associated with decreases in responding were considered *punishment*. It was noted that various schedule conditions gave rise to characteristic reproducible patterns of responding in time, yet little consideration was given to the criteria for identifying these different reproducible behavioral processes. These criteria are not absolute. They depend very much on the "state of the art" and the consensus of contemporaries.

In comparing performances in the earliest experiments on schedule-controlled behavior maintained by food presentation with performances in more recent experiments, it is clear that progress has been made in achieving reproducibility and control of behavior. In general, this improvement in control of behavior is not because of any change in the properties of the food used to maintain behavior, although it might be said that there had been a change in the effect of the food. The change has come about because optimal parameters of various features in the situation have been combined, including the parameters of the consequent event, the location and nature of external stimuli, the types of keys used, the reliability of the controlling equipment, the conditions of deprivation, the training conditions, and the experience of the subject. Because various combinations of conditions will suffice and because no single feature is likely to be essential, it may not be always possible to explain the reasons for technical advances. In some instances, specific changes in current practices have been shown to be important. For example, if food-deprived rats are maintained at 60–65% of ad lib body weight rather than at 80%, characteristic schedule-controlled performances are more easily obtained. In the development of stimulus control, the location, intensity, and duration of the controlling stimuli and the schedule under which they are presented can result in "errorless" discriminations, whereas only slightly different conditions can result in a much slower development of control. Perhaps the most important ingredient of advances in experimental control is the explicit attempt by investigators to achieve greater control. After the initial work showing the possibility of errorless discriminations (Terrace, 1963), many other investigators

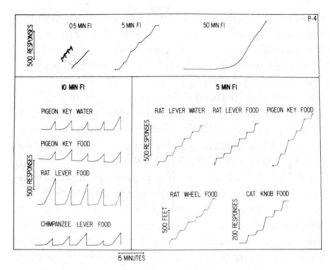

Fig. 5. Generality of characteristic FI performance (no responding, then acceleration to a maintained steady rate of responding). Ordinate—cumulative number of responses; abscissa—time. An FI schedule of presentation of food or water was in operation in all examples shown in this figure. Upper frame—individual pigeon (P-4) pecking plastic key (food). Three different durations of the fixed interval are shown; the general pattern persists despite the hundredfold change in the schedule parameter. Food presentations, ending each fixed interval, are marked by short diagonal strokes on the cumulative record. Lower left frame—performances under a 10-min FI schedule. Food or water presentations, ending each interval, are marked by the resetting of the recording pen to the base line. Lower right frame—performances under a 5-min FI schedule. The species, the type of switch recording the response, and the reinforcer presented are indicated above the records. The pigeon pecked a plastic key with its beak; the rat and chimpanzee pressed a horizontal lever with their paws; the cat depressed a rounded knob with its paw. The rat turned the wheel by running; only a turn of 180° is reinforced, but the cumulative distance the wheel turns is recorded directly. (From Kelleher & Morse, 1968b.)

soon found it possible to develop discriminative performances very quickly. Given an explicit description of what behavior is to be achieved, the conditions sufficient to realize the result can usually be found.

Schedule-controlled patterns of responding give a meaningful way of comparing different species, different maintenance events, or other interventions. Schedule-controlled patterns appear to have great generality; they occur in diverse species with a variety of different maintenance events (Figure 5). Different schedule performances depend upon the particular maintenance conditions. Usually, subjects with similar past experience exposed to the same parameter values can be expected to respond comparably, although the actual rates of responding may differ somewhat (Waller & Morse, 1963). To produce the same response rate, the parameters of the schedule may have to be different for different individuals. The value of producing

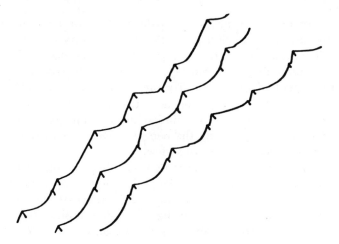

Fig. 6. Patterns of responding of three species (pigeon, rat, and monkey) under *mult* (multiple) FI FR schedules of reinforcement. (From Skinner, 1956. © 1956 by the American Psychological Association. Reprinted by permission.)

such comparable rates and patterns of schedule performances is that these reproducible temporal patterns represent an invariant behavioral process. Stevens (1951, pp. 20–21), discussing the importance of invariance as a tool of thought, concludes by saying: "The scientist is usually looking for invariance whether he knows it or not. . . . The delineation of the conditions of invariance for any phenomenon would tell us all we want to know about the matter." This same point of view is expressed by Skinner (1956, pp. 230–231) in commenting on Figure 6, which shows performances of a pigeon, rat, and monkey under a mult (multiple) FR FI schedule:

> Pigeon, rat, monkey, which is which? It doesn't matter. Of course, these three species have behavioral repertoires which are as different as their anatomies. But once you have allowed for differences in the ways in which they make contact with the environment, and in the ways in which they act upon the environment, what remains of their behavior shows astonishingly similar properties. Mice, cats, dogs and human children could have added other curves to this figure. And when organisms which differ as widely as this nevertheless show similar properties of behavior, differences between members of the same species may be viewed more hopefully. Difficult problems of idiosyncrasy or individuality will always arise as products of biological and cultural processes, but it is the very business of the experimental analysis of behavior to devise techniques which reduce their effects except when they are explicitly under investigation.

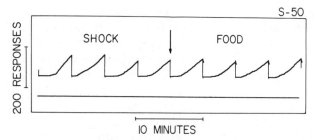

Fig. 7. Characteristic FI performance in the squirrel monkey under a multiple schedule of stimulus–shock termination and food presentation (Monkey S-50). The arrow indicates the change from the schedule of stimulus–shock termination to the schedule of food presentation. Left of the arrow—in the presence of a white light, electric shocks were scheduled to occur at 3-sec intervals starting after 5 min; the first response after 5 min terminated the stimulus-shock complex for 1 min. No shocks were delivered in the record segment shown. Right of the arrow—in the presence of a red light, the first response after 5 min was followed by food presentation and terminated the light for 1 min. Food presentations are indicated by short diagonal strokes on the cumulative record. The recording pen reset to the base line at the end of each fixed interval. The recorder did not run during the minute of darkness following each fixed interval. (From Kelleher & Morse, 1968b.)

One might note that the type of maintenance event, not specified in this example, is not critical. Figure 7 shows, for example, FI performances in a squirrel monkey maintained by the presentation of food and by the termination of a stimulus complex comprising a visual stimulus and an associated shock schedule (Kelleher & Morse, 1968b; Morse & Kelleher, 1966).

Schedule performances are invariant in part because techniques have been devised that produce invariance. By "delineating" the conditions of invariance for different species or for different maintenance events, there is a meaningful behavioral basis for comparing the effects of other independent variables. Of course, there are various bases, both formal and empirical, for making comparisons among different conditions, but a compelling argument can be made that comparisons among different events should be made on the basis of their similarities rather than their differences. The many different events that have been used to maintain or suppress behavior function similarly under appropriate conditions, but the conditions required for their suitability as reinforcers or punishers are different. Thus the essential aspect in studying events as reinforcers and punishers is not any inherent property of the events but rather the specification of the conditions under which events modify behavior. As we have noted, the experience of the individual and the schedule under which events are scheduled have often been neglected in favor of the more static properties of events. The value of dealing with reproducible behavioral processes has already been described. The next sections will consider some actual instances involving comparisons between different maintenance events that developed from practical applications in the field of behavioral pharmacology.

COMPARISONS OF THE EFFECTS OF DRUGS ON PERFORMANCES MAINTAINED BY DIFFERENT CONSEQUENCES

Although there was once considerable work comparing strengths of different drive states, in recent times interest in this topic has diminished. This change has resulted partly from the repeated finding that different schedule-controlled patterns of responding can be engendered in individual subjects with multiple schedules. Schedule performances embody a great deal of what traditionally has been called motivation (see the section on response-produced electric shocks near the end of the chapter). For other reasons, however, behavioral pharmacologists have long been interested in determining whether drugs have selective and specific effects on behavior controlled by noxious stimuli as compared with other events. Many investigators have compared the effects of drugs on behavior maintained by presentation of food with their effects on behavior maintained by termination (or postponement) of electric shock. Much of the interest in such comparisons derives from motivational interpretations of the clinical uses of drugs. After the development of the major and the minor tranquilizers, these drugs were soon used widely in the clinical treatment of psychiatric disorders involving agitation, apprehension, tension, or anxiety states. Consequently, it was generally accepted that the effects of these drugs on behavior would be understood in terms of their direct effects on underlying motivational states or drives.

Such motivational interpretations of the clinical uses of drugs promoted interest in experimental study of how drugs affect behavior controlled by noxious stimuli. It has been assumed that noxious stimuli control behavior by engendering an emotional state of fear or anxiety; changes in behavior after a drug have been explained as changes in this emotional state. Motivational interpretations have also been applied to the effects of drugs on behavior maintained by food presentation or water presentation; changes in behavior after drugs have been explained as changes in hunger or thirst.

Because hypothetical drive states, such as hunger or anxiety, are assumed to depend upon controlling environmental events, such as deprivation of food or presentation of electric shock, the generality of predictions about drugs affecting underlying motivational or emotional states can be evaluated in objective experiments. If drugs directly affect motivational states, the kind of effect a drug has on different behaviors should then depend on similarities or differences in the events controlling the behavior. Relevant experimental studies refute this view.

First, different patterns of responding maintained by the same event are selectively affected by drugs even when these patterns repeatedly alternate under a multiple schedule during the same session (see Kelleher & Morse, 1968b). In such instances, the differential effects of drugs cannot be attributed to the consequent event. The direction of the dependency of drug effects on schedule performance can differ among drugs. Barbiturates decrease responding under many parameter values of FI schedules at doses that do not decrease responding under FR schedules (Dews, 1955; Morse, 1962). Other drugs have the opposite effect: responding under FR schedules can be decreased by doses of amphetamines that increase responding under FI schedules (Kelleher & Morse, 1964; Smith, 1964).

Because the schedule can profoundly modify the effects of drugs, comparable schedules and comparable schedule-controlled patterns of responding must be established with different events (for example, food and electric shock) before there can be meaningful comparisons of the effects of drugs on responding controlled by these events. When schedule conditions and performances are comparable, many drugs have similar effects on behaviors controlled by different events. For example, in the rat responding under a FR 1 schedule of reinforcement, chlorpromazine decreases responding maintained by the presentation of food, intracranial stimulation, or heat. Appropriate doses of amphetamine increase responding maintained by the presentation of food, intracranial stimulation, or heat, while higher doses decrease responding (for details see Kelleher & Morse, 1968b).

Experiments by Weiss and Laties (1963) using heat as a reinforcer are particularly significant for the present discussion because they studied the effects of several drugs on skin and body temperature, as well as on frequency of responding maintained by heat presentation. The experiments were conducted with individual shaved rats in a small chamber in a refrigerated room; whenever the rat pressed a lever within the chamber, a lamp above the chamber delivered 2 sec of infrared heat. At certain temperatures, chlorpromazine decreased rates of responding even though it enhanced the rate at which temperature fell in the cold, and amphetamine increased rates of responding even though it caused the skin temperature to rise significantly. Noting that these effects are similar to those obtained when food or water is used to maintain behavior, Weiss and Laties (1963, p. 7) concluded that "the behavioral properties of these drugs are largely independent of the reinforcer that maintains the behavior, or, put another way, of the motivational state that supports it."

Some investigators have reported that chlorpromazine and reserpine have more marked effects on behavior maintained by electric shock than on behavior maintained by the presentation of food. Other investigators have reported that chlorpromazine has more marked effects on behavior maintained by presentation of food or intracranial stimulation than on behavior maintained by avoidance of electric shock. Still other studies comparing behaviors maintained by food and by electric shock found no difference in sensitivity to reserpine (for details see Kelleher & Morse, 1964, 1968b, 1968c). These results reflect on the difficulties involved in comparing behavioral effects of drugs on performances maintained with different reinforcers. In most of the studies the types and parameters of the schedules differed as well as the consequent events. When different reinforcers are presented according to different schedules, the effects of a drug may be largely determined by the schedule-controlled patterns of responding. For comparing the effects of drugs on behaviors maintained by different reinforcers, it is useful to start with similar schedules of reinforcement; however, there is still no a priori basis for equating such parameters as amounts of food and intensity of electric shock. It is unreasonable to presume that certain parameter values of one arbitrarily chosen schedule of food presentation will be comparable to the same parameters of an arbitrarily chosen schedule of electric shock termination.

The most satisfactory way to attack these problems is to obtain as nearly as possible identical patterns of responding maintained by different events and then to establish dose-effect relations for drugs on these patterns. Functional relations between drugs and behavior maintained by different schedules with each event can then be compared. Earlier it was noted that the conditions sufficient to realize a desired behavioral performance can usually be found. It is noteworthy that two different procedures for establishing comparable patterns of responding with formally comparable schedules of food presentation and electric shock termination have been developed.

Cook and Catania (1964) studied an FI schedule of electric shock termination in a group of squirrel monkeys. A pulsating electric shock of low intensity was continuously delivered, and the first response after 10 min terminated the shock; under this schedule, the rate of responding depended upon the intensity of the pulsating shock. Monkeys of another group were food-deprived and studied under an FI 10-min schedule of food presentation. The parameters of the schedules were selected to give comparable rates of responding, and response patterns characteristic of FI schedules were maintained under both food presentation and shock termination. Chlorpromazine and imipramine decreased rates of responding under both types of FI schedules, while selected doses of amphetamine, meprobamate, and chlordiazepoxide increased rates of responding. These results support the view that the behavioral effects of these drugs depend mainly upon schedule-controlled patterns of responding.

The other study directly compared the importance of type of reinforcer and schedule of reinforcement as determinants of the behavioral effects of drugs (Kelleher & Morse, 1964). Under some conditions the termi-

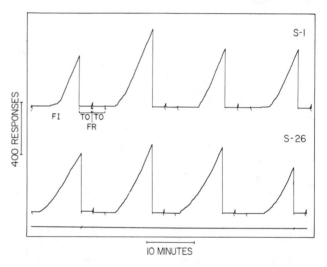

Fig. 8. Characteristic *mult* FI FR schedule performance maintained in squirrel monkeys by food presentation (upper record, monkey S-1) and by stimulus–shock termination (lower record, monkey S-26). The sequence of visual stimuli and corresponding schedules is the same in the upper and lower records. At the beginning of the records, the 10-min FI schedule was in effect in the presence of a white stimulus. At the termination of the FI component the recording pen reset to the bottom of the record, and a pattern of horizontal lines was present for 2.5 min; during this time-out (TO) period, responses had no programmed consequences. The next short diagonal stroke on the cumulative record indicates that the 30-response FR component was in effect in the presence of a red stimulus. Again, the cumulative recording pen reset to the bottom of the record at the termination of the FR component and was followed by the 2.5-min time-out component. This cycle was repeated throughout each session. At the bottom of the record for monkey S-26, the short diagonal strokes on the event line indicate electric shock (6.2 mA) presentation. (Modified from Kelleher & Morse, 1964.)

nation of a schedule complex, comprising a visual stimulus and an associated schedule of shock presentation, can maintain schedule-controlled patterns of responding characteristic of FI, FR, and *mult* FI FR schedules in the squirrel monkey (Morse & Kelleher, 1966). In one series of experiments, responding under such a *mult* FI FR schedule was compared with responding under a *mult* FR FI schedule of food presentation (Kelleher & Morse, 1964). Although maintained by different events, performances under the two multiple schedules were similar. Representative records for two monkeys are shown in Figure 8. The FR component of each multiple schedule sustained a high rate (about 2.3 responses per sec). The FI component of each multiple schedule was characterized by a pause (period of no responding) followed by acceleration of responding to a steady rate; the average rate in the interval was about .6 response per sec.

The effects of *d*-amphetamine on responding under each of the component schedules are shown in Figure 9. Except at the highest dose, *d*-amphetamine increased rates of responding under both FI schedules but decreased rates of responding under both FR schedules. Note that .3 mg/kg of *d*-amphetamine, which produced the maximum increase in rates of responding on both FI schedules (relatively low control rates), decreased rates of responding on both FR schedules (relatively high control rates). Many investigators have found that amphetamines tend to increase response output under schedules that maintain low rates of responding but tend to decrease response output under schedules that maintain high rates of responding. It is often assumed that decreases in responding maintained by food presentation are caused by anorexic effects of amphetamine even though such decreases occur under a variety of conditions. The similarity of the pairs of dose-effect curves in Figure 9 indicates that this interpretation is wrong. A mere decrease in responding after amphetamine, or any other drug, is not sufficient evidence of anorexia. Figure 9 shows that the effects of *d*-amphetamine depend more upon the type of schedule than upon the scheduled event (Kelleher & Morse, 1968b).

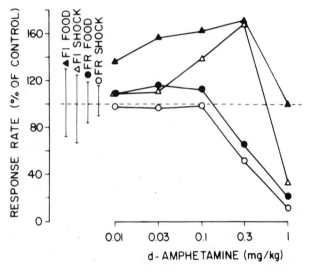

Fig. 9. Effects of *d*-amphetamine sulfate on rates of responding under multiple FI FR schedules of food presentation and stimulus–shock terminations. Three squirrel monkeys were studied on each multiple schedule. Each drug was given intramuscularly immediately before the beginning of a 2.5-hr session. At least duplicate observations were made on each monkey at each dose level. Summary dose-effect curves for the four component schedules were obtained by computing the means of the percentage changes in average response rates from control to drug sessions. The dashed line at 100% indicates the mean control level for each component. The vertical lines on the left of the figure indicate the ranges of control observations expressed as a percentage of the mean control value. Note the general similarity of the pairs of dose-effect curves for FI and for FR components. (Modified from Kelleher & Morse, 1964. © 1964 by the Society for the Experimental Analysis of Behavior, Inc.)

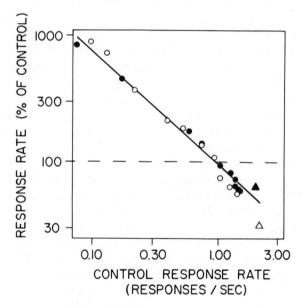

Fig. 10. Dependence of effect of *d*-amphetamine on predrug rate of responding in a squirrel monkey. Abscissa—average rate of responding in successive minutes of a 10-min FI schedule (circles) and under a 30-response FR schedule (triangles); ordinate—relative rate of responding after .3 mg/kg *d*-amphetamine, intramuscularly. Rates of responding were recorded separately during the FR component and during successive minutes of the FI component. Open and filled symbols indicate data from two different sessions. The line through the points was fitted by inspection. Based on data of a single monkey used in computing the averaged data under FI and FR schedules of stimulus-shock termination in Figure 9. (From Kelleher & Morse, 1968b. © 1968 by the Society for the Experimental Analysis of Behavior, Inc.)

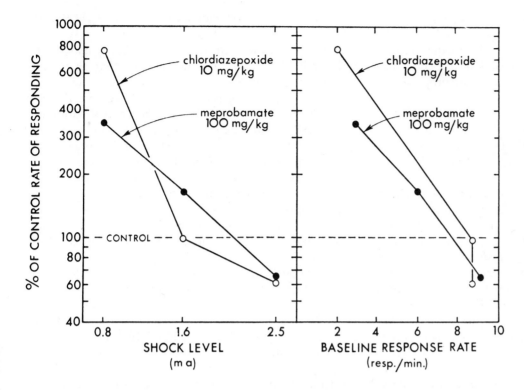

Fig. 11. Dependence of effect of chlordiazepoxide and meprobamate on intensity of electric shock or on predrug rate of responding in the squirrel monkey. Ordinate—relative rate of responding after oral doses of each drug; abscissa—shock intensity (left frame) and predrug rate of responding corresponding to each of the three shock intensities (right panel). (From Cook & Catania, 1964. Reprinted from *Federation Proceedings 23:* 832, 1964.)

There is a graded relation between the increase in low rates of responding and the decrease in high rates of responding after amphetamines. As shown in Figure 10, the relative response rate is an inverse linear function of the control rate. The two sets of data points are derived from the rates during complete sessions after *d*-amphetamine (.3 mg/kg, intramuscularly) and the corresponding rates during the previous control sessions under the multiple schedule of stimulus–shock termination. This same functional relation has been found in several different species under conditions in which different predrug rates of responding were engendered by different schedules of reinforcement, or by sampling different temporal periods of a single schedule. This model of amphetamine action suggests that observed increases and decreases in responding do not reflect qualitatively different processes.

In the experiments by Cook and Catania (1964) in which squirrel monkeys responded under an FI 10-min schedule of termination of electric shock, the effects of meprobamate and chlordiazepoxide depended upon the average predrug rate of responding, which in turn depended upon the intensity of the electric shock. The proportional increases in rate of responding were inversely related to predrug rates of responding for both drugs, except that the highest predrug rates were slightly decreased by both drugs (Figure 11). The rate-dependent effects of meprobamate and chlordiazepoxide appear similar to those of the amphetamines and barbiturates, but have not been as thoroughly studied.

In considering Figure 11 again, on the left side the drug effects are shown to depend upon electric shock intensity; on the right side they are shown to depend upon the control rate. The two functions are similar because variations in shock intensity changed the control rate. The function on the left has limited predictive generality, however, while that on the right fits these data into the broader context of rate-dependent effects. The advantage of describing these results in terms of rate dependencies is that they take on an applicability beyond the situation in which they were observed.

Although the actions of many drugs on behavior can be quantitatively related to the predrug rate of responding, this does not imply that all the behavioral effects of drugs can be interpreted as rate dependencies (see Kelleher & Morse, 1968b). Nevertheless, rate dependencies do operate widely and with profound effects. In any experiments in behavioral pharmacology, it is necessary to take into account the predrug rate in order to make valid predictions. Many of the seemingly qualitative differences in the effects of drugs on different performances result from a quantitative difference in predrug rates of responding.

The strong dependence of the effects of drugs on schedule-controlled behavior has implications that go beyond behavioral pharmacology. It indicates that behavioral processes such as reinforcement or punishment must be viewed in the context of ongoing behavior. Schedule-controlled behavior not only gives rise to organized, integrated performances but determines how other interventions will further modify behavior. Rates and patterns of schedule-controlled responding are, therefore, fundamental properties of behavior.

DRUG INJECTIONS AS CONSEQUENT EVENTS MAINTAINING BEHAVIOR

Experiments on the use of drugs as consequent or discriminative stimuli provide other instances in which the solution of practical problems in behavioral pharmacology has contributed to the study of behavior generally. During the past decade it has been demonstrated repeatedly that responding in experimental animals can be maintained by the intravenous injection of drugs from several different classes (for example, see Deneau, Yanagita, & Seevers, 1969). The injection of the drug thus functions as a reinforcer in these situations. As with any environmental event, drug injections maintain operant behavior only under certain conditions; as more information accumulates, the control over behavior improves. For example, rates of responding maintained by injections of cocaine or d-amphetamine are of the order of 50 times greater in current experiments than in some of the earliest ones (see Goldberg, 1973). Better control comes about through better specification of the relevant conditions.

Much of the research on the self-administration of drugs has been motivated by practical problems of drug abuse in man. One interest has been in developing animal models that would predict the abuse potential of drugs in man. The most commonly used procedure is to allow a subject to inject a given dose of a drug with each response for an extended period of time each day (3 to 24 hr). Such procedures are capable of distinguishing between many drugs that are likely to be abused in man and certain drugs that are unlikely to be abused. Comparing the levels of behavior maintained by different drugs provides practical information of limited generality—as, for example, in comparing the amounts eaten of oatmeal and Cream of Wheat. Under some conditions neither would be taken, and a starving person would take both. It is a mistake to consider drugs as having inherent reinforcing efficacies. In determining the characteristics of a drug as a reinforcer or punisher, the conditions that are sufficient to develop the same operant behavior should be determined. As with food or electric shock the capacity of a particular dose of drug to maintain behavior depends upon various conditions and may change over time. Doses of cocaine that will not maintain responding initially may do so in individuals with well-developed behavior (Goldberg, 1973). There are many examples of drug-taking behavior being modified by a subject's history. For example, Schlichting, Goldberg, Wuttke, and Hoffmeister (1971) found that the rate and pattern of responding maintained under FR schedules of d-amphetamine injections depended on whether rhesus monkeys had a history of responding maintained by cocaine, codeine, or pentobarbital. Thus rates and patterns of responding maintained by drug injections are a composite result of the history of the individual, the schedule of drug injection, and the dose of drug injected.

Previously we have used the term *metastable* to refer to two different stable patterns of responding maintained under the same schedule parameters, one before and one after an intervening treatment (Morse & Kelleher, 1966, 1970; Staddon, 1965). Instances of opposite effects of consequent events might be viewed as extreme cases of metastability. In an earlier section of this chapter it was noted that the drug nalorphine can both enhance behavior leading to its presentation and enhance behavior associated with its postponement (see Goldberg, Hoffmeister, & Schlichting, 1972). Intravenously injected drugs, like electric shocks, are presented directly to the subject, which makes it easier to use the same event in different ways. It may be of no fundamental significance that mainly "noxious events" have been shown to function in a variety of modes. The converse situation for drugs that are generally used as "positive" reinforcers has not been studied, but Smith and Clark (1972) have shown that there are conditions under which food delivery will be postponed by food-deprived subjects. Thus it seems clear that the maintenance of behavior by self-injected drugs is determined by various conditions, only one of which is the intrinsic properties of the drug itself.

Some conditions have been determined under which patterns of responding maintained by FR and FI schedules of drug injection are comparable to performances maintained by similar schedules of food presentation (Goldberg, 1973; Goldberg, Kelleher, & Morse, 1975). An important parameter in any experiment on drug self-administration is the dose, which may critically determine the level of responding under certain schedules. The amount of food has not seemed important in many studies with schedules of food presentation, but it is because the amount of food presented has been relatively constant and appropriate to the schedule parameters. When extreme amounts of food are presented or food delivery very intermittent, the amount of food presented becomes important (Morse, 1966; see Collier, Hirsch, & Kanarek, Chapter 2 in this volume).

Variations in drug dose and amount of food can have similar effects (Goldberg, 1973). For example, average rate of responding under 10- or 30-response FR schedules first increased and then decreased as the dose of cocaine injected was increased or as the amount of food presented was increased. Increasing the dose of cocaine or the amount of food resulted in a high rate of responding at the beginning of each session, but rates of responding decreased as the session progressed. The effects of varying the amount of drug or food were also studied under a second-order FI schedule of FR components, each terminating with a briefly presented visual stimulus. (A second-order schedule is one in which the behavior specified by a schedule contingency is treated as a unitary response that is itself reinforced according to some schedule—Kelleher, 1966; see Gollub, Chapter 10, and Zeiler, Chapter 8 in this volume.) Under the second-order schedule, response rates remained constant as the parameter value of the reinforcer was varied over a wide range. Again, the functions relating response rate to amount of drug or food were similar to one another, although they differed from the functions under simple FR schedules. The lower frequency of drug injection or food presentation under the second-order schedules limits cumulative effects that may decrease rates of responding (see also footnote 4). Once again, the way behavior is controlled by consequent events depends more upon the schedule than the type of scheduled event. Although injections of cocaine and presentation of food have very different properties, striking parallels between drug-maintained and food-maintained behavior can be obtained when they are studied under comparable schedules. Indeed, we may ask whether studies of this nature have implications for the abuse of food.

RESPONSE-PRODUCED ELECTRIC SHOCKS AS CONSEQUENT EVENTS MAINTAINING BEHAVIOR

The evidence is overwhelming that behavior is more controlled by the nature of the prevailing schedule than by the nature of the scheduled events. As noted earlier, compelling support for this view comes from experiments in which the same event has disparate or opposite effects on behavior when scheduled differently. The most thoroughly studied examples of such opposite effects are the maintenance and suppression of behavior by response-produced electric shock (discussed in earlier sections). Until recent years, response-produced electric shocks were seldom used under conditions in which they increased subsequent responding, yet numerous studies have shown diverse conditions under which key pressing is reliably maintained by response-produced electric shocks. Many of the features mentioned in earlier sections ("The Continuity of Behavior in Time" and "Ongoing Behavior") are important in developing such behavior; by having an existing level of ongoing responding and by scheduling the electric shocks intermittently, the schedules of shock presentation may come to modulate responding and develop schedule control.

Various studies have shown that responding can be maintained under FI schedules of electric shock delivery in squirrel monkeys trained under schedules of electric shock postponement that engender steady rates of responding. For example, McKearney (1968, 1969) studied squirrel monkeys trained under such an avoidance schedule. A 10-min FI schedule of response-produced electric shock was then introduced concurrently. Subsequently, when the schedule of electric shock postponement was eliminated and only the 10-min FI schedule of response-produced electric shock was in effect, a pattern of positively accelerated responding developed and was well maintained. Similarly, Byrd (1969) has shown in the cat that after a history of postponement of electric shocks, responding can be well maintained under an FI schedule of electric shock presentation. McKearney (1969) also studied a range of electric shock intensities and FI durations. As the fixed interval was decreased from 10 to 1 min, patterns of responding (as indicated by quarter-life values) were little affected, but rates of responding were inversely related to the FI duration. Responding ceased, however, when electric shocks were no longer scheduled and redeveloped when shocks were again presented under the FI schedule.

A study by Byrd (1972) has shown that responding can be established and maintained under second-order schedules of electric shock presentation. Again, in squirrel monkeys with a history of responding under schedules of electric shock postponement, characteristic FI patterns of responding were maintained under an FI 8-min schedule of electric shock presentation; a brief (1-sec) visual stimulus immediately preceded each electric shock. Performance was subsequently maintained under a second-order schedule in which the brief stimulus was presented under an FI 4-min schedule component; electric shock was delivered only after the completion of four FI components. Characteristic positively accelerated responding was engendered in the individual FI components. Patterns of responding maintained by presentation of the brief stimulus intermittently associated with delivery of an electric shock were similar to those maintained by brief stimuli intermittently associated with food presentation (see Gollub, Chapter 10 of this volume).

Under some conditions, the introduction of the FI schedule of shock presentation can be abrupt. For example, in one study, squirrel monkeys were trained to postpone electric shocks under schedules in which the period of time by which shock was postponed decreased with successive responses until a shock was delivered automatically (Kelleher & Morse, 1969). Certain parameters of this interlocking schedule of electric shock postponement engendered a stable pattern of positively accelerated responding between electric shocks (Figure 12, upper frame). A monkey trained under this schedule was then maintained under an FI 5-min schedule of electric shock presentation; the patterns of positively accelerated responding were more marked than they had been under the schedule of shock postponement (Figure 12, center and bottom frames).

An experiment was described earlier (see Figure 1) in which responding was both maintained and suppressed by the same response-produced electric shock (Kelleher & Morse, 1968a). This experiment is significant in showing that schedule conditions other than electric shock postponement can be used to develop FI performances with response-produced electric shock. Two monkeys were trained initially under a VI schedule of food presentation, and then FI schedules of electric shock presentation were superimposed on the schedule of food presentation. In one monkey, responding was initially suppressed under the combined schedule but subsequently recovered. Recovery from punishment has been frequently observed (Azrin & Holz, 1966). The rate of responding of the other monkey was more suppressed but later recovered after numerous changes in the schedules of shock presentation and after prolonged exposure to low shock intensities followed by gradually increasing shock intensities. Eventually, responding was enhanced in both monkeys under the combined schedules of food presentation and electric shock presentation and continued to be maintained when the food schedule was eliminated (for details see Kelleher & Morse, 1968a). As noted earlier (under "Disparate Effects of Consequent Events") in one experiment, the first response occurring after 10 min produced an electric shock, and each subsequent response during the 11th minute also produced a shock. A 1-min time-out period occurred at the end of the 11th minute. Clear patterns of positively accelerated responding developed during the

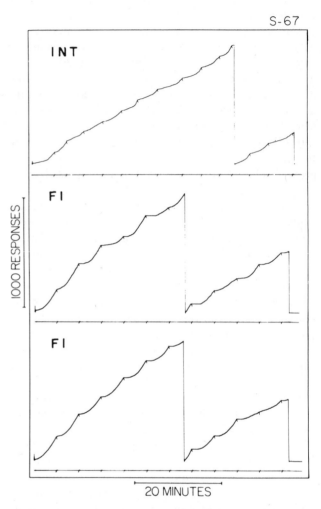

Fig. 12. Performances under an interlocking schedule of postponement of electric shocks (upper frame) and a FI 5-min schedule of presentation of electric shock (middle and bottom frames) (monkey S-67). Short diagonal strokes on both cumulative and event records indicate 3-mA shock presentations. The pattern of positively accelerated responding became more marked when response-produced shocks occurred under the FI schedule. (Modified from Morse & Kelleher, 1970.)

first 10 min of each cycle, whereas responding during the 11th minute of each cycle remained almost completely suppressed (see Figure 1). Studies of variations in shock intensity showed that the mean number of responses per session increased from 1,548 at a shock intensity of 1 mA to 4,227 at a shock intensity of 12.7 mA. During the entire study, responding in the 11th minute of each cycle was completely suppressed.

When the time-out period was eliminated so that each 11-min cycle was followed immediately by the start of the next cycle, performance was affected (Figure 13). An increase in responding during the early

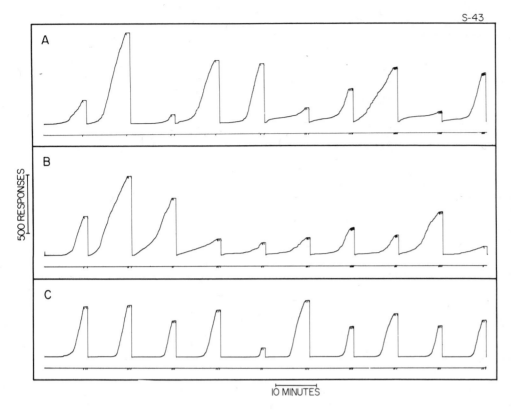

Fig. 13. Performance under a two-component FI 10-min FR 1 schedule of electric shock presentation without a time-out period separating 11-min cycles. Shock presentations are indicated by a diagonal stroke on cumulative and event records; the termination of one cycle (and the beginning of the next cycle) is indicated by the recording pen resetting to the base line. A–C—Sessions 186, 187, and 194. Note that there was less suppression during the FR 1 component when it was not followed by a time-out period than when it was (Figure 1). (From Kelleher & Morse, 1968a. © 1968 by the Society for the Experimental Analysis of Behavior, Inc.)

part of some cycles was a transient effect. Responding under the 1-response FR component in the 11th minute increased gradually and stabilized at a higher rate than had been maintained with the time-out; this resulted in a three- to fourfold increase in the number of shocks delivered. Thus the effects of electric shock in suppressing responding during the FR component were more pronounced when a time-out period followed that component. When scheduled shocks were omitted, responding gradually decreased to near zero; when electric shocks were scheduled again, the previous performance was gradually recovered (Figure 14). The extinction of performance under the two-component schedule appears to be similar to that occurring during extinction after FI schedules. The persistence of key pressing under this schedule contrasts with the rapid cessation of leash pulling described earlier (in the section headed "Characteristics of Responses").

Both maintenance and suppression of responding with response-produced electric shocks have also been observed under a multiple schedule (McKearney, 1972). In squirrel monkeys previously trained under a schedule of electric shock postponement, characteristic steady rates of responding were maintained under a VI 3-min schedule of electric shock presentation in the presence of a visual stimulus. Then an FR 1 schedule of electric shock presentation was in effect during certain 1- or 3-min periods associated with a different stimulus. Although the parameters of electric shock were identical in the two components of the multiple schedule, rates of responding were well maintained under the VI schedule but suppressed under the FR schedule.

The experiments by Kelleher and Morse (1968a) and by McKearney (1972) emphasize the importance of the schedule of electric shock presentation because identical electric shocks had opposite effects on responding under two different schedules. Responding was maintained by electric shocks presented under an FI 10-min schedule or a VI 3-min schedule and suppressed by electric shocks presented under an FR 1 schedule. The schedule of electric shock delivery determined whether its effects were characteristic of reinforcement or of punishment.

The effects of events that modulate behavior depend not only on the nature of the events and the schedule under which they are presented but also upon the experimental history of the individual. The historical determination of behavior does not necessarily imply any lack of modifiability. Although the conditions under which electric shocks came to con-

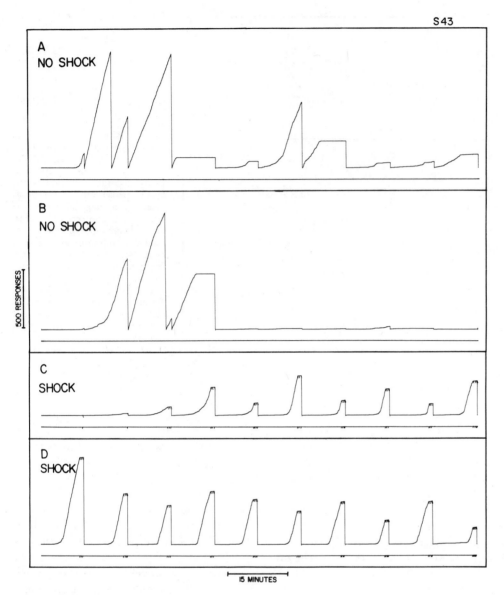

Fig. 14. The extinction and redevelopment of performance under the two-component *mult* FI 10-min FR 1 schedule of electric shock presentation without time-out periods. Recording as in Figure 13. A, B—Sessions 195 and 196, on extinction; C, D—Sessions 197 and 199, on a two-component shock schedule. (From Kelleher & Morse, 1968a. © 1968 by the Society for the Experimental Analysis of Behavior, Inc.)

trol behavior in the examples above were complex and depended on history, the maintained performances were under the control of the prevailing schedule of shock presentation.

A final example showing how historically determined behavior is modulated by current conditions is provided by a study in which a squirrel monkey had been trained to press one of two keys (key R) under a schedule of electric shock postponement, and responding on this key was then maintained under an FI 5-min schedule of electric shock presentation. Occasional responses occurred on the other key (key L) in every experimental session, although they had no programmed consequences. When the contingencies were reversed so that the FI schedule of electric shock presentation was in effect on key L and responding on key R had no programmed consequences, a period of transition followed. Responding on key R declined while responding on key L increased and became positively accelerated. Eventually, a characteristic FI pattern of responding was maintained on key L while low levels of responding occurred on key R (Figure 15). The changed contingency "shaped" a pattern of responding on key L. This example is important in showing that historically determined performances maintained by a schedule of electric shock presentation are not simply the temporal modulation of a highly stereotyped response pattern. The FI pattern of responding occurred on the key associated with the schedule of electric shock presentation.

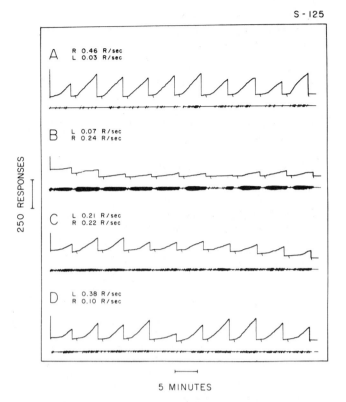

Fig. 15. Effects of changing the response key on which presentations of electric shock are scheduled under FI 5-min. Ordinate—cumulative number of key presses on key that produced electric shocks; abscissa—time. The recording pen reset to the base line with the presentation of electric shock and the beginning of a 1-min time-out period. Short diagonal strokes on the cumulative record indicate the end of the time-out; short diagonal strokes on the event record indicate key presses on the key that did not produce electric shocks. A—stable performance under FI schedule of shock presentation programmed on key R; B, C, D—Sessions 3, 18, and 55 under the FI schedule of shock presentation programmed on key L. The average rate of responding on key L gradually increased, while that on key R decreased after the contingency was changed. (Kelleher & Morse, unpublished observations.)

CONCLUSIONS

Valid concepts applicable to the scientific study of behavior evolved from discovering and controlling the determinants of orderly changes in responding. Important determinants of reinforcement and punishment are the parameters of consequent events, the quantitative properties of ongoing behavior, and the ways consequent events are scheduled. The scheduling of relations between behavior and consequent events brings diverse factors into operation in time as a dynamic coherent complex. The notions of schedule and of schedule-controlled behavior conveniently characterize the sequential interaction between behavior and environment.

Schedule control is the single most important property of operant behavior. Partly because of the conception of schedules as variations of a basic process of reinforcement rather than as the actual determinants of behavior, it has only slowly been appreciated that schedule-controlled behavior can determine the effects of consequent events. That the schedule of presentation of an event should determine the effect of the event is unexpected from traditional formulations; that it occurs suggests that traditional terms and time scales may be inappropriate. Diverse conditions will each result in characteristic reproducible and orderly behavioral performances. Even though it may not seem so at a superficial level, the discovery of the determinants of these diverse conditions gives a strong basis for generalizing about behavior. Reinforcement and punishment are best considered as reproducible behavioral processes.

Some consequent events that maintain behavior are especially forcing at particular parameter values, so that past experience is of little consequence; except when there is some ongoing behavior, certain bland events are relatively ineffective and other snappy events are likely to suppress behavior. Many of the activities that people engage in, such as growing peonies, sailing boats, and riding motorcycles, may tell more about the history of the individual (or his affluence) than can anything inherent in the activities themselves. Some ongoing behavior or past experience may be important in the development of behavior but not in its continued maintenance. For example, teaching programs shape behavior in a graded way; however, when the final level of competence is reached, the behavior at that time is no longer so critically dependent on slight gradations. Various devices and techniques are often used in initial development of lever pressing that are usually of no consequence after performances are well maintained. Traditionally, most experimental studies of reinforcement or punishment have used preemptive consequent events under conditions in which prior experience was not a critical determinant. Food presented to a highly deprived animal or a strong electric shock are immediately preemptive. Such consequent events are no better reinforcers than those that do depend upon history. In nonexperimental situations most behavior is maintained under conditions where history is important. One man is a lawyer, another a doctor; each "likes" his work and each is maintained by the environment. There is nothing about torts or about warts that is interesting to everyone. It is only under certain special circumstances that environmental consequences are especially forcing in engendering behavior. Even then, the conditions necessary for the development of behavior are more critical than the conditions necessary for its maintenance, implying that as soon as behavior develops, its history becomes important. In experimental situations behavior is often developed under forcing conditions where history is of little importance, but in nonexperimental situations most behavior is shaped from already existing behavior under conditions where the shaping sequence is important. How could it be otherwise? People are behaving all the time, and their behavior blends with the conditions of the current environment. In contrast, in the laboratory it is usually arranged so that there is no strong ongoing behavior before it is developed.

In recent years, it has become possible experimentally to study situations of increasing complexity and to extend the range of conditions sufficient to engender behavior into the domain of historical determinants. While some may view this as a messy pollution of well-established logical definitions, it brings the range of phenomena studied in laboratory settings closer to those of ordinary behavior. The concepts of historically determined and schedule-controlled behavior may seem unfamiliar and less precise than traditional formulations, but they are more valid.

REFERENCES

AZRIN, N. H. Some effects of two intermittent schedules of immediate and non-immediate punishment. *Journal of Psychology*, 1956, *42*, 3–21.

AZRIN, N. H. Punishment and recovery during fixed-ratio performance. *Journal of the Experimental Analysis of Behavior*, 1959, *2*, 301–305.

AZRIN, N. H. Effects of punishment intensity during variable-interval reinforcement. *Journal of the Experimental Analysis of Behavior*, 1960, *3*, 123–142.

AZRIN, N. H., & HOLZ, W. C. Punishment. In W. K. Honig (Ed.), *Operant behavior: Areas of research and application*. Englewood Cliffs, N.J.: Prentice-Hall, Inc., 1966.

AZRIN, N. H., HOLZ, W. C., & HAKE, D. F. Fixed-ratio punishment. *Journal of the Experimental Analysis of Behavior*, 1963, *6*, 141–148.

AZRIN, N. H., HUTCHINSON, R. R., & HAKE, D. F. Attack, avoidance, and escape reactions to aversive shock. *Journal of the Experimental Analysis of Behavior*, 1967, *10*, 131–148.

BLOUGH, D. S. New test for tranquilizers. *Science*, 1958, *127*, 586–587.

BYRD, L. D. Responding in the cat maintained under response-independent electric shock and response-produced electric shock. *Journal of the Experimental Analysis of Behavior*, 1969, *12*, 1–10.

BYRD, L. D. Responding in the squirrel monkey under second-order schedules of shock delivery. *Journal of the Experimental Analysis of Behavior*, 1972, *18*, 155–167.

CATANIA, A. C. Glossary. In A. C. Catania (Ed.), *Contemporary research in operant behavior*. Glenview, Ill.: Scott, Foresman, 1968.

CATANIA, A. C. On the vocabulary and the grammar of behavior. *Journal of the Experimental Analysis of Behavior*, 1969, *12*, 845–846.

CATANIA, A. C. The nature of learning. In J. A. Nevin (Ed.), *The study of behavior*. Glenview, Ill.: Scott, Foresman, 1973.

COOK, L., & CATANIA, A. C. Effects of drugs on avoidance and escape behavior. *Federation Proceedings*, 1964, *23*, 818–835.

DENEAU, G. A., YANAGITA, T., & SEEVERS, M. H. Self-administration of psychoactive substances by the monkey: A measure of psychological dependence. *Psychopharmacologia*, 1969, *16*, 30–48.

DEWS, P. B. Studies on behavior, I: Differential sensitivity to pentobarbital of pecking performance in pigeons depending on the schedule of reward. *Journal of Pharmacology and Experimental Therapeutics*, 1955, *113*, 393–401.

ESTES, W. K., & SKINNER, B. F. Some quantitative properties of anxiety. *Journal of Experimental Psychology*, 1941, *29*, 390–400.

FANTINO, E. Aversive control. In J. A. Nevin (Ed.), *The study of behavior*. Glenview, Ill.: Scott, Foresman, 1973.

FERSTER, C. B., & SKINNER, B. F. *Schedules of reinforcement*. New York: Appleton-Century-Crofts, 1957.

GOLDBERG, S. R. Comparable behavior maintained under fixed-ratio and second-order schedules of food presentation, cocaine injection, or d-amphetamine injection in the squirrel monkey. *Journal of Pharmacology and Experimental Therapeutics*, 1973, *186*, 18–30.

GOLDBERG, S. R., HOFFMEISTER, F., & SCHLICHTING, U. U. Morphine antagonists: Modification of behavioral effects by morphine dependence. In J. M. Singh, L. Miller, & H. Lal (Eds.), *Drug addiction*, Vol. 1: *Experimental pharmacology*. Mount Kisco, N.Y.: Futura, 1972.

GOLDBERG, S. R., HOFFMEISTER, F., SCHLICHTING, U. U., & WUTTKE, W. Aversive properties of nalorphine and naloxone in morphine-dependent rhesus monkeys. *Journal of Pharmacology and Experimental Therapeutics*, 1971, *179*, 268–276.

GOLDBERG, S. R., KELLEHER, R. T., & MORSE, W. H. Second-order schedules of drug injection. *Federation Proceedings*, 1975, *34*, 1771–1776.

HAKE, D. F., & CAMPBELL, R. L. Characteristics and response-displacement effects of shock-generated responding during negative reinforcement procedures: Pre-shock responding and post-shock aggressive responding. *Journal of the Experimental Analysis of Behavior*, 1972, *17*, 303–323.

HAWKINS, T. D., & PLISKOFF, S. S. Brain-stimulation intensity, rate of self-stimulation, and reinforcement strength: An analysis through chaining. *Journal of the Experimental Analysis of Behavior*, 1964, *7*, 285–288.

HERRNSTEIN, R. J., & SIDMAN, M. Avoidance conditioning as a factor in the effects of unavoidable shocks on food-reinforced behavior. *Journal of Comparative and Physiological Psychology*, 1958, *51*, 380–385.

HOLZ, W. C., & AZRIN, N. H. Interactions between the discriminative and aversive properties of punishment. *Journal of the Experimental Analysis of Behavior*, 1962, *5*, 229–234.

HUTCHINSON, R. R., AZRIN, N. H., & HAKE, D. F. An automatic method for the study of aggression in squirrel monkeys. *Journal of the Experimental Analysis of Behavior,* 1966, *9,* 233–237.

HUTCHINSON, R. R., AZRIN, N. H., & RENFREW, J. W. Effects of shock intensity and duration on the frequency of biting attack by squirrel monkeys. *Journal of the Experimental Analysis of Behavior,* 1968, *11,* 83–88.

HUTCHINSON, R. R., RENFREW, J. W., & YOUNG, G. A. Effects of long-term shock and associated stimuli on aggressive and manual responses. *Journal of the Experimental Analysis of Behavior,* 1971, *15,* 141–166.

KELLEHER, R. T. Conditioned reinforcement in second-order schedules. *Journal of the Experimental Analysis of Behavior,* 1966, *9,* 475–485.

KELLEHER, R. T., & MORSE, W. H. Escape behavior and punished behavior. Reprinted from *Federation Proceedings,* 1964, *23,* 808–817.

KELLEHER, R. T., & MORSE, W. H. Schedules using noxious stimuli, III: Responding maintained with response-produced electric shocks. *Journal of the Experimental Analysis of Behavior,* 1968, *11,* 819–838. (a)

KELLEHER, R. T., & MORSE, W. H. Determinants of the specificity of behavioral effects of drugs. *Ergebnisse der Physiologie,* 1968, *60,* 1–56. (b)

KELLEHER, R. T., & MORSE, W. H. Determinants of the behavioral effects of drugs. In D. H. Tedeschi & R. E. Tedeschi (Eds.), *Importance of fundamental principles in drug evaluation.* New York: Raven Press, 1968. (c)

KELLEHER, R. T., & MORSE, W. H. Schedules using noxious stimuli, IV: An interlocking shock-postponement schedule in the squirrel monkey. *Journal of the Experimental Analysis of Behavior,* 1969, *12,* 1063–1079.

KELLEHER, R. T., RIDDLE, W. C., & COOK, L. Persistent behavior maintained by unavoidable shocks. *Journal of the Experimental Analysis of Behavior,* 1963, *6,* 507–517.

MCKEARNEY, J. W. Maintenance of responding under a fixed-interval schedule of electric shock-presentation. *Science,* 1968, *160,* 1249–1251.

MCKEARNEY, J. W. Fixed-interval schedules of electric shock presentation: Extinction and recovery of performance under different shock intensities and fixed-interval durations. *Journal of the Experimental Analysis of Behavior,* 1969, *12,* 301–313.

MCKEARNEY, J. W. Maintenance and suppression of responding under schedules of electric shock presentation. *Journal of the Experimental Analysis of Behavior,* 1972, *17,* 425–432.

MCKEARNEY, J. W. Differences in responding under fixed-time and fixed-interval schedules of electric shock presentation. *Psychological Reports,* 1974, *34,* 907–914.

MORSE, W. H. Use of operant conditioning techniques for evaluating the effects of barbiturates on behavior. In J. H. Nodine & J. W. Moyer (Eds.), *Psychosomatic medicine: The first Hahnemann Symposium.* Philadelphia: Lea and Febiger, 1962.

MORSE, W. H. Intermittent reinforcement. In W. K. Honig (Ed.), *Operant behavior: Areas of research and application.* Englewood Cliffs, N.J.: Prentice-Hall, Inc., 1966.

MORSE, W. H., & KELLEHER, R. T. Schedules using noxious stimuli, I: Multiple fixed-ratio and fixed-interval termination of schedule complexes. *Journal of the Experimental Analysis of Behavior,* 1966, *9,* 267–290.

MORSE, W. H., & KELLEHER, R. T. Schedules as fundamental determinants of behavior. In W. N. Schoenfeld (Ed.), *The theory of reinforcement schedules.* Englewood Cliffs, N.J.: Prentice-Hall, Inc., 1970.

MORSE, W. H., MEAD, R. N., & KELLEHER, R. T. Modulation of elicited behavior by a fixed-interval schedule of electric shock presentation. *Science,* 1967, *157,* 215–217.

NEURINGER, A. J. Superstitious key pecking after three peck-produced reinforcements. *Journal of the Experimental Analysis of Behavior,* 1970, *13,* 127–134.

PREMACK, D. Toward empirical behavior laws, I: Positive reinforcement. *Psychological Review,* 1959, *66,* 219–233.

PREMACK, D. Reinforcement theory. In D. Levine (Ed.), *Nebraska symposium on motivation.* Lincoln: University of Nebraska Press, 1965.

PREMACK, D. Catching up with common sense, or two sides of a generalization: Reinforcement and punishment. In R. Glaser (Ed.), *The nature of reinforcement.* New York: Academic Press, 1971.

RACHLIN, H. *Introduction to modern behaviorism.* San Francisco: W. H. Freeman, 1970.

SCHLICHTING, U. U., GOLDBERG, S. R., WUTTKE, W., & HOFFMEISTER, F. d-Amphetamine self-administration by rhesus monkeys with different self-administration histories. *Proceedings of the European Society for the Study of Drug Toxicity,* 1970. Excerpta Medicine International Congress, Series 220, 1971, pp. 62–69.

SEGAL, E. F. Induction and the provenance of operants. In R. M. Gilbert & J. R. Millenson (Eds.), *Reinforcement: Behavioral analyses.* New York: Academic Press, 1972.

SIDMAN, M., HERRNSTEIN, R. J., & CONRAD, D. G. Maintenance of avoidance behavior by unavoidable shocks. *Journal of Comparative and Physiological Psychology,* 1957, *50,* 553–557.

SKINNER, B. F. On the conditions of elicitation of certain eating reflexes. *Proceedings of the National Academy of Sciences,* 1930, *16,* 433–438.

SKINNER, B. F. On the rate of formation of a conditioned reflex. *Journal of General Psychology,* 1932, *7,* 274–286.

SKINNER, B. F. Two types of conditioned reflex: A reply to Konorski and Miller. *Journal of General Psychology,* 1937, *16,* 272–279.

SKINNER, B. F. *The behavior of organisms.* New York: Appleton-Century-Crofts, 1938.

SKINNER, B. F. "Superstition" in the pigeon. *Journal of Experimental Psychology,* 1948, *38,* 168–172.

SKINNER, B. F. *Science and human behavior.* New York: Macmillan, 1953.

SKINNER, B. F. A case history in scientific method. *American Psychologist,* 1956, *11,* 221–233.

SKINNER, B. F. Operant conditioning. In W. K. Honig (Ed.), *Operant behavior: areas of research and application.* Englewood Cliffs, N.J.: Prentice-Hall, Inc., 1966.

SKINNER, B. F. *Contingencies of Reinforcement.* Englewood Cliffs, N.J.: Prentice-Hall, Inc., 1969.

SKINNER, B. F., & MORSE, W. H. Fixed-interval reinforcement of running in a wheel. *Journal of the Experimental Analysis of Behavior,* 1958, *1,* 371–379.

SMITH, C. B. Effects of d-amphetamine upon operant behavior of pigeons: Enhancement by reserpine. *Journal of Pharmacology and Experimental Therapeutics,* 1964, *146,* 167–174.

SMITH, J. B., & CLARK, F. C. Two temporal parameters of food postponement. *Journal of the Experimental Analysis of Behavior,* 1972, *18,* 1–12.

STADDON, J. E. R. Some properties of spaced responding in

pigeons. *Journal of the Experimental Analysis of Behavior,* 1965, *8,* 19–27.

STADDON, J. E. R., & SIMMELHAG, V. L. The "superstition" experiment: a reexamination of its implications for the principles of adaptive behavior. *Psychological Review,* 1971, *78,* 3–43.

STEINER, S. S., BEER, B., & SHAFFER, M. M. Escape from self-produced rates of brain stimulation. *Science,* 1969, *163,* 90–91.

STEVENS, S. S. Mathematics, measurement, and psychophysics. In S. S. Stevens (Ed.), *Handbook of experimental psychology.* New York: Wiley, 1951.

TERRACE, H. S. Discrimination learning with and without "errors." *Journal of the Experimental Analysis of Behavior,* 1963, *6,* 1–27.

WALLER, M. B., & MORSE, W. H. Effects of pentobarbital on fixed-ratio reinforcement. *Journal of the Experimental Analysis of Behavior,* 1963, *6,* 125–130.

WALLER, M. B., & WALLER, P. F. The effects of unavoidable shocks on a multiple schedule having an avoidance component. *Journal of the Experimental Analysis of Behavior,* 1963, *6,* 29–37.

WEISS, B., & LATIES, V. G. Effects of amphetamine, chlorpromazine, and pentobarbital on behavioral thermoregulation. *Journal of Pharmacology and Experimental Therapeutics,* 1963, *140,* 1–7.

ZEILER, M. D. Fixed and variable schedules of response-independent reinforcement. *Journal of the Experimental Analysis of Behavior,* 1968, *11,* 405–414.

ZIMMERMAN, D. W. Functional laws and reproducible processes in behavior. *Psychological Record,* 1963, *13,* 163–173.

8

Schedules of Reinforcement

the controlling variables*

Michael Zeiler

INTRODUCTION

Schedules of reinforcement are among the most powerful determinants of behavior. The effects of each type of schedule are systematic and orderly in individual organisms, and they are replicable within and across species (for an example see Skinner, 1959, p. 374, Figure 14). The particular performance generated depends on the schedule used, but each schedule has characteristic effects. In fact, one way to evaluate the adequacy of experimental control is by seeing if the behavior typical of specific schedules is reproduced (Sidman, 1960). Failure to obtain the expected performances indicates deficiency in the experimental laboratory.

Some psychologists have considered research on reinforcement schedules to be atheoretical, yet starting with Skinner (1938) and continuing with Ferster and Skinner (1957) and Morse (1966) there has been concern with theoretical analysis. Perhaps the pervasiveness of theory has not been generally recognized because the data have been so powerful that they demanded and received major attention, while the more conjectural theoretical efforts assumed secondary status. Typically, theory has not been formal or quantitative; it has been at a lower level, consisting of hypotheses about the essential controlling relations (but see Schoenfeld, Cole, Blaustein, Lachter, Martin, & Vickery, 1972, for a more formal taxonomic approach). The present purpose is to offer another such analysis.

The obvious origins of schedule research appear in Skinner's (1938) demonstration that a reinforcer does not have to follow every response in order to maintain responding, but that it need only occur intermittently. The importance of intermittent reinforcement eventually might have become apparent wtih discrete-trial procedures, but it happened immediately within Skinner's free operant paradigm. In research in which each response terminated a trial the focus tended to be on resistance to extinction under low-valued ratio schedules (the partial-reinforcement effect); in contrast, the free operant experiments emphasized the nature of performance under maintained reinforcement. The publication in 1957 of Ferster and Skinner's *Schedules of Reinforcement* represents the

---

* Preparation of this chapter and several of the experiments reported were supported by Research Grant GB-25959 from the National Science Foundation. I would like to thank M. J. Marr, W. H. Morse, and E. Davis for their comments.

beginning of the modern era of schedule research. This encyclopedia of schedules not only describes the performances occurring under many simple and compound schedules, but also pioneered in treating schedules as a distinct subject matter.

It became possible to use schedule performance to study the effects of other variables; for example, in behavioral pharmacology schedules provided a foundation for assessing the actions of drugs (see Harvey, 1971). But it soon became evident that schedules did more than establish reliable and recoverable base lines. The schedule itself played an important role in determining how the variables of primary interest operated. It served not just as a convenient vehicle for observing other processes at work but, for example, could determine whether a certain dosage of a given drug increased, decreased, or had no effect on the rate of responding (cf. Kelleher & Morse, 1968). Dews (1963) concluded:

> Schedule-controlled behavior does not merely provide a baseline for convenient study of other variables; it is itself close to the heart of the matter. This emphasis on the importance of schedules is not intended to imply that all of psychology should be reduced to a study of them. An influence can be all-pervading without being all-embracing. . . . It is suggested that schedule influences operate generally in psychology; that when these influences can operate, they will; and that a student of any problem in psychology—in motivation, generalization, discrimination, or the functions of the frontal lobes—ignores the consequences of the precise scheduling arrangements of his experiments at his peril. (p. 148)

The ubiquity of schedule effects means that an understanding of how the scheduling of reinforcers determines performance is of fundamental significance. Intermittent reinforcement organizes and maintains highly predictable extended sequences of behavior, and it also determines the effects of many other variables. The present chapter is an effort to describe how intermittent reinforcement operates to control behavior.

TYPES OF SCHEDULES

The word *reinforcement* refers to the effect of an operation; it does not describe an independent variable but is the interaction of an independent variable with behavior. By *reinforcement* is meant an increase in responding as a function of a stimulus event following the response. The stimuli having these effects are *reinforcing stimuli* or *reinforcers*. Schedules of reinforcement are the rules used to present reinforcing stimuli.

Time and Response Schedules

The most widely used schedules are defined in terms of time and responses. They may or may not require a particular response. All response-independent schedules are *time schedules,* and they are referred to as *fixed-time (FT)* or *variable-time (VT) schedules* depending on whether the interreinforcer time is fixed or changes from one reinforcer presentation to the next. Other schedules are response-dependent. Of these, the ones that only require responses are *ratio schedules,* and they are *fixed-ratio (FR)* or *variable-ratio (VR) schedules* depending on whether a fixed or variable number of responses is required. *Interval schedules* involve both response and temporal requirements, but they will be treated here as simple schedules. Interval schedules combine time schedules and a fixed-ratio schedule (FR 1): the first response emitted after a specific time has elapsed produces the reinforcer, and earlier responses have no scheduled consequences. In *fixed-interval (FI) schedules* the time is constant; in *variable-interval (VI) schedules* it varies. In VT, VI, and VR schedules the experimenter determines the precise sequence of interreinforcer times (VT, VI) or responses per reinforcer (VR). There also are schedules that provide reinforcer presentation after irregular time periods or irregular numbers of responses, but the precise sequences are not prespecified. Instead, each time period or response is equally eligible for reinforcement according to some probability. These schedules are known as *random-time (RT), random-ratio (RR),* and *random-interval (RI) schedules* depending on whether the probability of a reinforcer occurring refers to time alone, to responses alone, or to a response occurring at a certain time.

Response-independent schedules are here referred to as time schedules, despite earlier references to them as interval schedules preceded by an appropriate qualifying adjective (e.g., "free," "response-independent," "noncontingent"). Since interval schedules by definition require a response, to use them to refer to a response-independent arrangement is internally inconsistent and misleading. The time schedule designation avoids this ambiguity.

Differentiation Schedules

In differentiation schedules reinforcers are presented when a response or a group of responses displays a specified property. For example, responses might have to be emitted with a particular force, duration, or form (topography) or to occur in a certain locus. Differentiation schedules are involved in shaping new responses, but they also encompass certain unchanging requirements. *Interresponse-time (IRT) schedules* establish the time between successive responses as the requirement. If the time must equal or exceed the specified value, this is an IRT $> t$ schedule. If the response must occur before a specified time period elapses, this is an IRT $< t$ schedule. If the reinforcer is presented whenever a specified response has not occurred for a certain time period, this is an $\overline{R} > t$ schedule. The IRT $> t$, IRT $< t$, and $\overline{R} > t$ schedules all are differentiation schedules involving intervals between responses as a prerequisite for reinforcement. Since in an $\overline{R} > t$ schedule, not emitting a certain response is treated as if it was a response, reinforcement is manifested by a decreased frequency of the criterion response.

The IRT $> t$, IRT $< t$, and $\overline{R} > t$ designations replace DRL, DRH, and DRO. The problem with the old usage is that it confused a theoretical account of the effects of the schedules (differential-reinforcement-of-low-rate, differential-reinforcement-of-high-rate, differential-reinforcement-of-other [or not-] responding) with the simple description of the prescription for reinforcer delivery.

t–τ Schedules

Schoenfeld and his colleagues (Schoenfeld et al., 1972) have devised schedules based on temporal parameters combined with varying probability of reinforcement for single responses. The probability of reinforcer presentation occurring in any part of a repeating time cycle can be varied between 0.00 and 1.00, either dependent on or independent of a response. If the cycle duration is fixed and the probability of a reinforcer following the first response of a cycle is 1.00, it is equivalent to an FI schedule; if the probability of a reinforcer for the first response of a cycle is less than 1.00, it is an RI schedule. If the probability of reinforcement occurring for all responses is greater than 0.00 but less than 1.00, this is an RR schedule. These are limiting cases. Combinations of cycle lengths, periods of reinforcer availability, and probabilities of reinforcement for each response can be manipulated to generate numerous schedules.

Although Schoenfeld et al. (1972) have proposed t–τ schedules as a comprehensive schedule classification system, it does not incorporate fixed- and variable-ratio schedules directly. Response count does not enter into the specification of a schedule; probability of reinforcement is applied only to individual responses. Although performance typical of ratio schedules can be obtained by appropriate manipulation of the temporal parameters, this does not mean that response count is an irrelevant independent variable. Schedules still can be specified based on fixed and variable numbers of responses without reference to temporal parameters. Similar performances generated by ratio and t–τ schedules pose the challenge of finding characteristics common to both types. The t–τ schedules do not in themselves explain ratio performance.

Extinction

In an *extinction schedule* no reinforcer is presented. Extinction is not a schedule of reinforcement, but it is included here to provide a comprehensive list of common scheduling operations. The various schedules described so far (time, ratio, interval, differentiation, t–τ, extinction) can be combined in various ways to produce compound schedules. Together they comprise all reinforcement schedules known to date.

TYPES OF CONTROLLING RELATIONS: VARIABLES AND EFFECTS

Direct and Indirect Variables

A schedule states the conditions that must obtain for a reinforcer to be delivered. These prerequisites are formal properties. All schedules arrange that certain conjunctions of events must obtain at the moment of reinforcer presentation, although individual schedules differ in what these events must be. These formally imposed prerequisites are the *direct variables* imposed by a schedule. In ratio schedules, for example, presentation of the reinforcer depends on the execution of a certain number of responses, so that it is a formal requirement that this number of responses precede every reinforcer.

Other variables are not imposed directly. Although the time between successive reinforcer presentations is not specified by a fixed-ratio schedule, the characteristics of performance establish a certain time period.

And, although a time schedule does not require that any particular response occur, some behavior must precede the reinforcer. *Indirect variables* are those that are imposed without being explicitly prescribed by the schedule. One problem in a theoretical analysis of reinforcement schedules is to specify these indirect variables and when and how they influence performance.

It appears that any variable that occurs directly under one type of schedule can occur indirectly under others. For example, the time separating the reinforced response from the one preceding—the interresponse time (IRT)—is imposed at a specific value under $IRT > t$ and $IRT < t$ schedules. Under any schedule, however, some IRT precedes the reinforcer. Or interreinforcer time, which is specified directly under time schedules, arises indirectly under ratio schedules. This is not to say that the variable is necessarily exerting an effect under any schedule, but simply that it is imposed either directly or indirectly.

The fact that some schedules require what others permit provides a methodology for an experimental analysis of schedule effects. The hypothesis that an indirect variable (e.g., interreinforcer time) has effects under some schedule can be evaluated by studying how performance is affected when it is imposed as an explicit requirement (e.g., in time or interval schedules). When imposed directly it must produce the effects it is assumed to exert indirectly. This experimental strategy is in the tradition of Skinner (1938), Ferster and Skinner (1957), and Morse (1966).

Stereotypic and Dynamic Effects

Performance under a particular schedule is generally uniform among different subjects and in the same subject over prolonged periods of time. Each schedule accomplishes this by arranging certain interactions among characteristics of performance and the controlling direct and indirect variables.

These interactions can have two effects. The first is that certain characteristics of behavior may be repeated in the same form in the future. The production of repetitive stereotyped behavior is the defining attribute of reinforcement: the response preceding the reinforcer increases in frequency. The second effect is dynamic: performance changes from one instance to the next.

A Pervasive Stereotypic Effect: Response Dependency

When Skinner (1948) observed pigeons after giving them food every 15 seconds without regard to their

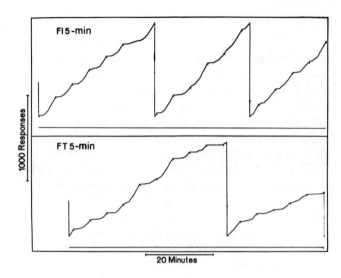

Fig. 1. Performance of a pigeon under FI 5-min and FT 5-min schedules. The response pen offset at food presentations. (From Zeiler, 1968.)

behavior, he found that each bird performed some consistent ritual. It seemed that this occurred because a particular behavior happened to occur in close temporal contiguity with food presentation (in chapter 5 of this volume Staddon offers a different interpretation). This temporal relation increased the probability of the response, even though the relation was adventitious. Additional research indicating many similarities between response-dependent and response-independent schedules suggests that the essential nature of the response-reinforcer relation is temporal (Herrnstein, 1966; Zeiler, 1972a). For example, as shown in Figure 1, both types of schedule can maintain the responses that precede them, and both have similar effects on how the responses are distributed in time (the pattern of responding). In addition, both bring responding under the control of the exteroceptive stimuli present when the reinforcer appears (Morse & Skinner, 1957). Such data imply that response-dependent reinforcer presentation increases the probability of the response because the dependency guarantees that the effective temporal relation will occur.

In all effective respondent-dependent schedules (except those involving delayed reinforcement) the specified response occurs close in time to the reinforcing event. The result of this contiguity is that the response is maintained at a substantial level. The precise rate and temporal patterning of the response are determined by the particular schedule. The delivery of a reinforcer following a single response is always an important determinant of the tendency to respond, but the schedule modulates the rate of responding and determines how successive occurrences of the response are distributed in time.

The Asymmetry of Reinforcement and Extinction

Herrnstein (1966) and Morse (1966) noted that behavior typically is acquired rapidly and lost slowly (although the loss is accelerated if there are numerous exposures to extinction). This asymmetry means that in all schedules a single reinforcer presentation generates numerous subsequent repetitions of the reference response. It is this property of reinforcement that is described by Skinner's (1938) concept of the reflex reserve.

Two experiments illustrate the large effects of a few reinforcer presentations. Skinner (1938, pp. 86–90) allowed rats to adapt to the experimental chamber and to the sound of the food magazine. He then presented a food pellet following one press and changed the schedule to extinction. As shown in Figure 2, more than 60 presses occurred before the response rate returned to the preconditioning level. Also, Neuringer (1970) demonstrated that pigeons given food for three successive key pecks emitted approximately 150 pecks in a subsequent extinction phase. A general effect of a reinforcing stimulus is to generate substantial quantities of the response that precedes it (a stereotypic effect).

Dynamic Effects

Some interactions between performance and controlling variables lead to change rather than to stereotypy. The important factor is the level of the variable in question. Consider, for example, the role of interreinforcer time in fixed-ratio schedules where it is an

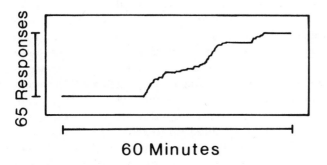

Fig. 2. Responding in a rat produced by a single food presentation. The first response was followed by a food pellet; later responses had no scheduled consequences. (Traced from Skinner, 1938, p. 87, Figure 15.)

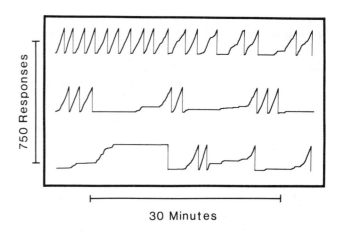

Fig. 3. Performance of a pigeon under an FR 150 schedule. The response pen reset at each food presentation.

indirect variable. If, for some reason, the interreinforcer time should lengthen, response rate might decrease. The consequence would be to increase interreinforcer time still further, thereby again reducing rate and producing an even longer interreinforcer time. Figure 3 illustrates such an effect, indicating that it is perhaps not felt immediately but may cumulate over several interreinforcer periods. Or an unusually short interreinforcer time might increase rate, thereby producing still shorter times and consequently increasing rate still further. An intermediate interreinforcer time, however, might not change the prevailing rate and therefore would recur in successive ratios. Variables operating in this way are said to have *dynamic effects*. Dynamic effects do not all change behavior in one direction. When variables are at a high level, they may operate to change behavior in such a way that a low level follows. This is the way the number of responses emitted per reinforcer presentation is hypothesized to operate under fixed-interval schedules; it will be discussed in detail in the next section.

Dynamic effects can only occur when the level of a variable is free to change, so they are typically effects of indirect variables. However, if the schedule requirements were to be changed depending upon the characteristics of performance, it would be possible to observe whether a direct variable has dynamic effects. Adjusting schedules, which will be discussed in a later section, have this provision.

Dynamic effects play an important part in determining the frequency of responding under schedules of intermittent reinforcement. They are particularly significant in schedules that maintain a high average number of responses per reinforcer presentations, but they also occur elsewhere. The fixed-interval schedule, which readily shows how these dynamic effects influence response frequency, provides the focus of the next section. The consideration of direct and indirect variables operating in fixed-interval schedules leads into the analysis of the determinants of response frequency under the other major schedules.

VARIABLES DETERMINING RESPONSE FREQUENCY

Although interval schedules require only a single response per reinforcer presentation, they maintain many more. At moderate and large parameter values, a fixed-interval schedule will maintain a larger average number of responses than can be maintained by ratio schedules. For example, Ferster and Skinner (1957, pp. 518–520) correlated one stimulus with an FI 5-min schedule and another with an FR 275 schedule (multiple FI 5-min FR 275). Responding was severely strained under the fixed-ratio schedule with periods of 80 minutes and more occurring without a response. However, if the fixed-interval stimulus was introduced during the pauses, more than 275 responses often were emitted within the 5-min period. In general, it is difficult to maintain responding with fixed-ratio schedules higher than FR 300 even after prolonged exposure to lower values. Yet an average of 300 responses per reinforcer presentation is maintained routinely with fixed-interval schedules. Figure 4 shows cumulative records for the same pigeon under

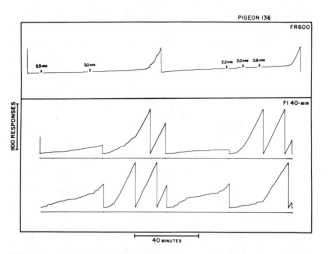

Fig. 4. Cumulative records for the last session of training of a pigeon with FR 600 and the first session with the FI 40-min schedule. The response pen reset at 1100 responses and with food presentation. Offsets of the event pen on the FI record indicate when food became available for the next response. Breaks in the FR record indicate periods with no responses.

the last session of FR 600 and the immediately succeeding session involving an FI 40-min schedule. The bird was studied under FR 1000 as well. The FR 1000 schedule (not shown) did not sustain responding, i.e., the bird responded infrequently during sessions as long as 16 hours and never completed a ratio. Responding was maintained with FR 600, but there were very long pauses and many hours between successive food presentations. With the FI 40-min schedule, however, there was an average of well over 1000 responses in each 40-min period. Ferster and Skinner (1957) show numerous records with several thousand responses occurring in an interval with no sign of strained behavior.

Why can a fixed-interval schedule maintain so many responses? An answer to this question helps to reveal the variables responsible for response rate under both interval and ratio schedules.

Response Number in Fixed-interval Schedules: The Herrnstein and Morse (1958) Experiment

An important factor in the ability of fixed-interval schedules to maintain a high average number of responses per reinforcer is simply that they require only one. Herrnstein and Morse (1958) drew attention to this apparent paradox in their investigation of a conjunctive fixed-interval, fixed-ratio schedule. Since, in a conjunctive schedule, the reinforcer is delivered when both individual schedule requirements have been met, the direct effects of the schedule involved both the minimum number of responses specified by the fixed-ratio component and the minimum interreinforcer time followed by a single response specified by the fixed-interval component. In a conjunctive FI 15-min FR 40 schedule, for example, a reinforcer is presented following the first response after 15 minutes if at least 39 responses have occurred earlier. Otherwise, the reinforcer is presented as soon after 15 minutes as the 40th response is emitted. The conjunctive FI FR schedule imposes minimum response requirements on the fixed-interval schedule, the minimum value depending on the parameter of the fixed-ratio component. (It also imposes a minimum interreinforcer interval in a fixed-ratio schedule.) Herrnstein and Morse maintained the interval value at 15 minutes and varied the ratio value from zero (a simple fixed-interval schedule) up to 240.

The left panel of Figure 5 shows the average number of responses per 15-min interval under each ratio requirement. As the ratio was increased, the number of responses per interval decreased. Both birds emitted close to 300 responses per interval with the simple

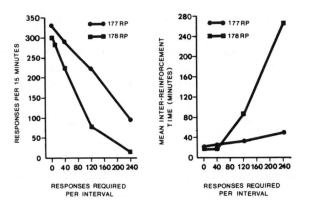

Fig. 5. The left panel shows the number of responses per 15 min; the right panel shows the mean interreinforcer time. (Data from Herrnstein & Morse, 1958. © 1958 by the Society for the Experimental Analysis of Behavior Inc.)

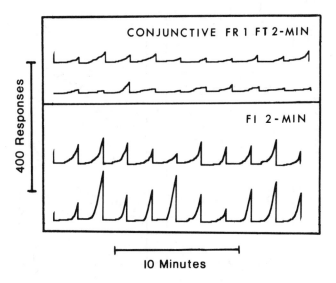

Fig. 6. Performance of a pigeon under a conjunctive FR 1 FT 2-min schedule compared with an FI 2-min schedule. The response pen reset at each food presentation.

fixed-interval schedule, but averaged 100 or less when food presentation required 240 responses. When 240 responses were required, one bird took more than 4 hours to obtain food (right panel), yet without the ratio requirement an average of more than 240 responses was emitted in 15 minutes (left panel).

These data indicate that an important factor in fixed-interval performance is that the schedule does not require more than one response. It is important, though, that this response be in close temporal contiguity to the reinforcer. A conjunctive FT FR 1 schedule also requires a single response, but it does not guarantee that it immediately precede the reinforcer. The data shown in Figure 6 corroborate Morgan's (1970) and Shull's (1970) reports that such a schedule maintains responding, but at a substantially lower level than a comparable fixed-interval schedule. If the response requirement is entirely eliminated by changing a fixed-interval to a fixed-time schedule, responding will eventually either fall to a low level or cease (Herrnstein, 1966; Zeiler, 1968). The responding maintained by a fixed-interval schedule evidently involves something other than the simple requirement of a single response per reinforcer presentation and/or the temporal regularity of the reinforcing stimulus.

Herrnstein and Morse attributed the high average frequency of responding on the fixed-interval schedule to the dynamic effect of the indirect variable *number of responses per reinforcer*. Consider the following hypothesis: The number of responses in an interval is determined by the number of responses in preceding intervals. High-response intervals (many responses per reinforcer) generate few responses in subsequent intervals; low-response intervals (few responses per reinforcer) generate many responses subsequently. This is a *dynamic effect*, because the value obtaining at one time can produce a different value later which will then itself determine the next value and so forth. It is an effect of an *indirect variable*, because the schedule does not specify how many responses (beyond one) must occur.

According to this hypothesis, a high frequency of responding in an interval is caused by preceding low-response intervals. The simple fixed-interval schedule allows as few as one response, but the addition of a fixed-ratio requirement means that there must be at least the number of responses specified by the ratio. Therefore, imposing a fixed-ratio requirement reduces responding by preventing a dynamic effect responsible for high numbers of responses.

The role of variation in the number of responses per reinforcer is evident from comparisons of variable-ratio and fixed-ratio schedule. Ferster and Skinner (1957, pp. 407–410) established responding under a VR 360 schedule, and they then changed the schedule to FR 360. There were more responses under the variable ratio; in fact, the fixed ratio did not always maintain responding. At the same average number of responses per reinforcer, therefore, variable numbers can maintain more responses than fixed numbers.

The maximum number of responses per reinforcer can be restricted without affecting the ability of a schedule to sustain responding. Neuringer and Schneider (1968) used an FI 30-sec schedule in which each response prior to the last produced a blackout (an intertrial interval). By varying the duration of the

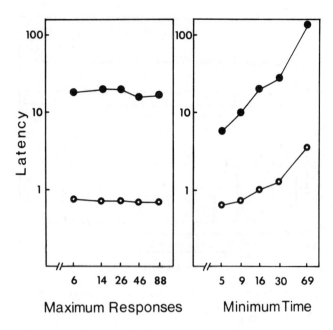

Fig. 7. Latency in seconds of the pigeons' first response after food presentation (filled points) and the time between successive subsequent responses (open points). (Left) Maximum number of responses per reinforcer on an FI 30-sec schedule. (Right) Minimum interreinforcer time on an FR 15 schedule. (Data from Neuringer & Schneider, 1968.)

blackout and measuring the interval in real time (by adding the blackout durations to the time spent responding), they restricted the total number of responses that could occur. For example, if the blackout duration was 4.96 sec, no more than six responses could occur. As in the ordinary fixed-interval schedule, the reinforcer could follow a single response. The left panel of Figure 7 shows that blackout durations ranging from .34 sec (maximum of 88 responses per reinforcer) to 4.96 sec (maximum of six responses) did not change the latency of each response. To the extent that this discrete-trial procedure involving intertrial intervals of different durations is related to the typical fixed-interval schedule, it shows that behavior is unaffected by restricting the maximum number of responses. The important factor, as shown by Herrnstein and Morse (1958), is that the possibility of few responses be preserved.

Cyclicities in Responding

Skinner (1938, pp. 123–126) found that responding under fixed-interval schedules varied in four ways. There were oscillations in the number of responses per session (first-order deviations); response frequency changed from one interval to the next in each session (second-order deviations); response rate changed within individual intervals (third-order deviations); individual responses tended to occur in groups (fourth-order deviations). First-order deviations have not received attention subsequently, while fourth-order deviations may occur with all schedules (Blough, 1963; Skinner, 1938). The distinctive characteristics of fixed-interval performance are the second- and third-order deviations. The third-order deviation—the pattern of responding or the distribution of responses in the time between successive reinforcer presentations—is a most important characteristic of different schedules and will be treated separately. The second-order deviations—the varying number of responses per interval—are of main concern now. Other investigators have also found that this deviation remains after extended exposure to fixed-interval schedules (Cumming & Schoenfeld, 1958; Dews, 1970). A satisfactory explanation of fixed-interval performance must explain the variability in response number per interval. This variability is illustrated in Figure 8.

Dews (1970) has shown that under an FI 3-min schedule the number of responses in an interval can vary over nearly a 50-fold range. In analyzing the relations among the number of responses emitted in 200 consecutive 3-min fixed intervals, Dews found two interesting phenomena. The first was shown by classifying intervals in terms of which of six class intervals described the number of responses. There was a general tendency for intervals with many responses to follow intervals with many responses. After an un-

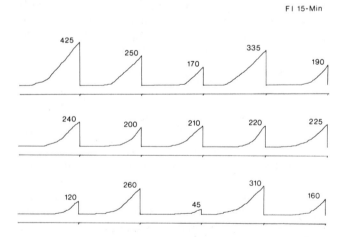

Fig. 8. Performance of a pigeon under an FI 15-min schedule. The response pen reset at each food presentation. Offsets of the event pen indicate when the 15-min interval timed out. The numerals adjacent to each interval indicate the number of responses in the interval to the nearest five responses as measured from the record.

predictable number of high-response intervals, one or more low-response intervals occur and the cycle repeats. There may also be a series of intervals having about the mean number of responses per interval. As Dews says, there is "irregular periodicity that was seen as a waxing and waning of the prevailing numbers of responses in sequence of intervals" (p. 59). It seems evident, therefore, that the relations controlling the number of responses in successive intervals may not operate immediately from one interval to the next but instead are cumulative effects over at least several intervals.

A second kind of cyclicity was revealed by ignoring the absolute number of responses and considering only the direction of change from one interval to the next. Dews found an alternation pattern in which intervals tended to be preceded and followed by intervals having more responses. "A second-order effect, alternation, was occurring during the session to a slight degree but . . . quantitatively this effect was small (and as a matter of fact, inconsistent from subject to subject)" (p. 58). Shull's (1971) data on sequential relations among initial pause durations can be interpreted as also showing a small alternation tendency on the assumption that pause duration and response number covary. Randolph and Sewell (1968) found that low-response intervals do tend to be followed by intervals with many responses, but that there is not an equally strong tendency for many responses to be followed by few. In general, then, there is a long-term effect of number of responses per reinforcer felt over several intervals and a more immediate but smaller effect seen from one interval to the next.

Herrnstein and Morse's (1958) explanation of fixed-interval responding in terms of the dynamic effects of the number of responses per reinforcer suggests that there should be oscillation in response number in successive intervals. In fact, the hypothesis that response number has dynamic effects seems to originate in Skinner's (1938) and Ferster and Skinner's (1957) attempts to explain the cyclicities. According to these views, intervals containing few responses generate intervals containing many responses, and these in turn generate few responses which then produce many responses and the cycle repeats. Apparently, the effects of a high response interval are not immediately to generate few responses in the next interval. Instead, effects seem to reveal an accumulation over several successive intervals.

In fixed-interval schedules, number of responses per reinforcer operates indirectly and its role must be inferred. However, fixed-ratio schedules establish number as an explicit independent variable and thereby disclose its effects on behavior. What happens when number of responses per reinforcer is manipulated directly?

Number of Responses and Fixed-Ratio Performance

Felton and Lyon (1966) and Powell (1968) extended Ferster and Skinner's (1957) investigations of the effects on pigeons of varying the fixed-ratio value. Both found that the duration of the initial pause increased as the ratio increased. In some subjects the postpause rate decreased with increases in the ratio, and in others the changes were less clear. Thus overall response rate (total responses divided by pause time plus the time spent responding) depends on, but is not linearly related to, the number of responses per reinforcer.

This relation corresponds to that hypothesized to account for response number fluctuations with fixed-interval schedules and to the results reported by Herrnstein and Morse (1958) with conjunctive FI FR schedules. Here, too, a small number of responses per reinforcer generated subsequent high average rates and many responses generated lower average rates. Since the hypothesized indirect effects were consistent with those found when the variable was imposed directly, the conclusion that the number of responses per reinforcer operates as an indirect determinant gains plausibility.

The fixed-ratio schedule does not allow the number of responses to have dynamic effects, because the number is held constant. Instead, it reveals how behavior is related to response number. With sufficiently high constant numbers (high ratios), a point is reached at which overall response rate drops and responding is poorly maintained in the absence of special histories. The precise nature of these histories is not well understood.

Interreinforcer Time

In general, at values under which fixed-ratio schedules maintain responding readily, the responses are emitted at higher rates than occur with fixed-interval schedules generating about the same average number of responses per reinforcer. This conclusion is derived from Ferster and Skinner's (1957) separate experiments involving fixed-ratio and fixed-interval schedules. If this is in fact the case, the number of responses per reinforcer cannot be the sole determinant of response rate, because response number can be the same under both types of schedule while rate varies.

The reason that equal responses per reinforcer can generate higher rates on ratio than on interval schedules lies in the relation of responding to the time between reinforcer presentations (interreinforcer time). The interreinforcer time is a function of response rate with ratio schedules, but its minimum is specified by the parameter value of interval schedules. When interreinforcer time is controlled on ratio schedules, response rate is affected markedly. Consider again Herrnstein and Morse's (1958) conjunctive FI FR schedules, but this time from the point of view of the ratio component. Interreinforcer time is not free to decrease to less than 15 min because of the FI 15-min requirement. Consequently, the minimum value is controlled. Also consider that Felton and Lyon (1966) found that under simple FR 150 schedule birds averaged somewhat more than 200 seconds to emit 150 responses. Herrnstein and Morse, in contrast, found that with a conjunctive FI 15-min FR 120 schedule the shortest average interreinforcer time was more than 30 min (Figure 5, right panel). The importance of leaving the minimum interreinforcer time uncontrolled to obtain high rates under ratio schedules seems evident. This was also shown by Neuringer and Schneider (1968). They used an FR 15 schedule in which each response before the last produced a blackout period, while the fixed-ratio schedule held the number of responses constant. The right panel of Figure 7 shows that the longer the interreinforcer time (the longer the blackouts), the longer was the latency of each response. These data are further evidence that the relation between response and reinforcer rates is one reason for the high rates under ratio schedules.

Variable-ratio schedules of moderate value maintain a high and fairly constant rate of responding (Ferster & Skinner, 1957, Chapter 7). As in the case of fixed-ratio schedules, the high rates depend on the circular relation between response rate and interreinforcement time. This was shown by Ferster and Skinner (pp. 399–407) in the following way.

Pigeons were matched in their stable response rates under a variable-interval (VI 5-min) schedule. Then one bird was changed to a variable-ratio schedule in which the number of responses per reinforcer was chosen to match the number emitted on the variable-interval schedule. The second bird was yoked to the first. When the first received food, the second obtained food for its next response. No other responses were required for the second bird. This generated a variable-interval schedule for the second bird, with interreinforcer time under the VI schedule matching that achieved for the first bird under VR. For one pair of birds the variable-ratio schedule generated two- to threefold higher rates than did the yoked variable-interval schedule. Interreinforcer time could not be responsible for the difference since it was the same; instead, the important factor had to be the dependence of interreinforcer time on response rate for the ratio bird.

A second effect occurred for another pair of birds. Responding could not be maintained under the variable-ratio schedule after the change from the initial variable interval. That one pair of birds revealed a higher rate under VR than VI while the other stopped responding under VR is not contradictory. When responding is well maintained by a ratio schedule, the rate is higher than with an interval schedule generating comparable numbers of responses per reinforcer; however, interval schedules will maintain a number of responses per reinforcer that cannot be sustained by ratio schedules.

Responding in interval and ratio schedules, in summary, reflects the operation of the number of responses per reinforcer and the interreinforcer time. The response number characteristics of interval schedules arise from the dynamic role of varying numbers of responses per reinforcer combined with constant interreinforcer times; the rate characteristics of ratio schedules arise from constant numbers of responses per reinforcer combined with behavior-dependent interreinforcer times. The parameters of each of these schedules are important in determining the performance engendered, because they establish the levels of the variables either directly or indirectly.

Tandem Schedules with FI and FR Components

The present analysis cannot explain why tandem FI FR schedules should have the effects that they sometimes do. In such a schedule, completion of a fixed-interval requirement initiates the ratio requirement, and completion of the ratio then produces the reinforcer. There are no stimulus changes correlated with the different schedule components. Ferster and Skinner (1957, pp. 416–422) found that a tandem FI 45-min FR 10 schedule increased response rate above that occurring with an FI 45-min schedule. Note that the tandem schedule places restrictions on both the minimum interreinforcer time and the minimum number of responses per reinforcer. The rate increase, therefore, is unexpected. Ferster and Skinner (p. 429) also showed that responding was maintained when the ratio component was increased to FR 400. Parametric analyses are necessary to show whether rate increases are general effects or occur only when the interval component is so large that it maintains a high average number of responses per reinforcer by itself.

The Relation Between Responses Per Reinforcer and Interreinforcer Time

Experiments studying the effect of fixed-ratio size on response rate consistently have confounded the direct effects of responses per reinforcer with the indirect effects of interreinforcer time. As ratio size was increased, the birds took more time to obtain each reinforcer. Therefore, increased interreinforcer time rather than, or in addition to, increased response number may have produced the lower overall rate. Changes in both variables occurred in Herrnstein and Morse's (1958) experiment as well. Under the conjunctive FI FR schedule any time the ratio requirement had not been met by the time the 15-min interval had elapsed, interreinforcer time increased. The right panel of Figure 5 shows that interreinforcer time did increase as a function of the size of the ratio, and the left panel shows that response rate decreased accordingly. The effects observed by Herrnstein and Morse may have been due to responses per reinforcer, to interreinforcer time, or to some combination of the two.

Neuringer and Schneider's (1968) attempt to separate the two variables was only partially successful. When they maintained an FR 15 schedule while varying interreinforcer time, they found that, as the time increased, response latency (time to the first response) increased as well (Figure 7, right panel). This demonstrated the role of interreinforcer time independent of the numbers of responses. Further, when they controlled interreinforcer time by establishing an FI 30-sec schedule while limiting the number of responses that could be emitted, latency was the same independent of response number (Figure 7, left panel). Thus they demonstrated that restricting the maximum number of responses had no significant effect on responding. They did not, however, control how few responses could occur, i.e., the minimum number of responses per reinforcer. Since the minimum number was unrestricted under all conditions, there was no interference with the property now hypothesized to induce high rates, and consequently no effect was observed.

An experiment by Crossman, Heaps, Nunes, and Alferink (1974) showed that minimum number of responses exerted effects with interreinforcer time controlled. They arranged a multiple schedule in which the first component was a ratio of FR 25, FR 50, or FR 100 and the second involved an FR 2 schedule with the 2 responses separated by a blackout. A computer recorded the time spent in the first component (interreinforcer interval). It then also recorded the latency of the first response of the second component and adjusted the duration of the blackout so that it ended when the latency plus the blackout equaled the interreinforcer interval of the first component. The next response produced food. The result was that the interreinforcer time was the same in both components, but one required 25, 50, or 100 responses whereas the other required 2.

Interreinforcer time in the first component increased as the ratio was raised. Figure 9 shows that the latency to the first response of both components increased as well. Since the response requirement was constant at two in the second component, interreinforcer time clearly was relevant. In addition, however, the latency was always shorter under the 2-response requirement than with the 25-, 50-, or 100-response requirement even though interreinforcer times were matched in both. In other words, response number was important independent of interreinforcer time. Although the response-produced blackouts in this and Neuringer and Schneider's experiment probably exerted distinctive effects that themselves still need to be isolated, the experiments do suggest that both in-

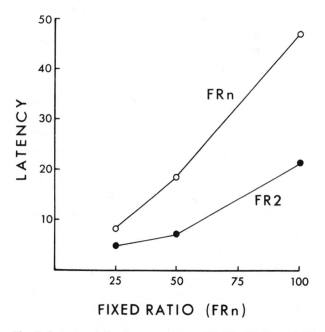

Fig. 9. Latency of the first response on FR 25, FR 50, and FR 100 schedules and on FR 2 schedules equated for interreinforcer time. (Data from Crossman et al, 1974.)

The Regenerating Power of Interval Schedules

The interval schedule tends to have the number of responses per reinforcer regress toward the mean. When responding is strong and many responses occur, the number of responses per reinforcer becomes high, and responses subsequently occur less frequently. When responding is weak, this means few responses per reinforcer and a subsequent high response rate. The occurrence of a reinforcer when the tendency to respond is low may have another related effect: should the organism stop responding for a time exceeding the interval parameter value, the next response will be followed by the reinforcer and responses will be regenerated.

Ratio schedules do not share this regenerating characteristic: no matter how much time elapses without a response, a reinforcer will not occur following the next instance, unless it just happens that the next one ends the ratio. Because ratio schedules do not provide a reinforcer just when it is needed to revive weak behavior, they are usually involved when a response is poorly maintained (Morse, 1966, p. 86).

If this regenerating potential is important, a variable-ratio schedule that matched a high-valued fixed-interval schedule in the sequence of response numbers per reinforcer would not maintain responding as well as the fixed interval. The variable-ratio schedule does not automatically adjust the response requirement downward when performance weakens. Since a correspondence between weak behavior and a low ratio would be entirely fortuitous, the variable-ratio schedule lacks a perfectly tuned regenerating characteristic. The only relevant information appears in Ferster and Skinner's (1957) comment about variable-ratio schedules: "As in all schedules requiring a number of responses, the bird will stop responding altogether if the average number goes beyond a certain value" (p. 391). In contrast, there is no apparent limit to how high an average number of responses can be achieved with interval schedules. If higher rates should occur on the variable-ratio schedule, however, it would suggest that the regenerating potential is not important.

The IRT>t schedule has the same built-in regenerating property as interval schedules. Under IRT>t schedules, whenever responding becomes weak enough that the organism pauses beyond the parameter value, the next response is followed by the reinforcer. As would be expected, therefore, these schedules also maintain many responses (e.g., Herrnstein & Morse, 1957).

ADJUSTING FIXED-RATIO SCHEDULES

Research involving adjusting fixed-ratio schedules further supports the hypothesis that schedules will maintain a large average number of responses if they provide a reinforcer whenever responding weakens. In an adjusting fixed-ratio schedule, the ratio requirement is changed based on some behavioral criterion. For example, Ferster and Skinner (1957, pp. 718–720) imposed an FR 160 schedule. Whenever the bird paused for 2 min or more before making the first response, the schedule became FR 1. This meant that whenever the FR 160 schedule failed to support responding, a single response produced the reinforcer. The adjusting schedule maintained a high response rate without long pauses; only occasionally did the FR 1 condition operate. Comparisons with other data suggest that the average rate was higher than might be expected with an FR 160 schedule alone.

In a second experiment (pp. 720–721) Ferster and Skinner employed a continuously adjusting schedule. (Actually, it was an interlocking schedule, since, in a given component one parameter decreased as a function of the other.) Whenever the initial pause was less than 25 sec, the ratio increased by 5 responses. During the first 25 sec the ratio decreased slowly unless there was a response (the rate of decrease is not specified). Responding was maintained in three birds with ratios of 445, 600, and 650 responses respectively. Such ratio values do not sustain behavior easily; for them to do so, it appears necessary to adjust requirements to the ongoing behavior.

The most systematic study of adjusting schedules was that of Kelleher, Fry, and Cook (1964, Experiment 1) with squirrel monkeys. It differed from the Ferster and Skinner experiments in that pausing affected the ratio requirement in a subsequent rather than in the current component (by Ferster and Skinner's definition, it was an adjusting as opposed to an interlocking schedule). A session began with an FR 10 schedule. If two successive postreinforcement pauses were shorter than time t, the ratio changed to the next higher value. Sixteen ratio values increased in steps from FR 10 to FR 1000. If two successive pauses exceeded t, the ratio decreased by one step (except that one pause exceeding t would reduce the ratio from FR 1000 to FR 870). The ratio remained constant if two successive pause durations were alternately longer and shorter than t. The values of t were 1, 2, 4, 8, and

15 min. Kelleher et al. pointed out that under simple fixed-ratio schedules, performance usually shows long pauses with schedules higher than FR 100. With the adjusting schedule, the average maintained fixed-ratio value increased with increases in t, but all levels of t produced averages higher than 100 responses per reinforcer. Average ratio values over 200 were typical with t values from 2 to 8 min, and the average number of responses was over 400 when t was 15 min. So a fixed-ratio schedule that lessens the response requirement when responding weakens maintains a substantial level of responding.

INTERLOCKING FIXED-RATIO, FIXED-INTERVAL SCHEDULES

A schedule that would seem to adjust ratio requirements to the momentary strength of responding is the interlocking fixed-ratio, fixed-interval schedule. In such a schedule, the fixed-ratio value decreases as time elapses since the preceding reinforcer and reaches FR 1 when the interval has elapsed. The rate of decrease in the ratio value is a function of the interval parameter: longer intervals mean slower decreases. If responses are emitted at a high rate, the reinforcer occurs after a number of responses close to the initial ratio value; if responding is slow, the reinforcer occurs after fewer responses.

Parametric data on interlocking FR FI schedules were reported by Berryman and Nevin (1962). Unfortunately, from the point of view of the present argument, the ratio value used (FR 32) itself maintained responding quite well. Combining the FR 32 schedule with a fixed-interval schedule in an interlocking FR FI reduced the overall rate of responding, with the amount of decrease positively related to the interval value. Apparently, the possibility of a reinforcer occurring when behavior weakens is unnecessary with small ratio schedules; under these conditions the occasional delivery of a reinforcer via an interval schedule seems to suppress responding. An interlocking FI FR schedule should markedly increase responding if the ratio schedule is so large that it does not maintain behavior very well by itself. This prediction has not yet been tested.

RESPONSE PATTERNING: THE TEMPORAL ORGANIZATION OF BEHAVIOR

Different schedules have distinctive effects on the way responses are distributed in the time between successive reinforcer presentations. These patterns of responding are stable and characteristic of the schedule.

The fixed-interval pattern is Skinner's (1938) third-order deviation from responding at a steady rate. Skinner describes it as follows: "Deviations of a third order appear as depressions in the rate of elicitation after the periodic reconditioning of the reflex. They are followed typically by compensatory increases, so that the total rate is unchanged" (p. 125). Much subsequent research has confirmed that there typically is a pause followed by responding. Postpause responding may display either continuous positive acceleration, positive acceleration changing to a steady high rate, or an abrupt transition from no responding to a high rate (e.g., Cumming & Schoenfeld, 1958; Ferster & Skinner, 1957; Schneider, 1969). Responding under variable-interval and random-interval schedules is fairly constant between successive reinforcers. Catania and Reynolds (1968) found that the precise nature of the variable-interval pattern depended on how the constituent intervals were selected and how they were distributed. Response rate can be either positively accelerated, negatively accelerated, or approximately linear depending on the distribution of interreinforcer intervals. Ratio schedules also produce characteristic patterns. With fixed-ratio schedules, there is a pause followed by a transition to responding at a high rate; the pause duration is a function of the fixed-ratio size (e.g., Felton & Lyon, 1966; Powell, 1968). Frequently, the transition is abrupt, but sometimes there is positive acceleration, and at times responding may slow somewhat at the end of the ratio (Ferster & Skinner, 1957). Under moderately valued schedules (e.g., FR 30) the rate is often very stable after the initial transition (Gott & Weiss, 1972; Weiss & Gott, 1972). Variable-ratio and random-ratio schedules tend to produce responding at a high steady rate, at least as judged from cumulative records (Ferster & Skinner, 1957; Schoenfeld et al., 1972). What variables are responsible for the patterns engendered by each schedule?

Temporal Placement of the Reinforcing Stimulus

A differentiating characteristic of interval schedules is the regularity of reinforcer presentation in relation to time. In fixed-interval schedules the reinforcer occurs at regular times (given that response rate is sufficiently high—as it invariably is—to produce the reinforcer close to when it becomes available), and in variable-interval and random-interval schedules it occurs irregularly. The placement of the stimulus in time plays a major role in determining the pattern of responding.

Interval and Time Schedules

Shifting from an interval to a time schedule maintains the temporal placement of the reinforcing stimulus while changing the tendency to respond. Interval and time schedules can be matched for minimum interreinforcer interval, but they differ in their ability to maintain a specific response. Time schedules maintain a lower response rate than do interval schedules (Appel & Hiss, 1962; Herrnstein, 1966; Zeiler, 1968). In fact, it is not unusual for the response to stop altogether under time schedules.

Interval and time schedules do, however, maintain the same pattern of responding (see Figure 1). One experiment (Zeiler, 1968) studied the effects of changing from variable to fixed schedules and vice versa; the transitions involved both interval and time schedules. If the preceding schedule was of the same type in terms of reinforcer regularity, the same pattern was maintained; if the schedules were of different types, the pattern changed accordingly. In this respect it made no difference whether the schedules were interval or time, although there were large effects on response rate. The temporal pattern of reinforcer deliveries controlled the pattern of responding.

Interval and time schedules generate similar patterns despite the differences they produce in the behavior occurring at the moment of reinforcer presentation (the interval schedule guarantees that it be a specific response, whereas the time schedule allows the response to vary). These observations are not in accord with analyses of patterning that stress the importance of the events occurring in close contiguity with the reinforcer. Dews (1969) provides an additional indication that the precise quantitative relations obtaining between responses and reinforcers do not control patterning. Dews compared performance on a fixed-interval schedule with that occurring when a small fixed-ratio requirement or a short delay of reinforcement was added to the end of the interval. Some of these manipulations changed the rate of responding, but none affected the pattern. As long as the temporal placement of the reinforcing stimulus was not markedly disturbed, the pattern was unchanged.

Quantitative Measurement of Temporal Placement of the Reinforcing Stimulus

Fixed and variable schedules can be differentiated in terms of variability of interreinforcer time (interval and time schedules) or number of responses per reinforcer (ratio schedules). With the fixed schedules, the parameter value indicates where each reinforcer is located; however, with variable schedules, the parameter indicates only the average location. (In random schedules there is no indication of the location but simply information about the probability of reinforcer presentation at any moment or for any response.) In an attempt to describe responding under variable-interval schedules, Catania and Reynolds (1968) have related response rate at a given point in postreinforcer time to the availability of the reinforcer at that point. They proposed two measures of temporal placement of the reinforcer: (1) *probability of reinforcement;* and (2) *local rate of reinforcement.*

PROBABILITY OF REINFORCEMENT

One measure of reinforcement density within a time period is how often reinforcers occur in a given interval relative to how often the interval occurs. Catania and Reynolds (1968) call this *probabilty of reinforcement,* or reinforcements per opportunity. Consider a variable-interval 1-min schedule with the following 20 interreinforcer intervals occurring in some irregular order: 3, 7, 10, 22, 28, 30, 42, 45, 50, 54, 62, 65, 66, 67, 85, 90, 95, 105, 134, and 140 sec. These individual intervals can be categorized in successive 20-sec class intervals as shown in column (a) of Table 1. The result is seven class intervals. Column (b) shows the number of reinforcers in each of these class intervals. Not each class interval has an equal opportunity for occurrence, since each can only occur when a shorter interval is not in force. For example, the 21–40-sec class interval exists only when one of the three members of the 0–20-sec class is not in effect, whereas the 121–140-sec class interval can only occur if no individual interval less than 121 sec is in force. Column (c) shows the number of opportunities for each class interval in each cycle of the 20 individual interreinforcer intervals. The probability of reinforcement for each class interval is computed by dividing column (b) by column (c). These probabilities are shown in column (d); they represent the probability of a reinforcer presentation in that region of time since the last reinforcer, given that the region has been reached.

Catania and Reynolds (1968) studied a number of different types of variable-interval schedules differentiated by the way the individual interreinforcer intervals were selected. All of these had the same mean value; i.e., each was a particular-valued variable-interval schedule, but they all differed in the probabil-

Table 1 Quantitative Measurement of Reinforcer Placement in VI Schedules

(a) Class Intervals (sec)	(b) Number of Reinforcers	(c) Opportunities	(d) Probability of Reinforcer Presentation	(e) Time Spent in Interval (sec)	(f) Local Rate of Reinforcement (Reinforcers/hr)
0–20	3	20	.150	360	30.0
21–40	3	17	.176	298	36.2
41–60	4	14	.286	228	63.2
61–80	4	10	.400	136	105.9
81–100	3	6	.500	87	124.1
101–120	1	3	.333	44	81.8
121–140	2	2	1.000	32	225.0

ity of reinforcement occurring with respect to successive class intervals. In three types of VI (arithmetic, linear, constant probability), reinforcement probability in an interval and the response rate in that interval (local response rate) both increased as time elapsed. However, in two other types (geometric, Fibonacci), local response rate decreased as probability of reinforcement increased. Therefore, probability of reinforcement in an interval cannot generally explain local response rate under variable-interval schedules.

LOCAL RATE OF REINFORCEMENT

Catania and Reynolds devised another measure of reinforcer density. This measure takes into account not simply how often a given class interval occurs, but also how much time is spent in that interval relative to the number of reinforcer presentations. Consider the 0–20-sec class interval in Table 1. Except when the 3-, 7-, or 10-sec interreinforcer intervals are in effect, the interval lasts for 20 sec. (This computational procedure is modified slightly from Catania and Reynolds by not splitting the time between successive classes.) This will occur in 17 of the 20 interreinforcer intervals, yielding a total time of 340 sec spent in the 0–20-sec class interval. In addition, the organism will spend 3 sec in that class interval when the 3-sec interval is scheduled, 7 sec when the 7-sec interval is in effect, and 10 sec when the 10-sec interval prevails. Over the 20 interreinforcer intervals, therefore, the 0–20-sec class interval will be in effect for a total of 360 sec. The time spent in each class interval is shown in column (e) of Table 1. The 21–40-sec class interval will be in effect a total of 298 sec, because there will be 3 intervals in which the class is never reached, 14 in which it will be in effect for the entire 20 sec (the 14 interreinforcer intervals longer than 40 sec), and a total of 18 sec (divided among the 22-, 28-, and 30-sec intervals) in which the class begins but is terminated prior to 40 sec. The computations for the other class intervals are equivalent. The *local rate of reinforcement* (column f) is computed by dividing the number of reinforcers presented in a class interval (column b) by the total time spent in that interval (column e).

Figure 10 depicts the local rate of reinforcement and the rates of responding at successive time periods after reinforcer presentation in several types of variable-interval schedule (Catania & Reynolds, 1968). The correspondence between local response rate and local rate of reinforcement was closer than the correspondence between local response rate and probability of reinforcement. The fit is not exact, primarily because of departures at low and intermediate values, but the curves do not diverge as they sometimes do for probability of reinforcement.

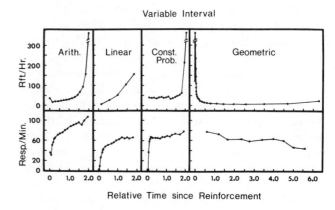

Fig. 10. Local rate of reinforcement (upper panels) in reinforcements per hr and local rate of responding (lower panels) on four different types of variable-interval schedule. Time units on the abscissa are interreinforcer times relative to the average interreinforcer interval (the VI value). (Data are for pigeons from Catania & Reynolds, 1968.)

Local Rate of Reinforcement and the Fixed-interval Pattern

Catania and Reynolds (1968, Experiment 4) found that the local rate of reinforcement analysis did not describe fixed-interval performance. Note that with fixed-interval schedules the local rate of reinforcement is 0.00 for all class intervals save the last, when it is 1.00. Yet substantial responding occurs prior to the end of the interval.

Several theorists have proposed that fixed-interval performance constitutes two phases, one corresponding to the period of not responding (the pause period) and the other corresponding to the period of responding (the work period). This general concept originated with Skinner (1938) and has been elaborated by Schneider (1969) and Shull, Guilkey, and Witty (1972). Schneider noted, as Shull (1970) later confirmed, that the work period is of variable duration (the period of pausing varies from one interval to the next). He suggested, therefore, that the work period is correlated with a variable-interval schedule, whereas the pause period is a period of extinction. According to Schneider, the pattern observed under a fixed-interval schedule is the outcome of extinction followed by a variable-interval schedule.

Schneider's account suggests the following application of Catania and Reynolds' (1968) local rate of reinforcement analysis. Define the interreinforcer intervals by measuring the time spent responding in each individual fixed interval. The only difference from VI is that the interreinforcer intervals are calculated from behavior rather than imposed directly. Compute the local rates of reinforcement from these values. For example, if, under an FI 5-min schedule the organism began responding 3 min prior to the end of a particular interval, the value of 180 sec would be assigned to that interval. Consider 10 such intervals having the values of 5, 30, 40, 65, 100, 110, 115, 130, 145, and 160 sec. Column (a) of Table 2 shows these values arranged into 20-sec class intervals, and column (b) shows the total amount of time spent in each. For example, if responding began 65 sec before reinforcer presentation, 20 sec was spent in each of class intervals 0–20, 21–40, and 41–60, and 5 sec was spent in interval 61–80. No time was spent in any of the longer classes. The number of reinforcers obtained in each class interval appears in column (c). For example, if responding began 30 sec before the end of the fixed interval, the reinforcer occurred in the 21–40-sec class. The local rate of reinforcement for each class interval (column d) was obtained by dividing column (c) by column (b).

Table 2 Local Rate of Reinforcement in FI Schedules

(a) Class Intervals (sec)	(b) Time Spent in Interval (sec)	(c) Number of Reinforcers	(d) Local Rate of Reinforcement (Reinforcers/hr)
0–20	185	1	19.5
21–40	168	2	42.9
41–60	140	0	0.0
61–80	124	1	29.0
81–100	109	1	33.0
101–120	83	2	86.7
121–140	49	1	73.5
141–160	23	2	313.0

The local response rate in a given class interval is the total number of responses occurring in that interval divided by the total time spent in that interval. This procedure is analogous to that used with variable-interval schedules by Catania and Reynolds, except that the segments are defined with respect to the onset of responding in each interval.

Figure 11 shows the local rate of responding and the local rate of reinforcement computed as described above for 150 successive reinforcer presentations under an FI 5-min schedule. The detailed correspondence between the two curves is not close, although generally both curves increase for three of the four birds. The curves resemble those found by Catania and Reynolds with arithmetic variable-interval schedules. Hence fixed-interval performance follows no more (but also no less) precisely from a local rate of reinforcement analysis than does variable-interval performance. The conceptualization of fixed-interval

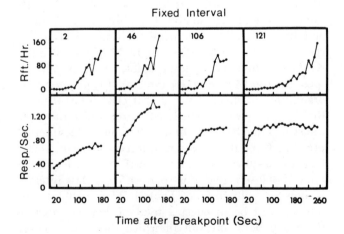

Fig. 11. Local rate of reinforcement in reinforcements per hr and local rate of responding on a FI 5-min schedule in pigeons. The reference point is the break point. See text for a detailed explanation. (Davis & Zeiler, unpublished data.)

performance as a combination of an extinction and a variable-interval schedule does not conflict with what is known about variable-interval performance. Whether this will help in understanding either fixed-interval or variable-interval behavior is still unclear. One is now confronted with explaining variable-interval performance, and it perhaps may be best understood as a combination of fixed-interval schedules.

Patterning Under Ratio Schedules

Ratio schedules establish certain inevitable relations between time and the reinforcing stimulus, although these are indirect rather than direct effects of the schedule. In fixed-ratio schedules the time that elapses from the first opportunity to respond until the reinforcer appears depends on ratio size and response rate. A reason for the initial pause and for its direct relation to ratio size (Felton & Lyon, 1966; Ferster & Skinner, 1957; Powell, 1968) may be the relation between one reinforcer and the time until the next. The pause might be attributed to the zero probability of reinforcement for the first response, but then it is difficult to understand why the first response should ever occur. Since the differential presentation of the reinforcer with respect to time always produces responding prior to the time the reinforcer is available, a pause followed by responding occurs. The importance of the interreinforcer interval is further implied by Killeen's (1969) finding that pausing was about the same in a fixed-ratio schedule and in an interval schedule yoked to it in terms of interreinforcer time. The shorter pause under variable-ratio schedules would follow from the occasional occurrence of the reinforcer close in time to the preceding one. Given the possibility of temporal control, it would be of interest if Catania and Reynolds' (1968) local rate of reinforcement analysis of variable-interval performance would apply equally well to behavior under variable-ratio schedules. This account of pausing followed by responding under ratio schedules is similar to that offered by Skinner (1938), Ferster and Skinner (1957), and Morse (1966).

Temporal Placement and Not Responding

Staddon's (1970, 1972) experiments provide further evidence that the pattern of responding depends on the temporal placement of the reinforcing event in relation to responses. During some intervals food was available in the first 60 sec following a food presentation; during other intervals it was only available after 60 sec. Under one condition any food presentation available in the first 60 sec occurred only if a key peck had not occurred for 10 sec ($R > 10$ sec). If the food was available after 60 sec, it was produced by pecking according to a variable-interval schedule. Under another procedure the schedule orders were reversed: a peck was required in the first 60 sec, and the $\overline{R} > t$ schedule was in effect thereafter.

The first procedure produced pauses followed by a substantial rate of key pecking, and the second produced pecking followed by pausing. Thus the temporal placement of the reinforcing event with respect to two different forms of behavior determined the probability with which each occurred at a given point in time.

The Components of Temporal Placement

The temporal pattern of reinforcers explains the pattern of responding on different schedules. *Temporal placement* refers to the occurrence of reinforcers in time in relation to some reference point, e.g., the last reinforcer presentation or the beginning of a trial. Attempts to further analyze temporal placement have focused on two processes: temporal discrimination and delay of reinforcement.

THE THEORETICAL BACKGROUND

The use of delayed reinforcement to explain patterning in sequences originated with Hull's (1932) account of why rats chose the shorter of two paths to the same goal and why they ran faster in the first section of a short alley than in the first section of a longer alley. Because the distance to reward differs, responding is reinforced with different delays. On the assumption that habit strength is inversely related to delay, choice of the shorter path or faster running in the shorter alley indicates that sequences of responses are influenced by their temporal remoteness from the reinforcing stimulus.

In 1952 Hull distinguished between experiments involving short and long alleys and those involving a delay period imposed after a single response. The first type presents reinforcers immediately upon the completion of the final response of the entire sequence (i.e., upon entering the goal box), so that the reinforcer is delayed with respect to earlier parts of the sequence. Hull described such procedures as involving a gradient of reinforcement within a chain (chaining delay). The second procedure imposes delay after the terminal response; it does not involve intrinsic delays due to the relations between early and later parts of sequences (nonchaining delay).

Spence (1956) pointed out that Hull distinguished chaining and nonchaining delay procedurally but not theoretically. Spence, in contrast, believed them to be the outcome of different processes. He proposed that behavior in the chaining situation was due to the similarity of goal box stimuli to stimuli occurring earlier in the chain. Response decrements in the nonchaining situation were attributed to other responses emitted during the delay period, and because they occur closer in time to the reinforcer these other responses compete with the target response. Whereas Hull believed that response strength was the outcome of delayed reinforcement in both chaining and nonchaining delay situations, Spence maintained that the two situations had little in common and that neither represented a direct functional relation between response strength and delay.

Dews's (1962) interpretation of fixed-interval schedules is very similar to Hull's analysis of chaining delay, and Dews, like Hull, used data from nonchaining-delay experiments to support the hypothesis. Skinner (1938), on the other hand, separated the two situations. His explanation of fixed-interval performance resembled Spence's account of chaining delay. It drew heavily on elapsed time as a stimulus; i.e., responding depends on the similarity of the temporal stimuli at any point to the temporal stimulus correlated with reinforcer presentation. This account emphasized stimulus properties rather than a theoretical gradient of reinforcement. Since Skinner also dealt with nonchaining delay in terms of competing adventitiously reinforced responses, his accounts of both chaining and nonchaining delay are similar to Spence's.

In the case of chaining delay, then, the issue is whether responding depends on the proximity to the end of the chain (Hull, Dews) or on the similarity of the conditions at any point to those present at the moment of reinforcer presentation (Skinner, Spence). Is fixed-interval performance due to the effect of a gradient of reinforcement on response strength, or does it depend on the time since the beginning of the interval in relation to the total interval duration? An answer to this question would indicate whether delay of reinforcement or temporal discrimination is the major controlling aspect of the temporal placement of reinforcement.

Temporal Discrimination

The term *temporal discrimination* has a confusing history. Sometimes it has been used as a process to explain behavior—e.g., the fixed-interval pattern is the outcome of the discrimination of time. But this shifted the problem to an explanation of how time comes to be discriminated, and it has never gone beyond a reiteration of the independent variables; e.g., it happens when reinforcement occurs at a certain point in time. Thus the process interpretation simply tacks on *temporal discrimination* to the relation between the independent variable and observable performance. A more meaningful usage of *temporal discrimination* proposes that elapsed time may function as a stimulus. A testable implication is that the time elapsing from the start of an interval has discriminative properties. Since, in a fixed-interval schedule, responding is never reinforced just after the interval begins, this period may serve as a discriminative stimulus controlling a low rate of responding. The same is true of fixed-ratio schedules, because responding just after reinforcer presentation is never followed by another reinforcer. The analysis can also be extended to patterning under variable schedules, where a reinforcer does sometimes occur just after the preceding one. The period immediately following reinforcer presentation does not come to function as a negative discriminative stimulus, and responses are emitted at a more stable rate.

Experiments on Temporal Discrimination

Catania (1970) described several experiments dealing with the discrimination of time. The temporal discrimination experiment is identical to other experiments on stimulus control, differing only in that time is the stimulus dimension manipulated. In a study of wavelength discrimination, the experimenter correlates certain wavelengths with a reinforcing stimulus and others with different consequences; in a study of temporal discrimination, different time durations are selectively correlated with the reinforcer.

In a temporal discrimination experiment, Stubbs (1968) had the center member of a three-key display transilluminated with white light for 1 of 10 durations. Which of the two side keys was then correlated with reinforcer availability depended on the preceding duration: if the center key had been lit for 1 of the 5 shorter durations, responses to one of the keys produced food. If it had been lit for one of the longer durations, responses to the other key produced food. By plotting responding to each key as a function of the preceding white key duration, Stubbs was able to compute the Weber fraction for discrimination of time. There was clear differential responding with respect to duration as the antecedent stimulus. Another example of a temporal discrimination experiment was provided by Reynolds and Catania (1962). Pigeons were exposed to a dark key for durations ranging from 3 to 30 seconds. When the key was then illuminated, responding was reinforced only if the preceding dark key duration had been a specific value (e.g., 3 sec). The birds responded at the highest rate following the duration correlated with reinforcer availability and at progressively lower rates with increasingly different durations. Clearly, duration can have discriminative properties.

Delay of Reinforcement

Delay of reinforcement describes the time from a response until the reinforcer appears. Dews (1962) hypothesized that delay of reinforcement is a determinant of fixed-interval patterning, since the reinforcer follows not only the last response in the interval, but also earlier ones, albeit with longer delays. Responses occurring closest to the reinforcing stimulus are subjected to the shortest delay; responses more remote from reinforcement are subjected to longer delays. "The progressive increase in rate of responding through the fixed interval would be based on a declining retroactive rate-enhancing effect of the reinforcing stimuli as the delay between response and reinforcement is increased" (Dews, 1962, p. 373).

Studies of Delayed Reinforcement

In order to evaluate the possibility that delay of reinforcement influences fixed-interval performance, it is necessary to observe its direct effects. Such research has manipulated the delay interval by having the reinforcer occur at varied times after the response. The experiments have differed in whether or not responses during the delay period reset the delay timer and in whether or not there was a distinctive stimulus correlated with the delay period.

A distinctive stimulus correlated with the delay usually eliminates responding during that period; thus it makes little difference whether or not responses reset the delay timer. Responding may either decrease as a function of delay (e.g., Hamilton, 1929; Pierce, Hanford, & Zimmerman, 1972) or be maintained with delays as long as 24 hr (Azzi, Fix, Keller, & Rocha e Silva, 1964; Ferster, 1953; Ferster & Hammer, 1965). These correlated stimulus conditions would not, in any event, seem to be relevant to fixed-interval performance, since the fixed-interval schedule provides no delay stimulus.

In the absence of distinctive stimuli, there is a difference depending on whether or not responses during the delay period reset the delay timer. If each response prolongs the delay (reset condition), responding typically declines with increased delays (Azzi et al., 1964; Dews, 1960; Skinner, 1938, pp. 139 ff.). This procedure also has little relevance to fixed-interval schedules when the presumed delay period for each response is unaffected by subsequent responses.

The situation most nearly equivalent to fixed-interval schedules is one without delay stimuli and resets. Dews (1960) arranged delays of 10, 30, or 100 sec between a key peck and food delivery. Responding was maintained with the 100-sec delay, but at a lower rate than with the 10-sec delay. Of the two birds given the 30-sec delay, one had a higher rate at 30 sec than at 10 sec, and the other had a lower rate at 30 sec. To some extent, then, the function relating response rate to delay of reinforcement corresponds to the hypothesized role played by delay in fixed-interval performance.

Explicit delays of reinforcement added to fixed-interval schedules have large effects whether responses do (Skinner, 1938, pp. 139–150) or do not (Dews, 1969) reset the delay timer. Skinner used either an FI 4-min or an FI 5-min schedule with delays of reinforcement ranging from 0 to 8 sec in 2-sec steps. Rate declined 33% with a 2-sec delay and more than 50% with 8 sec; in fact, Skinner concluded that the 8-sec delay probably did not maintain responding at all. Dews added a 1-sec delay of reinforcement to an FI 3-min schedule. Because responses did not reset the delay timer, the actual delay could range from 0 to 1 sec (Dews mentions that the average delay was about 250 msec). Response rate was about half that occurring with immediate reinforcer presentation. These data suggest that a reinforcing stimulus has a small effective range in time. If delays as short as 1 sec sharply reduce response rate, the high average level of responding maintained minutes or even hours prior to the appearance of the reinforcer under fixed-interval schedules cannot be attributed to the delay of reinforcement gradient. Morgan (1970) drew the same conclusion from his comparison of fixed-interval schedules with a conjunctive fixed-time, fixed-ratio schedule that maintained the same single-response requirement and interreinforcer interval, but did not guarantee that a response be contiguous with the reinforcer. Skinner's, Dews's, and Morgan's experiments demonstrate that substantial responding is maintained only if there is very close temporal contiguity between the final response and the reinforcer.

Delay of Reinforcement in Schedules Involving Response Number

Delay of reinforcement may operate when several responses must precede each reinforcer presentation. Catania (1971) required a sequence of responses to either one or two keys. If all of the responses except the first had to be to one key (key A), while the first response had to be to the other key (key B), the rate of responding to key B decreased as the number of subsequent key A responses was increased from 1 to 11. In another experiment, the sequence was always four responses. In one set of conditions the last response and two of the other three had to be to key A, while the remaining response had to be to key B. The closer the key B response was to the reinforcer, the higher was the rate of responding to key B. Catania attributed the results to the differential delay of reinforcement inherent in his procedures. The closer key B responses were to the reinforcer, the shorter the delay and hence the higher the response rate.

Catania (1971) observed that when the required sequence of responses was changed, the interreinforcer time increased substantially at first but then decreased. The decrease implies that the probability of the specifically required sequence increased. Yet Catania reported that stereotyped sequences did not occur. Perhaps the changes in interreinforcer time are attributable to changed interactions between two independent responses occurring at different rates. They could also be due to modification of the emitted response unit.

Interval Relativity

Further consideration indicates that temporal discrimination and delay of reinforcement actually are not distinguishable in interval schedules. The temporal relations in two types of experimental arrangement are shown in Figure 12 (derived from Jenkins, 1970). The free operant procedure describes the typical fixed-interval or fixed-time schedule in which the prevailing exteroceptive stimuli do not change until the reinforcer appears. Some event (time zero, or T_0) marks the beginning of the interval; often this event is the end of a reinforcer presentation accompanied by a stimulus change such as the illumination of the key and/or houselight. The originating event also could be the end of a blackout period, or any other stimulus that marks the onset of the interval. There is then a continuous period (N-period) in which a reinforcer is not available. The completion of the interval (time completed, or T_c) occurs when the reinforcer appears. Any particular point within the N-period is referred to as N and can be localized either with respect to T_0 (the T_0–N interval) or T_c (the N–T_c interval). Another procedure involves discrete trials. Responding is not free to occur at any time, but is limited to periods marked by distinctive stimuli and separated by intertrial intervals during which responses have no scheduled consequences. In some trials (R-trials) a reinforcer is available; in others (N-trials) it is not. There can be a series of N-trials between successive R-trials (e.g., Dews, 1966a), or, as shown in Figure 12, there can be alternating N- and R-trials (e.g., Dews, 1962; Jenkins, 1970). The location of an N-trial is specified either by the time from the end of the preceding R-trial to the end of the N-trial (the R_0–N interval) or the time from the end of the N-trial to the beginning of the next R-trial (the N–R_c interval). The interreinforcer intervals are T_0–T_c in the free operant procedure and R_0–R_c in the trial procedure.

The T_0–N interval as the controlling factor appears in accounts that emphasize elapsed time as a discriminative stimulus (time from the beginning of the interval); the N–T_c interval is crucial for delay-of-reinforcement explanations (the time between a response and the next reinforcer presentation). It is clear from Figure 12, however, that the T_0–N and N–T_c intervals are not independent, given that the T_0–T_c interval (the total fixed interval) is held constant. Since the two are perfectly negatively correlated, their effects cannot be separated. In addition, two lines of evidence suggest that they must be considered together.

When Dews (1970) plotted relative rate in each

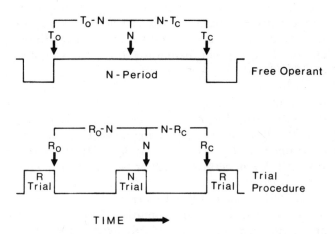

Figure 12. Temporal intervals. The upper segment (free operant) illustrates the typical fixed-interval schedule. T_0 indicates the stimulus change indicating the beginning of the interval. The stimulus continues until T_c, i.e., the presentation of the reinforcer that ends the interval. N is any point during the period between T_0 and T_c. The lower segment (trial procedure) illustrates the condition involving restricted opportunities to respond. R refers to trials in which a reinforcer is available, N to trials in which it is not.

one-fifth interval, curves for fixed intervals of 30 sec, 300 sec, and 3000 sec fell on top of one another. The relative patterns were independent of fixed-interval value. Even though equivalent fifths represented very different absolute time periods from the beginning or to the end of the fixed interval, relative position and patterning was constant.

Jenkins (1970) used a trial procedure to separate, absolute time from the beginning, and time to the end of the interval. The variables manipulated were the time from the end of one R-trial to the end of the N-trial (R_0–N interval) and the time from the end of the N-trial to the beginning of the next R-trial (the N–R_c interval). (Jenkins described the independent variables somewhat differently; he measured time from the beginning of each trial. The present description is used to facilitate the reanalysis of his data.) Table 3 shows eight conditions (columns a and b) and the results (column f).

Table 3 Intervals Studied by Jenkins (1970)

INTERVALS (max. duration in sec)			RELATIVE PROXIMITY		
(a)	(b)	(c)	(d)	(e)	(f)
R_0–N	N–R_c	R_0–R_c Interval	R_0–N/ R_0–R_c	N–R_c/ R_0–R_c	Average Responses on N-trials
54	8	62	.87	.13	6.7
154	8	162	.95	.05	8.6
54	108	162	.33	.67	3.3
154	108	262	.59	.41	3.5
154	8	162	.95	.05	12.9
154	207	361	.43	.57	6.7
54	20	74	.73	.27	6.1
154	20	174	.89	.11	8.6

All intervals are given in terms of their maximum duration in sec.

Neither the absolute R_0–N nor N–R_c intervals independently determined responding in the N-trials, since responding was not closely related to the value of either. But it is important to note that whenever there was a change in either the R_0–N or the N–R_c intervals, there was either a change in the other as well and/or a change in the time from the end of one R-trial to the beginning of the next (the R_0–R_c interval). Column (c) of Table 3 shows the R_0–R_c interval for each condition. Columns (d) and (e) show the R_0–N and N–R_c intervals as proportions of the R_0–R_c intervals, i.e., they describe the relative proximity of an N-trial to the overall interreinforcer period.

Although analyses based on the absolute quantitative data do not show very orderly results, the rank-order correlation between these relative proximity measures and responding on the N-trials was .88, with the sign being either positive or negative depending on whether the R_0–N or the N–R_c interval is used. In these eight conditions of Jenkins's discrete-trial procedure, as in the fixed-interval schedule, responding at any point during the interreinforcer interval was related to the proportion of the total interval that had elapsed (or was remaining) at that point.

Conclusion

The temporal location of a point in an interval can be specified from either the beginning or the end of an interval. Changes in the relative location of the point always mean relative changes in both the time from the beginning of the interval and the time to the end of the interval, and thus these two must be totally confounded. It cannot be asserted, therefore, that either of the periods is responsible for an effect. The important factor is the location of a given point relative to the overall duration of the interval (cf. Jenkins's, 1970, relative proximity principle).

SEQUENCES AND UNITS

The Chaining Hypothesis

Schedules of intermittent reinforcement impose order on the numerous responses that occur between successive reinforcers: the behavior generated has a sequential organization. Historically, it has been common to explain sequences in terms of response chaining. The essence of the chaining hypothesis is that each response provides the stimulus (or part of the stimulus complex) for the next response. These response-produced stimuli have an eliciting or discriminative stimulus function with respect to the next response, and they may have a reinforcing function with respect to preceding responses. Individual learning theories differ about whether the chain is composed of reflexes or of instrumental responses, but the concept of each response acting as a stimulus for the next is common to all.

Platt and Johnson (1971) reviewed data showing that behavior can have stimulus properties. Behavior under mixed FR FR schedules (two fixed-ratio schedules occur in some order, but with no exteroceptive stimulus indicating which one is in effect) shows differential sensitivity to the two ratio requirements. In one type of experiment, Rilling and McDiarmid (1965), Pliskoff and Goldiamond (1966), and others have shown that pigeons can make appropriate choices on the basis of the size of the fixed ratio just completed. In another type of experiment, Platt and Johnson (1971) delivered food to a rat only if the rat's approach to the food tray was preceded by N lever presses. Approaches prior to N lever presses resulted in a time-out and reset the response number requirement. The mean number of responses emitted per tray entry slightly exceeded the number required at all values of N. These data support the hypothesis that organisms can respond differentially to their own behavior.

In all these experiments different consequences were arranged following the emission of different numbers of responses. There is no evidence that responses function as discriminative stimuli in the absence of explicit differential reinforcement. Animals in extinction after fixed-ratio training will emit very long runs of responses before pausing (Ferster & Skinner, 1957, pp. 57–63); this provides no evidence for sensitivity to the number of responses previously required for reinforcer presentation. Data reported by Overmann and Denny (1974) suggest that the animals are controlled by the exteroceptive stimulus changes correlated with completion of the ratio rather than by response number. Control by response number appears to require that there be different schedules correlated with different numbers of responses; it does not arise automatically through the differential reinforcement of response number inherent in simple fixed-ratio schedules.

Chaining has been proposed as being involved in performance under fixed-interval schedules (Ferster & Skinner, 1957; Skinner, 1938), but this hypothesis no longer seems tenable. According to the chaining hypothesis, sequential changes in responding are due to the stimulus properties of preceding responses; consequently, the pattern should not survive interruptions in the flow of responses. Dews (1962, 1965a, 1965b, 1966a, 1966b) interpolated stimuli that disrupted responding at various points during fixed intervals. Although this should break the hypothetical chain, the basic fixed-interval pattern endured: when responding occurred, it was appropriate to the temporal location within the interval regardless of the response rate immediately preceding. Similar results have been obtained by others (Farmer & Schoenfeld, 1966; Ferster & Skinner, 1957, pp. 213 ff.; McKearney, 1970). Chaining, therefore, is not necessary for fixed-interval performance.

The chaining hypothesis has limited value. Keller (1966) objected to it as inherently untestable because it is based on purely inferred stimuli, while Lashley (1951) believed that the speed and precision with which many sequences are executed made it untenable to assume that each response is controlled by feedback from the preceding response. Data reported by Taub and Berman (1968) and Lashley (1917) show that precise sequences occur in organisms deprived of sensory feedback from their responses. If chaining occurs, perhaps it does so only under specialized conditions of differential reinforcement.

Response Units

THE SPECIFICATION OF A UNIT

Units other than the individual response might be affected by reinforcement and play a role in schedule-controlled performance. For example, Morse (1966) suggested the interresponse time as a reinforceable aspect of behavior, and Staddon (1967) proposed that the entire temporal pattern of responding may be a unit. The experimental evaluation of whether a certain form of behavior is a unit requires clarifying the different meanings of response units. (Although responses are emphasized here, a parallel case can be made for stimulus units.) Three different kinds of response unit can be distinguished. These are described here as *formal*, *conditionable*, and *theoretical* units.

One kind of response unit refers to the class of behavior that the experimenter prescribes as prerequisite for a reinforcer presentation; this is simply the operational definition of the measured response. This is the *formal response unit*. The formal unit is always unambiguous, but it need not be experimentally interesting or useful. To be so, a formal unit must obey a plasticity principle: its probability of occurrence should be affected by its consequences. Some formal units display this plasticity, whereas others do not. The term *operant* has been used to describe modifiable units; here they will be referred to as *conditionable response units*. Conditionable units, like formal ones, are unambiguous: if some behavior is required for reinforcer presentation and it increases in probability, it is a conditionable response unit.

The term *response unit* may also be used to refer to something inferred rather than observed directly. A response, a stimulus-response relation, or some cognitive activity, can be postulated to underlie observed performance. Inferred units are being used when it is asserted that organisms learn turning responses, or to approach certain locations in a maze, or interresponse times, or entire sequences of behavior. These inferred units will be referred to as *theoretical response units*.

The interresponse time illustrates the distinction between formal, conditionable, and theoretical units. If the interresponse time is specified as the requirement for the delivery of a reinforcing stimulus, it is the formal unit. If it should be altered by the imposition of these consequences, it is a conditionable unit. It is a theoretical unit when it is used to explain performance under a schedule in which some other behavior is specified as the formal unit. For example, in a fixed-ratio schedule the formal unit is the sequence of required responses. However, if the behavior that emerges is then explained as the outcome of differential reinforcement of short interresponse times, then the interresponse time is a theoretical unit. In other words, a theoretical unit is one that is hypothesized to underlie observed behavior.

Evaluating the plausibility of a particular theoretical unit requires a strategy analogous to that used to evaluate indirect variables: the hypothesized unit must be studied directly. This means that the theoretical unit must be specified as a formal unit. If it then proves to be conditionable, and if it is affected as it is hypothesized to be when it is used to explain a given performance, the theoretical construct gains plausibility.

Interresponse Time

An interresponse time (IRT) was initially conceptualized as a stimulus. Skinner (1938, pp. 247–284) described time since the preceding response as a discriminative stimulus controlling the emission of the next response, and Anger (1956) treated the interresponse time in the same way. Reynolds (1966) demonstrated that an IRT could indeed function as a discriminative stimulus by showing that if responding in the second component of a chained schedule was followed by food only if the IRT in the first component exceeded 18 seconds, response rate in the second component varied as a function of the preceding IRT. Thus the IRT as an antecedent event produced differential responding, i.e., it exerted stimulus control over responding.

Morse (1966) treated the IRT as a shaped and reinforced property of behavior rather than as an antecedent stimulus for a response. In the typical schedule of reinforcement in which IRTs are postulated as controlling behavior, the IRT is a property of emitted behavior and is not manipulated as a stimulus. Instead, stimulus properties are inferred from responding. If the IRT is treated as a differentiated response unit, unobservable stimuli need not be postulated as controlling observable performance. Given the one-to-one correspondence between response and inferred stimulus properties, however, the two treatments appear to be equivalent.

IRTs as Theoretical Units

Ferster and Skinner (1957) demonstrated that IRT reinforcement could explain the response rate differences in interval and ratio schedules. If responses tend to occur in bursts (Skinner's, 1938, fourth-order deviation from a steady rate), under ratio schedules it is likely that the response requirement will be met during a burst. Therefore, the IRT correlated with reinforcer presentation is likely to be in the short range of those emitted. Ratio schedules do in fact generate homogeneous sequences of short IRTs and those are the ones emitted at the moment of reinforcement (Gott & Weiss, 1972; Weiss & Gott, 1972). In interval schedules, however, it is more likely that the reinforcer will follow a period of pausing (more time elapses during a pause, hence making it more likely that the reinforcer will become available). Therefore, longer IRTs will be preferentially correlated with the reinforcing stimulus. Morse (1966) showed formally that more short IRTs will be reinforced on ratio than on interval schedules, and Dews (1969) confirmed that the terminal IRT in fixed-interval schedules is likely to be longer than the ones immediately preceding. Morse also developed a model for explaining patterning as the consequences of the relation between IRTs and reinforcement.

The selective reinforcement of IRTs accounts for what are otherwise puzzling data. Consider response rate under tandem FI FR schedules. Rate is higher than on a simple fixed-interval schedule (Ferster & Skinner, 1957). The addition of a fixed ratio at the end of the fixed interval makes it more likely that the reinforcer will follow a short IRT, and thereby preferentially reinforces short IRTs. If the emitted IRT distribution changes in the direction of the reinforced IRT distribution, it is to be expected that rate should increase with the tandem schedule.

Some data from t- and τ-schedules also fit an IRT analysis. In many of these schedules a reinforcer is available for a single response occurring at some point in time. Restricting the duration of the time period has large effects on response rate: rate increases as availability decreases. Morse (1966) has suggested that the period of reinforcer availability determines which IRTs are preferentially reinforced. The shorter the availability period, the more the schedule favors the reinforcement of short IRTs and the higher the consequent response rate.

The IRT as a Conditionable Response Unit

The IRT as a theoretical unit has the potential to explain major aspects of schedule-controlled performance. What is necessary, then, is to examine IRTs as formal response units and see if they are conditionable.

Tests of IRTs as conditionable responses derive from IRT > t and IRT < t schedules, which require that an IRT either exceed or be less than a certain value for a reinforcer to occur. Several experiments (e.g., Malott & Cumming, 1964; Richardson & Loughead, 1974; Staddon, 1965) have shown that if an IRT must exceed some value, the distribution of emitted IRTs changes in the appropriate direction. Similar results occur when a terminal IRT requirement is added to a variable-interval schedule, i.e., when the schedule is a paced VI or a tandem VI IRT > t (Anger, 1956; Shimp, 1967). Since the probability of the specific IRT that is required increases (although at long IRT requirements very few of the emitted IRTs may be long enough to produce the reinforcer), the IRT is a conditionable response unit.

Quantitative analyses of the effects of temporal differentiation schedules have shown similar results whether the unit involved was the IRT or some aspect of performance other than the interresponse time (Catania, 1970; DeCasper & Zeiler, 1974). Performance can be described by the power function $T = kt^n$, where T is the emitted duration, t is the required duration, and k and n are constants fit to the data. A small range of values of k and n are necessary to describe performance in most of these experiments. In fact, DeCasper and Zeiler have suggested that the effects of temporal differentiation schedules may be independent of particular response units and durations.

A problem in interpreting rate changes under IRT > t and other temporal differentiation schedules is that as the time parameter increases, the number of responses per reinforcer and average interreinforcer time both increase as well. If response rate is a function of reinforcer density, IRTs would change as well since they are the components of rate. Actually, however, this is not the major reason for the effects. Ferster and Skinner (1957, p. 460) found that adding an IRT > t requirement to a variable-interval schedule reduced rate without markedly affecting the average interreinforcer time. Richardson (1973) has also shown that interreinforcer time is not responsible for the IRT distributions in simple IRT > t schedules. Animals were given exactly the same temporal distributions of reinforcer presentations that they obtained under IRT > t, but without the IRT requirement (a variable-interval schedule yoked to the IRT > t schedule). The response rates and distributions of IRTs obtained under the IRT > t and yoked VI schedules differed greatly, showing that the specific differential reinforcement of IRTs was an important factor in IRT > t performance.

Alleman and Platt (1973) used what they termed a percentile reinforcement schedule involving IRT reinforcement. Platt (1973) has described such arrangements as shaping schedules: the prescribed behavior at any moment shifts with the nature of the behavior being emitted. In Alleman and Platt's experiments the critical aspects of performance were the emitted IRTs. Only IRTs more extreme than a certain proportion of the recently preceding IRTs were reinforced. Under some conditions, the requirement involved IRTs shorter than those preceding; under others, it involved longer IRTs. For example, the IRT might have to be shorter than 95% of the previous IRTs. The emitted IRT distribution then became progressively peaked at the lower end. A parametric study showed that when the IRTs had to be among the least frequent 5 or 10% the distribution shifted toward longer or shorter IRTs depending on which was required. These effects occurred even if the same number of responses per reinforcer were maintained over the range of percentile requirements. By selectively reinforcing extreme IRTs, the IRT distributions changed in the appropriate direction. Blough (1966) showed the complementary effect: variable IRTs were produced by always reinforcing the least frequent ones without regard to direction.

The data show, therefore, that an IRT is a conditionable response. It is reinforceable directly when it is specified as the formal response, and the changes in behavior are not attributable to changed reinforcer density.

IRTs and Reinforced IRTs

What do these data imply about behavior under schedules not specifying the value of terminal IRTs directly? Anger (1956) suggested that IRT reinforcement operates to control performance with such schedules. He found that under variable-interval schedules the frequency distribution of IRTs correlated closely with the frequency distribution of reinforced IRTs. Those IRTs that were most often correlated with the reinforcing stimulus occurred more frequently; the shapes of the IRT distributions corresponded with the shapes of the distribution of reinforcers per hour per IRT.

Later analyses have shown that this relation is probably not significant. Blough and Blough (1968) were the first to point out that the dependency of the reinforcer distribution on the IRT distribution is mathematically forced, because "on a VI schedule, the probability of reinforcement at a given IRT bin must increase with the number of responses in that bin" (pp. 26–27). Reynolds and McLeod (1970) showed that a correlation between emitted and reinforced IRTs holds regardless of the distribution of emitted IRTs.

Blough and Blough examined whether the distribution of reinforcers among various IRTs determined the IRTs emitted subsequently. If this were the case, it might be expected that the IRT distribution would shift in the direction of those IRTs that earlier had received the most reinforcers per hour. There was no indication that IRT distributions changed in this manner.

Anger (personal communication) suggests that IRT reinforcement occurs in the context of the increase in the frequency of a response due to reinforcement, the decrease due to nonreinforced responses, recovery of responses after a period of nonreinforcement, and perhaps a rate-enhancing effect of extinction as well. These factors interact to produce oscillations in emitted IRTs. Thus IRTs are the outcome of at least four influences rather than being simply due to frequency of reinforcement.

Since 1968 Shimp and his colleagues have been developing a systematic quantitative account of IRT reinforcement. The various experiments have involved a paced VI schedule (Anger, 1956; Ferster & Skinner, 1957), in which the reinforcer occurs following the first appropriate IRT emitted when a VI schedule has made the reinforcer available. Shimp's experiments have involved at least two IRT bands, each defined by a lower and upper bound. The procedure involves distinctive stimuli presented only during IRT bands that are eligible for reinforcement. Thus reinforcement occurs only during the stimulus, and the stimulus is correlated with the IRT requirements. The purpose of introducing stimuli in this way is to gain precise control over responding, but it seems possible that discriminative stimulus control may influence the performance in other ways as well. In any event, the dependent measure is the percentage of IRTs, P, falling in one of the bands. Considering the shorter class, P equals the number of IRTs in the short class divided by the number of IRTs in both classes.

In 1968 Shimp applied different relative frequencies or magnitudes of reinforcer presentation to 1.5–2.5-sec and 3.5–4.5-sec IRTs. The value of P was approximately linearly related to either relative frequency or magnitude of reinforcement, but it did not match either. Shimp (1969) found that with equal reinforcement frequency for both IRT classes P matched the *relative reciprocal* (term used by Hawkes & Shimp, 1974, here called RR) of the classes. The RR was computed by considering the lower bound of the short class ($t_{1,1}$) and the upper bound of that class ($t_{1,2}$) together with lower ($t_{2,1}$) and upper ($t_{2,2}$) bounds of the longer class. The relative reciprocal of the short class is:

$$\text{RR} = \frac{1/t_{1,1}/ + 1/t_{1,2}/}{1/t_{1,1}/ + 1/t_{1,2}/ + 1/t_{2,1}/ + 1/t_{2,2}/}$$

The values of RR and P matched when both IRT classes were reinforced equally. However, matching of RR and P seems only part of a general function which varies according to the absolute values of the short class of IRTs. Matching occurs when $t_{1,1}$ is in the 1–4-sec range, and departures occur at other values (Hawkes & Shimp, 1974).

Hawkes and Shimp review the series of experiments in some detail. What emerges is the possibility of a general function relating IRT reinforcement to behavior, and that the function interacts systematically with other variables to determine response rate. As the work has expanded to deal with more than two IRT classes, it has come increasingly into contact with what perhaps occurs under schedules of reinforcement not involving explicit IRT requirements (Shimp, 1973). This way of considering IRT reinforcement might show correspondences between what happens when IRTs are specifically required and when they are adventitiously correlated with the reinforcing stimulus on interval and ratio schedules.

Sequences as Response Units

Sequences as Theoretical Response Units

Skinner (1938) speculated that, in fixed-ratio performance, the effective response unit might involve all of the behavior extending between successive reinforcer presentation. Later, Mowrer and Jones (1945) reasoned that if ratios did in fact generate units composed of all of the responses, resistance to extinction should be a function of the number of units and a constant number of ratios would occur in extinction. Their failure, as well as Boren's (1961) and Weissman and Crossman's (1966), to obtain a perfect correspondence between the hypothesized units and number of responses in extinction seemed to oppose a response unit hypothesis. This failure could be due to the properties of extinction itself. Extinction is not a passive condition, but instead exerts effects of its own; these often include an initial intensification of responding prior to the well-known decrement (cf. Amsel, 1967; Morse, 1966). Also, extinction involves a change in stimulus presentations, and the way stimuli are presented in extinction can affect the number of responses emitted (Overmann & Denny, 1974). Despite these complications, predictions of the response unit hypothesis of resistance to extinction, although not completely accurate, were not totally out of line. In the Mowrer and Jones study, for example, the number of responses in extinction was linearly related to the number of responses previously required.

Data using a different schedule support the response unit analysis. Day and Platt 1972) used a fixed–constant number (FCN) schedule: rats had to emit a certain number of responses, but food was presented only if they approached the food tray after they had made those responses. Early approaches reset the response requirement. The schedules used were FCN 1, FCN 8, and FCN 32. In terms of the number of responses emitted in extinction, these data replicated those of Mowrer and Jones. However, it had been pointed out by Denny, Wells, and Maatsch (1957) that the number of responses in the ratio may not be the appropriate measure of the response unit. Instead, it would be the sequence of responses preceding each tray approach, and the important dependent variable in terms of resistance to extinction would be the number of approaches. Day and Platt found that in extinction the groups did not differ in the number of such approaches, and they concluded that the response unit hypothesis was tenable.

The stable sequences observed in successive components of second-order schedules involving fixed-ratio components fit a unitary response interpretation. In this research, a fixed-ratio sequence was treated as a single response unit, and it was reinforced according to some schedule. Findley (1962) used fixed-ratio components in a variety of complex schedules involving sequences of the same or of different responses and found that typical ratio patterns appeared in each component. Kelleher (1966) demonstrated that the ratio pattern was maintained when the first FR 20 completed after 10 min—an FI 10-min (FR 20) second-order schedule—resulted in food presentation. Lee and Gollub (1971) found the same when ratio performance was followed by a reinforcer on a fixed-ratio schedule, and Kelleher, Fry, and Cook (1964) also observed characteristic ratio performance when the fixed ratio was treated as a single response and was reinforced according to a DRL schedule. Marr (1971) has confirmed this finding with sequence schedules in which distinctive stimuli were correlated with each successive fixed-ratio component and the ratio performance produced the reinforcer according to either a fixed-interval or a fixed-ratio schedule. The component sequences resembled single responses in other ways. For example, Kelleher (1966) showed that with the FI 10-min (FR 20) second-order schedule the time taken to emit successive ratios shortened as the interval progressed. This can be compared with the shortening of successive interresponse times, when single responses are reinforced according to fixed-interval schedules. Shull, Guilkey, and Witty (1972) also found substantial similarity in the emission of successive fixed ratios and successive individual responses under fixed-interval schedules.

Sequences as Conditionable Response Units

Are sequences reinforceable units—that is, is their probability of occurrence a function of their consequences? To determine that and thereby to determine the plausibility of sequences as theoretical response units, it is necessary to impose the sequence as a formal unit and to observe whether it is conditionable. It is well to be cautious in concluding that a sequence is actually *required* by a schedule. For example, a ratio schedule imposes a sequence of n responses as a formal requirement, and it demonstrates that such a sequence is conditionable (reinforceable). It does not show that the particular pattern according to which ratios are emitted is conditionable, because the schedule does not require any particular pattern. Interval schedules specify nothing at all about sequences, since they require only a single response. Many responses may occur in highly organized form, but interval schedules do not demonstrate that either total interval performance or any portion of it other than the single response is a conditionable response unit.

Findley's (1962) and Kelleher, Fry, and Cook's (1964) procedures demonstrate the necessary conditions for observing that an aspect of schedule performance is conditionable. In their experiments, a reinforcer was presented at the completion of a fixed ratio only if the postreinforcement pause exceeded a minimum duration. They found that the pause durations changed in accordance with the requirements, so that pause behaved as a conditionable unit. These findings justify interpretation of the pause as a response unit on ordinary fixed-ratio schedules.

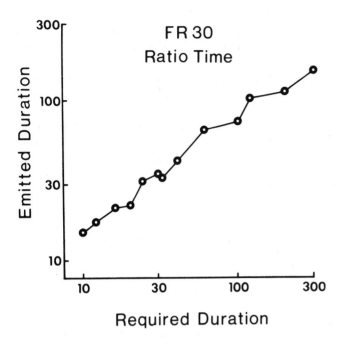

Fig. 13. Mean ratio time in seconds (initial pause time plus time spent responding) emitted by a pigeon as a function of the ratio time required for food presentation under an FR 30 schedule. (From DeCasper & Zeiler, 1974; Zeiler, 1970, 1972.)

This differential reinforcement procedure has been extended to other aspects of fixed-ratio performance. Figure 13 shows the effects of requiring that the duration of an entire ratio—i.e., the time from the first opportunity to respond until the completion of the ratio—must exceed some particular value. Other experiments investigated the effects of requiring that the duration be shorter than a specified value (Zeiler, 1970, 1972b). In all of the experiments, emitted durations were related to required durations by the same power function applicable to other temporal differentiation procedures (see page 224) (DeCasper & Zeiler, 1974). The duration of an entire ratio, therefore, is a reinforceable aspect of behavior. Since the total time taken to execute a ratio—the initial pause time plus the time spent responding—belongs not to any single response, but instead describes a property of the entire sequence, the experiments demonstrated that the ratio sequence can be shown to have unitary properties. More precisely, they showed that duration is a reinforceable aspect of the sequence. In one experiment (Zeiler, 1972b) the most orderly aspect of behavior was shown to be the overall duration of the ratios: the initial pause times and the rate of responding after the pause did not show equally predictable effects. The total sequence was more orderly than were either of the two major components.

TRANSITION STATES AND STEADY STATES

Since initial pause duration and overall duration of fixed-ratio sequences are conditionable, they could be reinforced under ordinary fixed-ratio schedules. If so, they could play a role in producing the stereotypy in pausing and interreinforcer time often observed in fixed-ratio performance. They cannot, however, be important in the development of steady-state behavior. If they were, the pause and ratio durations initially correlated with the reinforcer should tend to predominate. This does not usually occur. Consider a pigeon changed from one fixed-ratio schedule to a larger one. Immediately following the transition the pause is short and the ratio duration is also short. Eventually both durations lengthen despite these early duration-reinforcer relations. Apparently, other variables operate to establish the pause and ratio durations, and then they may come to operate as indirect determinants of performance once they have become more or less stable.

Figure 14 shows the frequency distributions of the duration of the pauses prior to the first response in the first 25 sessions of FR 30 after FR 1 training. Over

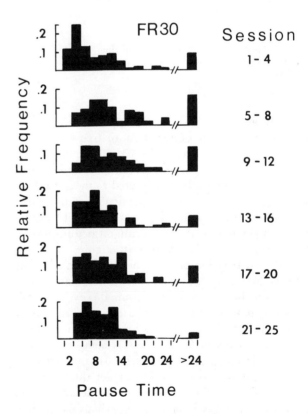

Fig. 14. Probability distribution of initial pause lengths (in seconds) in the first 25 sessions of an FR 30 schedule after an FR 1 history with pigeons. Each session consisted of 30 ratios.

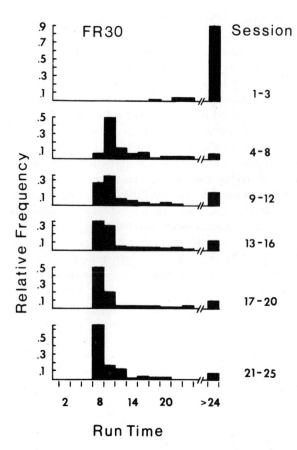

Fig. 15. Probability distribution of run-time lengths (seconds from the first to the last response) in the same sessions as in Figure 14.

the course of these sessions, it appeared that those pause durations that occurred more frequently (i.e., those that were most often followed 30 responses later by the reinforcing stimulus) became still more predominant. This could be interpreted as indicating the differential reinforcement of particular pause durations and the consequent increase in probability. Similar data were obtained for overall ratio duration. A very different effect is revealed in Figure 15, which shows the distribution of run times (the time from the 1st to the 30th response) for the same 25 sessions. The shorter run times came to predominate, even though they were not the times correlated with reinforcer presentation in the earlier sessions. It is not likely, therefore, that a specific run time is being reinforced in the development of simple fixed-ratio performance.

In conclusion, it is not clear whether the reinforcement of unitary properties operates to determine behavior under fixed-ratio schedules. Perhaps pause time and ratio duration are directly reinforced and run time is not. Or perhaps none of these aspects of performance is reinforced directly but develop their characteristics for other reasons. It may be, as Dews (1970) suggested, that "when a subject is exposed repeatedly to a consistent schedule, patterns of responding may become sufficiently consistent to enable particular aspects of the patterns themselves to be related reliably to the schedule. The very reliability of the relation may lead to the further strengthening of those particular aspects of the pattern" (p. 59). Perhaps unitary aspects of fixed-ratio performance do not play a role in establishing the final behavior, but do operate to maintain steady-state performance once it develops.

SUMMARY AND CONCLUDING REMARKS

The Controlling Variables

The preceding account of reinforcement schedules differs from those of Ferster and Skinner (1957) and Morse (1966) only in the variables that are given major emphasis. The general approach is basically the same: the assumption is that schedule-controlled behavior is multiply determined and that each hypothesized controlling variable must be studied directly to determine if it operates as expected.

Response rate and patterning appear to be controlled by different variables. This view differs somewhat from Ferster and Skinner's and Morse's in that they tended to deal with both characteristics simultaneously. A major departure is the present emphasis on factors other than the quantitative properties of the response occurring the moment of reinforcer presentation.

There are two types of variables responsible for performance, the *direct variables* specified by the schedule and the *indirect variables* that derive from performance. The variables have two types of effect, *stereotypic* and *dynamic*, differentiated by whether they tend to maintain the same behavior or to change performance. With respect to *response rate*, one significant factor is the particular *response dependency* that guarantees close temporal contiguity between a particular response class and the reinforcing stimulus. This variable operates directly under response-dependent schedules and indirectly under response-independent schedules, and it has the effect of maintaining or increasing the probability of the response that precedes the reinforcer. This is the most molecular aspect of the present approach. Other hypothesized variables encompass larger time periods and larger groups of responses. The *number of responses per reinforcer* and *interreinforcer time* were considered to be major factors. Also, the *availability of the reinforcer when responding weakens* may determine whether a given schedule will maintain many responses per reinforcer presentation. Thus responding under a given schedule reflects the conjunction of the response dependency, number of responses per reinforcer, interreinforcer time, and the regenerating power of the schedule. This account was able to deal with interval and ratio schedules and some complex schedules, but other complex schedules may involve additional variables.

Patterning was explained by a single variable, *the placement of the reinforcer in time*. In interval schedules the tendency to respond at any instant is determined by the location time relative to the overall interval duration.

Schedules that specify certain events as prerequisite for reinforcer presentation (e.g., a certain interresponse time or a certain behavioral sequence) reveal that such events can exert control over responding. Their role in the absence of such specification is unclear.

Some Reflections on Methodology

The rationale for the methodology advocated here is that the effects of hypothesized variables must be assessed by studying those variables directly. This approach has been followed consistently. Thus when number of responses per reinforcer was proposed as a source of control in fixed-interval performance, its mode of operation was assessed by reference to fixed-ratio schedules, which control it directly. The same procedure was followed with every hypothesized controlling variable. The approach has its limitations and potential pitfalls. Inherent in it is the idea that variables have relatively simple effects and that complicated interactions do not occur. Consider, for example, the assessment of number of responses per reinforcer by the use of ratio schedules. As the number (ratio size) is manipulated, interreinforcer time changes as well. Interreinforcer time is analyzed directly in interval schedules, but here responses per reinforcer will vary. If, in fact, the two variables interact in some complicated way, the function of either cannot be easily ascertained. Other as yet unknown experimental designs will be necessary to evaluate such interactions.

Another approach to the analysis of controlling variables is subtractive. A variable is prevented from operating (cf. Dews's work on interrupting the hypothesized response chain in fixed-interval schedules), and if the behavior is not disrupted, it is concluded that the variable is not important. This approach also requires caution. If a performance is actually overdetermined—i.e., if the behavior under a given schedule arises because several variables operate independently to produce the same performance—the elimination of one variable may not have a noticeable effect. Yet the variable may actually play a role. There are enough precedents (e.g., the sensory basis of maze learning, recovery of function in the brain) to warrant consideration of this possibility.

Schedules As Fundamental

Morse and Kelleher (1970) have maintained that schedules are fundamental determinants of behavior, because the particular events scheduled may be less important than is the schedule itself. In this sense, it is the schedule in relation to ongoing behavior that is fundamental in determining subsequent performance. There is another sense in which schedules are fundamental. If each schedule represents a particular conjunction of variables, the only way of arranging that conjunction is by establishing that schedule. Fixed-interval schedules establish (1) a response-reinforcer dependency involving a single response; (2) a nearly fixed interreinforcer time; (3) an unlimited range of possible number of responses per reinforcer in successive intervals; (4) a reinforcer following a single response when responding is not well maintained; (5) presentation of the reinforcer at a fixed time since the beginning of the interval. Only the fixed-interval schedule specifies that all of these conditions will occur. Each variable may be analyzed, and fixed-interval performance may be understood as the outcome of these component events, but the schedule is fundamental in that it alone can arrange these precise interactions. To the extent that the precise interaction of multiple variables is responsible for a distinctive performance, each schedule is a fundamental arrangement.

The problems faced by the experimenter interested in understanding schedule performance are difficult because of the complexities of the relationships. However, the fundamental role of schedules in psychology demands the attempt. It is impossible to study behavior either in or outside the laboratory without encountering a schedule of reinforcement: whenever behavior is maintained by a reinforcing stimulus, some schedule is in effect and is exerting its characteristic influences. Only when there is a clear understanding of how schedules operate will it be possible to understand the effects of reinforcing stimuli on behavior.

REFERENCES

Alleman, H. D., & Platt, J. R. Differential reinforcement of interresponse times with controlled probability of reinforcement per response. *Learning and Motivation*, 1973, *4*, 40–73.

Amsel, A. Partial reinforcement effects on vigor and persistence. In K. W. Spence & J. T. Spence (Eds.), *The psychology of learning and motivation* (Vol. 1). New York: Academic Press, 1967.

Anger, D. The dependence of interresponse times upon the relative reinforcement of different interresponse times. *Journal of Experimental Psychology*, 1956, *52*, 145–161.

Appel, J. B., & Hiss, R. H. The discrimination of contingent from noncontingent reinforcement. *Journal of Comparative and Physiological Psychology*, 1962, *55*, 37–39.

Azzi, R., Fix, D. S. R., Keller, F. S., & Rocha e Silva, M. I. Exteroceptive control of response under delayed reinforcement. *Journal of the Experimental Analysis of Behavior*, 1964, *7*, 159–162.

Berryman, R., & Nevin, J. A. Interlocking schedules of reinforcement. *Journal of the Experimental Analysis of Behavior*, 1962, *5*, 213–223.

Blough, D. S. Interresponse time as a function of continuous variables: A new method and some data. *Journal of the Experimental Analysis of Behavior*, 1963, *6*, 237–246.

Blough, D. S. The reinforcement of least-frequent interresponse times. *Journal of the Experimental Analysis of Behavior*, 1966, *9*, 581–591.

Blough, P. M., & Blough, D. S. The distribution of interresponse times in the pigeon during variable-interval reinforcement. *Journal of the Experimental Analysis of Behavior*, 1968, *11*, 23–27.

Boren, J. J. Resistance to extinction as a function of the fixed ratio. *Journal of Experimental Psychology*, 1961, *61*, 304–308.

Catania, A. C. Reinforcement schedules and psychophysical judgments: A study of some temporal properties of behavior. In W. N. Schoenfeld (Ed.), *The theory of reinforcement schedules*. Englewood Cliffs, N. J.: Prentice-Hall, Inc., 1970.

Catania, A. C. Reinforcement schedules: The role of responses preceding the one that produces the reinforcer. *Journal of the Experimental Analysis of Behavior*, 1971, *15*, 271–287.

Catania, A. C., & Reynolds, G. S. A quantitative analysis of the responding maintained by interval schedules of reinforcement. *Journal of the Experimental Analysis of Behavior*, 1968, *11*, 327–383.

Crossman, E. K., Heaps, R. S., Nunes, D. L., & Alferink, L. A. The effects of number of responses on pause length with temporal variables controlled. *Journal of the Experimental Analysis of Behavior*, 1974, *22*, in press.

Cumming, W. W., & Schoenfeld, W. N. Behavior under extended exposure to a high-value fixed interval reinforcement schedule. *Journal of the Experimental Analysis of Behavior*, 1958, *1*, 245–263.

Day, R. B., & Platt, J. R. Several tests of the response-unit hypothesis of extinction. Paper read at the meeting of the Psychonomic Society, 1972.

DeCasper, A. J., & Zeiler, M. D. Time limits for completing fixed ratios, III: Stimulus variables. *Journal of the Experimental Analysis of Behavior*, 1974, *22*, 285–300.

Denny, M. R., Wells, R. H., & Maatsch, J. L. Resistance to extinction as a function of the discrimination habit established during fixed-ratio reinforcement. *Journal of Experimental Psychology*, 1957, *6*, 451–456.

Dews, P. B. Free-operant behavior under conditions of delayed reinforcement, 1: CRF-type schedules. *Journal of the Experimental Analysis of Behavior*, 1960, *3*, 221–234.

Dews, P. B. The effect of multiple S^Δ periods on responding on a fixed-interval schedule. *Journal of the Experimental Analysis of Behavior*, 1962, *6*, 369–374.

Dews, P. B. Behavioral effects of drugs. In S. M. Farber & R. H. L. Wilson (Eds.), *Conflict and creativity*. New York: McGraw-Hill, 1963.

Dews, P. B. The effect of multiple S^Δ periods on responding on a fixed-interval schedule, II: In a primate. *Journal of the Experimental Analysis of Behavior*, 1965, *8*, 53–54. (a)

Dews, P. B. The effect of multiple S^Δ periods on responding on a fixed-interval schedule, III: Effects of changes in pattern of interruptions, parameters, and stimuli. *Journal of the Experimental Analysis of Behavior*, 1965, *8*, 427–435. (b)

Dews, P. B. The effect of multiple S^Δ periods on responding on a fixed-interval schedule, IV: Effect of continuous S^Δ with only short S^D probes. *Journal of the Experimental Analysis of Behavior*, 1966, *9*, 147–151. (a)

Dews, P. B. The effect of multiple S^Δ periods on responding on a fixed-interval schedule, V: Effects of periods of complete darkness and of occasional omissions of food presentations. *Journal of the Experimental Analysis of Behavior*, 1966, *9*, 573–578. (b)

Dews, P. B. Studies on responding under fixed-interval schedules of reinforcement: The effects on the pattern of responding of changes in requirements at reinforcement. *Journal of the Experimental Analysis of Behavior*, 1969, *12*, 191–199.

Dews, P. B. The theory of fixed-interval responding. In W. N. Schoenfeld (Ed.), *The theory of reinforcement schedules*. Englewood Cliffs, N.J.: Prentice-Hall, Inc., 1970.

Farmer, J., & Schoenfeld, W. N. Varying temporal placement of an added stimulus in a fixed-interval schedule. *Journal of the Experimental Analysis of Behavior*, 1966, *9*, 369–375.

Felton, M., & Lyon, D. O. The post-reinforcement pause. *Journal of the Experimental Analysis of Behavior*, 1966, *9*, 131–134.

Ferster, C. B. Sustained behavior under delayed reinforcement. *Journal of Experimental Psychology*, 1953, *45*, 218–224.

Ferster, C. B., & Hammer, C. Variables determining the effects of delay in reinforcement. *Journal of the Experimental Analysis of Behavior*, 1965, *8*, 243–254.

Ferster, C. B., & Perrott, M. C. *Behavior principles*. Englewood Cliffs, N.J.: Prentice-Hall, Inc., 1968.

Ferster, C. B., & Skinner, B. F. *Schedules of reinforcement*. Englewood Cliffs, N.J.: Prentice-Hall, Inc., 1957.

Findley, J. D. An experimental outline for building and exploring multioperant behavior repertoires. *Journal of the Experimental Analysis of Behavior*, 1962, *5*, 113–116.

Gott, C. T., & Weiss, B. The development of fixed-ratio

performance under the influence of ribonucleic acid. *Journal of the Experimental Analysis of Behavior*, 1972, *18*, 481–497.

Hamilton, E. L. The effect of delayed incentive on the hunger drive in the white rat. *Genetic Psychology Monographs*, 1929, *5*, 131–207.

Harvey, J. A. *Behavior analysis of drug action*. Glenview, Ill.: Scott, Foresman, 1971.

Hawkes, L., & Shimp, C. P. Choice between response rates. *Journal of the Experimental Analysis of Behavior*, 1974, *21*, 109–115.

Herrnstein, R. J. Superstition: A corollary of the principles of operant conditioning. In W. K. Honig (Ed.), *Operant behavior: Areas of research and application*. Englewood Cliffs, N.J.: Prentice-Hall, Inc., 1966.

Herrnstein, R. J., & Morse, W. H. Some effects of response-independent positive reinforcement on maintained operant behavior. *Journal of Comparative and Physiological Psychology*, 1957, *50*, 461–467.

Herrnstein, R. J., & Morse, W. H. A conjunctive schedule of reinforcement. *Journal of the Experimental Analysis of Behavior*, 1958, *1*, 15–24.

Hull, C. L. The goal gradient hypothesis and maze learning. *Psychological Review*, 1932, *39*, 25–43.

Hull, C. L. *A behavior system*. New Haven: Yale University Press, 1952.

Jenkins, H. M. Sequential organization in schedules of reinforcement. In W. N. Schoenfeld (Ed.), *The theory of reinforcement schedules*. Englewood Cliffs, N.J.: Prentice-Hall, Inc., 1970.

Kelleher, R. T. Chaining and conditioned reinforcement. In W. K. Honig (Ed.), *Operant behavior: areas of research and application*. Englewood Cliffs, N.J.: Prentice-Hall, Inc., 1966.

Kelleher, R. T., Fry, W., & Cook, L. Adjusting fixed-ratio schedules in the squirrel monkey. *Journal of the Experimental Analysis of Behavior*, 1964, *7*, 69–77.

Kelleher, R. T., & Morse, W. H. Determinants of the specificity of behavioral effects of drugs. *Ergebnisse der Physiologie*, 1968, *60*, 1–56.

Killeen, P. Reinforcement frequency and contingency as factors in fixed-ratio behavior. *Journal of the Experimental Analysis of Behavior*, 1969, *12*, 391–395.

Lashley, K. S. The accuracy of movement in the absence of excitation from the moving organ. *American Journal of Physiology*, 1917, *43*, 169–194.

Lashley, K. S. The problem of serial order in behavior. In L. A. Jeffress (Ed.), *Cerebral mechanisms in behavior*. New York: Wiley, 1951.

Lee, J. K., & Gollub, L. R. Second-order schedules with fixed-ratio components: Variation of component size. *Journal of the Experimental Analysis of Behavior*, 1971, *15*, 303–310.

Malott, R. W., & Cumming, W. W. Schedules of interresponse time reinforcement. *Psychological Record*, 1964, *14*, 211–252.

Marr, M. J. Sequence schedules of reinforcement. *Journal of the Experimental Analysis of Behavior*, 1971, *15*, 41–48.

McKearney, J. W. Rate-dependent effects of drugs: Modification by discriminative stimuli of the effects of amobarbitol on schedule-controlled behavior. *Journal of Experimental Analysis of Behavior*, 1970, *14*, 167–175.

Morgan, M. J. Fixed interval schedules and delay of reinforcement. *Quarterly Journal of Experimental Psychology*, 1970, *22*, 663–673.

Morse, W. H. Intermittent reinforcement. In W. K. Honig (Ed.), *Operant behavior: Areas of research and application*. Englewood Cliffs, N.J.: Prentice-Hall, Inc., 1966.

Morse, W. H., & Kelleher, R. T. Schedules as fundamental determinants of behavior. In W. N. Schoenfeld (Ed.), *The theory of reinforcement schedules*. Englewood Cliffs, N.J.: Prentice-Hall, Inc., 1970.

Morse, W. H., & Skinner, B. F. A second type of "superstition" in the pigeon. *American Journal of Psychology*, 1957, *70*, 308–311.

Mowrer, O. H., & Jones, H. Habit strength as a function of the pattern of reinforcement. *Journal of Experimental Psychology*, 1945, *35*, 293–311.

Neuringer, A. J. Superstitious key pecking after three peck-produced reinforcements. *Journal of the Experimental Analysis of Behavior*, 1970, *13* 127–134.

Neuringer, A. J., & Schneider, B. A. Separating the effects of interreinforcement time and number of interreinforcement responses. *Journal of the Experimental Analysis of Behavior*, 1968, *11*, 661–667.

Overmann, S. R., & Denny, M. R. The free-operant partial reinforcement effect: A discrimination analysis. *Learning and Motivation*, 1974, *5*, 248–257.

Pierce, C. H., Hanford, P. W., & Zimmerman, J. Effects of different delay of reinforcement procedures on variable-interval responding. *Journal of the Experimental Analysis of Behavior*, 1972, *18*, 141–146.

Platt, J. R. Percentile reinforcement: Paradigms for experimental analysis of response shaping. In G. H. Bower (Ed.), *Psychology of learning and motivation: Advances in research and theory* (Vol. 7). New York: Academic Press, 1973.

Platt, J. R., & Johnson, D. M. Localization of position within a homogeneous behavior chain: Effects of error contingencies. *Learning and Motivation*, 1971, *2*, 386–414.

Pliskoff, S. S., & Goldiamond, I. Some discriminative properties of fixed ratio performance in the pigeon. *Journal of the Experimental Analysis of Behavior*. 1966, *9*, 1–9.

Powell, R. W. The effect of small sequential changes in fixed-ratio size upon the post-reinforcement pause. *Journal of the Experimental Analysis of Behavior*, 1968, *11*, 589–593.

Randolph, J. J., & Sewell, W. R. A chained adjusting ratio schedule. *Psychological Reports*, 1968, *22*, 989–995.

Reynolds, G. S. Discrimination and emission of temporal intervals by pigeons. *Journal of the Experimental Analysis of Behavior*, 1966, *9*, 65–68.

Reynolds, G. S., & Catania, A. C. Temporal discrimination in pigeons. *Science*, 1962, *135*, 314–315.

Reynolds, G. S., & McLeod, A. On the theory of interresponse-time reinforcement. In G. H. Bower (Ed.), *The psychology of learning and motivation* (Vol. 4). New York: Academic Press, 1970.

Richardson, K. A test of the effectiveness of the differential-reinforcement-of-low-rate schedule. *Journal of the Experimental Analysis of Behavior*, 1973, *20*, 385–391.

Richardson, W. K., & Loughead, T. E. Behavior under large values of the differential-reinforcement-of-low-rate schedule. *Journal of the Experimental Analysis of Behavior*, 1974, *22*, 121–129.

Rilling, M. E., & McDiarmid, C. G. Signal detection in fixed-ratio schedules. *Science*, 1965, *148*, 526–527.

Schneider, B. A two-state analysis of fixed-interval responding in the pigeon. *Journal of the Experimental Analysis of Behavior*, 1969, *12*, 667–687.

Schoenfeld, W. N., Cole, B. K., Blaustein, J., Lachter, G. D., Martin, J. M., & Vickery, C. *Stimulus schedules: The t-τ systems.* New York: Harper & Row, 1972.

Shimp, C. P. The reinforcement of short interresponse times. *Journal of the Experimental Analysis of Behavior*. 1967, *10*, 425–434.

Shimp, C. P. Magnitude and frequency of reinforcement and frequencies of interresponse times. *Journal of the Experimental Analysis of Behavior*, 1968, *11*, 525–535.

Shimp, C. P. The concurrent reinforcement of two interresponse times: The relative frequency of an interresponse time equals its relative harmonic length. *Journal of the Experimental Analysis of Behavior*, 1969, *12*, 403–411.

Shimp, C. P. Synthetic variable-interval schedules of reinforcement. *Journal of the Experimental Analysis of Behavior*, 1973, *19*, 311–330.

Shull, R. L. The response-reinforcement dependency in fixed-interval schedules of reinforcement. *Journal of the Experimental Analysis of Behavior*, 1970, *14*, 55–60.

Shull, R. L. Sequential patterns in post-reinforcement pauses on fixed-interval schedules of food. *Journal of the Experimental Analysis of Behavior*, 1971, *15*, 221–231.

Shull, R. L., Guilkey, M., & Witty, W. Changing the response unit from a single peck to a fixed number of pecks in fixed-interval schedules. *Journal of the Experimental Analysis of Behavior*, 1972, *17*, 193–200.

Sidman, M. *Tactics of scientific research.* New York: Basic Books, 1960.

Skinner, B. F. *The behavior of organisms.* New York: Appleton-Century-Crofts, 1938.

Skinner, B. F. "Superstition" in the pigeon. *Journal of Experimental Psychology*, 1948, *38*, 168–172.

Skinner, B. F. A case history in scientific method. In S. Koch (Ed.), *Psychology: A study of a science* (Vol. 2). New York, McGraw-Hill, 1959.

Spence, K. W. *Behavior theory and conditioning.* New Haven: Yale University Press, 1956.

Staddon, J. E. R. Some properties of spaced responding in pigeons. *Journal of the Experimental Analysis of Behavior*, 1965, *8*, 19–27.

Staddon, J. E. R. Asymptotic behavior: The concept of the operant. *Psychological Review*, 1967, *74*, 377–391.

Staddon, J. E. R. Temporal effects of reinforcement: A negative "frustration" effect. *Learning and Motivation*, 1970, *1*, 227–247.

Staddon, J. E. R. Reinforcement omission on temporal go–no-go schedules. *Journal of the Experimental Analysis of Behavior*, 1972, *18*, 223–229.

Stubbs, A. The discrimination of stimulus duration by pigeons. *Journal of the Experimental Analysis of Behavior*, 1968, *11*, 223–238.

Taub, E., & Berman, A. J. Movement and learning in the absence of sensory feedback. In S. J. Freedman (Ed.), *The neuropsychology of spatially oriented behavior.* Homewood, Ill.: Dorsey Press, 1968.

Weiss, B., & Gott, C. T. A microanalysis of drug effects on fixed-ratio performance in pigeons. *Journal of Pharmacology and Experimental Therapeutics*, 1972, *180*, 189–202.

Weissman, N. W., & Crossman, E. K. A comparison of two types of extinction following fixed-ratio training. *Journal of the Experimental Analysis of Behavior*, 1966, *9*, 41–46.

Zeiler, M. D. Fixed and variable schedules of response-independent reinforcement. *Journal of the Experimental Analysis of Behavior*, 1968, *11*, 405–414.

Zeiler, M. D. Time limits for completing fixed ratios. *Journal of the Experimental Analysis of Behavior*, 1970, *14*, 275–286.

Zeiler, M. D. Superstitious behavior in children: An experimental analysis. In H. W. Reese (Ed.), *Advances in child development and behavior* (Vol. 7). New York: Academic Press, 1972. (a)

Zeiler, M. D. Time limits for completing fixed ratios, II: Stimulus specificity. *Journal of the Experimental Analysis of Behavior*, 1972, *18*, 243–251. (b)

9

Choice in Concurrent Schedules and a Quantitative Formulation of the Law of Effect*

Peter de Villiers

INTRODUCTION

Since the early 1960s there has been much operant conditioning research using continuous choice procedures. Several factors suggest the utility of these procedures for quantifying the effects of reward and punishment on behavior, the law of effect.

First, in continuous choice procedures (called *concurrent schedules*) two or more alternative schedules of reinforcement are simultaneously available and the animal continually chooses between responding to one alternative or the other. Thus the number of responses or amount of time the animal allocates to each alternative during an experimental session may be considered a measure of its preference. In this way

---

* The preparation of this chapter was supported by grants from the National Institute of Mental Health and the National Science Foundation to Harvard University. Thanks are due to many people for helpful suggestions, encouragement, and great patience, in particular to Bill Baum, Arturo Bouzas, Peggy Burlet, Jill de Villiers, Richard Herrnstein, Werner Honig, James Mazur, Arlene Pippin, John Staddon, Dan Weber, and James Wilkinson. I acknowledge my indebtedness to work by Peter Killeen for many of the points raised in the discussion, and to several graduate students in the Harvard University operant conditioning laboratory for permission to quote unpublished data.

choice can be used to quantify the relative reward value of different conditions of reinforcement.

Second, rates of responding to each of two alternatives are far more sensitive to the frequency and magnitude of reinforcement for each alternative than are response rates in a single response situation (Catania, 1963a; Herrnstein, 1961).

The most persuasive argument for any measure of response strength is an orderly relation between that measure and the frequency, duration, or immediacy of reinforcement. Relative performance and reinforcement measures obtained from concurrent schedules show just such an orderly relation. Many studies have shown that a simple linear "matching" relation holds between relative response rates (or time distribution) and relative frequency (Herrnstein, 1961), magnitude (Brownstein, 1971; Catania, 1963a) and immediacy of reinforcement (Chung & Herrnstein, 1967). This relation is described by the following equations:

$$\frac{R_1}{R_1 + R_2} \text{ or } \frac{T_1}{T_1 + T_2} = \frac{r_1}{r_1 + r_2} \text{ or } \frac{i_1}{i_1 + i_2} \text{ or } \frac{a_1}{a_1 + a_2} \quad (1)$$

where R_1 and R_2 are the number of responses per session to each of the two alternatives, T_1 and T_2 are the times spent responding on each schedule, and r_1 and r_2 are the frequencies of reinforcement for the alternative responses; i_1 and i_2 represent different immediacies (the reciprocal of the delay of reinforcement), and a_1 and a_2 different amounts of reinforcement for the two alternatives. From the matching relation, Herrnstein (1970) has formulated a powerful set of equations that describe the relation between response strength and reinforcement parameters in single-response situations as well as concurrent schedules.

This chapter is largely concerned with an evaluation of Herrnstein's equations as a quantification of the law of effect. After briefly describing concurrent schedule procedures, the chapter assesses the empirical basis and generality of the matching relation and its status as a general principle. Certain prerequisite conditions for matching are discussed, together with the role of procedural factors or more molecular processes. Herrnstein's (1970) quantitative formulation is then considered in detail—in particular, its ability to incorporate results of earlier runway studies in the tradition of Hull and Spence, and its relation to behavioral contrast phenomena. Finally, alternative or more general quantitative models of choice in concurrent schedules are discussed.

CONCURRENT SCHEDULES

Two different methods of programming concurrent schedules have generally been used. In one of these (Herrnstein, 1961), the animal switches back and forth between two spatially separated response keys or levers, each associated with a different reinforcement schedule. In the second (Findley, 1958), the animal switches between two schedules programmed on the same key by responding on a second changeover (CO) key; each schedule is correlated with a different stimulus. The first method will be referred to as a two-key or two-lever concurrent, the second as a CO-key concurrent schedule. The difference between the two procedures is illustrated in Figure 1.

In both procedures the two component schedules are programmed independently and continuously. If a reinforcement opportunity is programmed by a variable-interval (VI) schedule for response A while the animal is making response B, that reinforcement is held until the animal again makes response A. Consequently, the probability of reinforcement from one schedule increases with the time spent responding on the other schedule.

Fig. 1. Representation of two methods of programming concurrent schedules. The pigeon on the left is responding on a changeover-key concurrent schedule (Findley, 1958), the pigeon on the right on a two-key concurrent schedule (Herrnstein, 1961.)

When equal concurrent interval schedules are programmed in this way, rapid alternation between the two schedules is the dominant response pattern (Herrnstein, 1961; Skinner, 1950). This is conducive to the development of concurrent superstitions (Catania, 1966), the adventitious correlation of one response with reinforcement programmed for another. Responses to one alternative thus come partially under the control of the reinforcement schedule associated with the other. The best illustration of this comes from a study of one pigeon by Catania and Cutts (1963). Pecking at two keys was maintained by a concurrent VI 1-min VI 2-min schedule. Then the reinforcement for the VI 2-min key was discontinued (extinction). The pigeon continued pecking at a steady though somewhat reduced rate (about 15 responses per min) on the extinction key throughout the 12 1-hr sessions. Catania and Cutts reported similar results from 13 human subjects pressing two buttons on a concurrent VI 30-sec EXT schedule. Most of the subjects responded at a substantial rate on the button associated with extinction. Although never explicitly reinforced, responses on that button often occurred in close temporal proximity to reinforcement (increments of a counter) for the other button. Several early studies of concurrent schedules also found control of one response by the schedule for another (e.g., Sidman, 1958). Ferster and Skinner (1957, Chapter 13), for example, programmed a concurrent VI FI (fixed-interval) schedule, each schedule associated with a different key. On a single FI schedule almost no responding occurs early in the interval, but in the concurrent schedule considerable responding was maintained on the FI key early in the fixed interval, probably by accidental correlation with VI reinforcements for pecks on the other key.

To separate the two schedules a changeover delay (COD) is usually added to the concurrent schedule procedure (Herrnstein, 1961). The COD specifies the minimum time interval that must elapse between a CO and a subsequent reinforced response. In a two-key (or two-lever) concurrent procedure the COD is usually timed from the first response on a given key (or lever) after a CO (Herrnstein, 1961); in CO-key procedures it is usually timed from responses on the CO key (Catania, 1966). Alternatively, the COD can be programmed from the last response on a key before a CO (Findley, 1958), but since this selectively reinforces slow COs, the two other methods are preferred. Subsequent mention of the COD will refer to the first two methods of scheduling, unless otherwise specified.

The COD therefore insures a separation in time between response A and the reinforcement of response B, preventing the adventitious reinforcement of AB sequences. Its effectiveness in this respect is illustrated by a condition of the Catania and Cutts (1963) pigeon experiment in which a 1-sec COD was introduced. When the schedule for one key changed to extinction, responding on the extinction key rapidly declined to zero. Without the COD, responding on the extinction key continued at a steady rate. In the Catania and Cutts human experiment the introduction of a COD of between 2 and 15 sec in duration substantially reduced and in many cases eliminated responding on the extinction button.

The dominant patterns of responding on equal concurrent VI schedules with a COD shows runs of responses of roughly COD duration on one schedule alternating with runs of responses of similar duration on the other schedule. When unequal VI schedules are programmed concurrently, the duration of response runs maintained by the schedule programming more frequent reinforcement increases, and COs are less frequent (Catania, 1966). In the absence of the COD the switching response itself is a primary component of the behavior, and the main effect of changes in reinforcement is on switching; with a COD the main effect is on the rate of responding to each alternative.

Measurement of Choice or Preference

Response rates in concurrent schedules are usually calculated in terms of the number of responses made on each schedule divided by the total session time (minus time consumed by reinforcement)—i.e., overall response rates. Rate of responding to each alternative is calculated with respect to overall session time rather than the time the animal actually spends responding on each key because the concurrent schedules run continuously and the response alternatives are simultaneously available to the animal throughout the experimental session. Calculation of response rates with respect to the time that a given stimulus is in effect is more customary for multiple schedules, where each schedule runs and is available to the animal only in the presence of a particular stimulus. However, particularly in the CO-key concurrent schedule, the amount of time that the animal spends in the presence of the stimuli associated with each schedule can also readily be calculated. This enables the calculation of *local* response rates—i.e., the number of responses made on each schedule divided by the time spent responding on that schedule.

The relation between response rates and reinforcement frequencies in concurrent schedules is usually considered in terms of relative measures (Herrnstein, 1970): relative overall response rate [the number of responses made to one alternative divided by the total number of responses during the session—i.e., $R_1/(R_1 + R_2)$] and relative reinforcement frequency $[r_1/(r_1 + r_2)]$. Similarly, relative time distribution is measured in terms of the time spent in the presence of the stimulus associated with one schedule divided by the total session time $[T_1/(T_1 + T_2)]$. In two key concurrent schedules, the time distribution is calculated in terms of cumulative interchangeover time for each alternative. Exclusive preference for one alternative is shown by a relative response rate or relative time distribution of 1.00 or .00, indifference between the alternatives by relative values of .50. The relation between ratios of responses (R_1/R_2) or of time (T_1/T_2) and ratios of obtained number of reinforcements (r_1/r_2) for each of the alternative has also frequently been examined (e.g., Baum, 1974a; Baum & Rachlin, 1969; Staddon, 1968).

THE MATCHING RELATION IN CONCURRENT VI SCHEDULES— REINFORCEMENT FREQUENCY

In 1961 Herrnstein first demonstrated that when two independent VI schedules arranged reinforcements for concurrent responses and a COD was in effect, there was a matching relation between relative overall response rates and relative reinforcement frequency. Throughout his experiment the two VI schedules set an overall maximum rate of reinforcement at 40 per hr, but the number of reinforcements allocated to each key was systematically varied. At all distributions of the reinforcements, Herrnstein found that the

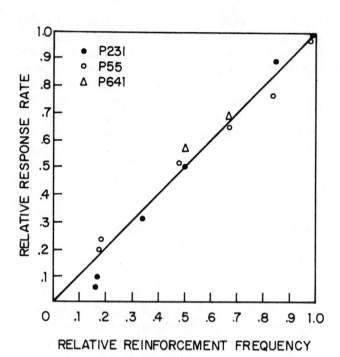

Fig. 2. The relative frequency of responding to one alternative in a two-key concurrent VI VI schedule as a function of the relative frequency of reinforcement for that alternative. The diagonal line shows matching between the relative frequencies. (Data from three pigeons, Herrnstein, 1961.)

pigeons' relative response rates approximately equalled the relative reinforcement frequencies for the two alternatives;

$$\frac{R_1}{R_1 + R_2} = \frac{r_1}{r_1 + r_2} \tag{2}$$

where R is response rate, r is reinforcement frequency, and the subscripts denote the two alternatives. The data from the three pigeons in the experiment are shown in Figure 2.

Response Matching

Since Herrnstein's 1961 study, matching between relative response rate and relative reinforcement frequency has been demonstrated in both kinds of concurrent schedule procedure and for several different species.

McSweeney (1975) reinforced pigeons' treadle presses on several two-treadle concurrent VI VI schedules with a 2-sec COD. The rate of reinforcement for one alternative remained constant at 30 food presentations per hr; the rate of reinforcement for the other varied from 15 to 120 per hr. For each of four pigeons, relative rate of responding in each component schedule matched the relative frequency of food that the schedule provided.

In an experiment by Baum (1972), a pigeon lived in the experimental situation. All of its food was obtained by pecking at two keys, each associated with a separate VI schedule. A 1.8-sec COD was in effect throughout the experiment. The bird was free to eat to satiation and one alternative alone was often sufficient to fulfill the bird's normal food requirements. Distribution of responses between the alternatives was therefore often unnecessary, but the pigeon nevertheless made thousands of responses on each key each day. For a wide range of relative reinforcement frequencies the proportion of pecks allocated to either key equaled the proportion of food obtained by pecks at that key.

In a subsequent experiment, Baum (1974b) extended the matching relation to wild pigeons in a more natural habitat. A version of the standard operant conditioning apparatus was placed in the attic of a wooden frame house in Cambridge, Massachusetts. A flock of about 20 free-ranging wild pigeons that inhabit the attic were trained to peck at two keys for access to grain. A narrow perch in front of the keys allowed only one pigeon at a time access to the keys and food, but the pecks of the group were treated as an aggregate. Over a wide range of concurrent VI VI schedules without a COD the pigeons' proportion of pecks at a key approximately equaled the proportion of grain presentations obtained from it.

Nevin (1969) used a two-key concurrent procedure, but presented the two keys simultaneously in discrete-choice trials. Independent concurrent VI schedules which ran during the intertrial interval as well as during the choice trials arranged reinforcements. When a reinforcer was scheduled for a key it was held and timing of the intervals in that schedule stopped until the next choice trial in which that key was chosen. The first peck in a trial terminated the trial: if a reinforcer had been scheduled for that key the response produced 4-sec access to grain. Choice trials without a peck lasted for 2 sec. The intertrial interval (ITI) was 6 sec long, during which time the keys were dark. Pecks during the ITI extended it for 6 sec from the last peck. The proportion of responses (choices) made by the pigeons to each key closely matched the proportion of reinforcements produced by each key in this discrete-trials procedure, as it does in concurrent VI schedules with continuous access to the keys.

Schroeder and Holland (1969) reported a further,

perhaps more exotic, confirmation of the response-matching relation with human subjects. Their subjects were required to monitor deflections of pointers on four dials arranged in a square with two on the left and two on the right. An eye movement camera recorded macrosaccadic eye movements scanning each of the dials. A fixation on a dial after looking away toward the other dials counted as one response. Looking horizontally or diagonally between the two pairs of dials was defined as a changeover. A change in fixation between two vertically arranged dials was therefore a response but not a changeover, while a change in fixation between left- and right-hand dials was both. Pointer deflections were delivered to the two left-hand dials on one variable-time (VT) schedule and to the right-hand dials on a second, independent VT schedule. Scheduled deflections were assigned with an equal probability to the upper or lower dial on each side. Signal presentation was contingent on looking toward the side for which it was scheduled, but was independent of which of the two dials on that side was being fixated.[1] When a short COD was programmed between crossover eye movements and signals, the pattern of scanning changed from fixating the four dials in succession or in a Z-shaped pattern to vertical scanning of the dials on either side with fewer crossovers. All reinforcements scheduled to occur before the COD timed out were held until the end of the COD and then delivered. With a 2.5-sec COD for one subject and 1.0-sec CODs for the others, all six subjects in the experiment matched relative scanning eye movement rates (number of fixations per min) on each side to the relative signal frequencies on each schedule.

Matching of Both Responses and Time

Catania (1963b) used a CO-key procedure so that time spent in each component could be accurately measured. With a 2-sec COD in effect, he found that pigeons approximately matched both the relative response rates and the relative amount of time spent in each component to the relative frequency of food. Similar results for pigeons were reported by Silberberg and Fantino (1970) using a two-key procedure, but with CODs varying between .88 and 3.5 sec. With rats as subjects and brain stimulation as the reinforcer Shull and Pliskoff (1967) also found that relative rate of lever pressing and time distribution matched the obtained distribution of reinforcements, but only when the COD was greater than 7.5 sec.

A different method for programming a CO-key concurrent schedule was used by Stubbs and Pliskoff (1969). One VI programmer arranged the reinforcements for both the schedules, each schedule being associated with a different color stimulus on the main response key. When a reinforcement was programmed, it was allocated to one schedule or the other according to different probabilities. Thus whenever a reinforcement opportunity was arranged for one schedule, no further reinforcements could be arranged for either schedule until the available reinforcement had been obtained. This procedure forces the subject to respond occasionally on both alternatives in order to obtain reinforcement for either alternative, even if one of the schedules is extremely unfavorable when compared with the other. The advantage of the Stubbs and Pliskoff procedure lies in insuring that the obtained relative reinforcement frequency must equal the scheduled relative frequency. On the other hand, the two alternative schedules are no longer independent of one another.

Stubbs and Pliskoff found matching for both relative response rates and relative time for three pigeons at five different relative reinforcement frequencies. Increasing the COD from 2 sec, the value at which matching was first obtained, through 32 sec produced little systematic change in relative response rates when relative reinforcement frequency was kept constant at .75. In this procedure, responding on the two schedules is somewhat constrained since the subject has to respond on the less favorable schedule in order to maintain the overall frequency of reinforcement. However, this requirement by no means forces the subject toward matching, and might be expected to favor indifference. Nevertheless, excellent matching was obtained.

In contrast to these results, Schmitt (1974) failed to find matching with humans in a conventional CO-key concurrent schedule procedure. Five subjects pressed a button for increments of a counter, each worth a number of cents, on one of two independent VI schedules each associated with a different stimulus light. They could change schedules by operating a toggle switch. A 1.5-sec COD stipulated the time that had to elapse after a changeover before a button press could be reinforced. In almost all of the experimental conditions relative response rates and relative time distribution did not match the relative frequency of reinforcement, the departure usually being toward indifference. Apart from the difference in subjects, reasons for the

---

[1] Reinforcement presentation was thus independent of the vertical scanning eye movements, but the schedule was not strictly a VT schedule since the reinforcements were contingent on looking toward the appropriate side.

discrepancy between these results and the studies on nonhuman species are not readily apparent.

Time Matching

In most of these studies, local response rates were found to be the same for each schedule, and response matching resulted from the matching of relative time distribution to relative reinforcement frequency. Brownstein and Pliskoff (1968) and Baum and Rachlin (1969) therefore argued that time and not response allocation underlies the matching relation.

Brownstein and Pliskoff (1968) demonstrated that the relative time spent in either component of a CO-key concurrent schedule matched the relative frequency of food provided in that component even in the absence of any key pecking for the food. The pigeons in their experiment changed the color of a stimulus light by pecking a single CO key, but the reinforcements in each component were delivered independently of the birds' behavior according to different VT schedules. The pigeons therefore chose between two different frequencies of food delivery each correlated with a different stimulus color. In this situation they matched the proportion of the session time spent in the presence of a color to the proportion of reinforcements associated with that stimulus:

$$\frac{T_1}{T_1 + T_2} = \frac{r_1}{r_1 + r_2} \qquad (3)$$

Baum and Rachlin (1969) pointed out that pigeons tend to peck at a constant rate when they are responding, with the majority of interresponse times (IRTs) falling between .3 and .5 sec (Blough, 1963). Long-term response rate varies with the duration of pauses between bursts of responses at the constant rate. With such a constant rate of responding, time spent responding determines the number of responses. Hence, Baum and Rachlin argued, time spent responding is the most general measure of response frequency for repetitive responses like key pecking or lever pressing.

Baum and Rachlin studied a response that can only be measured in terms of time spent responding: standing in a particular location. Standing on one or the other side of an experimental chamber was reinforced on two concurrent VI schedules. A 4.25-sec COD was signaled by the illumination of a white light in the chamber, during which time no reinforcement was presented. Post-COD standing on either side of the chamber was correlated with the illumination of either a red or green stimulus light, each associated with a different frequency of food presentation. When Baum and Rachlin plotted the results of this experiment in terms of Equation 3—i.e., the relative time spent in the presence of either the red or green stimulus—the data points from most of the pigeons systematically fell below the matching diagonal in a bowed curve. However, they found that the results could be expressed in terms of the following equation:

$$\frac{T_1}{T_2} = k \frac{r_1}{r_2} \qquad (4)$$

The ratio of the times spent on the two sides of the chamber was directly proportional to the ratio of the rates of reinforcement provided on the two sides. When the logarithms of the time ratios are plotted against the logarithms of the reinforcement ratios, Equation 4 specifies a linear function of the form $\log (T_1/T_2) = 1.00 \log (r_1/r_2) + \log k$, where 1.00 is the slope and $\log k$ the intercept of the function on the Y-axis when $\log (r_1/r_2) = 0$. The data from one of Baum and Rachlin's pigeons is shown in Figure 3, plotted in terms of both Equation 3 and the logarithmic form of Equation 4. The linear function of least squares fit to the log data is shown in the lower panel together with the percentage of the variance in the dependent variable accounted for by the function. The value of k is given by the antilog of the intercept; in this case $k = .54$. The slope of the function approximates 1.00 as specified by Equation 4.

When $k = 1.0$, Equation 4 is identical to the matching relation described by Equation 3. A k-value different from 1.0 signifies a constant proportional bias toward one side of the chamber or toward one schedule. Such a bias shows up as a constant displacement from the matching diagonal when the logs of the ratios are plotted against one another, as in the lower panel of Figure 3. Hence Equation 4 (proportional ratio matching) and its response equivalent,

$$\frac{R_1}{R_2} = k \frac{r_1}{r_2} \qquad (5)$$

are more general than Equations 2 and 3 (matching of relative proportions). They account for such factors as position or color preferences, or even preferences arising from qualitatively different reinforcers (see p. 252). The bias parameter k takes account of our imperfect knowledge of the reinforcers at work in the experimental situation. For example, in the Baum and Rachlin (1969) study there were two feeders. If they did not yield equal quantities of food, $k \neq 1.0$ to the extent that the units of r_1 and r_2 were not equiv-

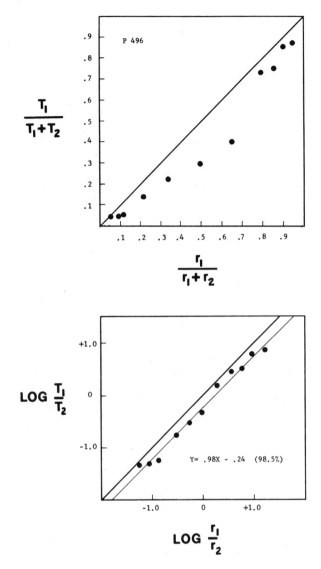

Fig. 3. Data from one pigeon in Baum and Rachlin's (1969) shuttlebox choice procedure plotted in terms of relative time and reinforcement distributions (top panel) and in terms of the logarithms of the time and reinforcement ratios (bottom panel). The heavy diagonal line represents perfect matching; the fine diagonal line plotted through the data points is the least-squares regression line for those points. The regression function and the percentage of data variance that it accounts for is given in the lower panel.

alent. Other biases can also be considered as reinforcers not identified in the independent variable. Baum (1974a) has therefore suggested that choice in concurrent schedules is best described by the ratio of responses or times spent responding as some function of the ratio of reinforcements. Where relative proportion matching is obtained, proportional ratio matching must also hold, but the converse is not necessarily true.

Baum (1975) recently reported time matching for humans in a vigilance task. Subjects were required to monitor red or green signals projected on a translucent plastic screen. The signals were arranged according to a single VI schedule and assigned as red or green with varying probabilities (cf. Stubbs and Pliskoff, 1969). By pressing down one of two telegraph keys the subjects illuminated the screen with either a green (left key) or red (right key) floodlight for the duration of the press, enabling them to detect the red or green signals. (Opposite colors made the signals visible.) As long as the appropriate floodlight was on, the signal remained on until it was turned off by pushing a button next to the depressed key. Turning off a signal incremented a "score" counter by 1. To reduce subjects' changeover rates a 2-sec COD was in effect and a response cost was programmed on a variable-ratio (VR) 3 for release of a key after it had been depressed. The response cost consisted of the increment by 1 of a second counter, the final tally of which was subtracted from the "score" counter to determine the overall session score. Pilot studies had indicated that the response cost was necessary to prevent subjects from simply alternating as rapidly as possible between the two keys.

To maintain the subjects' interest throughout the experiment it was given a gamelike appearance. As captain of a spaceship under enemy siege, the subject defended himself by detecting and destroying two types of enemy missiles: red ones and green ones. The colored floodlights represented the appropriate sensors; the response cost represented a "hit" by the enemy when a sensor was "deactivated." Subjects competed for a monetary bonus given for the highest session score (missiles detected minus "hits") for each block of five sessions.

With a 2-sec COD and a VR 3 response cost, two of the three subjects showed excellent matching between the ratio of the times for which each key was depressed and ratio of detections of each type of signal. The third subject was nearer indifference than predicted by matching, but when the response cost increased to a "hit" for every release, changeover rate declined and excellent matching was obtained over a wide range of signal ratios.

Assessment of the Empirical Evidence for Matching

How strong a generalization is the matching relation from the data just reviewed? Proportional ratio matching (Equations 4 and 5) specifies that the regression line relating log response or time ratios to log reinforcement ratio have a slope of 1.0. A slope greater

Table 1 Percentage of data variance accounted for by least-squares regression lines and best fit line of 1.0 slope relating log response ratio to log reinforcement ratio for both individual subjects and groups

INDIVIDUAL DATA	LEAST-SQUARES LINE	BEST FIT LINE OF 1.0 SLOPE	NO. OF POINTS	COD
Herrnstein (1961)				
P231	1.36X − .04 (99.0%)	1.00X − .12 (92.2%)	5	1.5 sec
P055	.80X − .01 (98.3%)	1.00X + .01 (92.3%)	5	1.5 sec
Catania (1963b)				
P117	.83X − .01 (90.5%)	1.00X − .02 (86.2%)	8	2 sec
P243	.77X + .01 (92.9%)	1.00X − .03 (87.2%)	8	2 sec
P294	.80X + .03 (90.3%)	1.00X (84.8%)	8	2 sec
Stubbs & Pliskoff (1969)				
P103	.86X + .08 (96.0%)	1.00X + .04 (93.7%)	4	2 sec
P104	1.24X − .01 (92.6%)	1.00X + .06 (89.1%)	4	2 sec
P108	.94X + .02 (98.4%)	1.00X + .01 (98.0%)	4	2 sec
Silberberg & Fantino (1970)				
A	.74X − .05 (99.9%)	1.00X − .06 (87.8%)	3	.88 sec
E	.77X − .06 (99.7%)	1.00X − .06 (91.0%)	3	.88 sec
C	.94X + .07 (48.0%)	1.00X + .04 (42.0%)	3	1.75 sec
B	.55X − .18 (61.0%)	1.00X + .10 (20.5%)	3	1.75 sec
G	.63X − .05 (99.0%)	1.00X + .10 (66.1%)	3	3.5 sec
H	.93X + .17 (99.8%)	1.00X + .16 (99.2%)	3	3.5 sec
Trevitt, Davison, & Williams (1972)				
P101	.52X + .02 (94.9%)	1.00X − .04 (10.9%)	4	3 sec
P102	1.01X − .15 (98.8%)	1.00X − .15 (98.5%)	4	3 sec
P105	.61X − .17 (91.5%)	1.00X − .21 (65.8%)	4	3 sec
P106	.73X − .04 (97.9%)	1.00X − .07 (85.5%)	4	3 sec
Baum (1972)				
A	.95X − .01 (99.4%)	1.00X − .01 (99.2%)	5	1.8 sec
McSweeney (1975)				
8422	.74X + .03 (93.8%)	1.00X − .04 (89.6%)	4	2 sec
8772	.89X − .01 (86.8%)	1.00X − .04 (85.6%)	4	2 sec
8845	1.01X − .03 (95.3%)	1.00X − .03 (95.1%)	4	2 sec
8927	.79X − .02 (84.2%)	1.00X − .08 (83.7%)	4	2 sec
GROUP DATA				
Herrnstein (1961)	1.11X − .02 (92.3%)	1.00X − .03 (91.4%)	12	1.5 sec
Catania (1963b)	.80X + .01 (90.7%)	1.00X − .02 (86.3%)	24	2 sec
Stubbs & Pliskoff (1969)	1.01X + .03 (92.5%)	1.00X + .04 (90.4%)	12	2 sec
Silberberg & Fantino (1970)	.85X + .04 (92.9%)	1.00X + .05 (90.0%)	18	.88–3.5 sec
Trevitt, Davison, & Williams (1972)	.76X − .10 (88.7%)	1.00X − .12 (80.7%)	16	3 sec
Baum (1974b)	1.03X + .05 (99.3%)	1.00X + .04 (99.1%)	5	no COD
McSweeney (1975)	.85X − .01 (87.2%)	1.00X − .02 (84.2%)	16	2 sec

Table 2 Percentage of data variance accounted for by least-squares regression lines and best fit line of 1.0 slope relating log time ratio to log reinforcement ratio for both individual subjects and groups

INDIVIDUAL DATA	LEAST-SQUARES LINE	BEST FIT LINE OF 1.0 SLOPE	NO. OF POINTS	COD
Catania (1963b)				
P117	.94X − .04 (94.8%)	1.00X − .05 (94.5%)	8	2 sec
P243	.76X − .06 (86.0%)	1.00X + .02 (77.2%)	8	2 sec
P294	.94X − .04 (93.4%)	1.00X − .05 (93.1%)	8	2 sec
Brownstein & Pliskoff (1968)				
P93	1.04X + .01 (98.6%)	1.00X + .01 (98.5%)	5	2 sec
Baum & Rachlin (1969)				
P334	.84X − .25 (97.3%)	1.00X − .24 (92.5%)	11	4.25 sec
P360	.63X − .12 (98.1%)	1.00X − .11 (64.4%)	11	4.25 sec
P488	1.09X − .29 (96.5%)	1.00X − .29 (95.4%)	11	4.25 sec
P489	1.15X − .49 (90.3%)	1.00X − .49 (88.8%)	11	4.25 sec
P490	1.29X − .06 (96.3%)	1.00X − .08 (91.5%)	11	4.25 sec
P496	.98X − .27 (98.5%)	1.00X − .26 (97.9%)	11	4.25 sec
Stubbs & Pliskoff (1969)				
P103	1.03X + .11 (97.5%)	1.00X + .12 (97.4%)	4	2 sec
P104	1.24X + .00 (92.8%)	1.00X + .07 (89.4%)	4	2 sec
P108	1.07X + .01 (99.0%)	1.00X + .03 (98.5%)	4	2 sec
Silberberg & Fantino (1970)				
A	.87X − .21 (99.7%)	1.00X − .21 (97.5%)	3	.88 sec
E	1.06X − .18 (96.2%)	1.00X − .18 (95.9%)	3	.88 sec
C	.58X + .45 (99.8%)	1.00X + .21 (48.6%)	3	1.75 sec
B	.84X − .12 (98.7%)	1.00X − .02 (90.2%)	3	1.75 sec
G	.97X − .08 (96.8%)	1.00X − .06 (96.6%)	3	3.5 sec
H	1.22X − .06 (96.3%)	1.00X − .01 (95.6%)	3	3.5 sec
Trevitt, Davison, & Williams (1972)				
P101	.60X − .02 (94.5%)	1.00X − .06 (35.0%)	4	3 sec
P102	1.11X − .08 (95.9%)	1.00X − .08 (95.0%)	4	3 sec
P105	.70X − .10 (94.0%)	1.00X − .12 (80.9%)	4	3 sec
P106	.98X − .08 (98.2%)	1.00X − .08 (98.1%)	4	3 sec
Baum (1975)				
Doug	1.16X − .08 (90.6%)	1.00X − .08 (82.8%)	10	2 sec
Noa	.98X + .03 (93.3%)	1.00X + .04 (92.6%)	10	2 sec
John I	.67X (96.1%)	1.00X + .01 (70.2%)	10	2 sec
John II	.94X + .15 (93.7%)	1.00X + .15 (93.3%)	11	2 sec
GROUP DATA				
Catania (1963b)	.89X − .01 (90.2%)	1.00X − .02 (88.7%)	24	2 sec
Brownstein & Pliskoff (1968)	.94X + .02 (97.5%)	1.00X + .02 (96.6%)	12	2–7.5 sec
Baum & Rachlin (1969)	1.01X − .24 (89.4%)	1.00X − .24 (89.0%)	66	4.25 sec
Stubbs & Pliskoff (1969)	1.11X + .04 (95.0%)	1.00X + .07 (94.0%)	12	2 sec
Silberberg & Fantino (1970)	1.07X − .05 (93.9%)	1.00X − .05 (93.4%)	18	.88–3.5 sec
Trevitt, Davison, & Williams (1972)	.88X − .08 (91.0%)	1.00X − .09 (89.4%)	16	3 sec
Baum (1975)	.93X (87.6%)	1.00X (85.6%)	30	2 sec

than 1.0 represents overmatching, a stronger preference for the schedule providing the more frequent reinforcement than that predicted by matching. A slope less than 1.0 represents undermatching, a weaker preference for the richer schedule than that predicted. In the following analysis a least-squares line of best fit was calculated for the data from all of the published experiments on concurrent VI VI schedules in which at least three different ratios of reinforcement frequency were studied. Data points showing exclusive preference for one or other schedule where the reinforcement ratio was either 0 or ∞ were excluded from the analysis, since neither of these can be expressed as a logarithm, although they are in keeping with the matching relation. To evaluate Equations 4 and 5 the percentage of data variance in the dependent variable accounted for by proportional ratio matching—i.e., by a line of 1.0 slope—was also calculated in each case. This analysis is shown in Table 1 for response ratios for both individual and group data. The group regression lines were calculated from all the data points provided by the subjects in that experiment. Table 2 shows the same analysis for time ratios.[2]

The matching relation accounts for over 80% of the data variance for 18 of the 23 individual subjects in Table 1 (response ratios), and for 22 of the 27 subjects in Table 2 (time ratios). It fails to account for a substantial proportion of the data for only 4 subjects, 2 in the Trevitt, Davison, and Williams (1972) study and 2 in the Silberberg and Fantino (1970) study. In fact, for the response ratios of the latter 2 pigeons, even the least-squares line accounts for little of the variance. A possible explanation for the marked deviation of these subjects from matching is considered later in this section.

Group data are important, especially for the studies in which only a few points were obtained for each subject. Here the matching relation accounts for over 80% of the variance in response ratios and for over 85% of the variance in time ratios for all the experiments. In all cases, the matching line is less than 8% worse than the regression line of least-squares fit.

Nevertheless, an important point in assessing the matching formulation is whether the deviations from matching are systematic. For time ratios (Table 2) there is no systematic deviation. The individual regression lines vary equally on both sides of matching, with a median slope of .98. For response ratios (Table 1) the slopes of the individual regression lines do tend toward undermatching, with a median slope of .80.

However, several methodological considerations must be taken into account in evaluating the data from some of the studies.

The strongest evidence for systematic undermatching comes from Trevitt et al. (1972). In this experiment four different concurrent VI VI values were studied in the course of an experiment on choice in two-key concurrent VI FI schedules. All of the data points for the concurrent VI VI schedule were obtained after long exposure to the different VI FI values, five VI FI conditions being studied before the first VI VI. In both the VI FI and VI VI conditions, both keys were illuminated with white light, and the FI schedule was always associated with the same key. During the VI VI procedure three of the four pigeons showed a bias toward the key that had been correlated with the VI schedule and preferred throughout the concurrent VI FI. All four pigeons showed regression lines for response ratios with very similar slopes to those obtained for them in the VI FI conditions. Both Trevitt et al. and Nevin (1971) demonstrated that regression lines relating response ratios to obtained reinforcement ratios on concurrent VI FI schedules have slopes of considerably less than 1.0. The prior exposure to concurrent VI FI schedules could therefore have affected the VI VI data in this study.

The Silberberg and Fantino (1970) study raises another consideration: control for order effects. The two pigeons that showed particularly marked undermatching, subjects B and C, were exposed to only three different relative reinforcement frequencies, with the same key providing more frequent reinforcement in each case. Subject B was successively exposed to relative reinforcement frequencies of .33, .20, and .11, subject C to relative frequencies of .67, .90, and .88. Any order effects in which the previous reinforcement conditions affected responding on the new reinforcement schedules (so-called hysteresis effects—Baum, 1974a; Stevens, 1957) could have produced the flat regression lines for the pigeons.[3]

Another major factor to be taken into account is the role of the COD in matching. Many studies (Brownstein & Pliskoff, 1968; Herrnstein, 1961; Shull & Pliskoff, 1967) have shown that a minimum COD duration is necessary for matching to be obtained, but

---

[2] In calculating the group regression line for Baum's (1975) data, the results from John I rather than John II were used, since the experimental parameters were the same for John I and the other two subjects.

[3] Undermatching in terms of a slope <1.0 does not necessarily mean that the subject is nearer indifference between the schedules than is predicted by the matching relation. A subject could actually respond more on the preferred key than matching predicts, yet still produce a regression line of slope <1.0. For example, if relative reinforcement frequencies of .50, .60, .70, and .80 were studied (i.e., if the same key always provided the more frequent reinforcement), relative response rates of .58, .66, .74, and .82 would produce a regression line with a slope flatter than 1.0. This was the case for the two pigeons that produced the flattest functions in the study by Silberberg and Fantino (1970).

there is no particular reason to believe that the same minimum COD value will suffice for all subjects. Just as there are individual and species differences in many discrimination tasks, it is likely that different COD values will be needed for individual subjects before they properly discriminate the two reinforcement schedules in a concurrent procedure. For example, a considerably longer minimum COD of 5 to 10 sec is apparently needed for rats (de Villiers & Millenson, 1972; Shull & Pliskoff, 1967) than for pigeons (about 1 to 3 sec—Catania, 1966; Herrnstein, 1961). Brownstein and Pliskoff (1968) reported that different COD values (between 2 and 7.5 sec) were needed to obtain matching for each of their three pigeons, and Schroeder and Holland (1969) needed a longer COD for one of their human subjects before matching was observed.

At all COD durations less than the minimum required for matching the subjects are nearer indifference between the two schedules and show a flatter function relating response and reinforcement ratios than that predicted by the matching relation—i.e., undermatching. Yet most studies have programmed the same short COD for all subjects, usually between 1 and 3 sec in duration. Therefore, it is not surprising that in most studies some subjects show regression lines with slopes less than 1.0. It is worth noting that only one of the studies shown in Tables 1 and 2 (Brownstein & Pliskoff, 1968) varied the COD duration for individual subjects until matching was obtained at the first relative reinforcement frequency. The only subject in that experiment for which three different relative reinforcement rates (besides 1.0) were studied produced a regression line relating time and reinforcement ratios with a slope of 1.04. The regression line for the group of three subjects, including all the data points, was $Y = .94X + .02$ (with 97.5% of the data variance accounted for)—close to perfect matching.

The matching relation, therefore, holds only under certain conditions. A COD of sufficient duration must be used for each subject, and the reinforcement schedules should be run in balanced order across the two keys to obviate order effects. Many of the studies cited in Tables 1 and 2 did not satisfy these conditions. Since most of the known factors that lead to systematic deviations from matching lead to undermatching (Baum, 1974a), this outcome will be obtained in experiments that fail to control for them.

The Role of the COD in Matching

The importance of the COD in the matching relation raises questions about the generality of matching. Indeed, it could be argued that the dependency of matching on a minimum COD duration severely limits the generality of the principle. This would follow if matching occurred only at certain arbitrary COD values. In fact, although different minimum COD values may be required for different species and even for different individual subjects, matching is found for all values of the COD greater than this minimum (Allison & Lloyd, 1971; Shull & Pliskoff, 1967; Stubbs & Pliskoff, 1969). The matching relation is therefore not an artifact of any particular COD duration, although it requires a minimum separation of the two schedules in time.

On the other hand, Pliskoff (1971) has argued that response or time distributions may themselves be by-products of changeover (CO) responding, which depends on both the COD duration and the relative reinforcement frequency. With a fixed COD duration, CO rate decreases as the relative reinforcement frequency diverges from .50; and with a fixed relative reinforcement frequency, CO rate decreases as the COD increases (Shull & Pliskoff, 1967; Stubbs & Pliskoff, 1969). But the results of Stubbs and Pliskoff's (1969) experiment do not support Pliskoff's conclusion that matching is determined by CO responding. They fixed the relative reinforcement frequency at .75, and although overall CO rate declined systematically with increasing COD duration, relative response rate and time allocation did not change. Matching was obtained at all COD values from 2 through 32 sec. This suggests that relative reinforcement frequency is the crucial variable in determining response and time matching.

Nevertheless, the role of the minimum COD values required for matching in concurrent schedules has still to be clarified. Catania (1966) and Herrnstein (1961, 1970) suggest that the COD separates the two schedules in time and so reduces the adventitious reinforcement of left-right or right-left response sequences. As mentioned earlier, Catania and Cutts (1963) showed that without a COD, responses to one alternative came partially under the control of the other reinforcement schedule. One function of the COD is therefore to prevent such concurrent superstitions by introducing a delay between a response to one alternative and the reinforcement from the other.

Pliskoff (1971) has suggested that the COD functions to punish the CO response since it specifies a period of time during which no response will be reinforced if the subject changes over. By thus decreasing CO rate, the COD separates the two schedules. Delays of increasingly longer duration produce larger decrements in CO rate, suggesting that increasing the COD may be comparable to increasing shock intensity in a punishment paradigm.

There are certain similarities between performances on concurrent schedules with CODs and those in which the CO response is explicitly punished by a shock or by a time-out from reinforcement. Todorov (1971) demonstrated that CO rate decreased and relative response rate increased as the intensity of shock or duration of time-out increased, as they do with increasing COD duration (Allison & Lloyd, 1971; Shull & Pliskoff, 1967).

However, the parallel breaks down under further scrutiny. Shull and Pliskoff (1967) observed that at all COD durations, relative response rates and time distributions continued to match the relative obtained reinforcement frequencies, and the local response rates tended to be the same on both schedules. On the other hand, Todorov (1971) found that with increasing punishment of the CO response, the relative rate of responding increased more rapidly than the relative time distribution, and the local rates of responding deviated more and more from equality. Relative reinforcement frequency did not change significantly as punishment increased, so that neither response nor time matching were obtained at time-out durations longer than 3 sec or at shock intensities higher than 4 mA.

In another procedure, Stubbs and Pliskoff (1969) programmed a fixed-ratio (FR) requirement of 20 responses on the CO key while the main key was darkened and the VI programmers stopped—i.e., the FR functioned like Todorov's time-out punishment. With the FR requirement in effect, relative response rate again overmatched the distribution of reinforcements and local response rates deviated from equality. These two experiments therefore fail to demonstrate any functional equivalence between the COD and direct punishment of the CO response.

It is nevertheless questionable whether these procedures constitute an adequate test of the hypothesis that the COD punishes changeovers. Since the reinforcement schedules did not run during the timeout or the FR contingent on the CO response, the punishers interacted with the VI schedules in a way that the COD does not. Similarly, the shock used as a punisher by Todorov could reduce the relative value of the food reinforcement (de Villiers & Millenson, 1972; Millenson & de Villiers, 1972). Pliskoff's (1971) punishment hypothesis therefore remains as a possible explanation of the COD's effects on responding.

Silberberg and Fantino (1970) proposed that the COD has a more complex role in the matching relation than simply separating the two schedules in time. They reported that response rates during the COD period following a CO were considerably higher than post-COD response rates. Relative response rates within the COD approximated .50 (indifference) while post-COD response rates overmatched the overall frequency of reinforcement. Only when these two response rates were added did overall relative response rate closely match relative reinforcement frequency. From these results, Silberberg and Fantino concluded that the matching relation depends on the interaction of COD and post-COD response patterns and on the perseverance of the COD response burst into the post-COD period on the preferred key. Since the probability of reinforcement on one VI schedule increases the longer the subject spends responding on the other schedule, they suggested that the high response rates during the COD on both keys reflect the increased local probability of reinforcement immediately after a CO.

Pliskoff (1971) similarly observed that with equal concurrent VI schedules, the response rate during the COD was higher than the post-COD response rate at all COD durations between .33 and 27 sec. But Pliskoff found that response rate during the COD was highest with a 1-sec COD and then declined as the COD increased, whereas the post-COD response rate was fairly constant at all COD values. Unfortunately, the same analysis has not been performed when relative reinforcement frequencies varied, but it suggests that the matching relation is not an artifact of the COD. The difference between COD and post-COD response rate decreases considerably as the COD lengthens, so response bursts during the COD must contribute a different relative amount to the overall rate of responding as the COD varies. Yet the matching of overall relative response rate to the relative frequency of reinforcement is maintained at all these COD durations (Shull & Pliskoff, 1967; Stubbs & Pliskoff, 1969).

Other results suggest that the high response rates generated during the COD are unnecessary for matching if the CO rate is low enough to separate the schedules in time. Kulli (unpublished data) showed that pigeons' CO rates systematically decreased with increasing body weight. Even without a COD, relative response rates matched relative reinforcement frequency when the birds were at 100 to 110% of their preexperiment ad libitum weights.

In brief, there is substantial evidence that a certain amount of separation and differentiation between the two reinforcement conditions is a necessary condition for matching in concurrent schedules and that this separation can be produced by several methods that reduce CO rate. However, any role played by the COD beyond merely producing this separation is not clear (cf. Kulli's data).

MAXIMIZING OR MATCHING

Shimp (1966, 1969a) has argued that matching is not fundamental, but is produced by more molecular interaction between choices and the probability of reinforcement. He scheduled reinforcements probabilistically for choices in a discrete-trial procedure (Shimp, 1966). A contingency similar to that in a VI schedule was employed in that a reinforcement programmed for a particular choice remained available until produced by the subject. The probability of reinforcement on one key therefore increased while the bird responded on the other key. Shimp found that both the initial postreinforcement choices and the sequential changes in choice probabilities between reinforcements corresponded to the differences in probability of reinforcement for each choice arranged by the schedule. He concluded that the overall matching found in concurrent VI schedules is a by-product of the subjects' tendency to maximize—i.e., to choose the alternative with the higher momentary probability of reinforcement on each choice trial.

However, discrete-trial experiments by Nevin (1969) and Herrnstein (unpublished data), using concurrent VI schedules, produced contrary results. Both Nevin and Herrnstein obtained matching, but sequential changes in choice probabilities and postreinforcement choices did not correspond to the momentary probability of reinforcement on each key. Nevin did find that choices were determined by changes in the relative frequency of reinforcement within sequences of trials between reinforcements, but as shown in Figure 4, Herrnstein found no relation between the pigeons' choices and the changing relative probability of reinforcement. Momentary maximizing is therefore not necessary for matching in concurrent VI schedules.

It is an empirical question whether matching can be explained by some combination of more molecular processes, but as Herrnstein (1970) has pointed out, there is no logical reason to assume that the matching relation must be explained at a molecular level. Choice behavior in concurrent schedules may be more orderly at the level of the matching equation than at the level of local response rate variations, sequences of choices, or relative changeover frequencies.

Nevertheless, the matching relation can perhaps be incorporated into a more general model of maximizing payoff per response. Indeed, Herrnstein and Loveland (1975) have argued that an implicit assumption of maximizing is present in our thinking about the interaction between reinforcement and behavior. It is an integral part of our conception of reinforcement that an animal engages in the more highly rein-

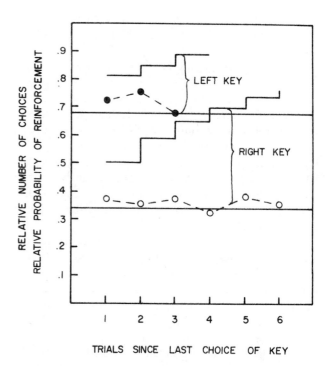

Fig. 4. The two step functions plot changes in the relative momentary probability of reinforcement with the number of trials since the last choice of each key in a discrete-trial concurrent VI VI schedule. The open and closed circles plot the relative number of responses on each key, averaged across two pigeons, as a function of the number of trials since the last choice of that key. The horizontal lines show the overall relative reinforcement rates on the two VI schedules. (Herrnstein, unpublished data.)

forced response when given a choice between two incompatible responses that differ in reinforcement. Herrnstein and Loveland suggest that in a choice between two VI schedules the animal adjusts its behavior to equalize the ratio of responses to reinforcements on each alternative, which produces matching:

$$\frac{R_1}{r_1} = \frac{R_2}{r_2}$$

$$\frac{R_1}{R_2} = \frac{r_1}{r_2}$$

and
$$\frac{R_1}{R_1 + R_2} = \frac{r_1}{r_1 + r_2} \qquad (6)$$

where R_1 and R_2 stand for responses to each of the two alternatives and r_1 and r_2 stand for the corresponding number of reinforcements. At any given moment, the animal performs that response which seems to have the most favorable response-to-reinforcement ratio. By responding to that alternative it drives its response-to-reinforcement ratio up toward that for the other alternative. When the other schedule offers the more favorable ratio, the animal switches to it. In choice between two unequal ratio schedules, where the experimenter fixes the response-to-reinforcement ratios, this maximization implies exclusive preference for the alternative with the smallest ratio of responses to reinforcements. In fact, Herrnstein (1958) and Herrnstein and Loveland (1975) have shown that on concurrent FR FR or VR VR schedules, pigeons will respond exclusively to the alternative with the shortest radio requirement, provided that the difference between the two ratios is larger than some minimum value.

This analysis of the role of maximizing in the matching relation leads to an interesting prediction for performance in concurrent VI VR schedules. According to the matching relation, an animal's response-to-reinforcement ratio on the VI schedule should come to equal the response-to-reinforcement ratio on the ratio schedule (see Equation 6). But should the VI schedule be short enough so that the obtained reinforcements per response for the VI schedule rise above the value fixed for the ratio schedule, responding to the ratio alternative should cease, since it no longer can offer the most favorable ratio of responses to reinforcements. Herrnstein (1970, 1971) showed that pigeons do match response ratios to reinforcement ratios on VI VR schedules over a wide range of schedule values. But once the VI was rich enough or the VR high enough so that the same rate of reinforcement could be obtained for fewer responses on the VI, responding on the VR tended to cease; that is, relative response rate drifted toward exclusive preference for the VI schedule.

TIME MATCHING AS THE FUNDAMENTAL MATCHING PROCESS

Brownstein and Pliskoff (1968), Baum and Rachlin (1969), and more recently Rachlin (1973) have all argued that matching of relative time allocation to the relative frequency of reinforcement is more basic than response matching in concurrent schedules. They demonstrated time matching in situations in which there were no response requirements apart from the allocation of time to the particular stimuli associated with each schedule. Baum and Rachlin (1969) proposed that even a series of repetitions of discrete responses such as key pecks or lever presses can be thought of as periods of time spent engaging in a continuous activity (key pecking or lever pressing), because these responses tend to be emitted in bursts of responses at a constant rate (Blough, 1963). The time spent pecking then determines the number of pecks emitted, and overall rate of responding over a session varies with the duration of pauses between the bursts.

The time spent in each component of a CO-key concurrent schedule, or cumulated interchangeover time in a two-key procedure, cannot directly measure the time spent responding as Baum and Rachlin define it, because it will always include time spent at other activities—e.g., grooming. These measures of time distribution between the two schedules will only be directly proportional to time spent responding if the proportions of time spent in other activities in each component were invariant across experimental conditions. Baum and Rachlin (1969) therefore suggest that the relative number of responses may provide the best measure of the relative time spent responding. As long as the time required for a response remains fairly constant, the number of responses will be directly proportional to time spent responding.

But it then becomes difficult, if not impossible, to distinguish empirically between response matching and matching in terms of time spent responding. While there are choice situations in which an analysis in terms of number of responses would be arbitrary (Baum & Rachlin, 1969; Brownstein & Pliskoff, 1968), there are also situations in which an analysis in terms of time would be arbitrary. Nevin (1969) and Herrnstein (unpublished data) both found response matching in discrete-trial procedures in which the pigeon had only occasional pecks at the key.

On the other hand, Rachlin (1973) argues that by allocating time to each schedule in a concurrent schedule procedure, the animal equalizes the local frequency of reinforcement for each alternative. Since *local* response rates are also equal on concurrent VI VI schedules (Catania, 1966; Killeen, 1972b; Shull & Pliskoff, 1967), overall response matching results from the matching of time allocation. But time allocation in the sense of equalizing local reinforcement frequencies refers to the total time spent in each component (or to cumulated interchangeover time), not to time spent responding as defined by Baum and Rachlin (1969). Local response and reinforcement rates are calculated in terms of the time spent in each component, and the evidence cited by Rachlin (1973) in support of his theory shows time matching in this sense (Catania, 1966; Killeen, 1972b; Shull & Pliskoff, 1967; Silberberg & Fantino, 1970).

But Herrnstein (1970, 1971) reported that pigeons matched relative response rates, but not the relative cumulated interchangeover time, to the relative reinforcement frequency in a two-key concurrent VI VR schedule. In this situation, rate of reinforcement is essentially independent of rate of responding on the VI but is directly proportional to response rate on the VR.[4] Since local rates of pecking on VR schedules are faster than those on VI schedules for the same frequency of reinforcement, matching cannot hold for both relative rate of responding and relative cumulated interchangeover time. For each of the 10 pigeons studied by Herrnstein, matching described relative rate of responding over a wide range of different VI and VR values, although local response rates were faster on the VR.

Herrnstein and Loveland (unpublished data) recently obtained similiar results in a CO-key concurrent VI VR procedure. The data are analyzed here in terms of Equations 4 and 5 (proportional ratio matching). All four pigeons in the study matched response ratios to obtained reinforcement ratios, but with a proportional bias toward the VR schedule; i.e., the pigeons responded a constant proportional amount more on the VR at all reinforcement ratios (except (0 or ∞). Figure 5 plots the logarithm of the response and time ratios against the logarithm of reinforcement ratios for each pigeon. The regression lines of best fit to these data and percentage of the variance accounted for are also shown. One pigeon matched both time and responses, but for three other birds the regression lines for time ratios are much flatter than those for response ratios. However, since the range of reinforcement ratios studied was narrow, the group data should also be examined, i.e., all the data points provided by the four pigeons. The least-squares regression lines for these data are $1.03X - 0.15$ for response ratios and $1.01X + 0.09$ for time ratios. Thus while the individual pigeons showed better response matching, the slopes for the group data functions were close to 1.0 for both responses and time.

La Bounty and Reynolds (1973) studied pigeons in a two-key concurrent FI FR schedule. This schedule has similiar properties to the VI VR schedule; local response rate is higher on the FR than the FI, and reinforcement rate on the FR is directly proportional to response rate. The experimenters report approximate matching between relative response rate and relative reinforcement frequency for four of six pigeons, but state that no pigeons matched relative

[4] It should be noted that relative reinforcement frequency in a concurrent VI VR schedule is not strictly an independent variable since reinforcement rate on the VR schedule is dependent on response rate on the VR. But this is often the case with short VI schedules as well, and the matching relation holds between relative reinforcement rate and *obtained*, not scheduled, relative reinforcement frequency.

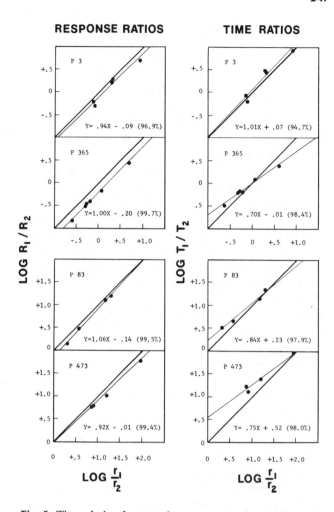

Fig. 5. The relation between log response ratio and log reinforcement ratio, and between log time ratio and log reinforcement ratio, for four pigeons responding on CO-key concurrent VI VR schedules. The heavy diagonals represent unbiased matching; the fine diagonals represent the regression lines fitted to the data by the method of least-squares. The percentage of the data variance accounted for by each regression line is also given. (Herrnstein & Loveland, unpublished data.)

time to relative reinforcement. They conclude that time matching is not more basic than response matching, since the latter can hold without the former. However, a different picture emerges when their data are reanalyzed in terms of proportional ratio matching, which accounts for bias toward one schedule. Time ratios in fact fit proportional ratio matching better than response ratios for four of the six pigeons. The slopes of the regression lines relating time ratios and reinforcement ratios for five of the pigeons were .88, .88, .99, .81, and .66; for response ratios they were .84, .79, .89, .75, and .86 for the same pigeons. All the pigeons showed a bias in time ratios toward the FI schedule, but the same bias was not found for response ratios. The sixth pigeon was either indifferent between the two schedules or else showed exclusive preference for the FR key. Thus in this study response matching was no better than time matching; both response and time distributions tended to somewhat undermatch the reinforcement distribution. A possible explanation of the undermatching found in concurrent FI FR schedules will be considered later in the chapter (under the heading "Applications of Herrnstein's Equations to Other Schedules").

To summarize, both response and time matching are found in concurrent schedules, and the best general conclusion at present is that the distribution of reinforcement in a concurrent schedule governs the distribution of behavior. Sometimes behavior is best measured in terms of the time allocated to each schedule, sometimes by the rate of responding. In some situations only one measure is appropriate (e.g., Baum & Rachlin, 1969; Brownstein & Pliskoff, 1968; Nevin, 1969), but why one measure sometimes works better than the other when both are available (Hollard & Davison, 1971) remains to be determined.

THE GENERALITY OF THE MATCHING RELATION

As Catania (1966) indicated in the first substantial review of choice in concurrent schedules, the significance of the matching relation depends on the range of conditions over which it occurs. We have already considered a substantial amount of evidence for matching to relative frequency of reinforcement in concurrent VI schedules, but does the matching relation hold for other reinforcement parameters (e.g., magnitude, immediacy, or quality of reinforcement); for different schedules besides the concurrent VI VI; or for negative reinforcement?

Magnitude of Reinforcement

The data on reinforcement magnitude are equivocal, both matching and undermatching being reported in studies of concurrent schedules. Catania (1963a) found that two of his three pigeons matched their distribution of responses to the relative durations of grain reinforcement provided by two equal VI schedules. But he examined only one relative reinforcement duration besides equality. Brownstein (1971) investigated choice between two pairs of unequal reinforcement durations in addition to equality in the time allocation procedure used by Brownstein and Pliskoff (1968). Three pigeons chose between two equal VI schedules of response-independent grain presentation by pecking at a CO key. Different COD durations (2, 5, and 7 sec) were scheduled for each bird. The slopes of the regression lines relating time ratios to reinforcement duration ratios were .70, 1.20, and .95 for the three pigeons. The pigeon for which the shortest COD was programmed (2 sec) was undermatching, and the pigeon with the 5-sec COD was overmatching. The regression line for the group data was .95X + .02. De Villiers and Millenson (1972) also reported response matching to relative duration of condensed milk reinforcement for three rats, but they only examined one relative duration (.75).

In a two-key concurrent schedule, Fantino, Squires, Delbruck, and Peterson (1972) varied the overall frequency of grain reinforcements while keeping the relative duration constant at .80 (1.5 and 6 sec). Relative response rates and the relative total reinforcer time on the 6-sec key increased as reinforcement became more frequent, because the pigeons spent more time responding on that key. Fantino et al. analyzed their data in terms of relative response rates and reported that the pigeons failed to match either relative hopper duration or relative total reinforcer time (hopper duration times the number of reinforcements on that key). But if the data are reanalyzed in terms of proportional ratio matching (Equation 5; repeated here for the reader's convenience),

$$\frac{R_1}{R_2} = k \frac{r_1}{r_2} \qquad (5)$$

which allows for bias toward one key, then matching is found (Baum, 1974a). A regression line of slope 1.08 and a k of 2.4 accurately describe the ratio data. The pigeons of Fantino et al. were therefore matching total reinforcer time, but with a constant proportional bias toward the 1.5-sec key. Such a systematic bias at all frequencies of reinforcement could arise if the time spent eating on the 6-sec reinforcement was in fact less than 4 times the 1.5-sec reinforcement.

The above results support response or time matching to reinforcement duration, but several other studies have failed to find matching to either relative duration or total reinforcer time. Walker, Schnelle, and Hurwitz (1970), using rats as subjects, varied the duration of access to sucrose solution and reported only poor matching between relative response rates and relative reinforcer durations. In a subsequent experiment, Walker and Hurwitz (1971) also varied the access to sucrose, but scheduled reinforcements by a single VI schedule (Stubbs & Pliskoff, 1969), thereby insuring that reinforcement frequency did not covary with reinforcement duration. They, too, found that preference for an alternative was less extreme than would be predicted by matching to the relative duration of reinforcement. However, in both these studies the COD was only 2 or 3 sec, too short for matching in concurrent schedules with rats. Moreover, the COD was programmed from the last response on a lever before a CO (Findley, 1958), making it functionally even shorter than the usual COD (Catania, 1966). Shull and Pliskoff (1967) and de Villiers and Millenson (1972) found that CODs longer than 5 sec were necessary before rats matched either frequency or duration of reinforcement.

Todorov (1973) studied concurrent schedules in which frequency and duration of reinforcement covaried. The pigeons in his experiment considerably undermatched the relative total reinforcer time, and frequency of reinforcement affected choice more than did duration. But this experiment used an extremely complex procedure. Three different pairs of VI schedules were programmed on the main key in randomized combinations, each pair in operation for 20 of the 60 reinforcements per session. The durations of reinforcement for the three different VI schedules were then varied in blocks of sessions. The procedure was therefore a multiple concurrent schedule, and it is difficult to assess the reinforcement interactions that such a schedule might produce. (Interactions in multiple schedules are discussed later in the chapter). Furthermore, Todorov used a 1-sec time-out contingent on a CO response in place of a COD. Whether the time-out is functionally equivalent to a COD (see p. 244) or whether it separated the schedules sufficiently is uncertain. The flat function relating relative response rate to relative total reinforcer time observed by Todorov is typical of the function found in the absence of a COD, so it is possible that the pigeons never fully distinguished the three different component schedules. However, Todorov did find that frequency of reinforcement had a greater effect on relative response rate than did reinforcement duration. This could represent either a problem of discrimination or a fundamental difference in the relationship between response strength and various reinforcement parameters. Mariner and Thomas (1969) argued that pigeons have difficulty discriminating between different hopper durations because they cannot tell that they are in the longer duration until the time of the shorter duration has passed. Mariner and Thomas failed to obtain peak shift[5] (Hanson, 1959) from pigeons in a wavelength discrimination with different hopper durations unless the two durations were signaled by hopper lights of different intensity. The peak shift is readily obtained when reinforcement frequency varies in a discrimination procedure (Dysart, Marx, McLean, & Nelson, 1974; Guttman, 1959). Thus pigeons might match relative reinforcement durations more closely if differential signals were provided for the hopper durations.

Schneider (1973) avoided a difficulty common to all these studies—that of determining whether the actual relative quantity of reinforcer obtained by the subjects equals that scheduled by the timers for hopper duration. He varied the number of food pellets provided during each reinforcement in a two-key concurrent schedule. A single VI schedule arranged the reinforcements, which were assigned with an equal probability to each key. A 1.5-sec COD operated throughout the experiment. Schneider noted that a fixed quantity of reinforcement on a key maintained more rapid responding when it was delivered frequently in small amounts than when it was delivered infrequently in large amounts. When reinforcement frequency remained constant the pigeons undermatched the relative quantity of reinforcement at three different pellet ratios (1:1, 1:3, and 1:7). Slopes of the regression lines relating log response ratios to log pellet ratios were .19, .41, .43, and .58 for the four pigeons. However, when the number of pellets per reinforcement remained constant, undermatching was also obtained for the same ratios of reinforcement frequency (slopes of .35, .46, .64, and .63). In view of the excellent matching reported by Stubbs and Pliskoff (1969) for frequency using the same scheduling procedure and a 2-sec COD, Schneider's result is surprising. The 1.5-sec COD was possibly too short for his pigeons, and it is unfortunate that he did not also study choice at longer COD durations.

Unpublished data from an experiment by de Villiers and Balboni suggest another reason why Schneider did not find matching to relative quantity of food. De Villiers and Balboni studied two rats responding on a two-lever concurrent VI schedule for different numbers of food pellets. A single VI 30-sec schedule arranged reinforcements which were assigned with equal probability (.50) to each lever. With one pellet of food for responding on the left lever and five pellets on the right, the COD was systematically increased from 5.5 through 15 sec. Relative response rate on the five-pellet lever increased between 5.5-sec and 7.5-sec COD duration but declined with further lengthening of the COD. Changeover rate decreased with increasing COD length. As the lower panel of Figure 6 indi-

[5] The peak shift is a displacement of the peak of a post-discrimination generalization gradient away from the stimulus associated with the higher frequency of reinforcement (S+) in the direction away from the stimulus associated with extinction or the lower frequency of reinforcement (S-).

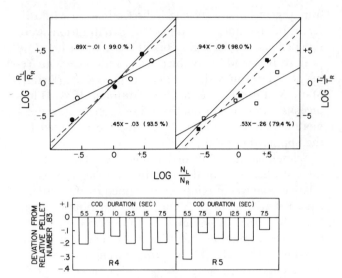

Fig. 6. (Top:) The mean log response ratios (left panel) and mean log time ratios (right panel) of two rats responding on a single-tape concurrent VI schedule plotted as a function of log pellet ratio N_L/N_R. The open symbols represent data from the condition in which relative frequency of reinforcement was kept constant at .50 and the relative number of food pellets for each alternative varied; the filled symbols represent the condition in which number of pellets per reinforcement was the same for both levers and relative frequency of reinforcement varied. The least-squares regression lines and the percentage of the data variance that they account for are given in the upper lefthand corner of each panel for frequency and the lower right-hand corner for number of pellets. (Bottom:) The bar graphs show the deviation from matching to relative pellet number (.83) (relative response rate minus relative number of pellets) for each rat as the COD duration varied. (From de Villiers & Balboni, unpublished data.)

cates, the smallest deviation from matching to the relative pellet number of .83 occurred at the 7.5-sec COD, and matching to relative pellet number was not observed at any COD value.

In the second condition of the experiment the COD was set at 7.5 sec and the number of food pellets for responding on each lever varied through the following sequence: 1:5, 3:3, 4:2, and 5:1. The VI 30-sec schedule continued to assign reinforcements with an equal probability to the two levers. The open symbols in the upper panels of Figure 6 show the mean log response ratios and mean log time ratios (cumulated interchangeover time) of the two rats plotted against the mean log pellet ratios. The least-squares regression lines fitted to the data were $.45X + .03$ (responses) and $.53X - .26$ (time). Slopes of the individual functions were .52 and .38 for responses, .62 and .46 for time ratios.

The upper panels of Figure 6 also give the mean response and time ratio data for the third condition of the experiment. With the same COD duration and three pellets for responding on each lever, the probability of reinforcement assignment to each lever was varied through the sequence: .50:.50, .15:.85, and .75:.25. Regression lines fitted to the mean data from the two rats were $.89X - .01$ (responses) and $.94X - .09$ (time): The slopes of the individual functions were .91 and .86 for responses, and .77 and 1.11 for time ratios. One rat therefore matched responses and the other rat approximately matched time allocation to the ratios of the obtained frequencies of reinforcement.

The results suggest that matching to relative magnitude of reinforcement does not hold in the Stubbs and Pliskoff (1969) single-tape scheduling procedure regardless of COD length and changeover rate. The single-tape procedure forces the animal to respond for some time on the alternative with the smaller reinforcer since half the reinforcement opportunities are scheduled for that side. Reinforcements assigned to that alternative must be obtained before the VI tape starts timing intervals again for either alternative. Increasing the COD reduces changeovers and separates the two alternatives in time, but it forces the animal to spend even longer responding on the alternative with the small reinforcer in order to restart the tape. Since the Stubbs and Pliskoff procedure, which varies relative frequency of reinforcement, does not force the animal toward the less frequently reinforced alternative to the same degree, matching is found at suitably long COD durations.

A recent experiment on magnitude of reinforcement by Iglauer and Woods (1974) used independently programmed VI 1-min schedules, thus avoiding the constraints on responding inherent in the single-tape procedure. They varied the dosage of intravenous cocaine injections available on each schedule, a parameter of reinforcement magnitude more immediately discriminable than duration. Drug dosage was manipulated by varying the volume of a constant-concentration cocaine solution injected over a constant time period. Reinforcers therefore differed in volume but not in concentration or duration. The full procedure was a modification of the standard two-lever concurrent schedule in that a single response on a center lever initiated the concurrent schedule on two adjacent levers. Responding on one lever produced a constant dose of .1-mg/kg/injection, while the dosage of cocaine associated with the other lever varied from .025 to .4 mg/kg/injection. During reinforcement, one of two pumps injected the cocaine solution for 35 sec, followed by a 5-min blackout of the chamber for the drug to take effect. At the end of the blackout a single response on the center lever again initiated the choice procedure. A 1.5-sec COD was in effect during the concurrent schedule component.

Since relative reinforcement frequency covaries to some extent with relative response rate in the two-tape procedure, Iglauer and Woods calculated the relative drug intake on the two levers. Drug intake represents the number of reinforcements received on a lever multiplied by the drug dose available on it. For both monkeys on the concurrent schedule, relative response rates matched relative drug intake over a wide range of values. Regression lines relating log response ratio to log drug intake ratio (excluding points of exclusive preference) were $1.08X - .06$ and $1.11X + .01$ for the two monkeys.

Two other monkeys responded in a concurrent chain schedule procedure (Autor, 1969; Herrnstein, 1964), in which responding during an initial two-lever concurrent VI VI schedule (choice link) led to one of two equal-valued single-lever FR schedules for cocaine (terminal links). These monkeys matched relative response rates during the choice link to their relative drug intake in the terminal links.

On a whole, these studies suggest that frequency of reinforcement may have a greater effect than magnitude on choice in concurrent schedules with short CODs, but the matching relation applies to total reinforcement received (amount times frequency) when appropriate concurrent schedule procedures are employed.

Immediacy of Reinforcement

The application of the matching relation was extended to immediacy of reinforcement (1/delay) by Chung and Herrnstein (1967). For four pigeons, VI reinforcement on one key (the standard key) was delayed for 8 sec, while on the other key (the experimental key) the delay of reinforcement on an equal VI schedule varied from 1 to 30 sec. For two other pigeons the standard key delay was 16 sec. During the delay of reinforcement the experimental chamber was blacked out. The slopes of the least-squares regression lines relating ratios of responses to ratios of immediacy of reinforcement on the two keys were .92 for the 8-sec standard delay group and 1.05 for the 16-sec group. The 16-sec pigeons showed a consistent bias toward the experimental key, but the slopes of both functions were close to perfect matching. In an earlier experiment, Chung (1965) had studied choice between immediate and delayed reinforcement in equal concurrent VI schedules. Chung and Herrnstein (1967) demonstrated that if a small constant (1.6 sec) was taken as the actual delay interval for what was nominally immediate reinforcement, Chung's pigeons were actually matching the relative reciprocal of delay on each key. The constant represents the time taken for the pigeon to lower its head to the feeder and begin eating.

On the other hand, Shimp (1969b, Experiment II) found that if pigeons in a similar choice procedure had to peck after the delay blackout to obtain reinforcement, two of the three birds still matched relative response rates to the relative reciprocal of blackout duration. Since there was now no time interval imposed between the last peck and food presentation, Shimp argued that the blackout and not the delay of reinforcement was crucial in Chung and Herrnstein's experiment. Shimp's procedure is much like requiring a lengthy prereinforcement interresponse time (IRT) stipulated by the blackout duration. Shimp (1969b, Experiment I) and Moffitt and Shimp (1971) demonstrated that in concurrent VI schedules in which different IRTs are required for reinforcement on the two schedules, pigeons match response rates to the relative reciprocal of IRT duration.

But experiments by Herbert (1970) do not support Shimp's interpretation of Chung and Herrnstein's results. Herbert used a single VI schedule and assigned the reinforcements with an equal probability to the two keys. In the first experiment, reinforcement for each key was delayed by a blackout, as in Chung and Herrnstein's study. Two relative delay values besides equality were examined. The slopes of regression lines relating ratios of responses to ratios of immediacy of reinforcement were .86, .73, and .86 for the three pigeons. The short 1-sec COD or the single-tape procedure (see p. 249) could account for the undermatching observed, especially for one bird. In a second experiment with the same pigeons, Herbert repeated Shimp's procedure requiring a response before food presentation after the blackouts. Only one of the three pigeons continued to approximate matching to the relative reciprocal of blackout duration; the other two were much closer to indifference at three different relative blackout durations. Matching was therefore considerably impaired by the added response requirement in this study.

In Herbert's third experiment reinforcement on one key was immediate, whereas it followed a blackout delay on the other key (as in Chung's 1965 procedure). But an equal number and duration of response-contingent blackouts were also programmed at variable intervals on the immediate key, independently of the reinforcement. Under these conditions, no pigeon matched the relative immediacy of reinforcement when a small constant was taken as the actual delay on the immediate key. When the relative frequency of reinforcement was fixed at .50, relative response rate on the key with immediate reinforcement increased as a linear function of increasing delay on the other key as opposed to the exponential function obtained by Chung (1965). On the basis of these results, Herbert questions Chung and Herrnstein's interpretation of their findings in terms of matching to relative immediacy of reinforcement. However, the pigeons in Herbert's third experiment did not choose between immediate and delayed reinforcement as was suggested; they actually chose between immediate reinforcement *plus* punishment by response-contingent time-out from food (blackout) and delayed reinforcement. The relation between this procedure and choice between two different delays of reinforcement (Chung & Herrnstein, 1967; Herbert, 1970, Experiment I), for which approximate matching is found, is unclear. The effects of punishment on choice in concurrent schedules is considered later in the chapter.

Nevertheless, the possibility remains that the pigeon's choice in Chung and Herrnstein's experiment was influenced more by rate of reinforcement than by the delay per se. Their procedure is formally similar to a concurrent chain schedule in which responding in an initial concurrent VI VI schedule leads to unequal-length terminal links (blackouts) ending with noncontingent food—i.e., different fixed-time (FT) schedules. The shorter terminal link (i.e., the shorter delay period) has the higher rate of reinforcement, and the relative frequency of reinforcement equals the relative reciprocal of blackout duration. Neuringer (1969) demonstrated that pigeons are indifferent between FT and FI terminal links in a concurrent chain schedule. This suggests that relative response rates in the choice link of a concurrent chain schedule should show the same functional relation to relative terminal link reinforcement frequency whether the terminal links are FT schedules (as in Chung and Herrnstein's study) or FI schedules. But Duncan and Fantino (1970) found greater preference for the shorter of two FI terminal links than was predicted by matching to the obtained relative frequency of reinforcement, although they investigated a range of FI durations similar to the delay duration employed by Chung and Herrnstein. Neuringer (1969) himself obtained undermatching between relative response rates in the choice link and the relative reciprocal of differing FI and FT terminal link durations. Thus the role of rate of reinforcement as opposed to delay in Chung and Herrnstein's results remains uncertain. (See Fantino, chapter 11 in this volume.)

Qualitatively Different Reinforcers

In all the above experiments the physical dimensions of a given reinforcer were varied. But what if the reinforcers differ in quality? In this case the subject may prefer one of the reinforcers over the other, even at equal frequencies of reinforcement. Hollard and Davison (1971) studied pigeons under two-key concurrent VI schedules with food as the reinforcer on one key and ectostriatal brain stimulation as the reinforcer on the other. A single VI schedule assigned reinforcements according to different proportions to the two keys (Stubbs & Pliskoff, 1969). The brain stimulation parameters were kept constant while the frequency of food reinforcement was varied. Although all the pigeons showed a constant proportional preference for the food at all frequencies of reinforcement, proportional ratio matching accurately described the relation between ratios of time spent responding for food or brain stimulation and ratios of the number of reinforcements of each kind. Individual regression lines relating the log of the time ratios to the log of the reinforcement ratios were: $Y = 1.05X + .74$; $Y = 1.01X + .27$; and $Y = .98X + .78$. On the other hand, all three pigeons produced regression lines relating response ratios to reinforcement ratios with a flatter slope than that predicted by matching, the individual slopes being .79, .65, and .83. Biased time matching but not response matching was therefore found for the different qualities of reinforcement.

Brown and Herrnstein (1975) have pointed out that the matching relation might not hold where the different reinforcers interact, as food and water do (Bolles, 1967). Since animals tend to drink following food consumption (Bolles, 1967), increasing the frequency of food reinforcement might enhance the value of a constant frequency of water reinforcement. On the other hand, Wood, Martinez, and Willis (1975) found that increasing the FR requirement in a concurrent FI (food) FR (food or water) schedule had different effects depending on whether the FR reinforcement was food or water. When both reinforcers were food, increasing the FR also increased the animal's responding on the FI; but when the FR reinforcer was water, responding on the FI for food was unaffected by changes in the FR. Systematic variation of the frequency of food and water reinforcers in concurrent schedules is necessary to determine the

Punishment and Choice in Concurrent Schedules

Few studies have quantified the effects of punishment on choice in concurrent schedules. Holz (1968) punished concurrent responses maintained by different frequencies of reinforcement in a two-key concurrent VI 1-min VI 4-min schedule. Each response on the two keys was punished by a brief electric shock. As the shock intensity increased, response rate on both keys progressively decreased. Nevertheless, at all shock intensities, as long as the pigeons continued to respond, the proportion of responses to each key matched the proportion of reinforcements obtained from that key. In Holz's procedure every response was punished, so the proportion of punishments equaled both the proportion of responses and the proportion of reinforcements on the two keys as long as the pigeon matched. If the shocks had been programmed so that this proportionality no longer held—e.g., by equal VI or FI punishment schedules—some interaction between the positive reinforcement and the punishment might be expected, and the simple matching relation might not hold. Azrin and Holz (1966) reported that when only one of the concurrent responses was punishment, the alternative response increased in frequency while the punished response was rapidly suppressed. However, no systematic study has yet quantified the interactions between punishing and rewarding consequences of responding in a concurrent schedule paradigm (cf. Rachlin & Herrnstein, 1969).

As discussed earlier, Todorov (1971) punished the CO response in a CO-key concurrent VI schedule with electric shock or time-out from reinforcement. Relative response rate and relative time allocation for the preferred schedule increased sharply as the shock intensity was increased or the time-out duration lengthened, but the relative reinforcement frequency did not also increase. The relative response and time measures therefore deviated more and more from matching in the direction of the preferred schedule as the punishment increased. This deviation from matching can be explained by the differences between the Holz (1968) and Todorov procedures. In the simple continuous punishment procedures used by Holz, each choice is punished in proportion to the number of responses made to it. However, in Todorov's procedure, each choice receives the same number of punishments per session, since the COs in both directions must be equal. Thus the less preferred choice receives disproportionately more punishment than the more preferred and is more suppressed.

De Villiers and Millenson (1972) also studied the interaction between positive reinforcement and aversive stimulation in a choice procedure. They superimposed a conditioned aversive stimulus (a conditioned suppression procedure—Estes and Skinner, 1941) on a two-lever concurrent VI schedule with different durations of reinforcement programmed for each response. They suggested that the aversiveness of the conditioned suppression procedure summated with the reinforcement for the two responses, subtracting a constant value from each. If this were the case, the relative reinforcing value of the preferred schedule would increase,

$$\frac{(r_1 - c)}{(r_1 - c) + (r_2 - c)} > \frac{r_1}{r_1 + r_2} \qquad (7)$$

where $r_1 > r_2$ and $r_2 \neq 0$, and so should the relative performance measures if matching to relative value were retained. In fact, de Villiers and Millenson found increased preference for the lever associated with the bigger reinforcement during the preshock stimulus. A similar interaction between the food reinforcement and the aversive value of the punishment could account for the increased preference for the more favored key in the Todorov (1971) study.

This interpretation of Todorov's results receives support from a recent experiment by de Villiers (unpublished data). Three pigeons responding on a two-key concurrent VI 1-min VI 3-min schedule for grain received intermittent punishment with brief electric shock for pecks at each key. Punishments were arranged by a single VI 15 sec schedule and assigned with an equal probability (.50) to each key, thus maintaining the relative frequency of punishment at .50. A 3-sec COD was programmed for food but not for punishment throughout the experiment. In the absence of punishment the pigeons closely matched relative response rates and relative time allocation (cumulated interchangeover time) to the relative frequency of reinforcement of .75. But with increasing intensity of punishment, the relative response and time distributions deviated more and more from matching toward the key with more frequent reinforcement. Overall response rate on the VI 3-min key was much more suppressed by punishment than that on the VI 1-min key. Figure 7 depicts the results from each pigeon.

Further systematic investigation of the effects of

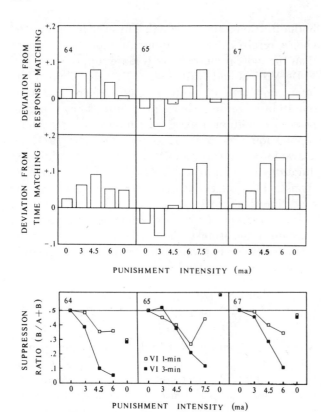

Fig. 7. Deviation of relative response rates (top panels) and relative time distribution (center panels) of three pigeons from relative frequency of reinforcement (relative frequency of responding or relative time minus relative frequency of reinforcement) on a concurrent VI 1-min VI 3-min schedule as a function of punishment intensity. Relative frequency of punishment was the same on each key. Shown in the lower panels are the suppression ratios for each key, calculated in terms of $B/(A+B)$, where B is response rate on a key in a particular punishment condition and A is response rate on the same key in the base line condition (no punishment). (From de Villiers, unpublished data.)

different punishment or conditioned suppression parameters on a wider range of relative reinforcement frequencies is needed to determine the function that relates the positive and negative consequences of choice. The sensitivity of concurrent performances to both positive reinforcement and punishment parameters (Catania, 1966; Holz, 1968) indicates that this paradigm could be very useful for study of the interactions between positive and aversive control of behavior.

Negative Reinforcement

Baum (1973) used the same shuttlebox situation as Baum and Rachlin (1969) and four of the pigeons from that study in a concurrent VI escape procedure. Standing on either side of the chamber was reinforced on two different VI schedules by a 2-min time-out from a train of shocks. There were sizable hysteresis effects, but proportional ratio matching, Equation 4, provided a good fit to the data for two of the four pigeons; i.e., those pigeons matched the ratio of time spent on each side of the chamber to the ratio of the frequencies of time-out provided on that side. The data from the other two pigeons deviated from the matching relation in opposite directions. For one pigeon, a regression line of greater slope than 1.0 fitted the time and reinforcement ratios, but this pigeon died after only the ascending series of schedule values. The data could therefore be affected by the strong order effects found in this experiment. The second pigeon undermatched the ratios of time-out frequencies, and Baum suggests that this may be due to the short COD used in the study (1 sec). This bird showed a constant high rate of COs at all schedule values and also undermatched ratios of positive reinforcement in Baum and Rachlin's earlier study when the COD was as long as 4.25 sec. But the equivalence of COD values for positive and negative reinforcement in concurrent schedules remains to be demonstrated, so this explanation is tentative.

Despite the difficulties involved in working with aversive contingencies, Baum's results suggest that subsequent research on concurrent schedules of negative reinforcement could be extremely fruitful. The matching relationship may provide a means of integrating both positive and negative reinforcement into the same conceptual framework (see also pp. 260 and 270).

Different Schedules of Reinforcement

Earlier in the chapter it was shown that the matching relation is readily extended to concurrent VI VR schedules (Herrnstein, 1970, 1971) and to concurrent FI FR schedules (La Bounty & Reynolds, 1973), though in the latter case the subjects tended to undermatch. In concurrent ratio schedules, on the other hand, matching cannot occur except trivially, since a ratio schedule fixes a proportionality between numbers of responses and numbers of reinforcements. In fact, for most pairs of ratio values on concurrent VR VR or FR FR schedules the subjects maximize reinforcements per response—i.e., respond exclusively to the alternative with the shortest ratio requirement (Herrnstein, 1964; Herrnstein & Loveland, 1975). The relation between maximizing and matching was discussed in an earlier section.

What about choice between concurrent interval schedules other than the concurrent VI VI? Both

Nevin (1971) and Trevitt, Davison, and Williams (1972) investigated choice in two-key concurrent VI FI schedules. Nevin reported that relative frequency of responding on the FI key depended on the relative frequency of reinforcement on that schedule, but did not match it. Instead, the ratio of responses on the FI to responses on the VI was a power function of the ratio of reinforcements for each schedule, with an exponent of approximately .50:

$$\frac{R_{FI}}{R_{VI}} = \frac{r_{FI}^{.5}}{r_{VI}^{.5}} \quad (8)$$

Two of his pigeons tended to favor the VI key while one favored the FI key.

The power function is more general than the matching relation described by proportional ratio matching (Equation 5). While proportional ratio matching specifies that the exponent shown in Equation 8 should be 1.0, the power function formulation allows the exponent to vary on both sides of 1.0. Thus it can account for both undermatching (slope <1.0) and overmatching (slope >1.0) to the reinforcement ratios. It should be noted that a suitable rescaling of the reinforcement variable—for example, by taking the square root of reinforcement frequency in the case of Equation 8—would give proportional ratio matching. The question of rescaling the reinforcement variable to give proportional ratio matching is discussed in more detail on pp. 275 ff.

Trevitt et al. (1972) also found a power function relation between the ratio of responses or time spent responding on each of the schedules and the ratio of reinforcements. All of their birds showed a consistent preference for the VI schedule. The exponents fitted to the Trevitt et al. data vary between .38 and .75 for response ratios, with an exponent of .62 for the averaged data. Similar slopes were found for each pigeon in control VI VI conditions, but the preference for the VI key was less marked. Comparing the VI FI and VI VI functions, Trevitt et al. therefore concluded that there was a constant proportional preference for the VI schedule in the VI FI choice. As discussed earlier, however, the VI VI data from this study are somewhat equivocal because of the long preexposure to the VI FI conditions during which the FI schedule was always associated with the same key; so the constant proportional preference for the VI may not be a general finding.

Nevertheless, both studies indicate that matching of response or time ratios does not occur in concurrent VI FI schedules. These ratios are related by a power function in choice between VI and FI schedules.

A study of choice in CO-key concurrent FI FI schedules (White & Davison, 1973) indicates that the pattern of responding is crucial in determining whether or not the matching relation holds in concurrent interval schedules. When typical VI performance was found on both FI schedules—i.e., a fairly constant response rate between reinforcements on each schedule—matching between response ratios and reinforcement ratios occurred. Similarly, when typical FI performance was found on both schedules—i.e., a postreinforcement pause followed by a rapidly accelerating response rate on each schedule—matching was also observed. However, when differing response patterns were generated by the two schedules, VI responding on the shorter FI schedule and FI responding on the longer schedule, a power function with an exponent close to .50 (individual exponents ranging from .38 to .57) related the response and reinforcement ratios on the two schedules. This exponent is the same as that found by Nevin (1971) for concurrent VI FI schedules.

Choice Between Interresponse Times

The pattern of responding on concurrent schedules can also be altered by reinforcing only particular bands of interresponse times (IRTs). In experiments by Staddon (1968) and Shimp (1968, 1969b) two classes of IRTs on a single key were differentially reinforced. The pigeons therefore chose between emitting two different IRTs on the same key, each associated with a different frequency of reinforcement. In Shimp's experiments, but not in that of Staddon, the two IRT bands were signaled by discriminative stimuli on the key.

It is difficult to characterize the reinforced operant in these paced schedules, since a large amount of collateral behavior is generated by such schedules (Kramer & Rilling, 1970). Nevertheless, orderly relations were obtained between response rates and reinforcement frequencies. Shimp (1968, 1969b) demonstrated that the relative frequency of each IRT approximately matched the relative reciprocal of its length, and the relative rate at which each of the two IRTs was emitted was a monotonically increasing function of its relative frequency of reinforcement. Staddon (1968) divided all of the responses made by his subjects into two component distributions under the control of the short and long IRT contingencies, respectively. The pigeons' allocation of responses to each of these distributions (response ratios derived from the component distributions) was related to the ratios of reinforcement of the two IRTs by a power function with an exponent of approximately .67 (a range of .59 to .77 for individual birds).

Moffitt and Shimp (1971) used a two-key concurrent procedure in which one class of IRTs was reinforced on one key and a second class of IRTs was reinforced on the other key. A single VI programmer arranged reinforcements for both keys, and these were assigned to each key according to different probabilities. In one experiment, the relative reinforcement frequencies were equal, but the lengths of the two reinforced IRTs varied. The relative rate of responding on a key approximately equaled the relative reciprocal of the length of the IRT reinforced on that key. In a second experiment, the relative reinforcement frequency for two particular IRTs, one on each key, was varied. The reinforced IRTs for one group of pigeons were the same as those used by Shimp (1968), 1.5 to 2.5 sec and 3.5 to 4.5 sec. For a second group of pigeons the reinforced IRTs were those used by Staddon (1968), 2 to 3 sec and 10 to 11 sec.

Monotonically increasing, negatively accelerated functions described the relation between relative response rate and relative reinforcement frequency for each key, similar to the functions obtained for the same IRTs by Shimp (1968) and Staddon (1968). If the data are plotted in terms of ratios of responses and reinforcements, the group of three pigeons exposed to the IRTs used by Staddon (1968) produce power functions with exponents of .73, .58, and .69, respectively. The group of pigeons exposed to the IRTs taken from Shimp's earlier experiment produce power functions with larger exponents, .91, .86, and .63, respectively, nearer the 1.0 exponent predicted by the biased matching relation. All of the pigeons showed a marked bias toward the shorter of the two IRTs, in keeping with the preference for shorter IRTs suggested by Shimp (1968). Choice between two concurrent IRTs therefore produces similar functions relating response ratios (or proportions) to IRT lengths and to reinforcement ratios (or proportions) whether the IRTs are programmed on two keys or together on one key.

The results of these experiments demonstrate that the closer together the two reinforced IRTs are in length, the higher the power function exponent and the closer the approximation to matching. Indeed, Shimp (1971) showed that when the same two bands of IRTs are reinforced on each key in a two-key concurrent schedule, close matching occurs between relative response rate on one key and relative reinforcement rate on that key. The matching relation therefore applies even in situations in which the pattern of responding on each key is constrained by paced schedules, provided that the response constraints are the same on the two keys. The more the constraints deviate from equality, the more relative response rates or response ratios deviate from matching.

Other experiments by Shimp (1970) and Hawkes and Shimp (1974) have established some of the boundary conditions for matching to the relative reciprocal of the reinforced IRTs. When two different signaled IRT bands are reinforced equally frequently on a single key, preference for the shorter of the IRTs increases from near indifference at very low overall rates of reinforcement until it reaches an asymptote approximating the matching-to-relative-reciprocal value between 20 and 30 reinforcements per hr (Shimp, 1970). Hawkes and Shimp (1974) concurrently reinforced two signaled IRT bands on a single key with equal frequencies. They maintained the relative reciprocal of the shorter IRT band at .70 but varied the absolute values of the two reinforced IRTs. Relative rate of emission of the two IRTs only matched the relative reciprocal of their lengths when the shorter IRT band was between 1.5 and 2.5 sec. This was roughly the lower bound of the shorter class of IRTs used in previous experiments that reported matching to the relative reciprocal (Moffitt & Shimp, 1971; Shimp, 1969b, 1971). When the lower bound of the shorter IRT band was less than 1.0 sec the pigeons were nearly indifferent between the two IRTs. And when both of the reinforced IRTs were longer than 2.5 sec the pigeons showed greater preference for the shorter IRT than was predicted by relative reciprocal matching.

To summarize, the matching relation applies in a wide range of choice situations, to several different parameters of reinforcement besides frequency, and to choice between several different schedules of reinforcement besides VIs. In concurrent VI FI and paced schedules, however, the slope of the function relating choice and reinforcement for each alternative differs from that predicted by matching, and even the generalized matching equations including a bias or preference parameter (Equations 4 and 5) do not handle the data. They account for deviations in the intercept of the function from that predicted by matching—i.e., for a consistent preference for one alternative—but not for deviations in slope from 1.0. In the next section of the chapter I shall consider how a quantitative formulation of the relation between response strength and reinforcement, derived from the matching relation, could account for the deviations from 1.0 slope found in these studies.

ABSOLUTE RATES OF RESPONDING AND A QUANTITATIVE LAW OF EFFECT

We have seen that in a wide range of choice situations the relative rate of responding is directly determined by the obtained relative frequency of reinforcement. However, the matching relationship between response proportions or ratios and the corresponding reinforcement proportions or ratios may not be the most fundamental way to quantify the relation between response strength and reinforcement. Response and reinforcement proportions or ratios remain invariant over large changes in overall response rate or reinforcement frequency. What about the absolute response rates in choice situations?

Herrnstein (1970) reasoned that the relative frequency of reinforcement should determine not only the relative response rates but also the absolute rates of responding. As Herrnstein pointed out, at every moment of possible action a set of alternative responses confronts the animal, so that each action is the outcome of a choice. No matter how the experimenter tries to control the extraneous sources of reinforcement for responses other than those stipulated in the experiment, the subject will always have distractions available, even if they are merely concerned with its own body or physiological processes. Thus even on single-response procedures the subject is in a concurrent situation, although the experimenter may monitor only one of the alternative responses and reinforcers.

Absolute response rate on single and concurrent schedules can therefore be considered a function of the frequency of reinforcement for that response relative to all the other sources of reinforcement for competing responses. Herrnstein (1970, 1971) suggested a direct proportionality between the overall relative frequency of reinforcement and the absolute rate of responding. For a situation containing n alternative sources of reinforcement he proposed a general equation of the form

$$R_1 = \frac{kr_1}{\sum_{i=0}^{n} r_i} \tag{9}$$

where R_1 is the rate of emission of the stipulated response and r_1 is the frequency or magnitude of reinforcement for that response. The parameter k represents the asymptotic response rate in the absence of any reinforcement for competing response—i.e., when r_1 equals Σr_i, the total amount of reinforcement from all sources in the situation. The parameter k can be thought of as the total amount of behavior sustained by all the reinforcement available to the animal in the experimental situation. It is measured in the same units as the stipulated response—e.g., in responses per min or running speed units' (see Herrnstein, 1974). The relation of Equation 9 to the matching equation then becomes clear:

$$\frac{R_1}{\sum_{i=0}^{n} R_i} = \frac{r_1}{\sum_{i=0}^{n} r_i}$$

$$k = \sum_{i=0}^{n} R_i \tag{10}$$

$$R_1 = \frac{kr_1}{\sum_{i=0}^{n} r_i}$$

Single Schedules—Frequency of Food Reinforcement

In a single-response procedure, Equation 9 becomes

$$R_1 = \frac{kr_1}{r_1 + r_e} \tag{11}$$

where R_1, r_1, and k are as specified for Equation 9. The parameter r_e represents the total reinforcement besides r_1 in the experimental situation[6]—i.e., all the other reinforcers that a subject brings with itself or finds in the experimental setting. The equation assumes that they can be given a value in terms of the units of reinforcement contingent on R_1; thus r_e is measured in terms of the same units as r_1, a frequency, amount, or concentration of reinforcement (Herrnstein, 1974).

Herrnstein (1970) tested this equation with data from two experiments investigating the effects of frequency of food on key-peck rate in pigeons. The best data come from an exhaustive study of single VI schedules by Catania and Reynolds (1968). Six pigeons were exposed to VI schedules with frequencies of reinforcement ranging from 8 to 300 reinforcements per

---

[6] In his 1970 paper "On the Law of Effect," Herrnstein used the expression r_o to mean all reinforcements besides r_1—i.e., $\Sigma r_i - r_1 = r_o$. But in his later paper (Herrnstein, 1974), he used r_o in a more restrictive sense of reinforcements that come spontaneously and are not conditional upon any responses. Therefore, r_e is used to denote more generally all reinforcements spontaneous or contingent on responses other than r_1—i.e., all extraneous sources of reinforcement (Herrnstein & Loveland, 1974). I shall follow the more recent usage of r_e throughout the chapter.

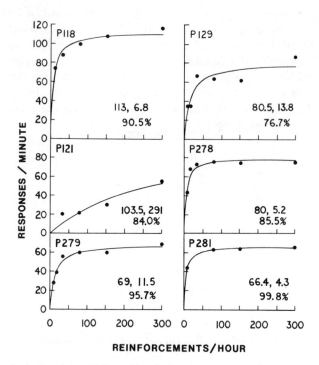

Fig. 8. Rate of responding as a function of frequency of food reinforcement for six pigeons responding on single VI schedules. The least-squares fit of Equation 11 to the data is plotted for each pigeon. The k- and r_e-values and the percentage of the variance in response rate accounted for by the functions are also shown. (Data from Catania and Reynolds, (1968) as plotted by Herrnstein, R. J. On the law of effect. *Journal of the Experimental Analysis of Behavior*, 1970. © 1970 by the Society for the Experimental Analysis of Behavior, Inc.)

hr. Figure 8 shows the least-squares fit of Equation 11 to the data from each of the pigeons. The values of k and r_e and the percentage of data variance accounted for by the equation in each case are given in the bottom right-hand corner of each panel. With a k of 66.3 responses per min and an r_e of 7.3 reinforcements per hr, the equation also accounts for 91.3% of the data variance when response rate is averaged across the pigeons for each VI value.

Chung (1966) reinforced pigeons' responses on a tandem FR 1 FIx schedule, where x represents a given duration after the first postreinforcement response. The first response after the postreinforcement pause started an FI timer, and the first response after the timer timed out produced food reinforcement. The length of the FI was varied, determining both rate of responding and rate of reinforcement. By this method, reinforcement rates of up to 2,000 per hr were obtained, many times the maximum value investigated by Catania and Reynolds (1968). Herrnstein (1970) demonstrated that Equation 11 also accounts for Chung's results, though with somewhat higher param-

eter values than those for Catania and Reynolds' subjects. With a k of 130 pecks per min and r_e of 210 reinforcements per hr, Equation 11 accounts for 94.7% of the variance in mean response rate for Chung's pigeons.

Can the equation be extended to other parameters of reinforcement besides frequency, and to other measures of response strength besides rate of key pecking? De Villiers and Herrnstein (in press) have carried out a comprehensive review of the literature on the relation between several measures of response strength (e.g., running speed in an alley or latency to respond in a discrete-trial situation, as well as the rate of emission of repetitive responses like key pecking or lever pressing) and several parameters of both positive and negative reinforcement. For each study the data were either taken from tables or estimated from figures. A least-squares fit of Equation 11 to the data from groups or individual subjects was performed, and the percentage of the variance in the dependent variable accounted for by the equation was calculated.[7]

Magnitude of Food Reinforcement

The most extensive study of magnitude of food reinforcement is that by Crespi (1942). Five groups of rats, 12 to 20 to a group, ran down a straight alley for different weights of dog chow, ranging from .02 to 5.12 grams. Equation 11 describes remarkably well the relation between the quantity of food and the mean running speed (1/time in sec) for each group of rats, accounting for 99.6% of the variance in running speed. Appendix A summarizes this and several other studies investigating the effects of magnitude of food reinforcement on response strength. In the study of Davenport, Goodrich, and Hagquist (1966), individual data were also available for four macaque monkeys lever-pressing for a varying number of pellets on a VI 1-min schedule. Once again the equation provides an excellent fit to the data, accounting for 99.9, 90.4, 90.1, and 96.6% of the variance in response rate for each monkey. For six of the remaining studies in Appendix A (Beier, 1958; Di Lollo, 1964; Hutt, 1954; Keesey & Kling, 1961, Experiment II; Logan, 1960, 12-hour group; Zeaman, 1949), which show group data from rats and pigeons, Equation 11 accounts for over

[7] A digital computer iteratively calculated the mean-squared deviation of obtained response rates from those predicted by Equation 11 for a wide range of k- and r_e-values varying on either side of those derived from a best fit by eye. The smallest mean-squared deviation thus obtained was subtracted from the total variance in response rate and the result divided by the total variance to determine the percentage of data variance accounted for by the equation.

90% of the variance in the measure of response strength in five cases, and for over 80% in the sixth. Since k in runway studies is measured in response speed units, 100/time in seconds to run the runway, it varies with runway length. Hence the k-values are not usually comparable across studies.

There are three exceptions to the remarkably good fit of Equation 11 to the data on magnitude of reinforcement. Keesey and Kling (1961, Experiment I) studied four pigeons key-pecking for different-sized chick-peas (varying from four quarter-peas to four whole peas) on a VI 4-min schedule. Catania (1963a) studied two pigeons key-pecking for three different durations of grain reinforcement (3, 4.5, and 6 sec) on a VI 2-min. Logan (1960, Experiment 55B) studied six rats per group receiving varying numbers of food pellets (1, 3, 6, and 12) for running down a straight alley. At 12 hr of food deprivation, running speeds of the groups conformed to Equation 11; but at 48 hr of deprivation running speed ceased to be a monotonic function of number of pellets. In the other two deviant studies (Catania, 1963a; Keesey & Kling, 1961, Experiment I) the experimenters observed minimal changes in response rate with increases in reinforcement magnitude. Two factors could possibly account for the insensitivity of key-peck rate to variations in reinforcement in these two studies. First, only a very narrow range of magnitudes was investigated, nowhere near the range studied by Crespi (1942) or the range of reinforcement in studies of frequency of food (Catania & Reynolds, 1968). Second, the pigeons were studied at high-drive levels in both experiments (as were the rats in the disconfirming condition of Logan's study). Herrnstein (1970) has argued that the reinforcement from sources other than r_1—namely, r_e—will be extremely small relative to r_1 itself under conditions of high drive. Response rates would therefore be very close to k over a fairly wide range of r_1-values, since r_1 would approximate Σr_i. The data variance in both pigeon studies was minimal.

In brief, Herrnstein's equation can be readily extended to the relation between response strength and magnitude of food reinforcement for several responses and species, though with a few exceptions.

Brain Stimulation

The magnitude of reinforcement from intracranial brain stimulation varies with several parameters of stimulation—e.g., the intensity, duration, or pulse frequency of the stimulation. But variations in response rate for brain stimulation on continuous reinforcement schedules do not provide an accurate measure of the magnitude of reinforcement, since the frequency of brain stimulation covaries with response rate on these schedules. At higher intensities or durations of stimulation, motor effects of the brain stimulation also tend to interfere with responding. Keesey (1962, 1964) therefore used a VI 16-sec schedule to investigate the effects of several parameters of stimulation of the posterior hypothalamus on rate of lever pressing in rats. Over a wide range of values, Equation 11 accurately depicts the relation between response rate and either the duration, intensity, or pulse frequency of the brain stimulation, accounting for 94.1, 92.9, and 96.9% of the data variance, respectively. The least-squares fit to the data from both of Keesey's studies is given in Appendix B.

Gallistel (1969) argued that lever-press rate on a VI schedule of brain stimulation might not be a valid measure of the magnitude of reinforcement, since response rate is also sensitive to the time since the last stimulation. To control for any variation in the aftereffects of the last brain stimulation, Gallistel gave all his subjects a series of 10 priming stimulations before they ran down a straight alley. Any differences in running speed should then be a function of the magnitude of the rewarding stimulation in the goal box. Nine rats, implanted in three different rewarding areas of the brain, ran the straight alley for a varying number of .01-msec pulses of electrical stimulation. Appendix B shows that the least-squares fit of Equation 11 accounts for a substantial proportion of the variance in running speed for each rat, even in some cases where there was little variation in running speed. The equation accounts for the behavior very well (i.e., better than 90%) for five out of the nine subjects.

Quality of Reinforcement

Numerous experiments have investigated the effects of different sugar concentrations on response strength. Guttman (1954) studied seven concentrations of sucrose (between 2 and 32%) and the same seven concentrations of glucose with rats lever-pressing on a VI 1-min schedule. The rats responded faster for sucrose than for glucose at each concentration, but Equation 11 accurately describes the relation between response rate and concentration for both reinforcers, accounting for 93.7 and 98.7% of the data variance.

Appendix C summarizes the data from this and several other studies on concentration of sucrose. In Guttman's (1953) experiment two different conditions were studied. In one a different group of about 20 rats was exposed to each concentration; in the other, 20 rats were exposed to all four concentrations. In both cases the equation accounts for over 90% of the variance in mean response rate. In analyzing the data from rhesus monkeys obtained by Conrad and Sidman (1956), response rates for the 60% sucrose solution were excluded because the experimenters report considerable satiation at this concentration. Two drive levels were used: 48 and 72 hr of food deprivation. As in the case of Logan's (1960) experiment on magnitude of reinforcement, the equation accounts for rather more of the variance in response rate at the lower drive level (96.2 versus 71.8%).

A pair of more extensive studies by Schrier (1963, 1965), also with rhesus monkeys and a lever-press response, used considerably shorter sessions to avoid satiation effects. Over a range of concentrations from 10 to 50%, the equation fits both the average and individual data remarkably well. For 10 of the 14 available individual functions, the variance accounted for was greater than 90%, and for none did it fall below 70%. For the three separate group averages, Equation 11 accounts for over 95% of the variance in each case.

Immediacy of Positive Reinforcement (1/Delay)

The most comprehensive data on delay of reinforcement in a single-response situation come from Pierce, Hanford, and Zimmerman (1972). Four rats responding on a VI 1-min schedule for food experienced delays of reinforcement varying from .5 to 100 sec. During the delay a cue light was illuminated and responding had no programmed consequences. Equation 11 again provides an accurate description of the results of Pierce et al., with immediacy of reinforcement (1/delay) as r_1. It accounts for 96.1% of the variance in mean response rate and for 80.8, 98.3, 78.9, and 97.4% of the variance for each of the four rats. The same rats were studied in a second condition in which the lever was retracted during the delay of reinforcement. The equation fits the data from this condition as well, accounting for 95.0% of the variance in mean response rate and for 97.8, 98.6, 94.9, and 92.9% of the individual data variances.

Appendix D gives the least-squares fit of the equation to several other studies on delay of reinforcement as well as that of Pierce et al. The Perin (1943) experiment is noteworthy in that it measured latency to lever press in a discrete-trial procedure as a function of delay of reinforcement. The equation here accounts for the relation between speed of responding (100/latency in sec) and immediacy of food presentation (1/delay). The remaining studies (Logan, 1960; Silver & Pierce, 1969) summarized in Appendix D also conform substantially to Equation 11. Both experiments used rats as subjects and food as reinforcement, but Logan measured speed in a runway and Silver and Pierce measured rate of lever pressing. In each case, including both high- and low-drive conditions in Logan's experiment, the equation accounts for over 90% of the variance in group data.

Frequency of Negative Reinforcement

De Villiers (1974) demonstrated that Herrnstein's equation for absolute response strength in single schedules of positive reinforcement can be extended to VI avoidance schedules, with shock-frequency reduction (shocks avoided per min) as the reinforcer for avoidance (Herrnstein, 1969; Herrnstein & Hineline, 1966). In de Villiers's experiment, lever-press responses canceled the delivery of shocks scheduled at variable intervals. If no lever press was made, all of the scheduled shocks were presented. The first response made after a scheduled shock, whether or not that shock had been presented, prevented the delivery of only the next scheduled shock. Extra responses between two scheduled shocks did not avoid further shocks. All the scheduled shocks could therefore be avoided if the rat responded at least once within every intershock interval, but the durations of the intervals varied unpredictably. On this VI avoidance schedule both received shock rate and shock-frequency reduction (scheduled shock rate minus received shock rate) can be measured, and response rate is not constrained by any fixed temporal relations between responses and shocks, as it is on the free operant avoidance schedules usually studied (Sidman, 1953, 1966).

Four rats were exposed to an ascending and descending series of VI avoidance schedules ranging from a VI 15-sec (four programmed shocks per min) to a VI 75-sec (.8 programmed shocks per min). A wide range of response rates was produced by each rat on the different schedules. Response rates are plotted against shock-frequency reduction (shocks avoided per min) for each rat in Figure 9. The least-squares fit of Equation 11 is shown for each animal. Where there were two determinations of response rate for a given VI value, the mean of the two was used in calculating the best fit of the equation. Equation 11 accounts for over 95% of the variance in response rate for each rat (see Figure 9). Reinforcement from extraneous sources, r_e, in VI avoidance schedules represents the reinforcements for freezing, crouching, defecating, etc. scaled in terms of their equivalent value in shocks avoided per min, the reinforcer for the avoidance response.

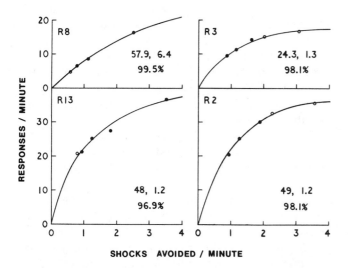

Fig. 9. Rate of responding as a function of shock-frequency reduction for four rats responding on single VI avoidance schedules. The least-squares fit of Equation 11 to the data is plotted for each rat. The k and r_e values and the percentage of the variance in response rate accounted for by the equation are also shown. Filled circles represent the mean response rate of two determinations for a given VI value; open circles represent single determinations. (de Villiers, 1974.)

Magnitude of Negative Reinforcement

Several experiments have investigated the effects of different amounts of voltage reduction between the alley and goal box on a rat's running speed in a straight runway. Three of these studies (Bower, Fowler, & Trapold, 1959; Campbell & Kraeling, 1953; Seward, Shea, Uyeda, & Raskin, 1960) are summarized in Appendix E. All of them used different groups of rats for each voltage reduction value. In fitting Equation 11, de Villiers and Herrnstein (in press) took running speed as the response measure and the reduction in voltage as the reinforcer. Extraneous reinforcement r_e is expressed as a voltage *reduction,* its value scaled in the units of the independent variable. Thus in the study of Bower et al. (1959) the value of the reinforcement for competing responses such as freezing or defecating is equivalent to a voltage reduction of 338 V. For all three experiments, Equation 11 accounts for over 85% of the data variance.

Woods and his co-workers (1965, 1966) used an interesting variant of the runway escape procedure. Their rats swam down a straight alley filled with very cold water in order to be placed in a goal box containing much warmer water. The independent variable was the increase in water temperature between the alley and goal box; the dependent variable was swimming speed (100/time in sec). Equation 11 accounts for these data very well, though it is not clear why parameter values in the two studies differ by as much as they do.

Dinsmoor and Hughes (1956) and Harrison and Abelson (1959) varied the duration of time-out from aversive stimulation contingent on a lever-press escape response. Dinsmoor and Hughes measured latency to lever press in a discrete-trial escape procedure and observed a monotonically increasing function relating speed of response (100/latency in sec) and duration of time-out. The equation accounts for 99.5% of the variance in speed of response for the rats that were escaping from a .2-mA shock. For the rats escaping from the stronger shock—.4 mA—variance in response speed was small and only about 75% of it was accounted for by the equation. Harrison and Abelson measured response rate on VI escape from a loud noise. They found substantial order effects and exposed only one rat to complete ascending and descending orders, but if response rates are averaged across the several determinations for each time-out duration, over 90% of the variance is accounted for by Equation 11.

Immediacy of Negative Reinforcement

Fowler and Trapold (1962) conducted a thorough study of delay of escape in a straight runway. Delay of voltage reduction in the goal box varied over five values between 1 and 16 sec for groups of five rats each. The observed relation between running speed in the runway (100/time in sec) and immediacy of escape (1/delay in sec) in the goal box conforms to Equation 11, 92.6% of the variance in running speed being accounted for by the equation with a k of 94.0 (running speed units) and an r_e of .06 (1/delay units). These results, together with other data from experiments varying delay of negative reinforcement, appear in Appendix F.

Tarpy (1969) had rats escape from electric shock by pressing either of two levers in a discrete-trial procedure. The experiment's main purpose was to investigate preference as a function of differential delays between a press on either lever and shutting off the shock. But de Villiers and Herrnstein (in press) tested Equation 11 with data from conditions in which the delay of escape was the same for both levers; 89.5% of the variance in response speed (100/latency in sec) for five delays between 1 and 16 sec (excluding the 0-delay condition) is accounted for. Tarpy and Koster (1970) varied delay of discrete-trial escape from electric shock by rats responding on a single lever. Using the three nonzero-delay values, 94.6% of the variance in response speed is accounted for by Equation 11. Leeming and Robinson (1973) also varied delay of escape from electric shock by rats, but the escape response was running from one compartment to the other in a shuttlebox. The equation accounts for 86.0% of the variance in speed to respond (100/latency in sec).

Finally, Appendix F also contains Moffatt and Koch's (1973) data from human subjects listening to a Bill Cosby comedy record. Occasionally the recording would stop and the subject could restart it by pressing a panel. The primary independent variable was the delay between the panel response and the onset of the recording. For the three nonzero delays studied, Equation 11 accounts for over 95% of the variance in speed of panel depression.

Summary

The remarkable generality of Herrnstein's equation is apparent from this survey. The behavior of rats, pigeons, monkeys, and (in the one case we found) people, is equally well accounted for, whether the behavior is lever pressing, key pecking, running speed, or response latency in a variety of experimental settings. The reinforcers can be as different as food, sugar water, escape from shock or loud noise or cold water, electrical stimulation of a variety of brain loci, or turning a comedy record back on. Out of 53 tests of Equation 11 on group data, the least-squares fit of the equation accounts for over 90% of the variance in the dependent variable in 42 cases, and for over 80% in another six cases. Out of 45 tests on individual data, the equation accounts for over 90% of the variance in 32 cases, and for over 80% in another seven cases. The literature appears to contain no evidence for a substantially different equation than Equation 11. Where the equation fails to account for most of the data variance, that variance is negligible in all cases but one. In the one exception (Logan, 1960, Experiment 55B) supposedly asymptotic running speed was a sharply nonmonotonic function of number of food pellets. Other experiments on pellet number, including one by Logan (1960), found monotonic functions, all conforming to Equation 11. This equation therefore provides a powerful but simple framework for the quantification of the relation between response strength and both positive and negative reinforcement.

Perhaps the most surprising feature of the close fit of the equation to the data is that it did not require any ad hoc transformations of the reinforcement variables. For example, studies of brain stimulation (Appendix B) or sucrose reinforcement (Appendix C) are well accounted for by Equation 11 by using ordinary physical scales for the independent variables, such as electrical pulses per second or percentage concentration by weight. In contrast, studies in psychophysics indicate that many dimensions of experience are not accounted for by the physical scales, unless they are transformed (Stevens, 1957). At least two explanations of the simplicity of the independent variables are possible.

First, some of the simplicity may reflect the relatively small ranges of the independent variable used in the studies. The range from 1 to 9 food pellets or .28 to 2.7 msec of brain stimulation is not quite an order of magnitude, while the usual psychophysical experiment uses several orders of magnitude. If such broad ranges of reinforcement could be used in studies of animal behavior, rescaling of the reinforcement variable might become necessary or a different equation might need to be formulated.

Second, several of the independent variables surveyed here have been shown to produce matching of relative response rate to relative reinforcement (see Equation 1) in concurrent schedules. Variables that obey Equation 1 should also obey Equation 11 (see pp. 257 and 266). Therefore the fit of Equation 11 to the data on frequency, magnitude, and immediacy of reinforcement only further confirms the matching relation for choice.

The Constancy of the k-parameter

In a recent paper Herrnstein (1974) suggests that the equation can be made even stronger. He argues that a formal implication of the matching relation is that for any given response the parameter k must remain constant across different qualities or quantities of reinforcement or changes in the animal's drive level, as long as the response topography does not change. The k-parameter is just a measure of behavior, such as responses per min, and represents the amount of behavior the observed response would show if there were no reinforcement for competing responses. When there are other sources of reinforcement, k measures the total frequency of all responses in units commensurate with the measure of the response being studied. The k-parameter is therefore simply "the modulus for measuring behavior" (Herrnstein, 1974), and the sole influence on its size is the chosen response form itself.

Several of the studies discussed above test the constancy of k across different qualities and quantities of reinforcement or across different drive levels. Only cases in which over 90% of the variance was accounted for by Equation 11 will be considered here, since the value of k is then well specified. When the equation was fitted to Guttman's (1954) data on the same eight rats lever-pressing for either sucrose or glucose, practically the same k-value was derived for the two reinforcers (15.6 versus 16.1 responses per min). The reinforcement from other sources (r_e) was much smaller for the sucrose function (7.1% versus 11.0%), in keeping with rats' preference for sucrose, the sweeter solution. Kraeling (1961) ran different groups of rats in a runway for sucrose solutions of varying concentration. Three separate functions relating running speed to sucrose concentration were found: one for each of three different durations of access to the sucrose in the goal box. The three k-values given by the least-squares fit of Equation 11 were 89.4, 87.9, and 88.7 running speed units, impressive confirmation of the constancy of k considering that different groups of rats ran in the different conditions. Logan (1960) ran groups of rats under both high- and low-drive levels (hours of deprivation) for different immediacies of food reinforcement. The k-values fitted to his data are 64.9 and 64.5. In the experiment of Seward et al. (1960), rats ran down an electrified runway for a reduction in voltage between the alley and goal box. For two different alley voltages, k-values of 161 and 146 running speed units were derived, about a 10% difference in k across drive levels. In the comparable experiment on escape from cold water (Woods & Holland, 1966), the rats swam from cold water to warmer water, and temperature increase was the reinforcement variable. For two different alley temperatures the k-values were 108 and 114 swimming speed units, an even better agreement between k-values than that found by Seward et al. (1960) for electric shock.

While the above studies support Herrnstein's hypothesis that k remains constant as reinforcement and drive values change, some of the data analyzed do not. In Keesey's (1964) experiment the same 10 rats lever-pressed on a VI 16-sec schedule for different durations of brain stimulation under two intensity conditions, 3.0 and 1.5 mA. In this case, the least-squares fit of Equation 11 produced a much larger k for the 3.0-mA condition (21.0 versus 14.9 responses per min), while r_e-values were very similar. In Schrier's (1965) experiment on monkeys lever-pressing for five different concentrations of sucrose, two different quantities, .33 and .83 cc, were investigated. The k-values for the mean response rates of the monkeys were 88 and 66.5 responses per min in the two conditions. Individual k-values also showed considerable variation across the two quantities (see Appendix C). Finally, the largest discrepancy was found in the experiment by Campbell and Kraeling (1953), in which rats ran down an electrified runway for reduction in voltage between the alley and goal box. The k-value derived for the more intense alley shock condition was over twice that derived for the less intense shock condition: 228 to 106 running speed units. The data on the constancy of k therefore remains equivocal, and further experiments must examine the range of conditions under which k does or does not remain constant.

ALTERNATIVE THEORIES OF RESPONSE STRENGTH

Shimp (1974) has argued against Herrnstein's equation as an adequate theory of response strength in VI schedules on the grounds that it neglects the role of the distribution of reinforced interresponse times (IRTs) in determining the overall response rate. Shimp points out that the mean rate of responding is the reciprocal of the mean of a distribution of IRTs, which is in turn determined by the distribution of reinforcements for those IRTs. He suggests that the pigeon in fact distributes its time among different IRTs according to how frequently each is reinforced relative to the others; i.e., the basic response is one of pausing between key pecks rather than key pecking per se.

Shimp (1974) studied three pigeons responding on a "synthetic" VI schedule (Anger, 1973; Shimp, 1973). Food reinforcement for key pecking was arranged by a single VI schedule and a programming device that assigned the reinforcements equally to each of ten classes of IRTs ranging from 1.0 to 6.0 sec in .5-sec classes. Overall reinforcement frequency was varied between 1 and 70 per hr by changing the VI schedule. Overall response rate on this schedule was a monotonically increasing, negatively accelerated function of overall reinforcement frequency, much like that observed with normal VI schedules by Catania and Reynolds (1968). Shimp argued that this overall response rate function could be decomposed into two time-allocation functions: (1) the time allocated by the pigeon to all of the reinforced IRTs as a function of overall reinforcement frequency—i.e., the percentage of session time taken up by all of the IRTs emitted in the range from 1.0 to 6.0 sec; and (2) the time allocated to any *particular* class of IRTs as a function of the reinforcement rate obtained by that class of IRTs—i.e., the number of emissions of that IRT class times its lower bound duration. At asymptotic overall response rate (over 20 reinforcements per hr) the relative amount of time allocated to a particular IRT class roughly matched its relative frequency of reinforcement. The pigeons spent about the same amount of time responding in each IRT class since each was assigned the same frequency of food; therefore, they made fewer of the long IRTs and more of the shorter ones. The asymptotic overall response rate in responses per min could therefore be predicted by a combination of the percentage of session time taken up by IRTs between 1.0 and 6.0 sec and the frequency of emission of each of the IRT classes in that range. This asymptote varies with the distribution of reinforcements across IRT classes; thus Shimp argues that there may be no such thing as a constant asymptotic response rate across reinforcement and drive conditions, as required by Herrnstein's theory. Given the distribution of reinforced IRTs, the experimenter could in fact predict the asymptotic response rate, since pigeons match the time allocated to each IRT class to its relative reinforcement frequency (provided that the overall reinforcement rate is above 20 per hr).

In assessing Shimp's argument against Herrnstein's molar formulation, however, several considerations should be taken into account. First, while Shimp (1973, 1974) and Anger (1956, 1973) have shown that an animal's behavior is sensitive to the differential reinforcement of particular IRTs, the extension of their analysis to responding on normal VI schedules is unclear. On VI schedules with a constant probability of reinforcement over time the differential reinforcement of IRTs is minimal unless the animal has a propensity to emit IRTs of a particular duration. Since pigeons tend to emit IRTs of about .3 to .5 sec duration (Blough, 1963), those IRTs may be differentially reinforced, but such an effect has not been conclusively demonstrated.

Second, Shimp's synthetic VI schedule had important differences from the normal VI. In his procedure the same 10 IRT classes were reinforced equally frequently at all VI values; but if differential reinforcement of IRTs takes place in a normal VI, different VI schedules should differentially reinforce different IRTs. Each mean response rate on the function relating responding to reinforcement frequency would therefore be the outcome of a different time-allocation function. Herrnstein's quantitative formulation accounts for the entire function, not only its asymptote.

Finally, there seems to be no way to extend Shimp's account of responding on VI schedules to the great wealth of data on other measures of response strength (e.g., running speed or latency) that Herrnstein's equation accounts for so well.

Catania (1973) has proposed an alternative equation for response strength based on assumptions about the excitatory and inhibitory effects of reinforcement on behavior. Whereas Herrnstein assumes that asymptotic response rate (k) for a given response is constant across different drive and reinforcement conditions, Catania assumes that responding increases linearly with increasing reinforcement,

$$R_1 = Kr_1 \qquad (12)$$

This effect combines with an inhibitory effect of total reinforcement on the response, whether the reinforcers originate from other sources or from the response itself (Catania, 1963b, 1969; Rachlin & Baum, 1969, 1972):

$$R_1 = Kr_1 \times \frac{C}{C + \Sigma r} \qquad (13)$$
$$= \frac{KCr_1}{C + \Sigma r}$$

where C is a constant that depends on the magnitude of the inhibitory effect of the reinforcers, and Σr is the total reinforcement obtained from all sources. Setting KC to a new constant k gives the following equation:

$$R_1 = \frac{kr_1}{C + \Sigma r} \qquad (14)$$

Here Σr includes only the specified sources of reinforcement, not extraneous unspecified sources as in Herrnstein's r_e. Thus when r_1 is the only scheduled reinforcement, $\Sigma r = r_1$ and Equation 14 is mathematically equivalent to Herrnstein's equation for single-response situations. The constant C is derived from the data, as is r_e. Catania's equation therefore accounts for as much of the data summarized in the earlier sections of the chapter as does Herrnstein's equation.

While there is not yet empirical data to distinguish between these two formulations, Catania (1973) argues that Herrnstein's equation assumes that the variety of reinforcers subsumed under r_e do not interact in any complex way with r_1, the scheduled reinforcer. But there is evidence for interaction between such reinforcers as food and water (Bolles, 1967). However, Catania's equation also fails to account for the data on choice between food and water reinforcers. In the experiment of Wood et al. (1975), rate of water reinforcement on an FR schedule did not affect rate of responding on a concurrently scheduled FI schedule for food, as it should if food and water simply sum in Σr in Equation 14. Therefore, neither equation readily handles interactions between reinforcers.

APPLICATION OF HERRNSTEIN'S EQUATIONS TO OTHER SCHEDULES

Herrnstein's equation for single schedules, Equation 11, applies best to VI schedules, in which the probability of a reinforcement being scheduled after one has been presented is approximately constant over time. Its extension to other schedules, such as FIs, is more difficult. Overall response rate on different FI schedules typically does not fit the equation very well. However, Schneider (1969) has argued for a two-state analysis of well-learned FI performance. In the first state, beginning immediately after reinforcement, response rate is very low and approximately constant over different FI values. At some variable time, on the average about two-thirds of the way through the FI, there is an abrupt transition (or break point) to a high and approximately constant response rate. Rate of responding in the second state is an increasing, negatively accelerated function of reinforcement frequency in that state, much like the function obtained for VI schedules. Schneider suggests that in a sense the pigeon is on a VI schedule in the second state, the interreinforcement intervals being determined by the bird's break point distribution. Herrnstein's equation actually provides an accurate account of second-state response rate in Schneider's experiment, though with somewhat higher parameter values than those usually found for pigeons on VI schedules. With a k of 147 responses per min and an r_e of 24 reinforcements per hr, the equation accounts for 92.2% of the variance in mean second-state response rate for Schneider's pigeons.

Several theorists have argued that the operation of at least two factors determines the pattern and rate of responding on schedules of intermittent reinforcement. Morse (1966) proposed that most schedule-controlled behavior results from the joint effects of reinforcement on response strength and the differential reinforcement of certain interresponse times (IRTs). Thus ratio schedules tend to maintain higher response rates than interval schedules for the same frequency of reinforcement possibly because there is more selection for long IRTs on interval than on ratio schedules (Killeen, 1969). Staddon (1972) similarly argued that responding on intermittent reinforcement schedules is determined by two factors: the relative frequency of reinforcement and the relative proximity of responses to reinforcement. The latter principle determines the temporal location of behavior under schedule control, accounting for the temporal pattern of responding typically found on FI and FR schedules, in which the relative proximity to reinforcement increases with time since the last reinforcement. On VI schedules with a random distribution of intervals, differential reinforcement of particular IRTs is minimized and the relative proximity of responses to reinforcement does not vary with post-reinforcement time. Consequently, response rate is fairly constant over time since reinforcement and is directly related to relative reinforcement frequency (see p. 258) (Catania & Reynolds, 1968). Staddon showed that these two factors can qualitatively account for many of the properties of behavior on FI, VI, FR, and VR schedules.

The data considered in the earlier sections of this chapter suggest that Herrnstein's equation provides an accurate quantitative formulation of one aspect of schedule-controlled behavior: the relation between response strength and relative reinforcement frequency or magnitude. Further research must specify the way this factor interacts quantitatively with other factors such as the relative proximity to reinforcement or differential reinforcement of IRTs to determine behavior on any given schedule.

Concurrent Schedules

Equation 11 can also be applied to absolute response rates in two-response concurrent schedules. The term r_e then breaks down into $r_2 + r_e$, where r_2 is the reinforcement rate associated with the second response. Thus:

$$R_1 = \frac{kr_1}{r_1 + r_2 + r_e} \quad (15)$$

where k and r_e are as already defined for Equation 11. Herrnstein (1970) demonstrated that this equation accounts for the absolute response rates obtained by Catania (1963b) for pigeons in a CO-key concurrent procedure. The fit of the equation to the data is shown in Figure 10. The left-hand panel shows response rate on each schedule as a function of reinforcement frequency for each when the total rate of reinforcement was held constant at 40 per hr. The right-hand panel shows response rate on each schedule when the reinforcement frequency on Schedule 2 was held constant at 20 per hr and that on Schedule 1 varied from 0 to 40 per hr. The straight line and two curves represent the plot of Equation 15 with k- and

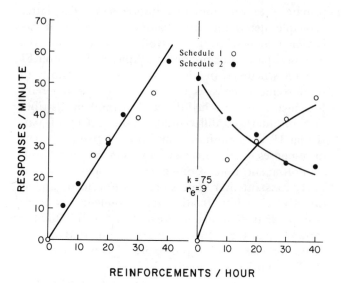

Fig. 10. The absolute rate of responding on each schedule as a function of the rate of reinforcement for each alternative in a CO-key concurrent VI VI schedule (Catania, 1963b). For the left panel, the overall frequency of reinforcement was held constant at 40 reinforcements per hr, while varying complementarily for the two alternatives. Each point is here plotted above the reinforcement rate at which it was obtained. For the right panel, the frequency of reinforcement for Schedule 2 was kept constant at 20 reinforcements per hr, while varying between 0 and 40 per hr for Schedule 1. The points here are plotted above the reinforcement rate on Schedule 1 at the time they were obtained. The values of k and r_e were used for the smooth curves in both panels. (Catania 1963b.)

$$\frac{R_1}{R_1 + R_2} = \frac{\dfrac{kr_1}{r_1 + r_2 + r_e}}{\dfrac{kr_1}{r_1 + r_2 + r_e} + \dfrac{kr_2}{r_2 + r_1 + r_e}} = \frac{r_1}{r_1 + r_2} \quad (16)$$

If the asymptotic response rates (k) or the r_e-values on the two schedules differ, however, the k-parameters or the denominators in Equation 16 will not cancel out, and matching will not be obtained. Herrnstein's formulation of the relation between absolute response rates and reinforcement therefore *predicts* deviations from matching in many cases. For example, in the paced schedules of Staddon (1968) and Moffitt and Shimp (1971), the reinforced IRTs were of different durations and hence the responses would differ in asymptotic response rate for the same frequency of reinforcement. They may also differ in their r_e-values, since more collateral behavior will be generated in the one case than in the other.

Similarly, Equation 15 might account for the deviation from matching with concurrent VI FI (Nevin, 1971; Trevitt et al., 1972) and FI FR (La Bounty & Reynolds, 1973) schedules. On FI or FR schedules, the value of r_e probably changes with the differing probability of reinforcement over time. While r_e should be fairly constant over time on a VI schedule, its value on an FI or FR schedule is likely to be high immediately following reinforcement, in the postreinforcement pause, and low immediately prior to reinforcement. Equal r_e-values for the two schedules in these procedures therefore cannot be assumed, as would be required for matching. If the differing mean r_e-values for each schedule could be ascertained, then the deviation from matching should be accounted for by Equation 15. However, until the application of Equation 11 (Herrnstein's equation for single schedules) is extended to FI and FR schedules, this explanation of the deviations from matching must remain speculative.

r_e-values as shown in the figure. The same parameter values were used for the functions in both panels. Only one data point deviates substantially from the plotted function, and the equation accounts for 91.0% of the variance in response rates in the left-hand panel and 90.3% of the variance in the right-hand panel.

Equation 15 was also fitted to the mean absolute response rates on each key from Chung and Herrnstein's (1967) study of choice between different immediacies of reinforcement. For the pigeons with an 8-sec delay on the standard key, the equation accounts for 90.5% of the variance in absolute response rate on the two keys. The k-value was 60 responses per min; r_e was .002 (1/delay units). The equation was not fitted to the data for the two pigeons with a 16-sec standard delay since they showed a consistent bias toward the variable-delay key. These data therefore also provide substantial confirmation for Herrnstein's system of equations.

Equation 15 predicts matching in concurrent schedules, since the denominators and k-parameters cancel out when relative response rate and reinforcement frequency are calculated:

Multiple Schedules and Behavioral Contrast

In Equation 15 two reinforcement schedules are assumed to exert their full effect on each response, since the schedules are simultaneously available to the subject. Numerous operant conditioning experiments, however, reveal interactions of a lesser magnitude between *successive* reinforcement conditions and the response rates they maintain.

Reynolds (1961a) first demonstrated that response rate in the first component of a multiple schedule depends not only on the frequency of reinforcement in that component, but also on the reinforcement in the second component. He trained one group of pigeons on a multiple VI VI schedule and another group on a multiple VR VR, component duration for both groups being 3 min. In both cases, the rate of responding in the first component of the schedule increased considerably when reinforcement was discontinued in the second component, although the reinforcement frequency in the first component was unchanged. Reynolds called the effect "behavioral contrast." Subsequent research has confirmed the phenomenon of behavioral contrast and extended it to different species even if the responses or the reinforcers in the two components are different in kind (Beninger, 1972; Premack, 1969). Reynolds (1961b, 1963) himself demonstrated that a change in the relative reinforcement rate in each component of the schedule is the major determinant of stable contrast. As long as reinforcement in the interacting component was sustained at the same level, contrast failed to occur, whether or not the pigeons responded in that component (Reynolds, 1961b). Bloomfield (1967a) found that both positive (increased response rate) and negative (decreased response rate) contrast were determined by changes in the relative reinforcement frequencies. Response rate in the VI component of a multiple schedule varied inversely with the frequency of reinforcement in the second component, whether that component was a DRL or an FR schedule. Only the relative reinforcement frequency and not differences in response rates or patterns of responding on the two component schedules had any effect on the direction or degree of behavioral contrast observed (Bloomfield, 1967a). Response rate in the presence of a given stimulus is therefore determined by the frequency of reinforcement during all of the stimuli that successively control the subject's behavior (Reynolds, 1961b).

These results agree qualitatively with Herrnstein's (1970) general formulation of the law of effect; response rate is directly related to its relative reinforcement frequency. In addition, Herrnstein (1970) showed how a simple modification of Equation 15 could provide an accurate quantitative account of many stable interactions between response rate and reinforcement in multiple schedules. Since only one schedule operates in each component, interaction between multiple schedules is presumably less than that in concurrent schedules. Therefore, Herrnstein inserted an interactive parameter into Equation 15, the equation describing absolute response rate in concurrent schedules:

$$R_1 = \frac{kr_1}{r_1 + mr_2 + r_e} \quad (17)$$

The parameter m varies between 0 and 1.0 and represents the degree of interaction between the two reinforcement conditions. In concurrent schedules interaction is maximal, so m equals 1.0, and Equations 15 and 17 are identical. Matching then follows as shown in Equation 16. The modified equation is therefore proposed to account for both matching in concurrent schedules and behavioral contrast in multiple schedules.

Equation 16 accurately describes the stable behavioral contrast reported in several experiments that investigated a sufficient range of reinforcement frequencies or durations. For example, Lander and Irwin (1968) varied reinforcement frequency in a multiple VI 3-min VI x-min schedule and Nevin (1968) varied the duration of nonresponding required for reinforcement in the DRO component of a multiple VI 3-min DRO x. Rachlin and Baum (1969) manipulated the duration of reinforcement associated with one key from 1 to 16 sec while the VI schedule associated with a second key remained constant. Illumination of the key light signaled the availability of reinforcement on the key for which reinforcer duration varied; reinforcement on the constant VI schedule was unsignaled. Since the pigeons in Rachlin and Baum's study only responded on the signaled key when the key light was illuminated—i.e., when reinforcement was available—the conditions of stimulation, reinforcement, and responding on the two schedules were successive. Their procedure could therefore be considered a multiple VI 3-min CRF schedule, even though two response keys were used. In all three of these studies, response rate on the unchanged schedule varied inversely with the frequency or duration of reinforcement for the other schedule. With appropriate parameter values selected, the averaged group data from each of the studies never deviates by more than 6 responses per min from a perfect fit to Equation 17. For 15 of 18 independent data points the deviation of data from theory is less than 3 responses per min (approximately 6%) (Herrnstein, 1970).

The subjects in these experiments were pigeons and the reinforcer was access to food, but de Villiers (1972) extended Herrnstein's equation for behavioral contrast to rats responding on multiple random-interval (RI) avoidance schedules. Lever-press responses canceled the delivery of shocks scheduled at random intervals, and the scheduled rate of shock was varied in the two components of the multiple schedule. When shock-frequency reduction (scheduled shock rate minus received shock rate) was substituted for r_1 and r_2 in Equation 17 (Herrnstein, 1969; Herrnstein & Hineline, 1966), the equation provided an accurate

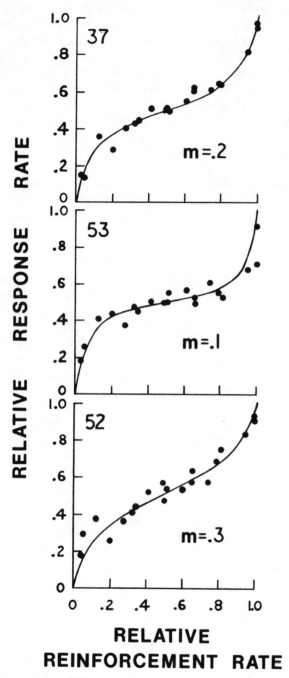

Fig. 11. The relative rate of responding as a function of the relative frequency of reinforcement in one component of a multiple VI VI schedule, for each of three pigeons. The smooth curves plot Equation 15, with $r_e = 0$ and m set to the values indicated. (From Reynolds, 1963.)

quantitative description of the long-term positive and negative contrast effects obtained in this study. The values of the k- and r_e-parameters calculated for each rat from the behavioral contrast data even predicted subsequent response rates on single RI avoidance schedules when inserted into Equation 11, Herrnstein's equation for single schedules. The deviation of observed from predicted response rate on the single schedules averaged only 5.5% of the observed response rate, and was never greater than 3 responses per min.

Equation 17 also makes predictions about relative response rates on multiple schedules. If $m < 1.0$, the predicted relation between relative response rate and relative reinforcement frequency is plotted by a family of curvilinear functions, the curvature of which depends on the magnitudes of r_1, r_2, r_e, and m (Herrnstein, 1970). An empirical test of this relation was provided by an experiment by Reynolds (1963) which systematically varied reinforcement rates in both components of a multiple VI VI schedule. Figure 11 shows the data from Reynolds's experiment and the relative response rate curve predicted by Equation 17 for the given parameter values. The value of r_e was set to zero for these curves, but the r_e-values typically obtained for pigeons on VI schedules would change the functions only minimally. Once again the theory provides a good fit to the data.

At this point, however, two limitations on the application of Equation 17 must be noted:

1. The equation not only assumes that a simple multiplicative mechanism governs the degree of interaction between the two reinforcement conditions, but it also assumes the most symmetrical of multiple schedules. It applies best to a schedule in which the response forms are the same in both components—i.e., in which they have equal asymptotic rates (k), in which the interaction is the same going from one component to the other in either direction (m), and in which extraneous sources of reinforcement are kept constant in the two components (r_e). Yet behavioral contrast occurs in multiple schedules in which many or all of these symmetries are violated (Premack, 1969). Such asymmetries would considerably complicate a quantitative analysis of the contrast effects, but it need not change the framework of the analysis—i.e., a framework which stresses relative reinforcement frequency (or magnitude) as a determinant of response strength.

2. Second, the equation is not intended to account for short-term contrast effects in multiple schedules such as those discussed by Terrace (1966a, 1966b, 1972) or even more transient changes in response rates reported by Nevin and Shettleworth (1966) and Bernheim and Williams (1967). Nevertheless, Herrnstein (1970) has indicated how Equation 17 could be easily modified to handle the contrast effects described by Terrace (1966a) by assuming that an extinction component is aversive (Terrace, 1966b) and adds a negative value to the denominator of the equation.

Matching in Multiple Schedules

Nevertheless, within the situations to which it directly applies, Equation 17 makes a number of interesting predictions. It not only predicts matching in concurrent schedules, but also predicts matching in multiple schedules under particular conditions.

First, if the reinforcement frequency in one component of the multiple schedule became extremely large relative to r_e and the scheduled reinforcement in other components, the denominators of the equations governing response rate in each of the components would approach equality. When the denominators are equal, matching is predicted (Equation 16). Data reported by Nevin in 1974 (cited by Herrnstein, 1970) test this prediction. Nevin studied pigeons in a three-component multiple schedule. Two of the components were conventional VI 1-min and VI 3-min schedules, each lasting for 1 min, and the third component consisted of a 30-sec blackout of the chamber separating the two VI components. The independent variable was the frequency of noncontingent reinforcement provided during the blackout. As predicted by Equation 17, response rates in the two VI components decreased steadily as reinforcement frequency in the blackout increased from zero to 360 per hr (Herrnstein, 1970). Furthermore, relative response rates in the VI components approached matching: .75 for the VI 1-min and .25 for the VI 3-min. Averaged over the four pigeons, relative response rate in the VI 1-min component went from .54 when there was no reinforcement in the blackout to .72 when the blackout reinforcement frequency was 360 per hr—i.e., 6 times the combined rate of reinforcement in the VI components. The denominators in Equation 17 for the two VI schedules therefore became more and more determined by the frequency of reinforcement in the blackout.

Second, similarly, if the values of r_1 and r_2 became extremely small relative to r_e, reinforcement from extraneous sources in the two components, the denominators in Equation 17 for each component would be determined by r_e. As the denominators approach equality, relative response rates should also approach matching.

Herrnstein and Loveland (1974) manipulated the relative importance of r_1 and r_2 by varying their pigeons' body weights. They argued that it is unnecessary to know the specific reinforcers that constitute r_e in order to conclude that r_e should become a larger fraction of the denominator as the pigeons get less and less hungry. Whatever reinforcers r_e contains, they should not covary with hunger the way r_1 and r_2 must. Equation 17 therefore predicts that a subject's performance in a multiple schedule should approach matching as the motivation for the scheduled reinforcer declines.

The basic procedure for the entire experiment was a multiple VI 1-min VI 4-min schedule with 2-min components. The body weight of the pigeons was systematically varied from 80 to 110% of their ad libitum weight at the beginning of the experiment. Finally, the pigeons responded on the multiple schedule with a cupful of food in the experimental chamber. For all five pigeons, absolute response rates declined steadily with increasing body weight. At the same time, relative response rate in each component asymptotically approached the matching value (.80 and .20, respectively). Two pigeons matched at 100% body weight and three pigeons matched at 110% body weight. With free food in the chamber, response rates dropped to low levels, between 5 and 15 responses per min; but the relative response rates for all five pigeons closely approximated matching.

Finally, Equation 17 predicts matching in multiple schedules when m approaches 1.0—i.e., when the interaction between the two components is maximal, as in concurrent schedules. The more the two reinforcement conditions are separated in time by long component durations, the less interaction there is likely to be between them, the smaller the contrast effect, and the greater the deviation from matching. On the other hand, the more the multiple schedule approximates a CO-key concurrent schedule with rapid alternations between the two reinforcement conditions, the larger the contrast effects and the closer the approximation to matching predicted by Equation 17.

Experiments by Shimp and Wheatley (1971) and Todorov (1972) provide a direct test of this prediction. They varied component duration in a multiple VI VI schedule with asymmetrical reinforcement frequencies. As component duration shortened, relative response rate increased for the richer VI and decreased for the other schedule. At the longer component durations (>10 sec), relative response rate undermatched relative reinforcement frequency on the richer VI, but with very brief components of 5 to 10 sec the relative response rate reached its maximal value and matching was observed. With 5-sec components, Shimp and Wheatley obtained matching to a wide range of relative reinforcement frequencies in the two components.

In a similar procedure, but with rats as subjects and multiple VI avoidance schedules, de Villiers (1974) demonstrated the same relation between relative response rate and relative frequency of negative reinforcement (shock-frequency reduction) as compo-

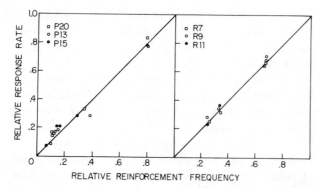

Fig. 12. The relation between relative response rate and relative reinforcement frequency for three pigeons responding on multiple VI VI food schedules with 5-sec components (Shimp & Wheatley, 1971) (left-hand panel); and for three rats responding on multiple VI VI avoidance schedules with 40-sec components (right-hand panel). The diagonal lines represent matching between the relative frequencies. (de Villiers, 1974.)

nent duration varied. At the longer component durations, relative response rate undermatched the relative shock-frequency reduction; but as component duration shortened, the relative response rate increased until it was maximal at 40-sec components. At this component duration matching was obtained for three different relative shock-frequency reduction values. Figure 12 summarizes the matching data from Shimp and Wheatley (1971) for positive reinforcement and from de Villiers (1974) for negative reinforcement.

Contrary Evidence

Certain limitations of Herrnstein's equation for multiple schedules have already been discussed. In addition, recent experiments indicate that several of its predictions are not supported by the data.

As Spealman and Gollub (1974) pointed out, Equation 17 predicts that the higher the reinforcement rate in an equal-valued multiple VI VI schedule, the larger the behavioral contrast found in the unchanged component when the second component is changed to extinction. When reinforcement frequencies in the two components are equal, $r_1 = r_2$ and Equation 17 can be rewritten as

$$R_1 = \frac{kr_1}{r_1 + mr_1 + r_e} \quad (18)$$

If reinforcement is no longer scheduled in the second component, response rate in the first component is governed by the following equation:

$$R_1' = \frac{kr_1}{r_1 + r_e} \quad (19)$$

where R_1' is response rate after behavioral contrast. The magnitude of behavioral contrast (percentage increase in responding in the unchanged component) is then calculated as follows:

$$\frac{R_1' - R_1}{R_1} \times 100 = \frac{\dfrac{kr_1}{r_1 + r_e} - \dfrac{kr_1}{r_1 + mr_1 + r_e}}{\dfrac{kr_1}{r_1 + mr_1 + r_e}} \times 100$$

$$= \frac{mr_1}{r_1 + r_e} \times 100 \quad (20)$$

According to this equation, the magnitude of behavioral contrast increases as r_1 increases, assuming that m and r_e are greater than zero and remain constant across the experimental conditions.

Spealman and Gollub (1974) tested this prediction with eight pigeons. Four of the pigeons responded on a multiple VI 30-sec VI 30-sec schedule, the other four on a multiple VI 180-sec VI 180-sec schedule. The components of the multiple schedules alternated every 180 seconds. The second-component schedule for each group of pigeons was then changed to extinction. Contrary to the prediction of Herrnstein's equation, the magnitude of behavioral contrast for the group with less frequent reinforcement (VI 180-sec) was greater than the contrast shown by all but one of the pigeons on the VI 30-sec. However, a critical assumption underlying the experiment is that the mean values of m and r_e do not differ across the two groups of pigeons, and this assumption may not be justified. It is plausible to suggest that extraneous sources of reinforcement (r_e) may be larger with less frequent contingent reinforcement and that the interaction between components (m) may be greater with more frequent reinforcement. But both of these effects would work in favor of the prediction by Equation 17 —greater behavioral contrast with more frequent reinforcement—and against the observed results.

Another prediction based on Equation 17 is that response rate on a multiple VI VI schedule will be lower than that on one of the VI schedules in isolation. Parameter R_1' in Equation 19 represents response rate on a single VI schedule (cf. Equation 11), and $R_1' > R_1$ in Equation 18 if $m > 0$. Herrnstein (1970) cited unpublished data from Terrace showing that pigeons' response rates on a single VI 60-sec schedule were higher than their response rates on a multiple VI 60-sec VI 60-sec schedule. De Villiers (1972) also found higher response rates on a single VI 15-sec avoidance schedule than in either component of a multiple VI 15-sec VI 15-sec avoidance schedule with rats. How-

Table 3 Mean absolute response rate in each component of the multiple schedule as a function of component duration, along with mean relative response rates and relative reinforcement frequencies for the component with more frequent reinforcement, for the studies of Shimp and Wheatley (1971) and Todorov (1972)

SHIMP AND WHEATLEY (1971)

Component Duration (in sec)	Responses/min VI 1-min	Responses/min VI 4-min	Relative Response Rate in VI 1-min	Relative Reinforcement Rate in VI 1-min
180	53.1	25.4	.68	.81
60	48.8	19.8	.71	.80
30	52.7	19.8	.73	.79
10	67.5	23.9	.74	.80
5	83.2	19.7	.81	.80
2	90.1	27.1	.77	.81

TODOROV (1972)

Component Duration (in sec)	Responses/min VI 30-sec	Responses/min VI 90-sec	Relative Response Rate in VI 30-sec	Relative Reinforcement Rate in VI 30-sec
300	47.3	31.9	.60	.74
150	52.7	32.1	.62	.75
40	52.9	26.8	.66	.75
10	57.2	23.6	.71	.75
5	58.4	27.0	.68	.75

ever, in a second experiment Spealman and Gollub (1974) found that neither the pigeons on the VI 30-sec nor the pigeons on the VI 180-sec schedules responded faster on those schedules in isolation than on multiple schedules with the same VIs as components.

One possible explanation of Spealman and Gollub's results is that m had gone to zero by this stage of their study. The single VI schedule was the fourth experimental condition, preceded and followed by a multiple VI VI schedule condition. Since the pigeons were run for long periods of time in each condition, as long as 70 30-min sessions, and the components of the multiple schedule were signaled by red versus green key lights throughout, m may well have approached zero by the end of the experiment. Equal rates of responding would then be expected for the single and multiple VI schedules. But if $m = 0$ in the last multiple-schedule condition of the experiment, response rate in that condition should be higher than that in the first multiple-schedule condition, where m was clearly greater than 0 (since substantial behavioral contrast was obtained). For only three of the seven pigeons run in the last multiple-schedule condition is that the case; for another three pigeons response rates are lower. Differences in component durations—180 sec in Spealman and Gollub's study versus 90 sec in Terrace's—might also explain the discrepancy in results, since m should be smaller with longer components; yet Spealman and Gollub obtained sizable contrast effects.

Finally, there is strong evidence that the process by which matching develops in multiple schedules with short components is different from that predicted by Equation 17. Provided that k and r_e do not change, the equation predicts that as component duration shortens and m approaches 1.0, response rates in both components should decrease. Lowest response rates should occur at the component duration where interaction is greatest and matching is obtained. Table 3 summarizes the average mean response rates in each component of the multiple schedule for the pigeons studied by Shimp and Wheatley (1971) and Todorov (1972). As component duration decreased, so did response rate in the component with less frequent reinforcement, until it reached its lowest value at the component duration where approximate matching was found. In contrast, response rate in the component with more frequent reinforcement increased with decreasing component duration, and was highest at the shortest duration. De Villiers (1972) found no clear relation between absolute response rates and component duration in his experiment on multiple VI avoidance schedules, but his results were affected by prolonged adaptation of the animals to the electric shock. This analysis and Spealman and Gollub's results therefore severely question the adequacy of Equation 17 as an account of the interactions between response rate and reinforcement frequency in multiple schedules.

AN ALTERNATIVE THEORY OF MATCHING AND BEHAVIORAL CONTRAST

In a recent paper, Rachlin (1973) raised two questions about the adequacy of Equation 17 in accounting for both behavioral contrast and matching. He argued first that the equation implies that the same process underlies matching in both multiple and concurrent schedules. Yet Killeen (1972a) found clear differences between the patterns of behavior that lead to matching in the two procedures.

In one experiment, Killeen divided his subjects into yoked pairs. Each pair contained a leader pigeon that was exposed to a CO-key concurrent schedule. Follower pigeons were yoked to the leaders so that the schedule in operation on the main key for these pigeons was determined by the changeovers of the leaders. Whenever a reinforcement was programmed for a response by the leader, it was also available for the follower. Killeen observed that leader and follower pigeons produced very similar patterns of responding, although the followers were on a true multiple schedule and had no control over alternation between the schedules. The absolute response rates were a little higher for the leader birds, but both groups of pigeons matched relative overall response rates to relative reinforcement frequency. The leader pigeons also matched the time they allocated to each schedule to the distribution of the reinforcements. The *local* rates of reinforcement in the concurrent and yoked conditions were therefore constant across the two component schedules. Killeen noted that the local response rates were also equal in both conditions so that relative local response rate matched relative local reinforcement frequency at .50. He concluded that in concurrent schedules the behavior observed is not so much response matching as it is equalizing. The pigeon adjusts the time spent in each component schedule so that the local reinforcement rates are equal. Overall relative response rate matching therefore results from the more basic process of time allocation. If this equalizing process is performed for, rather than by, the subject, as it was for the yoked pigeons, equal local response rates and overall response matching will be found even in multiple schedules.

In a second experiment, however, Killeen (1972a) showed that the response matching found in multiple VI schedules with brief components (Shimp & Wheatley, 1971; Todorov, 1972) is different in kind from that found in concurrent VI schedules. If component durations are fixed at equal values while reinforcements are programmed by unequal VI schedules in the two components, the subject can no longer equalize local reinforcement frequencies. The distribution of time to the two schedules is fixed by the experimenter so the local reinforcement rates approximate those set by the VI schedules in operation in each component. Local response rates therefore deviate from equality in the two components. With brief components, response rate–reinforcement interaction is maximal and the relative *local* response rate matches the relative *local* frequency of reinforcement provided by the two VI schedules.

From Killeen's results, Rachlin (1973) concluded that response matching in concurrent schedules results from the subject's distribution of time. Extra responses on the preferred schedule that lead to matching come from the extra time spent responding there, not from a higher local response rate. On the other hand, matching and behavioral contrast in multiple schedules are indicative of an increased response output when the relative reinforcement frequency is increased. Equation 17 fails to distinguish between these two processes.

Second, Rachlin argued that the equation does not account for both inhibitory and excitatory effects of reinforcement on responding. Rachlin and Baum (1972) found that free reinforcement scheduled at variable intervals inhibited key pecking maintained by a constant frequency of contingent reinforcement, in accordance with Herrnstein's equations. In sharp contrast with these results, several recent experiments have demonstrated excitatory effects of free reinforcement on a pigeon's key pecking.

For example, Staddon and Simmelhag (1971) presented food reinforcement to a pigeon at fixed time intervals, irrespective of the bird's behavior. They observed that after exposure to this procedure for a short period of time, pecking (at either the key or the walls of the chamber) began to predominate just prior to food presentation. Staddon (1972) argues that stimuli signaling the imminent presentation of food elicit pecking (as in autoshaping procedures—Brown & Jenkins, 1968; Gamzu & Williams, 1971), even if pecking has no effect on food presentation. Thus a base line response of key pecking is facilitated by a brief light stimulus signaling free food (LoLordo, 1971). Herrnstein and Loveland (1972) and Williams and

Williams (1969) report that a pigeon will peck at a brief stimulus signaling food even if the peck avoids or postpones the food presentation. There appears to be a special relation between pecking and food for a pigeon such that pecking becomes the dominant response in the bird's repertoire and tends to be emitted when food is imminent. Other responses that can be maintained by food reinforcement, such as treadle pushing, do not show the same special linkage to food for pigeons. LoLordo (cited by Staddon, 1972) reports that a base line of treadle pushing is suppressed by a light stimulus for free food because the pigeons peck at the signal key. Other research suggests that the special relation between pecking and food is species-specific for pigeons and that other responses may be linked to food reinforcement for other species (Breland & Breland, 1961).

Staddon and Simmelhag (1971) therefore define a class of "terminal responses" that bear a special relation to a particular reinforcer. These responses are excited by the mere presence of the reinforcer or by stimuli that signal its imminent presentation, and do not need to be selected for by the reinforcement contingencies. Different terminal responses may be linked to different reinforcers for a particular species. On the other hand, "interim responses" are not directly related to the reinforcer and tend to be emitted during periods of low reinforcement probability.

An experiment by Gamzu and Schwartz (1973) first raised the question of the relation between response elicitation in the presence of reinforcements and behavioral contrast. They presented free reinforcement to pigeons in both components of a multiple schedule. A color change of the key light signaled each component, but pecking the key had no programmed consequences. When the rate of free reinforcement was equal in the two components, no key pecking occurred. But when the rate of reinforcement in one component was reduced, the pigeons began to peck the key in the other component. Frequency of reinforcement in that component was unchanged, but it was now associated with a higher relative reinforcement rate. Gamzu and Schwartz observed that the number of responses made in the unchanged component approximated the increase in responding found in normal contrast experiments using similar rates of contingent reinforcement. They therefore suggested that normal positive behavioral contrast consists of the instrumental responding appropriate to the schedule in the unchanged component, plus the extra pecks elicited by the stimulus signaling a higher relative rate of reinforcement in that component. If a stimulus associated with a high frequency or probability of reinforcement alternates with a signal for low reinforcement rates, it elicits pecking in pigeons in both multiple schedules and autoshaping procedures.

Subsequent experiments have determined some of the conditions in which autoshaped pecking is produced in the Gamzu and Schwartz procedure. Redford and Perkins (1974) found that pigeons produced substantial rates of key pecking in the component associated with the higher relative frequency of free reinforcement only if the color stimuli signaling the two components were localized on the key. Substantial positive contrast was also found with pigeons pecking on a conventional multiple VI VI schedule when the schedule changed to multiple VI EXT (extinction) only if the component stimuli were localized on the key. When the components of the multiple schedule in both procedures were signaled by a change in the color of the houselight, none of Redford and Perkins's pigeons showed positive contrast or autoshaped pecking. This result is in keeping with an autoshaping account of positive contrast, since autoshaping of key pecking in standard procedures can only be obtained when the prefood stimulus is located on the response key (Wasserman, 1973). However, it should be noted that Redford and Perkins failed to get differential responding in the VI and EXT components of the multiple schedule when these were signaled by a change in the color of the houselight. They ran only five multiple VI EXT sessions, and those alternated with VI VI sessions. If their pigeons failed to discriminate the change in reinforcement conditions in the EXT component, behavioral contrast would not be expected to occur in the other component.

Schwartz (1973) demonstrated that key pecking is not elicited in the Gamzu and Schwartz procedure if the schedule components are signaled by the presence and absence of an auditory stimulus. Once key pecking was established with a change in key color signaling the components, however, it could be transferred from the control of the visual stimulus to a tone, although it was maintained at a somewhat reduced level. Subsequently, the pecking could be reinitiated by the tone signal after an extinction procedure. Schwartz suggests that for pigeons preexperimental relations exist among food, visual stimuli, and pecking, but not for auditory stimuli. Thus a pigeon's key peck cannot be autoshaped with an auditory prefood stimulus.

The results of two experiments by Keller (1974—cited by Rachlin, 1973) also support an autoshaping analysis of positive contrast. Pecking on one key (instrumental key) in the experimental chamber produced reinforcement according to a multiple VI 30-sec

EXT schedule. The stimuli associated with each component of the schedule, however, were presented on a second key (signal key). Pecking at either key in the VI component produced a feedback click; pecking in the EXT component produced no feedback. After training on the multiple VI 30-sec EXT schedule, the pigeons were run on a multiple VI 30-sec VI 30-sec schedule until responding was stable in both components. When reinforcement in the second component was again discontinued, only one of the three pigeons showed temporary behavioral contrast on the instrumental key in the VI 30-sec component; the other two pigeons showed no contrast on the instrumental key but began to peck the signal key in the unchanged component.

In Keller's second experiment there were three components in the multiple schedule, each associated with a different color key light on the signal key. The pigeons were trained on a multiple VI 1-min VI 1-min EXT schedule, and then the component schedules were varied. They were either a VI 1-min or EXT. None of the pigeons showed behavioral contrast on the instrumental key during a VI component when one or two of the other components was EXT; all three pigeons pecked at a substantial rate on the signal key during the VI components but not during the EXT components. Signal key response rate was highest when only one component was a VI. Rachlin (1973) concludes that if the signal and instrumental pecks were superimposed on a single key, as in normal multiple schedules, positive behavioral contrast would have been observed.

In view of these results, Rachlin (1973) suggests that whereas response matching in concurrent schedules is a by-product of a basic process of time allocation, matching and contrast in multiple schedules result from more direct excitatory and inhibitory effects of relative reinforcement frequency on responding. A stimulus associated with a higher relative reinforcement frequency elicits extra pecks, while a stimulus associated with a lower relative frequency inhibits pecking. In more general terms, Rachlin argues that "terminal" (Staddon & Simmelhag, 1971) or auto-shaped responses are excited during periods of high relative reinforcement frequency, while "interim" responses are inhibited. During periods of low relative reinforcement frequency the opposite process occurs: terminal responses are inhibited and interim responses excited. Hence both positive (excitatory) and negative (inhibitory) contrast effects occur. Matching is observed in both multiple and concurrent schedules because the two different processes that produce it are reactions to the same independent variable—the relative value (in most cases the relative reinforcement frequency) of the component schedules.

To the extent that Rachlin emphasizes relative reinforcement frequency as the major determinant of matching and contrast, his analysis is similar to Herrnstein's; but Rachlin stresses the differences between the underlying response rate and reinforcement interactions in multiple and concurrent schedules. His account of matching in multiple schedules is supported by the analysis of the response rate data from Shimp and Wheatley (1971) and Todorov (1972) given on p. 271, while Herrnstein's account is not. As the interaction between the components increases, Rachlin suggests that the pigeon's terminal response for food—pecking—should be facilitated in the period of high relative reinforcement frequency and more and more inhibited in the period of low relative reinforcement frequency. In fact, peck rate increased in the component with higher reinforcement frequency and decreased in the other component, with decreasing component duration in both studies.

However, Rachlin's theory of the processes producing the two kinds of response matching is itself inadequate in several respects. Response matching not only occurs in concurrent VI VI schedules where local response rates are equal in each schedule. It is found in concurrent VI VR schedules in which the local rates differ considerably on the two schedules and the subject cannot equalize both local response rates and reinforcement frequency (Herrnstein, 1970, 1971; Herrnstein & Loveland, unpublished data). It is also obtained in discrete-trial concurrent schedules where time allocation applies only arbitrarily (Nevin, 1969; Herrnstein, unpublished data). Hence more direct response matching occurs in concurrent schedules than Rachlin's theory implies.

Furthermore, the generality of Rachlin's explanation of behavioral contrast in multiple schedules is questionable. The results of an unpublished experiment by Bouzas question the generality of Keller's findings. Bouzas trained six pigeons on a multiple VI 1-min VI 1-min schedule with 30-sec components during which the instrumental key in the chamber was always white. In one experimental condition the components were signaled by a color change on a second (signal) key (i.e., Keller's procedure); in a second condition the components were signaled by the presence or absence of a tone. The six pigeons were studied in both conditions, three receiving Keller's procedure first and three receiving the tone condition first. When Bouzas discontinued the reinforcement in the second component, five of the six pigeons showed positive contrast in the first component in the tone condition. In the Keller procedure, four of the six pigeons showed positive contrast on the instrumental key in the absence of any pecking at the signal key. A fifth pigeon did peck at the signal key, but did not show contrast even when those extra pecks were added on the instrumental key. Bouzas then studied three of the pigeons in the Keller procedure with shorter component durations. The birds were trained on a multiple VI 1-min VI 1-min schedule with 10-sec components, and then switched to a VI 1-min VI 3-min. None of the pigeons showed contrast on the instrumental key in this procedure; but two of the three birds pecked the signal key a substantial amount during the VI 1-min component. Adding these extra pecks to response rate on the instrumental key produced positive contrast for these two birds. But the difference in results between the studies of Keller and Bouzas cannot be explained by component durations; Keller used 1-min and 2-min components, longer than either of the values used by Bouzas. Frequency of reinforcement could be a factor, as only one of Keller's three pigeons in his first experiment pecked at the signal key when he changed from a multiple VI 1-min VI 1-min to a multiple VI 1-min EXT schedule. Bouzas used VI 1-min schedules. On the other hand, Keller obtained signal key pecking from all three pigeons in the three-component multiple VI VI EXT schedule in which VI 1-min components were used.

The contrast effect found by Bouzas for the pigeons with the tone signal is also surprising in terms of an autoshaping analysis of contrast, since a pigeon's key peck can only be autoshaped with visual and not auditory stimuli. Similarly, LoLordo et al. (1974) found that a brief stimulus signaling free food only facilitated the base line key pecking if a visual signal was presented on the response key. An auditory prefood stimulus did not facilitate responding. But Westbrook (1973) also obtained positive contrast for six pigeons when the components of the multiple schedule were signaled by white noise versus a tone. The contrast effects found with auditory stimuli signaling components seem to be smaller than those found with visual stimuli on the key, but they are not readily explained by the autoshaping theory of contrast. (For a detailed discussion of the strengths and weaknesses of an autoshaping account, including a more detailed review of Keller's results, see chapter 3 by Schwartz and Gamzu in this volume.)

In brief, a large body of data on stable behavioral contrast and matching in multiple schedules can be accounted for by a particular view of response strength —namely, that the strength of a response is directly related to its relative frequency (or magnitude) of reinforcement. But it has become clear from the studies discussed here that no one analysis of behavioral contrast can handle all of the phenomena usually subsumed under that term. We must distinguish between short-term, transient effects that may be emotional in origin (Terrace, 1966b, 1972) and long-term, stable interactions between successive reinforcement conditions (Bloomfield, 1967b; Herrnstein, 1970). Other contrast effects seem to be related to excitatory effects of some reinforcers on particular responses (Gamzu & Schwartz, 1973; Staddon, 1972), and may even be species-specific. Indeed, there is no reason to believe that all of these contrast effects can be explained by the same process; many different phenomena may be involved.

DISCUSSION

Preceding sections of this chapter have considered a wide range of choice procedures in which a simple matching relation holds between relative performance measures and relative measures of reinforcement. They have shown how a quantitative theory of response strength derived largely from the matching relation can account for a remarkable range of data on response rate–reinforcement interactions in single, multiple, and concurrent schedules. But they have also indicated that some choice procedures do not produce the matching relation (Moffitt & Shimp, 1971; Nevin, 1971; Staddon, 1968; Trevitt et al., 1972; White & Davison, 1973). To what extent do these results weaken the matching relation as a quantitative law of choice in concurrent schedules?

Rachlin (1971) has argued that despite these empirical data, the matching relation "is not an empirical law but a statement of assumptions made prior to empirical test" (p. 249). It derives directly from our intuitions about unconstrained choice and as such it is not subject to disproof by empirical data. The theoretical matching law as formulated by Rachlin states that

$$\frac{T_1}{T_2} \text{ or } \frac{R_1}{R_2} = \frac{V_1}{V_2} \quad (21)$$

and

$$\frac{V_1}{V_2} = \frac{r_1}{r_2} \cdot \frac{a_1}{a_2} \cdot \frac{i_1}{i_2} \cdot \frac{x_1}{x_2} \quad (22)$$

where T represents the time allocated, R the number of responses made, and V the value of reinforcement consequent on each alternative; r is the reinforcement frequency, a the amount of reinforcement, i the immediacy of reinforcement, and x any other parameters of reinforcement for the two alternatives.

Rachlin believes that the matching law embodied in Equations 21 and 22 is a tautology or analytic statement about how reinforcing value should be measured. Wherever there are deviations from the simple matching relation (Equation 1), transformations on the independent variable dictated by obtained time (or response) ratios can make the law fit the data. A difference between programmed and obtained reinforcement (Premack, 1965) or the actions of unknown reinforcers (i.e., x_1 and x_2 in Equation 22) can always be invoked to minimize the deviation from matching. In these ways the theoretical matching law cannot be empirically disproved or supported. For Rachlin the value of the matching law lies in specifying the assumptions made in any choice experiment and circumscribing our search for hidden reinforcers so that matching will hold in choice situations.

A recent theoretical paper by Killeen (1972b), however, raises several arguments against Rachlin's approach to the matching relation. Killeen argues first that the empirical matching relation (Equation 1) must be distinguished from Rachlin's theoretical matching law (Equation 21). The empirical matching equations clearly are not examples of a law "not subject to empirical test," since concurrent schedule experiments could well have found some other relation between relative performance measures and reinforcement. On the other hand, Rachlin's matching law is indeed a tautology, since it assumes that time ratios define value ratios. But Killeen suggests that this only generates a redundant intervening variable —i.e., value. Since time ratios must equal value ratios, the former could be substituted for the latter whenever they occur, and the notion of value adds nothing to Rachlin's analysis. "The generality of Rachlin's law is uninteresting since it can be obtained in any situation where one cares to postulate an intervening variable equal to the data in question" (Killeen, 1972b, p. 491).

Rachlin asserts that Equation 21 is "derivable from the assumption that an organism choosing between alternatives is under no constraints except those the contingencies of reinforcement impose" (p. 249); it codifies our intuitions about choice. However, like Killeen (1972b), I do not see how this must follow, as many other relationships are possible. A far more complicated relation could hold between responding or time allocation and the reinforcement variables; why not $T_1 - T_2 = V_1 - V_2$ (see Lea & Morgan, 1972)? Moreover, it was the success of the empirical matching relation, not any intuitions about choice, that brought to the attention of researchers in operant conditioning the utility of the concurrent schedule procedure and the advantages of a relative measure of behavior in quantifying the law of effect. The value of an empirically based matching law lies in the extent to which it makes valid predictions in new situations, as well as in its utility for ordering data and pointing out anomalies. As Harré (1960) noted: "It is only when we begin to apply the law to cases further and further removed from the cases upon which it was based that we begin to run serious risks of a contrary case appearing and disconfirming the law" (p. 154). Three possibilities are open to us when the inevitable counterinstances to the matching law are found (Harré, 1960):

One, we can uphold the law and note the contrary case. "This will be the appropriate action when there are various doubts in the investigator's mind about the control of extraneous factors in the experimental set up" (Harré, p. 154). I have argued that this is the appropriate action in the case of studies by Schmitt (1974) for humans and Trevitt et al. (1972) for pigeons, and in the case of several experiments where undermatching probably resulted from a COD duration that was too short.

Two, we may merely state the limitations on the law (e.g., Boyle's law does not hold at very high pressures). In the present chapter I have stated some limitations on the application of the matching relation. Matching does not hold in the absence of a COD or when the COD is too short. Kulli's unpublished experiment showing matching in the absence of a COD at low drive levels (p. 244) suggests that rate of alternation between the schedules, and not the COD procedure per se, is the crucial factor. If the rate of alternation is too high, responses to one alternative come under partial control of the other reinforcement schedule.

White and Davison (1973) have suggested that the matching relation fails to hold when different patterns of responding are generated by the two schedules—e.g., on concurrent VI FI schedules (Nevin, 1971; Trevitt et al. 1972) or on concurrent paced schedules (Staddon, 1968; Moffitt & Shimp, 1971). In these cases the schedule contingencies tend to constrain response rates on the two schedules. When the patterns of responding are more similar—e.g., on concurrent FI FR schedules—the deviation from matching is much smaller (LaBounty & Reynolds, 1973); and when the response patterns are the same on the two keys, even though responding is paced by the reinforcement contingencies (Shimp, 1971), matching is obtained.

An important goal of future research will be the determination of further limitations on the matching relation. It will then be necessary to explain why matching does not hold in particular situations (see p. 266) and to assess the power of the matching law in terms of the range of situations for which it gives an accurate quantitative description of choice.

Third, we may attempt to "formulate a new generalization which will include all the results obtained under all sets of conditions that have been investigated" (Harré, p. 155). For example, Baum (1974a) generalized the matching equation to account for bias or inherent preference for one alternative. In this way he could account for data previously thought to contradict matching (e.g., Fantino et al., 1972). However, Baum's proportional ratio matching (Equations 4 and 5) does not handle "results obtained from all sets of conditions [of choice] that have been investigated." More general mathematical formulations of choice in concurrent schedules have therefore been suggested to replace the simple matching relation.

Killeen (1972b) proposed that an additive difference model of utility (Tversky, 1969) be considered a "working hypothesis" of the way in which different parameters of reinforcement determine choice:

$$\frac{T_1}{T_2} \text{ or } \frac{R_1}{R_2} = \frac{f_1(r_1)}{f_1(r_2)} \cdot \frac{f_2(a_1)}{f_2(a_2)} \cdot \frac{f_3(i_1)}{f_3(i_2)} \cdot \frac{f_4(x_1)}{f_4(x_2)} \quad (23)$$

where T, R, r, a, i, and x are as specified for Equations 21 and 22. This equation states that choice can be predicted by a particular concatenation of subjective scales of reinforcement. In the context in which each scale is derived, Equation 23 is true by definition, since the scales are defined by the choice behavior. But the equation becomes empirically falsifiable when extrapolations are made to new choice situations or when several subjective scales are combined (Killeen, 1972b). It also assumes that there are no interactions among the subjective scales, and this too is empirically testable.

Both the strength and weakness of Killeen's formulation lie in its great generality. Current research indicates that a simple linear scaling of reinforcement produces matching for a number of different reinforcement parameters. Then a far more parsimonious matching law than Equation 23 is possible. If the more general formulation embodied in Equation 23 does prove necessary to describe choice in concurrent schedules, then the variables that affect each reinforcement function will need to be specified. For example, the function relating time ratios to reinforcement frequencies seems to be different for choice between two VIs and choice between a VI and an FI schedule.

Staddon (1968, 1972) has argued that a power function relation between behavior and reinforcement ratios—i.e., a specific case of Killeen's equation—accurately describes all of the present data on choice in concurrent schedules:

$$\frac{T_1}{T_2} \text{ or } \frac{R_1}{R_2} = k \frac{r_1^n}{r_2^n} \quad (24)$$

where k is a parameter indicating any systematic bias toward one schedule. Equation 24 reduces to proportional ratio matching when the exponent is 1.0; but it also accounts for choice on paced schedules, concurrent VI FI and concurrent FI FR schedules in which exponents of less than 1.0 were obtained. Staddon (1972) suggests that the power function formulation is required in situations where there is an intrinsic preference for one of the responses or schedules of reinforcement apart from the frequencies of reinforcement associated with each.

Although it handles all of the data discussed in this chapter, the implications of the power function formulation must be further specified before its value relative to the simpler matching relation can be assessed. For example, the factors that lead to differences in the power function exponent have yet to be specified. In some situations in which subjects have a strong bias toward one or another of the reinforcers the exponent is near 1.0—i.e., the matching exponent (Hollard & Davison, 1971). Bias or intrinsic preference accounts for deviations in the intercept of the choice function from (0, 0), but not for differences in the exponent (Baum, 1974a). Furthermore, while Herrnstein (1970) has extended the matching relation to account for absolute as well as relative response rates, the implications of a power function formulation for absolute response rates (except where it reduces to the matching relation) are unclear.

Finally, as discussed earlier, Herrnstein's extension of the matching relation to absolute response rates may be used to account for some deviations from matching. For example, if values of k for two different response forms were previously determined in single schedules, it should be possible to predict the deviation from matching that would be observed in a concurrent schedule using those two responses (i.e., provided that the r_e-values were not too dissimilar for the two responses). There has been little quantitative investigation of choice between different response forms in concurrent schedules.

While there is thus general agreement about the empirical relation between response strength and relative reinforcement, there is yet to be a consensus on the best mathematical form for expressing it. It is only as the implications and predictions of each formulation are specified and empirically tested that their relative merits can be evaluated.

CONCLUSION

In 1971, Herrnstein prefaced a paper entitled "Quantitative Hedonism" with the statement: "The occasion for this article is the conviction that a precise statement of reinforcement may be at hand, growing out of the discovery that frequencies of alternative forms of behavior occur in the same proportion as the resulting reinforcements" (p. 400). Several precise quantitative statements of response rate–reinforcement interactions in concurrent, multiple, and single schedules have been discussed in this chapter. Although the chapter has concluded that the available formulations cannot yet be fully evaluated, it also indicates that during the past decade significant progress has been made toward the goal of a quantified law of effect encompassing both positive and negative reinforcement.

APPENDIX A

Least-squares fit of Equation 11 to the data from studies of magnitude of reinforcement. The values of k and r_e and the percentage of the variance in the dependent variable accounted for by the equation are shown.

CRESPI (1942): Running speed (100/time in sec) in a straight alley for five different weights of dog chow between .02 and 5.12 g. Groups of 7 to 21 rats per value.
$$k = 80 \text{ (running speed units)}$$
$$r_e = .2 \text{ (g of chow)}$$
$$99.5\%$$

ZEAMAN (1949): Speed (100/latency in sec) to leave the start box of a short runway for six different weights of cheese between .05 and 2.4 g. Groups of 8 to 10 rats per value.
$$k = 130 \text{ (100/latency in sec)}$$
$$r_e = .3 \text{ (g of cheese)}$$
$$82.1\%$$

HUTT (1954): Rate of lever pressing on a periodic-reinforcement 1-min schedule for three different weights of rat chow between 3 and 50 mg. Groups of 9 rats per value.
$$k = 12.4 \text{ (responses/min)}$$
$$r_e = 10.1 \text{ (mg of chow)}$$
$$99.6\%$$

BEIER (1958): Running speed (100/time in sec) in a straight alley for three numbers of pellets between 1 and 13 pellets. Groups of 6 rats per value.
$$k = 68.0 \text{ (running speed units)}$$
$$r_e = .67 \text{ (pellets)}$$
$$99.4\%$$

LOGAN (1960): Running speed (100/time in sec) in a straight alley for four different numbers of food pellets between 1 and 12 pellets. Groups of 6 rats per reinforcement value and drive level.

12 hr deprived
$$k = 45.1 \text{ (running speed units)}$$
$$r_e = .15 \text{ (pellets)}$$
$$90.0\%$$

48 hr deprived
$$k = 51.0 \text{ (running speed units)}$$
$$r_e = .15 \text{ (pellets)}$$
$$4.9\%$$

KEESEY & KLING (1961): Experiment I: Rate of key pecking on a VI 4-min schedule for four different numbers of peas between 1 and 4. Mean response rate of 4 pigeons, each exposed to all four values.
$$k = 118.6 \text{ (responses/min)}$$
$$r_e = .16 \text{ (peas)}$$
$$12.2\%$$

Experiment II: Rate of key pecking on a VI 4-min schedule for three different numbers of hemp seeds between 2 and 8 seeds. Mean response rate of 3 pigeons, each exposed to all three values.
$$k = 67.0 \text{ (responses/min)}$$
$$r_e = .45 \text{ (seeds)}$$
$$99.3\%$$

CATANIA (1963a): Rate of key pecking on a VI 2-min schedule for three different durations of access to grain between 3 and 6 seconds. Mean response rate of 3 pigeons, each exposed to all three values.
$$k = 64.6 \text{ (responses/min)}$$
$$r_e = .02 \text{ (sec of grain access)}$$
$$1.8\%$$

DI LOLLO (1964): Running speed (100/time in sec) in a straight alley for three different numbers of food pellets between 1 and 16 pellets. Groups of 16 rats per value.
$$k = 38.9 \text{ (running speed units)}$$
$$r_e = 1.0 \text{ (pellets)}$$
$$99.7\%$$

DAVENPORT, GOODRICH, & HAGGUIST (1966): Rate of lever pressing on a VI 1-min schedule for three different numbers of sucrose pellets between 1 and 9 pellets. Four macaque monkeys, each exposed to all 3 values.
Mean response rate of the four monkeys:
$$k = 21.7 \text{ (responses/min)}$$
$$r_e = 1.7 \text{ (pellets)}$$
$$100.0\%$$

Individual monkeys:

	k (responses/min)	r_e (pellets)	% of the variance accounted for
S36	16.5	2.0	99.9
S49	30.0	3.0	90.4
S57	26.0	1.4	90.1
S60	17.0	1.0	96.6

APPENDIX B

Least-squares fit of Equation 11 to the data from studies of the reinforcement magnitude of brain stimulation. The values of k and r_e and the percentage of the variance in the dependent variable accounted for by the equation are shown.

KEESEY (1962): Rate of lever pressing on a VI 6-sec schedule for six different durations (.28 to 2.65 msec), intensities (.5 to 4.0 mA) and pulse frequencies (23 to 138 pps) of hypothalamic brain stimulation. Mean response rates of 10 rats, each exposed to all six values of each parameter of brain stimulation.

Duration:
$k = 15.1$ (responses/min)
$r_e = .65$ (msec)
94.1%

Intensity:
$k = 20.4$ (responses/min)
$r_e = 2.0$ (mA)
92.9%

Pulse Frequency
$k = 25.0$ (responses/min)
$r_e = 145$ (pps)
96.9%

KEESEY (1964): Rate of lever pressing on a VI 16-sec schedule for five different durations (.25 to 2.0 sec) of posterior hypothalamic brain stimulation at two different intensities (3.0 and 1.5 mA). Mean response rates of 10 rats, each exposed to all five durations at both intensities.

3.0 mA
$k = 21.0$ (responses/min)
$r_e = .15$ (sec)
98.6%

1.5 mA
$k = 14.9$ (responses/min)
$r_e = .10$ (sec)
96.6%

GALLISTEL (1969): Running speed (100/time in sec) in a straight alley for four to six different numbers of brain stimulation puses (between 4 and 384 pulses per reinforcement. Nine rats, each exposed to several different stimulation values.

Individual rats:

	k (running speed units)	r_e (pulses of BS)	% of the variance accounted for
LH 22	107.5	1.2	76.0
LH 30	111.5	5.0	84.2
LH 35	94.2	2.5	96.5
LH 54	115.2	1.2	78.5
DBB 35	106.0	3.8	96.2
DBB 38	110.5	11.9	90.2
DBB 44	110.0	4.0	92.9
PH 35	108.0	18.0	77.8
PH 40	102.0	12.0	95.4

APPENDIX C

Least-squares fit of Equation 11 to the data from studies of sucrose and glucose concentration. The values of k and r_e and the percentage of the variance in the dependent variable accounted for by the equation are shown.

GUTTMAN (1953): Rate of lever pressing on a periodic-reinforcement 1-min schedule for four different concentrations of sucrose (4 to 32%). Mean response rates of 20 rats, each exposed to all four values; and mean response rate of groups of 20 rats per value.

Mean of rats:
$k = 8.5$ (responses/min)
$r_e = 4.2$ (% sucrose)
92.4%

Groups of rats:
$k = 11.5$ (responses/min)
$r_e = 11.5$ (% sucrose)
95.6%

GUTTMAN (1954): Rate of lever pressing on a VI 1-min schedule for seven different concentrations of sucrose and glucose (2 to 32%). Mean response rates of 8 rats, each exposed to all seven values of both reinforcers.

Sucrose:
$k = 15.6$ (responses/min)
$r_e = 7.1$ (% sucrose)
93.7%

Glucose:
$k = 16.1$ (responses/min)
$r_e = 11.0$ (% glucose)
98.7%

CONRAD & SIDMAN (1956): Rate of lever pressing on a VI 37-sec schedule for five different concentrations of sucrose (2.3 to 30%) at two drive levels (48 and 72 hr of deprivation). Mean of 3 monkeys, each exposed to all five concentrations at both drive levels.

48 hr deprivation:
$k = 16.3$ (responses/min)
$r_e = 3.7$ (% sucrose)
96.2%

72 hr deprivation:
$k = 17.6$ (responses/min)
$r_e = 1.7$ (% sucrose)
71.8%

KRAELING (1961): Running speed (100/time in sec) in a straight alley for three different concentrations (2.4 to 9.1%) and three different magnitudes 5 to 125 cc) of sucrose. Groups of 9 rats for each concentration and magnitude.

5 cc:
$k = 89.4$ (running speed units)
$r_e = 2.4$ (% sucrose)
100.0%

25 cc:
$k = 87.9$ (running speed units)
$r_e = 2.2$ (% sucrose)
99.2%

125 cc:
$k = 88.7$ (running speed units)
$r_e = 1.4$ (% sucrose)
95.6%

SCHRIER (1963): Rate of lever pressing on a VI 1-min schedule for five different concentrations of sucrose (10 to 50%). Mean response rates of 4 monkeys, each exposed to all five concentrations.

$k = 37.5$ (responses/min)
$r_e = 6.1$ (% sucrose)
95.4%

SCHRIER (1965): Rate of lever pressing on a VI 30-sec schedule for five different concentrations (10 to 50%) and two different magnitudes (.33 and .83 cc) of sucrose. Response rates of 8 and 6 monkeys, each exposed to all five concentrations, 6 of them exposed to both magnitudes.

Mean response rate of the 6 monkeys exposed to both magnitudes:

.33 cc:
$k = 88.0$ (responses/min)
$r_e = 16.1$ (% sucrose)
95.9%

.83 cc:
$k = 66.5$ (responses/min)
$r_e = 9.7$ (% sucrose)
96.3%

Individual data from the 8 monkeys with .33 cc of sucrose:

	k (responses/min)	r_e (% sucrose)	% of the variance accounted for
Ruth	109.1	17.0	94.3
John	61.9	6.9	85.7
Ken	91.0	21.5	98.6
Allan	55.2	.8	70.1
Karen	87.5	9.5	95.2
Joan	131.2	52.4	92.6
Leo	105.9	40.1	98.6
Mae	6.6	27.4	85.4

Individual data from the 6 monkeys with .83 cc of sucrose:

	k (responses/min)	r_e (% sucrose)	% of the variance accounted for
Ruth	82.4	5.5	84.9
John	77.2	6.0	97.0
Ken	86.5	20.0	97.7
Allan	61.9	7.5	90.8
Karen	68.2	11.2	93.3
Joan	45.8	65.0	98.3

APPENDIX D

Least-squares fit of Equation 11 to the data from studies of immediacy of positive reinforcement (1/delay in sec). The values of k and r_e and the percentage of the variance in the dependent variables accounted for by the equation are shown.

PERIN (1943): Speed of responding (100/latency in sec to lever press) in a discrete-trial situation with three different immediacies of reinforcement (2- to 10-sec delay). Groups of 25 rats per delay value.
$$k = 54.0 \text{ (100/latency in sec)}$$
$$r_e = .29 \text{ (1/delay in sec)}$$
$$93.2\%$$

LOGAN (1960, Experiment 55D): Running speed (100/time in sec) in a straight alley for five different immediacies of reinforcement (1- to 30-sec delay). Groups of 10 rats per delay value, each run at high and low drive.

High drive:
$$k = 64.9 \text{ (running speed units)}$$
$$r_e = .016 \text{ (1/delay in sec)}$$
$$99.1\%$$

Low drive:
$$k = 64.5 \text{ (running speed units)}$$
$$r_e = .075 \text{ (1/delay in sec)}$$
$$92.8\%$$

SILVER & PIERCE (1969): Rate of lever pressing on a VI 1-min schedule with five different immediacies of reinforcement (10- to 160-sec delay). Mean of 6 rats, each exposed to all five delay values.
$$k = 9.8 \text{ (responses/min)}$$
$$r_e = .02 \text{ (1/delay in sec)}$$
$$95.0\%$$

PIERCE, HANFORD, & ZIMMERMAN (1972): Rate of lever pressing on a VI 1-min schedule with five different immediacies of reinforcement (.5- to 100-sec delay), the delay of reinforcement being signaled by a cue light. Also three immediacies of reinforcement (10- to 100-sec delay) with the lever retracted during the delay. Mean response rates of 4 rats, each exposed to all of the delay values in both delay conditions:

Cue light:
$$k = 21.4 \text{ (responses/min)}$$
$$r_e = .04 \text{ (1/delay in sec)}$$
$$96.1\%$$

Lever retracted:
$$k = 106.0 \text{ (running speed units)}$$
$$r_e = .09 \text{ (1/delay in sec)}$$
$$95.0\%$$

Individual data from the cue-light condition:

	k (responses/min)	r_e (delay in sec)	% of the variance accounted for
R1	21.5	.03	80.8
R2	23.5	.15	98.3
R3	22.8	.02	78.9
R4	20.9	.07	97.4

Individual data from the retracted-lever condition:

	k (responses/min)	r_e (delay in sec)	% of the variance accounted for
R1	219.1	.63	97.8
R2	67.5	.80	98.6
R3	102.3	.23	94.9
R4	26.6	.04	92.9

APPENDIX E

Least-squares fit of Equation 11 to the data from studies of magnitude of negative reinforcement. The values of k and r_e and the percentage of the variance in the dependent variable accounted for by the equation are shown.

CAMPBELL & KRAELING (1953): Running speed (100/time in sec) in a straight alley for four different reductions in voltage (100 to 400 V) with a 400-V alley, and for three different voltage reductions (100 to 300 V) with a 300-V alley. Groups of 7 rats for each voltage reduction and each alley intensity.

400-V alley:
$$k = 228.0 \text{ (running speed units)}$$
$$r_e = 701.0 \text{ (V)}$$
$$92.9\%$$

300-V alley:
$$k = 106.0 \text{ (running speed units)}$$
$$r_e = 125.0 \text{ (V)}$$
$$98.9\%$$

BOWER, FOWLER, & TRAPOLD (1959): Running speed (100/time in sec) in a straight alley (250-V alley intensity) for three different reductions in voltage (50 to 200 V). Groups of 5 rats for each voltage reduction value.
$$k = 185.0 \text{ (running speed units)}$$
$$r_e = 338.0 \text{ (V)}$$
$$99.6\%$$

DINSMOOR & HUGHES (1956): Response speed (100/latency in sec to lever press) for four different durations of time-out (5 to 40 sec) from .2- and .4-mA shock. Groups of 5 rats per value of time-out and intensity.

.2 mA:
$k = 45.6$ (100/latency in sec)
$r_e = 89.4$ (sec time-out)
99.5%

.4 mA:
$k = 24.3$ (100/latency in sec)
$r_e = 6.7$ (sec time-out)
74.1%

HARRISON & ABELSON (1959): Rate of lever pressing for four different durations of time-out (2 to 20 sec) from loud noise (116 db.) One rat exposed to all four time-out durations.

$k = 3.1$ (response/min)
$r_e = .45$ (sec time-out)
91.4%

SEWARD, SHEA, UYEDA, & RASKIN (1960): Running speed (100/time in sec) in a straight alley for three different voltage reductions (65 to 315 V) with two different alley intensities (315 and 255 V). Groups of 9 rats for each voltage reduction and alley intensity.

315-V alley:
$k = 161.0$ (running speed units)
$r_e = 52.0$ (V)
97.7%

255-V alley:
$k = 146.0$ (running speed units)
$r_e = 35.0$ (V)
86.0%

WOODS, DAVIDSON, & PETERS (1964): Swimming speed (100/time in sec) in a cold-water tank (15°C water) for three different increases in water temperature (5 to 25°C). Groups of 10 rats per temperature increase.

$k = 163.0$ (swimming speed units)
$r_e = 18.0$ (°C)
93.6%

WOODS & HOLLAND (1966): Swimming speed (100/time in sec) in a cold-water tank for three different increases in temperature (4 to 16°C) with two different water tank temperatures (15 and 25°C). Groups of 16 rats for each temperature increase and water tank temperature.

25°C tank water:
$k = 108.0$ (swimming speed units)
$r_e = 1.3$ (°C)
85.9%

15°C tank water:
$k = 114.0$ (swimming speed units)
$r_e = 1.4$ (°C)
87.5%

APPENDIX F

Least-squares fit of Equation 11 to the data from studies of immediacy of negative reinforcement (1/delay in sec). The values of k and r_e and the percentage of the variance in the dependent variable accounted for by the equation are shown.

FOWLER & TRAPOLD (1962): Running speed (100/time in sec) in a straight alley (240-V alley intensity) with shock offset in the goal box delayed for five different delays between 1 and 16 sec. Groups of 5 rats per delay value.

$k = 94.0$ (running speed units)
$r_e = .06$ (1/delay in sec)
92.6%

LEEMING & ROBINSON (1973): Speed (100/latency in sec) of escape in a shuttlebox for five different immediacies of offset of a 420-V shock (1- to 16-sec delay). Groups of 10 rats per delay value.

$k = 39.4$ (100/latency in sec)
$r_e = .11$ (1/delay in sec)
86.0%

MOFFATT & KOCH (1973): Speed (1/latency in .01 sec) of panel depression to escape time-out from a comedy record for three different immediacies of reinstatement of the record (3- to 9-sec delay). Groups of 10 human subjects per delay value.

$k = 304.1$ (1/latency in .01 sec)
$r_e = 2.0$ (1/delay in sec)
96.6%

TARPY (1969): Speed (100/latency in sec) of lever-press escape response on either of two levers in a discrete-trial situation for five different immediacies of offset of a 200-V shock (1- to 16-sec delay). Groups of 10 rats per delay value.

$k = 98.1$ (100/latency in sec)
$r_e = .33$ (1/delay in sec)
89.5%

TARPY & KOSTER (1970): Speed (100/latency in sec) of lever-press escape response in a discrete-trial situation for three different immediacies of offset of a 200-V shock (1.5- to 6-sec delay). Groups of 10 rats per delay value.

$k = 45.5$ (100/latency in sec)
$r_e = .40$ (1/delay in sec)
94.6%

REFERENCES

ALLISON, T. S., & LLOYD, K. E. Concurrent schedules of reinforcement: Effects of gradual and abrupt increases in changeover delay. *Journal of the Experimental Analysis of Behavior*, 1971, *16*, 67–73.

ANGER, D. The dependence of interresponse times upon the relative reinforcement of different interresponse times. *Journal of Experimental Psychology*, 1956, *52*, 145–161.

ANGER, D. The effect upon simple animal behavior of different frequencies of reinforcement, II: Separate control of the reinforcement of different IRTs. *Journal of the Experimental Analysis of Behavior*, 1973, *20*, 301–312.

AUTOR, S. M. The strength of conditioned reinforcers as a

function of the frequency and probability of reinforcement. In D. P. Hendry (Ed.), *Conditioned reinforcement*. Homewood, Ill.: Dorsey Press, 1969.

AZRIN, N. H., & HOLZ, W. C. Punishment. In W. K. Honig (Ed.), *Operant behavior: Areas of research and application*. Englewood Cliffs, N.J.: Prentice-Hall, Inc., 1966.

BAUM, W. M. Choice is a continuous procedure. *Psychonomic Science*, 1972, *28*, 263–265.

BAUM, W. M. Time allocation and negative reinforcement. *Journal of the Experimental Analysis of Behavior*, 1973, *20*, 313–322.

BAUM, W. M. On two types of deviation from the matching law: Bias and undermatching. *Journal of the Experimental Analysis of Behavior*, 1974, *22*, 231–242. (a)

BAUM, W. M. Choice in free-ranging wild pigeons. *Science*, 1974, *185*, 78–79. (b)

BAUM, W. M. Time allocation in human vigilance. *Journal of the Experimental Analysis of Behavior*, 1975, *23*, 45–53.

BAUM, W. M., & RACHLIN, H. C. Choice as time allocation. *Journal of the Experimental Analysis of Behavior*, 1969, *12*, 861–874.

BEIER, E. M. *Effects of trial-to-trial variation in magnitude of reward upon an instrumental running response*. Unpublished doctoral dissertation, Yale University, 1958.

BENINGER, R. J. Positive behavioral contrast with qualitatively different reinforcing stimuli. *Psychonomic Science*, 1972, *29*, 307–308.

BERNHEIM, J. W., & WILLIAMS, D. R. Time-dependent contrast effects in a multiple schedule of food reinforcement. *Journal of the Experimental Analysis of Behavior*, 1967, *10*, 243–249.

BLOOMFIELD, T. M. Behavioral contrast and relative reinforcement in two multiple schedules. *Journal of the Experimental Analysis of Behavior*, 1967, *10*, 151–158. (a)

BLOOMFIELD, T. M. Some temporal properties of behavioral contrast. *Journal of the Experimental Analysis of Behavior*, 1967, *10*, 159–164. (b)

BLOUGH, D. S. Interresponse time as a function of continuous variables: A new method and some data. *Journal of the Experimental Analysis of Behavior*, 1963, *6*, 237–246.

BOLLES, R. C. *Theory of motivation*. New York: Harper & Row, 1967.

BOWER, G. H., FOWLER, H., & TRAPOLD, M. A. Escape learning as a function of amount of shock reduction. *Journal of Experimental Psychology*, 1959, *58*, 482–484.

BRELAND, K., & BRELAND, M. The misbehavior of organisms. *American Psychologist*, 1961, *16*, 681–684.

BROWN, P. L., & JENKINS, H. M. Auto-shaping of the pigeon's key-peck. *Journal of the Experimental Analysis of Behavior*, 1968, *11*, 1–8.

BROWN, R. W., & HERRNSTEIN, R. J. *Psychology*. Boston: Little, Brown, 1975.

BROWNSTEIN, A. J. Concurrent schedules of response-independent reinforcement: Duration of a reinforcing stimulus. *Journal of the Experimental Analysis of Behavior*, 1971, *15*, 211–214.

BROWNSTEIN, A. J., & PLISKOFF, S. S. Some effects of relative reinforcement rate and changeover delay in response-independent concurrent schedules of reinforcement. *Journal of the Experimental Analysis of Behavior*, 1968, *11*, 683–688.

CAMPBELL, B. A., & KRAELING, D. Response strength as a function of drive level and amount of drive reduction. *Journal of Experimental Psychology*, 1953, *45*, 97–101.

CATANIA, A. C. Concurrent performances: A baseline for the study of reinforcement magnitude. *Journal of the Experimental Analysis of Behavior*, 1963, *6*, 299–300. (a)

CATANIA, A. C. Concurrent performances: Reinforcement interaction and response independence. *Journal of the Experimental Analysis of Behavior*, 1963, *6*, 253–263. (b)

CATANIA, A. C. Concurrent operants. In W. K. Honig (Ed.), *Operant behavior: Areas of research and application*. Englewood Cliffs, N.J.: Prentice-Hall, Inc., 1966.

CATANIA, A. C. Concurrent performances: Inhibition of one response by reinforcement of another. *Journal of the Experimental Analysis of Behavior*, 1969, *12*, 731–744.

CATANIA, A. C. Self-inhibiting effects of reinforcement. *Journal of the Experimental Analysis of Behavior*, 1973, *19*, 517–526.

CATANIA, A. C., & CUTTS, D. Experimental control of superstitious responding in humans. *Journal of the Experimental Analysis of Behavior*, 1963, *6*, 203–208.

CATANIA, A. C., & REYNOLDS, G. S. A quantitative analysis of the responding maintained by interval schedules of reinforcement. *Journal of the Experimental Analysis of Behavior*, 1968, *11*, 327–383.

CHUNG, S.-H. Effects of delayed reinforcement in a concurrent situation. *Journal of the Experimental Analysis of Behavior*, 1965, *8*, 439–444.

CHUNG, S.-H. *Some quantitative laws of operant behavior*. Unpublished doctoral dissertation, Harvard University, 1966.

CHUNG, S.-H., & HERRNSTEIN, R. J. Choice and delay of reinforcement. *Journal of the Experimental Analysis of Behavior*, 1967, *10*, 67–74.

CONRAD, D. G., & SIDMAN, M. Sucrose concentration as reinforcement for lever pressing by monkeys. *Psychological Reports*, 1956, *2*, 381–384.

CRESPI, L. P. Quantitative variation of incentive and performance in the white rat. *American Journal of Psychology*, 1942, *55*, 467–517.

DAVENPORT, J. W., GOODRICH, K. P., & HAGGUIST, W. W. Effects of magnitude of reinforcement in *Macaca speciosa*. *Psychonomic Science*, 1966, *4*, 187–188.

DE VILLIERS, P. A. Reinforcement and response rate interaction in multiple random-interval avoidance schedules. *Journal of the Experimental Analysis of Behavior*, 1972, *18*, 499–507.

DE VILLIERS, P. A. The law of effect and avoidance: A quantitative relationship between response rate and shock-frequency reduction. *Journal of the Experimental Analysis of Behavior*, 1974, *21*, 223–235.

DE VILLIERS, P. A., & HERRNSTEIN, R. J. Toward a law of response strength. *Psychological Bulletin*, in press.

DE VILLIERS, P. A., & MILLENSON, J. R. Concurrent performances: A baseline for the study of conditioned anxiety. *Journal of the Experimental Analysis of Behavior*, 1972, *18*, 287–294.

DI LOLLO, V. Runway performance in relation to runway-goal-box similarity and changes in incentive amount. *Journal of Comparative and Physiological Psychology*, 1964, *58*, 327–329.

DINSMOOR, J. A., & HUGHES, L. H. Training rats to press a bar to turn off shock. *Journal of Comparative and Physiological Psychology*, 1956, *49*, 235–238.

DUNCAN, B., & FANTINO, E. Choice for periodic schedules of reinforcement. *Journal of the Experimental Analysis of Behavior*, 1970, *14*, 73–86.

DYSART, J., MARX, M. H., MCLEAN, J., & NELSON, J. A. Peak shift as a function of multiple schedules of reinforcement. *Journal of the Experimental Analysis of Behavior*, 1974, *22*, 463–470.

ESTES, W. K., & SKINNER, B. F. Some quantitative properties of anxiety. *Journal of Experimental Psychology*, 1941, *29*, 390–400.

FANTINO, E., SQUIRES, N., DELBRUCK, N., & PETERSON, C. Choice behavior and the accessibility of the reinforcer. *Journal of the Experimental Analysis of Behavior*, 1972, *18*, 35–43.

FERSTER, C. B., & SKINNER, B. F. *Schedules of reinforcement*. Englewood Cliffs, N.J.: Prentice-Hall, Inc., 1957.

FINDLEY, J. D. Preference and switching under concurrent scheduling. *Journal of the Experimental Analysis of Behavior*, 1958, *1*, 123–144.

FOWLER, H., & TRAPOLD, M. A. Escape performance as a function of delay of reinforcement. *Journal of Experimental Psychology*, 1962, *63*, 464–467.

GALLISTEL, C. R. The incentive of brain-stimulation reward. *Journal of Comparative and Physiological Psychology*, 1969, *69*, 713–721.

GAMZU, E., & SCHWARTZ, B. The maintenance of key-pecking by stimulus-contingent and response-independent food presentation. *Journal of the Experimental Analysis of Behavior*, 1973, *19*, 65–72.

GAMZU, E., & WILLIAMS, D. R. Classical conditioning of a complex skeletal response. *Science*, 1971, *171*, 923–925.

GUTTMAN, N. Operant conditioning, extinction, and periodic reinforcement in relation to concentration of sucrose used as reinforcing agent. *Journal of Experimental Psychology*, 1953, *46*, 213–223.

GUTTMAN, N. Equal-reinforcement values for sucrose and glucose solutions compared with equal-sweetness values. *Journal of Comparative and Physiological Psychology*, 1954, *47*, 358–361.

GUTTMAN, N. Generalization gradients around stimuli associated with different reinforcement schedules. *Journal of Experimental Psychology*, 1959, *58*, 335–340.

HANSON, H. M. Effects of discrimination training on stimulus generalization. *Journal of Experimental Psychology*, 1959, *58*, 321–334.

HARRÉ, R. *An introduction to the logic of the sciences*. New York: St. Martin's Press, 1960.

HARRISON, J. M., & ABELSON, R. M. The maintenance of behavior by the termination and onset of intense noise. *Journal of the Experimental Analysis of Behavior*, 1959, *2*, 23–42.

HAWKES, L., & SHIMP, C. P. Choice between response rates. *Journal of the Experimental Analysis of Behavior*, 1974, *21*, 109–115.

HERBERT, E. W. Two-key concurrent responding: Response-reinforcement dependencies and blackouts. *Journal of the Experimental Analysis of Behavior*, 1970, *14*, 61–70.

HERRNSTEIN, R. J. Some factors influencing behavior in a two-response situation. *Transactions of the New York Academy of Sciences*, 1958, *21*, 35–45.

HERRNSTEIN, R. J. Relative and absolute strength of response as a function of frequency of reinforcement. *Journal of the Experimental Analysis of Behavior*, 1961, *4*, 267–272.

HERRNSTEIN, R. J. Secondary reinforcement and rate of primary reinforcement. *Journal of the Experimental Analysis of Behavior*, 1964, *7*, 27–36.

HERRNSTEIN, R. J. Method and theory in the study of avoidance. *Psychological Review*, 1969, *76*, 49–69.

HERRNSTEIN, R. J. On the law of effect. *Journal of the Experimental Analysis of Behavior*, 1970, *13*, 243–266.

HERRNSTEIN, R. J. Quantitative hedonism. *Journal of Psychiatric Research*, 1971, *8*, 399–412.

HERRNSTEIN, R. J. Formal properties of the matching law. *Journal of the Experimental Analysis of Behavior*, 1974, *21*, 159–164.

HERRNSTEIN, R. J., & HINELINE, P. N. Negative reinforcement as shock-frequency reduction. *Journal of the Experimental Analysis of Behavior*, 1966, *9*, 421–430.

HERRNSTEIN, R. J., & LOVELAND, D. H. Food avoidance in hungry pigeons and other perplexities. *Journal of the Experimental Analysis of Behavior*, 1972, *18*, 369–383.

HERRNSTEIN, R. J., & LOVELAND, D. H. Hunger and contrast in a multiple schedule. *Journal of the Experimental Analysis of Behavior*, 1974, *21*, 511–517.

HERRNSTEIN, R. J., & LOVELAND, D. H. Maximizing and matching on concurrent ratio schedules. *Journal of the Experimental Analysis of Behavior*, 1975, *24*, 107–116.

HOLLARD, V., & DAVISON, M. C. Preference for qualitatively different reinforcers. *Journal of the Experimental Analysis of Behavior*, 1971, *16*, 375–380.

HOLZ, W. C. Punishment and rate of positive reinforcement. *Journal of the Experimental Analysis of Behavior*, 1968, *11*, 285–292.

HUTT, P. J. Rate of bar-pressing as a function of quality and quantity of food rewards. *Journal of Comparative and Physiological Psychology*, 1954, *47*, 235–239.

IGLAUER, C., & WOODS, J. H. Concurrent performances: Reinforcement by different doses of intravenous cocaine in rhesus monkeys. *Journal of the Experimental Analysis of Behavior*, 1974, *22*, 179–196.

KEESEY, R. E. The relation between pulse frequency, intensity, and duration and the rate of responding for intracranial stimulation. *Journal of Comparative and Physiological Psychology*, 1962, *55*, 671–678.

KEESEY, R. E. Duration of stimulation and the reward properties of hypothalamic stimulation. *Journal of Comparative and Physiological Psychology*, 1964, *58*, 201–207.

KEESEY, R. E., & KLING, J. W. Amount of reinforcement and free-operant responding. *Journal of the Experimental Analysis of Behavior*, 1961, *4*, 125–132.

KELLER, K. The role of elicited responding in behavioral contrast. *Journal of the Experimental Analysis of Behavior*, 1974, *21*, 249–257.

KILLEEN, P. Reinforcement frequency and contingency as factors in fixed-ratio behavior. *Journal of the Experimental Analysis of Behavior*, 1969, *12*, 391–395.

KILLEEN, P. A yoked-chamber comparison of concurrent and multiple schedules. *Journal of the Experimental Analysis of Behavior*, 1972, *18*, 13–22. (a)

KILLEEN, P. The matching law. *Journal of the Experimental Analysis of Behavior*, 1972, *17*, 489–495. (b)

KRAELING, D. Analysis of amount of reward as a variable in learning. *Journal of Comparative and Physiological Psychology*, 1961, *54*, 560–565.

KRAMER, T. J., & RILLING, M. Differential reinforcement of low rates: A selective critique. *Psychological Bulletin*, 1970, *74*, 225–254.

LaBounty, C. E., & Reynolds, G. S. An analysis of response and time matching to reinforcement in concurrent ratio-interval schedules. *Journal of the Experimental Analysis of Behavior*, 1973, *19*, 155–166.

Lander, D. G., & Irwin, R. J. Multiple schedules: Effects of the distribution of reinforcements between components on the distribution of responses between components. *Journal of the Experimental Analysis of Behavior*, 1968, *11*, 517–524.

Lea, S. E. G., & Morgan, M. J. The measurement of rate-dependent changes in responding. In R. M. Gilbert & J. R. Millenson (Eds.), *Reinforcement: Behavioral analyses*. New York: Academic Press, 1972.

Leeming, F. C., & Robinson, J. E. Escape behavior as a function of delay of negative reinforcement. *Psychological Reports*, 1973, *32*, 63–70.

Logan, F. A. *Incentive*. New Haven: Yale University Press, 1960.

LoLordo, V. M. Facilitation of food-reinforced responding by a signal for response-independent food. *Journal of the Experimental Analysis of Behavior*, 1971, *15*, 49–55.

LoLordo, V. M., McMillan, J. C., & Riley, A. L. The effects upon food-reinforced pecking and treadle-pressing of auditory and visual signals for response-independent food. *Learning and Motivation*, 1974, *5*, 24–41.

Mariner, R. W., & Thomas, D. R. Reinforcement duration and the peak shift in post-discrimination gradients. *Journal of the Experimental Analysis of Behavior*, 1969, *12*, 759–766.

McSweeney, F. K. Matching and contrast on several concurrent treadle-press schedules. *Journal of the Experimental Analysis of Behavior*, 1975, *23*, 193–198.

Millenson, J. R., & de Villiers, P. A. Motivational properties of conditioned anxiety. In R. M. Gilbert & J. R. Millenson (Eds.), *Reinforcement: Behavioral analyses*. New York: Academic Press, 1972.

Moffatt, G. H., & Koch, D. L. Escape performance as a function of delay of reinforcement and inescapable US trials. *Psychological Reports*, 1973, *32*, 1255–1261.

Moffitt, M., & Shimp, C. P. Two-key concurrent paced variable-interval schedules of reinforcement. *Journal of the Experimental Analysis of Behavior*, 1971, *16*, 39–49.

Morse, W. H. Intermittent reinforcement. In W. K. Honig (Ed.), *Operant behavior: Areas of research and application*. Englewood Cliffs, N.J.: Prentice-Hall, Inc., 1966.

Neuringer, A. J. Delayed reinforcement versus reinforcement after a fixed interval. *Journal of the Experimental Analysis of Behavior*, 1969, *12*, 375–383.

Nevin, J. A. Differential reinforcement and stimulus control of not responding. *Journal of the Experimental Analysis of Behavior*, 1968, *11*, 715–726.

Nevin, J. A. Interval reinforcement of choice behavior in discrete trials. *Journal of the Experimental Analysis of Behavior*, 1969, *12*, 875–885.

Nevin, J. A. Rates and patterns of responding with concurrent fixed-interval and variable-interval reinforcement. *Journal of the Experimental Analysis of Behavior*, 1971, *16*, 241–247.

Nevin, J. A. Response strength in multiple schedules. *Journal of the Experimental Analysis of Behavior*, 1974, *21*, 389–408.

Nevin, J. A., & Shettleworth, S. J. An analysis of contrast effects in multiple schedules. *Journal of the Experimental Analysis of Behavior*, 1966, *9*, 305–315.

Perin, C. T. A quantitative investigation of the delay-of-reinforcement gradient. *Journal of Experimental Psychology*, 1943, *32*, 37–51.

Pierce, C. H., Hanford, P. V., & Zimmerman, J. Effects of different delay of reinforcement procedures on variable-interval responding. *Journal of the Experimental Analysis of Behavior*, 1972, *18*, 141–146.

Pliskoff, S. S. Effects of symmetrical and asymmetrical changeover delays on concurrent performances. *Journal of the Experimental Analysis of Behavior*, 1971, *16*, 249–256.

Premack, D. Reinforcement theory. In D. Levine (Ed.), *Nebraska symposium on motivation*. Lincoln: University of Nebraska Press, 1965.

Premack, D. On boundary conditions of contrast. In J. T. Tapp (Ed.), *Reinforcement and behavior*. New York: Academic Press, 1969.

Rachlin, H. C. On the tautology of the matching law. *Journal of the Experimental Analysis of Behavior*, 1971, *15*, 249–251.

Rachlin, H. C. Contrast and matching. *Psychological Review*, 1973, *80*, 217–234.

Rachlin, H. C., & Baum, W. M. Response rate as a function of amount of reinforcement for a signalled concurrent response. *Journal of the Experimental Analysis of Behavior*, 1969, *12*, 11–16.

Rachlin, H. C., & Baum, W. M. Effects of alternative reinforcement: Does the source matter? *Journal of the Experimental Analysis of Behavior*, 1972, *18*, 231–241.

Rachlin, H. C., & Herrnstein, R. J. Hedonism revisited: On the negative law of effect. In B. Campbell & R. M. Church (Eds.), *Punishment and aversive behavior*. Englewood Cliffs, N.J.: Prentice-Hall, Inc., 1969.

Redford, M. E., & Perkins, C. C. The role of auto-pecking in behavioral contrast. *Journal of the Experimental Analysis of Behavior*, 1974, *21*, 145–150.

Reynolds, G. S. An analysis of interactions in a multiple schedule. *Journal of the Experimental Analysis of Behavior*, 1961, *4*, 107–117. (a)

Reynolds, G. S. Behavioral contrast. *Journal of the Experimental Analysis of Behavior*, 1961, *4*, 57–71. (b)

Reynolds, G. S. Some limitations on behavioral contrast and induction during successive discrimination. *Journal of the Experimental Analysis of Behavior*, 1963, *6*, 131–139.

Schmitt, D. R. Effects of reinforcement rate and reinforcer magnitude on choice behavior of humans. *Journal of the Experimental Analysis of Behavior*, 1974, *21*, 409–419.

Schneider, B. A. A two-state analysis of fixed-interval responding in the pigeon. *Journal of the Experimental Analysis of Behavior*, 1969, *12*, 677–687.

Schneider, J. W. Reinforcer effectiveness as a function of reinforcer rate and magnitude: A comparison of concurrent performances. *Journal of the Experimental Analysis of Behavior*, 1973, *20*, 461–471.

Schrier, A. M. Sucrose concentration and response rates of monkeys. *Psychological Reports*, 1963, *12*, 666.

Schrier, A. M. Response rates of monkeys under varying conditions of sucrose reinforcement. *Journal of Comparative and Physiological Psychology*, 1965, *59*, 378–384.

Schroeder, S. R., & Holland, J. G. Reinforcement of eye movement with concurrent schedules. *Journal of the Experimental Analysis of Behavior*, 1969, *12*, 897–903.

Schwartz, B. Maintenance of key pecking by response-independent food presentation: The role of the modality of the signal for food. *Journal of the Experimental Analysis of Behavior*, 1973, *20*, 17-22.

Seward, J. P., Shea, R. A., Uyeda, A. A., & Raskin, D. C. Shock strength, shock reduction, and running speed. *Journal of Experimental Psychology*, 1960, *60*, 250-254.

Shimp, C. P. Probabilistically reinforced choice behavior in pigeons. *Journal of the Experimental Analysis of Behavior*, 1966, *9*, 433-455.

Shimp, C. P. Magnitude and frequency of reinforcement and frequency of interresponse times. *Journal of the Experimental Analysis of Behavior*, 1968, *11*, 525-535.

Shimp, C. P. Optimum behavior in free-operant experiments. *Psychological Review*, 1969, *76*, 97-112. (a)

Shimp, C. P. The concurrent reinforcement of two interresponse times: The relative frequency of an interresponse time equals its relative harmonic length. *Journal of the Experimental Analysis of Behavior*, 1969, *12*, 403-411. (b)

Shimp, C. P. The concurrent reinforcement of two interresponse times: Absolute rate of reinforcement. *Journal of the Experimental Analysis of Behavior*, 1970, *13*, 1-8.

Shimp, C. P. The reinforcement of four interresponse times in a two-alternative situation. *Journal of the Experimental Analysis of Behavior*, 1971, *16*, 385-399.

Shimp, C. P. Synthetic variable-interval schedules of reinforcement. *Journal of the Experimental Analysis of Behavior*, 1973, *19*, 311-330.

Shimp, C. P. Time allocation and response rate. *Journal of the Experimental Analysis of Behavior*, 1974, *21*, 491-499.

Shimp, C. P., & Wheatley, W. L. Matching to relative reinforcement frequency in multiple schedules with short component duration. *Journal of the Experimental Analysis of Behavior*, 1971, *15*, 205-210.

Shull, R. L., & Pliskoff, S. S. Changeover delay and concurrent schedules: Some effects on relative performance measures. *Journal of the Experimental Analysis of Behavior*, 1967, *10*, 517-527.

Sidman, M. Avoidance conditioning with brief shock and no exteroceptive warning signal. *Science*, 1953, *118*, 157-158.

Sidman, M. By-products of aversive control. *Journal of the Experimental Analysis of Behavior*, 1958, *1*, 265-280.

Sidman, M. Avoidance behavior. In W. K. Honig (Ed.), *Operant behavior: areas of research and application*. Englewood Cliffs, N.J.: Prentice-Hall, Inc., 1966.

Silberberg, A., & Fantino, E. Choice, rate of reinforcement, and the changeover delay. *Journal of the Experimental Analysis of Behavior*, 1970, *13*, 187-197.

Silver, M. P., & Pierce, C. H. Contingent and noncontingent response rates as a function of delay of reinforcement. *Psychonomic Science*, 1969, *14*, 231-232.

Skinner, B. F. Are theories of learning necessary? *Psychological Review*, 1950, *57*, 193-216.

Spealman, R. D., & Gollub, L. R. Behavioral interactions in multiple variable-interval schedules. *Journal of the Experimental Analysis of Behavior*, 1974, *22*, 471-481.

Staddon, J. E. R. Spaced responding and choice: A preliminary analysis. *Journal of the Experimental Analysis of Behavior*, 1968, *11*, 669-682.

Staddon, J. E. R. Temporal control and the theory of reinforcement schedules. In R. M. Gilbert & J. R. Millenson (Eds.), *Reinforcement: Behavioral analyses*. New York: Academic Press, 1972.

Staddon, J. E. R., & Simmelhag, V. L. The "superstition" experiment: A re-examination of its implications for the principles of adaptive behavior. *Psychological Review*, 1971, *78*, 3-43.

Stevens, S. S. On the psychophysical law. *Psychological Review*, 1957, *64*, 153-181.

Stubbs, D. A., & Pliskoff, S. S. Concurrent responding with fixed relative rate of reinforcement. *Journal of the Experimental Analysis of Behavior*, 1969, *12*, 887-895.

Tarpy, R. M. Reinforcement difference limen (RDL) for delay in shock escape. *Journal of Experimental Psychology*, 1969, *79*, 116-121.

Tarpy, R. M., & Koster, E. D. Stimulus facilitation of delayed-reward learning in the rat. *Journal of Comparative and Physiological Psychology*, 1970, *71*, 147-151.

Terrace, H. S. Behavioral contrast and the peak shift: Effects of extended discrimination training. *Journal of the Experimental Analysis of Behavior*, 1966, *9*, 613-617. (a)

Terrace, H. S. Stimulus control. In W. K. Honig (Ed.), *Operant behavior: Areas of research and application*. Englewood Cliffs, N.J.: Prentice-Hall, Inc., 1966. (b)

Terrace, H. S. By-products of discrimination learning. In G. H. Bower (Ed.), *The psychology of learning and motivation* (Vol. 5). New York: Academic Press, 1972.

Todorov, J. C. Concurrent performances: Effect of punishment contingent on the switching response. *Journal of the Experimental Analysis of Behavior*, 1971, *16*, 51-62.

Todorov, J. C. Component duration and relative response rates in multiple schedules. *Journal of the Experimental Analysis of Behavior*, 1972, *17*, 45-50.

Todorov, J. C. Interaction of frequency and magnitude of reinforcement on concurrent performances. *Journal of the Experimental Analysis of Behavior*, 1973, *19*, 451-458.

Trevitt, A. J., Davison, M. C., & Williams, R. J. Performance in concurrent interval schedules. *Journal of the Experimental Analysis of Behavior*, 1972, *17*, 369-374.

Tversky, A. Intransitivity of preferences. *Psychological Review*, 1969, *76*, 31-48.

Walker, S. F., & Hurwitz, H. M. B. Effects of relative reinforcer duration on concurrent response rates. *Psychonomic Science*, 1971, *22*, 45-47.

Walker, S. F., Schnelle, J. F., & Hurwitz, H. M. B. Rates of concurrent responses and reinforcement duration. *Psychonomic Science*, 1970, *21*, 173-175.

Wasserman, E. A. The effect of redundant contextual stimuli on autoshaping the pigeon's keypeck. *Animal Learning and Behavior*, 1973, *1*, 198-206.

Westbrook, R. F. Failure to obtain positive contrast when pigeons press a bar. *Journal of the Experimental Analysis of Behavior*, 1973, *20*, 499-510.

White, A. J., & Davison, M. C. Performance in concurrent fixed-interval schedules. *Journal of the Experimental Analysis of Behavior*, 1973, *19*, 147-153.

Williams, D. R., & Williams, H. Auto-maintenance in the pigeon: Sustained pecking despite contingent non-reinforcement. *Journal of the Experimental Analysis of Behavior*, 1969, *12*, 511-520.

Wood, K. A., Martinez, E. S., & Willis, R. D. Ratio requirement and reinforcer effects in concurrent fixed-interval fixed-ratio schedules. *Journal of the Experimental Analysis of Behavior,* 1975, *23,* 87–94.

Woods, P. J., Davidson, E. H., & Peters, R. J. Instrumental escape conditioning in a water tank: Effects of variation in drive stimulus intensity and reinforcement magnitude. *Journal of Comparative and Physiological Psychology,* 1964, *57,* 466–470.

Woods, P. J., & Holland, C. H. Instrumental escape conditioning in a water tank: Effects of constant reinforcement at different levels of drive stimulus intensity. *Journal of Comparative and Physiological Psychology,* 1966, *62,* 403–408.

Zeaman, D. Response latency as a function of the amount of reinforcement. *Journal of Experimental Psychology,* 1949, *39,* 466–483.

10

Conditioned Reinforcement

schedule effects*

Lewis Gollub

INTRODUCTION

The topic of conditioned reinforcement has traditionally been concerned with the question whether a previously nonreinforcing stimulus could become a reinforcer through some conditioning operation.[1] The answer to such a question depends in large part on the way the reinforcement process is conceptualized. In the traditional view, reinforcement has been considered a static property of a stimulus. Stimuli could thus be categorized as reinforcers or nonreinforcers. If categorized as reinforcers they would be expected to increase or maintain the frequency of responses they follow.

More recent conceptions of the reinforcement process emphasize the dynamic nature of reinforcement (e.g., see Morse & Kelleher, chapter 7 of this volume). In this view, the reinforcement effect of a stimulus depends on many factors, such as the organism's deprivation, its past history of exposure to the stimulus, specific relations between the behavior elicited or controlled by a stimulus and the operant behavior under study (Premack, 1965), and, quite importantly, the schedule of stimulus presentation. In earlier treatments of conditioned reinforcement, however, the reinforcing effectiveness of the conditioned reinforcer was treated as a fixed property of the stimulus which could reveal itself under arbitrarily different conditions. The paradigm for studying conditioned reinforcement was a two-part experiment in which Part One consisted of "training," where a given type of association with a primary reinforcer was used to imbue some arbitrary stimulus with conditioned reinforcing properties, and Part Two was a "test" of whether the stimulus was, in the absence of the primary reinforcer, a conditioned reinforcer. The

---

* The author thanks W. H. Morse, who stimulated my early research on chained schedules, R. T. Kelleher, and A. C. Catania for provocative discussions over many years, and D. A. Stubbs for helpful comments on an earlier draft of this paper. A cordial environment for writing the review, and helpful support, were provided by Dr. T. Yanagita and K. Ando of the Central Institute for Experimental Animals, Kawasaki, Japan, while the author was on sabbatical leave from the University of Maryland. Thanks are due to S. Loftus, R. Crovo, and K. Flowers for help in preparing the manuscript. This work was supported, in part, by U.S.P.H.S. Research Grant MH-01604.

[1] This review deals only with positive reinforcement, i.e., operations involving the presentation of stimuli that increase the probability of responses they follow. Negative reinforcement is discussed in Chapters 7, 13, and 14. Further references in this chapter to reinforcement should always be understood to include only positive reinforcement.

major question was, "Under what conditions would a stimulus that was previously ineffective become a reinforcer?" In attempting to answer this question, the effect of the putative conditioned reinforcer was assessed during extinction with respect to primary reinforcement. The extinction techniques thus avoided the possible confounding of response maintenance by primary reinforcement in the test of the conditioned reinforcer.

In experiments with the extinction methods the effects of the putative conditioned reinforcer have generally been weak, sustaining either relatively few responses, or lasting for only a short time. This lability presumably resulted from the fact that the association with the primary reinforcer which established the conditioned reinforcer was, by definition, broken during the extinction test. (Detailed reviews of the experimental literature using extinction techniques can be found in Kelleher & Gollub, 1962; Miller, 1951; Myers, 1958; Wike, 1966.) In addition to their empirical frailty, the putative conditioned reinforcers were questioned on the grounds that the old response was maintained because of discriminative effects of the stimulus rather than reinforcing effects (see the previous reviews and Lott, 1967; Schuster, 1969; Wike, 1969). Thus, the question of whether an arbitrary stimulus can acquire a long-lasting reinforcement effect, and replace a primary reinforcer, frequently degenerated into inconclusive debate on alternative stimulus functions.

More recent experiments on conditioned reinforcement have emphasized response maintenance. In these procedures, responding is maintained by stimuli that have continued association with a primary reinforcer. Besides avoiding the traditionally intractable questions that arise in the context of extinction procedures, these newer techniques are also related more closely to the analysis of maintained responding generally, and the sequential properties of behavior in particular (cf. Kelleher, 1966a).

This review will be concerned primarily with the study of two paradigms, chained and second-order schedules of reinforcement. Both paradigms involve sequential response requirements, and the presentation of stimuli that bear a scheduled relationship to primary reinforcement. In both paradigms behavior is continually maintained by primary reinforcement.

CHAINED SCHEDULES OF REINFORCEMENT

In a chained schedule of reinforcement, a single primary reinforcement follows the completion of a sequence of individual schedule requirements, each of which is accompanied by a characteristic stimulus. For example, consider the sequence in a chained schedule in which a variable interval (VI) 2-min component precedes a fixed-interval (FI) 2-min component. A response key is initially lit green. After two minutes, on the average, the first peck changes the key color to red. The first peck that occurs two minutes or more after the key becomes red produces a small ration of food. The key then again becomes green, and the chain repeats.

A chained schedule (*chain*) is denoted by a list of the individual schedules in their order of occurrence; the component stimuli must also be described. Thus, the preceding example would be a *chain* VI 2-min FI 2-min with green and red lights on the response key. When the component schedules are identical, a further shorthand is sometimes used, which specifies the *number* of components, and the schedule in each (sometimes called the *unit schedule*). Thus, if both components of a two-component chain were FI 2-min, or a *chain* FI 2-min FI 2-min, the schedule could be denoted *chain* FR 2 (FI 2-min). This indicates that a primary reinforcer is presented after completion twice (fixed ratio 2, or FR 2) of the unit schedule requirement, FI 2-min. A characteristic stimulus is associated with each of the two components (cf. Kelleher, 1966a). The parentheses can be read as in mathematical functional notation, *a chain FR 2 of FI 2-min*. This notation is particularly helpful in contrasting results under chained schedules with those under other sequential schedules, such as tandem and second-order schedules.

Overview

Responding in individual components of chained schedules is primarily under the control of two variables: the component schedule and the temporal location of the component with respect to primary reinforcement (cf. Staddon, 1972). The analysis of chained schedules thus emphasizes two aspects of behavior: the temporal pattern of responding in each component, and the overall amount of responding in each component. In general, the pattern of responding in each component tends to resemble the pattern that occurs when responding under the same schedule produces primary reinforcement. Response rate increases from component to component towards primary reinforcement.

The major emphases of research on chained schedules have been the acquisition of responding under chained schedules (transition performances, cf. Sidman, 1960); parametric investigation of factors that determine the level of maintained responding; and, the analysis of the behavioral functions of the component stimuli of chained schedules.

Transition Performances Under Chained Schedules

In a noteworthy series of experiments, Ferster and Skinner (1957) examined transition and steady-state performances in pigeons under chained schedules following training on related simple and multiple schedules. They studied two-component chained schedules comprised of eight of the possible nine permutations of FI, FR, and VI schedule components.[2] Pigeons exposed to these schedules had previously been trained under related compound schedules with the same component stimuli. For example, a pigeon was exposed to a FI 1-min schedule with a blue key, alternating with a red key during which pecks had no consequences (EXT). The blue key light was presented independently of key pecks after varying durations of the red key light. This arrangement comprised a multiple (*mult*) schedule, *mult* EXT FI 1-min. A chained schedule was later arranged by presenting the blue light and its associated FI 1-min schedule dependent on a peck after varying durations of the red light that averaged 1 min, a VI 1-min schedule. The chained schedule was thus *chain* VI 1-min FI 1-min. Under the *mult* EXT FI 1-min schedule, very low rates of pecking occurred while the key was red, and pecking began a short time after the key became blue and continued until food presentation. Within the first hour under the chained schedule responding in the presence of the red key light had increased from near zero to about 15 pecks per minute, and increased still more in the second session. Responding in the terminal component (blue key light) was unchanged from the performance during the multiple schedule.

Ferster and Skinner (1957) also studied chained schedule performance after training on multiple schedules with food reinforcement in both components, e.g., a *mult* VI 3-min FI 1-min schedule. When performances in both components were stable, pecks in the presence of the VI 3-min stimulus produced not food, but rather the stimulus associated with the FI 1-min schedule (*chain* VI 3-min FI 1-min). Both birds exposed to this training regimen "substantially lost the performance on VI 3 formerly prevailing under the multiple schedule before developing a chained performance" (p. 660). In brief, when the stimulus presented in the initial component of the chained schedule had previously accompanied extinction, response rates increased under the chained schedule; when pecks in the component had previously produced food, pecking decreased under the chained schedule (cf. Ferster, 1953).

Transition performances have not been explored very extensively since Ferster and Skinner's observations. Gollub (1958) examined responding under 2- and 5-component chained schedules in pigeons that had previously been trained under comparable tandem schedules. In a tandem schedule, successive completion of two or more component schedules is required before primary reinforcement, but a single stimulus accompanies all components. In Gollub's experiments, the pigeons had never been exposed to the key light colors associated with the earlier components of the chained schedule. Gollub found that response rates in the initial component of 2-component chains decreased during the first and second sessions, compared to rates under the tandem schedule, and then increased, typically to a value higher than that attained in the initial component under the tandem schedule. One pigeon studied under tandem and chained schedules with five components had consistently lower rates in the initial chain component. Kelleher and Fry (1962) also found marked decreases in the response rate in the initial component within three sessions of *chain* FR 3 (FI 1-min) following 30 sessions under the comparable tandem schedule. Thus the changes in performance under chained schedules seem to depend on both the earlier experimental history of the organism (extinction versus food reinforcement) and the number of components in the chained schedule.

Such effects do not appear to depend on the specific training procedures, at least under some schedule values. A gradual increase to 60 sec in the interval durations of *chain* FI X FI X did not lead to terminal rates different from those attained by pigeons that were exposed to *chain* FI 60-sec FI 60-sec immediately after key peck acquisition (Gollub and Vogt, 1970). In a related study, Switalski and Thomas (1967) attempted to trace explicitly the development of stimulus control in the last 2 components of *chain* FR 3 (VI 40-sec) in pigeons. An unlit key marked the initial component, and a monochromatic light (550 nm) and a line were presented in the last 2 components, with counterbalanced orders for the two groups of pigeons. Stimulus generalization gradients for pecking were determined for line tilt, and wavelength, after the fifth and twelfth training sessions respectively. At both points in training, typical performance for a chained schedule was demonstrated. At the first generalization

[2] For definitions of these simple schedules of reinforcement, and descriptions of performances they generate, see Chapter 8.

test (after five training sessions) the generalization gradients were steeper for the terminal component than for the penultimate component. By the 12th session, about equal degrees of control were shown in each component by the chain. To paraphrase Switalski and Thomas (1967), stimulus control developed sequentially from the end of the chain forward.

Less attention has been paid to the temporal patterns of responding that develop under chained schedules. The evidence presented by Ferster and Skinner (1957), as well as in later reports, shows that although the temporal patterns within components of chained schedules resemble the patterns generated by the corresponding schedules of food reinforcement, there are also qualitative and quantitative differences. Responding to the initial components of chained schedules is more irregular, so that, for example the steady rate typically seen under VI schedules of food reinforcement is replaced by alternating periods of responding and pausing (*rough grain*). There are pauses at the beginning of both FI and VI initial components that are longer than those typically observed with food reinforcement. These effects have, unfortunately, not been subjected to experimental analysis.

Maintained Responding Under Chained Schedules

A major concern in research on chained schedules is the effect of the number, type, and quantitative requirements of the component schedules. Two effects are commonly reported. First, response rate tends to increase from earlier components to later components. Second, the rate of responding in a given component is determined by its separation from food presentation, and is higher when the component is followed by fewer components or when later components are short or require few responses. To some extent, number of components and the schedule requirement in each component appear to be interchangeable in determining temporal separation from food.

CHAINED INTERVAL SCHEDULES

Two experimental paradigms have been used to investigate the effects of duration of interval schedule. In one paradigm, only the terminal component is varied. In the second paradigm, all components are varied simultaneously.

On the basis of the data then available, Kelleher and Gollub (1962) concluded that the rate of responding in the initial component of 2-component chained schedules varied positively with the frequency or probability of food delivery in the terminal component. This relation holds both when food delivery is dependent on responding in the terminal component (Findley, 1962) and when food is presented independently (Kaufman & Baron, 1969).

In chained schedules with more than two components ("extended chained schedules," Kelleher & Gollub, 1962) the extent to which responding is sustained in the initial components also depends on the time that elapses from the end of the components to food reinforcement.

The profound effect on responding of the number and duration of fixed-interval components is illustrated in the following two experiments. In one experiment Gollub (1958) studied key pecking under chained schedules with 2, 3, 4, and 5 components, each of which was FI 30 sec. Responding in a given component was lower the farther the component was from food presentation. Figure 1 shows the mean rates of responding in each component as a function of the number of components intervening before food. A single curve connects the mean values. It can be seen that maintained response rate decreased steeply as

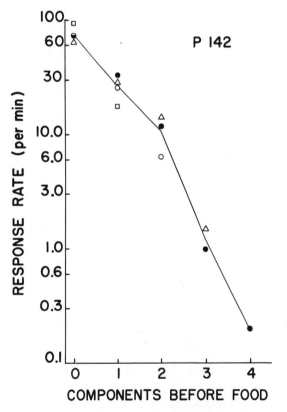

Fig. 1. Mean response rate in each component of chained schedules with 2, 3, 4, and 5 components, each FI 30-sec, plotted as a function of the number of components that intervene until the terminal component. The solid line connects the mean rates. Note that a logarithmic Y-axis is used. (Adapted from Gollub, 1958.)

a function of the increasing length of the chain.

Maintained response rates under three-, four-, and five-component chained schedules with different FI schedules in the components also were controlled largely by their separation from food reinforcement (Gollub, unpublished data). Figure 2 shows rates in each component of the following schedules, *chain* FR 3 (FI 45-sec), *chain* FR 4 (FI 30-sec), and *chain* FR 5 (FI 15-sec), plotted as a function of the mean time that the midpoint of each component preceded food presentation. To a first approximation, rate was a decreasing exponential function of time from reinforcement. These experiments show that response rate decreases rapidly as components are separated from food presentation by even modest amounts. Thomas (1967) also found that the earlier the component, the more profound the rate change as schedule value was varied in *chain* FR 3 (FI X) from 0.25 min to 2 min.

Complex behaviors can also be maintained under chained schedules. Boren and Gollub (1972) studied matching to sample in pigeons under *chain* FR 3 (FI X), where X was varied from 16 to 128 sec. The rate of matches (pecks to a side key whose color matched the previously displayed color on the center key) increased from beginning to end of chain, and showed an accelerating pattern (scallops) within components.

The effects of a given temporal separation are greater for FI component schedules than for comparable VI schedules. For example, Gollub (1958) showed that a 5-component chained schedule with a FI 1-min in each component generated extensive pauses, especially in the first two components; with VI 1-min components, steady responding was sustained even though the components were as distant from food as with FI components.

An experiment on 2-component chained schedules by Kendall (1967) suggests that the occasional presentation of short intervals in VI schedules constitutes the important difference between VI and FI components (cf. Catania & Reynolds, 1968). Kendall (1967) found higher rates in the first component of *chain* VI 1-min VI 1-min when the terminal VI 1-min schedule provided the first food delivery after 0.25 min than when the first food presentation was after 1.75 min.

CHAINED RATIO SCHEDULES

Two experimental paradigms have been used to study chained ratio schedules. These paradigms parallel those used with chained interval schedules. In one paradigm, changes in the response requirement are made in only one FR component, and all other components are held constant. The other components may be fixed ratio, or another schedule. In the second paradigm, in which all components are fixed ratio, all of the components are changed simultaneously.

An experiment of the first type was reported by Hanson and Witoslawski (1959). They showed that responding in the initial component of *chain* FI FR decreased as the number of responses required to produce food delivery in the second component was increased from 5 to 120 responses. Since increases in FR requirement produced correlated increases in the duration of the terminal component, changes in the initial component rate may reflect changes in the duration of the terminal component rather than in response requirement (cf. Killeen, 1969). Findley (1962) showed that changing the ratio requirement in only one component of *chain* FR FR FR affects responding in only the changed component and those preceding it, with quantitatively greater effects earlier in the chain.

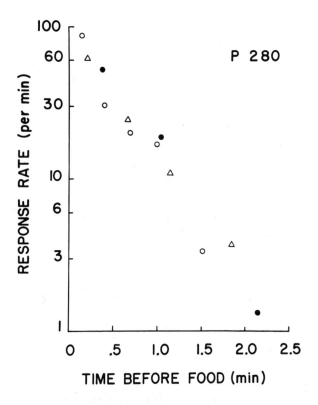

Fig. 2. Mean response rate in each component of *chain* FR 3 (FR 45-sec), plotted as filled circles, *chain* FR 4 (FI 30-sec), plotted as triangles, and *chain* FR 5 (FI 15-sec), plotted as open circles. Each value is plotted as a function of average time at which the midpoint of the component preceded food delivery. Note that a logarithmic Y-axis is used. (Gollub, unpublished data.)

An example of the second paradigm for studying chained FR schedules, in which the distribution of a given response requirement in different components is varied, was reported by Jwaideh (1973). She compared responding under 3- and 5-component chained FR schedules in which the total number of responses required for food presentation was constant. For different pigeons, the total number of pecks required was 60, 120, or 180. For example, one pigeon was studied under a *chain* FR 3 (FR 20) and *chain* FR 5 (FR 12). Post-reinforcement pauses were longer under the five-component chains than under the three-component chains. Response rates following the pause did not, however, vary systematically with different chained schedules. In a similar experiment, Ferster and Skinner (1957) found longer pauses before pecking began under *chain* FR 4 (FR 30) than under *chain* FR 15 FR 105. Segmenting a total number of responses into differing numbers of components seems to have a greater effect on responding than corresponding segmentation of an interval (cf. Figure 2).

Other Component Schedules

Experiments on chained FI or chained FR components generally reveal a monotonic increase in response rate from beginning to end of the chained schedule sequence. Such rate patterns are due to the specific component schedules, and are not necessary consequences of the chaining operation per se. Requiring a low rate in the terminal component can reverse the overall rate increase. Ferster and Skinner (1957) scheduled a *chain* FR 95 DRL 6-sec in which the ninety-fifth peck changed the key from red to purple; the first peck that was spaced six seconds or more from a preceding peck while the key was purple produced food delivery. High rates of responding followed a brief pause during the initial red light component, and a very low rate prevailed during purple until the DRL requirement was met. The entraining effect of periodic food delivery is thus only one factor in controlling regular patterns of responding under chained schedules.

Summary of Schedule Effects

Parametric investigations of chained interval and chained ratio schedules implicate three important factors controlling response rate: the type and the number of component schedules, and the requirement in each. These variables operate in the context of recurring food presentations (cf. Staddon, 1972). When the component schedules are all of the same type (e.g., all fixed ratio), the average response rates in the initial component is lowest and the rate increases throughout the chain until food presentation occurs. The response rate in a component is controlled primarily by the separation in time of that component from food presentation, so that number of components and the schedule requirement in each are interchangeable when these temporal relationships are constant, as under interval schedules. Changes in overall response rate are, however, modulated by the component schedules so that temporal patterns of responding in a component resemble those typically found under the same isolated schedule of food presentation.

Previous accounts of chained schedules (Ferster & Skinner, 1957; Kelleher & Gollub, 1962; Kelleher, 1966a) have appealed to a dual function of component stimuli as both discriminative stimuli that control a rate and pattern of responding appropriate to the component schedule, and conditioned reinforcing stimuli for behavior in a preceding component. This interpretation has proved to be exceedingly difficult to analyze experimentally, at least in part because unambiguous and independent measures of stimulus control and reinforcement strength are not currently available. The next section of this chapter reviews some of the ways in which stimulus factors have been investigated.

Stimulus Functions in Chained Schedules

Four types of manipulation have been used to study the role of stimuli in chained schedules: (1) Omitting stimulus changes with otherwise identical schedule contingencies (tandem schedule): (2) Changing the order of presentation of the component stimuli; (3) scheduling the sequence of stimuli independent of responding; and (4) presenting the component stimuli for brief, response-dependent exposures.

Tandem Schedules Compared to Chained Schedules

A tandem (*tand*) schedule is one "in which a single reinforcement is programmed by two schedules acting in succession without correlated stimuli" (Ferster & Skinner, 1957, p. 733). Thus, for every chained schedule there is a corresponding tandem schedule, with the same response requirements. The system for denoting tandem schedules is similar to that for chained schedules. Dissimilar component schedules are listed after the schedule abbreviation, thus, *tand* FI 2-min FR 5. When the same schedule appears in each component, a denotation like FR X (FI 1-min) is used. Note in this case that no special term is needed to indicate a

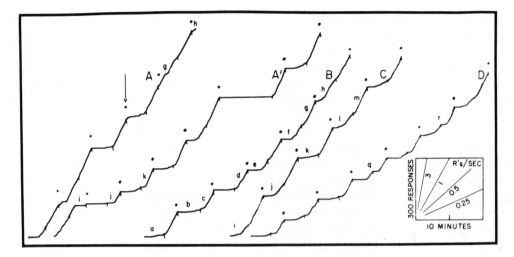

Fig. 3. *Tandem* and *chain* FI 3-min FI 2-min. Record A is the transition from tandem to chained schedule (at the arrow). Record A¹ is the continuation of that session. Records B, C, and D show further development in the chained schedule: Record B is from the second, C from the fourth, and D from the eighth session on the chained schedule. Pips indicate change from one schedule component to the next. Small dots above the record indicate food deliveries. (From Kelleher & Gollub, 1962. © 1962 by the Society for the Experimental Analysis of Behavior, Inc.)

tandem schedule since it can be described as a second-order schedule (cf. Kelleher, 1966a).

Gollub (1958) compared the performances of pigeons under tandem FI schedules with later performances of the same pigeons under the corresponding 2- and 5-component chained schedules. In all cases, the response rate in the terminal component of the chained schedule increased over that previously maintained in the terminal component of the tandem schedule. The rate in the initial component increased in two-component chains, but decreased with five components. The temporal pattern of responding also changed. Figure 3 shows the transition from *tand* FI 3-min FI 2-min to *chain* FI 3-min FI 2-min. A similar result for *chain* FR 3 (FI 1-min) components was reported by Kelleher and Fry (1962).

In some experiments, however, rates in tandem and chained schedules have not differed substantially. For example, Malagodi, DeWeese, and Johnston (1973) studied pigeons under *chain* FR 2 (FI 2-min) and *tand* FR 2 (FI 2-min), and found comparable average rates in both schedules. Appropriate temporal patterns of responding occurred under the chained schedule.

Performances can be studied under both tandem and chained schedules in each session if there is one stimulus for the tandem schedule and additional stimuli for the chained schedule components (multiple chained and tandem schedules, cf. Thomas, 1964). Gollub (1965) and Thomas (1967) obtained similar results studying multiple chained and tandem FI schedules. Thomas (1967) studied 3-component schedules with fixed intervals of .25 to 2.0 min. Generally, the rates of responding maintained in the terminal component of chained schedules were higher than in corresponding tandem schedules with the difference decreasing with increasing values of the fixed-intervals. The rates in the initial and middle components of the tandem schedules were higher than those under chained schedules, with the difference increasing with increasing interval duration.

Jwaideh (1973), in the experiment described above on chained and tandem FR schedules found that the pause after food presentation was generally longer for chained than for tandem schedules (cf. Ferster & Skinner, 1957). In addition, the rate after responding began (the running rate) in the first component was lower in chained than in tandem schedules in most cases, and the mean time to complete the required response number was greater for chained than tandem schedules, with the difference increasing with increasing total response requirement. Thomas (1964) also found lower average rates in the initial chain component of multiple chained and tandem FR schedules.

In summary, experiments comparing performance under tandem and chained schedules have yielded complex results. For two-component chains of FI schedules, the rate in the first component under chain was generally higher than tandem (Gollub, 1958), but not always (Malagodi, DeWeese, & Johnston, 1973).

Higher chained schedule rates have been interpreted as showing a conditioned reinforcing effect: responding that produces the terminal stimulus occurs at a higher rate than responding the same distance from food that does not change the stimulus conditions. Chains with more than two FI components have consistently shown lower rates in the initial component than occur under corresponding tandem schedules (Gollub, 1958; Kelleher & Fry, 1962). Similarly, rates were lower and pauses were longer in the initial component of three- and five-component chained FR schedules than in corresponding tandem schedules (Ferster & Skinner, 1957; Jwaideh, 1973; Thomas, 1964).

The comparison of chained and tandem schedules is more complicated, however, than might appear at first glance. Although schedules that are formally identical can be arranged, whether they are sufficiently comparable is a moot question. For example, in what sense is a FI component of a chained schedule in which its duration is marked precisely by a component stimulus comparable to a FI component of a tandem schedule without accompanying time markers? The concept of reinforcement contingencies implies that of discriminative stimuli (Skinner, 1969). Comparisons among schedules which are as different as tandem and chained may involve too many differences to illuminate specific aspects of control by either schedule.

Varying the Order of Stimuli in Chained Schedules

The discriminative and reinforcing functions of the component stimuli of chained schedules have been investigated by changing their order of presentation. Several experiments have used the following technique. Responding is first stabilized under a chained schedule. The order of stimuli is then changed, and the transition and stable performances under the new order are studied. In general, the results have shown strong control of response rate by the prevailing stimulus, so that high rates can be produced in early components of the chained schedule when a stimulus that has been presented previously toward the end of the chain is presented early. In addition, a stimulus that used to occur near the end of a chain can increase responding when it is presented as a consequence of responding in an earlier component.

After establishing performances under *chain* FR 3 (FI 1.5-min), Kelleher and Fry (1962) presented the three stimulus components in different orders on successive exposures to the chain. At first, the three colors controlled rates very similar to those maintained in their original chained schedule components. For example, the reverse order from the chained schedule produced a negatively accelerated pattern of responding. With continued exposure to the variable order of stimuli the pigeons responded at a more or less constant rate throughout each schedule sequence, with only brief pauses, if any, in the initial component. This pattern resembled that under the tandem schedule, with a single stimulus presented throughout the chain. After still further training, a new pattern of responding developed. Pauses after food were seldom longer than the scheduled interval (1.5 min), and miniature scallops comprised of a pause followed by accelerated responding typically occurred in both the middle and terminal components. Similar effects of reversing the order of component stimuli of chained FR schedules were reported by Jwaideh (1973) and by Ferster and Skinner (1957) with a continuously varying stimulus (an *added counter*).

The preceding experiments as well as others (Findley, 1962; Marr, 1971) on the effects of varying the stimulus sequence and the relationship of stimulus order to food presentation demonstrate that exposure to chained schedules develops strong discriminative control of responding by the component stimuli. This control is demonstrated by the maintenance of characteristic rates by each stimulus component when the stimulus is presented in a new sequence. These effects demonstrate little, however, about conditioned reinforcing effects of chained schedules. One other manipulation of stimulus order in chained schedules can provide relevant data here: scheduling the terminal stimulus in two or more different components of a chained schedule. Responding during the early presentation of that stimulus would show discriminative effects, independently of time of presentation. Responding in the presence of the stimulus component that *precedes* an early presentation of the terminal stimulus component would reflect the reinforcing effects of that stimulus as a consequence of responding.

Byrd (1971) studied the performances of pigeons on chained schedules with 3, 5, or 7 FI 1-min components in which the same key color was presented in the terminal component as in some earlier components (e.g., in the 1st, 3rd, and 5th, as well as in the 7th component). Different colors were presented in the other components. Strong rate-controlling effects of such repeated stimuli were demonstrated. In all cases, higher rates occurred during the early presentation of the repeated color than in the component that followed it. In one phase of the experiment Byrd (1971) presented one color (amber) in the 1st, 3rd, and 5th components of a 7-component chain, and unique colors in each of the other components. The rates in those components preceding amber (2nd and 4th) were compared with the rates previously maintained when the repeated stimulus also was paired with food, i.e., was presented in the 7th component. Rates were not higher under the latter condition. Byrd (1971) concluded that these results did not reveal a conditioned reinforcing effect of the component stimuli.

An unpublished experiment by Gollub indicates that chain component stimuli presented out of order can increase responding that produces these stimuli, but that these effects may be transient. Responding was maintained under *chain* FR 4 (FI 1.5-min). The color presented in the terminal component was then also presented in the second component. Responding increased immediately in both the initial and second components. Over the succeeding 27 sessions, however, responding in the initial component returned to its previous value, and responding in the second component also decreased markedly. Thus, an initial rate-enhancing effect of a chain component stimulus can disappear with continued training. With continued training, *white after orange* (or 1.5 min after food) gains different discriminative control from *white after blue* (or, 4.5 min after food). Byrd's (1971) pigeons had been exposed to presentation of the terminal stimulus at multiple locations in the chain for 115 sessions before the comparison mentioned above. It would not be surprising if control by the complex stimulus had developed by this time.

Clock Schedules

A major effect of the initial stimulus, especially in chains with more than two components, is discriminative. It controls very low rates. By definition, the initial stimulus component occurs furthest from the next food presentation, and responses in its presence are never followed promptly by food. Outside the chaining situation, such a stimulus would be referred to as S^Δ or S^-, and would normally control very low response rates (see Chapter 15).

An interesting comparison to chained schedules is the "added clock" of Ferster and Skinner (1957). They presented a spot of light on the key that grew progressively longer in a FI period reaching a maximum length when the next peck would produce food. The effects were quite dramatic. Zero response rates occurred in early parts of the interval, and were followed, often with a relatively rapid transition, by very high rates, sustained until food presentation. When the clock was "run backwards," with the long line presented immediately after food presentation and shrinking to a spot at the end of the FI period, response rates were maximal at the beginning of the interval, and decreased to zero as time passed. These results resemble effects reported by Jwaideh (1973) and Kelleher and Fry (1962) of comparable manipulations of chained schedule component stimuli. (See also Segal, 1962; Boren & Gollub, 1972.)

With pigeons on chained FI schedules, the early components frequently exceed their scheduled durations, since low rates with extensive pauses prolong them. The discrete-value "clock" of the chained schedule thus has settings with unequal durations. Tallen and Dinsmoor (1969) produced such a 3-valued clock by presenting the key colors to one pigeon that were simultaneously produced by a second pigeon under a *chain* FR 3 (FI) with FI values of 20-sec, 30-sec, or 45-sec (yoked-box technique). Responding under the clock schedule was confined almost entirely to the final stimulus (97.6–100% of all pecks), whereas pigeons under the chained schedule responded throughout the chain, with only 41.3–72% of their pecks in the terminal component, and the remainder of their pecks in the first two components.

In summary, responding occurs at very low rates in the presence of stimuli that are never associated with food. When responding in the presence of such stimuli is required for progression through the chain, response rates increase substantially. Such comparisons do not, however, distinguish the effects on responding of the response-dependent presentation of subsequent chain stimuli from the effects of the response requirement for the ultimate presentation of food. More comprehensive designs incorporating comparable tandem, chained, and clock procedures would help compare the discriminative effects of component stimuli (clock vs. chain) and the effects of the response dependencies (chain vs. tandem).

Brief Presentation of Component and Clock Stimuli

If component stimuli are reinforcers, a response that produces them even outside a chaining situation should be maintained. Hendry and Dillow (1966) found that clock stimuli from FI 3-min and FI 6-min maintained pecks on a second key, with presentation of the terminal stimulus maintaining the highest rate. Whether each clock stimulus alone could maintain pecking was not directly assessed.

Kendall (1972) investigated this question with a similar procedure. Pecks on one key produced food under FI 3-min. Pecks on a second key produced a

0.2-sec presentation of white, green, or red key-light in the first, second, and third minutes of the interval, respectively. In two later conditions of the experiment, pecks on the second key produced red during the last minute, and had no consequences during the first two minutes, or produced white and green during the first and second minutes, respectively. Figure 4 shows that pecks that produced time correlated stimuli were maintained only when red, the terminal minute stimulus, could be produced either as one of three stimuli, or as the only stimulus. When only the first two stimulus components could be produced, responding was not maintained. Whether green presented during the middle minute would alone sustain responding was not assessed. White, appearing when food was remote, might have suppressed pecks masking any rate-enhancing effect of response-dependent presentations of green (cf., Mulvaney, Dinsmoor, Jwaideh, & Hughes, 1974, for a direct demonstration of response suppression by S⁻). The experiment does show clearly that responses must produce the terminal clock stimulus at least part of the time to be maintained. Since the "information" concerning the occurrence of the terminal minute is the same whether a unique positive signal (red) is given or the lack of a negative signal (white or green) occurs, this experiment strengthens the line of argument that association with food or other positive reinforcers is necessary for the development of response maintaining effects by stimuli. Stimuli that provide the same "information" concerning elapsed time in the interval, but that have no close behavioral contiguity with food, did not sustain behavior (cf. Chapter 11).

Marr (1969) found the corresponding result for stimulus components of chained schedules with a complex one-key procedure. Briefly, higher rates were maintained by brief presentations of the terminal stimulus than by presenting the initial stimulus.

In summary, these experiments show that stimuli that are serially correlated with elapsed time in the interreinforcement interval of either fixed-interval or chained schedules control the rate of responses that produce them. Brief presentation of the terminal stimulus of a 3-component chain will maintain considerably higher rates than presentations of the first stimulus; presentation of the terminal stimulus alone will maintain as much responding as presenting all 3 clock stimuli; and presenting only the first 2 of 3 clock stimuli will not maintain responding.

Concurrent Chained Schedules

A discussion of chained schedules would not be complete without some consideration of concurrent chained schedules. (See Chapter 11 for a more comprehensive discussion of this topic.) This procedure has a basic appeal both for examination of the parameters of reinforcement in chained schedules (Kelleher & Gollub, 1962) and for scaling diverse reinforcement variables (cf. Baum & Rachlin, 1969).

The procedure was developed by Autor in his doctoral dissertation in 1961, and later published (Autor, 1969). The schedule can be conveniently divided into two parts. In the first (concurrent) part, two response keys are lighted. Equal VI schedules are associated with each key so that a peck occasionally produces the terminal component associated with that key. In the second (terminal component) part of the schedule, the color of the key changes, and the other key is not lit. Pecks in the terminal component produce food according to a schedule associated with that key. After food, the concurrently lit keys are again available.

Autor (1969) showed that the relative rates of responding during the concurrent part of the schedule were similar to the relative frequencies of reinforcement during the terminal components. This *matching* relationship occurred not only when food presentation in the terminal components was response-dependent under VI schedules, but also when food was presented occasionally and pecking was not permitted. Herrnstein (1964) extended these results by scheduling food presentations under variable-ratio (VR) schedules. He

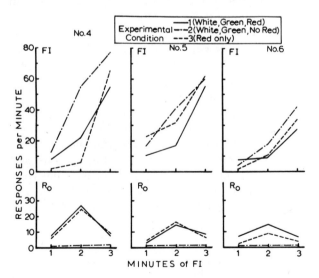

Fig. 4. Fixed-interval and observing response rates for each of the three birds in each of the three conditions. Fixed-interval rates are plotted in the upper panel and observing response rates in the lower panel for each bird. (From Kendall, 1972. © 1972 by the Society for the Experimental Analysis of Behavior, Inc.)

found that response proportions in the concurrent components tended to match more closely the relative temporal frequencies of food presentation than relative number of responses per food presentation. Because of the growing interest in studying the effects of reinforcement variables on relative measures of responding (Herrnstein, 1961), many papers followed these initial studies. Relative response rate was studied when the terminal components differed in: number of food presentations (Fantino & Herrnstein, 1968); FR versus VR schedules (Fantino, 1967); schedules of differential reinforcement of response rate (Fantino, 1968); amount and frequency of food presentation varying jointly (Ten Eyck, 1970); and FI versus VI schedules (Davison, 1969). In these and related studies, the relative rate of responding in initial concurrent links was used to scale *preference* or *value* (Baum & Rachlin, 1969; Killeen, 1972) of the terminal links. Concurrent chained schedules have even been used to study reinforcement variables in simple chained schedules themselves. In these experiments, two concurrent initial components lead either to a chained schedule or to a uniform stimulus providing food after about the same delay as the chained schedule. Schneider (1972) compared *chain* VI VI and *chain* FI FI schedules with corresponding tandem schedules. Duncan and Fantino (1972) compared *chain* FI FI with FI, and *chain* FR 3 (FI) with *chain* FR 2 (FI). Unfortunately, the two studies found strikingly different results. Schneider (1972) found essentially equal responding leading to chained and tandem schedules, whereas Duncan and Fantino (1972) found more responding leading to the less segmented schedule (FI versus *chain* FI FI, and 2-component versus 3-component chained schedules). Since only a small range of parameters was explored in terms of schedule type and schedule values, it would be premature to speculate on which procedural differences were responsible for the different results. As with many questions about chained schedules, further research is necessary to clarify the results.

Surprisingly, in view of the theoretical weight being placed on the relative rate data from concurrent chains the constraints in the basic paradigm have been little explored until recently. For example, in all seven studies on concurrent chained schedules mentioned earlier the schedules for terminating the concurrent components were equal (identical VI 1-min).

As it turns out, the schedules in the concurrent components are important determinants of the relative concurrent response rates. Fantino (1969) scheduled food presentations in terminal components according to VI 30-sec and VI 90-sec schedules. Identical pairs of schedules were used in the concurrent initial components. Over the experiment these were VI 40-sec, VI 120-sec, and VI 600-sec. The mean relative response frequency on the key associated with the VI 30-sec terminal component was 0.95, 0.81, and 0.60, respectively, as the initial schedules were varied. Thus, response distribution in the initial components depends in part on the absolute value of the equal, concurrent schedules. Alternative quantitative formulations of relative response rates in the concurrent components as a function of reinforcement variables in the terminal components must include some weighting for the concurrent schedule values (Davison & Temple, 1973; Fantino, Chapter 11 in this Volume; Squires & Fantino, 1971).

Quantitative models to describe behavior under concurrent chained schedules have grown increasingly complex as experimental variables have been extended beyond the initial limited values (see Fantino, Chapter 11 in this volume). In part this may reflect a terminological problem. It is a misnomer to call this experimental paradigm *concurrent chains*. Concurrent scheduling occurs for only part of the schedule. (For one exception, which was characterized by perhaps the most complex quantitative relationships in this field of research, see Fantino & Duncan, 1972.) This inaccurate terminology may have also distracted attention from what appears to be the crux of the matter: the organism is enmeshed in a complex set of contingencies, where, among other things, termination of the concurrent components not only is followed by one of the terminal components, but also delays the presentation of the alternative terminal component. Only recently has this point been appreciated (Duncan & Fantino, 1972). It is naive to consider concurrent chained schedules and related procedures as a simple technique for preference scaling of the terminal components.

In summary, the concurrent chains procedure, understood as a name and not a description, is a complex behavioral situation in which responding in the initial components is a function of the absolute and relative values of both the initial and terminal components. Much additional research is required to elucidate the individual sources of control in this situation.

Conditioned Reinforcement in Chained Schedules

The maintenance of responding under chained schedules has often been interpreted in terms of conditioned reinforcement (Ferster & Skinner, 1957; Gollub, 1958; Kelleher & Gollub, 1962). The preceding review indicates, however, that the strongest stimulus effects that are demonstrable in chained schedules are discriminative, i.e., the modulation of responding by prevailing stimulation due to previous reinforcement history in the presence of these stimuli. If reinforcement implies enhancement of responding by response-dependent stimuli, then only in certain circumstances (e.g., when *tand* FI FI is changed to *chain* FI FI) does response rate increase following response dependent presentation of temporally sequential stimuli. The difficulty in demonstrating clear reinforcement effects of stimulus components of chained schedules has led some writers to conclude that these stimuli are not reinforcers (e.g., Schuster, 1969). But response enhancement has been reported under certain conditions: in acquisition following tandem schedules, in repeated presentation of stimulus components, in comparisons of chained and equivalent serial stimulus (clock) schedules, and in a direct examination of how much responding is maintained by response-dependent presentations of component stimuli outside the chained schedule. Whether responding is enhanced, suppressed, or unchanged in a chained schedule compared to behavior under some procedurally related condition depends on the specific situations compared. Stimulus components of chained schedules may have complex behavioral effects that prevent an unambiguous prediction.

SCHEDULES OF BRIEF STIMULUS PRESENTATION

Extinction tests of conditioned reinforcement frequently involved brief presentation of a stimulus that had previously been associated with food, such as a magazine sound. As discussed above, interpretation of these experiments was often ambiguous. Few responses were maintained during extinction, at least in part because the association between stimulus and food was broken, and the reinforcing effectiveness of the stimulus was itself undergoing extinction.

More recently, techniques have been developed to study the effects on behavior of brief stimuli where food presentation continues. These techniques provide a chronic situation for the study of brief stimuli as maintaining events with some of the same advantages over extinction test procedures that the study of schedules of reinforcement has over the traditional extinction tests of *partial reinforcement*.

Two major classes of procedure have been developed in the study of response maintenance with brief stimuli. In one, presentations of the brief stimulus are scheduled as part of the schedule that arranges the presentation of food. These are second-order schedules (Kelleher, 1966a, b). In another procedure, the brief stimulus is presented according to an independent schedule that is concurrent with the schedule of food presentations (J. Zimmerman, 1963).

Second-order Schedules of Brief Stimulus Presentation

Kelleher (1966a) defined a second-order schedule in this way: "A second-order schedule is one in which the behavior specified by a schedule contingency is treated as a unitary response that is itself reinforced according to some schedule of primary reinforcement" (p. 181). This comprehensive definition applies to tandem schedules (no additional stimuli), chained schedules (different stimuli during each separate schedule), and schedules of brief stimulus presentation, in which a brief stimulus is presented according to the unit schedule contingency. For example, Findley and Brady (1965) presented food when a chimpanzee pressed a key 4000 times (FR 4000) in the presence of a red light. In the presence of a green light, food was also presented on the 4000th response; in addition, the food hopper was lighted (designated as S) for 0.5 sec after every 400 responses (FR 400:S). In the terminology of second-order schedules, the schedule of food presentation is denoted as FR 10 (FR 400:S). That is, food is delivered upon the tenth repetition of the FR 400 schedule. To facilitate description of these schedules, the schedule requirement for stimulus presentation will be referred to as the *unit schedule*.[3] The following review will consider the effects of different types of unit schedules on response rate and response pattern, and will then analyze some of the controlling variables.

Overview

Stimuli that are paired with food or other reinforcers can maintain long, orderly sequences of responding when they are presented according to second-order schedules. The pattern of responding is appropriate to the unit schedule, and the overall rate of respond-

---

[3] No standard vocabulary has emerged to describe the different parts of second-order schedules. It has been suggested that the schedule according to which the brief stimulus is presented (FR 400 in this present example) be called the *subordinate* schedule, and the schedule for arranging food (FR 10), the *superordinate*. The priority implied in such a nomenclature may not always apply, especially when schedules of the type FR (FI) are studied. In that case, the superordinate schedule would bear no important relationship to the ensuing behavior, which more closely resembles that under FI. Similarly, some have suggested *food* schedule, instead of superordinate. Again, it is the entire schedule, FR (FI), that arranges food presentation.

ing is frequently higher than that maintained by the corresponding second-order schedule without a brief stimulus (tandem schedule). The interpretation of these results is, however, subject to controversy. Increased rate under some circumstances can be attributed to discriminative effects of the brief stimulus with respect to food delivery. Other experiments have examined the relationship of brief stimulus to food presentation: no single temporal relationship seems necessary.

PATTERNS OF RESPONDING UNDER
SECOND-ORDER SCHEDULES OF
BRIEF-STIMULUS PRESENTATION

Fixed- and Variable-interval Unit Schedules. Long, orderly sequences of behavior can be maintained under second-order schedules of brief-stimulus presentation with FI unit schedules. Kelleher (1966b) scheduled food presentation to pigeons under FR 30 (FI 2-min:S) and FR 15 (FR 4-min:S) where S was a change in key color from blue to white for 0.7 sec. Under both schedules, the minimum time between food presentations was 60 min. For comparison, behavior was also studied under the corresponding tandem schedules. Three aspects of the results are important. First, under all four schedules (15 and 30 unit schedules, with and without brief stimulus presentations) behavior was well maintained over the one-hour periods separating food presentations. This is in marked contrast to the effects of chained schedules, in which substantial pauses usually occur when even 5 components of FI 1-min are scheduled (cf. Squires, Norborg, & Fantino, 1975). Second, the average rate of responding was low for first few unit schedule intervals, and then increased. This is illustrated by the cumulative records shown in Figure 5. Third, the brief stimulus controlled the temporal pattern of responding. There was usually a pause after each brief stimulus, followed by either a gradual or an abrupt acceleration to a moderately high rate until the next stimulus presentation. The maximal rate in each unit of the schedule sequences with the brief stimulus was generally higher than the maximal rate reached under the schedule without brief stimuli (11 out of 12 comparisons). This difference is illustrated in Figure 6 which shows mean response rates in successive quar-

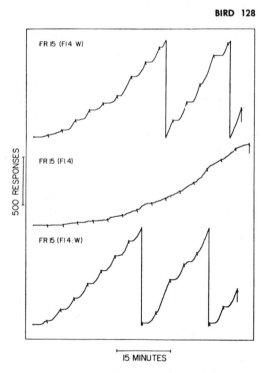

Fig. 5. Effects of omitting presentations of the white light at the end of each FI 4-min component (Bird 128). Each cumulative response record shows a sequence of 15 consecutive FI 4-min components; each sequence terminated with food reinforcement. Short diagonal strokes on the records designated FR 15 (FI 4-min:W) indicate 0.7-sec presentations of white light. Under the FR 15 (FI 4-min) schedule, there were no exteroceptive stimulus changes during the sequence; short diagonal strokes indicate the end of each FI 4-min component. (From Kelleher, 1966b. © 1966 by the Society for the Experimental Analysis of Behavior, Inc.)

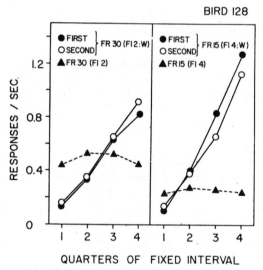

Fig. 6. Effects of omitting presentations of the white light on mean rates of responding in each quarter of the fixed-interval components (Bird 128). Each point is the median of the mean rates of responding in the last five sessions under each procedure. Solid circles: white light presented at termination of each fixed interval component; triangles: no exteroceptive stimulus change at termination of fixed-interval components; open circles: redetermination of effects of presenting white light. (From Kelleher, 1966b. © 1966 by the Society for the Experimental Analysis of Behavior, Inc.)

ters of the unit schedule interval under schedules with (circles) and without (triangles) brief stimulus presentations. Figure 6 also shows that the overall rate of responding, i.e., the mean number of responses per food presentation, was generally greater under the schedule of brief stimulus presentation than under the comparable tandem schedule. Boren (1973) found similar patterns of responding when pecks on a matching-to-sample procedure produced food under FR (FI:S) schedules.

Reinforcement omission, or percentage reinforcement of FI schedules, also involves second-order FI schedules. In this paradigm, responding is stabilized under a FI schedule, and food delivery is then omitted at the end of some percentage of the intervals. A time out (a period in which all lights in the experimental chamber are turned off) or other brief stimulus occurs instead. The sequence of intervals ending with and without food is irregular. The total schedule comprises a VR (FI:S), in that all intervals end in a brief stimulus (S) and after a variable number of these intervals, food also follows.[4] Staddon and Innis (1969) found that responding began much sooner in those 2-min fixed intervals which were preceded by time out than in those preceded by food. Mean response rates were therefore higher under the second-order schedule than under fixed-interval. The pause at the beginning of the interval varied with the duration of time out, which ranged from 2 to 32 seconds. Similar effects of omitted food delivery were demonstrated by Staddon (1970, 1972, 1974) and Kello (1972).

In a related experiment, Zeiler (1972) found that the smaller the percentage of intervals ending with food, the greater the responding earlier in the interval. As in a number of other experiments with this paradigm, Zeiler (1972) found that time out was an important factor in obtaining temporal control through the interval. In a related experiment, Zeiler (1972) studied the effects of presenting a 10-sec blackout after every interval in addition to either a 4-sec presentation of food or 4-sec time out that substituted for food. He found that responding was approximately equal in all intervals, whether they ended in food or not.

Response rate increases in the reinforcement omission experiments are not necessarily related directly to the occurrence of higher rates with schedules of brief stimulus presentation. In the former experiments,

---

[4] To be precise, this is a second-order schedule with unpaired stimulus, since time out does not precede food when the latter was presented. Some differences between paired and unpaired brief stimuli, and between blackout and other events as the brief stimulus, will be discussed later.

each food presentation typically follows between 2 and 4 unit schedule sequences, compared to as many as 64 in experiments on second-order schedules. Also, response rates in these experiments are generally compared to rates under a simple FI, or involve comparisons of performance following food with those following time out, whereas in Kelleher (1966a, b) and most other experiments, comparisons are made to tandem schedules. The two research paradigms thus cover different values of schedule, and make comparisons with different baselines. The research on reinforcement omission has, however, contributed to the analysis of interpretation of the behavioral function of the brief stimulus, to be discussed later.

Short, response-initiated fixed-interval unit schedules were studied by Neuringer and Chung (1967), Chung and Neuringer (1967), and Neuringer (1968). Chung and Neuringer (1967) studied a procedure in which a key peck started a fixed interval of 1 sec to 30 sec duration. The first peck after the interval elapsed produced either a 1-sec blackout (S) or, after variable intervals averaging one minute, food. The schedule can thus be notated VI 1-min (*tand* FR 1 FI X:S), with S unpaired with food. The pause before the first peck after blackout increased linearly with interval duration; the mean rate of responding during the fixed-interval period decreased as a negatively accelerated function of interval duration (cf. Starr & Staddon, 1974). In some parts of the experiment, food was scheduled after every unit schedule, a FR 1 (*tand* FR 1 FI X). Response rates under different values of the fixed interval were similar to those with VI 1-min in the second-order schedule, and the pause in these intervals was lower than when VI was scheduled. Chung and Neuringer (1967) reported similar rates for *tand* FR 1 FI schedules as for fixed ratio (FR 11). Thus, the contingencies of the short response-initiated interval schedules may make them more comparable to ratio than interval schedules.

Fixed-ratio Unit Schedules. Second-order schedules with fixed-ratio unit schedules of the form FR (FR:S) offer special circumstances for examining the behavioral properties of the brief stimulus. In such schedules, food is presented after a fixed number of responses, and performance can thus be compared to FR schedules with the same total response requirement. The added brief stimulus does not contribute additional response or temporal requirements, as with fixed-interval unit schedules, or with chained schedules.

The facilitatory effects of an added brief stimulus

under FR 10 (FR 400:S) in the chimpanzee and monkey were described earlier (Findley & Brady, 1965). Thomas and Stubbs (1967) found a similar effect with pigeons responding under FR 5 (FR 30:S) compared with FR 150.

Lee and Gollub (1971) studied second-order FR schedules of the form FR X (FR Y:S), with X·Y = 256. Values of X equal to 1, 2, 4, 8, 32, and 128 were presented in both ascending and descending orders. The brief stimulus was a 0.5-sec change in key light from red to green. Although 256 responses were required for food presentation under all conditions, the size of the unit schedule (or, conversely, the number of unit schedules and light flashes per food presentation) had dramatic effects on responding, as shown in Figure 7. The FR 256 schedule is represented by the extreme left point of each graph. Note that the highest median overall rates were obtained when the unit schedule was FR 64 or FR 128 (corresponding to 4 or 2 unit schedules per food presentation). Under the FR 2 unit schedule responding under the second-order schedule occurred at lower or equal rate to that under FR 256.

This parametric study indicates that global generalizations based on comparisons between a single second-order schedule of brief stimulus presentation and a corresponding FR schedule without a brief stimulus may be unwarranted, since performance depends on the specific scheduling of the brief stimulus. Parametric variation of schedule values is clearly necessary to determine functional properties in this complex situation.

The effects of different FR unit sizes was also investigated by Shull, Guilkey, and Witty (1972). They studied FI (FR) schedules in which 10 or 20 key pecks turned off the key light for 0.7 sec; pigeons were studied under FI 3 min, FI 6-min, and FI 12-min schedules, and corresponding second-order schedules. The FR unit schedules generated the *pause-run* response pattern typical of FR schedules of food presentation. Although Shull et al. (1972) did not present quantitative comparisons of rate, cumulative response records showed more responses per interval under FR 10 unit schedules than under simple FI, and more still under FR 20. Remarkably, despite these changes in rate and temporal organization of responding, the percent of the interval to the first response was not affected by interval duration, and increased only slightly as the behavior required for food presentation increased from 1 peck to 20 pecks. This result shows the strong temporal control of some features of responding by periodic food presentation, as well as control by the unit schedule.

Detailed measurement of responding within FR unit schedules shows the same pattern of interresponse times (IRT) within the unit schedule as that shown when food is presented under FR schedules (cf. Gott & Weiss, 1972). Kelleher (1966a) studied pecking in pigeons under a FI 10-min (FR 20:S) schedule. The time to the first peck in each group of 20 pecks was generally longer than other IRTs, and approximately equal IRTs characterized the next 19 pecks. Davison (1969), in an experiment with rats, only partly confirmed these results. Many differences in procedure between these studies makes a detailed comparison impossible.

THE ANALYSIS OF THE BEHAVIORAL FUNCTIONS OF BRIEF STIMULI

Two alternative behavioral functions have been proposed for the brief stimulus, reinforcing and discriminative. Compared to responding under identical schedules of reinforcement without brief stimulus presentation, increases in overall or local rates of a response that produce the brief stimulus, as in Kelleher (1966a, b), Findley and Brady (1965), and Lee and Gollub (1970), directly implicate a reinforcing function.

The brief stimulus also controls the temporal pat-

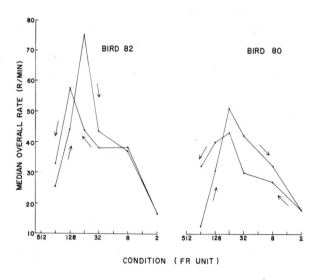

Fig. 7. Median overall response rates under each condition for Birds 82 and 80. Each pigeon was studied under FR X (FR Y:S) second-order schedules of brief stimulus presentation. A total of 256 responses was required for each food presentation such that X·Y = 256. The values shown are medians of the median rate in the last five sessions. Median rates within each session were calculated from a printed record of the time elapsing between food reinforcements. Arrows indicate the order in which the conditions were varied. (From Lee & Gollub, 1971.) © 1971 by the Society for the Experimental Analysis of Behavior, Inc.)

tern of responding. Unit schedules that terminate in a brief stimulus engender patterns similar to equivalent schedules of food presentation. The brief stimulus thus serves a discriminative function by controlling responding subsequent to its presentation.

Experimental analysis of the discriminative and reinforcing functions of brief stimuli has been attempted with several different techniques. The reinforcing effect has been examined with the concurrent chains procedure. Schuster (1969) scheduled as the terminal components of concurrent chained schedules, VI (FR 11:S) and VI, arguing that if S served a reinforcing function, its presentation in only one terminal component should enhance the total reinforcing effectiveness of that component. Instead, the pigeons had slightly higher rates in the initial component that did not produce the second-order schedule. This reverse preference may result from the fact that disparate response rates were generated in the terminal components (cf. Gollub, 1970; Moore & Fantino, 1975).

Another type of analysis of the reinforcing function of brief stimuli is related to the process by which conditioned reinforcers are established. Kelleher and Gollub (1962) argued that a conditioned reinforcer was established by simple contiguity of a stimulus with an effective reinforcer. (Alternatively, Keller & Schoenfeld, 1950, and others, have maintained that the conditioned reinforcer must be a discriminative stimulus for an operant, and still others have indicated an *informational* function, discussed at greater length in Chapter 11.) The pairing hypothesis, and to a lesser extent the discriminative stimulus hypothesis, have been tested in a series of studies that examined the effect of pairing the brief stimulus with food.

Pairing the Brief Stimulus with Primary Reinforcers. Kelleher (1966b) compared behavior under a second-order schedule of a brief stimulus paired with food with behavior under a second-order schedule of a stimulus not paired with food. In the former case, a white light was presented for 0.7 sec under a FR 15 (FI 4-min:S). Comparison conditions consisted of scheduling for 0.7 sec either an unlit key (D) or red key light (R) 14 times, with food alone presented after the fifteenth interval. In this case S was an unpaired stimulus.[5] The results for one of the three pigeons is shown in Figure 8. Mean response rate in each quarter of the FI in three replications with white key light paired with food are shown by circles. The rates with the other (unpaired) dark key are shown in the left panel, and those with (unpaired) red key, in the right panel. Both overall rates and rate changes within the FI period were different under the three conditions. Highest overall and terminal rates were obtained when the light that was paired with food was presented. Lowest mean rates, with little temporal control by the FI unit schedule, were obtained when a dark key was scheduled. The effects of the red light were intermediate: moderate mean rate, with some temporal control, although terminal rates in the interval were not as high as with the paired stimulus. One of three pigeons in the experiment responded almost as much with red as with white brief stimuli. Although Kelleher (1966b) interpreted these results as showing "that it may be necessary to present a stimulus in temporal contiguity with a reinforcing stimulus if the former stimulus is to become an effective conditioned reinforcer" (p. 484), he also indicated that the specific stimulus used and its previous associations with food, as well as the amount of training with an unpaired stimulus (here, 17 and 7 sessions, respectively) might be important parameters of the effect.

Subsequent experiments have confirmed some aspects of these results but have been equivocal about others. Over 20 studies have been concerned with the pairing operation of brief stimuli in second-order schedules. While the majority of comparisons have shown that a stimulus paired with food produced higher rates, or more pronounced control of rate changes by the unit schedule, or both, many of these studies have suffered from a serious methodological flaw: the stimulus paired with food was a physically different event from the unpaired stimulus. In some studies the difference was small (e.g., in Kelleher, 1966b, white key light *vs.* red key light) and the effect could reasonably be attributed to the pairing operation. In other studies the difference was considerable (presentation of a light in the feeder *vs.* a light on the key, de Lorge, 1969; Stubbs, 1969) and differences in

---

[5] It should be noted that the precise notation for the schedule of presentation of the unpaired stimulus is *tand* FR 14 (FI 4-min:S) FI 4-min. This notation emphasizes the existence of two differences between schedules of paired and unpaired stimuli: not only is the unpaired stimulus never followed directly by food, but food is delivered immediately after a response (FI 4-min), versus after a brief delay with a paired stimulus. In some experiments, e.g., Kelleher (1966b), food presentation under unpaired conditions is delayed by the duration of the brief stimulus, to match the key peck-food relation of the paired schedule. Another procedure, which would have certain formal advantages over those described previously, would be denoted *tand* FR 14 (FI 4-min:S_1) FI 4-min:S_2, where S_1 and S_2 refer to two different brief stimuli. That is, every interval would terminate with a brief stimulus, but the stimulus presented under the early components of the schedule would be different from the stimulus paired with food.

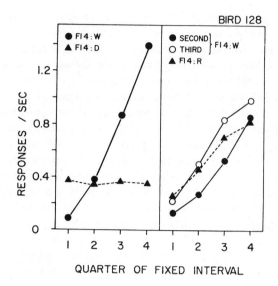

Fig. 8. Effects of presenting a stimulus that was not paired with primary reinforcement on mean rates of responding in each quarter of the fixed interval (Bird 149). Solid circles: white light terminated each component; triangles: dark key (left panel) or red light (right panel); open circles: final determination of points when white light terminated each component. (From Kelleher, 1966b. © 1966 by the Society for the Experimental Analysis of Behavior, Inc.)

effect could be due to any number of differences in the stimuli such as modality, location, intensity, previous exposures, and so on.

Three experiments reporting differences between paired and unpaired stimuli used the same stimulus in each condition, presented in different phases of the experiment. Hughes (1973) scheduled changes in key color and houselight for pigeons; D. W. Zimmerman (1969) scheduled a tone and a light for rats under conjoint schedules; Byrd (1972) scheduled a light for squirrel monkeys under a second-order schedule of electric-shock presentation. In four experiments when similar and presumably equivalent stimuli were presented, either paired or unpaired with food, higher rates were obtained with paired stimuli (de Lorge, 1967, 1969, 1971; Kelleher, 1966b).

Six studies reported equivalent effects using the same stimulus, both paired and unpaired, though of necessity the conditions were studied in separate phases of the experiment (Kelleher, 1966b, who found equivalent effects in one of three pigeons; Cohen & Stubbs, 1976; Stubbs, 1971, who reported 6 experiments; Hughes, 1973, with bright houselight as S; Stubbs & Cohen, 1972; Stubbs & Silverman, 1972, who used electric shock as the brief stimulus.)

What accounts for these conflicting results? A comparison of schedule types and schedule values, unit schedules, deprivation conditions, food presentation parameters, prevailing stimuli and briefly presented stimuli show extensive overlap among these studies (cf. Stubbs, 1971). No single variable distinguishes studies in which the pairing operation produced differential effects from those in which it did not. However, it is possible that a combination of some of these variables may be responsible for the differences.

Physical Properties of the Briefly Presented Stimulus. Stubbs (1971) demonstrated that the greater the number and type of events used as the brief stimulus, the greater the effect of the brief stimulus on temporal pattern of responding in FI unit schedules. He presented either a red key light, a white houselight, both, or a blackout, under nonpaired conditions. Greatest temporal rate changes were found with key light and houselight changes together, and least with blackout alone. Hughes (1973) found that a paired stimulus gave greater temporal rate changes (scallops) with FI unit schedules than did an unpaired stimulus, but found equivalent performances with a more intense stimulus. An electric shock to the pubis of pigeons likewise had identical effects whether paired with food or unpaired (Stubbs & Silverman, 1972). Similarly, Kello (1972) found greater control of pausing after omitted food presentations when a food magazine light accompanied blackout than with blackout alone.

The use of blackout as the brief stimulus has yielded varied results. In most experiments, blackout has been used as an unpaired stimulus, in the sense that food was presented immediately after the terminal peck under the second-order schedule. It can be argued, however, that a blackout is scheduled like a simultaneously paired stimulus, in the sense that key light and houselight are generally turned off during food presentation. This ambiguity in classification is possibly related to the inconsistent effects. Kelleher (1966b) found little patterning induced by a 0.7 sec change from blue key to dark key in an otherwise unlit chamber. Stubbs and Cohen (1972) found that a 2-sec blackout that was scheduled as a *paired* stimulus produced less patterning in FI 48-sec unit schedules than key light and houselight changes that were either paired or unpaired. On the other hand, Neuringer and Chung (1967) got effective control of responding with 0.25 to 7-sec blackouts under FR 11 or brief, response-initiated FI schedules. The effects of blackouts as brief stimuli under second-order schedules may thus depend on the unit schedule that is studied (cf. Starr & Staddon, 1974).

A second parameter that determines the effect of a brief stimulus is its duration. Byrd (1972) studied second-order schedules in squirrel monkeys in which the terminal maintaining event was a brief electric shock (cf. Morse & Kelleher, 1970). A blue light was scheduled under FR 4 (FI 4-min:S) for 0.1 to 10 sec. As duration of the brief stimulus increased, mean response rate decreased, with lowest rates early in the interval and least variability at the 1-sec duration. Cohen, Hughes, and Stubbs (1973) varied stimulus duration from 0.5 to 8 sec on VI 240-sec (FI 48-sec:S). There was relatively less responding early in the intervals under longer durations, and a clear trend of decreasing rate with increasing duration of the stimulus. A third effect requires special consideration.

Cohen, Hughes, and Stubbs (1973) found that in both pigeons responding was more positively accelerated within FI units during the second exposure to durations of 0.15 and 2 sec than during the first. This implies the existence of a partial irreversibility due either to extensive exposure to brief stimulus procedures or prior exposure to a long value (8 sec). Effects in other studies have been reversible. Hughes (1973) found pairing effects even when the order of presentation of paired and nonpaired conditions was controlled. Thus, history alone may not determine the effects of pairing, but history in combination with some other variables may be crucial (cf. Marr & Zeiler, 1974).

Discriminative Effects of the Brief Stimulus. Under second-order schedules with FI and FR unit schedules, the brief stimulus can be expected to serve a discriminative function: responses immediately after it are never reinforced. The stimulus thus controls a low or zero rate after its occurrence, as does food in a FI or FR schedule with primary reinforcement (cf. Staddon, 1974). Paired and unpaired stimuli are equivalent with respect to nonreinforcement of immediately subsequent responses.

In the balance of response-dependent rate-enhancing effects and response-independent rate-decreasing effects of brief stimuli, the latter are often predominant in the stable state. The former are often stronger either early in training, or when the stimuli are less intense and therefore less effective as discriminative stimuli. In fact, all the variables that are relevant to the development of stimulus control (stimulus salience as determined by modality, intensity, and previous training conditions) would be expected to affect the control by scheduled brief stimulus presentations (cf. Starr & Staddon, 1974).

Two recent experiments have shown changes in control by brief stimuli with repeated training. Marr and Zeiler (1974) first scheduled a brief stimulus unpaired with food under four procedures. Its presentations had minimal effect. After six procedures in which the stimulus was paired with food presentation, it was again scheduled unpaired with food. It now controlled responding nearly as well as when it was paired. Thomas and Blackman (1974) compared VI 66-sec (FI 10-sec:S) and VI 66-sec (VI 10-sec:S), where S was a change in key light from white to red for 3 sec, with comparable tandem schedules. Response rates were higher under both schedules of brief stimulus presentation, but pauses after the stimulus occurred only with the FI unit schedule. This result is consistent with the fact that food could occur at any time after the stimulus under the VI, whereas it could not occur for 10 sec under the FI.

The critical analysis of the behavioral function of the brief stimulus resembles the inconclusive debates that characterized the analysis of conditioned reinforcement in extinction procedures. Although discriminative effects were demonstrated in old response procedures, there has been no agreement on whether response acquisition on new response procedures can be ascribed unambiguously to conditioned reinforcement (Wike, 1969, but see Schuster, 1969; Longstreth, 1971).

Second-order schedules of brief stimulus presentation were developed, among other reasons, "to determine whether a brief stimulus that was occasionally contiguous with food delivery would maintain responding" (Kelleher, 1966b). Such a possibility would permit chronic investigation of conditioned reinforcement, since food presentation is continued in these schedules. The possibility that at least some rate increases under second-order schedules arise from discriminative effects of the brief stimulus (Fantino, Chapter 11 of this volume) also challenges an explanation in terms of reinforcement. Thomas and Blackman (1974) concluded that it was "difficult to see how the reinforcement hypothesis is to be differentiated from the discriminative hypothesis in terms of the performances maintained by brief stimuli in second-order schedules. Both hypotheses suggest that the way in which brief stimuli are scheduled may be crucial and both hypotheses are consistent with data" (p. 105).

BRIEF STIMULI SCHEDULED DURING EXTINCTION

One of the classic methods for testing the effectiveness of a stimulus as a conditioned reinforcer is to make its presentation dependent on a response in the absence of food (an extinction test). Because the stimulus was no longer paired with food, its effects eventually disappeared, although intermittent scheduling during the training phase could extend its effectiveness (D. W. Zimmerman, 1959). Both Zimmerman (1959) and Kelleher (1961) showed that the schedule under which the brief stimulus was produced, with food completely omitted, determined rate and temporal pattern of responding.

Several additional experiments have extended this paradigm. Thomas (1969) prolonged the effect of a briefly presented stimulus complex associated with food delivery. He scheduled brief presentations in the presence of one key color and longer presentations in the presence of a second color. The two colors alternated during sessions. For example, when a triangle was projected on the key, food was presented for 4 sec under FR 120. When the key was green, food was presented for 0.3 sec, a duration too short to allow eating. Substantial amounts of responding occurred when the key was green, with pauses after each presentation that were shorter than the pauses when pecks produced accessible food. When responses during green had no effect (EXT) or when they produced a 0.3 sec change in key color to red, a stimulus that was not associated with food presentation, very little responding was sustained. When 4 sec of food access was scheduled only when no pecks had occurred for 20 sec (DRO 20-sec) and brief (0.3 sec) operations of the feeder occurred on every tenth peck (FR 10), the pigeon responded faster when not receiving food than when it did. Thomas and Johanson (1970) obtained similar effects with a key-light change as the brief stimulus, rather than stimuli intimately associated with food. Thus, in both these experiments, responding was maintained by presentation of stimuli paired with food in the presence of a key color that was never directly associated with food (cf. Herrnstein & Loveland, 1972).

Token Reinforcement. A token is a small physical object that is delivered to an organism under some schedule. In the presence of another stimulus, a specified response involving the token, such as inserting it into a receptacle, is followed by presentation of food, juice, etc. This procedure resembles both chained schedules and second-order schedules of brief-stimulus presentation. The schedule of token delivery is the unit schedule, and the schedule for exchange specifies when behavior under the unit schedule is followed by food. The accumulating number of tokens is also a stimulus that is correlated with the possibility of food presentation, especially when food is scheduled after a given number of tokens. The number of accumulated tokens could have effects similar to those of chained schedule (or clock and counter) component stimuli.

In earlier experiments (Kelleher, 1957a,b, 1958) chimpanzees received poker chips which later were exchanged for foods and liquids. Similar procedures have recently been developed for use with rats (Malagodi, 1967 a,b; Waddell, Leander, Webbe, & Malagodi, 1972). As in second-order brief-stimulus schedules, the schedule of token delivery engenders consistent patterns of responding. Substantial rates are sustained at times considerably removed from food presentation. As in chained schedules, however, extended pauses occur when the stimulus conditions (i.e., number of tokens) are those correlated with zero probability of food presentation. Responding can be instated almost immediately by presenting, independently of responding, a large number of tokens (Kelleher, 1958). The stimulus conditions then resemble those typically prevailing closer to the end of the schedule sequence.

Malagodi (1967a,b) developed token reinforcement procedures with rats. Bar presses produced glass marbles under FR or VI schedules. According to an exchange schedule, in the presence of a characteristic stimulus, insertion of each marble into a receptacle was followed by delivery of a food pellet. Moderately low rates were maintained when food was available after 2 or 10 marbles had been delivered, a FR (VI) schedule. When a marble was produced under FR 20, a brief pause followed by high rates of bar pressing followed each marble delivery. Waddell et al. (1972) also scheduled marble delivery under a FR 20 unit schedule; the opportunity for food-reinforced marble insertion followed a marble delivery at a fixed time after the last food delivery, under a FI (FR) schedule. Even though every marble had always been exchanged for one food pellet, as the FI duration increased, the response rate, and therefore the number of marbles delivered, decreased. Cumulative records of responding under FI values of 1.5 min, 4.5 min, and 9.0 min show high local rates alternating with pauses after each marble delivery or food presentation, with longer pauses typically following the latter. Overall response rate between food presentations had an increasing trend, so that responding showed effects of both FI and FR schedules. A direct comparison of corresponding chained schedules, schedules of brief stimulus presentation, schedules of token delivery, and tandem schedules should be informative.

Concurrent and Conjoint Schedules of Brief Stimulus Presentation

The analysis of the role of the added stimulus in second-order schedules of brief stimulus presentation is complicated because a fixed relationship of the stimulus to food presentation may establish discriminative control. Reinforcing effects of a stimulus paired with food may be revealed less ambiguously in concurrent and conjoint schedules of brief stimulus and food presentation in which the temporal relation of the stimulus to food is irregular, since the two events are scheduled independently. When the schedules are associated with different operanda, they will be called concurrent schedules, and when they are associated with a single operandum, conjoint (Catania, 1968).

Sustained responding by brief stimulus presentations that are scheduled concurrently with food has been demonstrated under several conditions. In one group of experiments, by J. Zimmerman and his colleagues, pecking on one key produced for 0.5 sec the same stimulus complex that ordinarily accompanied food delivery: the key became dark, the houselight was turned off, a light in the feeder compartment was turned on, and a solenoid operated and raised a tray of food. A mechanical shutter covered the feeder opening in later experiments, preventing access to food. Accessible food, presented for 3 to 4 sec, was either scheduled concurrently, for pecks on a second key, or conjointly, under a variable-time (VT) schedule. In most of the experiments pecks on the key that produced the brief stimulus postponed the delivery of accessible food for 6 sec. This delay presumably attenuated the direct effects of food on pecking.

A series of five publications showed that rates of pecking between 3 and 10 min were maintained by the 0.5 sec magazine stimulus complex. J. Zimmerman and Hanford (1966) found considerably higher rates in the presence of a blue key light where pecks produced the food-paired stimulus complex on FI 1-min than in a yellow key light, where pecks had no consequences. Accessible food was presented independently of pecking under a VT 3-min schedule. J. Zimmerman, Hanford, and Brown (1967) found that the rate of pecking increased as the frequency of pecks producing the food-paired stimulus increased.

The food-paired stimulus also sustains responding for considerable periods of time after its pairing with food is eliminated. J. Zimmerman (1969) found that pecking was maintained in two pigeons by presentation of the brief stimulus for 24 and 32 50-min sessions. J. Zimmerman and Hanford (1967) found similar maintenance for as long as 16 sessions. Together with Thomas's (1969) and Kelleher's (1961) demonstrations of extensive maintenance of responding by food magazine stimuli, these results indicate that stimuli with extensive histories of contiguous association with food gain powerful maintaining control when presented as behavioral consequences.

In addition to the parametric investigation of frequency of presentation of brief stimuli, the effects of different schedules on temporal pattern of responding have been investigated. The schedules used include FI, VI, FR, DRL, and extinction. In general, the temporal pattern under each schedule resembled that typically generated by the same schedule of accessible food, although at considerably lower rates. Thus, schedules of response-produced stimuli paired with food appear to engender responding in a similar fashion to that maintained by traditional positive reinforcers, such as food and water.

Response maintenance under concurrent and conjoint schedules of brief stimulus presentation could be due to a direct effect of delayed presentation of accessible food. Two types of results argue against this possibility, however. First, multiple schedules of brief stimulus presentation control appropriate response rates. If pecks in the presence of one key color do not produce the brief stimulus while pecks in a different key color do (J. Zimmerman, 1963; J. Zimmerman & Hanford, 1966), the latter stimulus controls higher rates, even though responses in the presence of both colors are followed by delayed food. Moreover, this effect readily reverses when the correlation of schedule and stimulus is reversed (J. Zimmerman & Hanford, 1967; Hamm and Zimmerman, 1972).

Second, the food-paired brief stimulus complex maintains higher rates than a nonpaired stimulus (Hamm & Zimmerman, 1972; J. Zimmerman & Hanford, 1966, 1967). This comparison is compromised, however, because the nonpaired stimulus differed in many ways from the food-paired stimulus. A comparison in which both stimuli were arbitrary would permit a less ambiguous test of the role of association with food.

Other experiments have opposed the effects of food presentation under one schedule with brief-stimulus presentation under another schedule presented conjointly. The behavior controlled by the conjointly presented brief stimulus is chosen such that it reduces the frequency of food presentation. Randolph and Sewell (1965) scheduled food under DRL 20-sec and DRL 30-sec, and conjointly scheduled brief presentation of the feeder light and offset of key and houselight under FR 10. Response rate under the conjoint schedule was higher with brief stimulus presentations than without it, especially on the DRL 30-sec schedule. Stubbs (1967) also found greater rate increases with longer DRL values. Similarly, when Clark and Sherman (1970) arranged for non-matching-to-sample responses to produce a food-paired stimulus, the frequency of matching decreased by 30–40%, even though only matches produced food. Responses early in the fixed-interval period were also increased when bar pressing by rats produced a stimulus paired with water under a VI schedule (D. W. Zimmerman, 1969), or under a shorter FI than the one that arranged water delivery (D. W. Zimmerman, 1971). When the brief stimulus was presented independently of responding under a VT schedule, only small changes in responding were observed (D. W. Zimmerman, 1971).

As previously mentioned, some experiments on conjoint schedules have found minimal effects of brief stimuli. Neuringer and Chung (1967) found no rate increases with *conjoint* FR 10:S VI 1-min:food. Similarly, a 0.7-sec blackout paired with food enhanced responding only slightly under *conjoint* FR:S FI:food schedules according to Shull, Guilkey, and Witty (1972). Stubbs (1971) also found no significant effects of a brief-stimulus unpaired with food presented under FI 60-sec, with food presented under VI 240 sec. A second-order schedule with the same components engendered substantial patterned responding whether the brief stimulus was paired or unpaired with food.

The results of experiments on concurrent and conjoint schedules of brief-stimulus presentation indicate that stimuli that precede and/or accompany food presentation can often increase the rate of responses that produce them. Although the effects with concurrent schedules are often quantitatively small, they are sustained over long periods of time and can continue when food is no longer available.

One inference from these experiments has important implications for the further study of rate enhancing effects of brief stimuli. It appears that such effects can best be obtained when the response that produces the brief stimulus is under minimal control by food reinforcement. Thus, the clearest sustained effects are obtained when the response never produces food, as in the concurrent schedules, or is less strongly controlled by the schedule of food reinforcement, as in long DRL schedules or early in the fixed-interval period. Stated another way, the effects of the brief stimulus can be masked by the effects of food reinforcement, or by ongoing high response rates. When food delivery controls responding rather strongly, only discriminative effects of lower rate after the stimulus may appear. This seems the most frequent result in the majority of studies on second-order schedules, and it is an important consideration for experiments designed to test whether a stimulus paired with food delivery is a more effective reinforcer than one that is unpaired (cf. Cohen & Stubbs, 1976).

CONDITIONED REINFORCEMENT IN
SECOND-ORDER SCHEDULES OF BRIEF
STIMULUS PRESENTATION

The preceding review has shown that second-order schedules of brief stimulus presentation engender consistent and well maintained patterns of responding. Such patterns depend on the presentation of brief stimuli, but may reflect primarily their discriminative effects due to a consistent relation of the stimulus to subsequent food presentation. Whether a reinforcing (rate enhancing) effect is obtained depends on the baseline performance and schedule for presenting the brief stimulus. Response maintenance or enhancement can be observed most reliably during initial exposure to certain schedules of stimulus presentation. Since the focus of many experiments with these procedures has been steady state performance, some of these experiments provide poor evidence for a maintained conditioned reinforcing effect. When the relation of the stimulus to food is less regular, or when control of the response by food presentation is weak, as in the presence of stimuli that control low rates, rate enhancing effects can be observed, and are sustained. Striking instances are during extinction (Thomas, 1969), or when a concurrent or conjoint response does not produce food (J. Zimmerman, 1963, and related papers), and during periods of low rate in FI (D. W. Zimmerman, 1971) and FR schedules (Findley & Brady, 1965).

CONCLUDING REMARKS

The concept of conditioned reinforcement has been used as both an explanatory term in analyses of operant behavior in general, and as a concept to organize a variety of behavioral procedures. A reflex orientation which emphasized close temporal relationships predisposed early workers to interpret response acquisition or maintenance with delayed or intermittent reinforcement in terms of immediate consequences of behavior. Experimental paradigms were arranged to demonstrate these effects. Stimuli associated with effective reinforcers (e.g., food) were shown to prolong performance when primary reinforcers were omitted, to reduce the decrement caused by a delay between behavior and reinforcer, or even to serve as the sole consequence in acquisition of a new operant (cf. Miller, 1951; Myers, 1958). More detailed analyses have revealed, however, that these stimuli can also be serving discriminative function.

More recent results with chained schedules and

second-order schedules of brief-stimulus presentation also reveal strong discriminative effects of putative conditioned reinforcers. This has led some writers to be extremely skeptical about a rate-enhancing function of such stimuli (e.g., Schuster, 1969; Longstreth, 1971).

It is hardly a novel discovery, however, that stimuli have multiple functions (cf. Skinner, 1938). Different functions may be revealed differentially by various experimental procedures or under parametric manipulation. The fact that a behavioral effect depends on the schedule of presentation of a stimulus is not unique to conditioned reinforcers. The behavioral effects of drugs similarly depend on schedules and baseline performance (Dews, 1955; Kelleher & Morse, 1968).

The concept of conditioned reinforcement has played an important role in the development of practical techniques of behavioral control (Ayllon & Azrin, 1968; O'Leary & Drabman, 1971). The detailed analysis of some of these procedures reveals that relevant stimuli have other, and sometimes more important effects than response enhancement. Such results should not, however, lead us to neglect rate-enhancing effects under appropriate conditions. It would indeed be ironic if, at the same time that use of conditioned reinforcement techniques becomes a commonplace in the applied analysis of human behavior the results of limited experimental paradigms were taken as disproving the existence of conditioned reinforcement. The trends in experimental analysis reviewed here indicate that schedules can greatly modulate conditioned reinforcing effects.

REFERENCES

Ayllon, T., & Azrin, N. H. *The token economy: A motivational system for therapy and rehabilitation.* Englewood Cliffs, N.J.: Prentice-Hall, Inc., 1968.

Autor, S. M. The strength of conditioned reinforcers as a function of frequency and probability of reinforcement. In D. P. Hendry (Ed.), *Conditioned reinforcement.* Homewood, Ill.: Dorsey Press, 1969.

Baum, W. M., & Rachlin, H. C. Choice as time allocation. *Journal of the Experimental Analysis of Behavior,* 1969, *12,* 861–874.

Boren, M. C. P. Fixed-ratio and variable-ratio schedules of brief stimuli in second-order schedules of matching to sample. *Journal of the Experimental Analysis of Behavior,* 1973, *20,* 219–233.

Boren, M. C. P., & Gollub, L. R. Accuracy of performance on a matching-to-sample procedure under interval schedules. *Journal of the Experimental Analysis of Behavior,* 1972, *18,* 65–77.

Byrd, L. D. Responding in the pigeon under chained schedules of food presentation: The repetition of a stimulus during alternate components. *Journal of the Experimental Analysis of Behavior,* 1971, *16,* 31–38.

Byrd, L. D. Responding in the squirrel monkey under second-order schedules of shock delivery. *Journal of the Experimental Analysis of Behavior,* 1972, *18,* 155–167.

Catania, A. C. (Ed.) *Contemporary research in operant behavior.* Glenview, Ill., Scott, Foresman, 1968.

Catania, A. C., & Reynolds, G. S. A quantitative analysis of the behavior maintained by interval schedules of reinforcement. *Journal of the Experimental Analysis of Behavior,* 1968, *11,* 327–383.

Chung, S.-H., & Neuringer, A. J. Control of responding by a percentage reinforcement schedule. *Psychonomic Science,* 1967, *8,* 25–26.

Clark, H. B., & Sherman, J. A. Effects of a conditioned reinforcer upon accuracy of match-to-sample behavior in pigeons. *Journal of the Experimental Analysis of Behavior,* 1970, *13,* 375–384.

Cohen, S. L., Hughes, J. E., & Stubbs, D. A. Second-order schedules: Manipulation of brief-stimulus duration at component completion. *Animal Learning and Behavior,* 1973, *1,* 121–124.

Cohen, S. L., & Stubbs, D. A. Discriminative properties of briefly presented stimuli. *Journal of the Experimental Analysis of Behavior,* 1976, *25,* 15–25.

Davison, M. C. Successive interresponse times in fixed-ratio and second-order fixed-ratio performance. *Journal of the Experimental Analysis of Behavior,* 1969, *12,* 385–389.

Davison, M. C., & Temple, W. Preference for fixed-interval schedules: An alternative model. *Journal of the Experimental Analysis of Behavior,* 1973, *20,* 393–403.

de Lorge, J. Fixed-interval behavior maintained by conditioned reinforcement. *Journal of the Experimental Analysis of Behavior,* 1967, *10,* 271–276.

de Lorge, J. The influence of pairing with primary reinforcement on the maintenance of conditioned reinforcement in second-order schedules. In D. P. Hendry (Ed.), *Conditioned reinforcement.* Homewood, Ill.: Dorsey Press, 1969.

de Lorge, J. The effects of brief stimuli presented under a multiple schedule of second-order schedules. *Journal of the Experimental Analysis of Behavior,* 1971, *15,* 19–25.

Dews, P. B. Studies on behavior. I. Differential sensitivity to pentobarbital of pecking performance in pigeons depending on the schedule of reward. *Journal of Pharmacology and Experimental Therapeutics,* 1955, *113,* 393–401.

Duncan, B., & Fantino, E. The psychological distance to reward. *Journal of the Experimental Analysis of Behavior,* 1972, *18,* 23–34.

Fantino, E. Preference for mixed- versus fixed-ratio schedules. *Journal of the Experimental Analysis of Behavior,* 1967, *10,* 35–43.

Fantino, E. Effects of required rates of responding upon choice. *Journal of the Experimental Analysis of Behavior,* 1968, *11,* 15–22.

Fantino, E. Conditioned reinforcement, choice, and the psychological distance to reward. In D. P. Hendry (Ed.), *Conditioned reinforcement.* Homewood, Ill.: Dorsey Press, 1969.

Fantino, E., & Duncan, B. Some effects of interreinforcement time upon choice. *Journal of the Experimental Analysis of Behavior,* 1972, *17,* 3–14.

Fantino, E., & Herrnstein, R. J. Secondary reinforcement and number of primary reinforcements. *Journal of the Experimental Analysis of Behavior,* 1968, *11,* 9–14.

Ferster, C. B. Sustained behavior under delayed reinforcement. *Journal of Experimental Psychology,* 1953, *45,* 218–224.

Ferster, C. B., & Skinner, B. F. *Schedules of reinforcement.* Englewood Cliffs, N.J.: Prentice-Hall, Inc., 1957.

Findley, J. D. An experimental outline for building and exploring multi-operant behavior repertoires. *Journal of the Experimental Analysis of Behavior,* 1962, *5,* 113–166.

Findley, J. D., & Brady, J. V. Facilitation of large ratio performance by use of conditioned reinforcement. *Journal of the Experimental Analysis of Behavior,* 1965, *8,* 125–129.

Gollub, L. R. *The chaining of fixed-interval schedules.* Unpublished doctoral dissertation, Harvard University, 1958.

Gollub, L. R. Responding maintained by chained and tandem fixed-interval schedules of reinforcement. *American Psychologist,* 1965, *20,* 554.

Gollub, L. R. Information on conditioned reinforcement: A review of *Conditioned reinforcement,* edited by Derek P. Hendry. *Journal of the Experimental Analysis of Behavior,* 1970, *14,* 361–372.

Gollub, L. R., & Vogt, C. P. Acquisition of responding on chained schedules: Gradual compared to abrupt introduction of the chain. *Psychonomic Science,* 1970, *18,* 299–301.

Gott, C. T., & Weiss, B. The development of fixed-ratio performance under the influence of ribonucleic acid. *Journal of the Experimental Analysis of Behavior,* 1972, *18,* 481–497.

Hamm, H. D. & Zimmerman, J. Differential maintenance of concurrent operants with conditioned reinforcement in a free feeding situation. *Psychological Record,* 1972, *22,* 497–508.

Hanson, H. M., & Witoslawski, J. J. Interaction between the components of a chained schedule. *Journal of the Experimental Analysis of Behavior,* 1959, *2,* 171–177.

Hendry, D. P., & Dillow, P. V. Observing behavior during interval schedules. *Journal of the Experimental Analysis of Behavior,* 1966, *9,* 337–349.

Herrnstein, R. J. Relative and absolute strength of response as a function of frequency of reinforcement. *Journal of the Experimental Analysis of Behavior,* 1961, *4,* 267–272.

Herrnstein, R. J. Secondary reinforcement and the rate of primary reinforcement. *Journal of the Experimental Analysis of Behavior,* 1964, *7,* 27–36.

Herrnstein, R. J., & Loveland, D. H. Food-avoidance in hungry pigeons, and other perplexities. *Journal of the Experimental Analysis of Behavior,* 1972, *18,* 369–383.

Hughes, J. E. *Second-order schedules: A new procedure.* Paper presented at the Eastern Psychological Association, Washington, 1973.

Jwaideh, A. R. Responding under chained and tandem fixed-ratio schedules. *Journal of the Experimental Analysis of Behavior,* 1973, *19,* 259–267.

Kaufman, A., & Baron, A. Conditioned reinforcing and aversive aspects of the stimuli defining the components of a two-component chain. *Genetic Psychology Monographs,* 1969, *80,* 151–201.

Kelleher, R. T. Conditioned reinforcement in chimpanzees. *Journal of Comparative and Physiological Psychology,* 1957, *50,* 571–575. (a)

Kelleher, R. T. A multiple schedule of conditioned reinforcement with chimpanzees. *Psychological Reports,* 1957, *3,* 485–491. (b)

Kelleher, R. T. Fixed-ratio schedules of conditioned reinforcement with chimpanzees. *Journal of the Experimental Analysis of Behavior,* 1958, *1,* 281–289.

Kelleher, R. T. Schedules of conditioned reinforcement during experimental extinction. *Journal of the Experimental Analysis of Behavior,* 1961, *4,* 1–5.

Kelleher, R. T. Chaining and conditioned reinforcement. In W. K. Honig (Ed.), *Operant behavior: Areas of research and application.* Englewood Cliffs, N.J.: Prentice-Hall, Inc., 1966. (a)

Kelleher, R. T. Conditioned reinforcement in second-order schedules. *Journal of the Experimental Analysis of Behavior,* 1966, *9,* 475–485. (b)

Kelleher, R. T., & Fry, W. T. Stimulus functions in chained fixed-interval schedules. *Journal of the Experimental Analysis of Behavior,* 1962, *5,* 167–173.

Kelleher, R. T., & Gollub, L. R. A review of conditioned reinforcement. *Journal of the Experimental Analysis of Behavior,* 1962, *5,* 543–597.

Kelleher, R. T., & Morse, W. H. Determinants of the specificity of behavioral effects of drugs. *Ergebnisse der Physiologie: Biologischen Chemie und Experimentellen Pharmakologie.* 1968, *60,* 1–56.

Keller, F. S., & Schoenfeld, W. N. *Principles of psychology.* New York: Appleton-Century-Crofts, 1950.

Kello, J. E. The reinforcement-omission effect on fixed-interval schedules: Frustration or inhibition? *Learning and Motivation,* 1972, *3,* 138–147.

Kendall, S. B. Some effects of fixed-interval duration on response rate in a two-component chain schedule. *Journal of the Experimental Analysis of Behavior,* 1967, *10,* 341–347.

Kendall, S. B. Some effects of response-dependent clock stimuli in a fixed-interval schedule. *Journal of the Experimental Analysis of Behavior,* 1972, *17,* 161–168.

Killeen, P. Reinforcement frequency and contingency as factors in fixed-ratio behavior. *Journal of the Experimental Analysis of Behavior,* 1969, *12,* 391–395.

Killeen, P. The matching law. *Journal of the Experimental Analysis of Behavior,* 1972, *17,* 489–495.

Lee, J. K., & Gollub, L. R. Second-order schedules with fixed-ratio components: Variation of component size. *Journal of the Experimental Analysis of Behavior,* 1971, *15,* 303–310.

Longstreth, L. E. A cognitive interpretation of secondary reinforcement. In J. K. Cole (Ed.), *Nebraska Symposium on Motivation* (Vol. 19). Lincoln: University of Nebraska Press, 1971.

Lott, D. F. Secondary reinforcement and frustration: A conceptual paradox. *Psychological Bulletin,* 1967, *67,* 197–198.

Malagodi, E. F. Acquisition of the token reward habit in the rat. *Psychological Reports,* 1967, *20,* 1335–1342. (a)

Malagodi, E. F. Fixed-ratio schedules of token reinforcement. *Psychonomic Science,* 1967, *8,* 469–470. (b)

Malagodi, E. F., DeWeese, J., & Johnston, J. M. Second-order schedules: A direct comparison of chained, brief-stimulus, and tandem procedures. *Journal of the Experimental Analysis of Behavior,* 1973, *20,* 447–460.

MARR, M. J. Second-order schedules. In D. P. Hendry (Ed.), *Conditioned reinforcement.* Homewood, Ill.: Dorsey Press, 1969.

MARR, M. J. Sequence schedules of reinforcement. *Journal of the Experimental Analysis of Behavior,* 1971, *15,* 41–48.

MARR, M. J., & ZEILER, M. D. Schedules of response-independent conditioned reinforcement. *Journal of the Experimental Analysis of Behavior,* 1974, *21,* 433–444.

MILLER, N. E. Learnable drives and rewards. In S. S. Stevens (Ed.), *Handbook of experimental psychology.* New York: Wiley, 1951.

MOORE, J., & FANTINO, E. Choice and response contingencies. *Journal of the Experimental Analysis of Behavior,* 1975, *23,* 339–347.

MORSE, W. H., & KELLEHER, R. T. Schedules as fundamental determinants of behavior. In W. N. Schoenfeld (Ed.), *The theory of reinforcement schedules.* Englewood Cliffs, N.J.: Prentice-Hall, Inc., 1970.

MULVANEY, D. E., DINSMOOR, J. A., JWAIDEH, A. R., & HUGHES, L. H. Punishment of observing by the negative discriminative stimulus. *Journal of the Experimental Analysis of Behavior,* 1974, *21,* 37–44.

MYERS, J. L. Secondary reinforcement: A review of recent experimentation. *Psychological Bulletin,* 1958, *55,* 284–301.

NEURINGER, A. J. Varying reinforcement frequency on a percentage-reinforcement schedule. *Psychonomic Science,* 1968, *11(5),* 163–164.

NEURINGER, A. J., & CHUNG, S.-H. Quasi-reinforcement: Control of responding by a percentage reinforcement schedule. *Journal of the Experimental Analysis of Behavior,* 1967, *10,* 45–54.

O'LEARY, K. D., & DRABMAN, R. S. Token reinforcement programs in the classroom: A review. *Psychological Bulletin,* 1971, *75,* 379–398.

PREMACK, D. Reinforcement theory. In D. Levine (Ed.), *Nebraska Symposium on Motivation* Vol. 13. Lincoln: University of Nebraska Press, 1965.

RANDOLPH, J. J., & SEWELL, W. R. Competitive conditioned reinforcement during differential reinforcement of low rates. *Psychonomic Science,* 1965, *3,* 411–412.

SCHNEIDER, J. W. Choice between two-component chained and tandem schedules. *Journal of the Experimental Analysis of Behavior,* 1972, *18,* 45–60.

SCHUSTER, R. H. A functional analysis of conditioned reinforcement. In D. P. Hendry (Ed.), *Conditioned reinforcement.* Homewood, Ill.: Dorsey Press, 1969.

SEGAL, E. F. Exteroceptive control of fixed-interval responding. *Journal of the Experimental Analysis of Behavior,* 1962, *5,* 49–57.

SHULL, R. L., GUILKEY, M., & WITTY, W. Changing the response unit from a single peck to a fixed number of pecks in fixed-interval schedules. *Journal of the Experimental Analysis of Behavior,* 1972, *17,* 193–200.

SIDMAN, M. *Tactics of scientific research.* New York: Basic Books, 1960.

SKINNER, B. F. *The behavior of organisms: An experimental analysis.* New York: Appleton-Century-Crofts, 1938.

SKINNER, B. F. *Contingencies of reinforcement: A theoretical analysis.* Englewood Cliffs, N. J.: Prentice-Hall, Inc., 1969.

SQUIRES, N. K., & FANTINO, E. A model for choice in simple concurrent and concurrent-chains schedules. *Journal of the Experimental Analysis of Behavior,* 1971, *15,* 27–38.

SQUIRES, N. K., NORBORG, J., & FANTINO, E. Second-order schedules: Discrimination of components. *Journal of the Experimental Analysis of Behavior,* 1975, *24,* 157–171.

STADDON, J. E. R. Temporal effects of reinforcement: A negative "frustration" effect. *Learning and Motivation,* 1970, *1,* 227–247.

STADDON, J. E. R. Reinforcement omission on temporal go-no-go schedules. *Journal of the Experimental Analysis of Behavior,* 1972, *18,* 223–229.

STADDON, J. E. R. Temporal control, attention, and memory. *Psychological Review,* 1974, *81,* 375–391.

STADDON, J. E. R., & INNIS, N. K. Reinforcement omission on fixed-interval schedules. *Journal of the Experimental Analysis of Behavior,* 1969, *12,* 689–700.

STARR, B. C., & STADDON, J. E. R. Temporal control on periodic schedules: signal properties of reinforcement and blackout. *Journal of the Experimental Analysis of Behavior,* 1974, *22,* 535–545.

STUBBS, A. Competitive conditioned reinforcement and efficient differential reinforcement of low rate performance. *Psychonomic Science,* 1967, *8,* 299–300.

STUBBS, A. Contiguity of briefly presented stimuli with food reinforcement. *Journal of the Experimental Analysis of Behavior,* 1969, *12,* 271–278.

STUBBS, D. A. Second-order schedules and the problem of conditioned reinforcement. *Journal of the Experimental Analysis of Behavior,* 1971, *16,* 289–313.

STUBBS, D. A., & COHEN, S. L. Second-order schedules: Comparison of different procedures for scheduling paired and nonpaired brief stimuli. *Journal of the Experimental Analysis of Behavior,* 1972, *18,* 403–413.

STUBBS, D. A., & SILVERMAN, P. J. Second-order schedules: Brief shock at the completion of each component. *Journal of the Experimental Analysis of Behavior,* 1972, *17,* 201–212.

SWITALSKI, R. W., & THOMAS, D. R. The development of stimulus control in a three-member chained schedule. *Psychonomic Science,* 1967, *9,* 391–392.

TALLEN, R. R., & DINSMOOR, J. A. Conditioned reinforcement in chain fixed-interval schedules. *Proceedings of the 77th Annual Convention of the American Psychological Association,* 1969, *4,* 823–824.

TEN EYCK, R. L., JR. Effects of rate of reinforcement-time upon concurrent operant performance. *Journal of the Experimental Analysis of Behavior,* 1970, *14,* 269–274.

THOMAS, G., & BLACKMAN, J. Quaisreinforcement: Control of behavior by second-order interval schedules. *Learning and Motivation,* 1974, *5,* 92–105.

THOMAS, J. R. Multiple baseline investigation of stimulus functions in an FR chained schedule. *Journal of the Experimental Analysis of Behavior,* 1964, *7,* 241–245.

THOMAS, J. R. Chained and tandem fixed-interval schedule performance and frequency of primary reinforcement. *Psychological Reports,* 1967, *20,* 471–480.

THOMAS, J. R. Maintenance of behavior by conditioned reinforcement in the signaled absence of primary reinforcement. In D. P. Hendry (Ed.), *Conditioned reinforcement.* Homewood, Ill.: Dorsey Press, 1969.

THOMAS, J. R., & JOHANSON, C. Maintenance of fixed-interval responding by conditioned reinforcement in multiple schedules. *Psychonomic Science,* 1970, *19(3),* 135–136.

THOMAS, J. R., & STUBBS, A. Stimulus control of temporally

spaced responding in second-order schedules. *Journal of the Experimental Analysis of Behavior,* 1967, *10,* 175–183.

WADDELL, T. R., LEANDER, J. D., WEBBE, F. M., & MALAGODI, E. F. Schedules interactions in second-order fixed-interval (fixed-ratio) schedules of token reinforcement. *Learning and Motivation,* 1972, *3,* 91–100.

WIKE, E. L. *Secondary reinforcement: Selected experiments.* New York: Harper & Row, 1966.

WIKE, E. L. Secondary reinforcement: Some research and theoretical issues. In W. J. Arnold & D. Levine (Eds.), *Nebraska Symposium on Motivation* (Vol. 17). Lincoln: University of Nebraska Press, 1969.

ZEILER, M. D. Fixed-interval behavior: Effects of percentage reinforcement. *Journal of the Experimental Analysis of Behavior,* 1972, *17,* 177–189.

ZIMMERMAN, D. W. Sustained performance in rats based on secondary reinforcement. *Journal of Comparative and Physiological Psychology,* 1959, *52,* 353–358.

ZIMMERMAN, D. W. Concurrent schedules of primary and conditioned reinforcement in rats. *Journal of the Experimental Analysis of Behavior,* 1969, *12,* 261–268.

ZIMMERMAN, D. W. Rate changes after unscheduled omission and presentation of reinforcement. *Journal of the Experimental Analysis of Behavior,* 1971, *15,* 261–270.

ZIMMERMAN, J. Technique for sustaining behavior with conditioned reinforcement. *Science,* 1963, *142,* 682–684.

ZIMMERMAN, J. Meanwhile . . . back at the key: Maintenance of behavior by conditioned reinforcement and response-independent primary reinforcement. In D. P. Hendry (Ed.), *Conditioned reinforcement.* Homewood, Ill.: Dorsey Press, 1969.

ZIMMERMAN, J., & HANFORD, P. V. Sustaining behavior with conditioned reinforcement as the only response-produced consequence. *Psychological Reports,* 1966, *19,* 391–401.

ZIMMERMAN, J., & HANFORD, P. V. Differential effects of extinction on behavior maintained by concurrent schedules of primary and conditioned reinforcement. *Psychonomic Science,* 1967, *8,* 103–104.

ZIMMERMAN, J., HANFORD, P. V., & BROWN, W. Effects of conditioned reinforcement frequency in an intermittent free feeding situation. *Journal of the Experimental Analysis of Behavior,* 1967, *10,* 331–340.

11

Conditioned Reinforcement

choice and information*

Edmund Fantino

INTRODUCTION

Three Conceptions of Conditioned Reinforcement

Kelleher and Gollub (1962) and Kelleher (1966) have reviewed the important techniques that have been used to study conditioned reinforcement. Chained schedules and other second-order schedules occupy large portions of these reviews, and their continuing importance in the study of conditioned reinforcement has again been emphasized in the preceding chapter by Gollub. Over the past decade two additional techniques have become increasingly popular and important in the assessment of conditioned reinforcement: the study of observing responses (after Wyckoff, 1952, 1969), which has evaluated the reinforcing strength of stimuli that signal the availability of, or provide information about, primary reinforcement; and the study of choice for stimuli associated with schedules of primary reinforcement (after Autor, 1960, 1969). In this chapter I discuss research with these techniques and the important implications of this research for the theory of conditioned reinforcement. I begin by introducing the theories and distinguishing among them on conceptual grounds and in terms of empirical predictions. The three most viable conceptions of how a neutral stimulus acquires strength based on its relationship to primary reinforcement appear to be the following: (1) the *pairing hypothesis*, which states that the simple pairing of a stimulus with a primary reinforcer imparts conditioned reinforcing strength to that stimulus; (2) the *delay reduction hypothesis*, which states that the strength of a stimulus as a conditioned reinforcer is a function of the reduction in time to reinforcement correlated with the onset of that stimulus; (3) the *uncertainty reduction hypothesis*, which states that the strength of a stimulus is a function of its informativeness about primary reinforcement, i.e., how much un-

---

* The unpublished research mentioned herein and the preparation of this chapter were supported by National Institutes of Health Grant No. 20752-4 to the University of California, San Diego. Several individuals made detailed constructive suggestions of a prior draft, especially the editors and James Dinsmoor, as well as Bill Baum, David Case, Mike Davison, Joe Farley, Steve Hursh, Jed Rose, Ben Williams, and Mike Zeiler. Finally, I thank the members of my seminar on conditioned reinforcement early in 1974: Steve Buck, Mark Fridovich, John Hale, Cheryl Logan, Jay Moore, Jim Norborg, Nancy Squires, and especially Tibor Safar.

certainty reduction it provides about reinforcement.[1]

When applied to observing responses, the pairing and delay reduction hypotheses are both forms of a more general hypothesis, the *conditioned reinforcement hypothesis,* which may be most clearly distinguished from the uncertainty reduction hypothesis by the assertion that only stimuli having positive associations with primary reinforcement should reinforce observing responses (Dinsmoor, Browne, & Lawrence, 1972). The uncertainty reduction hypothesis, on the other hand, states that stimuli associated with negative outcomes should also be reinforcing; the conditioned reinforcement hypothesis requires that these stimuli be aversive—or at least not positively reinforcing. Much of the work on observing responses concerns these opposing predictions. As we shall see, virtually all of the evidence supports the conditioned reinforcement hypothesis.

The pairing and delay reduction versions of the conditioned reinforcing hypothesis may be distinguished in terms of temporal factors relating the conditioned reinforcing stimulus and the primary reinforcer. According to the pairing hypothesis, the degree of contiguity between the stimulus and the primary reinforcer determines the strength of that stimulus as a conditioned reinforcer. Contiguity has been measured often as the interval between the offset of the stimulus and the onset of the primary reinforcer. By this measure any stimulus that is perfectly contiguous with the primary reinforcer—i.e., with a 0-sec interval between the offset of the stimulus and the onset of the reinforcer—should be maximally effective as a conditioned reinforcer. As many studies, including those of observing and choice, suggest, a stimulus associated with a higher rate of primary reinforcement—as in a fixed-interval (FI) 10-sec schedule—is generally a more effective conditioned reinforcer than one associated with a lower rate (as in an FI 60-sec schedule), despite the fact that both stimuli are perfectly contiguous with the primary reinforcer in the sense noted. Thus a pairing hypothesis based on this view of contiguity, henceforth the *traditional pairing hypothesis,* is inadequate. A more viable measure of contiguity in these cases, therefore, is the interval between the *onset* of the stimulus and the onset of the primary reinforcer. This measure (time/reinforcement) is closely related to the rate of reinforcement in the presence of the stimulus. More generally, a pairing view will fare best if it is couched in terms of reinforcement density (i.e., number of reinforcements/unit time) in the presence of a given stimulus. A pairing hypothesis based on reinforcement density states that conditioned reinforcing strength will be determined by the rate of primary reinforcement in its presence. Such a pairing hypothesis, which bears only superficial similarity to the traditional pairing hypothesis, I shall call the *reinforcement density hypothesis.*[2]

The delay reduction hypothesis also states that the reinforcing strength of a stimulus is determined, in part, by the length of the interval between the onset of the stimulus and the onset of the primary reinforcer. But this interval length must be considered *relative to the length of the interval measured from the onset of the preceding stimulus to the onset of the same primary reinforcer.* In other words, the contribution of contiguity to the conditioned reinforcing strength of a stimulus must be considered in the context of how remote primary reinforcement had been *prior* to the onset of the stimulus. The greater the percentage improvement, in terms of contiguity, to primary reinforcement correlated with the onset of the stimulus, the greater its conditioned reinforcing strength. Thus a stimulus associated with an FI 30-sec schedule should be a stronger reinforcer if it is preceded by a 60-sec period of nonreinforcement than if it is preceded by a 10-sec period of nonreinforcement, since in the first case the onset of the 30-sec interval is correlated with a ⅔ reduction in time to primary reinforcement (of an original waiting time of 90 sec, only 30 sec—or ⅓—remains once the stimulus correlated with the interval schedule appears), but in the second case only with a ¼ reduction in time to primary reinforcement (of an original waiting time of 40 sec, 30 sec—or ¾—still remains once the stimulus correlated with the interval schedule appears). Neither the traditional pairing hypothesis nor the reinforcement density hypothesis distinguishes between these two cases. While there is no direct evidence bearing on this prediction, the results of Taus and Hearst (1970) and of Byrd (1971) suggest that the delay reduction hypothesis would be supported. The data from each of these studies show that the discriminative strength of a stimulus (in terms of rate of responding in its presence) increases with the duration of a preceding period of nonreinforcement even though the temporal relation of the stimulus to reinforcement is unchanged. Since the conditioned reinforcing strength

---

[1] Two of the more important traditional hypotheses which have proven less viable than the pairing hypothesis are the *discriminative stimulus hypothesis* (Keller & Schoenfeld, 1950) and the *cue strength hypothesis* (Wyckoff, 1959). These have been ably reviewed in a previous volume (Kelleher, 1966) and will not be discussed here. The discriminative stimulus hypothesis has also been reviewed in the preceding chapter.

[2] A phrase suggested by Dr. James Dinsmoor.

of a stimulus often covaries with its discriminative strength, the prediction made above by the delay reduction hypothesis would likely be borne out.

I should make clear that none of the hypotheses requires that production of the stimuli affect the occurrence of reinforcement. In terms of the delay reduction hypothesis, for example, a stimulus correlated with a reduction in time to primary reinforcement should be a conditioned reinforcer, i.e., it should maintain responses (such as observing or choice responses) whether or not these responses affect the temporal distribution of reinforcement.

The delay reduction hypothesis will be developed more fully as we go on. Research on observing responses is equally compatible with both the delay reduction and the reinforcement density hypotheses. As we shall see, however, research on choice clearly favors the delay reduction hypothesis. Thus, for simplicity, I shall stress the delay reduction hypothesis when discussing observing, though the reader should be aware that similar experimental outcomes are required by the reinforcement density hypothesis. Research on observing responses shows that the uncertainty reduction hypothesis is untenable. Thus it will be seen that only the delay reduction hypothesis of conditioned reinforcement is consistent with what is known about observing and choice.

The Pairing Hypothesis

The pairing hypothesis, which is more parsimonious than either the delay reduction or uncertainty reduction hypotheses, even when formulated in terms of reinforcement density, has a rich history. We shall consider it and some of its inadequacies before discussing the work on observing and on choice, at which time the two newer hypotheses will be more fully developed and evaluated. As the reviews of Kelleher and Gollub (1962), Kelleher (1966), and Nevin (1973) have concluded, the pairing hypothesis (after Hull, 1943) is the most viable of the traditional viewpoints of conditioned reinforcement. By the time of Nevin's (1973) review, however, it was clear that the pairing hypothesis had serious shortcomings, as Nevin himself pointed out. Some of these shortcomings also apply to the reinforcement density version of the pairing hypothesis—as I shall note below.

The pairing hypothesis is supported by the common observation that a stimulus paired with unconditioned reinforcement acquires the properties of a reinforcer (e.g., Nevin, 1973). It now appears that pairings or contiguity is effective only so long as a correlation exists between the stimulus and reinforcer. For example, Rescorla (1967, 1968, 1972) has shown that in Pavlovian fear conditioning when the probability of an unconditioned stimulus (US) in the presence of a conditioned stimulus (CS) is held constant, the degree of conditioned suppression may be sharply influenced by manipulating the probability of the US *in the absence* of the CS; when the probability of a US presentation is equal in both the presence and absence of the CS, no suppression occurs despite the fact that the number of pairings is kept constant. This result points to a conclusion that will gain support throughout this chapter whether we are discussing stimulus-reinforcer pairings, stimulus-reinforcer correlations, or other stimulus-reinforcer relations: The context in which stimulus-reinforcer events are embedded affects the strength imparted to the stimulus by the reinforcer. For example, in both the observing response and concurrent chains paradigms we shall see that a stimulus will reinforce behavior (observing responses in the first case, choice in the second) only when it is correlated with a reduction in the average time to primary reinforcement, regardless of the absolute temporal relation between the stimulus and primary reinforcement.

The most striking evidence *for* the pairing hypothesis has come from studies investigating three types of second-order schedules, considered in the previous chapter: tandem, brief-stimulus, and chained schedules. On a tandem schedule, the same stimulus is present throughout. A brief-stimulus schedule is the same as a tandem schedule, except that the end of each component is signaled by the brief presentation of a second stimulus. Each component of a chained schedule is associated with a different stimulus. The differences in the responding maintained by these three types of second-order schedules have been explained by the conditioned reinforcing properties of the brief stimuli or the stimuli comprising the chained schedule (e.g., Kelleher, 1966). According to this view, the brief-stimulus presentations occurring at the end of each schedule component are effective conditioned reinforcers because they are intermittently paired with primary reinforcement. Similarly, the terminal-link stimulus of a chained schedule is an effective conditioned reinforcer because it is contiguous with primary reinforcement. Studies of second-order schedules have demonstrated increments in responding relative to that maintained on tandem control schedules. It appeared, then, that pairing sufficed to create effective conditioned reinforcers.

The relevance of the second-order schedule data for the pairing hypothesis of conditioned reinforcement (and indeed for conditioned reinforcement in general) has been called into question more recently by the experiments of Stubbs (1971), Stubbs and Cohen (1972), and Squires, Norborg, and Fantino (1975). Stubbs showed that brief stimuli presented at the end of each component of a second-order schedule enhanced responding even when they were always omitted at the end of the component preceding primary reinforcement. Despite the fact that these brief stimuli were never paired with primary reinforcement, they were just as effective in maintaining behavior as were paired brief stimuli. This result is also inconsistent with the reinforcement density version of the pairing hypothesis since primary reinforcement occurs frequently, i.e., with high density, in the presence of the paired but not the unpaired brief stimulus. In Stubbs's experiment the pairing procedure consisted of the simultaneous pairing of the brief stimulus and food. Stubbs and Cohen (1972) found comparable results with pairing procedures in which the brief stimulus preceded food. Specifically, they found similar behavioral effects with (1) a simultaneous pairing procedure, (2) a procedure in which the brief stimulus preceded and overlapped food, and (3) a procedure in which the brief stimulus preceded but did not overlap food.

Squires et al. (1975) tested the following alternative explanation of the difference in responding maintained by tandem, chain, and brief-stimulus schedules: Stimuli which signal the relative unavailability of reinforcement suppress responding in the early components of second-order schedules in which primary reinforcement is never available. Thus responding in the early portions of a tandem schedule is better maintained than responding on a comparable chain schedule because the visual stimuli in the chain are more effective cues for nonreinforcement (and hence nonresponding) than are the temporal cues present in the tandem schedule. On the other hand, brief-stimulus presentations should be reliable cues for nonreinforcement in the subsequent component only if the subject is sensitive to the number of brief-stimulus presentations that have occurred since the previous primary reinforcement. Since number may be a much less effective cue than color, at least in pigeons, Squires et al. (1975) reasoned that a brief-stimulus schedule may be one in which pigeons have difficulty discriminating among the components of the schedule, making the brief-stimulus schedule functionally a schedule of reinforcement in which each component is reinforced a certain percentage of the time (this position has much commonality with that of Neuringer & Chung, 1967).

In order to test this proposition, Squires et al. exposed pigeons to a series of second-order schedules in which the completion of a fixed number of FI components (on the "main" response key) was required for primary reinforcement. For example, in Experiment 1, brief (2-sec) stimulus presentations on a second key (the "brief-stimulus key") followed the completion of each FI component (on the main key). In addition, during the final brief-stimulus presentation preceding primary reinforcement, a response was required on the second key in order to produce primary reinforcement. Prior to the end of the final component, responses to the brief-stimulus key had no consequences. Such responding did serve as a measure of the extent to which the brief-stimulus components were discriminated from one another. Squires et al. examined behavior on the following second-order schedules: FR 1 (FI 120-sec), FR 2 (FI 60-sec), FR 4 (FI 30-sec) FR 8 (FI 15-sec). They found that responding occurred on the brief-stimulus key on virtually every brief-stimulus presentation. As Figure 1 shows, even when inappropriate responding on the brief-stimulus key (i.e., responses to the brief stimulus prior to the final component) produced a 15-sec blackout and returned the subject to the beginning of the second-order schedule, none of the pigeons learned to withhold these responses; consequently, subjects received food only rarely in this condition. Results were different when different key colors were associated with each component of the second-order schedule. In such a chain schedule, brief-stimulus key pecks were confined to the last component, i.e., to the only component in which they were effective.

These results suggest that pigeons do not discriminate between the components of second-order schedules in the absence of differential cues. Squires et al. (1975, p. 170) note:

> Another possibility is that the mechanism underlying conditioned reinforcement is stimulus generalization, so that the more similar are the conditioned and primary reinforcers, the more effective will be the conditioned reinforcer. Since the paired and unpaired stimuli were identical in their similarity to primary reinforcement, their effects should have been the same. When the paired stimulus more closely resembles the primary reinforcer than does the unpaired stimulus it will, by this hypothesis, differentially enhance response rates. In support of this hypothesis, a study by Malagodi, DeWeese, and Johnston (1973) demonstrated the clear superiority of paired brief stimuli over unpaired brief stimuli (each added at the end of each component of a chain schedule as in our Experiment 3) when the paired brief stimuli were brief hopper presentations. J. Zimmerman and his co-workers (Zim-

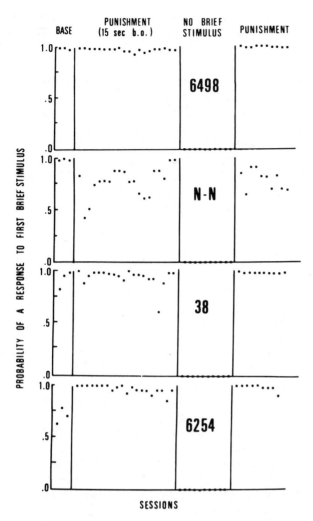

Fig. 1. Probability of a brief-stimulus key response during the first brief-stimulus presentation following primary reinforcement for the last three sessions of base line (no punishment), 20 sessions in which those responses were followed by a 15-sec blackout and return to the start of the first component ("punishment"), 10 sessions in which the brief-stimulus key was not illuminated during the usual time of the first brief-stimulus presentation, and 10 sessions more of the punishment condition. Data for each of four pigeons. (From Squires et al., 1975. © 1975 by the Society for the Experimental Analysis of Behavior, Inc.)

merman, 1969; Zimmerman and Hanford, 1966, 1968) have also maintained considerable responding when consequence of responding was the production of a short hopper presentation (too short to allow eating) and delay of longer hopper presentations. The apparent superiority of a brief hopper presentation to other paired brief stimuli may be attributed to its resemblance to the primary reinforcer [i.e., presentation of grain]. This effectiveness may either be due to the consequent conditioned reinforcing effects of those stimuli, or due to the failure to discriminate whether the hopper presentations will be short or [sufficiently] long [to permit ingestion of grain]. The latter explanation would be similar to the failure-to-discriminate hypothesis suggested above. . . . The differences in these two explanations (conditioned reinforcement *vs* generalization) is crucial because the latter explanation obviates any need for a separate *conditioned* reinforcement concept under these circumstances. The utility of the concept of conditioned reinforcement lies in the prediction that an arbitrary stimulus may become a conditioned reinforcer. If only those stimuli that [at the instant they are presented] cannot be discriminated from primary reinforcement are effective, a separate concept is no longer required.

. . . Although it may still be possible to invoke conditioned reinforcement as an explanatory mechanism for the behavior on different second-order schedules, at the present time . . . it is more parsimonious to explain the behavior in terms of the discriminative properties of the stimuli and of the salience of the stimuli for the particular organism.

The present analysis and the results of Squires et al. (1975) suggest that behavior is well maintained on second-order schedules because of "conditioned confusion"[3] rather than the effectiveness of the paired stimulus as a conditioned reinforcer. Thus what had been the most impressive support for the pairing hypothesis—behavior on second-order schedules—may turn out not to be support for it at all. Additional results, which will be described in the context of choice (e.g., Schuster, 1969; Squires, 1972) are also inconsistent with the pairing hypothesis. While the pairing hypothesis may have served us well, it appears to be time to discard or modify it in the light of recent research.

While most of the enhanced responding on second-order schedules may be due to a discrimination failure, as Squires et al. maintain, the high rates of responding engendered by this failure probably mask some real, albeit small, effect of pairing. The effects of pairing may become manifest when sufficiently sensitive procedures, such as multiple schedules (as in de Lorge's work, 1971), are employed. Nonetheless, most of the response enhancement that sometimes occurs on second-order schedules now appears to depend on pairing only in the following complex sense: When the subject cannot discriminate either among components of a second-order schedule or between brief stimuli and primary reinforcement, poor temporal control results and response rates are en-

---

[3] I thank Dr. Jim Norborg for turning this phrase.

hanced; paired brief stimuli may impair such discriminations. Depending on the stimuli selected and on the schedule of reinforcement, discrimination (and hence temporal control) on unpaired brief-stimulus schedules may be superior to that on paired brief-stimulus schedules. If so, response rates on the paired schedule would exceed that on the unpaired schedule. If discrimination among components or between unpaired stimuli and primary reinforcement is poor, however, response rates on the paired and unpaired schedules would be equivalent.

OBSERVING RESPONSES AND CONDITIONED REINFORCEMENT

In Wyckoff's (1952) observing response procedure, periods during which key pecking was reinforced with food according to FI schedules alternated with periods of extinction. The response key remained white throughout both periods, unless the pigeon pressed a pedal which turned the key red or green. When the two colors were correlated with the schedule in effect, much more pedal pressing was maintained than when the stimuli and schedules were uncorrelated. Wyckoff referred to the pedal presses as "observing responses," i.e., responses resulting in the presentation of a pair of discriminative stimuli. Other early studies of observing responses include those of Prokasy (1956) and Kelleher (1958).

One important explanation of observing responses stresses the information obtained from them and stipulates that uncertainty reduction reinforces observing behavior. A second explanation stresses the conditioned reinforcing strength of the stimulus correlated with the more positive outcome. Some form of the first interpretation—which has been called the *uncertainty reduction hypothesis*—has been favored by Berlyne (1957, 1960), Bloomfield (1972), Hendry (1969b), Lieberman (1972), Schaub (1969), and Schaub and Honig (1967), among others, while some form of the second interpretation—which has been called the *conditioned reinforcement hypothesis*—has been favored by Dinsmoor, Browne, and Lawrence (1972), Jenkins and Boakes (1973), Kelleher and Gollub (1962), Kendall (1973a), and Mulvaney, Dinsmoor, Jwaideh, and Hughes (1974), among others.

There are many differences among these general interpretations, not all of which can concern us here. We should point out, however, that the uncertainty reduction and conditioned reinforcement hypotheses can have much in common. In particular, a conditioned reinforcement hypothesis can specify that the strength of the stimulus associated with the more positive outcome depends upon an informative function. Consider two possible hypotheses about conditioned reinforcement strength: One, the traditional pairing hypothesis, states that the conditioned reinforcing strength of the stimulus derives from the pairing of the stimulus with primary reinforcement irrespective of any informative function; a second describes the conditioned reinforcing strength of the stimulus in terms of its informativeness about the immediacy of primary reinforcement. This second statement is more compatible with the uncertainty reduction hypothesis, though it remains distinct from it in at least one important respect, as we shall see below. The uncertainty reduction hypothesis may or may not be described in terms of conditioned reinforcement. In principle, it is compatible with conditioned reinforcement, since one could say: "A stimulus which becomes a conditioned reinforcer does so because it reduces uncertainty." Or one may eschew the term *conditioned reinforcement*, stating instead that information about reinforcement—i.e., uncertainty reduction per se—is a primary reinforcer.

Whatever the form of the conditioned reinforcement or uncertainty reduction hypotheses, however, the two hypotheses may be distinguished, as Dinsmoor et al. (1972), Jenkins and Boakes (1973), and others have pointed out: "The assertion that the negative value as well as the positive value of the informative stimulus variable reinforces the observing response is what distinguishes the uncertainty reduction hypothesis from the conditioned reinforcing hypothesis of observing behavior" (Jenkins & Boakes, 1973, p. 198).

In this section we shall first consider evidence on the question whether information about negative outcomes is reinforcing. We shall then summarize evidence from observing response studies which have varied the probability of the positively valued alternative in order to develop a quantitative formulation of observing behavior. The resultant hypothesis of observing behavior will be a form of the conditioned reinforcement hypothesis consistent with the theory of conditioned reinforcement suggested by studies of choice behavior to which I shall then turn.

Are Negative Stimuli Reinforcing?

As Bloomfield (1972) has stated:

Another way in which information-transmission theory confronts reinforcement-contiguity theory in the field of secondary reinforcement is through the function assigned to signals that precede a negatively valued environmental event. According to contiguity theory, a signal of that kind must become aversive, or at least much less reinforcing than the other cues available. The information hypothesis, on the contrary, requires that "bad news" be just as much "news" as "good news" and so does not differentiate these two cases. (p. 194)

There is also the position that predicts intermediate results: the negative stimuli should be reinforcing, but less so than the positive stimuli (Hendry, 1969b; Schaub, 1969). In either case, the negative stimuli should be reinforcing, not aversive. It should be added that the conditioned reinforcement hypotheses would also assign conditioned reinforcing value to "bad news" if the news could be acted on to increase the likelihood of negative reinforcement (in an escape or avoidance procedure) or of positive reinforcement (in an alternative response procedure). As far as I know, the experiments suggested by these latter predictions have not been carried out.

Three studies have been widely cited as evidence that "bad news" is reinforcing (Lieberman, 1972; Schaub & Honig, 1967; Schaub, 1969). Schaub and Honig's procedure consisted of alternation between periods of reinforcement and extinction for both "master" pigeons and yoked control pigeons. In reinforcement periods, pecks at a white key by the master subjects were reinforced on a variable-interval (VI) 1-min schedule and also produced a change in the color of the key from white to red—for 1.5 sec—on a fixed-ratio (FR) 3 schedule. In extinction periods, pecks at the white key were never followed by primary reinforcement, but pecks did produce a change in the color of the key from white to green (also on an FR 3 schedule). Yoked subjects received the same cues independent of their responding. Schaub and Honig found that the master pigeons pecked at a high rate during extinction periods (although not at as high a rate as in the reinforcement periods), suggesting that the production of the green stimulus (associated with extinction) reinforced responding during the extinction period. The yoked subjects generally responded only during reinforcement periods. Schaub (1969) then conducted a more elaborate study with the same basic procedure, except that responding could produce only a single stimulus: either the positive stimulus, associated with the VI schedule, or the negative stimulus, associated with extinction. He found that when subjects could produce only positive stimuli (i.e., when responding was completely ineffective during extinction periods), they responded more in extinction than did yoked control subjects (who again received key light changes whenever the experimental subjects produced them). In a later portion of his experiment, Schaub provided response-independent stimuli which made the response-produced stimuli redundant for the experimental birds. This eliminated performance differences between the experimental and control subjects. When the response-independent stimuli were then eliminated, response rates during extinction increased for the experimental birds, suggesting that responding was reinforced by the response-produced negative stimuli when they were no longer redundant.

As Dinsmoor (Dinsmoor, Flint, Smith, & Viemeister, 1969; Dinsmoor et al., 1972), Wilton and Clements (1971b), and Bloomfield (1972) have pointed out, however, the Schaub studies are not completely convincing. In Schaub and Honig (1967), for example, responding in the procedure with only negative stimuli may have been maintained by the occasional presentation of the positive stimulus after the period of extinction terminated (a possible interpretation of the results raised first by Schaub and Honig). Moreover, in either of the Schaub studies the absence of stimulus change after three responses may have signified that the positive component was in effect. Dinsmoor et al. (1972) made observing behavior effective on an aperiodic schedule of reinforcement (either VI 1-min or VI 2-min schedules) on which the absence of stimulus change was the *usual* consequences of a peck to the observing key (and hence could not reduce uncertainty). Thus the only significant uncertainty reduction was provided by stimulus change. In addition, observing responses were made on a different key than food responses. If the uncertainty reduction hypothesis were correct, observing responding should be maintained equally well if its only consequence were production of the negative stimulus (correlated with an extinction period on the food key) or if its only consequence were production of the positive stimulus (correlated with responding on an interval schedule of positive reinforcement). On the other hand, if the conditioned reinforcement hypothesis were correct, observing responding should be maintained only if the positive stimulus were sometimes produced.

Dinsmoor et al. (1972) found that observing behavior was well maintained when only the positive stimulus could be produced, as shown in the left panel of Figure 2, but that responding was eliminated when the only consequence of pecking the observing key was production of the stimulus signifying extinction periods (the center panel of Figure 2). Finally, when both stimuli were available, pigeons' observing behavior was maintained at an intermediate rate, raising the possibility that production of the

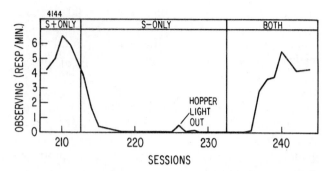

Fig. 2. Rate of observing on successive sessions by one pigeon (4144) when observing responses produced S+ only (left panel), S− only (center panel), or both stimuli (right panel). (From Dinsmoor et al., 1972. © 1972 by the Society for the Experimental Analysis of Behavior, Inc.)

negative stimulus had actually been punishing. The data shown in Figure 2, for one of Dinsmoor's pigeons, were typical for each of the five pigeons in the experiment, except that for one bird results in the left and right panels were comparable.

Several other studies have supported the contention of Dinsmoor et al. (1972) that negative stimuli do not reinforce observing behavior (e.g., Blanchard, 1975; Dinsmoor, Browne, Lawrence, & Wasserman, 1971; Dinsmoor, et al., 1969; Jenkins & Boakes, 1973; Kendall, 1973a; Mulvaney, Dinsmoor, Jwaideh, & Hughes, 1974). For example, Dinsmoor et al. (1971) used a procedure in which pigeons could produce a display of either the positive or negative discriminative stimulus on a key as long as they stood on a pedal. They left the pedal, however, as soon as the negative stimulus appeared. Mulvaney et al. (1972) studied two pigeons in an observing procedure with three keys. During alternating periods of unpredictable duration, responding on the center (food) key was reinforced on a VI schedule or was never reinforced. In the absence of observing, the color of all three keys was yellow. On identical but independent VI observing schedules, responding on either of the two side keys produced either a positive stimulus (green) on all three keys, if the VI food schedule were in effect, or a negative stimulus (red) on all three keys, if extinction were in effect. In the critical stage of the experiment, the negative stimulus could not be produced by responding on one of the two side keys; responding on the other side key continued to produce both positive and negative stimuli. The subjects responded at a higher rate on the key that produced only the positive stimulus, suggesting that the negative stimulus punished responding that produced it.

Blanchard (1975) studied eight pigeons on a single-key, discrete-trials observing procedure. Pecks during a trial produced colored key lights which signaled whether the trial would end with response-independent reinforcement or with no reinforcement. These stimuli were produced on a VI schedule which began operating at the onset of the trial. A procedure was employed which permitted the bird to produce S+ on those trials in which reinforcement would be delivered with or without producing S− on nonreinforced trials. In one condition, only a response preceded by at least 6 sec of nonresponding could produce S−, while any response that satisfied the VI requirement produced S+. In another condition, this contingency was reversed. Thus the pigeons could selectively produce only S+ (or only S−) by adjusting their interresponse times appropriately. The pigeons generally produced fewer negative stimuli in the course of training, which indicates that S− was punishing observing behavior.

Auge (1974) has extended these observations to a situation in which both alternatives involved primary reinforcement, but in which one was more positive than the other. He studied mixed fixed-ratio, fixed-interval schedules and found that observing behavior is maintained by the occasional presentation of the stimulus signaling the shorter delay to reinforcement (i.e., the schedule with the shorter inter-reinforcement interval). Observing responses produced stimuli signaling whether an FI 30-sec or an FR X schedule was in effect. When the stimulus signaling the FI schedule was eliminated, observing behavior was maintained when the FI 30-sec schedule alternated with the low-valued FR (e.g., 20 or 30) but not with large FRs (e.g., 100, 140, or 200). The converse was true when the stimulus signaling the FI 30-sec schedule was the only one that could be produced by observing responses: observing behavior was only maintained when the FI 30-sec schedule alternated with large FRs. In other words, only stimuli associated with the shorter delay to primary reinforcement maintained observing behavior (a result consistent with those from an earlier study by Kendall & Gibson, 1965). Auge (1973) has also shown that observing responding is maintained by the stimulus signaling the larger of two reinforcement magnitudes but not by the stimulus signaling the smaller.

Lieberman's (1972) study provides more convincing evidence for the uncertainty reduction hypothesis than Schaub's (1969). Nonetheless, his results are also interpretable in several ways, some of which have been discussed by Dinsmoor et al. (1972) and by Mulvaney et al. (1974). In Lieberman's basic procedure, a variable-ratio (VR) schedule alternated with extinction and no exteroceptive stimuli were associated with the two types of components. Hence the schedule was mix VR EXT. Observing responses on a different lever produced 6 sec of exposure to a stimulus associated with the component in effect. In one experiment, the VR value was varied between 5 and 100 and the effects on observing responding were studied. Lieberman reasoned that a conditioned reinforcement view of observing responding required a decrease in the rate of observing responding as the VR value increased (and hence the density of primary reinforcement associated with the positive stimulus decreased). Instead, an increase was noted (particularly between the conditions in which the VR requirement was 5—resulting in about three responses per minute—and 25—resulting in about 5 responses per minute). While the result is indeed consistent with an information view of observing behavior, it is also consistent with other possibilities. In the first place, Lieberman's procedure was essentially a concurrent schedule of food-reinforced responding and observing responding. From what is known about interactions on concurrent schedules (e.g., Catania, 1966), it would be expected that the greater the VR value for food-reinforced responding, the more responding should be maintained by any concurrently available schedule (in this case, observing responding). For this reason, more observing responding was maintained with higher VR values on the food-reinforced lever. In addition, in the VR component, where about three responses per second were emitted, an observing response delayed primary reinforcement as a result of the changeover delay (COD) requirement in effect. A COD was used to minimize interaction between responding on the two levers; thus primary reinforcement could not be obtained for a food lever response until at least 1½ sec after any response on the observing response lever. This delay was comparable to the time required for the subject to obtain primary reinforcement on a VR 5. Since this delay would be more noticeable with lower VR values, the failure to obtain an increase in observing responding with such values is not surprising.

Similar arguments and others may be leveled against the remaining portions of Lieberman's experiment (see also Dinsmoor et al., 1972, p. 80). As a last example, consider the main result of his final experiment (which in my opinion is the most interesting), in which observing responding during the extinction component of *MIX* VR 50 EXT no longer produced the negative stimulus ("S−") after the first ten (base line) sessions (although the positive stimulus —the "S+"—could be produced during the VR component). The result, averaged over five monkeys, is shown in Figure 3. Lieberman argues plausibly that the decline in observing response rates during the extinction component after the S− is removed suggests that the S− had been a conditioned reinforcer. However, the decline is also compatible with the notion that observing behavior had been maintained by stimulus change. If responding during the extinction component is reinforced by stimulus change, then less responding should occur once stimulus change is no longer available. Moreover, as Dinsmoor et al. (1972) have pointed out:

> To show that the light had been functioning as a reinforcer, Lieberman then eliminated it from his procedure and found that this led to a sharp decline in the frequency with which observing responses were recorded during the extinction component. But the situation without the light was not entirely comparable to the situation with the light. During the baseline determination, the presence of the tone or the light indicated that an observing response would have no consequence; conversely, the absence of the tone or the light set the occasion for observing. When the light was eliminated from the procedure, there was no stimulus to prevent the animal from responding during the 6-sec period when the light would otherwise have been present. To maintain comparability with the baseline procedure, Lieberman did not record these responses. But some of them may have been responses that under the baseline procedure would have been postponed until after the light had terminated and that would therefore have been recorded. Note that Schaub (1969), using a different recording procedure, did not find a corresponding decline in observing when he

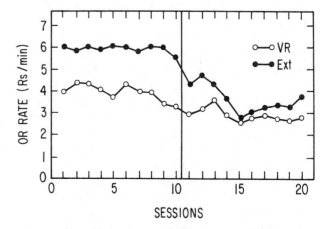

Fig. 3. Rate of observing (averaged over five subjects) on successive sessions before and after removal of the S− in the final experiment. (From Lieberman, 1972.)

withheld S− (Experiment 2a). It is difficult to see any way in which the data can safely be compared with and without the light in Lieberman's experiment. (p. 80)

Thus while Lieberman's results are interesting and constitute the only truly provocative support of the notion that bad news is reinforcing, they do not permit a reasonably unambiguous conclusion. Moreover, in view of the large body of unambiguous evidence suggesting that observing behavior is maintained only by stimuli correlated with positive reinforcement, it appears best to suspend judgment on the significance of Lieberman's results.

In conclusion, observing behavior is maintained by the stimulus associated with any of the following: (1) the presence of a schedule of positive reinforcement (as opposed to extinction—e.g., Dinsmoor et al., 1971; Wyckoff, 1952); (2) the shorter of two delays to reinforcement (e.g., Auge, 1974; Kendall & Gibson, 1965); (3) the larger of two magnitudes of reinforcement (e.g., Auge, 1973); (4) the absence of a schedule of punishment (e.g., Dinsmoor et al., 1969). Observing behavior is not maintained when there are no differential outcomes (e.g., Kendall, 1972; Wilton & Clements, 1971a) or when only the stimulus associated with the less valued of the two outcomes may be observed (Dinsmoor et al., 1972). Thus the weight of evidence clearly favors the conditioned reinforcement view of observing behavior over the uncertainty reduction view. Or in terms of our earlier discussion, the uncertainty reduction hypothesis is tenable only when restricted to uncertainty reduction which provides information that primary reinforcement is forthcoming. In that case, however, the hypothesis becomes indistinguishable from a conditioned reinforcement hypothesis that describes the strength of a stimulus in terms of its relation to primary reinforcement. Moreover, as Gollub (1970), Eckerman (1973), and McMillan (1974) have pointed out, the appeal of the information hypothesis, expressed in terms of uncertainty reduction, depends upon the quantitative predictions of information theory (Shannon & Weaver, 1949; Wiener, 1948). Once these predictions are shown to be incorrect when applied to the study of observing responses, there seems to be little reason to "save" a modified version of the uncertainty reduction hypothesis in favor of one based on conditioned reinforcement. I now turn to studies which have tested quantitative implications of the uncertainty reduction hypothesis by examining the strength of observing as a function of changes in the likelihood of the positive stimulus.

Studies Varying the Likelihood of Positive Stimuli

Several investigators have tested implications of the uncertainty reduction hypothesis by varying the probability that observing responses will lead to positive stimuli (and, subsequently, positive reinforcement). According to the uncertainty reduction hypothesis, the amount of observing behavior should be described by the symmetrical function shown in Figure 4A. This inverted U-shaped function describes the average amount of information transmitted by both the positive and negative stimuli as a function of the probability of the positive stimulus. Since the function is symmetrical, observing should be just as strong when the probability of the positive stimulus is p as when it is $1 - p$ (e.g., when $p = .20$ and $.80$). Figure 4B illustrates a function based only upon the amount of information transmitted by the positive stimulus. In intuitive terms, this function says that observing will increase as a function of the uncertainty reduction conveyed by stimuli associated with positive outcomes; the more unlikely the good news is, the more reinforcing when it does come. This function also implies that negative stimuli do not affect observing. This implication is responsible for the asymmetry.

If this asymmetrical function accurately describes observing, then more observing should occur when $p = .20$ than when $p = .80$. Wilton and Clements (1971b) tested this prediction. In their experiment, responding on an FI schedule produced both a stimulus signaling whether or not reinforcement was forthcoming and the delayed outcome of the trial: either nonreinforcement or response-independent reinforcement. Thus the same response was required to advance to the trial outcome stage as well as to produce stimuli correlated with the specific outcome. The probability of the positive stimulus (and hence reinforcement) was .80 in one condition and .20 in the other. For each of the six pigeons in the one comparison made by Wilton and Clements, more observing occurred when $p = .20$ than when $p = .80$. This result suggests that the symmetrical function is incorrect and supports the asymmetrical function. Note that this result is consistent with those discussed in the previous section: stimuli correlated with negative outcomes do not appear to maintain observing. It should be noted that Wilton and Clements did not include a control condition in which responses advanced the subject to the trial outcome stage (as in their actual procedure) but did *not* produce observing stimuli. Nor did they include a condition in which the subject advanced to the trial outcome stage whether or not it made an observing response. With-

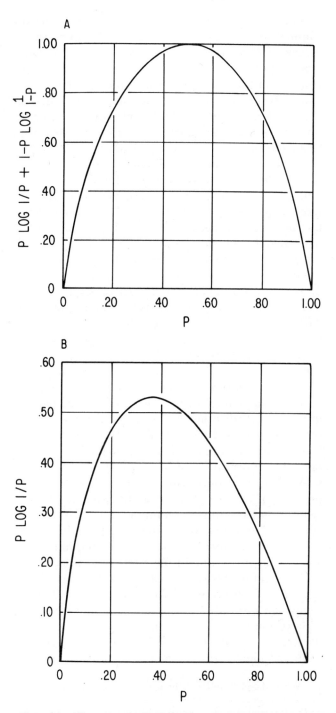

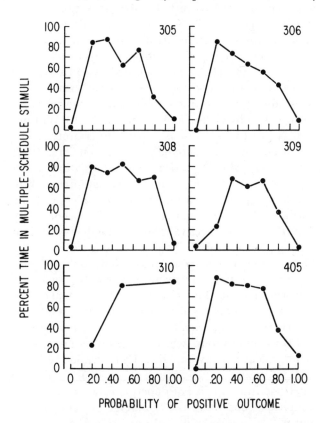

metrical function have been reported by McMillan (1974), McMichael, Lanzetta, and Driscoll (1967), Hendry (1965), and Eckerman (1973). In perhaps the most comprehensive study, McMillan (1974) allowed pigeons to convert a mix VI EXT schedule of food reinforcement to a corresponding multiple schedule (*mult* VI EXT). McMillan varied the probability that the VI component was in effect between the following values: .00, .20, .35, .50, .65, .80, and 1.00. His principal finding is shown in Figure 5. The data for one pigeon (310) are inconsistent with either of the functions under discussion. Of the remaining five, the data from four (all except 309) suggest an asymmetrical function similar to that in Figure 4B. Certainly, McMillan's data do not support a symmetrical function.[4]

Eckerman (1973) and McMillan (1974) have raised an intuitive objection to the Wilton-Clements hypothesis. They question the significance of considering the informativeness of positive signals in isolation. Indeed, it is *logically* impossible to have only

Fig. 4. (A) The amount of information transmitted by both S+ and S− as a function of the probability of S+. (B) The amount of information contributed by S+ to the average amount of information, again as a function of the probability of S+. (Adapted from Wilton & Clements, 1971b. © 1971 by the Society for the Experimental Analysis of Behavior, Inc.)

Fig. 5. Percentage of time spent in the presence of the multiple-schedule stimuli as a function of the probability of the positive stimulus. (Adapted from McMillan, 1974. © 1974 by the Society for the Experimental Analysis of Behavior, Inc.)

[4] McMillan's study also reports interesting data arguing against the discriminative stimulus hypothesis of conditioned reinforcement.

out these controls it is not clear what maintained responding in their study.

Fortunately, other data consistent with the asym-

positive information. Certainly, a meaningful application of information theory requires consideration of both positive and negative outcomes. There is also empirical evidence *against* the appropriateness of an asymmetrical observing response function. In the first place, Kendall (1973b) found that observing behavior was better maintained when the probability of a positive outcome was .25 than when it was .50 or .75. But according to Figure 4B, the amount of uncertainty reduction is equal when $p = .25$ and .50 (in each case, $p \log [1/p] = .50$). Similarly, Steiner (1970) found as much or more observing behavior when the probability of a positive outcome was .1 than when it was .5, an outcome opposite to that suggested by the shape of the function of Figure 4B. Most significantly, the function shown in Figure 4B has a telling empirical shortcoming when dealing with experiments on the effects of negative outcomes. As I discussed above, convincing evidence that the stimuli associated with negative outcomes actually *punish* observing behavior has been supplied recently by Mulvaney et al. (1974) and Blanchard (1975). This evidence undermines the rationale for the asymmetrical function—namely, the assumption that negative outcomes do not affect observing. Wilton (1972) has modified his own view to suggest that the appearance of negative stimuli punishes observing behavior rather than having no effect (as suggested by Wilton and Clements, 1971b). Wilton's view is just the opposite of a pure uncertainty reduction view (held by Berlyne, 1960; Bloomfield, 1972; and others) which specifies that information about negative events should be positively reinforcing. Wilton does not propose a quantitative theory specifying how punishing the negative stimuli are, except to say that they are less effective in controlling behavior than are the positive stimuli. In practice, this will have the effect of moving the peak of the function in Figure 4B toward a lower probability value by some unspecified amount. This change appears to make Wilton's later hypothesis consistent with the results of Blanchard (1975), Kendall (1973b), Steiner (1970), and Dinsmoor's group, which are inconsistent with the Wilton-Clements hypothesis. Thus while Wilton's (1972) newer hypothesis may be less valuable than his older one in that it is both nonquantitative and more complex, it does have the advantage of being consistent with more of the data. In any case, the new Wilton theory is not only manifestly inconsistent with the uncertainty reduction hypothesis (based on the function shown in Figure 4A) but, in stressing both the reinforcing and punishing functions of signals, it has more in common with the conditioned reinforcement hypothesis than with information views.

The results reviewed in this section may be accounted for in terms of a conditioned reinforcement theory of observing behavior (such as that of Dinsmoor's group), as McMillan has most recently suggested. Our argument begins with the fact that mixed schedules of reinforcement are less reinforcing, as measured in choice procedures, than equivalent multiple schedules (e.g., Bower, McLean, & Meacham, 1966; Hendry, 1969c; Hursh & Fantino, 1974), whatever the likelihood of the positive component, except at the end points: when $p = 1.0$ and $p = 0$, the multiple and mixed schedules are equivalent. For intermediate values, the difference in conditioned reinforcing strength between the multiple and mixed schedules should increase as p decreases.[5] Thus, conditioned reinforcing strength should increase monotonically as the probability of a positive outcome decreases, until the function approaches $p = 0$ (extinction), at which point observing should not occur. At the same time, as the probability of a positive outcome becomes very small, observing should decline since it is rarely reinforced. The observing response function generated by these two factors should resemble an asymmetrical inverted U-shaped function.

The delay reduction hypothesis makes comparable qualitative predictions. For example, consider one of the schedules used by McMillan (1974), a mixed VI 70-sec EXT schedule with equiprobable 40-sec components. Observing responses changed this mixed schedule to the equivalent multiple schedule. In the presence of the mixed schedule, the average delay to reinforcement at the beginning of a trial is 140 sec. Whereas production of the negative stimulus is not correlated with reduction in delay to reinforcement, and should not maintain observing, the onset of the positive stimulus is correlated with an average reduction of 70 sec (since it is correlated with the VI 70-sec component), or one-half the average time correlated with the mixed schedule, and should maintain observing. The lower the probability of the VI component, the greater the reduction in delay to primary

[5] When the probability of the positive component is high, the mixed schedule value is close to that of the positive outcome. As the probability of the positive outcome decreases, the mixed schedule value approaches that of the negative outcome. Many studies of how subjects average positive and negative outcomes (e.g., Bower, McLean, & Meacham, 1966; Davison, 1969, 1972; Fantino, 1967; Fantino & Navarick, 1974; Herrnstein, 1964b; Hursh & Fantino, 1973; Killeen, 1968a; Navarick & Fantino, 1974) have shown that the positive outcome is weighted far more heavily than the negative in choice. Since the discrepancy between the positive outcome on the multiple schedule and the value of the mixed schedule is greater, the more unlikely the positive outcome, it follows that preference for the multiple schedule should be an inverse function of the likelihood of the positive outcome.

reinforcement correlated with the positive stimulus. For example, when the probability of the positive outcome is .1, the delay to reinforcement in the presence of the mixed schedule is 700 sec and the reduction in time to reinforcement signified by the positive signal is 630 sec or $630/700 = .9$ the average delay signified by the mixed schedule. This particular view of conditioned reinforcement is appealing because it is consistent with the results of the experiments on choice that will be discussed in the next section of the chapter. Note that this conditioned reinforcement view—like that of Dinsmoor's group—requires that the probability of observing behavior increase as the likelihood of the positive outcome decreases, until some unspecified maximum point is reached. The descending part of the curve makes good sense, of course: when p is sufficiently low, observing behavior is rarely reinforced and should decline.

Observing Responses: Present Status

The clearest conclusion that may be drawn from the results and theories that have been discussed thus far is that the uncertainty reduction hypothesis of observing behavior (e.g., Bloomfield, 1972) is incorrect. Rather drastic modifications of this hypothesis which assume that negative signals are ineffective (e.g., Wilton & Clements, 1971b) or punishing (Wilton, 1972) make the uncertainty reduction view largely equivalent to those stipulating that observing behavior is maintained by conditioned reinforcement (e.g., Dinsmoor et al., 1969, 1972; Jenkins & Boakes, 1973). One form of the conditioned reinforcement hypothesis is inconsistent with some of the observing response data. In particular, a hypothesis that requires a stimulus to maintain observing behavior when it is paired or contiguous with primary reinforcement would have difficulty handling Auge's (1973, 1974) results: primary reinforcement was obtained in both components of the multiple schedules studied in his experiments, but observing behavior was maintained in only one component. In addition, as Wilton and Clements (1971a) have argued, the fact that little observing responding is maintained when reinforcement is available on every trial is also difficult to reconcile with the pairing hypothesis: as both stimuli in their continuous reinforcement condition were consistently paired with primary reinforcement, they should be strong conditioned reinforcers and should maintain observing behavior as well as they do in the condition in which reinforcement is available in the presence of only one of the two stimuli. Kendall (1972) obtained results similar to those of Wilton and Clements (1971a) with multiple delays of reinforcement; more observing responding was maintained when one of two 15-sec delays was increased to 120 sec. While these results are indeed incompatible with the traditional pairing hypothesis, they are completely consistent with both the reinforcement density and the delay reduction hypotheses. When both components are correlated with the same reinforcement density, the stimulus of the mixed schedule is also correlated with the same reinforcement density. Since observing does not produce a stimulus correlated with a higher density of reinforcement, observing should not occur. Similarly, neither multiple-schedule stimulus is correlated with a reduction in time to reinforcement (relative to the mixed-schedule stimulus) when the schedules are equal. Hence observing should not occur according to the delay reduction hypothesis. These hypotheses predict that only the more positively valued of two stimuli should maintain observing behavior, as Branch (1970) has hypothesized, and as the results from Dinsmoor et al. (1972) and Auge (1974) suggest, since the less positive stimulus is correlated with an increase, rather than a reduction, in average time to primary reinforcement (and a decrease, rather than an increase, in reinforcement density). Such stimuli should be aversive rather than reinforcing according to the delay reduction and reinforcement density hypotheses.

In addition, these hypotheses predict that when each of two stimuli are associated with a reduction in delay to primary reinforcement (or an increase in reinforcement density), both should maintain observing responding, and that more observing responding should be maintained by the stimulus associated with the greater reduction in time to reinforcement. For example, consider a procedure in which observing responses change a mixed FI 20-sec FI 40-sec FI 180-sec schedule to the equivalent multiple schedule. According to the delay reduction hypothesis, the stimuli associated with both the FI 20-sec and FI 40-sec schedules should maintain observing behavior (since the average time to reinforcement in the mixed schedule equals 80 sec) with more observing responding maintained by the FI 20-sec stimulus. If the schedule were changed to *MIX* FI 20-sec FI 120-sec FI 180-sec, however, only the stimulus associated with the FI 20-sec component of the multiple schedule should reinforce observing. (Since the average time to reinforcement in the mixed schedule is now 107 sec, the middle-valued stimulus—associated with FI 120-sec—no longer represents a reduction in time to reinforcement.) The reinforcement density hypothesis makes equivalent predictions.

Whether or not the form of the conditioned reinforcement hypothesis specified by the delay reduction hypothesis proves correct, it is clear that the conditioned reinforcement explanation of observing behavior (e.g., Blanchard, 1975; Dinsmoor et al., 1972; Jenkins & Boakes, 1973; Mulvaney et al., 1974) is more consistent with the data than the uncertainty reduction explanation (e.g., Berlyne, 1957; Bloomfield, 1972; Lieberman, 1972). We now turn to studies of choice behavior. The picture that emerges from the choice literature is consistent with the one we have drawn from the study of observing responses.

CHOICE AND CONDITIONED REINFORCEMENT

The Delay Reduction Hypothesis

The delay reduction hypothesis was developed (Fantino, 1969b) to integrate data from a series of experiments on choice and conditioned reinforcement begun by Autor (1960) and continued by many others in the subsequent sixteen years (cf. Fantino & Navarick, 1974; Hendry, 1969). When applied to choice procedures, the delay reduction hypothesis states that (1) organisms will choose the stimulus correlated with the greatest reduction in time to primary reinforcement and (2) preference will be greater the larger the difference in the delay reductions correlated with the chosen alternatives. Usually, the delay reduction hypothesis has been applied only in this sense of improvement in temporal proximity to reinforcement. Obviously, other variables such as punishment and the probability and magnitude of reinforcement affect conditioned reinforcement. The delay reduction hypothesis may be broadened readily to encompass improvement in reinforcer amount and probability and in punishment reduction, as I suggest below.

First, consider a subject operating a two-levered gambling device with the following payoff structure: Pulls on either lever are reinforced (according to equal VI schedules) by access to one of two sets of flashing lights, each correlated with the delivery of a response-independent dollar bill. The dollar is delivered after 5 min in the presence of one set of flashing lights, but after only 1 min in the presence of the other lights. After the dollar is received, the subject may again pull the levers leading to the flashing lights and more dollar bills. Pulls on one lever (when effective—as determined by the VI schedule) always lead to the same outcome. Choice is measured by the relative rates of lever pulling leading to the two outcomes. Obviously, many theories of choice or conditioned reinforcement—including a reinforcement density hypothesis, such as that considered when discussing observing—would require that the subject prefer the lights correlated with the 1-min delay. *How much* the 1-min delay is preferred, however, depends upon an additional factor we have yet to specify: the size of the equal VI schedules leading to the outcomes. Consider the following three values for the equal VIs: 1, 6, and 36 min. With VI 1-min schedules the average interval between the onset of a trial and receipt of the dollar is 3½ min as long as the subject is responding on both levers. It takes ½ min, on the average, for concurrent VI 1-min schedules to arrange reinforcement; the average wait in the presence of the flashing lights (½ × 1 min + ½ × 5 min) is an additional 3 min. But by responding exclusively on the lever leading to the shorter delay, the subject can receive a dollar every 2 min (1 min on the appropriate VI 1-min plus the 1-min delay). Indeed, for concurrent VIs of 4 min or less, the subject will increase his or her earnings by exhibiting exclusive preference for the 1-min delay: only that outcome is correlated with a reduction in waiting time to reinforcement. With VI schedules greater than 4 min, however, both outcomes are correlated with delay reduction and the subject should respond on both levers. For example, with VI 6-min schedules it takes an average of 6 min to obtain a dollar (an average of 3 min of responding on the levers and 3 min in the presence of the flashing lights) if the subject responds on both levers, but 7 min if responses are made exclusively on the lever with the shorter delay. Here the 5-min delay represents a reduction of 1 min (i.e., the onset of the flashing lights correlated with the longer delay brings the subject 1 min closer in time to the dollar than he had been while in the choice phase) whereas the 1-min delay represents a 5-min reduction. Thus the short-delay outcome represents a reduction 5 times greater than the alternative outcome. The longer the VIs, the smaller this ratio. Hence, with the VI 36-min schedules, the delay reductions for the 1- and 5-min outcomes are 20 min and 16 min, respectively, a ratio of just 5:4.

In summary, the delay reduction hypothesis states that subjects' choice for the more preferred of two alternatives should increase, the shorter the choice phase: with sufficiently short VIs only one outcome represents an improvement in terms of temporal proximity to reinforcement; as the VIs are made progressively longer, both outcomes represent improvement and the subject should shift away from exclusive preference toward indifference. Note that a reinforcement density hypothesis assumes the choice will depend only on the relative rates of reinforcement during the two outcomes and that choice should therefore be independent of the length of the choice phase (Autor, 1960, 1969; Herrnstein, 1964a). As we shall see, data instead support the delay reduction hypothesis.

Since probability of reinforcement is closely analogous to frequency (probabilities of obtaining a dollar may be substituted for waiting times as the outcomes in the example above) and since punishment is conceptually and empirically symmetrical with reinforcement (though opposite in sign—cf. Fantino, 1973, for a review) there is no need to illustrate how the delay reduction hypothesis applies to these variables. We shall consider choice for reinforcer magnitudes, however. Assume you are walking in a foreign city and are hungry. You know of two fine restaurants to which you had once been taken. You enjoy both but have a preference for one. You anticipate it will take about X min to track down each restaurant. Do you decide to dine at whichever you find first or will you hold out for the preferred one? I predict your decision would be based, in part, on the size of X (corresponding to the duration of the choice phase): the shorter the choice phase, the more likely you are to persist in finding the preferred restaurant. If X is very large, you are more likely to behave indifferently to the two. If this assumption is correct, then temporal context affects choice in the same way whether the outcomes differ with respect to rate or magnitude of reinforcement. Doug Navarick and I supported this notion recently in an analogous experiment with pigeons choosing between 4.5 and 1.5 sec access to grain: as the duration of the choice phase decreased—relative to the duration of the outcome phase—choice for the larger reward increased.

Before discussing the delay reduction hypothesis and its implications more fully and rigorously and presenting supporting data, we should review briefly the concurrent chains procedure developed to study conditioned reinforcement and used to test the delay reduction hypothesis.

The Concurrent Chains Procedure

This procedure, which is described fully below, involves measuring choice by rate of response during two equal VI schedules, each leading to a different conditioned reinforcer. Since the concurrently available VI schedules are equal, differences in response rates can be assumed to reflect differences in the reinforcing effectiveness of the stimuli being chosen, i.e., the stimuli associated with the terminal links of the chain. The independent variable is some manipulation of the relation between the conditioned and the primary reinforcer. The dependent variable is the relative strength of the two conditioned reinforcers as measured in the equal initial links: the number of choice responses made for one conditioned reinforcer divided by the total number of choice responses made for both conditioned reinforcers.

Beginning with Autor (1960, 1969), the concurrent chains procedure has been used extensively in the study of both choice and conditioned reinforcement. While some investigators have used it primarily to study choice, others have emphasized its relevance for conditioned reinforcement. Indeed, the same dependent variable can be taken as both a measure of choice and of conditioned reinforcement. Before outlining the procedure we should point out its potential strengths and weaknesses.

The procedure is a good one for studying choice between different schedules of reinforcement because, unlike simple concurrent schedules, the measure of choice is not confounded with the rates of responding generated by the schedules chosen. For example, response rates on VR schedules tend to be much higher than on FI schedules. If we took the relative rates of responding on a simple concurrent VR FI schedule as our measure of choice, therefore, we would be stacking the deck in favor of the VR schedule. Such a procedure would be more obviously inappropriate if we were comparing choice between a ratio schedule and a schedule which *required* low rates of responding. Perhaps to avoid such confusion of choice with the response rates generated by the schedules being chosen, Autor developed the concurrent chains procedure diagramed in Figure 6. In this procedure, the organism (normally a pigeon) responds on two concurrently available keys, each illuminated by the same stimulus. Responses on each key occasionally produce another stimulus, correlated with entry into the terminal link of the chain on that key. Entry into the two terminal links generally occurs at the same rate. Once the subject enters one terminal link the other key becomes dark and inoperative. Responses in the presence of the terminal-link stimuli are reinforced with food. In most experiments the initial links are reinstated after the subject obtains a single reinforcement in a terminal link. The independent variable has generally involved some difference in the conditions arranged during the two terminal links. The dependent variable is the measure of choice: the responses in the initial links.

Another advantage of the concurrent chains procedure is that it keeps the number of primary rein-

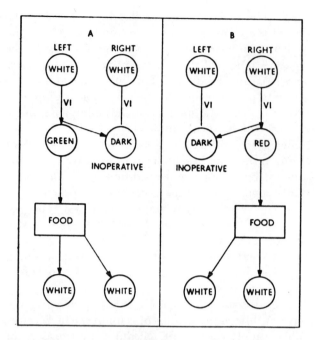

Fig. 6. The concurrent chains procedure. Panel A indicates the sequence of events when responses on the left key are reinforced; panel B presents the analogous sequence on the right key. Responses in the presence of the colored lights (the stimuli of the terminal links) are reinforced with food according to some schedule of reinforcement (generally, the independent variable). The measure of choice is the relative rate of responding in the presence of the concurrently available white lights. Typically, equal VI schedules arrange access to the terminal links. (Adapted from Fantino, 1969b. © 1969 by the Society for the Experimental Analysis of Behavior, Inc.)

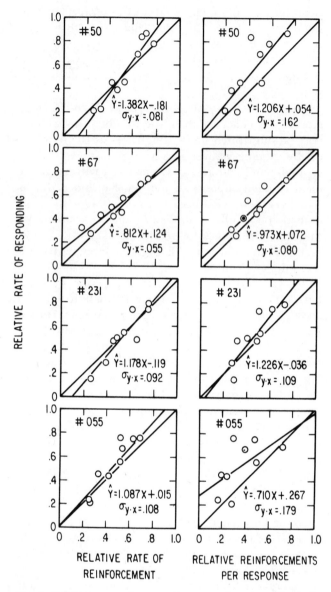

Fig. 7. Relative rate of responding as a function of relative rate of primary reinforcement (left panels) and the relative probability of primary reinforcement (right panels). The diagonal line from the origin to (1.0, 1.0) represents the locus of perfect matching between relative response rates and relative reinforcements. The other line represents the linear regression line through the data points. Each graph shows the calculated linear equation and the standard deviation around the regression line. (Adapted from Herrnstein, 1964a. © 1964 by the Society for the Experimental Analysis of Behavior, Inc.)

forcements for responding on each key close to the number intended by the experimenter over a wide range of preference for pecking one key or the other. If a subject responded exclusively on one key, for example, all primary reinforcements would be delivered on that key. Because of the nature of concurrently available VI schedules, however, the subject produces a higher rate of entry into the terminal links (and typically a higher rate of primary reinforcement) if it responds on both keys. In practice, this assures that the terminal link of each key will be entered equally often, even while the dependent variable—relative response rate in the initial links—is varying over a wide range. Thus the effects of number of reinforcements are not confounded with those of the intended independent variable. The procedure is also useful for studying conditioned reinforcement for two additional reasons. Normally, the effects of a conditioned reinforcer are examined in the absence of primary reinforcement in order to avoid possible confounding between the two reinforcing effects. In the terminal link of concurrent chains, a primary reinforcement schedule can be maintained, and the conditioned reinforcer does not therefore suffer extinction. Secondly, choice situations are known to be very sensitive to experimental manipulations (e.g., Catania, 1963, 1966; Herrnstein, 1961; Rachlin, 1967), and this favors experimental differentiations among the strengths of different conditioned reinforcers.

Most of the work with the concurrent chains procedure has examined the dependence of choice upon parameters of the interreinforcement interval (IRI), the interval between the conditioned reinforcement (i.e., a reinforced choice response) and the unconditioned reinforcement (i.e., food). This is also the material most relevant to our theoretical treatment of conditioned reinforcement and to the integration of results from concurrent chains studies with those from studies of observing responses: both sets of results indicate that the strength of a conditioned reinforcer is determined primarily by the increase in proximity to primary reinforcement correlated with the conditioned reinforcer (the delay reduction hypothesis). We shall not, therefore, discuss other variables which have been shown to affect preference in the concurrent chains procedure such as magnitude of reinforcement (e.g., Schwartz, 1969; Ten Eyck, 1970) or number of reinforcements (Fantino & Herrnstein, 1968; Squires & Fantino, 1971).

Choice with Aperiodic Schedules in Terminal Links

Although all the research we shall summarize supports the notion that choice is determined by the extent of reduction in delay to primary reinforcement correlated with the alternatives, the early work was consistent with a somewhat simpler interpretation which was accepted for nearly a decade. Specifically, both Autor (1960, 1969), using VI, VR, and response-independent schedules in the terminal links, and Herrnstein (1964a), using VI and VR schedules, found that the relative rates of choice responding (the number of initial-link responses on one key divided by the total number of initial-link responses on the two keys) matched the relative rates of reinforcement (the rate of reinforcement on one key divided by the sum of the two rates of reinforcement) in the two terminal links. This relation may be summarized by the following equation:

$$\frac{R_L}{R_L + R_R} = \frac{1/t_{2L}}{1/t_{2L} + 1/t_{2R}} \quad (1)$$

in which R_L and R_R represent the number of responses during the initial links on the left and right keys, respectively, and t_{2L} and t_{2R} represent the average durations of the left and right terminal links.

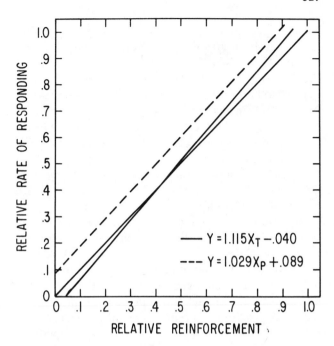

Fig. 8. Average linear regression lines for relative rate of responding during choice phase as a function of the relative rate of reinforcement (solid line crossing the diagonal line) and the relative probability of reinforcement (dashed line). The diagonal line from the origin to (1.0, 1.0) represents the locus of matching between choice and relative reinforcements. The subscripts of X in the equations (T and p) correspond to the independent variables of relative rate (X_T) and relative probability (X_p). (Adapted from Herrnstein, 1964a. © 1964 by the Society for the Experimental Analysis of Behavior, Inc.)

Figures 7 and 8 show Herrnstein's basic results: the relation of choice responding to both the relative rates of reinforcement and the relative reinforcements per response (in the terminal link) for individual birds (Figure 7) and the averaged data (Figure 8). As Figure 8 shows most clearly, choice responding matched relative frequency of reinforcement more closely than relative probability of reinforcement. In this sense, Herrnstein's study went beyond that of Autor in showing that the relative rate of primary reinforcement, rather than its relative probability, controlled the effectiveness of the conditioned reinforcers correlated with the terminal links of concurrent chains.

Fantino (1969a, 1969b) suggested an alternative (now called the delay reduction hypothesis) to Equation 1 which was also consistent with these data. Specifically:

$$\begin{aligned}\frac{R_L}{R_L + R_R} &= \frac{T - t_{2L}}{(T - t_{2L}) + (T - t_{2R})} \quad \text{(when } t_{2L} < T, t_{2R} < T)\\ &= 1 \quad \text{(when } t_{2L} < T, t_{2R} > T) \quad (2)\\ &= 0 \quad \text{(when } t_{2L} > T, t_{2R} < T)\end{aligned}$$

where T represents the average-delay-to-primary reinforcement *from the onset of either initial link* and t_{2L} and t_{2R} again represent the average durations of the left and right terminal links, respectively. Note that when entry into either terminal link produces an *increase* in the average delay to primary reinforcement (either $t_{2L} > T$ or $t_{2R} > T$), Equation 2 requires the organism to emit all its choice responses to the other key. In other words, Equation 2 specifies when the organism should respond exclusively on one key. Of course, the case in which both t_{2L} and t_{2R} are greater than T is impossible.

Equation 2 implies that the relative rate of responding in the initial links matches the reduction in the average delay to primary reinforcement correlated with entry into one terminal link relative to the reduction correlated with entry into the other. In other words, the greater the improvement, in terms of temporal proximity to reinforcement, correlated with the onset of the stimulus, the more effective it will be as a conditioned reinforcer. Like Equation 1, Equation 2 assumes that the conditioned reinforcing effectiveness of a stimulus will be a function of its proximity to primary reinforcement (t_{2L} and t_{2R} in Equations 1 and 2). Unlike Equation 1, Equation 2 requires consideration of the temporal context in which this proximity is embedded. For example, an implication of Equation 1 is that the organism's preference for one conditioned reinforcer over another should be invariant regardless of the rate of entry into the terminal links, at least when the initial links are equal. In particular, if t_{2L} and t_{2R} were equal to 30 and 90 sec, respectively, Equation 1 requires a choice proportion of .75 for t_{2L} regardless of the value of the initial-link schedules. But one may question why the organism should ever choose to enter the longer terminal link (t_{2R}) if it can obtain almost immediate access to the shorter one. The more inaccessible the two terminal-link schedules—i.e., the longer the initial links—the more the organism should be indifferent to their difference, since with very long initial links, entrance into either terminal link should be highly reinforcing (just, as we saw earlier, observing is more frequent the less likely a positive outcome). Specifically, Fantino (1969a) speculated that with sufficiently long initial links, organisms should be indifferent between the different terminal links and that with sufficiently short initial links the organism should respond exclusively to the side leading to the shorter terminal link. If this is true, then only for a particular band of intermediate values should the distribution of choice responses match the distribution of reinforcements obtained in the terminal links (as required by Equation 1). Equation 2 also predicts the circumstances under which the organism should respond exclusively for the shorter terminal link: *When entry into one terminal link fails to bring the organism closer in time to primary reinforcement that terminal link will not be entered.* In terms of conditioned reinforcement, a stimulus that is *not* correlated with a reduction in average delay to reinforcement should not be a conditioned reinforcer regardless of how contiguous the onset of the stimulus may be to primary reinforcement (just as observing is not well maintained by stimuli correlated with positive reinforcement but with a decrease in proximity to reinforcement—e.g., Auge, 1974). Thus when either value of t is greater than T, entry into the longer terminal link actually moves the organism further from primary reinforcement, and the stimulus correlated with entry into that terminal link should not be a conditioned reinforcer.

Since Autor's and Herrnstein's data were consistent with both Equations 1 and 2, Fantino (1969b) tested the two equations by varying T while holding t_L and t_R constant. Specifically, Fantino used three different pairs of identical VI schedules to arrange entry into the two terminal links which were always VI 30-sec and VI 90-sec. When the pair of initial-link schedules of intermediate duration was in effect (VI 120-sec), the choice proportions in the initial links matched the relative rates of reinforcement in the terminal links (Equation 1), a result consistent with both formulations. With shorter or longer initial-link durations, however, the distribution of choice responses no longer matched the relative rates of reinforcement, but continued to be well described by Equation 2. In addition, Fantino utilized two schedules in which both the initial and terminal links were unequal: chain VI 90-sec VI 30-sec vs. chain VI 30-sec VI 90-sec. Choice data from this procedure were also consistent with Equation 2.

The results from this experiment are shown in Table 1. These data show that for 15 out of 16 cases in which Equations 1 and 2 describe different choice proportions, Equation 2 provides a closer fit to the obtained data. Moreover, for each of the 16 points, Equation 2 accounts for the direction of the deviations from Equation 1. Thus for each of the 10 cases in which Equation 2 requires a higher choice proportion than Equation 1, columns (i) and (iv) in section B of Table 1 show that Equation 1 underestimates these proportions. Similarly, for each of the six cases in which Equation 2 requires a lower choice proportion than Equation 1, column (ii) in section B of Table 1 shows that Equation 1 overestimates these proportions. The data in column (iv) in section A of

Table 1 provide partial support for the prediction that the organism will cease responding for entrance into the longer terminal link when such entry moves him further in time from primary reinforcement. This prediction is supported in that there was a very strong preference for the shorter terminal link and, for two of the six birds, exclusive preference was reached.

There is a prediction of Equation 2 that seemed doubtful. Whenever the terminal-link durations t_{2L} and t_{2R} are equal, a choice proportion of .50—i.e., indifference—is required no matter what the initial-link values are, since the two terminal-link stimuli are correlated with the same degree of reduction in average delay to reinforcement. Instead, one might expect that preference would vary with the relative values of the initial links, since the rates of both primary reinforcement, $\left(\dfrac{1}{t_{1L} + t_{2L}} \text{ and } \dfrac{1}{t_{1R} + t_{2R}}\right)$ and conditioned reinforcement $\left(\dfrac{1}{t_{1L}} \text{ and } \dfrac{1}{t_{1R}}\right)$ are different

Table 1*

A. *Proportion of choice responses to key providing higher rate of reinforcement in terminal link for each pigeon in each of four conditions. The average proportion for each condition and the proportions required by Equations 1 and 2 are listed below the line. All VI values listed are in seconds.*

	(i) Chain VI 90 VI 30 vs. chain VI 30 VI 90	(ii) Chain VI 600 VI 30 vs. chain VI 600 VI 90	(iii) Chain VI 120 VI 30 vs. chain VI 120 VI 90	(iv) Chain VI 40 VI 30 vs. chain VI 40 VI 90
Pigeon 1	.97	.66	.74	.93
Pigeon 2	1.00	.56	.77	1.00
Pigeon 3	.83	.63	.87	1.00
Pigeon 4	.98	.63	.70	.89
Pigeon 5	—	.57	.97	.96
Pigeon 6	—	.53	.82	.92
Avg. Proportion	.94	.60	.81	.95
Equation 1	.75	.75	.75	.75
Equation 2	.90	.55	.75	1.00

B. *The deviations of the choice proportions above from the proportions required by Equations 1 and 2 for each pigeon for conditions (i)–(iv). For each of the sixteen points in which Equations 1 and 2 make different predictions, the smaller deviation is underscored. Column (v) on each side gives the mean of the absolute deviations for each pigeon. The means of the absolute deviations for each condition are listed below the line.*

	Equation 1					Equation 2				
	(i)	(ii)	(iii)	(iv)	(v)	(i)	(ii)	(iii)	(iv)	(v)
Pigeon 1	+.22	−.09	−.01	+.18	.12	+.07	+.11	−.01	−.07	.06
Pigeon 2	+.25	−.19	+.02	+.25	.18	+.10	+.01	+.02	0	.03
Pigeon 3	+.08	−.12	+.12	+.25	.14	−.07	+.08	+.12	0	.07
Pigeon 4	+.23	−.12	−.05	+.14	.14	+.08	+.08	−.05	−.11	.08
Pigeon 5	—	−.18	+.22	+.21	.20	—	+.02	+.22	−.04	.09
Pigeon 6	—	−.22	+.07	+.17	.15	—	−.02	+.07	−.08	.06
Mean of absolute deviations	.20	.15	.08	.20	.16	.08	.05	.08	.05	.06

*(From Fantino, 1969b. © 1969 by the Society for the Experimental Analysis of Behavior, Inc.)

for the two keys when the value of the initial-link VI schedules (t_{1L} and t_{1R} on the left and right, respectively) are unequal. Therefore, a critical test of the generality of Equation 2 assesses whether indifference holds when the initial links are unequal for the two keys with t_{2L} equal to t_{2R}.

Squires and Fantino (1971) supplied this test and suggested that an additional variable, which takes into account the rate of primary reinforcement on each key separately, should be incorporated into Equation 2:

$$\frac{R_L}{R_L + R_R} = \frac{r_L(T - t_{2L})}{r_L(T - t_{2L}) + r_R(T - t_{2R})} \quad \text{(when } t_{2L} < T, t_{2R} < T\text{)}$$
$$= 1 \quad \text{(when } t_{2L} < T, t_{2R} > T\text{)} \quad (3)$$
$$= 0 \quad \text{(when } t_{2L} > T, t_{2R} < T\text{)}$$

where $r_L = n_L/(t_{1L} + n_L t_{2L})$, which is the rate of primary reinforcement on the left key (n_L is the number of primary reinforcements obtained during one entry into the terminal link of the chain on the left key); and $r_R = n_R/(t_{1R} + n_R t_{2R})$, the rate of primary reinforcement on the right key. Equation 3 has the additional advantage of predicting matching in choice behavior with concurrent VI schedules (Herrnstein, 1970), i.e., when $t_{2L} = t_{2R}$.

Figure 9 illustrates the predictions made by Equations 1 through 3 in two concurrent chains situations. Figure 9a illustrates the case, studied by Autor (1960), Herrnstein (1964a), and Fantino (1969b), in which the terminal-link schedules are unequal (VI 30-sec and VI 90-sec in the example). Figure 9a shows the predictions made by each of the three equations as the value of the (equal) initial links increases. Figure 9b illustrates the type of schedule studied by Squires and Fantino (1971) in which the two terminal links are equal but the initial links are unequal. While Equations 1 and 2 require choice proportions of .50 regardless of the difference between the two initial links, Equation 3 requires an increase in choice proportions on the key with the constant initial-link VI value as the size of the initial-link VI schedule increases on the other key.

Squires and Fantino's results unequivocally supported Equation 3. Nonetheless, for the sake of clarity, we shall discuss the simpler, unmodified version in this chapter. This is acceptable since Equations 2 and 3 make similar predictions with equal initial links, and since virtually all studies of concurrent chains schedules have used equal initial links.

Thus data from these procedures suggest that the strength of a conditioned reinforcer is a function of the reduction in average delay to reinforcement correlated with one conditioned reinforcer, relative to the reduction in average delay to reinforcement correlated with the other. The delay reduction formulation is also useful in making ordinal predictions for binary choice, i.e., whether one schedule will be preferred to another, when the terminal links consist of schedules other than VIs. This formulation must be restricted largely to VI schedules, however, where precise quantitative predictions are required. These restrictions (which also apply to the reinforcement density formulation represented by Equation 1) depend, in part, on two characteristics of choice. First, short interreinforcement intervals are weighted more heavily than long ones in choice, a fact consistent with the relative contribution to observing behavior made by the more positive stimulus as opposed to either the less positive or negative stimulus. Thus Herrnstein (1964b), using the concurrent chains procedure, found that pigeons strongly preferred a VI schedule with an average interreinforcement interval of 15 sec to an FI 15-sec schedule. Comparable results were reported by Bower et al. (1966), Davison (1969, 1972), Fantino (1967), Hursh and Fantino (1973), Killeen (1968a), and Navarick and Fantino (1975). Since variable schedules are preferred to fixed schedules providing the same reinforcement density (and the same mean delay reduction), an appropriate principle of transforming variable schedules into their fixed equivalents, and vice versa, would be necessary if a single quantitative model were to describe choice proportions for both types of schedules. Choice between two schedules could then be described by first converting the schedules into their VI equivalents and then applying Equation 3. But no adequate general principle of transformation has been found. In the second place, when different types of schedules are arranged in the terminal links of concurrent chains, choice is likely to fail tests of strong stochastic transitivity (Navarick & Fantino, 1972, 1974, 1975). One implication of such intransitivities is that a general principle of transformation *cannot* be found. The issues here are thorny, and the interested reader can find a complete account in Fantino and Navarick (1974). For our present purpose it is sufficient to note

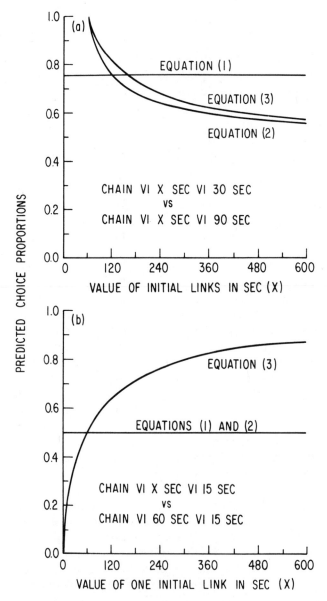

Fig. 9. The predictions of Equations 1, 2, and 3. In (a) the choice proportions (for the VI 30-sec terminal-link schedules) required by the three equations are plotted against the value of the equal initial links (VI X-sec). In (b) the choice proportions for the key with the VI 60-sec schedule in the initial link required by each of the three equations are plotted against the initial-link value on the other key (VI X-sec). (Adapted from Squires & Fantino, 1971. © 1971 by the Society for the Experimental Analysis of Behavior, Inc.)

that the delay reduction hypothesis is consistently superior to the reinforcement density hypothesis in accurately describing choice.

Up to now we have considered only the temporal duration of the terminal links (i.e., t_{2L} and t_{2R}, or what we have called the interreinforcement interval or IRI). Events *during* the IRI also affect choice and would probably affect observing in the same way, as we shall point out, though in most cases this has not been assessed. (In general, I predict that if one stimulus is preferred to another, it should maintain observing responses which change a mixed schedule, composed of both stimuli, to the corresponding multiple schedule.) We consider these effects in the next section.

Events During the Terminal Links

Neuringer (1969), in an interesting concurrent chains experiment, compared choice between reinforcement on an FI schedule and reinforcement after an interval in which the key was dark and inoperative. He found indifference between the FI and the response-independent schedules when the duration of the terminal links was equal. From his own and related data (including Anger, 1956; Autor, 1960; Dews, 1962, 1965; Herrnstein, 1964a; Killeen, 1968b; Neuringer & Schneider, 1968), Neuringer concluded that "these studies, together with the present findings, suggest the following hypothesis: the probability (or rate, or latency) of a response is controlled by the interval between that response and reinforcement (a) independently of the number of other responses intervening in the interval, and (b) independently of whether such intervening responses are required or prohibited" (p. 382).

Others, including Rachlin and Herrnstein (1969) and Schneider (1972) have also suggested that organisms should be indifferent between two terminal links whose overall durations are equal. In other words, given equal initial links, choice proportions should approximate .50 as long as the durations of the terminal links are also equal. This result would be consistent with all the models of choice we have considered thus far. For example, in Neuringer's experiment the stimuli associated with each terminal link are correlated with identical reductions in time to reinforcement. It might seem surprising, however, if choice were so simply and directly dependent on the size of the terminal links (t_{2L} and t_{2R} in Equations 1–3) irrespective of events occurring during them. Indeed, there are important exceptions to this generalization. These are considered in this section.

ADDITION OF STIMULI PAIRED WITH REINFORCEMENT

Schuster (1969) reported an important study testing the notion that stimuli paired with primary reinforcement will serve as conditioned reinforcers. Brief-stimulus presentations paired with primary reinforcement at the end of each terminal link were made available (on an FR 11 schedule) during one of two terminal links. The brief-stimulus presentations were therefore superimposed on the terminal-link food schedule. The main dependent variable was the rate of choice responding in the concurrently available initial links. Rate of primary reinforcement in the two terminal links was identical and was available on VI 30-sec schedules. Therefore, if the stimuli paired with food reinforcement were conditioned reinforcers, the pigeons should prefer to enter the terminal link with the superimposed schedule of brief stimuli. Schuster found that while the superimposed brief stimuli increased response rates in the terminal link, this terminal link "was eventually chosen less often. This result was consistent with a functional analysis, since, on the key with the superimposed schedules, the brief stimuli were correlated more often with nonreinforcement" (p. 234).

As Fantino (1969a), Gollub (1970), and Squires (1972) have observed, Schuster's conclusion is rendered ambiguous by the potential effects of the brief-stimulus presentations on terminal-link response rates. In particular, the high response rates generated by superimposed brief stimuli might have created an aversion for that terminal link which might have masked any conditioned reinforcing effect. Squires (1972) repeated Schuster's experiment in a way that avoids the confounding factor present in the earlier experiment: whereas Schuster had scheduled the superimposed brief stimuli on an FR schedule, Squires scheduled them on a VI. Squires found no consistent preference or aversion for the schedule with superimposed brief-stimulus presentations. Thus when the high rates of terminal-link responding, confounded in Schuster's work with brief-stimulus presentations, are eliminated, a preference for the schedule providing the brief stimuli still fails to develop.

It must be noted, however, that the superimposed brief stimuli are conditioned reinforcers only in the sense of the pairing hypothesis introduced and dismissed earlier. They certainly are not reinforcers in the informational sense (as Schuster rightly pointed out), nor are they correlated with a reduction in average time to reinforcement. Nor are they likely to maintain observing, though this has yet to be assessed.

In any case, although Squires's results are consistent with Neuringer's conclusion that choice is unaffected by events occurring during the IRI, results from three other types of experiments are not.

The Effects of Required Rates of Responding

Fantino (1968) demonstrated that high response rate requirements (such as schedules differentially reinforcing high rates, or DRH) are apparently aversive, at least when compared with a simple FI that provides reinforcement at the same rate and on the same proportion of trials. Other studies, however, have failed to demonstrate the effects of response rates upon choice (for example, Herrnstein, 1964a; Killeen, 1968b, 1971; Neuringer, 1969, discussed above). Moore and Fantino (1975) shed some light on these ostensibly conflicting findings. They noted that studies on the response rate problem fell into three categories: (1) those using aperiodic schedules in which response rates were varied but particular response rates were not required (Herrnstein, 1964a; Killeen, 1968b)—for example, Killeen's pigeons were indifferent between a VI schedule and a comparable response-independent schedule, although large differences in response rates were maintained by the two schedules; (2) those using periodic schedules in which response rates were varied but particular response rates were not required (Neuringer, 1969; Killeen, 1971); and (3) those in which particular response rates were required on periodic schedules (Fantino, 1968). Moore and Fantino examined preference for additional schedules falling into each of the three categories and replicated the prior results: only when particular response rates were required on periodic schedules did subjects choose the schedule without the response rate requirement. In addition, choice was unaffected when particular response rates were required on aperiodic schedules. These results suggested that response requirements influence choice to the extent that responses must be emitted during discriminable periods of nonreinforcement, as in the early portion of a periodic schedule. Moore and Fantino confirmed this notion by showing that pigeons preferred a periodic response-independent schedule to a periodic, response-dependent schedule that included a requirement to respond early in the terminal link even though responding produced reinforcement only later. It is likely that observing would also be maintained by the stimulus of the response-independent schedule, i.e., that subjects would respond to change a mixed into a multiple schedule if one component required responses during discriminable periods of nonreinforcement.

The Effects of Stimulus Sequences

Fantino (1969a) suggested that if two schedules of equal duration were segmented differently, the organism would prefer the one composed of fewer discriminable components. In other words, a simple FI 2X should be preferred to a chain FI X FI X schedule. Duncan and Fantino (1972) support this suggestion, showing that choice for a schedule is substantially reduced by the chaining operation. Their procedure is schematized and their main finding, preference for simple FI schedules over two-link chains with equivalent durations, is shown in Figure 10. Note that the obtained terminal-link durations were close to the scheduled ones (Xs close to .50 in Figure 10b), especially with the longer terminal links, for which the largest preferences were found. Thus these results cannot be explained in terms of reinforcement rates.

Duncan and Fantino (1972) concluded that preference for the simple FI could be attributed either to the additional stimulus or to the additional response requirement associated with the chain FI FI, but that whether the results were due to stimulus or response aspects of the chaining operation (or both), the results pointed to the insufficiency of reinforcement rates (or delay reductions) in determining choice. In order to tease apart the role of stimulus and response aspects of the chaining procedure, one portion of an experiment by Wallace (1973) assessed choice between chain FT X FT X and a simple FT 2X schedule. If stimulus aspects were responsible for the large preferences obtained by Duncan and Fantino, then preferences should be comparable in this procedure which is identical except for the absence of a response requirement in the terminal links. On the other hand, if response factors were sufficient to explain the large preferences obtained by Duncan and Fantino, then the results should reveal indifference between the chain and the simple FT schedules. Wallace found a clear and consistent preference for the simple FT schedule. Nonetheless, preferences were far smaller than they had been in the Duncan and Fantino study. This result suggests that both stimulus and response factors were responsible for the large preferences obtained by Duncan and Fantino (and replicated in a different portion of the Wallace study). It is possible, of course, that response factors are effective only insofar as they increase the degree of stimulus control.

Taken together, these results suggest that choice in the concurrent chains procedure may not be accurately described by considering simply the relative size of the terminal links, if the terminal links are segmented and are arranged according to periodic (as opposed to aperiodic) schedules of reinforcement.[6] Apparently, the initial-link stimulus of a chain FI FI or chain FT FT schedule is a more effective signal that the organism is temporally distant from primary reinforcement than is the stimulus associated with an FI or FT schedule, even though the durations and, therefore, the average delays to primary reinforcement are equal. Apparently, the subjective delay (or the "psychological distance") to primary reinforcement is greater in the segmented schedule. It should be acknowledged that these results not only limit the scope of the delay reduction hypothesis (as well as that of

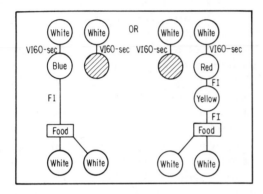

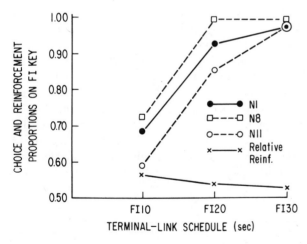

Fig. 10. (Top) Pictorial representation of the experimental procedure used by Duncan and Fantino (1972). The left portion of the figure indicates the sequence of events when responses on the left key were reinforced; the right portion indicates the sequence of events when responses on the right key were reinforced. The terminal links consisted of a simple FI schedule on one of the keys and a chain FI FI schedule on the other key. (Bottom) The mean choice proportions for each bird on the FI key as a function of the size of the intervals in the terminal links. The x's indicate the relative rate of reinforcement on the FI key. (Adapted from Duncan & Fantino, 1972. © 1972 by the Society for the Experimental Analysis of Behavior, Inc.)

[6] Schneider (1972) found no difference between chain and tandem VI schedules. The difference between his finding and that of Duncan and Fantino (1972) and Wallace (1973) is probably due to his use of VI schedules. For a discussion, see Duncan and Fantino (1972).

other formulations of choice in the concurrent chains procedure), but are consistent with the pairing hypothesis, dismissed as inadequate earlier, in the following sense: contiguity with primary reinforcement may sometimes enhance the effectiveness of a conditioned reinforcer. In terms of observing responses, these results suggest that subjects would respond to convert mixed FI 2X (chain FI X FI X) or mixed FT 2X (chain FT X FT X) schedules to their multiple-schedule equivalents. Again, these experiments have not been done.

Differential Discriminative Stimuli in the Terminal Links

Several experimenters have shown that organisms prefer multiple schedules of reinforcement to equivalent mixed schedules (e.g., Bower et al., 1966; Hendry, 1969b; Hursh & Fantino, 1974). Both Bower et al. and Hendry found uniformly large preferences for the multiple schedules. But responding in the initial links in their experiments was reinforced on FR schedules which, unlike concurrent VI schedules, are likely to lead to exclusive responding to one of the concurrent stimuli; this in turn means that most trials ended with the multiple-schedule terminal link. This bias may have contributed to the magnitude of the preference for the multiple schedule. Hursh and Fantino (1974) obtained reliable but much smaller preferences for the multiple schedule with VI 60-sec schedules in the choice phase and showed that the degree of preference could be manipulated by varying the size of the initial-link schedules (i.e., the shorter the choice phase, the larger the preference).

This preference for multiple over mixed schedules can be understood in terms of the well-established finding that the presence of short interreinforcement intervals has a disproportionate influence on choice (Davison, 1969, 1972; Fantino, 1967; Herrnstein, 1964b; Hursh & Fantino, 1973; Killeen, 1968a; Navarick & Fantino, 1975). In mixed schedules of reinforcement, no stimuli correlated with a short delay occur at the beginning of the terminal links, even on that half of the trials in which the shorter delay is scheduled. On multiple schedules, on the other hand, stimuli correlated with the short delay are immediately available on half of the trials. The occurrence of these stimuli are responsible for preference of the multiple schedule over the mixed schedule.

The results reviewed here suggest that even when different terminal links provide the same distribution of interreinforcement intervals, subjects will choose the link in which different stimuli are correlated with differing delays of reinforcement. Such preference, and its interpretation in terms of the reinforcing strength of stimuli correlated with positive outcomes, is consistent with the data and theory on observing responses, reviewed earlier.

Summary

The results considered in the last three sections all suggest that while terminal-link duration (the interreinforcement interval or IRI) is a crucial determinant of choice, events during the IRI must also be considered in any complete account of choice in the concurrent chains procedure. Stated in terms of conditioned reinforcement on periodic schedules, the results from the section on events during the IRI suggest that the strength of a stimulus as a conditioned reinforcer depends not only on the reduction in average delay to reinforcement correlated with its onset but also on whether response rate is constrained in its presence, on the number of additional stimuli intervening between it and primary reinforcement, and on the presence of differential discriminative stimuli in the terminal links (as in the mixed- vs. multiple-schedule comparison). Results from each of the three areas reviewed have been firmly established only with periodic (FR, FI, and FT) schedules, as opposed to aperiodic (VR, VI, and VT) schedules, suggesting the following: since clearly discriminable periods of nonreinforcement are not present in aperiodic schedules, differences between aperiodic schedules are likely to be less salient and to have less effect upon choice than comparable differences between periodic schedules. Thus while the delay reduction hypothesis of conditioned reinforcement is consistent with all of the data from the observing response and concurrent chains literature when only the size of the IRI is manipulated, some events occurring during the IRI must also be considered for a complete account of choice. It is likely that these same events would have comparable effects on observing responses.

CONCLUSIONS

The research on observing behavior suggests that information per se is not reinforcing. While drastically modified versions of the information hypothesis —stressing "good news" only—can be made to fit most of the observing response data, such accounts are often indistinguishable from conditioned reinforcement hypotheses such as the delay reduction hypothesis and the reinforcement density hypothesis. Moreover, the information hypotheses all seem to lack any specification of the importance of temporal variables, which are critical for the maintenance of operant behavior.

A more viable possibility is that organisms will respond to produce stimuli correlated with a reduction in delay to primary reinforcement (whether or not the observing response actually affects time to reinforcement). Studies of choice behavior with the concurrent chains procedure are also consistent with this delay reduction hypothesis: when an organism chooses between two stimuli correlated with different reductions in delay to primary reinforcement, its choice of either stimulus is a monotonic function of the relative reduction in average time to reinforcement correlated with that stimulus. If a stimulus is not correlated with a reduction in delay to primary reinforcement, it will not maintain a significant amount of responding in either the observing response or concurrent chains procedures—i.e., the stimulus will not be a conditioned reinforcer.

REFERENCES

Anger, D. The dependence of interresponse time upon the relative reinforcement of different interresponse times. *Journal of Experimental Psychology,* 1956, *52*, 145–161.

Auge, R. J. Effects of stimulus duration on observing behavior maintained by differential reinforcement magnitude. *Journal of the Experimental Analysis of Behavior,* 1973, *20*, 429–438.

Auge, R. J. Context, observing behavior, and conditioned reinforcement. *Journal of the Experimental Analysis of Behavior,* 1974, *22*, 525–533.

Autor, S. M. *The strength of conditioned reinforcers as a function of frequency and probability of reinforcement.* Unpublished doctoral dissertation, Harvard University, 1960.

Autor, S. M. The strength of conditioned reinforcers as a function of frequency and probability of reinforcement. In D. P. Hendry (Ed.), *Conditioned reinforcement.* Homewood, Ill.: Dorsey Press, 1969.

Berlyne, D. E. Uncertainty and conflict: A point of contact between information theory and behavior theory concepts. *Psychological Review,* 1957, *64*, 329–333.

Berlyne, D. E. *Conflict, arousal, and curiosity.* New York: McGraw-Hill, 1960.

Blanchard, R. The effect of S− on observing behavior. *Learning and Motivation,* 1975, *6*, 1–10.

Bloomfield, T. M. Reinforcement schedules: Contingency or contiguity. In R. M. Gilbert & J. R. Millenson (Eds.), *Reinforcement: Behavioral analysis.* New York: Academic Press, 1972.

Bower, G., McLean, J., & Meacham, J. Value of knowing when reinforcement is due. *Journal of Comparative and Physiological Psychology,* 1966, *62*, 184–192.

Branch, M. N. The distribution of observing responses during two VI schedules. *Psychonomic Science,* 1970, *20*, 5–6.

Byrd, L. D. Responding in the pigeon under chained schedules of food presentation: The repetition of a stimulus during alternate components. *Journal of the Experimental Analysis of Behavior,* 1971, *16*, 31–38.

Catania, A. C. Concurrent performances: Reinforcement interaction and response independence. *Journal of the Experimental Analysis of Behavior,* 1963, *6*, 253–263.

Catania, A. C. Concurrent operants. In W. K. Honig (Ed.), *Operant behavior: Areas of research and application.* Englewood Cliffs, N.J.: Prentice-Hall, Inc., 1966.

Davison, M. Preference for mixed-interval versus fixed-interval schedules. *Journal of the Experimental Analysis of Behavior,* 1969, *12*, 247–252.

Davison, M. Preference for mixed-interval versus fixed-interval schedules: Number of component intervals. *Journal of the Experimental Analysis of Behavior,* 1972, *17*, 169–176.

deLorge, J. The effects of brief stimuli presented under a multiple schedule of second-order schedules. *Journal of the Experimental Analysis of Behavior,* 1971, *15*, 19–25.

Dews, P. B. The effect of multiple S^Δ periods on responding on a fixed-interval schedule. *Journal of the Experimental Analysis of Behavior,* 1962, *5*, 369–374.

Dews, P. B. The effect of multiple S^Δ periods on responding on a fixed-interval schedule, III: Effect of changes in pattern of interruptions, parameters, and stimuli. *Journal of the Experimental Analysis of Behavior,* 1965, *8*, 427–435.

Dinsmoor, J. A., Browne, M. P., & Lawrence, C. E. A test of the negative discriminative stimulus as a reinforcer of observing. *Journal of the Experimental Analysis of Behavior,* 1972, *18*, 79–85.

Dinsmoor, J. A., Browne, M. P., Lawrence, C. E., & Wasserman, E. A. A new analysis of Wyckoff's observing response. *Proceedings of the 79th Annual Convention of the American Psychological Association,* 1971, 679–680. (Summary)

Dinsmoor, J. A., Flint, G. A., Smith, R. F., & Viemeister, N. F. Differential reinforcing effects of stimuli associated with the presence or absence of a schedule of punishment. In D. P. Hendry (Ed.), *Conditioned reinforcement.* Homewood, Ill.: Dorsey Press, 1969.

Duncan, B., & Fantino, E. The psychological distance to reward. *Journal of the Experimental Analysis of Behavior,* 1972, *18*, 23–34.

Eckerman, D. A. Uncertainty reduction and conditioned reinforcement. *Psychological Record,* 1973, *23*, 39–47.

Fantino, E. Preference for mixed- versus fixed-ratio schedules. *Journal of the Experimental Analysis of Behavior,* 1967, *10*, 35–43.

Fantino, E. Effects of required rates of responding upon choice. *Journal of the Experimental Analysis of Behavior,* 1968, *11*, 15–22.

Fantino, E. Conditioned reinforcement, choice, and the psychological distance to reward. In D. P. Hendry (Ed.), *Conditioned reinforcement.* Homewood, Ill.: Dorsey Press, 1969. (a)

Fantino, E. Choice and rate of reinforcement. *Journal of the Experimental Analysis of Behavior,* 1969, *12*, 723–730. (b)

Fantino, E. Aversive control. In J. A. Nevin & G. S. Reynolds (Eds.), *The study of behavior.* Glenview, Ill.: Scott, Foresman, 1973.

Fantino, E., & Herrnstein, R. J. Secondary reinforcement

and number of primary reinforcements. *Journal of the Experimental Analysis of Behavior*, 1968, *11*, 9–14.

Fantino, E., & Navarick, D. Recent developments in choice. In G. H. Bower (Ed.), *The psychology of learning and motivation* (Vol. 8). New York: Academic Press, 1974.

Gollub, L. R. Information on conditioned reinforcement. A review of *Conditioned reinforcement* (D. P. Hendry, Ed.). *Journal of the Experimental Analysis of Behavior*, 1970, *14*, 361–372.

Hendry, D. P. *Reinforcing value of information.* NASA Technical Report 65-1. Space Research Laboratory, University of Maryland, 1965.

Hendry, D. P. (Ed.). *Conditioned reinforcement.* Homewood, Ill.: Dorsey Press, 1969. (a)

Hendry, D. P. Introduction. In D. P. Hendry (Ed.), *Conditioned reinforcement.* Homewood, Ill.: Dorsey Press, 1969. (b)

Hendry, D. P. Reinforcing value of information: Fixed-ratio schedules. In D. P. Hendry (Ed.), *Conditioned reinforcement.* Homewood, Ill.: Dorsey Press, 1969. (c)

Herrnstein, R. J. Relative and absolute strength of response as a function of reinforcement. *Journal of the Experimental Analysis of Behavior*, 1961, *4*, 267–272.

Herrnstein, R. J. Secondary reinforcement and the rate of primary reinforcement. *Journal of the Experimental Analysis of Behavior*, 1964, *7*, 27–36. (a)

Herrnstein, R. J. Aperiodicity as a factor in choice. *Journal of the Experimental Analysis of Behavior*, 1964, *7*, 179–182. (b)

Herrnstein, R. J. On the law of effect. *Journal of the Experimental Analysis of Behavior*, 1970, *13*, 243–266.

Hull, C. L. *Principles of Behavior.* New York: Appleton-Century-Crofts, 1943.

Hursh, S. R., & Fantino, E. Relative delay of reinforcement and choice. *Journal of the Experimental Analysis of Behavior*, 1973, *19*, 437–450.

Hursh, S. R., & Fantino, E. An appraisal of preference for multiple *versus* mixed schedules. *Journal of the Experimental Analysis of Behavior*, 1974, *22*, 31–38.

Jenkins, H. M., & Boakes, R. A. Observing stimulus sources that signal food or no food. *Journal of the Experimental Analysis of Behavior*, 1973, *20*, 197–207.

Kelleher, R. T. Stimulus producing responses in chimpanzees. *Journal of the Experimental Analysis of Behavior*, 1958, *1*, 87–102.

Kelleher, R. T. Chaining and conditioned reinforcement. In W. K. Honig (Ed.), *Operant behavior: Areas of research and application.* Englewood Cliffs, N.J.: Prentice-Hall, Inc., 1966.

Kelleher, R. T., & Gollub, L. R. A review of positive conditioned reinforcement. *Journal of the Experimental Analysis of Behavior*, 1962, *5*, 543–597.

Keller, F. S., & Schoenfeld, W. N. *Principles of psychology.* New York: Appleton-Century-Crofts, 1950.

Kendall, S. B. Effects of informative stimuli with multiple delays of reinforcement. *Psychonomic Science*, 1972, *29*, 41–42.

Kendall, S. B. Redundant information in an observing-response procedure. *Journal of the Experimental Analysis of Behavior*, 1973, *19*, 81–92. (a)

Kendall, S. B. Effects of two procedures for varying information transmission on observing responses. *Journal of the Experimental Analysis of Behavior*, 1973, *20*, 73–83. (b)

Kendall, S. B., & Gibson, D. A. Effects of discriminative stimulus removal on observing behavior. *The Psychological Record*, 1965, *15*, 545–551.

Killeen, P. On the measure of reinforcement frequency in the study of preference. *Journal of the Experimental Analysis of Behavior*, 1968, *11*, 263–269. (a)

Killeen, P. Response rate as a factor in choice. *Psychonomic Science*, 1968, *12*, 34. (b)

Killeen, P. Response patterns as a factor in choice. *Psychonomic Science*, 1971, *22*, 23–24.

Lieberman, D. A. Secondary reinforcement and information as determinants of observing behavior in monkeys (*Macaca mulatta*). *Learning and Motivation*, 1972, *3*, 341–358.

Malagodi, E. F., DeWeese, J., & Johnston, J. M. Second-order schedules: A comparison of chained, brief-stimulus, and tandem procedures. *Journal of the Experimental Analysis of Behavior*, 1973, *20*, 447–460.

McMichael, J. S., Lanzetta, J. T., & Driscoll, J. Infrequent reward facilitates observing responses in rats. *Psychonomic Science*, 1967, *8*, 23–24.

McMillan, J. C. Average uncertainty as a determinant of observing behavior. *Journal of the Experimental Analysis of Behavior*, 1974, *22*, 401–408.

Moore, J., & Fantino, E. Choice and response contingencies. *Journal of the Experimental Analysis of Behavior*, 1975, *23*, 339–347.

Mulvaney, D. E., Dinsmoor, J. A., Jwaideh, A. R., & Hughes, L. H. Punishment of observing by the negative discriminative stimulus. *Journal of the Experimental Analysis of Behavior*, 1974, *21*, 37–44.

Navarick, D. J., & Fantino, E. Transitivity as a property of choice. *Journal of the Experimental Analysis of Behavior*, 1972, *18*, 389–401.

Navarick, D. J., & Fantino, E. Stochastic transitivity and unidimensional behavior theories. *Psychological Review*, 1974, *81*, 426–441.

Navarick, D. J., & Fantino, E. Stochastic transitivity and the unidimensional control of choice. *Learning and Motivation*, 1975, *6*, 179–201.

Neuringer, A. J. Delayed reinforcement *versus* reinforcement after a fixed interval. *Journal of the Experimental Analysis of Behavior*, 1969, *12*, 375–383.

Neuringer, A. J., & Chung, S. Quasi-reinforcement: Control of responding by a percentage reinforcement schedule. *Journal of the Experimental Analysis of Behavior*, 1967, *10*, 45–54.

Neuringer, A. J., & Schneider, B. A. Separating the effects of interreinforcement time and number of interreinforcement responses. *Journal of the Experimental Analysis of Behavior*, 1968, *11*, 661–667.

Nevin, J. A. Conditioned reinforcement. In J. A. Nevin & G. S. Reynolds (Eds.), *The study of behavior.* Glenview, Ill.: Scott, Foresman, 1973.

Prokasy, W. F. The acquisition of observing responses in the absence of differential external reinforcement. *Journal of Comparative and Physiological Psychology*, 1956, *49*, 131–134.

Rachlin, H. The effect of shock intensity on concurrent and single-key responding in concurrent-chain schedules. *Journal of the Experimental Analysis of Behavior*, 1967, *10*, 87–93.

Rachlin, H., & Herrnstein, R. J. Hedonism revisited: On the negative law of effect. In B. Campbell & R. M. Church (Eds.), *Punishment and aversive behavior*. Englewood Cliffs, N.J.: Prentice-Hall, Inc., 1969.

Rescorla, R. A. Pavlovian conditioning and its proper control procedures. *Psychological Review*, 1967, 74, 71–80.

Rescorla, R. A. Probability of shock in the presence and absence of CS in fear conditioning. *Journal of Comparative and Physiological Psychology*, 1968, 66, 1–5.

Rescorla, R. A. Informational variables in Pavlovian conditioning. In G. Bower (Ed.), *The psychology of learning and motivation* (Vol. 6). New York: Academic Press, 1972.

Schaub, R. E. Response-cue contingency and cue effectiveness. In D. P. Hendry (Ed.), *Conditioned reinforcement*. Homewood, Ill.: Dorsey Press, 1969.

Schaub, R. E., & Honig, W. K. Reinforcement of behavior with cues correlated with extinction. *Psychonomic Science*, 1967, 1, 15–16.

Schneider, J. W. Choice between two-component chained and tandem schedules. *Journal of the Experimental Analysis of Behavior*, 1972, 18, 54–60.

Schuster, R. H. A functional analysis of conditioned reinforcement. In D. P. Hendry (Ed.), *Conditioned reinforcement*. Homewood, Ill.: Dorsey Press, 1969.

Schwartz, B. Effects of reinforcement magnitude on pigeon's preference for different fixed-ratio schedules of reinforcement. *Journal of the Experimental Analysis of Behavior*, 1969, 12, 253–259.

Shannon, C. E., & Weaver, W. *The mathematical theory of communication*. Urbana: University of Illinois Press, 1949.

Squires, N. K. *Preference for conjoint schedules of primary reinforcement and brief-stimulus presentation*. Unpublished doctoral dissertation, University of California, San Diego, 1972.

Squires, N., & Fantino, E. A model for choice in simple concurrent and concurrent-chains schedules. *Journal of the Experimental Analysis of Behavior*, 1971, 15, 27–38.

Squires, N., Norborg, J., & Fantino, E. Second-order schedules: Discrimination of components. *Journal of the Experimental Analysis of Behavior*, 1975, 24, 157–171.

Steiner, J. Observing responses and uncertainty reduction, II: The effect of varying the probability of reinforcement. *Quarterly Journal of Experimental Psychology*, 1970, 22, 592–599.

Stubbs, A. D. Second-order schedules and the problem of conditioned reinforcement. *Journal of the Experimental Analysis of Behavior*, 1971, 16, 289–313.

Stubbs, A. D., & Cohen, S. L. Second-order schedules: Comparison of different procedures for scheduling paired and non-paired brief stimuli. *Journal of the Experimental Analysis of Behavior*, 1972, 18, 403–413.

Taus, S. E., & Hearst, E. Effects of intertrial (blackout) duration on response rate to a positive stimulus. *Psychonomic Science*, 1970, 19(5), 265–267.

Ten Eyck, R. L. Effects of rate of reinforcement-time upon concurrent operant performance. *Journal of the Experimental Analysis of Behavior*, 1970, 14, 269–274.

Wallace, R. F. *Conditioned reinforcement and choice*. Unpublished doctoral dissertation, University of California, San Diego, 1973.

Wiener, N. *Cybernetics*. New York: Wiley, 1948.

Wilton, R. N. The role of information in the emission of observing responses and partial reinforcement acquisition phenomena. *Learning and Motivation*, 1972, 3, 479–499.

Wilton, R. N., & Clements, R. O. Observing responses and informative stimuli. *Journal of the Experimental Analysis of Behavior*, 1971, 15, 199–204. (a)

Wilton, R. N., & Clements, R. O. The role of information in the emission of observing responses: A test of two hypotheses. *Journal of the Experimental Analysis of Behavior*, 1971, 16, 161–166. (b)

Wyckoff, L. B., Jr. The role of observing responses in discrimination learning. *Psychological Review*, 1952, 59, 431–442.

Wyckoff, L. B., Jr. Toward a quantitative theory of secondary reinforcement. *Psychological Review*, 1959, 69, 68–78.

Wyckoff, L. B., Jr. The role of observing responses in discrimination learning. In D. P. Hendry (Ed.), *Conditioned reinforcement*. Homewood, Ill.: Dorsey Press, 1969.

Zimmerman, J. Meanwhile . . . back at the key: Maintenance of behavior by conditioned reinforcement and response-independent primary reinforcement. In D. P. Hendry (Ed.), *Conditioned reinforcement*. Homewood, Ill.: Dorsey Press, 1969.

Zimmerman, J., & Hanford, P. V. Sustaining behavior with conditioned reinforcement as the only response-produced consequence. *Psychological Reports*, 1966, 19, 391–401.

Zimmerman, J., & Hanford, P. V. Differential effects on extinction of behaviors maintained by concurrent schedules of primary and conditioned reinforcement. *Psychonomic Science*, 1968, 8, 103–104.

12

Conditioned Suppression and the Effects of Classical Conditioning on Operant Behavior

Derek Blackman

INTRODUCTION

A defining feature of studies of classical conditioning is that the delivery of stimuli and the relationship between them are controlled by the experimenter independently of a subject's behavior (Black & Prokasy, 1972, p. xi). Pavlov (1927) was, of course, the first systematically to investigate the effects of such procedures on behavior. He presented one event (the conditioned stimulus: CS) regularly in a fixed temporal relationship with a second event (the unconditioned stimulus: US) which reliably elicited a response (the unconditioned response: UR). He found that eventually the CS came to produce behavior (the conditioned response: CR) which was similar to the UR. Pavlov's measures of this conditioning of an acquired reflex were simple but adequate. For example, when the UR was salivation caused by an irritant placed on the tongue, the CR was measured in terms of the number of drops of saliva resulting from the presentations of the CS. In this way conditioned responses were measured as they developed from a zero value on the first presentations of the CS to an asymptotic value when the stimulus was repeatedly presented with the US.

This chapter considers the effects of procedures of this nature in which events which signal the delivery of a US such as food or a shock are presented independently of an animal's behavior. However, the discussion is confined to experiments in which the effects are measured by the changes they produce in behavior which is maintained by response-dependent reinforcement. The dependent variable in such studies is provided by a comparison of the frequency with which *operant* responses are emitted during the Pavlovian CS and in its absence. A typical experimental situation is shown in diagramatic form in Figure 1. The top line shows the presentation of a continuous stimulus (e.g., a light) which is associated with a schedule of reinforcement. The fourth line shows the operant responses (e.g., lever presses) which are emitted during this discriminative stimulus, and the bottom line depicts the delivery of resultant response-dependent reinforcers according to an intermittent schedule, such as a variable-interval schedule. During the discriminative stimulus, and therefore while the subject is emitting operant responses, a second stimulus, such as a tone, is presented: this is shown in the second line of Figure 1. This second stimulus signals the delivery of a Pavlovian US such as electric shock (third line). The sec-

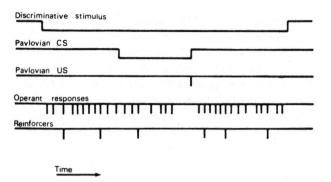

Fig. 1. Diagram representing typical experimental arrangements in the studies discussed in this chapter.

ond and third lines therefore depict in this case a typical Pavlovian delayed conditioning procedure, which is superimposed on a situation in which operant behavior is maintained by occasional reinforcement. The only behavioral measure in this experiment is provided by the operant responses depicted in Figure 1. This is the case in most of the experiments discussed in this chapter, although in some studies *additional* measures are taken of autonomic activity (respondent behaviors) which occur during the CS or after the US, such as changes in heart rate.

The experiments to be discussed differ from conventional classical conditioning experiments, then, in two important ways. First, the behavioral measures are provided by operant rather than by traditional respondent behavior. Second, when the Pavlovian CS is presented, the subject is at that time emitting a pattern of behavior which is recognized (and controlled) by the experimenter. These differences in emphasis have not, however, prevented the collection of data of considerable importance for classical conditioning. Moreover, such experiments have brought a number of theoretical issues into sharp focus.

Clearly, there are many different interactions which may be studied within the general procedure discussed above. As Rescorla and Solomon (1967) have pointed out, the operant behavior may be maintained by a schedule of positive or of negative reinforcement, and the Pavlovian US may be either appetitive or aversive. These various interactions will be reviewed in this chapter. However, most of the research conducted in this area has studied the effects of an aversive US (specifically, shock) with the Pavlovian procedure introduced when operant behavior is maintained by schedules of food or water reinforcement. It is here that the most developed theoretical implications are to be found, and it is this area of research and discussion to which we therefore turn first. No attempt will be made in this chapter to provide a comprehensive review of the truly vast body of literature reporting experiments in which Pavlovian procedures have been superimposed on operant behavior. The discussion is deliberately and strenuously selective, in the hope that general principles and problems may emerge more directly and more clearly.

THE ESTES-SKINNER PROCEDURE AND THE MEASUREMENT OF ITS EFFECTS

In 1941 Estes and Skinner reported the results of a study in which they exposed rats to an intermittent schedule of food reinforcement which would now be described as fixed-interval (FI) 4 min. When the rats' lever-pressing behavior had stabilized, a tone was presented for a period of 3 min (5 min in later conditions). As each period of tone ended, an unavoidable and inescapable shock was delivered to the rats through the grid floor. The delivery of both tone and shock was programmed independently of the rats' behavior, and the temporal relation between them makes it possible to term the procedure classical conditioning: the tone is thus a Pavlovian CS and the shock is a US. Unfortunately, the intensity of the shock was not reported in this early paper, but it must have been relatively mild because Estes and Skinner mentioned that it produced no noticeable disturbance in operant behavior when it was first delivered. However, as the repeated pairings of tone and shock continued, behavior during the tone became disrupted. The rate of responding during the tone fell until it was about one-third the rate during the same period "in control experiments." This is illustrated by cumulative records taken during the experiment, which show clearly the decrease in operant response rate during the period of tone in comparison with rates before and after the tone. The general finding that food-reinforced operant behavior decreases in frequency during a preshock stimulus has since been widely replicated in many different experimental conditions. The effect is sometimes called *conditioned suppression* (see detailed reviews by Davis, 1968, and Lyon, 1968). It is illustrated by the segments of cumulative record shown in Figure 2 (from Blackman, 1974) which show the operant behavior of a rat exposed to a variable-interval (VI) 30-sec schedule of food reinforcement, the delivery of which is shown by brief hatchmarks in the usual way. In the middle of successive 7-min periods, an auditory stimulus was presented for 1 min, during the whole of which time the pen on the cumulative recorder was deflected downward, although it could still be stepped across the paper by an operant response.

At the end of each of these 1-min periods, a very brief shock was delivered. The record at the top of Figure 2 shows that the responding maintained by the VI schedule was completely eliminated during the preshock signal, for the record is horizontal during the 1-min deflection. Immediately after the shock, the animal resumed the steady rate of operant responding maintained by the schedule. The lower segment of the record shows that during another two 1-min periods of the noise the rat did not stop responding completely, although the response rate was lower during the noise than in its absence. Since the VI schedule remained in operation during these periods, responses might still occasionally be followed by a reinforcer (shown by a brief *upward* hatchmark on the record). Figure 2 therefore depicts complete conditioned suppression (top) and partial conditioned suppression (bottom) of operant behavior during a CS (noise) terminated by a US (shock).

In this area of research, it has been generally accepted that an appropriate measurement is a comparison between response rates during a CS and in its absence rather than the absolute reduction of response rates during the CS. This measurement is achieved by means of a *suppression ratio* or *inflection ratio,* but unfortunately there has been no general agreement about the best way to make this calculation. One simple method is to present the rate during the CS as a direct proportion of a control rate of responding (e.g., Stein, Sidman, & Brady, 1958). In this case, complete conditioned suppression is depicted by a ratio of 0; if there is no effect on response rate attributable to the CS, the suppression ratio is 1.0, and if the response rate *increases* during the CS, the ratio is greater than 1.0. However, another widely used ratio (e.g., Kamin, 1965; Rescorla, 1968) expresses the rate during the CS as a proportion of the sum of control and CS response rates. This results in a figure of 0 for complete suppression, .5 for no suppression, and greater than .5 for acceleration of responding during a CS. The use of these different calculations, and of others, is a potential confusion in this area of research (see Lyon, 1968). Moreover, as will be discussed later, the use of any relative rate measure such as these is not without its problems (Lea & Morgan, 1972).

INVESTIGATIONS OF CLASSICAL CONDITIONING PARAMETERS

Many investigators have found that the amount of conditioned suppression (however the suppression ratio is calculated) is a function of conventional parameters in classical conditioning (Davis, 1968). To mention two simple examples, Annau and Kamin (1961) showed that the amount of conditioned suppression in rats is an increasing monotonic function of the intensity of the shock US, and Kamin and Schaub (1963) have shown a similar effect of the intensity of the CS. Rescorla and Solomon (1967) have suggested that "it might very well turn out that instrumental responding is as sensitive, or perhaps even more sensitive, a measure of the effects of Pavlovian conditioning procedures than are the traditionally measured conditioned visceral or motor reflexes themselves." Although Rescorla and Solomon considered this possibility "somewhat ironic," it is certainly true that the conditioned suppression paradigm has been widely and successfully used in order to develop our understanding of classical procedures in general. Reviewing a great deal of such work carried out in his own laboratory, Kamin (1965) has claimed that "we are measuring respondent behavior indirectly, with a surprising quantitative sensitivity." It is not possible to review here the large body of literature in this tradition. However, as one example of current work,

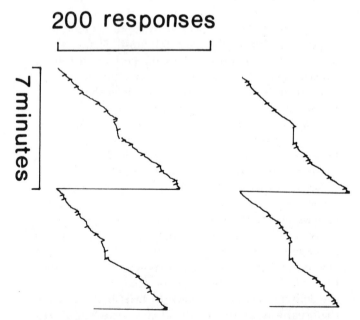

Fig. 2. Cumulative records illustrating the effects on operant behavior of a stimulus ending with an unavoidable shock (conditioned suppression). The response pen is offset during the preshock stimulus; hatchmarks denote reinforcement.

Rescorla's investigations of the necessary and sufficient conditions for a stimulus to become a classical conditioned stimulus may be cited.

Rescorla's important work grew out of his theoretical discussion of the appropriate control procedures for Pavlovian conditioning (Rescorla, 1967). In this paper, he suggested that conventional procedures did not allow for the measurement of appropriate base lines against which to assess accurately the strengths of a conditioned response developed by Pavlovian procedures. For example, in some experiments the stimulus which becomes the conditioned stimulus has first been presented in such a way that it is explicitly never paired with the unconditioned stimulus. The temporal contingency between the CS and the US is then introduced in the conditioning phase of the experiment. Rescorla argued that traditional control procedures such as this fail to provide an unconfounded measure of the effects of the experimental contingency between the stimuli. He suggested that the only way in which this could be achieved was by means of what he termed a "truly random" control procedure. With this control procedure, the stimulus which is to become the CS and the US are first presented at the frequencies to be used in the conditioning phase, but entirely independently; it is therefore possible for them to be occasionally presented together *by chance*. Hence occasional contiguity between the two stimuli may occur, but no reliable contingency exists between them at this stage of the experiment.

Rescorla's empirical work has subsequently developed these ideas. He has shown, for example, that mere contiguity between two stimuli is in fact not sufficient for Pavlovian conditioning to develop. If a stimulus is to become a CS and thus elicit a CR, it now seems that it must, in simple terms, provide a subject with "information" about the occurrence of the US. In his truly random control, the occurrence of a CS provides no information about the occurrence of a US, for the probability of a US is the same both when a CS is presented and when it is not. On the other hand, in traditional delayed conditioning experiments, the occurrence of a CS provides information that a US is about to be presented; moreover, no US is presented without a preceding CS. One of Rescorla's elegant experiments (1968) has used the conditioned suppression paradigm to investigate the effects of these and of various intermediate relationships between a CS and a US, and its results are summarized in Figure 3. The CS was a 2-min presentation of a tone, and the US was shock. Small groups of rats were exposed to various relationships between these stimuli. The probability of a shock in a period

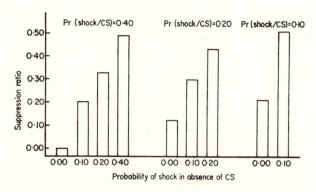

Fig. 3. Median suppression ratios for groups of rats as a function of the probability of shock in the presence and absence of the CS. A ratio of 0.00 denotes complete suppression, and .50 shows that the CS has no effect. (From Mackintosh, 1974, after Rescorla, 1968.)

of tone was specified for different groups as .40, .20, .10, or 0 (i.e., no shocks were delivered). Within these groups, subgroups of animals were exposed to varying probabilities of shock in periods when the tone was absent. Rescorla then measured the effects of the tone after these training conditions by superimposing the tone (without shocks) on food-reinforced operant behavior and measuring its disruptive effects. The dependent variable was expressed as a median suppression ratio, this being calculated by the formula which yields a ratio of 0 for complete conditioned suppression and .5 for no disruptive effect. Figure 3 shows the effects of the tone on the first day on which it was superimposed on the operant behavior of the various groups (four presentations for each rat). If the probability of a shock was the same both in the presence and the absence of a tone (Rescorla's truly random procedure), the tone had no suppressive effect. Thus suppression ratios are consistently at a value of approximately .5 whether the probability of a shock in the presence and in the absence of the tone was .40, .20, or .10. On the other hand, if shocks had initially occurred *only* during a period of tone (so that the probability of shock in the absence of the tone was 0), the tone caused relatively severe suppression of operant behavior. The amount of this suppression increases with greater probabilities of shock *during* the tone, for when the probability of shock in the tone was .10, .20, or .40, suppression ratios were approximately .20, .10, and 0 respectively. Figure 3 shows, then, that the tone suppressed operant behavior to the extent that it had been differentially associated with the occurrence of a shock, that is, in proportion to the difference between the probability of shock during the tone and its probability in the absence of the tone. The degree of classical conditioning increased as the probability of the US during the CS became greater than the probability of the US in the absence of the CS, and not simply as the former value increased.

Rescorla has developed his account of the necessary and sufficient conditions for classical conditioning far beyond the basic idea indicated above (see, for example, Rescorla, 1969; Rescorla & Wagner, 1972), but it is not necessary to provide a more complete description here. Rescorla's important work on classical conditioning is based closely on his use of the conditioned suppression procedure. This procedure makes it possible to measure behavior (in the form of operant response rates) throughout both non-CS and CS periods, whatever the probability of the US in either of them. The demands for a sensitive and reliable dependent variable to show the effects of the quantitative differences in Rescorla's independent variables is met by the indirect measurement of classical conditioning through the frequency of *operant* responses.

Our understanding of classical conditioning procedures has therefore been significantly advanced by studies of their effects on operant behavior. The examples discussed here are representative of a very large body of research which has been carried out within this general strategy, and they illustrate its contemporary impact. The procedure has consistently proved to be robust, reliable, and sensitive, and so any inherent ironies may surely be readily tolerated by researchers in the field of classical conditioning.

INVESTIGATIONS OF OPERANT CONDITIONING PARAMETERS

In the research discussed in the previous section, the emphasis was placed on the way in which the processes of classical conditioning may be investigated by means of conditioned suppression procedures. The operant behavior which provides the only dependent variable in these studies is usually maintained by a simple schedule of intermittent reinforcement. Typically, a variable-interval schedule is used for this purpose, for, of course, such schedules maintain operant behavior over considerable periods of time, and the generally moderate and consistent rates of responding which they generate make it easy for the experimenter to measure any suppressive effect of a CS (as in Figure 2, for example). Also, of course, partial suppression of behavior maintained by a variable-interval schedule may have only minimal effects on the frequency of reinforcement obtained. If the operant behavior of the subjects in various experimental groups is controlled by an identical procedure, we have seen that it is indeed possible to further the analysis of the necessary and sufficient conditions for classical conditioning to occur and to measure its strength as a function of specified independent variables. However, the amount of conditioned suppression during a preshock stimulus is not determined solely by such Pavlovian variables as the parameters of the conditioned and unconditioned stimuli and the contingencies between them. In this section other important variables are discussed which are related to the maintenance of the operant response on which the classical conditioning procedure is imposed.

Anything which affects the nature or strength of operant behavior may also affect the amount of disruption produced by a specified conditioned stimulus when it is superimposed on that behavior. This is perhaps not surprising, since conditioned suppression can be regarded as the result of pitting classical against operant conditioning effects. An important study which emphasizes this was reported by Stein, Sidman, and Brady (1958), who investigated the effects of varying the duration of a preshock stimulus through a range of 30 sec to 50 min and also examined the effects of varying the interval between successive stimulus presentations. Considerable variation was found in the amount of conditioned suppression produced by different combinations of these variables. However, neither of them proved to be a critical determinant in itself: instead, there was a high negative correlation between the amount of suppression and the *relative* duration of the preshock stimulus, i.e., the proportion of time in any session during which the CS was present. In considering ways in which this somewhat abstract temporal value might control the amount of conditioned suppression, Stein et al. noted that the behavior of the rats in their study was suppressed only to the extent that they did not thereby miss more than 10% of the total number of reinforcements which could be set up by the VI schedule. So, when a preshock stimulus (of any duration) was present for a relatively high proportion of the experimental session, complete suppression of operant behavior would have produced a substantial reduction in the number of reinforcements obtained. In these situations, only partial suppression of behavior was observed during the preshock stimulus. However, if a relatively short preshock stimulus was presented only rarely, the subjects could "afford" to suppress completely and yet still obtain at least 90% of the total possible reinforcers, and indeed complete suppression was observed in such situations.

Carlton and Didamo (1960) reported a study based

on that of Stein et al. (1958), but they varied the length of their experimental sessions so that the number of reinforcers actually obtained by subjects was constant throughout the various conditions of the experiment. Again it was found that the amount of conditioned suppression decreased as the relative duration of the preshock stimulus increased. Carlton and Didamo suggested that this reduction in the suppressive effect was due to "changes in response output which minimise the decline in reinforcement rate." This suggestion implies that behavior which is reinforced only occasionally will be less resistant to the suppressive effects of a preshock stimulus, for a "decline in reinforcement rate" resulting from suppression during a fixed preshock stimulus might not be so readily detected. An experiment by Lyon (1964) supports this hypothesis. Using pigeons as subjects, Lyon superimposed a preshock stimulus on both components of a multiple schedule in which two frequencies of reinforcement were programmed (*mult VI 1-min VI 4-min*). It was found that the pigeons' behavior was more suppressed during the preshock stimulus when it was superimposed on the lower frequency of reinforcement than when it occurred during the component with the higher reinforcement frequency. Lyon therefore suggested that behavior which is reinforced relatively frequently is more resistant to disruption by a conditioned suppression procedure than is behavior which is reinforced only rarely. This has been corroborated by Blackman (1968b), who used response-pacing procedures (Ferster & Skinner, 1957) which controlled responding at approximately equal rates in two components of a multiple schedule, but in which the frequencies of reinforcement were controlled by two different VI schedules. This made it possible to identify the effects of reinforcement frequency on conditioned suppression more unequivocally than did Lyon's (1964) study, for in the latter the different frequencies of reinforcement produced different control response rates, a possible confounding effect.

If the conditioned suppression phenomenon is conceptualized as the outcome of a competition between a classically conditioned response with a fixed strength and the tendency to emit operant responses which are occasionally reinforced, the relative resistance of behaviors which result in frequent reinforcement may not seem surprising. Less predictable, however, is the finding that, when reinforcement frequency is controlled, rates of responding are differentially susceptible to conditioned suppression during a preshock stimulus. Blackman has shown in a series of experiments (1966, 1967, 1968b) that high rates of responding are more suppressed during a preshock stimulus than are lower rates which obtain the same frequency of reinforcement. This conclusion was prompted by suppression ratios, but since these are relative measures of the responding during a preshock stimulus, it seemed possible that the differences in suppression ratio might have been merely artifacts of the different base line response rates. For example, if the absolute number of responses emitted during a preshock stimulus was constant whatever the base line response rates, then suppression ratios would inevitably suggest less suppression in the condition in which the preshock stimulus was superimposed on the lower rate. This was not the case, however. For example, in many conditions the absolute response rates during a preshock stimulus were higher when it was superimposed on the lower control rate than when it was superimposed on the higher control rate (Blackman, 1968b, Table 6). So, for example, one subject (rat 1) emitted 89 responses per min in the control conditions of one component (A) of a multiple schedule and 36 responses per min in the control conditions of the other component (B). The schedules in both components provided 2 reinforcements per min on average, but different response-pacing requirements were in operation in each component. During a 1-min period of tone which ended with a .5-mA shock the suppression ratios (response rate during CS divided by response rate in absence of CS) for this rat were .04 on component A and .60 on component B. These ratios reflected a mean rate of 5 responses per min in the preshock stimulus when it was superimposed on component A (high control rate) and 22 responses per min during the same preshock stimulus when it was superimposed on component B (lower control rate). Hence the relative differences in control response rates were reversed during the preshock stimulus, which supports the view based on suppression ratios that lower rates of responding are more resistant to disruption by a preshock stimulus than are higher rates.

The amount of conditioned suppression depends in part, then, on the frequency of reinforcement and on the rate of operant responding. The effects of classical conditioning procedures may therefore be dependent on the schedule of reinforcement on which they are superimposed. The importance of schedules in determining the behavioral effects of other independent variables requires no emphasis here, for it has been demonstrated in many other contexts, such as the effects of drugs (e.g., Kelleher & Morse, 1968) and the effects of unsignaled aversive stimuli (e.g., McKearney, 1972).

The effects of conditioned suppression procedures

have now been investigated with all the principal schedules of reinforcement. Lyon and Felton (1966a) studied pigeons' behavior maintained by variable-ratio (VR) schedules. They had expected that as the mean ratio requirement was increased from 50 to 100 to 200, the subjects would show more conditioned suppression, because the overall frequency of reinforcement would fall. In fact, however, the results of their experiment were inconclusive, for they found that the behavior maintained by all the VR schedules was quite insensitive to the conditioned suppression procedure. This may be because reinforcements were contingent upon the continued and sustained emission of responses with this schedule in a way that is not the case with variable-interval schedules. Fantino (1973) has pointed out that partial suppression during a preshock stimulus superimposed on a variable-interval schedule can have, within limits, virtually no effect on the rate of reinforcement. This is clearly not the case with ratio schedules. Fantino therefore regards the results of Felton and Lyon as being "readily interpretable." However, Blackman (1966) reported an experiment using rats as subjects in which VR 100 behavior was far from resistant to conditioned suppression: all three rats showed virtually complete conditioned suppression when the shocks (.5 mA, .2 sec) were introduced. Another three animals were "yoked" to these first three, i.e., reinforcements were made available to them by the delivery of reinforcements to the VR animals, so that they were in effect on a VI schedule with a mean interreinforcement interval identical to that of the ratio animals. These VI animals did not show such severe conditioned suppression, which emphasizes the susceptibility of the ratio animals to conditioned suppression in this experiment, in contrast to the resistance shown by Lyon and Felton's pigeons. The reasons for these inconsistencies remain obscure; one hesitates to invoke species differences, especially as pigeons and rats appear to be used interchangeably in other studies of conditioned suppression. Perhaps Fantino's (1973) suggestion that "it would have been interesting [in the Lyon and Felton study] to note whether conditioned suppression would have been obtained with high shock intensities" is useful, for it is possible that the shocks used by Lyon and Felton would not have suppressed other patterns of behavior in these pigeons.

The effects of conditioned suppression procedures have also been investigated with fixed-ratio and fixed-interval schedules. Lyon (1964) found that the effects of a preshock stimulus superimposed on FR 150 behavior in pigeons depended on how far the bird was advanced in its sequence of behavior when the stimulus was presented. If this occurred just after reinforcement, Lyon observed complete suppression during the stimulus. If, when the stimulus was introduced, the bird had emitted more than 60 responses in the required sequence of 150, it continued responding until the next reinforcement and then suppressed completely until the end of the stimulus. If the stimulus began when the bird was between 20 and 60 responses into the required sequence, immediate suppression was sometimes seen and on other occasions the animal continued to respond until the next reinforcement was obtained. The initial resistance to suppression when the bird had completed more than 60 responses may perhaps be taken as support for Lyon and Felton's (1966a) report that variable-ratio behavior in pigeons is resistant to suppression, for with the variable schedule the imminence of the next reinforcement may always be as close as in those conditions of Lyon's fixed-ratio experiment when the behavior was found to be resistant to suppression. Similarly, with variable-ratio schedules, the birds do not show postreinforcement pauses as they do on FR 150. Another study by Lyon and Felton (1966b) found that birds exposed to FR 25 (and to a lesser extent FR 50) did begin to respond again *after* a reinforcement had been obtained during a preshock stimulus. The birds therefore often obtained several reinforcements during the stimulus, and so to that extent could also be described as resistant to conditioned suppression.

The crucial relationship between the onset of a preshock stimulus and the imminence of reinforcement has also been suggested with fixed-interval schedules. For example, Blackman (1968a) discussed the behavior of one subject (rat 1) which was exposed to a FI 20-sec schedule. A 1-min preshock stimulus was presented in such a way that the next reinforcement became available 5 sec after its onset (and, therefore 25 and 45 sec after the onset). When the shock which ended this stimulus was of .5 mA for .2 sec, the rat responded long enough into the stimulus to obtain the first two of these reinforcements (i.e., for 25 sec), and then suppressed completely until the end of the stimulus. When the shock was increased to 1.6 mA, responding continued only long enough for the first reinforcement to be obtained (i.e., for 5 sec). With a shock setting of 3.0 mA for .5 sec, all responding was suppressed immediately the preshock stimulus was presented, even though a reinforcement would become available only 5 sec later. A study by Lyon and Millar (1969) also suggests that the imminence of reinforcement in an FI schedule may attenuate conditioned suppression. In the interreinforcement intervals of an FI 2-min schedule, a preshock stimulus of 30 sec was presented 30, 60, or 90 sec after the preceding reinforcement. It was found that there was marked suppression of responding during the stimulus when it was presented early in the interval, but no suppression when the stimulus occurred late in the interval.

Preshock stimuli have also been superimposed on behavior maintained by a schedule which differentially reinforces a very low rate of responding (DRL). In some circumstances it has been shown that responding on this schedule increases in frequency during a preshock stimulus. For example, Blackman (1968a) exposed rats to a multiple schedule, of which one component was a DRL 15-sec schedule and the other generated higher response rates. In all conditions of the experiment, this second pattern of behavior was suppressed during a preshock stimulus. However, when the stimulus ended with a relatively mild shock (.2 mA for .5 or 1.0 sec), the DRL behavior increased in frequency during its presentation, although with higher intensities of shock the more usual suppressive effect was found. The acceleration of DRL responding during a stimulus which ends with a mild shock is illustrated in Figure 4, which shows the cumulative records of three rats exposed throughout each experimental session to a DRL 15-sec schedule. A tentative suggestion has been made (Blackman, 1968a) that the acceleration effect on the DRL responding was attributable to a disruption of the collateral behavior which appeared to mediate the lever-pressing behavior. These stereotyped sequences of behavior were not formally measured in the experiment, but they characterized the DRL behavior in control conditions. During the preshock stimulus, however, the collateral behaviors seemed to be quickly disrupted, and lever pressing then occurred in their absence and at a higher frequency than in control conditions.

In an experiment which employed a two-lever situation (Blackman, 1970a), rats were exposed to a schedule in which a response on lever B was followed by reinforcement if a preceding response on lever A had been made at least 5, 10, or 15 sec before. When a preshock stimulus was superimposed on the behavior generated by this schedule, it was found that the frequency of timing attempts, i.e., of A-to-B sequences, decreased during the stimulus. This had also been found in a similar experiment by Migler and Brady (1964). When the delay required was 5 sec, there was no change in the distribution of A-to-B times during the preshock stimulus. Thus although the frequency of timing attempts decreased, their accuracy was not impaired, again replicating a finding by Migler and Brady (1964). However, when the required A-to-B delay was 10 or 15 sec, the distribution of A-to-B times changed during the preshock stimulus, there being more shorter intervals. Also noticeable (especially with the 15-sec-delay requirement) was an increased proportion of inappropriate B responses, i.e., B responses which were made without a preceding A response to initiate a timing attempt. The disruption of timing efficiency and the increase in appropriate B responses led in one case to an overall acceleration of B responses in comparison with control conditions, in spite of the decreased frequency of appropriate timing attempts. This accelerative effect may be analogous to the acceleration reported with a single-lever DRL schedule. A generally similar effect was reported by Blackman and Scruton (1973a), who superimposed a preshock stimulus on a two-lever counting schedule. In this case, rats were required to make at least a specified number of successive responses on lever A before switching to lever B to produce reinforcement, and there was a shift to shorter sequences of responses on lever A during the preshock stimulus.

Hearst (1965) has reported a deterioration in discriminative control as a result of the Estes-Skinner procedure. He superimposed a preshock stimulus on periods of intermittent reinforcement, and found that the operant behavior was suppressed in the usual way during this stimulus. However, the rats were also exposed to periods when no reinforcement was possible (extinction). The preshock stimulus never occurred during periods of extinction, but the deterioration in discriminative control reported by Hearst took the form of an increase in responding during these periods. Hearst related this finding to the Pavlovian concept of disinhibition. However, it should perhaps be mentioned that two subsequent experiments have

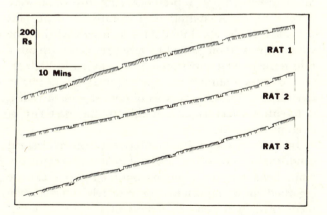

Fig. 4. The accelerative effects of a preshock stimulus on responding maintained by a schedule which differentially reinforces a low rate of lever pressing (DRL 15 sec). The response pen is offset during the preshock stimulus; hatchmarks denote reinforcement. (Unpublished data of Sanger & Blackman.)

failed to replicate his findings (Blackman & Scruton, 1973b; Weiss, 1968). In the former case, there was no increase in responding during periods of extinction, even when the preshock stimulus was subsequently presented during extinction periods as well as during the periods of intermittent reinforcement. The reasons for these potentially important inconsistencies between experiments are not clear as yet.

It is clear that the amount of suppression produced by a given preshock stimulus depends crucially on the nature of the schedule which maintains the operant behavior on which it is superimposed. Indeed, in some circumstances (albeit limited to fairly stringent timing schedules) a preshock stimulus will lead to an increase in the rate of food-reinforced operant responding. Certain familiar schedules of reinforcement, particularly variable-interval, provide a base line of behavior against which the effects of classical conditioning parameters can be readily assessed. However, it is also the case that, when classical conditioning procedures are held constant, substantial differences in the effects of a conditioned stimulus may emerge as a function of the precise schedules of reinforcement which maintain the operant behavior, differences not only of degree but even on occasion of direction.

MEASUREMENT OF CONDITIONED SUPPRESSION

We have already noted that most workers have measured conditioned suppression by comparing the response rate during the preshock stimulus with the control rate of responding, i.e., in the absence of the preshock stimulus. We may continue to regard the different formulae which have been used to make such a comparison as no more than tedious and potentially confusing. However, Hoffman (1969) and Millenson and de Villiers (1972) have suggested that the use of relative measures has not been adequately justified. A relative measure may make it easy to compare conditioned suppression of different patterns of operant behavior, but this entails an arbitrary assumption: "Measurement by relative suppression presupposes that under constant experimental conditions the warning signal will produce the same relative decrement independent of the rate of the responding at the moment of the warning signal presentation" (Hoffman, 1969, p. 68). There is now ample evidence that this assumption is false, as shown in the previous section. Suppression ratios obtained in experiments in which the same preshock stimulus is superimposed on different rates of operant behavior are not identical (Blackman, 1966, 1967, 1968b). Such a finding offers the investigator two very different interpretations (Blackman, 1972):

1. A suppression ratio may always reflect accurately the strength of a classically conditioned response elicited by the conditioned stimulus. In other words, the more severe the disruption of operant behavior (as expressed by a suppression ratio), the greater is the strength of the CR. If this is true, different strengths of CR are developed by a uniform procedure when it is superimposed on different operant response rates. Why this should be so remains unexplained, although it has often been suggested in a more general context that the effects of any independent variable depend on the nature of ongoing behavior as controlled by schedules of reinforcement (e.g., Dews, 1963).

2. A standard classical conditioning procedure may always result in a CR of uniform strength. Different suppression ratios describing the effects of a preshock stimulus on different patterns of operant behavior may then result from the fact that this uniform conditioned response interacts differently with these patterns of behavior. According to such a view, the suppression ratio is therefore not an uncontaminated reflection of the strength of a CR.

It is difficult to decide between these alternatives, and initial preferences may reflect whether one's basic allegiance is to the study of classical conditioning or of operant conditioning processes. Given this problem of interpreting suppression ratios, however, it would seem only prudent to support inferences based on these ratios by absolute data whenever possible. Thus in the case discussed in the previous section, suppression ratios suggested that high response rates were more disrupted by a preshock stimulus than were lower rates of responding. Corroborative evidence was provided by the absolute data, which showed that the stimulus was accompanied by fewer responses (in absolute terms) when superimposed on normally high response rates than when superimposed on normally lower rates. These two forms of data suggested that a differential effect is attributable to the patterns of operant behavior.

In many cases of interactions between a classical conditioning procedure and different patterns of operant behavior, the dilemma outlined above can be regarded as unimportant, for research interest may focus principally on the details of schedule control and its disruption. The matter can be of great practical significance, however, as may be illustrated by an example. Figure 5 shows data obtained from one rat which was exposed to a FR 10 schedule of food rein-

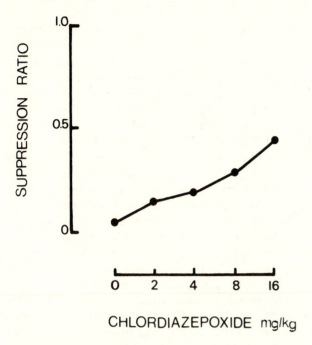

Fig. 5. The effects of various dosages of chlordiazepoxide on conditioned suppression of a rat's responding on a FR 10 schedule. Complete suppression = 0; no effect = 1.0. (Unpublished data of D. Sanger.)

forcement. When this behavior had stabilized, a conventional conditioned suppression procedure was introduced, the details of which are not important here. The rat was then tested after various injections of the minor tranquilizer chlordiazepoxide. Figure 5 plots the suppression ratios which were obtained with the various doses, these being calculated by Stein, Sidman, and Brady's (1958) formula: SR = CS rate/Control rate. It seems clear that increasing doses of the drug have an increasingly attenuating effect on conditioned suppression. However, with a relative measure such as this, these changes may be produced *either* by changes in response rate during the CS or by changes in its absence. Figure 6 shows the absolute response rates in these two periods after each dosage of the drug. The open points display the drug's effects on response rates during the preshock stimulus (FR 10/CS), and the closed points show response rates in its absence. Clearly, the effects of the drug are by no means as simple as at first they may have seemed on the basis of the suppression ratios in Figure 5. In fact, the ratios change as a result of changes in response rates both within the CS and in control conditions. With lower dosages, increases occur in both response rates. The differences between the effects of 8 mg/kg and 16 mg/kg, however, can be seen to be almost entirely due to differences in control rates, with little change in CS rates. The dilemma outlined earlier therefore

appears: does the orderly effect of increasing dosage on suppression ratios reflect (1) progressive reductions in the strength of the underlying conditioned response, or (2) merely contaminations produced by a changing control base line, with the strength of the conditioned response remaining unchanged? Although it may be difficult to answer such a question, it is surely clear that informed interpretation of the drug's effects demands absolute as well as relative data. Nevertheless, experimental reports continue to emphasize suppression ratios and frequently fail to supplement these by absolute rates in the presence and absence of a conditioned stimulus.

A further complication arises whenever any simple measure of conditioned suppression is reported, whether this be in the form of relative or of absolute response rates during a preshock stimulus. We have noted previously that a stimulus which ends with a shock is a conditioned stimulus within the Pavlovian delayed conditioning paradigm. With traditional Pavlovian procedures, some form of temporal discrimination usually develops within such a CS, the conditioned

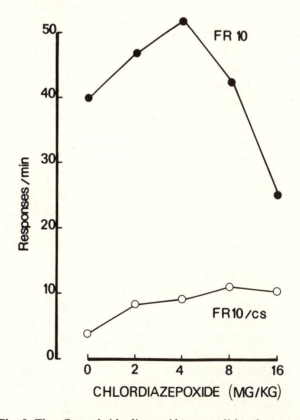

Fig. 6. The effects of chlordiazepoxide on conditioned suppression. The data are those which are expressed in the form of suppression ratios in Figure 7, but are here plotted in absolute terms, i.e., as response rates during the preshock stimulus (FR 10/CS) and rates in its absence (FR 10). (Unpublished data of D. Sanger.)

response eventually being characteristically elicited only toward the end of the CS (i.e., just before the US). A similar temporal discrimination has sometimes been reported with conditioned suppression. For example, Hendry and Van Toller (1965) reported that initial sustained suppression throughout a preshock stimulus was superseded by a pattern in which the suppression occurred only in the second half of the stimulus. In some cases, response rates during the first half of the stimulus in fact *increased* in comparison with control conditions. However, such temporal patterning has not been reported consistently in the literature, even in studies in which a preshock stimulus has been superimposed on operant behavior repeatedly. For example, Stein et al. (1958) remark that the type of response patterning within a fixed preshock stimulus was "not necessarily invariant from one stimulus presentation to the next." This is a further example of an inconsistency in the literature which has not yet been resolved. The development of temporal patterning may depend on a number of variables, such as the relative duration of the preshock stimulus, the intensity of the shock, the number of conditioning trials, and the nature of the schedule which maintains the operant behavior.

Unrecorded temporal patterning within a preshock stimulus could have a considerable contaminating effect on reported results. Millenson and Leslie (1974), for example, argue that a drug which appears to alleviate or enhance conditioned suppression might do so principally by affecting the nature of any such temporal discrimination. There would appear to be two ways of counteracting this possible contamination. The first is to vary the duration of the preshock stimulus from trial to trial, although still ending each stimulus presentation with a shock. Millenson and Hendry (1967) found that such a procedure did result in consistently suppressed responding during the stimulus. An alternative expedient is to use a conditioned stimulus of fixed duration in the usual way, but to deliver shocks at unpredictable moments throughout the stimulus and not merely as the stimulus ends. This procedure has been used occasionally. For example, Azrin (1956) included it (termed by him "VI uncorrelated shock"), and his cumulative records reveal consistent suppression throughout the stimulus associated with shock. More recently, Bond, Blackman, and Scruton (1973, Experiment 2) used the procedure. In this experiment the response rates were not entirely consistent throughout the stimulus associated with shock, but the inconsistencies may have resulted from the suppressive effects of the procedure on adjunctive licking which had reliably developed in this experiment: certainly, there was no evidence of an orderly temporal patterning during the stimulus.

Of course, the delivery of shocks at unpredictable moments during a stimulus is strongly reminiscent of Rescorla's procedures reviewed earlier, although in these studies shocks and another stimulus were associated only before operant conditioning occurred, and only the CS was subsequently superimposed on operant behavior. Nevertheless, a complication even in presenting shocks at random moments during a stimulus emerges from one of Rescorla's studies (1968). He found that response rates were not consistently suppressed even when the conditioned stimulus was superimposed on variable interval behavior. There was greater suppression during the *initial* parts of the stimulus, with less in the later parts (i.e., the opposite of Hendry & Van Toller's 1965 results using a conventional preshock stimulus). Rescorla suggested that this effect may reflect the fact that the onset of a CS is more discriminable than its continued presence. A second possibility mentioned by Rescorla, however, brings us full circle, for he suggests that his differential suppression within a CS may be

> an artifact of the measuring technique. A VI schedule of reinforcement is such that the longer [a subject] has refrained from pressing, the higher the probability that its next press will be reinforced. Thus the longer [the subject] suppresses, the more "pressure" the base-line operant schedule places on it to respond. (Rescorla, 1968, p. 5)

Rescorla therefore goes on to suggest that the strength of the classically conditioned response may be constant throughout the CS: only the tendency to emit an operant response changes. This suggestion is clearly based on the second interpretation of conditioned suppression discussed toward the beginning of this section.

The measurement of conditioned suppression is fraught with difficulties, some of which pose interesting dilemmas. There is scope for ambiguity even when responding is totally suppressed during a preshock stimulus. For example, Lyon (1965) claimed that a change in base line response rate is not sufficient to change the amount of conditioned suppression. However, in the first phase of his experiment, Lyon used a procedure which resulted in complete conditioned suppression, and he then found that complete suppression still occurred when the base line response rate was increased. Subsequent research (e.g., Blackman, 1968b) has shown that increases in base line response rate lead to an *increase* in the amount of conditioned suppression. Since this effect could not be shown in Lyon's experiment because of a "ceiling effect," he was therefore led to a general conclusion which was false. Problems of measurement in studies of conditioned suppression must therefore be borne in mind constantly in this area of research. Sometimes a simple suppression ratio in one sustained experimental situation may not be the most useful measure. For example, Fleshler and Hoffman (1961) investigated the stimulus generalization of conditioned suppression with pigeons. First, complete conditioned suppression was obtained during a 1000-Hz tone which preceded a shock. Then tones of different frequencies were presented in a generalization test in extinction conditions (i.e., no tone ended with shock). At first, the stimulus generalization gradient, which was measured by suppression ratios, was flat, there being almost complete conditioned suppression during all the tones. However, as testing proceeded, the gradient sharpened, the suppression ratios during the tones which were most different from the previous CS showing that these stimuli were the first to lose their control over behavior. Thus the flat gradient first obtained did not reflect uniform effects of the different test stimuli on behavior, and Fleshler and Hoffman's extinction procedure made it possible to identify their different degrees of behavioral control in spite of an initial "ceiling effect."

Although no simple measure of conditioned suppression is entirely satisfactory, many problems of interpretation may be overcome by using measures of absolute response rates during a preshock stimulus as well as the relative measures provided by suppression ratios, and in some circumstances by using repeated tests in changing conditions (as in Fleshler & Hoffman's 1961 experiment). The most important conclusion to be prompted, however, is that the most appropriate measure of conditioned suppression in any experiment should always be considered carefully.

SOME INTERPRETATIONS OF CONDITIONED SUPPRESSION

Why is positively reinforced operant behavior usually suppressed during a stimulus which is associated with shock? Three major explanations for this phenomenon will be considered here: operant behavior is suppressed because (1) other behaviors resulting from the procedure interfere with it; (2) the procedure generates an emotional state which affects the underlying motivational state of the subject; (3) the procedure allows for occasional adventitious punishment of the operant behavior. It is not always easy to keep these three accounts separate, and any attempt to do so results in some arbitrary decisions. The discussion continues to be confined to the effects of a preshock stimulus on food-reinforced behavior. The extension of the theories to other examples of classical conditioning effects on operant base lines will be considered subsequently.

The Interference Hypothesis

The possibility that other behaviors interfere with ongoing operant behavior to produce conditioned suppression has been suggested in terms both of competing respondent behavior and of competing operants, although the former has received by far the more attention.

We have seen in a preceding section of this chapter that conventional Pavlovian conditioning parameters such as the intensity of the CS and the US determine the severity of conditioned suppression, so that the phenomenon has been frequently studied as an example of Pavlovian conditioning. Kamin (1965) has expressed a widely held view that "the most obvious assumption has been that the interference with behavior, which serves as our measure, is largely the result of incompatibility between respondents elicited by S_1 [the pre-shock stimulus] and the ongoing behavior."

The empirical status of this interfering respondents hypothesis is open to some doubt. First, it is necessary to specify the behaviors said to be conditioned during the preshock stimulus which are supposed to interfere with the operant behavior. Second, it remains necessary to show why and how any such behaviors are incompatible with the emission of an operant such as pressing a lever. There are several obvious contenders in answer to the first of these questions, but surprisingly little systematic work has been carried out in an attempt to monitor changes in autonomic activities to see if their intensities vary with the amount of suppression of operant behavior. On a gross level, traditional signs of autonomic activity such as defecation, urination, piloerection, and freezing of motor activity have frequently been discussed in the context of conditioned suppression. In an early experimental program by Brady and his associates (see, for example, Brady, 1951) the effects of a preshock stimulus were measured either in terms of the suppression of operant behavior with one group of animals or in terms of gross changes in these autonomic activities. Similarly, Hunt and Brady (1955) commented on such activity during a stimulus which precedes an unavoidable shock. There seems little doubt that signs of autonomic activity such as these do characteristically accompany the early stages of many conditioned suppression experiments. However, Millenson and de Villiers (1972) have suggested that these signs seem to decrease with continued testing, although their comment is based on informal observations which deserve to be quantified systematically. Certainly in later stages of experiments suppression of operant behavior does appear to persist when gross signs of autonomic arousal are minimal or nonexistent.

There have been many studies of other more constrained respondent changes resulting from the delivery of a preshock stimulus (see, for example, the review by Weiskrantz, 1968). Two experimental programs which have related such changes to simultaneous suppression of operant behavior are particularly interesting. In the first of these (de Toledo & Black, 1966) the heart rates of rats were recorded. It was found that changes in heart rate did occur during the preshock stimulus, but they developed less quickly than did the suppression of operant responding. Moreover, the changes in heart rate were much more variable and of shorter duration than the operant suppression. This finding has been supported in a study by Brady, Kelly, and Plumlee (1969), in which the heart rate and blood pressure (both systolic and diastolic) of rhesus monkeys were monitored throughout the development and maintenance of conditioned suppression. During the preshock stimulus, there were certainly changes in these autonomic indicators. Again, however, suppression of the operant behavior developed before any detectable and reliable changes in heart rate and before changes in blood pressure. It was impossible to identify any consistently similar variations in the dependent variables in this study: with one subject changes in heart rate even appeared to be inversely related to the amount of conditioned suppression of operant behavior. On frequent occasions the two measures of blood pressure showed divergent patterns of conditioned reactions. The results of this experiment are illustrated by data from one subject in Figure 7. This shows the percentage changes in each of the four behavioral measures, expressed for each of the successive minutes of the 3-min preshock stimulus. Selected conditioning trials are shown. Reliable suppression of operant behavior developed before any consistent disruption in autonomic activities. The lack of consistent covariation between the measures can also be seen. This monkey also shows the development of a temporal discrimination in the conditioned suppression of operant behavior, as discussed earlier. This began to develop by the 16th trial, and eventually took the form of only slight suppression in the first minute of the stimulus, with almost total suppression in the second and third minutes. However, measures of autonomic activity fail to show this biphasic pattern. It is also worth noticing that on some trials (e.g., trials 18 and 31 of those shown) lever pressing occurred more frequently in the first minute of the stimulus than in control conditions—the effect reported by Hendry and Van Toller (1965) and discussed earlier. Again, there is no characteristic patterning of autonomic activity which reflects this distribution of operant responses during the preshock stimulus.

On the basis of their data, Brady and his associates concluded that the operant and autonomic effects of their experiment were causally independent, although doubtless related in complex ways. In the most general terms, they suggested that their finding "reflects unfavorably upon theoretical formulations that emphasize either the causal interdependence of behavioral and physiological events or the primacy of either one."

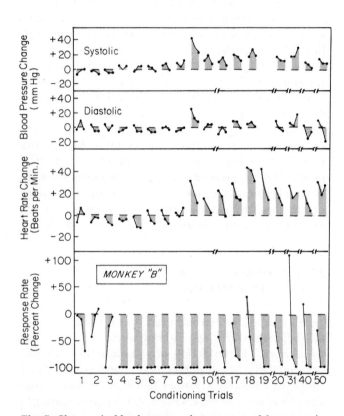

Fig. 7. Changes in blood pressure, heart rate, and lever-pressing response rate of a rhesus monkey during the 3 min of a preshock stimulus. The zero points represent control values in the absence of the preshock stimulus. (From Brady, Kelly, & Plumlee, 1969.)

Of course, in the context of the interference hypothesis of conditioned suppression it would always be possible to suggest that experimenters have failed to measure those respondents which do have a disruptive effect on operant behavior. Nevertheless, the evidence at present points unequivocally to the conclusion that conditioned respondents may accompany but do not cause conditioned suppression. In any case, even if some respondent were to be identified which varied in direct proportion to variations in operant responding, it would be by no means clear why it should be physically incompatible with that responding, the second necessary step if the interference theory is to be convincing. Further difficulties for this hypothesis are presented by the differential disruption of various frequencies and patterns of operant responding which was reviewed in an earlier section, for it is not obvious why any interfering respondent behavior should be more incompatible with some patterns and frequencies of operant responding than with others. This is, of course, particularly true when operant response rates are similar but reinforcement frequencies differ. Nevertheless it would certainly be of great interest to monitor autonomic changes when a preshock stimulus results in differential suppression of operant behavior. For example although operant and respondent behavior may not be functionally related on a 1:1 basis during a preshock stimulus, it would be interesting to discover whether the two classes of behavior are relatively resistant to disruption in the same circumstances (e.g., in situations which generate low operant response rates or with high reinforcement frequencies). Experiments such as this might have the greatest relevance in the general study of the relationships between autonomic processes and operant behaviors and of the relationship between physiological events and directly observable behaviors.

There remains one pattern of behavior not yet fully discussed but whose occurrence during a preshock stimulus might certainly be physically incompatible with lever pressing. Rats frequently crouch or "freeze" when shocked, and such behavior might occur during a preshock stimulus. Discussion of this possibility has been delayed, since it would be difficult to assert that this would necessarily be an example of a competing *respondent*. Leaving aside the question of whether such skeletal behaviors can be classically conditioned (see Chapter 3), it is possible that they might develop or be maintained as a result of their consequences, and hence should be regarded as competing *operant* behavior. In other words, adopting certain postures such as "freezing" might minimize the aversiveness of a shock when it is delivered, as Weiskrantz (1968) has suggested.

"Freezing" behavior during a preshock stimulus has been investigated with pigeons by Stein, Hoffman, and Stitt (1971). They used ethological recording techniques to measure general behavior which occurred in addition to operant key pecking and found that there was a marked decrease in all overt activity (including key pecking) during the stimulus. In this experiment it is unlikely that such a general inhibitory effect in behavior was maintained by an unprogrammed instrumental contingency, since the shock was delivered through wing bands.

Whether any "freezing" responses during a preshock stimulus should be regarded as competing respondents or competing operants, this general interpretation of conditioned suppression is open to the objections discussed above. As with other putative competing responses, even if they occur reliably and consistently, it is not clear whether they interfere with recorded operants and thereby cause their suppression or are merely a reflection of the same process which causes such suppression.

Motivational Explanations

Many researchers have suggested that a preshock stimulus produces a change in the motivational state of a subject, which in turn leads to conditioned suppression. In recent years, Estes (1969 p. 80) has suggested that

> a stimulus which has preceded a traumatic event, e.g., shock, . . . acquires the capacity of inhibiting the input of amplifier elements from sources associated with hunger, thirst and the like. If then, while the animal is performing an instrumental response for, say, food reward, this conditioned stimulus is presented, the facilitative drive input will be reduced and so also the probability or rate of the instrumental response.

A preshock stimulus may therefore be said to produce anxiety, which can be regarded as a motivational force which reduces positive motivation for reinforcement and thereby decreases the frequency of operant behavior.

A similar argument may also be developed from the description of conditioned suppression as resulting from a "conditioned emotional response" (CER). Thus Hunt and Brady (1951) hypothesized "an internal state underlying the behavioral reaction," and Kamin also used the term "CER" frequently (e.g., 1965). However, it is not consistently clear whether either Hunt and Brady or Kamin wish to emphasize the adjective *emotional* sufficiently to demand that their theories be considered under the present heading rather than the previous one; for Kamin, at least, has consistently conducted research which could be said rather to emphasize the "conditioned . . . response" as the behavioral outcome of Pavlovian conditioning rather than as a motivational state. In their interesting paper, Millenson and de Villiers (1972) suggest that this "failure to consider that the CER is an emotional phenomenon" has been a barrier to the adequate understanding of the effects we have been discussing. These writers seek to develop Skinner's (1938) statement that emotion is "a state of strength comparable in many respects with a drive" (p. 407) and to argue that conditioned suppression results from "a negative drive activity," a view similar to that of Estes. Thus "when the signal for shock [is] presented the rat's hunger might be temporarily suspended and 'suppression' is the natural consequence of food (as well as all other positive reinforcers) having temporarily lost its reward value" (Millenson, 1971, p. 229).

A motivational decrement theory such as this directs research attention to questions somewhat different from those discussed so far. Clearly, a stimulus which precedes a shock of a given intensity will have a greater suppressive effect, according to this theory, if it is superimposed on behavior which is relatively weakly motivated. In this context, Millenson and de Villiers (1972) discuss experiments in which they varied the deprivation conditions for subjects exposed to a preshock stimulus. The results for one of these are shown in Figure 8. Groups of rats were exposed to a random-interval 60-sec schedule of food reinforcement in two conditions on each day: first when 9 hr food-deprived (prefeeding) and then after being given 8–15 g of free food (postfeeding). In both conditions, a stimulus of variable length (Millenson & Hendry, 1967) ended with an unavoidable shock. The panel on the left in Figure 8 shows that mean rates of responding in the safe periods (i.e., in the absence of the preshock stimulus) were consistently higher in the prefeeding condition that in the postfeeding condition. The preshock stimulus suppressed both these patterns of behavior, the effect being dependent on the intensity of the shock delivered in the various phases of the experiment. The absolute decrease in response rate was greater in the prefeeding condition. However, the panel on the right in Figure 8 shows that in terms of a suppression ratio (CS/Control rate), the postfeeding condition appears to show the greater relative suppression at all shock intensities, the effect being clearer at .2 and .1 mA, where it is less contaminated by a ceiling effect produced by severe disruption of behavior. The data of this study are presented in terms of both absolute and relative response rates, and it can therefore be seen that the *lower* control response rates (postfeeding) are the *more* suppressed in terms of suppression ratios. Since, with pacing procedures in which the deprivation conditions are held constant, lower rates of responding are the *less* disrupted (Blackman, 1968b), it seems reasonable to conclude with Millenson and de Villiers that the suppressive effects of their preshock stimulus are related directly to the value of the reinforcers. Thus "emotion" has a greater disruptive effect on behavior which is less strongly motivated.

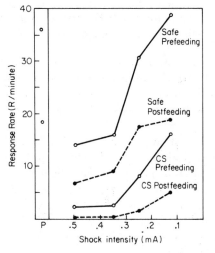 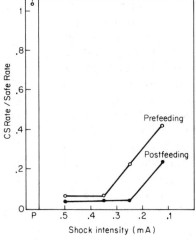

Fig. 8. The effects of a preshock stimulus on random-interval behavior in rats. The rats were tested when 9 hr food-deprived (prefeeding) and shortly after 8–15 g of free food (postfeeding). On the left are shown response rates during the CS and in its absence (safe) in both conditions. On the right are shown the resulting suppression ratios. (From Millenson & de Villiers, 1972.)

Millenson and de Villiers (1972) also reported an interesting change in relative preference when a preshock stimulus is superimposed on behaviors which are maintained by a concurrent schedule of reinforcement. Rats were exposed to a situation in which they could always press one lever for occasional access to 1.5-sec milk reinforcement or press another lever for access to the same reinforcer for 4.5 sec. In control conditions, an asymmetric performance was observed, rats showing some preference for the second lever. During a preshock stimulus which was superimposed on this concurrent schedule, the preference was enhanced, there being more suppression (in relative terms) of the responding on the 1.5-sec lever than on the 4.5-sec lever. This is further support (it is argued) for a drive decrement theory of conditioned suppression, since the increase in preference results from the greater suppressive effect of a conditioned emotional response on the less motivated behavior.

Motivational theories suggest research which might not arise from other conceptual schemes. Empirical data such as those of Millenson and de Villiers are therefore welcome and challenging. However, as with all such theories, there are potential disadvantages in the motivational view of conditioned suppression with its appeal to states which cannot be measured directly. For example, the differential effects of a preshock stimulus on behavior maintained by various schedules (discussed in the section on operant conditioning parameters, above) may too easily be translated into motivational terms in a way which can be difficult to refute. If a pattern of behavior proves to be susceptible to conditioned suppression, this can be taken as evidence that motivation is weak. On the other hand, behavior which is resistant to conditioned suppression can readily be described as strongly motivated. Since behavior which is reinforced frequently is less disrupted by a preshock stimulus, motivation can be said to vary with reinforcement frequency in a way that seems acceptable. Similarly, animals can be described as weakly motivated in the postreinforcement pause on a fixed-ratio schedule, thus handling Lyon's (1964) conditioned suppression data discussed earlier. But it has also been argued (Millenson & de Villiers, 1972) that because high rates of responding are relatively susceptible to conditioned suppression, they may be weakly motivated. This view may seem initially less plausible. It is true that Fantino (1968) has shown that animals prefer situations in which they are allowed to obtain reinforcement by responding at unpaced rates to situations in which they are required to respond at high rates. This might appear to be the independent evidence of the strength of motivation generated by different schedules which is clearly required to support the motivational theory of conditioned suppression. However, on this basis Fantino's experiment does not suggest a reason why low rates of responding are even more resistant to conditioned suppression than unpaced moderate rates, since he found that the latter are preferred in choice situations.

The idea that conditioned suppression results from an underlying emotional state has proved attractive in psychopharmacology. It has been argued that this behavioral manifestation of anxiety or of a conditioned emotional response may prove useful in the analysis of drugs which are presumed to act specifically on such states. Hence the effects on conditioned suppression have been reported of many drugs such as "tranquilizers" and barbiturates which have been used in clinical practice in an attempt to alleviate anxiety states. These reports have recently been reviewed by Millenson and Leslie (1974), who point out the considerable advantages of the conditioned suppression procedure in this context. First, as is the case with most operant conditioning experiments, experimental sessions may continue for long periods, thereby allowing the time course of a drug's effects to be measured. (See also Thompson & Boren, Chapter 18 of this volume.) Second, by choosing the parameters of the conditioned suppression experiment judiciously, it is possible to establish partial suppression during a preshock stimulus, thereby providing a behavioral base line which is sensitive to either alleviating or enhancing effects of a drug on anxiety. Third, and perhaps most important, since the procedure includes both signaled periods when anxiety is presumed to be suppressing behavior and periods of safety from aversive stimuli, it is possible to provide a within-sessions control for any side effects which a drug might have on overall motivation, on sensory function, or on locomotor activity.

An early experiment by Brady (1956) has been widely cited as illustrating the potential of this technique. Brady, using rats as subjects, established partial conditioned suppression of intermittently reinforced operant behavior during a preshock stimulus and then investigated the effects of amphetamine and of reserpine. Brady claimed that both these drugs had specific effects "in the affective sphere," i.e., on the conditioned emotional response. Thus amphetamine strengthened the CER, for in comparison with saline conditions the drug produced a decrease in the number of responses emitted during the preshock stimulus, in spite of what Brady described as a nonspecific side effect on the behavioral base line taking the form of an overall *increase* in control response rates. Similarly, it was argued that reserpine attenuated the CER: despite a nonspecific decrease in overall response rate, the number of responses during the preshock stimulus was greater than on saline days.

Unfortunately, subsequent work in this area has not consistently produced similarly encouraging data, and some signs of gloom have emerged as to the general usefulness of conditioned suppression as a model of anxiety in this context (e.g., Davis, 1968; Kelleher & Morse, 1964). Failures to produce clear-cut effects have led to interestingly different interpretations on occasion. Thus Kinnard, Aceto, and Buckley (1962) were led to conclude that conditioned suppression is not a model of anxiety. On the other hand, Ray (1964) concluded from essentially similar results that it *is* a model of anxiety, and that therefore "tranquilizing" drugs do not have a specific effect on anxiety.

It seems likely that the conditioned suppression phenomenon is a simple model of anxiety only on a superficial level. We have seen some of its complexities in preceding sections, and these must surely complicate the analysis of any drug's effects. Thus Appel (1963) has shown that a dosage of reserpine which reliably reduced conditioned suppression when the shock intensity was .8 mA failed to produce consistent effects when the shock was increased only to 1.0 mA. Similarly, the response rates during the preshock stimulus in Brady's (1956) experiment may have been changed not only by any specific effect of the drugs on the CER but also by the "nonspecific" side effects of the drugs: for example, the increased overall response rates produced by amphetamine may themselves have produced the relative decrease in response rates during the preshock stimulus (Blackman, 1972). Or again, since amphetamine is known to be an anorexic agent, the relative susceptibility of behavior to suppression after its administration may be the result of a relatively low motivational state in the subject on those days (Millenson & Leslie, 1974). Finally, any attenuating or enhancing effects of a drug on the amount of conditioned suppression may merely be the outcome of a drug's rate-dependent effects on the two rates of responding during and in the absence of the preshock stimulus (Wuttke & Kelleher, 1970).

Despite the complexities of the situation, Millenson and Leslie (1974) have suggested that the effects of drugs on conditioned suppression have not been as inconsistent as has sometimes been supposed. They consider the reported effects of chronic and acute doses of various drugs separately and conclude that minor tranquilizers (benzodiazepines, barbiturates, and meprobamate) have a relatively consistent effect in alleviating suppression in acute doses; on the other hand, it seems that phenothiazines and reserpine alleviate suppression fairly consistently in studies in which they are administered chronically.

The final experiment to be considered in this short review of drug effects was reported by Miczek (1973) and suggests that an emotional substrate of conditioned suppression may indeed be specifically affected by some drugs. Miczek reports that chlordiazepoxide alleviates conditioned suppression of behavior maintained by a VI schedule. His report presents data (shown on the right in Figure 9) in terms both of suppression ratios and of base line response rates following various injections of the drug, and in this case it seems that the dose-related alleviation of conditioned suppression is not contaminated in any gross way by any changes in behavioral base lines. Even more important evidence, however, is to be found in the effects of the drug administered to other animals exposed to a slightly different situation. These rats were also trained on a VI schedule. In their case, however, a stimulus was superimposed which ended

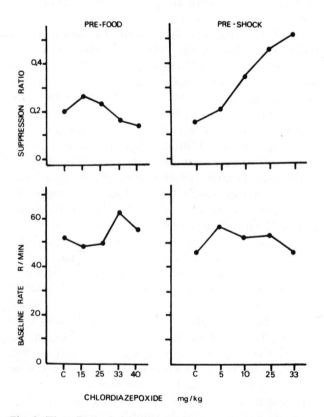

Fig. 9. The effects of chlordiazepoxide on suppression during a stimulus which precedes food (left) or shock (right). Suppression ratios are shown at the top and base line response rates below. Notice that the schedules of dosages are not identical in the two conditions. (Redrawn from Miczek, 1973.)

not with a shock but with the delivery of free food. Operant behavior was suppressed during this stimulus in much the same way as occurs during a preshock stimulus (this finding of "positive conditioned suppression" is reviewed in the next section of this chapter). Miczek reports, however, that this suppression of operant behavior was not attenuated by injections of chlordiazepoxide (see the left panels in Figure 9). These results suggest the drug has a specific effect on anxiety, rather than simply exerting different effects on different rates of responding regardless of the nature of the US signaled by the CS.

Studies of drug effects on conditioned suppression usually attempt to identify specific effects on the emotional states which are thought to produce the suppression. It may be recognized that these rather vaguely defined emotional states may be regarded as conditioned responses and might therefore have been discussed in the context of the interference hypothesis—i.e., emotion (anxiety) is a classically conditioned response which disrupts ongoing operant behavior. However, most drug studies do not attempt to identify the interfering conditioned emotional response per se, and that is why they have here been discussed in the context of a motivational theory.

The Punishment Hypothesis

In the conditioned suppression procedure a stimulus is superimposed on ongoing behavior and ends with a shock which is delivered regardless of what the subject does. *Punishment*, however, is defined as the "reduction of the future probability of a specific response as a result of the *immediate* delivery of a stimulus" (such as a shock) after that response (Azrin & Holz, 1966, emphasis added). It has been suggested that there are no fundamental differences between the processes that lead to these two forms of suppression. On the one hand, it has been argued (e.g., by Estes, 1944) that responding which is explicitly followed by shock is suppressed by the process outlined above in the motivational theory of conditioned suppression. Thus the shock is associated with certain external cues: these become conditioned stimuli by a Pavlovian procedure, and so behavior is suppressed as a result of a conditioned emotional response. This account has few advocates today as a theory of punishment (Azrin & Holz, 1966). However, the opposite theory has also been presented—that conditioned suppression results from an occasional chance contiguity between operant behavior and the delivery of a shock. This theory has been discussed at some length by Lyon (1968), and since there have been relatively few recent experiments explicitly designed to test it, will be dealt with only briefly here.

Clearly, shocks delivered "independently" of behavior may occasionally be associated with behavior in this way. Gottwald (1967) has shown that the amount of conditioned suppression on any trial is affected by the proximity of shock to a response on the previous trial. However, there are a number of reasons to doubt that conditioned suppression is principally caused by adventitious punishment. One of the most important of these is represented in Rescorla's work reviewed earlier. In his experiments, the association of a stimulus with shock is accomplished "off the base line," i.e., before operant training is begun. Subsequently only the conditioned stimulus is superimposed on operant behavior, and there is therefore no opportunity for any adventitious contiguity between shock and response. Yet, of course, conditioned suppression does occur during the CS in these experiments. Hoffman and Barrett (1971), using observational techniques and initial association of a stimulus with shock "off the base line," have also failed to support the punishment hypothesis with pigeon subjects, since again conditioned suppression developed when possible contiguity between shock and responding was minimized. There is also a good deal of evidence that the development of conditioned suppression may be accompanied at a gross level by more signs of autonomic disturbance than is punished behavior (Hunt & Brady, 1955). In addition, Annau and Kamin (1961) have claimed that a shock of .28 mA was sufficient in their experiment to suppress behavior when used in a punishment procedure, but not when used in the conditioned suppression procedure. Orme-Johnson and Yarczower (1974) used a yoking procedure, in which pigeons were exposed either to a discriminated punishment procedure or to one which delivered the same number of shocks independently of behavior. They reported that the latter procedure produced suppression while the former produced none. Moreover, the stimulus associated with shock in the conditioned suppression procedure acquired conditioned punishing effects, while the discriminative stimulus for the punishment procedure did not.

Lyon (1968) has argued that "punishment and conditioned suppression do not represent a behavioral dichotomy but specific points on a behavioral continuum," a suggestion that it is difficult to refute unequivocally. Differences between the effects of the two procedures may always be interpreted in such a way. However, considerable procedural differences between punishment and conditioned suppression inevitably present difficulties in comparing them, not least because suppression of responding has a consequence in reducing shock frequency in the former case but not the latter. It therefore seems unrewarding to try to reduce either one to the other, and this is perhaps why there is little current research with this emphasis.

A BRIEF REVIEW OF SOME OTHER CLASSICAL-OPERANT INTERACTIONS

The problems and questions arising from the study of interactions between classical and operant conditioning have been illustrated so far exclusively by studies in which stimuli associated with shock have been superimposed on operant behavior maintained by food or water reinforcement. We now turn to consider briefly some other procedures.

For some time, motivational theories of conditioned suppression gained considerable support from their apparent ability to handle data describing the effects of signaling an unavoidable shock when an animal's operant behavior is maintained by a schedule of shock avoidance. For example, Rescorla and Solomon (1967) have argued that the laws of Pavlovian conditioning are "the laws of emotional conditioning or laws of acquired drive states" and that "conditioned emotional states change [the subject's] motivation level and thus can serve either as motivators or reinforcers of instrumental responses." They therefore make the general assertion that aversively motivated operant behavior will increase in frequency during a stimulus which precedes an unavoidable shock, since this conditioned emotional state will summate with the motivation maintaining avoidance behavior. Studies by Sidman, Herrnstein, and Conrad (1957), Kelleher, Riddle, and Cook (1963), and Waller and Waller (1963) all showed that free operant avoidance did increase in frequency in this way during a stimulus which preceded the delivery of an unavoidable shock. However, more recently there has been a number of reports of conditioned suppression even of avoidance behavior (e.g., Blackman, 1970b; Bryant, 1972; Hurwitz & Roberts, 1969; Pomerleau, 1970; Roberts & Hurwitz, 1970; Scobie, 1972). It seems that suppression of avoidance behavior may occur if the unavoidable shock is discriminable from avoidable shocks (e.g., of a different intensity), or if such suppression does not increase the overall frequency of shocks, either because the avoidance schedule is suspended during the warning signal or because the response-shock times of the schedule are relatively long in comparison with the duration of the signal. At present, it is not easy to predict precisely the circumstances in which suppression will be the rule, but it is difficult to fit examples such as these into any traditional motivational theory. On the other hand, an interference hypothesis should in principle be as capable of handling suppression of avoidance behavior as of coping with suppression of positively motivated behavior. The problem with this theory, however, is that it offers little in the explanation of any *acceleration* of avoidance behavior during a conditioned stimulus.

Rescorla and Solomon (1967) also predicted on the basis of their motivational theory that, in their terms, any appetitively motivated behavioral base line will increase in frequency during an appetitive Pavlovian conditioned stimulus. In other words, food-reinforced operant behavior should increase in frequency during a signal that ends with presentation of free food. We have seen already, however (Miczek, 1973), that conditioned *suppression* may occur during such a stimulus. For example, using rats as subjects Azrin and Hake (1969), Meltzer and Brahlek (1970), and Hake and Powell (1970) have all reported suppression of responding during a stimulus lasting 10 or 12 sec and ending with the presentation of free food. Similarly, suppression has been reported with monkeys during prefood stimuli (Kelly, 1973a, 1973b; Miczek & Grossman, 1971). It is difficult to see how the Rescorla and Solomon (1967) account of classical-operant interactions can handle such findings. It is intriguing, however, to see the vigor with which other theoretical accounts of the more traditional conditioned suppression during a preshock stimulus have been extended to this so-called positive conditioned suppression. In their study, Azrin and Hake (1969) used either food or water as the reinforcer for operant behavior and delivered "free" food, water, or intracranial stimulation at the end of their stimulus. In general, they found suppression during the stimulus with all the combinations of reinforcer and US which they tested. They suggested that such suppression was the result of a "general emotional state" and argued that suppression during a pre*shock* stimulus is another example of the effects of such a state, rather than a model of a specific anxiety state. Azrin and Hake do not specify the nature of this general emotional state, but it would seem to be basically similar to Skinner's concept of emotion (1938, p. 407).

Kelly (1973a) has attempted to monitor any changes in autonomic activity in monkeys which might be conditioned during a prefood stimulus, with a view to evaluating the interfering respondents hypothesis in the context of positive conditioned suppression. Using the same experimental techniques to monitor cardiovascular activity as Brady, Kelly, and Plumlee (1969) had employed in their study of preshock stimuli, Kelly was again unable to detect any systematic covariation of changes in autonomic activity and operant suppression. He therefore dismisses the idea that positive conditioned suppression is caused by interfering respondents produced by the Pavlovian aspects of the procedure.

One difficulty in considering a theory of positive conditioned suppression in terms of interfering respondents is that the status of the free food as a Pavlovian unconditioned stimulus is by no means clear. In all the studies in this area, except when brain stimulation ended a stimulus in Azrin and Hake's (1969) study, the delivery of the "free" event seems to act more as a discriminative stimulus setting the occasion for an approach response to a particular part of the experimental chamber than as a stimulus which unconditionally elicits some response. This observation serves to emphasize the possibility that positive conditioned suppression might be produced by interfering *operants,* a recurring theme in this research (Farthing, 1971). Thus it may be that recorded operant responding decreases because the subject makes preparatory approaches to the food cup which maximize the speed of taking up the free food when it is delivered, although most reports in this area claim that such behaviors could not be detected. Also, whether suppression or acceleration of responding develops during a prefood stimulus, the possibility must be considered that this is superstitiously reinforced by the delivery of the free food—an analogue of the punishment hypothesis of the effects of preshock stimuli. However, the evidence for superstitious reinforcement in this context is not strong (see Staddon, 1972).

The effects of prefood stimuli are being shown increasingly to depend on the parameters of the situation and on the nature of the behavior on which they are superimposed. Thus Meltzer and Brahlek (1970) reported acceleration of rats' variable-interval behavior during a 120-sec prefood stimulus, but, as noted, suppression during a 12-sec stimulus. Henton and Brady (1970) trained monkeys on a DRL 30-sec schedule and found no effect of a prefood stimulus of 20 or 40 sec, but they found *acceleration* during a prefood stimulus lasting 80 sec. Kelly (1973b) also found acceleration of monkeys' DRL behavior during a 60-sec prefood stimulus; his experiment, however, also made it possible to compare this effect with that of the same prefood stimulus on random ratio behavior. This revealed a schedule-dependent effect, for the latter behavior was suppressed during the stimulus.

Smith (1974), using pigeons, investigated the contribution of various response rates and reinforcement frequencies to the effects of prefood stimuli of various lengths. He found that both high and low response rates were *increased* during a 5-sec prefood stimulus. With longer stimuli, high rates were suppressed, but low response rates were unaffected. With two of the three subjects, high response rates were less suppressed when they obtained high frequencies of reinforcement rather than lower frequencies. It is clear from this study that there are considerable similarities in the variables which control the amount of suppression during a prefood stimulus, as here, and during a preshock stimulus (e.g., Blackman, 1968b).

There appears to be an important species-dependent effect when relatively short prefood stimuli are used in experiments. Although the above review suggests that the behavior of rats and monkeys is consistently suppressed in such conditions, LoLordo (1971) has found that pigeons' response rates increase. Similarly, Smith (1974) found increases in various behavioral base lines during a 5-sec prefood stimulus with his pigeons. In a recent study, LoLordo, McMillan, and Riley (1974) have thrown considerable light on this anomaly. They found that if the operant response being studied was key pecking, response rates increased if the prefood stimulus was a change in the illumination of the key. However, if the prefood stimulus was a nonlocalized tone, there was no acceleration. Similarly, there were no consistent effects of a tone or light prefood stimulus if the operant was treadle pressing rather than key pecking. The authors interpret these results as suggesting that the accelerative effect dependent on a localized prefood stimulus is an example of an autoshaped and automaintained response (Brown & Jenkins, 1968). This suggestion has the immediate effect of bringing the discussion toward the work of Gamzu and Schwartz (1973), who have developed the view that key-pecking rates of pigeons may depend on a summation of pecking maintained by instrumental contingencies per se and pecking which is supported by automaintenance. Since autoshaping and automaintenance have been discussed in the context of classical rather than operant conditioning (Jenkins & Moore, 1973), the work of Gamzu and Schwartz (1973) and its extension to phenomena such as behavioral contrast (e.g., Keller, 1974) is clearly relevant to the study of interactions between classical and operant conditioning. However, since they are discussed elsewhere (Chapter 3), these ideas are not developed here.

It can be seen then that there has been much recent work on the effects of prefood stimuli on operant behavior. Some studies have even reported that such stimuli may have suppressive effects on behavior maintained by an avoidance schedule (e.g., Davis & Kreuter, 1972; Henton, 1972). In general terms, studies of the effects of prefood stimuli have developed in a similar way to those of preshock stimuli. In both cases, the parameters of the procedure and the nature of the behavioral base lines on which it is superimposed are crucial, and this makes it impossible to make general assertions that a given preevent stimulus will have simply suppressive or enhancing effects on behavior. There is at present no adequate general theory, whether this be couched in terms of a general emotional state, conditioned drives, competing respondents or operants, or superstitious reinforcement of different rates by the delivery of free food. In short, research in this area may be said to mirror almost exactly the problems which have been discussed in the context of preshock stimuli throughout this chapter.

CONCLUSION

The procedures we have considered in this chapter have an apparent simplicity that can obscure the very real complexities both of measurement and of interpretation. In particular, the appropriate measurement of the disruption of operant behavior by classical conditioning procedures poses great problems. There is a real danger that describing these effects in terms of a relative rate during the conditioned stimulus can obscure important aspects of the situation. In spite of this, we have seen that the measurement of Pavlovian conditioning processes through what is usually regarded as their indirect effects on operant behavior has been widely recognized as being unusually sensitive and thereby productive. On the other hand, attempts to monitor any autonomic effects which might be supposed to be *directly* conditioned by the Pavlovian aspects of the procedure have been generally disappointing: autonomic changes often do occur during the conditioned stimulus, but they in no sense appear to reflect the orderliness of the indirect operant effects which one might suppose to be mediated by the classical conditioning of autonomic processes. Faced with this problem, it has been argued that it is a rather ill-specified conditioned emotional response (CER) which is the direct outcome of the Pavlovian aspects of the conditioning procedure. Some workers have preferred to describe this CER as conditioned anxiety, a term which has a degree of superficial validity in a situation in which a stimulus precedes an unavoidable aversive event. However, more recently the idea of a general emotional state has been revived, of which the traditional conditioned emotional response is said to be but one example. A further theory suggests that disruptive effects of a conditioned stimulus result from the conditioning of a motivational state which interacts with the motivation which supports the base line operant behavior. Yet a further possibility is that disruption of operant behavior during a preevent stimulus is the outcome of poorly controlled instrumental contingencies and hence reflects the strength of other interfering operants or the result of adventitious punishment or reinforcement.

Whether disruptions of operant behavior are thought to reflect underlying classical or operant conditioning effects or the development of changed motivational states, it is quite clear that the effects of any preevent stimulus depend critically on the nature of the behavioral base lines on which they are superimposed. The effects of classical conditioning procedures on operant behavior are therefore schedule-dependent, as are the effects of so many other independent variables. The differing degrees of susceptibility to disruption by a Pavlovian conditioned stimulus pose further questions: do these differences reflect different strengths of an underlying conditioned response, or is this strength determined solely by CS–US parameters so that different degrees of suppression reflect the resistance to disruption of different patterns of operant behavior? Similar problems of interpretation arise from the effects of drugs on disruptions of operant behavior during a conditioned stimulus and clearly return us to the problem of appropriate measurement.

In spite of the many problems of measurement and interpretation which have been discussed in this chapter, studies of the effects of classical conditioning procedures on operant behavior have long played an honorable role in learning theory. A problem in reviewing this research, however selectively, is that it has been related at various times to many theoretical controversies in psychology, and these general issues have been mentioned only briefly here. The procedure has proved to be successful in providing a sensitive dependent variable for the study of the necessary and sufficient conditions for the development of an acquired reflex. However, research using this procedure has also provided empirical evidence which has been related to motivational theories of behavior and the role of classical conditioning in motivation, to the study of emotion, to the relations between physiological events and overt behavior, to the study of the effects of potential anxiolytic agents, and to many other important problems. Indeed, perhaps one of the most important features of these studies is that they provide a focus for discussion between workers of different theoretical persuasions. In this light, it seems almost symbolic that the amount of conditioned suppression in a specified situation is a function of both classical and operant conditioning parameters, and that this disruption seems at present not to be a direct reflection of underlying physiological or autonomic processes. This complexity emphasizes that no one approach to the problems discussed here can be thought of as dominant. Hearst and Jenkins (1975) have recently suggested that identifying the different forms of learned behavior which develop in specified circumstances is at present preferable to the espousal of any universal theory of learning. The results reviewed in this chapter support this view.

REFERENCES

Annau, Z., & Kamin, L. J. The conditioned emotional response as a function of intensity of the US. *Journal of Comparative and Physiological Psychology*, 1961, *54*, 428–432.

Appel, J. B. Drugs, shock intensity, and the CER. *Psychopharmacologia*, 1963, *4*, 148–153.

Azrin, N. H. Some effects of two intermittent schedules of immediate and non-immediate punishment. *Journal of Psychology*, 1956, *42*, 3–21.

Azrin, N. H., & Hake, D. F. Positive conditioned suppression: Conditioned suppression using positive reinforcers as the unconditioned stimuli. *Journal of the Experimental Analysis of Behavior*, 1969, *12*, 167–173.

Azrin, N. H., & Holz, W. C. Punishment. In W. K. Honig (Ed.), *Operant behavior: Areas of research and application*. Englewood Cliffs, N.J.: Prentice-Hall, Inc., 1966.

Black, A. H., & Prokasy, W. F. (Eds.). *Classical conditioning*, Vol. 2: *Current research and theory*. Englewood Cliffs, N.J.: Prentice-Hall, Inc., 1972.

Blackman, D. E. Response rate and conditioned suppression. *Psychological Reports*, 1966, *19*, 687–693.

Blackman, D. E. Effects of response pacing on conditioned suppression. *Quarterly Journal of Experimental Psychology*, 1967, *19*, 170–174.

Blackman, D. E. Conditioned suppression or acceleration as a function of the behavioral baseline. *Journal of the Experimental Analysis of Behavior*, 1968, *11*, 53–61. (a)

Blackman, D. E. Response rate, reinforcement frequency, and conditioned suppression. *Journal of the Experimental Analysis of Behavior*, 1968, *11*, 503–516. (b)

Blackman, D. E. Effects of a pre-shock stimulus on temporal control of behavior. *Journal of the Experimental Analysis of Behavior*, 1970, *14*, 313–319. (a)

Blackman, D. E. Conditioned suppression of avoidance behaviour in rats. *Quarterly Journal of Experimental Psychology*, 1970, *22*, 547–553. (b)

Blackman, D. E. Conditioned anxiety and operant behaviour. In R. M. Gilbert & J. D. Keehn (Eds.), *Schedule effects: Drugs, drinking, and aggression*. Toronto: University of Toronto Press, 1972.

Blackman, D. E. *Operant conditioning: An experimental analysis of behaviour*. London: Methuen, 1974.

Blackman, D. E., & Scruton, P. M. Conditioned suppression of counting behavior in rats. *Journal of the Experimental Analysis of Behavior*, 1973, *19*, 93–100. (a)

Blackman, D. E., & Scruton, P. M. Conditioned suppression and discriminative control of behavior. *Animal Learning and Behavior*, 1973, *1*, 90–92. (b)

Bond, N. W., Blackman, D. E., & Scruton, P. M. Suppression of operant behavior and schedule-induced licking in rats. *Journal of the Experimental Analysis of Behavior*, 1973, *20*, 375–383.

Brady, J. V. The effect of electroconvulsive shock on a conditioned emotional response: The permanence of the effect. *Journal of Comparative and Physiological Psychology*, 1951, *44*, 507–511.

Brady, J. V. Assessment of drug effects on emotional behavior. *Science*, 1956, *123*, 1033.

Brady, J. V., Kelly, D., & Plumlee, L. Autonomic and behavioral responses of the rhesus monkey to emotional conditioning. *Annals of the New York Academy of Science*, 1969, *159*, 959–975.

Brown, P. L., & Jenkins, H. M. Auto-shaping of the pigeon's key peck. *Journal of the Experimental Analysis of Behavior*, 1968, *11*, 1–8.

Bryant, R. C. Conditioned suppression of free-operant avoidance. *Journal of the Experimental Analysis of Behavior*, 1972, *17*, 257–260.

Carlton, P. L., & Didamo, P. Some notes on conditioned suppression. *Journal of the Experimental Analysis of Behavior*, 1960, *3*, 255–258.

Davis, H. Conditioned suppression: A survey of the literature. *Psychonomic Monograph Supplements*, 1968, *2* (14, Whole No. 30), 283–291.

Davis, H., & Kreuter, C. Conditioned suppression of an avoidance response by a stimulus paired with food. *Journal of the Experimental Analysis of Behavior*, 1972, *17*, 277–285.

Dews, P. B. Behavioral effects of drugs. In S. M. Farber & R. H. L. Wilson (Eds.), *Conflict and creativity*. New York: McGraw-Hill, 1963.

de Toledo, L. E., & Black, A. H. Heart rate: Changes during conditioned suppression in rats. *Science*, 1966, *152*, 1404–1406.

Estes, W. K. An experimental study of punishment. *Psychological Monographs*, 1944, *57* (Whole No. 263).

Estes, W. K. Outline of a theory of punishment. In B. A. Campbell & R. M. Church (Eds.), *Punishment and aversive behavior*. Englewood Cliffs, N.J.: Prentice-Hall, Inc., 1969.

Estes, W. K., & Skinner, B. F. Some quantitative properties of anxiety. *Journal of Experimental Psychology*, 1941, *29*, 390–400.

Fantino, E. Effects of required rates of responding upon choice. *Journal of the Experimental Analysis of Behavior*, 1968, *11*, 15–22.

Fantino, E. Emotion. In J. A. Nevin (Ed.), *The study of behavior: Learning, motivation, emotion, and instinct*. Glenview, Ill.: Scott, Foresman, 1973.

Farthing, G. W. Effect of a signal previously paired with free food on operant response rate in pigeons. *Psychonomic Science*, 1971, *23*, 343–344.

Ferster, C. B., & Skinner, B. F. *Schedules of reinforcement*. Englewood Cliffs, N.J.: Prentice-Hall, Inc., 1957.

Fleshler, M., & Hoffman, H. S. Stimulus generalization of conditioned suppression. *Science*, 1961, *133*, 753–755.

Gamzu, E., & Schwartz, B. The maintenance of key-pecking by stimulus-contingent and response-independent food presentation. *Journal of the Experimental Analysis of Behavior*, 1973, *19*, 65–72.

Gottwald, P. The role of punishment in the development of conditioning suppression. *Physiology and Behavior*, 1967, *2*, 283–286.

Hake, D. F., & Powell, J. Positive reinforcement and suppression from the same occurrence of the unconditioned stimulus in a positive conditioned suppression procedure. *Journal of the Experimental Analysis of Behavior*, 1970, *14*, 247–257.

Hearst, E. Stress-induced breakdown of an appetitive discrimination. *Journal of the Experimental Analysis of Behavior*, 1965, *8*, 135–146.

Hearst, E., & Jenkins, H. M. *Sign-tracking: The stimulus-reinforcer relation and directed action.* Austin, Texas: Psychonomic Society, 1974.

Hendry, D. P., & Van Toller, C. Alleviation of conditioned suppression. *Journal of Comparative and Physiological Psychology*, 1965, *49*, 458–460.

Henton, W. W. Avoidance response rates during a pre-food stimulus in monkeys. *Journal of the Experimental Analysis of Behavior*, 1972, *17*, 269–275.

Henton, W. W., & Brady, J. V. Operant acceleration during pre-reward stimulus. *Journal of the Experimental Analysis of Behavior*, 1970, *13*, 205–209.

Hoffman, H. S. Stimulus generalization versus discrimination failure in conditioned suppression. In R. M. Gilbert & N. S. Sutherland (Eds.), *Animal discrimination learning.* New York: Academic Press, 1969.

Hoffman, H. S., & Barrett, J. Overt activity during conditioned suppression: A search for punishment artifacts. *Journal of the Experimental Analysis of Behavior*, 1971, *16*, 343–348.

Hunt, H. F., & Brady, J. V. Some effects of electroconvulsive shock on a conditioned emotional response ("anxiety"). *Journal of Comparative and Physiological Psychology*, 1951, *44*, 88–98.

Hunt, H. F., & Brady, J. V. Some effects of punishment and inter-current "anxiety" on a simple operant. *Journal of Comparative and Physiological Psychology*, 1955, *48*, 305–310.

Hurwitz, H. M. B., & Roberts, A. E. Suppressing an avoidance response by a pre-aversive stimulus. *Psychonomic Science*, 1969, *17*, 305–306.

Jenkins, H. M., & Moore, B. R. The form of the auto-shaped response with food or water reinforcers. *Journal of the Experimental Analysis of Behavior*, 1973, *20*, 163–181.

Kamin, L. J. Temporal and intensity characteristics of the conditioned stimulus. In W. F. Prokasy (Ed.), *Classical conditioning.* Englewood Cliffs, N.J.: Prentice-Hall, Inc., 1965.

Kamin, L. J., & Schaub, R. E. Effects of conditioned stimulus intensity on the conditioned emotional response. *Journal of Comparative and Physiological Psychology*, 1963, *56*, 502–507.

Kelleher, R. T., & Morse, W. H. Escape behavior and punished behavior. *Federation Proceedings*, 1964, *23*, 808–817.

Kelleher, R. T., & Morse, W. H. Determinants of the specificity of the behavioral effects of drugs. *Ergebnisse der Physiologie*, 1968, *60*, 1–56.

Kelleher, R. T., Riddle, W. C., & Cook, L. Persistent behavior maintained by unavoidable shocks. *Journal of the Experimental Analysis of Behavior*, 1963, *6*, 507–517.

Keller, K. The role of elicited responding in behavioral contrast. *Journal of the Experimental Analysis of Behavior*, 1974, *21*, 249–257.

Kelly, D. D. Long-term prereward suppression in monkeys unaccompanied by cardiovascular conditioning. *Journal of the Experimental Analysis of Behavior*, 1973, *20*, 93–104. (a)

Kelly, D. D. Suppression of random-ratio and acceleration of temporally spaced responding by the same preward stimulus in monkeys. *Journal of the Experimental Analysis of Behavior*, 1973, *20*, 363–373. (b)

Kinnard, W. J., Aceto, M. D. G., & Buckley, J. P. The effects of certain psychotropic agents on the conditioned emotional response behavior pattern of the albino rat. *Psychopharmacologia*, 1962, *3*, 227–230.

Lea, S. E. C., & Morgan, M. J. The measurement of rate-dependent changes in responding. In R. M. Gilbert & J. R. Millenson (Eds.), *Reinforcement: Behavioral analyses.* New York: Academic Press, 1972.

LoLordo, V. M. Facilitation of food-reinforced responding by a signal for response-independent food. *Journal of the Experimental Analysis of Behavior*, 1971, *15*, 49–56.

LoLordo, V. M., McMillan, J. C., & Riley, A. L. The effects upon food-reinforced pecking and treadle-pressing of auditory and visual signals for response-independent food. *Learning and Motivation*, 1974, *5*, 24–41.

Lyon, D. O. Some notes on conditioned suppression and reinforcement schedules. *Journal of the Experimental Analysis of Behavior*, 1964, *7*, 289–291.

Lyon, D. O. A note on response rate and conditioned suppression. *Psychological Record*, 1965, *15*, 441–444.

Lyon, D. O. Conditioned suppression: Operant variables and aversive control. *Psychological Record*, 1968, *18*, 317–338.

Lyon, D. O., & Felton, M. Conditioned suppression and variable ratio reinforcement. *Journal of the Experimental Analysis of Behavior*, 1966, *9*, 245–250. (a)

Lyon, D. O., & Felton, M. Conditioned suppression and fixed ratio schedules of reinforcement. *Psychological Record*, 1966, *16*, 433–440. (b)

Lyon, D. O., & Millar, R. D. Conditioned suppression on a fixed interval schedule of reinforcement. *Psychonomic Science*, 1969, *17*, 31–32.

Mackintosh, N. J. *The psychology of animal learning.* 1974 Academic Press, London, New York, San Francisco.

McKearney, J. W. Schedule-dependent effects: Effects of drugs, and maintenance of responding with response-produced electric shocks. In R. M. Gilbert & J. D. Keehn (Eds.), *Schedule effects: Drugs, drinking, and aggression.* Toronto: University of Toronto Press, 1972.

Meltzer, D., & Brahlek, J. A. Conditioned suppression and conditioned enhancement with the same positive UCs: An effect of CS duration. *Journal of the Experimental Analysis of Behavior*, 1970, *13*, 67–73.

Miczek, K. A. Effects of scopolamine, amphetamine, and benzodiazepines on conditioned suppression. *Pharmacology, Biochemistry, and Behavior*, 1973, *1*, 401–411.

Miczek, K. A., & Grossman, S. Positive conditioned suppression: Effects of CS duration. *Journal of the Experimental Analysis of Behavior,* 1971, *15,* 243–247.

MIGLER, B., & BRADY, J. V. Timing behavior and conditioned fear. *Journal of the Experimental Analysis of Behavior,* 1964, *7,* 247–251.

MILLENSON, J. R. A motivation-reinforcement theory of emotion. *Studia Psychologica,* 1971, *13,* 222–238.

MILLENSON, J. R., & DE VILLIERS, P. A. Motivational properties of conditioned anxiety. In R. M. Gilbert & J. R. Millenson (Eds.), *Reinforcement: Behavioral analyses.* New York: Academic Press, 1972.

MILLENSON, J. R., & HENDRY, D. P. Quantification of response suppression in conditioned anxiety training. *Canadian Journal of Psychology,* 1967, *21,* 242–252.

MILLENSON, J. R., & LESLIE, J. The conditioned emotional response (CER) as a baseline for the study of antianxiety drugs. *Neuropharmacology,* 1974, *13,* 1–9.

ORME-JOHNSON, D. W., & YARCZOWER, M. Conditioned suppression, punishment, and aversion. *Journal of the Experimental Analysis of Behavior,* 1974, *21,* 57–74.

PAVLOV, I. P. *Conditioned reflexes* (trans. G. V. Anrep). London: Oxford University Press, 1927.

POMERLEAU, O. F. The effects of stimuli followed by response-independent shock on shock-avoidance behavior. *Journal of the Experimental Analysis of Behavior,* 1970, *14,* 11–21.

RAY, O. S. Tranquilizer effects as a function of experimental anxiety procedures. *Archives Internationales de Pharmacodynamie et de Therapie,* 1964, *153,* 49–68.

RESCORLA, R. A. Pavlovian conditioning and its proper control procedures. *Psychological Review,* 1967, *74,* 71–80.

RESCORLA, R. A. Probability of shock in the presence and absence of CS in fear conditioning. *Journal of Comparative and Physiological Psychology,* 1968, *66,* 1–5.

RESCORLA, R. A. Conditioned inhibition of fear. In N. J. Mackintosh & W. K. Honig (Eds.), *Fundamental issues in associative learning.* Halifax: Dalhousie University Press, 1969.

RESCORLA, R. A., & SOLOMON, R. Two-process learning theory: Relationships between Pavlovian conditioning and instrumental learning. *Psychological Review,* 1967, *74,* 151–182.

RESCORLA, R. A., & WAGNER, A. R. A theory of Pavlovian conditioning: Variations in the effectiveness of reinforcement and nonreinforcement. In A. H. Black & W. F. Prokasy (Eds.), *Classical conditioning,* Vol. 2: *Current Research and Theory.* Englewood Cliffs, N.J.: Prentice-Hall, Inc., 1972.

ROBERTS, A. E., & HURWITZ, H. M. B. The effect of a preshock signal on a free-operant avoidance response. *Journal of the Experimental Analysis of Behavior,* 1970, *14,* 331–340.

SCOBIE, S. R. Interaction of an aversive Pavlovian conditional stimulus with aversively and appetitively motivated operants in rats. *Journal of Comparative and Physiological Psychology,* 1972, *79,* 171–188.

SIDMAN, M., HERRNSTEIN, R. J., & CONRAD, D. G. Maintenance of avoidance behavior by unavoidable shocks. *Journal of Comparative and Physiological Psychology,* 1957, *50,* 553–557.

SKINNER, B. F. *Behavior of organisms.* New York: Appleton-Century-Crofts, 1938.

SMITH, J. B. Effects of response rate, reinforcement frequency, and the duration of a stimulus preceding response-independent food. *Journal of the Experimental Analysis of Behavior,* 1974, *21,* 215–221.

STADDON, J. E. R. Temporal control and the theory of reinforcement schedules. In R. M. Gilbert & J. R. Millenson (Eds.), *Reinforcement: Behavioral analyses.* New York: Academic Press, 1972.

STEIN, L., SIDMAN, M., & BRADY, J. V. Some effects of two temporal variables on conditioned suppression. *Journal of the Experimental Analysis of Behavior,* 1958, *1,* 154–162.

STEIN, N., HOFFMAN, H. S., & STITT, C. Collateral behavior of the pigeon during conditioned suppression of key pecking. *Journal of the Experimental Analysis of Behavior,* 1971, *15,* 83–93.

WALLER, M. B., & WALLER, P. F. The effects of unavoidable shocks on a multiple schedule having an avoidance component. *Journal of the Experimental Analysis of Behavior,* 1963, *6,* 29–37.

WEISKRANTZ, L. Emotion. In L. Weiskrantz (Ed.), *Analysis of behavioral change.* New York: Harper & Row, 1968.

WEISS, K. M. Some effects of the conditioned suppression paradigm on operant discrimination performance. *Journal of the Experimental Analysis of Behavior,* 1968, *11,* 767–775.

WUTTKE, W., & KELLEHER, R. T. Effects of some benzodiazepines on punished and unpunished behavior in the pigeon. *Journal of Pharmacology and Experimental Therapeutics,* 1970, *172,* 397–408.

13

Negative Reinforcement and Avoidance*

Philip N. Hineline

INTRODUCTION

This chapter deals with behavior that is maintained when it removes, reduces, or prevents stimulation. The stimulation is called aversive on the basis of this functional relation with behavior. Through the same functional relation, the removal or reduction of stimulation is defined as negative reinforcement. As the title suggests, many of the experiments to be described here were initially designed and interpreted as *avoidance,* with this term taken both as a convenient category of procedures for shaping and maintaining behavior, and as a presumably valid category of behavior or behavioral processes. However, avoidance will not be my organizing principle. The everyday meaning of this term is too general to assist analysis. Defined more precisely as the prevention, rather than the reduction or removal of aversive stimulation, *avoidance* applies to only a few of the procedures and data to be included here. Further, within psychology the term has been identified mainly with one theory, and with experimental procedures oriented to that theory. The history of the interplay between avoidance theory and experiments has been thoroughly documented by Herrnstein (1969) and by Bolles (1973) and will not be recounted here. I will, however, sketch the theory, initially noting some reasons for departing from it. Later I will occasionally indicate how the present approach relates to it or differs from it.

In brief, avoidance theory has required that some stimulus, called a warning stimulus or conditioned stimulus, be paired with primary aversive stimulation such as electric shock. Through this pairing the warning stimulus is said to become aversive. Then, an overt response that is allowed to prevent the shock can also produce an immediate effect, terminating the warning stimulus. In some versions of the theory, the warning stimulus is identified as a Pavlovian conditioned stimulus, producing a conditioned internal response; removal of the stimulus then terminates the conditioned response. In all versions, responding is said to be reinforced by its immediate effects, and only incidentally to prevent the primary stimulation. Paradoxically this is to assert that avoidance (as prevention of absent aversive stimulation) is not a basic process; rather that

---

* This manuscript was written with the support of funds from a PHS research grant MH-18432 from the National Institute of Mental Health to the author, and of a Summer Research Fellowship from Temple University.

such prevention is always the byproduct of escape from a present conditioned stimulus.

The present account departs from traditional theory, partly because warning stimuli are sometimes not aversive as predicted by the theory. Also, warning stimuli have multiple properties that the theory does not predict. These facts will be documented below.

There are more general reasons for taking a different approach. Avoidance theorizing has conformed to a prejudgement that the reduction of aversive stimulation must be immediately discriminable upon occurrence of a response, if that reduction is to reinforce the response. Thus in the prototypical procedure sketched above, the warning stimulus is included to provide an immediately discriminable effect. When avoidance procedures have not provided explicit immediate consequences, their interpretations have focused on plausible surrogates for the warning stimulus. The surrogates have been drawn from overt behavior, or covert behavior, or internal time-correlated stimuli, but have always been said to function in a manner like that described above for externally-supplied warning stimuli. Explanation of avoidance, then, has been mainly an explanation of how an animal bridges gaps in time between a response and the consequent non-occurrence, or reduced occurrence of the aversive stimulation. This focus came prior to any appreciable examination of the range of situations in which negative reinforcement is effective.

In defense of the strategy of beginning with theoretical notions of mechanism, it can be argued that the theory provides a means for summarizing and organizing data. Further, when carried out with precision as in mathematical models, this approach carries with it a formal evaluation of explanatory assumptions. However, when applied to avoidance theory this increased rigor has been accompanied by restriction to small ranges of data, gathered with impoverished sets of procedures (e.g. Hoffman, 1966; Theios, 1971). The more common, verbal postulations of avoidance mechanisms deal with more data, but as Hoffman (1966) and Church (1973) have noted, these accounts have at best been informal and imprecise. In both cases, the focus on questions of mechanism has tended to constrain the range of procedures that are studied.

The present account is still concerned with organizing principles. However, I will focus on external controlling variables. Traditional avoidance procedures will be included, as part of a continuum that includes situations where behavior is maintained by immediate consequences, as well as situations where its apparent controlling consequences are remote in time. I will begin by describing two experiments. One illustrates the fact that procedures conventionally labeled and studied as avoidance are very limited representatives of what this term might include. The second experiment suggests that negatively reinforced behavior may be more similar to its positively reinforced counterpart than is customarily assumed. I will then consider the forms that negative reinforcement procedures have taken, first defined in discrete-trial procedures, and then extended to free-operant procedures in which only the aversive stimuli are manipulated. Next, I will consider procedures in which cues are added, providing for stimulus control of negative reinforcement, and changing the way in which intermittent aversive stimulation affects behavior. Finally, I will deal with some issues related to the shaping of particular responses with negative reinforcement.

The following are some major points: The fundamental operations in negative reinforcement procedures have been shock-delay and shock-deletion. In shock-delay, the timing schedules for shock are reset by responses. In shock-deletion, the timing schedules proceed independently, but responses can cancel shock deliveries. In both of these, shock-frequency reduction appears to be a major controlling variable. When additional stimuli are provided, their functions depend on which procedural features they are correlated with. For example, added cues can control behavior through correlations with contingencies of reinforcement, irrespective of the presence or absence of shock. Added cues can also control behavior through their correlation with differing rates of shock. A distinction can be made between reinforcement due to a change of situation, and reinforcement due to shock-frequency reduction within a situation. Added stimuli can also be used to isolate particular variables such as shock-frequency reduction and short-term delay of shock. For the initial shaping of behavior with negative reinforcement, one may encounter apparent constraints on conditioning. However, this "characterization by deficit" is of little help. Additional principles may be needed to describe the maintenance of the ongoing stream of behavior upon which negative reinforcement must operate.

TWO ILLUSTRATIVE EXPERIMENTS

Broadening the Range of Avoidance Experiments

Consider first an experiment that suggests a way to systematically generate and examine a rich variety of behavioral situations that might be called avoid-

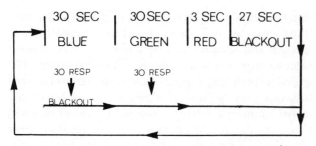

Fig. 1. Schema for a procedure using aversively maintained multiple operants. With no responding, the sequence progresses as indicated at the top of the diagram, with shocks accompanying the three-sec red light. As indicated, ratio schedules in effect during the red and green conditions permit shock-deletion and blackout for greater portions of the fixed 90-sec cycle. (After Krasnegor, Brady, & Findley, 1971. © 1971 by the Society for the Experimental Analysis of Behavior, Inc.)

ance. The experiment, by Krasnegor, Brady, and Findley (1971), used Rhesus monkeys, and was based on an abortable sequence of events diagrammed in Figure 1. Initial training was accomplished in phases, with the final procedure involving three stimuli in sequence on a recurring 90-sec cycle. If the confined monkey did not press a lever, a blue light was present for 30 sec, followed by a green light for 30 sec, followed by a 3-sec red light that was accompanied by three, brief, inescapable shocks, followed by 27 sec of darkness, or timeout, until the beginning of the next cycle. Thirty responses in the presence of either the green light or the blue light, with the count starting from zero at each stimulus change, produced timeout for the remainder of the 90-sec cycle. If fewer than 30 responses occurred in both the blue and green 30-sec periods, the red 3-sec light appeared with its 3 inescapable shocks. Thus, sufficiently rapid and persistent responding during either the blue or green light could abort the sequence, producing timeout for the remainder of the current 90-sec cycle. Stable performances were obtained in which the subjects received few shocks. One monkey responded primarily in the presence of the green light, which was the situation proximal to the red light and shocks. The other monkey completed the ratios about equally often in the proximal and distal (green and blue) situations. When the size of either response requirement was varied while the other was held constant, the performances of both monkeys gave similar functional relationships. As shown by a comparison of the two parts of Figure 2, responding in the distal situation dropped off more quickly as a function of fixed ratio size in that situation (Figure 2B) than it did in the proximal situation when that ratio was increased (Figure 2A). The main effect of varying the response requirements in the proximal or distal situations was to transfer the behavioral output toward the one requiring fewer responses, with a bias toward responding in the situation closer to shock.

This experiment indicates a promising approach for investigators who wish to make "avoidance" a primary concern. Krasnegor, Brady, and Findley's procedure could be expanded or extended, not only to examine a wider range of response requirements, but also to examine "reversing chains" in which responding in a proximal situation would reinstate a more distal situation. For example, the procedure described above could be modified so that responding in green would put the subject back in the presence of the blue light. I shall describe experiments with this feature later, in the context of stimulus control. One might also study choice and preference within this type of procedure by use of branching reverse sequences, such that differing, more-or-less distal situations could be made contingent upon different responses. This follows a strategy similar to that outlined by Findley (1962) for the study of appetitively-maintained behavior. The resulting procedures would more closely resemble what is commonly called "avoidance" than have traditional avoidance procedures.

Comparing Negative with Positive Reinforcement

My second illustrative experiment is by Kelleher and Morse (1964), who compared responding main-

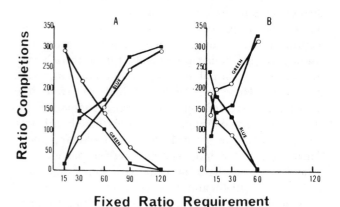

Fig. 2. Part A shows results of manipulating the fixed-ratio requirement in the proximal (green) stimulus while the ratio size in the distal (blue) stimulus remained constant at FR 30. Each data point represents the mean number of ratio completions for the last five sessions at each value of the ratio in green. Part B shows results of manipulating the FR requirement in the distal (blue) stimulus while the ratio requirement in the proximal (green) stimulus remained constant at FR 30. Each data point represents the mean number of ratio completions for the last five sessions at each value of the ratio in blue. The differing data points (filled squares vs. open circles) denote different monkeys. (After Krasnegor, Brady, & Findley, 1971. © 1971 by the Society for the Experimental Analysis of Behavior, Inc.)

tained by food presentation with responding maintained by termination of situations, denoted by distinctive visual cues, in which intermittent shocks occurred. The latter consequence can also be characterized as production of a discriminable shock-free situation. Three squirrel monkeys were trained on conventional multiple schedules of positive reinforcement in which a 10-min fixed-interval (FI) schedule alternated with a fixed-ratio (FR) schedule that required 30 responses. The schedules were accompanied by white and red lights, respectively, and exposures to these schedules were separated by timeout periods denoted by a visual pattern of horizontal bars. Three similar monkeys were trained on an analogous pair of schedules of negative reinforcement: in the FI schedule, brief shocks were scheduled to occur once per sec, beginning when the white light had been present for 10 min; the first response after the 10-min period produced the pattern of horizontal bars which denoted a situation with no shocks, and no response contingency. In the presence of the red light, brief shocks were scheduled to occur once every 30 sec; the 30th response in the presence of this light terminated the light and also produced the timeout stimulus. As shown in Figure 3, patterns of key-pressing maintained by these alternating FI and FR schedules were nearly identical for the appetitively-maintained and the aversively-maintained procedures. With this accomplished Kelleher and Morse administered D-amphetamine and chlorpromazine, separately and with systematic variation of doses. A detailed description of the drugs' effects is given in Chapter 7 of this book. For the present purpose, these effects can be easily summarized: While the two drugs had differing effects on behavior, the shock-maintained and food-maintained responding were very similarly affected by a given drug. In these situations the kind of consequences maintaining the behavior were less important than the specific pattern of behavior. This result recommends that appetitive/aversive distinctions not be taken for granted, nor too much predicated on them. Negatively-reinforced behavior and behavior characterized as avoidance may have much in common with behavior not so categorized. Nevertheless, the procedures for negative reinforcement differ formally from those of positive reinforcement, and the effects of negative reinforcement procedures will be the main concern here.

NEGATIVE REINFORCEMENT WITHOUT ADDED CUES

The Escape Procedure

A simple procedure for negative reinforcement is that of escape. In this procedure an aversive stimulus is presented and some aspect of the subject's behavior, which the experimenter specifies as a response, can terminate that stimulus. The stimulus is identified as aversive if the result of its termination is an increased probability or decreased latency of the response when that stimulus is again present. In most experiments on negative reinforcement the aversive stimulus has been electric shock. Other stimuli, such as intense light (Keller, 1941), loud noise (Harrison & Tracy, 1955), rotation (Riccio & Thach, 1966), temperature change (Weiss & Laties, 1961), and centrifugal force (Clark, Lange, & Belleville, 1973) have been used with varying success in aversive conditioning procedures, but the present chapter will deal mostly with shock since it has been almost universally used in systematic work.

In the escape procedure, behavior in the absence of an aversive stimulus has no effect on its subsequent recurrence. Such responding is typically ignored. Thus, escape conditioning is aptly described as a discrete-trial procedure, where the presence of the aversive stimulus defines a trial during which the subject's behavior is under study. Yet, while a trial is easily identified it is not a simple event. Three of its components will be distinguished here; as shown in Part I, of Figure 4, they coincide in time on the prototypical escape procedure, but can be viewed as independent. In the discussion that follows, these features will provide a basis for relating the escape procedure

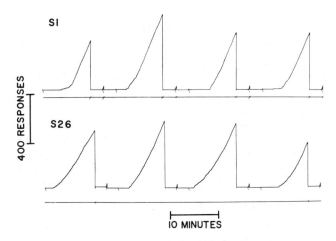

Fig. 3. Performance maintained by reinforcement with food (upper records) compared to performance maintained with electric shock (lower records) under multiple FI FR schedules. The large excursions were produced when the 10-min FI schedules were in effect; the smaller excursions were produced on the 30-response fixed-ratio schedules. At reinforcement, either through food delivery or shock prevention, the cumulative recording pen reset to the bottom of the record. (From Kelleher & Morse, 1964.)

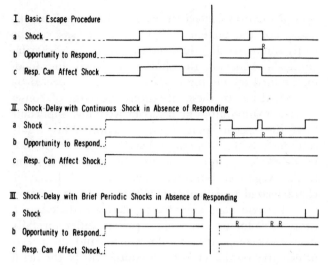

Fig. 4. Diagram illustrating three features as they apply to each of three procedures, with and without responding. Time is indicated linearly from left to right; upward displacement of a line indicates when a given feature is in effect. An "R" indicates occurrence of a response. Part I illustrates the basic escape conditioning procedure. Part II illustrates a shock-delay procedure in which failure to respond results in continuous shock. Part III illustrates a more typical shock-delay procedure of the kind devised by Sidman (1953), in which the RS interval is twice the SS interval.

to other negative reinforcement procedures and for interrelating those procedures. The escape trial includes: a) An aversive situation. In the basic escape procedure the aversive situation is defined by continuous presence of the aversive stimulus. b) An opportunity for responses to occur and to be counted. In the basic escape procedure the opportunity is often controlled by closing a door or removing a response lever; typically the opportunity for responding is terminated with the first response of the trial. c) An occasion when the specified response can affect the occurrence of aversive stimulation. One can relate these features to those of positive reinforcement situations: a) Providing an aversive situation is a manipulation that potentiates reinforcement. This feature identifies it as a "drive operation," analogous to deprivation procedures that are often used to potentiate positive reinforcement. Of course its discriminative properties differ from those of a deprivation procedure; I will discuss these properties later. b) The opportunity for responses to occur and be counted is typically terminated with the occurrence of one response. Given that the opportunity coincides with c), the occasion during which reinforcement is "set up" or available, this limited opportunity provides for continuous reinforcement (crf), or reinforcement on FR 1. To the extent that in positive reinforcement situations the observed response is precluded during positive reinforcement—key-pecking is improbable when the grain hopper is accessible—typical negative reinforcement and positive reinforcement situations are similar. They differ in that positive reinforcement durations are usually shorter than negative reinforcement durations.

Free Operants and the Escape Paradigm

Although the escape procedure of textbooks is usually described as requiring only a single response to terminate the shock and to produce an intertrial interval, where neither a), b) nor c) is operative, Dinsmoor and his colleagues have demonstrated schedules of negative reinforcement superimposed on the basic escape procedure. They allowed the opportunity for responding whenever the shock was present. Features a) and b) coincide as before, but c), the period during which responses could affect shocks, was restricted (Dinsmoor, 1967). As in appetitive schedules, reinforcements were set up during only parts of the periods when responding could occur. The resulting behavior on basic ratio and on interval schedules resembled that of comparable schedules of positive reinforcement.

So far I have said little about intervals when neither a) nor c) is operative. Of course, these intertrial intervals are of only peripheral interest if they include no opportunity to respond and other behavior is not observed. However, if a completely free operant is allowed and responding can and does occur between trials that it cannot affect, we have a situation that can be compared with other free-operant procedures. The shock can function as a discriminative stimulus, delineating the availability of reinforcement as well as providing the basis for it. This resembles an appetitive discrimination procedure where in the presence of a discriminative stimulus (S^d), responses are reinforced according to some schedule, with extinction in the absence of the discriminative stimulus (S^Δ). Keehn (1966) has noted patterns of intertrial responding that suggest such an interpretation, with discrete-trial negative reinforcement procedures seen as S^d–S^Δ discrimination procedures.

The Escape/Avoidance Distinction, and a Preview of the Present Approach

Sometimes in appetitive discrimination procedures, a delay contingency is imposed during S^Δ so that responding during this time prevents the onset of S^d. Such a delay contingency can be added to the escape procedure as well, and it has been done most simply in one version of the well-known shock-delay procedure devised by Sidman (1953)—the version with a shock-shock interval of zero. As diagrammed in Part II of Figure 4, in the absence of responding continuous shock is delivered. A response can terminate this shock for a period known as the response-shock (RS) interval; such a response is negatively reinforced by removal of shock. In addition, the opportunity to respond is continually present, and responses in the absence of shock delay the onset of shock. The shock will resume only if the response-shock interval elapses without an intervening response to restart the timing of this interval. In the appetitive case such a delay contingency reduces the future probability of the response to which it is applied. In the aversive case it has the opposite effect; responding in the absence of shock is maintained by delaying the onset of shock. In the present development of procedures the added delay feature introduces a new level of complexity. In previous procedures, whenever a response occurred it either removed the aversive stimulus or had no effect on aversive stimulation. Now, different consequences are produced by different classes of responses.

Within the tradition of aversive conditioning the presence vs. absence of shock has been the major distinction between escape and avoidance. Escape responses remove shock; avoidance responses prevent its occurrence. The validity of this distinction has been supported by experiments in which two different responses were independently maintained, one by removal of shock, and the other by delay or prevention of shock (e.g., Boren, 1961; Mowrer & Lamoreaux, 1946). The present account replaces this aspect of the escape/avoidance distinction with a more general concept of multiple contingencies of reinforcement under stimulus control. Instead of the $S^d - S^\Delta$ discriminations of the escape procedure (shock vs. no shock) where responses are reinforced in the presence of one stimulus and extinguished in the presence of another, there are two S^ds. A response in the presence of shock both removes the shock and produces a shock-free interval. Responses in the absence of shock delay it, extending the shock-free interval. As with the escape/avoidance distinction, if these two consequences are made contingent upon separate responses, the separate responses will be independently maintained. The separate effects, however, are not seen as resulting from distinct processes. Rather, they result from the fact that in discriminably different stimulus situations, different responses are reinforced. In this respect, it is like a positive reinforcement procedure where the presence of one light denotes a given schedule of reinforcement, and the presence of another light denotes a different schedule of reinforcement. Thus to the extent that the different negative reinforcement contingencies operate independently, denoted by distinctive cues, I will treat them like those of any other multiple-contingency procedure.

Later I will describe procedures that use intermittent brief shocks, producing situations that are not easily discriminable, but that involve differing reinforcement contingencies. In dealing with these I will distinguish between A) reinforcement by reduction of the density of aversive stimulation within a situation, and B) reinforcement by discriminable change of situation. Both categories include procedures that have been called "avoidance." The placing of a given procedure in category A) or category B) will depend upon added cues as well as upon characteristics of the aversive stimulation itself. The reasons for making this distinction will become evident later. For the immediate present, I shall describe procedures that cut across both escape and avoidance. These procedures require no special cues other than the shocks themselves. They involve shock-delay or shock-deletion, based on fixed or on variable time intervals.

The Continuum of Shock Density or Frequency

Electric shock continuously delivered may not be continuously received. For example, if it is grid shock the animal may produce intermittency by jumping up and down. Nevertheless the escape procedure is treated as a clear case of negative reinforcement by removal of shock. The experimenter may even arrange an escape procedure by explicitly presenting intermittent pulses of shock several times per second, rather than presenting it continuously. But if shock is presented several times per second, why not just twice per second, or once per second, or even less frequently? At some point we tend to stop labeling it continuous shock, and call it a stream of shocks. Responses are reinforced by interruption of (escape from) a stream of shocks. But as the pulses of shock are spaced out still further, to one every five, ten, or twenty seconds, we tend to characterize suspension of this situation not as removal of shock, or as interruption of a stream of shocks, but as reduction in shock frequency or density. One aspect of the shock delivery procedure that affects this characterization is the variability of the time between pulses of shock. Regularly spaced shocks seem to be appropriately characterized as streams or sequences until they become quite far apart. Irregularly spaced shocks are difficult to specify without reference to a distribution, whose measure of central tendency translates into frequency or density. Frequency and density are nearly equivalent. One stresses the number of shocks per unit time; the other stresses the time between events, but can also refer to the intensity and duration of those shocks.

Shock-Delay Procedures

The various forms of Sidman's well-known free-operant shock-delay procedure (Sidman, 1953) illustrate the density continuum. Diagrammed in Part III of Figure 4, the procedure is a more general form of the "escape-avoidance" procedure described above. In the absence of responding, instead of continuous shock, brief shocks are delivered periodically. These shocks are typically from 0.1 to 0.5 sec in duration, and are separated by the shock-shock (SS) interval. The shock-shock interval ranges from zero to more typically 3, 5, 10, or 20 sec. A single response interrupts this sequence for a time known as the response shock (RS) interval. With no additional intervening responses, occurrence of the next shock reinstates the SS interval as the determinant of shock delivery. However, if additional responses occur before the RS interval has elapsed, each one "resets the clock," restarting the timing of the RS interval. In the terms of the preceding pages, a short SS interval denoting virtually continuous shock might be considered as defining the aversive situation, while the RS interval defines its absence. A response during the brief SS interval produces a relatively long RS interval, effectively removing shock as in a standard escape procedure. However, in procedures where the SS interval approaches the RS interval, the term "escape" no longer seems appropriate; a response during a long SS interval can be said to delay shock just as responses during the RS interval do.

While the SS and RS intervals do not cleanly distinguish escape from avoidance, or even define the presence versus absence of aversive situation, they do have distinguishable effects on behavior. The effect of each is partly determined by the value assigned to the other. For example, Sidman (1962a) has noted that acquisition of lever-press responding is more easily achieved if the SS interval is substantially shorter than the RS interval. Leaf (1965) documented this effect with a between-group comparison in which each animal was run for only one session. Using a 20-second RS interval combined with SS intervals of 1, 3, 5, 10, or 20 seconds, he found consistent acquisition with SS intervals of 5 sec or less. Acquisition was less consistently obtained with the SS interval of 10 sec; and an SS interval equaling the 20-sec RS interval was only marginally effective. In contrast, Clark and Hull (1966) reported reliable acquisition with equal RS and SS intervals of 60 sec or more. However, in unpublished work I have been unable to replicate this latter result.

Once responding is established, RS and SS intervals affect response rates somewhat differently, as shown by one of Sidman's early experiments (Sidman, 1953). Sidman measured overall response rates while he varied the RS interval, holding the SS interval constant for each series of RS values, and changing the SS interval between series. In this way he obtained a family of functions for each subject; data from one of the rats is presented in Figure 5. With SS intervals of 5 sec or greater, maximal response rates occurred when the RS interval was equal to or slightly shorter than the SS interval. Response rates dropped off gradually as the RS interval was increased beyond the SS interval, giving plots that were concave upward. Response rates dropped off more quickly as the RS interval was decreased, giving plots that were concave downward, tending sharply toward zero with small RS values. With smaller SS intervals, where there was lit-

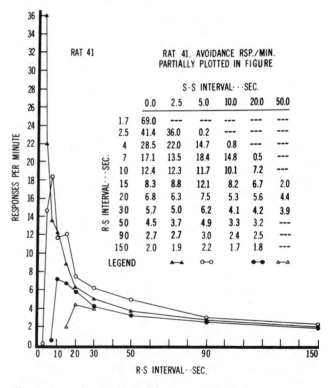

Fig. 5. One subject's rates of lever-press responding as response-shock intervals were varied in relation to constant shock-shock intervals. Each column of the table indicates a series obtained, in irregular order, with a given SS interval. Some of the series shown in the table are plotted in the curves. (After Sidman, 1953.)

tle room to manipulate the RS interval at values below the SS interval, only the concave-upward portion of the curve was obtained.

More recently, Clark and Hull (1966) examined the maintenance of overall response rates by procedures with equal RS and SS intervals, varying these intervals together. While they used preselected rats that had produced especially low shock rates during prior experimentation, the general features of their results agree with other less complete, but comparable data. As shown by the open symbols on the left side of Figure 6, increases in the RS = SS interval between 10 sec and 60 sec produced decreases in response rate according to a roughly hyperbolic function, transformed to roughly linear plots by using the reciprocals of the intervals. Clark and Hull noted that transformations other than the reciprocal, such as semilog and log-log transformations also produced approximately linear plots of response rate as a function of RS = SS interval. They found no compelling basis for selecting one of these transformations over another.

When Sidman (1953) held the SS interval constant at 2.5 seconds, varying the RS interval through larger values he obtained response rate changes comparable to those obtained by Clark and Hull. This is demonstrated by the plot with asterisks on the left side of Figure 6. These points were obtained by replotting a representative set of Sidman's data from Figure 5, in terms of reciprocals of the RS interval. Thus, as Sidman concluded from the experiment represented by Figure 5, the SS interval apparently has little effect in determining the shape of the rate versus RS function, provided that the RS interval is not substantially smaller than the SS interval. This is not a surprising outcome for well-conditioned animals that eliminate most shocks; the few shocks that they receive would be initiated by the Response-Shock timer. The results obtained by Clark and Hull with equal RS and SS intervals show relationships that would be expected on any schedules in which the RS interval exceeds the SS interval, at least for animals that eliminate most shocks.

The right side of Figure 6 shows shock rates that correspond to the response rates just considered. The open points indicate roughly linear increases in received shock rates as Clark and Hull increased the maximum possible shock frequency. However, for most animals, received shock rate was not simply a percentage of maximum shock rate. Clark and Hull reported that as the maximum shock rate was reduced to low values—corresponding to long SS = RS intervals—the percent shock reduction increased and more responses were emitted per shock received.

This is supported by plots on the right side of Figure 6 that tend toward zero to the right of the origin. The departure from a simple percentage relationship was not large. It appears reliable, however, for Sidman (1953) also reported a comparable effect when increasing the RS interval and using the reciprocal of the RS interval in place of maximum shock frequency.

SHOCK-DELETION PROCEDURES

A different type of negative reinforcement procedure provides continuous opportunity to respond and also incorporates much of the continuum, from pulse streams to widely spaced shocks. Instead of providing for a response to reset the timing interval and thus delay shock, these procedures allow a response to cancel or delete an impending shock without affecting the time cycles for shock delivery. The basic characteristics are readily evident in a fixed-cycle procedure described by Sidman (1966). As the label implies, the procedure is based on a timing cycle that progresses independently and constantly, regardless of the subject's behavior. With no responding, each timing cycle ends with a brief inescapable shock and starts again. The first response in a cycle cancels the shock due at

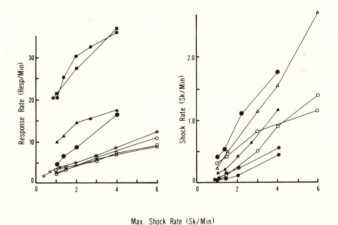

Fig. 6. Response rates and obtained shock rates as functions of the maximum shock rates possible under shock-delay and shock-deletion procedures. Each open symbol represents a pair of equal shock-shock and response-shock intervals on Sidman's shock-delay procedure, as used by Clark and Hull (1966). Differently shaped data points represent performances of different rats. The plot with asterisks shows response rate as a function of the reciprocal of the RS interval (which, for this set of intervals does not equal maximum shock rate), with the SS interval held constant at 2.5 sec. These data, obtained by Sidman (1953), are taken from Figure 5. The plots with filled symbols show response rates and received shock rates as functions of maximum shock rates on a shock-deletion procedure based on variably spaced shocks (after de Villiers, 1974). Most points show the mean of two determinations for a given VI schedule: one from an ascending, and one from a descending series of VI values.

the end of that cycle; additional responses during the cycle have no effect. Thus, as indicated in Part I of Figure 7, the opportunity to respond is continuous, but the occasion for a response to affect shock is limited to one effective response per cycle. This procedure has not been studied as extensively or as systematically as has the shock-delay procedure, but it is clearly effective for producing and maintaining lever-press responding. The fixed-cycle shock-deletion procedure is similar to the shock-delay procedures considered above in that both use fixed shock-shock intervals, and both allow frequent responding to eliminate all shocks. The two procedures differ in that all responses on the delay procedure affect shock, while on the deletion procedure not all responses are effective. They also differ with respect to which relations between responding and shock are fixed, and which are variable. In the delay procedures the interval between response and shock is fixed. The amount of shock reduction resulting from each response varies with the subject's spacing of responses. In deletion procedures the subject's spacing of responses affects the interval between response and shock, but the amount of shock reduction is tightly controlled; an effective response eliminates exactly one shock. Closely spaced responses are relatively ineffective in both: A response that closely follows another can produce only a small increment in shock delay. There is a low probability of deleting shock, since it is likely to fall in the same cycle as the earlier response.

Shock-delay procedures need not use constant time intervals. Indeed, Sidman and Boren (1957a) modified the basic delay procedure by changing the response-shock interval after each shock. This procedure readily produced both acquisition and maintenance of lever–pressing. Bolles and Popp (1964) used a delay procedure in which the response-shock interval was constant but the shock-shock interval varied from one shock to the next, with a mean value slightly under seven seconds. They compared acquisition on this procedure to that on a standard delay procedure where the RS interval was 15 sec and the SS interval was constant at five sec. This was a between-subject comparison, and their small number of rats prohibited concluding that the variable shock-shock interval was superior to the fixed one. However, the observed differences were clearly in that direction. In unpublished work I have found consistently good acquisition and maintenance of lever pressing on a procedure where both the response-shock and shock-shock interval varied randomly after each response and each shock. Clearly, fixed intervals are not critical to the effectiveness of the shock-delay procedures.

The shock-deletion contingency, where timing cycles are independent of behavior, is also readily adapted to variable shock-shock intervals, as shown by de Villiers (1974). His procedure was identical to Sid-

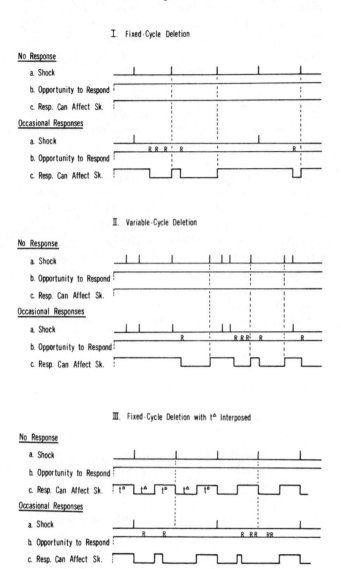

Fig. 7. Diagrams showing the relations between features of shock-deletion procedures. A given feature is in effect when its corresponding line is displaced upward. A straight line indicates that a given feature is continuously in effect. An "R" indicates the occurrence of a response. Part I illustrates a procedure based on fixed-cycle shock delivery (after Sidman, 1966). Part II illustrates a procedure that is formally identical except it is based on variable-cycle shock delivery (after de Villiers's 1974 "variable-interval" shock deletion). Part III illustrates a fixed-cycle procedure with imposed t^Δ periods when responding cannot affect the impending shock. On this procedure, t^D indicates periods when responding is effective. In this example t^Δ and t^D are of equal duration. Their relative durations can be varied (after Hurwitz & Millenson, 1961). In all three parts of the figure, sequences of events with and without responding are portrayed. The dashed lines identify points at which responding has resulted in deletion of shock.

man's fixed-cycle shock-deletion procedure described above, except that the shock-shock interval varied from cycle to cycle. In the absence of responding the rats received brief shocks, irregularly spaced so that the probability of a shock was roughly constant over time. The first response in an SS interval deleted the shock due at the end of that interval; additional responses within the interval had no effect. When the time for a (deleted) shock was passed, the next response would again be effective. A plausible sequence of events on this procedure, showing shocks delivered by identical random scheduling sequences with and without responding, is shown in part II of Figure 7. De Villiers first established responding with a schedule whose mean shock-shock interval in the absence of responding was 15 sec. He then varied this mean interval between 15 sec and 60 sec, over blocks of sessions. The resulting response rates are plotted individually for the four rats, with the filled symbols in Figure 6. These plots represent combined data from increasing and decreasing series, which de Villiers presented separately. With maximum shock frequency as an independent variable common to the two types of procedures, de Villiers's results are readily compared with the results obtained with fixed shock-delay procedures by Clark and Hull (1966). Interestingly, although absolute response rates are much higher for two of de Villiers's four animals, response rates versus maximum shock rate gave roughly similar functions in both cases. The "received shock frequency" plots for the two procedures show even greater similarity than the response rate plots. However, systematic relationships based on responses emitted per shock received and percent shock reduction as a function of maximum shock frequency observed on shock-delay procedures both by Sidman and by Clark and Hull were not consistently obtained on this procedure.

Shock-Frequency Reduction as a Controlling Variable

While response-shock intervals, shock-shock intervals, and maximum shock rate are straightforward as independent variables, none of these by itself adequately describes the consequence of responding when procedures are based on brief intermittent shocks. De Villiers addressed the problem of specifying the consequence of responding with a single expression, and at the same time provided evidence for functional similarity between positive and negative reinforcement. He also provided an additional means for comparing the effects of shock-delay and shock-deletion procedures. De Villiers started with a relationship that

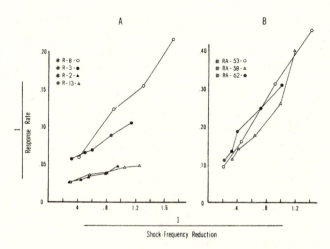

Fig. 8. Reciprocals of response rates plotted against reciprocals of shock-frequency reductions on shock-delay and shock-deletion schedules. Part A shows data obtained by de Villiers (1974) with a variable-cycle shock-deletion procedure. Part B shows data obtained by Clark and Hull (1966) with shock-delay schedules in which SS and RS intervals were held equal as they were varied over blocks of sessions. These plots are based on the same data that were presented in Figure 6.

Herrnstein had derived in studies of concurrent schedules of positive reinforcement and then developed to relate the rate of responding to the rate of reinforcement on single VI schedules (Herrnstein, 1970). A detailed treatment of this formulation can be found in Chapter 9 of the present volume. For the present purpose, suffice it to say that Herrnstein's equation predicts a linear relationship between the reciprocal of response rate and the reciprocal of the rate of reinforcement.[1] Since assessment of linearity is simpler than other forms of curve fitting, the response rates are plotted as reciprocals in Figure 8, using the data from Figure 6. For both de Villiers's data and those of Clark and Hull, shock-frequency reduction was computed for each animal on each schedule by subtracting the obtained shock rate from the shock rate that would occur with no responding. Part A of Figure 8 shows that this formulation describes the performance of each of de Villiers's four animals well; each plot is linear although the slopes differ for different animals. De Villiers tried substituting received shock in place

---

[1] The expression involved here is: $R_1 = \dfrac{k\,r_1}{r_1 + r_0}$, where R_1 is the rate of responding; r_1 is the frequency of reinforcement contingent on that response; k is the response rate if no alternative responses were reinforced; and r_0 is the sum of reinforcement frequencies contingent on responses other than that described by R_1 (whether or not these are measured by the experimenter). If this equation is inverted it predicts a linear relation between performance and reinforcement:

$$\frac{1}{R_1} = \frac{1}{k} + \frac{r_0}{k r_1}.$$

of shock-frequency reduction, but found this produced greater departures from linearity. Interestingly, responses of two of Clark and Hull's three animals show a comparable degree of linearity when plotted in the same way, as shown in Part B of Figure 8. De Villiers has argued that a linear relationship would not be expected on fixed shock-delay procedures since short-term effects of spaced responding would override the overall effects of reinforcement frequency. Perhaps the equating of relative reinforcement rate to shock-frequency reduction can be done more generally than de Villiers proposed.

Both de Villiers and Clark and Hull varied shock-frequency reduction only by manipulating the maximum shock frequency which could occur in the absence of responding. Their experiments implicate shock-frequency reduction mainly on the basis of its fitting a particular function when plotted in relation to response rates on these procedures. Other studies have more directly indicated shock-frequency reduction as a controlling variable, by manipulating this variable independently of the maximum shock frequency. The first instance of this was accomplished inadvertently by Sidman (1962a). Rats were concurrently exposed to two independent shock-delay schedules, using separate response levers. Each schedule was controlled by a single timer that was reset by responses on its appropriate lever, recycling as it delivered shock when no such responses had occurred. Hence, considered separately, each schedule was a conventional shock-delay procedure with equal RS and SS intervals. However, the two timers delivered indistinguishable shocks, so they combined to produce irregular shock sequences. Even when the two timers were given equal settings the rats tended to respond mostly on one lever, receiving frequent shocks from the schedule that required responses on the other lever. The rats' choice not to distribute responses on the two levers effected a lower limit to shock-frequency reduction. When two timers were given unequal settings, responding to the one with the greater interval would produce longer delays of individual shocks, but would result in relatively higher overall shock frequencies due to the continual recycling of the other timer. Responding to the lever with the shorter timer would produce shorter delays of individual shocks, but if this responding was sufficiently frequent it would result in relatively lower overall shock frequencies. With these unequal settings, the rats tended to respond exclusively on the lever that gave a shorter shock-delay per response, but which permitted a greater decrease in overall shock frequency. This experiment then led Sidman to propose shock-frequency reduction as a critical variable.

Following this lead, Herrnstein and Hineline (1966) devised a procedure that permitted direct and independent manipulation of both maximum shock frequency and the amount of shock-frequency reduction that responding could produce. This procedure, diagrammed in Figure 9, was based on two independent random schedules for delivering brief shocks. The schedules were generated by independently sampling two probability distributions once every two seconds. Averaging over longer time periods, the frequency of scheduled shocks was roughly constant over time, but the two schedules could have differing frequencies. In the absence of responding, the schedule with higher probability controlled the delivery of shock. A response transferred control to the schedule with lower probability, where the control remained until that schedule delivered a shock, at which time the control transferred back to the schedule with higher probability. Thus, one probability or the other was operative depending on whether a response or a shock had occurred last. On this procedure, a response could reduce shock frequency by a specified amount, but it could not impose a shock-free period, for shocks could and did occur immediately after some responses. This procedure permitted direct experimental manipulation of response-contingent shock-frequency reduction. Acquisition was reliably obtained even when the two shock schedules had probabilities as close as 0.2 vs. 0.3, giving mean shock frequencies of six and nine shocks per minute. However, the Herrnstein and Hineline experiment was mainly a study of acquisition, and included only a few combinations of shock frequencies,

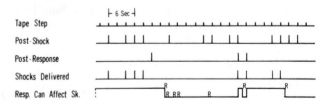

Fig. 9. Diagram showing the relations between features of a procedure for response-contingent shock-frequency reduction. The punched tape advances at regular 2-sec intervals. Deflections on the lines marked "post-shock" and "post-response" indicate holes in these respective channels of the tape; probability of a hole is constant for a given channel, but the probability can differ between channels. Shocks are shown as deflections on the line indicated. "R" indicates a response. The delivery of shock coincides with the occurrence of a hole in the tape channel currently in control, which correlates with whether a response can affect shock. Control is changed from one channel to the other by a shock if a response has occurred since the last shock, and by a response if a shock has occurred since the last response. (From Herrnstein & Hineline, 1966. © 1966 by the Society for the Experimental Analysis of Behavior, Inc.)

permitting no detailed analysis of response rate as a function of shock-frequency reduction. More systematic data would be of interest, especially in relation to the work of de Villiers described just above.

Returning to schedule classification, Herrnstein and Hineline's procedure resembles the shock-deletion procedure described earlier (Part I of Figure 6), in that the time-base of the shock-delivery schedule proceeds independently of behavior. No clocks are reset as would occur in shock-delay procedures. Unlike the earlier shock-deletion procedure, an effective response deletes shock only probabilistically, as determined by the difference between the two random shock-delivery schedules. This procedure also differs from the earlier shock-deletion procedures in that a response reduces the probability of shock, not only until the end of the timing cycle when a shock is deleted, but until a shock is delivered by the low frequency schedule. The amount of exposure to the low frequency shock schedule is determined by that schedule as well as by the amount of responding.

If control were to revert to the high-frequency schedule at the end of a timing cycle irrespective of whether a shock had been deleted, the procedure would fit a descriptive system that has recently been gaining some currency. This formulation has been described by Church (1969), Catania (1971), Seligman, Maier, and Solomon (1971), and by Gibbon, Berryman, and Thompson (1974), as a means for defining the degree of contingent relations between responding and rewarding stimuli or noxious stimuli. Neffinger and Gibbon (1975) have used the formulation to generate negative reinforcement procedures with added cues. It could also be used to increase the generality of uncued shock-deletion procedures that have been described above (Part I of Figure 6) and enable these, like Herrnstein and Hineline's procedure, to manipulate shock frequency reduction independently of absolute shock frequency. The formulation simply is this: in any given time period, probability of shock, given a response, can be manipulated independently of the probability of shock given no response in that time period. On the standard, fixed-cycle shock-deletion procedure (Part I of Figure 6), the probability of shock given no response is 1.0; the probability of shock given a response is zero. This need not be the case; either probability can be manipulated between these values. So long as the probability of shock given a response is smaller than the probability given no response, negative reinforcement can occur. The possible shock frequencies are determined jointly by probabilities per cycle, and cycle length. Cycle length sets the maximum shock frequency. Also, cycle length, independently of probability, determines the minimum response rate needed to achieve a given degree of shock-frequency reduction. On Herrnstein and Hineline's procedure, the minimal shock frequency could be achieved by a minimum of one response after each shock. On the probabilistic fixed-cycle shock-deletion procedures just outlined, a minimum of one response per cycle is required to achieve the minimal shock frequency, no matter when specific shocks have occurred.

I noted earlier that shock density is an alternative specification to shock frequency. Density differs from frequency, partly in emphasizing the spacing between shocks rather than shocks per unit time, but also because it can encompass the duration and intensity of shocks as well as the frequency of shock onset. For example, if shocks were to occur every five seconds, a reduction in either the duration or the intensity of shocks would count as a density reduction even though shock frequency remained constant. Powell and Peck (1969) demonstrated the potency of such a density reduction with a procedure that illustrates an interesting hybrid between shock-delay and shock-deletion. Their schedule resembled shock-deletion in that the time-based shock delivery schedule proceeded independently of behavior. However, the effects of responding were metered through a response-shock interval identical to that of a shock-delay schedule, as follows: Brief shocks were delivered every five seconds. Responses started a 20-second timer with the same contingent relationship as for Sidman's delay procedure. However, instead of delaying shocks, starting this timer reduced the intensity of the one-per-five-second shocks. So long as 20 seconds did not elapse without a response, all shocks were delivered at the lower intensity. Powell and Peck found acquisition with this procedure to be more rapidly and reliably achieved than with a standard shock-delay procedure with $SS = 5$ and $RS = 20$.

Schedules of Negative Reinforcement Based On Intermittent Shocks

The shock-delay procedures considered so far have provided for every occurrence of the response to be effective. As will be seen below, schedules of reinforcement are easily achieved by imposing a ratio requirement or by limiting the access to reinforcement. On the shock-deletion procedures already described, there have been intervals when responses were ineffective. However, these were periods of reinforcement, when impending shock had already been cancelled or reduced in probability. Disabling the response lever at these times is analogous to disabling the lever in the presence of a food reinforcer in appetitive procedures. Schedules of reinforcement by shock-deletion require modifying response effectiveness at other times as well.

Hurwitz and Millenson (1961) did this, examining the maintenance of responding while they systematically varied the access to reinforcement in the face of uncancelled shocks. Their procedure, diagrammed in Part III of Figure 7, was conceived within a formulation developed by Schoenfeld and his associates (Schoenfeld and Cole, 1972). The formulation uses two time periods, designated t^Δ and t^D, which alternate continually to produce fixed cycles. Positive reinforcement on this schedule is customarily delivered immediately upon occurrence of the first response in t^D. Additional responses during t^D are ineffective, as are those during t^Δ. In the negative reinforcement case arranged by Hurwitz and Millenson, the first response during t^D deleted a shock that was scheduled to occur at the end of t^D. With t^Δ equal to zero, as was the case during initial training in Hurwitz and Millenson's experiment, this procedure is identical to the simple fixed-cycle shock-deletion procedure diagrammed in Part I of Figure 7. As t^Δ is increased to values greater than zero, the procedure becomes one in which the shock-deletion periods are alternated with periods during which responding cannot affect the impending shock. Hurwitz and Millenson held the sum of t^Δ and t^D constant at 30 seconds, and systematically increased t^Δ, changing its value every few sessions. The resulting response rates and shock rates are shown in Figure 10, each giving a systematic relation between response rate and the relative time that reinforcement was accessible. When most of the cycle was spent in t^D, response rates were low, and many shocks were received. The response rate function obtained by Hurwitz and Millenson resembles a comparable function obtained by Hearst (1960) with analogous manipulations of a $t^\Delta - t^D$ schedule based on positive reinforcement. The two curves differ in the location of maximum rate, but not in their general shapes.

Sidman (1962b) reported virtually identical results with the same procedure, using a 15-second cycle. However, when he departed from the usual $t^\Delta - t^D$ procedures and moved the access period to the middle of the cycle, responses continued to be most probable near the end of the cycle, where shock was due. Sufficient mid-cycle responses occurred to produce a few shock deletions, but response rates soon dropped to near zero. The eventual decrement in overall performance can be attributed either to the fact that placing access to reinforcement at mid-cycle permitted shocks to occur immediately after some responses—late in the cycle when no response had occurred during the access period—or simply to a decrement in shock-frequency reduction.

More recently, Kadden, Schoenfeld, and Snapper (1974) studied $t^\Delta - t^D$ schedules of shock-deletion in which the probability of shock with a response in t^Δ, and the probability of shock if no response occurred during t^D, were manipulated independently. They used Rhesus monkeys as subjects, and after initial shaping of the response with removal of continuous shock, the sum of $t^\Delta + t^D$ was always 60 seconds. They established stable response rates with a series of temporal combinations ($t^D = 45$ sec, then 30 sec, then 6 sec) in which probability of shock was 1 given no response, and zero if a response occurred. These features resemble the procedures by Hurwitz and Millenson, and by Sidman, described just above. Kadden et al. then independently varied the probability of shock

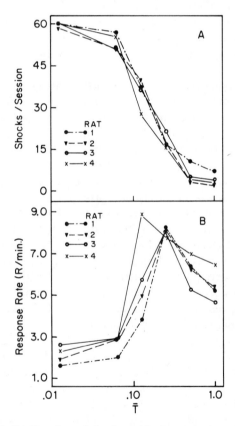

Fig. 10. (A) Number of shocks received per session; (B) lever-press response rates for four rats as a function of the temporal schedule parameter $\overline{T}$. $\overline{T}$ is defined as $t^D/(t^D + t^\Delta)$ and represents here the relative portion of a 30-second shock-shock interval in the period during which the first response resulted in deletion of the next shock due. (From Hurwitz and Millenson, 1961. © 1961 by the American Association for the Advancement of Science.)

given a response and the probability of shock given no response, presenting the values in different orders for different monkeys. Responding always ceased when the probability of shock was greater if a response occurred than if no response occurred. Also, responding ceased or dropped to very low levels when the probability of shock given no response was reduced, provided that the probability of shock given a response was greater than zero. Responding was more persistent when the probability of shock given a response was kept at zero; the monkeys seldom paused long enough to encounter the new consequences of not responding.

Kadden, Schoenfeld, and Snapper's procedure fits the contingency analysis of probabilistic fixed-cycle shock-deletion schedules that I noted earlier (p. 375). However, the insertion of large t^Δ periods into the cycle makes the procedure an interval schedule of reinforcement as well as a probabilistic contingency manipulation. Indeed, the patterns of responding within cycles revealed fixed-interval scheduling effects when shock deliveries permitted response patterns to stay in synchrony with the timing cycle. Thus, when probability of shock given a response exceeded zero, but was not high enough to eliminate responding, response rates increased as time for the t^D period (as well as the possibility of another shock) approached.

Shock-delay procedures have been adapted to produce schedules even more closely resembling the traditional basic positive reinforcement schedules. Verhave (1959) imposed ratio schedules on a shock-delay procedure. He pretrained the animals with conventional shock-delay procedures, starting with SS = 3 and RS = 30 sec, and then moving to SS = RS = 30 sec. He then imposed ratio requirements so that more than one response was required during a given RS or SS interval, to delay the next shock. The response requirement was increased from two up to eight. Response rates increased concomitantly over those obtained when single responses could delay shock. Then, holding the ratio constant at eight, Verhave varied the RS interval, and found a functional relation similar to those obtained in experiments by Sidman (1953) and by Clark and Hull (1966) where every response could delay shock (see Figure 6 above). Of course the absolute response rates were substantially higher than in these studies with a ratio of one.

Sidman (1966) reported a shock-delay experiment that he called fixed-interval avoidance. In the absence of responding, the procedure resembled the $t^\Delta - t^D$ procedure of Hurwitz and Millenson already described. A fixed interval when responses could not affect shock (t^Δ) was followed by a fixed period in which responding could affect an impending shock.

Delivery of the shock started this cycle over. On Sidman's procedure responding could change the cycle length. Each response in the "effective" period (corresponding to t^D on Hurwitz and Millenson's procedure) delayed the shock and extended that period; response-shock intervals were in effect until responding lapsed and shock occurred, reinstating the "t^Δ" period. Using a t^Δ of 60 sec and a response-shock interval of 6 sec, Sidman observed an acceleration of response rate within the t^Δ period. This pattern, which is characteristic of fixed-interval schedules was also observed in the experiment by Kadden et al. (1974), described above. The pattern indicates a degree of discrimination of nonreinforcement during the t^Δ period. Hurwitz and Millenson did not find systematic changes in response rate within the t^Δ periods. This difference of results is attributable to the fact that on Sidman's procedure, each t^Δ period began with a shock, providing a discriminable cue that was not consistently present on Hurwitz and Millenson's procedure. The experiment by Kadden et al. confirmed that cuing function of shock.

Sidman's fixed-interval procedure and the $t^\Delta - t^D$ procedure of Kadden et al. are not entirely comparable to fixed-interval positive reinforcement procedures, for the periods when responses cannot affect shock are also periods when no shocks can occur. The basis for reinforcement is missing, along with the access to reinforcement. In positive reinforcement procedures the basis for reinforcement is continually present. Hence, the negative reinforcement procedures would have been more comparable to positive reinforcement schedules if shocks were delivered during the t^Δ periods. Similar issues arise in defining the extinction of negatively reinforced behavior.

Extinction After Negative Reinforcement

Extinction is the discontinuation of reinforcement, with continued opportunity to respond. One expects that responding will return to levels that occurred prior to conditioning. By convention, a basic or "reference" extinction procedure implies a situation in which prior conditioning occurred, unchanged except for the withholding of reinforcement. Depending on its prior scheduling, the absence of reinforcement may or may not produce a situation strikingly different from that during prior conditioning. While this degree of difference most likely will affect how quickly the process of extinction occurs, the degree of difference is irrelevant to the definition of an extinction procedure or process. Extinction, whether quick or slow, is still extinction.

The experiments described below will illustrate the following points regarding extinction after negative reinforcement: Two different types of extinction procedures have been proposed. The more traditional one simply involves the discontinuation of shock. However, it has been recently argued that this removes reinforcement only indirectly, through suspension of the drive operation upon which reinforcement was based. By this view, discontinuing all shocks is analogous to providing food continuously during extinction of food-reinforced responding. An alternative type of extinction procedure involves continued presentation of shocks while eliminating the effects of responses on shock. Proponents of this as a reference procedure argue that discriminability of the extinction situation is an issue in defining the extinction of negative reinforcement, especially if one focuses on the contingent relation between responding and reinforcement rather than merely the delivery or nondelivery of reinforcement. Finally, the fact that delivery of *free* or noncontingent shocks may induce responding in a way inconsistent with usual notions of negative reinforcement, further complicates the definitions and interpretations of extinction of negatively reinforced behavior.

Alternative Procedures for Extinction

To extinguish responses that were conditioned with shock-delay procedures in which responding could reduce the shock frequency to zero, some experimenters have simply deactivated the shock generator. Thus, for example, Shnidman (1968) eliminated all shocks after rats had been trained with a few four-hour sessions of shock-delay with SS = 5 sec and with RS = 20 or 40 sec, each rat being exposed to both values. The shock generator was deactivated three hours after the beginning of a session that continued beyond its usual 4-hour limit, if necessary until response rate declined to zero for 15 min. Response rates dropped to zero within an hour for two of three rats, and within two hours for the third. Using a similar extinction procedure, Boren and Sidman (1957) found greater persistence of responding. After first subjecting their rats to 100 or more hours of initial training with SS and RS intervals of 20 sec, they alternated periods of conditioning and extinction. The 6-hour sessions were divided into two periods, with normal conditioning for the first part of each session, and with the shock generator off during the second part of each session. Responding during extinction declined in an orderly fashion over a few sessions, but in most cases did not reach zero.

Some animals' responding also declined during the conditioning periods, indicating overall extinction, but other animals continued to respond during the conditioning periods. In these latter cases the periods when the shock generator was off clearly were discriminated from the periods when it was on, even though no added exteroceptive stimuli were supplied. Boren and Sidman suggested the occurrence of unshocked nonavoidance could account for their results, but the experiment does not permit one to distinguish this from a discrimination based directly on the shocks themselves.

The elimination of all shock produces confounded changes in two of the three basic features I have used for analyzing negative reinforcement procedures. The aversive situation is removed, and access to reinforcement is therefore modified indirectly. This is especially obvious in relation to escape procedures, where conditioning is based on removal of continuous shock. Reinforcement of a particular response is impossible if the reinforcer (absence of shock) is continuously present. In principle, the confounding is no different for procedures based on intermittent shocks, although special procedures are required to determine whether a reduction in responding reflects discrimination of the absence of shock or of the absence of contingent relations between responses and shock.

Davenport, Coger, and Spector (1970), following a related paper by Davenport and Olson (1968), stated the implications of eliminating all shocks. They argued that removal of all shocks is either suspension of the drive operation, or else it constitutes reinforcement of all behavior since whatever the organism does is followed by shock omission, a consequence that during prior conditioning was restricted to the avoidance response. To provide an alternative extinction procedure Davenport, Coger, and Spector trained rats with 10 hours of exposure to a standard shock-delay procedure (SS = 15, RS = 15). Then they delivered a shock every 15 sec irrespective of behavior, starting this extinction procedure an hour after a session had begun. Four of the five animals virtually ceased responding within 90 min of the noncontingent shock procedure: the fifth had responded primarily immediately after shocks during conditioning (reducing its shock frequency by only 6 percent), and simply continued in this pattern of post-shock responding. Thus, extinction appeared to be achieved with suspension of the negative reinforcement contingency while maintaining the basis for negative reinforcement. In principle, reinforcement could have been delivered at any moment.

This procedure did not deal with the implications

of subjects avoiding more or less well during conditioning. Some people, having taken this into account, focus the definition of extinction on the contingency between response and reinforcement, rather than simply on the discontinuation of reinforcement (analogous considerations also apply to positive reinforcement.) To the extent that in the animal's history shocks have set the occasion for reinforcement, the elimination of shocks during extinction is as much a change of cues as it is a discontinuation of the relation between responding and reinforcement. On the other hand, to the extent that the subject's prior performance has completely eliminated shocks during training, the reintroduction of maximal shock frequency during extinction produces a situation in extinction that little resembles recent sessions of conditioning. Coulson, Coulson, and Gardner (1970) pointed this out, suggesting that in this context a proper extinction procedure would be delivery of a pattern of shocks similar to that observed during the training sessions that just preceded extinction. They carried this out after pretraining with a shock-delay procedure (SS = 5, RS = 30). They recorded the exact sequence of shocks received by each animal during its final conditioning session and subsequently delivered the same pattern to produce an extinction procedure based on noncontingent shocks, which they compared to extinction with all shocks deleted. In the latter condition, responding dropped quickly to zero; with the "matched shock" extinction procedure responding declined over some 6 to 15 sessions, but typically not to zero.

Although they reported a somewhat slower decline in response rate for extinction with noncontingent shocks matching the shocks of avoidance conditioning, the results of Coulson, Coulson, and Gardner (1970) are not directly comparable to those obtained by Davenport, Coger, and Spector (1970). The two studies used different conditioning parameters, and different amounts of training prior to extinction. A more direct comparison of these procedures has been achieved in my laboratory by G. D. Smith (Smith, 1973). He first trained rats with a shock-delay procedure (SS = 5, RS = 20) until they met a fairly rigorous performance criterion: over 75% of scheduled shocks avoided, and stable responding assessed over a 2-week period. All animals were then exposed to three different procedures that eliminated negative reinforcement: shock omission; delivery of noncontingent shock every five seconds, which matched the shock-shock interval of the previous training program; and a pattern of shocks that matched the given animal's final conditioning session. Exposures to the various "extinction" procedures lasted five 100-min sessions each, and retraining to the same stability criteria was carried out after each exposure to nonreinforcement. All animals were exposed to the shock-omission procedures before exposure to the other two procedures. Then after retraining, some rats were given the "maximum shock frequency" of noncontingent shock, while others were exposed to the "matched-shock" procedure. After retraining, each rat was then exposed to the other noncontingent shock procedure, and then retrained and reversed again. Figure 11 shows performance of a representative animal from each of the two sequences of procedures.

Even with prior avoidance training to a stringent criterion, turning off the shock generator produced precipitous declines in responding. In contrast, responding persisted throughout five-day exposures to extinction procedures based on noncontingent delivery of shocks. On the matched-shock procedure all animals showed a progressive decline in responding over the five-session exposure, indicating an extinction process and suggesting that more extended exposure to this procedure would have resulted in low levels if not complete cessation of responding. The results of noncontingent shock delivered according to the fixed shock-shock interval were more variable, usu-

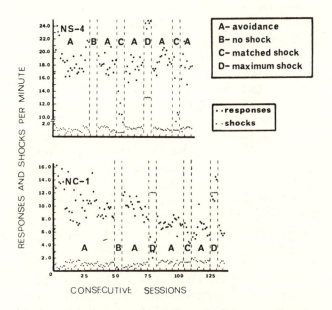

Fig. 11. Responses and shocks per minute as a function of sessions for a representative rat from each of two procedural sequences. Responses and shocks are indicated by separate symbols as noted in the Figure. Each data point represents the mean rate for a single session. Transitions from one experimental procedure to another are indicated by dashed lines drawn through individual plots. The order in which individual rats were exposed to extinction procedures is also indicated in the individual graphs. (From G. D. Smith, 1973.)

ally showing a persistent high rate of responding, but occasionally showing low consistent rates. Reconditioning, while accomplished after exposure to each extinction procedure, was most disrupted after the matched-shock procedure, but virtually immediate after the shock-omission procedure. Stressing these latter results, Smith (1973) argued for match-shock as the "reference" extinction procedure, and agreed with Davenport et al. (1970) and Coulson et al. (1970) that the traditional procedure of omitting all shocks constitutes a suspension of the drive operation, and is only indirectly a removal of the negative reinforcement contingency.

The resulting treatment of extinction still has to deal with the fact that the responding of different subjects is extinguished in the presence of different absolute shock rates corresponding to, and thus confounded with the effectiveness of prior conditioning.

Effects of Noncontingent Shocks

While the reasons for using noncontingent shock as the basis for extinction are quite compelling, the persistence of responding on such extinction procedures complicates the analysis of behavior in animals with histories of negative reinforcement based on shock. Such persistence is well illustrated in rats trained on the shock-frequency reduction procedure based on randomly spaced shocks, that I have already described (Herrnstein & Hineline, 1966). While extinction was indeed achieved by delivering noncontingent shocks, it often took many sessions. For example, one animal emitted some 20,000 responses at a slowly-decreasing rate over some 12,000 min accumulated in 100-min sessions. In light of this, it is difficult to know whether experiments presented as "maintenance of responding by noncontingent shocks" are indeed what the description implies, or whether the effects so reported are merely modulations of responding that is undergoing extinction. For example, Hurwitz, Roberts, and Greenway (1972) drew conclusions regarding the response-maintaining effects of response-independent shocks on the basis of only one hour on the noncontingent shock procedure, after more than 200 hours of preliminary training.

Other studies have been carried out further, with a variety of interesting results. For example, Powell and Peck (1969) found that after training with shock-intensity reduction, noncontingent shocks maintained subsequent responding even when it was varied over a fairly wide range of intensities and frequencies. Powell (1972) examined effects of noncontingent shocks on responding after more conventional Sidman shock-delay procedures, and found that periodic noncontingent shock produced responding in 8 of 13 rats, some persisting for as long as 180 hours of exposure to a given procedure. Aperiodic shocks produced somewhat less persistent responding, a result consistent with observations by Kadden (1973) using rhesus monkeys. According to Powell, the temporal relations of responses to shock in his study indicated that much of the responding was shock-elicited, presumably reflecting attacks on the lever. However, even though it has a reflex-like time relation to the noncontingent shock, this responding appears to be related to the prior avoidance conditioning. When shock-delay training on a second lever was interposed before the noncontingent shock procedure was begun, the responding that persisted during the subsequent noncontingent shock procedure occurred almost entirely on the lever first used for shock reduction. This suggests that the shock was functioning both as a discriminative and as an eliciting stimulus.

An analysis by Hake and Campbell (1972) of responding produced by noncontingent shocks complicates the picture still further. Using a fixed-interval escape procedure with squirrel monkeys, they observed two patterns of lever-press responding. One pattern, post-shock responding, suggested elicitation; the other showed characteristics of maintenance by the fixed-interval schedule. When they changed the situation, making two operanda available—a key whose pressing was reinforced on the FI schedule and a hose conveniently available for biting—they found that the post-shock responding was confined to the bite hose, while the FI responding occurred on the key. So far, this appears to be a nice test of Powell's (1972) notion that the post-shock responding differed functionally from other responding, being shock-elicited rather than an unextinguished responding based on negative reinforcement. However, when Hake and Campbell made the bite hose unavailable, post-shock responding was then observed on the key. Clearly, this was not a biting response; they still classified it as shock-elicited aggressive responding, but displaced to whatever manipulandum was available.

Finally, McKearney has shown that in animals with negative reinforcement histories one can readily maintain responding even with response-produced shocks provided that the probability of a response producing shock is not too high. High-probability response-produced shock suppresses responding (McKearney, 1972; Powell, 1972). Thus, clearly, the effects of shock delivered to animals with histories of negative reinforcement demand further analysis and will receive further experimentation (cf. chapter 7 of this volume by

Morse & Kelleher). For present purposes, it suffices to note that long after it has been discontinued, shock reduction can affect an animal's responses to shock. An experimenter purporting to demonstrate negative reinforcing effects in animals with histories of prior negative reinforcement must acknowledge the possible effects of shock delivery, which result from prior as well as current response-contingent relationships.

NEGATIVE REINFORCEMENT WITH ADDED CUES

So far, I have focused on procedures where shock is the only exteroceptive stimulus manipulated within conditioning sessions. In some of these procedures the addition of other cues would be superfluous, for the shock itself denotes the opportunity to respond and the availability of reinforcement, as well as producing the aversive situation. However, if shocks are brief and intermittent, if not all responses in the presence of shock are effective, or if responding in the absence of shock can affect subsequent shock delivery, then added stimuli such as tones or lights become of interest. The germinal idea for the present discussion of added stimuli comes from Keehn (1966), from Sidman (1966), and from Herrnstein (1969). They have suggested or argued that such added stimuli should be considered as discriminative stimuli denoting the availability of negative reinforcement. In addition, Baum (1973a) has provided a key concept, identifying situation transitions as reinforcements. I attempt to go beyond these in distinguishing several interrelated functions of added cues in negative reinforcement situations. I shall start with multiple schedule experiments where cues correlate with whole conditioning procedures, including aversive situations, accessibility of reinforcement, and periods of shock reduction produced on a given procedure. Later will come cues denoting more limited aspects of negative reinforcement procedures, such as particular shock-presentation schedules, opportunity to respond, and limited periods when responding can affect shock.

Added Cues Denoting Multiple Contingencies

A simple multiple schedule can be achieved by correlating a reinforcement procedure with one stimulus, correlating extinction with another, and alternating the two stimuli. This was accomplished by Bersh and Lambert (1975). They initially conditioned lever-press responding in rats, with 32 sessions of exposure to a procedure of the kind devised by Herrnstein and Hineline (1966), which I have described previously. In the absence of responding, randomly spaced shocks were delivered at a mean inter-shock time of 5.7 sec. A response resulted in another random distribution of shocks, still giving a fairly constant moment-to-moment probability of shock, but with an average of 20 sec until the next shock. With delivery of this shock, the higher shock frequency was reinstated. These 100-min sessions of initial training were accomplished in a darkened chamber. Next a light was provided as a discriminative stimulus (S^D), accompanying the same procedure as before. This light was present for four-min periods, alternating with periods of darkness during which shocks were delivered according to the high-frequency shock schedule, independently of any responding (Darkness = S^Δ). The duration of the S^Δ period was determined by a delay contingency; a return to light and its correlated access to reinforcement could not occur until 20 sec had elapsed without a response. Later in training this delay requirement was extended to 40 and then to 60 sec for some animals. Finally, two of the rats were placed on an extinction procedure in which the high shock frequency occurred independently of responding, and whether or not the light was on.

Figure 12 shows a representative performance on this procedure. Response rates in darkness came under control of nonreinforcement, dropping far below those in the presence of the light. These reduced rates developed systematically, and often fairly quickly, even though the shock frequency in darkness was substantially higher than that in light, and darkness had accompanied the initial conditioning. During extinction of the discriminative responding, with noncontingent shocks delivered on the average of every 5.7 sec regardless of responding or stimulus condition, the response rates slowly moved together as responding decreased in the presence of the light. The plots for initial conditioning and for the discrimination are fairly representative for all animals. However, the data for the final extinction procedure is not representative, for the other animal exposed to this procedure persisted with high response rates in the presence of the light, and low response rates in its absence. The persistence of the discrimination under these circumstances is somewhat surprising, given the selective extinction that produced the discrimination in the first place. It is less surprising in comparison with another experiment that used noncontingent shocks after histories of negative reinforcement. Appel (1960) placed rats on a discrimination procedure similar to that of Bersh and Lambert but with negative reinforcement provided by a shock-delay procedure. His

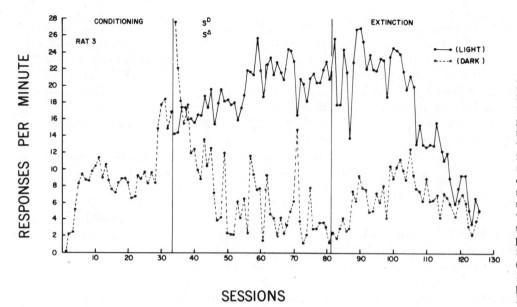

Fig. 12. Responses per minute for Rat 3 during initial conditioning, with response-contingent shock-reduction in darkness; discrimination training, with response-contingent shock-reduction in light and noncontingent shock in darkness; and extinction, with noncontingent shock in both light and darkness. Data points connected with broken lines indicate responding in darkness; data points connected with solid lines indicate responding in light. (After Bersh & Lambert, 1975. © 1975 by the Society for the Experimental Analysis of Behavior, Inc.)

animals failed to show discriminative control when the extinction component included delivery of noncontingent shocks. Systematic comparisons would be needed to identify critical features for establishing this type of discrimination.

The multiple schedules studied by Bersh and Lambert and that studied by Appel involved reinforcement in one component and nonreinforcement with delivery of noncontingent shocks in the other. De Villiers (1972, 1974) has studied multiple schedules with shock deletion procedures based on different shock frequencies in the different components. In both of de Villiers's experiments the basic procedures were the same as in his experiment described above. In the absence of responding, shocks were delivered at irregular intervals, with a roughly constant probability of shock from moment-to-moment. He specified these in terms of the mean interval between shocks. The first response within any scheduled shock-shock interval cancelled the shock due at the end of that interval; additional responses within that interval had no effect. In his earlier experiment, de Villiers (1972) demonstrated contrast effects in addition to basic multiple schedule effects. He first provided identical shock-deletion schedules in the presence and absence of a buzzer that alternated, on for three min and off for three min. Then the schedule was changed in one component, providing for greater or less shock-frequency reduction by increasing or decreasing the maximum shock frequency. The response rate changed in that component, in a direction directly related to the change in shock-frequency reduction. Thus, if shock frequency increased, so did responding (and the amount of shock reduction). The contrast effect was revealed by response rate changes in the opposite direction in the presence of the alternate stimulus where the schedule had remained unchanged. De Villiers showed that these contrast effects could be summarized by an equation that Herrnstein (1970) had developed to deal with behavioral contrast in multiple schedules of positive reinforcement.

Extending the study of stimulus control, de Villiers (1974) examined responding on similar multiple schedules, but used separate levers and cue lights for the different component schedules. This permitted further examination of shock-frequency reduction as a controlling variable. He also varied the frequency with which the components of the multiple schedule alternated within a session. This latter manipulation permitted a detailed comparison with multiple schedules of positive reinforcement. With positive reinforcement it has been found (e.g., Todorov, 1972) that rapid alternation between components of a multiple schedule produces relative response rates that are nearly proportional to their relative rates of reinforcement. Also with positive reinforcement, less frequent alternation between components produces smaller differences between response rates on the different components. De Villiers (1974) found very similar relationships for multiple schedules of negative reinforcement, with amount of shock-frequency reduction corresponding to rate of reinforcement. This is shown in Figure 13, where different panels (bounded by vertical lines) correspond to different pairs of component schedules in the multiple schedule. The horizontal line in each panel of the figure indicates the relative shock-frequency reduction produced on the right lever, averaged over exposures to

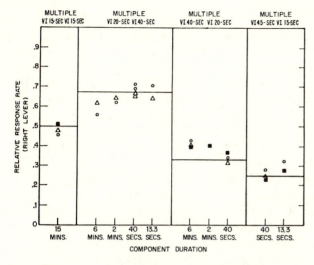

Fig. 13. Mean relative response rates of each rat for the last six sessions of each experimental condition. The mean relative shock-frequency reduction for each multiple schedule is shown by the horizontal solid lines. The data points of differing shapes designate performances of different rats. (From de Villiers, 1974.)

a given pair of values. Shock-frequency reduction was computed by subtracting the obtained shock frequency from the frequency that would have occurred in the absence of responding. For each schedule component, this measure of "r" was substituted into the equation, $\frac{r_r}{r_r + r_l}$ where r_r and r_l are reinforcement rates on the right and left components, respectively. When the component schedules were alternated every 40 sec, the relative response rates closely matched the relative amounts of shock-frequency reduction. When the component schedules were alternated more slowly, response rates were more nearly equal in the two components, giving relative values closer to 0.5. This effect was similar to one seen in pigeons run on similar schedules of positive reinforcement, as noted above.

I noted earlier that de Villiers found, when applying Herrnstein's (1970) relative reinforcement frequency equations to responding on single variable-interval schedules, that good fits to the matching relation were obtained when reinforcement rate was defined as degree of shock-frequency reduction. Obtained shock frequency also provided a fair approximation to the data (as it should, being correlated with magnitude of shock frequency reduction), but shock-frequency reduction provided a better fit in every case. On the multiple schedules considered here, relative shock-frequency reduction was more simply related to relative response rate than was received shock rate. I also noted earlier that since de Villiers's shock-frequency reduction procedures allowed responding to reduce shock frequency to zero, he could manipulate shock frequency reduction only by varying the "background" or maximum shock frequency, that which would occur only in the absence of responding. A more powerful test of shock-frequency reduction would be to hold background shock frequency constant and manipulate the minimum shock frequency produceable by responding, including other values as well as zero.

Wertheim (1965) also studied multiple schedules of negative reinforcement, but used shock-delay procedures. In addition to demonstrating potent stimulus control of responding, and contrast effects, he found that the relative response rate was correlated quite strongly with relative frequencies of shock delivery. However, the use of his procedures for a comparison of shock frequency with shock-frequency reduction is problematical since he used shock-shock intervals of zero, giving continuous shock in the absence of responding.

Added Cues and the Escape Paradigm

My discussion of negative reinforcement procedures began with the escape paradigm, and evolved away from it. A response in the presence of continuous shock removes that shock, producing a shock-free interval. Negative reinforcement is clearly the offset of the shock; specifying the shock-free interval is no problem. However, there is a continuum between continuous shock and sequences of intermittent brief shocks. The escape paradigm providing for response-produced shock-free intervals is effective across much of this continuum, but it is not clear how to specify the effective consequence when the duration of the interval between brief shocks approaches that of the response-produced shock-free interval. The analysis confronts a "figure-ground" problem: A response can be considered as deleting or delaying a specific shock, or the situation can be treated as one and continuous, with responses reducing the overall aversiveness of the situation. The experimental procedure may specify shock-deletion or shock-delay, but the effective variable may well be shock-frequency reduction.

When cues are used in multiple schedules such as those just considered, an added stimulus is correlated with a whole procedure. It accompanies not only a schedule of shock presentation and the contingency or schedule of reinforcement whereby responding can affect the shock presentation, but also the periods of shock reduction that responding produces. The cue does not simplify interpretation of the procedure and its effects; the cue merely delimits the periods during which the procedure operates. If, however, the cue correlates only with particular features of a conditioning procedure, it does enter into the interpretation of the procedure's effects.

The first examples to be considered here are experiments in which the cue correlates perfectly with the shock-presentation schedule. Onset and offset of the cue provide distinct boundaries to a sequence of intermittent shocks, permitting interpretation to rely again on the escape paradigm of negative reinforcement. Dinsmoor and Bonbright (reported in Dinsmoor, 1967) directly compared such a procedure to a standard escape procedure that used continuous shock. They used a multiple schedule, consisting of white noise accompanied by intermittent brief shocks, alternating with continuous shock of lower intensity in the absence of the white noise. In both situations, the same variable-interval schedule was in effect, with the removal of the continuous shock, or of noise plus intermittent shock, contingent upon lever-pressing. By independently adjusting the shock intensities in the two components of the multiple schedule, they produce virtually indistinguishable patterns of lever-pressing in the two components. These performances were identically affected by administration of chlorpromazine at various doses. Thus, in this situation, behavior that removed continuous shock was equivalent to that which removed intermittent shocks and correlated white noise. This should come as no great surprise after the results of Kelleher and Morse (1964) who compared the effects of drug administrations on closely similar food-maintained and shock-maintained lever-press performances. As described at the beginning of this chapter, they found that drug effects were determined more by the specific patterns of behavior than by the types of reinforcement maintaining those patterns.

Procedures using cues correlated with intermittent shocks have often been characterized as "reinforcement by removal of a stimulus paired with shock," (e.g., Azrin, Holz, Hake, and Ayllon, 1963; Dinsmoor, 1967; Kelleher and Morse, 1964), which of course describes the immediate response consequence. However, this characterization implies that on these procedures, the effects of shock on responding are entirely mediated by the correlated stimulus. One must still consider possible direct effects that the intermittent shocks and their deletion may have on behavior, independent of the correlated stimulus. Morse and Kelleher acknowledge this in their more recent description of these procedures by characterizing them as reinforcement by "termination of schedule complexes" (Morse & Kelleher, 1966), the schedule complex being the combination of intermittent shocks and correlated stimulus. They found evidence for direct effects of shocks. When developing fixed-interval schedules of negative reinforcement, they found that when intermittent shocks were delivered throughout the interreinforcement interval the positive-accelerating rates commonly identified with this schedule ("fixed-interval scallop") failed to appear. They obtained the characteristic fixed-interval performance only by allowing the interval to elapse before the intermittent shock began, as described above in the procedure for Figure 3. It is likely that the direct effects of intermittent shocks delivered during the interval are akin to the effects of noncontingent shocks delivered during extinction after conditioning with shock-delay procedures (e.g., McKearney, 1969).

Dinsmoor (1962) systematically examined some direct effects of shocks and shock-deletion, correlated with a cue and cue-removal. He compared rats' performances on two procedures, both of which could be called VI 30-sec schedules of negative reinforcement. Both schedules of reinforcement were superimposed on identical schedules of intermittent shock, specified by their mean shock-shock intervals. In both procedures responding could produce fixed shock-free periods during which any scheduled shocks were deleted. Responses during these shock-free periods had no effect.[2] In one procedure an added light and tone denoted the presence of the schedule of intermittent shocks and the shock-free periods, respectively. In the other procedure, no added cues were provided. Initial training was accomplished with fixed shock-deletion periods of 60 sec, and with mean shock-shock intervals varying from day to day, between 7.5 and 120 sec. The duration of shock-free periods was also systematically manipulated over sessions, between 15 and 240 sec for one animal, and between 30 and 240 sec for the other two. Thus, in some sessions a reinforced response could produce a shock-free period that exceeded the average shock-shock interval; in other sessions it could not. In some sessions the correlated lights and tones were used. In other sessions there were no exteroceptive cues other than the shocks themselves. In all sessions a variable interval schedule provided a mean interreinforcement time of 30 sec if the animal responded sufficiently often in the presence of the shock schedule. This time was computed by subtracting the reinforcement (shock-free) periods from the total time.

[2] This is similar to what I have previously called a shock-deletion procedure. However, since the duration of the shock-deletion period is based on time, independent of the shock-delivery schedule, I will refer to this consequence of responding simply as a shock-free period.

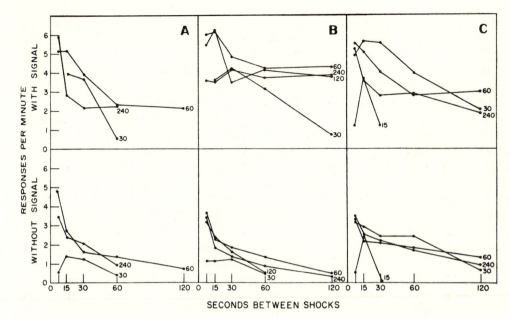

Fig. 14. Families of curves showing the mean rate of bar pressing by each rat as a function of the mean interval between successive shocks. The values identifying each curve represent the number of seconds for which shocks were deleted by an effective response. A, B, and C denote individual rats. (From Dinsmoor, 1962. © 1962 by the Society for the Experimental Analysis of Behavior, Inc.)

As indicated by Figure 14, response rates were much higher with added cues. However, there was also substantial responding when the cues were not provided, especially when the mean shock-shock interval was less than 30 sec. Dinsmoor found that shock-free periods with durations of 30 sec or less tended to be less effective than longer values, except when the average shock-shock interval was extremely short. Above 30 sec, the duration of the shock-free period had little systematic effect whether or not the correlated cues were supplied. Relative response rates in the presence and absence of the shock schedule indicated discriminative control by the added cues. When performances were stable, fewer than 10% of the responses typically occurred during the shock-free periods, while without the cues these percentages were much higher. Thus considered in total, Dinsmoor's experiment indicates both discriminative control by the correlated cues and potent reinforcing effects of the immediate response-contingent stimulus change that these cues provide, but it also indicates the likelihood of some behavioral control by the shocks, independent of the cues.

Stimuli correlated with intermittent shocks enhance the flexibility with which negative reinforcement can be scheduled. This was demonstrated in the experiment by Kelleher and Morse (1964), described early in the present chapter, showing characteristic fixed-interval and fixed-ratio schedule effects in squirrel monkeys. In elaborating on the techniques used for development of such performances, Morse and Kelleher (1966) also summarized a number of characteristics that behavior on these procedures has in common with behavior on comparable positive reinforcement schedules.

Azrin, Holz, Hake, and Allyon (1963) provided another striking demonstration of such effects, with ratio schedules. First, they exposed squirrel monkeys to four 6-hour preliminary sessions consisting of 5-min periods of intermittent shock (with the mean SS interval increased over sessions, from 15 sec to 2 min) correlated with bright light and silence, alternated with 5-min shock-free periods accompanied by tone and dimmed lights. They noted that this pretraining is similar to magazine training sessions in experiments using positive reinforcement. Subsequently, they made 30-sec shock-free periods, with correlated stimuli, contingent on responding. Responding during shock-free periods was ineffective. The shock-delivery schedule continued to be accompanied by the bright light and silence. Moving from continuous reinforcement, they found extremely stable and persistent fixed-ratio performances with ratios of 25 and 50, and maintained substantial, though less stable responding with ratios as high as FR 300.

Azrin et al. then held the ratio requirement at 50, and varied the shock-delivery schedule and the duration of response-produced shock-free periods. They found that under some conditions the duration of the cued shock-free period is less critical a variable than Dinsmoor's (1962) results indicated. Over hundreds of hours of conditioning, changes in relative duration of the shock-free periods produced by responding had very little effect on performance. For example, with a mean shock-shock interval of ten minutes, and the duration of the cued shock-free period reduced to ten seconds, only a slight reduction in overall response rate was observed. Responding was also maintained, although at a lower overall rate, when the shock-free periods were as brief as two seconds. At the same time, the absolute shock rate correlated with the bright light and silence seemed not to be critical either, provided that the shock frequencies were changed gradually. For example, when every 25th response (FR 25) produced a 30-sec timeout, and the shock-shock interval was increased gradually by giving 18 hours or more of exposure to each value, response rates remained virtually unchanged with the mean shock-shock interval approaching one hour. To be sure, it must be emphasized that these are maintenance data, resulting from very gradual changes in experimental conditions. More sudden changes in shock frequency or timeout duration did result in performance decrements. Also, these results were obtained with monkeys, whereas most experiments on negative reinforcements have used rats.

These experiments by Azrin et al. suggest that a critical and potent feature of the cued escape paradigm is the stimulus change occurring at the onset of a shock-free period. Frequencies and patterns of responding revealed schedule control by this event, with only minor or limiting effects attributable to overall shock frequency, shock-frequency reduction, or duration of the stimulus-correlated shock-free periods. This tentative conclusion gains further support from an experiment by W. M. Baum (1973b) who studied pigeons' time allocation in shock-correlated stimulus situations, as influenced by how frequently cued shock-free periods were initiated in those situations. The experiment is also of interest because it demonstrates another quantitative similarity between positive and negative reinforcement. It can also be related to the functions obtained by de Villiers (1972, 1974) described earlier.

Baum's experiment used an experimental chamber whose floor was made of two platforms. If the pigeon stood on one platform, a red light was on; if the pigeon stood on the other, a green light was on; standing on both platforms simultaneously was accompanied by a white light, and a move from one platform to the other produced the white light for one second. All of these lights were accompanied by brief shocks delivered once per sec. When either the red or the green light was on, as determined by the bird's position, two variable-interval programming timers were running which could initiate two-minute shock-free periods, with all lights off. The two variable-interval timers typically had differing mean intervals, and each could initiate a shock-free period in the presence of only one color. When the scheduled interval on one timer elapsed in the presence of the color associated with the other timer, the first timer's shock-free interval was not delivered until immediately after the color changed. These procedural features closely resemble those of an experiment by Baum and Rachlin (1969) using the same chamber, with concurrent schedules of food delivery instead of schedules of shock deletion. In that experiment, Baum and Rachlin had found that the ratio of times spent on two sides of the chamber was proportional to the ratio of the corresponding frequencies of positive reinforcement. Formally, this matching relation is virtually identical to the repeatedly-verified matching relation describing relative response rates (e.g. key-pecks per minute) as a function of relative frequencies of positive reinforcement (Herrnstein, 1970).

Figure 15 shows the results obtained on Baum's procedure, including individual data points for each of four pigeons, showing relative time allocations as a function of relative frequencies with which cued shock-free periods were initiated in the presence of

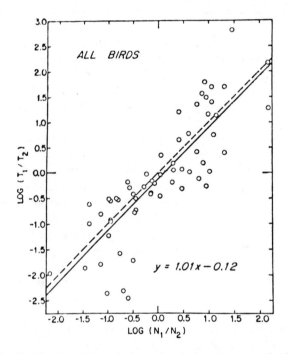

Fig. 15. The logarithm of the ratio of time spent on the left to time spent on the right as a function of the logarithm of the ratio of number of shock-free periods obtained on the left to number of shock-free periods obtained on the right. The data from four birds are presented; each data point represents a value obtained from an individual bird. The solid line was fitted by the method of least squares. The broken line has a slope of one, and passes through the origin; it represents the performance of perfect matching. (From W. M. Baum, 1973b. © 1973 by the Society for the Experimental Analysis of Behavior Inc.)

the red and green lights. While there was considerable variability, the least-squares fit of the points on Figure 15 closely matches the line indicating a matching relation. The birds' relative times spent on the two sides of the chamber, excluding shock-free periods and changeover periods, matched the relative frequencies with which cued shock-free periods were produced on the two sides, again excluding the shock-free periods themselves.

In introducing this experiment and in discussing its results, Baum made the plausible assumption that with a constant shock frequency in the shock situation, and a constant duration of shock-free periods, frequency of escape from the shock situation is directly related to magnitude of shock-frequency reduction. Thus he interpreted the matching relation shown in Figure 15 as showing reduction in rate of aversive stimulation to be the critical parameter of, or even more strongly, the definition of, negative reinforcement. He also stated that it demonstrated a quantitative function relating behavior to shock-frequency reduction that was comparable to that obtained by de Villiers (1972, 1974) which I described earlier. The problem with this interpretation is that in Baum's procedure the frequency with which shock-free periods were initiated in the presence of the red or the green light, and from which the independent variable of Figure 15 was derived, was not proportional to shock-frequency reduction in the presence of those stimuli. If we simply look at shock frequency in the presence of the red light versus that in the presence of the green light, disregarding shock-free periods as Baum did when computing the relative reinforcement rates, we find no difference. They were both equal to one shock per second. If instead the shock-free periods are included when computing shock frequencies on the two sides, relative shock-frequency reduction does equal the relative frequency of shock-free periods, provided that this latter measure also includes the durations of the shock-free periods. On this basis it is possible for the birds' relative time allocations to match the relative reductions in shock frequency. However, a plot comparable to Figure 15, but using shock-frequency reductions computed from the data given in the appendix of Baum's article in place of the frequency of timeout production, gave a much less orderly function. Thus, the measures plotted in Figure 15 were well chosen, but the resulting function does not show the relation of time allocation to magnitude of shock-frequency reduction. Rather, the birds' relative time allocations matched the relative frequencies, in the situations where shocks occurred, of onset of highly discriminable shock-free intervals.

Reinforcement Achieved by Shock Reduction Within a Situation, Contrasted with Reinforcement by Change of Situations

The variable-cycle shock-deletion procedures used as components of multiple schedules by de Villiers (1972, 1974) identified shock-frequency reduction as a controlling variable, as I described earlier. The contrast between de Villiers's experiments and the one by Baum that I have just described, points up two distinct modes of negative reinforcement. In de Villiers's experiments, as in other multiple schedules, the presence of a given cue could be said to define a situation. Responding within that situation reduced the shock frequency within the situation but did not remove the situation itself. In Baum's experiment, responding did not affect shock frequency in the situation itself; rather, it occasionally produced a change of situation, to one in which shock frequency was lower. It is tempting to identify these two modes of reinforcement with the familiar labels of avoidance and escape, but they do not conform to these labels as commonly understood. The effects of both can be based on averaging events over time. Neither is reducible to the other, although there must be boundary procedures that resemble both, when the response-produced stimulus change is not clearly discriminable. In some ways, the relationship between these two modes of reinforcement resembles the relationship between magnitude and frequency of positive reinforcement, as follows.

Herrnstein (1970) pointed out that the matching relation for relative frequency of positive reinforcement can be expected to hold only if reinforcement magnitudes are equal, or if some mathematical adjustment is made to deal with their inequality. In addition Herrnstein suggested that a matching function obtained with equal reinforcement frequencies but varied reinforcement magnitudes, could be used for the scaling of reinforcement magnitude to make valid such a mathematical adjustment. Very tentatively, the analogous treatment of negative reinforcement can be spelled out by accepting Baum's specification of frequency of negative reinforcement in terms of the frequency with which shock-free periods (changes of situation) are initiated. Magnitude of reinforcement could be either the duration of shock-free period or the magnitude of change in shock schedule or in shock intensity that accompanies the change of situation.

In addition, the shock frequencies and intensities prior to change of situation could be treated as magnitudes of drive operation, tightly defined as operations that potentiate reinforcement operations. De Villiers's experiments with multiple schedules could be seen as potential scaling procedures to permit the use of varying magnitudes of reinforcement within Baum's procedure. However, we must still contend with the distinction between magnitude of reinforcement as achieved by varying background shock frequency and as achieved by holding that frequency constant and varying response-produced lower frequencies.

MULTIPLE RESPONSE PATTERNS PRODUCED BY SHOCK-DELAY PROCEDURES

The experiments described above identify controlling features of negative reinforcement mainly through long-term parametric relations between these features and overall response rates. A more direct approach has also been used, based on manipulation and observation of short-term response patterns, rather than on curve-fitting with overall rates. For example, using a shock-delay procedure Sidman (1966) found that when the shock-shock and response-shock intervals differ (SS=20, RS=40), the spacing of responses within those intervals differs accordingly. Thus differing RS and SS intervals are discriminable, and as they alternate the animals respond appropriately to each. When the SS interval approaches zero, and thus is extremely short relative to the RS interval, responses during the shock-shock interval can be said to remove shock, producing a distinct change of situation. Responses during the RS interval are maintained on a much lower range of the shock-density continuum; their consequent shock-delay or shock-frequency reduction can be characterized as further reduction within a less aversive situation.

A distinctive pattern of responding has frequently been noted that is related to, although not entirely confined to post-shock periods. This responding has been characterized as "bursting." Ellen and Wilson (1964) described it in detail, contrasting it with the spaced responding or "continual-responding pattern" characteristic of the response-shock interval. There have been repeated suggestions that this burst pattern is adventitiously maintained by shock removal, an interpretation well supported by an experiment by Boren (1961) which illustrates another method for separate study of shock-removal and shock-delay. He introduced a second lever into a shock-delay situation. One lever worked only during the response-shock interval; the other lever worked only during the shock-shock interval. Using a shock-shock interval of zero (continuous shock), Boren found that the burst pattern, even though occurring partly in the RS interval, was entirely confined to the shock-removal lever, the one operative only during the (zero) SS interval.

The use of two concurrently recordable responses permitted a dissociation of effects of reinforcement by shock-removal from effects of reinforcement by shock-delay even when some of these effects (bursts) were not explicitly prescribed by the schedule. By itself this experiment requires a distinction between the two response classes only because they are controlled by different parts of the shock-frequency continuum. However, it complements the preceding experiments by de Villiers and by Baum, supporting a distinction between change of situation and reduction of aversiveness within a situation.

CONCURRENT SCHEDULES, WITH REINFORCEMENT BY SHOCK-DELAY AND BY REMOVAL OF THE SHOCK-DELAY PROCEDURE

Verhave (1962) explicitly arranged for concurrent but separate control of behavior by these two aspects of negative reinforcement. He used several procedures; in all of them, responses could delay shocks (SS=3, RS=30). In each, some responses could produce a "timeout" period, accompanied by a tone, in which both the shocks and the shock-delay contingency were absent.[3] In an initial experiment the onset of the timeout period was made contingent upon the same lever-press that delayed shock, but with a fixed-interval schedule. Verhave found no indications of control by the fixed-interval schedule. However, in a later experiment where the cue-correlated timeout periods were made contingent upon pressing a second lever, they had very clear effects. In this experiment, initial training was accomplished by partitioning the conditioning chamber to provide access only to the shock-delay lever. After responding was stable on this procedure, and after irregularly spaced tone presentations to ensure that the tone by itself had no effect on responding, the second lever was made accessible. Depressions of this lever produced 10-min timeout periods accompanied by the tone. Figure 16 portrays some of the results with the cumulative records indicating responses and shocks on the shock-delay lever. Downward deflections of the underlying event records indicate timeout periods, each produced by a response on the second lever. The first panels show the first session in which responding could produce the timeout periods. The first response-produced timeout oc-

---

[3] Within the present chapter the term "timeout" is reserved for shock-free periods that accompany suspension of a shock-delay contingency that would permit responding to extend shock-free intervals. It should be recognized that other authors have applied the term to any clearly discriminable shock-free period.

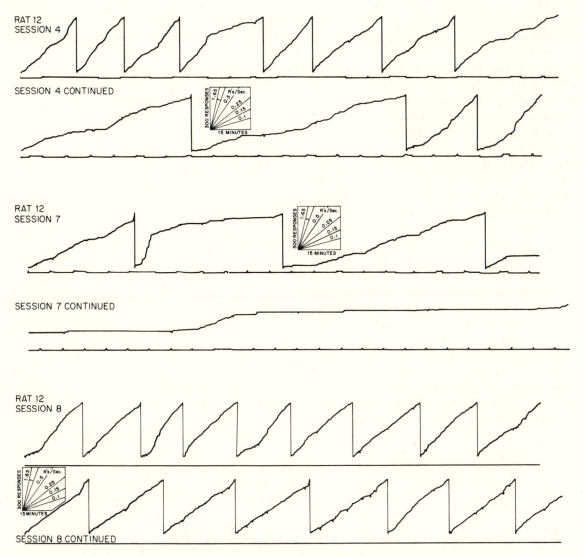

Fig. 16. Cumulative records showing performance on a shock-delay procedure, with associated event records showing performance on a lever that produced timeout from the shock-delay procedure. Shocks are indicated by pips on the cumulative record. Timeout periods are indicated by downward deflections of the event record. The top two panels show the fourth session of shock-delay training, the first session in which the timeout procedure was in effect. The middle pair of panels shows performance during the fourth session in which the timeout procedure was in effect; the bottom pair shows performance in the next session, during which the timeout procedure was discontinued, producing extinction on the second lever while the shock-delay procedure continued. (After Verhave, 1962. © 1962 by the Society for the Experimental Analysis of Behavior, Inc.)

curred very early in the session, perhaps facilitated by the similarity of the two levers located under identical pilot lights. Responding on the delay lever persisted undiminished throughout that timeout period. This responding during timeout did not begin to diminish until the fourth and fifth timeouts, which followed one another closely, suggesting a strengthening of responding on the timeout lever. Response rates during timeout periods did not become reliably lower until close to the 11th timeout, which was after more than 100 minutes of exposure to the timeout situation. In general, responding on the delay lever decreased and frequency of timeout production increased over the next few hours of conditioning; the seventh six-hour session indicates the typical pattern, more shock-delay responding and a slightly lower frequency of timeout production early rather than late in the session. When the timeout lever was deactivated, responding quickly recovered on the shock-delay lever (bottom 2 panels of Figure 16). In additional experiments, Verhave imposed ratio schedules on the timeout lever. When fewer than ten responses were required to produce a timeout, responding persisted on the timeout lever; when the ratio exceeded ten, two of three animals reverted to responding exclusively on the delay lever. So long as responding persisted on the timeout lever, enough accompanying responses were emitted on the delay lever that few shocks were received even though the ratio took some time to complete.

Verhave concluded that for his subjects the timeout was an effective but rather weak reinforcer similar in its effects to food for a minimally deprived organism. It seems more directly analogous to a situation with effective deprivation but with two kinds of food reinforcers available, one slightly preferred to the other. Sidman (1962c) studied the effects of a similar procedure with monkeys. He found that responding was readily maintained when cued time-out periods were contingent upon higher ratios, but that there were substantial interactions between responding on the shock-delay lever and the chain-pull response that produced timeout periods. It is likely that the animals' prior histories of positive reinforcement were important in maintaining the behavior with higher ratios. The species difference may also have contributed to the differing persistence on ratio schedules.

CONCURRENT REINFORCEMENT
WITH STIMULI DENOTING
SHOCK-FREE PERIODS

The notion of a shock-free situation has little meaning except in the context of other contrasting situations where shocks occur at least sometimes. This fact and its significance have been stressed by Rescorla (1967), mainly in relation to Pavlovian conditioning. He has advocated replacing traditional stimulus-pairing procedures with stimulus-correlation procedures. In procedures where cue presentation is determined independently of shock presentation, cues have zero correlation with shock, as do cues in experiments where there are no shocks. In only a trivial sense do the latter denote shock-free periods. Positively correlated cues are those for which the probability of shock is greater in their presence (or immediately following their occurrence) than in their absence. Negatively correlated cues include those I have already described as cues correlated with or denoting shock-free periods. Shock probability is greater in their absence than in their presence. Frequently, stimulus correlation procedures are accomplished apart from operant reinforcement procedures, but assessed through their effects on baselines of operant behavior. In the first of these that I will describe, the effects to be measured were concurrent reinforcing effects superimposed on shock-delay procedures.

As noted above, Verhave (1962) found that a separate response, rather than the shock-delay response, was needed for demonstrating concurrent reinforcing effects of a timeout stimulus correlated with absence both of the shock-delay contingency and shock. Rescorla (1969) used a two-response procedure to demonstrate that at least to some degree responding maintained by shock-delay is sensitive to concurrent reinforcing effects of a stimulus correlated only with absence of shocks. Using dogs, he established panel-press responding with the shock-delay procedure (SS=10, RS=30). Responding on either of two panels could eliminate all shocks, but responding exclusively on either panel for two minutes made that panel inoperative until a response had occurred on the other panel. Then in three pretest sessions with the delay procedure still in effect but without the two-min limitation, he made brief (0.5 seconds) tones of 400 Hz and 1200 Hz each separately contingent on presses of different panels, with the positions reversed midway through the pretesting period. Panel pressing was unaffected by these tone presentations, however, five intervening sessions of conditioning with a Pavlovian procedure changed this. With the response panels removed, a 2-sec darkening of the chamber was sometimes followed by shock 8 sec later; at other times it was followed in 7 sec by a tone, but with shock omitted. Negatively correlated with shock, the tone was either 400 Hz or 1200 Hz, depending on the animal. Subsequently the animals were re-exposed to the same procedure used during pretesting, with panel presses producing brief tone presentations as well as shock-delay. During this testing, responding clearly predominated on the panel that produced the tone that for the given animal had been negatively correlated with shock in the Pavlovian procedure. The stimulus denoting absence of shock had a reinforcing effect revealed in response preference. However, consistent with Verhave's (1962) results when using a single response, the reinforcing effect was not evident in absolute rates.

Weisman and Litner (1969) devised a more potent procedure for demonstrating reinforcing effects of a stimulus whose negative correlation with shock was established during separate, Pavlovian conditioning sessions. The stimulus had clear concurrently reinforcing effects on a single response maintained by a shock-delay schedule. Using rats, they established a wheel-turning response with a delay procedure of SS=5, RS=20 sec, and then divided their subjects

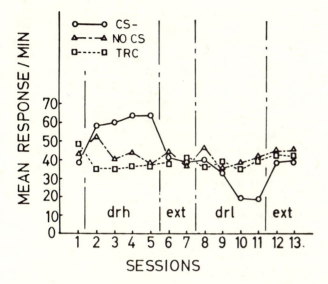

Fig. 17. Mean responses per minute for baseline, differential reinforcement of high rate (drh), differential reinforcement of low rate (drl), and extinction sessions. These reinforcement contingencies refer to the presentation of a tone, contingent upon changes in rates of responding that was, all the while, maintained by a shock-delay procedure. During intervening sessions in a separate chamber, the tone was presented in different relations to shock for two of the three groups: randomly, or unrelated for TRC; negatively correlated, for CS–. For the third group (no CS) only shocks were presented during the intervening sessions. (After Weisman & Litner, 1969. © 1969 by the American Psychological Association. Reprinted by permission.)

into three groups, run on identical procedures during alternate "test" days, but differing in their treatments on the intervening days. For one group (CS–, using Pavlovian terminology in Figure 17), 5-sec presentations of a 400 Hz tone were correlated with shock-free periods. For another (TRC in Figure 17, for "truly random control" after Rescorla (1967), tones and shocks were presented independently, so that the probability of shock was equal in either presence or absence of tone. The third group received the same number of shocks, but the tone was not presented ("No CS") on the intervening days in the second chamber.

During the test sessions, which included continued training with the shock-delay procedure, presentations of the tone were made contingent upon changes in response rate. First came differential reinforcement of high rates (drh). During the first 30 min of the initial drh session the number of responses per 5 seconds required to produce the tone was gradually increased from 4 to 10, where it remained. During the final 30 min of the second test session and test sessions 3–5, the criterion of 10 or more responses per 5 sec remained in effect. During the shock-delay sessions on test days 6 and 7 the tone was not presented. These sessions were included to observe extinction of any conditioned reinforcement effects generated under the drh procedure.

During test sessions 8–11, if zero or one response occurred in a 5-sec interval the 400–Hz tone was presented in the succeeding 5-sec interval. Thus, during these sessions responding at a low rate produced the tone. As with the drh procedure, only the rate of responding in the absence of the tone could affect the presentation of the tone, but responses occurring at any time during the session postponed shock. Again, during shock-delay sessions administered on test days 12 and 13 the tone was not presented. These sessions were included to observe extinction of any conditioned reinforcement effects generated during the drl procedure.

As shown in Figure 17, for rats exposed to tones denoting shock-free periods during intervening sessions, lever-pressing maintained by the shock-delay contingency was increased by the drh schedule and decreased by the drl schedule of tone presentation. Rats for which the tone had not been correlated with absence of shock in the intervening days did not show any such reinforcing effects of contingent tone presentation.

Dinsmoor and Sears (1973) used dimensional control by an added cue to reveal reinforcing effects of the cue correlated with shock-free periods. In addition, the cue's negative correlation with shock was accomplished by presenting it in synchrony with a shock-delay procedure by a technique similar to one developed by Rescorla (1968). Dinsmoor and Sears used pigeons, and the shock-delay procedure (SS = 5, RS = 20 sec) contingent upon treadle-pressing. In addition to the 20-sec response-shock interval, each response produced a 1000 Hz tone of 5-sec duration, which ensured repeated presentation of the tone during shock-free periods. After 58 training sessions, a test procedure was introduced during the final 60 min of every third 90-min session. In this testing, tones of various frequencies were made contingent upon the response; responding was also examined in additional sessions where no tones were presented. As indicated by Figure 18, all birds responded maximally when the response-produced tone had a frequency of 1000 Hz, as in training. For two of the three birds, response rates dropped substantially when the frequency of the tone was varied. Across birds, the degree of decrement produced by changing tone frequency was correlated with the degree of decrement observed when the tone was deleted entirely (open data points in Figure 18). Noncontingent presentations of the 1000 Hz tone resulted in relatively little responding. The

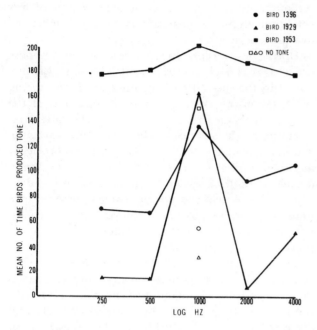

Fig. 18. The mean number of times the response-contingent tone was produced by each of three pigeons during the final 60 min of each test session, in which tones of various frequencies were presented, contingent on responses. The open symbols indicate a comparable measure for periods when no tone was presented. Training occurred with the tone of 1000 Hz; other frequencies used during testing are also indicated on the abscissa. (After Dinsmoor and Sears, 1973.)

effects of varying the frequency of these response-produced tones are not readily attributable to the degree of stimulus change produced by responding, or to the degree of difference between stimuli correlated with the presence of shock (silence) and the response-produced stimulus. Rather, they are attributable to the physical differences between the response-produced stimuli and the stimulus that was previously correlated with shock-free periods immediately following responses.

Each of the four preceding experiments has demonstrated simultaneous control of behavior by shock-delay (shock-frequency reduction without distinctive change of situation) and by reinforcement based on clearly discriminable changes of situation. Verhave (1962) found that a response independent of the shock-delay contingency was sensitive to concurrent reinforcing effects of stimuli correlated with absence of shocks (and of the shock-delay contingency), while the shock-delay response was insensitive to these effects. Rescorla (1969) found a choice measure to be more sensitive than absolute response rate measures for demonstrating concurrent reinforcement effects. However, Weisman and Litner (1969) showed that if the cues correlated with shock-free periods are made contingent specifically upon changes in response rate, the delay-maintained response itself is sensitive to reinforcement by the cue correlated with shock-free periods. In these last two experiments the correlations between cues and shock-free periods were established and maintained in separate training sessions, and thus required special test sessions to demonstrate their effects. Dinsmoor and Sears (1973) demonstrated a method for assessing concurrent reinforcement effects of a stimulus whose negative correlation with shock was established within the shock-delay procedure itself, although the stimulus change always coincided with the initiation of shock-delay.

Discriminative Properties of Cues Added to Shock-Delay Procedures

I have been emphasizing the reinforcing properties of stimuli denoting shock-free periods. At the same time, discriminative properties, revealed by behavior in the presence of the stimuli, have sometimes been observed. These appeared to be closely correlated with the reinforcing properties. For example, Dinsmoor and Sears (1973), when gathering the data shown above in Figure 18, found that the frequency of responding in the presence of a given tone frequency was inversely related to the response rate maintained by response-contingent presentation of that tone frequency. A similar, though less systematically examined effect was observed in the experiment by Verhave (1962) on reinforcing effects of timeout from a shock-delay procedure. There, responding on the shock-delay lever during timeout from the shock-delay procedure decreased as responding increased on the separate lever that produced the timeout periods. This relationship appears roughly similar for both Dinsmoor and Sears's and Verhave's experiments even though the durations of the stimuli denoting shock-free periods differed drastically—5 sec versus 10 min—and one denoted absence of an entire procedure while the other denoted the momentary absence of shock within a similar procedure.

In the experiments that follow, discriminative effects of cues paired with presence and absence of shock were the main focus of study.

CUES SUPERIMPOSED ON SHOCK-DELAY PROCEDURES

Rescorla and LoLordo (1965), with dogs as subjects, found that when a cue had been correlated with shock-free periods in a separate situation, superimposing the cue on a baseline of shock-delay responding produced a decrease in responding in its presence. This finding was replicated in rats by Weisman and Litner (1969). With analogous procedures these two studies also demonstrated increased response rates in the presence of stimuli that had separately been presented in positive correlation with shock. Extrapolations based on these results must be done with caution, for Pomerleau (1970) showed that either enhancement or suppression could be produced by a cue paired with shock, depending on the duration of the cue. Brief cues apparently produce the simplest effects, since they are less affected by the shock frequency produced by the ongoing shock-delay schedule.

Of special interest for the present analysis is an experiment by Rescorla (1968) demonstrating effects of cue-shock correlations established within an ongoing shock-delay procedure. Using different groups Rescorla trained dogs with an SS interval of 10 sec and an RS interval of 30 sec contingent upon a free-operant shuttle response. For some animals a tone was presented for 5 sec after each response; for others, the 5-sec tone came on 25 sec after a response. For a third group of dogs the 5-sec tones were presented at random. None of these tone presentations had any apparent effects on acquisition, but when the tones were then deleted while the shock-delay procedure remained in effect, response rates increased for the group that had received tone immediately after responses. Finally, the shock-delay procedure was suspended (no shocks delivered) and the tones were presented noncontingently. Greatly decreased response rates were observed in the presence of the tone for animals that had previously received tones immediately after responses. In contrast, animals that had previously received the tone 25 sec after responses showed greatly enhanced response rates in the presence of the tone.

Rescorla interpreted his results as supporting traditional two-factor avoidance theory, in which a classically-conditioned response termed "fear" is said to generate the operant response, and removal or inhibition of that classically-conditioned response is said to reinforce the operant response. Thus, the tone immediately following responses would be a fear inhibitor, and that presented just before shock (25 sec after response) would be a fear elicitor, each with appropriate effects on shock-delay responding. Others (e.g. Anger, 1963) have argued that on this type of procedure the cue itself becomes aversive through its correlation with shock. It then generates the response, with its removal reinforcing the response. Either way, the experiments just described (Rescorla, 1968, 1969; Weisman and Litner, 1969), demonstrated results consistent with the two-factor view. Clearly, Pavlovian-cue relations are imbedded in cued negative reinforcement procedures. We have seen that the role of such cue relations can profitably be studied with the aid of Pavlovian procedures applied outside the negative reinforcement sessions, and some of their results can be predicted from principles of Pavlovian conditioning.

However, the conditioned aversive or "fear generating," and thus response-generating role of cues correlated with shock has come into question. For example, Bolles, Stokes, and Younger (1966) and Bolles and Grossen (1969) found that responding was not very effectively maintained by removal of a stimulus paired with shock unless the shock was also deleted. Kamin, Brimer, and Black (1963) used a separate procedure outside a negative reinforcement situation to independently examine conditioned properties of a cue that was paired with shock in the negative reinforcement situation. This separate procedure was the well-known "conditioned anxiety," or conditioned suppression procedure of Estes and Skinner (1941). Using subjects at various stages of training with negative reinforcement, Kamin et al. took the cue that had accompanied shock during that training, and presented it noncontingently during food-reinforced responding. The cue produced least suppression of appetitive responding in animals for which the cue was most effective for maintaining negatively-reinforced responding. This result runs strongly counter to predictions of the two-factor formulation, which would require that a stimulus producing greater fear would be more effective, both for negative reinforcement and for suppression of appetitive behavior.

Cues Inserted in Shock-Delay Procedures: "Warning Stimuli"

The most telling evidence against the traditional two-factor formulation comes from procedures in which preshock cues, often called "warning stimuli," are introduced into shock-delay procedures. Some of these experiments have not received the attention they deserve, so they are presented in detail here. First was an experiment by Sidman (1955) who pretrained cats and rats in his noncued shock-delay procedure (SS = 20, RS = 20) and then introduced a 5-sec preshock cue (light) that could be either delayed or removed. That is, responses less than 15 sec apart delayed both the onset of the light and of the shock (RL interval = 15 sec; RS interval = 20 sec). Responses in the presence of the light terminated it and delayed the shock. If no response occurred the light terminated with the brief shock, initiating shock-light and shock-shock intervals identical to the response-light and response-shock intervals. With this procedure most of the responding came to occur in the presence of the light, with only 25 to 30 percent of the responses typically occurring in its absence, mainly in post-shock bursts. There was some tendency for response rates to increase as time for the light onset approached, but these rates were very low relative to response rates in the presence of the light. Ulrich, Holz, and Azrin (1964) used a similar procedure with a buzzer instead of a light. The response-buzzer interval was 15 sec; the response-shock interval was 20 sec, both comparable to Sidman's experiment. They used a shorter shock-shock interval of five sec. In the absence of responding the buzzer was on continuously, accompanied by a shock every five seconds. They found an even greater concentration of responding in the presence of the pre-shock cue, with only a very low, constant rate of responding in its absence. When they shortened the response-buzzer interval, responding continued to be concentrated in the period immediately after buzzer onset.

If the preshock cue were to be considered a conditioned aversive stimulus whose removal could reinforce responding, one might expect that on these procedures the animals' responding would be maintained by its delay as well as by its removal, comparable to responding maintained by shock-delay when no cue is provided. That did not happen; the animals usually did not delay the warning stimulus. To preserve the notion of conditioned aversive stimuli one could say that the warning stimulus became only moderately aversive. Its removal could maintain responding, but its delay could not.

Whatever its plausibility this reinterpretation is challenged by an experiment by Field and Boren (1963) who provided "warning stimuli for warning stimuli." Their underlying procedure was an "adjusting avoidance schedule" (Sidman, 1962d), where in the absence of responding brief shocks occurred every 5 sec, and each response produced 10 sec of shock-free time. These 10-sec periods were cumulative up to 100 sec. Field and Boren used two sets of stimuli in this procedure. One was a series of 11 pilot lights spaced evenly in a line on the wall above the lever. Each lamp in ordinal sequence accompanied a specific 10-sec period within the 100-sec range. The 11th light, directly above the lever, was on during the shock-shock interval. The light most distant from the lever was on when the next shock was not due to occur for 100 sec. The second set of 11 stimuli was a series of click rates ranging from 57.7 per sec during the shock-shock interval, to zero when shock was 100 sec distant. Figure 19 shows typical performances with auditory and visual stimuli combined, with visual and auditory stimuli separated, and with no added warning stimuli. With both sets of stimuli (top panel), the rat typically responded so that shock was kept 30 to 50 sec away. When there were no added stimuli (bottom panel), shock was typically kept 90 to 100 sec away, with occasional lapses. Most interesting are the intermediate cases: performance with the auditory stimuli was very similar to that with both auditory and visual stimuli; performance with light alone was intermediate between that for both stimuli and that for no added cues. Light plus clicker can reasonably be assumed to be a more distinctive cue than light alone. Thus, with the more salient or discriminable stimu-

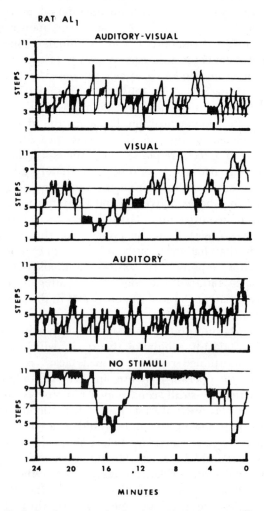

Fig. 19. Strip chart records showing one rat's responding with both classes of multiple warning stimuli, with each class of stimuli alone, and with no warning stimuli. The pen records the position of the stepping relay, hence the temporal proximity of the shock is indicated in 10-sec increments. On these records time runs from right to left. (From Field & Boren, 1963.)

lus changes, the animals maintained a closer proximity to shock. Field and Boren interpreted their results in terms of degree of stimulus control, and of stimulus generalization. They argued that with more highly discriminable stimuli, characterized by a relatively sharp gradient, the animals could maintain the relatively closer proximity to shock without incurring an increase in shock frequency. An interpretation in terms of conditioned aversive stimuli could probably handle these results with certain added assumptions. However, a simple and direct application of this approach would seem to predict the opposite results. When more clearly discriminable stimulus changes were provided one might expect facilitation of responding that prevented the conditioned aversive stimuli. Instead, the responding shifted toward stimuli more closely associated with shock.

Grabowski and Thompson (1972) obtained similar results with monkeys. They used lights correlated with successive time segments of SS and RS intervals on conventional shock-delay procedures.

Additional experiments by Sidman and Boren (1957 b & c) and by Sidman (1957) more directly illustrate the discriminative rather than aversive role of preshock stimuli inserted into shock-delay procedures. In one of these, Sidman and Boren (1957b) compared performance on two procedures, one of which was described just above (Sidman, 1955). On that procedure, responding that delayed shock could also delay or remove a tone presented 5 sec before a shock was due. As noted above, most responding occurred in the presence of the tone instead of delaying it. The comparison procedure also used shock-delay and cue-delay, with pretraining on a conventional procedure whose shock-shock and response-shock intervals both equal to 20 sec. Similar to the above procedure, a 4-sec light preceded all shocks; responses in its absence delayed its onset by 16 sec while delaying shock by 20 sec. However, responses in the presence of the light had no effect either on light or on shock; once the light came on the impending shock was unavoidable. When this procedure was introduced to animals pretrained with no warning stimuli, responding in the dark, which was now the only effective responding, initially increased but then decreased over sessions. The final stable levels were not systematically related to response rates during initial conditioning on the uncued shock-delay procedure; some rates were higher than initially, others were lower. Any responding that initially occurred in the presence of the light decreased systematically to very low levels. Additional control procedures assessed possible effects of variable light durations and varying correlations of light and shock in the comparison procedure where responses could terminate the light. Taking all of these into account, it was clear that while both procedures satisfied the conditions for formation of a Pavlovian discrimination, only in the case of the cue denoting unavoidable shock did the cue function as a conditioned aversive stimulus. However, even there we could treat it just as a stimulus correlated with the suspension of the shock-delay contingency: responding in its presence decreased; responding in its absence could still delay shock, and that responding persisted. Absence of the light in this case, was a stimulus correlated with access to reinforcement, and responding persisted in the presence of that stimulus even though it was not paired with shock.

A second experiment by Sidman and Boren (1957c) argues even more strongly for discriminative properties of a preshock cue within delay procedures. After pretraining on the standard noncued shock-delay procedure with SS and RS intervals of 20 sec, a cue was added. So long as 15 sec did not elapse between responses, it was identical to the familiar cued shock-delay procedure (Sidman, 1955). Responses could delay the onset of the cue light, as determined by a response-light interval of 15 sec analogous to the usual shock-delay contingency. However, if the animal paused, allowing the cue light to come on, a response-shock interval of 5 sec was in effect such that responses delayed the shock but also extended the duration of the cue light. With a shock, the cue light was turned off, reinstating the 15-sec response-light contingency. With the transition to this schedule from uncued shock-delay (SS = RS = 20 sec), responding in the presence of the light increased temporarily over that of the comparable time periods in the pretraining schedule and then dropped well below that in the dark. For three of four rats, responding in the dark on the 15-sec light-delay schedule increased slightly over that for comparable time periods in the prior schedule. For all rats the terminal response rate in the absence of the light substantially exceeded that in the presence of the light. In short, the animals frequently waited through the light, took the shock, and then responded more rapidly, delaying the renewed onset of the light.

This result suggests that the low response rates (pauses) in the presence of the cue light in the sequential procedure were reinforced by termination of the stimulus and its associated contingency, even though the shock whose reduction provided the basis for maintaining the whole performance accompanied the termination of that light.

The shift of responding within a sequential procedure, from a more demanding to a less demanding component is reminiscent of the effects observed by Krasnegor, Brady, and Findley (1971), which were described earlier in the present chapter. It indicates that the reinforcing or aversive properties of a cue-defined situation can be strongly affected by the scheduled reinforcement contingencies in that situation, apart from correlated shock delivery *per se*. The similarity of the two experiments is revealed by parametric manipulations with the Sidman and Boren procedure. These manipulations, reported by Sidman (1957), make the controlling features of that procedure even more clear. First, the response-light interval was held constant while the response-shock interval, operative in the presence of the light, was manipulated. Response rates varied in both the presence and absence of the light, so that more time was spent in the condition permitting lower response rates. Complementary results are shown in Figure 20; these were obtained by holding the response-shock interval constant at 10 sec and varying the response-light interval from 10 to 20 sec. As the figure shows, when the two intervals were equal at 10 sec, most responding occurred in the presence of the light, directly delaying shock. However, when the response-light interval was increased, performance changed and the animal spent most of its time in the dark, with responding again maintained by associated less stringent performance requirement. These functions are very similar to those of Krasnegor et al. (1971), shown in Figure 2.

In a follow-up experiment, Sidman and Boren (1957b) moved animals from a schedule of this kind, with a RL interval of 15 sec and a RS interval of 10 sec in the presence of the light, to a procedure that differed in that the cue light and the associated response-shock interval did not terminate with the first shock. Once on, the light remained on for five min, accompanied by ten-sec response-shock and shock-shock intervals, independently of shocks taken during this period. Response rates in the absence of the light and maintained by the light-delay contingency, were slightly higher than in the comparable procedure where cue presentation terminated whenever a shock was delivered. Response rates in the presence of the lights were very high relative to rates on the comparable procedure where the light terminated with shock. Low rates were no longer reinforced by a return to less stringent response requirements.

The Several Properties of Added Cues, and Their Implications for Two-Factor Theory

Returning to the terms of my earlier analysis of negative reinforcement procedures without added cues, the preshock, or "warning" stimulus added to a shock-delay or shock-deletion procedure is correlated with several key procedural features. The added cue accompanies the opportunity to respond, and is correlated with a frequency or probability of shock. It also denotes periods when responding is especially effective, and thus is correlated with the availability of reinforcement. Accordingly, behavioral effects of a warning stimulus are confounded. The preshock cue cannot be seen as simply providing a classically conditioned surrogate for the shock, for several effects of the cue are independent of its relation to shock. A change in availability of reinforcement contingent upon behavior in the presence of a cue can markedly change that behavior. It can also change behavior that affects the onset of the cue. The manipulation of one correlated feature may affect changes in behavior directly, or indirectly by shifting control to a different correlated feature. In short, the familiar warning stimulus, traditionally used to simplify interpretation of negative reinforcement, is an added feature of great complexity.

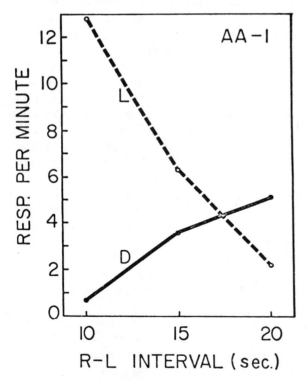

Fig. 20. Rate of responding in the light (L) and in the absence of the light (D) for rat AA-1 as a function of the interval by which responses in the dark could delay the light (the RL interval). The RS interval, by which responses during the light could delay shocks, was constant at 10 sec. (From Sidman, 1957.)

Traditional two-factor theory of the form that postulates internal mediating responses classically conditioned to the warning stimulus, encounters the above problems and more. These conditioned responses, with their own cue properties, must themselves be multiply correlated with the various aspects of the conditioning procedure. Further, as Black (1971) has argued in exhaustive detail, there is no reliable principle for *a priori* selection or identification of a mediating response. The closer one comes to identifying a physiological index of a classically conditioned response or process that might mediate the operant behavior, the greater the likelihood that the index is an instrumentally conditioned artifact of the operant procedure. At the same time, the less susceptible the proposed mediator is to problems of artifact, the less adequate it is to account for the operant behavior. In addition, if one is concerned with mediation of performance, a phasic reflex response is far too primitive to mediate the lawful but complex behavior produced by the procedures we have been considering. In principle the Pavlovian model can encompass more enduring responses. In practice a proposed diffuse but unitary process identified by a facile label such as "fear" is likely to provide superficial interpretation. As Myer (1971) has argued, present evidence does not indicate that there is a single, unitary, mediating process based on pairing of stimuli with shock.

This is not to belittle the role of cues in negative reinforcement procedures, nor to disregard all aspects of the Pavlovian paradigm as it applies to these procedures. The correlation of cues with presence or absence of shocks, as systematized by Rescorla and his colleagues (e.g. Rescorla & Wagner, 1972) provide the basis for the most comprehensive formulation of stimulus combination now available. However, instead of characterizing the positive or negative correlation of a cue with shock as production or inhibition of a Pavlovian response, it is proposed here that in operant behavior, the role of cues correlated with shocks is better characterized as affecting the averaging of shock over time.

This averaging need not be construed in terms of the subject's internal mechanism, but rather in terms of what methods for summarizing the independent variables lead to the simplest functional relationships. For example, comparison of periodic with aperiodic events suggests that equivalencies cannot be based on arithmetic averaging. In the case of concurrent chain schedules of positive reinforcement, an aperiodic sequence of reinforcements is preferred over a periodic sequence of events with the same overall frequency (e.g. Herrnstein, 1964); it appears that short interreinforcement times have disproportionately great effects (see also Fantino, Chapter 11 in this volume). For the aversive case, Bolles and Popp (1964) found indications that on a shock-delay procedure, a variable shock-shock interval produced acquisition more reliably than did a fixed shock-shock interval with approximately the same mean value. If this is interpreted as effectively shortening the shock-shock interval, the results are comparable to those obtained by Leaf (1965), showing better acquisition with small shock-shock intervals. Thus we have both an appetitive and an aversive example suggesting that arithmetic averaging is inappropriate.

Whatever the method of averaging, the onsets and offsets of added cues appear to enhance or even change the boundaries of time intervals over which intermittent events are effective. With respect to intermittent shocks accompanied by tones and lights, we might consider the onset or offsets of the added cues as influencing the behavioral effects of shock in much the same way that, in visual pattern perception boundary lines can influence the way that dots in the visual field are grouped. If the lines fall between areas with differing but homogeneous densities of dots, the differences between these homogeneous areas will be enhanced. If on the other hand, there is a continuous gradient of density of dots, drawing a line across the gradient will effectively separate the areas. The observer will report the pattern not as a gradual gradient, but rather as a group of areas with separate, more-or-less homogeneous but different densities. So, analogously, presentation or removal of a tone or light may influence the way that a series of brief electric shocks will be averaged. This function is implicit in my distinguishing between shock-frequency reduction within a cue-defined situation and a change of cue-defined situations with differing shock frequencies. The onset or offset of a continuous cue provides a boundary for a group or groups of irregularly spaced shocks.

The effect of cues on averaging of intermittent shocks is illustrated quite clearly in an experiment by Badia, Coker, and Harsh (1973). For initial training, they exposed rats to a variable-time schedule of brief, noncontingent, and nonreduceable shocks. The probability of shock was fairly constant over time, with a mean shock-shock interval of four min. In addition, each shock was preceded by a five-sec tone. After three sessions of exposure to this signaled shock procedure, shocks occurred without the tone unless the animal responded. A response turned on a cue light for three minutes, during which shocks were preceded by the tone. Quick acquisition of responding occurred once an animal made contact with this contingency. The animals consistently responded, producing the situation defined by the cue light, in which shocks were reliably preceded by the five-second tone.

After stable responding was established, Badia et al. varied the shock frequency in the signaled condition, using mean shock-shock intervals of 2, 1.0, or 0.5 min. Meanwhile, they held the shock frequency in the unsignaled condition constant at one shock per four min. By not pressing the lever, the animals could always maintain this condition in which shock frequency remained at one shock per four min. All rats persisted in responding when signaled shocks averaged one per two min, and three of four animals persisted when signaled shocks averaged one per min. That is, responding was maintained by production of a situation in which signaled shocks occurred four times as frequently as the unsignaled shocks that would occur in the absence of responding. A control experiment, with all shocks unsignaled, established that the various shock frequencies were discriminable by the animals.

The interpretation given these results by Badia et al. was that the addition of preshock warning signals effectively provided substantial shock-free intervals in the absence of those signals. Most responses produced the light-correlated situation denoting shock-free periods; the averaging or integrating of intermittent shocks occurred only within the boundaries established by the warning stimuli. In addition, it is clear that the preshock "warning signals" did not increase the aversiveness of the more molar situation defined by the presence of the cue light, as might be expected if they were to be interpreted simply in terms of conditioned aversiveness. To the contrary, they decreased the aversiveness of that situation. Characterized as affecting integration of shocks over time, they can be said to have produced discriminable shock-free intervals. Recall that Dinsmoor and Sears (1973) demonstrated dimensional control by stimuli denoting shock-free intervals, independently of stimuli denoting availability of shock or setting the occasion for the response. They, and a number of others (e.g. Bolles, 1970; Rescorla, 1969) have argued for the potency of discriminable shock-free intervals in reinforcing behavior. An attractive feature of the stimuli denoting shock-free periods for the analysis of behavior is not only their apparent potency as reinforcers, but also their comparatively low degree of confounding with various aspects of negative reinforcement procedures. Denoting "timeout" periods, their simplicity contrasts with other stimuli that are multiply correlated with opportunities to respond, access to reinforcement, and shock probability, frequency, or density.

Cues Denoting Limited Response Opportunity, Apart from the Aversive Situation

Free-operant procedures for examining negative reinforcement have permitted study of schedule effects that were inconceivable within traditional escape and avoidance procedures. They have produced diverse but orderly behavioral phenomena that complement those produced by positive reinforcement. At the same time, response patterns on schedules of negative reinforcement have sometimes been attributed to contingencies or principles that are not readily manipulable or testable within a free-operant situation itself. The behavior often interacts with a schedule in such a way as to prohibit clean manipulation of the critical variable. Analysis of such contingencies has required a redeparture from the free-operant paradigm to special forms of limited-opportunity procedures. I shall examine the use of limited-opportunity schedules for addressing three questions regarding negative reinforcement. One deals with the isolation of the contingency between response and shock, independently of shock frequency and responses rate. Another deals with the role of temporal discriminations in behavior on shock-delay procedures. The third question concerns the relative contributions of short-term shock-delay and long-term shock-frequency reduction. Interestingly, Shimp (1973) has argued for the positive reinforcement case that an analysis of the variables operative in standard schedules of reinforcement often requires a departure from those schedules. Some such analyses have used limited-opportunity procedures very much like those to be considered here (e.g. Jenkins, 1970).

Isolating Contingency and Frequency

When discussing shock-deletion procedures without added cues, I noted that a contingency between response and shock-deletion can be efficiently specified in terms of two probabilities. These are the probability of shock if a response occurs, and the probability of shock given no response. As pointed by Church (1969), Catania (1971) and several others, the degree of contingency can be described as the difference between the two probabilities. However, in uncued free-operant procedures this specification tells only part of the story, for one must also specify the interval for which the probability operates. For example, in a standard fixed-cycle shock-deletion procedure, the probabilities are specified in relation to the shock-shock interval. An example is shown in part I of Figure 7, where the probability of shock given a response is zero, and the probability given no response is one. In schedules defined under the $t^\Delta - t^D$ schedules devised by Schoenfeld and his associates (e.g. part III of Figure 7; also, see Kadden, Schoenfeld, & Snapper, 1974), the probabilities are specified in relation to t^D, which is a portion of the shock-shock interval. Within either of these situations, the duration of the period for which the probabilities are specified has strong implications. That period determines both the maximum possible shock rate, and the minimum response rate required to achieve a given amount of shock reduction. In uncued situations these are both powerful variables.

The confounding of rate with contingency can be mitigated by adding a cue that coincides with the period for which the probabilities are specified. Cue duration is still a variable to be considered, but to some degree it can be moved to the background along with overall response and shock rates. If the cue is removed by a response, no more than one response can occur per cue presentation. The shock can be limited to a maximum of one per cue as well so that both can be described by probabilities instead of frequencies.

Neffinger and Gibbon (1975) have reported an experiment that separates frequency and contingency in this way. Using rats, they superimposed a tone on a basic fixed-cycle shock-deletion procedure that was virtually identical to that diagrammed above in part I of Figure 7. With no responding, a 0.5 sec shock was delivered every 20 sec; a tone was on during the intervening 19.5 sec during which a response could affect shock. A response in the presence of the tone terminated the tone, and deleted the shock due at the end of that cycle. The tone came on again when the shock had been deleted, starting a new 20-sec cycle.

The addition of the tone converted this to a discrete-trial procedure. At least Neffinger and Gibbon treated it as such, for they ignored responses in the absence of the tone. They trained their rats with the conventional probabilities: probability of a shock was zero if a response had occurred; probability of a shock given no response was one. Also, in this training they discarded approximately 70 percent of their animals, which failed to meet a stringent performance criterion. Then the two probabilities were manipulated independently, but with interspersed retraining at the original values. The left panel of Figure 21 shows the effects of decreasing the probability of shock given no

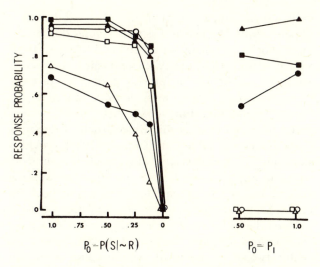

Fig. 21. The left panel shows response probability as a function of the conditional probability of shock given no response, $P(Sk/\sim R)$, while the probability of shock given a response, $P(Sk/R)$, was constant at zero. The right panel shows response probabilities when the shock probabilities for responding and for not responding were equal, at values greater than zero. Each plot represents a different rat. Data are taken from the final three days of exposure to the schedule values, and the functions are plotted from left to right in the order in which the probability values were studied. (After Neffinger & Gibbon, 1975. © 1975 by the Society for the Experimental Analysis of Behavior, Inc.)

response, while holding the probability of shock given a response constant at zero. With this manipulation, response probabilities remained relatively high until the probability of shock given no response was very low.

The right panel of Figure 21 shows the effects of subsequently eliminating the contingency, by making the probabilities of shock equal whether or not the rats responded. The performances separated into two distinct classes: some animals quit responding; others responded persistently. With further analysis, Neffinger and Gibbon argued that one class was sensitive only to contingency; the other was sensitive both to contingency and to absolute shock density. Interestingly, these two classes of animals could not be distinguished in the left side of the figure, or in original training. As the authors noted, the distinctness of two classes of performance may have resulted partly from their stringent subject selection procedures.

THE ROLE OF TEMPORAL
DISCRIMINATIONS IN BEHAVIOR ON
SHOCK-DELAY PROCEDURES

It is well established that subjects trained on a shock-delay schedule distribute their responses nonrandomly in time. The momentary probability of a response typically increases as time elapses during the shock-shock or response-shock interval (Anger, 1963; Sidman, 1966). Gibbon (1972) delineated some characteristics of the timing process needed to produce these response distributions, arguing that it has "scalar" properties, functioning with units proportional to the intervals being timed (such as response-shock intervals). Libby and Church (1974) provided additional evidence for the scalar property, showing with a free-operant shuttle response, that rats' spacing of responses is proportional to the response-shock interval. Some interpretations of the conditioning process have been founded upon the observed response distributions. For example, Anger (1963) used it to enable two-factor theory to explain conditioning on uncued shock-delay procedures. He proposed that the animal's internal stimuli correlated with times close to the response-shock interval become aversive through pairing with shock. When responses occur these were said to be replaced with other internal time-correlated stimuli that are not closely paired with shock. Responding, then, was said to be reinforced by removal of conditioned aversive stimuli whose temporal properties are referenced to the response that produces the shock-delay, establishing a "time-zero."

Rescorla (1968) supported a two-factor interpretation by demonstrating the potential for Pavlovian conditioning based on features of the shock-delay procedure. These features involve the pairing of responses and shocks in fixed time relations. He pretrained his subjects on a shock-delay procedure (SS = 10, RS = 30) and then gave independent training with a Pavlovian trace conditioning procedure in which onset of a 5-sec tone preceded unavoidable shock in the same time relationship as the response-shock interval of the shock-delay procedure. That is, shock followed the offset of tone by 25 sec. Then, when he superimposed the tone upon the ongoing shock-delay procedure, he found response acceleration in phase with the 25-sec tone-shock interval, showing that the temporal features of the Pavlovian procedure affected responding maintained by shock-delay. Rescorla presented this as evidence for a mediating emotional response which would normally be conditioned to feedback stimuli from the shock-delay response.

I have argued above that preshock stimuli are better characterized as discriminative stimuli, rather than as conditioned aversive or emotion-producing stimuli. Dinsmoor and Sears (1973) provided such an account, proposing a "fading trace" initiated by each response and denoting shock-free periods. They supported their interpretation with the demonstration, illustrated above in Figure 21, of dimensional control by stimuli paired with shock-free short post-response times.

By all three accounts—Anger, Rescorla, and Dinsmoor and Sears—the animal's spacing of responses in time reflects an underlying process fundamental to the reinforcement of responding on the shock-delay procedure. However, there is another likely interpretation of the spaced responding. A shock-delay procedure, viewed as a procedure for reinforcement by shock-frequency reduction, provides differential reinforcement of spaced responding. Within the response-shock interval, the more widely spaced the responses, the greater the magnitude of reinforcement for a given response. This view suggests that the production of spaced responding is a second-order process, not critical to the maintenance of responding *per se,* but affecting only the distribution of responses. Sidman (1966) supported this latter view with a variety of arguments. Some of his supporting data came from concurrent schedules; some came from demonstrations that temporal discriminations often do not appear until after responding is well established.

Hineline and Herrnstein (1970) addressed the question with an experiment that eliminated the possible differential reinforcement based on shock-frequency reduction. The experiment used a modified version of the fixed-cycle shock-deletion procedure described earlier (part I of Figure 7). As before, brief shocks occurred every 20 sec, defining a 20-sec cycle. Also as in the free-operant fixed-cycle procedure, the first lever-press within a cycle cancelled the shock due at the end of that cycle. In addition, the lever was retracted from the chamber immediately after the response permitting only one response per cycle, and was re-extended to initiate the new cycle; a buzzer was correlated (positively or negatively for different animals) with presence of lever, also denoting the opportunity to respond. Thus, each response eliminated only one shock, no matter where it occurred within the 20-sec cycle. The beginning of a cycle was cued either by a shock or by stimulus changes correlated with insertion of the lever into the chamber. Distributions of responses within the cycle were compared to inter-response time distributions and shock-response time distributions of a conventional shock-delay procedure with shock-shock and response-shock intervals of 20 seconds.

As expected, animals on the shock-delay schedule frequently showed temporal discriminations, indicated by increasing probabilities of responding late in the response-shock interval. Animals on the fixed-cycle schedule with limited response opportunity sometimes showed greatest probability of response late in the cycle, indicating a timing process. But sometimes the probability of response decreased with time during the cycle, and sometimes it was fairly constant, indicating randomly spaced responding. These changes were not correlated with changes in number of shocks deleted. The changes in distribution of responses within a cycle were sometimes sudden, but more often were gradual and systematic. One of the widest and most systematic changes of response distribution is shown in Figure 22. In this figure, the slope of each function is the important feature. Positive slopes indicate timing, with the momentary probability of response increasing with time since trial (cycle) onset. A horizontal slope indicates randomly spaced responding, with the momentary probability of response constant over time. This rat clearly showed slowly shifting response distributions, with continuity of performance from week to week, but with wide swings in the distribution of responses within the 20-sec cycles. The distribution of responding was unrelated to proficiency of performance, for the animal took fewer than one percent of the possible shocks in any session.

The data of this experiment clearly revealed that processes producing spaced responding need not be critical to the maintenance of responding. This challenges the two-factor interpretations, since the stimulus change initiating each cycle should have provided excellent cues for temporal conditioning. Dinsmoor and Sears's interpretation of timing is perhaps least challenged by this experiment, given that a warning stimulus (presence of lever, and correlated buzzer) was present until the shock-deleting response had occurred, and the response produced the same feedback whenever it occurred. However, their interpretation still would not predict the observed gradual changes in spacing of responses within a cycle, from timing to non-timing and back again.

On the other hand, Sidman's notion regarding the basis for spaced responding is not supported either, for the experiment shows that spaced responding need not be based on differential reinforcement through shock-frequency reduction. The experiment does support Sidman's contention that spacing of responding is a second-order process, and that Pavlovian pairings with temporal stimuli or stimulus traces is not necessary to the maintenance of responding. As I described earlier, Neffinger and Gibbon (1975) used a procedure similar to that of Hineline and Herrnstein (1970), except that their lever did not retract when responses occurred. They too found the distributions of responding to be unrelated to proficiency of performance, and concluded that timing is more collateral than causal in behavior on shock-delay procedures.

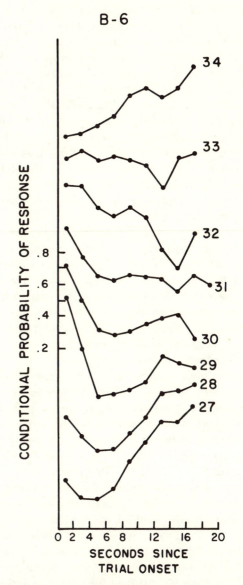

Fig. 22. Changes in conditional probability of response as a function of time since the beginning of a cycle (or trial) for one rat. The figure is based upon eight consecutive weeks during conditioning with the fixed-cycle shock-deletion procedure, and limited response opportunity. The conditional probabilities were computed by dividing the number of responses in a 2-sec class interval by the number of opportunities for response in that class interval. The computation compensates for the fact that each response in a given class interval eliminated the opportunity for response intervals later in that class interval. To clarify the continuity of performance changes, plots for successive weeks, numbered at the right of the figure, are displaced upward, in consecutive order. The size of scale indicated on the ordinate is valid for all plots. Absolute values for the 0-2 sec class interval, for the successive weeks, were .32, .45, .76, .72, .70, .55, .45, and .22, respectively. (From Hineline & Herrnstein, 1970. © 1970 by the Society for the Experimental Analysis of Behavior, Inc.)

Dissociation of Shock-Delay and Shock-Frequency Reduction

Two variables have been confounded in nearly all procedures for negative reinforcement. Responding reduces overall shock-frequency or density, and at the same time it produces short-term delay of shock, a shock-free interval. Even the random-shock procedures of Herrnstein and Hineline (1966) and of de Villiers (1972, 1974) can be described in terms of average time between response and shock, contrasted with time between shocks in the absence of responding. Such a translation is mathematically tautological, in that average delay is merely the reciprocal of shock frequency. Still, it is also a change in emphasis from molar, long-term controlling relations to short-term controlling relations.

In the experiment described just above, the molar and molecular features of behavior were dissociable in that the molar features—degree of shock-frequency reduction, or probability of response per trial—were stable while the microstructures of performance were highly unstable. The experiments that follow focus on *procedural* dissociation of the molecular and molar aspects of negative reinforcement.

In these experiments the opportunity to respond was again limited, to permit precise control of the delay between response and shock with no intervening responses to complicate the relationship. Delivery of a shock at times between response opportunities permitted the shock frequency to be manipulated somewhat independently of short-term delay. The first such procedure (Hineline, 1970) provided for responses to produce shock-delay without affecting overall shock frequency. As shown in part I of Figure 23, the procedure was based on fixed 20-sec cycles. Time specifications within a cycle began with insertion of the lever into the chamber. In the absence of responding the lever was accessible for alternate 10-sec periods, with a shock occurring at the eighth second of the lever's presence. A response prior to that point produced immediate removal of the lever and delayed the shock from the 8th to the 18th second of the cycle. There was still one shock per 20 sec. This procedure maintained responding in each of five rats exposed to it, two of which had prior training with a conventional cued shock-delay procedure, and three of which were experimentally naive.

These results are compared with a second experiment, using the procedure diagrammed in part II of Figure 23. In the absence of responding this procedure was identical to the one just described: 20-sec repeated cycles began with insertion of the lever into the chamber; a shock occurred at the eighth second, and the lever retracted at the 10th second for the remainder of the cycle. As before, a response removed the lever and delayed the shock. However, this was accomplished by production of a 10-sec interval with the lever out, and a shock occurring 8 sec after the response. There was still one shock per cycle, but responses shortened the cycle, increasing overall shock frequency. Response rates of the two rats with previous training decreased systematically to negligible levels, within five sessions and nine sessions respectively. Eleven naive rats placed directly on this procedure never responded on more than 30 percent of the cycles. Typically, responding rose to 20 or 25 percent of the cycles during a few of the early sessions, and then systematically decreased to zero.

The first of these two experiments indicates that short-term shock-delay can function as a reinforcer independently of overall shock frequency. The procedure used a variable response-shock interval (10 to 18 sec, depending on the placing of the response within a cycle), and constant shock frequency. In the second experiment, apparently shock-delay was not sufficiently potent to override an opposing change in shock frequency. This procedure provided a shorter, constant response-shock interval (8 sec), as well as increased shock frequency contingent upon responding. A complicating feature of both procedures was the delivery of shocks sometimes in the presence of the lever and sometimes in its absence. While shock frequencies in the presence and in the absence of the lever (each accumulated over all cycles) did not indicate this as the source of response strength,[4] another set of procedures was devised to eliminate possible confounding effects of these relative shock frequencies.

The revised procedure (Hineline, 1969) permitted complete dissociation of the opportunity to respond from the situation in which shocks occur. It also permitted wider ranges of shock-delay and shock frequency. As shown in Part III of Figure 23, all variants of the procedure were identical if no response occurred. That sequence of events is portrayed just above the dotted line in the figure: a cycle began with insertion of the lever into the chamber; it retracted at the 10th sec, a shock (1.0 sec; 0.8 mA) was

---

[4] Two of the three naive animals placed on the constant frequency procedures persistently responded so as to produce substantially higher shock rates in the absence of the lever than in its presence. Herrnstein (1969) showed that the principle of shock-frequency reduction under stimulus control can account for this experiment if the computation of shock frequencies is based only on stimulus exposures (presence or absence of lever) during which shock occurred.

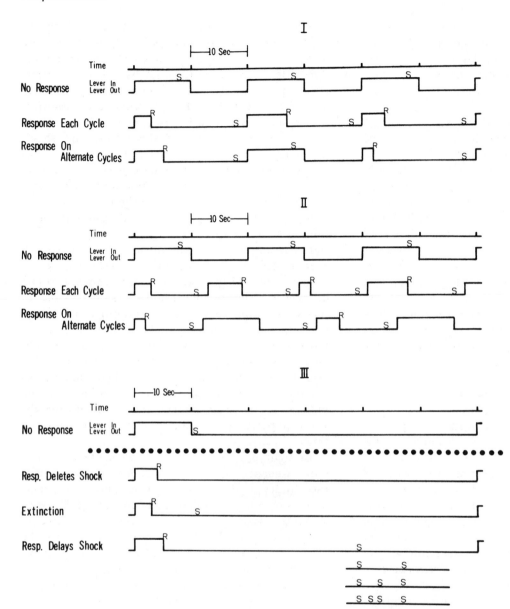

Fig. 23. Diagrams for three shock-delay procedures with response opportunity limited in order to isolate shock-delay from shock-frequency. Time is represented linearly from left to right, as indicated on the top line of each diagram. Upward displacement of a line indicates insertion of the lever at the beginning of a cycle. Downward displacement indicates retraction of the lever. An "S" marks the delivery of a shock; an "R" indicates the occurrence of a response. (From Hineline, 1969, 1970.)

delivered at the 11th second, and a new cycle began with reinsertion of the lever at the 60th second.

A sequence of procedures was run; each provided a different consequence for responding. The first was a shock-deletion procedure. If a response occurred, the lever retracted immediately and no shock was delivered on that cycle. The second was an extinction procedure. If a response occurred, the lever retracted immediately, but the shock was still delivered at the 11th sec. The third was a shock-delay procedure with constant overall shock frequency. If a response occurred, the lever retracted immediately and the shock was delayed from the 11th to the 39th sec. This was followed by shock-delay procedures where the delay was achieved at the expense of increases in overall shock frequency. These procedures were identical to the third procedure, except that one, two, three, or four additional shocks were delivered in cycles where the response occurred. For two shocks per response, the shocks occurred at the 39th and 47th secs of the cycle. The larger numbers of shocks were added with the spacing indicated at the bottom of the diagram, filling in the interval between the 39th and 47th secs.

Each rat was first trained until stable on the first, shock-deletion procedure. Next, each rat was placed on the second (extinction) procedure until responding decreased to less than 5 percent of the trials. The third procedure, shock-delay, was instituted next; if a rat failed to respond on this he was reconditioned on the shock-deletion procedure and then moved to the shock-delay procedure. If a rat developed stable responding on the third procedure, the final sequence was instituted, providing two, three, four, and then five shocks per response.

One of the six rats responded on over 90% of the cycles on the initial, shock-deletion procedure. The others stabilized at approximately 80%, 75%, 70%, 20%, and one animal seldom responded at all, even with hand-shaping. All animals' responding ceased within a very few sessions of exposure to the second procedure where a shock occurred at the 11th second independently of responding. Only two animals resumed responding when transferred directly from this to the shock-delay procedure, the two that had responded most on the initial, shock-deletion procedure. The others failed to respond on the third procedure even after reconditioning with shock deletion. These two were then run on procedures in which responses delayed shock but increased shock frequency. As the number of shocks per response was increased every five sessions, from two, three, four, and then to five shocks per response, they continued to respond on nearly all cycles.

Thus, in some animals, delay of shock maintained responding even when it produced a fivefold increase in overall shock frequency. However, these animals had prior training on a shock-deletion procedure, and although their responding had subsequently been extinguished with a noncontingent shock procedure, the results should be interpreted with some caution. Response-contingent shocks, and sometimes even noncontingent shocks, can maintain responding in animals with histories of negative reinforcement (e.g. McKearney, 1972; Powell, 1972).

In order to be sure that prior negative reinforcement based on combined shock-delay and shock-frequency reduction would not contaminate the dissociation of these two variables, the initial, shock-deletion phase has been eliminated from subsequent experiments with the same set of procedures with 60-second cycles. These experiments have encountered difficulties of conditioning that have also sometimes been reported with more conventional negative reinforcement procedures. Hence, while the following, rather autobiographical series will tell something about the contributions of shock-delay and shock-frequency reduction to negative reinforcement, it will also illustrate strategies that have been used to deal with difficulties of initial conditioning with negative reinforcement. This will prepare the way for a discussion of special considerations regarding initial conditioning with negative reinforcement.

In an unpublished experiment, twelve naive rats were placed on the procedure diagrammed by the bottom line of Figure 23. The only response consequences were lever-removal and shock-delay. None of the twelve acquired stable lever-pressing. Hand-shaping with some animals, by making lever-removal and shock-delay contingent upon successively closer movements toward the lever, resulted in their hovering over the lever and spending most of their time near it, but did not produce reliable lever-pressing. The animals often tended to remain motionless during the 10-sec opportunity period, moving around at other times.

In light of these results, supplementary positive reinforcement was used, in a manner similar to that used by Riess (1970) with a conventional shock-delay procedure, and by Giulian and Schmaltz (1973) with a discrete-trial, cued shock-deletion procedure, to bring the animals' behavior into contact with the delay contingency without a history of shock reduction. In collaboration with G. D. Smith, several variants of this approach were used on a few animals with moderate success. One is described here; it demonstrated the clear and reliable, but weak reinforcing effects of delay-of-shock with constant shock frequency. The sequence of procedures and results is shown in

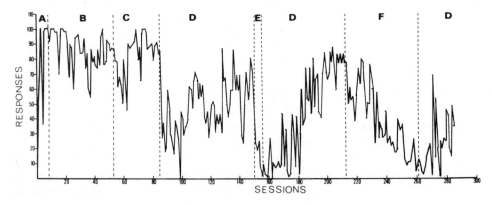

Fig. 24. Lever-presses per session for rat DS-6, on a sequence of procedures: A) Responses produce food with no shocks delivered; B) Responses produce food and delay of shock; C) Same as B, but free access to food in home cage; D) Discontinue positive reinforcement; responses produce shock delay only; E) One shock delivered at the 16th sec of each cycle; F) One shock delivered at the 47th sec of each cycle.

Figure 24. Prior to training the rats were food-deprived; then lever-pressing was established and maintained with delivery of sweetened condensed milk as reinforcer (part A of Figure 24). Then a slightly modified version of the shock-delay procedure described above (part III of Figure 23) was added, with shock intensities increased by increments over sessions (part B of Figure 24). This shock-delay procedure differed from that diagrammed in Figure 23, in that: with no response the shock occurred at the 16th instead of the 11th sec; responding delayed the shock until the 47th sec; whenever it occurred, shock was preceded by a three-second tone. These changes were made to minimize response-opposing effects of signaled versus unsignaled shocks (e.g. Badia et al., 1973), since shock immediately preceded by lever removal could be said to be signaled shock, while the delayed shock could not. When shock intensities were increased to 1.0 mA, a level that supports lever-press responding on conventional shock-delay procedures, food deprivation was discontinued by giving free access to lab chow in the home cage, but delivery of condensed milk contingent upon lever-presses was continued (part C in Figure 24). When body weights had recovered to normal free-feeding levels, the positive reinforcement was discontinued (condition D in Figure 24), and when performance was stabilized to the point of showing no consistent trends, two control or extinction procedures were used to insure that indeed it was shock delay that maintained the responding. First, (condition E) all shocks were delivered at the 14th sec, independently of responding. This procedure was comparable to the extinction procedure of the preceding experiment, and the results were similar; responding dropped quickly to negligible levels. Reinstatement of the shock-delay procedure produced a slow, systematic, but variable reacquisition over some 40 sessions. In the next control procedure (condition F), all the shocks were delivered noncontingently at the delayed position, the 47th sec of the cycle. On this procedure responding slowly but consistently declined toward zero, until reversed by a return to the shock-delay procedure which again produced, slow, variable, but systematic reacquisition. Thus, in an animal with no history of response-produced shock deletion, delay of shock appeared to be an unconfounded but fairly weak reinforcer. Several animals on this procedure did not persist in responding when the shock intensities were raised; others responded at lower levels when the positive reinforcement was discontinued.

It is clear from the procedural diagrams of Figure 23 that the fixed-cycle procedure separating the opportunity to respond from the periods when shocks occur permits complete independence of shock-delay and shock-frequency changes made contingent upon responding. This flexibility was used in a recent experiment by Lambert, Bersh, Hineline, and Smith (1973), pitting shock-frequency reduction against shock delay, with a different part of the range of time values permitted by a 60-sec cycle. In the absence of responding the lever was available for 10 sec, and then five brief shocks were delivered, one per second, between the 11th and 15th sec. A response during the first 10 sec retracted the lever and deleted the five later shocks, but produced one immediate shock. Thus, responses could reduce shock frequency at the expense of reducing shock delay to zero. Two rats placed directly on this procedure initially responded on approximately 60 percent of the cycles for the first few sessions; then their responding dropped systematically to zero by session 13. Two other animals, trained with a procedure where a response could terminate the stream of five shocks, also ceased responding on the procedure permitting only shock frequency reduction with contingent zero-delay shock. Thus, shock frequency reduction also appeared to be a weak reinforcer when pitted against a reduction in shock-delay.

Perhaps the weakness of these reinforcing effects should be interpreted in light of a notion advanced by Jenkins (1970), with reference to limited-opportunity positive reinforcement procedures. It is a notion very similar to the one I advanced earlier, regarding the effects of cues on the averaging of shocks over time:

> The possibility exists that distinctively different occasions for nonreinforcement and reinforcement confine or localize the effect of reinforcement while more similar occasions extend the interval over which delayed reinforcement supports a prior response. (Jenkins, 1970, p. 105)

To the extent that this is true, confining the response opportunity to a clearly discriminable situation distinct from the effects of the response weakens the reinforcing effect of either short-term delay or shock-frequency reduction.

The reinforcing effect may be weak for another reason, however. Acquisition of lever-pressing with conventional shock-delay procedures is most easily accomplished with short shock-shock intervals. Perhaps the change to long cycle length, attractive because it permits longer delays, is relatively ineffective because it imposes a low basal shock rate. If the conventional shock-delay procedures, providing both shock-delay and shock-frequency reduction within the situation where the response occurs, are ineffective for producing initial acquisition of lever-pressing with similar long intervals, then the weak effects in Figure 24, and in the work by Lambert et al. (1973) are not surprising.

One strategy for studying weak reinforcing effects is to use a response more easily conditioned than the lever-press. A likely candidate is a shuttle response, which has been shown to be readily strengthened with shock reduction (Bolles, 1970; Riess, 1971; Riess & Farrar, 1972). In unpublished work, J. Harman and I have recently verified the usefulness of this approach by subjecting four rats to a shock-delay procedure with a shock-shock interval of 60 sec, and an RS interval of 120 sec. With a free-operant shuttle response, all animals quickly and consistently reduced their shock frequencies to less than one per 10 min. Lambert et al. (1973), using the shock-frequency reduction procedure with nondelayed shock described above, found a shuttle response to be maintained slightly more easily than lever-pressing. In an additional unpublished experiment, J. Harman and I used a shuttle response in conjunction with the shock-delay procedure diagrammed at the bottom of Figure 23. Moderate to low response rates were obtained, comparable to those of the latter parts of Figure 24. The shuttle response did not require the addition of positive reinforcement early in training to produce these effects. Thus again, shock-delay and shock-frequency had independently isolable but weak reinforcing effects when response opportunity was discriminably separated from the situation in which shocks occurred.

Earlier in this chapter we saw that in the case of weak reinforcing effects of timeout from the shock-delay procedures, a two-response or choice situation provided more sensitive measures than did measures based on maintenance of a single response. Further, in positive reinforcement studies of reinforcement magnitude and frequency, choice procedures provided by concurrent chains have also proven especially sensitive. It may be that choice procedure would provide an effective strategy for the isolation of shock-frequency reduction and short-term shock delay as well, permitting systematic assessment of the relative potency of differing magnitudes of each.

CONSIDERATIONS REGARDING INITIAL ACQUISITION

Operant conditioners have tended to emphasize maintenance of responding and of response patterns, rather than initial acquisition of control over particular responses by reinforcement. With positive reinforcement, conceptual concern over initial acquisition has been allayed by appeal to the principle of shaping. This principle, of response selection through reinforcement of successive approximations to a specified response, was convincingly demonstrated in Skinner's early work, and is routinely replicated in undergraduate laboratories. Over the years the assumed generality of this principle has been occasionally challenged (e.g. Breland & Breland, 1961), but only recently has that challenge become a central topic supported by systematic work on autoshaping (Brown & Jenkins, 1968) and other response-selection effects (e.g. Staddon & Simmelhag, 1971).

The present chapter has also emphasized maintenance rather than acquisition, partly because an integrative account of negative reinforcement analogous to that of positive reinforcement seems needed at this time. Also, as argued by Morse and Kelleher (1966), it appears that once control over a response with negative reinforcement is achieved, the effects of scheduling negative reinforcement are much like those of scheduling positive reinforcement. However, initial acquisition with negative reinforcement has consistently been of more concern than with positive, probably because using the former, experimenters have often encountered difficulty in producing a chosen response. The difficulties have tended to arise in relation to particular species, and to particular responses.

Species Differences in Acquisition

According to informal laboratory lore, "monkeys and dogs avoid better than rats do," and until very recent years the behavior of pigeons seemed virtually immune to negative reinforcement based on shock reduction. However, it is impossible to deduce exactly comparable situations for different species and choose apparatus configurations, shock intensities, and cue intensities or modalities on the basis of the subjects' differing shapes and receptors. Hence, it is difficult to devise valid cross-species comparisons. The case of pigeons is especially instructive in this regard.

In view of several unpublished, unsuccessful attempts to produce or maintain key-pecking with shock-delay or shock-reduction, Rachlin and Hineline (1967) devised a shaping procedure based on termination of trains of shock pulses with slowly increasing intensity. They successfully, if arduously, shaped the key-peck response and maintained repetitive responding within a limited range of fixed-ratio and fixed-interval schedules (Hineline & Rachlin, 1969a, b). More recently, Ferrari, Todorov, and Graeff (1973) developed these shaping procedures further and maintained stable key-peck responding with a shock-delay procedure. Using an SS interval of two seconds, manipulations of the RS interval resulted in performance changes similar to those observed by Sidman with rats (Sidman, 1953). However, they too reported the need for hours of tedious shaping during the initial training. Schwartz and Coulter (1971) found that key-pecking established with positive reinforcement did not readily transfer to negative reinforcement. However, more recently, Lewis, Lewin, Stoyak, and Muehleisen (1974) were able to transfer control of key-pecking from positive reinforcement to negative reinforcement based on termination of a cue and deletion of frequent irregularly spaced shocks, and Foree and LoLordo (1974) succeeded in a similar transfer, to a shock-delay procedure with added cues.

It is clear, however, that with the pigeon, responses other than key-pecking are more easily established with negative reinforcement. Hoffman and Fleshler (1959) found a head-lifting response to be slightly more susceptible to shock-reduction, and MacPhail (1968) obtained reliable, high-probability shuttle responding with pigeons on a cued shock-deletion procedure. Later, Smith and Keller (1970) and Foree and LoLordo (1970) easily accomplished conditioning with free-operant shock-delay procedures contingent upon a foot-treadle response. Klein and Rilling (1972) have built upon this by manipulating the parameters of shock-delay and of shock intensity, replicating in considerable detail the results obtained with the lever-press in rats (Boren, Sidman, & Herrnstein, 1959; Sidman, 1953). As described above, Dinsmoor and Sears (1973) used the same schedule and response to demonstrate dimensional control by response-produced stimuli, and Klein and Rilling (1974) also used the treadle-press in pigeons to study generalization effects with tones accompanying the shock-delay component of a multiple schedule.

This brief history shows that some aspects of observed species differences in behavioral processes originate as much in the method used for examining them, as in any differing capacities of different species. In addition, it points up the importance of response specification for ease of conditioning, a consideration that has had considerable impact on recent interpretations of negative reinforcement.

Response Differences: Apparent Susceptibility to Reinforcement

I just reviewed evidence that in pigeons treadle-press or shuttle responses have been more easily brought under control of negative reinforcement than has the key-peck, which is so readily controlled by positive reinforcement. Earlier, I noted comparable observations by Riess and Farrar (1972) that in rats a shuttling response is usually acquired with negative reinforcement more rapidly and reliably than is a repetitive lever-press response. Further along similar lines, Keehn (1967) observed that the response of running in a wheel was acquired more quickly with a shock-delay contingency than was a lever-press response. Bolles (1970) found differences in acquisition on a shock-deletion procedure, when comparing the responses of running in a wheel, turning, or rearing.

Bolles (1970) has discussed these differences in relation to "species-specific defense reactions." He noted that in the genetic histories of small animals, random "trial-and-error" patterns of behavior must have been maladaptive in aversive situations or situations accompanied by intense or novel stimulation. While the first inappropriate response producing loss of food leaves an animal still hungry, an inappropriate response in an aversive situation may very well leave the animal dead. Bolles proposed that in such situations the responses of freezing, fighting, or fleeing would be most generally adaptive, so animals that tended to behave in these ways in these situations would tend to survive and reproduce. In their offspring, these behavior patterns could be expected to predominate in aversive and novel situations. This line of reasoning can lead to two interpretations that are not mutually exclusive. One proposes that particular responses are especially associable or conditionable with a particular stimuli. The other analyzes the differences in terms of the operant levels of various responses in aversive situations. Bolles has clearly implied that the former is more important, arguing that negative reinforcement is basically selection from among species-specific defense reactions; other responses are deemed unconditionable. From this viewpoint, the conditioning of a particular response with negative reinforcement can only be achieved to the extent that the response is part of a species-specific defense reaction. Seligman and Hager (1972), developing an earlier discussion by Seligman (1970), have opted for a similar interpretation. They used a concept of "preparedness" to make explicit the proposed susceptibility of a response to the effects of (or in their terminology, the associability of a response to) a particular reinforcer.

Both of these interpretations relate well to the apparent differences of conditionability described above. They also account for Bindra and Anchel's (1963) demonstration that immobility can readily be conditioned with a shock-removal contingency, and the observation by Keehn (1967) that lever-holding is more readily produced and maintained with negative reinforcement than is repeated lever-pressing. Both immobility and lever-holding can be components of the species-specific response of freezing. The first interpretation outlined above is especially supported by an experiment by Foree and LoLordo (1973). They found that after a combined light and tone were used as a cue in an appetitive situation the light had stronger effects on behavior, whereas after the same light and tone were used as a cue in a negative reinforcement procedure the tone had stronger effects on behavior.

However, attributing species differences in conditioning to species differences in associativity or susceptibility to reinforcement does have some drawbacks. First, as Schwartz (1974) has pointed out, any independent assessment of such "preparedness" of a response must be made with existing conditioning procedures. Different procedures will give differing results, and any attempt to standardize the measures of "preparedness" will necessarily standardize a set of "fundamental" conditioning procedures. This would be counter to current critical examinations of common conditioning concepts, and would impose an arbitrariness more difficult to assess than that of the "arbitrary response."

Second, the "species-specific" label draws our attention away from the fact that these reactions and their conditionability, however common and stereotyped among members of a species, have ontogenetic as well as genetic origins. I wonder, for example, about the degree to which the conditionability of a rat's running in an aversive situation originated in its interactions with littermates during the early weeks of life. The label "species-typical" would be more appropriate. This term would remind us that we have not closed the question of the origins of an animal's behavioral characteristics, while still suggesting that we look to genetic factors for part of the answer.

Third, in appealing to genetic determination one appeals to a largely unspecified sequence of events. To be sure, one can breed animals that tend to respond in this way or that, but this only establishes the plausibility of the explanation. To the extent that species-typical reactions are specified and studied independently, with adequate identification of the circumstances under which they will occur, their use is easily justified. However the genetic explanations tend to be used in a post hoc fashion when all else has failed. The independent specification usually is not available, and one can thus choose convenient properties for the genetically determined behavior. More directly testable explanations are sometimes available in which the relative ease of conditioning of a particular response is explained in terms of attributes of the response itself. For example, Keehn (1967) noted that the relatively slow acquisition of lever-press responding, compared to wheel running, may occur because in the latter a continued response pattern is permitted, while the former requires repeated production and discontinuance of a response pattern. He compared acquisition of running with acquisition of lever-holding, and found these two responses equally conditionable with negative reinforcement.

Finally, as Ferrari, Todorov, and Graeff (1973) have pointed out, any comparison of conditionability or associability of different responses must be made on the basis of optimal procedures for each response. This brings us inevitably to the other aspect of Bolles's formulation, the role of shock-produced behavior in determining the operant levels of different responses. Optimal procedures must accommodate or eliminate this behavior.

Competing, Shock-Produced Behavior

Any intense, novel, or aversive stimulus is likely to produce behavior that helps to determine the repertoire of responses available for reinforcement. This is especially relevant in negative reinforcement procedures since, by definition, such stimulation must be present, highly probable, or impending when the to-be-reinforced response is emitted. This contrasts with positive reinforcement situations, where the critical stimulus is presented *after* the response is emitted. Effects of noncontingent aversive stimulation have been reviewed by Myer (1971), who abstracted some useful principles. He noted, for example, that proximally received stimuli usually produce skeletal behavior that tends to remove the stimulation. Distally received stimuli—in themselves aversive or paired with aversive stimuli—tend to produce cessation of movement.

Thus electric shock, while providing the basis for reinforcement, produces behavior patterns that must interact with the responses that experimenters have chosen to reinforce. Sometimes facilitation occurs, but often competition or disruption occurs instead. Specific competing patterns have been described and discussed by experimenters who had difficulty in conditioning particular responses with negative reinforcement. For example, a number of experimenters have observed shock-produced freezing and lever-holding (e.g. Dinsmoor, 1967; Feldman & Bremner, 1963; Keehn, 1967). Smith, Gustavson, and Gregor (1972) used high-speed photography to examine the pigeon's response to unsignaled shock, and found that the shock produced head-flexions—movements in the direction opposite to that required for key-pecking. Shock-elicited aggressive patterns such as biting the manipulandum have also been observed and measured (Azrin, Hutchinson and Hake, 1967; Azrin, Rubin and Hutchinson, 1968; Pear, Moody and Persinger, 1972; Powell, 1972). The use of intermittent shocks or cues correlated with these shocks may not eliminate competing behavior, for as Hoffman (1966) and Myer (1971) have noted, the preshock warning stimulus commonly used in shock-deletion procedures fits a paradigm for conditioned suppression of active skeletal behavior. As Estes and Skinner (1941) demonstrated, appetitively maintained behavior is suppressed in the presence of a stimulus that has been paired with shock. While after initial conditioning has been achieved with negative reinforcement, such a stimulus may enhance active responding (e.g. Rescorla, 1968), its effect during initial conditioning is to produce crouching and freezing.

Each of these shock-produced behavior patterns has been seen as interfering with initial attempts to bring lever-press responding under control of negative reinforcement. I have also found evidence that in rats the disruption persists beyond initial conditioning (Hineline, 1966). The persisting disruption is revealed in a commonly-observed "warm-up" effect, whereby even after they have achieved proficient performance, rats continue to take many shocks early in sessions. In this experiment rats were conditioned with a shock-delay procedure (SS = RS = 20). Direct observation of subjects showing pronounced warm-up revealed that patterns of freezing and lever-holding were clearly evident early in the sessions, when most shocks were received, but not later in sessions. In a subsequent set of procedures, the possible disruptive effects were examined indirectly, by making positive reinforcement and shock-delay both contingent upon presses of the shock-delay lever. The schedule of positive reinforcement (VI 40 sec), when used alone prior to shock-delay training, produced performances with few interresponse times exceeding 20 sec until satiation late in the sessions. Thus, if there were no disruption virtually all early session shocks should have been eliminated by the addition of positive reinforcement. For rats with extensive prior training the added positive reinforcement failed to eliminate the disproportionately high shock frequencies early in sessions. Animals with less extensive training showed some reduction of warm-up with the added positive reinforcement. However, four of five animals continued to show at least some warm-up, indicating transient disruption of lever-pressing. To the extent that these results implicate competing behavior as disrupting negatively reinforced responding early in all sessions, competing responses are relevant to maintenance of the conditioned response, as well as to its initial acquisition. Experimenters have often tacitly acknowledged this by discarding data from the initial parts of all sessions, even in studies of long-term maintenance.

Negative Reinforcement and the Ongoing Behavioral Stream

Whichever aspect of the shock-produced competing responses one chooses to stress, one must come to grips with their ontogenetic as well as their phylogenetic origin. Furthermore, since they affect the operant level, or "behavioral stream" (Schoenfeld, 1969) upon which negative reinforcement must operate, one must consider specifically how they are maintained in a given situation.

Of course, operant conditioning principles partly describe the shaping of the behavioral stream. These principles can be used to explicitly study the maintenance of the "competing behavior." For example, Keehn and Walsh (1970) have examined reinforcement of lever-holding, and Bolles and Riley (1973) have carefully examined reinforcement and punishment, as well as elicitation of a freezing response. In some cases operant principles have been used to specifically eliminate the competing behavior. For example, Forgione (1970) improved the acquisition of repeated lever-pressing by identifying and eliminating reinforcement that inadvertently had been made contingent upon short-latency post-shock responding. Feldman and Bremner (1963) eliminated freezing and lever-holding by making brief shock contingent upon these responses, while making shock-delay contingent upon repeated pressing.

Initial training procedures for bringing a particular response under control of negative reinforcement are "little transfer experiments." The result of one conditioning procedure produces the operant level for the next procedure to act upon. Therefore it is not surprising that the effects of negative reinforcement are very different once an organism's behavior has been brought under control of *some* negative reinforcement procedure. The situation is analogous to the teaching of swimming. Once one swimming technique is brought under control of water-filled situations, which involves eliminating many incompatible water-produced responses, it is relatively easy to train any of a variety of swimming patterns.

However, some components of the behavioral stream clearly are produced in ways not subsumed under principles of reinforcement and punishment. Usually the species-typical patterns have been characterized as elicited even though they may include complex response patterns. Elicitation plays a role, as Bolles and Riley (1973) have demonstrated, but it is somewhat inadequate in that it implies a passive organism that does nothing except when goaded. The ethologists' concept of "releasing stimuli" for particular classes of behavior is only slightly less limiting. It more readily encompasses complex behavior patterns, but still tends to characterize the controlling environment as made up of discrete, single stimuli.

To be sure, single stimuli are important, but animals are also sensitive to temporal configurations of environmental objects and events. Temporal patterns of environmental events interact with patterns of ongoing behavior. Perhaps we shall come to deal with these interactions in terms of modulation (Gibbon & O'Connell, 1973; Morse & Kelleher, 1970), periodicity and aperiodicity (Kadden, 1973), autocorrelation, closed and open loops, and/or contingency and noncontingency as expressed in a statistical, rather than a merely associative sense (Baum, 1973). Concepts such as these may help us understand how some procedures that were designed to reinforce a specific response are actually more effective for producing behavior that competes with that response. It is not yet clear whether these developing concepts will come to subsume what we now call reinforced as well as what we call non-reinforced behavior. Perhaps the operations we now treat as discrete and unitary will be of interest mainly as ends of continua such as those suggested by Catania (1971). Whatever reformulations occur, they must also deal with interrelations described here, between responding and the response-contingent reduction of stimulation.

REFERENCES

Anger, D. The role of temporal discriminations in the reinforcement of Sidman avoidance behavior. *Journal of the Experimental Analysis of Behavior*, 1963, *6*, 447–506.

Appel, J. B. The aversive control of operant discrimination. *Journal of the Experimental Analysis of Behavior*, 1960, *3*, 35–48.

Azrin, N. H., Holz, W. C., Hake, D. F., & Ayllon, T. Fixed-ratio escape reinforcement. *Journal of the Experimental Analysis of Behavior*, 1963, *6*, 449–456.

Azrin, N. H., Hutchinson, R. R., & Hake, D. F. Attack, avoidance and escape reactions to aversive shock. *Journal of the Experimental Analysis of Behavior*, 1967, *10*, 131–148.

Azrin, N. H., Rubin, H. B., & Hutchinson, R. R. Biting attack by rats in response to aversive shock. *Journal of the Experimental Analysis of Behavior*, 1968, *11*, 633–639.

Badia, P., Coker, C., & Harsh, J. Choice of higher density signalled shock over lower density unsignalled shock. *Journal of the Experimental Analysis of Behavior*, 1973, *20*, 47–55.

Baum, W. M. The correlation-based law of effect. *Journal of the Experimental Analysis of Behavior*, 1973, *20*, 137–153. (a)

Baum, W. M. Time allocation and negative reinforcement. *Journal of the Experimental Analysis of Behavior*, 1973, *20*, 313–322. (b)

Baum, W. M., & Rachlin, H. C. Choice as time allocation. *Journal of the Experimental Analysis of Behavior*, 1969, *12*, 861–874.

Bersh, P. J., & Lambert, J. V. The discriminative control of free-operant avoidance despite exposure to shock during the stimulus correlated with nonreinforcement. *Journal of the Experimental Analysis of Behavior*, 1975, *23*, 111–120.

Bindra, D., & Anchel, H. Immobility as an avoidance response, and its disruption by drugs. *Journal of the Experimental Analysis of Behavior*, 1963, *6*, 213–218.

Black, A. H. Autonomic aversive conditioning in infrahuman subjects. In Robert F. Brush (Ed.), *Aversive Conditioning and Learning*. New York: Academic Press, 1971.

Bolles, R. C. Species-specific defense reactions and avoidance learning. *Psychological Review*, 1970, *77*, 32–48.

Bolles, R. C. The avoidance learning problem. In G. H. Bower (Ed.), *The Psychology of Learning and Motivation* (Vol. 6). New York: Academic Press, 1973.

Bolles, R. C. & Grossen, N. E. Effects of an informational stimulus on the acquisition of avoidance behavior in rats. *Journal of Comparative and Physiological Psychology*, 1969, *68*, 90–99.

Bolles, R. C. & Popp, R. J. Parameters affecting the acquisition of Sidman avoidance. *Journal of the Experimental Analysis of Behavior*, 1964, *7*, 315–321.

Bolles, R. C. & Riley, A. L. Freezing as an avoidance response: Another look at the operant-respondent distinction. *Learning and Motivation*, 1973, *4*, 268–275.

Bolles, R. C., Stokes, L. W., & Younger, M. S. Does CS termination reinforce avoidance behavior? *Journal of Comparative and Physiological Psychology*, 1966, *62*, 201–207.

Boren, J. J. Isolation of post-shock responding in a free operant avoidance procedure. *Psychological Reports*, 1961, *9*, 265–266.

Boren, J. J., and Sidman, M. A discrimination based upon repeated conditioning and extinction of avoidance behavior. *Journal of Comparative and Physiological Psychology*, 1957, *50*, 18–22.

Boren, J. J., Sidman, M., & Herrnstein, R. J. Avoidance, escape, and extinction as functions of shock intensity. *Journal of Comparative and Physiological Psychology*, 1959, *52*, 420–425.

Breland, K., & Breland, M. The misbehavior of organisms. *American Psychologist*, 1961, *16*, 661–664.

Brown, P. L., & Jenkins, H. M. Auto-shaping of the pigeon's key-peck. *Journal of the Experimental Analysis of Behavior*, 1968, *11*, 1–8.

Catania, A. C. Elicitation, reinforcement, and stimulus

control. In R. Glaser (Ed). *The Nature of Reinforcement*. New York: Academic Press, 1971.

Church, R. M. Response Suppression. In Campbell, B. A. & Church, R. M. (Eds.), *Punishment and Aversive Behavior*. New York: Appleton-Century-Crofts, 1969.

Church, R. M. Laws of learning. (Review of *Aversive Conditioning and Learning* by Robert F. Brush). *Contemporary Psychology*, 1973, *18*, 322–323.

Clark, F. C. & Hull, L. D. Free-operant avoidance as a function of the response-shock-shock = shock interval. *Journal of the Experimental Analysis of Behavior*, 1966, *9*, 641–647.

Clark, F. C., Lange, K. O., & Belleville, R. E. Behavioral regulation of gravity: schedule effects under escape-avoidance procedures. *Journal of the Experimental Analysis of Behavior*, 1973, *20*, 345–353.

Coulson, G., Coulson, V., & Gardner, L. The effect of two extinction procedures after acquisition on a Sidman avoidance contingency. *Psychonomic Science*, 1970, *18*, 309–310.

Davenport, D. G., Coger, R. W. and Spector, O. J. The redefinition of extinction applied to Sidman free-operant avoidance responding. *Psychonomic Science*, 1970, *19*, 181–182.

Davenport, D. G. & Olson, R. D. A reinterpretation of extinction in discriminated avoidance. *Psychonomic Science*, 1968, *13*, 5–6.

de Villiers, P. A. Reinforcement and response rate interaction in multiple random-interval avoidance schedules. *Journal of the Experimental Analysis of Behavior*, 1972, *18*, 499–507.

de Villiers, P. A. The law of effect and avoidance: a quantitative relationship between response rate and shock-frequency reduction. *Journal of the Experimental Analysis of Behavior*, 1974, *21*, 223–235.

Dinsmoor, J. A. Variable-interval escape from stimuli accompanied by shocks. *Journal of the Experimental Analysis of Behavior*, 1962, *5*, 41–47.

Dinsmoor, J. A. Escape from shock as a conditioning technique. In M. R. Jones (Ed.), *Miami Symposium on the Prediction of Behavior: 1967; Aversive Stimulation*. Coral Gables, Fla.: University of Miami Press, 1968.

Dinsmoor, J. A., & Sears, G. W. Control of avoidance by a response-produced stimulus. *Learning and Motivation*, 1973, *4*, 284–293.

Ellen, P., & Wilson, A. Two patterns of avoidance responding. *Journal of the Experimental Analysis of Behavior*, 1964, *7*, 97–98.

Estes, W. K. & Skinner, B. F. Some quantitative properties of anxiety. *Journal of Experimental Psychology*, 1941, *29*, 390–400.

Feldman, R. S., and Bremner, F. J. A method for rapid conditioning of stable avoidance bar pressing behavior. *Journal of the Experimental Analysis of Behavior*, 1963, *6*, 393–394.

Ferrari, E. A., Todorov, J. C., & Graeff, F. G. Nondiscriminated avoidance of shock by pigeons pecking a key. *Journal of the Experimental Analysis of Behavior*, 1973, *19*, 211–218.

Field, G. E., & Boren, J. J. An adjusting avoidance procedure with multiple auditory and visual warning stimuli. *Journal of the Experimental Analysis of Behavior*, 1963, *6*, 537–543.

Findley, J. D. An experimental outline for building and exploring multi-operant behavior repertoires. *Journal of the Experimental Analysis of Behavior*, 1962, *5*, 113–166.

Foree, D., & LoLordo, V. Signalled and unsignalled free-operant avoidance in the pigeon. *Journal of the Experimental Analysis of Behavior*, 1970, *13*, 283–290.

Foree, D., & LoLordo, V. M. Attention in the pigeon: differential effects of food-getting versus shock-avoidance procedures. *Journal of Comparative and Physiological Psychology*, 1973, *85*, 551–558.

Foree, D., & LoLordo, V. M. Transfer of control of the pigeon's key peck from food reinforcement to avoidance of shock. *Journal of the Experimental Analysis of Behavior*, 1974, *22*, 251–259.

Forgione, A. G. The elimination of interfering response patterns in lever-press avoidance situations. *Journal of the Experimental Analysis of Behavior*, 1970, *13*, 51–56.

Gibbon, J. Timing and discrimination of shock density in avoidance. *Psychological Review*, 1972, *79*, 68–92.

Gibbon, J., Berryman, R., & Thompson, R. L. Contingency spaces and measures in classical and instrumental conditioning. *Journal of the Experimental Analysis of Behavior*, 1974, *21*, 585–605.

Gibbon, J., & O'Connell, M. E. Acquisition and maintenance of responding by rats under non-contingent shock. Paper read at the Annual Meeting of the Eastern Psychological Association, 1973, Washington, D.C.

Giulian, D., & Schmaltz, L. W. Enhanced discriminated bar-press avoidance in the rat through appetitive preconditioning. *Journal of Comparative and Physiological Psychology*, 1973, *83*, 106–112.

Grabowski, J., & Thompson, T. Response patterning on an avoidance schedule as a function of time-correlated stimuli. *Journal of the Experimental Analysis of Behavior*, 1972, *18*, 525–534.

Hake, D. F., & Campbell, R. L. Characteristics and response-displacement effects of shock-generated responding during negative reinforcement procedures: pre-shock responding and post-shock aggressive responding. *Journal of the Experimental Analysis of Behavior*, 1972, *17*, 303–323.

Harrison, J. M., & Tracy, W. H. The use of auditory stimuli to maintain lever-pressing behavior. *Science*, 1955, *121*, 373–374.

Hearst, E. Multiple schedules of time-correlated reinforcement. *Journal of the Experimental Analysis of Behavior*, 1960, *3*, 49–62.

Herrnstein, R. J. Aperiodicity as a factor in choice. *Journal of the Experimental Analysis of Behavior*, 1964, *7*, 179–182.

Herrnstein, R. J. Method and theory in the study of avoidance. *Psychological Review*, 1969, *76*, 49–69.

Herrnstein, R. J. On the law of effect. *Journal of the Experimental Analysis of Behavior*, 1970, *13*, 243–266.

Herrnstein, R. J., & Hineline, P. N. Negative reinforcement as shock-frequency reduction. *Journal of the Experimental Analysis of Behavior*, 1966, *9*, 421–430.

Hineline, P. N. The warm-up effect in avoidance conditioning. Unpublished Doctoral Dissertation, Harvard University, 1966.

Hineline, P. N. One shock now or five shocks later. Paper read at the Annual Meeting of the Eastern Psychological Association, Philadelphia, 1969.

Hineline, P. N. Negative reinforcement without shock reduction. *Journal of the Experimental Analysis of Behavior*, 1970, *14*, 259–268.

HINELINE, P. N., & HERRNSTEIN, R. J. Timing in free-operant and discrete-trial avoidance. *Journal of the Experimental Analysis of Behavior*, 1970, *13*, 113–126.

HINELINE, P. N., & RACHLIN, H. Notes on fixed-ratio and fixed-interval escape responding in the pigeon. *Journal of the Experimental Analysis of Behavior*, 1969, *12*, 397–401. (a)

HINELINE, P. N., & RACHLIN, H. Escape and avoidance of shock by pigeons pecking a key. *Journal of the Experimental Analysis of Behavior*, 1969, *12*, 533–538. (b)

HOFFMAN, H. S. The analysis of discriminated avoidance. In W. K. Honig (Ed.), *Operant Behavior: Areas of Research and Application*. Englewood Cliffs, N.J.: Prentice-Hall, Inc., 1966.

HOFFMAN, H., & FLESHLER, M. Aversive control with the pigeon. *Journal of the Experimental Analysis of Behavior*, 1959, *2*, 213–218.

HURWITZ, H. M. B., & MILLENSON, J. R. Maintenance of avoidance behavior under temporally defined contingencies. *Science*, 1961, *133*, 284–285.

HURWITZ, H. M. B., ROBERTS, A. E., & GREENWAY, L. Extinction and maintenance of avoidance behavior using response-independent shocks. *Psychonomic Science*, 1972, *28*, 176–178.

JENKINS, H. M. Sequential organization in schedules of reinforcement. In W. N. Schoenfeld (Ed.), *The Theory of Reinforcement Schedules*. Englewood Cliffs, N.J.: Prentice-Hall, Inc., 1970.

KADDEN, R. M. Facilitation and suppression of responding under temporally defined schedules of negative reinforcement. *Journal of the Experimental Analysis of Behavior*, 1973, *19*, 469–480.

KADDEN, R. M., SCHOENFELD, W. N., & SNAPPER, A. G. Aversive schedules with independent probabilities of reinforcement for responding and not responding by Rhesus monkeys: II. Without Signal. *Journal of Comparative and Physiological Psychology*, 1974, *87*, 1189–1197.

KAMIN, L. J., BRIMER, C. J., & BLACK, A. H. Conditioned suppression as a monitor of fear of the CS in the course of avoidance training. *Journal of Comparative and Physiological Psychology*, 1963, *56*, 497–501.

KEEHN, J. D. Avoidance responses as discriminated operants. *British Journal of Psychology*, 1966, *57*, 375–380.

KEEHN, J. D. Running and bar pressing as avoidance responses. *Psychological Reports*, 1967, *20*, 591–602.

KEEHN, J. D., & WALSH, M. Barholding with negative reinforcement as a function of press- and release-shock intervals. *Learning and Motivation*, 1970, *1*, 36–43.

KELLEHER, R. T., & MORSE, W. H. Escape behavior and punishment behavior. *Federation Proceedings*, 1964, *23*, 808–817.

KELLER, F. S. Light aversion in the white rat. *Psychological Record*, 1941, *4*, 235–250.

KLEIN, M., & RILLING, M. Effects of response-shock interval and shock intensity on free-operant avoidance responding in the pigeon. *Journal of Experimental Analysis of Behavior*, 1972, *18*, 295–303.

KLEIN, M., & RILLING, M. Generalization of free-operant avoidance behavior in pigeons. *Journal of the Experimental Analysis of Behavior*, 1974, *21*, 75–88.

KRASNEGOR, N. A., BRADY, J. V., & FINDLEY, J. D. Second-order optional avoidance as a function of fixed-ratio requirements. *Journal of the Experimental Analysis of Behavior*, 1971, *15*, 181–187. © 1971 by the Society for the Experimental Analysis of Behavior, Inc.

LAMBERT, J. V., BERSH, P. J., HINELINE, P. N., & SMITH, G. D. Avoidance conditioning with shock contingent upon the avoidance response. *Journal of the Experimental Analysis of Behavior*, 1973, *19*, 361–367.

LEAF, R. C. Acquisition of Sidman avoidance responding as a function of S–S interval. *Journal of Comparative and Physiological Psychology*, 1965, *59*, 298–300.

LEWIS, P., LEWIN, L., STOYAK, M., & MUEHLEISEN, P. Negatively reinforced key pecking. *Journal of the Experimental Analysis of Behavior*, 1974, *22*, 83–90.

LIBBY, M. E., & CHURCH, R. M. Timing of avoidance responses by rats. *Journal of the Experimental Analysis of Behavior*, 1974, *22*, 513–517.

MACPHAIL, E. M. Avoidance responding in pigeons. *Journal of the Experimental Analysis of Behavior*, 1968, *11*, 629–632.

MCKEARNEY, J. W. Fixed-interval schedules of electric shock presentation: extinction and recovery of performance under different shock intensities and fixed-interval durations. *Journal of the Experimental Analysis of Behavior*, 1969, *12*, 301–313.

MCKEARNEY, J. W. Maintenance and suppression of responding under schedules of electric shock presentation. *Journal of the Experimental Analysis of Behavior*, 1972, *17*, 425–432.

MORSE, W. H., & KELLEHER, R. T. Schedules using noxious stimuli. I. Multiple fixed-ratio and fixed-interval termination of schedule complexes. *Journal of the Experimental Analysis of Behavior*, 1966, *9*, 267–290.

MORSE, W. H., & KELLEHER, R. T. Schedules as fundamental determinants of behavior. In W. N. Schoenfeld (Ed.), *The Theory of Reinforcement Schedules*. Englewood Cliffs, N.J.: Prentice-Hall, Inc., 1970.

MOWRER, O. H., & LAMOREAUX, R. R. Fear as an intervening variable in avoidance conditioning. *Journal of Comparative and Physiological Psychology*, 1946, *39*, 29–50.

MYER, J. S. Some effects of noncontingent aversive stimulation. In Robert F. Brush (Ed.), *Aversive Conditioning and Learning*. New York: Academic Press, 1971.

NEFFINGER, G. G., & GIBBON, J. Partial avoidance contingencies. *Journal of the Experimental Analysis of Behavior*, 1975, *23*, 437–450.

PEAR, J. J., MOODY, J. E., & PERSINGER, M. A. Lever attacking by rats during free operant avoidance. *Journal of the Experimental Analysis of Behavior*, 1972, *18*, 517–523.

POMERLEAU, O. F. The effects of stimuli followed by response-independent shock on shock-avoidance behavior. *Journal of the Experimental Analysis of Behavior*, 1970, *14*, 11–21.

POWELL, R. W. Some effects of response-independent shocks after unsignalled avoidance conditioning in rats. *Learning and Motivation*, 1972, *3*, 420–441.

POWELL, R. W., & PECK, S. Persistent shock-elicited responding engendered by a negative-reinforcement procedure. *Journal of the Experimental Analysis of Behavior*, 1969, *12*, 1049–1062.

RACHLIN, H., & HINELINE, P. N. Training and maintenance

of keypecking in the pigeon by negative reinforcement. *Science*, 1967, *157*, 954–955.

Rescorla, R. A. Pavlovian conditioning and its proper control procedures. *Psychological Review*, 1967, *74*, 71–80.

Rescorla, R. A. Pavlovian conditioned fear in Sidman avoidance learning. *Journal of Comparative and Physiological Psychology*, 1968, *65*, 55–60.

Rescorla, R. A. Establishment of a positive reinforcer through contrast with shock. *Journal of Comparative and Physiological Psychology*, 1969, *67*, 260–263.

Rescorla, R. A., & LoLordo, V. M. Pavlovian inhibition of avoidance behavior. *Journal of Comparative and Physiological Psychology*, 1965, *59*, 406–412.

Rescorla, R. A., & Wagner, A. R. A theory of Pavlovian conditioning: variations in the effectiveness of reinforcement and nonreinforcement. In A. H. Black & W. F. Prokasy (Eds.), *Classical Conditioning II: Current Research and Theory*. Englewood Cliffs, N.J.: Prentice-Hall, Inc., 1972.

Riccio, D. C., & Thach, J. S. Rotation as an aversive stimulus for rats. *Psychonomic Science*, 1966, *5*, 267–268.

Riess, D. A shaping technique for producing rapid and reliable Sidman barpress avoidance. *Journal of the Experimental Analysis of Behavior*, 1970, *13*, 279–280.

Riess, D. Shuttle boxes, Skinner boxes, and Sidman avoidance in rats: acquisition and terminal performance as a function of response topography. *Psychonomic Science*, 1971, *25*, 283–286.

Riess, D., & Farrar, C. H. Unsignalled avoidance in a shuttle box: a rapid acquisition, high-efficiency paradigm. *Journal of the Experimental Analysis of Behavior*, 1972, *18*, 169–178.

Schoenfeld, W. N. "Avoidance" in behavior theory. *Journal of the Experimental Analysis of Behavior*, 1969, *12*, 669–674.

Schoenfeld, W. N., & Cole, B. K. *Stimulus schedules: the t–t systems*. New York: Harper & Row, 1972.

Schwartz, B. On going back to nature: a review of Seligman and Hager's Biological Boundaries of Learning. *Journal of the Experimental Analysis of Behavior*, 1974, *21*, 183–198.

Schwartz, B., & Coulter, G. A failure to transfer control of key pecking from food reinforcement to escape from and avoidance of shock. *Bulletin of the Psychonomic Society*, 1971, *1*, 307–309.

Seligman, M. E. P. On the generality of laws of learning. *Psychological Review*, 1970, *77*, 406–418.

Seligman, M. E. P., & Hager, J. L. *Biological Boundaries of Learning*. Englewood Cliffs, N.J.: Prentice-Hall, Inc., 1972.

Seligman, M. E. P., Maier, S. F., & Solomon, R. L. Unpredictable and Uncontrollable Aversive Events. In F. R. Brush (Ed.), *Aversive Conditioning and Learning*, New York: Academic Press, 1971.

Shimp, C. P. Synthetic variable-interval schedules of reinforcement. *Journal of the Experimental Analysis of Behavior*, 1973, *19*, 311–330.

Shnidman, S. R. Extinction of Sidman avoidance behavior. *Journal of the Experimental Analysis of Behavior*, 1968, *11*, 153–156.

Sidman, M. Two temporal parameters in the maintenance of avoidance behavior by the white rat. *Journal of Comparative and Physiological Psychology*, 1953, *46*, 253–261.

Sidman, M. Some properties of the warning stimulus in avoidance behavior. *Journal of Comparative and Physiological Psychology*, 1955, *48*, 444–450.

Sidman, M. Conditioned reinforcing and aversive stimuli in an avoidance situation. *Proceedings of New York Academy of Sciences*, 1957, 534–544.

Sidman, M. Reduction of shock frequency as reinforcement for avoidance behavior. *Journal of the Experimental Analysis of Behavior*, 1962, *5*, 247–257 (a).

Sidman, M. Classical avoidance without a warning stimulus. *Journal of the Experimental Analysis of Behavior*, 1962, *5*, 97–104 (b).

Sidman, M. Timeout from avoidance as a reinforcer: a study of response interaction. *Journal of the Experimental Analysis of Behavior*, 1962, *5*, 423–434 (c).

Sidman, M. An adjusting avoidance schedule. *Journal of the Experimental Analysis of Behavior*, 1962, *5*, 271–277 (d).

Sidman, M. Avoidance behavior. In W. K. Honig (Ed.), *Operant Behavior: Areas of Research and Application*. Englewood Cliffs, N.J.: Prentice-Hall, Inc., 1966.

Sidman, M., & Boren, J. J. The use of shock-contingent variations in response-shock intervals for the maintenance of avoidance behavior. *Journal of Comparative and Physiological Psychology*, 1957, *50*, 558–562 (a).

Sidman, M., & Boren, J. J. A comparison of two types of warning stimulus in an avoidance situation. *Journal of Comparative and Physiological Psychology*, 1957, *50*, 282–287. (b)

Sidman, M., & Boren, J. J. The relative aversiveness of warning signal and shock in an avoidance situation. *Journal of Abnormal and Social Psychology*, 1957, *55*, 339–344. (c)

Smith, G. D. Extinction of free-operant avoidance in rats. Unpublished Doctoral Dissertation, Temple University, 1973.

Smith, R. F., Gustavson, C. R., & Gregor, G. L. Incompatability between the pigeons' unconditioned response to shock and the conditioned key-peck response. *Journal of the Experimental Analysis of Behavior*, 1972, *18*, 147–153.

Smith, R., & Keller, F. Free-operant avoidance in the pigeon using a treadle response. *Journal of the Experimental Analysis of Behavior*, 1970, *13*, 211–214.

Staddon, J. E. R., & Simmelhag, V. L. The "superstition" experiment: a reexamination of its implications for the principles of adaptive behavior. *Psychological Review*, 1971, *78*, 3–43.

Theios, J. Mathematical models for aversive conditioning. In R. F. Brush (Ed.), *Aversive Conditioning and Learning*. New York: Academic Press, 1971.

Todorov, J. C. Component duration and relative response rates in multiple schedules. *Journal of the Experimental Analysis of Behavior*, 1972, *17*, 45–59.

Ulrich, R. E., Holz, W. C., & Azrin, N. H. Stimulus control of avoidance behavior. *Journal of the Experimental Analysis of Behavior*, 1964, *7*, 129–133.

Verhave, T. Technique for differential reinforcement of rate of avoidance responding. *Science*, 1959, *129*, 959–960.

Verhave, T. The functional properties of a time out from

an avoidance schedule. *Journal of the Experimental Analysis of Behavior,* 1962, *5,* 391–422.

WEISMAN, R. C., & LITNER, J. S. Positive conditioned reinforcement of Sidman avoidance behavior in rats. *Journal of Comparative and Physiological Psychology,* 1969, *68,* 597–603.

WEISS, B., and LATIES, V. G. Behavioral thermoregulation. *Science,* 1961, *133,* 1338–1344.

WERTHEIM, G. A. Behavioral contrast during multiple avoidance schedules. *Journal of the Experimental Analysis of Behavior,* 1965, *8,* 269–278.

14

By-Products of Aversive Control*

R. R. Hutchinson

INTRODUCTION

The concept of aversive control is familiar to all psychologists who work with operant methods, and commonly refers to the conditioning procedures of escape, avoidance, and punishment. Under such conditions, it has often been found that secondary or "by-product" performances are generated. This chapter discusses some of the secondary effects of aversive control and describes how these may be functionally related to aversive control procedures.

The concept of aversive control connotes the application of aversive stimuli in a manner such that its consequences affect performance. Aversiveness is assessed by the capacity of a stimuli to support responses which eliminate or reduce such stimulation, or alternatively by its capacity to suppress performances maintained by other stimuli. Thus, aversive stimuli are often referred to as negative reinforcers or punishers. It is in such a context that the concept of by-products of aversive control has developed. When a stimulus is thought of as having properties defined by its capacity to alter behavior through a contingent relation with that behavior, simultaneous influences upon behavioral processes other than by contingent influence have typically been discussed as by-product, secondary, or adjunctive influences of the stimulus. Yet attention to the contingent control of certain environmental stimuli, is not a sufficient reason to consider other performances or effects which are produced simultaneously and non-contingently by such stimuli, to be secondary in nature. Only recently has it become understood that aversive stimuli may produce complex chains of reactions directly, and that though these performances may be seen in environments where the contingent control of some behavior is being studied, such direct effects are also present in environments where no contingency arrangements are present.

Recent work shows that aversive stimulation produces complex, highly coordinated performance sequences in a wide range of species. These performances

---

* The assistance of G. Emley, E. Hallin, N. Murray, V. Pufpaff, B. Snowden, S. Crawford, K. Dinzik, G. Pierce, I. Wing, S. Carpenter, T. Sammons, N. Hunter, D. Mann, T. Proni, V. Lane, P. Reynolds, L. Peebles, D. Marine, and R. Sewell was essential to this work. Financial support came from the Department of Mental Health of the State of Michigan, National Science Foundation grant GB-33620X, Office of Naval Research grant N00014-70-A-0183-0001, and National Aeronautics and Space Administration grant NGR-23-014-002.

are reliably produced and constant during extended periods of observation. Though such behaviors may be modified in learning paradigms, their expression is fundamentally dependent neither upon historical nor contemporary response-contingent environmental events. Recent findings in our laboratory suggest that such reactions produced by aversive stimuli may partially form the basis for the complex performances which often result from the application of response-contingent procedures.

METHODS

The methods employed for the work described in the present chapter, are in the main, described in detail in earlier publications. It may be useful, however, to describe several experimental guidelines which have emerged over a number of different studies, designed to measure behavioral sequences not usually undergoing response-contingent control.

By the very nature of aversive stimulation, vigorous attempts by subjects to escape or avoid full or direct stimulus contact is likely. To prevent unwarranted stimulus variability, apparatus must be designed to insure stable long-term contact as experimentally specified. Stimuli should be brief to prevent momentary variations in posturing and orientation which can produce marked alterations in stimulus intensity. Additionally, continuous feedback to the experimenter regarding contact dimensions such as skin resistance, electrode pressures, etc., must be routinely available on a moment-to-moment basis.

Response-sensor mechanisms must be located appropriately within the experimental space so as to make optimal contact with performances as they occur. No control via reinforcement of successive response approximations ("shaping") or contingency management is possible in such experiments. The experimenter records the behavior where he finds it. Constant attempts at improving the suitability of contact surfaces and feedback stimuli are required, as are sensors which are indestructible and operate reliably over hundreds of thousands of occurrences. It is also necessary to tailor chamber spaces to suit an individual subject's physical and behavioral variations.

Figure 1 illustrates an apparatus which we have designed for testing biting attack responses in mice. The mouse here shown while biting a small protruding nylon object is restrained in a small plexiglas tube. The tube is removable from the apparatus so that most subject preparation can be accomplished in the home colony. Subsequent to placement in the testing apparatus, the subject's tail is cleansed and placed under two contact electrodes at the rear of the apparatus. In front of the subject is an object (in most cases a small bit of flexible nylon) attached to a variable force and displacement sensor. A standard telegraph key has proved useful for this purpose. The method has been suitable for the study of effects of genetic variations, drug influences, and social living conditions on attack behavior. Figure 2 is an illustra-

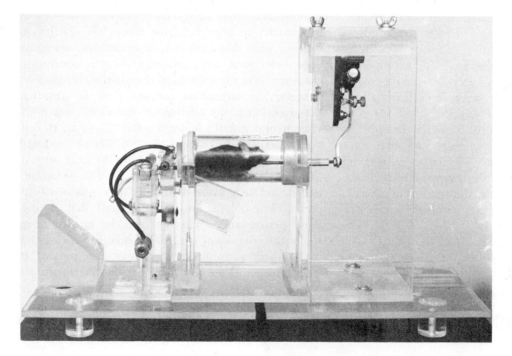

Fig. 1. Photograph of apparatus used for testing the effects of aversive stimulation on biting attack by mice. The subject shown here biting a protruding nylon object is partially restrained in a cylindrical capsule mounted at the center of the apparatus. The subject's tail is lightly taped to a plexiglas rod. Two brass electrodes rest upon cleansed and prepared portions of the tail. The nylon bite object is attached directly to a telegraph key which allows force and displacement adjustments.

Fig. 2. Apparatus used for testing effects of aversive stimulation upon manual manipulative, biting attack, and drinking reactions in the squirrel monkey. The subject is restrained by a waist-lock assembly and is seated on two plexiglas rods. The tail is placed in a stockade device. Two brass electrodes rest upon cleansed and prepared portions of the distal section of the tail. A rubber hose may be connected between two pipe stanchions located external to the right and left walls of the test space. Compressive forces possible only by biting attack are recorded via an air flow switch mounted at the rear of the intelligence panel. A response lever may be seen mounted on the lower left hand quadrant of the removable front intelligence panel. In studies where chain pulling was measured, the chain is suspended from the chamber ceiling.

tion of the apparatus used for the study of squirrel monkey subjects. The chamber was originally developed by Drs. D. F. Hake and N. H. Azrin at Anna State Hospital for work on shock-avoidance behavior (Hake & Azrin, 1963; Hake, 1968) and incorporates a number of helpful features for the study of elicited behavior. Gross physical movement of the subject is controlled such that an aversive stimulus can be applied precisely through electrodes upon a shaved portion of the tail which is restrained under a stockade. The upper torso and limbs are left unrestrained so that a considerable range of behavior is possible. In studies of biting attack, a rubber hose is suspended several inches in front of the subject approximately at head level. Bites on the rubber hose produce sufficient air displacement to trigger an air flow switch mounted on the rear of the panel, but grasping, tugging, and pulling have too little effect to trip the switch. A drink tube and drinkometer to record drinking can be mounted on the panel either in front of, or to the left of the subject. Response levers, chains, etc., can be mounted suitably for manual response contact.

The human testing paradigms have been used to study the phyletic continuity process of aggression and anger. These paradigms in earlier tests with other species revealed the effects of social contingencies, symbolic communication upon operant and respondent processes, and the effect of several drugs upon aggressive reactions.

Studies with humans have required preliminary development of force transducers inserted directly into the mouth. These devices have allowed perfection of the methods of recording biting contractions externally and without awareness by the subjects. Electrodes are placed over the temporalis and masseter muscles at positions illustrated in Figure 3. The muscles controlling the eccentric and concentric occlusal patterns contract, i.e., biting occurs, during both the presentation of aversive stimuli and subsequent to the withdrawal of positive reinforcers (Hutchinson & Pierce, 1971; Pierce, 1971; Proni, 1973). Small needle electrodes are used rather than surface electrodes, as these allow far more precise, noise-free recordings of electromyographic (EMG) potentials which covary with bite contraction force (Hutchinson & Pierce, 1971).

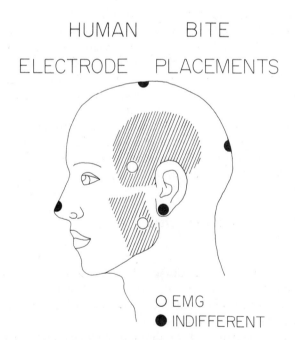

Fig. 3. Schematic illustration of electrode placement positions for recording of temporalis and masseter electromyographic activity. The indifferent electrodes are paralleled electrically to provide a balanced reference. The electrode on the nose is a silver disc. Standard clip electrodes are used on each ear. All other electrodes are standard ¼" subdermal EEG needle electrodes.

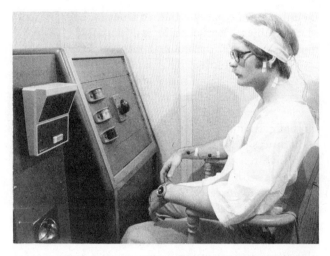

Fig. 4. Photograph of the actual test space for assessing biting and other motor responses by human subjects subsequent to aversive stimulation. Electrode leads from head recording areas are provided strain relief under a standard athletic bandage wrapped loosely around the forehead and returned to an input box at the rear of the chair. Other recording electrodes are evident on the forearm and wrist. On the intelligence panel of the console are signal lights and response buttons. At center left is an intercom for continuous communications with the experimenter or other subjects during social procedures. A magazine cup for delivery of coins is also provided. The test chamber is linked visually via a window arrangement with an identical test space. The two spaces may be linked or separated.

EMG recordings from the forearm, neck, and other areas allow confirmation of differential activity of the temporalis and masseter muscles relative to these latter muscle groups at different times. An actual test setting of a human subject is shown in Figure 4. After preparation for an experimental session a subject is seated in electrostatically and acoustically isolated test space where various stimuli and responses may be recorded. Test spaces are arranged in pairs to allow, when experimentally desirable, visual and auditory contact with partners in social experiments.

BEHAVIOR CAUSED BY AVERSIVE STIMULATION

This section will discuss the present state of our understanding of several major classes of behavioral sequences as they relate to the occurrence of aversive stimulation and to one another. Historically, our laboratory has worked to develop methods and techniques for the objective long term study of aggression-attack sequences in animals and man. The departure point for this work is the series of studies by Ulrich, Azrin, and their colleagues (Azrin, Hake, & Hutchinson, 1965; Azrin, Hutchinson, & Hake, 1963; Azrin, Hutchinson, & Sallery, 1964; Hutchinson, Azrin, & Hake, 1966; Ulrich, & Azrin, 1962; Ulrich, Hutchinson, & Azrin, 1965).

As experience has been gained in the sensing of complex reactions in several species, it has become apparent that the aggression-attack reaction to aversive stimulation is only one of several identifiable behavioral sequences and patterns which relate to one another and to aversive stimulation in a reliable fashion.

Numerous studies have shown that the delivery of an intense aversive, noxious, or unpleasant stimulus will produce, in a variety of species, movement toward, contact with, and possibly destruction of, animate or inanimate objects in the environment (Ulrich & Azrin, 1962; Ulrich, Hutchinson, & Azrin, 1965). Figure 5 illustrates some temporal and intensive relations which have been recorded from several species following delivery of a noxious or aversive stimulus. Shortly after the stimulus event, attack or biting begins at a high intensity. Repetitions of this response are likely with the frequency and intensity gradually falling over a period of seconds or minutes (Azrin, Hutchinson, & Sallery, 1964; Hutchinson, Azrin, & Renfrew, 1968).

If aversive stimuli are repeatedly delivered in a discriminable temporal pattern a display of aggression-attack reactions assumes additional features. During the period prior to an ensuing aversive stimulus (and at a discriminable temporal period after aversive stimuli) additional biting attack reactions will occur. Figure 6 illustrates this temporal pattern for one species and subject. Biting attack reactions occur for a period before the occurrence of an aversive stimulus, but usually cease just before shock (Hutchinson & Emley, 1972; Hutchinson, Renfrew, & Young, 1971).

Although aggression-attack sequences often occur in reaction to conditional stimuli, more recent studies have shown that other reaction sequences are also likely. These reactions include sensory scanning, manual manipulation, and locomotion sequences (Hutchinson & Emley, 1972; Hutchinson, Renfrew, & Young, 1971). Figure 7 illustrates the automatic recording of shock-induced lever pressing in a squirrel monkey and noise-induced movement by a human. During the presentation of a conditional stimulus, activities occur at a progressively increasing rate until just before the aversive stimulus, when all reactions cease.

Sensory scanning, and locomotion and manual manipulative behaviors are prepotent to attack reactions during the period prior to unconditional stimulus occurrence (Hutchinson & Emley, 1972; Hutchinson & Emley, 1973). Figure 8 shows the records of a

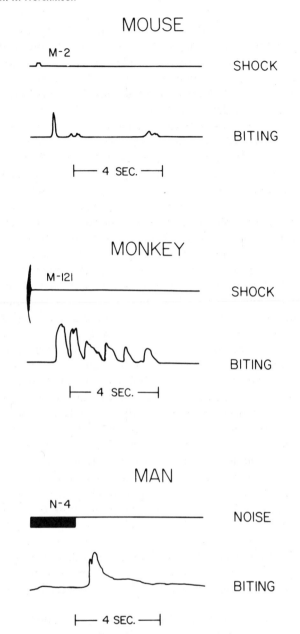

Fig. 5. Automatic recordings of biting responses by a mouse, a squirrel monkey, and an adult male human subsequent to aversive stimulation. The mouse subject was of the Swiss–Webster strain. Shock was via tail electrodes, at 600 v for 200 msec. Biting attack upon a nylon object began shortly thereafter. The nylon bite object was connected to a Statham force transducer, the output of which was amplified and recorded by a Grass Model 5 polygraph. Static peak force required to produce excursions as seen here is approximately 35 g. The squirrel monkey was shocked for 200 msec via tail electrodes. The pressure tracing of biting was obtained from a Statham P23 pressure transducer, the output of which was amplified and displayed by a Grass Model 5 polygraph. The human subject was stimulated with 110 db of 2000-Hz tone. Speakers were mounted on either side, and several feet to the front of the subject. Biting, in the form of nonfunctional, concentric occlusion, began shortly thereafter. Responses were recorded with subdermal EEG electrodes. Signals were amplified, integrated, and recorded by a Grass Model 5 polygraph.

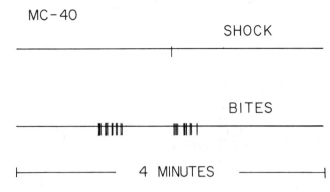

Fig. 6. Reconstruction of actual event records obtained from one squirrel monkey subject of biting attack responses both prior and subsequent to aversive stimulation. Shock was 400 v, delivered for 200 millisec each four min.

monkey and a human male when the separate reaction classes could each occur. Lever presses of the monkey, and movements of the torso and upper limbs of the male human, progressively increase in frequency during a period of conditional stimulus de-

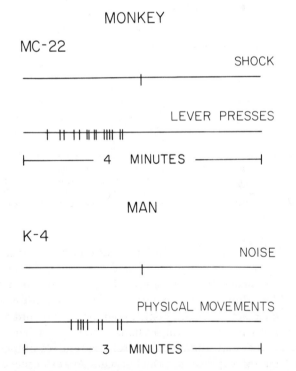

Fig. 7. Reconstruction of actual event records obtained from a squirrel monkey subject and an adult male human during periods of aversive stimulation. For the squirrel monkey, electric shock was 400 v for 200 msec delivered every 4 min. The response lever was mounted on the intelligence panel immediately ahead of and to the left of the subject. For the human, aversive stimulation was 2 seconds of 2000-Hz pure tone delivered each 3 minutes at an intensity of 110 db (measured at the amplifier output transformer). Aversive stimulation is preceded by progressively increasing and then decreasing frequencies of manual responding and/or the physical movements of upper torso or arms.

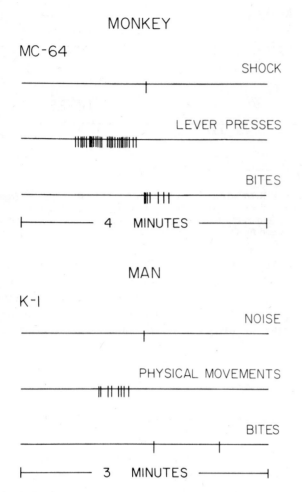

Fig. 8. Reconstruction of actual event records obtained for a squirrel monkey subject and an adult male human. For each subject simultaneous records of pre-aversive stimulus manual manipulative or movement reactions and post-aversive stimulus biting was obtained. Parameters of aversive stimulation were as described previously.

livery, but immediately prior to unconditional stimulus delivery these reactions cease. Following delivery of the unconditional stimulus biting reactions occur.

The addition of apparatus suitable for sensing a second reaction of different topography is not only a technical exercise. Such a change alters the environment and may influence the relative and combined behavioral expressions which occur. An example of the influence of a change in features of the environment (established at the convenience of the investigator to allow simultaneous sensing and recording of several responses) upon the several reactions which may occur is illustrated by the upper graph in Figure 9. In Figure 9, the aggression-attack reactions of biting a rubber hose, and the manual-manipulative and sensory-scanning reactions involved in pulling a chain, are influenced by the presence or absence of the opportunity to bite (Hutchinson & Emley, 1972; Hutchinson, 1970). The pair of cumulative records obtained on Day 5, for a squirrel monkey subject illustrates that chain-pulling responses occurred predominately before the deliveries of electric shocks. Immediately before shock delivery, chain pulling was absent. Subsequent to shock delivery, biting attack occurred and then progressively diminished. Later, for a series of tests, the rubber hose was removed from the chamber for the entire session. Both post-shock and pre-shock chain pulling increased. These effects can be noted on Day 22 and Day 34. After replacement of the hose, performance returned to the earlier pattern. An exaggerated illustration of this dual effect of interaction between the pre-event and post-event behaviors is illustrated in the lower graph of Figure 9. Here for a squirrel monkey subject, tests were conducted of the interactions between hose biting and lever pressing. Studies of such interactions are important in understanding the separate processes for two reasons. On the one hand, the elimination of the opportunity to engage in biting attack reactions subsequent to the delivery of the aversive stimulus generated greater numbers of anticipatory or pre-shock manual manipulative reactions—an effect similar to only one other condition known to us—that produced by an increase in shock intensity or duration. Thus, preventing attack subsequent to aversive stimulation is functionally similar to increasing the intensity of an aversive stimulus. This suggests the possibility that the influences of a biting attack are similar to those of shock reduction (Hutchinson, Renfrew, & Young, 1971). At a more speculative level, this effect may account for at least a portion of the reinforcement inherent in biting attack sequences which has been reported in previous studies (Azrin, Hutchinson, & McLaughlin, 1965).

Of greater relevance to the present discussion is the second effect noted: removal of the opportunity to attack caused an increase in post-shock manual manipulative and sensory scanning responses of chain pulling and lever pressing. We have repeatedly found that post-shock manual responses have increased when the opportunity to attack was absent, to a level almost identical in absolute number with the frequency of post-shock attack responses which occurred during periods when a hose was present (Hutchinson, 1970; Hutchinson & Emley, 1972). Conversely, the provision of opportunity to attack causes a shift from post-shock manual manipulative and sensory scanning responses to biting attack. When allowed, attack reactions are prepotent over other locomotor and manipulative reactions subsequent to aversive stimulation: this is the

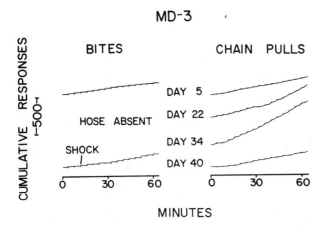

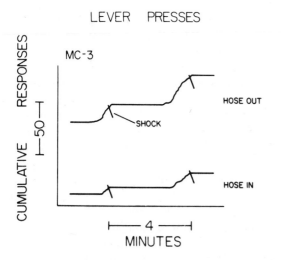

Fig. 9 (upper). Cumulative response records for biting attack and chain pulling by one squirrel monkey subject before, during, and after removal of the opportunity to engage in biting attack responses. During the period illustrated on Days 22 and 34 while the bite hose was removed from the test chamber, the subject demonstrated increased pre-shock chain-pulling response bursts equivalent to response bursting of biting attacks during previous periods of hose availability. Subsequent to return of the opportunity to attack, performance returned to original levels. (lower). Cumulative response record segment showing magnified illustration of the increase of pre-shock lever presses and the instatement of post-shock lever-press burst reactions subsequent to the removal of the opportunity to attack. The inter-shock interval was 4 min.

suggestion presented, but it does not take into account several features of the testing apparatus and methods employed in the studies. First, the testing environments all include features of physical or social restraint. For infrahuman subjects, cage arrangements have stockades or other restraint devices which guarantee contact between an applied aversive stimulus and the organism. Additionally, the stimulus is delivered for only a brief instant to minimize the possibility

that any movements or other efforts by the subject might be followed by a reduction or termination of the stimulus and thus be reinforced. With the human testing techniques, actual reliable contact between an aversive stimulus and the subject is provided by the recruitment of volunteers who are fully informed of the noxiousness which may occur. In addition the volunteers are assured that no unreasonable or potentially hazardous stimulation will be used, that financial remuneration will be received, that only mild noxious stimuli will be used, and that escape is always immediately available. In summary, for both animals and humans, the testing paradigms have been designed to eliminate a class of reactions which is known to be highly probable during or immediately subsequent to the occurrence of an aversive stimulus, e.g., physical movement and escape from the noxious stimulus. Innate reactions of flinching, jumping, and running immediately after application of an aversive stimulus are thoroughly documented in the literature (Brogden, Lipman, & Culler, 1938; Campbell & Teghtsoonian, 1958; Liddell, 1934). Also, in more recent studies, it has been shown that an experimentally learned escape reaction will become prepotent over aggression-attack sequences (Azrin, Hutchinson, & Hake, 1967; Ulrich, 1967).

Are there reactions which are equally or more potent than attack sequences in environments where no reinforcement for such non-attack behavior occurs? In fact the temporal primacy of locomotor and manual manipulative reactions over aggression-attack behaviors has been observed. A minority of subjects in our laboratory continue to make a small number of manual responses for long periods subsequent to shock delivery and before attack, even when attack opportunity is present. Figure 10 is an illustration of the high speed event records obtained for both lever presses and biting attacks. Whereas lever presses dominate before shock delivery, the typical pattern of biting attacks predominates after shock delivery. The important feature of this illustration, however, is the

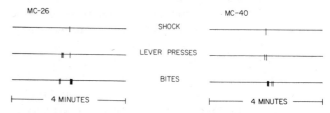

Fig. 10. Reconstruction of actual event records obtained for two squirrel monkey subjects of lever-press responding and biting attacks. Note that lever presses which occur subsequent to shock delivery, occur prior to ensuing episodes of biting attack.

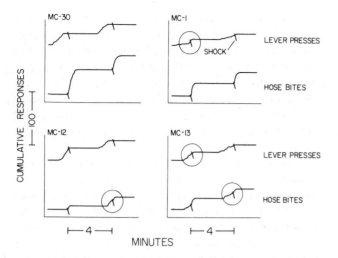

Fig. 11. Cumulative response record segments for simultaneously recorded manual manipulative and aggressive attack sequences for four different squirrel monkey subjects. The general pattern for each subject is a relatively greater probability of pre-shock manual manipulative responding and a relatively greater probability of post-shock biting attack responding. Individual differences from these general patterns are circled and are discussed in the text.

temporal position of the manual behaviors which do occur following shock. When such manual responses occur, they predominately occur immediately after shock and before the biting attack responses. Thus, even in environments where there has been no reinforcement for long periods of time, a number of subjects continue to engage in locomotion, manual manipulation, and sensory scanning reactions immediately after shock and before the aggressive-attack reaction sequences.

Considerable individual variation in the temporal and intensive patterns of the reaction sequences is typically observed (Hutchinson & Emley, 1972; Hutchinson, Renfrew, & Young, 1971). Figure 11 is an example of four subjects. For each subject, the relative probability of manual manipulations is greatest before shock and the relative probability of biting attack greatest after shock. For several subjects, there is also a tendency toward the brief absence of all reactions immediately prior to shock. Each subject, however, provides a slightly different variant on these general statements. Subject MC-30 illustrates a relatively clear temporal differentiation of these reaction patterns. MC-1 shows some post-shock as well as pre-shock lever pressing. MC-12 shows some pre-shock biting attack in addition to greater pre-shock lever pressing. MC-13 shows both post-shock lever pressing and pre-shock biting attack. Currently our understanding of these processes does not allow us to be certain whether these differences depend on constitutional or on technical differences in our handling methods or recording apparatus. Nevertheless, the general pattern is clear. Manual manipulative, locomotor, and sensory scanning responses occur prior to noxious stimulation, but cease immediately before aversive stimulation. Following the aversive stimulus, tendencies towards locomotion, sensory scanning, and manual manipulation are later followed by aggression-attack sequences.

The behavioral sequences which occur both before and after aversive stimulation may vary even when stimulus parameters are held constant. Two separate and opposite processes, habituation or facilitation, can occur even with invariant features of aversive stimuli. If aversive stimuli are relatively mild and/or frequent, the reaction sequences show progressive reductions in amplitude and frequency over successive occurrences of the stimulus (Hutchinson, Renfrew, & Young, 1971; Ulrich & Azrin, 1962). Figure 12 (upper panel) illustrates the cumulative response records of post-shock attack behaviors over a series of relatively mild and frequent shock occurrences. Successive shocks result in progressively fewer attacks.

The repetitive, but infrequent delivery of intense aversive stimuli can result in increased responses or facilitation, rather than habituation. Figure 12 (lower panel) illustrates for one squirrel monkey subject the effect of infrequent, intense shock deliveries upon pre-shock lever pressing and post-shock biting attack. The rate of both responses increases progressively until responding is almost continuous. Some time is always necessary for the development of this response facilitation effect; somewhere between 20 and 40 minutes seems to be the necessary amount of time for several species tested. Once the process is begun it is possible to terminate all aversive stimulation, yet continue to observe the occurrence of these reactions for hours and even days (Hutchinson & Emley, 1972; Hutchinson, Renfrew, & Young, 1971).

Due to the processes of habituation and facilitation, a momentary measurement of the amplitude or frequency of display of reactions is not a reliable estimate of the current level of "aversiveness" to which the organism is exposed, since, depending upon the history of aversive stimulus encounter, the subject's current reactions may be excessive or diminished by considerable degree relative to what another subject or the same subject would have shown at an earlier time.

Further experiments have found that additional reaction sequences are influenced by the occurrence of aversive stimulation. After the delivery of an aversive stimulus, a series of manual manipulative and locomotive responses, or after a series of biting attack

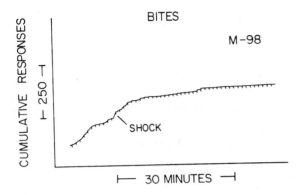

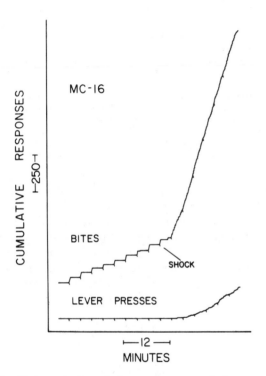

Fig. 12 (upper). Cumulative response record for one squirrel monkey subject during a session where frequent and relatively mild aversive stimulation was delivered. Habituation of responding over successive shock episodes is evident. Shocks were 100 msec duration, 100 V intensity, delivered once each minute. **(lower).** Cumulative response record for one squirrel monkey subject where biting attack reactions and manual lever pressing responses were simultaneously recorded during response facilitation over successive shock occurrences. Shock was 400 v delivered for 200 msec every 4 min.

reactions, subjects begin drinking (Hutchinson & Emley, unpublished research). Figure 13 (upper graph) presents event recordings for two subjects during a period before and after electric shock delivery. For each subject the typical pattern of manual manipulative and locomotor reactions (in this case lever presses) is apparent for both subjects during the pre-aversive stimulus period. This behavior is absent for a brief period immediately before the aversive stimulus occurs. After shock delivery there is a rapid flurry of biting attacks. Following this, both subjects show a series of lick responses which first increase and then decrease over ensuing seconds. Figure 13 (lower panel) shows in cumulative record form, the response patterns for lever presses, bites, and licks for one subject. Pre-shock lever pressing increases up until almost time for shock delivery, but shows a tendency for reduction immediately before shock. Subsequent to shock, a rapid series of biting attack reactions occurs. Following this, a negatively accelerated burst of water licking responses takes place.

Figure 14 shows the temporal distribution of manual manipulative and locomotor responses, biting at-

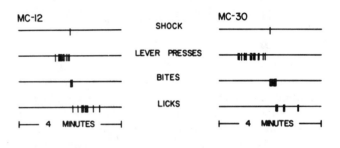

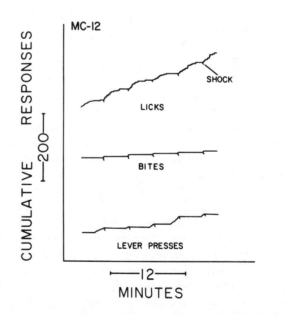

Fig. 13 (upper). Reconstruction of actual event records obtained for two squirrel monkey subjects when manual lever pressing, biting attacks, and water licking were each simultaneously measured during periods of aversive stimulation. Following biting attack, subjects begin drinking for several seconds. **(lower).** Cumulative response record segments for one squirrel monkey subject of manual lever pressing, biting attacks, and water licking during periods of aversive stimulation.

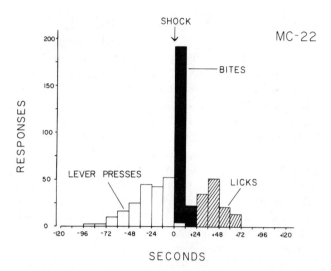

Fig. 14. Temporal distribution of manual lever pressing, biting attack reaction and water intake responses prior and subsequent to aversive stimulation. Responses are totalled over 12-sec intervals. Shock was delivered at "0" seconds.

tack responses, and licking responses averaged across an entire session for one subject. Here, in the individual intershock intervals, lever pressing shows a progressive increase in the period before shock. As the minimum class intervals are 12 seconds, no abrupt termination of responding in the few seconds prior to shock is evident, although this is frequently seen in individual records. Subsequent to shock delivery, a brief series of lever presses occurs, followed immediately by biting attacks upon the rubber hose. This attack reaction subsides progressively and then water licking responses occur first at a higher and then at a lower frequency falling over some seconds to zero.

Limiting or expanding other response opportunities has effects on the magnitude or frequency of drinking responses which are similar to those previously described for lever pressing and biting. Removing the opportunity to attack, by removing the rubber hose from the chamber, increases the number of licks and the amount of water consumed. These reaction shifts remain for as long as the environment is altered. Figure 15 portrays the effect for one subject in successive experimental sessions where the hose first was present then removed for several days and then returned to the chamber. Removal of the hose, and thus the opportunity to attack caused biting attacks to again quency of licking subsequent to shock. Return of the opportunity to attack caused biting attacks to again occur as before. Licking responses were reduced to their original level.

Drinking reactions are also influenced by the temporal pattern and intensity of shock delivery in a

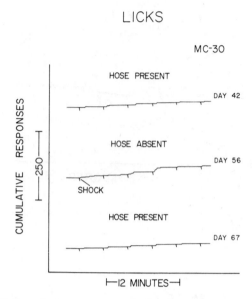

Fig. 15. Cumulative response record segments of fluid intake responses for one squirrel monkey subject before, during and subsequent to removal of the opportunity to attack. Intake responses and the amount of fluid consumed are increased in the absence of attack opportunity.

manner similar to that already illustrated for pre-shock manual responses and post-shock biting attack reactions. If intense aversive stimuli are delivered infrequently, licking responses will begin to occur at a far greater rate and in an almost continuous episode as compared with earlier occasions. Figure 16 displays for one subject, this facilitation of drinking re-

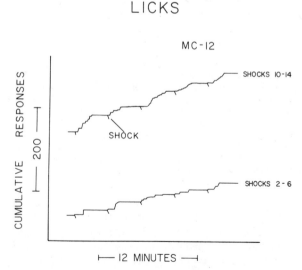

Fig. 16. Cumulative response record segments of fluid intake responses for one squirrel monkey subject in early and later portions of a period of aversive stimulation showing development of response facilitation.

actions when continuing, infrequent, intense, and aversive stimuli are presented.

From the foregoing discussion and illustrations, it is evident that occurrence of aversive stimuli can influence a series of complex motor reactions for a period after aversive stimulation and, through conditioning, to stimulus periods prior to the delivery of a particular ensuing aversive stimulus. Further, there is a predictable ordering of the frequencies or tendencies for various reaction sequences to occur, both prior to, and after aversive stimulus delivery. During conditional stimulation, locomotor, manual manipulative, and sensory scanning reactions occur at a progressively increasing frequency until some period immediately before the aversive unconditional stimulus delivery. During that same period, occurrence of aggression-attack sequences and drinking reactions can occur, though these are of lesser strength than the locomotor and manual manipulative reactions. Immediately prior to unconditional stimulus delivery, all reaction tendencies cease, a period of behavioral arrest or suppression occurs. After the occurrence of an unconditional aversive stimulus, locomotor, manual manipulative, and sensory scanning responses are maximal for a brief period. Subsequent to this time, aggression-attack reaction sequences develop to a high frequency and then gradually return to zero. Later yet, and subsequent to attack reactions, drinking responses occur, first, at a progressively increasing and then a gradually decreasing frequency over ensuing seconds and minutes. These sequential relationships are sketched symbolically in Figure 17.

Manual manipulation, arrest, attack, and drink reactions may or may not occur in the particular stimulus context present at the time a subject is responding. Sometimes, only partial sequences will occur since alternate response reaction classes may, through reinforcement, completely or substantially displace in time and strength the basic reaction patterns noted.

Each of these reaction types involves a complex sequence of coordinated movements, frequently involving many muscle groups in concert with sensory scanning processes acting upon particular objects or places in the environment. So far, our findings suggest that these reactions, though flexible and capable of considerable modification, nevertheless tend to occur in an essentially identical fashion in many members of the same species. Additionally, individual subjects show great consistency between successive behavioral episodes over long periods. Such species specificity, coupled with uniformity across successive instances makes it tempting to refer to these reactions as reflexes or innate reactions. We have refrained from this for several reasons. We have little evidence regarding the portions or features of these performances which may be independent of learning. Also, the modification of these reaction sequences which comes about from alterations in post-response environment (reinforcement) implies a reliance on feedback that is perhaps not a common feature of other processes referred to as reflexive or innate, and has been little emphasized in connection with them.

BEHAVIOR CAUSED BY AVERSIVE STIMULI IN ESCAPE PARADIGMS

Operant conditioning procedures involving aversive control may be divided into the response-produced-stimulus-offset ("escape") and response-produced-stimulus-onset ("punishment") paradigms. In escape conditioning or performance paradigms some aspect of behavior results in the termination of either the conditional aversive stimulus or the unconditional aversive stimulus. Often where the conditional stimulus is terminated the paradigm is defined as avoidance conditioning—a reference to the fact that such responding also avoids occurrence of the unconditional stimulus. For both unconditional-stimulus and conditional-stimulus escape, the response occurs in the presence of an identifiable unique aspect of the environment. As such, the reaction sequences which will occur can be predicted, at least in part, by knowledge of how behavior is influenced directly by aversive stimuli as described in the previous section.

Several general behavioral relationships are observed during escape/avoidance-learning and performance. During presentation of the conditional stimu-

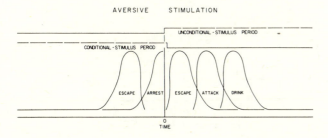

Fig. 17. Schematic illustration of the sequential features of behavioral processes produced by aversive stimulation. During the conditional stimulus period, locomotor, manual manipulative and visual scanning responses are progressively elevated. In a more imminent temporal position to unconditional stimulation, behavioral reactions are arrested or suppressed. Subsequent to unconditional stimulus delivery, manual manipulative, locomotor and visual scanning responses are increased. Subsequent to this, aggression-attack sequences occur. At yet a later point in time, fluid intake responses begin.

lus, locomotor, manual manipulative, and visual scanning reactions will be likely (Brogden, Lipman, & Culler, 1938; Miller, 1948; Mowrer & Lamoreaux, 1942). As the conditional stimulus continues toward the time ordinarily corresponding to introduction of the unconditional stimulus, behavior will initially increase in probability and then decrease (Anger, 1963; Hoffman, 1966; Sidman, 1955). After the occurrence of the unconditional stimulus, a brief period of heightened probability of manipulative, locomotor, and visual scanning responses will be evident (Sidman, 1958; Hoffman, 1966). Later yet, or in situations where escape reactions are not reinforced, aggression-attack sequences will occur (Azrin, Hutchinson, & Hake, 1967). Each of these patterns is similar to that described in the previous section where such performances were shown to result from conditional and unconditional stimulation directly. Figure 18 (upper panel) presents a segment from a cumulative record of one subject on a Sidman avoidance schedule, during a portion of the session when the unconditional aversive stimulus actually did occur twice. The rapid post-stimulus burst of lever pressing behavior frequently reported in this circumstance, is evident. The lower graph of Figure 18 presents a segment from two simultaneous cumulative records obtained from another subject on similar experimental parameters, except that a bite hose was placed in the test chamber. For this animal, the opportunity to engage in attack sequences, caused a total displacement of the post-stimulus lever-pressing behavior by a flurry of biting attacks on the rubber hose (Azrin, Hutchinson, & Hake, 1967). In numerous avoidance sessions where the attack opportunity is present we have observed that subjects typically show a nearly or totally complete shift in the post-shock reaction sequences to that pattern shown in the lower graph of Figure 18. As suggested on the basis of data presented in earlier sections, biting may somehow serve to reduce the effect of shock. Coupled with an essentially zero reinforcement probability for bursting responses on the lever, this may produce alteration of the two performances seen in the lower portion of Figure 18.

The literature also shows that escape or avoidance behavior is often absent or infrequent early in a testing session even after learning seems stable in earlier tests. This daily or weekly recurrent absence of initial strength coupled with the progressive increase in responding over subsequent shocks during testing has been referred to as "warm up" (Hoffman, 1966; Hoffman, Fleshler, & Chorny, 1961). In the previous section the similar facilitation of shock-produced performances by repetitive shock deliveries was illustrated.

Thus the temporal and intensive patterns of manual and locomotor behaviors observed on schedules involving escape-avoidance procedures are similar or identical to those observed routinely when such contingencies are not in effect. Therefore, to what extent are the performance elements, normally observed under escape and/or avoidance training and learning procedures, attributable to the contingencies rather than as a direct result of contact with conditional and unconditional aversive stimuli? This question can only be answered conclusively, it seems to me, by a

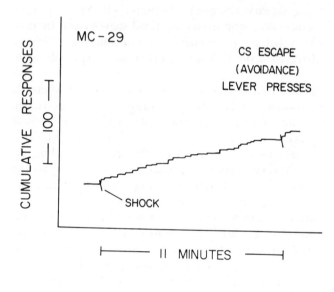

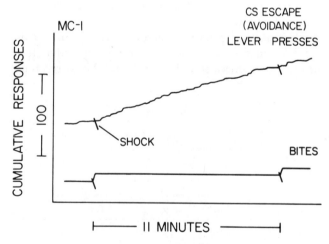

Fig. 18 (upper). Cumulative response record segments during Sidman avoidance conditioning for one squirrel monkey subject. Subsequent to shock delivery, a brief flurry of lever presses occurs. Avoidance parameters were response-shock interval, 30 sec, shock-shock interval, 30 sec, shock intensity 400 v 200 millisec duration. **(lower)** Cumulative response record segments during a Sidman avoidance program. Simultaneously recorded manual lever pressing and biting attacks for one squirrel monkey subject are shown. Note that subsequent to shock delivery, the flurry of responding occurs upon the bite hose.

careful three-part experimental sequence. Subjects must first be exposed for an extended period to the conditional and unconditional stimuli in the absence of any contingencies. Subsequent to this, contingencies may be introduced and shifts in performance noted. To establish the certainty of the contingency's long term influences, at a later time a return to original noncontingent stimulation must be arranged. Unfortunately, these conditions are almost never met experimentally. Typically, a shift in some feature of the contingencies or in their temporal or interlocking character, has been the primary experimental manipulation and a shift from one level of performance to another has been the observed result. Such tests are helpful, but they leave unanswered the question of what topographic and intensive features of behavior are independent of, or dependent on, contingencies per se. In our studies we typically do not find that subjects respond at high continuous response rates during response-independent stimulus presentation. A shift to avoidance conditions from response-independent shock usually produces large increments in response rate. An example of such an effect may be seen in Figure 19. Here selected segments of cumulative records under three successive experimental conditions are displayed. This particular subject had a two-year history of response-independent shock every four minutes for one hour sessions. During this period a variety of tests were performed using this behavioral baseline. The baseline behavioral pattern is shown as the uppermost segment of Figure 19. At this point avoidance conditioning was begun. By Day 22 of the avoidance program a high steady rate of nearly shock-free responding was occurring. In subsequent tests the subject was returned to response-independent shock conditions and behavior was observed over an extended period. The rate of responding gradually fell to the level seen in the bottom segment of Figure 19. Two features of these results are important. First, it took a long time for performance to stabilize at a lower level after exposure to avoidance conditioning; second, the level at which performance stabilized was 10–15 times greater than it had been before the avoidance training. Each of these results has also been noted in earlier studies (Kelleher, Riddle, & Cook, 1963; Sidman, 1960).

BEHAVIOR CAUSED BY AVERSIVE STIMULI IN PUNISHMENT PARADIGMS

In punishment paradigms, presentation of the conditional or unconditional stimulus is contingent upon

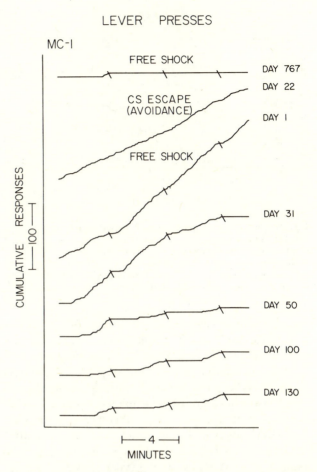

Fig. 19. Cumulative response record segment for one squirrel monkey subject during response-independent shock, Sidman avoidance conditioning, and subsequent response-independent shock sessions. Avoidance conditioning results in a large increase in manual responding compared to initial response-independent shock baseline performance. Subsequent to avoidance, responding gradually falls until it stabilizes but at a level of responding many times greater than prior to avoidance learning.

the occurrence of some response. Since in this paradigm the unconditional stimulus and the conditional stimulus are not present during a response, but only afterward, the ongoing response rate will be determined by other conditions which are present, such as food deprivation, food reinforcement schedule, etc. Generally, since the establishment of a contingency between a response and an unconditional aversive stimulus simultaneously places a negative reinforcement contingency on behaviors other than the to-be-punished response (Dinsmoor, 1954), and since, as has been shown in the prior section, the terminal effect of conditional stimuli is to produce depression or an absence of behavior, any responding which results in the occurrence of unconditional stimulation will be reduced. After the actual occurrence of an uncondi-

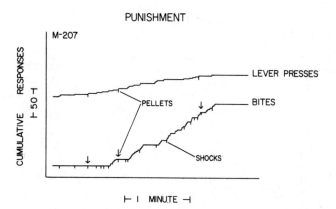

Fig. 20. Cumulative response record segments for one squirrel monkey subject during variable-interval food reinforcement and simultaneous continuous punishment of manual lever pressing. Biting attack episodes occur subsequent to shock deliveries. Data are reconstructions of event records obtained from R. E. Ulrich, Western Michigan University, Kalamazoo, Michigan.

tional stimulus, however, other reaction sequences ordinarily produced by unconditional aversive stimulation will be observed. Figure 20 presents the simultaneous cumulative records of a subject on a variable-interval food-reinforcement schedule and simultaneous continuous shock punishment for lever pressing. Also, the opportunity to attack a rubber hose was present. Note that bursts of biting attack tend to occur after the delivery of electric shocks (Ulrich, personal communication). Whether fluid intake responses are increased subsequent to the occurrence of punishment by an unconditional stimulus is unknown to me.

When responding is maintained and produced by arrangements other than positive reinforcement schedules, additional interactions with punishment programs can occur. When unconditional or conditional aversive stimulation is made contingent on performances which have been generated by aversive stimulation (either by escape-avoidance routines, or by response-independent shock application), the results can appear confusing. Sometimes in these situations, the contingent application of conditional aversive stimulation can actually elevate behavior. Figure 21 presents selected cumulative record segments for two squirrel monkey subjects during response-independent shock delivery programs and subsequent response-contingent shock delivery schedules. The two records show the simultaneous results for pre-shock manual manipulative responses and post-shock biting attacks. In the case of subject MC-30, during response-independent shock delivery (labeled *No Punishment*) lever pressing occurred at a progressively increasing rate until just before shock when behavior was absent. Subsequent to shock delivery, biting attacks occurred,

first at a high rate and then at a decreasing rate. The subject who experienced shock delivery contingent upon lever pressing (labeled *Punishment*), produced the pattern illustrated, one seen in numerous other subjects in the laboratory. Generally, no lever pressing occurred during the first few minutes of the response-independent shock delivery sessions, nor on the first day when shocks were response produced. At about seven minutes into the first punishment session the initial lever press occurred and produced a shock. Subsequent to this shock a flurry of biting attacks occurred. For this subject, no further lever presses occurred during any session for the next 20 punishment sessions. A quite different performance is illustrated in the right hand column, for subject MC-5. This subject had a much higher rate of pre-shock manual responding during the response-independent shock sessions. The consistent pattern was a progressively increasing lever press rate up to almost the instant of shock delivery, with at most only a very brief pause prior to shock occurrence. Further, little or no biting occurred subsequent to shock. Introduction of punishment contingencies produced an actual increase in pre-shock lever pressing. By Day 20 on this procedure, in fact, an increase in responding under contingent shock conditions was evident. Results similar to those for MC-5 have also been reported in recent experiments (Morse, Mead, & Kelleher, 1967; Stretch, Orloff, & Dalrymple, 1968) in other laboratories and have served as the evidential base for a theoretical position

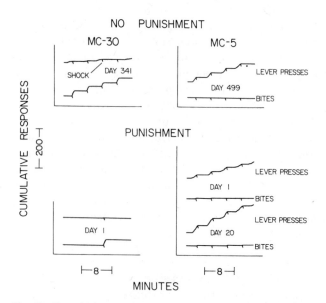

Fig. 21. Cumulative response record segments obtained simultaneously for manual lever pressing and biting attack reactions for two squirrel monkey subjects prior to and during punishment of lever pressing.

that electric shock and other aversive stimuli, can serve as positive reinforcer-like events, depending upon the schedule of presentation of such events. However, other interpretations are possible. Figure 21 shows prompt and total cessation of responding for one subject (MC-30) when shifted from a response-independent shock schedule to a response-contingent shock schedule. Figure 22, on the other hand, shows that reinstatement of response-independent shock procedures for subject MC-30 produced a gradual, but progressive return of responding to a pattern and level identical to that observed prior to punishment conditions. In the case of subject MC-5 and others displaying similar high response rate patterns, additional experiments have been conducted. Figure 23 presents full cumulative records for MC-5 through a series of experimental tests involving successive alterations in the fixed-interval shock punishment schedule, and finally followed by a return to response-independent shock procedures. No other response maintenance procedures (such as food, time out from shock, etc.) are ever a part of these experiments. In the left hand column, the upper tracing illustrates final performance under response-independent shock conditions. Over a series of months, the fixed-interval value of the punishment schedule was gradually reduced from four minutes to two minutes, one minute, 15 seconds, and finally to 5 seconds. During these tests responding was not reduced, rather, overall rate of response increased. Throughout these tests, it was noted that not on a single instance was responding low enough to cause shock to be delayed more than a few seconds, as compared to when shock would have occurred on a response-independent shock baseline. The high frequency of responding exhibited by MC-5 caused the shock delivery to occur without change, just as though scheduled by a clock without regard to behavior. For reasons unknown to us, this situation was altered for the first time at point A on Day 18 of the 5-sec FI punishment condition, shown in the center column of Figure 23. On the next day (Day 19) the pattern of performance was immediately different from the beginning of the session. No responding occurred for almost 4 minutes. The first response produced a shock. This happened three more times during session 19. Subsequently, no responding was observed during any of the 50 additional punishment test sessions.

A return to response-independent shock conditions also produced for this subject, a gradual increase in responding until it assumed the same temporal and intensive pattern initially displayed prior to punishment testing. This behavior which might have been interpreted as "maintained" by the response-produced shock contingency, was in fact, a shock-produced-response performance. Previous reports of similar effects have in all cases inadvertently employed one or more of several different collateral response-producing or response-reinforcing procedures. Frequently these studies have employed an avoidance history (Byrd, 1969; Kelleher & Morse, 1968; McKearney, 1968; Stretch, Orloff, & Dalrymple, 1968). In the previous section we saw that an avoidance history, even long past, could markedly increase the response generating effects of subsequent response-independent shock delivery schedules. Other experiments have employed free-shock baselines (McKearney, 1969; Morse, Mead, & Kelleher, 1967). In this and earlier sections we have shown that free shock can generate responding. In still other experiments, simultaneous reinforcement (Azrin, Holz, Hake, & Ayllon, 1963) procedures such as time out from shock (McKearney, 1970; Morse & Kelleher, 1970), or previous food reinforcement histories have been used (Morse & Kelleher, 1970). Such procedures produced high levels of responding neces-

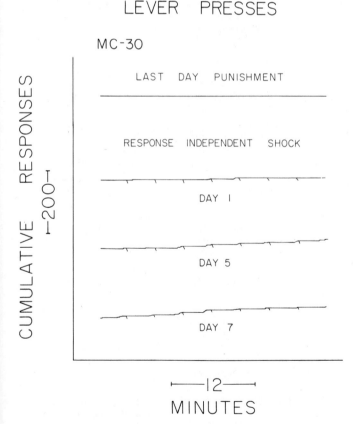

Fig. 22. Cumulative response record segments for one squirrel monkey subject during final testing of punishment for manual responding and subsequent response-independent shock conditions. Responding gradually recovers upon removal of the punishment contingency.

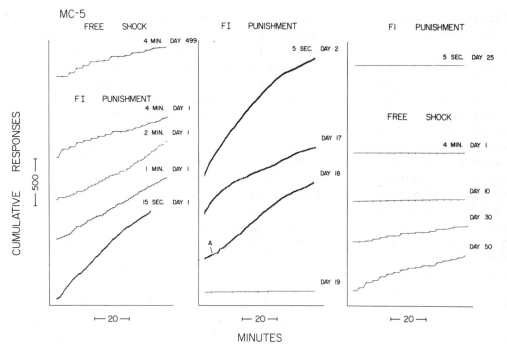

Fig. 23. Cumulative response records for one squirrel monkey subject during stable performance on response-independent shock and during a series of experiments where manual lever pressing was punished. Later yet, the subject was returned to response-independent shock conditions. Whereas punishment, particularly at long intervals, appears to increase responding temporarily, behavior is eventually totally suppressed. Return to response-independent shock produces a gradual reinstatement of performance.

sary to both compete with the response-suppressing effects of the punishment schedule and/or to generate behavioral patterns which obscure or eliminate discriminable episodes of shock reduction following absence of responding. Each of these practices can confuse the outcome of a particular study and cloud understanding of the basic behavior-generating effects of aversive stimulation.

REFERENCES

ANGER, D. The role of temporal discriminations in the reinforcement of Sidman avoidance behavior. *Journal of the Experimental Analysis of Behavior*, 1963, 6, 477–506.

AZRIN, N. H., HAKE, D. F., & HUTCHINSON, R. R. Elicitation of aggression by a physical blow. *Journal of the Experimental Analysis of Behavior*, 1965, 8, 55–57.

AZRIN, N. H., HOLZ, W. C., HAKE, D. F., & AYLLON, T. Fixed-ratio escape reinforcement. *Journal of the Experimental Analysis of Behavior*, 1963, 6, 449–456.

AZRIN, N. H., HUTCHINSON, R. R., & HAKE, D. F. Pain-induced fighting in the squirrel monkey. *Journal of the Experimental Analysis of Behavior*, 1963, 6, 620.

AZRIN, N. H., HUTCHINSON, R. R., & HAKE, D. F. Attack avoidance and escape reactions to aversive shock. *Journal of the Experimental Analysis of Behavior*, 1967, 10, 131–148.

AZRIN, N. H., HUTCHINSON, R. R., & McLAUGHLIN, R. The opportunity for aggression as an operant reinforcer during aversive stimulation. *Journal of the Experimental Analysis of Behavior*, 1965, 8, 171–180.

AZRIN, N. H., HUTCHINSON, R. R., & SALLERY, R. D. Pain-aggression toward inanimate objects. *Journal of the Experimental Analysis of Behavior*, 1964, 7, 223–228.

BROGDEN, W. J., LIPMAN, E. A., & CULLER, E. The role of incentive in conditioning and extinction. *American Journal of Psychology*, 1938, 51, 109–117.

BYRD, L. D. Responding in the cat maintained under response-independent electric shock. *Journal of the Experimental Analysis of Behavior*, 1969, 12, 1–10.

CAMPBELL, B. A., & TEGHTSOONIAN, R. Electrical and behavioral effects of different types of shock stimuli on the rat. *Journal of Comparative and Physiological Psychology*, 1958, 51, 185–192.

DINSMOOR, J. A. Punishment: I. The avoidance hypothesis. *Psychological Review*, 1954, 61, 34–46.

HAKE, D. F. Actual versus potential shock in making shock situations function as negative reinforcers. *Journal of the Experimental Analysis of Behavior*, 1968, 11, 385–403.

HAKE, D. F., & AZRIN, N. H. An apparatus for delivering pain-shock to monkeys. *Journal of the Experimental Analysis of Behavior*, 1963, 6, 297–298.

HOFFMAN, H. S. The analysis of discriminated avoidance. In W. K. Honig (Ed.), *Operant behavior: areas of research and application*. Englewood Cliffs, N.J.: Prentice-Hall, Inc., 1966, 499–530.

HOFFMAN, H. S., FLESHLER, M., & CHORNY, H. Discriminated bar-press avoidance. *Journal of the Experimental Analysis of Behavior*, 1961, 4, 309–316.

HUTCHINSON, R. R. Effects of post-shock attack opportunity upon pre-shock manipulative responding. Paper presented at Psychonomic Society, 1970.

HUTCHINSON, R. R., AZRIN, N. H., & HAKE, D. F. An automatic method for the study of aggression in squirrel monkeys. *Journal of the Experimental Analysis of Behavior*, 1966, 9, 233–237.

HUTCHINSON, R. R., AZRIN, N. H., & RENFREW, J. W. Effects of shock intensity and duration on frequency of biting attack by squirrel monkeys. *Journal of the Experimental Analysis of Behavior*, 1968, 11, 83–88.

HUTCHINSON, R. R., & EMLEY, G. S. Schedule-independent factors contributing to schedule-induced phenomena. In R. M. Gilbert, & J. D. Keehn (Eds.), *Schedule Effects: Drugs, Drinking, and Aggression*. Toronto: University of Toronto Press, 1972, 174–202.

HUTCHINSON, R. R., & EMLEY, G. S. Effects of nicotine on avoidance, conditioned suppression and aggression response measures in animals and man. In W. L. Dunn (Ed.), *Smoking Behavior: Motives and Incentives*. Washington, D.C.: V. H. Winston, 1973, 171–196.

HUTCHINSON, R. R., & PIERCE, G. E. Jaw clenching in humans: Its measurement and effects produced by conditions of reinforcement and extinction. Presented at American Psychological Association, 1971.

HUTCHINSON, R. R., RENFREW, J. W., & YOUNG, G. A. Effects of long-term shock and associated stimuli on aggressive and manual responses. *Journal of the Experimental Analysis of Behavior*, 1971, *15*, 141–166.

KELLEHER, R. T., & MORSE, W. H. Schedules using noxious stimuli, III. Responding maintained with response-produced electric shocks. *Journal of the Experimental Analysis of Behavior*, 1968, *11*, 819–838.

KELLEHER, R. T., RIDDLE, W. C., & COOK, L. Persistent behavior maintained by unavoidable shocks. *Journal of the Experimental Analysis of Behavior*, 1963, *6*, 507–517.

LIDDELL, H. S. The conditioned reflex. In F. A. Moss (Ed.), *Comparative Psychology*. Englewood Cliffs, N.J.: Prentice-Hall, Inc., 1934.

MCKEARNEY, J. W. Maintenance of responding under a fixed-interval schedule of electric shock presentation. *Science*, 1968, *160*, 1249–1251.

MCKEARNEY, J. W. Fixed-interval schedules of electric shock presentation. Extinction and recovery of performance under different shock intensities and fixed-interval durations. *Journal of the Experimental Analysis of Behavior*, 1969, *12*, 301–313.

MCKEARNEY, J. W. Responding under fixed-ratio and multiple fixed-interval fixed-ratio schedules of electric shock presentation. *Journal of the Experimental Analysis of Behavior*, 1970, *14*, 1–6.

MILLER, N. E. Studies of fear as an acquirable drive: I. Fear as motivation and fear-reduction as reinforcement in the learning of new responses. *Journal of Experimental Psychology*, 1948, *38*, 89–101.

MORSE, W. H., & KELLEHER, R. T. Schedules as fundamental determinants of behavior. In W. N. Schoenfeld (Ed.), *The theory of reinforcement schedules*. Englewood Cliffs, N.J.: Prentice-Hall, Inc., 1970, 139–185.

MORSE, W. H., MEAD, R. N., & KELLEHER, R. T. Modulation of elicited behavior by a fixed-interval schedule of electric shock presentation. *Science*, 1967, *157*, 215–217.

MOWRER, O. H., & LAMOREAUX, R. R. Avoidance conditioning and signal duration—a study of secondary motivation and reward. *Psychological Monographs*, 1942, *54*, 5, 247.

PIERCE, G. E. Effects of several fixed-ratio schedules of reinforcement and of extinction upon temporalis and masseter muscle contractions in humans. Masters thesis, Western Michigan University, 1971.

PRONI, T. J. The effect of changes in response-independent pay upon human masseter EMG. Masters thesis, Western Michigan University, 1973.

SIDMAN, M. Some properties of the warning stimulus in avoidance behavior. *Journal of Comparative and Physiological Psychology*, 1955, *48*, 444–450.

SIDMAN, M. Normal sources of pathological behavior. *Science*, 1960, *132*, 61–68.

SIDMAN, M. Some notes on "bursts" in free-operant avoidance experiments. *Journal of the Experimental Analysis of Behavior*, 1958, *1*, 167–172.

STRETCH, R., ORLOFF, E. R., & DALRYMPLE, S. D. Maintenance of responding by fixed-interval schedule of electric shock presentation in squirrel monkeys. *Science*, 1968, *162*, 583–586.

ULRICH, R. E. Interaction between reflexive fighting and cooperative escape. *Journal of the Experimental Analysis of Behavior*, 1967, *10*, 311–317.

ULRICH, R. E., & AZRIN, N. H. Reflexive fighting in response to aversive stimulation. *Journal of the Experimental Analysis of Behavior*, 1962, *5*, 511–520.

ULRICH, R. E., HUTCHINSON, R. R., & AZRIN, N. H. Pain-elicited aggression. *Psychological Record*, 1965, *15*, 111–126.

15

Stimulus Control and Inhibitory Processes*

Mark Rilling

OVERVIEW

A reinforcer never occurs in a vacuum, isolated from outside influences. Environmental events, the *stimuli* of stimulus control, are present before, during, and after the occurrence of the reinforcer. The rapid solution of major substantive problems in the area of stimulus control is due in large measure to the elegance of techniques for reliably assessing the control of behavior by these environmental events. These techniques are considered in the following section.

The third section considers the influence of a number of specific factors on the characteristics of the empirically obtained stimulus-generalization gradient. Discussed are the effects of the schedule of reinforcement during training and a microanalysis of the generalization gradient in terms of interresponse times.

Discrimination training is one of the most powerful determinants of stimulus control. The fourth section defines the various types of discrimination training and gives particular attention to the measurement and interpretation of inhibitory phenomena. Spence's theory of discrimination learning is reexamined in the context of recent evidence on the impact of discrimination training on stimuli varying within a single dimension on the stimulus-generalization gradient. In addition, the newer dynamic models of stimulus control are considered as they apply to inhibitory phenomena.

The basic assumption in the fifth section is that the determinants of inhibitory phenomena are independent of whether the discriminative stimuli are selected from a single or two independent dimensions. This section examines the effect on inhibitory phenomena of amount of training, sequence of the discriminative stimuli, and schedule of reinforcement. The joint effect of the response rate and incentive differences between the two components of the multiple schedule on the shape of the generalization gradient is also considered.

The phenomenon of errorless learning has played a major role in theories of stimulus control. It refers

---

* Preparation of this chapter and the author's research was supported in part by NIMH grant No. 5 R01 MH 18342. I thank the many graduate and undergraduate students at Michigan State University for their comments on an earlier version of this chapter. I am especially indebted to Vern Honig, Tom Kodera, John Staddon, Herb Terrace, Dave Thomas, Stan Weiss, and many other colleagues for their constructive comments and guidance in our pursuit of a clearer understanding of stimulus control.

to discriminations in which the rate of responding during (S−) is negligible from the first session of discrimination training. Errorless learning was considered an exception to the basic laws of discrimination learning in that S− was apparently neutral, rather than acquiring inhibitory properties during errorless discrimination training. In the sixth section data are presented which indicate that basic inhibitory phenomena are in fact obtained following errorless learning.

THE DEFINITION AND MEASUREMENT OF STIMULUS CONTROL

The Vocabulary of Stimulus Control

STIMULUS CONTROL

Stimulus control is observed when a change in a particular property of a stimulus produces a change in some response characteristic, as in the rate or probability with which a response occurs. For example, the onset of a light is said to control behavior if responding occurs at a higher (or lower) rate in the presence of the light than in its absence.

The rationale for introducing the new term *stimulus control* stems from the semantic confusion which Brown (1965) noted as existing between the terms *discrimination* and *generalization*. To illustrate this, suppose different rates of responding to a red stimulus and to a green stimulus are established. Then the data can be described as indicating a discrimination between red and green—or, with the logically equivalent statement, as indicating a failure to generalize between red and green. Therefore, theoretical attempts to explain generalization as a failure to discriminate, or discrimination as a failure to generalize, may involve the fallacy of using different words to describe the same behavioral process. This problem is avoided when *discrimination* and *generalization* are defined as opposite ends of the single continuum of *stimulus control*.

Nondifferential and differential reinforcement are two training procedures which are frequently employed in experiments on stimulus control. In *nondifferential reinforcement*, a response is equally reinforced in the presence of all the stimuli in the environment, so that the consequences of responding remain identical independent of stimulus change. This procedure is typically employed to obtain base line levels of responding to stimuli that subsequently are differentially reinforced. *Differential reinforcement* is a class of training procedures in which responses are unequally reinforced. When differential reinforcement depends upon the stimuli in the environment, as in most experiments in stimulus control, the procedure is called *discrimination training*. In discrimination training, certain stimuli predict occasions when a class of responses is reinforced and other stimuli predict occasions when those responses are not reinforced or when they are reinforced according to a different schedule. Stimuli that are correlated with periods of reinforcement are often designated *positive stimuli* (S+), while those stimuli which are correlated with periods of extinction are designated *negative stimuli* (S−).

THE STIMULUS-GENERALIZATION GRADIENT

At the completion of discrimination training, different rates of responding are typically associated with each stimulus. However, it is not apparent how the organism will respond to test stimuli that have not been previously presented. It is not clear to what properties of the stimulus the organism is responding. To answer these questions, the stimulus may be varied along its various dimensions. For example, in a discrimination between red and green, dimensions such as the size of the stimulus, its luminance, and its wavelength may have acquired control over responding. The *dimension of generalization* is the continuum along which a particular property of a stimulus is varied during a test for stimulus control. Physical dimensions such as the wavelength of a light, the frequency or intensity of a tone, or line orientation are usually selected. A *stimulus-generalization gradient* is the function obtained when the total number of responses to each of the stimulus values presented during the generalization test are plotted against the dimension of generalization.

Techniques for Obtaining a Stimulus-generalization Gradient

A stimulus-generalization gradient is employed to determine the properties of the stimuli that have acquired control over responding. Responding may decrease, increase, or remain unchanged during a stimulus-generalization test. A variety of procedures have been developed for obtaining stimulus-generalization gradients. No single procedure is appropriate for all experimental problems, and the shape of the gradient depends upon the procedure employed. The advantages and disadvantages of each procedure are detailed in the sections that follow. Note that in each of these procedures, specific training is usually given with respect to only one or two stimuli on a dimension prior to the stimulus-generalization test. Consequently, most of the stimuli presented during the generalization test are novel.

TRANSIENT OR EXTINCTION METHODS

In the *single-stimulus method,* a response is reinforced in the presence of one stimulus. In a subsequent test, extinction to a single test stimulus occurs. A separate, independent group is required for each data point on the stimulus-generalization gradient, which is obtained by averaging the total number of responses during extinction for each animal in the group. While single-stimulus tests can be used with operant methods, and have indeed been studied by Hiss and Thomas (1963), the advantages of presenting all test values to each individual subject are so great that this method has been used almost exclusively.

Skinner developed the *multiple-stimulus method* for assessing generalization which was first reported in 1950. In a report prepared in 1944 but not published until 1965, Skinner described a precursor of the most common method for obtaining generalization gradients with operant methods. The classic study reported by Guttman and Kalish (1956) incorporated many aspects of Skinner's procedure and determined the direction of subsequent research in stimulus generalization.

Guttman and Kalish selected the visual spectrum as the stimulus dimension to exploit the excellent color vision of pigeons. During training, the response key was illuminated with a monochromatic light source. Responses on the key were reinforced with food on a variable-interval (VI) 1-min schedule of reinforcement. After a substantial rate of responding was established, generalization testing was carried out during extinction in a session which began with several reinforcements to the training stimulus. During the generalization test, 11 different-colored stimuli, including the training stimulus, were randomly presented on the key each for 60 sec. Each stimulus was repeated 12 times within the test in an attempt to average out the differences due to the slow decrease in the response rate produced by extinction. After the first generalization test, the birds were retrained with reinforcement and a second generalization test identical to the first was administered.

When Guttman and Kalish administered this second generalization test, the generalization gradient from the second test showed fewer total responses than the gradient obtained from the first test. This illustrates a major disadvantage of the extinction methods: the measurement of generalization is contaminated by the effects of extinction. Optimal assessment of stimulus generalization requires comparison with a behavioral base line which is both stable and recoverable. Unfortunately, responding during extinction lacks both of these characteristics. The rate of responding decreases, eventually to zero, and repeated exposures to extinction reduce the number of responses obtained.

The advantage of the multiple-stimulus method is that a stimulus-generalization gradient is obtained from a single organism and averaging of data from different organisms is not required.

MAINTAINED GENERALIZATION METHODS

Procedures in which a constant rate of responding is maintained by reinforcement are generally preferred to transient or transition procedures in which the rate of responding is changing, as described above. Several investigators (D. Blough, 1969, 1975; P. Blough, 1972; Malott, Malott & Glenn, 1973; Pierrel, 1958) have employed *maintained generalization procedures.* The session is divided into trials of generally short duration—e.g., 20 sec. On training trials responding is reinforced intermittently in order to maintain a base line rate of responding. On test trials, responding is never reinforced, and a generalization gradient is obtained during each session by presenting the test stimuli in random order. As long as the animal fails to discriminate test from training trials, responding occurs during the test trials even though reinforcement never occurs. As D. Blough (1969) has shown, the technique is extremely powerful, since hundreds of generalization gradients can be obtained from the same animal over a period of many months. A typical finding with the maintained procedure (P. Blough, 1972) is that the stimulus-generalization gradient around the training stimulus gradually becomes sharper within the sensory limits of the organism. This method is very useful when closely spaced stimuli are used in the test.

A disadvantage of maintained procedures is that several weeks of pretraining are required to establish a constant rate of responding on the base line schedule of reinforcement before a stimulus-generalization gradient can be obtained. Another disadvantage is that when the test stimuli are spaced far apart, a discrimination between training and test stimuli is acquired and responding to the test stimuli rapidly falls to zero. In this latter case, the extinction technique may be more appropriate. Whether the maintained procedures will eventually replace the transient procedures of obtaining the gradient during extinction remains to be seen.

Simultaneous or Concurrent Methods

The methods just described are appropriate for assessing stimulus control in successive discriminations. Stimulus generalization is also measured in simultaneous discriminations. In a simultaneous discrimination two stimuli are presented to the organism at the same time: S+, correlated with reinforcement, and S−, correlated with extinction. When a discrete-trial procedure is employed, each response to S+ is reinforced and each response to S− (or error) produces a time-out during which the onset of the next trial is delayed. When responses at two different locations are intermittently reinforced in the presence of two different stimuli, the procedure is called a concurrent schedule of reinforcement. During a *concurrent generalization test*, a variety of test stimuli are presented at two locations during extinction, and the number of responses to each stimulus which occur at each location are recorded. As employed by D. Blough (1973) and Catania, Silverman, and Stubbs (1974), this procedure produces two stimulus-generalization gradients, one for each stimulus location.

A second procedure, described by Honig, Beale, Seraganian, Lander, and Muir (1972), employs a concurrent schedule with an explicit changeover or advance response. Two discriminative stimuli, S+ and S−, are presented alternately at one location so that only one stimulus is present at a time. A second response, at a different location, terminates the current stimulus and produces the next stimulus in a predictable series. The advantage of this procedure is that it expands the range of dependent variables to include the *time* as well as the number of responses in the presence of each stimulus (or class of stimuli). This procedure has been employed by Honig et al. and Beale and Winton (1970) to measure generalization of the pigeon's response of terminating a stimulus associated with extinction.

The Analysis of Data from a Generalization Test: Absolute vs. Relative Gradients

A generalization gradient based on the total number of responses obtained during extinction is called an *absolute generalization gradient*. An absolute gradient is the simplest method of presenting generalization data. However, some important experimental questions require a comparison of different conditions and cannot be answered with absolute gradients. Suppose that an experimenter wants to compare the amount of generalization produced by two conditions which produce an extreme difference in the total number of responses during extinction. For instance, two different schedules of reinforcement may produce drastic differences in the rate of responding during extinction for two different groups of subjects. A relative stimulus-generalization gradient can be used to compare conditions in such cases, and also when individual absolute gradients differ substantially in their mean rates.

In a *relative gradient*, the number of responses to each test stimulus is expressed as a percentage of the total responses to all stimuli. Relative gradients are also sometimes plotted as a proportion of responses made to the training stimulus. When relative gradients are averaged, equal weight is given to each gradient. In constructing a relative gradient, the experimenter assumes that a given absolute decrement is psychologically greater against a base line of low responding to the training value than against a high base line. Comparisons can be made between the slopes of relative gradients since the gradients have been equated for the differences in the number of responses obtained during the generalization test. However, as Morgan (1969) points out, conclusions about slopes and differences are safest when absolute as well as relative gradients intersect.

Control for Stimulus Preferences

Suppose an experimentally naïve pigeon is placed in an experimental chamber which contains a key which can be illuminated with various stimuli. The bird's responses on the key are not reinforced, but various stimuli are projected on the key and the number of responses to each stimulus are recorded. Most investigators assume that such a procedure will produce a flat gradient with few or no responses to each stimulus and conclude that no stimulus preferences are present. This conclusion is probably incorrect. Some species exhibit marked preferences for certain stimuli which are determined by hereditary and developmental rather than by reinforcement variables. If these effects are not considered, the results of a stimulus-generalization test may be misinterpreted. For example, by measuring the unconditioned pecking behavior of newly hatched gull chicks which were presented with various monochromatic stimuli, Hailman (1969) obtained a preference function resembling a stimulus-generalization gradient. Several reviewers—e.g., Hinde & Hinde (1973); Seligman & Hager (1972); Shettleworth (1972)—have stressed that the experimenter must consider the constraints which the organism's heredity, anatomy, and development impose upon the behavior of an organism in a learning experiment.

SOME DETERMINANTS OF GENERALIZATION GRADIENTS

Nondifferential Reinforcement

A VI schedule of positive reinforcement is often employed to sustain a moderate rate of responding prior to the generalization test in each of the techniques for measuring stimulus generalization. In these techniques the schedule of reinforcement is usually held constant at VI 1-min, at least when pigeons serve as subjects. However, by manipulating the schedule of reinforcement in effect prior to the generalization test, Hearst and his colleagues discovered that the schedule of reinforcement is one of the most potent determinants of the slope of a stimulus-generalization gradient. Different schedules of reinforcement produce widely divergent absolute gradients because they differ in their resistance to extinction. Therefore, relative gradients are employed to compare the effects of schedule of reinforcement on the slope of the generalization gradient.

Hearst, Koresko, and Poppen (1964) found that relative gradients obtained after differential reinforcement of low rate (DRL) training were much flatter than gradients obtained after VI training. On a DRL schedule an interresponse time greater than t sec produces reinforcement, while an interresponse time less than t sec is extinguished. In a second experiment, Hearst, Koresko, and Poppen (1964) trained each group of animals on a different value of a VI schedule. The longer the mean value of a VI schedule, the lower the response rate and frequency of reinforcement. Generalization was measured during extinction with the multiple-stimulus method. Figure 1 shows that a VI 4-min schedule produces a rather flat relative gradient, indicating that more generalization is observed with long VI schedules than with the short VI 1-min schedule which is usually employed in generalization experiments. These data demonstrate that the slope of a stimulus-generalization gradient can be drastically altered by manipulating the temporal distribution of food deliveries while holding stimulus variables constant.

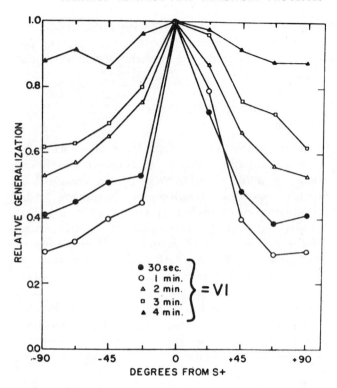

Fig. 1. Gradients of relative generalization for five groups of pigeons in which each group received training on a different value of a VI schedule prior to the generalization test. The S+ was a vertical line (0°) for all subjects. In general, the gradient becomes flatter as the value of the VI schedule increases. (From Hearst, Koresko, & Poppen, 1964. © 1964 by the Society for the Experimental Analysis of Behavior, Inc.)

Thomas and Switalski (1966) compared stimulus generalization following variable-ratio (VR) and VI training. In order to equate the two schedules for the frequency and pattern of reinforcement, pairs of pigeons were matched through a yoking procedure. The time required by a pigeon on VR training to complete each ratio determined the interval at which its yoked pigeon on VI training was reinforced. Thus when one pigeon's response was reinforced on the VR schedule, the next response of the VI bird was also reinforced. The VR schedule generated a higher rate of responding than the VI schedule, but the gradient for the VR group was slightly flatter than the VI gradient.

What is the explanation for these results? A simple explanation is that each response is determined to some extent by previous responses (factor A) and to some extent by external stimuli (factor B), where $A + B = 1$ (i.e., complete determination). When factor A is important, as on DRL and (perhaps) ratio schedules, then factor B is correspondingly less so; hence the flatter gradients. While this hypothesis is an attractive device for integrating data on the effects of schedules of reinforcement on stimulus generalization, the explanation remains post hoc until a method is developed for measuring the extent to which a response is determined by previous responses.

Microstructure of the Stimulus-generalization Gradient

This subsection provides a review of the summation or averaging procedures that are employed on the data obtained during a stimulus-generalization test. The basic question is whether all responses are equivalent. The question has been divided into three subsidiary questions which will be considered in turn: (1) Does the shape of the gradient depend upon the amount of time which has preceded the response? (2) Does the shape of the gradient change during the test session? (3) Is the gradient an artifact of inappropriate averaging of responses of different topographies?

IRT ANALYSIS OF THE STIMULUS-GENERALIZATION GRADIENT

An interresponse time (IRT) analysis of the rate of responding is a useful technique for determining the essential characteristics of stimulus control. One of D. Blough's (1969) experiments neatly illustrates the contribution of responses within various IRT categories to the shape of the stimulus-generalization gradient. Pigeons were intermittently reinforced for responses to a 582-nm stimulus, and the data for generalization were obtained with a maintained procedure by randomly presenting a series of adjacent wavelengths during extinction.

Three stimulus-generalization gradients were obtained by dividing the number of responses into four IRT categories or class intervals: .6 to 1.0 sec, 1.0 to 2.0 sec, 2.0 to 4.0 sec, and greater than 4.0 sec. Few responses occurred between 0 and .6 sec because the key was darkened during this period to provide stimulus feedback for each response. The dependent variable, IRTs/OP was the conditional probability that a response fell within one of the four IRT categories.

Figure 2 clearly indicates that the stimulus on the key acquires control over the pecking response only within an IRT range of 2.0–4.0 sec. The figure shows a fairly flat gradient and complete generalization for IRTs within the .6–1.0-sec and 1.0–2.0-sec categories. In other words, the stimulus on the key does not control the rate of responding when an animal responds with IRTs less than 2.0 sec.

Similar data have been obtained with the lever-pressing response of rats by Crites, Harris, Rosenquist, and Thomas (1967). However, an experiment by White (1973) has restricted the generality of this phenomenon. Stimulus control over the responding of pigeons was acquired by responses in all IRT class intervals, including those of less than 2.0 sec. White's procedure differed from Blough's in a number of significant respects. The generalization test in White's experiment was preceded by differential reinforce-

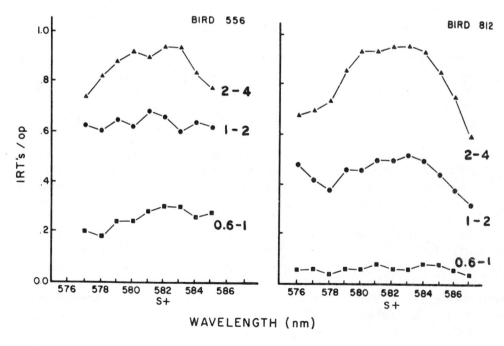

Fig. 2. Maintained gradients obtained following reinforcement of responding at 582 nm, showing the probability of a response as a function of wavelength and interresponse time (IRT). The numbers next to each function indicate the IRT class intervals in sec. The overall level of the curves varies with the number of responses in the class interval. The significant aspect is that the gradients with the class interval between 2 and 4 sec is steeper than the flat gradients obtained between .6 and 1 sec. (From D. Blough, 1969. © 1969 by the Society for the Experimental Analysis of Behavior, Inc.)

ment, while Blough employed nondifferential reinforcement. Additional research is necessary to specify the conditions under which stimulus control is acquired or is not acquired over responses following various IRTS. The data base of this research should be broadened by employing responses other than pecking. For example, Hemmes (1973) has shown that pigeons acquire a discrimination between a red or a white houselight located above the ceiling of the experimental chamber when responses on a foot treadle located on the floor of the chamber are reinforced with food. It would be interesting to know if stimulus control over the treadle response depends upon the duration of the preceding IRT.

Blough's experiments, like those discussed in the preceding section, imply that the sensitivity of a response to stimulus variation depends upon the amount of time which has elapsed since the preceding response.

Steepening of the Stimulus-generalization Gradient During Extinction

In the multiple-stimulus method, each stimulus is presented several times in extinction during the generalization test. In general, fewer responses are obtained with each successive presentation of the same stimulus. Several experiments (Friedman & Guttman, 1965; Thomas & Barker, 1964) have demonstrated a steepening of the relative stimulus-generalization gradients during extinction. Friedman and Guttman analyzed the changes in the generalization gradient which occurred during testing by dividing the total number of responses during extinction into successive quarters. A relative generalization gradient was constructed for each of the four quarters. The gradients became steeper as extinction progressed because the rate of responding dropped to zero more rapidly for the stimuli which were remote from the training stimulus while responding to the training stimulus decreased less rapidly. Thus a long generalization test in which each stimulus is presented many times is biased toward a steep gradient, while a short generalization test with few stimulus presentations is biased toward a flat gradient. While the magnitude of the bias is small, caution is required in interpreting differences in the slopes of the gradients from different experiments because the differences could be due to comparing generalization test sessions of different lengths.

Why does the generalization gradient become steeper as extinction progresses? A plausible explanation is based on an IRT analysis. When the rate of responding is high, short IRTs predominate, while long IRTs emerge when the rate of responding is low. Since the rate of responding slows during extinction, IRTs become longer. Blough's data demonstrated that responses preceded by long IRTs may acquire more stimulus control than do responses preceded by short IRTs. Since long IRTs predominate toward the end of a stimulus-generalization test carried out during extinction, the gradient should become steeper.

The Stimulus-generalization Gradient: Fact or Artifact?

Several investigators (Migler, 1964; Migler & Millenson, 1969; Ray & Sidman, 1970; Stoddard & Sidman, 1967, 1971) view the stimulus-generalization gradient as a continuous function, consisting of varying proportions of discrete elements. The proportions can vary continuously, but the elements (IRTs or whatever) are discrete or "quantal." Consider the reduced number of responses to an intermediate test stimulus. The same number of responses could be produced by a constant, intermediate rate of responding or by averaging brief periods of responding at the previously reinforced rate with long periods containing few or no responses. These investigators employed simultaneous methods for assessing stimulus control following discrimination training in which responses at more than one location were reinforced. In general, the test stimuli controlled the relative frequency of the two responses that were reinforced during training so that a mixture of the two responses was obtained at intermediate test stimuli. Mixing of different responses is likely to occur during stimulus generalization when two incompatible responses have been reinforced during simultaneous discrimination training prior to the generalization test, so simultaneous methods are well suited to the measurement of competing responses during generalization.

Collins (1974) obtained IRT distributions of the pecking response of pigeons while generalization was measured with the multiple-stimulus method during extinction. Following single-stimulus training in which responding to a 554-nm stimulus was reinforced on a VI schedule, the number of responses in the longer IRT class intervals (>6 sec) increased systematically with divergence from S+, while the frequency of responses with short IRTs decreased. Following successive discrimination training between two stimuli, the IRT distribution for an intermediate test stimulus was a mixture, in varying proportions, of the response patterns conditioned in the presence of S+ and S−.

Using rats as subjects, Weiss (1972b) measured IRT distributions in the presence of a light associated with a DRL schedule and a tone associated with a VR schedule. The absence of the light or tone was associated with extinction. After a low rate of responding was established on the DRL schedule and a high rate of responding was established on the VR schedule, the tone and light were presented simultaneously as a compound stimulus during extinction. An IRT analysis of responding during the compound stimulus revealed few patterns of responding during the compound stimulus that were not present during the individual presentations of the light and the tone.

All of these experiments, which employed a wide variety of methods for assessing stimulus control, are in agreement that the presentation of an intermediate test stimulus following discrimination training between two stimuli does not produce a constant, intermediate rate of responding. A significant component of the original behaviors which were conditioned during training remains during generalization testing. Therefore, as Weiss (1972b) points out, the stimulus-generalization gradient is probably a product of the mixing of a small number of response classes. The task of the microanalysis of stimulus control is to determine and isolate the variables responsible for the mixture of responses which result in the stimulus-generalization gradient.

A microanalysis of the generalization gradient in terms of interresponse times or competing responses is compatible with research whose goal is to determine the effects of various variables upon the shape of the stimulus-generalization gradient. It is to this body of research that attention is now directed.

INFLUENCE OF DISCRIMINATION TRAINING ON THE GENERALIZATION GRADIENT

One of the main problems in the discrimination learning of animals is to specify the conditions under which a change in a stimulus produces a change in the probability with which a response occurs. A general finding (see the reviews by Thomas, 1969, 1970) is that nondifferential reinforcement produces a flatter stimulus-generalization gradient than does differential reinforcement. Discrimination training is one of the most effective procedures for increasing the slope of the stimulus-generalization gradient.

Two Types of Discrimination Training

The term *discrimination training* is very broad, since there are many different procedures which share the defining characteristic of an S+ which is correlated with reinforcement and an S− which is correlated with extinction. Switalsky, Lyons, and Thomas (1966) have developed useful terminology for classifying the types of discrimination training on the basis of the relationship between the discriminative stimuli (S+ and S−) and the stimulus dimension on which the generalization gradient is obtained.

The first type is *intradimensional training*, which occurs when S+ and S− are selected from the same stimulus dimension and a generalization test is carried out within that dimension. A common example of intradimensional training is a successive discrimination in which responding is reinforced in the presence of one wavelength, S+, and extinguished in the presence of another wavelength, S−. Other dimensions frequently used are the frequency of an acoustic stimulus and orientation of a line.

An important characteristic of intradimensional training is that it is impossible to vary the psychological distance of a test stimulus from S+ without also varying its psychological distance from S−. Therefore, intradimensional training is employed when the experimenter wants to study the *interaction* between reinforcement at S+ and extinction at S− on responding to each stimulus.

The second type of discrimination training is *interdimensional training* which occurs when S+ is equally distant psychologically from each of the stimuli on the S− dimension or when S− is equally distant from each of the stimuli on the S+ dimension. When two dimensions are *psychologically independent*, each stimulus from the S+ dimension is equally distant psychologically from each of the stimulus on the S− dimension. Interdimensional training is employed when the experimenter wants to compare responding to stimuli similar to S− with responding to stimuli similar to S+, under conditions where the two kinds of responding are assumed to be independent. Two separate generalization gradients for the S+ and S− dimensions may be obtained with interdimensional training, thereby avoiding the interaction obtained with intradimensional training. This rationale for interdimensional training was stated by Jenkins (1965) and is described in greater detail in monographs by Hearst, Besley, and Farthing (1970) and Hearst (1972).

Silence, the absence of S+ or S−, is a stimulus at the end point of the intensity (loudness) dimension which is often employed in interdimensional training. For example, suppose that silence is the stimulus that is employed as S⁻ and a tone of 1,000 Hz is employed as S⁺. If intensity and frequency are independent dimensions, then the frequency of the tone may be varied during a stimulus generalization test without changing the psychological distance between the test values from the S⁺ dimension and S⁻.

The stimuli for the early experiments in interdimensional discrimination training were a priori assumed to be psychologically independent dimensions. However, psychological independence is an empirical concept, and a preliminary experiment is required to demonstrate the stimuli that appear independent to the experimenter are also functionally independent, as indicated by the behavior of the organism. A test for psychological independence is conducted as follows. First a response is reinforced in the presence of a stimulus from the *A*-dimension without the presentation of a stimulus from the *B*-dimension. Then a stimulus-generalization gradient is obtained by presenting test stimuli from the *B*-dimension. If a horizontal gradient is obtained, the stimulus from the *A*-dimension is independent of the *B*-dimension. The converse experiment could be carried out by first training with stimulus *B* and then testing on the *A*-dimension to determine if stimulus *B* is independent of the *A*-dimension.

Giurintano, Schadler, and Thomas (1972) conditioned the pecking response of different groups of pigeons in the presence of stimuli that are a priori independent of the dimension of line orientation: a white light, a green light, and a white dot. Then each group was given a stimulus-generalization test in which the angle of a white line on a dark background was varied. A preexperimental preference for a particular orientation was not obtained. Training with the white or dim light produced a preference for vertical, while training with the dot produced a preference for 30°. Only the green stimulus resulted in no preferred orientation and therefore was functionally orthogonal to the angle of the line. Using a similar procedure, Selekman (1973) conditioned pecking in the presence of a white key and obtained a nonhorizontal gradient on the wavelength dimension. The pigeons demonstrated a preference for short wavelengths between 510 and 560 nm. These data demonstrate that an experiment is necessary to determine if the two dimensions employed in interdimensional training are functionally independent. Complete functional independence is probably an ideal state, and it is unlikely that any two dimensions are completely independent. By determining an organism's preference for certain stimuli, the experimenter may consider this response bias in selecting the most appropriate stimuli for interdimensional training. Thus, for example, the experimenter may deliberately design the experiment to counteract the anticipated bias in order to make such an outcome more convincing.

Comparing Nondifferential with Differential Reinforcement

The effects of nondifferential and differential training procedures on stimulus generalization are illustrated by a widely cited experiment of Jenkins and Harrison (1960). The data from a subsequent experiment of Jenkins and Harrison (1962) extend these results comparing the effects of interdimensional and intradimensional training on the slope of the stimulus-generalization gradient. In their first experiment, one group of pigeons was given nondifferential training in which a 1,000-Hz tone signaled that a VI schedule of reinforcement was in effect. No training stimulus explicitly correlated with extinction was introduced until the generalization test. A second group was given interdimensional training in which S⁺ was a 1,000-Hz tone and S⁻ was silence. The tone and silence were randomly presented so that the animals learned to respond in the presence of the tone and not to respond in the absence of the tone.

The individual gradients for a representative bird from each group which received each type of training are shown in Figure 3. During generalization, the test stimuli were tones widely separated in frequency from the training stimulus, as well as silence. The relative gradient following nondifferential training demonstrated weak stimulus control, since the gradient was relatively flat with a maximum at S⁺.

In contrast with nondifferential training, interdimensional training produced a steeper gradient with a clear maximum at 1,000 Hz and over 20% of the total responses occurring to the training stimulus for each animal. Following interdimensional training, the frequency of the tone during the test systematically controlled the rate of pecking. Why does the frequency of the tone acquire control over responding when the only source of discrimination training is between the presence and absence of the tone? Clearly, differential reinforcement is more effective than nondifferential reinforcement in activating stimulus control, but the question has no adequate answer.

In a second experiment, Jenkins and Harrison (1962) obtained much steeper generalization gradients when several of the birds were given additional intradimensional training between two closely spaced tones

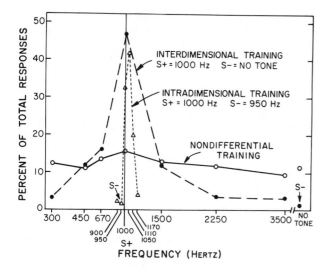

Fig. 3. Representative individual generalization gradients of total frequency obtained from pigeons following three training conditions. The open circles show a relatively flat gradient obtained after nondifferential reinforcement in the presence of a 1,000-Hz tone. The closed circles show that a steeper gradient was obtained following interdimensional training in which S+ was a 1,000-Hz tone and S− was no tone. The open triangles show that the steepest gradient was obtained following intradimensional training in which S+ was a 1,000-Hz tone and S− a 950-Hz tone. (Adapted from Jenkins & Harrison, 1960. © 1960 by the American Psychological Association, and reprinted by permission. And Jenkins & Harrison, 1962. © 1962 by the Society for the Experimental Analysis of Behavior, Inc.)

rather than between a tone and the absence of the tone as in their original experiment. Notice in Figure 3 that following intradimensional training between an S+ of 1,000 Hz and an S− of 950 Hz, the maximum did not occur at S+, but occurred instead at 1,050 Hz. This phenomenon is called the *peak shift* and is the general result of intradimensional training. In the peak shift, the peak or mode of the generalization gradient occurs at a test stimulus which is displaced from S+ in a direction away from S−. The significance of this important phenomenon is discussed later.

In an earlier review of the Jenkins and Harrison experiment, Terrace (1966c) concluded that "differential reinforcement was necessary to establish stimulus control" (p. 281). However, this conclusion was not correct since Jenkins and Harrison obtained weak stimulus control following nondifferential reinforcement. In addition, Thomas and Setzer (1972) showed reliable auditory frequency generalization gradients in both rats and guinea pigs following nondifferential reinforcement. The finding that auditory stimuli acquire good stimulus control during nondifferential reinforcement with food for rats and guinea pigs and poor control for pigeons may reflect a difference between either the ontogeny or the inherited propensities of the subjects in these experiments. Therefore, the effect of nondifferential reinforcement on stimulus control depends upon the stimulus dimension, reinforcer, and species of the subject. (See Mackintosh, chapter 16 in this volume.)

Using pigeons and visual stimuli, Switalski, Lyons, and Thomas (1966) and Lyons and Thomas (1967) compared the effects of interdimensional nondifferential reinforcement and interdimensional differential reinforcement on the slope of the stimulus-generalization gradient. In the Lyons and Thomas study, the stimuli were a white vertical line on a black background and a 555-nm light. When responding to both stimuli was equally reinforced, the gradients for wavelength were flattened. Following interdimensional training between 555 nm (S+) and the vertical line (S−), the gradients for wavelength were steepened.

Interdimensional training does not guarantee stimulus control over the behavior of the organism by the dimension selected by the experimenter, but it is more effective than nondifferential reinforcement. When compared with interdimensional training, intradimensional training between stimuli which are closely spaced on the stimulus dimension further sharpens the stimulus-generalization gradient.

Effects of Intradimensional Training

THE POSITIVE PEAK SHIFT

The classic peak shift experiment was performed by Hanson (1959). Four groups of pigeons were given intradimensional training on the wavelength dimension with the same S+, 550 nm. The groups differed only with respect to the S− employed: 555, 560, 570, and 590 nm. The experimental groups were trained on the discrimination until the response rate during S− reached zero. The number of sessions required to reach this discrimination criterion increased as the difference between S+ and S− decreased. Following discrimination training, each animal was given a generalization test with stimuli which ranged from 480 to 620 nm.

The results for these groups plus a control group that received nondifferential reinforcement with S+ only are presented in Figure 4. The peak of the generalization gradient for the four experimental groups did not occur at S+, 550 nm. Rather, the peak occurred at 540 nm, a stimulus that the birds had never seen until the generalization test. This is the *positive peak shift*, which is usually called simply the peak shift. Extrapolation of the gradient obtained with S− at 555 nm suggests that the peak would have

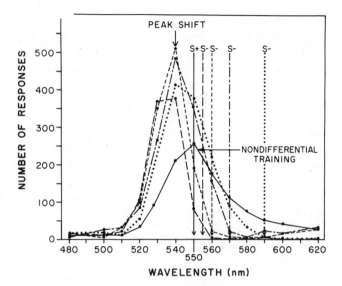

Fig. 4. Effects of intradimensional discrimination training on the stimulus-generalization gradient for different groups of pigeons. For all groups, S+ was 550 nm. Four groups received discrimination training with S− at 555, 560, 570, or 590 nm, respectively, as indicated by the vertical arrows. A control group (solid curve) received nondifferential reinforcement at 550 nm and showed a maximum at S+. The groups given discrimination training showed a positive peak shift with the maximum displaced from S+ to 540 nm. (From Hanson, 1959. © 1959 by the American Psychological Association. Reprinted by permission.)

occurred at 535 nm if that test stimulus had been presented, and extrapolation of the gradient with S− at 590 nm suggests a peak shift at 545 nm. Hanson's data suggest that the magnitude of the peak shift depends upon the difference between S+ and S−. Most subsequent experiments (see the review by Purtle, 1973, p. 410) agree that the closer the spacing between S+ and S−, the greater the probability of obtaining a peak shift. Successful research on the determinants of the peak shift requires the inclusion of several test stimuli which are spaced closely to S+.

Figure 4 also shows that the experimental groups emitted more responses in the vicinity of S+ than did the nondifferential control group. This difference may simply reflect the fact that the control group received only five days of nondifferential reinforcement followed by the generalization test, while the experimental groups received up to 25 additional days of discrimination training prior to the generalization test. Alternatively, the increased output in the vicinity of S+ may reflect the occurrence of behavioral contrast. When *behavioral contrast* occurs during discrimination training, the rate of responding to S+ is elevated relative to a base line of nondifferential reinforcement prior to the stimulus-generalization test. The higher rate to S+ carries over to the generalization test and produces a higher rate of responding to the stimuli in the vicinity of S+. When behavioral contrast is assessed with a control group, the control group should receive the same amount of exposure to S+ as the experimental group.

Discrimination training reduced the number of responses in the vicinity of S− as compared with the control group. This produced asymmetrical gradients with more area on the side of S+ that was away from S−. The *area shift* is an index of a gradient in which more than 50% of the area of the gradient lies on the side of S+ away from S−. The area shift is based on the assumption that the theoretical excitatory gradient around S+ is symmetrical. The area shift is more sensitive to the effects of intradimensional training than is the peak shift, since some animals which do not show a peak shift may still show an area shift (Terrace, 1966c, p. 328). However, the peak shift is superior to the area shift as a dependent variable. Area shifts must be interpreted with caution, since an asymmetric gradient may reflect chance variability, stimulus preferences, or lack of excitation in the vicinity of S−. In Hanson's experiment the area shift, the percentage of responses below 550 nm increased as the difference between S+ and S− decreased.

One of the most convincing demonstrations of the peak shift was a study by Thomas and Williams (1963) which employed an S− located between *two* S+ stimuli. The S− was 560 nm which alternated successively with an S+ of 540 and 580 nm. The postdiscrimination gradient showed a double peak shift with the two maximums located at 530 and 590 nm. This study clearly demonstrates that the peak of the gradient shifts away from S−.

A comprehensive review of the literature on the peak shift by Purtle (1973) indicates that the phenomenon has been obtained following intradimensional discrimination training on a variety of dimensions with several species of organisms, including humans. Notwithstanding the generality of the phenomenon, research on the determinants of the peak shift is confronted with the problem of individual differences. Published articles are filled with restrictive statements such as "only one of the four subjects displayed the peak shift" or "three of the five birds produced the peak shift," etc. When the stimuli are spaced closely along the stimulus dimension, more responses may by chance occur to a test stimulus other than S+ producing an artifactual peak shift. The optimal parameters for producing the peak shift should be determined. One problem is that the measurement of the peak shift during extinction with the Guttman and Kalish technique may increase the variability of the data. The use of a maintained procedure may increase the reliability of the phenomenon.

The Negative Peak Shift

A *negative peak shift* occurs when the minimum of the generalization gradient occurs at a test stimulus which is displaced from S− in a direction away from S+. Careful examination of Figure 4 shows that several of the experimental groups showed a negative peak shift. However, reliable measurement of the negative peak shift was difficult in Hanson's experiment due to the low response output for test stimuli in the vicinity of S−.

Guttman (1965) solved the problem of the zero rate of responding in the vicinity of S− by nondifferentially reinforcing responses to a range of spectral stimuli that were subsequently employed in the generalization test. This was followed by intradimensional discrimination training between S+ and S− to a criterion less strict than Hanson's. Then a generalization test was administered during extinction. The results of this experiment, presented in Figure 5, show both a positive and a negative peak shift. The data in Figure 5 represent an average for six animals given intradimensional discrimination training on the wavelength dimension. The minimum did not occur at S−, test stimulus 11, but was displaced beyond S+ away from S− to test stimulus 14. This is a negative peak shift of 15 nm on the wavelength dimension.

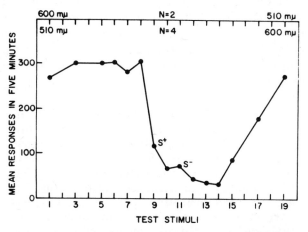

Fig. 5. A stimulus-generalization gradient illustrating both a positive and a negative peak shift. Responding to the test stimuli was nondifferentially reinforced. Then the rate of responding to S− was reduced by intradimensional discrimination training. Finally generalization was measured by presenting the test stimuli during extinction. The maximum did not occur at S+, test stimulus 9, but was displaced to test stimulus 8, a positive peak shift. The minimum did not occur at S−, test stimulus 11, but was displaced to test stimulus 14, a negative peak shift. (From Guttman, 1965.)

Similarly, the maximum did not occur at S+, test stimulus 9, but was displaced beyond S+ away from S− to test stimulus 8.

Stevenson (1966) has also obtained a negative peak shift with a method which involves testing over only the half of the stimulus dimension centered around S−. When stimuli in the vicinity of S+ were not presented, the rate of responding in the vicinity of S− was much higher than in Hanson's experiment. The advantage of Stevenson's procedure is that a negative peak shift can be obtained after the birds meet a strict criterion of no responding to S− without previously reinforcing responses to any of the test stimuli except S+. Stevenson's experiment demonstrates that the presentation of S+ during the generalization test is not necessary for the negative peak shift.

Since most of the research has concentrated on the positive peak shift, the negative peak shift has been a neglected experimental phenomenon. More research is needed to determine the correlation between these two phenomena of intradimensional discrimination training. The simplest assumption is that the determinants of the positive and negative peak shifts are identical.

Additive and Suppressive Summation

In the experiments on the positive and negative peak shifts, the continuum was defined by a dimension of a stimulus. Weiss (1972a) defines a *stimulus set* in terms of the on and off states of two discriminative stimuli: a tone (T) and a light (L). The set extends from the all-off extreme ($\overline{T} + \overline{L}$) through the one-stimulus on conditions (T + $\overline{L}$) or ($\overline{T}$ + L) to the all-on extreme (T + L). The preceding peak shift experiments employed two-component multiple schedules in which each component was associated with the on state of a stimulus. Weiss argues that consideration of the rate of responding and conditions of reinforcement in the off as well as the on states is essential for a complete understanding of a stimulus control. Therefore, Weiss employs three-component multiple schedules in which the third component is associated with the all-off extreme of the ordered stimulus set.

Typically rats are intermittently reinforced for pressing a lever in these experiments. Consider a three-component multiple schedule in which responding is reinforced in the presence of a tone (T + $\overline{L}$) and a light ($\overline{T}$ + L), while responses are extinguished in the absence of the tone and light ($\overline{T} + \overline{L}$). Responding is maintained at approximately equal rates in the tone and the light. After discrimination training, stimulus control is assessed in a compounding test in which the tone and the light are presented separately and, in addition, the tone-plus-light compound stimulus is presented for the first time. The typical outcome of this type of experiment is *additive summation,* in which more responses are obtained to the compound stimulus than to either of the single training stimuli alone.

Weiss (1972a, p. 194) explained additive summation as follows. When $\overline{T} + \overline{L}$ is associated with extinction, the response which is conditioned is response cessation (R_1). When responding is reinforced in the presence of $T + \overline{L}$, the behavior which is conditioned consists of a mixture of the response controlled by the tone (R_2) and response cessation (R_1) which is controlled by the absence of the light. Similarly, the $(\overline{T} + L)$ stimulus controls a mixture of behavior controlled by the light (R_3) and response cessation (R_1) controlled by the absence of the tone. During presentation of $T + L$, additive summation occurs because responding consists of a mixture of responses controlled by the light (R_2) and responses controlled by the tone (R_3). The mixture of R_2 and R_3 produces a higher rate of responding than the mixture of either R_2 or R_3 with R_1. According to this formulation the habits conditioned in $\overline{T} + \overline{L}$ are influencing the behavioral control in $T + \overline{L}$ and $L + \overline{T}$ through $\overline{L}$ and $\overline{T}$, respectively. Therefore, according to Weiss, the response rate and reinforcement frequency determined by the $\overline{T} + \overline{L}$ contingency sets the *conditioning context* within which control is acquired by $T + \overline{L}$ and $L + \overline{T}$.

Now consider a second experiment in which responding is reinforced in the absence of the light and tone and responding is reinforced at a lower rate or punished in the presence of a tone and light. The typical outcome of this experiment is called *suppressive summation,* in which fewer responses are obtained to the compound stimulus than to either training stimulus alone. Weiss also explained suppressive summation in terms of a mixture of responses controlled by each stimulus element.

Additive summation is analogous to the positive peak shift, since in each case the maximum rate of responding is controlled by a stimulus removed from S^+ in a direction away from S^-. Similarly, suppressive summation is analogous to the negative peak shift. Weiss (1971) noted that these phenomena are functionally similar in the sense that each has the same determinants. Weiss (1972a) summarizes the effects of conditioning context as follows:

> Compounding the *same* schedule-associated stimuli might lead to additive summation under one set of circumstances, suppressive summation under another or even averaging in a third complex schedule context.... [This means] that absolute properties cannot be attributed to the schedule-associated behaviors without due regard to the total schedule context of which they are a part. (p. 206, italics in original)

Effects of Interdimensional Training

EXCITATION, INHIBITION, AND DIMENSIONAL CONTROL

Hearst, Besley, and Farthing (1970) define *excitatory* and *inhibitory stimuli* as follows:

> An "excitatory stimulus" is a stimulus . . . that develops during conditioning . . . the capacity to increase response strength above the level occurring when that stimulus is absent. An "inhibitory stimulus" is a stimulus that develops during conditioning the capacity to decrease response strength below the level occurring when that stimulus is absent. (p. 376)

Consider a hypothetical experiment in which interdimensional training is employed with S^+ correlated with reinforcement and S^- correlated with extinction. After discrimination training, a test is required to determine if S^+ has acquired the capacity to increase responding, and a separate test is required to determine if S^- has acquired the capacity to decrease responding. As the following quotation illustrates, Hearst et al. distinguish these tests from procedures for obtaining a stimulus-generalization gradient.

> The term "excitatory dimensional control," in our view, would be applied when new stimulus values that lie at progressively greater distances along a specific dimension from an excitatory stimulus show a graded decremental effect. The term "inhibitory dimensional control" would be applied when new stimulus values at progressively greater distances from an inhibitory stimulus show a graded incremental effect on the strength of an operant response. It is important to point out that an incremental gradient around some stimulus value is *necessary but not sufficient* for defining inhibitory dimensional control. The specific stimulus at which responding is minimal must also be shown to be inhibitory by some independent test, since it is logically possible that such a stimulus is relatively

"neutral" and the other values progressively more excitatory. (p. 377)

Stimulus-generalization gradients are classified as excitatory or inhibitory on the basis of whether responding decreases or increases with increasing distance from the training stimulus. An *excitatory* or *decremental* stimulus-generalization gradient has a maximum at or near S+. The number of responses to a test stimulus decreases with increasing distance from S+. An *inhibitory* or *incremental* stimulus-generalization gradient has a minimum at or near S−. The number of responses to a test stimulus increases with the distance from S−. Excitatory gradients measure generalization of reinforcement while inhibitory gradients measure generalization of extinction.

The Measurement of Inhibitory Stimulus Control

This section describes four techniques that have been developed for the measurement of inhibitory stimulus control following interdimensional discrimination training. As Rescorla (1969a, 1969b) and Hearst (1972) have pointed out, a variety of different experimental operations are used to define a conditioned inhibitor. Furthermore, the measurement of conditioned inhibition is more difficult to measure than is conditioned excitation, thus necessitating special control procedures to avoid confounding conditioned inhibition with other behavioral processes. Paralleling the research on conditioned inhibition, a variety of methods have emerged for the measurement of inhibitory stimulus control. These include (1) resistance to extinction, (2) resistance to reinforcement, (3) combined cue or summation tests, and (4) stimulus reduction.

Resistance to Extinction

Three groups of investigators (Honig, Boneau, Burstein, & Pennypacker, 1963; Jenkins & Harrison, 1962; Schwartzbaum & Kellicut, 1962) independently developed interdimensional procedures to measure generalization of extinction independently of generalization of reinforcement. For example, Honig et al. ran two similar studies in which interdimensional discrimination training was given to one group of pigeons with S+ as a homogeneous white key and S− as a black vertical line bisecting the white key. For the other group, S+ was a vertical line on the key and S− was the white key. After differential responding was well established, stimulus generalization was measured by presenting the line at various angles with the Guttman and Kalish technique.

If the effects of extinction generalize, S− should show the fewest responses and the number of responses to a test stimulus should increase with increasing distance from S−. For the groups with the line correlated with S−, Figure 6 shows that an inhibitory gradient was obtained around S−. With S+ correlated with reinforcement, an excitatory or decremental gradient was obtained. This experiment is one of the clearest demonstrations of parallel generalization for extinction and reinforcement.

The major advantage of interdimensional training for the measurement of inhibitory dimensional control is that the stimuli can be varied along the S− dimension without interacting with S+. Excitatory gradients around S+ and inhibitory gradients around S− can be compared with this procedure. Notice in Figure 6 that more responses were obtained during the generalization test when the orientation of the line was employed as the S+ dimension. The major weakness of the extinction procedure is that when very few responses are obtained during the generalization test along the S− dimension, a "floor effect" makes detection of inhibition extremely difficult.

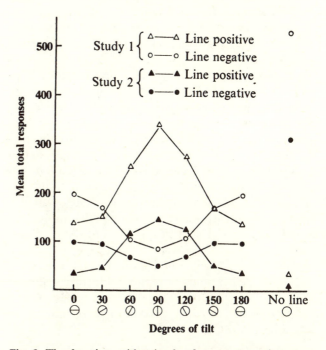

Fig. 6. The functions with triangles demonstrate excitatory or decremental gradients of stimulus control and were obtained following interdimensional training between a vertical line (S+) and no line (S−). The functions with circles demonstrate inhibitory or incremental gradients of stimulus control and were obtained following interdimensional training between a vertical line (S−) and no line (S+). (From Honig, Boneau, Burstein, & Pennypacker, 1963.)

Resistance to Reinforcement

Hearst, Besley, and Farthing (1970) adapted the method of retardation of the development of a conditioned response from Rescorla's (1969a) analysis of inhibition in classical conditioning. This procedure substantially increased the reliability of the inhibitory gradient. Rather than measuring the resistance to *extinction* on the S− dimension, as in the extinction methods, the resistance to *reinforcement* on the S− dimension is obtained. First, behavior is extinguished to S− during interdimensional discrimination training. Then, during the generalization test, responses to all of the test stimuli are reinforced on a VI schedule. The procedure is repeated for several successive daily sessions. The procedure assumes that the resistance of a response to the effects of reinforcement, in the presence of a former S−, provides an index of the inhibitory properties of that stimulus. For example, an animal will acquire a response to a novel stimulus more rapidly than to a stimulus to which responding has been previously extinguished. The advantage of the resistance-to-reinforcement method is that it eliminates the problem of the zero base line which occurs when no responses are obtained during the generalization test. A limitation of the procedure is that equal rates of reinforcement are required in the presence of each test stimulus. Otherwise, differences in response rate during testing could be attributed to differential reinforcement.

Rilling, Caplan, Howard, and Brown (1975) demonstrated the effectiveness of the resistance-to-reinforcement procedure in elevating responding to the S− dimension following errorless learning in which the rate of responding to S− was essentially zero throughout discrimination training. The results of this procedure for 15 successive days of generalization testing are illustrated in Figure 7. For both birds, the slope of the inhibitory gradient remained essentially unchanged during many sessions. While individual variability was observed in the shape of the gradients during the early sessions, the inhibitory gradients showed no tendency to invert and became excitatory with extended training as reported by Hearst, Besley, and Farthing (1970). Therefore, the resistance-to-reinforcement procedure reliably measures inhibitory stimulus control.

Combined Cues or Summation

Combined-cue tests are also designed to elevate response output to the S− dimension during the generalization test. Many investigators—e.g., Rescorla (1969a)—regard summation as the most direct method

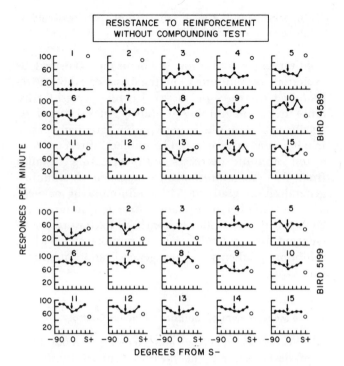

Fig. 7. Rate of responding to each test stimulus during each of the 15 days of generalization testing with the resistance to reinforcement procedure for birds 4589 and 5199. (From Rilling, Caplan, Howard, & Brown, 1975. © 1975 by the Society for the Experimental Analysis of Behavior, Inc.)

of measuring inhibition, especially when a classical conditioning paradigm is employed. In this method, S+ is presented simultaneously with test stimuli from the S− dimension. The assumption is that if the test stimulus has inhibitory properties, its presentation should produce a decrement in the presence of a stimulus associated with reinforced responding. In a study by Lyons (1969), using a combined-cues technique, S+ was a monochromatic light of 550 nm and S− was a white vertical line on a black background. During a stimulus-generalization test, the angle of the line was varied, but each test stimulus from the S− dimension was superimposed upon S+. Surprisingly, *excitatory* generalization gradients were obtained with the *peaks* at S−. In a similar experiment using a combined-cues test in which lines at various angles were superimposed upon S+, Davis (1971) obtained evidence for the inhibitory property of the line, since all such compound stimuli produced lower rates of responding than S+ alone. However, for some birds maximum responding occurred when S− was combined with S+. These data are anomalous, since S− was an inhibitory stimulus, while a decremental gradient was obtained around S−.

However, Drexler and Terrace's unpublished data

suggest that Lyons's and Davis's failure to obtain inhibitory stimulus control may have been due to a high rate of responding to S− prior to the stimulus-generalization test. These studies indicate that adequate interpretation of stimulus-generalization gradients requires data showing the rates of responding to S+ and S− during the acquisition of the discrimination prior to the generalization test.

At present, the combined-cues method is the least satisfactory procedure for measuring inhibitory dimensional control. Superimposing S+ upon S− may not produce the desired increase in responding in the presence of S− during the generalization test, as Yarczower (1970) noted. The presence of S+ may overshadow stimuli from the S− dimension and produce a flat gradient. Furthermore, the measurement of inhibition is dependent upon the strength of reinforced responding, so that the detection of inhibition is more likely when the reinforced behavior is weak and susceptible to disruption than when the reinforced behavior is strong and resistant to disruption. Consistent with this view, Yarczower and Evans (1974) found that an increase in the amount of training was accompanied by a reduction in the amount of external inhibition to a novel stimulus.

STIMULUS-REDUCTION OR
ADVANCE PROCEDURE

The fourth technique for measuring inhibitory stimulus control is stimulus reduction. Several investigators (Rilling, Askew, Ahlskog, & Kramer, 1969; Rilling, Kramer, & Richards, 1973; Terrace, 1971) have demonstrated that pigeons acquire a response that terminates and thereby reduces the duration of the stimulus associated with extinction. These data indicate that a stimulus associated with the absence of reinforcement may become a conditioned aversive stimulus. As Honig, Beale, Seraganian, Lander, and Muir (1972) point out, none of the current definitions of *inhibition* deals with the possibility that it may be defined by a reduction in the duration of S−. Rather, the definitions concentrate upon a reduced rate of responding in the presence of a stimulus as the criterion for inhibition. Unfortunately, this had led most investigators to neglect duration as a parameter of an inhibitory stimulus.

SELECTING A METHOD FOR ASSESSING
INHIBITORY STIMULUS CONTROL

Rescorla (1969a) and Hearst (1972) argue that the "most direct" method is the best, and they lean toward the combined-cues test as the method of choice. The problem here is that no criterion is employed for ranking procedures on a scale of "directness." The combined-cues test is probably employed more frequently because of its historical precedent in Pavlov's work. An empirical criterion should be employed in selecting a procedure for measuring inhibitory stimulus control. The most sensitive procedure is usually the best choice. Hearst's (1972) point that experimenters should employ a variety of methods and compare the results of different procedures is worthy of further emphasis. It seems likely that the results of such research will demonstrate that the different measures of inhibitory stimulus control are not always highly correlated.

Spence's Theory of Discrimination Learning

ASSUMPTIONS AND
QUALITATIVE PREDICTIONS

Spence's (1937) analysis of what is now called intradimensional learning has become a classic. Although this theory evolved before the development of operant techniques, it provides the best explanation for the effects of intradimensional training on the postdiscrimination gradient. The theory includes the following five assumptions:

1. Reinforcement of responding to a stimulus (S+) produces an excitatory tendency to respond to S+.
2. Excitation generalizes around S+.
3. Extinction of responding to a stimulus (S−) produces an inhibitory tendency opposite to the tendency associated with S+.
4. Inhibition generalizes around S−.
5. The predicted response to any test stimulus is obtained by subtracting the amount of inhibition to the stimulus from the amount of excitation to the stimulus.

Spence developed his theory to account for transposition, which is observed in a simultaneous discrimination when the subject prefers to S+ a novel stimulus which is displaced from S+ in a direction away from S−. Riley (1968) has provided a thorough review of the theories and research on the transposition problem. However, the transposition experiments did not provide a crucial test of Spence's theory, since the hypothetical gradients of excitation and inhibition were never directly measured.

Spence's theory is easily extended to successive discrimination experiments. Following intradimensional training, the postdiscrimination gradient is the resultant of the interaction between excitation and inhibition. Therefore, the number of responses emitted to each test stimulus during a generalization test is obtained by subtracting the amount of generalized inhibition to S− from the amount of generalized excitation to S+.

Spence's algebraic summation or gradient-interaction theory produces the following major predictions about the shape of the postdiscrimination gradient following intradimensional discrimination training:

1. The maximum or peak of the generalization gradient occurs at a test stimulus which is displaced from S+ in a direction away from S−. This is the positive peak shift.
2. The minimum of the generalization gradient occurs at a test stimulus which is displaced from S− in a direction away from S+. This is the negative peak shift.
3. The magnitude of the peak shift increases as the difference between S+ and S− is reduced. The peak shift is not obtained with a large difference between S+ and S−, since there is no overlap or interaction between the excitatory and inhibitory gradients.
4. The peak shift does not occur if the inhibitory gradient is flat or horizontal. Subtracting a constant from the excitatory gradient yields a predicted gradient with the peak at S+.
5. Rate of responding to S+ is reduced by discrimination training relative to the single-stimulus base line. Therefore, the number of responses to each stimulus in the postdiscrimination gradient should be less than the number of responses in the excitatory gradient obtained following single-stimulus training.

MATHEMATICAL CONSTRAINTS ON
SPENCE'S THEORY

When Spence (1937) first proposed his theory, he was forced to speculate about the theoretical shape of the excitatory and inhibitory gradients. This was a weakness which he readily acknowledged. His approach was essentially intuitive, illustrated with graphs of convex hypothetical generalization curves which have been reproduced in most learning texts. Critics have pointed out that not all excitatory and inhibitory functions generate the predictions described above. For example, Hull (1943) noted that exponential or concave gradients fail to predict the peak shift. In addition, Hebert and Krantz (1965) and D. Blough (1969) have shown that linear or tent-shaped gradients also fail to predict peak shifts.

What relationship between the excitatory and inhibitory gradients is necessary and sufficient for a

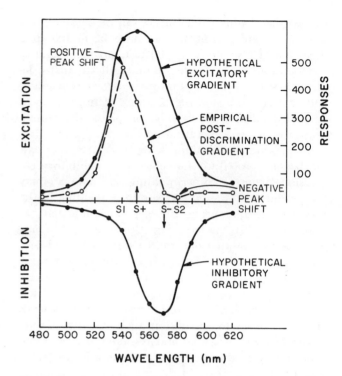

Fig. 8. Post hoc prediction of the postdiscrimination gradient using Spence's algebraic summation theory. The empirical postdiscrimination gradient was obtained by Hanson (1959) with S+ at 550 and S− at 570 nm. The empirical gradient is obtained by subtracting the hypothetical inhibitory gradient from the hypothetical excitatory gradient. The hypothetical functions were selected to yield the positive peak shift, in which the peak of the empirical gradient was displaced from 550 nm to 540 nm and the negative peak shift in which the minimum was displaced from 570 to 580 nm. (Original figure prepared by Marty Klein.)

quantitative prediction of the positive and negative peak shifts? To answer this consider Figure 8, which presents one of Hanson's (1959) empirical postdiscrimination gradients from Figure 4 of this chapter, which shows both positive and negative peak shifts. Hypothetical gradients of excitation and inhibition which sum algebraically to yield Hanson's data were devised post hoc. These are also presented in Figure 8. The hypothetical gradient of excitation has a maximum at S+, and the hypothetical gradient of inhibition has a minimum at S−.

On the empirical postdiscrimination gradient, maximal responding occurred to S1, a stimulus displaced from S+ in a direction away from S−. Minimal responding occurred to S2, a stimulus displaced from S− in a direction away from S+. It can be proven mathematically[1] that in order to obtain a positive peak shift from S+ to S1, the slope of the inhibitory gradient between S+ and S1 must be *steeper* than the slope of the excitatory gradient between S+ and S1.

[1] I thank Marty Klein for developing this proof.

Similarly, a necessary and sufficient condition for the negative peak shift from S⁻ to S2 is that the slope of the excitatory gradient between S⁻ and S2 be *steeper* than the slope of the inhibitory gradient between S⁻ and S2.

The next problem is the selection of a family of curves which best fit the excitatory and inhibitory gradients obtained after interdimensional training. Since theorists (e.g., Rescorla, 1969a; Spence, 1936, 1937) define *excitation* and *inhibition* as opposite behavioral processes, excitatory and inhibitory gradients from the same family are most appropriate. Gaussian discriminal distributions, of which the bell-shaped normal distribution curve is the most familiar example, are the best mathematical model for describing the shape of the excitatory and inhibitory gradients obtained after interdimensional training. (See Blough, 1969, and Nunally, 1967, for further discussion of these distributions.) Blough (1967, 1969) obtained bell-shaped gradients by presenting several test stimuli which were spaced closely to the training stimulus. Sharp peaks in published gradients may just reflect a lack of data points in the vicinity of S⁺.

In order to predict the positive and negative peak shifts simultaneously, and still have some positive values in the postdiscrimination gradient, either the entire excitatory gradient must be further from the abcissa than the inhibitory gradient or the inhibitory gradient must be a flatter bell than the excitatory gradient. Empirical evidence (Hearst, 1968, 1969b; Honig et al., 1963; Jenkins & Harrison, 1962) suggests that inhibitory gradients are indeed flatter than excitatory gradients. Jenkins (1965, pp. 58–59) implies that flatter inhibitory gradients must be the case when stimulus control along the S⁻ dimension is measured by the number of responses (such as key pecking) which are reinforced during S⁺. There are two subclasses of responses, other than key pecking, which must be considered: (1) incompatible responses, such as turning away from the key, which are presumably conditioned during S⁻, and (2) all other responses. In plotting the inhibitory gradient, only a decrease in the subclass of incompatible responses which appears as an increase in the response that is reinforced in S⁺ contributes to the slope of the inhibitory gradient. An increase in all other responses lowers the overall level of responding and flattens the inhibitory gradient.

Quantitative Tests of Spence's Theory

Appetitive base lines. The hypothetical nature of the excitatory and inhibitory gradients is a major weakness of Spence's theory. The development of interdimensional training techniques has removed this ambiguity, since the shape of the excitatory and inhibitory gradients can be empirically determined. The methodology for the prediction of the peak shift from gradients of excitation and inhibition has been developed by Hearst (1968, 1969b).

The basic design involves three groups which are given successive discrimination training. The preexcitation group is given interdimensional training with an S⁺ selected from the dimension of generalization and an orthogonal S⁻. Discrimination training is followed by a generalization test which produces an empirical excitatory gradient. The preinhibition group is given interdimensional training with an S⁻ selected from the dimension of generalization and an orthogonal S⁺. The generalization test produces an empirical inhibitory gradient. The third group is given intradimensional training with the S⁺ of the preexcitation group and the S⁻ of the preinhibition group. A generalization gradient is also obtained after intradimensional training.

Hearst's analysis does not assume that the gradient obtained after intradimensional training has the same form as those obtained after interdimensional training. In fact, intradimensional gradients are often asymmetric, while interdimensional gradients are often symmetrical. The analysis simply predicts the postdiscrimination gradient for the intradimensional group by subtracting the inhibitory gradient from the excitatory gradient.

One problem is that the absolute gradients vary greatly in the mean total number of responses to the test stimuli due to the occurrence of behavioral contrast during the acquisition of the discrimination. When the groups were equated in Hearst's study (1968) by converting the absolute gradients to relative gradients, a reasonably good fit was obtained between a predicted and the obtained postdiscrimination gradient by subtracting the relative inhibitory gradient from the relative excitatory gradient. Unfortunately, the analysis was weakened by Hearst's failure to obtain a peak shift for the group that received intradimensional training.

Hearst (1968, 1969b) employed the dimension of the angle of the line in his experiments. Using the design developed by Hearst, Marsh (1972) employed the wavelength dimension to see if the subtraction of an empirical inhibitory gradient from an excitatory gradient produced a predicted gradient including the peak shift which corresponded to the gradient obtained after intradimensional training. Marsh's predicted postdiscrimination gradient displayed a peak shift and showed a rough correspondence to the actual postdiscrimination gradient. Thus the data derived from an appetitive base line provide some support for the gradient-interaction theory proposed by Spence.

Aversive base lines. In contrast with the extensive literature on the influence of environmental stimuli on behavior maintained by schedules of positive reinforcement, very little is known about the influence of environmental stimuli on behavior maintained by schedules of negative reinforcement, although Sidman (1966, p. 494) demonstrated stimulus control of free operant avoidance behavior. The earlier experiments in the stimulus control of behavior maintained by aversive stimuli were analyzed by Hearst (1969a) in a pioneering paper which concluded that similar laws of generalization applied to positive and negative reinforcement. Hearst found that the parameters of the base line rather than the type of behavioral base line determined the shape of the stimulus-generalization gradient.

Basing their experiment upon Hearst's design, Klein and Rilling (1972) investigated the prediction of gradients following intradimensional training with an aversive base line. Pigeons were trained to press a treadle on a shock-postponement schedule in which brief 4-mA shocks followed one another at 5-sec intervals (S–S interval) unless the treadle was pressed. After a treadle press, the next shock occurred after 20 sec (R–S interval). After avoidance responding stabilized, auditory discriminative stimuli were introduced. The positive stimulus (S+) was associated with the avoidance schedule, while the negative stimulus (S−) was associated with extinction of avoidance without shocks. For the excitatory group, S+ was a 1,000-Hz tone and S− was noise; for the inhibitory group, S+ was noise and S− was a 1,500-Hz tone; and for the intradimensional group, S+ was a 1,000-Hz tone and S− was a 1,500-Hz tone. After reaching a criterion for the acquisition of the discrimination, each group was given an identical stimulus-generalization test along the frequency dimension.

Two types of generalization tests were employed: resistance to extinction, in which there were no scheduled shocks; and resistance to (negative) reinforcement, in which one avoidable shock occurred 5 sec after the beginning of each test *tone* presentation if the animal failed to respond during the first 5 sec. The resistance-to-negative-reinforcement procedure was developed as an analog to the procedure developed by Hearst et al., for positive reinforcement, in order to elevate the rate of responding along the S− dimension. This technique is also similar to Hoffman's (1966, pp. 516–517) use of noncontingent shocks between stimulus presentations which increased stimulus control in a conditioned suppression paradigm.

The relative gradients for the three groups are presented in Figure 9. The left panel shows the gradients obtained with shock, and the right panel shows the gradients obtained without shock. For Group I, the excitatory group, in which S+ was 1,000 Hz and S− was noise, the peak of the gradients occurred at S+. For Group II, the inhibitory group, in which S+ was noise and S− was 1,500 Hz, an inhibitory gradient with a minimum at S− was obtained. For Group III,

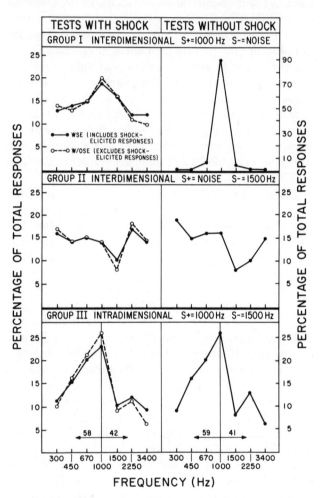

Fig. 9. The upper panel presents the relative excitatory gradients obtained for Group I. The center panel presents the relative inhibitory gradients obtained for Group II. The lower panel presents the relative postdiscrimination gradients. The gradients on the left are the results of tests conducted with avoidable shocks. In these gradients, the solid-lined gradients (WSE) include shock-elicited responses, while the broken-lined gradients (W/OSE) exclude shock-elicited responses. The gradients on the right are from tests conducted without scheduled shocks. Tones are spaced at approximately equal intervals along a log scale. Note that the ordinate scale for the Group I no-shock gradient (upper right) differs from the other ordinate scales. (From Klein and Rilling, 1974. © 1974 by the Society for the Experimental Analysis of Behavior, Inc.)

the intradimensional condition, in which S+ was 1,000 Hz and S− was 1,500 Hz, an asymmetric gradient with a maximum at S+ and a minimum at S− was obtained. Only one of the four birds in the intradimensional group showed a peak shift. When pecking was reinforced with food, Jenkins and Harrison (1962) obtained a peak shift with an S+ of 1,000 Hz and an S− of 950 Hz. Possibly the difference between S+ and S− in the Klein and Rilling experiment may have been too large to obtain a peak shift.

The left panel of Figure 10 illustrates how the inhibitory gradient was subtracted from the excitatory gradient to yield a derived postdiscrimination gradient (PDG). The right panel of Figure 10 shows that reasonable agreement was obtained between the predicted PDG 1 and the empirical relative gradient obtained from Group III, since four of the seven points matched almost exactly. The prediction is improved further by converting to proportions in PDG 2.

Figure 9 shows that the relative excitatory gradient was much steeper for the tests without shock than for the tests with shock. Actually, very few responses to each test stimulus were obtained for the excitatory gradients without shock. The predictions in Figure 10 would have been much worse had the data for the tests without shock been employed, but the tests with shock probably provide a more accurate picture of the generalization process.

In general, the results of the experiments of Hearst, Marsh, and Klein and Rilling support Spence's gradient-interaction theory and suggest that the determinants of generalization on appetitive and aversive base lines are similar.

Dynamic Models of Stimulus Control

While Spence's theory integrates much of the data on stimulus control, it is inadequate in accounting for a growing number of phenomena. In some cases, responding is found to be enhanced in the presence of a stimulus near an S−, and responding is diminished in the presence of a stimulus near an S+. Several dynamic models have been developed (D. Blough, 1975; Rescorla & Wagner, 1972; Wagner & Rescorla, 1972) which incorporate such phenomena that are not easily handled by Spence's theory. The basic assumptions of their model are stated by Rescorla and Wagner (1972) as follows:

> The effect of a reinforcement or nonreinforcement in changing the associative strength of a stimulus depends upon the existing associative strength, not only of that stimulus, but also of other stimuli concurrently present. It appears that the changes in associative strength of a stimulus as a result of a trial can be well-predicted from the composite strength resulting from all stimuli present on that trial. If this composite strength is low, the ability of a reinforcement to produce increments in the strength of component stimuli will be high; if the composite strength is high, reinforcement will be relatively less effective. Similar generalizations appear to govern the effectiveness of a nonreinforced stimulus presentation. If the composite associative strength of a stimulus compound is high, then the degree to which a nonreinforced presentation will produce decrements in the associative strength of the components will be large; if the composite strength is low, the effect of a nonreinforcement will be reduced. (p. 73)

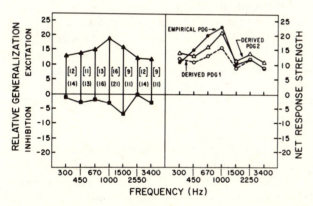

Fig. 10. (Left) Relative gradients of excitation (closed triangles) and inhibition (squares). The excitatory gradient is the WSE gradient of Figure 9 (upper left). The inhibitory gradient is calculated from the WSE gradient of Figure 9 (center left). The numbers in the square brackets alongside the vertical lines between the gradients represent the algebraic sum of the two points that the particular line connects. The numbers in parentheses along the same vertical lines were obtained by transforming the numbers in square brackets to a scale of 100. (Right) Empirical (closed-circles) postintradimensional discrimination gradient (PDG) of relative generalization from Figure 9 (WSE), compared with PDGs derived from the calculations on the left. The values on derived PDG 1 are from the square brackets on the left, while the values on derived PDG 2 are from the parentheses on the left. (From Klein & Rilling, 1974. © 1974 by the Society for the Experimental Analysis of Behavior, Inc.)

Two experiments by D. Blough (1975) illustrate the utility of a dynamic model of stimulus control. In these experiments the rate of responding to stimuli along a continuum is observed. Associative strength is manipulated by associating a moderate rate of reinforcement with each stimulus on the continuum which produces an above-zero base line. A decremental gradient is obtained by increasing the frequency of reinforcement in the presence of one stim-

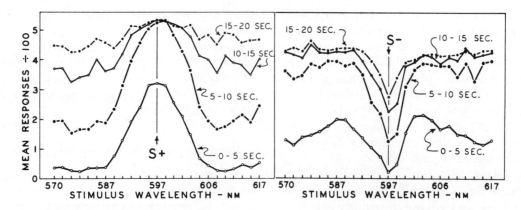

Fig. 11. (Left) A family of excitatory gradients for one bird classified by breaking down the 20-sec interval into four 5-sec periods. The gradients become flatter as the end of the interval approaches. (Right) A family of inhibitory gradients for one bird classified within the FI 20-sec base line. Note the "shoulders" to the left and right of 597 for the 0–5-sec functions and the apparent ceiling effect in curves collected during the last two quarters of the trial interval. The excitatory gradients were obtained by increasing the probability of reinforcement in the presence of 597 relative to the other test stimuli, and the inhibitory gradients were obtained by decreasing the probability of reinforcement at 597 nm. (From Blough, 1975. © 1975 by the American Psychological Association. Reprinted by permission.)

ulus, while an incremental gradient is obtained by decreasing the frequency of reinforcement.

The base line was an FI 20-sec schedule and responses were recorded within 5-sec intervals: 0–5, 5–10, and 15–20 sec from the onset of the fixed interval. The probability of food at the end of the interval was .1. The moderate rate of reinforcement for all of the stimuli assured an above-zero base line prior to generalization testing. The most important aspect of this procedure is that an excitatory gradient was obtained by increasing the probability of reinforcement during 597 nm, S+; and following a return to the base line, an inhibitory gradient was obtained by decreasing the probability of reinforcement to 597 nm, now an S−. These results are presented in Figure 11. Responses are shown separately for each of the four 5-sec periods within the 20-sec trial interval. The FI schedule was selected to avoid a "ceiling effect" in which the rate of responding is so high that it is not influenced by the value of the test stimulus. Generalization was measured each day with a maintained procedure in which several test trials were included within each session.

In Figure 12 the probability of reinforcement was four times higher for the long-wavelength trials than it was for the reinforcer that ended short-wavelength trials. The rate of responding immediately to the right of the boundary between reinforcement probabilities is accentuated relative to the other stimuli receiving the same probability of reinforcement, while the rate of responding to the left of the boundary is attenuated relative to the other stimuli receiving the same probability of reinforcement. Thus the boundary between reinforcement conditions for multiple stimuli on a continuum is an important determinant of inhibitory stimulus control. These data confirm experiments of Catania and Gill (1964) and Farthing (1974). Blough has developed a dynamic mathematical model, similar to that of Rescorla and Wagner (1972), that provides an excellent fit to these data. This

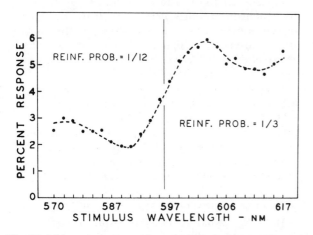

Fig. 12. Mean relative rate of responding for three birds. Data were obtained during discrimination training in which reinforcement was four times as frequent in the conditioned reinforcer that ended long-wavelength trials as it was in the conditioned reinforcer that ended short-wavelength trials. Note the trough and peak to the left and right of the dividing line between low and high reinforcement. (From Blough, 1975. © 1975 by the American Psychological Association. Reprinted by permission.)

phenomenon is also analogous to the Mach bands obtained in visual perception which are produced by differences in luminance between adjacent regions of the stimulus.

In Blough's experiments, each stimulus presentation was followed by an interval of 5–12 sec during which any responses on the dark key were extinguished. Weiss's research on stimulus compounding suggests that what is learned when the discriminative stimuli are "off" is an important determinant of stimulus control. Therefore, perhaps Blough's results would have been different without the dark key.

One of the controversial issues in stimulus control, as Hearst et al. (1970) point out, has been the search for a neutral zone between excitation and inhibition. They point out that an incremental gradient around S− does not indicate whether that stimulus is neutral or inhibitory. It could be argued that a concept of inhibition is not necessary to explain Blough's data, since the behavior could also be explained in terms of reduced excitation. It would be useful to extend Blough's procedure to interdimensional training to determine if the combination of S− with S+ produces a decrement in responding. Such a procedure would establish that S− is an inhibitory stimulus.

Blough's data suggest that inhibition occurs relative to a base line probability of reinforcement in the presence of the background stimuli. There is, therefore, no point of absolute neutrality, only increments or decrements from the base line of nondifferential reinforcement. Stimuli associated with reduced rates of reinforcement demonstrate some of the same inhibitory phenomena as do stimuli associated with extinction. An important empirical question is the extent to which similar functional relationships are obtained between these two conditions.

DETERMINANTS OF THE PEAK SHIFT AND INHIBITORY STIMULUS CONTROL

Historically, the peak shift was investigated before interdimensional training led to the discovery of the inhibitory stimulus-generalization gradient. Consequently, much more is known about the determinants of the former than of the latter. Hearst's three-group design provides the most promising framework for a quantitative analysis of the relationship between interdimensional and intradimensional training. Unfortunately, experiments which compare the two types of discrimination training under equivalent conditions are rare. However, the available data (Hearst, 1969b; Klein & Rilling, 1974; Marsh, 1972) suggest that the determinants of the peak shift and the inhibitory gradient are identical.

Since Klein and Rilling obtained inhibitory gradients on an avoidance base line, it appears that the peak shift and inhibitory control do not depend on whether responding is maintained by an appetitive or an aversive base line.

In the sections which follow, a unified theory of the peak shift and inhibitory dimensional control will be presented. Consideration will be given to those variables which fail to produce the peak shift and inhibitory dimensional control. This analysis sheds some light on the necessary and sufficient conditions for these effects.

Amount of Training

Most theories of discrimination learning, including those of Spence (1936) and Hull (1943), predict that the excitatory and inhibitory gradients become steeper as a function of the amount of discrimination training. If the determinants of the peak shift and inhibitory stimulus control are the same, the probability of obtaining the peak shift should also increase as a function of the amount of training. Empirical investigation of the influence of the amount of training, defined by the number of sessions, indicates that this variable is indeed one of the most important determinants of the peak shift and inhibitory stimulus control. It is not clear at present, though, which aspects of this variable—e.g., number of reinforcements, duration of exposure to the discriminative stimuli, number of alternations between S+ and S−, etc.—are critical in determining the slope of the generalization gradient.

INTRADIMENSIONAL TRAINING

Thomas (1962) observed the acquisition of the area peak shift by administering a short generalization test to each subject following every even-numbered session of discrimination training. After only 30 min of exposure to S−, a reliable shift in the area of the gradient was observed, sometimes even before the rates of responding to S+ and S− began to separate. The magnitude of the area shift increased as a negatively accelerated function of the amount of training.

Once the effects of short amounts of training were determined, investigators turned to the effects on the peak shift of training extended over many sessions. Terrace (1966a) administered generalization tests following the 15th, 30th, 45th, and 60th sessions of discrimination training between two wavelength stimuli with: 580 nm (S+) and 506 nm (S−). The peak of the first gradient occurred at 600 nm, a peak shift of 20 nm. During the next two generalization tests, the magnitude of the peak shift *decreased* to 10 nm, and by the last generalization test, the peak shift had disappeared and the peak reverted back to S+. Positive behavioral contrast also decreased with extended training. In *positive behavioral contrast,* the response rate in the constant component increases when the response rate in the variable component is decreased by extinction. These data led Terrace to the conclusion that determinants of behavioral contrast and of the peak shift are identical.

Data obtained in subsequent experiments disprove Terrace's interpretation. Dukhayyil and Lyons (1973) determined the effects of 105 days of intradimensional training on behavioral contrast and the peak shift. As in Terrace's experiment, generalization tests were administered at regular intervals. While no bird showed a peak shift on each test, a majority of the birds showed a peak shift after 105 days of training. Substantial fluctuations in the rate of responding to S+ were obtained. Therefore on a day-by-day basis, the occurrence of the peak shift is not correlated with the existence of contrast (i.e., with response rate in S+). Both behavioral contrast and the peak shift are obtained after extended discrimination training.

Interdimensional Training

In an independent groups design, Hearst and Koresko (1968) administered a generalization test following different amounts of training in which responding in the presence of S+ was nondifferentially reinforced. The shallow excitatory gradient which was obtained on the second day of training became progressively steeper through 14 days of training.

In the Hearst and Koresko study, the acquisition of the response was confounded with the acquisition of dimensional stimulus control, since both processes occurred simultaneously. These processes were isolated by Schadler and Thomas (1972). In order to firmly establish the response, pecking the key was first nondifferentially reinforced during 10 daily 30-min sessions in the presence of a white key that was orthogonal to angularity, the dimension of stimulus control. Then generalization gradients were obtained after 0, 5, 10, or 20 min of nondifferential training in the presence of a single white vertical line on a black background. Dimensional control by angularity was acquired rapidly and approached asymptote after 20 min of nondifferential training. The Schadler and Thomas study demonstrated that the acquisition of response strength and the acquisition of stimulus control over responding are distinct, separable behavioral processes. Once the response is acquired, control by a stimulus associated with reinforcement may develop in a matter of minutes.

Farthing and Hearst (1968) determined how the amount of interdimensional training affected generalization of extinction. After seven sessions of nondifferential reinforcement which established the pecking response, five groups of pigeons received from 1 to 16

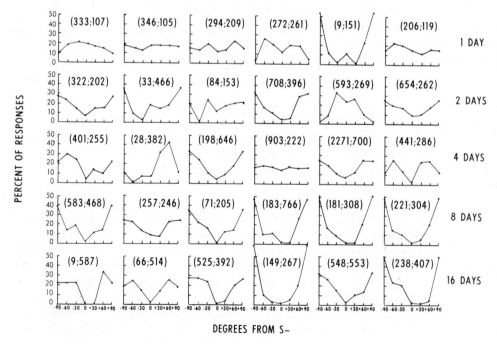

Fig. 13. Relative gradients of inhibition for individual birds in five groups that received from 1 to 16 days of discrimination training prior to the stimulus-generalization test. The probability of obtaining an inhibitory gradient within each group increases with the amount of training. The numbers in parentheses for each bird indicate, on the left, the total responses to the six-line test stimuli, and, on the right, the number of test responses to S+ (no line). (From Farthing & Hearst, 1968. © 1968 by the Society for the Experimental Analysis of Behavior, Inc.)

days of discrimination training. The S⁺ was a plain white field and S⁻ was a white field bisected by a black vertical line. Following discrimination training, each animal was given a generalization test in extinction, during which the angle of the line was varied. Figure 13 shows the relative gradient obtained from each bird. At least one steep inhibitory gradient was obtained at each condition of days of training. The basic effect of the independent variable was to increase over days the probability of obtaining an inhibitory gradient from each session. By Day 8, the probability was 1.0.

Hearst (1971) found that an inhibitory gradient obtained after 64 sessions of prolonged discrimination training had essentially the same shape as those obtained after 8 or 16 hours. Selekman (1973) replicated Farthing and Hearst's experiment, adding a correction procedure in which each response to S⁻ extended its duration. He found no relationship between the number of sessions and the slope of the inhibitory gradient which formed during the first session of discrimination training. Using stimulus compounding as an index of inhibition, Yarczower and Curto (1972) found that S⁻ suppressed positively reinforced responding during the first 10 min of discrimination training.

Thus in both the excitatory and inhibitory case, it appears that stimulus control is acquired in minutes rather than hours. The failure to find a relation between the amount of interdimensional training and the amount of inhibition appears related to the use of conditions that measure inhibition hours or sessions after inhibitory stimulus control has reached asymptote.

Aversive Baselines

Rilling and Budnik (1975) determined the influence of the amount of discrimination training on the acquisition of excitatory and inhibitory stimulus control in a treadle-press avoidance paradigm. During 21 days of interdimensional discrimination training, generalization was measured daily with a maintained procedure by randomly substituting each of six test frequencies for the 1,000-Hz training stimulus. Groups 1 and 2 were designed to measure the acquisition of excitatory stimulus control by associating the 1,000-Hz tone (S⁺) with a schedule of free operant avoidance and noise (S⁻) with extinction. Groups 3 and 4 were designed to measure the acquisition of inhibitory stimulus control by associating the noise (S⁺) with free operant avoidance and the 1,000-Hz tone (S⁻) with extinction.

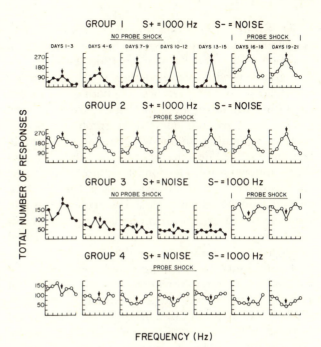

Fig. 14. Acquisition of gradients of excitation and inhibition. Groups 1 and 2 show the development of the excitatory gradient around S⁺, while Groups 3 and 4 show the development of the inhibitory gradient around S⁻. Each gradient was formed by adding the total number of responses to each stimulus across three days of training. Each data point is a sum for the three birds in each group. The closed circles show the gradients obtained without a probe shock, while the open circles show the gradients obtained with the addition of an unavoidable probe shock during each test stimulus. For Groups 1 and 3, the probe shock was present during sessions 16–21. For Groups 2 and 4, the probe shock was presented from the beginning of discrimination training. The arrow indicates the 1,000-Hz stimulus for each group. Note the different ordinate scales for Groups 1 and 2 and for Groups 3 and 4. The frequencies employed were from left to right: 300, 450, 670, 1,000, 1,500, 2,500, and 3,400 Hz. (From Rilling & Budnik, 1975. © 1975 by the Society for the Experimental Analysis of Behavior, Inc.)

The gradients are presented in Figure 14. For Group 1, an increasing number of responses to the 1,000-Hz tone (designated by an arrow) was observed as a function of the number of days of training. This increase indicates the birds' discrimination of the test stimuli, which were always presented during extinction, from the 1,000-Hz training stimulus, which was usually associated with the avoidance schedule. As discrimination training progressed, the gradients became steeper. The addition of the unavoidable shocks in Session 16 flattened the generalization gradient by elevating responding to the test stimuli more than responding to S⁺. For Group 2, unavoidable probe shock elevated responding to the test stimuli in comparison with Group 1. The steepening of the excitatory gradient with training was much less pronounced than in Group 1.

For Group 3, the acquisition of the discrimination is reflected in a rapid decrease in the number of responses to S− and flat gradients for Sessions 7–15. Flat gradients with low responding to the test stimuli are difficult to interpret because both neutral and inhibitory stimuli produce the same outcome in such situations. When the unavoidable probe shocks increased responding, inhibitory gradients emerged in Sessions 16–21. The emergence of the inhibitory gradients following introduction of the probe shocks reemphasized the equivocal nature of a flat stimulus-generalization gradient with a low response output. For Group 4, in which the probe shocks were present from Day 1, inhibitory gradients were obtained throughout discrimination training.

These results show striking parallels between positive and negative reinforcement for the acquisition of stimulus control and support Hearst's views that similar laws of generalization apply to positive and negative reinforcement. Both the excitatory and inhibitory gradients become steeper during the acquisition of the discrimination.

Summary

The amount of training has a similar influence on the acquisition of stimulus control following interdimensional and intradimensional discrimination training and supports a unified treatment of the two types of discrimination training. The acquisition of the response has often been confounded with the acquisition of stimulus control. When these processes are separated by providing nondifferential reinforcement of the response prior to discrimination training, excitatory and inhibitory stimulus control is acquired within minutes rather than hours. While more data on the minimum amount of training necessary for stimulus control would be desirable, the data suggest that the probability of obtaining the peak shift and inhibitory gradient increases in the course of discrimination training. Extended training has little influence once the necessary and sufficient conditions for the inhibitory gradient or peak shift have been established.

Stimulus Sequences and Massed Extinction

Spence's theory of discrimination learning does not explicitly consider sequential variables, such as frequency of alternation of S+ and S−. For Spence, the relevant variable determining inhibition is the amount of exposure to S−. In massed extinction, the subject is exposed to a single relatively long presentation of S− which contrasts with the distributed extinction obtained in a successive discrimination when S+ and S− are briefly presented in alternate or random sequences. Spence's theory of discrimination learning predicts a peak shift following massed extinction.

As it turns out, however, the sequential presentation of S+ and S− is essential for the peak shift and inhibitory stimulus control, a finding that Spence's theory of discrimination learning fails to predict. When S+ and S− were selected from the wavelength dimension, Honig, Thomas, and Guttman (1959) found that after 20 or 40 min of massed extinction to S−, the peak of the generalization gradient occurred at S+. A peak shift was obtained following an equivalent amount of exposure to each stimulus when the stimuli were presented alternately. Yarczower and Switalski (1969) also obtained no peak shift following massed extinction using goldfish as the experimental organism. Weisman and Palmer (1969) compared massed extinction and an equivalent amount of discrimination training with interdimensional presentations of the discriminative stimuli. The birds receiving massed extinction showed a flat gradient along the S− dimension, while an inhibitory gradient with the minimum at S− was obtained following successive discrimination training.

The typical successive discrimination is a mixture of four possible transitions: S+S+, S−S−, S+S−, and S−S+. The results of the above experiments indicate that the identical transitions, S+S+ and S−S−, are not effective in producing the peak shift and inhibitory stimulus control. In a well-designed and carefully controlled experiment, Ellis (1970) compared the effectiveness of the two opposite transitions: S+S− and S−S+. One group experienced a single S+S− alternation within each of several daily sessions, while the other group experienced a single S−S+ alternation. Ellis obtained a peak shift for the birds that received a transition between massed extinction and massed reinforcement, but the peak shift was absent for the group that received massed reinforcement followed by massed extinction. These data suggest that S−S+ transition is the necessary and sufficient condition for the peak shift. It would be interesting to replicate this experiment with interdimensional training to determine if the S−S+ transition is also necessary and sufficient for inhibitory stimulus control.

An experiment by Rosen and Terrace (1975) confirmed the absence of the peak shift and inhibitory stimulus control following massed extinction in the presence of intradimensional and interdimensional stimuli. These investigators found that the peak shift and inhibitory stimulus control were reinstated by the interpolation for 3 min between massed extinction and generalization testing of each of the following procedures: (1) the presentation of S+ *with* reinforced responding; (2) the presentation of S+ *without* reinforced responding; and (3) the presentation of food independently of responding in the presence of the dark key.

Yarczower (1974) found that, as compared with a group that received a generalization test without any extinction sessions, massed extinction sharpened control by the S+ stimulus. Although Yarczower's results are at variance with some of the earlier experiments, the data are in agreement with the finding that, although massed extinction may sharpen an excitatory gradient, it reduces the probability of obtaining inhibitory phenomena such as the peak shift and inhibitory stimulus control.

These experiments demonstrate that extinction of responding in the presence of S− is not inevitably followed by a peak shift or inhibitory stimulus control. The relevant variable seems to be the number of transitions from S− to S+.

Stimulus Context and Memory

Contextual stimuli are stimuli within the experimental apparatus that remain uncorrelated with the contingencies of reinforcement in the experimental chamber. Potential contextual stimuli are the lamps that illuminate the chamber (houselights), the level of the background noise, and the walls and floor of the chamber. Since these stimuli are not usually varied systematically during the course of an experiment, most investigators have assumed that they acquire no control over responding. However, contextual stimuli play a significant role in models of the inhibitory process (e.g., Wagner & Rescorla, 1972) and a theory of forgetting as retrieval failure (Spear, 1971). Therefore, it was inevitable that investigators would reassess the role of these background stimuli in the stimulus control of behavior.

Miller (1972) employed an *ABA* sequence of discrimination reversals to assess the role of stimulus context on stimulus control. Each of the three major experimental groups received identical conditions of discrimination training and generalization testing. In Phase 1, the discriminative stimuli were 576 nm (S+) and 555 nm (S−), while during Phase 2 the discriminative stimuli were reversed. In the third phase, each pigeon received a stimulus-generalization test on the wavelength dimension.

The groups differed with respect to the stimulus context. For Group $C_1C_1C_1$, the stimulus C_1 remained present throughout the three phases. For Group $C_1C_2C_2$, the stimulus context changed from C_1 to C_2 during Phase 2 and remained constant during the stimulus-generalization test. For Group $C_1C_2C_1$, the stimulus context changed from C_1 to C_2 during Phase 2 and reverted back to C_1 during generalization testing. Miller changed the stimuli gradually rather than abruptly between phases in order to avoid the loss of responding with changes in the contextual stimuli. The question of primary interest is whether the peak shift was appropriate to the discriminative stimuli of Phase 1 or Phase 2.

The main results of Miller's experiment are presented in Figure 15. For Group $C_1C_1C_1$, a bimodal gradient with maximums at 549 and 559 was obtained. The peak shift at 549 is appropriate for the final phase of discrimination training, while the peak at 559 reflects generalization from the S+ employed during the first phase. For Group $C_1C_2C_2$, the peak shift at 549 nm is appropriate to the contextual stimuli present during Phase 2 and generalization testing.

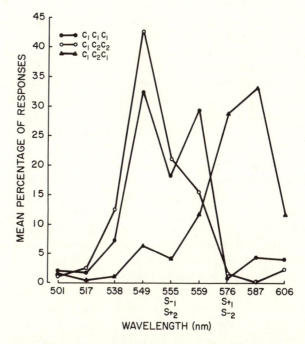

Fig. 15. Dependence of the peak shift upon the discriminative and background stimuli present during discrimination training and the generalization test. When the background stimuli remained constant, Group $C_1C_1C_1$, a bimodal gradient with maximums at 549 and 559 was obtained. With the presence of C_2 during reversal training and generalization testing, Group $C_1C_2C_2$, a peak shift occurred at 549 nm away from S_2^-. With the presence of C_1 during initial discrimination training and generalization testing, Group $C_1C_2C_1$, a peak shift occurred at 587 nm away from S_1^-, rather than the negative stimulus present during reversal training immediately prior to the generalization test, S_2^-. (Redrawn from Miller, 1972.)

The most dramatic influence of the contextual stimuli was obtained for Group $C_1C_2C_1$, in which the contextual stimuli present during generalization testing were associated with Phase 1 of discrimination training. This group yielded a peak shift at 587 nm appropriate to Phase 1. For this group, interference from Phase 2 was eliminated by manipulating the contextual stimuli. The contextual stimuli enabled the subjects to store the memory for the discriminative stimuli of Phase 1 independently of the memory for the discriminative stimuli of Phase 2. Although the contextual stimuli are presumably neutral since they are present during both S+ and S−, they exert powerful control over responding.

Miller's research demonstrates that paradigms originally developed for research on information processing in humans are also relevant to the stimulus control of behavior in infrahuman organisms and that the location of the peak of the stimulus-generalization gradient is a sensitive index of interference.

Schedules of Reinforcement

Variables associated with the schedule of reinforcement during discrimination training influence inhibitory stimulus control and the peak shift to a significant degree. For example, most experiments on stimulus control have employed a multiple schedule in which S+ was associated with reinforcement and S− with extinction. The alternation of these stimuli in a successive discrimination produces successive periods of responding at relatively high or low rates.

Whenever multiple schedules of reinforcement are utilized, two potential sources of influence on inhibitory phenomena are observed. One relates to the interaction between the relative rates of responding emitted to each stimulus. The other derives from the incentive contrast produced by the difference between the density of reinforcement in the two components. The following sections will deal with such questions as: (1) How much of a difference between the two rates of responding is necessary before inhibitory phenomena are produced? (2) Is inhibitory stimulus control present when a discrimination is established by different rates of reinforcement during the two stimuli? (3) If this is so, how much of an incentive difference between the reinforcers in the two components is necessary?

Fixed-interval Schedules

Every student of operant behavior is familiar with the scalloped pattern of responding produced by the fixed-interval (FI) schedule. The rate of the reinforced response is zero immediately after reinforcement and accelerates rapidly through the interval until the response is reinforced. This pattern is produced by the alternation of a period of extinction with a period of reinforcement availability. Staddon (1969) suggested that a stimulus-generalization test conducted by varying the stimulus present throughout the interval should produce inhibitory stimulus control at the beginning of the interval and excitatory stimulus control at the end of the interval. This is exactly the result obtained in an elegant experiment by Wilkie (1974).

Responses in the presence of a vertical line (0°) were reinforced on FI 3-min for two birds and FI 6-min for the third bird. In order to increase stimulus control by the line, each reinforcement was followed by a blackout of 10 min. Generalization was measured by randomly varying the angle of the line during different intervals. Each stimulus was present throughout the interval. An essential component of Wilkie's experiment was a maintained procedure in which responses were reinforced as usual throughout the generalization test.

The generalization gradients in the left-hand panel of Figure 16 show that an inhibitory gradient with a minimum at the vertical line was obtained from each bird during the first third of the interval, while an excitatory gradient was obtained during the last third. During the middle of the interval, the rate of responding was not influenced by the angle of the line. These results are dependent upon maintaining responding during the generalization test with reinforcement at the end of the interval. The right-hand panel of Figure 16 demonstrates that a family of excitatory gradients were obtained when the test was carried out during extinction with the omission of reinforcement.

Wilkie's results support the theory of temporal control developed by Staddon (1974). When food is delivered on a schedule with a constant period, Staddon predicts that food acquires inhibitory aftereffects that decay with the passage of time. Therefore, a stimulus associated with the termination of food acquires inhibitory stimulus control.

Multiple Schedules: Response Rate and Incentive Interactions

Under the typical conditions of discrimination training, a *mult* VI extinction schedule produces a peak shift following intradimensional training and an inhibitory gradient following interdimensional training. The data reviewed in this section demonstrate that the peak shift and inhibitory stimulus control

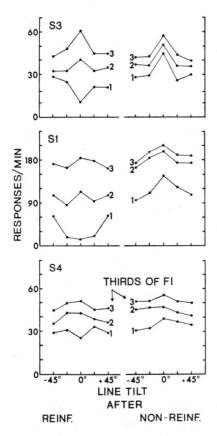

Fig. 16. Response rate in the presence of the lines at different angles during successive thirds of the fixed intervals that followed 0° intervals ending in reinforcement (left-hand panels) or nonreinforcement (right-hand panels). When responding is reinforced, an inhibitory gradient is obtained at the beginning of the interval and an excitatory gradient is obtained at the end of the interval. Rate is averaged for each of the three birds over five test sessions. (From Wilkie, 1974. © 1974 by the Society for the Experimental Analysis of Behavior, Inc.)

are also obtained under a wide range of conditions in which responding is reinforced during *each* of the two components. *Incentive* variables are the properties of the reinforcer that determine its effectiveness in maintaining responding. The delay, frequency of occurrence, magnitude, or intensity of a positive or negative reinforcer are incentive variables that combine with the rate of responding to determine the probability of the peak shift and the amount of inhibitory stimulus control. The relative incentive value of two schedules of reinforcement is operationally defined by the organism's degree of preference for the stimuli associated with each schedule when they are presented simultaneously. Measuring this preference requires an independent condition which unfortunately is rarely employed in experiments on stimulus control.

The analysis was suggested by some work of Weiss (1971, 1974) and Weiss and Van Ost (1974) in the area of stimulus compounding. Weiss (1974) formulated a model of stimulus control in which response and incentive properties conditioned to tone and light combine to produce the behavior resulting in T + L. Maximum additive summation occurs when T + L is composed of stimulus elements associated with an increase in both response and reinforcement rates. For maximum suppressive summation, T + L is composed of stimulus elements associated with a decrease in both. When only one factor is operating, response or reinforcement, while the other is constant over multiple-schedule components, T + L should control only moderate summation. When response and reinforcement properties are conflicting, one increasing and the other decreasing, minimal or no summation should occur to T + L. Since summation and peak shift are sensitive to many of the same variables, it could prove useful to apply Weiss's formulations to predictions of peak shift and inhibitory stimulus control.

Some new terminology must be introduced before translating from the stimulus-compounding to the stimulus-generalization paradigm. For the many cases in which a successive discrimination is established by reinforcing responding at different rates during each of the two components of a multiple schedule, the notation of S+ and S− is inadequate. In the convention followed here, the stimulus associated with *constant* conditions of reinforcement during prediscrimination and discrimination training is *S1*, and the stimulus associated with a *change* in the conditions of reinforcement is *S2*, whether the change is an increase or decrease in reinforcement density. Thus the rate of responding during S2 may either increase or decrease during the acquisition of the discrimination depending upon the nature of the change in reinforcement. In the special multiple schedule in which extinction is introduced after a period of nondifferential reinforcement, S+ corresponds to S1 and S− to S2.

Translating from the stimulus-compounding to the stimulus-generalization paradigm, the theory predicts that the probability of the peak shift and an inhibitory gradient is maximized when S1 controls a higher response rate and reinforcement frequency than S2. When S1 is associated with a change in only one of these variables, the probability of the peak shift and an inhibitory gradient is less. Finally, when S1 is discriminative for an increase in the response rate, but signals a decrease in the frequency of reinforcement, the probability of the peak shift and inhibitory gradient is minimized or eliminated.

The frequency of reinforcement during S1 and S2 has been specified and carefully controlled in many experiments. Therefore, the frequency of reinforcement rather than a direct measure of the incentive value or response strength is employed in the analysis of these experiments. The assumption made in this analysis is that the frequency of reinforcement is directly related to incentive value and may therefore serve as an estimate of the incentive value, although the correlation between the two remains to be verified. It is reasonable to assume that other variations in reinforcement affecting preference—e.g., delay, magnitude, and intensity—would act similarly in determining incentive differences.

Table 1, which is an adaptation of one Weiss (1974) presented in his analysis of response and incentive variables in the results of stimulus compounding, presents the results of stimulus-generalization tests following discrimination training in a number of studies. These experiments are classified with respect to the reinforcement and response rates in S2 as compared to S1. S1 is the stimulus associated with *constant* conditions of reinforcement during prediscrimination and discrimination training. S2 is the stimulus associated with a *change* in the conditions of reinforcement and/or response requirements, whether these changes are increases or decreases.

The response rate and reinforcement frequency in S2 may each decrease, increase, or remain unchanged during the acquisition of the discrimination. This yields a 3×3 matrix with nine cells. Each cell is subdivided according to whether intra- or interdimensional training was employed. For each experiment, the schedule associated with S1 is given first, followed by S2 in parentheses. The outcomes predicted by extrapolation of Weiss's theory are indicated within each cell as the probability of the peak shift following intradimensional training. The probability of an inhibitory gradient following interdimensional training is also presented. Each cell contains investigations meeting the response and reinforcement relations indicated for S1 and S2. In general, the fit is excellent, and, with the exceptions noted in the footnotes, the experiments support the predictions from Weiss's model.

The upper left cell, in which both the response rate and frequency of reinforcement during S2 decreased, was the starting point of this research effort. Hanson's (1959) original experiment, where responding in S2 was reduced through extinction while a VI schedule remained operative in S1, is the extreme arrangement for this cell. Guttman (1959) extended Hanson's original experiment on the peak shift with intradimensional discrimination training on a *mult* VI 1-min VI 5-min schedule instead of a *mult* VI 1-min extinction schedule. A peak shift away from the stimulus associated with the VI 5-min schedule was obtained during a stimulus-generalization test. The shape of the postdiscrimination gradient in Guttman's experiment was virtually identical to that obtained in Hanson's experiment, so the VI 5-min schedule was as effective as extinction in producing the peak shift. This result was confirmed by Terrace (1968) and by Wheatley and Thomas (1974). Since the peak shift was obtained when each discriminative stimulus was associated with a schedule of reinforcement, extinction during S2 is not necessary for the production of the peak shift.

Using intradimensional training Dysart, Marx, McLean, and Nelson (1974) systematically varied the frequency of reinforcement during S2 from VI 1-min through VI 5-min to extinction using a separate group of pigeons for each condition. Within each group, the probability of obtaining a peak shift away from S2 increased as a function of the decrease in the relative frequency of reinforcement associated with S2. Since the correlation between the rate of responding and the rate of reinforcement during S2 was +.97, it was not possible to specify which of these factors was responsible for the peak shift.

Among the most impressive evidence for a relative interpretation of the peak shift was a study by Wheatley and Thomas (1974) in which four of six pigeons showed a peak shift away from the VI 24-sec component of a *mult* VI 12-sec VI 24-sec schedule. The best predictor of the peak shift in their experiment was a discrimination index, responses to S1 divided by total responses. A poor discrimination index in the study by Yarczower, Dickson, and Gollub (1966) may explain why this study was the only failure to obtain a peak shift for the experiments in the upper left cell of Table 1. Wheatley and Thomas conclude that, given a good index of discrimination between S1 and S2, a peak shift is obtained away from S2 when S2 is associated with a high frequency of reinforcement, *provided* S1 is associated with a still higher frequency.

The Wheatley and Thomas study was carried out with a two-component multiple schedule. Suppose, following Weiss, that a three-component schedule is employed—e.g., *mult* VI 12-sec VI 24-sec EXT, with extinction associated with the absence of the discriminative stimuli. By this temporal manipulation of the stimulus context it seems possible that the peak shift would not be obtained.

Weisman (1969) ran a parallel interdimensional

Table 1 Results of Stimulus-generalization Experiments Classified According to Response Rate and Reinforcement Rate Differences Between S2 and S1

		RESPONSE RATE IN S2 COMPARED WITH S1		
		Decrease	*No Change*	*Increase*
REINFORCEMENT RATE IN S2 COMPARED WITH S1 *Decrease*	PREDICTION INTRADIMENSIONAL TRAINING	MAXIMUM PEAK SHIFT VI 1′ (VI 5′) Guttman (1959) Terrace (1968) Wheatley & Thomas (1974) VI 30″ (VI 1′)[a] VI 1′ (VI 2′) or (VI 5′) Dysart et al. (1974) VI 30″–DRL 4″ (VI 4′–DRL 8″) Yarczower et al. (1966)[a] VI 12″ (VI 24″) or (VI 60″) Wheatley & Thomas (1974)	MODERATE PEAK SHIFT VI 2.5′ (VI 5′) Wheatley & Thomas (1974)[a] VI 30″–DRL 4″ (VI 3′–DRL 2″) Yarczower et al. (1966)[a]	MINIMAL PEAK SHIFT No data
	PREDICTION INTERDIMENSIONAL TRAINING	MAXIMUM INHIBITORY GRADIENT VI 1′ (VI 5′) Weisman (1969)	MODERATE INHIBITORY GRADIENT No data	MINIMAL INHIBITORY GRADIENT No data
No Change	PREDICTION INTRADIMENSIONAL TRAINING	MODERATE PEAK SHIFT VI 1′ (DRL 6″) VI 1′ (VI 1′ + punishment) Terrace (1968) VI 1′ (DRO 50″) Yarczower et al. (1968) VI 1′–6″ Reinf. (VI 1′–2″ Reinf.) Mariner & Thomas (1969) VI 1′ (VI 1′ + delay) Wilkie (1972) VI 1′ (VT 1′) Huff et al. (1975)	MINIMAL PEAK SHIFT VI 1′ (DRL 6″) Terrace (1968)	MODERATE PEAK SHIFT No data
	PREDICTION INTERDIMENSIONAL TRAINING	MODERATE INHIBITORY GRADIENT VI 1′ (DRL) or (DRO) Weisman (1969, 1970) VI 1′ (VT 1′) Weisman & Ramsden (1973) VI 1′ (VI 1′ + delay) Richards (1973)	MINIMAL INHIBITORY GRADIENT VI 1′ (VT 1′) Weisman & Ramsden (1973)	MODERATE INHIBITORY GRADIENT No data
Increase	PREDICTION INTRADIMENSIONAL TRAINING	MINIMAL PEAK SHIFT VI 30″–DRL 4″ (DRO 10″) Yarczower et al. (1968)	MODERATE PEAK SHIFT No data	MAXIMAL PEAK SHIFT VI 5′ (VI 1′) Terrace (1968)[b] VI 1′–2″ Reinf. (VI 1′–6″ Reinf.) Mariner & Thomas (1969)
	PREDICTION INTERDIMENSIONAL TRAINING	MINIMAL INHIBITORY GRADIENT No data	MODERATE INHIBITORY GRADIENT No data	MAXIMAL INHIBITORY GRADIENT No data

[a] A peak shift was not obtained.
[b] Only one of the three birds showed a peak shift.
The Schedule Associated with S1 is Given First Followed by S2 in Parentheses.
SOURCE: Predictions adapted from Weiss's (1974) two-factor combinational model of stimulus control.

experiment on a multiple VI 1-min and VI 5-min schedule. A shallow inhibitory gradient on the dimension of line orientation was obtained for each of the animals where the rate of responding to S2 was reduced by a shift from VI 1-min to VI 5-min. If the determinants of the peak shift and the inhibitory gradient are identical, then, extending Wheatley and Thomas (1974), some pigeons should demonstrate an inhibitory gradient around a stimulus associated with a VI 24-sec schedule following interdimensional training on a *mult* VI 12-sec VI 24-sec schedule. Additional data are needed to determine the limits of inhibitory stimulus control following interdimensional training with various schedules associated with S1 and S2.

Spence viewed inhibition in absolute rather than relative terms and always identified inhibition with extinction. One of the major conclusions from the experiments in the upper left cell in Table 1 is that the peak shift and inhibitory stimulus control are determined by the relative rates of reinforcement during S1 and S2. Richards's unpublished experiment demonstrated that S2, a stimulus associated with a VI 1-min schedule in which reinforcement was delayed for 10 sec, was inhibitory and produced a decrement in responding when presented simultaneously with S1 in a combined-cues test. The amount of inhibition was less than was obtained when S2 was associated with extinction. These data reduce the appeal of Spence's original formulation and require a relative theory which assumes that S2 becomes an inhibitory stimulus when it is associated with a less favorable schedule of reinforcement.

In the experiments in the upper left cell of Table 1, the reduction in the frequency of reinforcement during S2 was confounded with a reduction in the rate of responding during S2. Therefore, the next logical step was to hold the frequency of reinforcement constant during S1 and S2 while reducing the rate of responding in the presence of S2. The experiments in which this procedure was employed are indicated in the middle cell of the "Decrease" column in Table 1. The evidence from these experiments is quite consistent: both the peak shift and inhibitory gradient are obtained. Therefore, reduction in reinforcement frequency during S2 is not necessary for these phenomena. Reduction of the response rate alone might be adequate. However, an equal frequency of reinforcement during S1 and S2 does not imply that the incentive values of S1 and S2 were identical. Although the relative incentive values of S1 and S2 were not measured in any of these experiments, it is likely that S1 is preferred to S2 when each

response to S2 is punished (Terrace, 1968), when the magnitude of reinforcement during S2 is smaller than S1 (Mariner & Thomas, 1969), when reinforcement during S2 is delayed (Richards, 1973; Wilkie, 1972), or when reinforcement during S2 is independent of responding (Huff, Sherman, & Cohn, 1975). Additional data are needed to determine if VI schedules are preferred to the DRL, (DRO), and VT schedules employed by Terrace (1968), Yarczower, Gollub, and Dickson (1968), Weisman (1969, 1970), and Weisman and Ramsden (1973). No data are available to determine if the peak shift and inhibitory stimulus control are obtained when the relative incentive values of S1 and S2 are identical.

A study by Yarczower et al. (1968), in the lower left cell of Table 1, suggests that the peak shift does not occur when the frequency of reinforcement during S2 is increased, but the rate of responding is decreased. The paucity of data in this cell indicates the lack of research under these conditions.

The "No Change" column of Table 1 presents data for experiments in which the rate of responding during S1 was identical to the rate during S2 so that differential responding between these stimuli was not present prior to the stimulus-generalization test. The data are remarkably consistent. Independently of the reinforcement rate during S2, the peak shift and inhibitory stimulus control are not obtained.

Weiss predicts that incentive differences alone should produce a moderate probability of the peak shift and inhibitory stimulus control when the rates of responding to S1 and S2 are identical. The Wheatley and Thomas (1974) and Yarczower et al. (1966) experiments fail to support this prediction, but we do not know if these subjects were discriminating the reinforcement differences between components, a necessary precondition for establishing different incentive values.

The "Increase" column of Table 1 indicates that in only two experiments has the discrimination been acquired by increasing the response rate during S2 while a lower rate is maintained during S1. The lower right cell indicates that the peak shift has been obtained by increasing both the frequency of reinforcement and response rate during S2 in the experiments of Terrace (1968) and Mariner and Thomas (1969). However, the data from these experiments are not as consistent as those in the upper left cell of Table 1. Perhaps this is because it is easier to establish a discrimination between S1 and S2 by decreasing rather than increasing the rate of responding during S2.

In general, these data support the conceptual framework developed by Weiss (1971, 1972, 1974) through his work in stimulus compounding, suggesting that incentive and rate differences between S1 and S2 combine to produce the peak shift and inhibitory stimulus control. Thus when the incentive parameters of S1 and S2 are held constant, the greater the index of discrimination between S1 and S2, the higher the probability of obtaining the peak shift or inhibitory stimulus control. When S1 and S2 control comparable response rates, this formulation predicts that the greater the incentive difference between S1 and S2, the higher the probability of obtaining the peak shift or inhibitory stimulus control. However, since it appears that these two variables might combine, the greatest probability of peak shift and the largest inhibitory effects are predicted for the upper left and lower right cells on Table 1 where large incentive and rate differences between S1 and S2 are established during discrimination training. Although this analysis was limited to positive reinforcement, similar results are predicted for responding maintained by negative reinforcement. The extent to which these variables determine the peak shift and inhibitory stimulus control awaits the results of further parametric research, but a glance at Table 1 indicates a remarkable consistency in the data from many different laboratories.

CONCURRENT SCHEDULES

In a concurrent schedule, two discriminative stimuli are presented at separate locations and responding to each stimulus is reinforced independently. Concurrent schedules are ideally suited for experiments designed to measure the influence of incompatible responses on the peak shift and inhibitory stimulus control. Although Spence's theory of discrimination learning was designed for the simultaneous paradigm, one of the ironies of research based on his theory is that some of the data that best fit Spence's theory were obtained from a successive paradigm.

Catania (1969) has developed a theory of inhibition which removes much of the mystery from this phenomenon by specifying the experimental procedures which produce the inhibited and inhibiting events. Consider the case in which a stimulus is presented on each of the left and right keys and responding on each key is reinforced according to a concurrent schedule. According to Catania, reinforcement of a response on the left key inhibits responding on the right key by increasing the probability of a further response on the left key. Similarly, reinforcing a response on the right key inhibits responding on the left key. As Catania puts it, "the rate of a reinforced response is inhibited by the reinforcement of other responses" (p. 741). The advantage of Catania's formulation is that it treats reinforcement (e.g., of a response on the left key) as the causal variable which produces inhibition (of responding on the right key). However, the "inhibition" of one response by the reinforcement of another does not necessarily imply that the stimulus controlling that response, or the lack of it, is an inhibitory stimulus. This requires an independent test for an inhibitory stimulus.

D. Blough (1973) obtained a peak shift on both the right and left keys following successive intradimensional training by reinforcing a response on the opposite key during S⁻. On the right key, stimuli of 550 and 559 nm were presented alternately as in the usual multiple schedule. The left key was always illuminated with a white diamond. Responses on the right key were reinforced in the presence of 550 nm and extinguished in the presence of 559 nm. On the left key the contingencies were reversed. Responses on the left key were reinforced in the presence of 559 nm (when it appeared on the right key) and extinguished in the presence of 550 nm. After discrimination training, two stimulus-generalization gradients were obtained by recording the number of responses to the left and right keys while the wavelength of the stimulus on the right key was varied.

The left panel of Figure 17 shows the gradients obtained from responses on the left key, and the right panel shows the gradients from the right key. The left panel of Figure 17 shows a peak shift for

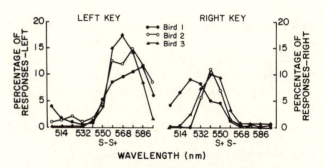

Fig. 17. (Left) Left-key generalization gradients from individual birds trained with VI reinforcement for pecks at the left key during 559 (S⁺) and extinguished during 550 (S⁻). On the left key, a positive peak shift with more responding to the longer wavelengths occurred. (Right) Right-key generalization gradients from individual birds reinforced for pecks on the right key during 550 nm (S⁺) and extinguished during 559 nm (S⁻). On the right key, a positive peak shift with more responding to the shorter wavelengths occurred. (From D. Blough, 1973.)

each of the birds with the maximum displaced from S+ (559 nm) toward a longer wavelength. The right panel shows a peak shift for each of the birds with the maximum displaced from S+ (550 nm) toward the short wavelengths.

In a similar experiment with interdimensional training, Catania, Silverman, and Stubbs (1974) obtained an inhibitory gradient on the left key by reinforcing responses on the right key when S− was present on the left key. Inhibitory processes have also been successfully investigated by Beale and Winton (1970), Winton and Beale (1971), and Honig et al. (1972), who measured generalization with a concurrent procedure in which an "advance" or changeover response was employed.

The experiments of D. Blough (1973) and Catania, Silverman, and Stubbs (1974) provide excellent support for Catania's theory of inhibition of one response by reinforcement of another response. However, it is important to emphasize that in Blough's experiment the peak shift was obtained when S+ alternated with S− in a successive discrimination on the same key. It is interesting to note that the peak shift was not obtained in experiments—e.g., Honig (1962, 1967)—in which S+ and S− were presented on different keys. When S+ was located on one key and S− on a different key, the probability of the peak shift might have decreased as a function of the distance between the keys, since this made the comparison of S+ with S− more difficult. The advantage of the concurrent procedures, which reinforce a response on the left key when extinction is in effect on the right key, is that the competing response is brought under experimental control.

ERRORLESS LEARNING RECONSIDERED

The previous sections described the influence of discrimination training on the shape of the generalization gradient and demonstrated the variables that have been established as the determinants of the peak shift and inhibitory stimulus control. This section considers the influence of a special type of discrimination training, "errorless" discrimination training, on stimulus control and inhibitory processes. *Errorless learning* refers to the class of discriminations in which the rate of responding to S− approaches zero from the first session of discrimination training. The major reason for the extensive interest in errorless learning is that it is considered an exception to the basic laws of discrimination learning developed in the previous sections.

What is Errorless Learning?

THE DEFINITION OF ERRORLESS LEARNING

The "error" of errorless learning is the occurrence during S− of the response that is reinforced during S+. The definition of an *error* depends upon the criteria employed for defining *response*. Consider the pecking response of the pigeon, which is the typical response in most experiments in errorless learning. This response consists of an orientation toward the key, an approach to the key, and a peck on the key. A response is usually defined automatically by a force of about 20 g on the key, and other components of the response are typically not recorded. The number of errors may be increased by relaxing the criterion for a response to include approach responses which do not contact the key, and the number of errors may be decreased by increasing the force of the peck required to activate the key or by restraining the animal from contacting the key. For example, a pigeon which made zero pecks on the key could be converted into a subject which learned with errors by counting near-misses, pecks around the key, etc.

Ethological analyses using procedures developed by Staddon and Simmelhag (1971) reveal a number of potentially interesting responses and response sequences which are modified during errorless discrimination training. These analyses indicate that errorless discrimination training procedures are effective in eliminating the terminal peck response from the sequence of observing and approach responses to S−. For example, Wessells (1974, Experiment III) obtained an errorless discrimination without fading using an autoshaping procedure. On half of the trials, a white light, (CS+), on the left key was immediately followed by food. On the other trials, a green key light, (CS−), was not followed by food. Wessells recorded three key-directed behaviors during each trial: (1) an orienting response described as "looking at the key," (2) an approach response defined as any movement toward the key, and (3) the peck at the key. Wessells found that the emergence of the pecking response was always preceded by an orientation-approach sequence. During S− isolated approach responses increased rapidly during the first few trials of discrimination training and then decreased, while during S+ the approach toward the key consistently increased. The orientation response behaves exactly as the traditional theory of discrimination predicts. During S+, the orientation response is maintained by reinforcement, while the response extinguishes during S−.

In order to obtain more data on the behaviors which are observed during the acquisition of an errorless discrimination, Rilling, Caplan, and Brown's unpublished study recorded the three responses specified by Wessells during errorless autoshaping and subsequent sessions of discrimination training in which the duration of each component was gradually increased to 1 min. After autoshaping, responses during S+ were reinforced on a VI 30-sec schedule. For 10 of the 12 birds in the experiment, the following sequence of responses emerged during successive S+ trials: an observing response appeared earliest, followed by an approach to the key, which was finally followed by pecks on the key. A hierarchy of responses was observed during S−. For each of the birds, the probability of an observing response was greater than the sum of the approach and key-peck responses during S−. The difference in behavior between S+ and S− is that reliable pecking does not emerge from the approach response during S−. Although many of the birds were errorless with respect to pecks on the key, they were not "errorless" with respect to the response of approaching the key. The responses for one of the errorless pigeons are presented in Figure 18.

Since the definition of an *error response* during S− is arbitrary, it follows that the definition of *errorless learning* is also arbitrary. Researchers of errorless learning tend to differentiate cases of learning without errors from cases of learning with errors based upon the absolute number of errors produced throughout the experiment. Terrace (1972) described subjects exhibiting few errors (on the order of 25 or fewer for the parameters of his experiment) as performing fundamentally the same as subjects which made no errors at all. Both groups were labeled "errorless," as they appeared distinct from subjects which made substantially more nonreinforced responses during S−.

This classification is theoretically useful if the performance of those subjects which make zero or a few errors, however defined, during S− is fundamentally different from those subjects which make many errors. The data reviewed in this section demonstrate that this classification is *not* useful, because few phenomena of discrimination learning depend reliably upon the rate of responding during S−. Therefore, the distinction between learning without errors and learning with errors is arbitrary. A more fruitful strategy may be to isolate those variables that determine the rate of responding during S− and to develop theories that predict these rates. This strategy avoids the embarrassing question of how many errors are necessary before errorless learning becomes errorful learning.

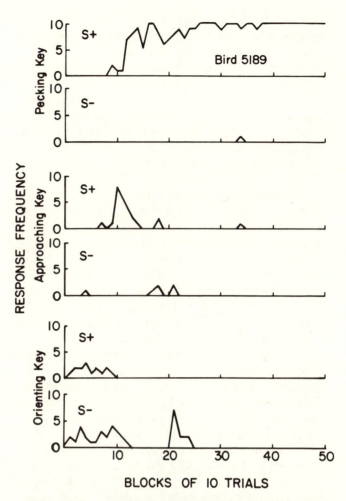

Fig. 18. Number of responses pecking the key, approaching the key, and orienting toward the key during S+ and S− for bird 5189 during the acquisition of a "errorless discrimination." During S+ orienting and approaching the key preceded the emergence of pecking, while during S− orienting and approaching the key were *not* followed by pecking. (From Rilling, Caplan, & Brown, unpublished data.)

ERRORLESS LEARNING AS THE
TRANSFER OF STIMULUS CONTROL

One of the most potent determinants of the number of errors during the acquisition of a discrimination is the physical similarity between S+ and S−. For example, when S+ was a green and S− a dark key, Kodera and Rilling (1975) obtained fewer errors than when S+ was a green and S− a red key. As Terrace (1973) points out, the failure to respond to the dark key is presumably a transfer from the discrimination training that took place in the animal's environment prior to the experiment. Pigeons are reinforced for pecking at brightly colored bits of grain, but are not reinforced for pecking at dark holes. These experiments suggest that interdimensional training often produces fewer errors than intradimensional training because of the greater similarity of the stimuli in the intradimensional case.

Therefore, special techniques are necessary to establish an errorless discrimination when S+ and S− are similar as in intradimensional training. In *fading*, a property of a stimulus is gradually changed on successive trials to transfer control of responding from one property of a stimulus to another. For example, in the experiment which initiated the current interest in errorless learning, Terrace (1963a) first established an errorless discrimination between a red S+ and a dark S− by beginning with a dark key with a duration of 1 sec. In Phase 1, the duration of the dark key was lengthened from 1 to 30 sec. In Phase 2, the discrimination was transferred from a dark key, S−, to a green S− by reducing the duration of the dark key to 1 sec and gradually increasing the intensity of the chromatic S− to match that of S+. In Phase 3, the duration of the green S− was gradually increased from 1 to 30 sec to match the duration of S+.

Regrettably, fading remains a part of the art rather than the science of operant conditioning. Many investigators—e.g., Rilling, Kramer, and Richards (1973), Karpicke and Hearst (1975)—have obtained more errors than Terrace reported in attempts to obtain errorless discriminations. The parameters of fading which are necessary for errorless learning remain uninvestigated. How rapidly should the intensity and duration of S− be increased in order to obtain optimal errorless discrimination learning? Furthermore, the effectiveness of fading is rarely compared with appropriate control conditions in which fading is not employed. The procedural variables which are responsible for errorless discrimination learning have been neglected in the rush to compare errorless learning with learning with errors.

In a second experiment Terrace (1963b) compared three procedures for transferring stimulus control from the wavelength dimension to the line-orientation dimension. In the first phase of the experiment, the pigeons acquired an errorless discrimination between red (S+) and green (S−), and in the second phase the discrimination was between a vertical line (S+) and a horizontal line (S−). Transfer was accomplished by several procedures. In the *abrupt procedure*, the red stimulus on the S+ trials was replaced with a vertical line and the green stimulus on the S− trials was replaced with a horizontal line. In the *superimposition-only procedure*, the vertical line was superimposed on red and the horizontal line was superimposed on green for five sessions before the lines were presented alone. In the *superimposition and fading procedure*, the vertical and horizontal lines were superimposed upon the chromatic stimuli for five sessions, but the intensities of the red and green lights were gradually reduced within one session until they were no longer visible to the human observer. A fourth group received discrimination training between the vertical and horizontal lines without pretraining on the discrimination between red and green.

The results of this experiment are presented in Figure 19, which shows that the total number of errors during S− depended upon the method of transfer from the red-green to the vertical-horizontal discrimination. The superimposition and fading procedure produced errorless transfer, while the abrupt procedure produced the most errors. This experiment demonstrates that both fading and superimposition independently facilitate transfer of stimulus control and supports an interpretation of errorless learning as a transfer of stimulus control from one dimension to another.

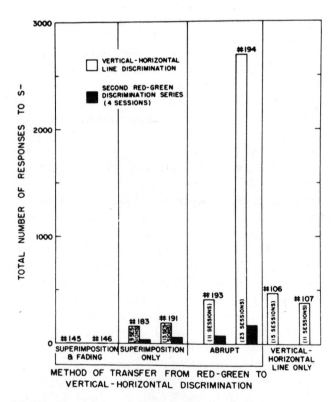

Fig. 19. The number of errors made by each bird during the acquisition of a vertical-horizontal discrimination following errorless red-green discrimination training. Errors during a second series of red-green discrimination sessions are also indicated. (From Terrace, 1963b. © 1963 by the Society for the Experimental Analysis of Behavior, Inc.)

TERRACE'S THEORY OF ERRORLESS LEARNING

Errorless learning has been observed occasionally for many years, but has remained little more than a laboratory curiosity and incidental observation. For example, Skinner (1938, pp. 203–206) established a brightness discrimination in rats without errors by introducing S− during the first session of training. Errorless learning was also observed by Schlosberg and Solomon (1943).

The popularization of programmed instruction by Skinner in the late fifties and early sixties led to intense interest in errorless learning. Skinner argued that one of the major advantages of programmed instruction was that the student is seldom wrong. In 1961, he eloquently advocated training procedures which produce as few errors as possible. This was accomplished through stimulus generalization by changing each successive question only slightly from one frame to the next. Although Skinner offered no data, errors presumably had aversive consequences which might lead to escape behavior. Skinner's theory that optimal learning is accomplished by maximizing positive reinforcement and minimizing aversive consequences forms a background for the theory of errorless learning developed by Terrace.

Most of the research in errorless learning is not concerned with the transfer of stimulus control. Rather, it is concerned with testing Terrace's theory that the phenomena of errorless learning are fundamentally different from the phenomena obtained when the discrimination is acquired with errors.

Terrace has consistently argued that errorless learning is fundamentally different from learning with errors. In discussing the results of his original experiment, Terrace (1963a) wrote, "Discriminations acquired with zero, or a near zero, number of responses to S−, can be clearly distinguished from discriminations acquired with large amounts of responding to S− by criteria other than the number of acquisition responses to S−" (p. 23). The theory was subsequently refined by Terrace (1966b) to specify that S− functions as a neutral stimulus following errorless discrimination learning, while S− functions as an aversive and inhibitory stimulus following learning with errors. A similar distinction between the two different types of discrimination learning is maintained in the most recent version of this theory (Terrace, 1972).

Terrace distinguishes the product of discrimination learning from the by-product of discrimination learning. The *product* of differential reinforcement is the acquisition of a higher rate of responding to S+ than to S−. For convenience, Terrace (1972) has classified other behavioral phenomena which occur during the acquisition of a discrimination as *by-products* of discrimination learning. The by-products of discrimination learning include behavioral contrast, emotional and aggressive behavior during S−, aversive properties of S−, inhibitory properties of S−, and the positive and negative peak shift. Terrace (1972) set out to assess whether each of the by-products had similar underlying mechanisms which would be the case if they covaried as a function of the same variables. Terrace's theoretical position is simply stated: "None of [the by-products of discrimination learning] occurs following discrimination learning without errors" (p. 251). This is reiterated in each of his papers on errorless learning (Terrace, 1963a, 1963b, 1964, 1966a, 1966b, 1966c, 1968, 1972, 1973). As the review of the literature in this section will show, each of the by-products of discrimination learning, except the peak shift, has been obtained following errorless discrimination learning. Therefore, a revision of Terrace's theory is required.

Rilling and his students (Kodera & Rilling, 1975; Rilling & Caplan, 1973, 1975; Rilling, Caplan, Howard, & Brown, 1975; Rilling, Kramer, & Richards, 1973) have carried out a series of experiments which demonstrate that the by-products of discrimination learning bear little relationship to the occurrence or nonoccurrence of errors during S−. These experiments suggest that the parameters which most readily produce one by-product—e.g., extinction-induced aggression—may not produce another—e.g., behavioral contrast. Only the peak shift and inhibitory stimulus control appear to have identical underlying mechanisms. Therefore, the theory which explains behavioral contrast may differ from the theory that explains extinction-induced aggression, and so on. It follows that the best strategy for research is to identify those variables which produce each behavioral phenomenon and to develop separate theories for each. Whether a behavioral process is classified as a by-product or not is irrelevant for the task of isolating its determinants.

What Is Learned in Errorless Learning?

This section demonstrates how errorless learning modifies the behavior of the organism. The experiments were designed to determine if it is necessary to modify traditional theories of discrimination learning for the errorless case. The procedures employed are: (1) observations of aggressive behavior, (2) escape from S⁻, and (3) assessment of inhibitory stimulus control.

Aggressive Behavior During Errorless Learning

Azrin, Hutchinson, and Hake (1966) developed the standard procedure for measuring extinction-induced aggression between pigeons in the experimental laboratory. They alternated periods in which each response was reinforced with periods of extinction. In addition to the experimental pigeon, a second, partially restrained pigeon was also present at the rear of the experimental chamber. Azrin et al. found that the probability of attack against the target pigeon was low when the opportunity to eat was available. However, when the opportunity for reinforcement was withdrawn, the probability of aggression was high. The duration of attack was a direct function of the number of food reinforcements and decreased as a function of the time since the withdrawal of the opportunity to eat. With a high degree of consistency, they found that attack occurs at the moment of transition from reinforcement to extinction, which led them to suggest that the interruption of eating produced the aggression.

In the typical procedure for measuring aggression during extinction, a substantial number of responses on the key are observed. This raises the question of whether the aggression is produced from the frustration which occurs as a by-product of the nonreinforced responses, as Terrace argued (1966c, 1971, 1972), or by the withdrawal of the opportunity for reinforcement. If aggression occurred during an errorless S⁻, then nonreinforced responses are not necessary for this species-specific behavior. This would argue instead that withdrawal of reinforcement is the crucial determinant of aggression. In order to obtain quantitative data on the phenomenon of extinction-induced aggression during errorless learning, Rilling and Caplan (1973) trained pigeons to discriminate without errors between a green light as S⁺ and a dark key as S⁻. The opportunity to attack a restrained target bird was also present. During discrimination training, the rate of attack in the presence of the dark key was higher for each animal than the operant level, even though most of the animals acquired the discrimination without errors. Furthermore, the rate of attack did not decrease during 45 sessions of discrimination training. These data demonstrate that attack during S⁻ also occurs during errorless discrimination training and fails to confirm Terrace's theory.

The procedure developed by Azrin et al. only detects the final component of the attack sequence. Rilling and Caplan (1973) photographed some of the species-specific precursors of the attack response, flight behaviors, and the actual attack response for two birds that were errorless throughout the experiment. For pigeons, the first response in the sequence is bowing, which frequently precedes attack. In bowing, following erection of the head and body, the bird ruffles the feathers of the neck and bows the head toward the ground while walking in circles and emitting cooing calls. The second response, illustrated in part A of Figure 20, is attack intention in which, while standing upright, the bird raises the feathers of its neck and pecks in an open space in front of its opponent while vibrating its wings. The final response is attack itself. Part B shows an attack response for bird 5. Part C shows an attack response by bird 1. Part D shows bird 5 immediately after an attack terminated. While these preattack behaviors are difficult to measure automatically, they are reliably obtained during an errorless S⁻ in the presence of a target pigeon.

Fig. 20. Photographs taken during S⁻ of two pigeons that acquired a discrimination without errors. Section A illustrates attack intention and B illustrates attack for bird 5. Section C shows attack for bird 1 and D shows bird 1 shortly after an attack response. (From Rilling & Caplan, 1973. © 1973 by the Society for the Experimental Analysis of Behavior, Inc.)

The data of Azrin et al. (1966) and Rilling and Caplan (1973) suggest that the withdrawal of the opportunity for reinforcement is one of the primary determinants of extinction-induced aggression. The probability of attack is highest immediately following the termination of S+ and decreases thereafter. Furthermore, high rates of attack during extinction occurred only during those sessions in which S+ and S− alternated, but did not occur in sessions in which S− was presented alone. Extinction per se did not induce aggression. This suggests that the less the incentive contrast between S+ and S−, the less the amount of aggression obtained. In a subsequent experiment, Rilling and Caplan (1975) found that the frequency of reinforcement during S+ was a determinant of extinction-induced aggression during errorless discrimination learning. A VI 30-sec schedule induced a higher rate of attack during extinction than a VI 5-min schedule.

The results of these experiments demonstrate that the aggression-inducing properties of S− are not primarily due to the contingencies of reinforcement prevailing during S−, but are a contrast effect determined by the contingencies prevailing during S+.

Escape from S−

Rilling, Askew, Ahlskog, and Kramer (1969) conducted a series of experiments which demonstrated that an escape paradigm can be used to detect the aversive properties of S− in a successive discrimination. In their procedure, a successive discrimination was programmed on one key. A peck on a second key produced a time-out which terminated S− or S+ and darkened the chamber. During the acquisition of the discrimination, time-outs occurred during S−. The probability of a time-out was highest early in S−, a finding which paralleled the occurrence of attack behavior in a similar situation (Azrin, Hutchinson, & Hake, 1966; Rilling & Caplan, 1973). These data support the assertion that the time-out response is an escape response and an index of the aversive properties of the stimuli present when the response occurs.

One of Skinner's arguments in favor of learning without errors is that errors make the situation so aversive that the learner tends to escape from the environment in which learning is supposed to occur. Rilling, Kramer, and Richards (1973) designed an experiment to test directly Skinner's interpretation of errorless learning using the escape procedure of Rilling et al. (1969). In a successive discrimination four groups of pigeons were trained to discriminate between red and green. Following the design of Terrace's (1963) original experiment, the groups differed with respect to the procedure used to introduce S−: early-progressive, early-constant, late-progressive, and late-constant. The aversive properties of S− were measured using the escape procedure of Rilling et al. (1969) in which a single peck at a second key terminated S− for 10 sec and darkened the chamber.

Figure 21 shows the number of errors and time-outs for each animal in each of the four conditions. The data in the upper panel are ordered from left to right by ranking the animals from least to most errors. The lower panel shows the number of time-outs for the corresponding bird in the upper panel. The procedures for introducing S− had a significant effect on the number of responses to S− during the acquisition of the discrimination. The constant procedure

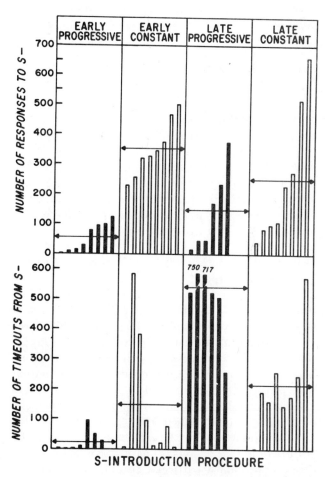

Fig. 21. (Upper panel) Total number of responses to S− for each animal during all sessions of discrimination training. (Lower panel) Total number of time-outs from S− during the 10 final sessions of discrimination training. The arrows between panels indicate the mean for each group. Note the lack of correlation between the number of responses to S− and the number of time-outs from S−. (Rilling, Kramer, & Richards, 1973.)

produced more errors than the progressive procedure. The procedures for introducing S− also had a significant effect on the number of time-outs from S−. However, here late introduction of S− produced more time-outs from S− than early introduction of S−.

In interpreting the results of an experiment in which pigeons escaped from S−, Terrace (1971) concluded that "the occurrence of nonreinforced responding to S− is the crucial factor in rendering S− aversive." Therefore, Terrace predicts that a positive correlation is obtained between the number of errors and an index of the aversiveness of S−. Figure 21 demonstrates that, within each condition, the number of responses to S− is a poor predictor of the number of time-outs from S−. To the extent that time-outs from S− are an index of the aversive properties of S−, these data do not support the view that the aversiveness of a stimulus is directly proportional to the number of unreinforced responses emitted in its presence.

Inhibitory Stimulus Control

Independent tests for inhibition. One of the first experiments to suggest that an errorless S− is inhibitory was an experiment of Marsh and Johnson (1968). In the first phase of the experiment, an errorless successive discrimination between red and green was established with a fading procedure. In the second phase of the experiment, the reinforcement contingencies for S+ and S− were reversed, so that the previously positive stimulus was extinguished and the previously negative stimulus was reinforced. Four of the five subjects did not respond to S+ (the former S−) more than once during five days of reversal training. A control group that did not receive errorless training acquired the reversal rapidly. Therefore, a history of errorless learning appears to retard the detection of changes in the reinforcement contingencies. As compared to a subject that has acquired a discrimination with errors, the errorless bird is at a relative disadvantage in coping with an environment in which the conditions of reinforcement change.

As mentioned earlier, Hearst, Besley, and Farthing (1970) argue that an independent test is necessary to demonstrate that a particular stimulus is inhibitory. Two procedures have been developed for such tests. In the combined-cues test, S− is an inhibitory stimulus if its combination with S+ produces a decrement in responding. In the resistance-to-reinforcement test, S− is an inhibitory stimulus if the acquisition of a conditioned response is retarded. Using both of these tests, Wessells (1973) demonstrated that an errorless S− was inhibitory.

Wessells established errorless learning with an autoshaping paradigm. On a CS+ trial, the key was illuminated with a green light for 6 sec and always followed immediately by food independently of the pigeon's behavior. On a CS− trial, the key was illuminated with a white vertical line on a black background which was *never* followed by food. Half of the trials were CS+ trials and half were CS− trials. The key was dark between trials. During Phase 1, pecking on the key emerged during CS+ for each bird, while the birds were errorless during CS− using a criterion of 25 or fewer errors. The tests for inhibition were carried out during the second phase of the experiment.

Four groups were employed in Wessells's experiment. Group 1 received 80 presentations each of CS+ and CS− in Phase 1, while Group 2 received 200 presentations each of CS+ and CS−. In Phase 2, Groups 1 and 2 received a test in which the resistance to autoshaping of the former CS− was measured. On half of the trials, the former CS− was presented on the left key while a novel stimulus was presented on the right key on the other trials. For each bird, a peck at the key with the novel stimulus emerged earlier than pecks at the key with the former CS−. The amount of inhibition was a function of the number of conditioning trials: the birds with 400 differential conditioning trials showed more inhibition than the groups receiving only 160 trials.

Group 3 also received 400 differential conditioning trials followed by a combined-cues test in which CS−, the white line, was superimposed upon CS+, the green background. Group 4 was a control group for the possible unconditioned suppressive effects of the white line. Combining the CS− with the CS+ completely suppressed responding for the birds that received errorless differential conditioning. In contrast, combining the novel white line with CS+ produced only a slight decrement in responding. The results of Wessells's experiment are a convincing demonstration that an errorless S− acquires inhibitory properties. A negative contingency between the CS− and the unconditioned stimulus (food), so that the CS− predicts the absence of food, appears sufficient to account for the development of conditioned inhibition (see Rescorla, 1969a).

Using an errorless autoshaping procedure similar to that employed by Wessells (1973), Wilkie and Ramer (1974) found that an errorless S− is more resistant to autoshaping than an S− with errors. Therefore, as measured by the resistance-to-reinforcement procedure, an errorless S− is *more* inhibitory than an S− with errors. Clearly, an errorless S− is not a neutral stimulus, as was first proposed by Terrace (1966).

Generalization following errorless intradimensional training. The evidence that S− remains a neutral stimulus following errorless learning is based on two experiments of Terrace (1964, 1966) in which a stimulus-generalization test was administered following errorless discrimination learning. In one of the most widely cited experiments, Terrace (1964) established an errorless intradimensional discrimination with an early-progressive procedure. S+ was 540 nm and S− was 580 nm. During a generalization test which was administered following 14 days of discrimination training, the peak of the gradient for all three errorless birds occurred at S+. When a late-constant procedure was employed, a peak shift was obtained for two of the three subjects. These data led Terrace to conclude that S− is a neutral stimulus when the discrimination is acquired without errors. While Terrace attributed the difference between the groups to the number of errors during S−, an equally plausible interpretation is that the probability of obtaining the peak shift depends upon the procedure for introducing S−.

The peak shift is the only phenomenon of stimulus control which has not yet been obtained following errorless discrimination training. In view of the evidence cited above that S− functions as an inhibitory stimulus following errorless learning, it seems likely that the peak shift might occur following intradimensional errorless learning. The problem is to select values of S+ and S− which are spaced closely enough to permit the observation of the peak shift yet which do not preclude errorless learning.

Generalization Following Errorless Interdimensional Training. When a stimulus-generalization test is administered following interdimensional discrimination learning, an inhibitory gradient is usually obtained around S−. Two experiments of Terrace (1966b, 1972) are apparently exceptions to this generalization. In the first experiment, a single group of birds were trained to discriminate between a white vertical line (S+) and a wavelength of 580 nm (S−) using traditional discrimination-training procedures. Substantial individual differences in the number of responses to S− were obtained. Flat gradients with virtually zero responses to each test stimulus were obtained for those subjects that acquired the discrimination with the lowest rates of responding to S−. Inhibitory gradients with a minimum at S− were obtained for those subjects that acquired the discrimination with the highest rates of responding to S−. These data led Terrace to conclude that inhibitory stimulus control was absent following errorless learning.

These experiments have been extensively criticized by subsequent investigators. Bernheim (1968) pointed out that the post hoc method of dividing the subjects into groups with and without errors biased the errorless group toward pigeons that did not respond to wavelength and therefore virtually guaranteed a zero base line. Terrace attempted to meet this criticism in a second experiment (Terrace, 1972) in which a fading procedure was used to train the discrimination without errors. As was the case in the first experiment, the gradients obtained from the errorless group were flat. Birds that acquired the discrimination without the fading procedure responded to S− and demonstrated inhibitory gradients during the stimulus-generalization test.

A second criticism that applies equally to both experiments is that virtually no responses were emitted to each test stimulus by the errorless birds. Deutsch (1967) and Hearst, Besley, and Farthing (1970, p. 388) noted that the assessment of stimulus control by the S− dimension is ambiguous when stimulus values far from S− produce zero responding, because a "floor effect" prevents the detection of a minimum in responding at S−. Hearst et al. pointed out that the assessment of stimulus control by the S− dimension requires an elevation in the overall level of responding to each of the stimuli during the stimulus-generalization test. If Terrace's interpretation is correct, the gradient should remain flat when elevated.

In an experiment designed to verify the Hearst et al. interpretation of Terrace's experiment, Rilling, Caplan, Howard, and Brown (1975) compared the resistance-to-reinforcement and combined-cues techniques for elevating responding to the test stimuli from the S− dimension. Discrimination training began with autoshaping to increase the probability of errorless learning. The positive stimulus was a green key light that was followed immediately by food after 8 sec, while the negative stimulus was a black vertical or horizontal line that was never immediately followed by food. Autoshaping was followed by eight days of successive discrimination training during which responding to S+ was reinforced on a VI schedule. After identical conditions of discrimination training, three different types of generalization tests were employed: resistance to extinction with compounding, resistance to reinforcement without compounding, and resistance to reinforcement with compounding. In the compounding tests, various line angles were presented on a green background. In the tests without compounding, these same line angles were presented without the green background. Terrace's experiments employed resistance to extinction without compounding.

Figure 22 presents the average number of responses to each of the test stimuli during days 1-5 of generalization testing for each of the groups. An inhibitory gradient with a minimum at S⁻ was obtained for the two groups tested with the resistance-to-reinforcement procedure. Therefore, stimulus control was acquired by the S⁻ dimension even though the discrimination was acquired with a very low rate of responding to S⁻. More responses were obtained during the compound test than during the noncompound test, because compounding produced responses early in generalization that were reinforced on the VI schedule. A flat gradient above the zero base line was obtained for the experimental group that was tested during extinction with the compound stimuli, indicating that inhibitory stimulus control by the angle of the line was not obtained for this condition of testing.

These results emphasize that flat gradients with zero responses to each test stimulus, such as those obtained by Terrace (1966, 1972), are an equivocal outcome. Deutsch (1967) and Hearst et al. (1970) were correct in their initial criticism of Terrace's experiment that a "floor effect" prevented the detection of inhibitory stimulus control. A rate of responding to the test stimuli greater than zero is necessary for the assessment of inhibitory stimulus control. In the Rilling et al. experiment, the resistance-to-reinforcement procedure was the more sensitive index of inhibitory stimulus control. Similar results have been obtained by Karpicke and Hearst (1975).

Behavioral Contrast

The phenomenon of behavioral contrast receives particular emphasis here, as its investigation (Terrace, 1963a) formed the basis for Terrace's theory of errorless discrimination learning.

The four training groups—early-progressive, early-constant, late-progressive, and late-constant—differed considerably in terms of the number of responses emitted to S⁻, with the subjects of the early-progressive group displaying errorless or nearly errorless performance. Substantially more errors to S⁻ were observed for the other three groups. Terrace subsequently attributed special significance to the distinction between discrimination learning with and without errors based on other differences between early-progressive birds and the others. The most basic of these differences was the absence of behavioral contrast in the early-progressive group. From this observation, Terrace (1972) concluded that behavioral contrast does not occur if the discrimination is acquired without errors.

In contrast with Terrace's interpretation, Reynolds (1961), Friedman and Guttman (1965), Taus and Hearst (1970), Vieth and Rilling (1972), and Sadowsky (1973) obtained behavioral contrast from pigeons when a blackout, during which the chamber was completely dark, was employed as S⁻. While the number of errors during S⁻ was not always recorded in these experiments, the blackout presumably functioned as an errorless S⁻, since pigeons readily dis-

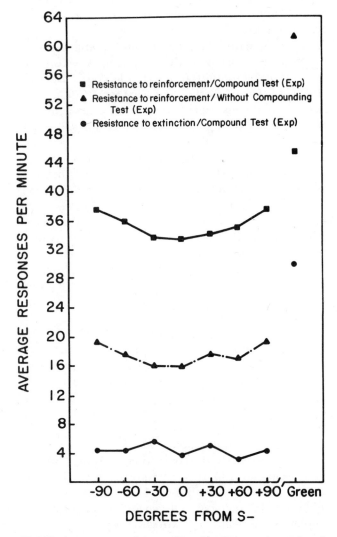

Fig. 22. Average rate of responding for the experimental and control groups to each of the test stimuli during days 1-5 of generalization testing. (From Rilling, Caplan, Howard, & Brown, 1975. © 1975 by the Society for the Experimental Analysis of Behavior, Inc.)

criminate a blackout from an illuminated key associated with reinforcement. These data suggest that nonreinforced responding to S− plays a minor role in the production of behavioral contrast.

Since the early-progressive group failed to display behavioral contrast in Terrace's experiment, an alternative interpretation, which logically must be entertained, is that some aspect of this procedure precluded the observation of contrast. In Terrace's (1963a) design, it is impossible to partition the effects on behavioral contrast of learning the discrimination with or without errors from the immediate effects of the specific training procedure employed. Consequently, Kodera and Rilling (1975) systematically replicated Terrace's original experiment in errorless learning. However, a dark key was used as S− with a green key as S+, rather than the red and green stimuli used by Terrace. This substitution of S− stimuli produced errorless acquisition of the discrimination in many pigeons from groups in addition to those receiving early-progressive discrimination training.

At the completion of the experiment, all eight birds of the early-progressive group were still errorless, using a criterion of 25 or fewer total responses to S− for classifying a bird as errorless. Six of the eight pigeons in the early-constant group were errorless, three of the late-progressive group, and four of the late-constant group. These data clearly confirm Terrace's finding that the early introduction of S− was very effective in reducing the number of errors during discrimination training. The progressive groups differed from the constant groups in errors only during the first five days of discrimination training when S− was faded in for the progressive groups. The progressive groups made significantly fewer total errors during the first five days of discrimination training than did the constant groups. During the first five days of discrimination training, the early-progressive group emitted fewer responses to S− than did the early-constant group.

Figure 23 shows the mean daily rates of responding to S+ throughout the various phases for each of the four groups. Of primary importance was the observation that behavioral contrast occurred in all four groups. The increase in rate was, in general, slightly greater following a transition from base line to discrimination than was the subsequent decrease following the opposite transition. Figure 23 also reveals a trend for the late groups to exceed the early groups in the mean amount of behavioral contrast produced. While time of S− introduction was a more powerful variable than the method of introducing S−, the constant group's introduction of S− tended to produce

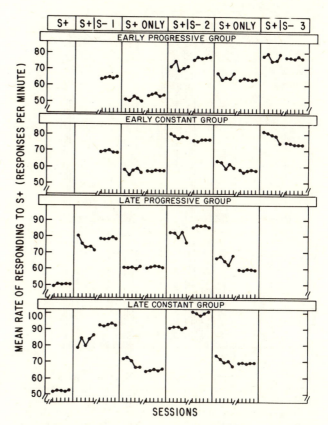

Fig. 23. Mean rate of responding to S+ for the early-progressive, early-constant, late-progressive, and late-constant training groups. Because the early introduction of S− precluded an initial phase of base line training, the data for the early groups are displaced to the right to place them in phase with the data for the late groups. In the top column, S+ refers to the baseline; S+|S− 1, S+|S− 2, and S+|S− 3 refer respectively to the first, second, and third phases of discrimination training. All comparisons of the magnitude of behavioral contrast are based upon this configuration of the data. (From Kodera & Rilling, 1975. © 1975 by the Society for the Experimental Analysis of Behavior, Inc.)

more contrast than did the progressive group's S− introduction.

In his original experiment, Terrace (1963a) observed a close relationship between the occurrence of errors during S− and behavioral contrast during S+ and went on to argue that behavioral contrast was produced by nonreinforced responding during S−. This interpretation of behavioral contrast predicts a positive correlation between the number of errors during S− and the magnitude of behavioral contrast during S+.

Figure 24 compares the number of responses during S− (upper panel) with the magnitude of behavioral contrast during S+ (lower panel). The left panels compare the number of errors during the first phase of discrimination training with the amount of behavioral contrast exhibited during the first discrim-

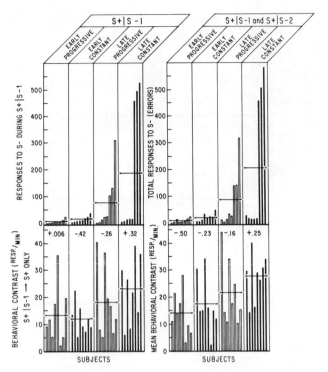

Fig. 24. Relationships between responding during S⁻ (errors) and the magnitude of behavioral contrast produced. The bars within each panel are ordered with respect to the total number of errors produced during S⁺|S⁻ 1 (the first discrimination phase). Arrows within each panel mark the group mean for that measure. The left half of this figure depicts the relationship between the number of errors made during S⁺|S⁻ 1 and the amount of behavioral contrast observed for each pigeon. The right half of the figure presents the relationship between the total number of errors occurring during the first two phases of discrimination training and the mean behavioral contrast produced overall. Spearman rank-order correlation coefficients for each group are indicated by the numbers appearing just below the error data. (From Kodera & Rilling, 1975. © 1975 by the Society for the Experimental Analysis of Behavior, Inc.)

ination-training phase. The right panels relate the total number of errors made throughout the experiment with the mean behavioral contrast produced by each subject. The birds are ordered according to the number of errors made during the first discrimination phase. The group means are indicated by horizontal arrows.

A direct relationship between errors and behavioral contrast within groups would be represented by a rank-ordering of the amount of behavioral contrast from least to most within each of the four conditions, reflecting the symmetry of the error data. Clearly, no such relationship is visible in the data of Figure 24. Pigeons that produced the fewest errors in each condition were as likely to show the greatest amount of contrast as were those that produced the greatest number of errors. Spearman rank-order correlation coefficients between the number of errors and the amount of behavioral contrast are indicated in Figure 24 for each group. None of these correlations was significant.

In other aspects the Kodera and Rilling experiment confirms the results obtained in Terrace's experiment. The major discrepancy between the two studies is the occurrence of behavioral contrast following early-progressive training in the Kodera and Rilling study. Another important difference is that many of the birds in the early-constant, late-progressive, and late-constant groups were also errorless, yet demonstrated behavioral contrast. Which differences in procedure are responsible for Terrace's failure to observe behavioral contrast in the early-progressive group? His original experiment included a red key as S⁺ and a green key as S⁻. Behavioral contrast is widely assumed to be independent of whether the stimuli used as S⁺ and S⁻ lie on the same or different dimensions, since contrast is obtained after both inter- and intradimensional training. Using a separate group of pigeons trained on the early-progressive procedure of the main experiment, Kodera and Rilling substituted a red S⁻ for the dark key. The mean magnitude of behavioral contrast was 23.2 responses per min for the red group as compared with 15.3 responses per min for the group with a dark key as S⁻. These results suggest that the magnitude of behavioral contrast is greater following intradimensional training than following interdimensional training. In any event, Terrace's use of a red S⁻ did not preclude the occurrence of contrast.

A more significant difference between the two studies was Terrace's use of 3-min components during S⁺ and S⁻ while Rilling and Kodera used 1-min components. Using a group of pigeons for whom the duration of S⁺ was 3 min, which also decreased the number of alternations between S⁺ and S⁻ from 25 to 8, the magnitude of behavioral contrast following early-progressive training decreased to only 7.8 responses per min and contrast was not obtained from each bird. The total duration of S⁺ remained constant in these experiments. These data suggest that Terrace's failure to obtain behavioral contrast was due in part to the use of stimulus components with a duration of 3 min. This is coupled with the fact that Terrace's data were subject to more random daily fluctuation than were those of Kodera and Rilling (1975), who obtained more stable response rates through the imposition of response stability requirements before instituting changes in training conditions. What is not clear is whether the attenuation in the behavioral contrast was due to increased duration of S⁺ or to the decrease in the number of alternations between S⁺ and S⁻.

Errorless Learning in Perspective

Errorless learning is the transfer of stimulus control from one dimension associated with S⁻ to another, provided the transfer is obtained with a zero rate of responding to the new S⁻ from the first session of transfer. When the pecking response of the pigeon is reinforced during S⁺, errorless discrimination-training procedures are effective in eliminating the terminal peck response from the sequence of observing and approaching S⁻. Therefore, the behavior of the organism during S⁻ is modified or conditioned by errorless discrimination training.

Errorless learning includes the tail with few errors of the distribution of total errors for the acquisition of a discrimination. Since the definition of an *error response* is arbitrary, it follows that the definition of *errorless learning* is also arbitrary. Extensive research has demonstrated that the behavior of subjects with few errors is not fundamentally different from the behavior of subjects with many errors, except for the difference in errors.

Escape from S⁻, aggression during S⁻, conditioned inhibition, inhibitory stimulus control, and behavioral contrast have all been obtained independently of whether the discrimination was acquired with or without errors. Therefore, a theoretical classification based on the distinction between learning with errors and learning without errors is not useful.

By concentrating upon the number of errors, investigators have overlooked key determinants of the many phenomena produced by differential reinforcement. The research of Rilling and his students demonstrates that the manner of presentation of conditions during discrimination learning, not the production of errors, determine the so-called by-products of discrimination learning.

Two procedural variables that have been identified are: (1) the time in the subject's experimental history at which S⁻ is introduced (e.g., early or late), and (2) the rapidity with which S⁻ is introduced (e.g., progressively or abruptly). The data indicate that S⁻ is more aversive, as measured by escape behavior (and more behavioral contrast is observed during S⁺), when S⁻ is introduced late in training. While data are not yet available, the previous findings suggest that conditioned inhibition and inhibitory stimulus control are also greater when S⁻ is introduced late in training. The time of S⁻ introduction is a more powerful variable than the method of introducing S⁻. Abrupt introduction of S⁻ produces more behavioral contrast than gradual introduction. This analysis suggests that conditioned inhibition and inhibitory stimulus control are also greater when S⁻ is introduced abruptly.

Frequency of reinforcement during S⁺ affects behavior during S⁻. Aggressive behavior during extinction is induced by the withdrawal of the stimulus associated with reinforcement, rather than by the change in the consequences of the pecking response during extinction. The higher the frequency of reinforcement during S⁺, the higher the rate of attack during S⁻. Since conditioned inhibition is a contrast phenomenon produced by the absence of reinforcement, this variable may have a similar influence on conditioned inhibition and inhibitory stimulus control.

A pigeon that has acquired a discrimination with a procedure in which S⁻ is introduced gradually and early in training may show "errorless learning" and less aggression and more escape and behavioral contrast than a pigeon that has acquired the same discrimination but with a S⁻ introduced abruptly and late in training. However, the organism that has acquired the discrimination without errors is retarded in detecting changes in the response-reinforcer relationship in the presence of S⁻ as compared to an organism that mastered the discrimination with errors. When inhibition is measured with a resistance-to-reinforcement procedure, more conditioned inhibition is obtained for the birds that acquired the discrimination without errors than for the birds that acquired the discrimination with errors. Therefore, errorless learning is clearly not the best learning for an organism exposed to a changing environment.

SUMMARY

The acquisition of stimulus control in a successive discrimination occurs as follows. In discrimination training, certain stimuli predict occasions when a class of responses is reinforced, and other stimuli predict occasions when those responses are not reinforced or when they are reinforced according to a different program. By definition, stimulus control requires different rates or patterns of responding in the presence of each stimulus. Following the acquisition of a discrimination, a test is necessary to determine which aspects of the training stimuli have acquired control over responding. The stimulus-generalization gradient is the primary index of stimulus control. Gradients are obtained by extinction or steady-state methods in which the stimuli are presented singly or simultaneously.

In intradimensional training, the interaction between reinforcement at S+ and extinction at S− is reflected in the stimulus-generalization gradient as the positive and negative peak shifts. These processes are separated in interdimensional training in which an excitatory gradient is obtained around S+ and an inhibitory gradient is obtained around S−. Following interdimensional training, the normal distribution curve provides the best fit to empirically obtained gradients of excitation and inhibition. For the variables that have been investigated to date, the determinants of the peak shift and the inhibitory gradient are identical.

A functional analysis reveals a wide range of variables that determine inhibitory stimulus control. Once the reinforced response is acquired, inhibitory control by stimuli associated with the absence of reinforcement may develop rapidly in a matter of minutes. Extended training has relatively little influence once the necessary and sufficient conditions for inhibitory stimulus control have been established. Inhibitory stimulus control requires relatively brief successive alternations of the discriminative stimuli, as opposed to massed presentations, and the presence during the generalization test of the background stimuli present during training. The determinants of the peak shift and inhibitory stimulus control are independent of whether responding is positively or negatively reinforced.

Extinction is not necessary for the acquisition of inhibitory stimulus control. Stimuli associated with less favorable schedules of reinforcement demonstrate some of the same inhibitory phenomena as do stimuli associated with extinction. Inhibitory control is a relative rather than an absolute property of a discriminative stimulus.

In the many cases in which responding is reinforced differently in the presence of S1 and S2, stimulus control is dependent upon the combination of the discriminative and incentive properties of the stimuli. When the response rates to S1 and S2 are identical, the peak shift and inhibitory stimulus control are not obtained. The greater the index of discrimination between S1 and S2, the higher the probability of obtaining a peak shift. Provided a discrimination between S1 and S2 is established, the peak shift and inhibitory stimulus control are obtained even though the frequencies of reinforcement in S1 and S2 are identical. Inhibitory phenomena are maximized by large incentive and rate differences between S1 and S2.

Some theories of the peak shift and inhibitory stimulus control have focused upon a single primary determinant such as nonreinforced responding during extinction. Such theories are an inadequate oversimplification, since an experimental analysis demonstrates multiple determinants of inhibitory phenomena. Spence's theory of discrimination learning provides a simple integrated account of the peak shift and inhibitory stimulus control. However, Spence's theory fails to account for the effects of conditioning context, the relativity of inhibitory stimulus control, the effects of transitions between S− and S+, and enhanced responding within a spatially defined dimension.

The time is ripe for the development of new quantitative theories that integrate the extensive data reviewed in this chapter. The extension to operant behavior of theories of Pavlovian differential conditioning may lead to a single integrated formulation of stimulus control. Many of the questions raised by investigators of human cognition and information processing are the same questions asked by investigators in stimulus control. The extent to which these developments are relevant to research on stimulus control remains to be determined.

REFERENCES

Azrin, N. H., Hutchinson, R. R., & Hake, D. F. Extinction-induced aggression. *Journal of the Experimental Analysis of Behavior,* 1966, *9*, 191–204.

Beale, I. L., & Winton, A. S. W. Inhibitory stimulus control in concurrent schedules. *Journal of the Experimental Analysis of Behavior,* 1970, *14*, 133–137.

Bernheim, J. W. Comment. *Psychonomic Science,* 1968, *11*, 327.

Blough, D. S. Stimulus generalization as signal detection in pigeons. *Science,* 1967, *158*, 940–941.

Blough, D. S. Generalization gradient shape and summation in steady-state tests. *Journal of the Experimental Analysis of Behavior,* 1969, *12*, 91–104.

Blough, D. S. Two-way generalization peak shift after two-key training in the pigeon. *Animal Learning and Behavior,* 1973, *1*, 171–174.

Blough, D. S. Steady-state data and a quantitative model of operant generalization. *Journal of Experimental Psychology: Animal Behavior Process,* 1975, *104*, 3–21.

Blough, P. M. Wavelength generalization and discrimination in the pigeon. *Perception and Psychophysics,* 1972, *12*, 342–348.

Brown, J. S. Generalization and discrimination. In D. I. Mostofsky (Ed.), *Stimulus generalization.* Stanford: Stanford University Press, 1965.

Catania, A. C. Concurrent performances: Inhibition of one response by reinforcement of another. *Journal of the Experimental Analysis of Behavior,* 1969, *12*, 731–744.

Catania, A. C., & Gill, C. A. Inhibition and behavioral contrast. *Psychonomic Science,* 1964, *1*, 257–258.

Catania, A. C., Silverman, P. J., & Stubbs, D. A. Concurrent performances: Stimulus-control gradients during schedules of signalled and unsignalled concurrent reinforcement. *Journal of the Experimental Analysis of Behavior,* 1974, *21,* 99–108.

COLLINS, J. P. *Generalization and decision theory.* Doctoral dissertation, University of Massachusetts, 1974.

CRITES, R. J., HARRIS, R. T., ROSENQUIST, H., & THOMAS, D. R. Response patterning during stimulus generalization in the rat. *Journal of the Experimental Analysis of Behavior,* 1967, *10,* 165–168.

DAVIS, J. M. Testing for inhibitory stimulus control with S− superimposed on S+. *Journal of the Experimental Analysis of Behavior,* 1971, *15,* 365–369.

DEUTSCH, J. A. Discrimination learning and inhibition. *Science,* 1967, *156,* 988. (Technical comment.)

DUKHAYYIL, A., & LYONS, J. E. The effect of over-training on behavioral contrast and the peak shift. *Journal of the Experimental Analysis of Behavior,* 1973, *20,* 253–263.

DYSART, J., MARX, M. H., MCLEAN, J., & NELSON, J. A. Peak shift as a function of multiple schedules of reinforcement. *Journal of the Experimental Analysis of Behavior,* 1974, *22,* 463–470.

ELLIS, W. R. Role of stimulus sequences in stimulus discrimination and stimulus generalization. *Journal of Experimental Psychology,* 1970, *83,* 155–163.

FARTHING, G. W. Behavioral contrast with multiple positive and negative stimuli on a continuum. *Journal of the Experimental Analysis of Behavior,* 1974, *22,* 419–425.

FARTHING, G. W., & HEARST, E. Generalization gradients of inhibition after different amounts of training. *Journal of the Experimental Analysis of Behavior,* 1968, *11,* 743–752.

FRIEDMAN, H., & GUTTMAN, N. Further analysis of the various effects of discrimination training on stimulus generalization gradients. In D. I. Mostofsky (Ed.), *Stimulus generalization.* Stanford: Stanford University Press, 1965.

GIURINTANO, L. P., SCHADLER, M., & THOMAS, D. R. Angularity preferences and stimulus orthogonality in pigeons. *Psychonomic Science,* 1972, *26,* 273–275.

GUTTMAN, N. Generalization gradients around stimuli associated with different reinforcement schedules. *Journal of Experimental Psychology,* 1959, *58,* 335–340.

GUTTMAN, N. Effects of discrimination formation on generalization measured from the positive-rate baseline. In D. Mostofsky (Ed.), *Stimulus generalization.* Stanford: Stanford University Press, 1965.

GUTTMAN, N., & KALISH, H. I. Discriminability and stimulus generalization. *Journal of Experimental Psychology,* 1956, *51,* 79–88.

HAILMAN, J. P. Spectral pecking preference in gull chicks. *Journal of Comparative Psychology,* 1969, *67,* 465–467.

HANSON, H. M. Effects of discrimination training on stimulus generalization. *Journal of Experimental Psychology,* 1959, *58,* 321–334.

HEARST, E. Discrimination learning as the summation of excitation and inhibition. *Science,* 1968, *162,* 1303–1306.

HEARST, E. Aversive conditioning and external stimulus control. In B. A. Campbell & R. M. Church (Eds.), *Punishment and aversive behavior.* New York: Appleton-Century-Crofts, 1969. (a)

HEARST, E. Excitation, inhibition, and discrimination learning. In N. J. Mackintosh & W. K. Honig (Eds.), *Fundamental issues in associative learning.* Halifax: Dalhousie University Press, 1969. (b)

HEARST, E. Contrast and stimulus generalization following prolonged discrimination training. *Journal of the Experimental Analysis of Behavior,* 1971, *15,* 355–363.

HEARST, E. Some persistent problems in the analysis of conditioned inhibition. In R. A. Boakes & M. S. Halliday (Eds.), *Inhibition and learning.* New York: Academic Press, 1972.

HEARST, E., BESLEY, S., & FARTHING, G. W. Inhibition and the stimulus control of operant behavior. *Journal of the Experimental Analysis of Behavior,* 1970, *14,* 373–409.

HEARST, E., & KORESKO, M. B. Stimulus generalization and the amount of prior training on variable-interval reinforcement. *Journal of Comparative and Physiological Psychology,* 1968, *66,* 133–138.

HEARST, E., KORESKO, M., & POPPEN, R. Stimulus generalization and the response-reinforcement contingency. *Journal of the Experimental Analysis of Behavior,* 1964, *7,* 369–380.

HEBERT, D. L., & KRANTZ, J. A. Transposition: A re-evaluation. *Psychological Bulletin,* 1965, *63,* 244–257.

HEMMES, N. S. Behavioral contrast in pigeons depends upon the operant. *Journal of Comparative and Physiological Psychology,* 1973, *85,* 171–178.

HINDE, R. A., & STEVENSON-HINDE, J. (Eds.). *Constraints on learning.* New York: Academic Press, 1973.

HISS, R. H., & THOMAS, D. R. Stimulus generalization as a function of testing procedure and response measure. *Journal of Experimental Psychology,* 1963, *65,* 587–592.

HOFFMAN, H. S. The analysis of discriminated avoidance. In W. K. Honig (Ed.), *Operant behavior: Areas of research and application.* New York: Appleton-Century-Crofts, 1966.

HONIG, W. K. Prediction of preference, transposition, and transposition-reversal from the generalization gradient. *Journal of Experimental Psychology,* 1962, *64,* 239–248.

HONIG, W. K. Prediction of preference, transposition, and transposition-reversal from the generalization gradients. In G. A. Kimble (Ed.), *Foundations of conditioning and learning.* New York: Appleton-Century-Crofts, 1967.

HONIG, W. K., BEALE, I., SERAGANIAN, P., LANDER, D., & MUIR, D. Stimulus and response reduction: Two aspects of inhibitory control in learning. In R. A. Boakes & M. S. Halliday (Eds.), *Inhibition and learning.* New York: Academic Press, 1972.

HONIG, W. K., BONEAU, C. A., BURSTEIN, K. R., & PENNYPACKER, H. S. Positive and negative generalization gradients obtained after equivalent training conditions. *Journal of Comparative and Physiological Psychology,* 1963, *56,* 111–116.

HONIG, W. K., THOMAS, D. R., & GUTTMAN, N. Differential effects of continuous extinction and discrimination training on the generalization gradient. *Journal of Experimental Psychology,* 1959, *58,* 145–152.

HUFF, R. G., SHERMAN, J. E., & COHN, M. Some effects of response-independent reinforcement on auditory generalization gradients. *Journal of the Experimental Analysis of Behavior,* 1975, *23,* 81–86.

HULL, C. L. *Principles of behavior.* New York: Appleton-Century-Crofts, 1943.

JENKINS, H. M. Generalization gradients and the concept of inhibition. In D. I. Mostofsky (Ed.), *Stimulus generalization.* Stanford: Stanford University Press, 1965.

JENKINS, H. M., & HARRISON, R. H. Effect of discrimination training on auditory generalization. *Journal of Experimental Psychology*, 1960, *59*, 246–253.

JENKINS, H. M., & HARRISON, R. H. Generalization gradients of inhibition following auditory discrimination learning. *Journal of the Experimental Analysis of Behavior*, 1962, *5*, 435–441.

KARPICKE, J., & HEARST, E. Inhibitory control and errorless discrimination learning. *Journal of the Experimental Analysis of Behavior*, 1975, *23*, 76–83.

KLEIN, M., & RILLING, M. Generalization of free-operant avoidance behavior in pigeons. *Journal of the Experimental Analysis of Behavior*, 1974, *21*, 75–88.

KODERA, T., & RILLING, M. Procedural antecedents of behavioral contrast: A reexamination of errorless learning. *Journal of the Experimental Analysis of Behavior*, in press.

LYONS, J. Stimulus generalization as a function of discrimination learning with and without errors. *Science*, 1969, *163*, 490–491.

LYONS, J., & THOMAS, P. R. Effects of interdimensional training on stimulus generalization, II: Within-subjects design. *Journal of Experimental Psychology*, 1967, *75*, 572–574.

MALOTT, K., MALOTT, R. W., & GLENN, M. F. Maintaining responding during stimulus generalization testing in extinction. *Journal of the Experimental Analysis of Behavior*, 1973, *19*, 199–209.

MARINER, R. W., & THOMAS, D. R. Reinforcement duration and the peak shift in post-discrimination gradients. *Journal of the Experimental Analysis of Behavior*, 1969, *12*, 759–766.

MARSH, G. Prediction of the peak shift in pigeons from gradients of excitation and inhibition. *Journal of Comparative and Physiological Psychology*, 1972, *81*, 262–266.

MARSH, G., & JOHNSON, R. Discrimination reversal following learning without "errors." *Psychonomic Science*, 1968, *10*, 261–262.

MIGLER, B. Effects of averaging data during stimulus generalization. *Journal of the Experimental Analysis of Behavior*, 1964, *7*, 303–307.

MIGLER, B., & MILLENSON, J. R. Analysis of response rates during stimulus generalization. *Journal of the Experimental Analysis of Behavior*, 1969, *12*, 81–87.

MILLER, J. T. *The effect of contextual cue change during reversal training on post-discrimination generalization gradients.* Doctoral dissertation, University of Colorado, 1972. (University Microfilms No. 73–18, 582)

MORGAN, M. J. Book review of animal discrimination learning. In R. M. Gilbert & N. S. Sutherland (Eds.), *Quarterly journal of experimental psychology*, 1969, *21*, 291–292.

NUNNALLY, J. C. *Psychometric theory.* New York: McGraw-Hill, 1967.

PIERREL, R. A. Generalization gradient for auditory intensity in the rat. *Journal of the Experimental Analysis of Behavior*, 1958, *1*, 303–313.

PURTLE, R. B. Peak shift: A review. *Psychological Bulletin*, 1973, *80*, 408–421.

RAY, B. A., & SIDMAN, M. Reinforcement and stimulus control. In W. N. Schoenfeld (Ed.), *The theory of reinforcement schedules.* Englewood Cliffs, N.J.: Prentice-Hall, Inc., 1970.

RESCORLA, R. A. Pavlovian conditioned inhibition. *Psychological Bulletin*, 1969, *72*, 77–94. (a)

RESCORLA, R. A. Conditioned inhibition of fear. In N. J. Mackintosh & W. K. Honig (Eds.), *Fundamental issues in associate learning.* Halifax: Dalhousie University Press, 1969. (b)

RESCORLA, R. A., & WAGNER, A. R. A theory of Pavlovian conditioning: Variations in the effectiveness of reinforcement and non-reinforcement. In A. Black & W. F. Prokosy (Eds.), *Classical conditioning* (Vol. 2). Englewood Cliffs, N. J.: Prentice-Hall, Inc., 1972.

REYNOLDS, G. S. Behavioral contrast. *Journal of the Experimental Analysis of Behavior*, 1961, *4*, 57–71.

RICHARDS, R. W. Stimulus generalization and delay of reinforcement during one component of a multiple schedule. *Journal of the Experimental Analysis of Behavior*, 1973, *19*, 303–309.

RILEY, D. A. *Discrimination learning.* Boston: Allyn & Bacon, 1968.

RILLING, M. Effects of timeout on a discrimination between fixed-ratio schedules. *Journal of the Experimental Analysis of Behavior*, 1968, *11*, 129–132.

RILLING, M., ASKEW, H. R., AHLSKOG, J. E., & KRAMER, T. J. Aversive properties of the negative stimulus in a successive discrimination. *Journal of the Experimental Analysis of Behavior*, 1969, *12*, 917–932.

RILLING, M., & BUDNIK, J. E. Generalization of excitation and inhibition after different amounts of training on an avoidance baseline. *Journal of the Experimental Analysis of Behavior*, 1975, *23*, 207–215.

RILLING, M., & CAPLAN, H. J. Extinction-induced aggression during errorless discrimination learning. *Journal of the Experimental Analysis of Behavior*, 1973, *20*, 85–91.

RILLING, M., & CAPLAN, H. Frequency of reinforcement as a determinant of extinction-induced aggression. *Journal of the Experimental Analysis of Behavior*, 1975, *23*, 121–129.

RILLING, M., CAPLAN, H., HOWARD, R., & BROWN, C. H. Inhibitory stimulus control following errorless discrimination learning. *Journal of the Experimental Analysis of Behavior*, 1975, *24*, 121–133.

RILLING, M., KRAMER, T. J., & RICHARDS, R. W. Aversive properties of the negative stimulus during learning with and without errors. *Learning and Motivation*, (New York: Academic Press, Inc., 1973) *4*, 1–10.

ROSEN, A. P., & TERRACE, H. S. On the minimal conditions for the development of a peak-shift and inhibitory stimulus control. *Journal of the Experimental Analysis of Behavior*, 1975, *23*, 385–414.

SADOWSKY, S. Behavioral contrast with timeout, blackout, or extinction as the negative condition. *Journal of the Experimental Analysis of Behavior*, 1973, *19*, 499–507.

SCHADLER, M., & THOMAS, D. R. On the acquisition of dimensional stimulus control by the pigeon. *Journal of Comparative and Physiological Psychology*, 1972, *79*, 82–89.

SCHLOSBERG, H., & SOLOMON, R. L. Latency of response in a choice discrimination. *Journal of Experimental Psychology*, 1943, *33*, 22–39.

SCHWARTZBAUM, J. S., & KELLICUT, M. H. Inverted generalization gradients about a nonreinforced stimulus. *Psychological Reports*, 1962, *11*, 791–792.

SELEKMAN, W. Behavioral contrast and inhibitory stimulus

control as related to extended training. *Journal of the Experimental Analysis of Behavior*, 1973, *20*, 245–252.

SELIGMAN, M. E. P., & HAGER, J. L. (Eds.). *Biological boundaries of learning.* Englewood Cliffs, N.J.: Prentice-Hall, Inc., 1972.

SHETTLEWORTH, S. J. Constraints on learning. In D. S. Lehrman, R. A. Hinde, & E. Shaw (Eds.), *Advances in the study of behavior.* New York: Academic Press, 1972.

SIDMAN, M. Avoidance behavior. In W. K. Honig (Ed.), *Operant behavior: Areas of research and application.* Englewood Cliffs, N.J.: Prentice-Hall, Inc., 1966.

SKINNER, B. F. *The behavior of organisms.* New York: Appleton-Century-Crofts, 1938.

SKINNER, B. F. Are theories of learning necessary? *Psychological Review*, 1950, *57*, 193–216.

SKINNER, B. F. Why we need teaching machines. *Harvard Educational Review*, 1961, *31*, 377–398.

SKINNER, B. F. Stimulus generalization of an operant: A historical note. In D. I. Mostofsky (Ed.), *Stimulus generalization.* Stanford: Stanford University Press, 1965.

SKINNER, B. F. *Contingencies of reinforcement: A theoretical analysis.* Englewood Cliffs, N.J.: Prentice-Hall, Inc., 1969.

SPEAR, N. E. Forgetting as retrieval failure. In W. K. Honig & P. H. R. James (Eds.), *Animal memory.* New York: Academic Press, 1971.

SPENCE, K. W. The nature of discrimination learning in animals. *Psychological Review*, 1936, *43*, 427–449.

SPENCE, K. W. The differential response in animals to stimuli varying within a single dimension. *Psychological Review*, 1937, *44*, 430–444.

STADDON, J. E. R. Inhibition and the operant. A review of sensory inhibition by G. V. Bekesy & Mach Bands: Quantitative studies on neural networks in the retina by F. Ratliff. *Journal of the Experimental Analysis of Behavior*, 1969, *12*, 481–489.

STADDON, J. E. R. Temporal control, attention, and memory. *Psychological Review*, 1974, *81*, 375–391.

STADDON, J. E. R., & SIMMELHAG, V. L. The "superstition" experiment: A reexamination of its implications for the principles of adaptive behavior. *Psychological Review*, 1971, *78*, 3–43.

STEVENSON, J. G. Stimulus generalization: The ordering and spacing of test stimuli. *Journal of the Experimental Analysis of Behavior*, 1966, *9*, 457–468.

STODDARD, L. T. & SIDMAN, M. The effects of errors on children's performance of a circle-ellipse discrimination. *Journal of the Experimental Analysis of Behavior*, 1967, *10*, 261–270.

STODDARD, L. T. & SIDMAN, M. The removal and restoration of stimulus control. *Journal of the Experimental Analysis of Behavior*, 1971, *16*, 143–154.

SWITALSKI, R. W., LYONS, J., & THOMAS, D. R. Effects of interdimensional training on stimulus generalization. *Journal of Experimental Psychology*, 1966, *72*, 661–666.

TAUS, S. E. & HEARST, E. Effects of intertrial (blackout) duration on response rate to a positive stimulus. *Psychonomic Science*, 1970, *19*, 265–267.

TERRACE, H. S. Discrimination learning with and without errors. *Journal of the Experimental Analysis of Behavior*, 1963, *6*, 1–27. (a)

TERRACE, H. S. Errorless transfer of a discrimination across two continua. *Journal of the Experimental Analysis of Behavior*, 1963, *6*, 223–232. (b)

TERRACE, H. S. Wavelength generalization after discrimination learning with and without errors. *Science*, 1964, *144*, 78–80.

TERRACE, H. S. Behavioral contrast and the peak shift: Effects of extended discrimination training. *Journal of the Experimental Analysis of Behavior*, 1966, *9*, 613–617. (a)

TERRACE, H. S. Discrimination learning and inhibition. *Science*, 1966, *154*, 1677–1680. (b)

TERRACE, H. S. Stimulus control. In W. K. Honig (Ed.), *Operant conditioning: Areas of research and application.* Englewood Cliffs, N.J.: Prentice-Hall, Inc., 1966. (c)

TERRACE, H. S. Discrimination learning, the peak shift, and behavioral contrast. *Journal of the Experimental Analysis of Behavior*, 1968, *11*, 727–741.

TERRACE, H. S. Escape from S−. *Learning and Motivation*, 1971, *2*, 148–163.

TERRACE, H. S. By-products of discrimination learning. In G. H. Bower (Ed.), *The psychology of learning and motivation* (Vol. 5). New York: Academic Press, 1972.

TERRACE, H. S. Conditioned inhibition in successive discrimination learning. *Transactions of the New York Academy of Sciences* (Series II), 1973, *35*, 39–50.

THOMAS, D. R. The effects of drive and discrimination training on stimulus generalization. *Journal of Experimental Psychology*, 1962, *64*, 24–28.

THOMAS, D. R. The use of operant conditioning techniques to investigate perceptual processes in animals. In R. M. Gilbert & N. S. Sutherland (Eds.), *Animal discrimination learning.* New York: Academic Press, 1969.

THOMAS, D. R. Stimulus selection, attention, and related matters. In J. H. Reynierse (Ed.), *Current issues in animal learning.* Lincoln: University of Nebraska Press, 1970.

THOMAS, D. R., & BARKER, E. G. The effects of extinction and "central tendency" on stimulus generalization in pigeons. *Psychonomic Science*, 1964, *1*, 199–121.

THOMAS, D. R., & SETZER, J. Stimulus generalization gradients for auditory intensity in rats and guinea pigs. *Psychonomic Science*, 1972, *28*, 22–24.

THOMAS, D. R., & SWITALSKI, R. W. Comparison of stimulus generalization following variable-ratio and variable-interval training. *Journal of Experimental Psychology*, 1966, *71*, 236–240.

THOMAS, D. R., & WILLIAMS, J. L. A further study of stimulus generalization following three-stimulus discrimination training. *Journal of the Experimental Analysis of Behavior*, 1963, *6*, 171–176.

VIETH, H. A., & RILLING, M. E. Comparison of timeout and extinction as determinants of behavioral contrast: An analysis of sequential effects. *Psychonomic Science*, 1972, *27*, 281–282.

WAGNER, A. R., & RESCORLA, R. A. Inhibition in Pavlovian conditioning application of a theory. In R. A. Boakes & M. S. Halliday (Eds.), *Inhibition and learning.* New York: Academic Press, 1972.

WEISMAN, R. G. Some determinants of inhibitory stimulus control. *Journal of the Experimental Analysis of Behavior*, 1969, *12*, 443–450.

WEISMAN, R. G. Factors influencing inhibitory stimulus control: Differential reinforcement of other behavior during discrimination training. *Journal of the Experimental Analysis of Behavior,* 1970, *14,* 87–91.

WEISMAN, R. G., & PALMER, J. A. Factors influencing inhibitory stimulus control: Discrimination training and prior nondifferential reinforcement. *Journal of the Experimental Analysis of Behavior,* 1969, *12,* 229–237.

WEISMAN, R. G., & RAMSDEN, M. Discrimination of a response-independent component in a multiple schedule. *Journal of the Experimental Analysis of Behavior,* 1973, *19,* 55–64.

WEISS, S. J. Discrimination training and stimulus compounding consideration of nonreinforcement and response differentiation consequences of S^Δ. *Journal of the Experimental Analysis of Behavior,* 1971, *15,* 387–402.

WEISS, S. J. Stimulus compounding in free-operant and classical conditioning: A review and analysis. *Psychological Bulletin,* 1972, *78,* 189–208. (a)

WEISS, S. J. Free-operant compounding of high- and low-rate discriminative stimuli: An interresponse time analysis. *Learning and Motivation,* 1972, *3,* 469–478. (b)

WEISS, S. J. Discriminative and incentive interactions in composite-stimulus control of free operant behavior. Paper presented at the 82nd Annual Convention of the American Psychological Association, 1974.

WEISS, S. J. & VAN OST, S. L. Response discriminative and reinforcement factors in stimulus control of performance on multiple and chained schedules of reinforcement. *Learning and Motivation,* 1974, *5,* 459–472.

WESSELLS, M. G. Errorless discrimination, autoshaping, and conditioned inhibition. *Science,* 1973, *182,* 941–943.

WESSELLS, M. G. The effects of reinforcement upon the pre-pecking behaviors of pigeons in the autoshaping experiment. *Journal of the Experimental Analysis of Behavior,* 1974, *21,* 125–144.

WHEATLEY, K. L., & THOMAS, D. R. Relative and absolute density of reinforcement as factors influencing the peak shift. *Journal of the Experimental Analysis of Behavior,* 1974, *22,* 409–418.

WHITE, K. G. Post-discrimination generalization as a function of interresponse time. *Animal Learning and Behavior,* 1973, *1,* 297–301.

WILKIE, D. M. The peak shift and behavioral contrast: Effects of discrimination training with delayed reinforcement. *Psychonomic Science,* 1972, *26,* 257–258.

WILKIE, D. M. Stimulus control of responding during a fixed interval reinforcement schedule. *Journal of the Experimental Analysis of Behavior,* 1974, *21,* 425–432.

WILKIE, D. M., & RAMER, R. G. Errorless discrimination established by differential autoshaping. *Journal of the Experimental Analysis of Behavior,* 1974, *22,* 333–340.

WILTON, R. N. & CLEMENTS, R. O. Behavioral contrast as a function of the duration of an immediately preceding period of extinction. *Journal of the Experimental Analysis of Behavior,* 1971, *16,* 425–428.

WINTON, J. S. W. & BEALE, I. L. Peak shift in concurrent schedules. *Journal of the Experimental Analysis of Behavior,* 1971, *15,* 73–81.

YARCZOWER, M. Behavioral contrast and inhibitive stimulus control. *Psychonomic Science,* 1970, *18,* 1–3.

YARCZOWER, M. Discriminative effects of massed extinction. *Journal of the Experimental Analysis of Behavior,* 1974, *22,* 161–168.

YARCZOWER, M., & CURTO, K. Stimulus control in pigeons after extended discrimination training. *Journal of Comparative and Physiological Psychology,* 1972, *80,* 484–489.

YARCZOWER, M., DICKSON, J. F., & GOLLUB, L. R. Some effects on generalization gradients of tandem schedules. *Journal of the Experimental Analysis of Behavior,* 1966, *9,* 631–639.

YARCZOWER, M., & EVANS, G. "Combined cue" test of conditioned inhibition in pigeons. *Journal of Comparative and Physiological Psychology,* 1974, *87,* 261–266.

YARCZOWER, M., GOLLUB, L. R., & DICKSON, J. F. Some effects of discriminative training with equated frequency of reinforcement. *Journal of the Experimental Analysis of Behavior,* 1968, *11,* 415–423.

YARCZOWER, M., & SWITALSKI, R. Stimulus control in the goldfish after massed extinction. *Journal of the Experimental Analysis of Behavior,* 1969, *12,* 565–570.

16

Stimulus Control

attentional factors*

N. J. Mackintosh

INTRODUCTION

Experimental subjects do not respond, nor do experimenters arrange contingencies of reinforcement, in a vacuum. In experiments on both classical and operant conditioning, the experimenter delivers reinforcers only in the presence of a specific set of stimuli. This is most obviously true of classical experiments, where the availability of reinforcement is always signaled by the presentation of a specific conditional stimulus (CS). But it is equally true of operant experiments, for operant responses are reinforced only when they occur in a specific situation. At the least they are reinforced only in the experimental chamber. Often, they are reinforced only during certain periods of an experimental session, with these being marked by the presentation of explicit discriminative stimuli signaling that some class of responses will be reinforced according to a particular schedule.

If the experimental situation or the experimenter's discriminative stimulus or CS is changed in one or more ways, it is common to observe an apparently correlated change in the subject's behavior. A pigeon that receives food on a variable-interval schedule for pecking at a key illuminated with green light will peck at a lower rate if the color of the light is changed to red. A dog salivating upon every presentation of a 1,000-Hz tone signaling the delivery of food may salivate less profusely if a 2,000-Hz tone is presented. If a change in a particular stimulus is always followed by a change in the probability, amplitude, latency, or rate of a particular response, we may say that this stimulus exercised some control over that response. The term *stimulus control* has come to be used as a convenient shorthand expression for describing such an observed relationship between changes in external stimuli and changes in recorded behavior.

In the hands of some writers, the term *stimulus control* has been characterized as "relatively neutral" and as one to be preferred to "traditional concepts of generalization and discrimination" (Terrace, 1966, p.

---

* The preparation of this chapter was supported by grants from the National Research Council of Canada and the U.K. Science Research Council. I am indebted to Vicky Gray for permission to cite the results of unpublished research and to A. Dickinson, G. Hall, and the editors of this volume for their extensive and valuable comments on an earlier draft.

271). It is, of course, possible to reserve the term *stimulus control* solely to refer to the slope of a generalization gradient, but it is neither clear that it is particularly profitable to do so nor obvious that it has always been used in this purely descriptive sense. In the present chapter, at any rate, the term will not be used in this strictly neutral way. To say that a particular stimulus has acquired control over a subject's behavior, I shall assume, is tantamount to saying that this stimulus has been established as a signal for reinforcement, or as a signal that a certain class of responses will be reinforced.[1] Evidence that a stimulus has been successfully established as a signal for reinforcement may be provided in a variety of ways. One way is to show that changes in some features of the stimulus result in correlated changes in behavior. Another way would be to show that the removal of the stimulus resulted in the cessation of the subject's responses. Yet other measures of control are possible: the rate of subsequent discrimination learning, when the original stimulus continues to signal reinforcement and a second stimulus signals nonreinforcement, would be equally acceptable measures of the control gained by the stimulus.

The slope of a generalization gradient, therefore, is only one of several potential measures of stimulus control. It is not even necessarily the best or most sensitive measure. Thus if an experimenter observes a flat gradient of generalization when he varies some aspect of the training situation, he is not entitled to conclude that this aspect had gained no control over his subject's behavior. He may say, if he wishes, that this aspect exerted no control over responding on this series of test trials, but this, of course, is no more than a redescription of the outcome of the data. The flat gradient is not necessarily evidence that this stimulus failed to acquire control over behavior; it may simply imply that the testing procedure is inadequate to demonstrate such control. Flat gradients are often, for example, consequences of ceiling or floor effects. Farthing and Hearst (1970) trained pigeons on a discrimination between a vertical line displayed on a blue background and a horizontal line on a green background. When given a series of nonreinforced test trials to the component stimuli as well as to various compounds, they responded at so low a rate to vertical and horizontal lines presented on black backgrounds that it was impossible to detect any evidence of significant control by the orientation of the line. Other tests, however, revealed a substantial difference in the readiness to respond to vertical and horizontal lines (see also Zentall, 1972).

Conversely, a subject with a very high probability of responding in the training situation may continue to respond on all test trials, and thus show a flat gradient of generalization because of a ceiling effect. This may happen only rarely in experiments which study rate of key pecking in pigeons, for rate of responding is a relatively unbounded measure of response strength. Where more bounded measures are used, such as the proportion of trials on which a response occurs, or measures of conditioned suppression in aversive conditioning, there is clear evidence that ceiling effects may obscure the control actually gained by a stimulus, which is only displayed during the course of an extended series of test trials (e.g., Gray & Mackintosh, 1973; Hoffman & Fleshler, 1961).

A second reason why the control gained by one stimulus may not be revealed in a generalization test is that other aspects of the experimental situation may have gained even stronger control over responding. If these other stimuli remain unchanged during the course of testing, they may maintain a constant rate of responding and thus "mask" the control actually acquired by the stimulus varied during testing. The concept of masking is one that will play a central role in later sections of this chapter. For the present, it will be sufficient to provide a brief example. Newman and Baron (1965) trained pigeons to peck a response key illuminated with a white vertical line on a green background. When given a generalization test to other orientations of the line, still shown on a green background, the pigeons responded at a relatively constant rate to orientations of the line as far as 45° on either side of vertical. Several later studies, however, while confirming this finding, have shown that under conditions where a significant level of responding can be maintained in the absence of the colored background, a reliably sloping gradient of generalization can be observed when different orientations of the line are shown on a black background (Freeman & Thomas, 1967; Newman & Benefield, 1968; Thomas, Svinicki, & Svinicki, 1970).

The flat gradient in the first case reflects more about the control over responding acquired by the colored background than about the *lack* of control acquired by the line. A particular feature of the reinforced stimulus display may indeed acquire control over responding, but this control may be masked dur-

---

[1] A stimulus may also gain control if it is established as a signal for the omission of a reinforcer or as a signal that certain responses will not be reinforced. The phenomena of inhibitory control, discussed by Rilling in chapter 15, are not specifically discussed here. It seems reasonable, however, to expect that many of the principles derivable from studies of excitatory stimulus control will apply equally to the case of inhibitory control.

ing a subsequent test, because the unchanged presence of another set of features insures a uniform rate of responding on all test trials.

The behavior of a subject in a generalization test, therefore, does not necessarily provide a simple or direct measure of the control acquired by the stimulus during earlier training. This point has a number of important implications. It may not always be easy, for example, to determine whether differences in the slope of a generalization gradient following different experimental treatments reflect differences in the control acquired as a consequence of those treatments, or the effects of those treatments on the host of other variables that may affect test performance. If different treatments produce substantially different rates of responding, differences in test performance may reflect ceiling or floor effects influencing one gradient more than the other. If different treatments produce substantial differences in resistance to extinction, then, since it is known that gradients become progressively steeper during the course of extinction (Hoffman & Fleshler, 1961; Jenkins & Harrison, 1960; Thomas & Barker, 1964), their effect on generalization gradients may be simply attributed to this factor rather than to their effect on stimulus control per se.

Examples of one or more of these possibilities will recur in what follows. It will be important to remember that generalization gradients provide but one of several methods of measuring stimulus control and that the assessment of stimulus control is necessarily an indirect affair. We do not observe stimulus control in the data of a generalization test. We may infer that a stimulus has acquired control over a subject's behavior by noting a correlation between changes in stimuli and changes in responding. But the inference is not always easy.

CONDITIONS AFFECTING THE ESTABLISHMENT OF STIMULUS CONTROL

The study of stimulus control has for a long time centered around the question of the sufficient and necessary conditions responsible for the observation of a sloping gradient of generalization when some feature of the training situation is varied. As Terrace (1966) noted, one aspect of this issue was the objection raised by Lashley and Wade (1946) against what they called a "Pavlovian theory of generalization." Lashley and Wade argued that Hull and Spence had followed Pavlov in supposing that the reinforcement of a response in the presence of a particular stimulus was sufficient to establish a center of excitation, and that this excitation would spread to other stimuli in proportion to their similarity to the training stimulus. Sloping gradients were an automatic consequence of reinforcement in the presence of a particular stimulus. Although this view can be seriously attributed neither to Hull nor to Spence, it is fair to acknowledge that Lashley and Wade's paper, by stressing the point that sloping gradients might *not* be an automatic consequence of the delivery of reinforcement in the presence of a particular stimulus, did provide valuable impetus in initiating research designed to uncover the conditions necessary and sufficient for the establishment and demonstration of control by any set of stimuli.

Intrinsic Differences in the Salience of Stimuli

These are important questions. Perhaps even more important, however, is the realization that they may not admit of any one, general answer. There is no reason to suppose that a single set of conditions, sufficient and necessary for the establishment of stimulus control in one case, will hold for all stimuli, responses, reinforcers, or subjects. The control exercised by a particular stimulus over the behavior of a particular subject will obviously depend on that subject's sensory apparatus; pigeons are more likely than rats, for example, to be controlled by the wavelength of a discriminative stimulus. Equally, the amount of training required to establish control by a particular stimulus will surely vary from stimulus to stimulus, and in a situation where a number of different stimuli are equally correlated with reinforcement, some will acquire greater control over responding than others. These are not surprising observations. No one would deny that some stimuli appear to be more effective for some subjects than are others. It may even be useful to characterize such differences as consequences of differences in the "salience" of particular stimuli to particular subjects, provided that the circular nature of the definition is appreciated. There are, however, less obvious, and therefore rather more interesting, constraints on the generality of possible answers (Shettleworth, 1972).

Nature of Response and Reinforcer

Dobrzecka, Szwejkowska, and Konorski (1966) have shown that the features of an auditory stimulus which come to control the responses of a dog may depend upon the nature of the response required by the experimenter. Dogs were placed in a stand and exposed to two discriminative stimuli, a metronome in

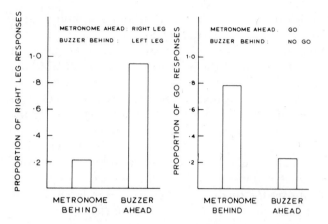

Fig. 1. Results of experiment by Dobrzecka et al. (1966). In the left panel are shown the results from dogs trained to respond with different legs to qualitatively different auditory stimuli, located in different positions. When tested with the stimuli in reversed positions, they reverse their responses. The right panel shows the results from dogs trained either to raise or not to raise their right leg. When tested with the position of metronome and buzzer reversed, they continue to respond as before.

front and a buzzer sounded from behind. One group was required to raise their right foreleg in response to one stimulus and their left foreleg in response to the other; a second group was trained on a go–no go discrimination, being required to raise their right foreleg to one stimulus and to refrain from responding in the presence of the other. Subjects were then tested by reversing the positions of the metronome and buzzer. The results of these test trials are shown in Figure 1. It can be seen that if animals were required to learn which foot to raise, the location of the signal had acquired control over responding, while animals required to learn the go–no go discrimination had learned to respond to the metronome and not respond to the buzzer, regardless of the position from which they were sounded.

Thus although the dogs were perfectly well able to discriminate both between the locations of the buzzer and of the metronome, and between the quality of the sound produced by each source, responding was controlled in one case only by the qualitative difference, and in the other case only by the difference in location. The selective control observed cannot be attributed to differences in the salience of the two cues, if this is understood to refer to the physical characteristics of a stimulus and to the subject's sensory capacities.

The work of Garcia, Revusky, Rozin, and others has suggested that when a particular reinforcing event follows the ingestion of food, the feature of the food which will be established as a signal for reinforcement will depend on the nature of the reinforcer

(Garcia & Ervin, 1968; Revusky & Garcia, 1970; Rozin & Kalat, 1971). Rats appear to associate the flavor of food or water with subsequent poisoning, and the visual or other external features accompanying its ingestion with a reinforcer such as electric shock. In a study that is, in effect, rather similar in design to that of Dobrzecka et al., Garcia and Koelling (1966) gave rats the opportunity to drink water having a particular flavor and whose ingestion was accompanied by a particular set of visual and auditory stimuli. One group received an electric shock, either immediately or after a delay, contingent on drinking this water; a second group was made sick either by an injection of lithium chloride or by X-irradiation. The results of a series of test trials, in which the flavor and the visual and auditory cues were separately presented, are shown in Figure 2. The shocked animals showed a marked reduction in their consumption of water accompanied by these visual and auditory stimuli, but no aversion to the specific flavor used in training; poisoned rats, on the other hand, showed an aversion to the flavor of the water they had been exposed to, but none to the visual and auditory stimuli accompanying its ingestion.

The specific features of food or drink that are associated with subsequent poisoning may differ from one group of animals to another. Predatory birds, for example, associate the visual characteristics of their prey with its unpalatable taste (Brower, 1969); this is, of course, a feature of their behavior responsible for the evolution of visual Batesian mimicry among prey

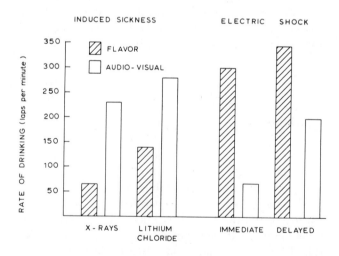

Fig. 2. Rate of drinking during test trials when rats have been punished for drinking water with a particular flavor and whose ingestion was accompanied by a particular set of audiovisual stimuli. The flavor of the water was established as the effective signal when induced sickness was the aversive reinforcer, but the audiovisual stimuli became the effective signal if electric shock was the aversive reinforcer. (After Garcia & Koelling, 1966.)

species. Other birds have been shown to associate the visual characteristics of water, rather than its taste, with subsequent poisoning (Wilcoxon, Dragoin, & Kral, 1971). How far these differences between different species may be attributed merely to differences in sensory capacity is not at present certain. The important point is that in Garcia and Koelling's experiment, as in that of Dobrzecka et al., one component of a compound stimulus acquired control over behavior under one condition, while the other component acquired control under a second condition.

Garcia's findings reflect an apparent dependency between specific stimuli and specific reinforcers, but they should not necessarily be regarded simply as a consequence of the specialized nature of the system regulating food intake. Foree and LoLordo (1973), for example, found that the elements of a compound stimulus that gained control over responding in pigeons depended on whether responding was being reinforced by the presentation of food or by the avoidance of electric shock. On a series of discrete trials, signaled by the combined illumination of a red light and the presentation of a 440-Hz tone, pigeons were trained to press a treadle either to obtain food or to avoid shock. When tested with these components in isolation, subjects reinforced with food tended to respond only in the presence of the light, while those reinforced by the avoidance of shock responded more to the auditory than to the visual component. At the very least, these results suggest that the well-known difficulty of establishing control over food-reinforced key pecking in pigeons by an auditory stimulus (see below) cannot be entirely attributed to defects in the birds' sensory system.

Garcia and Ervin (1968) and Rozin and Kalat (1971) have argued that the rat's readiness to associate flavors with illness is a prime example of an adaptive specialization in learning. One can hardly doubt that such learning is of adaptive significance in the life of a relatively omnivorous animal, but to point to the adaptive significance of a particular characteristic is not the same as specifying the causal factors responsible for its appearance in any particular individual. There may be genetically determined constraints on the probability that different stimuli will become signals for different reinforcers. It is also possible, however, that a subject's prior experience of correlations between events in its environment may affect the probability of certain events being established as signals for others. It is possible, for example, that an adult rat has had a lifetime's experience in which gastric changes have been correlated with changes in recently experienced tastes, but uncorrelated with changes in auditory or visual stimuli, or that an adult pigeon has an extensive experience of correlations between changes in visual stimuli and changes in the probability of food, but no correlation between auditory changes and the availability of food. Before accepting Garcia and Rozin's inference, therefore, it is important to see how far prior experience can affect the establishment of stimulus control.

Prior Experience

Although numerous experimenters have exposed animals to a variety of different experiences with particular sets of stimuli, before training them to respond to those, or similar, stimuli, they have only rarely been concerned to provide answers to the questions raised by the results discussed in the preceding section. It will be necessary to survey rapidly some of the other questions posed, and answers provided, before returning to this issue.

EARLY EXPERIENCE: LASHLEY AND WADE'S HYPOTHESIS

One of Lashley and Wade's theses was that a change in some aspect of the training situation would produce a correlated change in the subject's behavior only if that subject had some prior experience of variation along this stimulus dimension. "The 'dimensions' of a stimulus," they wrote, "are determined by comparison of two or more stimuli and do not exist for the organism until established by differential training" (Lashley & Wade, 1946, p. 74). The implication that has been investigated in a number of studies is that animals deprived of all experience of variations along a particular stimulus dimension by restricted conditions of rearing will produce flat gradients of generalization along that dimension.

Some results reported by Peterson (1962) appeared to provide some initial support for this suggestion. Peterson trained two groups of young ducklings to peck a key illuminated with sodium light of 589 nm and then tested them for generalization to other wavelengths. Two birds reared in normal illumination showed orderly and sloping wavelength gradients with a peak at 589 nm. Four other birds, however, had been reared in individual cages diffusely illuminated by sodium light, and had thus received little or no experience of variations in wavelength before the generalization test. All four birds showed flat wavelength gradients. Peterson's results have been thought to imply that "a necessary condition for obtaining a generalization gradient of wavelength whose slope is greater than zero is prior exposure to white light. White light presumably allowed differential reinforcement with respect to different wavelengths to occur prior to the generalization test" (Terrace, 1966, p. 279).

As I shall argue below, it is questionable whether this conclusion necessarily follows from Peterson's results. For the moment, however, it will be enough to question the reliability and generality of those results. Tracy (1970) has attempted to replicate Peterson's experiment with a larger number of subjects, but with at best only partial success. He did, indeed, find that birds reared in monochromatic sodium light showed somewhat flatter gradients than those reared in normal illumination, but the main results of his experiment, shown in Figure 3, leave no doubt that their responding was moderately well controlled by changes in wavelength. Tracy further showed that the difference between the gradients of these two groups may have been partly a consequence of the effect of rearing on preferences for different wavelengths. The right-hand panel of Figure 3 shows wavelength gradients of control and experimental subjects following reinforcement in the presence of a white vertical line on a black key. It can be seen that even without any prior reinforcement in the presence of 589 nm, the sodium-reared birds showed a greater preference for shorter wavelengths than did the controls. It is in this region of the spectrum, as the left-hand panel of Figure 3 shows, that their gradients were flatter than those of controls following wavelength training.

Ganz and Riesen (1962), in a study with monkeys published at about the same time as Peterson's experiment, presented data suggesting that monkeys reared in complete darkness might initially generalize a trained response relatively completely to wavelengths other than that to which they were trained to respond. Dark-reared and control subjects were trained to press a response key for sucrose solution while exposed to monochromatic light projected to their right eye. When tested with other wavelengths, interspersed with reinforced retraining trials with the original stimulus, control subjects showed an orderly, sloping gradient from the first day of testing, while those reared in the dark produced an initially flat gradient, which gradually became steeper during the course of successive test sessions. The results of the first test session, therefore, suggest that dark rearing may initially flatten generalization gradients in monkeys.

Several later experiments, however, employing other subjects, such as chicks or Japanese quail, have completely failed to substantiate Ganz and Riesen's or Peterson's results. Neither rearing in monochromatic light nor rearing in total darkness has been found to have any significant effect on the slope of wavelength gradients in these subjects (Malott, 1968; Rudolph & Honig, 1972; Rudolph, Honig, & Gerry, 1969).

The conclusion must be, then, that prior experience of variation along a particular stimulus dimension is not a necessary condition for the establishment of control by a stimulus falling on that dimension. Extended rearing under restricted conditions, of course, might interfere with the normal development of the neural mechanisms underlying stimulus analysis, and it is possible that such an effect might be more pronounced in primates than in birds. But as a general rule, it is clear that artificial restrictions on a subject's prior experience do not necessarily disrupt the normal development of simple perceptual analysis, and do not prevent the normal establishment of stimulus control under appropriate training conditions.

Nonreinforced Exposure to a Single Stimulus: Latent Inhibition

In Tracy's (1970) experiment with ducklings, there was some suggestion that monochromatic rearing might have had some tendency to flatten the gradient of wavelength generalization. Although this appears to have been largely due to a change in the unconditional preference for different wavelengths, there is another factor that might have been responsible for such an effect. Numerous studies have now established that repeated exposure to a particular stimulus in the

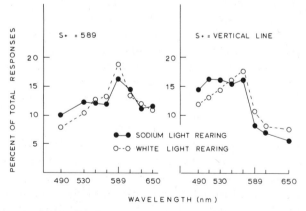

Fig. 3. Relative gradients of wavelength generalization in ducklings reared either in white light or in monochromatic sodium light (589 nm). The left panel shows gradients obtained after reinforcement for responding to 589 nm. The right panel shows gradients after reinforcement for responding to a vertical white line. (After Tracy, 1970. © 1970 by the Society for the Experimental Analysis of Behavior, Inc.)

absence of reinforcement may significantly impair the subsequent establishment of control by that stimulus when it is presented either as a CS or as a discriminative stimulus.

This finding was first clearly reported by Lubow and Moore (1959), who termed the effect "latent inhibition." In their experiment, goats and sheep received 10 nonreinforced presentations of a stimulus that later served as a CS signaling shock to the foreleg. These animals acquired a conditioned flexion response significantly more slowly than control subjects who received no preexposure to the CS. Lubow and Moore suggested that this interference with the acquisition of a conditioned flexion response might have been a consequence of the establishment of some incompatible response during preexposure. A subsequent experiment provided little support for this suggestion (Lubow, 1965), and it has been convincingly disproved by the results of several later experiments (Halgren, 1974; Reiss & Wagner, 1972; Rescorla, 1971). In all of these studies, nonreinforced preexposure to a stimulus interfered with both excitatory and inhibitory conditioning to that stimulus. In Rescorla's experiment, for example, rats were given nonreinforced preexposure to a tone before the start of conditioned emotional response (CER) conditioning. When the tone signaled shock, preexposed subjects showed poorer conditioning than controls; but if a light was used to signal shock, and a tone-light compound to signal the omission of shock, preexposed animals not only learned to suppress to the light as rapidly as controls, they also continued to suppress to the tone-light compound longer than the controls.

The implication is that nonreinforced exposure to a stimulus may interfere with the establishment of that stimulus as a signal either for reinforcement or for the omission of reinforcement. If the effect of such exposure were simply to condition a response incompatible with the required conditioned response (CR), it should obviously facilitate, rather than interfere with, the development of conditioned inhibition. Latent inhibition is, moreover, a quite general phenomenon, having been observed in a variety of classical conditioning preparations (Lubow, 1973), as well as in studies of operant discrimination learning (Hearst, 1972; Mellgren & Ost, 1969). It is certain, therefore, that prior experience with a particular stimulus will significantly affect the establishment of control by that stimulus—although the effect is not that which Lashley and Wade would have predicted. Exposure to a particular set of stimuli, so far from being a necessary condition for the establishment of control by those stimuli, may interfere with the establishment of control. Monochromatic rearing, as in Peterson's (1962) and Tracy's (1970) experiments, may reduce the slope of gradients of wavelength generalization, not because it abolishes the experience of variations in wavelength, but because it insures that the wavelength used in training is not readily established as a signal for reinforcement.

Exposure to Various Correlations
Between Stimuli and
Reinforcement

In experiments stimulated by Lashley and Wade's assumptions about the importance of early experience, as in studies of latent inhibition, exposure to a particular stimulus is scheduled without any correlated exposure to reinforcement. There is, however, another group of studies which has systematically analyzed the effects of exposure to different correlations between stimuli and reinforcers on the subsequent acquisition of control by those stimuli. Among the earliest and best known of such experiments are those of Lawrence (1949, 1950) on the acquired distinctiveness of cues, in which transfer between simultaneous and successive discriminations in the rat was shown to depend on the relationship between the relevant stimuli of the two problems. Later studies of intradimensional and extradimensional shifts, in which, having learned one problem, animals are shifted to a second, where the relevant stimuli are either from the same dimension as, or from a different dimension from, those relevant in the first problem, have confirmed that experience of a correlation between a particular set of stimuli and reinforcement will selectively increase the probability that similar stimuli will subsequently gain control over responding in a new situation (Shepp & Eimas, 1964; Shepp & Schrier, 1969).

An experiment by Thomas, Mariner, and Sherry (1969) suggests that the principle of acquired distinctiveness may be used to counteract the difficulty of establishing auditory control over food-reinforced key pecking in pigeons. They confirmed the finding, first reported by Jenkins and Harrison (1960), that nondifferential reinforcement of a pigeon's key pecks in the presence of a 1,000-Hz tone would result in essentially flat gradients of generalization when the frequency of the tone was varied between 300 and 3,500 Hz. For 100 days before the start of key-peck training, however, a second group of pigeons received their daily ration of food in their home cages always signaled by a 1,000-Hz tone. All birds in this group showed a steep and orderly gradient of generalization along the auditory frequency dimension, with a peak of responses at 1,000 Hz. It would be of considerable interest to see whether similar results could be obtained if the auditory stimuli established as signals for food during preexperimental treatment were not exactly the same as the tone presented during key-peck training. This would suggest that the results of Thomas et al. represented a general change in the probability of auditory stimuli gaining control over food-reinforced behavior.

Foree and LoLordo (1973), it will be recalled, found that although a visual stimulus was more likely than an auditory stimulus to gain control over food-reinforced responding in pigeons, this ordering was reversed when subjects were required to make the same response in order to avoid shock. Is it possible that this differential sensitivity to visual stimuli as signals for food, and to auditory stimuli as signals for shock, is related to the normal early experience of the pigeon via a process similar to that observed in experiments on acquired distinctiveness? For this to be true, it would be necessary to assume that experience of a correlation between a particular class of stimuli and a particular class of reinforcer would selectively alter the distinctiveness of those stimuli as signals for those reinforcers. It is possible that in the pigeon's normal experience the availability of food is more reliably signaled by visual than by auditory stimuli (as noted by Jenkins & Harrison, 1960), but if this is to help explain Foree and LoLordo's results, it must be assumed that this enhances the distinctiveness of visual stimuli as signals for food, but not as signals for shock.

There is, in fact, some evidence of precisely such a reinforcer-specific change in the distinctiveness of particular stimuli. Mackintosh (1973) found that if rats were exposed to uncorrelated presentations of a tone and shock, subsequent conditioning between tone and shock was severely retarded, although the tone could be rapidly established as a signal for water. Conversely, exposure to uncorrelated presentations of tone and water retarded subsequent tone-water conditioning, without having a comparable effect on tone-shock conditioning. Thus a stimulus that has in the past signaled no change in the probability of one reinforcer will be established as a signal for that reinforcer only with difficulty, but may readily serve as a signal for another reinforcer.

Conclusions

There is, then, evidence that prior exposure to a particular correlation between a stimulus and a reinforcer may affect the control over responding acquired by that stimulus during subsequent experimental training. Exposure to a positive correlation between a stimulus and reinforcer may increase the control gained by that stimulus; unreinforced presentations of a stimulus or exposure to uncorrelated presentations of a stimulus and reinforcer may decrease the control gained by that stimulus when subsequently paired with reinforcement. There is, however, little reason to accept Lashley and Wade's contention that prior exposure to a set of stimuli, in and of itself, without regard to the relationship between those stimuli and reinforcement experienced during such treatment, is a particularly important determinant of generalization gradients. There is certainly no evidence to support the view that prior exposure to variations along a stimulus dimension is a necessary prerequisite for the establishment of control by that dimension. While the ability of a stimulus to acquire control over a subject's behavior depends on that subject's past experience, therefore, there is no reason to suppose that the perception of stimulus relations is always dependent on exposure to variations in that stimulus. For at least some subjects and some stimulus dimensions, the perceptual system is already organized to respond differentially and in an orderly manner to variations along that dimension. This is not to say that the dimensions of stimuli to which animals respond correspond exactly to the physical dimensions, such as wavelength, visual intensity, or auditory frequency, which are manipulated by experimenters. It is obvious that we know very little about the dimensions along which animals are capable of classifying their environment.

EXPERIMENTAL PROCEDURES: NONDIFFERENTIAL REINFORCEMENT AND DISCRIMINATION TRAINING

Much of the experimental analysis of stimulus control in operant experiments has consisted of attempts to specify the training procedures required to establish control by particular stimuli. The volume of research conducted is testimony to the conclusion that no single set of conditions appears sufficient and necessary for all stimuli, subjects, or experimental situations. Experimental conditions apparently sufficient to establish control by visual stimuli over a pigeon's food-reinforced behavior, as we have seen, are not sufficient to establish auditory control over this behavior. Many investigators have ignored the possible contribution of differences in salience or past experience, and have attempted to show that these differences in outcome are more apparent than real.

If, it is argued, visual and auditory stimuli gain control at different rates, this is because the *effective* schedules of reinforcement associated with such stimuli are not the same. One suggestion, as we shall see below, is that a localized visual stimulus will gain control where a diffuse auditory stimulus will not, because the probability of the subject's being stimulated by the visual stimulus will be correlated with the occurrence of responding and therefore with the probability of reinforcement, while the auditory stimulus will impinge on the subject whether or not he is responding.

Nondifferential Reinforcement

Jenkins and Harrison's (1960) experiment established beyond question that the nondifferential reinforcement of a subject's responses in the presence of a particular stimulus was not always sufficient to insure that changes in that stimulus would result in any change in the subject's behavior. This observation has been taken by some as their point of departure. Terrace (1966), for example, has argued that nondifferential reinforcement is never sufficient to establish stimulus control and that apparent exceptions to this rule are always cases where, inadvertently or implicitly, differential reinforcement was in fact scheduled. Although this position turns out to be rather difficult to discredit, I shall argue that it is in fact wrong and that even if we ignore differences in past experience, the most important cause of differences in stimulus control is not any difference in the opportunity for differential reinforcement, but a difference in the extent to which such control is masked by the presence of other stimuli.

THE HYPOTHESIS OF IMPLICIT DIFFERENTIAL REINFORCEMENT

One might have thought that there would be numerous examples of sloping gradients of generalization obtained without the necessity of programming differential reinforcement by discrimination training. Pavlov (1927) reported several differences in responding to training and test stimuli in experiments on salivary conditioning in dogs and also observed systematic changes in rate of salivation to test stimuli progressively less similar to the training stimulus. Subsequent experiments have reported reliably sloping gradients along such dimensions as auditory frequency after classical conditioning in pigeons (Hoffman & Fleshler, 1961) and rabbits (Moore, 1972). A classical conditioning experiment, however, necessarily involves differential reinforcement between the presence and absence of the CS. The subject is, in effect, trained on a discrimination between the experimental situation alone, signaling nonreinforcement, and the experimental situation plus CS, signaling reinforcement. Thus differential reinforcement correlated with the presence and absence of the CS may be responsible for the sloping gradient observed when some aspect of the CS is varied.

Experiments on instrumental learning do not, it may be thought, necessarily involve any such differential reinforcement correlated with the presence and absence of a discriminative stimulus. The subject may be placed in the apparatus and responding may be reinforced in the continuous presence of some specific stimulus, which may then be varied in order to test for generalization. Certainly, the classic study of Guttman and Kalish (1956) on wavelength generalization in pigeons at first sight seems to approximate to this description. Birds were reinforced for pecking a key illuminated with a light of a single wavelength and were then tested with a series of new wavelengths. It is, however, not difficult to point to at least two possible sources of differential reinforcement implicit in Guttman and Kalish's procedure (Heinemann & Rudolph, 1963; Terrace, 1966). First, they programmed brief, 10-sec intertrial intervals during which the key was dark and the schedule of reinforcement not in effect. Whether or not the birds responded during these blackouts, it remains true that the illumination of the key with light of a given wavelength, during which food was available, was contrasted with the absence of illumination, when food was not available. Guttman and Kalish's use of a stimulus localized on the pigeon's response key may have permitted a second source of implicit differential reinforcement. Since reinforcement was contingent on pecking the key, it follows that at the moment of reinforcement subjects must always have just pecked the key, and therefore been exposed to the wavelength projected onto the key. At times when they were not pecking, and therefore not exposed (or not so closely exposed) to this wavelength, reinforcement was never delivered. Implicitly, therefore, reinforcement may have been correlated with variations in the subjects' exposure to wavelength.

The first of these suggestions can definitely be ruled out. Although the use of a blackout between stimulus presentations may have some effect on the slope of generalization gradients, it is not a necessary condition for the establishment of reliable stimulus control. Thomas, Svinicki, and Svinicki (1970) and Thomas, Ernst, and Andry (1971), for example, observed relatively steep gradients along the dimension of line orientation after pigeons had been reinforced for pecking a key continually illuminated with a vertical line.

The second suggestions seem intuitively plausible, but although there is some evidence that the localization of a discriminative stimulus on the subjects' manipulandum may sharpen generalization gradients, such results are open to alternative explanations, and there is ample evidence that such localization is not necessary. Heinemann and Rudolph studied brightness generalization in pigeons after training them to peck a key of a particular brightness. Under ordinary conditions, they observed relatively steep gradients; but when the entire front wall of the pigeons' chamber was made equal in brightness to the response key, the brightness gradient was essentially flat. Heinemann and Rudolph attributed this outcome to a reduction in the opportunity for differential reinforcement, since, they argued, during training subjects would have been exposed to a stimulus of the same brightness as the response key even when not pecking. It is equally possible, however, that it is a consequence of the relative indiscriminability of large areas of brightness; in the absence of any contrast, changes in brightness of the entire front wall of the chamber during testing may have been difficult for subjects to detect.

It is, at any rate, quite certainly possible to observe sloping gradients correlated with changes in relatively diffuse stimuli not localized on any response key. Hearst (1962) trained monkeys to press a lever for food in the presence of a continuous overhead light. Subsequent variations in the intensity of the light resulted in reliably sloping gradients. Mrs. V. Rege, working in my laboratory, has trained pigeons to peck an unilluminated key in the presence of an overhead, continuously illuminated red or blue light. Subsequent generalization tests in extinction revealed reliably sloping gradients when the color of the overhead light was changed. Finally, Rudolph and Van Houten, in an unpublished study, have shown that it is possible to obtain reliable control by a diffuse auditory stimulus in pigeons without explicit discrimination training. They trained pigeons to peck a key illuminated with white light and, once pecking was established, gradually faded out the illumination of the key until the pigeons were pecking in the dark. Under these circumstances, a 1,000-Hz tone, continuously present, could be shown to exert significant control over responding: they observed reliably sloping gradients of generalization when the frequency of the tone was varied over a series of test trials. This study has a number of important implications which will be discussed later. For the present, it provides another instance of good control by a stimulus not located on the subject's manipulandum.

The burden of these experiments seems quite clear. The localization of a stimulus on or near the subjects' manipulandum is not a necessary prerequisite for that stimulus to gain control over responding in the absence of explicit differential reinforcement. The theorist who wishes to maintain that implicit differential reinforcement is necessary for the establishment of stimulus control must therefore fall back onto a new line of argument. This may not, of course, be impossible. One might still argue that even when the discriminative stimulus is apparently quite diffuse, subjects are still implicitly exposed to differential reinforcement for responding in its presence. If a pigeon is required to peck a key in the presence of an overhead light or a tone, for example, the precise stimuli to which it is exposed will change while it is executing a response. Thus it could be argued that the stimuli impinging on the subject at the moment of pecking will differ, in some subtle ways, from those to which it is exposed when not responding: the presence of standing waves might cause a discriminable change in the intensity of an auditory stimulus at the moment of responding.

One may wonder whether this possibility is susceptible of disproof. Moreover, the claim that the establishment of stimulus control requires differential reinforcement within the experimental situation must not only resort to a considerable amount of special pleading; if pressed too far, it also seems headed toward some logical inconsistency. The implication is that in the absence of such differential reinforcement, no stimuli from the experimental situation would ever gain control over responding. And yet the mere fact that subjects are reinforced in the experimental situation means that differential reinforcement is programmed between that situation and their home cage. Thus if no feature of the experimental situation could be shown to have acquired control over responding, this would show that differential reinforcement was certainly not *sufficient* to establish control. It may, of course, be impossible to predict which particular feature or features will acquire control, and there is obviously no guarantee that the controlling stimuli will include those which the experimenter chooses to vary in a subsequent generalization test. But if differential reinforcement is necessarily programmed whenever an animal receives its daily ration of food in the experimental situation, and not outside, then it is surely implausible to suppose that further differential reinforcement *within* the experimental situation is necessary for the establishment of stimulus control. The difference in schedule of reinforcement between the experimental situation and the home cage should presumably be sufficient to establish control over responding by some features of the apparatus.

MASKING

Since instrumental responses are typically reinforced only in a particular situation, some aspects of that situation should gain control over responding. Since evidence of control over a pigeon's food-reinforced responses by such stimuli as tones is often hard to come by, it remains to consider why nondifferential reinforcement within the experimental situation is not sufficient to establish control by all features of the situation.

The simplest solution to this problem is surely that proposed by Hull (1952, pp. 64–69). If a pigeon's responses are reinforced in the presence of a set of stimuli $S_1, S_2, S_3, \ldots S_n$, where S_1 represents a 1,000-Hz tone, S_2 the illumination from the response key, and S_3 the illumination from the houselight, a generalization test to other frequencies of the tone, S_1', S_1'' etc., will vary only S_1 and leave all other stimuli, $S_2, S_3, \ldots S_n$ constant. To the extent that some of these other stimuli have gained control over responding, they will continue to control a high rate of responding on all test trials. Their presence, therefore, may mask the control actually gained by the tone.

As was briefly noted earlier, a pigeon reinforced for pecking at a key containing a white line on a colored background may show relatively little control by the line when tested with other orientations shown on the same-colored background, but produce a steep gradient of generalization if the lines are displayed without colors on a black background (Freeman & Thomas, 1967; Newman & Benefield, 1968). Thus some of the stimuli displayed on the pigeon's response key may mask the control gained by other stimuli on the key. Van Houten and Rudolph (1972) and Rudolph and Van Houten (unpublished) have extended these observations by showing that stimuli presented on a pigeon's response key may mask control by such relatively diffuse stimuli as a flow of air or a tone of particular frequency. In the former experiment, pigeons were reinforced for pecking a key illuminated with white light in the presence of a 30-mph flow of air from a source behind the response key. When the speed of this airflow was varied between 30 and 0 mph in a subsequent generalization test, three out of four birds continued to respond at a relatively constant rate, with only one bird showing evidence of reliable control by this stimulus. In a second group, however, trained to peck an unilluminated key in a dark box, all four birds show excellent control by the airflow stimulus in the subsequent generalization test. Moreover, if birds were required to learn a discrimination between two different velocities of airflow, they learned much more rapidly when the chamber was dark than when the key was illuminated with white light. Thus the presence of an illuminated response key would mask the appearance of control by this nonvisual, relatively unlocalized stimulus.

Rudolph and Van Houten confirmed the conclusions of this first study in a second experiment using auditory stimuli. Birds trained to peck an illuminated key in the presence of a 1,000-Hz tone generalized almost completely to other frequencies of tone. This group, therefore, replicated Jenkins and Harrison's (1960) results. As briefly noted above, however, a second group, trained to peck a dark key in the presence of a tone, showed a reliable and steep gradient when tested with other frequencies. The results are shown in Figure 4.

It is clear that the presence of visual stimuli may mask control by stimuli from other modalities in the pigeon. The general conclusion suggested by these experiments, then, is that failures of stimulus control are more plausibly attributed to the presence of other stimuli which mask control by the experimenter's stimulus than to the absence of implicit differential reinforcement. Variations in entirely diffuse stimuli may result in sloping generalization gradients, and

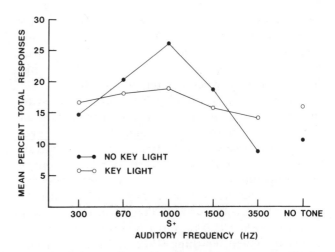

Fig. 4. Relative gradients of auditory frequency generalization in pigeons after responses to 1,000 Hz have been reinforced, either in the dark, or with an illuminated key light. (After Rudolph & Van Houten, unpublished data.)

the removal of potential masking stimuli reliably increases the slope of such gradients.

Overshadowing

Rudolph and Van Houten's studies, as they themselves recognized, are open to an alternative interpretation. Control by the frequency of a tone or the velocity of a flow of air may not just be masked by the constant presence of the key light during testing. The presence of this more salient visual stimulus during acquisition may have prevented such auditory or tactile stimuli from acquiring control in the first place. Such a possibility was envisaged by Lashley and Wade (1946) when they argued that a flat gradient of generalization obtained when one feature of the training situation was varied might signify that the subject had attended to some other feature of the situation during training.

We do not need to subscribe without reserve to Lashley and Wade's theoretical analysis in order to accept the possibility of an effect such as this. That the presence of a more intense or salient stimulus may interfere with the acquisition of control by a less intense or salient stimulus was first reported by Pavlov (1927, pp. 141–143), who termed the effect "overshadowing." He reported that dogs given classical conditioning with a compound CS containing one intense and one weak component might show essentially no conditioning to the weak component presented alone on a test trial, "although it is obvious . . . that the ineffective component . . . could easily be made to acquire powerful conditioned properties by independent reinforcement outside the combination" (p. 142). Evidence of overshadowing has been reported in a variety of other situations: in CER conditioning by Kamin (1969), in discrete-trial simultaneous discrimination learning by Lovejoy and Russell (1967), and in discrete-trial successive discrimination learning by Miles and Jenkins (1973).

The principle of masking, as defined here, states that the presence of one stimulus, A, may obscure the *expression* of control by a second stimulus, B, even though it can be shown (by testing with B in the absence of A) that B has acquired significant control over responding. The principle of overshadowing states that the presence of A may interfere with the *acquisition* of control by B. The distinction between the two can best be illustrated by reference to a concrete experiment. Farthing (1972) trained two groups of pigeons on a successive discrimination. For one group, a vertical line on a red background served as S+, and a green key light served as S−. For the second group, the color projected onto the key was the same on both positive and negative trials, and the only stimulus correlated with the availability of reinforcement was the presence or absence of the line. After acquisition, generalization tests were given to other orientations of the line, displayed on either a red or a black background. The results of these generalization tests are shown in Figure 5. The difference in the performance of both groups between test trials when the lines were shown on a colored background and those trials when they were presented on an uncolored ground may be taken as evidence of a masking effect. The presence of the colored background significantly decreased the control over responding displayed by the line in both groups. Superimposed on this effect, however, there is also a clear difference *between* the gradients produced by the two groups, regardless of the type of test trial. Even when the lines were displayed on a black background, subjects for whom the difference between positive and negative trials in acquisition had been marked both by differences in color and by the presence of the line showed significantly less control by line than did subjects for whom the presence of the line was the only signal for reinforcement. The presence of the additional wave-

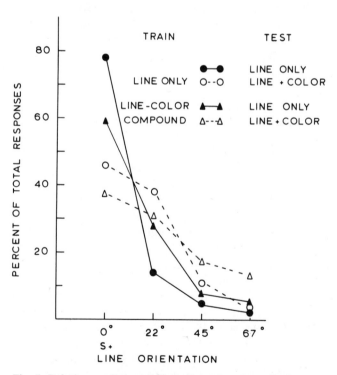

Fig. 5. Relative gradients of line-orientation generalization in pigeons trained either on a line-orientation discrimination or on a compound wavelength and line-orientation discrimination. The lines were shown with- or without a colored background. (After Farthing, 1972.)

length cue during training reduced the control acquired by the line during this phase of the experiment.

In Rudolph and Van Houten's studies, the illumination of the key light was the stimulus that interfered with control by tones or airflows. The nature of this stimulus makes it impossible to determine whether they were observing masking, overshadowing, or a combination of the two. For in order to prove that the key light had actually overshadowed these other stimuli, it would be necessary to show that its presence on test trials had not merely been masking control. But in order to show this, it would be necessary to conduct test trials with the key light dark. If pigeons have been trained to peck an illuminated key, however, they will, unless there is another source of illumination, stop pecking when the key is abruptly darkened. In the absence of responding, it is impossible to assess the degree of control acquired by any stimulus.

This difficulty does not detract from the main conclusion suggested by this body of research: a major reason why some stimuli fail to show significant control over responding is that they are either overshadowed or masked by the presence of more salient stimuli. This conclusion has the further virtue, as we shall see, of explaining why discrimination training is frequently necessary to establish control by relatively unsalient stimuli. A great deal of research has been devoted to an examination of the effects of various discriminative procedures on stimulus control, and it is time to turn to this question.

Intradimensional Discrimination Training

Although, as was argued above, differential reinforcement within the experimental situation may not be necessary for the acquisition of stimulus control, this should not be taken to imply that such differential reinforcement has no effect on control. On the contrary, discrimination training has powerful and important effects on generalization.

Pavlov (1927) reported the most obvious instance of this effect of discrimination training on generalization. If a particular tone was established as a classical CS for food, the presentation of other tones would also elicit salivary CRs. In order to prevent the occurrence of such generalized CRs, Pavlov stated, it was necessary to continue reinforcement in the presence of the original CS and to present the other tones without reinforcement. Discriminative conditioning between neighboring stimuli would thus sharpen the gradient of generalization between them. Numerous other studies have examined the effects of providing discrimination training between two stimuli falling along a particular dimension on subsequent generalization to other values of that dimension. Such intradimensional discrimination training has sharpened gradients of auditory frequency generalization in experiments on galvanic skin response (GSR) conditioning in human subjects (Hovland, 1937), eyelid conditioning in rabbits (Moore, 1972), and key pecking in pigeons (Jenkins & Harrison, 1962), and similar results have been reported for brightness generalization in rats (Schlosberg & Solomon, 1943) and wavelength generalization in pigeons (Honig, 1962; Honig, Thomas, & Guttman, 1959). The results of the study by Honig et al. are shown in Figure 6.

The generally accepted explanation of this result has been some version of that proposed by Pavlov himself. Reinforcement in the presence of one stimulus and nonreinforcement in the presence of another are said to decrease responding to stimuli falling between S+ and S− because the tendency to respond produced by reinforcement at S+, which generalizes to these intervening stimuli, is counteracted by a tendency not to respond, produced by nonreinforcement at S−, which also generalizes to the intervening stimuli. The resulting postdiscrimination gradient is a consequence of the interaction between the "excitatory" gradient centered round S+ and the "inhibitory" gradient centered round S−, an analysis first formally proposed by Spence in 1937.

There is, however, good reason to believe that

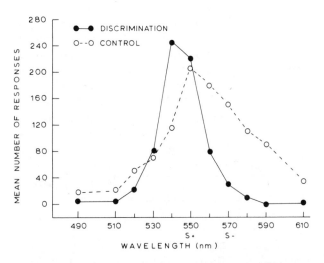

Fig. 6. Absolute gradients of wavelength generalization in pigeons. Control subjects received reinforcement for responding to S+ (550 nm), while for discrimination subjects, reinforced trials to S+ were alternated with nonreinforced trials to S− (570 nm). After Honig et al., 1959. © 1959 by the American Psychological Association. Reprinted by permission.)

such an interaction between hypothetical excitatory and inhibitory gradients, although of considerable importance, is not sufficient to account for all features of the postdiscrimination gradient. As Figure 6 shows, the effect of nonreinforcement at S− is not only to increase the slope of the gradient between S+ and S−, it also sharpens the gradient on the other side of S+. This decline in responding to stimuli so far removed from S− is difficult to attribute to the generalization of any inhibitory tendency not to respond to S−. A similar effect can be observed in several other studies of intradimensional discrimination training (e.g., Hanson, 1959; Jenkins & Harrison, 1962; Moore, 1972). It seems probable that discrimination training has further effects responsible for this additional sharpening of generalization gradients. This conclusion is amply confirmed by studies of interdimensional discrimination training, where changes in the slope of postdiscrimination gradients cannot be attributed to any interaction between excitatory and inhibitory tendencies.

Interdimensional Discrimination Training

Jenkins and Harrison (1960) were the first to use interdimensional training to examine the effects of differential reinforcement on the slope of a generalization gradient, uncomplicated by interactions between excitatory and inhibitory tendencies. They trained pigeons on a discrimination between the presence and absence of a 1,000-Hz tone and then tested for generalization along the dimension of auditory frequency. Although, as noted above, nondifferential reinforcement resulted in a relatively flat frequency gradient, reinforcement in the presence of the tone, randomly alternated with nonreinforcement in its absence, resulted in steep and reliable gradients in all subjects.

Jenkins and Harrison's results have been confirmed and extended in a number of subsequent studies. Newman and Baron (1965), Switalski, Lyons, and Thomas (1966), and Lyons and Thomas (1967) have shown that giving pigeons training between the presence and absence of a line or specific wavelength on the response key significantly sharpens generalization gradients of orientation or wavelength. Moore (1972) has reported that rabbits given differential eyelid conditioning with a tone as CS+ and a light as CS− show a steeper gradient of auditory frequency generalization than a control group simply given reinforced trials with CS+ alone. Several studies of conditioned reinforcement in rats may be taken to imply a similar effect (e.g., Notterman, 1951). There is no question, then, but that differential reinforcement between the presence and absence of a specific stimulus will increase the slope of a generalization gradient measured when some feature of that stimulus is subsequently varied.

The important feature of interdimensional training is that the stimulus correlated with nonreinforcement during initial acquisition is presumably equidistant from all test stimuli. Thus the increase in the slope of the postdiscriminative gradient cannot be attributed to the differential generalization of inhibitory tendencies to different stimuli. Jenkins and Harrison accepted that the type of analysis proposed by Hull (1952) provided the most plausible explanation of their data. As noted above, Hull's argument amounted to saying that if a pigeon were nondifferentially reinforced for responding in the presence of a 1,000-Hz tone, then although the frequency of the tone might be established as a signal for reinforcement, the potential control acquired by the tone might be masked by innumerable other features of the situation, each of which was as well correlated with the delivery of reinforcement as was the tone itself. These other features remain constant during a test for auditory frequency generalization, and would therefore maintain a constant rate of responding. By providing differential reinforcement between the presence and absence of the tone, the experimenter insures that at least some of these other features are now less well correlated with reinforcement than is the frequency of the tone. If these differences in the "validity" of different features result in reliable differences in their control over responding, then interdimensional training may sharpen generalization gradients because it effectively reduces control by incidental stimuli that would otherwise mask the stimuli varied by the experimenter.[2]

Rudolph and Van Houten's unpublished experiment, described earlier, provides the first line of evidence to support this analysis. In their replication of Jenkins and Harrison's study they showed that it was the presence of visual stimuli, such as the key light, that prevented the tone from exercising control over responding; pigeons trained and tested in the dark showed orderly and steep gradients of auditory frequency generalization.

The second point that requires investigation is whether interdimensional auditory discrimination training can indeed suppress control by such masking

---

[2] As noted above, a particular stimulus may fail to control behavior after nondifferential reinforcement not because its control is masked by other, unvarying stimuli, but because it is overshadowed by these other more salient stimuli. This possibility does not, of course, affect the present argument.

visual stimuli. Miles, Mackintosh, and Westbrook (1970) trained pigeons on a discrete-trial discrimination with a tone as S+ and white noise as S−, but with the response key illuminated with light of a particular wavelength on both positive and negative trials. Key color, therefore, served as a potential masking stimulus, and, indeed, when subjects were initially given S+ trials only, they showed strong control by the color of the key, responding consistently on test trials to the color they were trained with and not responding when the color was changed. The effect of auditory discrimination training, however, was to weaken this control by color; after nine sessions of tone-noise discrimination training, subjects responded consistently only to the tone and showed a significantly greater tendency to respond on test trials to the changed key color.

The results of Miles et al. have been replicated in subsequent unpublished experiments by Miles. Once again interdimensional auditory discrimination training led to a significant flattening of the generalization gradient obtained when the color of the key was changed; in this replication, moreover, subjects were tested in silence, so that the decrease in control by color could not have been due to any increase in control by tone. Blough (1969) has also reported data showing that a stimulus common to both positive and negative trials of a discrete-trial discrimination will lose control over responding. It is reasonable, then, to argue that differential reinforcement between any arbitrary pair of stimuli will tend to reduce control by other stimuli common to both positive and negative trials, and that the frequently observed sharpening of generalization gradients resulting from such discrimination training is a consequence of this suppression of control by such incidental stimuli which might otherwise act as effective masking stimuli.

Even if this is accepted as an explanation of the effects of interdimensional training, it must be clear that the principle itself stands in need of explanation. Why should discrimination training between the presence and absence of a tone, for example, reduce the control exercised by visual stimuli common to both positive and negative trials? Hull argued that this was simply a consequence of the new schedule of reinforcement correlated with such incidental stimuli. If we schematize the tone as T and the light as L, then nondifferential reinforcement in the presence of the tone consists of a series of TL+ trials, while interdimensional training consists of a series of TL+ trials alternating with L− trials. In the former case, L is consistently reinforced; in the latter, L is equally often reinforced and not reinforced. This deterioration in the schedule of reinforcement associated with L should, Hull argued, be sufficient to reduce the control it acquires.

As Jenkins and Harrison (1960) and Wagner (1969) have pointed out, this is a distinctly implausible suggestion. By comparison with consistent reinforcement, it is true, differential reinforcement results in a decline in the correlation of an incidental stimulus with reinforcement, but it is unlikely that this decline would in and of itself be sufficient to have any drastic effect on the control such a stimulus acquires. Even the relevant stimuli in typical free operant schedules are only intermittently correlated with reinforcement; and it is well known that in discrete-trial situations a 50% schedule of reinforcement is sufficient to establish highly reliable responding. An important series of studies by Wagner, Logan, Haberlandt, and Price (1968) has confirmed that in such discrete-trial situations the schedule of reinforcement associated with an incidental stimulus common to positive and negative trials of a discrimination is not, as such, sufficient to explain why such a stimulus fails to acquire control over responding. Three experiments were conducted, one employing instrumental discrimination learning in rats, a second conditioned suppression in rats, and the third eyelid conditioning in rabbits; but the basic design of each of these experiments was identical. For subjects in the discrimination group (hereinafter called Group TD, for true discrimination), reinforced trials to a tone-light compound (T_1L+) alternated with nonreinforced trials to another tone-light compound (T_2L-). The light, it should be noted, was common to both positive and negative trials, and when tested with L alone, subjects showed little or no tendency to respond. Discrimination training between T_1 and T_2 had apparently prevented L acquiring significant control. Instead of comparing this discrimination group with a nondifferentially reinforced group, however, Wagner et al. used a control group that also received T_1L and T_2L trials and also received reinforcement on only 50% trials. The important difference for this group (hereinafter called Group PD, for pseudodiscrimination training) was that the delivery of reinforcement was uncorrelated with T_1 and T_2. In this PD group, L acquired strong control over responding in spite of the fact that the actual schedule of reinforcement associated with L was exactly the same as in Group TD. Thus it is not the schedule of reinforcement associated with an incidental stimulus during discrimination training that suppresses control by such a stimulus, but the fact that there are other stimuli better correlated with reinforcement. It is not its absolute validity or correlation with reinforcement that is the most important determinant of the control gained by a stimulus, but its relative validity compared to that of other available stimuli.

This conclusion is of profound importance, for it implies some interaction between the control over responding acquired by different stimuli. If incidental stimuli fail to acquire control, not simply because they are imperfectly correlated with reinforcement, but because other stimuli are better correlated, this suggests that stimuli may compete for the acquisition of control. In the experiments of Wagner et al. the auditory stimuli acquired little control over responding in the PD groups, thus enabling the light to gain substantial control. In the TD groups, on the other hand, the auditory stimuli, being perfectly correlated with reinforcement, acquired strong control and thus prevented the acquisition of control by the light. We may say that the light failed to gain control because it was overshadowed by a better predictor of reinforcement.

The term *overshadowing* is usually used in Pavlov's original sense to refer to the effect of the presence of a salient stimulus on the acquisition of control by an equally valid but less salient stimulus. The extension of the term to cover the case where, of two equally salient stimuli, the more valid may interfere with the acquisition of control by the less valid implies a parallel between the two effects. There certainly seems to be some resemblance, and, as we shall see later, similar theoretical analyses have been applied to both effects. Whether differences in validity have the same effect as differences in salience, however, is for present purposes less important than the acceptance of the general principle that it is not the absolute validity of a stimulus that determines its control, but whether it is accompanied by other, more valid predictors of reinforcement.

This principle provides the most plausible interpretation of the effects of interdimensional discrimination training on the acquisition of stimulus control. Differential reinforcement will result in the overshadowing of a potentially wide range of stimuli common to positive and negative trials, which might otherwise mask, or even themselves overshadow, the stimuli in which the experimenter is interested. There is, however, one very important corollary to this analysis. Discrimination training between the presence and absence of a discriminative stimulus may indeed result in the overshadowing of all incidental stimuli, but this does not guarantee that the aspect of the discriminative stimulus subsequently varied in a generalization test will be that which gains control over the subjects' behavior. One more salient aspect may still overshadow another. If, therefore, discrimination training is given between the presence and absence of a compound stimulus, not all features of that compound will necessarily acquire good control. The experiment by Farthing (1972), described earlier, showed that if pigeons receive differential reinforcement between a vertical line on a red key and no line on a green key, the presence of the wavelength difference between positive and negative trials significantly reduced the control over responding acquired by the line.

It is even more important to note that overshadowing of one aspect of a discriminative stimulus by another during interdimensional training may not require the explicit use of a compound stimulus. An experimenter may give interdimensional training between the presence and absence of a vertical line and then test for control by the line by varying its orientation on a series of test trials. But the line may be characterized in many other ways—as having, for example, a particular size, height, width, and brightness. There is no guarantee that the feature varied by the experimenter will be the one to have gained control over the behavior of the subject. Interdimensional discrimination training may still not insure control by the particular feature varied during the generalization test.

A number of studies illustrate the validity of this line of reasoning. Boneau and Honig (1964) found that when pigeons were given conditional discrimination training with one of the conditional stimuli being the presence or absence of a vertical line on the key, they still showed a relatively flat gradient in a subsequent generalization test along the dimension of line orientation. Williams (1973) found that interdimensional discrimination training between the presence and absence of a series of clicks emitted at a rate of 2.45 per sec was not sufficient to produce a sloping gradient to other click frequencies. Since pigeons were well able to learn a discrimination between two click rates, and, having done so, showed a reliable and steep gradient of generalization when tested with other rates, the failure of interdimensional training to establish control by click rate cannot be attributed to an inability to detect such differences. As Williams argued, it is most plausibly regarded as a consequence of overshadowing; other features of the clicks, such as their intensity or individual frequencies, were as well correlated with reinforcement, as was their rate, and by virtue, presumably, of their greater initial salience, may have overshadowed, or at least masked, control by rate.

Unfortunately, neither Boneau and Honig nor Williams tested the prediction that other features of their discriminative stimuli had acquired control over responding. Williams did not measure generalization along the dimension of intensity, nor Boneau and Honig along the dimensions of brightness or line length. An experiment by Mackintosh (1965), however, provides some relevant evidence. Rats received interdimensional training between the presence and absence of a white circle of a particular size displayed on the window of a jumping stand. Subsequent tests between the original circle and one of a different size revealed relatively poor control by the specific size of the circle used in original training. The feature of the situation that had gained most control over responding was the brightness difference between a door containing a white circle and one containing no circle. Animals trained with the circle positive, showed a strong preference for the larger (i.e., brighter) of two circles, regardless of their absolute sizes; while animals trained to respond to a blank door, with the white circle negative, showed a stronger preference for the smaller (i.e., less bright) of two circles, again regardless of their absolute sizes.

Extradimensional Training

In intradimensional training, subjects are exposed to differential reinforcement correlated with stimuli differing along the dimension subsequently varied in a generalization test. In interdimensional training, differential reinforcement is correlated with the presence or absence of a specific stimulus, some aspect of which is then varied in a generalization test. But discrimination training can be programmed between a pair of stimuli quite unrelated to the set of stimuli varied during generalization testing. One can examine the effect of discrimination training between different wavelengths on the acquisition of control by a line or by a tone. Such a test requires, of course, that responding at some point be reinforced in the presence of the line or tone. Two procedures which have been adopted for the provision of such reinforced experience are illustrated in Table 1. In the first, successive-stage procedure, subjects are initially trained on, say, a wavelength discrimination and are then reinforced for responding to a vertical line. In the second, concurrent procedure, the line is present during the course of wavelength discrimination training, appearing on both positive and negative trials. Since the two procedures may pose rather different problems for theoretical analysis, they will be treated separately.

SUCCESSIVE-STAGE EXTRADIMENSIONAL EXPERIMENTS

That extradimensional training between one pair of stimuli might enhance the control apparently

Table 1 Schematic Representation of Two Designs for Studies of Extradimensional Discrimination Training and Generalization

DESIGN	GROUP	TRAIN		TEST
		STAGE 1	STAGE 2	
Successive-stage	Discrimination	Blue + Green −	Vertical +	*Line-Orientation Generalization*
	Control (Pseudodiscrimination)	Blue +/− Green +/−		
Concurrent	Discrimination	Vertical on Blue + Vertical on Green −		*Line-Orientation Generalization*
	Control (Pseudodiscrimination)	Vertical on Blue +/− Vertical on Green +/−		

gained by an entirely different stimulus was first clearly shown by Honig (1969). Honig trained one group of pigeons on a discrimination between different key colors (Group TD), while a second group received the same sequence of stimuli uncorrelated with reinforcement (Group PD). Both groups were then reinforced for pecking at a set of vertical lines on the response key and finally received a generalization test along the dimension of orientation. Group TD showed a significantly steeper gradient than Group PD. Results clearly related to Honig's have been reported by Eck, Noel, and Thomas (1969), who found that pigeons given PD training with one set of stimuli in stage 1 learned a new discrimination between a new set of stimuli in stage 2 significantly faster than subjects receiving PD training in stage 1. Similarly, Frieman and Goyette (1973) confirmed that training on one discrimination would facilitate the learning of a second, independent problem.

The argument of the preceding section was that discrimination training sharpens generalization gradients by effectively neutralizing incidental stimuli that would otherwise interfere with the acquisition or expression of control by the test stimulus. At first sight, Honig's (1969) results seem inconsistent with any such analysis: it is hard to see why wavelength discrimination training should have had any effect on control by a subsequently presented stimulus. Wagner (1969), however, has shown how this type of analysis may be relevant to the understanding of extradimensional training. The critical assumption is that there may be incidental situational stimuli present during all stages of training. If these stimuli are neutralized during initial TD training, and if this effect transfers to stage 2 of the experiment, they will no longer compete for control with the new set of discriminative stimuli manipulated by the experimenter. In PD groups, on the other hand, such situational stimuli will gain control of responding in stage 1 and continue to control behavior in stage 2. Wagner (1969) reported the results of an experiment on eyelid conditioning in rabbits, which provided evidence of just such an effect. The design of his experiment is shown in Table 2. A TD group was given discrimination training between two lights (L_1 and L_2); on separate trials they also received reinforcement signaled by a tone (T). This procedure produced steeper auditory gradients around T than those obtained from a PD group, which was treated identically in the presence of T but for whom L_1 and L_2 were randomly associated with reinforcement. These results, therefore, replicated those obtained by Honig. Wagner also, however, provided an explicit incidental vibratory stimulus (V) common to all trials; thus the actual

Table 2 *Design of Experiment by Wagner (1969)*

GROUP	TRAIN	TEST
TD	L_1V+, L_2V-, T_1V+	T_1, T_2, etc.
PD	$L_1V\pm$, $L_2V\pm$, T_1V+	T_1, T_2, etc.

L_1, L_2 = Lights; T_1, T_2 = Tones; V = Vibratory stimulus

stimuli to which subjects were exposed were compounds, L_1V, L_2V, and TV. Test trials with V alone indicated that it had acquired less control over responding in Group TD than in Group PD. This feature of Wagner's design thus enabled him to show that the increase in control by T in Group TD was accompanied by a decrease in control by V.

Wagner's results make it possible to maintain that discrimination training always increases control by one set of stimuli by suppressing control by others. The only new assumption required is that the incidental stimuli suppressed during the course of discrimination training remain suppressed when the original discriminative stimuli are removed. A minor modification of Honig's design, however, produces data which are more problematic. Thomas, Freeman, Svinicki, Burr, and Lyons (1970, Experiments 1 and 2) confirmed Honig's finding that birds given TD color training before reinforced exposure to a vertical line would show a steeper gradient to other orientations of the line than a PD group.[3] In the experiments of Thomas et al., however, unlike Honig's, the vertical line was shown in stage 2 compounded with one of the discriminative stimuli from stage 1. Birds initially given TD or PD training with green and red stimuli, with green signaling a variable-interval (VI) schedule for the TD group, were reinforced in stage 2 for responding to a vertical line superimposed on a green background, before being tested for generalization to other orientations of the line on a black background.

Although this change in procedure appears relatively minor, it might be expected to have had substantial consequences. In analyzing Honig's results, it was suggested that TD training might suppress control by incidental situational stimuli, and that this loss of control by potentially competing stimuli might then enable the vertical line to gain more control

[3] Thomas et al. also obtained similar results when TD and PD training were given with two different line orientations, and subjects were then reinforced for responding to a single wavelength, followed by a generalization test to other wavelengths. For ease of exposition in what follows, however, it will be simpler to concentrate on their first experiment and assume that TD and PD training is given with two wavelengths and that subsequent training is given with a vertical line.

over responding than in the PD group. Wagner's experiment confirmed that an explicitly manipulated incidental stimulus would indeed gain less control over responding if presented in conjunction with stimuli correlated with reinforcement and nonreinforcement (in a TD group) than with stimuli uncorrelated with reinforcement (in a PD group). The change in procedure introduced by Thomas et al., however, involved presenting in stage 2 the vertical line itself in conjunction with one of the discriminative stimuli of stage 1. This might be expected to have *reduced* the control acquired by the vertical line in the TD group. The principle of overshadowing exemplified in Wagner's data implies that TD training will result in the suppression of control by any stimulus presented in conjunction with the relevant discriminative stimuli. Although this may include situational stimuli, it is hard to see why it should not also have included the vertical line in the experiment of Thomas et al. Nevertheless, in that experiment, as in Honig's, TD training resulted in an apparent increase in control by the vertical line.

It is not only a theoretical principle of possibly limited importance, such as that of overshadowing, and the results of rather different experiments, such as Wagner's, that appear to conflict with the data of Thomas et al. For the design of their experiments is in fact very similar to the design of experiments on "blocking," and blocking has been reliably observed in studies of free operant discrimination learning in pigeons, with designs extremely similar to that employed by Thomas et al. Johnson (1970), for example, initially trained pigeons on a vertical-horizontal discrimination and then gave compound discrimination training with the vertical line superimposed on a blue background and the horizontal line superimposed on a yellow background. In a subsequent generalization test such birds showed reliably less control by wavelength than a control group that had received no training on the vertical-horizontal discrimination in stage 1. Thus prior discrimination training on the vertical-horizontal problem reduced rather than enhanced the control by stimuli subsequently compounded with the original discriminative stimuli. Although similar blocking effects have not always been observed in similar experiments with pigeons (e.g., Farthing & Hearst, 1970), there is no doubt that the majority of similar studies have reported similar results (Chase, 1968; Miles, 1970; vom Saal & Jenkins, 1970).

Why should pretraining on one component of a compound sometimes reduce control by a second component, as in studies of blocking, and sometimes enhance control by a second component, as in the studies by Thomas et al.? There are, in fact, several differences between the design of the two types of experiment. Thomas et al. compared groups given TD or PD training in stage 1, while Johnson compared a TD group with an untreated control group. An experiment by Freeman (1967, cited by Honig, 1970), however, suggests that in this situation at least, this difference is of no consequence.[4] A second difference is in the treatment of all subjects in stage 2. In experiments where TD training enhances control by the added component, animals are exposed to a single compound stimulus and reinforced for responding in its presence; in experiments where blocking is observed, animals receive discrimination training between pairs of compound stimuli. Mackintosh and Honig (1970) have explicitly compared these two procedures by running in a single study the two pairs of group shown in Table 3. As can be seen from Fig-

[4] Whether this is always true is a question discussed later.

Table 3 *Design of experiment by Mackintosh and Honig (1970)*

	GROUP	STAGE 1	STAGE 2	TEST
Blocking	TD	V+; H−	VB+, HY−	Wavelength generalization
	Control	−		
Enhancement	TD	V+; H−	VB+	Wavelength generalization
	Control	−		

V = Vertical line; H = Horizontal line; Y = Yellow; B = Blue

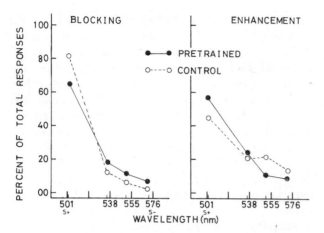

Fig. 7. Relative gradients of wavelength generalization in pigeons. The groups whose data are shown in the left panel received discrimination training between vertical and horizontal lines superimposed on backgrounds of 501 and 576 nm; those in the right panel were reinforced for responding to a vertical line on the 501-nm background. (After Mackintosh & Honig, 1970. © 1970 by the American Psychological Association. Reprinted by permission.)

ure 7, they found it possible to replicate both Johnson's finding of blocking and the finding of enhancement by Thomas et al. When stage 2 involved a discrimination between two lines shown on a colored background, pretraining on the line-tilt discrimination reduced the control acquired by color. When stage 2 involved the nondifferential reinforcement of responding to a vertical line on a colored background, however, pretraining on the line-tilt discrimination tended to enhance the control gained by color. It seems probable, therefore, that the decisive factor determining the outcome of such experiments is whether stage 2 involves reinforcement for responding in the presence of a single compound or discrimination training between two compound stimuli.

The occurrence of blocking is entirely consistent with the principle of overshadowing. In studies of overshadowing, the more salient or valid member of a compound stimulus may reduce the control acquired by the other component. In blocking, the validity of one element is increased by previously establishing it as a signal for reinforcement, and such pretraining reduces the control acquired by the other element. Why, then, should pretraining on one component apparently increase the control acquired by the other in the enhancement design? The answer must be related to Mackintosh and Honig's finding that enhancement occurred instead of blocking only when subjects received nondifferential reinforcement for responding to the stimulus subsequently varied during generalization testing. The control group in this design, therefore, received no discrimination training at any stage of the experiment and, as can be seen from Figure 7, gave a flatter gradient than any other group in the experiment. If, as we have argued, discrimination training suppresses control by incidental stimuli, it is possible that the flat gradient shown by this control group was a consequence of masking by these incidental stimuli. The suppression of incidental stimuli in the TD group by prior training on the line-tilt discrimination, then, may have been more than enough to compensate for the partial overshadowing of the test stimulus that resulted from its presentation in conjunction with the more valid line tilt. In the blocking design, on the other hand, both TD and control groups received discrimination training in stage 2. In neither group, therefore, should incidental stimuli have succeeded in masking control by wavelength, and the only effect observed was the overshadowing of wavelength by the previously trained component.

This may well seem an unduly elaborate analysis. In particular, one could take objection to the argument that enhancement occurs because the overshadowing of potentially masking situational stimuli is sufficient to outweigh the overshadowing of the test stimulus. Against this, however, it can reasonably be insisted that if such apparently contradictory results as enhancement and blocking depend upon relatively minor differences in experimental procedure, an adequate analysis is likely both to be complex and to appeal to a conflict between opposing processes. It is possible, nevertheless, that enhancement is not a consequence of differences between the overshadowing of incidental and test stimuli. It may be necessary to appeal to an entirely new set of principles. Thomas (1970) has argued that enhancement indicates the operation of a much more general process of attentiveness which may affect the control acquired by any set of stimuli. Discrimination training, he suggests, may insure that animals learn

> the validity of external stimuli as signifying events or contingencies of significance for the welfare of the organism. In this way the benefits of discrimination training would not be specific to the dimension or dimensions varied in training but might generalise to other aspects of the training stimulus as well. By the same token, nondifferential training might serve to teach the animal the insignificance of external stimuli and/or the futility of behaving differentially in their presence, and this learning might generalise to stimuli not involved in the initial training. (p. 324)

Some light on these different interpretations may be shed by examining a further set of experimental results, those obtained in the second type of extradimensional study referred to in Table 1. It is time to consider these studies.

Concurrent Extradimensional Experiments

In successive extradimensional experiments, the stimulus whose control is assessed is presented separately from the extradimensional discriminative stimuli. In concurrent extradimensional experiments, the test stimulus is presented, in conjunction with the discriminative stimuli, during the course of discrimination training. It is, in other words, an explicit, incidental stimulus, common to positive and negative trials. Several recent studies of free operant discrimination learning by pigeons have examined the effect of such extradimensional training on the acquisition of control by such a stimulus and have yielded relatively consistent results. Thomas et al. (1970, Experiments 3 and 4), for example, gave pigeons TD or PD training with two wavelengths, with a vertical line appearing on the response key on all trials; they then tested the birds for generalization to other orientations of the line presented on a black background. Just as TD wavelength training had enhanced control by a *subsequently* presented line, so in these studies TD training enhanced control by a line present during the course of TD training.

Thomas (1970) has argued that this finding provides definitive evidence that any principle of overshadowing must at best be subservient to a much more important general effect of discrimination training. There is, of course, no doubt that these results are not what the principle of overshadowing would lead one to expect. This is hardly surprising, for they are the exact opposite of the results reported by Wagner et al. (1968), which earlier provided the impetus for the application of the principle of overshadowing to the effects of differential reinforcement. Wagner et al. concluded that the control acquired by a stimulus reinforced on 50% of trials was adversely affected by the presence of other, more valid signals of reinforcement. In their experiments, TD training between two tones *reduced* the control displayed by a light common to positive and negative trials. The design of their studies is exactly the same as that of Thomas et al., with tones instead of wavelengths, and a light serving as the incidental stimulus instead of a vertical line. And yet the two sets of studies produced diametrically opposed results.

Wagner et al. replicated their findings in three separate experiments. There is equally no doubt about the reliability of the results of Thomas et al. They have been confirmed in subsequent studies by Bresnahan (1970) and Turner and Mackintosh (1972) and in a series of unpublished experiments conducted at Dalhousie University by Dr. V. Gray. An understanding of the causes of this discrepancy, therefore, is a necessary prerequisite to any adequate theoretical analysis.

In pursuit of his argument that the major effect of discrimination training is an increase in general attentiveness, insuring an increase in control by all stimuli, Thomas (1970) has sought to dispute the validity of the data given by Wagner et al. and has suggested that their conclusions are a mistaken inference from an inappropriate test procedure. Wagner et al. assessed the degree of control gained by the incidental visual stimuli in their experiments by measuring the amount of responding that occurred when that stimulus was presented alone, without the auditory discriminative stimuli. In the experiments of Thomas et al. and in subsequent replications of their work, the control exercised by the incidental stimulus has been assessed by varying some aspect of that stimulus and measuring the slope of the resulting generalization gradient. It is possible that these measures might not coincide. Subjects in a PD group might respond at a higher rate to the incidental stimulus presented alone, because they were less disrupted than were TD subjects by the removal of the discriminative stimuli. Simultaneously, however, PD subjects might also respond at a substantially higher rate when some aspect of the incidental stimulus was varied in a generalization test. The former measure was taken by Wagner et al. to imply stronger control by the incidental stimulus. The latter might imply less.

Thomas, Burr, and Eck (1970) trained rats in a free operant situation with results that appeared to provide some support for this argument. Rats were trained to press a lever in the presence of two compound stimuli, T_1L_1 and T_2L_1; for TD animals T_1L_1 signaled a VI schedule of reinforcement and T_2L_1 signaled extinction; for PD animals each compound signaled reinforcement and extinction equally often. As is shown in Figure 8, when subjects were tested with L_1 alone and with a dimmer light, L_2, TD animals responded significantly less to L_1 than did PD animals, thus apparently showing less control by the light and confirming the results of Wagner et al. However, since they also responded very much less to L_2 than did PD animals, they in fact made a higher proportion of their total test responses to L_1 than did the

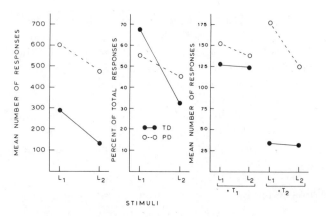

Fig. 8. Effects of true (TD) and pseudo (PD) auditory discrimination training on generalization to different light intensities. The first and second panels show absolute and relative gradients in rats tested to the lights alone, where L_1 is the light intensity used in training. The third panel shows absolute gradients of generalization when rats were tested with the lights shown in conjunction with the auditory stimuli, where T_1 was S+ and T_2 was S- for the TD group. (After Thomas et al., 1970. © 1970 by the American Psychological Association. Reprinted by permission.)

PD animals. On this measure, therefore, they showed a steeper relative gradient along the dimension of light intensity and may be said to have shown more control by the light. Thomas, Burr, and Eck thus claimed that there was no real discrepancy between the results reported by Wagner et al. and those originally reported by Thomas et al. They further argued that the only proper measure of control by an incidental stimulus is the slope of a relative generalization gradient when some feature of that stimulus is varied, and that the reason why TD animals in their experiment had responded at a lower rate to L_1 than did PD animals was simply because they were more disrupted by the removal of the auditory discriminative stimuli. They thus argued that the results of all of these studies were consistent with the proposition that TD training increases control by an incidental stimulus common to positive and negative trials.

There are, however, features even of their own data that suggest some caution in accepting Thomas, Burr, and Eck's conclusion, and the results of other experiments leave little doubt that neither their arguments nor their data can be accepted in their entirety. In the first place, there are grave problems involved in the interpretation of relative generalization gradients when these are based on widely differing absolute rates of responding. As Figure 8 shows, in Thomas, Burr, and Eck's experiment there is little or no difference between TD and PD groups in the slope of the absolute gradient. The reason why the relative gradient is steeper for the TD group is that it is derived from a lower absolute level of responding. To say that this represents a greater difference in the "true" response strength to L_1 and L_2 is, in effect, to say that the difference between 280 and 150 responses is really greater than the difference between 600 and 480. There is certainly no a priori reason why this should be true, and it is not difficult to think of reasons, such as a ceiling effect obscuring the true response strength to L_1 in Group PD, which would suggest exactly the opposite conclusion. Furthermore, as is also shown in Figure 8, when another pair of TD or PD groups was tested with L_1 and L_2, but this time presented in conjunction with T_1 and T_2, the PD animals now appear to have shown a steeper absolute gradient than the TD animals. Thomas, Burr, and Eck ignore these data, and merely assert, without citing statistical support, that "subjects responded approximately as much to compounds including L_2 as they did to those including L_1."

There are, moreover, several experiments which have shown that the discrepancy between the data of Wagner et al. and those of Thomas et al. cannot be resolved by pointing to differences in their procedures for measuring control. Even if the control exercised by an incidental stimulus is assessed by varying some aspect of it in a generalization test, it is possible to confirm the finding by Wagner et al. that TD training may reduce, rather than enhance, such control. What, then, is the basis for this difference in outcome? Perhaps the most obvious difference between the studies by Wagner et al. and Thomas et al. is that in each of their experiments Wagner et al. employed either an instrumental or a classical discrete-trial procedure, while the studies by Thomas et al. and subsequent replications of their results have all employed free operant procedures. Turner and Mackintosh (1972) first suggested that this might be an important factor and presented data showing that pigeons given discrete-trial discrimination training might show a flatter gradient than a PD group around a stimulus common to positive and negative trials. Gray and Mackintosh (1973) confirmed this result. They trained pigeons on a series of discrete trials to peck a key illuminated with a vertical line on all trials. For TD birds, positive trials were signaled by a tone and negative trials by white noise; for PD birds the tone and noise each signaled reinforcement on 50% of trials. The results of generalization tests, conducted in silence, to other orientations of the line are shown in Figure 9. It can be seen that in this experiment all measures agree in showing greater control by the line in PD animals than in TD animals: the PD group responded at a higher rate to the vertical line and also showed

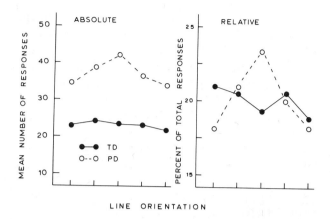

Fig. 9. Absolute and relative gradients of line-orientation generalization in pigeons following TD or PD training using a discrete-trial procedure. (After Gray & Mackintosh, 1973.)

steeper absolute and relative gradients along the dimension of line orientation.

It is clear, therefore, that regardless of the procedure used to assess control, discrimination training in a discrete-trial situation may decrease, rather than increase, the control gained by an incidental stimulus common to positive and negative trials. Thomas's results are of less generality than he has supposed.

Analysis of the Effects of Extradimensional Training

If the use of free operant or discrete-trial procedures is the critical variable determining the effects of discrimination training on control by incidental stimuli, it remains to attempt some interpretation of this difference. There are numerous differences between the two procedures. Which are the important ones, and how do they come to affect the outcome of these experiments?

In free operant discriminations, responses to S+ are usually reinforced on variable-interval schedules, typically on VI 1-min schedules in the experiments of concern here. In discrete-trial discriminations, on the other hand, reinforcement is typically available on all S+ trials. It is possible that this marked difference in the schedule of reinforcement associated with S+ has an important effect on the experimental outcome. If it is accepted that discrimination training suppresses control by incidental stimuli by insuring that other stimuli are relatively more valid signals of reinforcement, the magnitude of this effect will necessarily depend on the difference in the validity of incidental and discriminative stimuli. The more precisely the presence of a discriminative stimulus signals the availability of reinforcement, the more successfully it will overshadow an incidental stimulus. The S+ of a discrete-trial discrimination, signaling the immediate delivery of reinforcement on every trial, is surely a better predictor of reinforcement than is an S+ associated with a variable-interval schedule in a free operant discrimination. Thus TD training should be more effective in suppressing control by incidental stimuli in typical discrete-trial studies than in typical free operant experiments. There is, unfortunately, no evidence to support or refute these speculations. It should be noted, moreover, that although it may explain the direction of the difference between discrete-trial and free operant experiments, this suggestion will not explain why TD training in a free operant experiment should actually increase the control displayed by an incidental stimulus.

In the preceding section, the argument was advanced that discrimination training might increase control by stimulus A because it suppressed control by another stimulus B, which would otherwise have overshadowed or masked control by A. Following this line of reasoning, Turner and Mackintosh (1972) argued that the repetitive nature of responding on typical free operant schedules might provide a source of stimuli that came to control behavior and could therefore mask control by an incidental stimulus in a PD group. If these response-produced stimuli lost control as a consequence of TD training, an exteroceptive incidental stimulus might be able to exercise more control over responding. Even if discrimination training resulted in some overshadowing of this incidental stimulus by the relevant discriminative stimuli, it would also suppress control by response-produced stimuli, and this latter unmasking effect might be even more important.

A study by Hall and Honig (1974) provides some support for this suggestion. They first gave pigeons TD or PD training with red and green overhead lights serving as discriminative stimuli and then reinforced them for pecking at a set of vertical lines on the response key, before finally testing for generalization to other orientations of the line. One pair of TD and PD groups had been required to peck the key during initial TD and PD training, and these groups confirmed the results of Thomas et al., in that initial TD training enhanced control by the lines. The second pair of groups, however, had received free reinforcement not contingent on key pecking during their initial exposure to the TD or PD schedules. These groups, after being subsequently autoshaped to peck the vertical line and then given VI reinforcement for several sessions, showed no difference whatsoever in the slope of their generalization gradients when tested with other orientations of the line. The only obvious difference between the two pairs of groups was that where TD training increased control by the lines, animals were repetitively pecking at a response key during exposure to the TD or PD schedule. When this one factor was changed, there was no suggestion of an enhancement effect.

These results are certainly consistent with the idea that TD training may enhance control by some set of exteroceptive stimuli only to the extent that such training suppresses control by stimuli associated with repetitive instrumental responding. The implication is that such response-produced stimuli, if not neutralized by discrimination training, may mask or even overshadow control by an exteroceptive stimulus. There is, of course, nothing novel in the suggestion that free operant schedules of reinforcement may enable stimuli associated with the repetitive nature of responding to gain control over the subject's behavior.

> Under a variable interval schedule of reinforcement, for example, the organism often responds at a nearly constant rate for long periods of time. All reinforcements therefore occur when it is responding at that rate, *although this condition is not specified by the equipment*. The rate becomes a discriminative and, in turn, a reinforcing stimulus, which opposes any change to a different rate. (Skinner, 1966, p. 25)

The point has been documented by Blough's (1963) studies of pigeons trained to peck a key illuminated with a given wavelength on variable-interval and differential reinforcement of low rate (DRL) schedules. The probability of pecking within a very brief interval of a preceding peck was found to be essentially unaffected by changes in the wavelength projected onto the key. Such pecks, Blough concluded, were controlled more by the occurrence of preceding pecks than by any exteroceptive discriminative stimulus. Both Hearst (1969) and Ray and Sidman (1970) have gone so far as to argue that free operant schedules of reinforcement may be inappropriate for the study of exteroceptive stimulus control. The probability of initiating a response (as in a discrete-trial procedure) may be a better measure of the role of exteroceptive discriminative stimuli than is the probability of continuing to respond.

Turner and Mackintosh's argument required only that some set of incidental stimuli, more prevalent in free operant than in discrete-trial procedures, should be responsible for the masking of control by a specific incidental stimulus in PD subjects. Whether or not these masking stimuli are a product of repetitive responding is still open to question. A further set of results, however, confirms that much of the effect observed in the experiments of Thomas et al. is undoubtedly a consequence of such masking of control in the PD group (Honig, 1969, 1974; Turner & Mackintosh, 1972). The design of Turner and Mackintosh's experiment is shown in Table 4. Pigeons initially received TD or PD training between different key colors signaling variable-interval and extinction schedules, with a vertical line on the key on all trials. In the control condition, TD or PD groups were subsequently reinforced for responding to a plain red key and were then tested for generalization to other orientations of the line on a black background. As in other studies, the TD group showed the steeper gradient. In the experimental condition, however, both TD and PD subjects received several sessions of TD training with a new pair of wavelengths and with no line on the key, before being tested for generalization along the dimension of line orientation. In these groups, there was no difference between the gradients of subjects initially given TD training and those given PD training. Additional TD training on a new pair of stimuli increased the control displayed by the line in PD subjects to the point where their generalization

Table 4 *Design of Experiment by Turner and Mackintosh (1972)*

GROUP		STAGE 1	STAGE 2	TEST
Control	TD	BV+, GV−	R+	Orientation
	PD	BV±, GV±		Generalization
Experimental	TD	BV+, GV−	R+, Y−	Orientation
	PD	BV±, GV±		Generalization

B = Blue; G = Green; R = Red; Y = Yellow; V = Vertical line

gradient was indistinguishable from that of TD subjects.

That TD training with a new pair of stimuli can sharpen, for PD subjects, the gradient around a *previously* presented incidental stimulus implies that the typically flat gradient produced by PD subjects in free operant experiments cannot be a consequence of any failure of that incidental stimulus to *acquire* control. It must be due to a masking of such control by stimuli, which can then be neutralized by subsequent discrimination training. Honig (1969, 1974) has demonstrated the converse of these results. Just as subsequent TD training can sharpen the gradient of PD subjects, so subsequent PD training can flatten the gradient of TD subjects. Honig also showed that this flattening can itself be reversed by further TD training. The generality and reliability of these results, therefore, leave little doubt that at least part of the difference between TD and PD gradients observed in the experiments of Thomas et al. and in subsequent experiments represents nothing more than the masking of control in PD subjects by other irrelevant stimuli.

Is this a sufficient account of the effects of extradimensional discrimination training? Thomas (1970), as we noted earlier, has insisted that it is necessary to appeal to a process of general attentiveness, brought into play by discrimination training, which can affect control by all stimuli. An increase in general attentiveness will increase the control acquired not only by relevant stimuli and subsequently presented stimuli, but also by incidental stimuli, present but irrelevant during the course of discrimination learning. It is important to see whether recourse to such an analysis is necessitated by the data.

There is good reason to question whether Thomas's analysis is *sufficient* to account for the data we have been considering. It is clear that discrimination training in discrete-trial situations does not increase control by incidental stimuli. It is equally clear that the effect observed in free operant experiments is due not so much to an increase in the control actually acquired by the incidental stimulus as to an increase in the probability that the control acquired by such stimuli during training will in fact be displayed in the test situation. It is possible, nevertheless, that discrimination training does have the sort of general effect postulated by Thomas, in addition to the more specific effects suggested here, and that these general effects serve to counteract more selective processes. The evaluation of this possibility must be a rather problematic affair. Some results obtained with pigeons by Gray, however, provide some support for such a compromise by showing that discrimination training might not reduce control by a specific incidental stimulus, even if masking effects have been controlled.

The present argument has been that discrimination training always tends to suppress control by relatively less valid stimuli but that this effect might not always be observed because such training has also suppressed control by other, potentially masking stimuli. It follows that if discrimination training could somehow be given to PD subjects so as to neutralize these other masking stimuli, this basic overshadowing effect would become apparent. Gray (personal communication) attempted to test this prediction by training pigeons to peck a vertical line superimposed on a blue or green background. For a TD group, the color of the background was correlated with the availability of reinforcement; for a PD group, no such correlation existed. For both groups, however, these trials were interspersed with trials on which the key light was white (with no line), and responding was not reinforced. From the outset of the experiment, therefore, the "PD" group received discrimination training, with the line on colored backgrounds signaling occasional reinforcement and a plain white key signaling nonreinforcement. Since the line was the best single predictor of reinforcement, it should have acquired strong control over responding. In the TD group, on the other hand, the color of the key was an even more reliable predictor of reinforcement and, by the principle of relative validity, should have overshadowed the line. There was no suggestion of such an effect: the slope of the line-tilt gradient was, indeed, marginally steeper in the TD group than in the PD group.

DISCUSSION

The argument to this point has been complex and possibly tortuous. Before attempting to assess the further theoretical implications of this argument, therefore, it may be as well to recapitulate briefly the main outline.

Recapitulation

If a change in a particular stimulus results in a correlated change in a subject's behavior, we may say that this stimulus controls the subject's behavior. In any situation, it is obvious some stimuli will gain control more rapidly than others, while yet other stimuli may apparently fail to gain control. We may categorize these differences as differences in salience.

The simplest possible account of stimulus control

would be to say that the reinforcement of a particular response in the presence of a given set of stimuli will insure that all those stimuli will gain control over that response at a rate determined by their salience. We have seen that this is an oversimplification: a stimulus may gain control without necessarily displaying that control in a particular test situation. This is often because a change in one feature of the situation leaves other controlling features unchanged: the responding maintained by these latter features may prevent the experimenter from detecting the control gained by the former. The unchanged features serve to mask control, which can readily be detected by testing in their absence. This masking effect is of no great theoretical significance in itself[5]; its importance lies in the fact that the experimenter may fail to recognize its presence and thus fail to appreciate the reasons for apparent failures of stimulus control. It is clear, for example, that if a pigeon's key pecks are nondifferentially reinforced in the presence of a tone, the tone is well able to acquire control over responding. The absence of control by the tone may simply be a consequence of masking by the key light. It is also probable that responding on most free operant schedules of reinforcement is at least partially under the control of previous responses, which may mask control by exteroceptive stimuli. There is indeed direct evidence that this is true of some of a pigeon's key pecks. Experimenters need to remind themselves that the experimental situations in which they place their subjects contain a multiplicity of features, and that a failure to detect control by one feature may reflect nothing more than the control gained by others.

A more salient stimulus might not only mask the expression of control by another, it might also prevent the less salient stimulus from acquiring control in the first place. This principle of overshadowing also applies to the case where stimuli differ in validity rather than in salience: a stimulus which is reliably correlated with the occurrence of reinforcement may prevent one less well correlated from acquiring control over responding. Whenever discrimination training is programmed, constant features of the experimental situation become less well correlated with reinforcement than the discriminative stimuli. The principle of overshadowing, therefore, implies that the discriminative stimuli will prevent these situational stimuli from acquiring control, and this may explain the effect of discrimination training on stimulus control. Nondifferential reinforcement in the presence of a tone, for example, will produce little control by the tone, because other, more salient stimuli, such as the key light, will either mask or overshadow the tone. Differential reinforcement between the presence and absence of the tone, however, will suppress control by the key light and other situational stimuli and prevent their masking the tone. Whenever animals are exposed to differential reinforcement, therefore, stimuli correlated with these changes in reinforcement will tend to acquire control over behavior, and in so doing will prevent other less valid stimuli from gaining control, even if these other stimuli are intrinsically more salient. Since these other stimuli may include such features as the shape and size of the apparatus, a background masking noise, the time of day, or the occurrence of previous responses, it is not surprising that differential reinforcement should have such pervasive effects and should so reliably enhance the control gained by discrete features of the experimental situation, such as stimuli on a pigeon's response key.

Whether this principle is sufficient to explain all effects of discrimination training on stimulus control is still an open question. In some situations, discrimination training, so far from enhancing control by relevant stimuli only at the expense of irrelevant stimuli, appears to enhance control by the latter also. It may be possible to reconcile this observation with the principle of overshadowing by arguing that discrimination training suppresses control by other irrelevant stimuli which might mask the control gained by the particular incidental stimulus manipulated by the experimenter. It is also possible, however, that discrimination training has additional, more general effects on stimulus control.

Theoretical Analysis

The argument throughout this chapter has been theoretical in the sense that I have not listed a set of empirical conditions known to affect the slope of generalization gradients, but have rather attempted to reach an understanding of the principles governing those effects. The principles invoked, however, themselves stand in need of explanation. In particular, it is important to consider how overshadowing and general attentiveness can be incorporated into theoretical analyses of learning.

OVERSHADOWING

There can be no gainsaying the fundamental importance of overshadowing. The presence of a more salient or more valid stimulus is apparently able to

---

[5] This is, perhaps, an exaggeration. An adequate explanation of masking requires at least some assumptions about the effects of adding together different sources of response strength. For one set of possible assumptions, see Hull (1952, p. 66).

interfere with the acquisition of control by less salient or less valid stimuli. This observation contradicts the basic assumption, common to most traditional theories of learning, that all stimuli present at the moment of reinforcement will gain control over behavior, with any differences in the control acquired by different stimuli being a consequence of their own salience or absolute validity. The occurrence of overshadowing implies, on the contrary, some interaction or competition between stimuli for control of behavior.

One possible explanation of overshadowing is to appeal to what Thomas (1970) has called an "inverse hypothesis." The assumption is that there is a fixed upper limit to the control that can be gained by any set of stimuli, and that this must be shared between all stimuli present in the experimental situation. The greater the control acquired by one subset of the available stimuli, therefore, the less will be available for others. One expression of this inverse hypothesis is to be found in theories of selective attention (Lovejoy, 1968; Sutherland & Mackintosh, 1971), which assume an inverse relation between the probabilities or strengths of attention to different sets of stimuli. The term *attention* is here used not in the sense employed by Honig (1970) to delimit a class of experimental operations, nor yet in the sense employed by Terrace (1966) to refer to residual variability in experimental data. The meaning of the term is quite precisely defined, by its use in a formal model, to refer to a parameter whose value determines first the amount of change in associative strength of a stimulus as a consequence of reinforcement and nonreinforcement and, secondly, the extent to which the subjects' behavior will be actually controlled by that stimulus rather than by another at any particular moment.

The inverse hypothesis may also be derived from a theory of associative competition (Rescorla & Wagner, 1972; Revusky, 1971). Following a suggestion of Kamin (1969), Rescorla and Wagner have argued that changes in the associative strength of one component of a compound depend upon the current associative strength of all other components. This will insure that the asymptotic associative strength of one component of a reinforced compound will be inversely related to the asymptotic strength of other components. Overshadowing of an auditory by a visual component is a consequence of the fact that the visual component, by virtue of its greater salience or better correlation with reinforcement, acquires associative strength more rapidly than the auditory component and thus reduces the associative strength available for conditioning to the latter.

Overshadowing seems a sufficiently reliable phenomenon to require some version of the inverse hypothesis for its explanation. It is not possible, as has been attempted by Thomas (1970), to dismiss all instances of overshadowing or blocking as artifacts susceptible of alternative explanation. Nevertheless, Thomas's point is worth serious consideration, even if not always for the reasons he advances. There have, in fact, been several reported failures of overshadowing, both in instrumental learning (e.g., Sutherland & Andelman, 1967) and in classical conditioning (e.g., Schnur, 1971). Mackintosh (1974), indeed, has suggested that on the basis of the available evidence overshadowing requires either marked differences in salience between overshadowing and overshadowed cues or a difference in their correlation with reinforcement. A weak or poorly correlated stimulus will be overshadowed by another more salient or more valid one, but it will not itself detract from conditioning to the stronger stimulus; nor indeed is there much evidence that two salient or equally correlated stimuli will overshadow one another. If this conclusion is substantiated by further research, it will require some modification of the rather rigid interpretation of the inverse hypothesis postulated by theories of selective attention or limited associative capacity.

Before leaving the topic of overshadowing, it is worth showing that it provides a simple explanation of one result which has not been considered so far. We have documented the finding that in free operant situations an incidental stimulus may show stronger control over responding following TD training than after PD training. There is good evidence that a major part of this difference is due to the difference between the TD group and subjects receiving simple, nondifferential reinforcement, even if this is programmed in an unchanging stimulus situation (e.g., Bresnahan, 1970; Honig, 1969; Turner & Mackintosh, 1972). We have not considered whether PD training would produce any different level of control from that produced by simple nondifferential reinforcement. The question is whether, for example, nondifferential reinforcement of a pigeon's key pecks in the presence of a vertical line and an unchanging wavelength would result in stronger control by the line than would the same schedule of reinforcement in the presence of the line, but with random variations in wavelength. Although some studies have suggested that these two procedures may have relatively similar effects on control in such a situation (e.g., Thomas et. al., 1970, Experiment 5), there are other studies which have rather clearly shown that the PD treatment may result in significantly flatter generalization gradients (Bresnahan, 1970; Honig, 1969, 1974; Tomie, Davitt, & Thomas, 1973).

Tomie et al. have inferred from this difference that animals learn to be inattentive to all stimuli when exposed to variations in one set of stimuli uncorrelated with variations in reinforcement. It is equally possible, however, to interpret such a result in terms of Rescorla and Wagner's (1972) account of overshadowing. If the flat gradients of PD subjects are a consequence of control by some set of masking stimuli, then the more control such stimuli acquire, the flatter these gradients will be. But if stimuli compete for the acquisition of control, then the control acquired by masking stimuli must be inversely related to the control acquired by any other stimuli explicitly manipulated by the experimenter. A single constant wavelength will acquire control more rapidly than will a randomly varying pair of wavelengths. In the former case, therefore, potential masking stimuli will have less chance to acquire control and will be less able to mask control by other stimuli subsequently varied in a generalization test.

GENERAL ATTENTIVENESS

A large part of Thomas's argument against the inverse hypothesis was based on the assertion that evidence for a process of selective attention is far outweighed by evidence for a process of general attentiveness. Although this claim may be exaggerated, there are sufficient problems with attempts to attribute all effects of discrimination training to the overshadowing of incidental stimuli so that it becomes important to see whether any more precise characterization can be provided of this concept of general attentiveness. What are the factors which operate to prevent the relevant stimuli of a discrimination problem from overshadowing, and thus reducing control by, incidental stimuli common to both positive and negative trials? A simple suggestion, which should be considered, even if it must also in the end be dismissed, is that discrimination training establishes a set of observing or orienting responses which increase control by other stimuli located in proximity to the discriminative stimuli. Pigeons trained to discriminate between two wavelengths projected onto a response key will learn to look at the key and will thus learn about any other stimuli, such as a line, that also appear on the key. Venerable as this suggestion may be, in the present context it is neither plausible nor empirically substantiated. It is hard to see how, even in the absence of explicit discrimination training, a pigeon could learn to direct responses at a key without looking at it. Moreover, several studies of extradimensional transfer have used stimuli not located on the response key, without this having any apparent effect on the outcome of the experiment. In one experiment, Thomas et al. (1970) gave pigeons TD or PD training with different floor tilts serving as the discriminative stimuli and found that TD training resulted in reliably better control by the wavelength projected onto the key. Hall and Honig (1974) found differences in the control gained by a set of lines projected onto the response key after pigeons had received TD or PD training between different overhead lights. Conversely, Gray (personal communication) has shown that if pigeons are given TD or PD training with different wavelengths, with a tone present on all trials, TD subjects will show better control by the tone in a subsequent generalization test.

Thomas (1970) noted that results such as these ruled out the possibility that enhancement could be simply due to the establishment of appropriate observing responses and concluded that "a central attentional mechanism seems required" (p. 327). If subjects are exposed to a correlation between changes in stimuli and changes in reinforcement, the assumption seems to be that they will come to expect that future changes in stimulation will also be correlated with changes in reinforcement. There is a certain plausibility to this idea, but it should be recognized as no more than an intuitive and disturbingly vague proposal. Certainly no attempt has yet been made to specify a formal model with the required properties. Until such a day, it may be worth seeing whether more prosaic processes are sufficient to account for the observed data.

A more neutral description of those data may help to suggest one possible set of ideas. Extradimensional enhancement is said to occur if subjects, given a generalization test after TD training between two wavelengths with a vertical line always present, respond relatively infrequently to other orientations of the line, whereas subjects given PD training continue to respond at a relatively constant rate regardless of the orientation of the line. If subjects are to show good control by the stimuli varied in a generalization test, they must either never respond, or rapidly stop responding, to the majority of test stimuli. Since it is only rarely that subjects do not respond at all to any test stimulus, one determinant of the slope of most generalization gradients will be the rate at which responding extinguishes to such stimuli. This point is documented by the observation, noted earlier, that generalization gradients become progressively steeper in the course of testing in extinction.

It may therefore be parsimonious to attribute at least some of the difference between TD or PD gradients to a simple difference in the resistance to extinction engendered by the two schedules. There is, in fact, independent evidence that discrimination training may result in the more rapid extinction of responding to S+ than does partial reinforcement in the presence of that stimulus (Jenkins, 1961), and several reasonably well-defined theoretical analyses are available to explain such an effect. Amsel's theory of partial reinforcement and persistence (Amsel, 1962, 1972) is readily applied to the present set of data. Animals exposed to a PD schedule may be assumed to have learned that responding in the face of occasional periods of nonreinforcement will be later reinforced. Responding will therefore persist in the fact of a series of nonreinforced test trials. After TD training, on the other hand, subjects may learn that responding during periods of nonreinforcement will not be reinforced, and they will therefore stop responding during a generalization test. Although Amsel has not applied his analysis specifically to the case of generalization tests, he has presented an account of discrimination learning which implies that prior exposure to a schedule of partial reinforcement will retard the acquisition of a successive discrimination by retarding the extinction of responses to S− (Amsel & Ward, 1965). Amsel and Ward's original analysis assumed that such effects would be confined to situations where the discriminative stimuli remained unchanged between discrimination training and prior exposure to partial reinforcement. Several subsequent experiments, however, have shown that this is incorrect and that differences between partial reinforcement and either consistent or differential reinforcement transfer virtually without loss even when the discriminative stimuli are changed (e.g., Flaherty & Davenport, 1972; Galbraith, 1973).

Such transfer is readily explained by an extension of the analysis applied to the "generalized partial reinforcement effect" (Amsel, Rashotte, & MacKinnon, 1966; Brown & Logan, 1965). Animals exposed to partial and consistent reinforcement in different alleys respond persistently over a series of extinction trials even if extinction is conducted in the previously consistently reinforced alley. Although animals that receive only consistent reinforcement in one alley rapidly stop running if extinguished in that alley, exposure to partial reinforcement in another situation is sufficient to insure persistent responding in extinction. Amsel refers to this finding as a case of mediated generalization. The events that control behavior in extinction are assumed to be stimuli arising from the delivery or omission of reinforcement: animals reinforced for responding persistently in the face of nonreinforcement in one situation will continue to do so when exposed to nonreinforcement in a new situation.[6]

In this analysis, the specific discriminative stimuli, in whose presence animals receive partial or consistent reinforcement, are viewed as providing a context in which habits of persistence or its converse are established. Thus examples of extradimensional transfer of TD or PD training are explained not by saying that animals attribute significance to external stimuli and generalize this to other stimuli, but rather by saying that limited changes in contextual stimuli may not disrupt patterns of behavior that have previously been established under particular conditions of reinforcement. It seems probable that there must be some limits to this generalization. There may be better transfer of persistence to a nonreinforced generalization test, if animals have been partially reinforced in the presence of uncorrelated variations in external stimuli, than if such training has been given in an unchanging stimulus situation. This would provide an alternative explanation of the previously noted finding that PD training may result in even flatter generalization gradients than exposure to a comparable schedule of reinforcement in the presence of a single, unchanging stimulus.

Concluding Comments

It is worth stressing one point in conclusion. Whatever the merits of rival explanations of stimulus selection and overshadowing on the one hand, and of rival explanations of general attentiveness on the other, the distinction between the principles of general and selective changes in controlling stimuli may be difficult to maintain both in fact and in logic. To say that discrimination training produces a "set to discriminate," which encourages differential responding to all stimulus dimensions, may seem to imply some theoretical assumptions quite distinct from those im-

---

[6] Amsel himself has always assumed that the subject's emotional reactions to nonreinforcement provide the source of stimulation which controls persistent behavior. This identification does not affect the logic of the argument. In discrete-trial situations, where responding on one trial is reinforced after a preceding nonreinforced trail, it may be as appropriate to assume that the memory of such an outcome, rather than the frustration conditioned by that outcome, comes to control behavior (Capaldi, 1967). In the present context, it might be more appropriate to make some entirely different identification. The important point is that a free operant PD or nondifferential schedule reinforces a steady rate of responding, even after relatively prolonged periods of nonreinforcement. As soon as TD subjects learn the discrimination, they do not receive reinforcement after responding through such prolonged periods of nonreinforcement. It does not matter how such periods of nonreinforcement are detected.

plied by theories of overshadowing. It is, however, possible to argue that evidence of a general effect of discrimination training is always a consequence of the suppression of control by other stimuli which were not measured by the experimenter.

In the preceding section, an analysis of general attentiveness was proposed which suggested that PD subjects show less control by stimuli varied in a generalization test than do TD subjects, because they have been reinforced for responding at a steady rate through periods of nonreinforcement and continue to do so during testing. In effect, this amounts to saying that they show relatively little control by the test stimuli, because their behavior is controlled by other events. This analysis, therefore, would seem to be a special case of the general proposition advanced earlier: procedures which increase the control exercised by one set of stimuli achieve their effects by decreasing the control exercised by others. If, as a consequence of discrimination training, subjects are ready to attribute changes in reinforcement to changes in external stimuli, as Thomas has suggested, this may simply be because they have learned that such changes are not dependent on the time of day, their own motivational state, the occurrence of preceding responses or reinforcers, or yet other events which the experimenter has not even suspected.

REFERENCES

AMSEL, A. Frustrative nonreward in partial reinforcement and discrimination learning. *Psychological Review*, 1962, *69*, 306–328.

AMSEL, A. Inhibition and mediation in classical, Pavlovian, and instrumental conditioning. In R. A. Boakes & M. S. Halliday (Eds.), *Inhibition and learning*. London: Academic Press, 1972.

AMSEL, A., RASHOTTE, M. E., & MACKINNON, J. R. Partial reinforcement effects within subject and between subjects. *Psychological Monographs*, 1966, *80* (20, Whole No. 628).

AMSEL, A., & WARD, J. S. Frustration and persistence: Resistance to discrimination following prior experience with the discriminanda. *Psychological Monographs*, 1965, *79* (4, Whole No. 597).

BLOUGH, D. S. Interresponse time as a function of continuous variables: A new method and some data. *Journal of the Experimental Analysis of Behavior*, 1963, *6*, 237–246.

BLOUGH, D. S. Attention shifts in a maintained discrimination. *Science*, 1969, *166*, 125–126.

BONEAU, C. A., & HONIG, W. K. Opposed generalization gradients based upon conditional discrimination training. *Journal of Experimental Psychology*, 1964, *66*, 89–93.

BRESNAHAN, E. L. Effects of extradimensional pseudodiscrimination and discrimination training upon stimulus control. *Journal of Experimental Psychology*, 1970, *85*, 155–156.

BROWER, L. P. Ecological chemistry. *Scientific American*, 1969, *220*, 22–29.

BROWN, R. T., & LOGAN, F. A. Generalised partial reinforcement effect. *Journal of Comparative and Physiological Psychology*, 1965, *60*, 64–69.

CAPALDI, E. J. A sequential hypothesis of instrumental learning. In K. W. Spence & J. T. Spence (Eds.), *The psychology of learning and motivation* (Vol. 1). New York: Academic Press, 1967.

CHASE, S. Selectivity in multidimensional stimulus control. *Journal of Comparative and Physiological Psychology*, 1968, *66*, 787–792.

DOBRZECKA, C., SZWEJKOWSKA, G., & KONORSKI, J. Qualitative versus directional cues in two forms of differentiation. *Science*, *153*, 87–89. © 1966 by the American Association for the Advancement of Science.

ECK, K. O., NOEL, R. C., & THOMAS, D. R. Discrimination learning as a function of prior discrimination and nondifferential training. *Journal of Experimental Psychology*, 1969, *82*, 156–162.

FARTHING, G. W. Overshadowing in the discrimination of successive compound stimuli. *Psychonomic Science*, 1972, *28*, 29–32.

FARTHING, G. W., & HEARST, E. Attention in the pigeon: Testing with compounds or elements. *Learning and Motivation*, 1970, *1*, 65–78.

FLAHERTY, C. F., & DAVENPORT, J. W. Successive brightness discrimination in rats following regular versus random intermittent reinforcement. *Journal of Experimental Psychology*, 1972, *96*, 1–9.

FOREE, D. D., & LOLORDO, V. M. Attention in the pigeon: Differential effects of food-getting versus shock-avoidance procedures. *Journal of Comparative and Physiological Psychology*, 1973, *85*, 551–558.

FREEMAN, F. *The effect of extradimensional discrimination training on the slope of the generalization gradient.* Unpublished master's thesis, Kent State University, 1967.

FREEMAN, F., & THOMAS, D. R. Attention vs. cue utilization in generalization testing. Paper presented at Midwestern Psychological Association, Chicago, 1967.

FRIEMAN, J., & GOYETTE, C. H. Transfer of training across stimulus modality and response class. *Journal of Experimental Psychology*, 1973, *97*, 235–241.

GALBRAITH, K. Fractional anticipatory goal responses as cues in discrimination learning. *Journal of Experimental Psychology*, 1973, *97*, 177–181.

GANZ, L., & RIESEN, A. H. Stimulus generalization to hue in the dark-reared macaque. *Journal of Comparative and Physiological Psychology*, 1962, *55*, 92–99.

GARCIA, J., & ERVIN, F. R. A neuropsychological approach to appropriateness of signals and specificity of reinforcers. *Communications in Behavioral Biology*, 1968, *1*, Part A, 389–415.

GARCIA, J., & KOELLING, R. A. Relation of cue to consequence in avoidance learning. *Psychonomic Science*, 1966, *4*, 123–124.

GRAY, V. A., & MACKINTOSH, N. J. Control by an irrelevant stimulus in discrete-trial discrimination learning by pigeons. *Bulletin of the Psychonomic Society*, 1973, *1*, 193–195.

Guttman, N., & Kalish, H. I. Discriminability and stimulus generalization. *Journal of Experimental Psychology*, 1956, *51*, 79–88.

Halgren, C. R. Latent inhibition in rats: Associative or nonassociative? *Journal of Comparative and Physiological Psychology*, 1974, *86*, 74–78.

Hall, G., & Honig, W. K. Stimulus control after extradimensional training in pigeons: A comparison of response contingent and noncontingent training procedures. *Journal of Comparative and Physiological Psychology*, 1974, *87*, 945–952.

Hanson, H. M. Effects of discrimination training on stimulus generalization. *Journal of Experimental Psychology*, 1959, *58*, 321–334.

Hearst, E. Concurrent generalization gradients for food-controlled and shock-controlled behavior. *Journal of the Experimental Analysis of Behavior*, 1962, *5*, 19–31.

Hearst, E. Aversive conditioning and external stimulus control. In B. A. Campbell & R. M. Church (Eds.), *Punishment and aversive behavior*. Englewood Cliffs, N.J.: Prentice-Hall, Inc., 1969.

Hearst, E. Some persistent problems in the analysis of conditioned inhibition. In R. A. Boakes & M. S. Halliday (Eds.), *Inhibition and learning*. London: Academic Press, 1972.

Heinemann, E. G., & Rudolph, R. L. The effect of discriminative training on the gradient of stimulus generalization. *American Journal of Psychology*, 1963, *76*, 653–658.

Hoffman, H. S., & Fleshler, M. Stimulus factors in aversive controls: The generalization of conditioned suppression. *Journal of the Experimental Analysis of Behavior*, 1961, *4*, 371–378.

Honig, W. K. Prediction of preference, transposition, and transposition-reversal from the generalization gradient. *Journal of Experimental Psychology*, 1962, *64*, 239–248.

Honig, W. K. Attentional factors governing the slope of the generalization gradient. In R. M. Gilbert & N. S. Sutherland (Eds.), *Animal discrimination learning*. London: Academic Press, 1969.

Honig, W. K. Attention and the modulation of stimulus control. In D. Mostofsky (Ed.), *Attention: Contemporary theory and analysis*. Englewood Cliffs, N.J.: Prentice-Hall, Inc., 1970.

Honig, W. K. Effects of extradimensional discrimination training upon previously acquired stimulus control. *Learning and Motivation*, 1974, *5*, 1–15.

Honig, W. K., Thomas, D. R., & Guttman, N. Differential effects of continuous extinction and discrimination training on the generalization gradient. *Journal of Experimental Psychology*, 1959, *58*, 145–152.

Hovland, C. I. The generalization of conditioned responses, I: The sensory generalization of conditioned response with varying frequencies of tone. *Journal of General Psychology*, 1937, *17*, 125–148.

Hull, C. L. *A behavior system*. New Haven: Yale University Press, 1952.

Jenkins, H. M. The effect of discrimination training on extinction. *Journal of Experimental Psychology*, 1961, *61*, 111–121.

Jenkins, H. M., & Harrison, R. H. Effect of discrimination training on auditory generalization. *Journal of Experimental Psychology*, 1960, *59*, 246–253.

Jenkins, H. M., & Harrison, R. H. Generalization gradients of inhibition following auditory discrimination learning. *Journal of the Experimental Analysis of Behavior*, 1962, *5*, 435–441.

Johnson, D. F. Determiners of selective stimulus control in the pigeon. *Journal of Comparative and Physiological Psychology*, 1970, *70*, 298–307.

Kamin, L. J. Predictability, surprise, attention, and conditioning. In B. Campbell & R. Church (Eds.), *Punishment and aversive behavior*. Englewood Cliffs, N.J.: Prentice-Hall, Inc., 1969.

Lashley, K. S., & Wade, M. The Pavlovian theory of generalization. *Psychological Review*, 1946, *53*, 72–87.

Lawrence, D. H. Acquired distinctiveness of cues, I: Transfer between discriminations on the basis of familiarity with the stimulus. *Journal of Experimental Psychology*, 1949, *39*, 770–784.

Lawrence, D. H. Acquired distinctiveness of cues, II: Selective association in a constant stimulus situation. *Journal of Experimental Psychology*, 1950, *40*, 175–188.

Lovejoy, E. *Attention in discrimination learning*. San Francisco: Holden-Day, 1968.

Lovejoy, E., & Russell, D. B. Suppression of learning about a hard cue by the presence of an easy cue. *Psychonomic Science*, 1967, *8*, 365–366.

Lubow, R. E. Latent inhibition: Effects of frequency of nonreinforced preexposure of the CS. *Journal of Comparative and Physiological Psychology*, 1965, *60*, 454–459.

Lubow, R. E. Latent inhibition. *Psychological Bulletin*, 1973, *79*, 398–407.

Lubow, R. E., & Moore, A. U. Latent inhibition: The effect of nonreinforced preexposure to the conditioned stimulus. *Journal of Comparative and Physiological Psychology*, 1959, *52*, 415–419.

Lyons, J., & Thomas, D. R. Effects of interdimensional training on stimulus generalization, II: Within-subjects design. *Journal of Experimental Psychology*, 1967, *75*, 572–574.

Mackintosh, N. J. Transposition after single-stimulus pretraining. *American Journal of Psychology*, 1965, *78*, 116–119.

Mackintosh, N. J. Stimulus selection: Learning to ignore stimuli that predict no change in reinforcement. In R. A. Hinde & J. Stevenson-Hinde (Eds.), *Constraints on learning*. London: Academic Press, 1973.

Mackintosh, N. J. *The psychology of animal learning*. London: Academic Press, 1974.

Mackintosh, N. J., & Honig, W. K. Blocking and attentional enhancement in pigeons. *Journal of Comparative and Physiological Psychology*, 1970, *73*, 78–85.

Malott, M. K. Stimulus control in stimulus-deprived chickens. *Journal of Comparative and Physiological Psychology*, 1968, *66*, 276–283.

Mellgren, R. L., & Ost, J. W. P. Transfer of Pavlovian differential conditioning to an operant discrimination. *Journal of Comparative and Physiological Psychology*, 1969, *67*, 390–394.

Miles, C. G. Blocking the acquisition of control by an auditory stimulus with pretraining on brightness. *Psychonomic Science*, 1970, *19*, 133–134.

Miles, C. G., & Jenkins, H. M. Overshadowing in operant conditioning as a function of discriminability. *Learning and Motivation*, 1973, *4*, 11–27.

Miles, C. G., Mackintosh, N. J., & Westbrook, R. F. Redistributing control between the elements of a compound stimulus. *Quarterly Journal of Experimental Psychology*, 1970, 22, 478–483.

Moore, J. W. Stimulus control: Studies of auditory generalization in rabbits. In A. H. Black & W. F. Prokasy (Eds.), *Classical conditioning*, Vol. 2: *Current research and theory*. Englewood Cliffs, N.J.: Prentice-Hall, Inc., 1972.

Newman, F. L., & Baron, M. R. Stimulus generalization along the dimension of angularity. *Journal of Comparative and Physiological Psychology*, 1965, 60, 59–63.

Newman, F. L., & Benefield, R. L. Stimulus control, cue utilization, and attention. Effects of discrimination training. *Journal of Comparative and Physiological Psychology*, 1968, 66, 101–104.

Notterman, J. M. A study of some relations among aperiodic reinforcement, discrimination training, and secondary reinforcement. *Journal of Experimental Psychology*, 1951, 41, 161–169.

Pavlov, I. P. *Conditioned reflexes*. Oxford: Oxford University Press, 1927.

Peterson, N. Effect of monochromatic rearing on the control of responding by wavelength. *Science*, 1962, 136, 774–775.

Ray, B. A., & Sidman, M. Reinforcement schedules and stimulus control. In W. N. Schoenfeld (Ed.), *The theory of reinforcement schedules*. Englewood Cliffs, N.J.: Prentice-Hall, Inc., 1970.

Reiss, S., & Wagner, A. R. CS habituation produces a "latent inhibition effect" but no active "conditioned inhibition." *Learning and Motivation*, 1972, 3, 227–245.

Rescorla, R. A. Summation and retardation tests of latent inhibition. *Journal of Comparative and Physiological Psychology*, 1971, 75, 77–81.

Rescorla, R. A., & Wagner, A. R. A theory of Pavlovian conditioning: Variations in the effectiveness of reinforcement and nonreinforcement. In A. H. Black & W. F. Prokasy (Eds.), *Classical conditioning*, Vol. 2: *Current research and theory*. Englewood Cliffs, N.J.: Prentice-Hall, Inc., 1972.

Revusky, S. The role of interference in association over a delay. In W. K. Honig & P. H. R. James (Eds.), *Animal memory*. New York: Academic Press, 1971.

Revusky, S., & Garcia, J. Learned associations over long delays. In G. H. Bower (Ed.), *The psychology of learning and motivation* (Vol. 4). New York: Academic Press, 1970.

Rozin, P., & Kalat, J. W. Specific hungers and poisoning as adaptive specializations of learning. *Psychological Review*, 1971, 78, 459–486.

Rudolph, R., & Honig, W. K. Effects of monochromatic rearing on spectral discrimination learning and the peak shift in chicks. *Journal of the Experimental Analysis of Behavior*, 1972, 17, 107–111.

Rudolph, R. L., Honig, W. K., & Gerry, J. E. Effects of monochromatic rearing on the acquisition of stimulus control. *Journal of Comparative and Physiological Psychology*, 1969, 67, 50–58.

Schlosberg, H., & Solomon, R. L. Latency of response in a choice of discrimination. *Journal of Experimental Psychology*, 1943, 33, 22–39.

Schnur, P. Selective attention: Effect of element preexposure on compound conditioning in rats. *Journal of Comparative and Physiological Psychology*, 1971, 76, 123–130.

Shepp, B. E., & Eimas, P. D. Intradimensional and extradimensional shifts in the rat. *Journal of Comparative and Physiological Psychology*, 1964, 57, 357–361.

Shepp, B. E., & Schrier, A. M. Consecutive intradimensional and extradimensional shifts in monkeys. *Journal of Comparative and Physiological Psychology*, 1969, 67, 199–203.

Shettleworth, S. J. Constraints on learning. In D. S. Lehrman, R. A. Hinde, & E. Shaw (Eds.), *Advances in the study of behavior*. New York: Academic Press, 1972.

Skinner, B. F. Operant behavior. In W. K. Honig (Ed.), *Operant behavior: Areas of research and application*. Englewood Cliffs, N.J.: Prentice-Hall, Inc., 1966.

Spence, K. W. The differential response in animals to stimuli varying within a single dimension. *Psychological Review*, 1937, 44, 430–444.

Sutherland, N. S., & Andelman, L. Learning with one and two cues. *Psychonomic Science*, 1967, 15, 253–254.

Sutherland, N. S., & Mackintosh, N. J. *Mechanisms of animal discrimination learning*. New York: Academic Press, 1971.

Switalski, R. W., Lyons, J., & Thomas, D. R. Effects of interdimensional training on stimulus generalization. *Journal of Experimental Psychology*, 1966, 72, 661–666.

Terrace, H. S. Stimulus control. In W. K. Honig (Ed.), *Operant behavior: Areas of research and application*. Englewood Cliffs, N.J.: Prentice-Hall, Inc., 1966.

Thomas, D. R. Stimulus selection, attention, and related matters. In J. H. Reynierse (Ed.), *Current issues in animal learning*. Lincoln: University of Nebraska Press, 1970.

Thomas, D. R., & Barker, E. G. The effects of extinction and "central tendency" on stimulus generalization in pigeons. *Psychonomic Science*, 1964, 1, 119–120.

Thomas, D. R., Burr, D. E. S., & Eck, K. O. Stimulus selection in animal discrimination learning: An alternative interpretation. *Journal of Experimental Psychology*, 1970, 86, 53–62.

Thomas, D. R., Ernst, A. J., & Andry, D. K. More on masking of stimulus control during generalization testing. *Psychonomic Science*, 1971, 23, 85–86.

Thomas, D. R., Freeman, F., Svinicki, J. G., Burr, D. E. S., & Lyons, J. Effects of extradimensional training on stimulus generalization. *Journal of Experimental Psychology Monograph*, 1970, 83 (1, Part 2).

Thomas, D. R., Mariner, R. W., & Sherry, G. Role of preexperimental experience in the development of stimulus control. *Journal of Experimental Psychology*, 1969, 79, 375–376.

Thomas, D. R., Svinicki, M. D., & Svinicki, J. G. Masking of stimulus control during generalization testing. *Journal of Experimental Psychology*, 1970, 84, 479–482.

Tomie, A., Davitt, G. A., & Thomas, D. R. Role of stimulus similarity in equivalence training. *Journal of Experimental Psychology*, 1973, 101, 146–150.

Tracy, W. K. Wavelength generalization and preference in monochromatically reared ducklings. *Journal of the Experimental Analysis of Behavior*, 1970, 13, 163–178.

Turner, C., & Mackintosh, N. J. Stimulus selection and irrelevant stimuli in discrimination learning by pigeons. *Journal of Comparative and Physiological Psychology*, 1972, 78, 1–9.

Van Houten, R., & Rudolph, R. The development of stimulus control with and without a lighted key. *Journal of the Experimental Analysis of Behavior,* 1972, *18,* 217–222.

vom Saal, W., & Jenkins, H. M. Blocking the development of stimulus control. *Learning and Motivation,* 1970, *1,* 52–64.

Wagner, A. R. Incidental stimuli and discrimination learning. In R. M. Gilbert & N. S. Sutherland (Eds.), *Animal discrimination learning.* London: Academic Press, 1969.

Wagner, A. R., Logan, F. A., Haberlandt, K., & Price, T. Stimulus selection in animal discrimination learning. *Journal of Experimental Psychology,* 1968, *76,* 171–180.

Wilcoxon, H. C., Dragoin, W. B., & Kral, P. A. Illness-induced aversions in rat and quail: Relative salience of visual and gustatory cues. *Science,* 1971, *171,* 826–828.

Williams, B. A. The failure of stimulus control after presence-absence discrimination of click-rate. *Journal of the Experimental Analysis of Behavior,* 1973, *20,* 23–27.

Zentall, T. Attention in the pigeon: Novelty effects and testing with compounds. *Psychonomic Science,* 1972, *27,* 31–32.

17

Animal Psychophysics*

Donald Blough
and
Patricia Blough

INTRODUCTION

This chapter concerns the assessment, by operant methods, of the sensory and perceptual capacities of nonverbal animals. Though behavioral methods have been used for such purposes since early in the century, modern operant techniques have markedly increased their efficiency. Many methodological variations have appeared; instrumentation has been vastly improved, and the number of species and problems studies has multiplied. Experimenters have successfully answered questions that would have been out of reach just a few years ago, and further rapid development is in prospect.

This burst of activity in animal psychophysics has been prompted in part by the rapid expansion of research on the anatomy and physiology of sensory processes. For such experiments, nonhuman organisms have, of course, been popular subjects. The resulting findings have called for corresponding psycho-

physical data from the same species, because a complete understanding of sensory functioning within a species requires interlocking anatomical, physiological, and behavioral data. A broad understanding of sensory functioning also requires cross-species comparisons. For example, when systems differ characteristically in structure, psychophysical data may reveal corresponding functional differences. Already such correspondences have contributed a good deal to our understanding of the way sensory systems work, and they suggest fascinating possibilities for future research.

This chapter will focus on research and methods that seek information regarding sensory and perceptual systems. Problems in some related areas of stimulus control, although they are sometimes considered part of "animal psychophysics," are treated elsewhere in this volume, and we shall not dwell on them. We shall stress studies that seek a functional relationship between a carefully defined response and a carefully controlled stimulus dimension, and our emphasis will be on methods that have been successful in describing such relationships. Thus more consideration will be given to studies that show how a response measure varies across a range of stimulus values than to studies

---

* Preparation of this chapter was partially supported by USPHS grant MY-02456. We thank Dr. Charles Shimp and the Psychology Department, University of Utah, for providing the facilities that we used during the writing of this chapter.

that simply inquire about an animal's ability to discriminate between two values. The more limited experiments have helped in the development of behavioral techniques, and have been useful in answering such questions as "Do cats have color vision?" However, detailed functional relationships may answer not only the question "Do they?" but also "What kind?" and "How much?"

Although this chapter will concentrate on operant techniques, it is well to remember that other behavioral methods, involving reflexes or classical conditioning, may best serve particular purposes. Indeed, for some species, operant methods simply may not work. In the frog, for example, psychophysical data are badly needed to supplement rapidly mounting data on visual anatomy and physiology, but as yet frogs have proven refractory to positive reinforcement techniques.

Within the operant paradigm, the choice of a method often hinges on the achievement of maximal stimulus control and simple, quantitative indices of this control. This means that operant methods favored for other purposes may be inappropriate in psychophysical research. For example, the rate of a free operant as exhibited on a cumulative record will rarely be seen in studies cited here; many experiments use discrete-trial methods in some ways resembling the mazes and jumping stands of earlier decades. However, the modern use of older methods involves a more thorough analysis of the situation than did earlier applications. Extraneous cues arising from many sources are carefully eliminated; competing sources of control are minimized, and appropriate orienting and fixating responses are often an integral part of the behavioral picture.

In the following pages we shall consider first some techniques used to measure sensory thresholds in animals and some approaches to the many problems that arise in this area. We shall next deal with perceptual and scaling studies. This research involves suprathreshold stimuli that raise special problems of stimulus control. Finally, we shall consider the role of signal detection theory in animal psychophysics, outlining relevant methods and examining the applicability and the usefulness of this approach.

MEASURING SENSORY THRESHOLDS

In threshold studies, the psychophysicist seeks an index of his subject's sensory capacity either in terms of the minimum perceptible stimulus strength or the minimum perceptible difference between two stimuli. With nonverbal subjects, such studies usually begin by establishing a discrimination between very different stimuli. Threshold determination involves the examination of the discriminative response to a range of stimulus strengths, and the threshold itself is taken to be the stimulus value or difference that yields some arbitrary criterion of discriminability.

The next two sections examine methods of achieving the stimulus-response relationship upon which threshold determination rests. First, we consider various response measures and their associated reinforcement contingencies, and then we deal with methods of stimulus presentation.

Response Measures

METHODS THAT USE A SINGLE RESPONSE MANIPULANDUM

Single-response methods may be chosen for several reasons. They are behaviorally and conceptually simple; they are relatively easy to instrument; and they keep the subject in a reasonably constant position. We shall distinguish between "go/no–go" methods, where the stimulus dimension controls a discriminated operant that is maintained by appropriate reinforcement contingencies, and the "conditioned suppression" methods, where the stimulus is paired with an aversive stimulus and controls the suppression of an ongoing operant.

Go/no–go Methods. To an operant psychologist, an attractive form of go/no–go procedure might be a simple multiple schedule in which discrimination is assessed from the relative response rates during positive stimulus (S^+) and negative stimulus (S^-) conditions. Unless special precautions are taken, however, this method has at least two important defects: (1) the occurrence of reinforcement in an S^+ period may act as a cue for responding, and (2) the appearance of the S^+ may act to reinforce responses in the preceding S^- period. A study by Raslear, Pierrel-Sorrentino, and Brissey (1975) shows how reinforcement cues may confound stimulus effects when variable interval and extinction alternate in a multiple schedule (*mult* VI EXT). This research examined discriminations of auditory intensity in the chinchilla, using the absence of sound as the S^+ and its presence, at varying intensities, as the S^-. Since the design included unreinforced as well as reinforced presentations of the S^+, the authors were able to assess the role of reinforcement as a cue. At large intensity differences, a measure based on unreinforced S^+ periods showed about the same discriminability as a measure based on reinforced S+ presentations. As intensity difference decreased, however, reinforcement cues appeared to assume more importance, so that the measure based on reinforced S+ presentations continued to show differential responding even at very small intensity differences.

The go/no–go paradigm may also be used in discrete-trial methods that program very short stimulus presentations and measure the probability that a single response will occur on each trial. This probability measure is often favored over response rate because of its relative simplicity and because response rate appears to be affected by complex nonstimulus factors. Furthermore, reinforcement cues cannot confound stimulus effects, since reinforcement terminates the trial.

As a rule, go/no–go methods employ the traditional reinforcement contingencies; that is, they program reinforcement of responses in the presence of the stimulus and their extinction in its absence. However, since subject chambers and manipulanda are usually designed with a view to facilitating the response, these procedures often favor excessive "false positive" responses. That is, subjects tend to err in the direction of responding when the stimulus is absent, rather than failing to respond when it is present. Signal detection theory has focused attention on these two types of error ("false alarms" and "misses") and suggests that an imbalance between them indicates a "biased" subject.

An experiment by Terman and Terman (1972) shows how a go/no–go situation may be modified in an attempt to discourage response bias. In a study of auditory intensity discrimination in rats, these authors introduced symmetrical contingencies for the two types of error. The rats were required to press a nose key in the presence of a standard stimulus and to withhold the response in the presence of a comparison intensity. Time-outs followed both failures to press during the standard stimulus presentation and the occurrence of presses during the comparison intensities. Positive reinforcement was also symmetrical; that is, it followed both "hits" (key responses to the standard stimulus) and "correct rejections" (withholding the response during the comparison stimulus presentations). Despite these contingencies, Terman and Terman found that their subjects tended to be biased in the direction of responding, for false alarms were more probable than misses. The authors suggest that differences in the topographies of the response for hits ("press") and correct rejections ("don't press") might account for some of the bias. The nose key response was more explicitly defined in terms of its topography and also differed in its temporal relation to signal onset, since it could occur any time during the 3-sec stimulus presentation and still produce reinforcement.

The discriminated avoidance response has also been used in psychophysical studies, especially with species that are not readily amenable to positive reinforcement procedures. In go/no–go avoidance a response is maintained because it removes a stimulus signaling shock or some other aversive event. Variations in the stimulus along some dimension yield corresponding changes in response probability, which describe a psychophysical function. A nice example of this procedure has been reported by Clack and Herman (1963), who used it to obtain a set of auditory thresholds in the monkey. Their sessions were divided into trials, each starting with the presentation of a white light. On some trials a tone followed the onset of this light; the tone signaled shock, and lever presses in its presence avoided the shock. A lever press in the presence of the tone was a hit, and was reinforced by shock avoidance. A press in the presence of the white light but in the absence of the tone was a false alarm and was punished by shock as, of course, were misses—failures to respond during the tone. A similar procedure has been used by Saunders (1969) in a study of auditory intensity discrimination in the cat, a species known for its finicky attitude toward food reinforcers.

Although the use of electric shock has been effective, it has certain disadvantages. Some species—pigeons, for example—require wires that may interfere with the animal's freedom of movement. More important is the possible disruptive effect of punishment on the subject's behavior. Nonetheless, one comparison between positive and negative reinforcement techniques (Sidley, Sperling, Bedarf, & Hiss, 1965) reports that, while the positive reinforcement method yielded more "cooperative" subjects, similar spectral sensitivity functions were generated by the two procedures.

Conditioned Suppression Method. Under suitable conditions an aversive signal will suppress the rate of an operant response, and the degree of this suppression may be used as a psychophysical response measure. The method involves the superposition on a base line operant of signals that terminate after a minute or so with a shock or other aversive event. As a result of such pairings, the signal itself acquires suppressing properties. The amount of suppression is measured by the change in the baseline response rate, and it usually is stated in terms of a ratio composed of rates before and after the introduction of the signal. A stable baseline is important, since pauses in the absence of the signal can be recorded as "false alarms." Variable-interval and variable-ratio schedules are frequently used to maintain such a baseline. (For an extensive discussion of the suppression method and related data see Blackman, Chapter 12 in this volume.)

The psychophysical function resulting from the suppression method describes the relationship between some dimension of the aversive signal and the amount of suppression that the signal produces. Many such functions have been acquired by Smith (1970) and his colleagues for a variety of species and sensory modalities. One study describes olfactory sensitivity in the pigeon (Henton, 1969). Using as a baseline the key-pecking response maintained on a variable-interval schedule, delivery of controlled amounts of amyl acetate was paired with shock at the birds' pubis bones. When a strong concentration of the odorant had acquired good suppressing properties, the concentration was gradually decreased. A psychophysical function related the odorant concentration to the suppression ratio.

A series of studies on the auditory sensitivity of neurologically mutant mice (Ray, 1970; Sidman, Ray, Sidman, & Klinger, 1966) examined the reliability and validity of the suppression method. This research produced such data as, for example, the finding that mice with inner-ear defects failed to suppress to auditory stimuli, although suppression to visual stimuli was still present. These studies support the reliability of the suppression method; the data replicated well within subjects, and agreement between subjects was also good. It should be noted, however, that while conditioned suppression is measured in terms of operant response rate, the phenomenon is generally considered an instance of classical conditioning (see Chap. 12). As with other differences between some of the methods we describe, we do not know the extent to which thresholds measured by suppression might differ from thresholds based on a discriminated operant. Even were such comparisons done, they may be difficult to interpret, because obtained thresholds may depend on so many aspects of the procedures used to measure them.

METHODS THAT USE TWO OR MORE RESPONSE MANIPULANDA

In most human psychophysics, the subject is instructed to give a specifically defined response on each trial—"yes" or "no," "brighter" or "dimmer," or the like—rather than to respond on some trials and to withhold the response on others. A comparable procedure with animals requires a manipulandum for each response alternative. An advantage of such symmetrical response requirements is that the experimenter can then distinguish "failures to respond" from "incorrect responses" and is thus unlikely to confuse poor attention, "freezing," and so forth with poor stimulus discriminability. Response bias may also be minimized to the extent that the alternative responses are comparable with one another and reinforcement contingencies are symmetrical.

Forced-choice Procedures. The most straightforward of the multiresponse techniques is the two-response forced-choice method, used extensively in visual psychophysics. Here, each of two stimuli appear near their associated response manipulanda, and the animal is reinforced for making the response corresponding to the "correct" stimulus, which might be defined as "the one that is illuminated," "the one that has the stripes," or perhaps "the one that is the brighter." The position of the correct stimulus should vary, of course, in such a manner that consistent responding to one of the manipulanda results in chance performance. Although this method is most frequently used for problems in vision, Wilson, Stamm, and Pribram (1960) successfully investigated tactual discrimination in monkeys by training their subjects to choose the coarser of two grades of sandpaper.

Frequently, a third, "observing" response is added to the forced-choice method, as in a series of studies on goldfish color vision described by Yager and Thorpe (1970). These investigators used tanks that contained two response keys at one end and an observing key at the other. A press on the illuminated observing key presented the stimulus and set up reinforcement on one of two response keys; the fish then swam to the other end of the tank and made its choice response. In their work on spectral sensitivity, Yager and Thorpe caused the observing response to illuminate one of the two choice keys with monochromatic light, and a response to this lighted key brought food. Following the choice response was an intertrial interval during which the entire tank was illuminated so as to produce chromatic adaptation conditions desired by the experimenters. Using a similar method, P. Blough (1971) assessed pigeon visual acuity at controlled target distances. Here, one purpose of the observing response was to force the bird to retreat a considerable distance from the target stimuli before each trial. Again, operation of an observing key at one end of the experimental chamber set up stimuli at the other end. One stimulus key was striped, the other

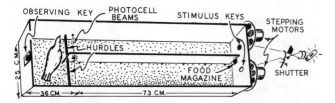

Fig. 1. An experimental chamber illustrating the use of an observing response combined with a two-key forced-choice task. To initiate a trial, the bird pecks the observing key, thus opening the shutter and illuminating the two stimulus keys. As the bird enters an alley leading to one of the two keys, it breaks a photocell beam, thus recording its choice and initiating the appropriate consequences. If the choice is correct, the shutter remains open until the bird pecks the stimulus key for food reinforcement. An incorrect choice closes the shutter at once. The purpose of the hurdles is to help delay the choice response. (From P. Blough, 1971. © 1971 by the Society for the Experimental Analysis of Behavior, Inc.)

blank, and pecks at the striped key produced reinforcement. Figure 1 shows that a vertical partition and photocell arrangement forced the bird to make its choice while it was still at the far end of the chamber.

Although it complicates the apparatus, a three- or four-response forced-choice procedure has desirable aspects. Additional choices extend the range between perfect and chance performance; for example, while chance performance is 50% for a two-response method, it falls to 25% for a four-response method. Three or more responses also allow the experimenter to ask that a subject choose the "different" stimulus. This more general paradigm may be useful for a variety of problems, at least for subjects capable of responding to the "difference" concept. DeValois and his colleagues have collected psychophysical data on monkey color vision with the multiresponse procedure, illustrated by a study of increment thresholds reported by Jacobs (1972). A tungsten source illuminated three response panels, and a monochromatic light was added to this background on one of the three panels. Squirrel monkey subjects were reinforced for responding to the panel with the added monochromatic light, whatever its wavelength. Each of the three panels was correct equally often. By varying wavelength and intensity of the added light, Jacobs measured sensitivity under these conditions across a broad range of wavelengths.

"Yes-no" Procedures. Forced-choice procedures using two or more keys may not be as subject to the effects of response bias as are less symmetrical paradigms. Unfortunately, successful use of forced-choice with animals probably necessitates the simultaneous presentation of two or more stimuli that can be adequately separated in space. When stimuli must occur in succession, as in most auditory tasks, human subjects may be instructed to choose the earlier or later stimulus, but a corresponding task is probably too difficult for most nonhuman animals. For such problems, the two-response "yes-no" task is a popular alternative. Here, a response to one manipulandum is reinforced if a specified condition is present (the "yes" response) and to another if the condition is absent (the "no" response). In this task, of course, response preferences may affect the data by altering the a priori ability of "yes" or "no" responses. A bias toward the "yes" key tends to drive the "threshold" down, while a bias toward the "no" key drives it up. Work of Irwin and Terman (1970) on auditory sensitivity in rats illustrates the use of this method. To start a trial, the rat positioned itself so as to break a photocell beam. This caused the lighting of two choice keys and also produced either noise alone or a tone added to noise. The animal was to press the left key for noise alone and the right key for noise plus tone. Electrical brain stimulation reinforced a correct response to either key; a time-out followed each error. One of the two rat subjects reached approximately 95% correct responses when the tone signal was strong; the other rat's best performance was about 85% correct. Despite the symmetrical reinforcement contingencies, both rats showed position preferences that increased as the signal became more difficult to detect.

Pigeons can learn a variation of the yes-no method that is reminiscent of DeValois's and Jacobs's use of forced choice with oddity problems. Birds respond to one key if two stimuli match and to another if the stimuli differ. Wright (1972) used this method to study pigeon wavelength discrimination. A center observing key contained a bipartite field whose halves could be illuminated by the same or by different monochromatic lights. A peck on this key illuminated two side keys, and a right-key response was then correct if the stimulus lights were the same, while a left-key response was correct if they differed. Both types of correct responses were reinforced, and errors produced time-outs. During each session, a single reference wavelength appeared with each of a number of comparison wavelengths. Unfortunately, it is not clear how well the birds discriminated "difference" on the center key as a concept apart from the specific wavelength differences to which they responded. That is, the report does not indicate whether the birds learned each new discrimination more quickly than the last. Evidently the task was difficult, however, for 6 out of 12 birds were eliminated from the study because of poor performances.

A variation of the yes-no procedure, described by

Stebbins (1970) and some of his colleagues, has been particularly successful in auditory psychophysics. Here, one manipulandum has both an observing function and a "no" function. Responses to this lever produce the auditory signal on a variable-interval or variable-ratio schedule. The subject must switch to another lever ("yes") during the signal to be reinforced; however, switching to this second lever either before or after the signal brings a time-out. Occasional "catch" trials, when no tone is presented, measure the probability of false alarms. Methods such as this have yielded clear auditory data for monkeys (Gourevitch, 1970; Stebbins, 1970) and bats (Dalland, 1970). The procedure has also been used to measure latencies, as we shall see in a later section. Figure 2 shows a set of psychophysical functions obtained by this method with monkey subject.

As we have indicated, the measures described above, though all useful, differ in their suitability for particular sensory modalities, in their ease of instrumentation, and very likely in their suitability for particular species. Unfortunately, we are generally unable to say whether they also differ with respect to the threshold measures that they yield. A few studies suggest that methodological differences may not be great; the experiments of Sidley et al. (1965), mentioned above, showed similar findings from a method based on positive reinforcement and one based on aversive control. Mentzer's (1966) research also failed to reveal any clear difference among thresholds obtained from yes-no, two-key forced-choice, and four-key forced-choice methods. Studies that make such comparisons are, however, rather difficult to interpret, since many aspects of each situation are chosen arbitrarily (e.g., stimulus placement, response force required, etc.), and effects of these parameters could obscure real methodological effects.

Adapting the Response to the Species

The animal psychophysicist often wishes to study species other than the rats, pigeons, or monkeys for which reinforcers, manipulanda, and general methodology have become standardized. Some species, such as the cat or the turtle, may be chosen because extensive sensory physiological data are available. Others, such as the bat or the sea lion, are of interest because of the special characteristics of a sensory system. Often, such "new" species are found to perform well in relatively standard situations: for example, turtles, squirrels, seals, and chinchillas all press keys or levers for appropriate consummatory rewards. But some species do not adapt well to such familiar tasks, and the experimenter must apply his imagination and his knowledge of the response repertoire of his subjects to the design of appropriate experimental arrangements. Research with bats, described by Dalland (1970), exemplifies this point. The experiment, inspired by the bat's use of echolocation in detecting prey, involved the assessment of the auditory response to very-high-frequency tones. Since the nonflying movements of bats are minimal and poorly adapted to the usual manipulanda, Dalland chose to measure gross bodily movements. An observing response required the bat to position itself on a platform in such a way as to break a photocell beam. In front of this platform was a tube from which the auditory signal emanated. Thus the observing response harmonized with the bat's natural tendency to orient toward sounds, and it also ensured constant position with regard to the stimulus. In this procedure, the bat was reinforced, in the presence of sound, for walking to a food cup. Figure 3 illustrates this arrangement. Since bats do not readily walk, this response had the advantage of reducing the probability of false alarms. Although extended response shaping was required, Dalland successfully measured tone thresholds through a range of high frequencies.

Naturalistic considerations also suggested a useful response in a study of visual acuity of sea lions. These animals emit a "barking" vocalization which the experimenters, Schusterman and Balliet (1970), brought under visual control, at first by associating the visual stimulus with a situation that tended to elicit the bark. Eventually they were able to test visual acuity

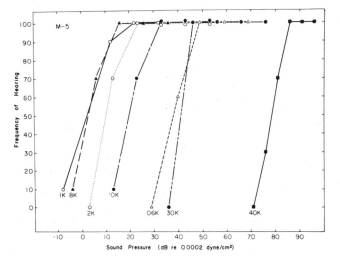

Fig. 2. A set of psychophysical functions for a single monkey showing the relation between frequency of hearing and sound intensity. Each curve describes this relationship for a different tone frequency. (From Stebbins, 1970.)

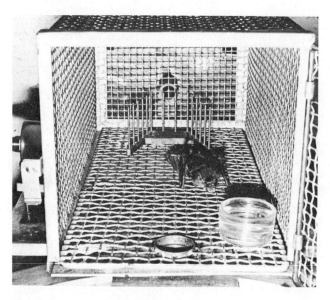

Fig. 3. Apparatus for obtaining audibility data for the bat. The bat positioned itself on the platform at the rear of the cage in such a way as to break a photocell beam. When a tone occurred the subject crossed the cage for food reinforcement. The tone came from the tube beyond the platform. (From Dalland, 1970.)

by requiring the sea lions to vocalize when a grating stimulus appeared but to remain silent when the stimulus was blank. An important advantage of vocalization as a response is that it is not tied to a spatial location. The authors thus were able to test acuity at various controlled target distances.

Not only an animal's response repertoire, but also the conditions under which the responses ordinarily occur may bear on the choice of psychophysical methodology. The cat, for example, has a reputation for recalcitrance in operant situations, but this reputation may be due more to obtuse experimenters than to obstinate animals. Recent studies indicate that positive reinforcement methods are quite feasible if the cat is sufficiently hungry and if its task is properly designed. Berkley (1970), for example, found that the natural tendency for the cat to use its paws, though apparently ideal for lever pressing, was actually an obstacle to visual control, since cats tend to watch their paws as they use them. Berkley's successful apparatus employed a nose key, which the cat could press only after it had placed its head through a hole too small to include the paws. The author reported rapid success in training visual discriminations with this apparatus, and found it more easily automated than some earlier methods used with cats.

Less obvious, but possibly of great importance, are considerations of stimulus-response associability related to the "preparedness" notion of Seligman (1970).

A report by Nye (1973) suggests, for example, that the pigeon's key peck is poorly controlled by laterally placed visual stimuli, although performance on an identical discrimination is excellent when the stimuli are located in the bird's frontal field of view. This find, if confirmed, illustrates the subtlety of species idiosyncrasies with which the animal psychophysicist may have to cope.

Methods of Stimulus Presentation

The experimenter's goal, in threshold studies, is typically to estimate the stimulus value that can be detected 50% of the time. Preliminary work is usually necessary so that stimuli may be chosen over a range that will include the threshold value and across which stimulus and response values will systematically covary. In working with human subjects, experimenters commonly omit stimuli far above or below threshold, since such presentations are inefficient. In animal work, however, some signals must be of known detectability if reinforcement contingencies are to be effective in training the animal and in maintaining its behavior during testing. Thus there must be a number of "wasted" trials, during which the stimulus is well above or below threshold. Experimenters have adapted, with this modification, most of the well-known human psychophysical methods, which prescribe the spacing of stimuli around threshold and the order of stimulus presentation.

Testing with a Broad Range of Stimulus Values

To obtain complete psychophysical functions, experimenters usually choose a stimulus set that extends in regular steps from values that are almost always detected to values that are very rarely detected. Once chosen, these stimuli may be presented in ascending order of strength (or increasing difference between standard and comparison, when a difference threshold is sought), descending order, or in random order. In animal work, descending order is perhaps the most popular, for it seems best to start with an easy discrimination and proceed to those more difficult. This procedure thus incorporates a "shaping" or "fading" aspect. Although this method resembles the psychophysical method of limits, stimuli tend to be more widely spaced than in a human experiment, and each stimulus value is apt to occur in blocks of several trials before a new value is introduced. The block method is desirable because performance may change somewhat over trials, and a number of trials may be necessary to yield a reliable indication of performance. In the study of pigeon acuity, illustrated in Figure 1, trial blocks were very large; altogether each block included 256 trials and occupied two experimental sessions. As is true of many animal studies, this procedure required the birds to reach a criterion level of performance at a strong signal (wide stripes) before proceeding with progressively weaker signals. The research affirmed the importance of these easy sessions, for performance on easy discriminations tended to be poor following sessions at the most difficult discriminations.

Hodos and Bonbright (1972) describe a procedure that employed much smaller blocks of descending stimuli. The study neatly incorporates warm-up trials and checks on the subject's discrimination performances. Pigeon subjects discriminated a standard light from lights of varying comparison intensities. Each session began with a 20-trial warm-up with a large intensity difference (.8 log units). The next 20 trials constituted an "assessment" period, at the same large intensity difference, to determine the subject's basic performance level. If the bird's error rate was greater than 10% during this period, no new comparison values were introduced, and the entire session was devoted to training. If performance met criterion, however, the data were recorded and further sets of 20-block trials occurred, each at a smaller intensity difference than the last. After testing at the smallest difference, the warm-up condition at .8 log-unit difference was repeated. Then a final descending series began. The authors state that "the warm-up period between the first and second descending series of stimuli served to dissipate extreme response biases that developed . . . during the later, more difficult discriminations of the first sequence and would otherwise be carried over into the earlier discriminations of the second sequence" (p. 473).

Some animal studies have used series of ascending stimulus values, usually along with descending series. Used alone, the ascending order may generate a high rate of false alarms (Dalland, 1970). It may also yield higher thresholds than the descending series (e.g., Mishkin & Weiskrantz, 1959; Terman, 1970), although Smith (1970) found similar thresholds by the two methods in his conditioned suppression procedure. As in human psychophysics, it seems appropriate to average the results of ascending and descending series when both are used.

A set of stimulus values may also occur in random order. This procedure has yielded orderly psychophysical functions, and we might expect it to maintain the basic discrimination most effectively, because easy discriminations are mixed with more difficult ones. In the monkey auditory work of Stebbins, which we described earlier, audiometric functions from the method of limits and the method of constant stimuli appear very similar. The pigeon acuity study (P. Blough, 1971) compared a random stimulus method with a descending series method, and again the two yielded similar thresholds. However, performance on the easy discriminations was somewhat worse for the random stimulus method, despite the fact that warm-up sessions and gradual introduction of less detectable stimuli preceded sessions based on random presentation. Another disadvantage of random ordering is that it tends to commit the experimenter to a set of stimulus values that may later turn out to be inappropriate.

As we have said, a *threshold* is generally defined as a stimulus value associated with a criterion response probability. Because the criterion is rarely met exactly, the actual threshold value usually comes from interpolation on a graph that relates the stimulus and response measures. In methods that use a broad range of stimulus values, this graph will usually show a wide range of response probabilities, extending from chance to nearly perfect performance. To arrive at a threshold figure, many experimenters simply connect the two points on either side of their threshold criterion and interpolate appropriately. A second procedure, which makes use of more of the data, is to fit a function to all of the points and then proceed with the interpolation. (A transformation which makes the function approximately linear is helpful for this purpose, since a straight-line fit is relatively easy to achieve either statistically or by eye.) This second procedure is more complicated, but is worth the trouble when the data are variable, since inclusion of all points contributes to the reliability of the threshold estimate.

Threshold Tracking

The methods just described are inefficient, in a sense, because they include many trials on which the stimulus is well above threshold. In tracking methods (also known as "staircase," "up-down," or "titration" methods), most stimuli presented are near threshold, so there are fewer wasted trials. However, tracking methods may require long training and relatively complex apparatus.

Tracking has been used with a number of sense modalities in a variety of species. An early application in animal psychophysics produced data on dark adaptation in pigeons (D. Blough, 1958, 1961). The paradigm was essentially two-manipulandum, yes-no, although the session was not divided into trials. Pecks on the "no" key (key B) were reinforced when a stimulus patch was dark, and pecks on the "yes" key (key A) were correct when the stimulus was illuminated. Correct key B responses were reinforced with food, and key A responses were maintained because they occasionally turned out the stimulus light, thus setting the occasion for key B reinforcement. Variable-interval and variable-ratio requirements helped to prevent control of pecking by temporal or numerical factors; that is, reinforcement had no close relationship to elapsed time or to number of responses emitted. Threshold tracking resulted from this procedure because responses on the "no" key raised the intensity of the stimulus and responses on the "yes" lowered it; thus a well-trained subject kept the stimulus light near its threshold value, and a continuous record of intensity followed the threshold through time.

The tracking procedure raises special problems of stimulus control, some of which have been discussed by Blough (1958) and more recently by Clack and Harris (1963) and Rosenberger (1970). It is necessary, for example, to discourage the subject from simply responding alternately to the keys until reinforcement occurs. An effective means of discouraging this strategy is to have incorrect responses increase the ratio by which reinforcement is programmed. Another potential problem is the deterioration of stimulus control that may occur when a discrimination remains difficult over a long period of time. To compensate for this, Clack and Harris increase signal strength to a relatively high level following reinforcement to provide a "warm-up" period.

The tracking idea is readily adaptable to several of the response paradigms that we have previously described. For example, a combination of tracking and conditioned suppression is described by Ray (1970) and by Rosenberger (1970). Here, degree of response suppression controlled signal strength. When suppression exceeded some criterion, signal strength decreased; when suppression no longer met the criterion, signal strength increased. A threshold could be derived from the stimulus values, since these were correlated with response suppression.

In trialwise tracking methods, the stimulus value may change following each presentation (the "staircase" method) or following a block of trials. Thorpe (1971) used the latter procedure in a study of goldfish spectral sensitivity. Stimulus intensity decreased when the number of correct responses per block exceeded a criterion and increased when the number fell below the criterion. The block method bases each stimulus change on more response information than does the single-trial staircase method, and one comparison of the methods reports that the block procedure indeed yields less variable data (Moskowitz & Kitzes, 1966). The staircase method, however, provides more threshold indications per unit time, and this may be an overriding factor when sensitivity is to be followed through time.

Are thresholds found by the tracking method comparable to thresholds from other methods? In Blough's method, reinforcement contingencies for the two keys were asymmetrical, since food was contingent only on "no" responses (Saslow, 1967). Since "no" responses increase the signal's strength, the resulting thresholds could be spuriously high. Some confirmation of such an effect comes from Clack and Harris (1963), who noted that their rats tended to maintain the auditory stimulus at suprathreshold levels. Rosenberger (1970) identified another possible difficulty with tracking: when the animal controls the signal, responses may not be reinforced with equal probabilities at all signal strengths. Thus the tendency to switch from key A to key B could become stronger in the presence of certain signals than for others, with a distortion of threshold data resulting.

Direct comparisons between tracking and other methods are rare. Symmes (1962), in his studies of flicker discrimination in monkeys, reported that a technique much like Blough's generated lower critical flicker-fusion frequencies (higher thresholds) than did a go/no-go method using comparable target parameters. However, Stebbins (1970) found that auditory thresholds generated by his version of the tracking method were very close to those yielded by a method of limits and a method of constant stimuli. Perhaps Stebbins's failure to find differences had to do with his modification of the technique. While Blough and Symmes provided direct reinforcement only for responses appropriate to the signal's absence, Stebbins also reinforced with food responses appropriate to the signal's presence, whatever its strength, and punished (by a time-out) failure to report a signal. These contingencies perhaps favor a stronger "yes" response and thus a lower threshold than the less symmetrical reinforcement procedure. Such differences among various versions of the tracking method seem to preclude any blanket statement comparing this method with others.

The definition of *threshold* is somewhat less standardized in the tracking method than in the other methods we have described. Basically, the experimenter seeks the stimulus value at which the probability of switching from the "yes" to the "no" response, and vice versa, is greatest. This may be done visually, by drawing horizontal lines that bisect various subsets of data and averaging the stimulus values represented by these lines (Clack & Harris, 1963). Alternatively, reversal points—those stimulus values at which the subject switches from key A to key B—may be averaged. Rosenberger (1970) has described a method for treating data from discrete-trial procedures.

Some Methodological Problems

Sensory data are most informative when variations in the response measure depend solely on changes in stimulus conditions or sensory states. Though a certain amount of variability from other sources is inevitable, the contribution of nonstimulus factors may be reduced considerably by careful experimental design. The sections below outline some stimulus control problems and methods that have been successful in coping with them. We shall consider these problems in the relatively well-defined context of threshold research, but it will be evident that most of the discussion is equally applicable to the suprathreshold and scaling research to be covered later. In some instances, we shall return to these maters in the later discussion.

FIXATION AND ATTENTION

The achievement of good control by an accurately specified stimulus requires that a subject be appropriately oriented and attentive. In most human psychophysics the subject's physical orientation is adjusted with the utmost care, but with animals such control is often quite crude. Nonetheless, researchers have worked out methods for achieving at least some control over this variable. An obvious method is physical restraint (as in the monkey restraining chair), but we stress behavioral methods here.

When a single manipulandum is used, an animal subject's orientation may remain roughly constant. In an olfactory study with rats, Goff (1961) required that the rats press the response lever only with their left paws; this condition helped to maintain the rat in a relatively constant position with respect to a device that delivered the odorant. More explicit control of orientation may be achieved through the use of an observing response, upon which stimulus presentation is contingent. In her study of pigeon acuity, for example, P. Blough (1971) used an observing response to position the birds at an appropriate distance from the stimulus targets. Other researchers have required their subjects to insert their heads through holes in order to view a visual stimulus, and, in some auditory work, orientation has been controlled by requiring the animal to press an appropriately placed lever to turn on the tone. As we have seen, in his audiometric works Dalland (1970) required his bats to break a photocell beam to produce the tone stimulus (see Figure 3). Because tone intensity varied with distance from its source, the control of the subject's position during stimulus presentation was crucial in this case.

The training of visual fixation was an important feature of studies by Scott and Milligan (1970) on the motion aftereffect in monkeys. This effect requires a preexposure condition in which the subject fixates on the center of a rotating target for a few seconds. Humans perform this task readily with the aid of verbal instructions. With monkeys, however, lengthy training was required. Using infrared light reflected from the subject's cornea, an observer monitored eye position and gradually shaped the required fixation. Although this method apparently succeeded, the constant presence of a human observer makes it inefficient for many types of research. Automated techniques that precisely control eye position will be a boon to visual psychophysics with animals.

Although various fixating and orienting responses can be trained, good stimulus control requires, by definition, an attentive subject. Thus in psychophysical studies, a subject's failure to respond to a signal may result from a failure of attention as well as failure of the stimulus to exceed threshold. One procedure that appears to favor attention is the programming of aversive consequences for incorrect responses. Such a consequence is the time-out, a period during which stimuli do not occur and responses are ineffective. Time-outs are usually programmed to follow false positive responses, but in an effort to achieve symmetrical consequences, experimenters may also program time-outs to follow failures to report the positive stimulus. Occasionally a stronger punishment appears to be helpful. Gourevitch (1970) sometimes combined shock with time-out in order to improve stimulus control in his auditory experiments with monkeys. Shock should be used with caution, however, because it can cause serious response disruption. Still another method that may make the subject "stop and look" is the elimination of reinforcement for any response that follows stimulus onset with very short latency. In two-key designs, a changeover delay operates in a similar fashion to discourage rapid alternation between keys. In this procedure, reinforcement is withheld if the time between operation of the keys is less than some minimum. Many experimenters also cause responses to require a certain amount of effort, as in the substitution of a short fixed ratio for a single "yes" or "no" response. Observing responses, when made to the critical stimulus, may be programmed to require multiple responses, presumably resulting in an increased exposure to the appearance of the stimulus.

Despite the effectiveness of such techniques, most animal subjects are not "perfectly attentive"—that is, on some trials they make errors even on easy discriminations. Psychophysical functions reflect such errors by approaching an asymptote below 100% correct at the strongest signal values. Criteria of stable performance, measured during warm-up trials or "catch" trials, help the experimenter to estimate the degree of such inattention and, if necessary, take measures to reduce it. In addition, the experimenter may use a correction for attention, such as that suggested by Heinemann, Avin, Sullivan, and Chase (1969). This correction, based on the upper and lower asymptotes of a sigmoidal psychophysical function, assumes that the subject is inattentive on a certain proportion of the trials and that the probability of being inattentive does not vary with signal strength. The second part of this assumption is somewhat questionable as a general rule, since there is evidence that performance on easy discriminations tends to deteriorate after a series of trials on difficult discriminations. Perhaps behavior associated with attentiveness extinguishes during difficult discriminations.

EXTRANEOUS CUES

Animal subjects have an annoying ability to devise response strategies different from those intended by the experimenter. These strategies are sometimes based on extraneous cues provided by poorly designed apparatus. Stimulus systems must be free of transients such as sounds accompanying the onset and offset of the stimulus; auditory apparatus must control for the effects of standing waves; equipment must be designed so that easily confounded dimensions, such as visual luminance and wavelength, may be varied independently. The rise time of stimuli can act as a discriminable cue, so the onset and offset characteristics of the stimulus event should remain constant across stimulus values. Improved equipment has been an important factor in the growing quality of animal psychophysical studies, but there are occasions when even the most careful experimenter cannot be sure that he has perfect control over an extraneous variable. For example, in studies involving stimulus wavelength, even small luminance differences between monochromatic lights may confound the data. In such cases, the confounding factor may be varied at random over a small range in such a way that no particular value will be well correlated with reinforcement.

Stimulus preferences may also confound psychophysical data. For example, pigeons tend to respond more to some colors than to others, although the preferred color appears to differ among birds. In the auditory modality, the intensity dynamism effect may be considered a type of stimulus preference. Sadowsky (1966) has shown, for example, that rats discriminate more accurately when the positive stimulus is the more intense of two sounds. This effect appears to be consistent enough to require controls. Thus in their study of the auditory intensity difference limen, Raslear et al. (1975) made silence the positive stimulus so that dynamism effects could not account for the discrimination in this go/no-go task. An experimenter may cope with less predictable preferences by using a reasonable number of subjects, a high training criterion, and insightful data analysis.

Response bias is one of the worst plagues of the animal psychophysicist. In multiresponse designs, for example, position preferences are almost always a problem. These may be minimized by a correction procedure, such that incorrect responses are followed by the same stimulus or stimulus array until a correct response occurs. Analysis must omit these correction trials, of course, since they are nonrandom. The correction procedure may reduce but it does not eliminate effects of position preference, which appear to grow more pronounced as signal strength decreases (P. Blough, 1971; Terman, 1970). In a forced-choice design, the effects of such preferences are relatively benign, since the correct stimulus varies in position. In a yes–no task, however, preferences may affect the threshold by driving it up (if the preference is for the "no" response) or down (if the preference is for the "yes" response). Similarly, biases that favor responding or not responding may affect thresholds determined by a go/no-go procedure.

Sequential dependencies may also serve as unwanted sources of control. A strictly random determination of stimulus order is usually undesirable, since this procedure may generate a long series of identical trials, during which a position preference may become strengthened. Unfortunately, however, modified random series may include contingencies that some animals discriminate. Thus Terman (1970) reported that rats apparently discriminated the constraint that a given stimulus array could not occur more than three times in succession. When performance in a psychophysical task fails to reach chance level even at very low signal strengths, the experimenter may suspect (as Terman did) the operation of sequential or other nonstimulus cues.

Reinforcement Contingencies

We have discussed previously the role of special contingencies in maximizing attention and the role that reinforcement may inadvertently play as an extraneous discriminative stimulus. Other uses of reinforcement may also involve difficulties. For example, most threshold procedures program reinforcement for correct detections of the signal, regardless of its strength. This procedure avoids selective reinforcement of particular signal strengths and would seem to aid the subject in discriminating weak stimuli. However, when the stimulus is present but subthreshold,[1] the procedure may also provide reinforcement for responses that are, functionally, false alarms. Little research has been directed specifically at this problem, though Nevin (1970) found that increased relative reinforcement at weak signals produced an increased false alarm rate. Several studies indirectly suggest that reinforcement of positive responses to subthreshold signals may not seriously affect threshold data. The tracking procedure used by Stebbins (1970), for example, included a large proportion of weak signals and must have resulted in occasionally reinforced "yes" responses to sounds below threshold. Yet, as we have noted, these audibility functions were very much like those from methods that included a greater proportion of more intense tones. In connection with the conditioned suppression method, Ray (1970) discussed the effect of "unsignaled" shocks that presumably occurred following subthreshold sounds and reported that, when kept to a minimum, these did not seem to affect the data. Blough's version of the tracking method (1958) seemingly avoided the reinforcement of perceptually inappropriate responses, yet we have seen that this method may introduce other sorts of bias. Perhaps the advantages of reinforcing correct responses to weak but superthreshold signals outweigh the disadvantages of reinforcing "false alarms" to subthreshold stimuli.

Learning Effects

Performance on some psychophysical tasks may continue to improve for an exasperatingly long time. In the acuity work previously mentioned (P. Blough, 1971), successive psychophysical functions increased in steepness for many months. Mishkin and Weiskrantz (1959) also reported learning effects that lasted for a considerable time. The extent of such effects no doubt relates to the difficulty of the task. Experimenters should be alert to this problem and, when running a sequence of conditions, either counterbalance for order or first ascertain that their functions represent a stable asymptote.

Abstraction of the Stimulus

Animal subjects appear to differ in their ability to form concepts based on relational or abstract properties of stimuli. The efficiency of many experiments could be improved if, for example, all species could transfer readily among specific instances of "matching" or "oddity," but only primates, after long training, have been clearly seen to do this. Even matching or oddity within a specific dimension (color, for example) may be learned as a series of specific problems (Cumming & Berryman, 1961). However, Honig (1965) was able to establish "wavelength stimulus difference" as a controlling relation, apparently independent of specific wavelength stimuli. In this study, pigeons learned to peck the right one of two keys if both keys were illuminated by the same wavelength and to peck the left key if the wavelengths differed. The birds could not base their discrimination on any absolute wavelength difference because each wavelength appeared equally often on both keys and was paired equally often with itself and with a different wavelength. The birds also performed correctly with new wavelengths. Malott and Malott (1970) report similar generalized matching in single-key tests. There is no good evidence, however, that this "same-different concept" can transfer to a new stimulus dimension in the pigeon.

Because of the abstraction problem and others that we have outlined, the measurement of sensory thresholds is apt to be time-consuming and a continual challenge to the experimenter's ingenuity. Nonetheless, as we have seen, the patient application of well-tailored operant methods can yield remarkably detailed data on the sensory capacities of an animal subject. The use of such methods in the study of more complex perceptual phenomena raises exciting possibilities, but has produced many fewer data. We consider such research in the next section.

SUPRALIMINAL STIMULI

The following sections will consider research in psychophysical scaling and perception. The nature of

---

[1] We recognize that the "theshold" concept is questioned in modern psychophysics. In this discussion, however, we find it convenient to speak of "subthreshold" stimuli rather than developing a complex argument that assumes a continuum of stimulus effects to which response criteria are applied. The practical impact of the present argument remains essentially unchanged after transposition to the signal detection format.

these problems is more complex than those involving threshold determination, and successful studies are relatively few. Such experiments often involve abstract or poorly defined stimulus variables, and they tend to be modeled after human research that depends on relatively complicated verbal instructions and responses. Translating such problems into paradigms suitable for animal experimentation has been difficult compared to the task of designing threshold experiments. In a threshold study, for example, the experimenter may program reinforcement on the basis of the physical presence or absence of the signal. In suprathreshold experiments, however, there is a broad range of stimuli for which only the subject can define "correct" and "incorrect" responses. We cannot tell a subject in a scaling experiment what sound intensity is "twice as loud" as another, nor can we tell him in a perceptual study at what relative distance two sizes should look equal. Such stimulus control must carry over from training in which performance can be defined and reinforced. In a size-distance experiment, for example, the subject might be trained with equal physical sizes at equal distances. Test stimuli, which would include a variety of size and distance conditions, might either follow training presentations or be interspersed with them.

Perceptual Studies

What does an animal "see" when subjected to complex suprathreshold stimulation? As with human subjects, the question can often be translated, "What different sets of stimulus conditions yield the same response?" For example: "For what combinations of input parameters do two sounds seem equally loud?" (equal-loudness functions), "What combinations of arrowheads make two lines elicit the same response?" (Müller-Lyer illusion), "After exposure to which wavelengths does the subject respond to a neutral stimulus as though it were 550 nm?" (colored afterimage). Information is also gained from the *degree* to which responses are the same in different situations; for example, if a monotonic response measure is used, it may be possible to scale the similarity of a set of stimuli.

It is apparent that perceptual studies, as just formulated, are fundamentally studies of generalization or transfer, and operant generalization methods have been used increasingly in this area (Malott & Malott, 1970; Thomas, 1969). However, the precise method to use is not usually obvious. Shall the response measure be relatively built-in, like reaction time, or more subject to conditioning, like response rate? Will simple training in the presence of one stimulus suffice, or must training isolate one stimulus aspect or dimension and associate the response measure with this alone? We turn now to examples of research in which these questions have been answered in various ways.

Reaction Time Methods

When stimulus intensity increases, the response, whether reflex or learned, decreases in latency. This relationship has been used to equate stimuli for intensity, in much the same manner that lights may be equated for luminance by finding intensities that leave the pupil a constant diameter. Stebbins (1966) used the reaction time method to determine equal-loudness contours for the monkey, and in the same manner Moody (1969) found equal-brightness contours for the rat. In these experiments, the animals learned to release a lever as soon as a sound or light occurred. For a set of different frequencies (or wavelengths), those intensities that yielded constant reaction times were called equally loud or equally bright. The use of several criterion reaction times gave contours at several intensity levels. A set of curves from Moody (1970) appears in Figure 4.

We might look at one of these reaction time experiments in more detail, noting the steps taken to clarify the stimulus-response relationship. Moody (1969) trained his rats to enter a viewing tunnel set in the wall of an experimental chamber. At the far end of the tunnel, lights of various wavelengths could

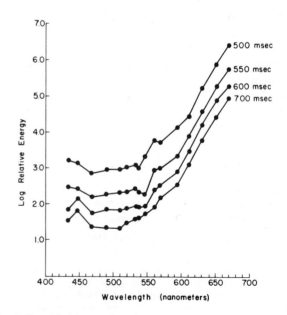

Fig. 4. Equal-brightness functions of the rat determined by the latency method. The criterion latency is indicated to the right of each curve. (From Moody, 1970.)

appear on a frosted glass screen. The rat encountered a response lever about halfway down the tunnel, and above this lever was a loudspeaker. The rat learned a response chain as follows: in the presence of white noise from the loudspeaker, press the lever; when a light appears on the glass screen, release the lever. Lever releases to the light produced water reinforcement. Since the light did not appear unless the lever was held down for an interval (.2 to 3.0 sec), the rat was in a relatively constant position when the light came on and was presumably ready to react. Stebbins (1966) assured constant conditions from trial to trial by restraining his monkeys in a chair and delivering reinforcements directly into the monkey's mouth. Variability in reaction time may be further reduced by adding a "limited hold" to the reinforcement contingency, such that if the subject waits too long to release its lever, no reinforcement is forthcoming even for "correct" responses. Moody discusses this and other methodological matters in his review of the method (Moody, 1970).

The reaction time method has the advantage that the relationship between the stimulus variable and response is built in. The necessary training, designed to shorten reaction time and reduce its variability, serves only to exhibit this unlearned relationship more clearly. The method thus avoids the difficult task of teaching an animal an arbitrary stimulus-response relationship and maintaining that relationship under novel test conditions. However, the reaction time method suffers the disadvantage that the unlearned stimulus-response relationship may not provide the information that the experimenter seeks. It has thus far been applied only to intensive dimensions, and on these it has not permitted one to say by how much one stimulus is louder or brighter than another, but only to indicate stimuli that are equal. It may be possible to surpass both of these limitations; Moody (1970) suggests that modified choice of discriminative situations may make reaction times applicable to qualitative dimensions. The possibility that a metric scale may be based on reaction time data is touched on below.

Simple Generalization Methods

At the present writing, generalization methods are the most widely used operant techniques in the study of animal perception. Of these, the simplest involves merely training an animal to respond in the presence of a given stimulus and then systematically varying the stimulus as the response extinguishes (Guttman & Kalish, 1956). The number of responses emitted to each stimulus value during the extinction test allows the values to be ranked according to their similarity to the training stimulus.

This simple generalization procedure frees the experimenter to choose the most convenient response and also the most informative set of test stimuli. The stimuli need not come from a physically defined "dimension" such as intensity; indeed, the generalization test may be designed to identify possible stimulus dimensions. Exemplifying the flexibility of the method with regard to response measures and test stimuli is a study of taste by Tapper and Halpern (1968). Rats were irradiated with gamma rays as they drank a chemical solution. Such irradiation makes the animal sick, and under suitable conditions a single exposure induces an aversion to the taste of the substance associated with irradiation. Thus in this case the response was a decrease in drinking. The test stimuli were a number of different chemical solutions; aversion (decreased drinking) generalized to some of these but not others. Tapper and Halpern suggest that the method may be a way to determine the dimensions along which taste quality is represented in the rat.

The work of Thomas and his colleagues (Thomas, 1969) on perception of the vertical exemplifies the use of generalization tests to clarify complex interaction of perceptual variables. In one such study, pigeons were trained to peck at a vertical line projected on a response key in a lighted box. When the birds were exposed successively to a number of lines set at different angles, they responded most to the line that was "visually vertical" (i.e., at right angles to the ceiling) even when the box was tilted around the bird while the floor remained horizontal. Birds trained in a dark box while standing on a horizontal floor, but tested in the dark on a floor tilted 24° to the left, responded most to a line tilted approximately the same amount to the left. The experiments suggest that visual cues predominate in the birds' perception of vertical, but when these are absent postural or kinesthetic cues may be used. Thomas relates these results to a similar work on "sensory-tonic" and "field-dependency" effects in human subjects.

The simple generalization test, with single-stimulus training followed by extinction, has serious limitations, however. Since the data are obtained during extinction, responses are relatively few and data points are variable. The procedure singles out no particular aspect of the stimulus, so the aspect to be tested may control the measured response weakly or not at all. For example, after simple exposure training, the wavelength of light on a pigeon's pecking key does control response probability; line tilt also does, though less strongly; tone frequency does not, without additional discrimination training. We turn now to the uses of such additional training.

Generalization After Differential Reinforcement

Perceptual studies commonly incorporate differential reinforcement, in order to improve upon the relatively weak and nonspecific control often generated by single-stimulus training. The simplest way to strengthen control is to reinforce responses in the presence of the stimulus and omit reinforcement in the absence of the stimulus. Jenkins and Harrison (1960) found this sufficient to bring the pigeon's pecking response under the control of tone frequency. When an interrupted tone ("beep-beep-beep . . .") was on continuously throughout a pigeon's key-pecking experience, the rate of pecking did not change when the frequency of the tone departed from its training value. However, when birds were trained to peck only when the tone was on and not when it was off—a discrimination presumably irrelevant to the frequency dimension—subsequent tests revealed strong control of response rate by tone frequency.

In the Jenkins and Harrison experiment, reinforcement in the presence of a stimulus, contrasted with nonreinforcement in its absence, may be said to "call the subject's attention" to the stimulus. However, no particular aspect of the stimulus was singled out. Jenkins and Harrison would probably have observed response changes to variations, for example, in the intensity or harmonic content of their tone stimuli, had these been tested. To increase control by a specific stimulus aspect, one may employ differential reinforcement of stimuli differing in this aspect alone. Such differential reinforcement during training may be accompanied by equal reinforcement of irrelevant stimulus variations. We mentioned an instance of this above: the equal reinforcement of randomly varying stimulus luminances, in studies where wavelength was crucial but luminance was irrelevant.

Studies of interocular transfer of line tilt illustrate these methodological points. They also illustrate the uncertainty about the nature of the controlling stimulus which may remain, even following differential reinforcement of a seemingly obvious aspect. Mello (1966) studied transfer of a tilt discrimination from one eye to the other by fitting pigeons with goggles that restricted vision to the anterior visual field of one eye. She then reinforced presentations on the pigeon's pecking key of a 45° line (S+) while presentations of the line tilted in the opposite direction (135°) went unreinforced (S−). During S− periods, pecks also delayed the return of the 45° S+. Following such training, "angle of tilt" would be expected to control pecking more than other aspects of the line, such as color, that were the same during both S+ and S− periods.

After this training period, Mello tested her birds with a series of line tilts. When tested with their trained eye uncovered, the birds responded most (as expected) to the 45° line to which they had been reinforced. With the untrained eye uncovered, however, they responded most to a tilt of 135°, the mirror image of the training pattern. This result could have interesting implications for the nature of the pigeon's stimulus processing mechanisms; Mello's comments on this matter concerned the representation in the brain of patterns viewed monocularly.

However, the interpretation of the mirror image data is open to conflicting interpretations, and these exemplify hidden assumptions that may underlie perceptual studies. Mello assumed, quite naturally, that angle of line tilt controlled behavior in the training and test situations. Corballis and Beale (1970) suggested, however, that the controlling stimulus in this situation may best be defined as "up" versus "down," rather than angle of tilt. A bird trained with its left eye covered has most of its left field of view occluded; if such a bird attended only to the right half of the stimulus key, a 45° line would be "stimulus in the upper part of the field" and a 135° line would be "stimulus in the lower part of the field." If, when the right eye was covered, the left eye similarly attended only to the left half of the key, the 135° line would now be "upper" and the 45° line "lower." Thus a discrimination between "upper" and "lower," performed with either eye, would cause the apparent mirror-image reversal reported by Mello. Corballis and Beale did tests with other sorts of line stimuli that seem to support their contention. We may conclude that the controlling aspects of even seemingly simple stimuli cannot be taken for granted; the experimenter may have one stimulus aspect in mind, and the animal subject another.

The interocular transfer experiments also suggest the importance of possibly unlearned perceptual factors in determining the nature of controlling stimuli. Another example from recent research concerns "features," or salient portions of visual patterns, which seem crucial to pigeons in determining the course of pattern discrimination learning (Sainsbury, 1971). This feature-dependent control would surely affect research on pattern perception in which birds peck at complex visual targets.

In some cases, such as the Tapper and Halpern taste research cited above, the dimensions of complex stimuli are admittedly unknown. The object of differential training then is not to call the subject's attention to a supposedly known dimension, but rather to establish control by known physical stimuli. Some experimenters then use generalization tests to identify the manner in which the subject classifies or dimensionalizes the stimuli. A good example of such work is a study by Sutherland (1969) on shape perception in rats, octopuses, and goldfish. Sutherland taught his subjects to discriminate between a square and either a horizontally oriented parallelogram or a vertically oriented parallelogram. He then presented a variety of shapes and recorded the percentage of trials on which the subjects gave the "square" response. These percentages were used to rank the test shapes with respect to their similarity to the square. From his inspection of this ranking, Sutherland concluded that octopuses seem to discriminate squares from parallelograms on the basis of the "presence or absence of thin horizontal or vertical segments," while rats discriminated on the basis of "oblique contours running in the same direction as the contours of the original parallelogram." (Goldfish seemed somewhere in between.) Sutherland incorporated these conclusions in a tentative receptive-field model of shape discrimination.

Generalization following differential training may not be simply a matter of recording the rate or probability of response to a set of test stimuli. Several manipulanda may be involved, and whole patterns of discriminative response may transfer to the test situation. A case in point is the measurement, by Scott and his co-workers (1963, 1970) of the spiral aftereffects in monkeys. We discussed previously the measures these investigators took to ensure the monkey's attention to and fixation upon a preexposure target. The training task was a discrimination between an expanding bright circle (right-hand lever correct) and a contracting circle (left-hand lever correct). Every second correct press produced a food pellet, while presses of the wrong lever yielded a mild shock. Following this differential reinforcement, a series of test stimuli yielded a psychometric function relating the percentage of left-lever responses to rate and direction of change in circle diameter. Preexposure to an "expanding" or "contracting" spiral shifted this function, as shown in Figure 5. Notably, the method provided a quantitative measure of the aftereffect; the rate of circle expansion or contraction at which the monkey judged the circle "stationary" was affected by preexposure in much the same way as in humans. How-

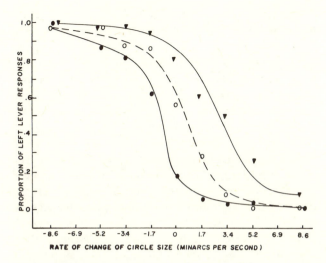

Fig. 5. Proportion of left-lever ("contracting") responses as a function of rate of change of circle diameter, following preexposure to three spiral conditions: stationary—open circles; counterclockwise rotation ("contracting")—filled circles; clockwise rotation ("expanding")—triangles. (From Scott & Powell, 1963. © 1963 by the American Association for the Advancement of Science.)

ever, the use of monkey subjects enabled the investigators to carry out a subsequent study of the effects of certain brain lesions on this perceptual phenomenon.

The spiral aftereffect experiments provide a good example of the problems caused by the experimenter's inability to define the "correct" test responses and hence his inability to maintain reinforcement during testing. To minimize the difference in reinforcement conditions between training and testing, Scott and Milligan (1970) sometimes reinforced correct responses during testing on trials when the circle was expanding or contracting so rapidly that its motion would override any aftereffect. One monkey apparently detected this contingency: "He seemed to discover that when the spiral was rotating, difficult discriminations never resulted in shock, and the animal responded with a stereotyped left lever response to all circles moving at less than 1.7 minarcs per second" (p. 354). The maintained generalization procedure, next to be described, accepts the development of discrimination in the testing situation as the price for a more copious flow of test data.

Maintained Generalization Procedures

A generalization test in extinction is often adequate to suggest the major characteristics of generalization gradients, especially if group averages are used.

However, for meaningful individual gradients showing some detail, it is necessary to increase overall responding by incorporating reinforcement into the test procedure. The simplest way to do this is to intersperse some reinforced training stimulus presentations among randomized test stimulus presentations. Usually, the reinforced trials can occur rather infrequently and still maintain responding.

Recently, P. Blough (1972) used the maintained procedure to investigate a number of regions on the visual wavelength continuum. Her data showed marked differences among spectral regions in the shape of the generalization gradients; the steepness of the gradient slopes were reasonably consistent with wavelength discriminability data (cf. Wright, 1972, discussed above). A set of these gradients appears in Figure 6. The figure also shows an important feature of the maintained procedure: the gradual sharpening of gradients around the reinforced stimulus. As an experiment continues over many hours, gradient steepness gradually approaches an asymptote that depends on the discriminability among the test stimuli. The maintained procedure thus represents a transition from "pure generalization" data, where the subject's response is relatively unconstrained by differential reinforcement, to "discriminability" data, where response is maximally constrained and limits are set by factors such as sensory acuity.

Because the maintained generalization gradient provides a continuous stream of quantitative data, it is useful for scaling and signal detection work, which requires a substantial data base. The procedure is advantageous also for the investigation of discriminative processes such as stimulus summation and attention, which are considered elsewhere in this volume (Chapter 16; cf. D. Blough, 1969, 1972). A serious disadvantage of the maintained procedure is that response to stimuli highly discriminable from S^+ may fall rapidly to an uninformative zero level. Thus the procedure is most useful with sets of quite similar stimuli.

Scaling

With one or two exceptions, meaningful scales of stimulus continua produced by animal subjects are still more a hope than a reality. We consider scaling here because of promising results from a few experiments, interesting methodological beginnings, and the potential usefulness of such data. Adequate scales may simplify our conception of the processes of behavioral control by aiding us to distinguish influences attributable to sensory or perceptual systems from those attributable to other variables. For example, we are in a better position to study discrimination learning if we can present our subject with sets of stimuli that are equally different, since the effects of other variables may then be isolated with more success (for such a use of scaling see D. Blough, 1972). Scales also tell us about the functioning of sensory processes themselves. For example, sensory transduction must be consistent with a power law of sensory magnitude, if that law is correct; similarly, color coding mechanisms must be consistent with the "color circle" such as that determined by Schneider for the pigeon (Schneider, 1972; see below).

Luce (1972) identifies three kinds of psychophysical measurement that we may use as a guide to animal work. First, and currently most promising in animal work, are studies that derive scales from ordinal data. In this kind of scaling, the response measure (for example, rate or probability) is used only to provide information about order; that is, for example, if stimulus A elicits 30 responses, B elicits 15 responses, and C elicits 14 responses, the method uses only the information that responses to A > responses to B > responses to C. Many quite different data sets (such as 30, 27, 1) would of course yield the same order. The method has the great advantage that nothing is assumed about the response measure except that it is monotonically related to the similarity or psychological distance between the corresponding stimuli.

Shepard, a major developer of this method (e.g., Shepard, 1966), applied his analysis to existing wave-

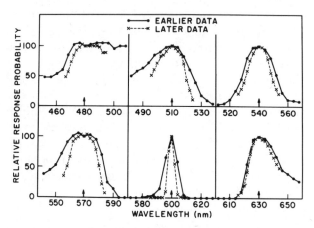

Fig. 6. Maintained wavelength generalization gradients around reinforced stimuli in six spectral regions. Responses to the value indicated by the arrow in each panel were intermittently reinforced. Other stimuli were presented in extinction. Data are averaged across three birds at two different stages of training. The points connected by solid lines are spaced at 4-nm steps were obtained somewhat earlier than those connected by dashed lines. (From P. Blough, 1972.)

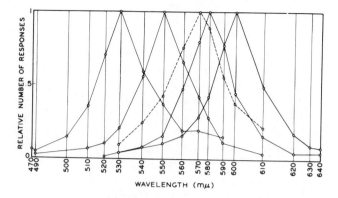

Fig. 7. Generalization gradients based on data from Guttman and Kalish (1956) (solid lines) and from Blough (1961) (broken lines). Note the uneven spacing of the wavelengths; their relative distances have been adjusted to increase the uniformity of the gradients. (From Shepard, 1965.)

length generalization data from pigeons (Shepard, 1965). He showed that a transformation of the wavelength scale would convert these gradients, which come from overlapping regions of the spectrum, to approximately the same shape. Some converted gradients appear in Figure 7; note that wavelengths on the abscissa are irregularly spaced, for units on this axis now represent psychological distance or similarity. The ordinate in Figure 7 is response frequency, but the wavelength scale would be unaffected by any y-axis transformation that preserved the order among the points. For example, after a logarithmic transformation of the ordinate, each gradient would still be the same shape as the others, even though this common shape would change. Thus such a transformation would not call for any change in the stimulus scale.

It is helpful to think of distance along the abscissa in Figure 7 as representing similarity, to the pigeon, among the various wavelengths. However, this particular scale does not actually represent similarity among hues very accurately. For one thing, stimulus luminance was not controlled in the experiments upon which the curves are based. More importantly, a single dimension is inadequate to represent the similarity among hues judged by human subjects, and evidently this is also true of pigeons. A more adequate two-dimensional map of hue for the pigeon has been developed by Schneider (1972), in the most extensive scaling job to be found in the animal literature to date. Schneider based this map on wavelength difference ratings from pigeons, using a method much like that employed by Honig (1965) to study the wavelength difference dimension. In Schneider's study, two wavelengths appeared as a split field on the center key of a three-key pigeon box. An observing peck at the split field lighted the side keys. If the two wavelengths were the same, a peck at the right key was correct, but if they were different, a peck at the left key was correct. Correct responses were always signaled by a feeder light flash, with food coming on 20% of the correct trials. The measure of dissimilarity of two stimuli was the percentage of left key pecks given when these stimuli appeared together.

Schneider used 12 wavelengths (66 pairs) spaced across the spectrum in one experiment and 15 wavelengths (105 pairs) in a second. The percentages of left-key pecks to all the pairs were ranked, the ranks averaged across birds, and the averages used to derive a two-dimensional spatial representation of the distance between the various stimuli. This representation appears in Figure 8. An appreciation of the relation between the raw data and this figure may be aided if one imagines straight lines drawn across the diagram to connect various pairs of wavelengths. A long line signifies that the pair elicited many "different" pecks; if the lengths of these lines were ordered from greatest to least, their order would (ideally) match the order of the ranked key-peck data. A provocative feature of this method is the extent to which mere rank-order information can determine the distance between points in a diagram such as Figure 8. The form of Schneider's function is also very interesting, for human ratings of color similarity also yield a roughly circular configuration, with long and short wavelengths perceptually similar. The diagram suggests that, despite important anatomical differences, the

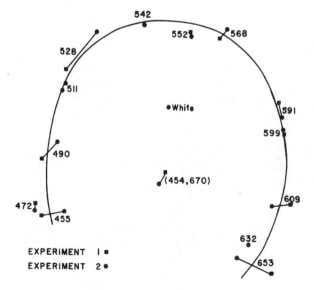

Fig. 8. A two-dimensional color space for the pigeon, based on the rank-ordering of wavelength pairs by "same-different" pecks. See text. (From Schneider, 1972.)

color mechanisms of the pigeon and man may be similar in some ways.

Direct scaling methods use more information from the response measure than simple rank order. In human psychophysics, magnitude estimation exemplifies these methods. In animal work, attempts have been made to use response rate for the same purpose. For example, Herrnstein and Van Sommers (1962) used rate in an attempt to scale visual stimulus intensity to the pigeon. In this study, pecking rate corresponded roughly to a human subject's assignment of numbers to stimulus intensities in the magnitude estimation procedure. To bring rate under the control of intensity, these investigators first trained birds to respond at different rates to several different visual intensities with increased rates required for higher intensities. New stimuli, in between the training stimuli in intensity, were found to elicit intermediate rates. These rates, taken as estimates of the magnitude of the intermediate stimuli, were roughly predicted by a power function relating intensity and magnitude.

As Boakes (1969a) points out, the Herrnstein and Van Sommers method for direct sensory scaling seems to depend on the establishment of a general relation ("the brighter the light, the faster I go") rather than on the attachment of specific rates to specific intensities. In other words, for the method to be effective, the response measure must change continuously and monotonically with the stimulus dimension under study. Furthermore, the function representing this change must not be tied to specific parameters of training, such as the particular response rates reinforced. It is not clear that either of these conditions is met in the Herrnstein and Van Sommers work; the results might, for example, represent the generalization to the test stimuli of the specific rates controlled by nearby training stimuli. In light of these objections, Boakes (1969a) recommends the indirect method of bisection, which makes fewer assumptions, and he has used this method with some success in the bisection, by pigeons, of a brightness interval (1969b). In this case, pigeons learned to peck right for a bright stimulus and to peck left if the stimulus was dim. The stimulus that produced equal pecking on each key was then assumed to bisect the brightness interval. Boakes's data suggest that a power function describes the relation between visual intensity and subjective magnitude in his pigeons. However, the prevalence of position preferences, which we discussed earlier, could seriously interfere with this method. Since these preferences tend to be most pronounced during difficult discriminations, they might be expected to affect response choice for intermediate stimuli. This effect may account for individual differences in the data from some of Boakes's birds.

Because operant response probability is easily conditionable and is subject to so many nonsensory influences, it seems unlikely that it can be used conveniently as a direct scaling measure. The relation between reaction time and intensity, on the other hand, seems largely built into the organism, and this measure may provide information on the transduction of intensity. As we have already seen, equal loudness and equal brightness contours have been successfully based on equal reaction times (Moody, 1969, 1970; Stebbins, 1966). Stebbins suggested that loudness for the monkey might be scaled in units of reciprocal response latency. Recent work with human subjects (Mansfield, 1970; Vaughan, Costa, & Gilden, 1966) suggests that human reaction time is a power function of intensity, just as are numerical magnitude estimates. Aikin (1973) compared reaction time scales with magnitude estimation scales for the same sets of auditory and visual stimuli and found them very similar. Perhaps reaction time scales may serve the function in animal psychophysics that magnitude estimation scales serve in human psychophysics, but much remains to be done before this correspondence can be accepted.

Biases introduced by training conditions and reinforcement contingencies clearly hamper direct scaling to animal studies. Probabilistic models of information processing, such as signal detection, hold out the hope that the effects of bias may be extracted from psychophysical data, and "pure" sensory scales might result. The d' value of detection theory, for example, could serve as the unit for a sensory scale which, if the assumptions of the theory were met, would be independent of reinforcement and other nonsensory biases. Though such scaling has not been attempted with animals, signal detection theory has played an increasingly important role in other areas of animal psychophysics, and we shall consider this matter in the following sections.

SIGNAL DETECTION THEORY IN ANIMAL PSYCHOPHYSICS

Experimenters who study sensory processes usually seek data that reflect stimulus effects unconfounded by variables that affect behavior through other channels, such as motivation, attention, or response bias. We have already discussed some procedural measures designed to minimize the impact of these other variables. Despite such techniques, however, confounding effects remain, and efforts to isolate them through appropriate data analysis continue to be part of psychophysical research. The theory of signal detection is a relatively recent mode of analysis that attempts to separate sensory from other influences, which are lumped together as "bias."

The theory of signal detection became popular largely because it seemed to account more adequately than did classical theory for the pattern of detection responses to weak stimuli. In the present operant context, we can express a major difference between signal detection theory and classical theory in terms of their assumptions about the nature of stimulus control. Classical theory says, in effect, that detection responses are entirely under stimulus control on most trials. A weak stimulus sometimes is below threshold, leading to a "no" response. Classical theory further assumes that on some percentage of the below-threshold trials (which experimenters try to minimize) unspecified nonstimulus variables cause the subject to emit a "yes." These "false alarms" are pure guesses, unrelated to the stimulus. Signal detection theory, on the other hand, holds that the stimulus controls response on all trials, but this control is shared with other (bias) variables. The theory incorporates a statistical scheme by which stimulus effects are, in effect, added to bias effects to determine response outcome.

The assumptions of detection theory lead to the prediction, widely confirmed in human experiments, that changes in signal strength on the one hand, and changes in bias on the other, affect the probability of a detection response in characteristic ways. The outcome of these changes is clarified by the sort of graph common to signal detection presentations, in which correct detections ("yesses" to a signal) are plotted against false alarms ("yesses" to non-signals). When a signal of constant strength is presented many times, while one or more other factors are varied (e.g., the relative reinforcement of "yes" and "no" responses), points along a "receiver operating characteristic" (ROC) or "isosensitivity" curve result. If signal strength changes, a new ROC curve is produced. Examples of such curves are shown in Figure 9. The most common form of signal detection theory predicts that these ROC curves will have the form shown in Figure 9A and that they will become straight lines, as in Figure 9B, when the coordinates are transformed into standard deviation units ("z-scores"). These diagrams separate graphically the two kinds of variables, signal and bias, with which the theory deals: signal changes move a data point from ROC curve to ROC curve, toward or away from the main diagonal; bias changes slide the point along a curve. The sensitivity

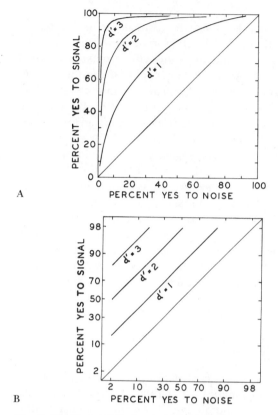

Fig. 9. Idealized ROC (isosensitivity) curves for two different signal intensities. The points along each curve represent different response biases, which modify the percentage of responses both to "noise" (no signal)—plotted on the abscissa—and to the signal—plotted on the ordinate. Panel A shows untransformed response probabilities; panel B shows the same data, but spacing on the coordinates is in terms of normal z-scores.

index d' measures the stimulus effect; it represents the distance of a curve from the diagonal. We cannot go further into the basic theory in this chapter; the reader unfamiliar with signal detection theory is urged to consult a reference such as Engen (1971) or the more comprehensive Green and Swets (1966).

The primary variables that affect performance, according to detection theory, are signal strength, signal probability, and reinforcement contingencies. Since these variables are easily manipulated in animal discrimination experiments, and because such studies may feasibly involve many thousands of responses, animal experimenters have been increasingly interested in using this sort of analysis. This has been done not only to clarify sensory processes, but also to investigate the assumptions of detection theory and to find out more about the actual interactions of the variables controlling behavior.

The use of animal subjects has led to some revisions in the rationale behind assumptions of detectability theory, if not in their form. For example, the human observer is usually assumed to be "fully informed" about the distribution of input events that he will encounter, and he is thought to make a rational decision leading to such a goal as "maximum number of correct responses." An analysis more congenial to most animal investigators is provided by Boneau and Cole (1967), who show that, if a subject adjusts its responses to "most food for least work," its contact with the reinforcement contingencies can provide information comparable to that available to the "fully informed" human observer. Detection theory also assumes that trials are statistically homogeneous; that is, essentially the same statistical processes control detection on every trial. This assumption is rather rarely mentioned in human studies, but must be carefully considered in animal work, where occasional "lapses of attention" seem almost inevitable. We shall return to this matter below.

Some Animal Studies Using Signal Detection Analysis

A number of recent studies have subjected animal data to signal detection analysis. Of these, however, few have used the analysis as an aid in determining sensory functions. One of the few is the wavelength discrimination study by Wright (1972), whose method was previously described. In this study, the pigeon made a choice peck at one key if two wavelengths were the same, and at another key if they differed. In order to provide the bias changes that are necessary to generate ROC curves, Wright varied the relative probability of reinforcement for responses to the two choice keys. Families of such curves arose from the use of a number of wavelength differences (corresponding to different "signal strengths") at each reference wavelength.

Wright organized his data by separating correct detections (pecks on the "different" key when the projected wavelengths differed) from false alarms (pecks on the "different" key when the wavelengths were the same). This pair of values was obtained for each set of wavelengths under each reinforcement condition, and such a pair provided the coordinates for a single point on a ROC diagram. Variation of reinforcement probability, with wavelength difference constant, provided the set of points for an isosensitivity (ROC) function; each wavelength difference provided a new function, as exemplified in Figure 4 by the data from Moody (1970). In Wright's data, the curves shift toward the upper left corner of the diagram as wavelength difference increases.

When correct detections and false alarms are scaled on normalized coordinates, the most common form of detection theory predicts that the ROC curve for each stimulus condition will be parallel to the main diagonal as shown in Figure 9B. The distance between the ROC curve and the diagonal then may be summarized by a single number, d', which represents the subject's sensitivity to the stimulus that yielded the line. However, most of Wright's data, like most results from human subjects, are best fit by lines that converge, so no single distance index can describe the bird's sensitivity for a given stimulus condition. A variety of measures have been used to cope with this situation (cf. Green & Swets, 1966). Wright adopted as his measure the distance of the ROC curve from the major diagonal at the point of "zero bias," that is, where the curve crosses a minor diagonal in a diagram such as that of Figure 9. From the d' values determined in this way, Wright constructed psychometric functions relating d' to wavelength difference at each reference wavelength that had been tested. From each of these functions he picked off that wavelength difference that yielded a d' of 2.0, and this set of wavelength differences yielded detailed discriminability functions.

In a more recent article, Wright (1974) used these results to develop a model of discrimination that brings signal detection theory together with more classic views of the psychometric function. He argues that when discrimination is measured under equal-bias conditions the psychometric function becomes a straight line if plotted with d' as a function of stimulus difference. Further, this straight line passes through the origin, so its slope provides the appropriate index of discriminability. Wright argues further that this conceptually simple picture has been obscured, in much psychophysical work, by procedures that introduce strong response bias. For example, human subjects have often been strongly cautioned not to give "false alarms" and thus have a strong bias against "yes" responses. We cannot delve further here into Wright's provocative article, but it clearly illustrates two central points: (1) the great significance of response bias and (2) the general utility of using animals in psychophysical work. It is most unlikely that Wright could have obtained from humans the very extensive results upon which his theory is based.

Studies by Clopton (1972) and Elsmore (1972) exemplify the manipulation of bias through changes in the probability of signal presentation rather than the probability of reinforcement. Clopton's monkeys discriminated increments in noise intensity, and his ROC curves are well fit by functions based on Rayleigh distributions rather than on the more usual normal distributions of noise and signal plus noise. The monkeys in Elsmore's experiment were trained to

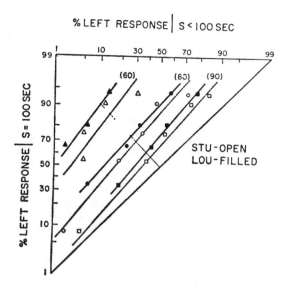

Fig. 10. Duration discrimination data from two monkeys. The animals discriminated 60, 80, or 90 sec from 100 sec. The points along each line represent different response biases induced by alterations in the relative probability that the short or long durations would be presented. (From Elsmore, 1972. © 1972 by the Society for the Experimental Analysis of Behavior, Inc.)

press one lever for a long stimulus duration and another lever for shorter durations. By changing the relative probability of the long and short durations, Elsmore successfully changed the bias toward the two levers, producing the rather nice data exemplified in Figure 10. Elsmore also analyzed the interaction between signal probability and the probability of reinforcement on the two levers. This analysis exemplifies the sort of interactions of variables that may operate in a detection situation, and we shall illustrate the main idea by a simple example. Suppose that a long-duration stimulus (the "signal") occurs on many trials and a short-duration stimulus occurs on relatively few. If the reinforcement schedule for the two stimuli is the same (as in this case), more reinforcements will be obtained for pressing the lever indicating "long duration." Elsmore showed that the "optimal response bias" that maximizes reinforcement probability under these circumstances is very close to the actual bias that he observed.

To obtain ROC curves through experimental manipulation of the subject's criterion, as exemplified above, one requires a great many trials at a number of values of the biasing variable. In human psychophysics, the "rating method" has been used to produce ROC curves more quickly. This method assumes, in effect, that a subject has a number of criteria at the same time, each controlling a response that indicates a degree of certainty about the signal. Thus if a signal is not strong enough to make the subject say, "Yes, I am very sure a signal was presented," or even, "Yes, a

signal was presented," it may still suffice to make him say, "Yes, a signal *might* have been presented." Each of these degrees of certainty, or *ratings*, represents the effect of a different bias and generates a point on the ROC curve for a given signal strength. D. Blough (1967) applied this method to animal subjects, treating the pigeon's rate of pecking as an index reflecting its rating of a stimulus. This study used stimuli on a wavelength continuum; the stimulus set included a single S+ value, presentations of which were interspersed with many S− presentations. If response rate was very low, the pigeon was considered to be "quite sure" that the reinforced stimulus was not present, while if the rate was high, the pigeon was "sure" that the reinforced stimulus was present. As in other methods, a single ROC curve corresponds to one particular stimulus ("signal") that differs from the S+ ("noise"). Each point along such a curve is based on the proportion of trials that yielded a given rate of response to the S+ (the *x*-coordinate of the point) or to the stimulus in question (the *y*-coordinate of the point). When plotted on normalized coordinates, these values produced quite linear ROC curves (Figure 11), but again the curves converged somewhat, rather than remaining parallel to the main diagonal. Response latency has also been used as a rating measure in animal work (e.g., Yager & Duncan, 1971).

Even in the absence of data necessary to generate complete ROC curves, the signal detection format, with "hits" plotted against "false alarms," can be a convenient way to display response bias and to estimate its interaction with apparent sensitivity. Terman (1970), for example, reinforced rats equally on two

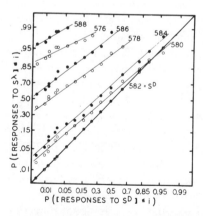

Fig. 11. ROC (isosensitivity) functions for a discrimination between a wavelength of 582 nm (considered "noise") and each of several other wavelengths ("signals"). The curves are produced by the "rating" method, where the coordinates of each point represent the probability that a given number of response (*i*) or fewer were made to the stimulus in question. When *i* is set at successively greater values, a set of points along one curve results. (From D. Blough, 1967. © 1967 by the American Association for the Advancement of Science.)

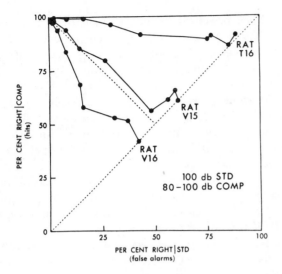

Fig. 12. Isobias functions for discriminations between a 100-db standard and comparison stimuli from 80 to 100 db. The rats differ in their degree of bias, but the amount of bias is relatively consistent in each. ROC curves cannot be plotted here because bias was not varied for fixed signal strengths. (From Terman, 1970. © 1970 by the Society for the Experimental Analysis of Behavior, Inc.)

levers for "correct detections" and "correct rejections," obtaining the "isobias" functions shown in Figure 12. Only signal intensity varied here, for there was no manipulation of bias upon which ROC curves could be based. Nonetheless, it is evident that each of the three rats, although run under symmetrical reinforcement conditions, had a relatively constant bias toward one lever or the other. Rat T16, for example, was strongly biased toward the right lever, as indicated by its high rate of false alarms at weak signal values. Despite such biases, Terman found that the rats gave very similar functions when the sensitivity index d' was plotted against stimulus intensity.

Nevin, one of the first to apply the signal detection method to animal data, has suggested that the paradigm may clarify the interactions of variables other than signal and bias (Nevin, 1970; Nevin, Olson, Mandell, & Yarensky, 1975). As we mentioned earlier, he reports cases in which d' appears to vary with reinforcement contingencies—despite the common assumption that this index is an unbiased index of sensory and input factors. Such research suggests the question with which we close this chapter: to what extent, and in what ways, is signal detection analysis of use in animal experimentation?

The Usefulness of Signal Detection Analysis in Animal Work

Under what circumstances, if any, should a researcher plan animal experimentation around the use of signal detection analysis? This question raises two more specific issues, which we shall consider in turn. First, does the interaction of "sensory" and "bias" factors that is implicit in the detection model correspond to the nature of discriminative control in psychophysical settings, and does signal detection isolate a measure of sensitivity that is truly independent of nonsensory variables? Second, is this measure practical to use, in terms of the time or the number of observations required to estimate it?

As we suggested above, a major impetus for detection analysis in human psychophysics was a failure of psychophysical data to correspond to the classical view that on any given trial a detection response is controlled either by sensory input, or by some error factor, but not by both. As our review suggests, animal data agree with human results in this respect. Animal ROC curves clearly suggest that the detection response is a joint function of sensory and other variables, as proposed in the detection model. For this reason, the detection paradigm may be useful to researchers interested in clarifying the nature of stimulus control. This sort of research is beyond the scope of this chapter, but see, for example, Nevin (1967, 1970), D. Blough (1967, 1972), Heinemann et al. (1969), and Chase and Heinemann (1972).

The available literature in this area suggests, however, that indices like d' must be interpreted with great care. The data of Heinemann et al. (1969), for example, indicate that animals may be inattentive to the stimulus on a significant proportion of trials. This is equivalent to saying that the classical view of detection is partly right, for, on some trials, sensory input plays no role in controlling the response. Thus a correction like the classical correction for false reports must be estimated and applied to the data, in effect removing the "inattentive" trials from the subsequent analysis.

Available animal data, like most results from human subjects, fail to follow the simplest version of detection theory, which predicts that ROC curves plotted on normalized coordinates will be straight lines parallel to the major diagonal. Instead, these lines converge in such a way that the sensitivity index d' cannot be determined unambiguously. As we saw above, Wright chose to estimate d' from the point at which his ROC curves crossed the minor diagonal; this method had the advantage of representing detection under conditions of "no bias"—that is, when equal numbers of incorrect responses were occurring on both keys. Many other solutions to the convergence problem may be found in the detection literature. Assumptions about the form of underlying distributions of sensory events may be altered, or nonparametric measures, such as the area under the ROC curve, may be employed (cf. Green & Swets, 1966).

Though various means may be employed within the framework of detection theory to deal with the convergence of ROC curves, one explanation for the phenomenon is rarely considered, for it strikes at a fundamental assumption of the theory. This explanation questions the independence of signal and bias variables. In other words, detection theory assumes that a given signal will produce a central effect which, though it varies statistically from moment to moment, is not affected by the variables that control bias. Unfortunately, the correctness of this assumption has not been firmly established either for human or animal data, and alternatives to it have been suggested (D. Blough, 1972; Pike, 1973).

The work of Nevin and his co-workers (1970, 1975) suggests procedural limits on the applicability of the detection paradigm. In these studies, the usual reinforcement contingencies produced a good separation of sensitivity and bias effects, as implied by the theory. However, when the usual correlation of reinforcement with stimuli was abandoned, this separation broke down. Such was the case, for example, when a "yes" response was occasionally reinforced in the presence of "noise" as well as in the presence of "signal." In such a circumstance, it is hardly surprising that the measure of sensitivity suffers since these ambiguous reinforcement contingencies lead to an ambiguous definition of the "correct" response. Such work is valuable in providing a broader context within which the area of applicability of signal detection may be identified.

Even if one assumes that d' is a relatively good measure of sensitivity under given conditions, one may ask if it is sufficiently better than other measures to justify its use. The most accurate way to estimate d', and a necessary procedure for some nonparametric indices, is to determine experimentally a large portion of an ROC curve. This takes a great deal of time. It seems that, biased though it may be, percentage correct remains an adequate measure for most studies having to do with sensory function. If the experiment can be cast into a forced-choice paradigm, in which the two responses are symmetrically related to the stimulus (e.g., "push the lever under the brighter panel"), and response preference is minimized, d' and percentage correct are virtually equivalent. To quote Green and Swets (1966): "If the observer's preference among alternatives is indeed negligible, . . . a satisfactory index of sensitivity is the percentage of correct response, or the value of d' that corresponds to this percentage" (p. 408).

Even under less favorable circumstances, such as a biased yes-no situation, the practical effects of nonsensory variables on a threshold estimate may be rather small. Irwin and Terman (1970) point out that, assuming an animal's sensitivity (d') to be constant, even a rather strong response bias will yield only a relatively small change in percentage correct. For example, if a subject incorrectly presses the "no" lever five times as often as he incorrectly presses the "yes" lever, his percentage correct for a given signal strength will be at most 4% lower than his percentage correct had he no response bias. The impact of this relatively small shift will be even less if bias remains relatively constant, for it is the difference in threshold across conditions, rather than its absolute value, that is usually of interest.

It appears, then, that in operant work concerned strictly with sensory processes, the determination of ROC curves probably does not add enough information to be worth its cost. Rather than focusing on the ROC curve, or on the d' measure, the experimenter should concentrate on the minimization of bias, and use the forced-choice procedure if possible. For work not strictly sensory, however, the signal detection paradigm may comprise a convenient framework. This framework may further the analysis of discriminative processes in animals, and animal experiments may provide efficient means for testing the detection model and its assumptions.

REFERENCES

AIKIN, L. C. *A comparison of reaction time and magnitude estimation methods for brightness and loudness.* Unpublished doctoral thesis, Brown University, 1973.

BERKLEY, M. A. Visual discriminations in the cat. In W. C. Stebbins (Ed.), *Animal psychophysics.* Englewood Cliffs, N.J.: Prentice-Hall, Inc., 1970.

BLOUGH, D. S. A method for obtaining psychophysical thresholds from the pigeon. *Journal of the Experimental Analysis of Behavior,* 1958, *1*, 31–43.

BLOUGH, D. S. Animal psychophysics. *Scientific American,* 1961, *205*, 113–122.

BLOUGH, D. S. Stimulus generalization as signal detection in pigeons. *Science,* 1967, *158*, 940–941.

BLOUGH, D. S. Attention shifts in a maintained discrimination. *Science,* 1969, *166*, 125–126.

BLOUGH, D. S. Recognition by the pigeon of stimuli varying in two dimensions. *Journal of the Experimental Analysis of Behavior,* 1972, *18*, 345–367.

BLOUGH, P. M. The visual acuity of the pigeon for distant targets. *Journal of the Experimental Analysis of Behavior,* 1971, *15*, 57–67.

BLOUGH, P. M. Wavelength generalization and discrimination in the pigeon. *Perception and Psychophysics,* 1972, *12*, 342–348.

BOAKES, R. A. Response continuity and timing behavior. In R. M. Gilbert & N. S. Sutherland (Eds.), *Animal dis-*

crimination learning. New York: Academic Press, 1969. (a)
BOAKES, R. A. The bisection of a brightness interval by pigeons. *Journal of the Experimental Analysis of Behavior,* 1969, *12,* 201–209. (b)
BONEAU, C. A., & COLE, J. L. Decision theory, the pigeon, and the psychophysical function. *Psychological Review,* 1967, *74,* 123–135.
CHASE, S., & HEINEMANN, E. G. Choices based on redundant information: An analysis of two-dimensional stimulus control. *Journal of Experimental Psychology,* 1972, *92,* 161–175.
CLACK, T. D., & HARRIS, J. D. Auditory thresholds in the rat by a two-lever technique. *Journal of Auditory Research,* 1963, *3,* 53–63.
CLACK, T. D., & HERMAN, P. N. A single-lever psychophysical adjustment procedure for measuring auditory thresholds in the monkey. *Journal of Auditory Research,* 1963, *3,* 175–183.
CLOPTON, B. M. Detection of increments in noise intensity by monkeys. *Journal of the Experimental Analysis of Behavior,* 1972, *17,* 473–481.
CORBALLIS, M. C., & BEALE, I. L. Monocular discrimination of mirror-image obliques by pigeons: Evidence for lateralized stimulus control. *Animal Behavior,* 1970, *18,* 563–566.
CUMMING, W. W., & BERRYMAN, R. Some data on matching behavior in the pigeon. *Journal of the Experimental Analysis of Behavior,* 1961, *4,* 281–284.
DALLAND, J. I. The measurement of ultrasonic hearing. In W. C. Stebbins (Ed.), *Animal psychophysics.* Englewood Cliffs, N.J.: Prentice-Hall, Inc., 1970.
ELSMORE, T. F. Duration discrimination: Effects of probability of stimulus presentation. *Journal of the Experimental Analysis of Behavior,* 1972, *18,* 465–469.
ENGEN, T. Psychophysics, I: Discrimination and detection. In J. W. Kling & L. A. Riggs (Eds.), *Woodworth and Schlosberg's experimental psychology* (3rd ed.). New York: Holt, Rinehart & Winston, 1971.
GOFF, W. R. Measurement of absolute olfactory sensitivity in rats. *American Journal of Psychology,* 1961, *74,* 384–393.
GOUREVITCH, G. Detectability of tones in quiet and in noise by rats and monkeys. In W. C. Stebbins (Ed.), *Animal psychophysics.* Englewood Cliffs, N.J.: Prentice-Hall, Inc., 1970.
GREEN, D. M., & SWETS, J. A. *Signal detection theory and psychophysics.* New York: Wiley, 1966.
GUTTMAN, N., & KALISH, H. I. Discriminability and stimulus generalization. *Journal of Experimental Psychology,* 1956, *51,* 79–88.
HEINEMANN, E. G., AVIN, E., SULLIVAN, M. A., & CHASE, S. Analysis of stimulus generalization by a psychophysical method. *Journal of Experimental Psychology,* 1969, *80,* 215–224.
HENTON, W. W. Conditioned suppression to odorous stimuli in pigeons. *Journal of the Experimental Analysis of Behavior,* 1969, *12,* 175–185.
HERRNSTEIN, R. J., & VAN SOMMERS, P. Method for sensory scaling with animals. *Science,* 1962, *135,* 40–41.
HODOS, W., & BONBRIGHT, JR., J. C. The detection of visual intensity differences by pigeons. *Journal of the Experimental Analysis of Behavior,* 1972, *18,* 471–479.
HONIG, W. K. Discrimination, generalization, and transfer on the basis of stimulus differences. In D. I. Mostofsky (Ed.), *Stimulus generalization.* Stanford, Calif.: Stanford University Press, 1965.
IRWIN, R. J., & TERMAN, M. Detection of brief tones in noise in rats. *Journal of the Experimental Analysis of Behavior,* 1970, *13,* 135–143.
JACOBS, G. H. Increment-threshold spectral sensitivity in the squirrel monkey. *Journal of Comparative and Physiological Psychology,* 1972, *79,* 425–431.
JENKINS, H. M., & HARRISON, R. H. Effect of discrimination training on auditory generalization. *Journal of Experimental Psychology,* 1960, *59,* 246–253.
LUCE, R. D. What sort of measurement is psychophysical measurement? *American Psychologist,* 1972, *27,* 96–106.
MALOTT, R. W., & MALOTT, M. K. Perception and stimulus generalization. In W. C. Stebbins (Ed.), *Animal psychophysics.* Englewood Cliffs, N.J.: Prentice-Hall, Inc., 1970.
MANSFIELD, R. J. W. *Intensity relations in vision: Analysis and synthesis in a nonlinear sensory system.* Unpublished doctoral thesis, Harvard University.
MELLO, N. K. Interocular generalization: A study of mirror-image reversal following monocular training in pigeon. *Journal of the Experimental Analysis of Behavior,* 1966, *9,* 11–16.
MENTZER, T. L. Comparison of three methods for obtaining psychophysical thresholds from the pigeon. *Journal of Comparative and Physiological Psychology,* 1966, *61,* 96–101.
MISHKIN, M., & WEISKRANTZ, L. Effects of cortical lesions in monkeys on critical flicker frequency. *Journal of Comparative and Physiological Psychology,* 1959, *52,* 660–666.
MOODY, D. B. Equal brightness functions for supra-threshold stimuli in the pigmented rat: A behavioral determination. *Vision Research,* 1969, *9,* 1381–1389.
MOODY, D. B. Reaction time as an index of sensory function. In W. C. Stebbins (Ed.), *Animal psychophysics.* Englewood Cliffs, N.J.: Prentice-Hall, Inc., 1970.
MOSKOWITZ, H., & KITZES, L. A comparison of two psychophysical methods using animals. *Journal of the Experimental Analysis of Behavior,* 1966, *9,* 515–519.
NEVIN, J. A. Effects of reinforcement scheduling on simultaneous discrimination performance. *Journal of the Experimental Analysis of Behavior,* 1967, *10,* 251–260.
NEVIN, J. A. On differential stimulation and differential reinforcement. In W. C. Stebbins (Ed.), *Animal psychophysics.* Englewood Cliffs, N.J.: Prentice-Hall, Inc., 1970.
NEVIN, J. A., OLSON, K., MANDELL, C., & YARENSKY, P. Relative reinforcement and signal detection. *Journal of the Experimental Analysis of Behavior,* 1975, *24,* 355–367.
NYE, P. W. On the functional differences between frontal and lateral visual fields of the pigeon. *Vision Research,* 1973, *13,* 559–574.
PIKE, R. Response latency models for signal detection. *Psychological Review,* 1973, *80,* 53–68.
RASLEAR, T. G., PIERREL-SORRENTINO, R., & BRISSEY, C. Concurrent assessment of schedule and intensity control across successive discriminations. *Journal of the Experimental Analysis of Behavior,* 1975, *23,* 247–254.
RAY, B. A. Psychophysical testing of neurologic mutant mice. In W. C. Stebbins (Ed.), *Animal psychophysics.* Englewood Cliffs, N. J.: Prentice-Hall, Inc., 1970.
ROSENBERGER, P. B. Response-adjusting stimulus intensity. In W. C. Stebbins (Ed.), *Animal psychophysics.* Englewood Cliffs, N.J.: Prentice-Hall, Inc., 1970.

SADOWSKY, S. Discrimination learning as a function of stimulus location along an auditory intensity continuum. *Journal of the Experimental Analysis of Behavior*, 1966, *9*, 219–225.

SAINSBURY, R. S. Effect of proximity of elements on the feature-positive effect. *Journal of the Experimental Analysis of Behavior*, 1971, *16*, 315–325.

SASLOW, C. A. *Animal psychophysics: An examination of the field.* Seattle: University of Washington, Report PRP–37N, 1967.

SAUNDERS, J. Behavioral discrimination of click intensity in cat. *Journal of the Experimental Analysis of Behavior*, 1969, *12*, 951–957.

SCHNEIDER, B. Multidimensional scaling of color difference in the pigeon. *Perception and Psychophysics*, 1972, *12*, 373–378.

SCHUSTERMAN, R., & BALLIET, R. F. Conditioned vocalizations as a technique for determining visual acuity thresholds in sea lions. *Science*, 1970, *169*, 498–501.

SCOTT, T. R., & MILLIGAN, W. L. The psychophysical study of visual motion aftereffect rate in monkeys. In W. C. Stebbins (Ed.), *Animal psychophysics*. Englewood Cliffs, N.J.: Prentice-Hall, Inc., 1970.

SCOTT, T. R., & POWELL, D. A. Measurement of a visual motion after-effect in the rhesus monkey. *Science*, 1963, *140*, 57–59.

SELIGMAN, M. E. P. On the generality of the laws of learning. *Psychological Review*, 1970, *77*, 406–418.

SHEPARD, R. N. Approximation to uniform gradients of generalization by monotone transformations of scale. In D. I. Mostofsky (Ed.), *Stimulus generalization.* Stanford, Calif.: Stanford University Press, 1965.

SHEPARD, R. N. Metric structures in ordinal data. *Journal of Mathematical Psychology*, 1966, *3*, 287–315.

SIDLEY, N. A., SPERLING, H. G., BEDARF, E. W., & HISS, R. H. Photopic spectral sensitivity in the monkey: Methods for determining and initial results. *Science*, 1965, *150*, 1837–1839.

SIDMAN, M., RAY, B. A., SIDMAN, R. L., & KLINGER, J. M. Hearing and vision in neurological mutant mice: A method for their evaluation. *Experimental Neurology*, 1966, *16*, 377–402.

SMITH, J. Conditioned suppression as an animal psychophysical technique. In W. C. Stebbins (Ed.), *Animal psychophysics*. Englewood Cliffs, N.J.: Prentice-Hall, Inc., 1970.

STEBBINS, W. C. Auditory reaction time and the derivation of equal loudness contours for the monkey. *Journal of the Experimental Analysis of Behavior*, 1966, *9*, 135–142.

STEBBINS, W. C. Studies of hearing and hearing loss in the monkey. In W. C. Stebbins (Ed.), *Animal psychophysics*. Englewood Cliffs, N.J.: Prentice-Hall, Inc., 1970.

SUTHERLAND, N. S. Shape discrimination in rat, octopus, and goldfish: A comparative study. *Journal of Comparative and Physiological Psychology*, 1969, *67*, 160–176.

SYMMES, D. Self-determination of critical flicker frequencies in monkeys. *Science*, 1962, *136*, 714–715.

TAPPER, D. N., & HALPERN, B. P. Taste stimuli: A behavioral categorization. *Science*, 1968, *161*, 708–709.

TERMAN, M. Discrimination of auditory intensity by rats. *Journal of the Experimental Analysis of Behavior*, 1970, *13*, 145–160.

TERMAN, M., & TERMAN, J. S. Concurrent variation of response bias and sensitivity in an operant-psychophysical test. *Perception and Psychophysics*, 1972, *11*, 428–432.

THOMAS, D. R. The use of operant conditioning technique to investigate perceptual processes in animals. In R. M. Gilbert & N. S. Sutherland (Eds.), *Animal discrimination learning.* New York: Academic Press, 1969.

THORPE, S. A. Behavioral measures of spectral sensitivity of the goldfish at different temperatures. *Vision Research*, 1971, *11*, 419–433.

VAUGHAN, JR., H. G., COSTA, L. D., & GILDEN, L. The functional relation of visual evoked response and reaction time to stimulus intensity. *Vision Research*, 1966, *6*, 654–656.

WILSON, M., STAMM, J. S., & PRIBRAM, K. H. Deficits in roughness discrimination after posterior parietal lesions in monkeys. *Journal of Comparative and Physiological Psychology*, 1960, *6*, 535–539.

WRIGHT, A. A. Psychometric and psychophysical hue discrimination functions for the pigeon. *Vision Research*, 1972, *12*, 1447–1464.

WRIGHT, A. A. Psychometric and psychophysical theory within a framework of response bias. *Psychological Review*, 1974, *81*, 322–347.

YAGER, D., & DUNCAN, I. Signal-detection analysis of luminance generalization in goldfish using latency as a graded response measure. *Perception and Psychophysics*, 1971, *9*, 353–355.

YAGER, D., & THORPE, S. Investigations of goldfish color vision. In W. C. Stebbins (Ed.), *Animal psychophysics*. Englewood Cliffs, N.J.: Prentice-Hall, Inc., 1970.

18

Operant Behavioral Pharmacology

Travis Thompson
and
John J. Boren

INTRODUCTION

Scientific interest in the behavioral actions of drugs is not new. For decades investigators have studied whether certain drugs could alter behavior in open field tests, T-mazes, straight alleys, pole climbing apparatuses, shuttle boxes, key pecking situations, and lever pressing devices. Often such studies attempted to elucidate drug effects on such phenomena as memory, learning, anxiety, or drives. Two problems became apparent from this body of research: (1) More sensitive and reliable behavioral procedures were needed to assess the behavioral actions of drugs. (2) Many of the early questions asked were clearly premature, if not misguided. An objective and operationally based conceptual framework within which to interpret the actions of drugs on behavior had to be formulated before such issues could begin to be considered.

Early infrahuman experiments were given impetus in the 1950s when chlorpromazine and reserpine, the first tranquilizers, were reported to be useful in treating certain psychiatric patients. These findings were made in the clinic and came more as a surprise than as the logical outcome of planned laboratory research. However, due in large part to these early clinical discoveries, further interest in laboratory research in behavioral pharmacology took a sharp upswing. In the late 1950s and early 1960s, the primary interest centered around two problems: (1) How can one discover new drugs with useful applications in psychiatry? (2) Is it possible to arrive at a more thorough understanding of these drugs through a laboratory analysis?

It became clear early on that operant techniques were among the most sensitive for measuring the behavioral action of drugs (Boren, 1966; Cook & Kelleher, 1963; Dews & Morse, 1961; Gollub & Brady, 1965; Sidman, 1959). The profusion of studies using operant techniques that followed led to the emergence of several journals to accommodate the burgeoning literature. In addition, textbooks on drugs and behavior were written (e.g., Iverson & Iverson, 1975; Rech & Moore, 1971; Thompson & Schuster, 1968) which involved major emphasis on the experimental analysis of operant behavior.

That operant baselines are sensitive indicators of drug action now seems uncontested. However, it is one thing to show that a behavioral system is sensitive to the manipulation of an independent variable (in this case, drug administration), and it is another to show that the resulting data are meaningful and significant. One of the major theses of the present chapter is that operant behavioral pharmacology has, by and large, succeeded in satisfying the two major requisites of a scientific domain concerned with the analysis of drug actions on behavior: (1) The provision of sensitive and reliable behavioral procedures; and (2) the provision of an objective, operationally based conceptual framework within which to interpret the results of experiments on the behavioral actions of drugs. It is our contention that one of the main purposes of operant behavioral pharmacology is to interpret the behavioral mechanisms by which these behavioral changes are brought about; that is, to express the scientific significance of findings concerning behavioral actions of drugs in terms of a more general set of principles.

Behavioral pharmacology, which has grown out of the integration of experimental psychology and pharmacology, is concerned with the behavioral actions of drugs. Its primary goal is the description of the behavioral mechanisms by which drugs alter behavior. A prerequisite to such a description is an understanding of the factors that control the behavior in question. To understand the way in which drugs alter behavior, it is first necessary to understand the factors which control behavior. It follows that a description of the interaction of drug variables with behavioral variables is an essential first step in understanding the behavioral mechanisms of drug actions (Thompson and Schuster, 1968). In general pharmacology, the "mechanism of action" of a drug refers to some "basic" process, typically physiological or biochemical, which mediates a drug's effect upon a particular response. In pharmacology, the term "response" refers to any change in the organism which can be reliably produced by a drug on repeated occasions. Within behavioral pharmacology such responses can be properly related only to *behavioral* mechanisms of action—that is, mechanisms describable in terms of basic behavioral processes.

It is important to keep in mind the principle that a drug cannot cause a biological system to respond in a qualitatively new way. That is, a drug may increase or decrease values of dependent variables but may not cause a fundamental change in the operation of the biological system. As a consequence, we must ask ourselves, "With which of the existing systems that regulate behavior is a drug interacting to produce the observed behavioral change?" This is the fundamental question to which we must address ourselves when we ask, "What is the *behavioral mechanism* by which this drug effect is brought about?"

The Problem of Sample Size

A common feature of the operant approach to behavioral pharmacology involves the intensive study of a single individual subject. The emphasis is on close observation and firm experimental control. If the experiment is successful, a subject will behave predictably from session to session and even from minute to minute. Thus, when an effective drug is administered in the middle of a session, a change from the dependable baseline behavior should be readily apparent in an individual subject. Furthermore, on different sessions, a range of drug dosages can be studied in the same subject with a sound basis for comparison.

The intensive study of the individual subject will be emphasized in this chapter and in other discussions of operant techniques. This might be labeled the "N of One" approach, and has sometimes been misunderstood. The approach is *not* simply to use a small number of subjects for its own sake. For example, someone might attempt a drug-behavior experiment with three subjects stabilized on a behavioral baseline. The first subject is given dose #1, the second subject is given dose #2, and the third subject is given dose #3. From such an experiment, one can do little more than estimate crudely the nature of the dose-response curve. Differences among subjects will be confounded with differences produced by the drug dosage so that one cannot tell which is which. A more informative use of three subjects would be to administer each dose on separate sessions to each of the subjects. Then with each individual, one could determine how the different doses modified this subject's behavior.

There is no simple rule for deciding on the number of subjects. The critical question is whether the experiment can be replicated, and the most straightforward answer comes from successful replications. If unknown and/or uncontrolled variables are operating in the experiment, replication will be difficult, and the experimenter will be aware of trouble with his technique. Thus, when the experimenter has reason to suspect uncontrolled variables, he is wise to use more than one subject.

There *are* circumstances where a single subject is adequate. Although opinions may differ on this matter, the circumstances are approximately as follows: (1) The experimenter is working in a well-controlled experimental situation with a thorough knowledge of his techniques and his subjects. Thus, the experimenter probably has the problem of uncontrolled variables well in hand. (2) The results from the single subject are in accord with previous data and fit plausibly into a well-understood body of knowledge. (3) The experimenter has studied other subjects with related procedures, and the results are consistent. Sidman's (1960) more extensive discussion of this matter under the topic of "systematic replication" is recommended to the interested reader.

Under these circumstances the probability of successful replication is high, so that additional subjects are unnecessary. The same amount of experimental time might be better spent in studying variations on the experiment rather that replicating. By the same token, if these circumstances do not hold, the use of additional subjects is indicated.

Why Experiment with Drugs?

The reasons for selecting a drug for an experimental study are no less complicated than the reasons for investigating any variable which affects behavior. However, at least a few of the more common reasons can be indicated:

CURIOSITY ABOUT THE BEHAVIORAL EFFECTS OF DRUGS

How will atropine affect conditioned avoidance behavior? Is behavior maintained by a fixed–interval schedule more sensitive to drugs than behavior maintained by a fixed-ratio schedule? Such questions are typical of those which a behavioral phamacologist might find interesting. Drugs can be powerful variables; they can eliminate behavior altogether or increase it manifold. Any drug might have an interesting or unusual action in a behavioral situation, and the fact that such a situation occasionally arises may be quite enough to maintain the activity of a scientist.

PRACTICAL UTILITY OF DRUGS IN HUMAN AFFAIRS

The use of drugs in treating human ills represents the most socially valuable application of pharmacology. As a result, a great deal of research is directed toward potential applications of drugs. For example, scientists in government and industrial laboratories study thousands of newly synthesized organic chemicals every year in the hope that they will discover a medically useful drug. There are also a number of other practical implications of drug research. In recent years, for example, increasing attention has been given to problems of behaviorally toxic effects of chemicals (Sparber, 1972; Spyker, Sparber, & Goldberg, 1972) administered during gestation or chronically in the adult animal (Weiss and Laties, 1969). Further, the seemingly evergrowing incidence of drug abuse has posed an enormous research problem for behavioral pharmacologists.

ANALYSIS AND VERIFICATION OF CLINICAL FINDINGS

A drug which is useful in the clinic is interesting to the research worker for several reasons. He may wish to understand more fully the mechanism responsible for the clinical effect than can be done conveniently and without danger in human patients. In the laboratory with animal subjects, he can readily perform surgery, administer toxic doses, or implant electrodes in an effort to understand the drug's action. In another case he may use the drug to determine whether the laboratory procedures are relevant to a clinical problem. For example, suppose a researcher has found a way to disrupt the complex conditioned behavior of guinea pigs by injecting an extract from the blood of psychotic patients and he wants to know if his experimental situation is related to the psychoses of human patients. If Drug A is known to affect the behavior of psychotic patients favorably, and if Drug A also reduced the extract-induced disruption of the behavior of the guinea pigs, then the researcher has reason to suspect that his behavioral technique might be useful in studying anti psychotic agents, such as drugs. However, he may be incorrect. Drug A may alter the disrupted behavior of the guinea pigs for entirely different reasons from those responsible for changing the behavior of psychotic patients, and the laboratory situation may bear only a superficial resemblance to clinical psychosis.

ANALYZING BEHAVIORAL PROCESSES

A drug can occasionally be found which has a certain main effect without seriously disrupting secondary effects. This drug can then be used as an analytical tool. For example, Dews (1955a) showed that behavior maintained by a fixed-interval (FI) schedule of reinforcement was much more sensitive to the effects of pentobarbital than was behavior maintained by a fixed-ratio (FR) schedule. In a related study, Herrnstein and Morse (1956) examined the effect of pentobarbital on similar tandem FI FR performance, where the behaviors generated by the two components of the schedule were joined in a single performance and could not be easily disentangled. When pentobarbital was given in a high dosage, the pause characteristic of fixed-interval behavior was sharply changed while the fixed-ratio behavior remained unchanged. Thus, the drug experimentally separated the two behaviors and gave the experimenters additional evidence that the complex tandem performance could indeed be properly analyzed into the simple components. As another example, Thompson and Pickens (1970) compared patterns of self-administration of stimulants and opiates by infrahuman subjects. They found that stimulants such as the amphetamines and cocaine were self-administered in a highly regular pattern with extremely narrow distributions of inter-response times. Opiates, on the other hand, engender a bimodal distribution of inter-response times which is far flatter and more variable.

Baseline Stability

The ideal behavioral baseline should be stable. *Stable* means that the behavior remains about the same from one observation period to another (i.e., from session to session or from hour to hour). For example, if an animal's lever-pressing rate to avoid a shock remained between 9.5 and 10.5 responses per minute over 20 sessions, then the behavior would surely be regarded as stable because of the low variability. One would have considerable confidence that the response rate in the next session would remain between 9.5 and 10.5 responses per minute. If a drug were given prior to this session and the response rate went up as little as 20 percent (to 12 responses/minute), one would still conclude that the drug had increased the rate because of the clear departure from the usual variability of the baseline.

Note the relation between the degree of stability and the magnitude of effect with which the experimenter can work. The greater the stability, the smaller the effect which can be reliably studied. For example, if the mean of 20 control values is 10.0 responses/minute and the range is ±.1 response/minute (a very stable baseline), then a 10 percent increase to 11 responses/minute following a drug injection would be considered a reliable effect. On the other hand, with the same mean and a range of ±5 responses/minute (a less stable baseline), a 10 percent "increase" above the mean would be well within the normal variation. Thus, a drug dose which was injected before the session would be considered ineffective. Statistical tests of significance can be used for a more formal analysis of this issue. By any analysis, however, greater baseline stability makes for easier evaluation of small drug effects.

Extreme baseline stability can be a mixed blessing. It is sometimes a hallmark of powerful control by determining variables which may make it hard to produce any departure. Simple escape behavior to an intense electric shock (e.g., the rat presses a lever to turn off a shock) is a case in point. This behavior is quite stable and typically occurs less than a second from the shock onset. However, a drug must produce a massive effect, such as making the rat severely ataxic, before the escape responding is reduced.

Another case where stability assumes secondary importance involves behavior which is interesting partly because it is inappropriate to or fails to meet the current environmental contingencies. Such behaviors are not likely to remain stable. However, a drug study of individual subjects in such situations is not necessarily difficult since the behavior frequently is temporarily stable or undergoes slow, systematic change. A drug which rapidly brings the behavior under the control of the current contingencies (a "therapy" effect) provides an interesting outcome. Morse and Herrnstein (1956) described a pigeon which was required to peck a key 160 times (FR 160) for a food reinforcement. For the conditions of the experiment the number of responses required was overly large, so that the bird sometimes paused half an hour or more before working for a reinforcement (a "strained" fixed-ratio performance). Methamphetamine not only greatly increased the bird's pecking rate immediately but the rate remained high the next day when the drug was no longer present. The high rate in the next session was presumably due to the unusually large number of reinforcements made possible by the drug's action on the previous day. Baseline stability, while it makes drug work more convenient and exact, need not be a critical consideration. Semi-stable procedures may permit useful observations which are not possible with the more conventional techniques.

PRINCIPLES OF DRUG ACTION

While the student of operant behavior is usually aware of behavioral factors in designing drug-behavior research, he may be unfamiliar with basic pharmacological variables. In attempting an understanding of the principles of pharmacology, it is well to keep in mind several basic classes of variables:

A. The type of drug
B. The route of administration
C. The relationship between the dose of drug administered and the magnitude of response
D. Absorption and distribution

E. Time course of drug effects
F. Distribution
G. Fate
H. Multiple administrations of the same drug.

The Type of Drug

It would clearly be useful if the many behavioral drugs could be arranged on the basis of common properties into a small number of categories. Thus, we could study, understand, and remember significant facts about the small number of categories rather than being confused by a mass of particulars. The only problem would seem to be the selection of appropriate criteria for the various categories. Unfortunately, no classification scheme turns out to be really satisfactory. For example, one logical choice for a classification criterion might be the mechanism of action, such as the locus of action within the CNS and the neurotransmitter involved. However, the information on most drugs is much too scanty and speculative to permit classification on this basis. Another more molar possibility might be to try to classify drugs as stimulants or depressants on the basis of whether the drug increases or decreases the response rate on some standard schedule of reinforcement. The problem with such categories is that drugs usually have more complex effects. For example, pentobarbital can increase fixed-ratio response rates at low doses and decrease rates at high doses (Waller and Morse, 1963). Is pentobarbital to be classed a stimulant or a depressant? Atropine increases the rate in the initial section of fixed-interval scallops and decreases the rate in the terminal section (Boren and Navarro, 1959). Should the atropine effect on the initial section be classed stimulant and on the terminal section depressant? Or should atropine, based on the entire effect, be called a disruptant? These examples illustrate an inherent problem with drugs: They have multiple and complex effects and they therefore resist classification into any one category.

Drugs are sometimes categorized by chemical structure. Classification by structure can be useful when several compounds with a similar structure have similar effects. The classical case for CNS drugs is the barbiturate structure. Amobarbital, pentobarbital, secobarbital, etc., are all used to induce sleep, and therefore, discussing these compounds as "barbiturates" is meaningful. However, we sometimes forget that drugs used in medical practice are often selected in a thoroughly biased way. In the laboratories of pharmaceutical manufacturers, organic chemists synthesize a great many compounds for possible therapeutic use, and a common starting point for the synthetic program is a known useful (and salable) drug. Thus, after the success of the first barbiturates (barbital and phenobarbital), over two thousand variations were synthesized. Furthermore, industrial pharmacologists screened the compounds for the ability to put mice or rats to sleep. Largely as the result of such activity, a number of hypnotic barbiturates were made available to the physician and to the pharmacologist. However, it would be utterly incorrect to think that all compounds with a barbiturate nucleus are hypnotic drugs. Indeed, there are countless barbiturates which are inactive as hypnotics or are toxic at hypnotic doses.

A similar case can be made for the phenothiazines, for which chlorpromazine is the model compound. After the clinical success of chlorpromazine in treating schizophrenic patients, countless phenothiazines were synthesized, and screening programs selected out the compounds which had chlorpromazine-like actions. The selected drugs were then usually tested in the same clinical situation for which chlorpromazine had been proven useful. As a result of this carefully biased selection procedure (and, of course, partly because variations of the phenothiazine structure yielded compounds with antipsychotic activity), we now have a group of structurally similar drugs with clinically similar effects. Nevertheless, there are many inactive phenothiazines which did not reach the market and are hardly known outside drug company laboratories.

There are other difficulties with classification by chemical structure. Compounds with similar effects (such as amphetamine and methylphenidate, or chlorpromazine and haloperidol) have quite different structures. Sometimes two compounds with only minor chemical differences (for example, one methyl group or one chlorine atom more or less) have substantially different pharmacological activity. Furthermore, the action of certain molecules separately may bear no relation to their action when combined. For example, the antipsychotic drug, perphenazine, is composed largely of joining phenothiazine to piperazine, both of which are used to destroy intestinal worms. For reasons such as these, it has not proved feasible to classify most drugs by chemical structure.

The common categorization of drugs is on the basis of their therapeutic effect. Table 1 lists a number of drugs affecting behavior and groups them in categories based upon therapeutic usage. These categories are subject to the advantages and disadvantages discussed above. However, the table serves to list representative behavioral drugs grouped according to a widely used classification.

TABLE 1   Representative Behavioral Drugs Classified According to Therapeutic Usage*

I. ANTIPSYCHOTIC DRUGS	V. HYPNOTICS
chlorpromazine (Thorazine)	pentobarbital (Nembutal)
triflupromazine (Vesprin)	secobarbital (Seconal)
trifluoperazine (Stelazine)	amobarbital (Amytal)
perphenazine (Trilafon)	phenobarbital (Luminal)
fluphenazine (Permitil, Prolixin)	methaqualone (Quaalude, Sopor)
thioridazine (Mellaril)	chloral hydrate (Somnos)
haloperidol (Haldol)	
	VI. HALLUCINOGENS (PSYCHOTOMIMETICS)
II. ANTIANXIETY DRUGS	LSD
meprobamate (Miltown, Equanil)	mescaline
chlordiazepoxide (Librium)	psilocybin
diazepam (Valium)	
	VII. ANALGESICS
III. ANTIDEPRESSANT DRUGS	morphine
imipramine (Tofranil)	meperidine (Demerol)
amitryptaline (Elavil)	methadone
isocarboxazid (Marplan)	heroin
nialamide (Niamid)	
phenelzine (Nardil)	VIII. OTHER PSYCHOTROPIC DRUGS
	atropine
IV. STIMULANTS	scopolamine
dl-amphetamine (Benzadrine)	cocaine
methamphetamine (Desoxyn, Methedrine)	reserpine
methylphenidate (Ritalin)	lithium carbonate
magnesium pemoline (Cylert)	tetrahydrocannabinol
caffeine	

* The generic or nonproprietary name is listed first, and the trade or proprietary name is listed second in parentheses.

Routes of Administration*

The pathway by which a drug is introduced into an organism is called *route of administration*. The more commonly used routes can be categorized as either *oral* or *parenteral* (any route outside the alimentary tract). The oral route is often used in infrahuman research because it readily allows the administration of insoluble or irritating compounds and because it facilitates comparison with human studies, which typically use the oral route.

With parenteral administration, the drug is injected directly into the desired site. Although there are other routes for parenteral administration, the ones most widely used in infrahuman research are subcutaneous, intramuscular, intraperitoneal, and intravenous. Since none of the drug can be lost by vomiting or destroyed by gastrointestinal fluids, the dosage is more certain in parenteral administration than in oral. In addition, the rate of absorption is usually more rapid.

* This section is based largely on Chapter 2 of Thompson and Schuster, 1968.

In subcutaneous (SC) injections the tip of the needle is inserted immediately under the skin where a solution is expelled. Intramuscular (IM) injections are accomplished by inserting the needle deep into a muscle mass and expelling a solution or suspension. Intraperitoneal (IP) administration is perhaps the most commonly used route in rats. The needle is inserted directly into the peritoneal cavity, providing rapid drug absorption. Intravenous (IV) administration is used when immediate action and maximal certainty of dosage is required. The tip and shaft of the needle are inserted into the lumen of a vein, and the drug is directly expelled into the vein. Generally only aqueous solutions, which will not damage blood and its constituents or produce local vascular irritation may be used.

The Dose-Response Relationship

According to a common notion, every drug has a "just right" dose which is standard, appropriate, and physiologically active. This notion may have some justification where a specific effect of a drug is desired. For example, when a physician must treat a patient for an acute bacterial infection, he will probably administer a "standard" dose of an antibacterial drug. On the basis of extensive experience he has probably selected this dose as being large enough to have a therapeutic effect on most patients and small enough to avoid undesirable side effects. Even in this restricted situation, however, the notion of the "just right" dose may be inappropriate where the dose happens to be too low for a particular infection or too large for a particular patient who is sensitive to the toxic side effects.

In a more general sense, the concept of the "just right" dose is quite misleading. It overlooks the fact that drugs, like most variables, can be applied at different levels under varying conditions to produce different effects. At the extreme ends of the dose range, every drug has a dose which is so low that it is ineffective and one which is so high that it is lethal. Between these two extremes are dose levels which are generally appropriate for a pharmacological study.

An observation fundamental to all pharmacology is the quantity of drug administered is related in an orderly way to the magnitude of the effect produced. The relation between the dose and the magnitude of effect is called the *dose-response (or dose-effect) relationship*. An example is shown in Figure 1. The data are from an experiment by Waller and Morse (1963) and show how pentobarbital affects two pigeons' key-pecking rates. The pecking response was maintained by reinforcement on a fixed-ratio (FR 30) schedule (i.e., every thirtieth peck produced grain). The dose-effect curves for both birds show an orderly increase in the response rate as a result of the intramuscular injection of 2 and 3 mg (total dose per pigeon). Three mg seemed to produce the maximum rate while the largest dose (5.6 mg) substantially decreased the response output. The dose-effect curve, taken as a whole, shows how pentobarbital over an effective dosage range quantitatively affects the FR 30 response rate.

Why is it important to determine a dose-response curve for a drug? Perhaps the major reason is that drugs often have different effects at different doses. Therefore, full knowledge of a drug's effects can be attained only if a full dosage range is studied. In the data shown in Figure 1, pentobarbital both increased and decreased the response rate—depending on the dose. As a general rule, any drug which will increase behavioral output at some intermediate dose will surely decrease output at some higher dose. The decrease will occur, if for no other reason, because a toxic effect can always be produced by excessively high dosages. The selection of one particular dose does not permit a valid statement of what the drug does. To return to the example of Figure 1, if one selected 3 mg of pentobarbital to study, one would be convinced that the drug was a "stimulant" which increased response output. If one chose 6 mg, one would be equally sure that the drug was a "depressant" which decreased response output. If one picked .01 mg, the drug would be classed inactive, and if one picked 100 mg, it would appear to be a deadly toxin.

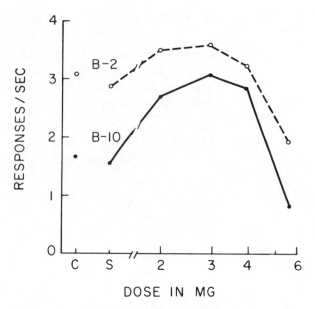

Fig. 1. The effects of pentobarbital on rate of responding on FR 30. The dose is plotted on a log scale while the rate is plotted on a linear scale. The dose-effect curves of two individual pigeons (B-2 and B-10) are shown. The points above "S" show the rate after saline injections (mean of two observations). The points above "C" show the non-injection control rates (mean of six to eight observations). The points for each dosage are the mean of two observations. The dosage is given in terms of number of mg injected. Since the birds weighed slightly more than 400 g, the dosage in mg/kg can be readily calculated (From Waller & Morse, 1963. © 1963 by the Society for the Experimental Analysis of Behavior, Inc.)

Even if two dosage levels were studied, the conclusion might be misleading. For example, one might choose two dosages, one on each side of a maximal level, and then find that they had almost the same effect. A logical but erroneous conclusion might be that increased dosage levels of this drug do not cause a greater effect and that the dose-response curve is relatively flat. Furthermore, it would be easy to select two doses from the left or the right side of the maximum. Thus, one might conclude that larger doses either increase the behavioral output or decrease it. One can guard against such conditions only by studying a number of doses distributed over the effective dosage range of the drug.

As another example of confirmation by other doses, suppose that the results from a low dose suggested ambiguously that the subject's ability to discriminate between a steady light and a flashing light had deteriorated slightly. To clarify this matter, the investigator might consider two alternative procedures. One is to study the low dose again to see if the small effect on the discrimination could be observed. If so, he would have greater confidence in the effect. In all probability, however, the effect will be as ambiguous as before (within the range of extreme control effects), so that a definite conclusion may still be difficult. A second alternative is to increase the dose (as one would normally do in determining a dose-response relationship) to determine whether the effect on the discrimination is increased. If the effect now emerges as large and clear, the investigator's confidence in the effect increases a great deal. This principle of experimental design is not limited to drug-behavior experiments. In the study of any independent variable where the effects are small, it is often more efficient to enlarge the effect by intensifying the variable than simply by replicating the small effect.

A further use of the dose-response curve is in the quantitative comparison of two or more drugs. The pharmacologist will frequently want to know which of two drugs is the more potent, or synonymously, which is the more active. In other words, he wants to know which drug produces a given effect at the smaller dosage. The first step is to determine a dose-response curve for each drug. Figure 2 illustrates several possible outcomes (assumed values) for Drugs A, B, and C. The figure might, for example, represent the decreases in the rate of avoidance responding produced by three depressant drugs. Comparison of Drugs A and B is easy. Drug A is clearly more potent than Drug B in the sense that equivalent effects are produced at lower doses by Drug A. The comparison is easy partly because the effective dosage ranges overlap very little but largely because the dose-effect curves are parallel. The parallel feature permits one to reach the same conclusion about potency regardless of the size of the effect. In Figure 2, Drug A is about eight times more potent than Drug B, regardless of whether the comparison is based on a 50 percent effect, a 25 percent effect, etc. Furthermore, because of the parallel curves, it is possible to calculate a single value for each drug which represents its potency.

The comparison of Drugs A and C is considerably more difficult. The dose-response curves are not parallel, and the effective dose ranges overlap. To be more specific, Drug C appears to be more potent at 1 and 2 mg/kg and less potent at 8 and 16 mg/kg. In such cases expression of potency in terms of the median effective dose (ED_{50}) of the two drugs is arbitrary and misleading. Statistical or computational devices do not help since the ambiguity is inherent in the data. The most convenient solution is to end the search for a single number which relates the potency of each drug and simply to recognize the characteristics of the two dose-response curves.

Note the likelihood of error if Drugs A and C were to be compared at a single dose of each instead of the full dose range. If 1 mg/kg were used, one would definitely conclude that Drug C was more potent; if 16 mg/kg were used, one would conclude equally definitely that Drug A was more potent. To gain complete and accurate information about a drug there is no substitute for a study which determines a full dose-response curve.

Absorption and Distribution

The amount of drug at the site of action determines the effect produced. Once a drug has been introduced into an organism, it is absorbed and distributed to many parts of the body, including the site of action. The amount of drug reaching the site of action is primarily dependent on the amount administered, its physical state, the character of the membranes the drug must pass, and the route that it must take to get from the site of administration to the site of action. The time taken to get from the site of administration to the site of action is largely determined by the rate of absorption.

The absorption rate, in turn, is primarily determined by the route of administration, the physical properties of the drug preparation, and the rate of

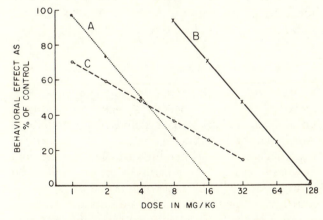

Fig. 2. Three possible dose-effect curves illustrating the comparison of potency.

administration. These are the manipulable factors that determine how rapidly a drug reaches the site of action. The absolute absorption rate can be expressed in terms of the change in concentration of the drug at the site of application over time. Figure 3 illustrates how theoretical absorption and excretion curves produce the concentration curve of the amount of drug at the site of action. This theoretical curve is modified by a set of variables, not all of which are readily controllable. The absolute rate of drug absorption from the site of administration can be considered a physicochemical relation between the drug and the transporting medium. The transporting medium (blood) is the primary factor regulating the absolute absorption rate.

Drugs tend to move from sites of high concentration to areas of lower drug concentration. However, movement of a drug from the site of administration along a concentration gradient very seldom limits absorption rate. Most frequently, the amount of blood flowing through tissue determines how rapidly a drug will be absorbed from surrounding tissue. Therefore, anything that modifies circulation—exercise, temperature, presence of other drugs—also alters rate of absorption. In intravenous administration, of course, absorption is not a limiting factor, and blood levels of a drug reach their maximal concentration immediately. Figure 4 presents the comparative durations of action curves for intramuscular, intravenous, subcutaneous, and oral routes of administration, in which serum concentrations of penicillin were determined for various periods following administration. Clearly, intramuscular administration most closely approximates intravenous administration, while oral administration and subcutaneous routes, though very slow, maintain serum drug levels for a longer period. Although intraperitoneal administration is associated with a duration curve similar to that obtained with the intramuscular route, it provides a slower but longer lasting peak drug concentration.

Time Course of Drug Effects

Many behavioral variables can be applied and removed almost instantaneously. A light can be turned on and off; a shock can be delivered and removed. Such events are public and easily observed so the experimenter knows when the variable is present and at what intensity. The situation is not as simple with a drug. Although the experimenter knows he has injected an animal with a drug, he does not know in advance when the drug will take effect, the drug concentration at the site of action, or how long the effect will last. For this sort of information concerning the drug's time course, the basic source is generally experimental and determined individually with each behavioral preparation.

Every drug has its own time course. As shown in Figure 4, there is a delay in onset of action, (with i.p. and i.m. routes) an increasing effect up to a peak, and finally a decreasing effect until the predrug state is again reached, where the drug has been matabolized or excreted. To illustrate such a relation, consider the study by Grove and Thompson (1970) dealing with the effects of pentobarbital on food-reinforced FR 120 schedule performance by rats. The top frame in Figure 5 shows baseline FR 120 performance on the left side, followed by the effects of a saline injection on the right side. A pause occurred, even after saline, as indicated at C on the cumulative record. The three sets of cumulative records below are labelled 5, 10, and 20, corresponding to the dosage in milligrams/kilogram. In general, pentobarbital suppressed the overall response rate by successively increasing pausing. At 5 mg/kg the drug increased pausing immediately after reinforcement; in addition, a series of pauses and bursts of responding occurred in later ratios (e.g., at E). At 10 mg/kg a pause in responding of 45 min duration

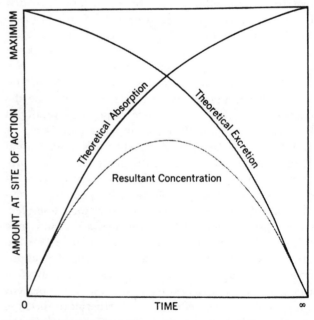

Fig. 3. Theoretical absorption and excretion curves, yielding a curve of concentration at the site of action. Although symmetrical curves of this type are theoretically possible, almost all decay curves are hyperbolic and bear little resemblance to the absorption curves. Similarly, the resultant curve of the actual amount reaching the site of action is never symmetrical and is modified by numerous factors, as discussed in the text (From Marsh, D. F., *Outline of Fundamental Pharmacology*, 1950. Courtesy of Charles C Thomas, Publisher, Springfield, Ill.)

occurred following the first reinforcement. Then about 50 responses were completed at an intermediate rate of about 30 responses per min. Responding was almost completely suppressed by the 20 mg/kg dose with slight responding resuming toward the end of the session. As can be seen from the foregoing example, the duration of action of a drug can be indicated by a period of disruption or alteration of the ongoing baseline performance. In this case the length of disruption and the dosage of the drug were closely correlated.

Distribution

When the drug concentration in the blood equals the concentration at the site of administration, absorption is said to be complete. This does not, however, imply that the drug has been equally distributed to all tissues of the body. The factors determining differential distribution are poorly understood, but some variables are known to be important. Drug molecules vary greatly in size, from methanol, with a molecular weight of 32, to some of the biological macromolecules with molecular weights of up to 4×10^7 (Bernal, 1958). Obviously such variability in molecular size is reflected in differential rates of distribution.

The solubility properties of the drug comprise another factor known to alter distribution. For example, thiobarbiturates are very fat soluble, and therefore

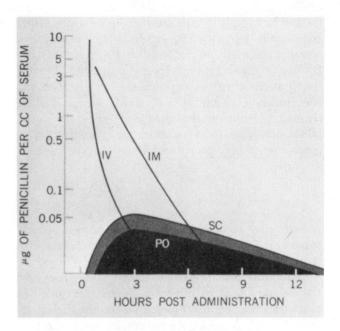

Fig. 4. Intravenous (IV), intramuscular (IM), oral (PO) and subcutaneous (SC) routes of administration and serum concentrations of penicillin. Three milligrams of penicillin G per kilogram of body weight were administered at various times to one individual, and the amounts of penicillin activity in the serum determined at time intervals. It is readily apparent that certain routes of administration greatly influence uptake and also elimination. Much drug is wasted by some routes, and more frequent administration of the drug is necessary if effective blood levels are to be maintained (From Marsh, D. F., *Outline of Fundamental Pharmacology*, 1950. Courtesy of Charles C Thomas, Publisher, Springfield, Ill.)

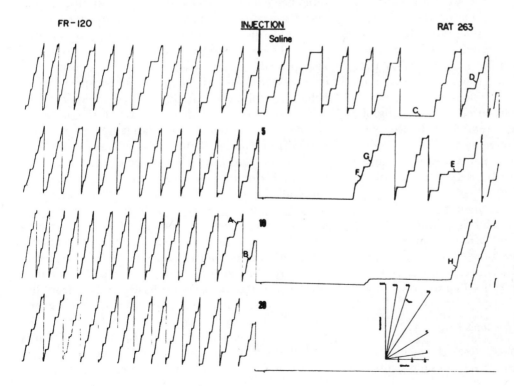

Fig. 5. Cumulative records illustrating the effects of saline, 5.0, 10.0, and 20.0 mg/kg ip of pentobarbital on food-reinforced FR 120 schedule performance. The primary effect of pentobarbital on FR performance was to exaggerate pausing, with minimal effects on running rate. (From Grove & Thompson, 1970.)

tend to be rapidly distributed in adipose tissue. Other compounds tend to have affinities for proteins of blood plasma, not on the basis of their solubility but because of their protein-binding properties. Finally, distribution to tissues depends on the presence and concentrations of the same or similar drugs in those tissues. Addition of the same drug or of its antagonists may lead to no increase in concentration in given tissues if receptor sites for that drug are already saturated.

Fate

Following absorption, a drug may undergo transformation in the body and be ultimately excreted either unchanged or as a biotransformation product. The biotransformations that a drug undergoes and the mechanism of its excretion are referred to as the *fate* of a drug. Figure 3 presented the theoretical excretion curve, revealing the assumption that the mechanisms of drug excretion are diametrically opposite to those of absorption. As a matter of fact, the routes of excretion are very seldom the simple inverse of those of absorption. It is worthwhile to consider briefly the most common routes of excretion; the kidney, the lungs, the skin, the bile duct, and the intestines.

Volatile agents, such as the anesthetic gases and alcohol, are excreted across the pulmonary membrane. We are all well aware that sodium chloride is excreted in part across the skin; however, few other compounds of significance are found on the skin surface. Organic arsenicals are among the drugs excreted across the bile duct, and certain agents like quinine, as well as some sterols, are excreted in the feces. The vast majority of drugs are excreted by the kidneys. Because of the central role of the kidneys in removing drugs from the body, proper functioning of these organs is of extreme importance in drug research. Renal damage may increase a drug's duration of action; it may even have lethal consequences at a dosage that would otherwise be well within a tolerable range.

Some drugs, such as the inhalant anesthetics, are excreted from the body in unchanged forms. Most drugs, however, undergo some chemical changes prior to excretion. The transformation of a drug with a specific biological action to an inactive form, or to a form with different effects, is called biotransformation.

Multiple Administrations of the Same Drug

In behavioral pharmacology research, where several replications of a procedure on the same animal are desirable, the investigator would much prefer minimal interaction between successive administrations of the same drug. At times, however, it is found that the dose required to produce the same effect must be increased on successive administrations. Or, when the same dose is repeated, the effect becomes smaller with each dose. When this occurs, it is said that *tolerance* has developed. Multiple administrations of the narcotic analgesics, barbiturates, and amphetamines are particularly likely to lead to the development of tolerance. Certain other chemically related drugs can, when administered in place of the original drug, produce a very similar response; at times, they can substitute for the original drug. Usually, as tolerance develops to the original drug, tolerance also develops to substitute drugs so that successively higher doses of such drugs are also required to produce the original effect. Under these conditions, it is said that *cross tolerance* has developed.

If discontinuing a drug which has been administered repeatedly and regularly precipitates a characteristic syndrome of illness (often including vomiting, diarrhea, convulsions, and even death), the animal has become *physically dependent* on the drug. If an animal reliably self-administers the drug when provided with the opportunity, the term *behavioral dependence* applies. Thus, an organism that is physically dependent may be behaviorally dependent as well, though the converse is not necessarily true. Humans who exhibit behavioral dependence without physical dependence are said to be habituated to the drug.

Another problem arises when a drug is readministered before the effects of the previous dose have disappeared. When a drug has not been entirely excreted or has not undergone complete transformation before a second dose is administered, *cumulation* results. Such factors as the presence of the necessary enzymes to carry out the transformation reaction, the normal functioning of the excretory mechanism (e.g., excretion by the kidney), or storage can affect the likelihood of cumulation. Under these conditions, the concentration of the drug in various tissues and fluid compartments progressively increases. In general, if a drug is administered repeatedly, a portion is transformed and excreted, but a certain amount remains. Cumulation rate depends on the interval between administrations and the dose. A typical cumulative effect is illustrated in Figure 6, where data from five administrations of the same dose of a drug are presented. While partial recovery occurs following each dosing, the level following the last administration is well above that seen on the first injection.

Obviously, a major consideration in gauging cu-

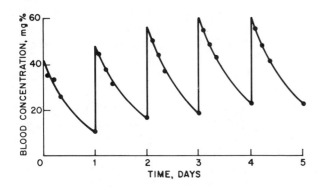

Fig. 6. The cumulation of the blood concentration of atrolactamide with time when the drug was readministered to a dog at 24-hour intervals. Note that on the fourth administration an essentially steady state has been achieved (From Historical background and general principles of drug action, by J. A. Wells. In V. A. Drill (Ed.), *Pharmacology in Medicine.* © 1958 by McGraw-Hill Book Company. Used with permission.)

mulative effects is interadministration interval. By spacing successive administrations sufficiently far apart, it is usually possible to avoid cumulation. However, the disappearance of the active compound or its metabolites does not necessarily indicate that a drug effect may still not exist. For example, the drug may cause morphological or biochemical changes in cells which may far outlast the presence of the active agent. In these cases, cumulative effects are not defined by the presence or absence of the drug but by the changes in the measured drug effect.

ANALYZING BEHAVIORAL MECHANISMS OF DRUG ACTION

Specificity of Drug Action

A fundamental problem in analyzing the ways in which drugs alter behavior is to determine the degree to which effects observed are specific to the drug and to the specific set of conditions investigated. In the following pages we will discuss some of the *minimal* conditions that must be satisfied in order to determine the specificity of drug action.

As indicated earlier, typically a small sample size will be used in analyzing the actions of drugs in operant behavioral pharmacology. The emphasis in these investigations is the reversibility of drug effects on the established behavioral baseline. In general, within-subject control procedures are used (that is, A B A designs will be employed) in which a given variable, such as a drug dose or a schedule value, will be ap-

plied and removed and repeated. This requires a high degree of reproducibility of the behavioral baseline. There are basically two approaches to the problem of the reliability of the baseline. One is the use of the A B A design in which the manipulation is repeatedly applied to the same baseline. It is sometimes difficult to re-establish the baseline once it has been shifted, such as under conditions of transition states (Sidman, 1960). In this case, another alternative is commonly used, involving multiple baselines. Two or more schedules may be conditioned under distinctive stimulus conditions which may be presented sequentially (such as in chains or multiple schedules), or concurrently (as in concurrent schedules or non-reversible options). For example, during one session a given performance can be evaluated by presenting the discriminative stimulus for that behavior (e.g., FR 40 on the right lever), while on another session a similar performance (FR 40 on the left lever) can be examined in the presence of a different stimulus to determine whether the measured effect can be replicated. Such schedules may be presented repeatedly with high reliability of performance during each schedule component. These procedures are not without their difficulties, because there may be interactions among components.

Assuming an effect of a drug is measured at a given dose of compound on a given behavioral baseline, the question then arises "Is the effect unique to that dose, or does it also occur at other doses?" Hence, as in any other area of pharmacology, it is necessary to administer at least three doses of the drug in question, typically using a logarithmic dosage regimen. A parallel question is: "Is the observed effect specific to the schedule value chosen?" Behavior maintained by reinforcement schedules which generate high response rates may be affected differently by a given drug, than schedules which generate low rates (cf. Dews, 1955a). Hence, it may be necessary to evaluate the effects of a drug at more than one schedule value. For example, Thompson, Trombley, Luke, and Lott (1970) studied effects of morphine on rats responding for food on FR 10, FR 20, and FR 40 schedules (Figure 7). Had a single schedule been studied (e.g., FR 10), it might have been concluded that in the dosage range investigated (1 to 6 mg/kg IP) morphine generates a rather flat dose-response curve. However, when a different schedule value is investigated (FR 40) a clearly inverse curvilinear function emerges. Hence, it is essential to study both a range of drug dosages and a range of schedule parameter values to obtain a complete picture of drug action.

Another useful control procedure involves experi-

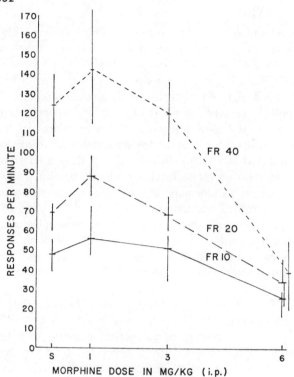

Fig. 7. Mean overall response rates on FR 10, FR 20, and FR 40 schedules treated with saline, 1.0, 3.0, and 6.0 mg/kg of morphine sulfate ip. Each mean is based on three values, and ranges are indicated by vertical lines. (From Thompson et al., 1970.)

mentally varying the rates of responding, while holding the reinforcement density constant. For example, subjects might be conditioned on a fixed-ratio schedule and the mean interreinforcement time is determined. Then the same animals would be conditioned on a multiple schedule including a variable-interval component having the same overall reinforcement density but which maintains a lower rate of responding (i.e., Mult FR VI). Under such conditions, differences might be presumed to be due to some property of the performance, such as rates of responding, rather than reinforcement density.

Yet another kind of control procedure may be necessary to evaluate whether the drug effects are specific to the particular behavioral consequence employed. For example, behavior maintained by food, water, or sexual reinforcement may not be affected in the same way by all drugs. Recent research on behavior maintained by electric shock presentation suggests that, at times, the nature of the consequence is less important than schedule considerations (Kelleher & Morse, 1968; see also chapter 7 in this volume). However, other research dealing with drug-maintained responding suggests that the generalization cannot be applied to all reinforcers (Thompson & Pickens, 1972).

Finally, it may be that drugs affect two behaviors differently because their *baseline rates differ*. For example, Dews (1958) has shown that amphetamines affect schedule-controlled performances differently, not so much because the reinforcement schedules differ *per se*, but because different schedules generate different patterns of inter-response times. In one study such a necessary control was accomplished by manipulating the baseline rate during one component of concurrent operants. Cherek and Thompson (1973) studied concurrent key pecking reinforced by access to food and by access to a target bird which could be attacked. In an initial study it was found that Δ^9 THC, the active ingredient in marijuana, had a more marked effect on the key pecking maintained by access to an attackable object. However, since the baseline rate of the two operants differed, it was necessary to complete a final manipulation in which the rate of pecking maintained by food was driven down by adding a DRL contingency to the FI food reinforced performance. Even when the rates were equated, Δ^9 THC had a much more marked effect on the operant reinforced by access to an attackable object (Figure 8).

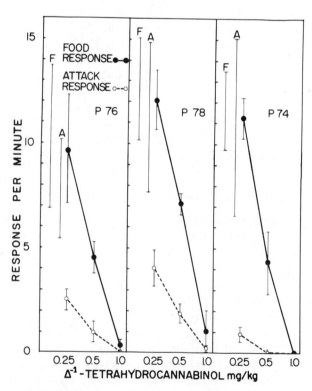

Fig. 8. Effects of Δ^1 tetrahydrocannabinol on key pecking maintained by access to food (solid) and a target bird (dashed) in three pigeons. Baseline rates of key-pecking maintained by the two reinforcers were equated prior to drug administration (From Cherek & Thompson, 1973.)

Behavioral Mechanisms By Which Drugs May Act

Arriving at an understanding of the mechanisms by which drugs modify behavior is as complex as the permutations and combinations of variables which interact at any moment in time to engender a particular performance. An approach to analyzing this quagmire of variables has been suggested elsewhere (Thompson and Schuster, 1968). The rate, pattern, and form of current operant behavior are determined by certain antecedent factors, the current stimulus conditions, and the maintaining consequences of behavior. Drugs, as independent variables, interact with any or all of these classes of factors to determine the particular behavioral outcome. A better grasp of the meaning of a particular finding in behavioral pharmacology can be had if one asks, "With which of these factors that regulate behavior has the drug interacted?" Has the drug altered the deprivation state (an antecedent variable), stimulus control (a current stimulus variable), response topography (a property of the response), or the reinforcer or schedule control (a consequent variable)? In the succeeding pages a number of studies are discussed within the foregoing framework. This is intended not to provide an exhaustive literature review, but rather an illustrated outline of research dealing with a particular class of variables.

Antecedent Variables

Among the more important antecedent variables which an organism brings to an experimental situation are its past history, and its deprivational state established by manipulations prior to the experiment. Terrace (1963a) demonstrated that pigeons were capable of acquiring a discrimination of color and the orientation of a line in an "errorless" fashion. An "error" was defined as the failure to respond to a stimulus correlated with reinforcement (an S^D) or a response to a stimulus correlated with non-reinforcement (an S^Δ). Errorless learning was established by starting discrimination training immediately after the response to S^D had been conditioned, and by progressively reducing the difference between the S^D and the S^Δ from an initial large difference to a relatively small, final difference. In a subsequent study Terrace (1963b) showed that pigeons that had learned a discrimination without errors, which appeared superficially the same as that established by the more typical method (involving the occurrence of many errors), responded in a dramatically different way to imipramine and chlorpromazine. Chlorpromazine and imipramine disrupted the pigeons' performances on a discrimination between vertical and horizontal lines only if the discrimination was learned with errors. Birds learning the discrimination in the errorless fashion exhibited no errors whatever in a dosage range from 1.0 to 17.0 mg of the two drugs.

A second class of antecedent variables involves interactions of drug effects with deprivation states. Singh and Manocha (1966) studied interactions of deprivation conditions and past reinforcement history in determining the effects of chlorpromazine. They found the effect of a given dose of chlorpromazine depended upon both the degree of deprivation and the amount of reinforcement history. That is, extensive past histories and high deprivation levels attenuated the effects of chlorpromazine. Deprivation states can be relevant wherein drugs serve as maintaining consequences as well. Meisch and Thompson (1973) studied the effects of food deprivation on lever pressing reinforced by ethanol in rats. Figure 9 shows the effect of increasing food deprivation levels on the disposition to respond for ethanol. In general, high rates of ethanol-reinforced responding were maintained as a function of increasing food deprivation, which also varied as a function of FR value. Woods, Downs, and Villarreal (1973) studied two methods of drug deprivation: Withdrawal of the drug and administration of a drug antagonist. The subjects were physically dependent rhesus monkeys who could self-administer a narcotic by pressing one lever and receive food by pressing a second lever. Both methods of inducing opiate withdrawal evoked nearly identical behavioral changes on food-reinforced responding. While food-reinforced behavior was disrupted by both drug deprivation procedures, responding on the drug lever was increased by both methods of induction. Thus, deprivation variables as antecedent procedures can be powerful in determining the actions of the drug.

As discussed earlier, on repeated administration of certain drugs, tolerance develops—that is, a higher dose of the drug is required to produce the same effect. Tetrahydrocannabinol (THC) is one such compound. McMillan and co-workers (1970, 1971) have studied the development of behavioral tolerance to THC in pigeons. The degree of past history of THC treatment can profoundly effect the degree to which the drug suppresses ratio-reinforced responding. Although a dose of 1.8 mg/kg of Δ^9 THC may be sufficient to totally suppress responding during the first 3–5 days of administration, after 30 days of administration of gradually increasing doses, pigeons' response rates following administration of 10 mg/kg may be close to normal control values.

A final class of antecedent variables involves the superimposition of a history of classical conditioning

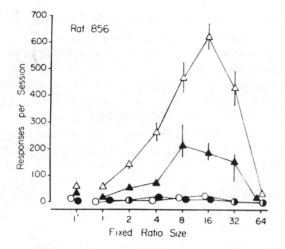

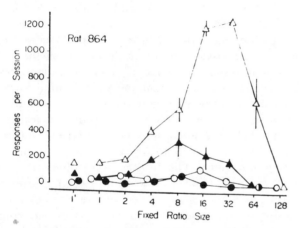

Fig. 9. Effect of FR size on responses per 6-hr session. Ordinate: responses plotted on a linear scale. Abscissa: FR size plotted on a logarithmic scale. Different scales were used on the ordinate. Open triangles: mean ethanol responses during food deprivation (n = 2); filled triangles: mean ethanol responses during food satiation (n = 3). Open circles: mean water responses during food deprivation (n = 4); filled circles: mean water responses during food satiation (n = 6). The height of the vertical lines indicates the range; absence of a vertical line at a particular point indicates that the range was within the area occupied by the symbol. The results for FR 1 on the left were obtained after completing the sequence of increasing FR values. (From Meisch & Thompson, 1973.)

on operant baselines. The widely noted placebo effect involves, at least in part, a conditioned effect due to environmental variables paired with drug administration. Pickens and Crowder (1967) studied the effects of a history of amphetamine injections on locomotor activity. After several pairings of the amphetamine injection with increased locomotor activity, the injection of saline was capable of producing a similar increase in general activity. Goldberg and Schuster (1967) studied conditioned suppression by a stimulus paired with nalorphine administration in rhesus monkeys physically dependent upon morphine. Physically dependent monkeys were first trained to press a lever for food reinforcement on an FR 10 schedule. A tone, initially neutral, was aperiodically presented five minutes before the intravenous injection of nalorphine. Nalorphine, because it is a morphine antagonist, can suddenly produce withdrawal symptoms. After several sessions, conditioned suppression of the food reinforced operant was observed during tone presentation prior to the administration of nalorphine. In a later study, Goldberg, Woods, and Schuster (1969) demonstrated increases in responding for morphine injections in physically dependent monkeys when a stimulus pair with nalorphine administration was presented. Using rhesus monkeys formerly dependent on morphine, Goldberg and Schuster (1969) demonstrated an increased sensitivity to nalorphine's operant suppressing effect as compared with control monkeys having no prior history of morphine exposure. Within the dosage range employed, nalorphine injections produced hypersensitivity in formerly dependent monkeys but not in controls. Such effects were observed to occur for as long as 60–120 days of complete abstinence from morphine, long after any possible residual effects of the drug could have persisted, and after physical dependence had disappeared.

Stimulus Variables

Environmental factors altering the stimulus control of operant behavior have been extensively studied and are described elsewhere in the present volume. The precise manner and the degree to which various classes of drugs alter or participate in stimulus control is a matter of some conjecture. That the drugs are capable of altering stimulus control is widely known. For example, LSD alters a visual stimulus discrimination in pigeons in a dose-dependent fashion (Becker, Appel, & Freedman, 1967). LSD is also known to effect the shape of a stimulus generalization gradient in rats (Dykstra and Appel, 1972). Further, the degree to which stimulus control is altered by a drug varies with the complexity of the discriminative stimulus (Dews, 1955b). However, it is one thing to show that a drug produces a dose-dependent change in the degree of stimulus control and another to describe the behavioral mechanism by which such an effect was brought about. One attempt at such an account was provided by Dykstra and Appel (1972) in which it was shown that the shape of a stimulus generalization gradient was changed after the administration of LSD. The authors noted that a dose of LSD which produces a change in the gradient did so only at relatively high rates of responding, suggesting that the change produced by the drug was more a rate-dependent effect of the drug than an effect specifically on stimulus control.

Laties and Weiss (1966) have suggested that the degree to which behavior is affected by drugs depends to a considerable degree on how much the baseline behavior is controlled by exteroceptive as opposed to interoceptive stimuli. They studied performance of pigeons on fixed-interval schedules in the presence of five one-minute discriminative stimuli (i.e., a clock condition). Their primary dependent variable was the distribution of responses over successive minutes of a clock as a function of doses of amphetamine, scopolamine, pentobarbital, chlorpromazine, and promazine. All of the drugs used produced substantial changes in the FI response distribution when the pigeons had no exteroceptive discriminative stimulus correlated with elapsed time. Providing the birds with an exteroceptive clock, however, modified the response distribution greatly and decreased sensitivity to amphetamine, scopolamine, and pentobarbital, although the sensitivity to chlorpromazine and promazine was largely unchanged. These findings suggest that the source of discriminative stimuli controlling the performance is important in determining the reaction to drugs, and further that it is relatively more important for some drugs than others. In another study (Laties, 1972), pigeons were trained on a chained and tandem FR 8 FR 1 reinforcement schedule in which eight pecks on one response key were followed by a single peck on the second key which produced access to grain. If the bird switched keys before the count of eight, the series of responses had to be started again. During one condition, no external stimulus change occurred following the eighth response (i.e., tandem condition). During the other condition a stimulus change invariably occurred following the eighth response (i.e., chain condition). The addition of the stimulus change made the subjects much more efficient in meeting the required minimum count before switching to the reinforcement key. That is, the chained schedule condition generated more efficient performance than the tandem schedule condition. Response rate, however, remained about the same. When a discriminative stimulus was not present (i.e., the tandem condition), chlorpromazine, d-amphetamine, and scopolamine led to premature switching to the reinforcement key. The addition of the external discriminative stimulus attenuated the effects of scopolamine and d-amphetamine most; chlorpromazine and promazine least.

Overton (1971) has studied the discriminative stimulus properties of an array of drugs using a T-Maze. On drug sessions animals pretreated with various behaviorally active drugs are reinforced for turning one direction in the maze, and on vehicle control days for turning the opposite direction. Certain CNS drugs, including the barbiturates and minor tranquilizers, exercise strong stimulus control, while phenothiazines such as chlorpromazine exercise rather weak stimulus control. Rats readily learn the correct turn at the choice point in a T-Maze when pretreated with a barbiturate, alcohol, or chlordiazepoxide, while requiring a relatively long period to acquire stimulus control when pretreated with a phenothiazine derivative. Taking this line of research one step further, Barry and Kubena (1972) studied discriminative stimulus characteristics of alcohol, marijuana, and atropine in rats. In their procedure rats were reinforced on a FR 5 schedule of food reinforcement for pressing one lever, while if they pressed the other lever they received painful foot shock. Under ethyl alcohol, atropine, and Δ^1 THC, rats rapidly learned to press the food lever under the appropriate drug or control condition and to avoid the lever which produced shocks. Tests for stimulus generalization were then conducted, in which rats trained under one drug condition were tested with various doses of the same or other drugs. The experimental question was "how similar are the stimulus properties of drug X to the drug used in training?" Lower doses of the drug used in training generally produce intermediate percentages of correct responding. However, when other drugs were administered, the results were more complex. Animals that had been trained under pentobarbital tended to respond correctly when tested under other depressants, such as chlordiazepoxide. Animals trained using atropine as the discriminative stimulus tended to respond correctly when receiving doses of other anticholinergic drugs such as scopolomine. The Δ^1 THC animals responded correctly only when other marijuana extracts were administered. If alcohol trained animals were administered chlorpromazine or d-amphetamine under generalization test conditions, incorrect responding tended to occur. When Δ^1 THC trained animals were administered various depressant, stimulant, or hallucinogenic drugs, incorrect or control responding tended to occur.

One of the earliest studies using an operant technique to analyze the discriminative stimulus properties of drugs was conducted by Cook, Davidson, Davis, and Kelleher (1960). Dogs, surgically prepared with intravenous catheters, were intravenously administered various doses of epinephrine, norepinephrine, or acetylcholine prior to a painful shock to the dog's limb. The dog could avoid the shock by lifting his limb during the discriminative stimulus period preceding the shock. Acetylcholine served as a highly effective discriminative stimulus, while l-epinephrine served as a relatively weak discriminative stimulus, taking approximately twice as long to establish control to a criterion of 100% correct responding.

One of the more elegant studies of discriminative control of operant behavior by a drug was conducted by Schuster and Brady (1964). In that study rhesus monkeys, also surgically prepared with an intravenous catheter, were infused with various doses of epinephrine in the presence of which lever pressing was reinforced on a fixed-ratio schedule of food presentation. When saline was injected, lever pressing had no consequence. The independent variable was the dosage of epinephrine administered, and the dependent variable was the percentage of epinephrine and saline control trials during which the subject met the response requirements for reinforcement. Figure 10 shows the acquisition curves. By one animal's 25th session, epinephrine exercised substantial stimulus control over the animal's behavior.

Harris and Balster (1971) first trained rats on multiple and mixed reinforcement schedules using exteroceptive discriminative stimuli. Subsequently, the same schedules were used in training with various drugs as discriminative stimuli instead of exteroceptive stimuli. Their findings essentially corroborated those of Overton, in that depressants such as chlordiazepoxide and ethyl alcohol were capable of establishing strong stimulus control (in this case over multiple schedule performance), whereas phenothiazine derivatives exercised little or no stimulus control. Similarly, hallucinogens such as psilocybin and LSD were very ineffective as discriminative stimuli.

CONSEQUENCE VARIABLES

Type of consequence: Positive reinforcement. The types of consequences of behavior and the schedules according to which they are presented appear to be fundamental determinants of behavior (Morse and Kelleher, 1970). Hence, one would expect that the effects of drugs would depend critically upon how the drugs interact with consequences and their schedules of presentation. Dews and Morse (1961) and Kelleher and Morse (1969) have argued the *type* of consequence is a relatively unimportant factor in determining the behavioral actions of drugs, whereas the *schedule* according to which various types of consequences are presented is of primary importance. There are several lines of evidence supporting this thesis.

Laties and Weiss (1963) studied the effects of amphetamine, chlorpromazine, and pentobarbital on the behavioral regulation of temperature. The rats, after being placed in a cold compartment, were trained to warm themselves by pressing a lever that turned on a heat lamp. Amphetamine, at a dose level that by itself did not increase the rate at which body temperature fell in the cold, increased the frequency with which the rats turned on the lamp even though the skin temperature was driven above normal. Chlorpromazine, at a dose level that accelerated heat loss in the cold, decreased the frequency with which the lamp was turned on. Pentobarbital produced only a transient depression directly correlated with base level. Behavioral thermoregulation was impaired by both amphetamine and chlorpromazine, the former by increasing and the latter by decreasing the optimal frequency of bursts of heat.

Waller and Waller (1962) studied the effects of chlorpromazine on behavior maintained by food reinforcement and shock avoidance in a multiple reinforcement schedule. There was no evidence that chlorpromazine had a differential effect on avoidance behavior or on food-reinforced behavior as a function of the type of reinforcer. At low doses, rates of responding on the food reinforcement component increased slightly whereas rates on the avoidance com-

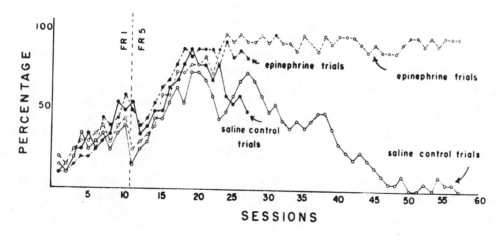

Fig. 10. Percentage of epinephrine and saline control trials in which the subject met the response requirements for reinforcement. (From Schuster & Brady, 1964.)

ponent remained relatively unchanged. At higher doses both components showed an approximately equal depression of responding. Kelleher and Morse (1964) studied the effects of d-amphetamine sulfate and chlorpromazine on rates of responding under multiple FI FR food and shock-escape schedules. Three squirrel monkeys were studied at each multiple schedule. Each drug was given IM immediately before the beginning of the 2½ hour session. Both amphetamine and chlorpromazine had similar effects on behavior maintained on a given schedule regardless of the type of consequence, i.e., whether it was shock avoidance or food reinforced. Similarly Cook and Catania (1964) studied the effects of drugs on food-reinforced and escape behaviors. They studied the performance of squirrel monkeys under FI 10-min schedules of food reinforcement or electric shock termination. In one group of food-deprived monkeys, the first key-pressing response after 10 min led immediately to food presentation. In the second group of monkeys, an intermittent electric shock of low intensity was continuously delivered to the grid floor of the experimental chamber. The first response after 10 min terminated the electric shock. These schedules of food presentation and shock termination are formally similar, and both engendered patterns of responding characteristic of FI schedules. With both types of reinforcers, chlordiazepoxide, meprobamate, imipramine, and chlorpromazine had similar effects. All of the foregoing data would seem to argue that the precise consequence of the behavior may be less important in determining the drug effect.

The foregoing remarks have to be modified under certain circumstances. For example, animals physically dependent on morphine derivatives and treated with antagonist drugs such as nalorphine or naloxone respond differently from animals that are not physically dependent. Naloxone and nalorphine have entirely different effects on morphine-reinforced responding in animals than on food-maintained responding. Similarly, Jacobs (1958) studied the effect of exogenous insulin on the choice between a 10% glucose solution and a 35% solution. The 10% solution was typically preferred by untreated rats. However, when insulin was administered prior to choice testing, the preference shifted to the 35% solution. That is, the more concentrated glucose solution was shown to be a more powerful reinforcer depending upon the insulin injection. Under such circumstances the type of consequence *is* of critical importance.

Another class of reinforcers which has received particular attention in behavioral pharmacology has been drugs themselves. Spragg (1940) and Masserman and Yum (1946), Headlee, Coppock, and Nichols (1955), and Beach (1957) were among the first to present experimental evidence that drugs could serve as reinforcers. These early studies set the stage for later experiments demonstrating more conclusively the reinforcing properties of an array of compounds. This literature has been reviewed recently, and the array of drugs that serves as reinforcing consequences is approximately the same as those that are associated with drug dependence in man (Schuster and Thompson, 1969; Thompson and Pickens, 1969; 1970). Among the drugs that have been shown to be self-administered are the narcotic analgesics, barbiturates, certain central nervous system stimulants such as amphetamine, cocaine, and cannabis, and some hallucinogens.

The development which was of critical importance in fostering research on drug reinforcement was development of the technology necessary to permit chronic intravenous injections of drug solutions in unrestrained or partially restrained animals (Pickens & Thompson, 1975; Schuster & Thompson, 1969). The intravenous route is especially important because it minimizes the delay of reinforcement between the occurrence of the operant and the onset of drug effect.

The fact that drugs serve as reinforcers for infrahuman subjects may be viewed by some to be an interesting, if somewhat curious, finding. However, the skeptical reader may ask why the reinforcing properties of drugs are of any general interest to those in the field of operant conditioning. There are three reasons, two practical and one theoretical. First, the basic processes which are involved in drug reinforcement in infrahuman subjects may be functionally comparable to those in humans who use and abuse drugs. If so, our approach to the problems associated with human drug dependence changes dramatically. Nearly all drugs which are commonly abused by humans are self-administered and serve as effective reinforcers for infrahuman subjects (Schuster and Thompson, 1969; Thompson and Pickens, 1969). This suggests that the principles and knowledge concerning the control of operant behavior by other reinforcers can now be brought to bear in the human situation, and so lead to a better understanding of the controlling variables of drug-maintained behavior in man.

A second and related reason why drug reinforcement is an interesting phenomenon is the possibility that the infrahuman drug self-administration laboratory may serve as a testing ground for future abuse potential of drugs introduced for human therapeutic purposes. As indicated above, thus far, all drugs which have been tested in infrahuman laboratory and which are actively self-administered by infrahuman subjects (e.g., rats and/or monkeys) are also known to be commonly abused by man. In the years to come, as new compounds are manufactured and about to be introduced into the clinic, testing in infrahuman drug self-administration laboratories may prove to be useful in predicting which compounds have the highest abuse potential and should be subject to special regulation.

A third reason for being interested in the drug reinforcement phenomena has to do with understanding basic mechanisms controlling behavior. Drugs as reinforcers have certain unusual, if not unique properties, which permit them to be used to study reinforcement phenomena difficult to study using other reinforcers. It is easy to obtain infrahuman subjects with no previous experience of drug reinforcers, so that interpretation of effects is not complicated by an unknown past history. In addition, infrahuman drug self-administration provides us with a way of studying mechanisms controlling behavior in the laboratory, including biochemical and physiological mechanisms, as well as an array of environmental variables, including reinforcement contingencies, stimulus control, and other classes of variables discussed throughout the present volume.

When research on drug self-administration by infrahuman subjects was first initiated, the main questions that were asked dealt with the types of drugs that served as reinforcers. It is now clear that it is the rule rather than the exception that drugs serve as powerful primary reinforcers for most infrahuman subjects. Now the questions that must be answered include the following: (1) Under what conditions do various classes of compounds serve as reinforcers and gain the greatest control over behavior? (2) To what extent do drug reinforcers have the same properties as other reinforcers? For example, do drugs lead to the establishment of schedule control in much the same fashion as other reinforcers (Thompson and Pickens, 1969)? To what extent do manipulations of reinforcement magnitude yield effects similar to the magnitude of other reinforcers such as food, water, or brain stimulation? Do histories of intermittent reinforcement or reinforcement with certain types of drugs affect the resistence to extinction? Similarly, do all drugs, controlling for the number of reinforcements, generate the same degree of resistance to extinction? What is the role of deprivation conditions in determining the control of behavior by various classes of drug reinforcers (e.g., those which produce physical dependence such as morphine, as contrasted with those which do not produce physical dependence such as cocaine)? To what degree are behaviors maintained by drug reinforcement subject to stimulus control in the same way as behaviors maintained by other reinforcers? Finally, what is the role of conditioned reinforcement in the overall control of drug-maintained responding? Once answers can be provided for the foregoing questions, it may be possible to begin to alter the degree to which drugs as reinforcers control behavior. In other words, solutions to problems of drug dependence may depend, to a significant degree, upon an understanding of the basic mechanisms by which drug reinforcement operates.

Punished Responding. Morse (1964) studied the effects of amobarbital and chlorpromazine on punished behavior of pigeons. Key pecking which was maintained by a variable-interval schedule of food reinforcement was also punished by brief electric shocks. Under this simultaneous food reinforcement and shock punishment schedule, responding was depressed to a low and fairly uniform rate that was inversely related to punishment intensity. Morse found that amobarbital partially restored responding suppressed by punishment, while chlorpromazine had no tendency to attenuate the suppressing effects of punishment. Other investigators using a variety of species, including the rat and monkey, have shown similar effects—namely that barbiturates and minor tranquilizers generally decrease the suppressing effects of punishment while amphetamines, morphine, chlorpromazine, and trifluoperazine usually do not attenuate the suppressing effects of punishing shock (Geller and Seifter, 1960, 1962; Kelleher and Morse, 1964, 1968; Morse, 1964; Wuttke and Kelleher, 1970). McMillan (1973) attempted to discover the mechanism by which various drugs attenuate the effects of punishment. The effects of a variety of compounds on key pecking responses punished by electric shock in a multiple FI 5 FI 5 punishment schedule were investigated using pigeons. Most of the drugs studied increased low rates of both punished and unpunished responses, while increasing higher rates or decreasing them. However, low rates of punished responding were sometimes increased more by pentobarbital, diazepam, and chlordiazepoxide than were matched rates of unpunished responding. In contrast d-amphetamine and chlorpromazine usually increased low rates of unpunished responding more than matched rates of punished responding. Thus, the effects of drugs on punished responding appeared to depend upon the control rate of punished responding; however, the rate-dependent effect of drugs on punished responding is not always the same as for unpunished responding.

A series of experiments conducted by Morse and Kelleher (1970) and McKearney (1972) have cast considerable doubt upon what has commonly been termed a "motivational" interpretation of the effects of drugs on operant behavior. In these experiments, squirrel monkeys were trained on schedules of electric shock presentation. Monkeys exposed to various reinforcement histories (typically unsignaled shock avoidance, but sometimes shock elicitation or variable-interval food-reinforced responding) were exposed to response-contingent painful electric shock. Under these conditions, after sufficient exposure to the schedule, lever-pressing performance stabilized and typical fixed-interval performance emerged. That is, a shock which under other certain circumstances would serve as an effective punisher appears to be maintaining behavior. Morse and Kelleher (1970) have explored the implications of schedules of shock presentation for a general understanding of the concept of reinforcement and reinforcement schedules. It has generally been found that drugs have effects on responding maintained by schedules of electric shock presentation that are indistinguishable from those on schedules of food-reinforced responding or water-maintained responding. This striking result was not only unexpected but is obviously incompatible with any simple notion one might have about "tranquilizing" or "anxiety reducing" effects of drugs as being the primary basis for determining their behavioral actions. One would assume that the motivational state associated with a schedule of shock presentation would not be at all like that under a schedule of food or water presentation.

SCHEDULE CONSIDERATIONS

The last class of variables which will be considered in the present context concerns the schedules according to which response consequences are presented. Dews (1955a) studied differential sensitivity to pentobarbital of key-pecking performance by pigeons using fixed-interval and fixed-ratio reinforcement schedules. Dews found that a dosage of pentobarbital which had a rate increasing effect on fixed-ratio 50 performance produced a markedly rate reducing effect on FI performance. Although Dews employed either an FI or an FR schedule throughout an entire session, other investigators have used multiple schedules, in which FI and FR components occurred randomly throughout each session (Morse and Herrnstein, 1956). With a multiple schedule the same subject can be studied under drug conditions in which responding is maintained by the same reinforcer but based upon different reinforcement schedules within a single session. Thus, differential effects of a given drug on these alternating patterns of responding can hardly be attributed to changes related to the reinforcer, but rather must be interpreted in terms of the reinforcement schedules.

In another study, Dews (1958) demonstrated schedule-dependent effects using methamphetamine. The number of responses made by pigeons in a fixed period of time was greatly increased by methamphetamine when the birds were conditioned using FI 15-min and FR 900 schedules. However, the rates were only slightly increased when the birds were conditioned using other schedules (VI 1-min and FR 50). The fact that the effect of drugs depends critically on the type of schedule and the schedule parameter is now widely recognized. For a number of years it was thought that the schedule *per se* was a fundamental determinant of the behavioral actions of drugs. However, Dews (1958) suggested that perhaps the mechanism by which schedule-dependent drug effects were brought about concerned the number and length of inter-response times generated by a given schedule. That is, schedules which generate short inter-response times, such as fixed-ratio schedules, will lead to rate decrements following amphetamine administration, while schedules which engender long inter-response times will tend to be associated with rate increases following amphetamine administration. This notion, which has come to be called the "rate dependency hypothesis," has considerable support involving an array of drugs. Kelleher and Morse (1969) have summarized the findings pertaining to rate dependent drug effects as follows: "The net effect of amphetamines on the average rate of responding under a schedule can be analyzed in terms of effects of rates of responding in different temporal periods of the schedule. . . . Whether amphetamine increases or decreases responding depends upon the pre-drug rate of responding as well as the dose. Evidence . . . indicates that pre-drug rates of one response or more per second are only decreased by increasing doses of amphetamine. Pre-drug rates of less than one response per second increased to a maximum and then decreased after increasing doses of amphetamine" (Kelleher and Morse, 1969). Rate dependent drug effects have been reported for the amphetamines, barbiturates, minor tranquilizers such as meprobamate and chlordiazepoxide and morphine (Kelleher, Fry, Deegan, & Cook, 1961; Richelle, Xhenseval, Fontaine, & Thone, 1962; Smith, 1964; Thompson, et al., 1970).

Some of the more convincing research done dealing with the rate dependency hypothesis involves detailed examination of performance within a given simple fixed-interval schedule. Smith (1964) studied the effects of d-amphetamine (.01–10.0 mg/kg IM) on a FI 5-min performance by pigeons. Specifically, Smith studied the effects on response rate during the *first* and *last minute* of each FI 5-min component of the schedule. He found that d-amphetamine markedly increased the low rates of responding characteristic of the first minute of the schedule and decreased the high rates of responding characteristic of the fifth minute of the schedule. At a dose of 3 mg/kg the maximum overall rate increase was observed. The rate of responding in the first minute was significantly increased and was significantly lower during the last minute. A dose of 10 mg/kg decreased overall response rates; however, this dose produced a greater increase in rate in the first minute than did the 3 mg/kg dose, but also produced a more marked decrement in rate during the last minute. In short, the change in overall responding produced by d-amphetamine was the net result of its rate increasing effects early in the interval and its rate decreasing effect during the latter portion of the fixed interval.

Although the rate dependency hypothesis appears to apply to a considerable range of schedule-controlled phenomena, there are several noteworthy exceptions. Responding that is maintained at a relatively low rate under punishment conditions does not seem to follow the rate dependent effect to the same degree as responding which is not under the control of punishment. Responding that is punished and therefore maintained at a low rate is often further decreased by amphetamine (Geller and Seifter, 1960). The rate dependency hypothesis would predict an increase in these low response rates. Under conditions in which the responding has not previously occurred or has no programmed consequence, amphetamine may have little tendency to enhance responding. Verhave (1958) studied bar pressing by untrained rats during 12 daily one-hour sessions in which responding had no programmed consequence. During the first session, all rats responded and the mean number of responses was 15.7. Over successive sessions, the mean number of responses showed an orderly decrement, such that by the seventh session the mean response rate was only .8 responses per hour, and three of the six rats did not respond at all. Methamphetamine (2 mg/kg S.C.) was administered before the eighth session. The rate dependency hypothesis would predict increases in these low response rates. However, the mean response rate remained at .8 responses per hour and four of the six subjects did not respond at all. Finally, Dews (1955b) studied the effects of methamphetamine on an animal which received extensive training on a simple discrimination, and found that methamphetamine in the dosage range .1 to 3 mg/kg IM had no rate increasing effect on responding in the presence of visual stimulus in which key pecking had no programmed consequence.

Thus, while the rate dependency hypothesis appears to apply to a wide array of experimental findings, there are certain situations in which it does not hold. The fact that rate dependency does occur under a number of circumstances, does not necessarily indicate the mechanism by which the rate dependency phenomenon is engendered. For example, amphetamine may attenuate or in some way alter the degree of stimulus control (Dews, 1955b; Laties and Weiss, 1966). In a related study Hearst (1964) has examined the effects of d-amphetamine on avoidance responses in monkeys. Hearst found that amphetamine flattened the generalization gradient, once again suggesting an alteration in stimulus control. Hill (1970) has presented data suggesting that one of the mechanisms by which amphetamines altered behavior is by changing reinforcing properties of stimuli paired with unconditioned reinforcement. In these investigations Hill has presented evidence suggesting that amphetamine increases the conditioned reinforcing properties of such stimulus events.

TRADITIONAL PROBLEMS FORMULATED WITHIN AN OPERANT FRAMEWORK

Acquisition and Extinction—Learning

In the introduction to this chapter it was suggested that early research dealing with drugs and behavior was sometimes misguided. Investigations designed to deal with drug effects on such phenomena as learning, motivation (e.g., fear, anger, hunger, etc.), or perception were often formulated so that no matter what the experimental outcome, it would be impossible to determine the mechanisms involved. The development of behavioral pharmacology over the past decade has begun to make it more profitable to ask experimental questions pertaining to these very complex issues. For example, when one is concerned with the effects of drugs on learning, as Dews has pointed out (1970), one is interested in more than a trivial change of behavior of a student in a classroom, such as the difference between being awake and sleeping during a learning task. Instead, operant behavioral pharmacology has focused attention on questions such as "In what way do various drugs effect the transition from one steady state to another?"

As an example of an operant approach to the study of drug effects on "learning," Stolerman (1971) studied the acquisition of lever pressing by rats on a continuous reinforcement schedule under saline, chlorpromazine, and chlordiazepoxide. He found that while both chlorpromazine and chlordiazepoxide reduced the rate of acquisition of the lever pressing response, there were significant differences both in the degree of the reduction and the mechanism underlying the differences. Heise and Lilie (1970) studied the effects of scopolamine, atropine, and d-amphetamine on elimination of responding on nonreinforced trials in a discrete-trial situation. Under one set of conditions, an exteroceptive stimulus indicated periods when responses would go unreinforced (i.e., S^Δ) while under other conditions there was no external S^Δ. Scopolamine impaired performance (that is, reduced the percentage of trial responses that were reinforced) to about the same extent when an external stimulus indicated a non-reinforcement as when the stimulus was absent. D-amphetamine, on the other hand, impaired performance only when there was no exteroceptive S^Δ. Barry and Kubena (1971) studied the effects of THC on acquisition of shock avoidance by rats. They found that acquisition of an avoidance response was improved when performed under the acute effects of high daily doses of THC beginning at an early stage of training. Facilitation of the acquisition of avoidance has also been found with various other drugs which, in common with THC, have a predominantly behavioral depressant effect, but impair well-established avoidance responses only at very high doses (Barry and Buckley, 1966). Meisch (1972) studied the development of ethanol as a reinforcer for rats, describing a procedure for establishing rapid acquisition of ethanol-controlled behavior. It has been shown previously that rats will self-administer ethanol solutions when they are substituted for water in a schedule-induced polydipsia procedure (Meisch & Thompson, 1971). In Meisch's experiment, sessions were run using a 4-hour polydipsia period preceded by a 2-hour period during which concurrent food reinforcement was not available. Responding for water, or for ethanol on experimental days, could occur at any time during the 6-hour session. Little or no responding occurred for water during the first 2-hour component, while high rates of water-reinforced responding were obtained during the subsequent 4-hour period. Following establishment of this pattern of water-reinforced responding, an 8% ethanol solution was presented on days alternating with water control days. Using the pattern of water responding as a baseline, Meisch was able to show the development of ethanol as a reinforcer by comparing the rate of ethanol responding during the first 2-hour component with the rate of water responding. Using this procedure it was possible to establish ethanol as an effective reinforcer with five exposures to the drug solution.

Griffiths and Thompson (1973, 1974) studied the effects of pentobarbital on the elimination of food-reinforced fixed-ratio responding by rats during extinction. In a series of studies, it was demonstrated that the administration of immobilizing doses of pentobarbital on the first day of extinction markedly reduces the overall number of responses to extinction. In a number of control procedures it was shown that it did not matter whether a series of pentobarbital doses was administered which decreased abruptly or very gradually, but rather merely whether the rate of responding was markedly suppressed during the first part of the first session of extinction. Figure 11 shows responses in extinction by animals treated with

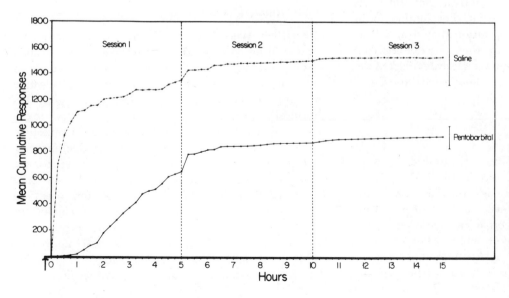

Fig. 11. Effects of 20 mg/kg i.p. pentobarbital on responding during extinction following matched FR 20 food reinforcement history (rats). Pentobarbital was administered at the arrow prior to extinction session, with no further drug administrations. Vertical bars at the right side of each curve indicate range of variability for each group (Griffiths & Thompson, 1973.)

pentobarbital prior to the beginning of a 5-hour extinction session. As can be seen, there was a very substantial difference in total responding to extinction as a function of a high immobilizing dose of pentobarbital during the first portion of the extinction session.

The foregoing studies indicate that it is possible to study phenomena falling within the rubric of "learning" but expressed in terms of concepts understandable within an operational experimental analysis of behavior. Transition states, such as acquisition and extinction or performance shift from one schedule to another, are subject to analysis within the framework of an experimental analysis of behavior.

Motivational Factors

Motivational variables have long been a major focus of many investigators in psychopharmacology. Psychiatrists and other practitioners working in psychopharmacology are interested in reducing anxiety, aggression, altering sex drives, and so forth. Laboratory investigators had hoped to find drugs which would selectively alter hunger or thirst. Within the framework of an experimental analysis of the behavioral actions of drugs, such phenomena are profitably approached by manipulating the type of consequences controlling behavior. Behavior reinforced by access to a target which can be attacked (Cherek, Thompson, & Heistad, 1973; Hutchinson, Azrin, & Hunt, 1968) provides a mechanism for studying the effects of drugs on aggressive behavior. Similarly, drugs' effects on food reinforced responding, on responding maintained by water, and responding to avoid painful shocks, are methods by which one can begin to understand the degree to which drugs have any selective effects on these motivational states. As indicated in our earlier discussion, considerable doubt has been cast upon the proposition that drug effects are primarily determined by the consequence controlling behavior, but are to a far greater degree dependent on the way in which those events are scheduled to be presented or avoided.

Sensation and Perception

A third major category of investigations concerning drug effects pertains to the way in which drugs alter perception or sensation. Drugs such as the hallucinogens, depressants, and even to some degree stimulants, are said to alter an organism's perception. An effort to understand the way in which drugs alter perception can be formulated, to a considerable degree, in terms of stimulus control. In an earlier section stimulus control was discussed with reference to drug effects. As can be seen, the locus of analysis is not within the central nervous system or the mind, but is expressed in terms of covariation between certain external stimulus events and systematic changes in behavior.

FUTURE OF BEHAVIORAL PHARMACOLOGY

The future of behavioral pharmacology appears to lie in two primary directions.

A Fine-Grained Laboratory Analysis of Behavioral Mechanisms of Drug Actions

Weiss (1970) and Weiss and Gott (1972) have provided a micro-analysis of drug effects on fixed-ratio performance and the temporal structure of behavior. Weiss and Gott found that amphetamine and imipramine shortened all inter-response times within a FR 30 reinforcement schedule while pentobarbital lengthened them. The effects observed were related to what Weiss and Gott called "the relatively unitary character of fixed-ratio performance and its inherent cohesiveness." Plots of the incidence of inter-response time greater than one second suggest that amphetamine and imipramine alter fixed-ratio cohesiveness whereas pentobarbital enhances it (i.e., either the ratio performance consisted of extremely short and extremely long inter-response times, or was totally disrupted at very high doses).

Applied Implications of Behavioral Pharmacology

Behavioral Toxicology

In 1969, Weiss and Laties wrote the first major review dealing with behavioral toxicology. They stated, "Many studies of the behavioral effects of drugs can be conceived of as attempts to determine selective toxicity in the context of a therapeutic aim. Behavioral toxicology is the study of the selective toxicity as the direct aim." (p. 320) A number of investigations have attested to the sensitivity of operant procedures in assessing behavioral actions of toxins. Armstrong, Leach, Belluscio, Maynard, Hodge, and Scott (1963) studied the effects of mercury vapor on performance on a multiple reinforcement schedule in pigeons, and found it was possible to produce reversible changes in the behavioral baseline before they could detect any overt pathology or gross behavioral disruption. Beard and Wertheim (1967) studied the effects of carbon monoxide on temporal discrimination in human subjects. They were able to detect the effect of relatively low concentrations of carbon monoxide (50 parts/million over a 90-min exposure). They also studied the effect of low concentrations of carbon monoxide on responding during a spaced reinforcement schedule in rats. The amount of carbon monoxide in the atmosphere necessary to produce a given change in performance was a function of the pause between the responses demanded of the schedule. That is, when a 30-sec pause was required, about 10 min of exposure to 100 parts/million was enough to diminish response rate more than two standard deviations below the control. With a 10-sec pause required, about 40 min of exposure was necessary to produce a comparable decrement in performance.

Drug Abuse

Another area of behavioral pharmacology with significant implications for applied matters is drug abuse. Thompson and Schuster (1968), Schuster and Thompson (1969), and Thompson and Pickens (1969) have provided a conceptual framework within which to better understand human drug dependence. That drugs serve as powerful reinforcers is now widely accepted, and efforts to understand and modify human drug dependence are emerging based on an operant interpretation. Much of the published research has dealt with alcoholism although some workers have begun to deal with problems of modifying the use of opiate compounds as well. Mello and Mendelson (1970) have studied drinking patterns during work-contingent and non-contingent alcohol acquisition in human alcoholics. Bigelow and co-workers (1972) investigated factors influencing alcohol consumption by chronic alcoholics. Bigelow, Cohen, Liebson, and Faillace (1972) studied establishment of controlled drinking by alcoholics. Volunteer chronic alcoholics were given access to substantial quantities of alcohol in situations where they earned the opportunity to participate in an enriched ward environment contingent on controlled drinking. The subjects overwhelmingly chose to drink moderately. In another study, Bigelow and Liebson (1972) examined response-cost factors controlling alcoholic drinking. Once again the subjects were given access to alcohol under experimental conditions. When a high ratio requirement was established for access to alcohol, alcohol drinking dropped to near zero. In another manipulation, when the number of tokens required to purchase drinks was markedly increased, if the subject drank more than two drinks per hour, a great reduction in alcohol consumption occurred. Pickens, Bigelow, and Griffiths (1973) studied alcohol consumption in a chronic alcoholic under controlled ward conditions. They studied the effects of a time-out contingency and the establishment of stimulus control on drinking by a chronic alcoholic over a one-year period. Using these procedures, it was possible to reduce the amount of alcohol consumed from 1.5 ounces per minute to approximately .2 to .3 ounces per minute.

One of the more impressive applied outgrowths of an operant interpretation of drug dependence has been Hunt and Azrin's (1972) work with chronic alcoholics in an outpatient setting. Using a combination of positive reinforcement for non-drug related behavior and time-out from positive reinforcement contingent on drinking, they have been able to establish extensive control over alcohol consumption by chronic alcoholics. In addition, the patients with whom they worked maintained a high degree of employment and maintained something approximating a normal home life following treatment. Liebson, Bigelow, and Flamer (1973) have used methadone as a reinforcer for consuming disulfuram, in combined alcoholics and heroin addicts. Disulfuram blocks alcohol metabolism and leads to vomiting following consumption of alcohol. In their technique, alcoholics were reinforced with methadone contingent on consuming their disulfuram. Boudin (1972) has developed a large scale program based on a system of positive reinforcement for participating in treatment programs involving a variety of contingency management control techniques for violation of the system.

Pre-Clinical and Clinical Extensions of Laboratory Findings

Behavioral pharmacology has now reached the point where it is meaningful to approach some questions concerning clinical therapeutic effects of behaviorally active drugs. Physicians have often used behaviorally active drugs based on the assumption that a drug functions independently of the environmental conditions under which the drug is administered.

In recent years interest has grown in the use of operant techniques in conjunction with drug therapy in various applied settings. Lindsley (1962) first demonstrated the applicability of operant conditioning techniques in the measurement of drug-behavior interactions in an applied human setting. Subsequently Hollis (1968) demonstrated a technique for measurement of differential behavioral effects of

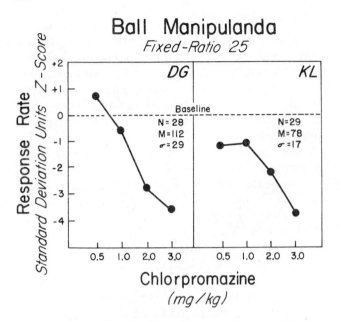

Fig. 12. Effects of chlorpromazine on rate of ball-manipulanda responding under fixed-ratio 25 schedule of positive reinforcement. Curves represent standard deviation units of change in response rate from control to drug sessions for subjects DG and KL. The dashed line at 0 units indicates the mean control level. (From Hollis & St. Omer, 1972.)

chlorpromazine in human retardates. More recently Hollis and St. Omer (1972) studied the effects of chlorpromazine (0.5–3.0 mg/kg) on operant responding by retardates in a controlled experimental situation. Figure 12 shows the effect of chlorpromazine on the rate of FR 25 responding for M & M reinforcement by two retarded subjects. The response rates are expressed as deviations in standard scores from the baseline rates. The data demonstrate a direct relation between the dose of chlorpromazine administered and the amount of response rate suppression of fixed-ratio performance. In another manipulation, Hollis and St. Omer studied the effects of chlorpromazine on response rates and response latency using a FR 400 schedule of positive reinforcement in two additional subjects. Figure 13 shows dose response curves of FR 400 performance across the dosage range of .25 to 1.0 mg/kg. As can be seen, once again there is an orderly relation between dose of chlorpromazine administered and suppression of operant responding, a finding comparable to those obtained with infrahuman subjects.

Strong, Sulzbacher, and Kirkpatrick (1973) studied the effects of diphenhydramine on facial grimacing in a classroom by a five-year-old boy, deficient in language and learning ability. Figure 14 shows the relationship between several manipulations of consequences following occurrence of grimacing in Experiment 1. In Experiment 2, data are presented from a baseline placebo and 12.5 and 25 mg doses of diphenhydramine. Both response-contingent consequences (loss of candy and self-recording) suppressed grimacing to near zero rate per minute, whereas diphenhydramine, which also had a rate reducing effect, did so to a considerably lesser degree. In another experiment, Sulzbacher (1972) studied the effects of d-amphetamine and methylphenidate on classroom behavior of children with learning difficulties. Figure 15 shows the effects of placebo, 5, and 10 mg of d-amphetamine on talking out in class and out-of-seat behavior during class. Figure 16 shows the effect of d-amphetamine on academic performance. Amphetamine had a marked rate-reducing effect on the inappropriate behavior, while producing a slight disruptive effect on academic responding. Methylphenidate, on the other hand, had a much less striking effect on talking out in class, a slight rate increasing effect on writing performance in the classroom, but little or no effect on arithmetic and reading behavior.

Recently attention has been given to the interaction between reinforcement contingencies and drug treatment in purely applied settings, such as in state mental hospitals. Paul, Tobias, and Holly (1972) studied the effects of a variety of behaviorally active drugs on psychotic behavior of chronic mental hos-

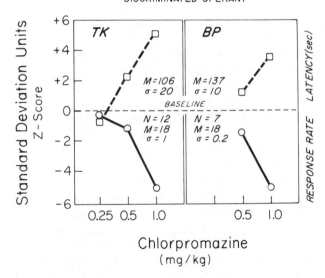

Fig. 13. Effects of chlorpromazine on cumulated latency and rate of left-leg responding under conditions of a simple discriminated operant on a fixed-ratio 400 schedule of positive reinforcement for subjects TK and BP. Curves represent standard deviation units of change in response latency and rate from control to drug sessions. The dashed line at 0 units indicates the mean control level. (From Hollis & St. Omer, 1972.)

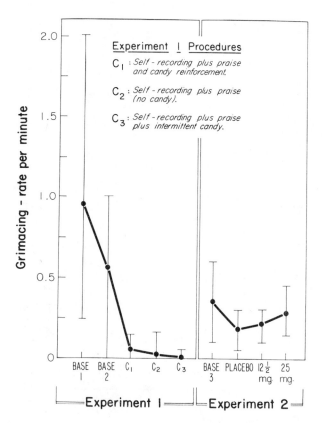

Fig. 14. Rate per minute of facial grimaces. Experiment 1 shows the effects of three different reinforcement contingencies. Experiment 2 compares the effects of two dosage levels of diphenhydramine with baseline (no drug) and placebo conditions. These data on drug effect were gathered about 2 hours after the medication was administered. (From Strong et al., 1974.)

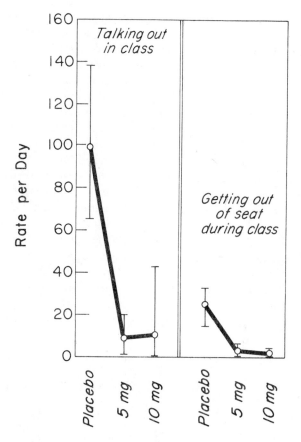

Fig. 15. Effects of d-amphetamine on Ralph's classroom behavior. The heavy lines connect the means of each condition. The light bars around each mean indicate the range of daily rates. (From Sulzbacher, 1972.)

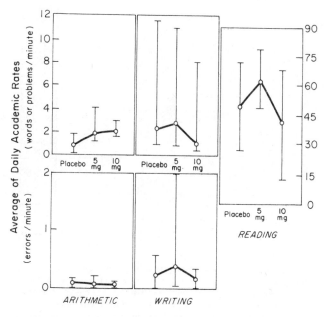

Fig. 16. Effects of d-amphetamine on the academic performance of Ralph. (From Sulzbacher, 1972.)

pital patients under conditions of milieu therapy and behavior modification in a state mental hospital. Although behavioral contingencies seem to have a significant effect in improving the behavior of psychotic patients, none of the drug therapies in any of the dosages administered had any statistically significant effect in improving behavior. McConahey and Thompson (1972) and McConahey (1973) studied the effect of chlorpromazine on the behavior of twenty-two moderately to severely retarded women in a state hospital. A multiple schedule was used in which token reinforcement was presented contingent upon adaptive behavior during a portion of the day, while during a comparable period of the day no programmed consequences were arranged. During alternate 28-day periods the residents received, in a randomly assigned order, either chlorpromazine or an identically appearing placebo. No overall significant differences were found between drug and placebo treatments in any of 25 behaviors recorded on all 22 patients over time. On the other hand, very large statistically significant differences were obtained on 22 of the 25 behavioral measures across all residents, comparing the reinforcement periods and the non-reinforcement periods of the multiple schedule. Figure 17 shows the total frequency of observations during which residents were sitting at a table working constructively at a learning task during periods when they were being reinforced (contingencies) as opposed to periods when they were not being reinforced (no contingencies), while being treated with placebo or chlorpromazine. There were no apparent differences due to the chlorpromazine and placebo treatments in the tendency to work constructively at a task, while there were very large differences between periods in which patients were reinforced with tokens as compared with those when they were not. Figure 18 shows similar data with the total frequency of residents raising their voices, a behavior frequently occurring preceding physical aggression. As can be seen there were no appreciable differences between the frequency of raising the voice during placebo and chlorpromazine treatments either with

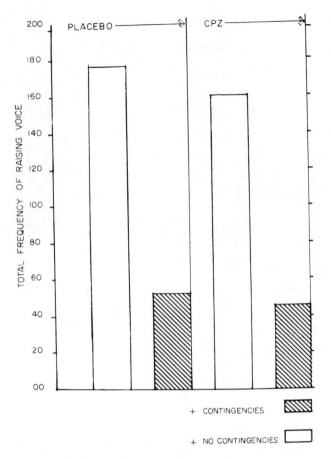

Fig. 18. Total frequency of instances of raising voice (a behavior frequently preceding physical aggressive acts) under the same four treatment conditions as indicated in Figure 17. (From McConahey 1972.)

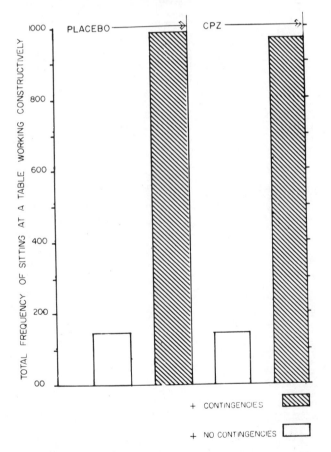

Fig. 17. Total frequency of instances of constructively working at a task (seated) by 22 retarded women during daily 45 minute periods under four treatment conditions: Token reinforcement (contingencies) plus placebo; token reinforcement plus chlorpromazine (CPZ); no programmed contingencies plus placebo; no programmed contingencies plus chlorpromazine. (From McConahey, 1972.)

or without reinforcement. However, when reinforcement occurred, there was an enormous reduction in the amount of raising voices both during placebo and chlorpromazine treatments.

Data from the foregoing studies suggest that it is possible to analyze some of the interactions between reinforcement conditions and drug-treatment conditions in a variety of applied settings involving disturbed children, children with learning difficulties, retardates and hospitalized psychiatric patients. The introduction of behaviorally active medication in a variety of applied settings must be predicated upon more careful attention to the interactions between drug treatment and the prevailing environmental contingencies.

REFERENCES

Armstrong, R. P., Leach, L. J., Belluscio, P. R., Maynard, E. A., Hodge, H. C., & Scott, J. K. Behavioral changes in the pigeon following inhalation of mercury vapor.

American Industrial Hygiene Association Journal, 1963, *24,* 366–375.

BARRY, H. & BUCKLEY, J. P. Drug effects on animal performance and the stress syndrome. *Journal of Pharmaceutical Sciences,* 1966, *55,* 1159–1183.

BARRY, H. & KUBENA, R. K. Discriminative stimulus characteristics of alcohol, marihuana and atropine. In J. Singh, L. Miller, & H. Lal (Eds.), *Drug Addiction: Experimental Pharmacology.* North Miami, Florida: Symposia Specialists, 1972.

BEACH, H. D. Morphine addiction in rats. *Canadian Journal of Psychology,* 1957, *11,* 104–112.

BEARD, R. R. & WERTHEIM, G. A. Behavioral impairment associated with small doses of carbon monoxide. *American Journal of Public Health,* 1967, *57,* 2012–2022.

BECKER, D. I., APPEL, J. B., & FREEDMAN, D. X. Some effects of lysergic acid diethylamide on visual discrimination in pigeons. *Psychopharmacologia,* 1967, *11,* 354–364.

BERNAL, J. D. Structure arrangements of macromolecules. *Discussions of the Faraday Society,* 1958, *25,* 6.

BIGELOW, G., COHEN, M., LIEBSON, I. & FAILLACE, L. A. Abstinence or moderation? Choice by alcoholics. *Behavior Research and Therapy,* 1972, *10,* 209–214.

BIGELOW, G. & LIEBSON, I. Cost factors controlling alcoholic drinking. *The Psychological Record,* 1972, *22,* 305–314.

BOREN, J. J. The study of drugs with operant techniques. In W. K. Honig (Ed.), *Operant Behavior: Areas of Research and Application.* Englewood Cliffs, N.J.: Prentice-Hall, Inc., 1966.

BOREN, J. J. & NAVARRO, A. P. The action of atropine, benactyzine, and scopolamine upon fixed interval and fixed ratio behavior. *Journal of the Experimental Analysis of Behavior,* 1959, *2,* 107–115.

BOUDIN, H. M. Contingency contracting as a therapeutic tool in the deceleration of amphetamine use. *Behavior Therapy,* 1972, *3,* 604–608.

CHEREK, D. & THOMPSON, T. Effects of tetrahydrocannabinol on schedule-induced aggression. *Pharmacology, Biochemistry and Behavior,* 1973, *1,* 493–500.

CHEREK, D. R., THOMPSON, T. & HEISTAD, G. T. Responding maintained by the opportunity to attack during an interval food reinforcement schedule. *Journal of the Experimental Analysis of Behavior,* 1973, *19,* 113–123.

COOK, L. & CATANIA, A. C. Effects of drugs on avoidance and escape behavior. *Federation Proceedings,* 1964, *23,* 818–835.

COOK, L. C., DAVIDSON, A., DAVIS, D. J. & KELLEHER, R. T. Epinephrine, norepinephrine, and acetylcholine as conditioned stimuli for avoidance behavior. *Science,* 1960, *131,* 990–991.

COOK, L. & KELLEHER, R. T. Effects of drugs on behavior. *Annual Review of Pharmacology,* 1963, *3,* 205–222.

DEWS, P. B. Studies on behavior: I. Differential sensitivity to pentobarbital of pecking performance in pigeons depending on the schedule of reward. *Journal of Pharmacology and Experimental Therapeutics,* 1955, *115,* 343–401. (a)

DEWS, P. B. Studies on behavior: II. The effects of pentobarbital, methamphetamine, and scopolamine on performances in pigeons involving discrimination. *Journal of Pharmacology and Experimental Therapeutics,* 1955, *115,* 380–389. (b)

DEWS, P. B. Studies on behavior: IV. Stimulant actions of methamphetamine. *Journal of Pharmacology and Experimental Therapeutics,* 1958, *122,* 137–147.

DEWS, P. B. Drugs in psychology: A commentary on Travis Thompson and Charles R. Schuster's *Behavioral Pharmacology. Journal of the Experimental Analysis of Behavior,* 1970, *13,* 395–406.

DEWS, P. B. & MORSE, W. H. Behavioral pharmacology. *Annual Review of Pharmacology,* 1961, *1,* 145–174.

DYKSTRA, L. A. & APPEL, J. B. Lysergic acid diethylamide and stimulus generalization: Rate-dependent effects. *Science,* 1972, *177,* 720–722.

GELLER, I., KULOK, JR., J. T., & SEIFTER, J. The effects of chlordiazepoxide and chlorpromazine on a punishment discrimination. *Psychopharmacologia,* 1962, *3,* 374–385.

GELLER, I. & SEIFTER, J. The effects of meprobamate, barbiturates, d-amphetamine and promazine on experimentally induced conflict in the rat. *Psychopharmacologia,* 1960, *1,* 482–492.

GELLER, I. & SEIFTER, J. The effect of mono-urethans, di-urethans and barbiturates on a punishment discrimination. *Journal of Pharmacology and Experimental Therapeutics,* 1962, *136,* 284–288.

GOLDBERG, S. R. & SCHUSTER, C. R. Conditioned suppression by a stimulus associated with nalorphine in morphine-dependent monkeys. *Journal of the Experimental Analysis of Behavior,* 1967, *10,* 235–242.

GOLDBERG, S. R. & SCHUSTER, C. R. Nalorphine: Increased sensitivity of monkeys formerly dependent on morphine. *Science,* 1969, *166,* 1548–1549.

GOLDBERG, S. R., WOODS, J. H. & SCHUSTER, C. R. Morphine: Conditioned increases in self-administration in rhesus monkeys. *Science,* 1969, *166,* 1306–1307.

GOLLUB, L. R. & BRADY, J. V. Behavioral pharmacology. *Annual Review of Pharmacology,* 1965, *5,* 235–262.

GRIFFITHS, R. R. & THOMPSON, T. Effects of chlorpromazine and pentobarbital on pattern and number of responses in extinction. *Psychological Reports,* 1973, *33,* 323–334.

GRIFFITHS, R. R., & THOMPSON, T. Pentobarbital facilitated extinction: Effects of different schedules of drug withdrawal. *Pharmacology, Biochemistry and Behavior,* 1974, *2,* 331–338.

GROVE, R. & THOMPSON, T. The effects of pentobarbital on performance maintained by an interlocking fixed-ratio fixed-interval reinforcement schedule. In T. Thompson, R. Pickens, & R. Meisch (Eds.), *Readings in Behavioral Pharmacology.* Englewood Cliffs, N.J.: Prentice-Hall, Inc., 1970.

HARRIS, R. T. & BALSTER, R. L. An analysis of the function of drugs in the stimulus control of operant behavior. In T. Thompson & R. Pickens (Eds.), *Stimulus Properties of Drugs.* Englewood Cliffs, N.J.: Prentice-Hall, Inc., 1971.

HEADLEE, C. P., COPPOCK, H. W. & NICHOLS, J. R. Apparatus and technique involved in a laboratory method of detecting the addictiveness of drugs. *Journal of the American Pharmaceutical Association,* 1955, *44,* 229–231.

HEARST, E. Drug effects on stimulus generalization gradients in the monkey. *Psychopharmacologia,* 1964, *6,* 57–70.

HEISE, G. A. & LILIE, N. Effects of scopolamine, atropine and d-amphetamine on internal and external control of responding on non-reinforced trials. *Psychopharmacologia,* 1970, *18,* 38–49.

HERRNSTEIN, R. J. & MORSE, W. H. Selective action of pentobarbital on component behaviors of a reinforcement schedule. *Science,* 1956, *124,* 367–368.

HILL, R. T. Facilitation of conditioned reinforcement as a mechanism of psychomotor stimulation. In E. Costa & S.

Garattini (Eds.), *Amphetamines and Related Compounds.* Proceedings of the Mario Negri Institute for Pharmacological Research, Milan. New York: Raven Press, 1970.

Hollis, J. H. Chlorpromazine: Direct measurement of a differential behavioral effect. *Science,* 1968, *159,* 1487–1489.

Hollis, J. H. & St. Omer, V. V. Direct measurement of psychopharmacologic response: Effects of chlorpromazine on motor behavior of retarded children. *American Journal of Mental Deficiency,* 1972, *76,* 397–407.

Hunt, G. M. & Azrin, N. H. Community reinforcement approach to alcoholism. Presented at the Annual Meeting of the American Psychological Association, Honolulu, Hawaii, Sept., 1972.

Hutchinson, R. R., Azrin, N. H. & Hunt, G. M. Attack produced by intermittent reinforcement of a concurrent operant response. *Journal of the Experimental Analysis of Behavior,* 1968, *11,* 489–495.

Iverson, S. & Iverson, L. *Behavioral Pharmacology.* London: Oxford University Press, 1975.

Jacobs, H. L. Studies on sugar preference: The preference for glucose solutions and its modification by injections of insulin. *Journal of Comparative and Physiological Psychology,* 1958, *51,* 304–310.

Kelleher, R. T., Fry, W., Deegan, J. & Cook, L. Effects of meprobamate on operant behavior in rats. *Journal of Pharmacology and Experimental Therapeutics,* 1961, *133,* 271–280.

Kelleher, R. T. & Morse, W. H. Escape behavior and punished behavior. *Federation Proceedings,* 1964, *23,* 808–817.

Kelleher, R. T. & Morse, W. H. Determinants of the specificity of the behavioral effects of drugs. *Ergebnisse der Physiologie,* 1968, *60,* 1–56.

Kelleher, R. T. & Morse, W. H. Determinants of the behavioral effects of drugs. In D. H. Tedeschi & R. E. Tedeschi (Eds.), *Importance of Fundamental Principles in Drug Evaluation.* New York: Raven Press, 1969.

Laties, V. G. The modification of drug effects on behavior by external discriminative stimuli. *Journal of Pharmacology and Experimental Therapeutics,* 1972, *183,* 1–13.

Laties, V. G. & Weiss, B. Effects of amphetamine, chlorpromazine and pentobarbital on behavioral thermoregulation. *Journal of Pharmacology and Experimental Therapeutics,* 1963, *140,* 1–7.

Laties, V. G. & Weiss, B. Influence of drugs on behavior controlled by internal and external stimuli. *Journal of Pharmacology and Experimental Therapeutics,* 1966, *152,* 388–396.

Liebson, I., Bigelow, G. & Flamer, R. Alcoholism among methadone patients: A specific treatment method. *American Journal of Psychiatry,* 1973, *4,* 483–485.

Lindsley, O. Operant conditioning techniques in the measurement of psychopharmacological response. In J. H. Nodine & J. H. Moyer (Eds.), *Psychosomatic Medicine.* Philadelphia: Lea and Febiger, 1962.

Marsh, D. F. *Outline of Fundamental Pharmacology: The Mechanics of the Interaction of Chemicals and Living Things.* Springfield: Charles C. Thomas, 1950.

Masserman, J. H. & Yum, K. S. An analysis of the influence of alcohol on experimental neurosis. *Psychosomatic Medicine,* 1946, *8,* 36–52.

McConahey, O. L. A token system for retarded women: Behavior modification, drug therapy and their combination. In T. Thompson and J. Grabowski (Eds.), *Behavior Modification of the Mentally Retarded.* New York: Oxford University Press, 1972.

McConahey, O. L. Effects on concurrent behavior modification and chlorpromazine administration in mentally retarded women. Unpublished doctoral dissertation, University of Minnesota, December, 1973.

McConahey, O. L. & Thompson, T. Concurrent behavior modification and chlorpromazine therapy in a population of institutionalized mentally retarded women. Paper presented at the Annual Meeting of the American Psychological Association, Washington, D.C., 1972.

McKearney, J. W. Schedule-dependent effects: Effects of drugs, and maintenance of responding with response-produced electric shocks. In R. M. Gilbert & J. D. Keehn (Eds.), *Schedule Effects: Drugs, Drinking, and Aggression.* Toronto: University of Toronto Press, 1972.

McMillan, D. E. Drugs and punished responding I: Rate-dependent effects under multiple schedules. *Journal of the Experimental Analysis of Behavior,* 1973, *19,* 133–145.

McMillan, D. E., Dewey, W. L. & Harris, L. S. Characteristics of tetrahydrocannabinol tolerance. *Annals of the New York Academy of Sciences,* 1971, *191,* 83–99.

McMillan, D. E., Harris, L. S., Frankenheim, J. M. & Kennedy, J. S. 1-Δ^9-transtetrahydrocannabinol in pigeons: Tolerance to the behavioral effects. *Science,* 1970, *119,* 501–503.

Meisch, R. Rapid development of ethanol as a reinforcer for rats. *Proceedings,* 80th Annual Convention, The American Psychological Association, 1972, 851–852.

Meisch, R. A. & Thompson, T. Ethanol intake in the absence of concurrent food reinforcement, *Psychopharmacologia,* 1971, *22,* 72–79.

Meisch, R. & Thompson, T. Ethanol as a reinforcer: Effects of fixed-ratio size and food deprivation. *Psychopharmacologia,* 1973, *28,* 171–183.

Meisch, R. A. & Thompson, T. Ethanol as a reinforcer: An operant analysis of ethanol dependence. In J. M. Singh & H. Lal (Eds.), *Drug Addiction, Vol. 3: Behavioral and Clinico-Toxicological Aspects.* Miami, Florida: Symposia Specialists, 1974.

Mello, N. K. & Mendelson, J. H. Experimentally induced intoxication in alcoholics: A comparison between programmed and spontaneous drinking. *Journal of Pharmacology and Experimental Therapeutics,* 1970, *173,* 101–116.

Morse, W. H. Effect of amobarbital and chlorpromazine on punished behavior in the pigeon. *Psychopharmacologia,* 1964, *6,* 286–294.

Morse, W. H. & Herrnstein, R. J. Effects of drugs on characteristics of behavior maintained by complex schedules on intermittent positive reinforcement. *Annals of the New York Academy of Sciences,* 1956, *65,* 303–317.

Morse, W. H. & Kelleher, R. T. Schedules as fundamental determinants of behavior. In W. N. Schoenfeld (Ed.), *The Theory of Reinforcement Schedules.* Englewood Cliffs, N.J.: Prentice-Hall, Inc., 1970.

Overton, D. A. Discriminative control of behavior by drug states. In T. Thompson and R. Pickens (Eds.), *Stimulus Properties of Drugs.* Englewood Cliffs, N.J.: Prentice-Hall, Inc., 1971.

Paul, G., Tobias, L. L. & Holly, B. L. Maintenance psychotropic drugs with chronic mental patients in the presence of active treatment programs: A "triple blind" withdrawal study. *Archives of General Psychiatry,* 1972, *27,* 106–115.

PICKENS, R., BIGELOW, G. & GRIFFITHS, R. An experimental approach to treating chronic alcoholism: A case study and 1 year follow-up. *Behavior Research and Therapy,* 1973, *11,* 321–325.

PICKENS, R. & CROWDER, W. F. Effects of CS-US interval on conditioning of drug response, with assessment of speed of conditioning. *Psychopharmacologia,* 1967, *11,* 88–94.

PICKENS, R. & THOMPSON, T. Intravenous preparations for self-administration by animals. *American Psychologist,* 1975, *30,* 274–276.

RECH, R. H. & MOORE, K. E. (Eds.), *An Introduction to Psychopharmacology.* New York: Raven Press, 1971.

RICHELLE, M., XHENSEVAL, B., FONTAINE, O., & THONE, L. Action of chlordiazepoxide on two types of temporal conditioning in rats. *International Journal of Neuropharmacology,* 1962, *1,* 381–391.

SCHUSTER, C. R. & BRADY, J. V. The discriminative control of a food-reinforced operant by interoceptive stimulation. *Pavlov Journal of Higher Nervous Activity,* 1964, *14,* 448–458.

SCHUSTER, C. R. & THOMPSON, T. Self-administration of and behavioral dependence on drugs. *Annual Review of Pharmacology,* 1969, *9,* 483–502.

SIDMAN, M. Behavioral pharmacology. *Psychopharmacologia,* 1959, *1,* 1–19.

SIDMAN, M. *Tactics of Scientific Research.* New York: Basic Books, 1960.

SINGH, S. D. & MANOCHA, S. N. The interaction of drug effects with drive level and habit strength. *Psychopharmacologia,* 1966, *9,* 205–209.

SMITH, C. B. Effects of d-amphetamine upon operant behavior of pigeons: Enhancement by resperine. *Journal of Pharmacology and Experimental Therapeutics,* 1964, *146,* 167–174.

SPARBER, S. B. Effects of drugs on the biochemical and behavioral responses of developing organisms. *Federation Proceedings,* 1972, *31,* 74–80.

SPRAGG, S. D. S. Morphine addiction in chimpanzees. *Comparative Psychology Monographs,* 1940, *15,* No. 7.

SPYKER, J. M., SPARBER, S. B. & GOLDBERG, A. M. Subtle consequences of methylmercury exposure: Behavioral deviations in offspring of treated mothers. *Science,* 1972, *177,* 621–623.

STOLERMAN, I. P. A method for studying the influences of drugs on learning for food rewards in rats. *Psychopharmacologia,* 1971, *19,* 398–406.

STRONG, C., SULZBACHER, S. I. & KIRKPATRICK, M. A. Use of medication versus reinforcement to modify a classroom behavior disorder. *Journal of Learning Disabilities,* 1974, *7,* 214–218.

SULZBACHER, S. I. Behavior analysis of drug effects in the classroom. In Semb, G. (Ed.), *Behavior Analysis and Education.* University of Kansas, 1972.

TERRACE, H. S. Discrimination learning with and without "errors". *Journal of the Experimental Analysis of Behavior,* 1963, *6,* 1–27. (a)

TERRACE, H. S. Errorless discrimination learning in the pigeon: Effects of chlorpromazine and imipramine. *Science,* 1963, *140,* 318–319. (b)

THOMPSON, T., GRIFFITHS, R. & PICKENS, R. Drug self-administration by animals: Some implications for human drug dependence. In F. Hoffmeister (Ed.), *Psychic Dependence,* Berlin: Springer, Verlag, 1973.

THOMPSON, T. & PICKENS, R. Drug dependence and conditioning. In H. Steinberg (Ed.), *Scientific Basis of Drug Dependence.* London: J. A. Churchill, 1969.

THOMPSON, T. & PICKENS, R. Stimulant self-administration by animals: Some comparisons with opiate self-administration. *Federation Proceedings,* 1970, *29,* 6–12.

THOMPSON, T. & PICKENS, R. Drugs as reinforcers: Schedule considerations. In R. M. Gilbert & J. D. Keehn (Eds.), *Schedule Effects: Drugs, Drinking, and Aggression.* Toronto: University of Toronto Press, 1972.

THOMPSON, T. & SCHUSTER, C. R. *Behavioral Pharmacology.* Englewood Cliffs, New Jersey: Prentice-Hall, Inc., 1968.

THOMPSON, T., TROMBLEY, J., LUKE, D. & LOTT, D. Effects of morphine on behavior maintained by four simple food-reinforcement schedules. *Psychopharmacologia,* 1970, *17,* 182–192.

VERHAVE, T. The effect of methamphetamine on operant level and avoidance behavior. *Journal of the Experimental Analysis of Behavior,* 1958, *1,* 207–219.

WALLER, M. B. & MORSE, W. H. Effects of pentobarbital on fixed-ratio reinforcement. *Journal of the Experimental Analysis of Behavior,* 1963, *6,* 125–130.

WALLER, M. B. & WALLER, P. F. Effects of chlorpromazine on appetitive and aversive components of a multiple schedule. *Journal of the Experimental Analysis of Behavior,* 1962, *5,* 259–264.

WEISS, B. Amphetamine and the temporal structure of behavior. In E. Costa & S. Garattini (Eds.), *Amphetamines and Related Compounds.* New York: Raven Press, 1970.

WEISS, B. & GOTT, C. T. A microanalysis of drug effects on fixed-ratio performance in pigeons. *Journal of Pharmacology and Experimental Therapeutics,* 1972, *180,* 189–202.

WEISS, B. & LATIES, V. G. Behavioral pharmacology and toxicology. *Annual Review of Pharmacology,* 1969, *9,* 297–326.

WELLS, J. A. Historical background and general principles of drug action. In V. A. Drill (Ed.), *Pharmacology in Medicine.* New York: McGraw Hill Book Company, 1958.

WOODS, J. H., DOWNS, D. A. & VILLARREAL, J. E. Changes in operant behavior during deprivation- and antagonist-induced withdrawal states. In L. Goldberg & F. Hoffmeister (Eds.). *Psychic Dependence.* Berlin: Springer-Verlag, 1973.

WUTTKE, W. & KELLEHER, R. T. Effects of some bezodiazepines on punished and unpunished behavior in the pigeon. *Journal of Pharmacology and Experimental Therapeutics,* 1970, *172,* 397–405.

19

Central Reinforcement

a bridge between
brain function and behavior*

Gordon Mogenson

and

Jan Cioé

INTRODUCTION

It was nearly 60 years after the brain was first stimulated electrically that it was shown that motivational effects could be elicited by such stimulation. This long delay following the historic experiments of Fritsch and Hitzig, who stimulated the motor cortex in 1870, was due in part to the facts that most of the experiments during this period were in anesthetized animals and that most investigators stimulated the cerebral cortex, which is motivationally neutral (Doty, 1969). In the early 1930s Hess performed important pioneering experiments in unanesthetized, freely moving animals. Although he observed that a variety of motivated behaviors could be elicited by stimulation of the hypothalamus and other subcortical structures, more than two decades passed before further developments occurred. The demonstration of central reinforcement, made possible by the use of stereotaxic surgical procedures for the implantation of chronic stimulating electrodes and by the use of operant techniques, provided the major impetus for the study of brain mechanisms of reinforcement and more generally for the study of brain-behavior relationships.

Positive central reinforcement was first reported by J. Olds and Milner (1954), who observed that rats receiving electrical stimulation of the septum returned to the place in an open field where they had been stimulated (Figure 1). When the animals could initiate the brain stimulation by pressing a lever they made this operant response at high rates for long periods of time. Central reinforcement, inferred from the brain self-stimulation phenomenon, immediately excited the interest and imagination of psychologists and other investigators. During the next few years central reinforcement was demonstrated with electrical stimulation of a number of subcortical structures in a variety of species, including man. Although the possible practical application of central reinforcement was recognized early (in 1955 McClelland suggested, in a humorous yet prophetic vein, that brain self-stimulation might be made readily available to perk us up, as an

---

* The authors wish to express their appreciation to Miss Anne Baxter and Mrs. Marianne Jeffery for typing the several drafts of the manuscript and to D. Baran, J. P. Huston, W. J. McClelland, P. M. Milner, A. G. Phillips, Ann Robertson, P. Russell, B. B. Schiff, and T. B. Wishart who read and commented on earlier versions of this article. The authors' research is supported by grants from the National Research Council of Canada and the Medical Research Council of Canada.

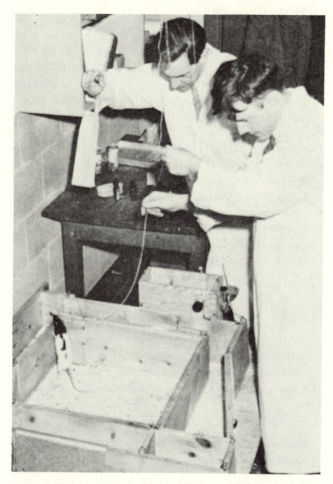

Fig. 1. This picture illustrates the discovery of central reinforcement by James Olds and Peter Milner. (From Hebb, 1972.)

"exotic coffee break") and although the possibilities for its use in the alleviation of abnormal behaviors clearly exist (Crichton, 1972), the major developments have been experimental and theoretical. Psychologists saw the relevance of central reinforcement to many of the issues and problems of the psychology of learning, and they were intrigued by the possibility that self-stimulation would permit the direct study of the neural substrates of reinforcement and lead eventually to an understanding of the basic mechanisms of motivation and learning. They were interested in comparing central reinforcement with conventional reinforcers to determine whether the self-stimulation phenomenon was interpretable in terms of drive reduction theory, the most popular behavioral theory at the time. The discovery of self-stimulation and central reinforcement reactivated a number of issues in the areas of motivation, reinforcement, and learning, and as we indicate later, the work that followed led to new conceptions of reinforcement.

Central reinforcement has also stimulated other areas of research. The self-stimulation procedure has been widely used in studying the effects of drugs on behavior, and research using central reinforcement has had a strong impact on the new disciplines of neuropharmacology and psychopharmacology. A number of studies have indicated that catecholaminergic neurons subserve brain self-stimulation. Self-stimulation is markedly reduced by drugs which inhibit the synthesis of catecholamines, deplete catecholamines from nerve terminals, or destroy catecholaminergic neurons, and is increased by drugs, such as amphetamine, which increase the synaptic release and prevent the reuptake of catecholamines (for a review see German & Bowden, 1974). Several years ago Stein postulated the noradrenergic hypothesis of reward and subsequently demonstrated that noradrenalin was released during self-stimulation, apparently due to the activation of noradrenergic fibers (Stein & Wise, 1969). Stein, Wise, and Berger (1972) have proposed that schizophrenia is the result of a biochemical disturbance (a deficit in the enzyme dopamine-β-hydroxylase) in which noradrenergic "reward" fibers are destroyed by the production of 6-hydroxydopamine, a neurotoxin.

The first successful conditioning of visceral responses was obtained with central reinforcement and opened the field of biofeedback. Central reinforcement enabled experimenters to deliver a reinforcement for the desired visceral response even though the animal was paralyzed and so was unable to approach or consume conventional reinforcers. It is necessary to induce paralysis in order to avoid the possibility that the visceral response is merely an artifact of the conditioning of skeletal movements. Di Cara and Miller (1968) demonstrated that blood pressure, blood flow, intestinal contractions, and other visceral responses were conditioned using stimulation of reinforcing sites in the hypothalamus. This field, although controversial, is an active area of investigation which may contribute eventually to an understanding and treatment of psychosomatic disorders.

Finally it should be mentioned that central reinforcement has stimulated research at the interface between psychology and ethology. This resulted from the observations that feeding (Hoebel & Teitelbaum, 1962; Margules & Olds, 1962), drinking (Mogenson & Stevenson, 1966), object carrying (Phillips, Cox, Kakolewski, & Valenstein, 1969), and other species-typical behaviors are elicited from the same brain sites as self-stimulation. Not only has this led to an ingenious theory of reinforcement (Glickman & Schiff, 1967) and vigorous investigation of self-stimulation behavior, but it has also helped to promote the discourse between psychologists and ethologists, a development which was long overdue.

METHODOLOGICAL CONSIDERATIONS

Following the initial demonstration of central reinforcement there was considerable research to delineate the regions of the brain subserving the phenomenon (e.g., J. Olds, 1956; M. E. Olds & J. Olds, 1963; Wetzel, 1968). Although the hypothalamus has been the most popular target, central reinforcing effects are also obtained from many other neural structures, throughout the limbic system (Milner, 1970) and the extrapyramidal motor system (e.g., Routtenberg & Malsbury, 1969). Appendix A indicates the diversity of brain structures shown to be at least mildly reinforcing and also illustrates the ubiquity of the phenomenon across species.

Experimental Procedures

In order to obtain central reinforcement it is necessary, of course, to place a stimulating electrode in or near one of the brain structures referred to in Appendix A. The operative procedure involved is relatively simple and straightforward, especially if the subject is one of the more hardy laboratory animals (e.g., rat or gerbil). The animal is first anesthetized and the top of the head shaved. After the head is positioned in a stereotaxic instrument an incision is made along the midline to expose the skull. Bone sutures are identified as a guide in directing the electrode to subcortical structures. A standard brain atlas (e.g., Pellegrino & Cushman, 1967) is used with reference to skull bone sutures in order to obtain three-dimensional coordinates for placement of the electrode in the desired structure. A hole is then drilled through the skull and the electrode is lowered to the desired depth by the micromanipulator of the stereotaxic carriage. The electrode is securely attached to the skull and anchoring screws placed around the electrode hole by acrylic cement. About one week is usually allowed for the animal to recover from the trauma of surgery before testing is begun; such a preparation can continue in use for many months.

Electrical stimulation provided by a stepdown transformer from a 60-Hz ac source is very effective for self-stimulation and was used extensively for several years. Commercial electronic stimulators have been used to deliver rectangular pulses which may be varied in pulse duration, frequency, and waveform as well as in intensity. The duration of a train of reinforcing stimulation is usually limited to less than 1 sec (.2 and .5 sec being the most popular), although in certain situations an operant response may be reinforced by several trains (e.g., Hawkins & Pliskoff, 1964). The details of the delivery system for the brain stimulation are dependent on the particular experimental situation, although typically the brain stimulation is delivered through wire leads from a commutator or other device which allows reasonable freedom of movement. When the desired response has occurred the central reinforcement is delivered either automatically or manually.

Central reinforcement has been demonstrated in several experimental situations (mazes, obstruction boxes, runways, shuttleboxes), but it has been studied almost exclusively with operant methodology. With operant techniques a high degree of environmental control is possible, and since the operant response causes little or no change in the environment the behavior is very stable (Honig, 1966, p. 4). When the operant response is maintained with central reinforcement the motivational state of the animal which results from the brain stimulation is relatively constant —unaltered by satiation effects, for example—so that the operant responding is stable for long periods of time.

Operant Rate as a Measure of Central Reinforcement

The Skinner box has been the most popular test for self-stimulation, and as a result rate of response has been widely adopted as the measure of central reinforcement. Response rate is not, however, always a reliable indicator of reinforcement strength. Hodos and Valenstein (1962) showed in a two-lever preference test (hypothalamic versus septal stimulation at various current intensities) that animals did not necessarily select the site of stimulation and current intensity that maintained the highest response rates. For example, rats preferred septal stimulation at a moderate current intensity to hypothalamic stimulation even though the hypothalamic stimulation maintained a higher response rate. Similarly, Davis, Davison, and Webster (1972) demonstrated in pigeons performing on concurrent variable interval (VI) schedules that the most highly preferred brain stimulation maintained low rates of responding. There is also evidence (Valenstein & Beer, 1962) that reinforcement strength as determined by competition of central reinforcement with other reinforcers such as food and shock avoidance is not the same as that indicated by response rate. Finally, Hawkins and Pliskoff (1964) have made the same point by using a two-member behavioral chaining procedure. In this procedure responding on a VI schedule on a single lever is reinforced by access to a second retractable lever which delivers central reinforcement on a continuous reinforcement (CRF) schedule. The rate of pressing on the first lever continued to increase at current intensities higher than those which maintained peak response rate on the second lever, thus indicating that the potency of central reinforcement cannot be assessed adequately by self-stimulation rates on a CRF schedule.

Valenstein (1964) has argued on the basis of these results that the rate of responding on a CRF schedule is a poor index of reinforcement strength. He has gone on to point out that there are logical difficulties in using an average CRF rate since there is the implicit assumption that reinforcement strength is homogeneous throughout the test session. Occasionally, this assumption is not justified with central reinforcement since some effects of the stimulation which persist may change the strength of the reinforcer after its administration (e.g., seizure activity—Mogenson, 1965; Newman & Feldman, 1964). Furthermore, central reinforcement, especially at higher current intensities, may elicit various respondents in an unconditioned manner (e.g., forced motor responses), which can disrupt the response rate even though these high current intensities are preferred over lower intensities which maintain higher response rates (Hodos & Valenstein, 1962).

Although the criticisms of Valenstein against a CRF rate of response as an index of central reinforcement appear justified in some situations, such a measure is meaningful in many others. Clearly, if a comparison is being made between diverse sites of stimulation, or if high intensities are employed, there is a real problem of distortion with a CRF response rate measure. It seems equally true, however, that in the majority of experiments there is little distortion as long as moderate current intensities are employed, as even Valenstein's data indicate (Hodos & Valenstein, 1962). The use of moderate intensities decreases the probability of both interfering motor responses and seizure activity. This situation is indeed fortunate since most of the work discussed in the comparison of central and conventional reinforcers (discussed in a later section) is based on the CRF response rate measure.[1]

[1] It might be useful at this point to establish two conventions: (1) the species should be understood to be rats unless otherwise indicated; and (2) the method used in a particular study involves a conventional operant response (such as lever pressing) on a CRF schedule unless a different method is specified. The use of these conventions will help to simplify the task of describing the many studies of self-stimulation.

The Advantages of Intermittent Schedules

It should be noted that many of the criticisms of the use of response rate as a measure of central reinforcement apply mainly when a CRF schedule is used. Intermittent schedules, which are preferable to the CRF schedule in most operant situations, produce a more stable pattern of behavior while still maintaining a sensitivity to environmental manipulations (Reynolds, 1968). Accordingly, intermittent schedules may be preferable for a behavioral analysis of self-stimulation. When the trains of pulses are spaced, the disruptive side effects of brain stimulation, such as forced motor responses and carry-over effects, are minimized. Using a two-lever chaining procedure, Hawkins and Pliskoff (1964) clearly showed that the response rate on the intermittently reinforced lever paralleled the results obtained with preference tests when current was manipulated. Moreover, by using intermittent schedules one retains the advantages of using a rate measure as the dependent variable (e.g., Honig, 1966, pp. 6–7; Skinner, 1966b, pp. 15–17). There has been, however, some problem in maintaining animals on a "reinforcement-poor" intermittent schedule using central reinforcement in a single-lever situation; the problem (as is discussed more fully in a later section) appears at least partially to be one of determining how much central reinforcement is equivalent to the standard amounts of food and water reinforcement commonly used. The advantages of an intermittent schedule also accrue to the use of concurrent schedules, which appear to be highly sensitive to changes in the magnitude of reinforcement, as opposed to single schedules, which are less so (Hollard & Davison, 1971). Such sensitivity may be particularly useful in analyzing the incentive properties of brain stimulation.

Another modification of intermittent schedules which has been successfully employed with central reinforcement is the progressive-ratio procedure described originally by Hodos (1961) for food reinforcement. In this procedure the animal is required to emit a progressively increasing number of responses in order to obtain each successive reinforcement. The "terminal ratio" is defined as the highest number of responses emitted before a pause of given duration, such as 15 sec, occurs. This is used as the dependent measure. Hodos (1965) demonstrated that the size of the terminal ratio is sensitive to long durations of rewarding brain stimulation. Keesey and Goldstein (1968) further modified this procedure by defining the "terminal ratio" as the highest level of stable ratio (FR) responding that a given reinforcement condition would maintain, and they were able to demonstrate that the functions relating this terminal ratio to a wide range of stimulus currents were monotonic at all brain stimulation sites tested. It appears that these more sophisticated behavioral techniques are potentially useful for the study of central reinforcement and for the analysis of the reinforcement process in general.

Although there are certain limitations in the use of a CRF schedule with central reinforcement, a CRF rate measure is still meaningful in most situations. When a comparison is being made between stimulation sites or when high current intensities are used there is the possibility of distortion of a CRF response rate measure. In most experiments there is little distortion, however, especially if moderate current intensities are employed.

Stein and Ray (1959) devised a CRF procedure which allows the animal to self-regulate the current intensity. Pressing one lever increases the current, whereas pressing a second lever decreases it. Interestingly, it was reported that high current levels which often produced disruptive motoric responses were selected. Modifications of this "titration" method have been used extensively in the analysis of drug effects on self-stimulation behavior (e.g., Stein, 1962).

Nonrate Measures of Central Reinforcement

As we have already mentioned, central reinforcement has been obtained in other experimental situations which do not utilize a rate measure. These procedures, however, also have drawbacks which have limited their usefulness. Hodos and Valenstein (1962) used a preference procedure in which animals choose between two conditions available on different levers, but this becomes extremely cumbersome when a large number of comparisons are to be made. This procedure, nonetheless, is quite useful in validating other procedures. The obstruction box technique employed by J. Olds (1960) is generally not as useful due to the inherent problems involved in repeated aversive foot shock as well as the apparent analgesic properties of some brain stimulation (Yunger, Harvey, & Lorens, 1973). A technique which has gained much more widespread use than either of those already mentioned was developed by Valenstein and Meyers (1964) and employs a shuttlebox. They have suggested that a shuttlebox situation, in which central reinforcement is continuously delivered as long as the animal remains on one side but not on the other, provides a measure of reinforcement value which minimizes the influence of activity level and performance capabilities. The measure used is the percentage of time spent receiving stimulation. Since the positive (brain stimulation) and neutral sides can be randomly interchanged, this measure is directly amenable to statistical evaluation. Some animals, however, self-administer very brief trains of central reinforcement and may spend less than 50% of the session (chance level) on the positive side, although these same animals repeatedly cross over and receive the stimulation (Cioé, personal observation). Independent measures of reinforcement strength indicate that stimulation will maintain a lever-press response as well as the operant of crossing in the shuttlebox. This effect, however, is not reflected in the time score, which limits the usefulness of this measure.

CENTRAL REINFORCEMENT COMPARED TO CONVENTIONAL REINFORCEMENT

In the study of central reinforcement, operant methods are both important and useful, as shown in the previous section; indeed, the area would probably not have undergone such rapid and fruitful expansion without operant techniques. In this section we would like to turn the discussion around and demonstrate the contribution that central reinforcement can make to an analysis of operant behavior. The main issue is this: does self-stimulation differ in any substantial and irreducible way from the more conventional reinforcers used before its discovery (e.g., food and water to a deprived animal, saccharine, etc.)? The initial view of this phenomenon was that the neural substrate of reinforcement had been discovered, and so it was argued that conventional and central reinforcement were essentially identical in nature (J. Olds, 1956). With further research, however, there emerged a growing number of apparent dissimilarities, and elaborate theories were developed to account for these differences. More recently, the similarities of conventional and central reinforcement have been stressed and the so-called differences attributed to procedural differences (e.g., Trowill, Panksepp, & Gandelman, 1969) and to the more rapid decay of stimuli that control central reinforcement (Lenzer, 1972). Conventional and central reinforcement will be compared in this section under the following headings: acquisition, extinction, secondary reinforcement, priming, intensity and persistence, partial reinforcement, and influence of drive state on self-stimulation. In each case, we shall attempt to show that when appropriate comparisons are made and equivalent conditions established, the two kinds of reinforcers do not differ substantially.

Acquisition

In the pioneering study of J. Olds and Milner (1954) it appeared that the rate of acquisition of the operant response for central reinforcement was unusually rapid compared to acquisition using conventional reinforcers. Subsequently this observation was confirmed by other investigators experienced with shaping animals using conventional reinforcers. A comparison of central and conventional reinforcers is not entirely justified, however, since the temporospatial relations between response and reinforcement are not the same (Gibson, Reid, Sakai, & Porter, 1965). For example, when water is used as the reinforcer of an operant response the animal must depress the lever, move to the dipper, and then drink: there is usually a spatial separation between the lever and the water which results in a delay of the consummatory act. With central reinforcement, however, there is no such delay in reinforcement. Gibson et al. attempted to equate the two situations by having animals that were receiving central reinforcement depress a lever which introduced a dry dipper that had to be contacted to trigger the stimulation, a situation comparable to the behavioral chaining procedure of Hawkins and Pliskoff (1964); either sugar water or brain stimulation was delivered immediately when the animal touched the dipper. Panksepp and Trowill (1967a) made the two situations even more similar by delivering chocolate milk via an intraoral fistula immediately after a lever press. It was found in both studies that when the conventional reinforcement was immediate, acquisition was as rapid as that found with central reinforcement. This finding is not surprising given the well-established importance of delay of reinforcement in other situations (Renner, 1964).

It is not clear what role temporospatial factors play in other test situations. For example, for the acquisition of a discrimination task there are conflicting reports as to whether or not there are significant differences in acquisition rate between central and conventional reinforcers. Kling and his associates (Kling & Berkley, 1968; Kling & Matsumiya, 1962; Terman & Kling, 1968) have failed to find significant differences. Sadowsky (1969), however, has demonstrated a faster rate of acquisition of a multiple schedule (i.e., an operant discrimination) with central reinforcement as compared to food pellets. None of these studies attempted to control for temporospatial differences between central and conventional reinforcers. Linholm and Keesey (1970), however, tried to control for these differences by imposing an arbitrary 1-sec delay of central reinforcement following performance of the operant (breaking a photobeam over the food cup). Despite such a control the acquisition rate for central reinforcement (both hypothalamic and septal stimulation) was superior as compared with sweetened condensed milk. The study therefore suggests a difference between central and conventional reinforcers—at least for a discrimination task—not attributable to differences in immediacy of delivery. Linholm and Keesey suggest, rather speculatively, that this effect may be related to differences in the duration of central and conventional reinforcers. Stimuli associated with ingestion occur following the presentation of food reinforcement, and as the food passes through the oral-esophygeal cavities the possibility of conditioning behaviors incompatible with the discriminative response increases, since these stimuli are present for a relatively long period of time. Central reinforcement, in contrast, usually involves a relatively short duration of stimulation with more distinctive onset-offset characteristics. Such an interpretation is not inconsistent with a view that stresses the similarities of central and conventional reinforcers; central reinforcement is a case in which the experimenter has greater control than usual over the duration of the stimuli associated with reinforcement, and appropriate manipulations would result in greater similarity in the effects of central and food reinforcement (e.g., Linholm & Keesey, 1968).

Extinction

Extinction occurs very rapidly when the operant response is reinforced by brain stimulation (Culberton, Kling, & Berkley, 1966; Deutsch & Howarth, 1963; J. Olds & Milner, 1954; Seward, Uyeda, & Olds, 1959), suggesting a second fundamental difference between central and conventional reinforcers (Figure 2). However, the earlier differences may have been due to difference in procedure; with conventional reinforcers the animal is usually food- or water-deprived, and there is a temporal delay between operant response and reinforcement; whereas with central reinforcement the animal is typically not deprived, and reinforcement is presented immediately.

Extinction occurs less rapidly with central reinforcement when animals are food-deprived (Deutsch & DiCara, 1967). Furthermore, extinction with conventional reinforcement occurs more rapidly when animals are not deprived (Panksepp & Trowill, 1967b). When central reinforcement and sugar water

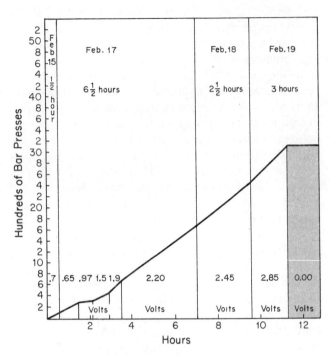

Fig. 2. When an operant response is maintained by central reinforcement, extinction occurs very rapidly as shown when the stimulation voltage is reduced to zero. (From Olds & Milner, 1954. © 1954 by the American Psychological Association. Reprinted by permission.)

were used with comparable testing conditions, extinction curves were similar (Gibson et al., 1965). It may be concluded that extinction with central reinforcement is comparable to extinction with a high-incentive conventional reinforcer presented with minimal delay to an animal sated or following a short deprivation period (Trowill, Panksepp, & Gandelman, 1969).

Secondary Reinforcement

The deprivation state of the animal may also be the variable which accounts for the mixed success of attempts to demonstrate secondary reinforcement using brain stimulation. Seward, Uyeda, and Olds (1959), Keys (1964), and Mogenson (1965) were all unable to establish secondary reinforcement, but these studies were conducted with nondeprived animals. Stein (1958), using a classical conditioning procedure, paired a tone with hypothalamic or septal stimulation and demonstrated that the tone possessed reinforcing properties due to its association with central stimulation. Similarly, Knott and Clayton (1966) were able to confirm Stein's results in addition to demonstrating that partial reinforcement (i.e., intermittent pairing of tone and central reinforcement) produces a more durable secondary reinforcement than does continuous reinforcement. Unfortunately, however, neither of these reports specifies the feeding schedule employed. The importance of this variable is indicated by DiCara (1966) as well as DiCara and Deutsch (1966). It was found that secondary reinforcement could be obtained using electrical stimulation of a brain area sensitive to the level of food deprivation (see J. Olds, 1958a) if the animals were in fact food-deprived; if food deprivation did not affect the rate of self-stimulation, no secondary reinforcement was obtained. It appears, therefore, that another apparent difference between central and conventional reinforcers is related to the level of deprivation rather than to the characteristics of the reinforcers.

Priming

J. Olds and Milner (1954) reported that following the rapid extinction to central reinforcement it was necessary to deliver noncontingent brain stimulation "to show that the current was turned on again" (p. 425) before lever pressing resumed. Furthermore, it has been reported that it is also necessary to deliver a few of these "free" stimulations at the start of a session to induce the animal to self-stimulate even though no formal extinction procedure has been introduced. This anomaly of central reinforcement has been emphasized by Deutsch and Howarth (1963); they have suggested that self-stimulation involves the activation of a drive system as well as a reinforcement system. Priming (i.e., delivery of "free" stimulation), it is suggested, induces the proper drive state so as to motivate the animal to lever-press; without the induction of this drive state the animal fails to start self-stimulating. Each stimulation, therefore, sets up the appropriate state in the animal so that the following stimulations are reinforcing and thereby responding is maintained.

Although there is a certain appeal to this view, which has led to some interesting experiments by Deutsch and his colleagues, it has been reported that many animals do not require priming to initiate self-stimulation (Trowill, Panksepp, & Gandelman, 1969). Furthermore, animals can be trained to continue lever-pressing after periods of nonreinforcement (Gandelman, Panksepp, & Trowill, 1968; Pliskoff, Wright, & Hawkins, 1965), indicating that central reinforcement "is not totally dependent on the time since the last stimulation" (Trowill et al., 1969, p. 291).

Intensity and Persistence

One of the more obvious features of brain self-stimulation is the astonishing vigor of the animal's behavior, which is frequently reflected in very high rates of responding. For example, Ray, Hine, and Bivens (1968) reported an average rate of 130 lever presses per min on a CRF schedule. It should be noted, of course, that part of the reason for such high rates with central reinforcement is that so little time is needed to "consume" the reinforcement—certainly much less time than is required to chew pellets or drink water. This leads to an artifact in the comparison of response rates based on a CRF schedule and in fact is one reason why it is more desirable to use an intermittent schedule for such comparisons. The differences in the time required to "consume" the reinforcement will only minimally affect such schedules.

Not only do animals emit relatively high response rates, but they continue to do so for relatively long periods of time. J. Olds (1958a) recorded 35 lever presses per min for 26 hr until the animal was exhausted and went to sleep (Figure 3), and Valenstein and Beer (1964) an average rate of 30 responses per min for a period of 20 days. Even telencephalic stimulation, which typically satiates more quickly than diencephalic stimulation, does so only after 4 to 8 hr

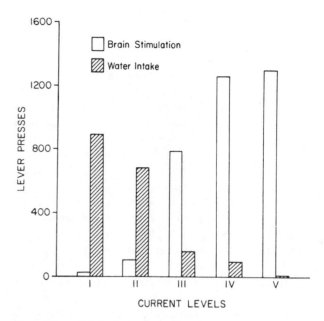

Fig 4. Water-deprived rats press lever for electrical stimulation of the hypothalamus in preference to lever-pressing for water as shown for current levels III, IV, and V. When the intensity of brain stimulation is low they show a preference for water. (Based on Morgan & Mogenson, 1966.)

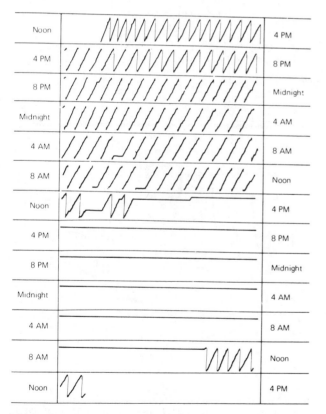

Fig. 3. Operant responding continues for very long periods of time when central reinforcement is used. This rat pressed the lever for more than 24 hr before going to sleep. (From Olds, 1958b. © 1958 by the American Psychological Association. Reprinted by permission.)

(J. Olds, 1958b). It is this characteristic—relative insatiability—of central reinforcement which is its most salient feature as compared to conventional reinforcers and which makes central reinforcement such a useful laboratory procedure.

The potency of central reinforcement and the degree to which it may be used to control an animal's behavior is most clearly demonstrated in test situations involving a choice between conventional reinforcers and reinforcing brain stimulation. Rats show a preference for the central reinforcement when it is in competition with food (Routtenberg & Lindy, 1965; Spies, 1965) or water (Falk, 1961; Mogenson, 1969b; Morgan & Mogenson, 1966; Phillips, Morgan, & Mogenson, 1970; Stutz, Rossi, & Bowring, 1971), even when food- or water-deprived for 24 or 48 hr (Figure 4). Rats ignored food and water ("self-starved") but lever-pressed for electrical stimulation of the medial forebrain bundle in the region of the hypothalamus (Routtenberg & Lindy, 1965). Animals also tolerate intense painful stimuli (Olds, 1960; Valenstein & Beer, 1962) or a cold ambient temperature (Carlisle & Snyder, 1970) in order to self-stimulate the hypothalamus.

Central reinforcement, although usually stronger than conventional reinforcement in competition tests, does not produce a rigid, inflexible pattern of responding. If the incentive characteristics of the alternative are high, the preference for central reinforcement disappears. When the alternative was a highly palatable saccharine-glucose solution, lever-press rates of more than 100 per min were recorded and rats showed an equal preference for this solution and electrical stimulation of the hypothalamus after being water- and food-deprived for 22 hr (Phillips, Morgan, & Mogenson, 1970). The relative preference for central and conventional reinforcement depends on the current intensity (Deutsch, Adams, & Metzner, 1964; Falk, 1961; Morgan & Mogenson, 1966), the length of water deprivation (Deutsch, Adams, & Metzner, 1964; Morgan & Mogenson, 1966), the duration of the test session, and the palatability of the conventional reinforcer (Phillips, Morgan, & Mogenson, 1970).

The results of the studies that have just been reviewed suggest that when deprivation period, intensity, and quality of the reinforcer are manipulated appropriately, central and conventional reinforcers are equally effective in controlling operant responses.

Partial Reinforcement

As mentioned earlier in the discussion of methodological problems, partial-reinforcement schedules may circumvent some of the difficulties involved in using response rate on a CRF schedule as a measure of relative reinforcement value. There are, however, repeated references in the literature suggesting that performance for central reinforcement is poorer than for conventional reinforcers on more complicated schedules. Sidman, Brady, Boren, Conrad, and Schulman (1955) reported obtaining successful performance on a variable-interval (VI) 16-sec schedule and a fixed-interval (FI) 7-sec schedule. Brodie, Moreno, Malis, and Brodie (1960) found that most of their monkeys would not respond to schedules exceeding fixed ratio (FR) 20, although one anomalous monkey performed an FR 150; Culberton, Kling, and Berkley (1966) reported that it took four times as long to train animals to respond on an FR 10 using central reinforcement than with water.

Other investigators (e.g., Brown & Trowill, 1970; Cantor, 1971; Pliskoff, Wright, & Hawkins, 1965) have managed to obtain performance for central reinforcement similar to that for conventional reinforcers by slight manipulations of the reinforcement procedure. Sidman et al. (1955) were the first to point out that performance on these schedules was related to the intensity of the brain stimulation; they further suggested that low-current stimulation was comparable to small amounts of reinforcement and that to obtain stable performance the "amount" of central reinforcement must be properly equated to conventional reinforcers. This line of argument was extended by Pliskoff and colleagues (Hawkins & Pliskoff, 1964; Pliskoff, Wright, & Hawkins, 1965; Pliskoff & Hawkins, 1967), who suggested that a standard food pellet was equivalent to several (5–20) brief trains of brain stimulation in terms of reinforcement strength. Using such a multiple-stimulation technique it has been possible to maintain FI 1-min and VI 1-min schedules (Brown & Trowill, 1970), and when combined with the two-member chaining procedure that equates temporospatial factors, performance was maintained on FI 10 min, FR 200, and differential reinforcement at low rates (DRL) 180-sec.

Cantor (1971) has also been able to obtain stable behavior with intermittent schedules (e.g., FR 200, VR 30, FI 3-min, VI 2-min, and DRL 20-sec), but using only single stimulations without an equating of temporospatial factors (Figure 5). The distinguishing

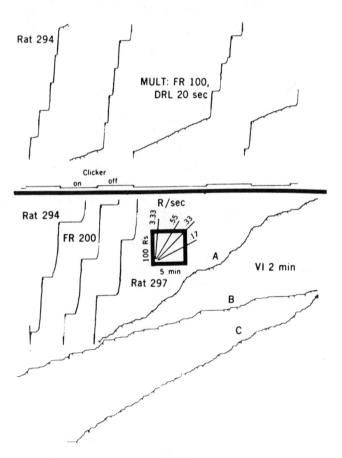

Fig. 5. Sample cumulative response curves for two rats. Rat 294 received a multiple schedule (FR 100, DRL 20-sec) and an FR 200; rat 297 is on a VI 2-min schedule. Reinforcement is indicated by oblique "pips." Brain stimulation for rat 297 was signaled on the record at A, unsignaled at B, and again signaled at C. (From Cantor, 1971. © 1971 by the American Association for the Advancement of Science.)

feature of his procedure was that the single stimulation was made predictable by preceding it with a brief, exteroceptive warning signal; when the animal depressed the bar a light came on and continued for 1 sec with the central reinforcement automatically occurring during the last .5 sec of the light. If this signal was withdrawn after mastery of the schedule, performance broke down. These results can also be viewed as enhancing the reinforcement value of central reinforcement since it has been found that predictable central reinforcement (i.e., signaled) is more reinforcing than unpredictable central reinforcement (i.e., unsignaled) (Cantor & LoLordo, 1970, 1972); the precise reason for this increase in reinforcement value is not certain.

It seems, once again, that what was initially considered a dramatic difference between central and more conventional reinforcers (i.e., maintenance of high intermittent schedules) can be viewed as an artifact of dissimilar procedures.

Influence of Drive State on Self-Stimulation

The effectiveness of food and water and other conventional reinforcers is enhanced when the animal is deprived to induce a central motive state. Is central reinforcement similarly enhanced by a central motive state produced either by deprivation of the primary reinforcer (e.g., food) or by electrical stimulation of certain areas of the brain—primarily the hypothalamus?

Early studies of the effects of food and/or water deprivation on self-stimulation rates (e.g., Brady, Boren, Conrad, & Sidman, 1957) were not conclusive, since the enhancement of rate obtained could have resulted from a general effect of deprivation on activity rather than a specific interaction between self-stimulation and the deprivation. Olds (1958a), however, was able to demonstrate with castrated male rats that some animals (medial electrode placements) showed increased self-stimulation rates when food-deprived whereas other animals (more lateral placements) showed an increased rate only when injected with androgen (male sex hormone). Not only is this a clear demonstration that general activity changes were not responsible for the enhanced response rates, but it also suggests that the effect of a particular deprivation or need state was specific to the site of stimulation.

In subsequent studies it was observed that feeding (Hoebel & Teitelbaum, 1962; Margules & Olds, 1962), drinking (Mogenson & Stevenson, 1966), copulation (Caggiula & Hoebel, 1966; Herberg, 1963), and other motivated behaviors could be elicited by electrical

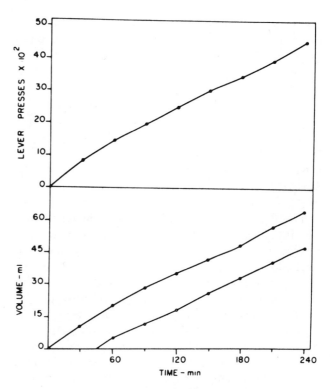

Fig. 6. Concurrent self-stimulation and elicited drinking for a period of 24 hr. The cumulative lever-press responses are shown in the top panel. In the low panel cumulative water intake (top line) and cumulative urine output (bottom line) are plotted. (From Mogenson & Stevenson, 1967.)

stimulation of brain sites effective for central reinforcement (Figure 6). The rate of self-stimulation of "feeding sites" was increased during food deprivation (Goldstein, Hill, & Templer, 1970; Margules & Olds, 1962) and following the injection of insulin which increases appetite (Hoebel, 1969). On the other hand, stomach distention, forced obesity, and injections of glucagon, procedures which reduce food intake, reduced the rate of self-stimulation of these brain sites.[2] Similarly, castration reduced, and the administration of androgens increased, the rate of self-stimulation of hypothalamic sites from which copulatory behavior could be elicited (Caggiula & Hoebel, 1966; Hoebel, 1969).

These studies suggest that central drive or motive states influence conventional and central reinforcement in a similar manner. According to Deutsch (1960) the reinforcement system functions in association with a drive system: during self-stimulation, both the reinforcement system and the drive system

---

[2] Water deprivation was reported not to change the rate of self-stimulation of hypothalamic "drinking sites" (Mogenson, 1969a). It is not clear why thirst fails to influence self-stimulation whereas hunger and sex drives enhance central reinforcement.

are activated concurrently. Hoebel (1969, 1971) has explained the results described in the previous paragraph by assuming several reinforcement systems—a hunger-reinforcement system, a thirst-reinforcement system, a sex-reinforcement system, etc., each in association with a particular drive.

SOME IMPLICATIONS OF COMPARING CENTRAL AND CONVENTIONAL REINFORCERS

From the comparisons that have been made thus far, it appears that central and conventional reinforcers are very similar if allowance is made for methodological and parametric differences in the experiments on which the comparisons are based. This is not to suggest that central and conventional reinforcers are identical. In fact, there is increasing recognition that conventional, peripheral reinforcers themselves are not identical or even homogeneous (Bolles, 1970; Shettleworth, 1972; Staddon & Simmelhag, 1971). How an animal's behavior is altered by a reinforcer, and what and how it learns, is subject to the constraints of its species-specific behavioral organization; as Skinner (1966a) pointed out several years ago, behavior is a function of phylogenic contingencies as well as ontogenic contingencies.

Central reinforcement may also not be homogeneous. It has been suggested that there are subsystems of reinforcement (Gallistel & Beagley, 1971), and it has also been suggested that they may be related to feeding, drinking, or other drives (Hoebel, 1969) or to various species-typical behaviors (Glickman & Schiff, 1967). Even if there is a single central reinforcement system (as assumed by Stein, 1969), it may be activated less directly or less strongly depending on the sites of stimulation. The electrical stimulation may activate other neural systems besides central reinforcement, and these "side effects" may alter its effectiveness in reinforcing operant responses.[3]

In any case, in view of the similarities of central and conventional reinforcers it may be asked whether there are any advantages in using central reinforcement which permit a unique contribution to the experimental analysis of behavior or to the better understanding of the mechanisms of reinforcement.

In terms of rate of operant responding and preference behavior, direct stimulation of appropriate brain sites is the most potent reinforcer available. It can be used without the undesirable contaminating effects of conventional reinforcers such as the stress of food deprivation or aversive peripheral shock and the satiating effects of the consummatory behavior. Self-stimulation may be considered a "pure operant"; it can be maintained for relatively long periods of time without excessive ingestion of food or water or other consequences which inhibit the operant behavior. It is the purest form of incentive whose effects have a rapid onset and rapid offset. Therefore, with the use of central reinforcement it is possible to have the greatest degree of behavioral control and to maintain this control for long periods of time. This characteristic of central reinforcement has made it a valuable tool in psychopharmacology and has made possible the pioneering studies of biofeedback (see this chapter's introduction).

In the hands of experts trained in operant technology, the purity, potency, and insatiability of central reinforcement permit a control of human behavior which is awesome to contemplate. The decision about the legitimate use of central reinforcement for behavior modification in the treatment of self-destructive tendencies and other abnormal behaviors or in the training of mentally retarded children will not be an easy one; Michael Crichton's recent novel *Terminal Man* (1972) highlights the ethical issues associated with the use of central reinforcement for such purposes. However, there is no question that the neurobehavioral technology is available for an impressive degree of control of man's behavior.

The other unique feature and advantage of central reinforcement is that it permits direct access to the mechanisms of the brain that subserve reinforcement. Although this may not appear important to those interested in reinforcement exclusively from the viewpoint of behavioral control, it does excite physiological psychologists and other neuroscientists concerned with the neural substrates of reinforcement, motivation, and learning. Self-stimulation experiments have implicated a number of brain structures which subserve reinforcement. Sophisticated experiments which combine electrophysiological, histological, and neurochemical techniques with operant techniques are beginning to elucidate the characteristics of the positive reinforcement system and its relationship with memory, motor, and perceptual systems (Gallistel, Rolls, & Greene, 1969; Rolls, 1972; Smith & Coons, 1970). This

---

[3] Reinforcing electrical stimulation may elicit various sorts of respondents such as integrated consummatory responses, forced motor movements, autonomic changes (e.g., heart rate and blood pressure), as well as endocrine changes (elevated ACTH), some of which may be entirely independent of the reinforcing character of the brain stimulation. Such spurious effects are believed to result from the simultaneous activation of a number of closely intermingled neural systems by the relatively indiscrete electrical stimulation.

active and interesting field of research promises to reveal the circuitry and the workings of the neural pathways that subserve both central and conventional reinforcers.

At the present time the exact neural basis for central reinforcement is still uncertain in spite of vigorous investigation for nearly two decades. This state of affairs has prompted Crow (1972c) to comment, "As a bridge between psychological theory and neurophysiology the value of the discovery [of central reinforcement] is limited by the fact that the anatomical pathways which must be activated to yield the response have not been identified" (p. 414). However, new developments in mapping neural pathways using histochemical techniques (to provide a chemical neuroanatomy of the hypothalamus and limbic system) may lead to the identification of the neural substrates of central reinforcement (discussed below).

THE NATURE OF CENTRAL REINFORCEMENT

An observer who sees an animal self-stimulate its brain for the first time is usually very impressed with this fascinating phenomenon. Typically he asks, "Why does the animal do that?" What is the nature and the mechanism of central reinforcement?

A number of explanations of self-stimulation have been proposed during the last 20 years. However, in spite of intensive and often ingenious research it is not possible to say with certainty whether any of these interpretations is correct. In this final section we first consider two of the most popular views and then present some speculations about the mechanisms of central reinforcement.

Central Reinforcement from the Viewpoint of Drive Theory and Response Reinforcement

When self-stimulation of the brain was discovered, and for several years thereafter, drive-reduction theory was the dominant theory of reinforcement and learning. It is not surprising that attempts were made to explain the self-stimulation phenomenon from this theoretical point of view (Miller, 1960), and studies of central reinforcement were undertaken with this theory in mind (Deutsch & Howarth, 1963).

In one of his earlier papers J. Olds (1956) proposed that positively reinforcing brain stimulation "must excite some of the nerve cells that would be excited by satisfaction of the basic drives—hunger, sex, thirst, and so forth" (p. 15). In accordance with drive-reduction theory, Olds was suggesting that central reinforcement is due to the brain stimulation mimicking (or activating neural systems concerned with) the reduction of one of the basic biological drives, which in turn reinforces the operant response. However, a few years later observations were made which suggested just the opposite: feeding (Hoebel & Teitelbaum, 1962; Margules & Olds, 1962), drinking (Mogenson & Stevenson, 1966), and copulatory (Caggiula & Hoebel, 1966; Herberg, 1963) behavior were elicited from the same electrode sites that were highly effective for self-stimulation.

Initially it seemed paradoxical that the animal pressed a lever to stimulate its hypothalamus making it seek food or water. Deutsch (1960) proposed that there is a distinctive reinforcement system of the brain activated during self-stimulation and that it functions in association with a drive system. He did not see any paradox, since he assumed that the reinforcement system and the drive system had to be activated concurrently. In other words, drive induction, produced either in a conventional manner (e.g., water deprivation) or by electrical stimulation of the brain, is a necessary condition for reinforcement. Glickman and Schiff's (1967) attempt to resolve this paradox involved a departure from drive-reduction theory and a different view of both the nature of reinforcement and the mechanisms by which feeding and drinking are elicited by electrical stimulation of the brain. They pointed out that the behaviors elicited from the same brain sites as self-stimulation (feeding, drinking, gnawing, copulating, etc.) are species-typical responses that contribute to adaptation to the environment and to survival. In the course of biological evolution animals endowed with the neurological apparatus to make these responses will survive and reproduce. According to Glickman and Schiff, reinforcement results from the activation, either by natural stimuli or by electrical stimulation of the brain, of neural pathways that initiate species-typical behaviors. They assumed that there is a single system which has conventional reinforcement and drive properties. In some ways, their proposal is a new version of Sheffield's (Sheffield, Roby, & Campbell, 1954) consummatory response theory, and they avoid the paradox referred to above by avoiding the use of terms like *hunger drive* or *drive reduction*. Unlike Deutsch, they do not assume a distinctive drive system.

Although self-stimulation and elicited drinking have been observed to occur concurrently (Mogenson, 1969a), the elicited drinking is not necessary for central reinforcement. The administration of amphetamine, which markedly reduced drinking elicited by hypothalamic stimulation, did not reduce, but rather increased dramatically, the rate of self-stimulation of the same hypothalamic site (Mogenson, 1968). Furthermore, by varying the parameters of stimulation, the "drive-eliciting" and central reinforcement effects of hypothalamic stimulation could be dissociated. Using a train of hypothalamic stimulation .5 sec or longer both self-stimulation and elicited drinking were observed, whereas with a train duration of .1–.2 sec self-stimulation occurred in the absence of elicited drinking (Figure 7). Lesions have also been used to dissociate the drive-inducing and the central reinforcement properties of hypothalamic stimulation; it has been shown that lesions of the substantia nigra selectively disrupt the elicited carrying of objects that occurred concomitantly with self-stimulation in a shuttlebox but did not interfere with self-stimulation per se (Phillips, 1973). Finally, it should be noted that the current intensity threshold to elicit feeding and drinking is below the threshold for self-stimulation when stimulus train durations of more than 1 sec are used (Coons & Cruce, 1968; Huston, 1971, 1972; Miller, 1960).

Central Reinforcement from the Viewpoint of Incentive Motivation

Electrical stimulation of the hypothalamus may elicit drinking and feeding not by activating systems for internal deficit signals, as suggested in the previous section, but by mimicking incentive stimuli (or "appetite-whetting" stimuli) associated with drinking and feeding; it is then not a paradox that animals self-stimulate "feeding sites" and "drinking sites." Certain stimuli, such as sweet and salty solutions, are particularly effective reinforcers (Pfaffman, 1960; Young, 1959), even in the absence of biological deficits and needs; a sensory stimulus "can function as a reinforcer in its own right" (Pfaffman, 1960, p. 255). Pfaffman has suggested that central reinforcement is due to the activation of neural pathways that normally transmit such incentive motivational stimuli.

The results of experiments by Pfaffman and Young, as well as those from peripheral self-stimulation experiments (Campbell, 1971), suggest that brain self-stimulation results from activating pathways of the brain that transmit signals from natural reinforcers. These include inputs from smell and taste and other exteroceptive stimuli, but also may include proprioceptive and interoceptive inputs. In higher animals "central reward pathways" are also activated by cognitive processes. Campbell (1971), after noting the pleasure one gets from mathematics, science, chess, or crossword puz-

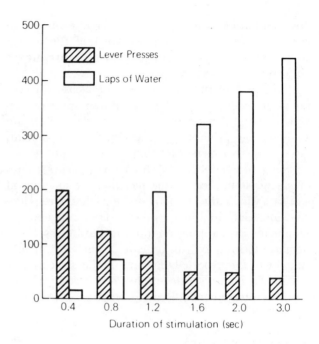

Fig. 7. The effect of varying the duration of hypothalamic stimulation on self-stimulation and elicited drinking. Elicited drinking occurs only when the duration is greater than .4–.5 sec. The fastest rates of self-stimulation occurred with the shortest duration of stimulation. (From Mogenson & Stevenson, 1966.)

zles, maintains that "only in the human brain can thinking activate the limbic pleasure areas" (p. 22). It appears that in man and other animals with complex brains, reinforcement and motivated behaviors depend on natural processes concerned with higher cognitive functions as well as those that process interoceptive, exteroceptive, and proprioceptive inputs.

Central Reinforcement as the Interaction of Incentive Stimuli and a Central Motive State

It is now generally acknowledged that there was too much emphasis in the past on the role of internal, deficit signals for the initiation of motivated behaviors and the so-called drives. A number of investigators have emphasized the importance of identifying and studying the influence of the various controlling stimuli for self-stimulation (Lenzer, 1972) and for other motivated behaviors (Flynn, Vanegas, Foote, & Edwards, 1970; Roberts, 1970). There is an increasing acceptance of the view that motivated behavior in general and reinforcement in particular depend on external as well as internal stimuli (Bindra, 1969; Mogenson & Huang, 1973). One of the best examples of the importance of this interaction of internal and external stimuli is the mislabeling of drive states that are initiated by internal stimuli in the absence of appropriate environmental signals as reported by Schachter (1967). It appears that the central motive state that subserves a particular motivated behavior depends on both internal, deficit signals and external signals.

Support for this view comes from studies of the effects of sensory stimuli on brain self-stimulation. Rats self-stimulated faster when induced by the brain stimulation to drink water, apparently because of the oral stimulation (Figure 8; see also Mogenson & Kaplinsky, 1970), and when the sensory stimulation was further increased by adding saccharine to the water they self-stimulated at a still faster rate (Phillips & Mogenson, 1968): external incentive stimuli enhanced central reinforcement. Even when the external stimulus is not response-contingent, self-stimulation is increased, as demonstrated when rats self-stimulated with a background odor present (Phillips, 1970). It appears, therefore, that the external stimulus is not enhancing response reinforcement but rather is enhancing or interacting with the central motive state induced by the electrical stimulation. Furthermore, when the current intensity is below threshold, rats will not respond unless water is available, so that oral stimulation accompanies self-stimulation (Mendelson, 1967; Mogenson, Morgan, Phillips, & Stevenson, 1968).

External stimuli are frequently most effective as motivational stimuli when they occur in the presence of a central motive state—for example, following a period of water or food deprivation. Stimulation of central reinforcement sites induces a motive state—it elicits feeding (Hoebel & Teitelbaum, 1962) and drinking (Mogenson & Stevenson, 1966)—so that the animal is more responsive to appropriate external stimuli (such as the sight of water or smell of food) and its behavior is appropriate to the situation. The brain stimulation also activates neurons concerned with the transmission and processing of external, motivational stimuli (Pfaffman, 1960). The rate of self-stimulation, and apparently the strength of central reinforcement, is increased either by the presence of appropriate external motivational stimuli (see previous paragraph) or by increasing the central motive state (by food deprivation—for example, J. Olds, 1958a). It follows, therefore, that the event designated reinforcement is the occurrence of external motivational stimuli in the presence of a central motive state.[4] This combination occurs when an animal encounters food or water in the presence of an appropriate drive state, and a similar combination is produced apparently by stimulation of certain brain sites which yield central reinforcement.

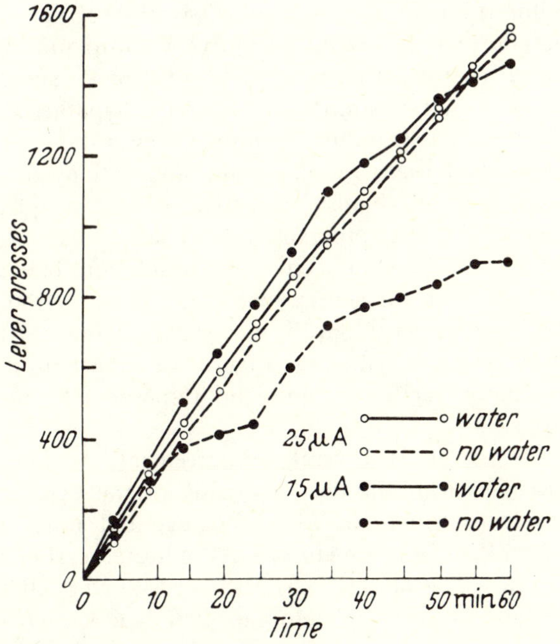

Rolls (1972) has obtained unit activity data which can be interpreted to support the view that the reinforcement of self-stimulation is primarily associated with incentive, motivational stimuli. Rolls reported that with self-stimulation from both the lateral hypothalamus and septum, neurons in the amygdala were activated. If stimulus-bound feeding and drinking could be elicited from the hypothalamic placements, not only was there neural activation of the amygdala but in addition cells in the midbrain were activated. This midbrain activity did not occur from sites which maintained self-stimulation only. Rolls has suggested that these midbrain neurons are associated with increased "arousal"—or, in our terms, they contribute to the central motive state. One could speculate further that activation of the neurons of the amygdala may be involved primarily with incentive stimuli, given the amygdala's involvement with sensory input, whereas the midbrain structures are more involved with the induction of a central motive state. It could be argued, therefore, that since self-stimulation occurred only when amygdaloid neurons were activated, central reinforcement depends primarily on activating neural elements concerned with incentive motivation.

Fig. 8. A rat self-stimulates and is induced by the hypothalamic stimulation to drink water. At the lower current intensity (15 µA) the rate of self-stimulation is faster when the animal is induced to drink. Self-stimulation is facilitated by the oral stimulation. (From Mogenson & Morgan, 1967.)

[4] These views are similar to those of Bindra (1968), who has made a comprehensive historical analysis of theories of conventional reinforcers and the changing emphasis in the treatment of motivation.

It is difficult, however, on the basis of these data to exclude the possibility that such reinforcing brain stimulation might also influence the central motive state so that the magnitude of the central reinforcement increases as the electrical stimulation has a greater effect on the central motive state. The data reviewed earlier which demonstrate increases in self-stimulation rates with appropriate changes in the central motive state would of course support the involvement of the central motive state in central reinforcement.

A Model for Central and Conventional Reinforcement

If central and conventional reinforcement are similar, as has been suggested in earlier sections, it should be possible to deal with both in relation to the same theoretical model. This will be attempted in this section.

The model shown in Figure 9, which we have selected for purposes of illustration, is a slight modification of the one proposed by Milner (1970). It assumes, as indicated above, that reinforcement results from an interaction of appropriate internal and external stimuli. External stimuli that are involved in incentive motivation have discriminative properties, but they also, along with internal, deficit stimuli, induce a central motive state. We are defining *reinforcement*, as indicated above, as the occurrence of incentive stimuli in the presence of a central motive state. We shall first describe how this model applies to a conventional reinforcer (i.e., water) and then go on to consider central reinforcement.

When an animal is deprived, water-deficit signals initiate behavioral activation and increased exploration. According to the model, exploratory activity results from these drive stimuli, increasing arousal which influences the motor facilitator, and from increased input to the response switch mechanism, which accounts for the variability of behavioral response. If the animal encounters water, which is an appropriate incentive stimulus, and drinks, the response-hold mechanism is activated and it in turn inhibits the response switch mechanism. The animal will then continue to drink, since this behavior keeps it in the presence of the incentive stimulus, until the drive stimuli are reduced by water intake (or inhibited by short-term satiety signals) and the influence of the arousal mechanism on the motor facilitator and the response-hold mechanism disappears.

How is central reinforcement explained by this model? One suggestion is that central reinforcement results from the simultaneous activation of pathways that normally transmit incentive stimuli and drive stimuli (pathways designated 1 and 2 in Figure 9), a proposal that is similar to Deutsch's hypothesis discussed earlier. Initially the animal presses the lever by chance and turns on the brain stimulation; the response-hold mechanism is activated and it quickly acquires the lever-press response. The response switch is then inhibited and the self-stimulation behavior may continue for a very long time. If extinction occurs rapidly, as is often the case when the brain stimulation ceases, it is because there is no longer input to the motor facilitator and the response-hold mechanism.

The strongest central reinforcement is obtained with electrical stimulation of sites of the hypothalamus from which drinking, feeding, and other motivated behaviors are elicited. As indicated earlier, the rate of self-stimulation is increased during elicited drinking (Mogenson & Morgan, 1967) and is increased further by adding saccharine to the water (Phillips & Mogenson, 1968). The rate of self-stimulation is also frequently increased by food deprivation (J. Olds, 1958a). Assuming that pathways 1 and 2 are being activated during concurrent self-stimulation and drink-

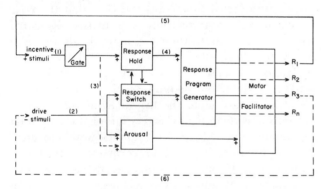

Fig. 9. A model of central and conventional reinforcement. Reinforcement is assumed to result from the interaction of a central motive state with appropriate incentive stimuli (see text). A central motive state is induced by internal deficit (pathway 2) stimuli and by external incentive (conditioned and unconditioned, pathway 1) stimuli. Many incentive stimuli have at least a weak arousing effect (pathway 3) and also influence the central motive state. Central reinforcement according to the model is due to the activation of pathway 1 or pathways 1 and 2 concurrently. When the response-hold mechanism is activated by appropriate inputs along the incentive pathway the response switch mechanism is inhibited, the response program generator sends a fixed command to the motor facilitator, and a stable behavior (R_1, such as lever pressing for brain stimulation) occurs. If this behavior is accompanied by appropriate stimuli (e.g., water or saccharine solution in rats that self-stimulate and drink concurrently—Mogenson & Morgan, 1967), the central reinforcement is facilitated (pathway 5). On the other hand, drive-reducing stimuli (gastric distention, elevated blood sugar) reduce reinforcement (pathway 6). (Adapted from Milner, 1970.)

ing or feeding, we suggest that the oral stimulation and the deprivation enhance central reinforcement by increasing the inputs along pathways 1 and 2, respectively.

Another possibility is that the central reinforcement is due to activation of only those pathways that transmit incentive stimuli (pathway 1). Certain conventional incentive stimuli seem to be effective reinforcers even in the absence of internal, deficit (drive) stimuli (Pfaffman, 1960). Perhaps this is because they have at least a weak arousal effect (see postulated pathway 3), thereby influencing the motor facilitator as well as the response-hold mechanism.

Central Catecholamine Pathways and Self-Stimulation

The region of the medial forebrain bundle as it passes through the lateral hypothalamus (LH) has been recognized for some time as the "hotspot" for self-stimulation (J. Olds & M. E. Olds, 1964). For a time it appeared that this might be because of the association of this region with drive systems such as feeding, drinking, etc. (Hoebel, 1969); Mogenson, 1969a). More recent evidence, however, suggests that the potent central reinforcement from stimulation of this region results from activating ascending noradrenergic and dopaminergic neurons which are densely concentrated here (German & Bowden, 1974).

The noradrenergic and dopaminergic pathways are shown in Figure 10. Using histofluorescence techniques a group of Swedish workers demonstrated that these neural pathways project from the midbrain and lower in the brainstem through the region of the lateral hypothalamus to the basal ganglia, limbic forebrain structures, and cerebral cortex (Fuxe, Hokfelt, & Ungerstedt, 1970; Ungerstedt, 1971). Self-stimulation results from stimulation of ascending noradrenergic neurons in the medial forebrain bundle (Stein, Wise, & Berger, 1972) as well as from stimulation of the locus coeruleus, the site from which fibers of the dorsal noradrenergic bundle originate (Crow, 1972b; Ritter & Stein, 1973) and from stimulation of the ventral noradrenergic neurons (Ritter & Stein, 1974). Self-stimulation has also been obtained from a number of sites known to contain dopaminergic neurons, such as the substantia nigra (Crow, 1972a; Phillips & Fibiger, 1973; Routtenberg & Malsbury, 1969) and the area adjacent to the intrapeduncular nucleus (Dreese, 1966). Furthermore, it has been reported that dopamine is released from dopaminergic terminals during self-stimulation (Arbuthnott, Crow, Fuxe, Olson, & Ungerstedt, 1970).

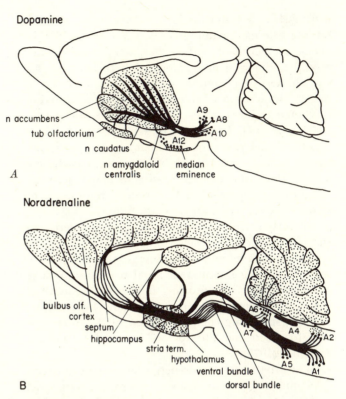

Fig. 10. Catecholaminergic pathways demonstrated with the histofluorescence technique which project from the midbrain and brainstem through the hypothalamus to limbic forebrain structures (tub. olfactorium, bulbus olf., septum, n. accumbens, n. amygdaloid centralis, hippocampus), basal ganglia (n. caudatus), and cerebral cortex. The locus coeruleus is at the site of the A6 cell bodies as shown in B. The substantia nigra and the interpeduncular nucleus are in the region of the A9 and A10 cell bodies shown in A. (From Ungerstedt, 1971.)

Experiments involving neuropharmacological manipulations of these catecholaminergic pathways also influence self-stimulation, providing additional evidence for their role in central reinforcement. Drugs such as alpha-methyl-*p*-tyrosine, which inhibit catecholamine synthesis, and reserpine, which deplete catecholamine stores, cause a decrement in self-stimulation (Cooper, Black, & Paolino, 1971; J. Olds, 1956; Poschel & Ninteman, 1966; Stein, 1962). On the other hand, drugs such as monoamine oxidase inhibitors, which increase catecholamine levels, and amphetamine or cocaine, which increase the synaptic release and block the reuptake of catecholamines, facilitate self-stimulation (Crow, 1970; Domino & Olds, 1972; Horowitz, Chow, & Carlton, 1962; M. E. Olds, 1970; Phillips & Fibiger, 1973; Poschel, 1969; Stein, 1962, 1964). Stein and Wise (1969) maintained that noradrenergic neurons have an exclusive role in self-stimulation. However, more recent neuropharmacological evidence has implicated dopaminergic neurons (Lippa, Antelman, Fisher, & Canfield, 1973). Convincing evidence for the role of dopaminergic neurons has been provided in experiments utilizing dopamine blockers and agonists. Pimozide and haloperidol, relatively selective blockers of dopaminergic receptors when given in low doses, cause a marked reduction in self-stimulation (Liebman & Butcher, 1973; Wauquier & Niemegeer, 1972). Rats will lever-press to self-administer, via a jugular catheter, a central dopamine-receptor stimulant, apomorphine. The self-infusion of apomorphine apparently reinforces lever pressing because it activates dopaminergic synapses of the "central reinforcement system" (Baxter, Glickman, Stein, & Scerni, 1974).

Recently there has been a good deal of interest in the physiological and behavioral effects of lesioning the noradrenergic and dopaminergic pathways. Since such studies suggest the functional relevance of these pathways and might provide some clues about their role in self-stimulation, they will now be reviewed briefly; for a more complete review of this literature see Mogenson and Phillips (1975) and Stricker and Zigmond (1975).

When the dorsal noradrenergic and the nigrostriatal dopaminergic pathways are damaged or destroyed with electrolytic lesions or more selectively with a neurotoxin, 6-hydroxydopamine, the tonic alertness and phasic behavioral arousal of the animal are disrupted (Chu & Bloom, 1973; Jones, Bobillier, Pin, & Jouvet, 1973). The animal is drowsy and somnolent, suffers from sensory neglect and disturbance of sensorimotor integration, and has difficulty in initiating behavior (Fibiger, Zis, & McGeer, 1973; Marshall & Teitelbaum, 1973; Stricker & Zigmond, 1975; Ungerstedt, 1971). Included in the behavioral deficits is a disturbance in feeding and drinking. The dorsal noradrenergic pathway which projects diffusely to the cerebral cortex inhibits cortical inhibitory neurons, thereby causing cortical activation and behavioral arousal (E. Roberts, 1974). The nigrostriatal dopaminergic pathway projects to extrapyramidal motor structures. When these pathways are damaged there are deficits in behavioral arousal, extrapyramidal motor functions, and affect (Stricker & Zigmond, 1975).

If these catecholamine pathways have an essential role in central reinforcement, as suggested earlier, damage or destruction of the pathways should cause a severe decrement in self-stimulation. This has been demonstrated using 6-hydroxydopamine, the neurotoxin which selectively destroys noradrenergic and dopaminergic neurons. When central catecholamine neurons are destroyed by administering 6-hydroxydopamine into the ventricles, self-stimulation of the lateral hypothalamus is markedly reduced (Breese, Howard, & Leahy, 1971; Phillips, unpublished observations; Stein & Wise, 1971).

The anatomical, neuropharmacological, and lesioning studies discussed in the previous paragraphs show that central reinforcement is associated with stimulation of brain catecholamine (CA) pathways. We now consider the implications of this relationship for understanding the mechanisms of brain self-stimulation.

As indicated above, the most popular explanations of brain self-stimulation were from the viewpoint of drive and incentive theories of motivation. It is not surprising, therefore, that the first attempt to deal with the role of CA pathways in central reinforcement was in terms of drive and incentive systems. Crow (1973) suggested that stimulation of the dopaminergic (DA) nigrostriatal pathway is reinforcing because it is involved in the processing of incentive stimuli. Olfactory projections go to the habenular nucleus and then to the interpeduncular nucleus where, according to Crow, they influence the dopaminergic neurons (A9 cells shown in Fig. 10). Self-stimulation of the DA pathway results from the activation of fibers that transmit olfactory incentive stimuli. Crow hypothesized also that the dorsal noradrenergic (NA) bundle subserves central reinforcement based on drive reduction. Anatomical evidence is again cited in support of the proposal, particularly the close relationship between dorsal NA neurons in the locus coeruleus (A6 cells shown in Fig. 9) and the nucleus of the tractus solitarius which receives gustatory input. Since gustatory stimuli are closely associated with the termination of gustatory behavior, Crow suggests that fibers of the dorsal NA pathway are activated by stimuli associated with drive reduction.

Crow's proposal to account for the role of CA pathways in self-stimulation emphasized sensory stimuli. Although olfactory and gustatory signals and pathways are stressed, the model might also be extended to deal with visual, auditory, proprioceptive, interoceptive, and other biologically significant stimuli known to be involved in reinforcement (Mogenson & Phillips, 1975). Crow's formulation will appeal to those who stress the sensory side of the nervous system and for whom the concepts of drive reduction and incentive have special significance. However, it does not deal with the relationship of the CA pathways to the neural systems for the initiation and motor control of behavior, a serious shortcoming for those who favor the views of Glickman and Schiff (1967) or Milner (1970) rather than those of Deutsch and Howarth (1963) or Pfaffman (1960). In the final section we consider the role of the CA pathways in brain self-stimulation from the viewpoint of their anatomical and physiological relationships with neural systems concerned with the motor control of behavior.

Central Reinforcement as the Inhibition by Catecholamine Pathways of the Neural Systems for the Motor Control of Behavior

The DA nigrostriatal pathway and the dorsal NA pathway project to the striatum, the cerebral cortex, and the cerebellum, structures which make important contributions to the motor control of behavior (Figure 11). Damage to these pathways, as indicated in the previous section, disrupts feeding, drinking, and other goal-directed behaviors; one of the most prominent deficits is in the initiation of responding. Although there has been considerable interest in the role of these pathways in feeding and drinking, because of their strategic location at the interface between neural systems concerned with the "intention to respond" and those concerned with "motor control" it is likely that they contribute to a variety of behaviors.

Motor control of behavior depends on complex in-

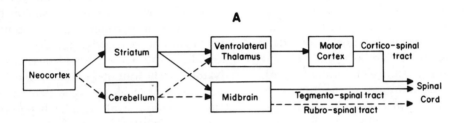

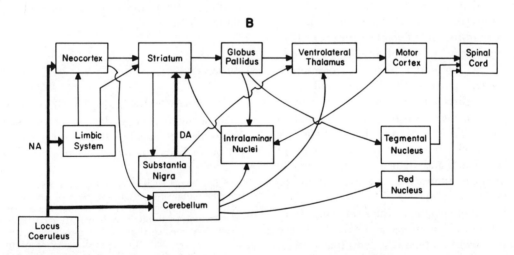

Fig. 11. The DA nigrostriatal pathway and the dorsal NA pathway project to key structures involved in the initiation and motor control of behavior—the striatum, the cerebral cortex, and the cerebellum.
(A.) Parallel systems project from the neocortex to the lower motor neurons of the spinal cord via the striatum and cerebellum. The striatum, which is in a position to sample activity in the motor cortex and cerebellum (via projections through the intralaminar nucleus of the thalamus), the limbic system, and the sensory and association cortex, has an important role in the translation of the "intention to respond" into the "command signals" for motor control. The cerebellum contributes to error detection through projections to the motor cortex (via the ventrolateral thalamus) and provides subroutines for the execution of the intended movement. (Based on Kemp & Powell, 1971.)
(B). The DA nigrostriatal pathway and the dorsal NA pathway exert inhibitory effects on the striatum, cerebral cortex, and cerebellum. According to Milner (1975), these inhibitory effects are the key to the central reinforcement from direct stimulation of these pathways, since these effects suppress response-inhibitory systems permitting the (reinforced) ongoing behavior to be protected and to continue. (From Mogenson & Phillips, 1975.)

terrelationships among a number of brain structures (Figure 11). It is not our purpose to consider the dynamic functioning of these structures and pathways (for further details see Kemp & Powell, 1971; Mogenson & Phillips, 1975). Instead we are concerned with the possibility that the anatomical and functional relationships of the DA and NA pathways with neural systems for motor control may provide some clues about their role in central and conventional reinforcement. Inhibitory effects are exerted by the DA nigrostriatal pathway and the dorsal NA pathway on the striatum, cerebral cortex, and cerebellum (Conner, 1970; Curtis & Crawford, 1969; Segal & Bloom, 1974). This may be surprising, since these pathways make important contributions to cortical activation and behavioral arousal (Jones et al., 1973; Jouvet, 1972). However, the electrophysiological and behavioral data are easily accounted for by the proposal that DA and NA axon terminals inhibit inhibitory interneurons, thereby causing the disinhibition of neurons concerned with cortical activation and motor control of behavior (E. Roberts, 1974). According to Roberts, the central nervous system consists of "genetically preprogrammed circuits which are released for action by neurons (command neurons) that are strategically located at junctions in neuronal hierarchies dealing with both sensory input and effector output" (p. 127). It has been suggested by several investigators (e.g., Glickman & Schiff, 1967) that such preprogrammed circuits for biting, chewing, swallowing, and other components of goal-directed behaviors are represented in the brainstem. Roberts suggests that "segmental command neurons, like the circuits they control, are largely inhibited from above, and that a decrease in inhibition allows command neurons to fire, thereby releasing the preprogrammed circuits over whose activity they preside" (p. 128).[5]

Milner (1975) has suggested that the inhibitory effects of the DA and NA neurons, and specifically the disinhibition they exert on neural systems that initiate and control behavior, are the key to understanding self-stimulation and central reinforcement. His proposal will now be presented.

It is well known that ongoing behavioral responses may be interrupted by a novel stimulus. Milner attributes this to the activation of a response-inhibitory system in the cerebral cortex.[6] The interruption of ongoing behavior by sensory stimuli does not occur, however, if the behavior is reinforced either by a conventional reinforcer or by central reinforcement. According to Milner, activation of the inhibitory catecholamine pathways, either by direct stimulation in the self-stimulation procedure or due to the central effects of conventional reinforcers, suppresses the response-inhibitory system so that the ongoing behavior is protected and maintained.

In an earlier section we emphasized a number of similarities between reinforcement obtained with conventional reinforcers and that from direct stimulation of the brain. Milner's ingenious hypothesis suggests a mechanism common to both conventional reinforcement and central reinforcement. Furthermore, it provides a role for drive and incentive stimuli as activators of the catecholamine "reward" neurons and at the same time links these neurons to neural systems for motor control. The hypothesis appears to provide a fruitful integration and synthesis of the previous hypotheses of central reinforcement that stressed sensory input (Deutsch & Howarth, 1963; Pfaffman, 1960) and response elicitation (Glickman & Schiff, 1967).

SUMMARY

The discovery of brain self-stimulation in the early 1950s aroused a good deal of enthusiasm among behavioral and neural scientists interested in the modification of behavior by experience and the underlying

---

[5] Roberts (1974), after reviewing the relevant evidence, hypothesizes that fibers of the dorsal NA pathway inhibit γ-aminobutyric acid (GABA) interneurons in the upper layers of the cerebral cortex, thereby influencing electroencephalographic cortical arousal and behavior. He also suggests that inhibitory GABA neurons in the striatum, which tonically inhibit preprogrammed neural circuits for patterned postural control and movements, could be inhibited by fibers of the DA nigrostriatal pathway.

[6] The increased activity and greater persistence of exploratory behavior following lesions of certain regions of the cerebral cortex and hippocampus indicate that these structures are part of a response-inhibitory system. Milner (1976) suggests that "arousal of any cortical activity produces a transient response inhibition" so that "the immediate effect of the presentation of a new stimulus is to interrupt the on-going response." Activation of the catecholamine pathways protects these responses from being suppressed, however, by inhibiting the response-inhibitory system. "Thus, food, for a hungry animal, not only elicits approach, chewing, swallowing, and so on, but sends inhibitory input to [the response-inhibitory system] to ensure that cortical outflow does not interfere with the performance." Similarly, direct electrical stimulation of the catecholamine pathways could prevent cortical outflow from disrupting the responses that preceded the central stimulation so that the self-stimulation behavior continues.

Milner's views could be easily integrated with those of Roberts (1974). Although Milner limits his analysis to disinhibition of cortical functions, it could be readily extended to include disinhibition of the striatum by the inhibitory effects of DA nigrostriatal neurons on striatal inhibitory interneurons. In other words, the response-inhibitory system postulated by Milner could be represented in the striatum as well as the cerebral cortex.

modifiability of the nervous system. The potent reinforcement of various operant responses by electrical stimulation of the hypothalamus, limbic structures, and other regions of the brain seemed to provide a means of studying directly the basic mechanisms of reinforcement and learning. A number of the subsequent studies appeared to demonstrate, however, some important differences between central and conventional reinforcers—in the rapidity of response acquisition, in the persistence and relative insatiability of responding, in extinction, when used in partial reinforcement programs, and when presented with secondary reinforcers. Some of these differences appeared to be anomalies when considered in relation to drive-reduction theory, the most widely accepted and influential theory of motivation and reinforcement at that time. Also, some of the experimental findings, such as the elicitation of drinking and feeding from self-stimulation sites, seemed paradoxical when considered from this theoretical point of view; for example, why should an animal perform a response which makes it thirsty when, according to the theory, reinforcement results from drive reduction?

In recent years, there has been less emphasis on drive theory and increasing interest in incentive motivation. Evidence from self-stimulation experiments has contributed to this trend, which has led to a completely different way of thinking about self-stimulation and central reinforcement, as well as about the broader field of motivation and conventional reinforcement. At the same time, it was demonstrated that the differences between central and conventional reinforcers were not really of a fundamental nature but were due primarily to procedural differences, particularly in the delay of reinforcement and the deprivation state of the animal. This recent concern with the similarities between central and conventional reinforcement, in contrast to the emphasis on differences in the past, has revitalized the view that self-stimulation can provide important insights about reinforcement and motivation.

Rate of self-stimulation, a widely used although imperfect index of central reinforcement, is increased by hunger, the administration of sex hormones, and other manipulations that induce or increase a central motive state. Self-stimulation is also increased by taste, smell, and other relevant incentive stimuli. These observations suggest that reinforcement involves an interaction of a central motive state with incentive stimuli.

Recently it was shown that central reinforcement is associated with stimulation of catecholamine pathways of the brain. It has been proposed that the nigrostriatal dopamine pathway transmits incentive stimuli, that the dorsal noradrenalin pathway transmits drive stimuli, and that these form the basis of central reinforcement. An alternative hypothesis has been derived from the observation that these catecholamine pathways exert inhibitory effects on the cerebral cortex, striatum, and other neural structures concerned with the initiation and motor control of behavior. The hypothesis was considered that stimulation of catecholamine pathways is reinforcing because they exert suppressive effects on response-inhibitory systems of the brain. This hypothesis not only accounts for conventional reinforcement but also integrates and synthesizes previous hypotheses of central reinforcement that emphasized sensory input and response elicitation.

APPENDIX A

Some examples of studies of self-stimulation from various sites and species

PYRIFORM CORTEX: Rat–Olds & Olds, 1963: Cat–O'Donohue & Hagamen, 1967.

CINGULATE GYRUS: Rat–Olds & Olds, 1963: Cat–O'Donohue & Hagamen, 1967.

HIPPOCAMPUS: Rat–Olds & Olds, 1963; Ursin, Ursin, & Olds, 1966: Cat–O'Donohue & Hagamen, 1967.

FORNIX: Rat–Olds & Olds, 1963: Cat–O'Donohue & Hagamen, 1967: Gerbil–Routtenberg & Kramis, 1967: Rabbit–Brunner, 1966.

SEPTUM: Rat–Olds & Olds, 1963: Cat–O'Donohue & Hagamen, 1967; Wilkinson & Peele, 1963: Monkey–Bursten & Delgado, 1958; Lilly, 1957: Man–Heath, 1963; Bishop, Elder, & Heath, 1963: Rabbit–Campbell, 1968.

OLFACTORY TUBERCLE: Rat–Olds & Olds, 1963: Cat–O'Donohue & Hagamen, 1967.

OLFACTORY BULB: Rat–Routtenberg, 1971; Phillips, 1970.

PREOPTIC: Rat–Olds & Olds, 1963; Olds, Travis, & Schwing, 1960: Cat–O'Donohue & Hagamen, 1967; Wilkinson & Peele, 1963: Monkey–McHugh, Black, & Mason, 1966.

LATERAL HYPOTHALAMUS: Rat–Olds & Olds, 1963: Cat–O'Donohue & Hagamen, 1967; Wilkinson & Peele, 1963: Monkey–Briese & Olds, 1964: Rabbit–Brunner, 1966: Goat–Persson, 1962: Squirrel–Wetzel & King, 1966; Wetzel, King, & Nowicki, 1967: Dog–Stark & Boyd, 1963; Bacon & Wong, 1972: Pigeon–David, Davison, & Webster, 1972; MacPhail, 1966; Webster & Beale, 1970.

VENTROMEDIAL HYPOTHALAMUS: Rat–Olds & Olds, 1963: Cat–O'Donohue & Hagamen, 1967.

MEDIAL FOREBRAIN BUNDLE: Rat–Olds & Olds, 1963; Olds, Travis, & Schwing, 1960: Cat–O'Donohue & Hagamen, 1967; Schnitzer, Reid, & Porter, 1965; Wilkinson & Peele, 1963: Gerbil–Routtenberg & Kramis, 1967.

ZONA INCERTA: Rat–Olds & Olds, 1963: Monkey–Briese & Olds, 1964: Squirrel–Wetzel & King, 1966; Wetzel, King, & Nowicki, 1967.

THALAMUS: Rat–Olds & Olds, 1963; Cooper & Taylor, 1967: Cat–O'Donohue & Hagamen, 1967; Grastyán & Angyán, 1967: Man–Heath, 1963; Bishop, Elder, & Heath, 1963: Squirrel–Wetzel, King, & Nowicki, 1967: Dog–Bacon & Wong, 1972.

CAUDATE NUCLEUS: Rat–Routtenberg, 1971; Olds, Travis, & Schwing, 1960: Cat–O'Donohue & Hagamen, 1967; Justesen, Sharp, & Porter, 1963: Monkey–Briese & Olds, 1964; Lilly, 1957: Man–Heath, 1963; Bishop, Elder, & Heath, 1963: Dog–Bacon & Wong, 1972: Dolphin–Lilly & Miller, 1962.

AMYGDALA: Rat–Olds & Olds, 1963: Cat–O'Donohue & Hagamen, 1967: Monkey–Briese & Olds, 1964: Man–Heath, 1963; Bishop, Elder, & Heath, 1963.

GLOBUS PALLIDUS: Rat–Olds & Olds, 1963: Cat–O'Donohue & Hagamen, 1967: Monkey–Routtenberg, Gardner, & Huang, 1971; Lilly, 1957.

PUTAMEN: Monkey–Lilly, 1957.

CENTRAL GREY: Rat–Cooper & Taylor, 1967.

VENTRAL TEGMENTUM: Rat–Olds & Olds, 1963; Olds & Peretz, 1960; Routtenberg & Malsbury, 1969: Cat–O'Donohue & Hagamen, 1967; Wilkinson & Peele, 1963.

SUBSTANTIA NIGRA: Rat–Crow, 1972a; Routtenberg & Malsbury, 1969: Cat–O'Donohue & Hagamen, 1967: Monkey–Briese & Olds, 1964: Gerbil–Routtenberg & Kramis, 1967.

RED NUCLEUS: Cat–O'Donohue & Hagamen, 1967.

LOCUS COERULEUS: Rat–Crow, 1972b.

FRONTAL CORTEX: Rat–Routtenberg, 1971; Routtenberg & Sloan, 1972: Cat–O'Donohue & Hagamen, 1967; Wilkinson & Peele, 1963.

BRACHIUM CONJUNCTIVUM: Rat–Routtenberg & Malsbury, 1969: Cat–O'Donohue & Hagamen, 1967: Monkey–Briese & Olds, 1964.

CEREBRAL PEDUNCLE: Rat–Olds & Olds, 1963: Squirrel–Wetzel, King, & Nowicki, 1967.

PALEOSTRIATUM: Pigeon–Goodman & Brown, 1966; MacPhail, 1966, 1967.

NEOSTRIATUM: Pigeon–MacPhail, 1966, 1967; Webster & Beale, 1970.

HYPERSTRIATUM: Pigeon–MacPhail, 1966, 1967.

ECTOSTRIATUM: Pigeon—MacPhail, 1966; Hollard & Davison, 1971.

PALLIDUM: Goldfish–Boyd & Gardner, 1962.

REFERENCES

ARBUTHNOTT, G. W., CROW, T. J., FUXE, K., OLSON, L., & UNGERSTEDT, U. Depletion of catecholamines in vivo induced by electrical stimulation of central monoamine pathways. *Brain Research,* 1970, *24,* 471–483.

BACON, W. E., & WONG, I. G. Reinforcement value of electrical brain stimulation in neonatal dogs. *Developmental Psychobiology,* 1972, *5,* 195–200.

BAXTER, L., GLUCKMAN, M. I., STEIN, L., & SCERNI, A. Self-injection of apomorphine in the rat: Positive reinforcement by a dopamine receptor stimulant. *Pharmacology, Biochemistry, and Behavior,* 1974, *2,* 389–391.

BINDRA, D. Neuropsychological interpretation of the effects of drive and incentive-motivation on general activity and instrumental behavior. *Psychological Review,* 1968, *75,* 1–22.

BINDRA, D. The interrelated mechanisms of reinforcement and motivation and the nature of their influence on response. In *Nebraska symposium on motivation.* Lincoln: University of Nebraska Press, 1969.

BISHOP, M. P., ELDER, S. T., & HEATH, R. G. Intracranial self-stimulation in man. *Science,* 1963, *140,* 394–396.

BOLLES, R. C. Species-specific defense reactions and avoidance learning. *Psychological Review,* 1970, *77,* 32–48.

BOYD, E. S., & GARDNER, L. C. Positive and negative reinforcement from intracranial stimulation of a teleost. *Science,* 1962, *136,* 648–649.

BRADY, J. V., BOREN, J. J., CONRAD, D., & SIDMAN, M. The effect of food and water deprivation upon intracranial self-stimulation. *Journal of Comparative and Physiological Psychology,* 1957, *50,* 134–137.

BREESE, G. R., HOWARD, J., & LEAHY, J. P. Effect of 6-hydroxydopamine on electrical self-stimulation of the brain. *British Journal of Pharmacology,* 1971, *43,* 255–257.

BRIESE, E., & OLDS, J. Reinforcing brain stimulation and memory in monkeys. *Experimental Neurology,* 1964, *10,* 493–508.

BRODIE, D. A., MORENO, O. M., MALIS, J. L., & BRODIE, J. J. Rewarding properties of intracranial stimulation. *Science,* 1960, *131,* 929–930.

BROWN, S., & TROWILL, J. A. Lever-pressing performance for brain stimulation on F-I and V-I schedules in a single-lever situation. *Psychological Reports,* 1970, *26,* 699–706.

BRUNNER, A. Facilitation of classical conditioning in rabbits by reinforcing brain stimulation. *Psychonomic Science,* 1966, *6,* 211–212.

BURSTEN, B., & DELGADO, J. M. R. Positive reinforcement induced by intracerebral stimulation in the monkey. *Journal of Comparative and Physiological Psychology,* 1958, *51,* 6–10.

CAGGIULA, A. R., & HOEBEL, B. G. "Copulation-reward" site in the posterior hypothalamus. *Science,* 1966, *153,* 1284–1285.

CAMPBELL, H. J. Acute effects of pregnene steroids on septal self-stimulation in the rabbit. *Journal of Physiology* (London), 1968, *196,* 134P–135P.

CAMPBELL, H. J. Pleasure-seeking brains: Artificial tickles, natural joys of thought. *Smithsonian,* 1971, *2,* 14–23.

CANTOR, M. B. Signaled reinforcing brain stimulation facilitates operant behavior under schedules of intermittent reinforcement. *Science,* 1971, *174,* 610–613.

CANTOR, M. B., & LOLORDO, V. M. Rats prefer signaled reinforcing brain stimulation to unsignaled ESB. *Journal of Comparative and Physiological Psychology,* 1970, *71,* 183–191.

CANTOR, M. B., & LOLORDO, V. M. Reward value of brain

stimulation is inversely related to uncertainty about its onset. *Journal of Comparative and Physiological Psychology*, 1972, *79*, 259–270.

CARLISLE, H. J., & SNYDER, E. The interaction of hypothalamic self-stimulation and temperature regulation. *Experientia*, 1970, *26*, 1092–1093.

CHU, N. D., & BLOOM, F. E. Norepinephrine containing neurones: Changes in spontaneous discharge patterns during sleeping and waking. *Science*, 1973, *179*, 908–910.

CONNER, J. D. Caudate nucleus neurones: Correlation of the effects of substantia nigra stimulation with iontophoretic dopamine. *Journal of Physiology* (London), 1970, *208*, 691–704.

COONS, E. F., & CRUCE, J. A. F. Lateral hypothalamus: Food current intensity in maintaining self-stimulation of hunger. *Science*, 1968, *159*, 1117–1119.

COOPER, B. R., BLACK, W. C., & PAOLINO, R. M. Decreased septal-forebrain and lateral hypothalamic reward after alpha-methyl-*p*-tyrosine. *Physiology and Behavior*, 1971, *6*, 425–429.

COOPER, R. M., & TAYLOR, L. H. Thalamic reticular system and central grey: Self-stimulation. *Science*, 1967, *156*, 102–103.

CRICHTON, M. *The terminal man*. Toronto: Bantam Books, 1972.

CROW, T. J. Enhancement by cocaine of intracranial self-stimulation in the rat. *Life Sciences*, 1970, *9*, 375–381.

CROW, T. J. A map of the rat mesencephalon for electrical self-stimulation. *Brain Research*, 1972, *36*, 265–273. (a)

CROW, T. J. Intracranial self-stimulation with electrodes in the region of the locus coeruleus. *Brain Research*, 1972, *36*, 275–287. (b)

CROW, T. J. Catecholamine-containing neurones and electrical self-stimulation, 1: A review of some data. *Psychological Medicine*, 1972, *2*, 414–421. (c)

CROW, T. J. Catecholamine-containing neurones and electrical self-stimulation, 2: A theoretical interpretation and some psychiatric implications. *Psychological Medicine*, 1973, *3*, 66–73.

CULBERTON, J. K., KLING, J. W., & BERKLEY, M. A. Extinction responding following ICS and food reinforcement. *Psychonomic Science*, 1966, *5*, 127–128.

CURTIS, D. R., & CRAWFORD, J. M. Central synaptic transmission: Microelectrophoretic studies. *Annual Review of Pharmacology*, 1969, *9*, 209–240.

DAVIS, A. H., DAVISON, M. C., & WEBSTER, D. M. Intracranial reinforcement in pigeons: An analysis using concurrent schedules. *Physiology and Behavior*, 1972, *9*, 385–390.

DEUTSCH, J. A. *The structural basis of behavior*. Chicago: University of Chicago Press, 1960.

DEUTSCH, J. A., ADAMS, D. W., & METZNER, R. J. Choice of intracranial stimulation as a function of delay between stimulations and strength of competing drive. *Journal of Comparative and Physiological Psychology*, 1964, *57*, 241–243.

DEUTSCH, J. A., & DICARA, K. Hunger and extinction in intracranial self-stimulation. *Journal of Comparative and Physiological Psychology*, 1967, *63*, 344–347.

DEUTSCH, J. A., & HOWARTH, C. I. Some tests of a theory of intracranial self-stimulation. *Psychological Review*, 1963, *70*, 444–460.

DICARA, L. V. Brain stimulation and secondary reinforcement. *Dissertation Abstracts*, 1966, *27*, 2157–B.

DICARA, L. V., & DEUTSCH, J. A. Secondary reinforcement as a function of drive in intracranial self-stimulation. *Proceedings of the 74th Annual Convention of the American Psychological Association*, 1966, 105–106.

DICARA, L. V., & MILLER, N. E. Instrumental learning of vasomotor responses by rats: Learning to respond differentially in the two ears. *Science*, 1968, *159*, 1485–1486.

DOMINO, E. F., & OLDS, M. E. Effects of D-amphetamine, scopolamine, chlordiazepoxide, and diphenylhydantoin on self-stimulation behavior and brain acetylcholine. *Psychopharmacology*, 1972, *13*, 1–16.

DOTY, R. W. Electrical stimulation of the brain in behavioral context. *Annual Review of Psychology*, 1969, *20*, 289–320.

DREESE, A. Importance du septème mésencéphalo-telencephalique noradrenergique comme substratum anatomique du comportement d'autostimulation. *Life Sciences*, 1966, *5*, 1003–1014.

FALK, J. L. Septal stimulation as a reinforcer of an alternative to consummatory behavior. *Journal of Experimental Analysis of Behavior*, 1961, *4*, 213–217.

FIBIGER, H. C., ZIS, A. P., & MCGEER, E. G. Feeding and drinking deficits after 6-hydroxydopamine administration in the rat: Similarities to the lateral hypothalamic syndrome. *Brain Research*, 1973, *55*, 135–148.

FLYNN, J. P., VANEGAS, H., FOOTE, W., & EDWARDS, S. Neural mechanisms involved in a cat's attack on a rat. In R. Whalen (Ed.), *Neural control of behavior*. New York: Academic Press, 1970.

FUXE, K., HOKFELT, T., & UNGERSTEDT, U. Morphological and functional aspects of central monamine neurons. *International Review of Neurobiology*, 1970, *13*, 93–126.

GALLISTEL, C. R., & BEAGLEY, G. Specificity of brain stimulation reward in the rat. *Journal of Comparative and Physiological Psychology*, 1971, *76*, 199–205.

GALLISTEL, C. R., ROLLS, E., & GREENE, D. Neuron function inferred from behavioral and electrophysiological estimates of refractory period. *Science*, 1969, *166*, 1028–1030.

GANDELMAN, R., PANKSEPP, J., & TROWILL, J. A. The effect of lever retraction on resistance to the extinction of a response rewarded with electrical stimulation of the brain. *Psychonomic Science*, 1968, *10*, 5–6.

GERMAN, D. C., & BOWDEN, D. M. Catecholamine systems as the neural substrate for intracranial self-stimulation: A hypothesis. *Brain Research*, 1974, *73*, 381–419.

GIBSON, W. E., REID, L. D., SAKAI, M., & PORTER, P. B. Intracranial reinforcement compared with sugar-water reinforcement. *Science*, 1965, *148*, 1357–1359.

GLICKMAN, S. E., & SCHIFF, B. B. A biological theory of reinforcement. *Psychological Review*, 1967, *74*, 81–109.

GOLDSTEIN, R., HILL, S. Y., & TEMPLER, D. I. Effects of food deprivation on hypothalamic self-stimulation in stimulus-bound eaters and noneaters. *Physiology and Behavior*, 1970, *5*, 915–918.

GOODMAN, I. J., & BROWN, J. L. Stimulation of positively and negatively reinforcing sites in the avian brain. *Life Sciences*, 1966, *5*, 693–704.

GRASTYÁN, E., & ANGYÁN, L. The organization of motivation at the thalamic level of the cat. *Physiology and Behavior*, 1967, *2*, 5–13.

HAWKINS, T. D., & PLISKOFF, S. S. Brain stimulation intensity, rate of self-stimulation, and reinforcing strength: An analysis through chaining. *Journal of Experimental Analysis of Behavior*, 1964, *7*, 285–288.

Heath, R. G. Electrical self-stimulation of the brain in man. *American Journal of Psychiatry,* 1963, *120,* 571–577.

Hebb, D. O. *A textbook of psychology* (2nd ed.). Philadelphia: Saunders, 1966.

Herberg, L. J. Seminal ejaculation following positively reinforcing electrical stimulation of the rat hypothalamus. *Journal of Comparative and Physiological Psychology,* 1963, *56,* 679–685.

Hodos, W. Progressive ratio as a measure of reward strength. *Science,* 1961, *134,* 943–944.

Hodos, W. Motivational properties of long durations of rewarding brain stimulation. *Journal of Comparative and Physiological Psychology,* 1965, *59,* 219–224.

Hodos, W., & Valenstein, E. S. An evaluation of response rate as a measure of rewarding intracranial stimulation. *Journal of Comparative and Physiological Psychology,* 1962, *55,* 80–84.

Hoebel, B. G. Feeding and self-stimulation. *Annals of the New York Academy of Science,* 1969, *157,* 758–778.

Hoebel, B. G. Feeding: Neural control of intake. *Annual Review of Physiology,* 1971, *33,* 533–568.

Hoebel, B. G., & Teitelbaum, P. Hypothalamic control of feeding and self-stimulation. *Science,* 1962, *135,* 375–377.

Hollard, V., & Davison, M. C. Preference for qualitatively different reinforcers. *Journal of Experimental Analysis of Behavior,* 1971, *16,* 375–380.

Honig, W. K. *Operant behavior: Areas of research and application.* New York: Appleton-Century-Crofts, 1966.

Horowitz, Z. P., Chow, M. I., & Carlton, P. L. Self-stimulation of the brain by cats: Effects of imipramine, amphetamine, and chlorpromazine. *Psychopharmacology,* 1962, *3,* 455–462.

Huston, J. P. Relationship between motivating and rewarding stimulation of the lateral hypothalamus. *Physiology and Behavior,* 1971, *6,* 711–716.

Huston, J. P. Inhibition of hypothalamically motivated eating by rewarding stimulation through the same electrode. *Physiology and Behavior,* 1972, *8,* 1121–1126.

Jones, B. E., Bobillier, P., Pin, C., & Jouvet, M. The effect of lesions of catecholamine-containing neurons upon monamine content of the brain and EEG and behavioral waking in the cat. *Brain Research,* 1973, *58,* 157–177.

Jouvet, M. Some monaminergic mechanisms controlling sleep and waking. In A. G. Karczmar & J. C. Eccles (Eds.), *Brain and human behavior.* Berlin: Springer-Verlag, 1972.

Justesen, R., Sharp, J. C., & Porter, P. B. Self-stimulation of the caudate nucleus by instrumentally naive cats. *Journal of Comparative and Physiological Psychology,* 1963, *56,* 371–374.

Keesey, R. E., & Goldstein, M. D. Use of progressive fixed-ratio procedures in the assessment of intracranial reinforcement. *Journal of Experimental Analysis of Behavior,* 1968, *11,* 293–301.

Kemp, J. M., & Powell, T. P. S. The connexions of the striatum and globus pallidus: Synthesis and speculation. *Philosophical Transactions of the Royal Society of London,* 1971, *262,* 441–457.

Keys, N. W. Secondary reinforcement and reinforcing intracranial stimulation. *Dissertation Abstracts,* 1964, *28,* 3436.

Kling, J. W., & Berkley, M. A. Electrical brain stimulation and food reinforcement in discrimination and generalization situations. *Journal of Comparative and Physiological Psychology,* 1968, *65,* 507–511.

Kling, J. W., & Matsumiya, Y. Relative reinforcement values of food and intracranial stimulation. *Science,* 1962, *135,* 668–670.

Knott, P. D., & Clayton, K. N. Durable secondary reinforcement using brain stimulation as the primary reinforcer. *Journal of Comparative and Physiological Psychology,* 1966, *61,* 151–153.

Lenzer, I. I. Differences between behavior reinforced by electrical stimulation of the brain and conventionally reinforced behavior: An associative analysis. *Psychological Bulletin,* 1972, *78,* 103–118.

Liebman, J. M., & Butcher, L. L. Effects on self-stimulation behavior of drugs influencing dopaminergic neurotransmission mechanisms. *Naunyn-Schmiedebergs Archiv für Pharmakologie und experimentelle Pathologie* (Berlin), 1973, *277,* 305–318.

Lilly, J. C. Learning elicited by electrical stimulation of subcortical regions in the unanesthetized monkey. *Science,* 1957, *125,* 748–749.

Lilly, J. C., & Miller, A. M. Operant conditioning of the bottlenose dolphin with electrical stimulation of the brain. *Journal of Comparative and Physiological Psychology,* 1962, *55,* 73–79.

Linholm, E., & Keesey, R. E. Discrimination learning as a function of the duration of rewarding hypothalamic stimulation. *Psychonomic Science,* 1968, *10,* 153–154.

Linholm, E., & Keesey, R. E. Faster rates of discrimination learning with centrally elicited reinforcement than with food. *Journal of Comparative and Physiological Psychology,* 1970, *72,* 318–327.

Lippa, A. S., Antelman, S. M., Fisher, A. E., & Canfield, D. R. Neurochemical mediation of reward: A significant role for dopamine? *Pharmacology, Biochemistry, and Behavior,* 1973, *1,* 23–28.

MacPhail, E. M. Self-stimulation in pigeons: The problem of "priming." *Psychonomic Science,* 1966, *5,* 7–8.

MacPhail, E. M. Positive and negative reinforcement from intracranial stimulation in pigeons. *Nature* (London), 1967, *213,* 947–948.

Margules, D. L., & Olds, J. Identical "feeding" and "rewarding" systems in the lateral hypothalamus of rats. *Science,* 1962, *135,* 374–375.

Marshall, J. F., & Teitelbaum, P. A comparison of the eating in response to hypothermic and glucoprivic challenges after nigral 6-hydroxydopamine and lateral hypothalamic electrolytic lesions in rats. *Brain Research,* 1973, *55,* 229–233.

McClelland, D. C. Some social consequences of achievement motivation. In *Nebraska symposium on motivation.* Lincoln: University of Nebraska Press, 1955.

McHugh, P. R., Black, W. C., & Mason, J. W. Some hormonal responses to electrical self-stimulation in the *Macaca mulatta. American Journal of Physiology,* 1966, *210,* 109–113.

Mendelson, J. Lateral hypothalamic stimulation in satiated rats: The rewarding effects of self-induced drinking. *Science,* 1967, *157,* 1077–1079.

Miller, N. E. Some motivational effects of brain stimulation and drugs. *Federation Proceedings,* 1960, *19,* 846–854.

MILNER, P. M. *Physiological psychology.* New York: Holt, Rinehart & Winston, 1970.

MILNER, P. M. Theories of reinforcement, drive and motivation. In L. L. Iverson, S. D. Iverson, & S. H. Snyder (Eds.), *Handbook of psychopharmacology.* (Vol. 7) New York: Plenum Press, 1976.

MOGENSON, G. J. An attempt to establish secondary reinforcement with rewarding brain stimulation. *Psychological Reports,* 1965, *16,* 163–167.

MOGENSON, G. J. Effects of amphetamine on self-stimulation and induced drinking. *Physiology and Behavior,* 1968, *3,* 133–136.

MOGENSON, G. J. General and specific reinforcement systems for drinking behavior. *Annals of the New York Academy of Sciences,* 1969, *157,* 779–797. (a)

MOGENSON, G. J. Effects of drugs on the preference between electrical stimulation on the lateral hypothalamus and water. *Psychonomic Science,* 1969, *17,* 13–14. (b)

MOGENSON, G. J., & HUANG, Y. H. The neurobiology of motivated behavior. In G. A. Kerkut & J. W. Phillis (Eds.), *Progress in neurobiology* (Vol. 1). Oxford: Pergamon Press, 1973.

MOGENSON, G. J., & KAPLINSKY, M. Brain self-stimulation and mechanisms of reinforcement. *Learning and Motivation,* 1970, *1,* 186–198.

MOGENSON, G. J., & MORGAN, C. Effects of induced drinking on self-stimulation of the lateral hypothalamus. *Experimental Brain Research,* 1967, *3,* 111–116.

MOGENSON, G. J., MORGAN, C. W., PHILLIPS, A. G., & STEVENSON, J. A. F. Studies of self-stimulation and drinking. Paper presented at 24th International Congress of Physiology, Washington, D.C., July 1968.

MOGENSON, G. J., & PHILLIPS, A. G. Motivation: A psychological construct in search of a physiological substrate. In A. N. Epstein & J. M. Sprague (Eds.), *Progress in psychobiology and physiological psychology* (Vol. 6). New York: Academic Press, 1976.

MOGENSON, G. J., & STEVENSON, J. A. F. Drinking and self-stimulation with electrical stimulation of the lateral hypothalamus. *Physiology and Behavior,* 1966, *1,* 251–254.

MOGENSON, G. J., & STEVENSON, J. A. F. Drinking induced by electrical stimulation of the lateral hypothalamus. *Experimental Neurology,* (New York: Academic Press, Inc., 1967), *17,* 119–127.

MORGAN, C. W., & MOGENSON, G. J. Preference of water-deprived rats for stimulation of the lateral hypothalamus rather than water. *Psychonomic Science,* 1966, *6,* 337–338.

NEWMAN, B. L., & FELDMAN, S. M. Electrophysiological activity accompanying self-stimulation. *Journal of Comparative and Physiological Psychology,* 1964, *57,* 244–247.

O'DONOHUE, N. F., & HAGAMEN, W. D. A map of the cat brain for regions producing self-stimulation and unilateral inattention. *Brain Research,* 1967, *5,* 289–305.

OLDS, J. Runway and maze behavior controlled by basomedial forebrain stimulation in the rat. *Journal of Comparative and Physiological Psychology,* 1956, *49,* 507–512.

OLDS, J. Effects of hunger and male sex hormone on self-stimulation of the brain. *Journal of Comparative and Physiological Psychology,* 1958, *51,* 320–324. (a)

OLDS, J. Satiation effects in self-stimulation of the brain. *Journal of Comparative and Physiological Psychology,* 1958, *51,* 675–678. (b)

OLDS, J. Differentiation of reward systems in the brain by self-stimulation techniques. In E. R. Ramey & D. S. O'Doherty (Eds.), *Electrical studies in the unanesthetized brain.* New York: Hoeber, 1960.

OLDS, J., & MILNER, P. Positive reinforcement produced by electrical stimulation of septal area and other regions of the rat brain. *Journal of Comparative and Physiological Psychology,* 1954, *47,* 419–427.

OLDS, J., & OLDS, M. E. The mechanism of voluntary behavior. In R. Heath (Ed.), *The role of pleasure in behavior.* New York: Harper, 1964.

OLDS, J. & PERETZ, B. A motivational analysis of the reticular activating system. *Electroencephalography and Clinical Neurophysiology,* 1960, *12,* 445–454.

OLDS, J., TRAVIS, R. P., & SCHWING, R. C. Topographic organization of hypothalamic self-stimulation functions. *Journal of Comparative and Physiological Psychology,* 1960, *53,* 23–32.

OLDS, M. E. Comparative effects of amphetamine, scopolamine, chlordiazopoxide, and diphenylhydantoin on operant and extinction behavior with brain stimulation and food reward. *Neuropharmacology,* 1970, *9,* 519–532.

OLDS, M. E., & OLDS, J. Approach-avoidance analysis of rat diencephalon. *Journal of Comparative Neurology,* 1963, *120,* 259–295.

PANKSEPP, J., & TROWILL, J. A. Intraoral self-injection, I: Effects of delay of reinforcement on resistance to extinction and implication for self-stimulation. *Psychonomic Science,* 1967, *9,* 405–406. (a)

PANKSEPP, J., & TROWILL, J. A. Intraoral self-injection, II: The simulation of self-stimulation phenomenon with a conventional reward. *Psychonomic Science,* 1967, *9,* 407–408. (b)

PELLEGRINO, L. J., & CUSHMAN, A. J. *A stereotaxic atlas of the rat brain.* New York: Appleton-Century-Crofts, 1967.

PERSSON, N. Self-stimulation in the goat. *Acta Physiologica Scandinavica,* 1962, *55,* 276–285.

PFAFFMAN, C. The pleasures of sensation. *Psychological Review,* 1960, *67,* 253–268.

PHILLIPS, A. G. Enhancement and inhibition of olfactory bulb self-stimulation by odours. *Physiology and Behavior,* 1970, *5,* 1127–1131.

PHILLIPS, A. G. The role of the substantia nigra in behavior elicited by electrical stimulation of the brain. Paper presented at the meeting of the Canadian Psychological Association, Victoria, B.C., June 1973.

PHILLIPS, A. G., COX, V. C., KAKOLEWSKI, J. W., & VALENSTEIN, E. S. Object-carrying by rats: An approach to the behavior produced by brain stimulation. *Science,* 1969, *166,* 903–905.

PHILLIPS, A. G., & FIBIGER, H. C. Substantia nigra: Self-stimulation and poststimulation feeding. *Physiological Psychology,* 1973, *1,* 233–236.

PHILLIPS, A. G., & MOGENSON, G. J. Effects of taste on self-stimulation and induced drinking. *Journal of Comparative and Physiological Psychology,* 1968, *66,* 654–660.

PHILLIPS, A. G., MORGAN, C. W., & MOGENSON, G. J. Changes in self-stimulation preference as a function of incentive of alternative rewards. *Canadian Journal of Psychology,* 1970, *24,* 289–297.

PLISKOFF, S. S., & HAWKINS, T. D. A method for increasing the reinforcement magnitude of intracranial stimulation.

Journal of Experimental Analysis of Behavior, 1967, *10,* 281–289.

PLISKOFF, S. S., WRIGHT, J. E., & HAWKINS, T. D. Brain stimulation as a reinforcer: Intermittent schedules. *Journal of Experimental Analysis of Behavior,* 1965, *8,* 75–88.

POSCHEL, B. P. H. Mapping of rat brain for self-stimulation under monoamine oxidase blockade. *Physiology and Behavior,* 1969, *4,* 325–331.

POSCHEL, B. P. H., & NINTEMAN, F. W. Hypothalamic self-stimulation: Its suppression by blockade of norepinephrine biosynthesis and reinstatement with methamphetamine. *Life Sciences,* 1966, *5,* 11–16.

RAY, O. S., HINE, B., & BIVENS, L. W. Stability of self-stimulation responding during long test sessions. *Physiology and Behavior,* 1968, *3,* 161–164.

RENNER, K. E. Delay of reinforcement: A historical review *Psychological Bulletin,* 1964, *61,* 341–361.

REYNOLDS, G. S. *A primer of operant conditioning.* Glenview, Ill.: Scott, Foresman, 1968.

RITTER, S., & STEIN, L. Self-stimulation of noradrenergic cell group (A6) in locus coeruleus of rats. *Journal of Comparative and Physiological Psychology,* 1973, *85,* 443–452.

RITTER, S., & STEIN, L. Self-stimulation in the mesencephalic trajectory of the ventral noradrenergic bundle. *Brain Research,* 1974, *81,* 145–157.

ROBERTS, E. Disinhibition as an organizing principle in the nervous system: The role of gamma-aminobutyric acid. *Advances in Neurology.* Raven Press, 1974, *5,* 127–143.

ROBERTS, W. W. Hypothalamic mechanisms for motivational and species-typical behavior. In R. E. Whalen (Ed.), *The neural control of behavior.* New York: Academic Press, 1970.

ROLLS, E. T. Activation of amygdaloid neurones in reward, eating, and drinking elicited by electrical stimulation of the brain. *Brain Research,* 1972, *45,* 365–381.

ROUTTENBERG, A. Forebrain pathways of reward in *Rattus norwegicus. Journal of Comparative and Physiological Psychology,* 1971, *75,* 269–276.

ROUTTENBERG, A., GARDNER, E. L., & HUANG, Y. H. Self-stimulation pathways in the monkey, *Macaca mulatta. Experimental Neurology,* 1971, *33,* 213–224.

ROUTTENBERG, A., & KRAMIS, R. C. "Foot-stomping" in the gerbil: Rewarding brain stimulation, sexual behavior, and foot shock. *Nature,* 1967, *214,* 173–174.

ROUTTENBERG, A., & LINDY, J. Effects of the availability of rewarding septal and hypothalamic stimulation on bar pressing for food under conditions of deprivation. *Journal of Comparative and Physiological Psychology,* 1965, *60,* 158–161.

ROUTTENBERG, A., & MALSBURY, C. Brainstem pathways of reward. *Journal of Comparative and Physiological Psychology,* 1969, *68,* 22–30.

ROUTTENBERG, A., & SLOAN, M. Self-stimulation in the frontal cortex of *Rattus norwegicus. Behavioral Biology,* 1972, *7,* 567–572.

SADOWSKY, S. Discriminative responding on associated mixed and multiple schedules as a function of food and ICS reinforcement. *Journal of Experimental Analysis of Behavior,* 1969, *12,* 933–945.

SCHACHTER, S. Cognitive effects on bodily functioning. In D. C. Glass (Ed.), *Neurophysiology and emotion.* New York: Rockefeller University Press and Russell Sage Foundation, 1967.

SCHNITZER, S. B., REID, L. D., & PORTER, P. B. Electrical intracranial stimulation as a primary reinforcer for cats. *Psychological Reports,* 1965, *16,* 335–338.

SEGAL, M., & BLOOM, F. E. The action of norepinephrine in the rat hippocampus, II: Activation of the input pathway. *Brain Research,* 1974, *72,* 99–114.

SEWARD, J. P., UYEDA, A., & OLDS, J. Resistance to extinction following cranial self-stimulation. *Journal of Comparative and Physiological Psychology,* 1959, *52,* 294–299.

SHEFFIELD, F. D., ROBY, T. B., & CAMPBELL, B. A. Drive reduction versus consummatory behavior as determinants of reinforcement. *Journal of Comparative and Physiological Psychology,* 1954, *47,* 349–354.

SHETTLEWORTH, S. J. Constraints on learning. In D. S. Lehrman, R. A. Hinde, & E. Shaw (Eds.), *Advances in the study of behavior* (Vol. 4). New York: Academic Press, 1971.

SIDMAN, M., BRADY, J. V., BOREN, J. J., CONRAD, D. G., & SCHULMAN, A. Reward schedules and behavior maintained by intracranial self-stimulation. *Science,* 1955, *122,* 830–831.

SKINNER, B. F. The phylogeny and ontogeny of behavior: Contingencies of reinforcement throw light on contingencies of survival in the evolution of behavior. *Science,* 1966, *153,* 1205–1213. (a)

SKINNER, B. F. Operant behavior. In W. K. Honig (Ed.), *Operant behavior: Areas of research and application.* New York: Appleton-Century-Crofts, 1966. (b)

SMITH, N. S., & COONS, E. E. Temporal summation and refractoriness in hypothalamic reward neurons as measured by self-stimulation behavior. *Science,* 1970, *169,* 782–785.

SPIES, G. Food vs. intracranial self-stimulation reinforcement in food-deprived rats. *Journal of Comparative and Physiological Psychology,* 1965, *60,* 153–157.

STADDON, J. E. R., & SIMMELHAG, V. L. The "superstition" experiment: A re-examination of its implications for the principles of adaptive behavior. *Psychological Review,* 1971, *78,* 3–43.

STARK, P., & BOYD, E. S. Effects of cholinergic drugs on hypothalamic self-stimulation response rates in dogs. *American Journal of Physiology,* 1963, *205,* 745–748.

STEIN, L. Secondary reinforcement established with subcortical stimulation. *Science,* 1958, *127,* 466–467.

STEIN, L. Effects and interactions of imipramine, chlorpromazine, reserpine, and amphetamine on self-stimulation: Possible neurophysiological basis of depression. *Recent Advances in Biological Psychiatry,* 1962, *4,* 288–308.

STEIN, L. Chemistry of proposive behavior. In J. T. Tapp (Ed.), *Reinforcement and behavior.* New York: Academic Press, 1969.

STEIN, L., & RAY, O. S. Self-regulation of brain stimulating current intensity in the rat. *Science,* 1959, *130,* 570–572.

STEIN, L., & WISE, C. D. Release of norepinephrine from hypothalamus and amygdala by rewarding medial forebrain bundle stimulation and amphetamine. *Journal of Comparative and Physiological Psychology,* 1969, *67,* 189–198.

STEIN, L., & WISE, C. D. Possible etiology of schizophrenia: Progressive damage to the noradrenergic reward system by 6-hydroxydopamine. *Science,* 1971, *171,* 1032–1036.

STEIN, L., WISE, C. D., & BERGER, B. D. Noradrenergic reward mechanisms, recovery of function, and schizophrenia. In J. K. McGaugh (Ed.), *The chemistry of mood, motivation, and memory.* New York: Plenum Press, 1972.

Stricker, E. M., & Zigmond, M. J. Recovery of function following damage to central catecholamine-containing neurons: A neurochemical model for the lateral hypothalamic syndrome. In J. M. Sprague & A. N. Epstein (Eds.), *Progress in psychobiology and physiological psychology* (Vol. 6). New York: Academic Press, 1976.

Stutz, R. M., Rossi, R. R., & Bowring, A. M. Competition between food and rewarding brain shock. *Physiology and Behavior,* 1971, *7,* 753–757.

Terman, M., & Kling, J. W. Discrimination of brightness differences by rats with food or brain-stimulation reinforcement. *Journal of Experimental Analysis of Behavior,* 1968, *11,* 29–37.

Trowill, J. A., Panksepp, J., & Gandelman, R. An incentive model of rewarding brain stimulation. *Psychological Review,* 1969, *76,* 264–281.

Ungerstedt, U. Stereotaxic mapping of the monoamine pathways of the rat brain. *Acta Physiologica Scandinavica,* 1971, Suppl. *367,* 1–48.

Ursin, R., Ursin, H., & Olds, J. Self-stimulation of hippocampus in rats. *Journal of Comparative and Physiological Psychology,* 1966, *61,* 353–359.

Valenstein, E. S. Problems of measurement and interpretation with reinforcing brain stimulation. *Psychological Review,* 1964, *71,* 415–437.

Valenstein, E. S., & Beer, B. Reinforcing brain stimulation in competition with water reward and shock avoidance. *Science,* 1962, *137,* 1052–1054.

Valenstein, E. S., & Beer, B. Continuous opportunity for reinforcing brain stimulation. *Journal of Experimental Analysis of Behavior,* 1964, *7,* 183–184.

Valenstein, E. S., & Meyers, W. J. Rate-independent test of reinforcing consequences of brain stimulation. *Journal of Comparative and Physiological Psychology,* 1964, *57,* 52–60.

Wauquier, A., & Niemegeer, C. J. Intracranial self-stimulation in rats as a function of various stimulus parameters, II: Influence of haloperidol, pimozide, and pipamperone on medial forebrain bundle stimulation with monopolar electrodes. *Psychopharmacology,* 1972, *27,* 191–202.

Webster, D. M., & Beale, I. L. Intracranial self-stimulation in the pigeon: The effects of current intensity. *Psychonomic Science,* 1970, *20,* 15–17.

Wetzel, M. C. Self-stimulation anatomy: Data needs. *Brain Research,* 1968, *10,* 287–296.

Wetzel, M. C., & King, J. E. Self-stimulation with monophasic current in the rock squirrel and rat. *Psychonomic Science,* 1966, *6,* 7–8.

Wetzel, M. C., King, J. E., & Nowicki, L. E. Some monophasic self-stimulation loci in the rock squirrel and rat. *Psychonomic Science,* 1967, *9,* 35–36.

Wilkinson, H. A., & Peele, T. L. Intracranial self-stimulation in cats. *Journal of Comparative Neurology,* 1963, *121,* 425–440.

Young, P. T. The role of affective processes in learning and motivation. *Psychological Review,* 1959, *66,* 104–125.

Yunger, L. M., Harvey, J. A., & Lorens, S. A. Dissociation of the analgesic and rewarding effects of brain stimulation in the rat. *Physiology and Behavior,* 1973, *10,* 909–913.

20

The Experimental Production of Altered Physiological States

concurrent and contingent behavioral models*

Joseph Brady
and
Alan Harris

INTRODUCTION

The development of laboratory behavioral approaches to the production of altered physiological states reflects the emergence of two general models for their experimental analysis. The more traditional *concurrent model* emphasizes the effects of prior-occurring or accompanying environmental-behavioral interactions on physiological processes. The early work of Pavlov and Cannon relating autonomic changes to environmental antecedents provides classical examples of such laboratory studies. Current applications of this model have extended the analysis of both respondent and operant conditioning effects upon a broad range of physiological processes (e.g., hormonal secretions). The more recent *contingent model,* in contrast, focuses on environment-behavioral interactions which follow physiological change and provide controlling consequences for instrumental conditioning effects involving visceral-autonomic responses. Applications of this model have shown, for example, that both increases and decreases in heart rate can be produced by experimentally-programmed environmental consequences (e.g., food delivery and/or shock avoidance) which follow such autonomic changes. Over the decade since the topic of behaviorally-induced physiological alterations was reviewed for the original volume on *Operant Behavior* (Brady, 1966), a substantial literature has emerged on instrumental visceral-autonomic conditioning. Both the laboratory and clinical descriptions of such phenomena provide convincing evidence of the extensive behavioral-environmental influences available for experimental analysis within the framework of this contingent psychophysiological model.

CONCURRENT MODELS

Early Studies

Research in this area has traditionally emphasized Pavlovian (i.e., respondent) conditioning processes concerned primarily with adjustments of the organism's "internal economy" (e.g., Cannon, 1915; Gantt, 1960; Pavlov, 1879), and an active experimental interest in such classical psychophysiology continues to be

* Supported by NHLI Grants HL-06945, HL-17958, HL-17970, and HL-17680.

reflected in contemporary research literature (Black, 1971; Figar, 1965; Harris & Brady, 1974). By the middle of the present century, however, reliable methods were developing for direct observation and measurement of a wide range of physiological processes in situations involving both classical respondents and instrumental or operant performances. In the middle 1960s, a review of this area (Brady, 1966) surveyed three major groups of laboratory operant conditioning studies related to the experimental production of altered physiological states.

Transient Physiological Changes

The first group of reports described relatively transient cardiorespiratory and neurophysiological changes which were for the most part confined to experimental periods during which the animal subjects were engaged in some required operant performance (e.g., Sidman shock-avoidance), and appeared to represent physiological responses related to stimuli produced by the instrumental behavior. Cardiorespiratory effects were found to accompany both appetitively and aversively maintained instrumental performances, but they seldom if ever endured beyond the limits of the specific experimental condition which provided the occasion for their appearance (Berlanger & Feldman, 1962; Eldridge, 1954; Hahn, Stern, & McDonald, 1962; Malmo, 1961; Perez-Cruet, Black, & Brady, 1963; Perez-Cruet, Tolliver, Dunn, Marvin, & Brady, 1963; Shapiro & Horn, 1955; Wenzel, 1961). Central nervous system effects described in electrophysiological studies involving instrumental conditioning procedures were found to be characterized by a similar transience (Anliker, 1959; Hearst, Beer, Sheatz, & Galambos, 1960; John & Killam, 1959; Porter, Conrad, & Brady, 1959; Ross, Hodos, & Brady, 1962) though the findings were suggestive of relationships involving behaviorally-induced autonomic and somatic changes.

Durable Physiological Alterations

The second group of studies called attention to more durable endocrinological and visceral-alimentary changes. The production of marked obesity in normal rats by controlling drinking behavior as a shock avoidance response (Williams & Teitelbaum, 1956), and the experimental elevation of alcohol ingestion levels in rhesus monkeys during and for prolonged periods following exposures to shock-avoidance conditioning (Clark & Polish, 1960) were represented as two of the more dramatic examples of relatively durable behaviorally-induced alimentary changes. Endocrinological effects associated with such instrumental conditioning procedures also appeared somewhat less transient than similarly induced cardiorespiratory alterations. The systematic analysis of such psychoendocrinological relations was extensively described in a series of studies providing at least a partial basis for the psychophysiological approach which has continued to characterize many aspects of the more recent developments in this research field (Mason & Brady, 1956; Mason, Brady, Polish, Bauer, Robinson, Rose, & Taylor, 1961; Mason, Brady, Robinson, Taylor, Tolson, & Mougey, 1961; Mason, Brady, & Sidman, 1957; Mason, Mangan, Brady, Conrad, & Rioch, 1961; Mason, Nauta, Brady, Robinson, & Sachar, 1961; Sidman, Mason, Brady, & Thach, 1962).

Chronic Somatic Effects

The third and final group of studies surveyed in the 1966 review dealt with the role of operant behavior in the production of chronic somatic changes of the type associated with gastric ulcers and systemic infections. The relatively few studies which had appeared in this area prior to the first *Operant Behavior* volume testified to the many difficulties presented by an experimental analysis of the behavioral factors involved. The observed somatic changes were generally irreversible. This imposed severe restrictions upon replications within individual animals, a procedure which has typically characterized operant research. In 1956, for example, Sawrey and Weisz first reported the production of gastric ulcers in rats exposed to an instrumental "conflict" procedure, though subsequent studies (Conger, Sawrey, & Turrell, 1958; Sawrey, Conger, & Turrell, 1956; Weisz, 1957) clearly suggested that multiple interacting factors, including food deprivation, "fear," shock, weight loss, and even social experience could not be readily teased apart in such "conflict"-produced alterations. A subsequent series of studies at the Walter Reed Medical Center in Washington was concerned with the production of peptic ulcers in rhesus monkeys who were exposed to recurrent instrumental avoidance performance requirements (Brady, 1958; Brady, 1963; Brady & Polish, 1960; Brady, Porter, Conrad, & Mason, 1958; Polish, Brady, Mason, Thach, & Neimeck, 1962; Porter, Brady, Conrad, Mason, Galambos, & Rioch, 1958) and these experiments confirmed the complexity of such effects. Two additional studies, however, one with humans (Davis & Berry, 1963) and one with animals (Rice, 1963), were able to provide further support for the indicated relationship between instrumental avoidance performances and gastro-intestinal changes.

And at least two other reports (Rasmussen, Marsh, & Brill, 1957; Simson, 1958) had appeared by the mid 1960's relating the incidence of infectious and other disease processes to instrumental performance requirements involving escape and avoidance in laboratory animals.

RECENT DEVELOPMENTS

Over the past decade, the endocrine and cardiovascular systems have continued to provide a major focus for laboratory behavioral studies within the framework of traditional concurrent models for the production of altered physiological states. Some attention has also been directed to gastro-intestinal processes, central nervous system effects, and related physiological states. Significant methodological advances related to the continuous measurement and recording of blood pressure (Perez-Cruet, Plumlee, & Newton, 1966; Swinnen, 1968; Werdegar, Johnson, & Mason, 1964) have contributed in an important way to the progressive development of better models. Increasing use of long-term preparations (Brady, 1965; Findley, Brady, Robinson, & Gilliam, 1971; Forsyth, 1969; Herd, Morse, Kelleher, & Jones, 1969) has provided for more extended observation and experimental manipulation. Behavioral procedures of established effectiveness, including conditioned suppression (Estes & Skinner, 1941) and free-operant avoidance (Sidman, 1953) have received increasing attention in psychophysiology. Progressively more precise analysis of the observed interactions highlights the developments to be reviewed in the remainder of this section.

Endocrine and Cardiovascular Changes

Systematic increases in plasma 17-hydroxycorticosteroid (17-OH-CS) levels during acquisition of conditioned suppression (i.e., "conditioned emotional response" or CER) have now been described, for example, in the rhesus monkey (Mason, Brady, & Tolson, 1966). Presentations of a 5-min tone were terminated contiguously with brief foot shock (5 ma for 0.2 sec); these were superimposed upon a lever-pressing performance maintained by food on an intermittent reinforcement schedule (VI 60″). Only one tone-shock pairing was programmed during each of seven separate experimental sessions. Each CER "acquisition" trial was programmed 15 min after the start of the animal's daily lever-pressing session and blood samples were drawn immediately before and immediately after each 30-min session. Progressive decreases in the lever pressing rate during tone presentations (i.e., conditioned suppression) over the course of the 7 CER acquisition trials were accompanied by progressive increases in 17-OH-CS levels (as compared to lever-pressing control sessions with no tone-shock pairings). Essentially the same CER procedure has also been studied in chronically catheterized rhesus monkeys monitored for heart rate and blood pressure changes during both acquisition and long-term maintenance of conditioned suppression using a 3-min clicker presentation as the CS (Brady, Kelly, & Plumlee, 1969). Over the course of the first 8 to 10 clicker-shock pairings, all 5 animals in the experiment showed consistent and systematic decreases in both heart rate and blood pressure during the clicker. However, continued daily pairings of clicker and shock, superimposed upon the lever-pressing performance, produced abrupt and sustained reversals in both the direction and the magnitude of the cardiovascular response, usually commencing at about trial 9 or 10 as shown in Figure 1. Significantly, these changes were observed to persist as large magnitude increases in heart rate and both systolic and diastolic blood pressure in response to the behaviorally suppressing clicker presentations for from 50 to 100 daily conditioning trials.

The results of these more extended studies emphasize the differential temporal course of the skeletal and autonomic components of the CER development. The cardiovascular changes (i.e., heart rate and blood pressure decreases) accompanying the initial conditioning trials probably reflected the reduction in motor activity (i.e., suppression of lever-pressing rate) which developed in response to the clicker over the first 8 to 10 trials. The later-appearing "conditioned cardiac respondent" could be considered to have developed only after this initial "suppression" stage and to have been maintained in the form of sustained cardiovascular activation (i.e., increased heart rate and blood pressure) during clicker presentations over the extended course of the experiment. Such an account could, to some extent at least, reconcile recurrent conflicting reports regarding the direction of heart rate changes in response to the CS in CER studies (DeToledo, 1971; DeToledo & Black, 1966; DeVietti & Porter, 1970; Nathan & Smith, 1968; Parrish, 1967; Smith & Nathan, 1967, Smith & Stebbins, 1965; Stebbins & Smith, 1964; Sutterer, Howard, Loth, & Obrist, 1970; Williams, 1969). In addition to the obvious problems associated with species differences (i.e., studies with monkey subjects generally report heart rate increases while rat studies usually describe heart rate decreases during conditioned suppression), these

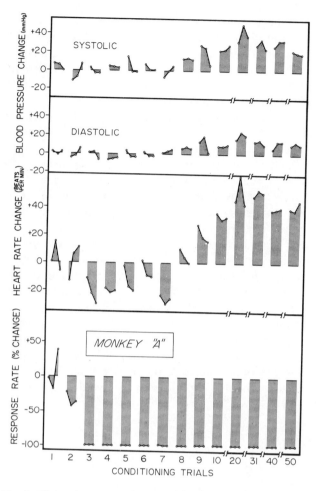

Fig. 1. Minute-by-minute changes in blood pressure, heart rate, and lever-pressing response rate for Monkey A on successive three-min, clicker-shock trials during acquisition of the conditioned emotional response. The zero points represent control values calculated from the three-min interval immediately preceding the clicker. (From Brady et al., 1969.)

more recent findings, involving biphasic cardiovascular changes in the course of CER development and maintenance, strongly suggest that the temporal course of such experimental observations may be an important source of variability. More importantly, the results of these studies would seem to support the view that significant aspects of the behavioral and autonomic effects described are not causally dependent. Rather, it would appear that the cardiovascular and skeletal changes are more accurately represented as independently conditioned effects of the same experimental procedures. This characterization of emotional conditioning (i.e., CER) would seem to have important implications for the validity of theoretical formulations which emphasize either the causal interdependence of behavioral and physiological events in the "emotion" process or the primacy of either one (Brady, 1975).

The extended analysis of behaviorally induced endocrine and cardiovascular changes over the past decade has focused even more intensively upon conditioned avoidance models, predominantly of the free-operant or Sidman variety using well-standardized 20-sec RS and 2-sec SS intervals. There have been several reconfirmations (Brady, 1965, 1967) of the two-fold to four-fold elevations in 17-OH-CS levels associated with even relatively brief, shock-free experimental exposures to such avoidance contingencies. Furthermore, marked differences in the hormone response were observed (Mason, Brady, & Tolson, 1966) when the free-operant avoidance procedure included a discriminable exteroceptive warning signal or when "free" shocks were superimposed upon the performance baseline. Significantly, the corticosteroid response was consistently reduced during "discriminated" avoidance sessions including an exteroceptive auditory stimulus presented 5 sec before shock whenever 15 sec had elapsed since a previous response, though removal of the "warning signal" resulted in the immediate reappearance of the steroid elevations. Conversely, superimposing "free" or unavoidable shocks (at the rate of approximately 2 or 3 per hour) upon a well-established avoidance performance without a "warning signal" was observed to produce more than a 100% increase over the elevated corticosteroid levels evident during the regular nondiscriminated Sidman avoidance procedure.

Significant advances have also been made during the past decade in determining the endocrine and cardiovascular consequences of free-operant avoidance performance requirements during long-term studies of months and even years. A report by Brady (1965), for example, describes the effects of repeated exposure to continuous 72-hour avoidance over periods up to and, in some cases, exceeding one year, upon patterns of thyroid, gonadal, and adrenal hormone secretion in a series of five chair-restrained rhesus monkeys. Two of the five monkeys participated in the 72-hour avoidance experiment on six separate occasions over a 6-month period with an interval of approximately 4 weeks intervening between each exposure. The remaining three animals performed on a schedule which repeatedly programmed 72-hour avoidance cycles followed by 96-hour non-avoidance or "rest" cycles (3 days "on" and 4 days "off") for periods up to and exceeding one year.

The two animals exposed to repeated 72-hour avoidance at monthly intervals for 6 months showed a progressively increasing lever-pressing response rate with each of the six successive 72-hour avoidance sessions, all illustrated in Figure 2. During the initial 72-hour avoidance experiment with these two animals, response rates averaged 16 and 18 per minute, respectively. Response-rate values for these same monkeys during the sixth 72-hour avoidance experiment averaged 28 and 27 resp/min, respectively. In contrast, shock frequencies over this same period showed a sharp decline within the first two 72-hour avoidance cycles. Hormone changes related to the repeated 72-hour avoidance cycles showed consistent and replicable patterns over the 6-month experimental period for both animals. During the initial experimental sessions, as shown in Figure 2, both monkeys showed approximately three-fold elevations in 17-OH-CS levels during 72-hour avoidance and returned to near baseline levels about 6 days afterwards. The remaining four monthly experiments were characterized by substantial, though diminished steroid responses (approximately two-fold elevations in 17-OH-CS levels) during avoidance, with essentially the same 6-day period required for recovery of basal levels. Significant changes related to the extended avoidance performance were also observed in catecholamine, gonadal, and thyroid hormone levels, with recovery cycles extending in some instances (thyroid) for 3 weeks following the 72-hour avoidance period. A detailed experimental and interpretive analysis of such multiple hormone changes induced by exposure to the 72-hour Sidman procedure has been provided in an exhaustive multiauthored monograph (Mason et al., 1968) describing this most systematic series of laboratory studies yet to appear in the psychoendocrine literature.

The three remaining monkeys described in the Brady (1965) report as performing on the 3 days "on," 4 days "off" avoidance schedule showed an initial increase in lever-pressing response rates for approximately the first 10 avoidance sessions similar to that seen with the two animals described above. By approximately the 20th weekly session with these animals, however, lever-pressing response rates during the 72-hour avoidance period had decreased to a value well below that observed during the initial avoidance sessions, and the performance tended to stablize at this new level for the ensuing weeks of the experiment. In contrast, shock frequencies for all animals quickly approximated a stable low level within the first two or three exposures to the avoidance schedule

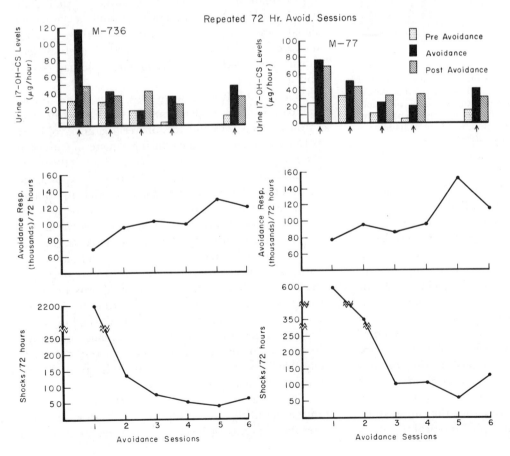

Fig. 2. Steroid levels, avoidance response rates, and shock frequencies for animals M-736 and M-77 during 6 monthly 72-hour avoidance sessions. (From Brady, 1965.)

and seldom exceeded a rate of 2 shocks per hour for the remainder of the experiment. Food and water intake, however, remained relatively stable throughout the entire course of the study. The typical pattern, exemplified by monkey M-157, is illustrated in Figure 3. The initial 72-hour avoidance sessions were characterized by progressive increases in lever-pressing and elevations in 17-OH-CS levels. In the succeeding weeks, 17-OH-CS levels gradually declined but rose again by the 30th week. The general pattern obtained with M-157 was replicated with only minor variations in the two additional animals on this same experimental program. Perhaps the most consistent and striking observation in all three monkeys was the change in responsivity of the pituitary-adrenal system to the avoidance stress with continued exposure to this procedure over extended time periods. These findings are somewhat at variance with the repeated observations in many previous acute studies of a close positive relationship between steroid elevations and avoidance performance. These more extended studies, in contrast, suggest that continued exposure to repeated performance requirements on the time schedule programmed in this experiment may produce a dissociation between the avoidance performance and the 17-OH-CS response. Although a definitive analysis of such relationships is not possible on the basis of these data alone, a critical role of the temporal parameters (work-rest cycles) is clearly indicated. Certainly, related findings (Mason et al., 1968) on the course of recovery for a broad range of hormone measures provide additional support for this focus upon temporal factors in the experimental analysis of behaviorally induced physiological states.

A trend toward more extended periods of experimental observation and measurement has also been apparent in concurrent avoidance studies focusing upon cardiovascular changes, particularly in primates. Both rhesus (Forsyth, 1969) and squirrel monkeys (Herd, Morse, Kelleher, & Jones, 1969) have been reported to develop hypertensive blood pressure levels with recurrent exposure to free-operant avoidance requirements for periods up to and exceeding 12 months. Chair-restrained baboons (Findley, Robinson, & Gilliam, 1971) performing on a discrete-trial fixed ratio instrumental escape-avoidance procedure, how-

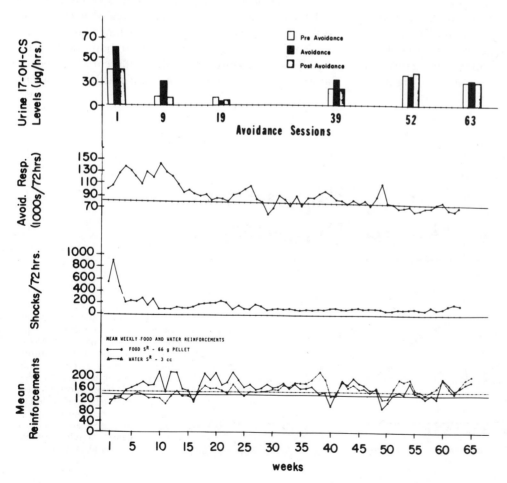

Fig. 3. Steroid levels, avoidance response rates, shock frequencies, and food and water intake levels for animal M-157 throughout 65 weekly 72-hour avoidance sessions. (From Brady 1965.)

ever, were not found to maintain elevated blood pressure levels over the year or more during which they participated in the study (Findley, Brady, Robinson, & Gilliam, 1971). During two six-hour periods each day (separated by rest, feeding, and sleep intervals), the animals were required to respond on an FR 100 schedule to terminate a red light presented intermittently (average interval 5 min) and associated with occasional unavoidable shocks. Indeed, the baboons in this extended study did show substantial pressure increases during the actual escape-avoidance performance intervals within the daily experimental sessions, and there were some periods during the first several months on the program characterized by general elevations in both blood pressure and heart rate as illustrated in Figure 4. But a significant differentiating feature of the schedule requirements in these latter studies generated substantial ratio performances on a rather heavy Lindsley manipulandum and the persistent cardiac output (i.e., heart rate) elevations attendant upon the recurrent 24-hour exposure to this high "work-activity" level do not appear to have been a prominent feature of the studies by Forsyth (1969) and Herd et al., (1969) involving more conventional (i.e., non-fixed ratio) free-operant avoidance procedures. Indeed, this characteristic of the behavioral-cardiovascular interaction pattern may well have played a critical role in the long-term return to normotensive pressure levels illustrated in Figure 4 for the baboons studied by Findley, Brady, Robinson, & Gilliam (1971).

A recent series of studies at the Johns Hopkins University School of Medicine on cardiovascular changes associated with operant avoidance procedures (Anderson & Brady, 1971, 1972, 1973a, 1973b; Anderson, Daley, Findley, & Brady, 1970; Anderson & Tosheff, 1973) provides further evidence which is at least consistent with the relationship between muscle activity and the dynamic interplay of cardiac output and peripheral resistance suggested by Findley et al. (1971). The focus of Anderson's studies with dogs has been upon continuous monitoring of blood pressure and heart rate during free-operant (panel press) shock avoidance, and, significantly, during a *pre-avoidance* period of fixed duration systematically programmed to precede the required avoidance performance. Under these conditions, a unique divergence between heart rate and blood pressure changes was observed during pre-avoidance intervals up to 15 hours in length, with virtually all animals showing a characteristic systolic and diastolic pressure increase and either a decrease or no change in heart rate. Comparisons involving similar performance requirements on a variable interval food reinforcement schedule revealed a markedly different pre-performance cardiovascular pattern characterized by systematic increases in both heart rate and blood pressure. And this differential "preparatory" pattern has now been confirmed both between

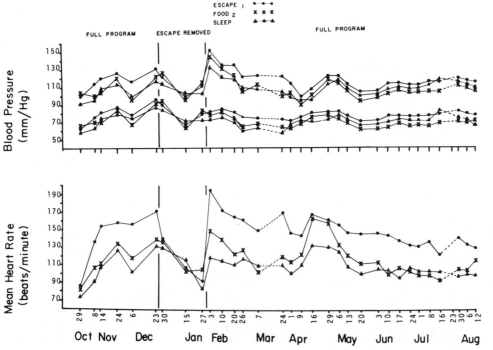

Fig. 4. Mean systolic blood pressure (top three lines in upper section), mean diastolic blood pressure (bottom three lines in upper section), and mean heart rate (bottom section) for baboon Sport plotted at approximately weekly intervals during the course of the experiment for each of the three major activity cycles. (From Brady et al., 1971.)

individual animals maintained separately on each of the procedures, and "within" the same animal alternately performing on the avoidance and food reinforcement schedule, as shown in Figure 5. The bar graph to the left shows the average blood pressure, heart rate, and panel response rate for dog Simon during consecutive 10-min intervals for 10 "avoidance" sessions and illustrates the divergent change in heart rate and blood pressure which occurs during the one-hour pre-avoidance period. The middle graph shows the same measures for the same dog taken during 10 subsequent "food" sessions illustrating the characteristic concordance between heart rate and blood pressure increases in the course of the preperformance hour. And finally, the bar graph to the right shows Simon's recovery of the pre-avoidance pattern during a single "avoidance" session following exposure to the 10 "food" sessions shown in the middle graph.

Direct measurements of cardiac output in such dogs prepared with aortic flow probes during exposure to the avoidance performance have indicated that the pre-avoidance pressure changes are attributable to increased peripheral resistance while the pressure increases during the avoidance performance *per se* occur under conditions of increased cardiac output and decreased peripheral resistance. Additional beta adrenergic blockade studies with the drug propranolol during the same experimental procedure confirm the role of sympathetic arousal in the sustained pressure elevations *during* avoidance but suggest that factors other than sympathetic mediation may be involved in the progressive pre-avoidance pressure increases (Anderson & Brady, 1973b).

The results of these experiments establish firm relationships between a broad range of endocrine and cardiovascular response processes and free-operant behavioral performances. Both general and specific support for these findings has now been provided by numerous published reports with rodents, carnivores, and primates (Banks, Miller, & Ogawa, 1966; Black, 1959; Black & Dalton, 1965; Brady, 1967, 1969, 1970a, 1970b, 1971, 1972, 1974; Brady, Anderson, Harris, & Stephens, 1973; Brady, Findley, & Harris, 1971; Brady, Harris, & Anderson, 1972; Brady & Nauta, 1972; Brown, Schalch, & Reichlin, 1971; Brush & Levine, 1966; Coover, Goldman, & Levine, 1971; Forsyth, 1968, 1971, 1972; Forsyth & Harris, 1970; Forsyth, Hoffbrand, & Melmon, 1971; Frazier, Weil-Melherbe, & Lipscomb, 1969; Granger, 1970; Graham, Cohen, & Shmavonian, 1967; Higgins, 1971; Hokanson, DeGood, Forrest, & Brittain, 1971; Jennings, Averill, Opton, & Lazarus, 1970; Jolley, 1970; Kelleher, Morse, & Herd, 1972; Krahenbuhl, 1971; Laforge, 1971; Lawler, Meyers, & Obrist, 1972; Levine, Gordon, Peterson, & Rose, 1970; Malcuit, Ducharme, & Berlanger, 1968;

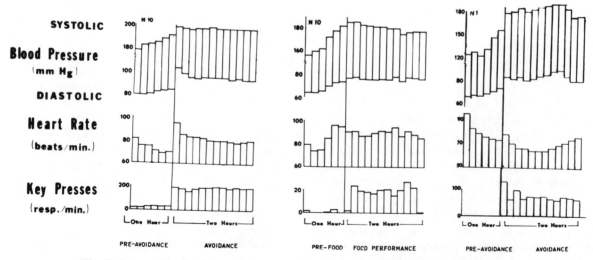

Fig. 5. Average blood pressure, heart rate, and panel response rate during consecutive 10-min pre-performance and performance intervals for 10 "avoidance" sessions (left panel), 10 "food" sessions (middle panel), and one additional "avoidance" session (right panel) following exposure to the 10 "food" sessions (middle panel) with the same dog (Simon). (From Brady et al., 1973.)

Miller, Banks, & Caul, 1967; Miyata & Soltysik, 1968; Morse, Herd, Kelleher, & Gross, 1971; Rose, Mason, & Brady, 1969; Soltysik & Kowalski, 1960; Stern & Word, 1962; Stoyva, Forsyth, & Kamiya, 1968; Swadlow, Hosking, & Schneiderman, 1971; Vanderwolf & Vanderwart, 1970; Weiss, Stone, & Harrel, 1970). In many respects, the changes in absolute levels of selected hormones and autonomic activity can be viewed as reflecting relatively undifferentiated consequences of arousal states associated with behavioral responses under aversive conditions. The reliable temporal course of visceral and steroid changes under such conditions and the quantitative relations between degree of behavioral involvement and at least short-term physiological response levels has been well documented. In addition, the organism's behavioral history would appear to be critical in determining the nature and extent of autonomic-endocrine response to such performance situations. Clearly however, the most meaningful level of analysis for such hormone and visceral response processes in relationship to more chronic emotional interactions would appear to be the broader patterning or balance of secretory and visceral change in many interdependent autonomic and endocrine systems which in concert regulate metabolic events. Indeed, it would appear that such autonomic-endocrine response patterns can be usefully differentiated in relationship to the historical and situational aspects of behavioral events. This differential analysis may well provide a first step in the direction of identifying distinguishable intraorganismic consequences which are associated with both episodic and persistent behavioral interactions.

Gastrointestinal Effects

While the obvious constraints imposed upon laboratory studies of behaviorally induced somatic pathology have continued to limit the range of experimental activity in this general area over the past decade, the recent research literature does reflect an abiding concern with the effects of environmental interactions upon the gastrointestinal system (Ader, 1971; Smith & Hain, 1970). Of particular interest would seem to be the rather extended analysis of factors which influence the incidence of peptic ulcers in rodents and primates under aversive behavioral control. Some further support for the efficacy of "conflict" and related procedures in the production of gastric lesions in laboratory rats has been provided by studies focusing upon approach-avoidance methods and comparisons involving individual and group "stress" exposure (Lower, 1967; Sawrey, 1964; Sawrey & Long, 1962; Sawrey & Sawrey, 1963, 1964a, 1964b, 1966), but replication and confirmation of the reported relationships continue to present problems (Ader, Beels, & Tatum, 1960; Ader, Tatum, & Beels, 1960; Pare, 1964). Similarly, recurrent descriptions of avoidance performance effects upon the gastrointestinal system have characteristically presented something less than a consistent picture with regard specifically to the conditions under which ulcers are most likely to occur. The reported incidence of peptic ulcers in rhesus monkeys intermittently exposed to free-operant shock-avoidance requirements (Brady, Porter, Conrad, & Mason, 1958) has proven difficult to repeat under some laboratory conditions (Folz & Miller, 1964) including those under which the study originated (Brady, 1964). Additionally, several investigations with laboratory rats in escape-avoidance situations have failed to find an incidence of gastric lesions in experimental animals which exceeded that of controls, and in some instances, yoked control animals receiving unavoidable shocks showed a greater degree of ulceration than their avoiding partners (Moot, Cebulla, & Crabtree, 1970; Pare, 1971; Weiss, 1971a).

To some extent, a clarification and at least partial reconciliation of these apparently conflicting developments in the delineation of behavioral effects upon the gastrointestinal system has been suggested by Weiss in a systematic series of published experimental reports from the Rockefeller University in New York (Weiss, 1970, 1971a, 1971b, 1971c). These studies started with the observation that laboratory rats which received intermittent tail shock following presentation of a 10-second beeping tone developed significantly less gastric ulceration than animals receiving the same shock without the "predictability" provided by the pre-aversive "warning" stimulus. Weiss then examined the effects of adding an operant escape-avoidance ("coping") panel-press to the procedure. Under these conditions, markedly fewer gastric lesions were found in the experimental animals when compared with "helpless" controls similarly exposed to warning signals and shocks (1 per min for 21 hours) but without escape-avoidance "coping." The interactions between warning signals and the escape-avoidance responses were tested in a subsequent experiment in which rats received electric shock that was preceded by either a warning signal, a series of signals providing an "external clock," or no signal at all. Under all three conditions, animals which could avoid and/or escape shock developed less ulceration than did yoked "helpless" animals. In addition, there was a clear difference in favor of the warning signal condition reducing ulceration as compared to the no-signal controls regardless of whether they were "helpless" or could escape/avoid the shock.

On the basis of this rather mammoth 180-rat experiment, Weiss theorized that the incidence of peptic ulcers may be a function of the interaction between strength of the escape-avoidance performance (i.e., the frequency of "coping" responses) and the probability of discriminable response-contingent signals associated with the absence of aversive stimuli (i.e., "feedback" about shock-free conditions). In these terms, the incidence of peptic ulcers in monkeys performing on free-operant avoidance is accounted for by the fact that they respond frequently in the absence of warning stimuli, and that the "safe" signals produced by these responses are not readily discriminable as "feedback" stimuli. The yoked-control monkeys, in contrast, characteristically emitted "avoidance" responses only infrequently, received only a few shocks well-distributed in time (due to the high performance rates of the experimental animals), and were found to be free of gastrointestinal pathology. Some further confirmation of this formulation has been provided by Weiss in a subsequent series of experiments which showed that the frequency of ulcers was increased in avoidance rats punished with shock for responding (i.e., "coping" response in high strength plus weak "feedback" about shock-free conditions), and decreased in animals producing a brief tone with each shock-postponing panel-press (i.e., strong "feedback" about shock-free conditions).

It is perhaps worth noting (though a bit out of place in the "physiological systems" organization of this chapter) that Weiss and his colleagues at the Rockefeller University have also found hormonal and body weight changes which reflect the interactions suggested by the ulcer studies, and that levels of brain norepinephrine are increased in escape-avoidance animals and decreased in non-performing ("helpless") shocked rats (Weiss, 1972; Weiss, Stone, & Harrel, 1970).

Central Nervous System Interactions

Electrophysiological changes continue to provide a hazy focus for a handful of studies over the past decade involving the use of operant methodology in the analysis of behaviorally-induced central nervous system alterations. Sidman avoidance performance in the rat, for example, has been reported (Bremner, 1964) to change irregular hippocampal EEG activity such that regular 5-7 cps theta activity appears just prior to and during lever pressing. Significantly, however, alteration of this theta pattern by direct electrical stimulation did not disrupt the concurrent avoidance behavior, indicating clearly that the correlated hippocampal theta activity was not essential to the performance. Food-maintained instrumental pedal-pushing in the dog has also been found to produce an increase in hippocampal theta rhythms accompanied by a highly correlated acceleration in heart rate (Konorski, Santibanez-H, & Beck, 1968). Large amplitude spindle electrocorticogram activity topographically restricted to the parieto-occipital region has as well been reported in the cat during lever pressing on a variable interval schedule for milk reward (Marczynski, Rosen, & Hackett, 1968), and systematic changes in the cortical evoked activity (auditory and visual cortex) of the cat have been related to the rate of discriminative avoidance acquisition (Saunders, 1971).

Several studies involving depth recording of both single and multiple neural unit activity during operant performances have been reported in the brain physiology literature over the past several years. Single neurons in the midbrain tegmentum of rats have been shown to respond discriminatively (i.e., increased firing rates) to tones following a lever press, signaling food, water, or no reinforcement under differential deprivation conditions (Phillips & Olds, 1969). EEG potential and amplitude changes in the reticular formation and amygdala of Wistar rats have also been shown to differ as a function of food reward and nonreward during a discriminated lever pressing performance using auditory signals (Norton, 1970). Multiple unit activity recorded from implanted monopolar macroelectrodes in the reticular formation, thalamus, cochlear nucleus, inferior colliculus, medial geniculate, and auditory cortex of the cat during discriminative instrumental avoidance training with tone as a warning signal has also been shown to reflect the sequential development of neuronal conditioning (Halas, Beardsley, & Sandlie, 1970). The process was observed to start with the reticular formation and progress upward from the cochlear nucleus to the auditory cortex. While one would be hard put to support an interpretation of these findings in terms of direct operant control of such neurophysiological events, some evidence has been produced for distinguishable neural activity patterns during classical, instrumental, and discrimination learning using the same multiple unit model (Beardsley, 1969). In this regard, for example, a recent study of EEG discriminators of delayed matching to sample behavior in *Macaca nemestrina* has shown that coherence values associated with correct responses were generally higher than those for incorrect responses in the frequency bands 1-3, 3-4, 5-7, and 8-13 Hz (Campeau, Adey, Durham, Tolliver, Ringler, & Kanner, 1971). The authors suggest that such elevated electrophysiological coherences may be a condition for optimal performance under these operant circumstances.

The relationship between electrical signs of "expectancy" in the brain as reflected in the EEG contingent negative variation (CNV) wave form (Walter, 1966) and operant performance requirements has received increasing experimental attention in several recently reported studies (Delse, Marsh, & Thompson, 1972; Donchin, Gerbrandt, Leifer, & Tucker, 1972; Peters, Knott, Miller, VanVeen, & Cohen, 1970; Rebert, 1972; Tecce, 1972). Without belaboring the details of the several stimulus and response variable analyses (e.g., task difficulty, pitch discrimination accuracy, reaction time) which have been described, the general conclusion that a widespread and protracted negative potential in the frontal cortex can be associated with discriminative stimulus control of minimal instrumental response tendencies (Hefferline, 1958) seems now to be well established both clinically and experimentally. Quantitative relations between the CNV measure as a predictor and the properties of the operant response (i.e., accuracy, latency, etc.) however, remain to be worked out in more precise detail. The range and variability of such performance-related brain electrical activity changes must also be extended to include the "contingent positive variation" wave form (large 180-300 microvolt positive steady potential shift associated with high-voltage alpha activity over the posterior marginal gyrus) reported to be associated with response-produced food reinforcement in deprived cats (Marczynski, York, & Hackett, 1969).

A few reports over the past several years have suggested that behaviorally induced changes in the chemical constitution of the brain may be systematically related to operant performance requirements under at least some aversive control conditions. The work of Hyden as reviewed recently by Deguchi (1969) in relationship to biochemical research on learning generally supports the finding that RNA in Dieter's nucleus of the rat is both increased and changed in composition as a function of wire-climbing, and that similar changes are observed in cortical cells when transfers in "handedness" training are required. Instrumental escape and avoidance training have also been reported to increase the incorporation of uridine into polyribosomes of the mouse brain and produce higher poly- and monosome ratios as compared to both yoked (receiving shocks only) and non-yoked control mice (Uphouse, MacInnes, & Schlesinger, 1972a, 1972b). It also seems possible that the shock-avoidance-induced hyperthermia in instrumentally trained rats recently described by Delini-Stula (1970) as enduring over an extended series of extinction trials may be related directly or indirectly to such changes in brain chemistry.

CONTINGENT MODELS

Technological and Methodological Developments

Research over the past decade concerned with the effects of conditioning procedures on physiological responses has focused prominently upon contingency relationships between antecedent visceral and glandular changes on the one hand, and experimentally programmed environmental consequences (e.g., food delivery and/or shock avoidance), on the other. Studies within the framework of this instrumental conditioning paradigm have clearly emphasized some physiological response systems (e.g., cardiovascular) more than others. This uneven distribution of measures reflects the technological and methodological developments which have paced the emergence of an operational laboratory psychophysiology. It is appropriate to acknowledge at least some of the major innovations and refinements upon which this burgeoning research domain depends. Particularly noteworthy have been the technical advances in the recording and measurement of heart rate (Blizard & Welty, 1970; Brener, 1965; DeToledo & Black, 1965; Ferraro, Silver, & Snapper, 1965; Fitzgerald, Vardaris, & Teyler, 1968; Krausman, 1970; Pare, Isom, & Reus, 1970; Perez-Cruet, Tolliver, Dunn, Marvin, & Brady, 1963; Ramsay, Pomerleau, & Snapper, 1968), blood pressure (DiCara, Pappas, & Pointer, 1969; Forsyth & Rosenblum, 1964; Herd & Barger, 1964; Krausman, 1969; Krausman, Ehrlich, & Brady, 1972; Perez-Cruet, Plumlee, & Newton, 1966; Swinnen, 1968; Werdegar, Johnson, & Mason, 1964), hormone levels (Mason et al., 1968), and electromyographic activity (Dixon, DeToledo, & Black, 1969; Hefferline, Keenan, Harford, & Birch, 1960) in both restrained and free-moving animals. As these and other psychophysiological developments (Brown, 1967) have increased the ease and accessibility of visceral and autonomic measurement techniques, an ever-broadening range of biological events has been exposed to experimental scrutiny in relationship to behavioral conditioning procedures.

Early History

Studies concerned with the analysis of instrumental visceral-autonomic conditioning represent a relatively recent development in the experimental production of altered physiological states with laboratory roots originating in the work of Neal Miller and his students at Yale in the mid-1960s, (e.g., Miller, 1969). Indeed, several earlier reports with human subjects (Crider, Shapiro, & Tursky, 1966; Fowler & Kimmel, 1962; Johnson, 1963; Kimmel & Hill, 1960; Kimmel & Kimmel, 1963; Lisina, 1958; Razran, 1961; Shapiro, Crider, & Tursky, 1964; Shearn, 1962) had foretold of such "operant" learning effects involving visceral and autonomic processes, and an extensive literature on "voluntary" physiological control by Yoga meditation and breathing techniques (Anand & Chhina, 1961; Anand, Chhina, & Singh, 1961; Bagchi & Wenger, 1959; Wenger & Bagchi, 1961; Wenger, Bagchi, & Anand, 1961) has long been available. But the experimental analysis of such instrumental autonomic conditioning effects in the animal laboratory has clearly activated a new research area in the investigation and application of such "visceral learning" phenomena.

Recent Past Reports

The earliest reported animal learning experiments on instrumental autonomic conditioning involved an attempt by Miller and Carmona (1967) to change the rate of *salivation* in a water-deprived dog by reinforcing both increases and decreases in this antecedent autonomic response with a contingent environmental consequence (i.e., water reward). Although the results of this study showed clearly that such autonomic responses could be controlled by operant procedures, attention was focused upon the possible role of skeletal muscle activity as a "mediator" of the observed visceral changes. Since the curarization technique used to control such skeletal muscle mediation produced direct effects upon salivation, an experiment by Trowill (1967) explored the operant control of *heart rate* in curarized laboratory rats using rewarding electrical brain stimulation (medial forebrain bundle at the level of the posterior hypothalamus) as a reinforcing consequence. Although the actual changes were small, both increases and decreases in heart rate were successfully conditioned. A subsequent study by Miller and DiCara (1967) showed that the magnitude of the instrumentally conditioned heart rate response could be influenced dramatically (producing changes approximating 20% of the basal values) by a "shaping" procedure which required the animals to meet a progressively more difficult criterion in order to obtain the rewarding brain stimulation. In addition, this experiment also demonstrated that such operant autonomic changes could be brought under discriminative control of the specific stimulus complex which provided the occasion for reinforcement of the response either of raising or lowering the heart rate. In a further confirmation of this instrumental heart rate conditioning effect, Hothersall and Brener (1969), using curarized rats and electrical brain stimulation reward, incorporated a feedback light whenever the prescribed criterion was met, and extended their investigation to include a demonstration of operant extinction when the instrumentally conditioned heart rate response was no longer reinforced with brain stimulation.

Mediational Events

Persistent concern with the degree of skeletal involvement in such instrumental autonomic conditioning was reflected in a series of experiments by Black (1967a) with dogs initially trained on a lever-pressing shock-avoidance task and subsequently curarized for operant conditioning of either *electromyographic* or heart rate responses. The level of curarization insured little or no overt movement but did not completely eliminate the EMG response. The results showed that the instrumentally conditioned heart rate changes were closely associated with the conditioned EMG changes which readily transferred to affect the performance in the non-curarized state. In a later report, however, Black (1968) concluded that the heart rate response could be conditioned independently of overt movement, without conceding that the operant autonomic changes occurred in the absence of some central event related to the initiation and performance of skeletal motor responses. Miller and DiCara (1967) had in fact hypothesized that such central activity (e.g., motor cortex impulses), classically conditioned to elicit heart rate changes, might account for the demonstrated autonomic effects. A control procedure, however, involving strong tail shocks (3 ma) produced smaller heart rate increases (10%) than did instrumental conditioning (20%), suggesting that such indirect skeletal mediation was unlikely to account for the observed heart rate changes. They further showed (DiCara & Miller, 1968a) that the completely curarized rat (i.e., no EMG responses from the gastrocnemius muscle) could learn to both increase and decrease heart rate as an operant shock-avoidance response, thus establishing that the instrumental autonomic conditioning effect was not an artifact of the electrical brain stimulation reinforcer. The results of this study also showed that discriminative control over the conditioned heart rate change could be developed and maintained by a stimulus which always preceded shock presentation. Such instrumentally learned heart rate changes have also been shown to persist in the absence of reinforced practice trials over extended periods (e.g., 3-month retention tests), and they can be relearned after extinction (DiCara & Miller, 1968d).

Response Specificity

Transfer of learning effects have also been demonstrated in a series of studies by DiCara and Miller (1969a, 1969b) in which heart rate changes instrumentally conditioned under curare were subsequently (one week later) observed in free-moving rats, and additional training in the noncurarized state was shown to produce changes of even greater magnitude. Similar transfer was also demonstrated from the noncurarized to the curarized state, and the differences in respiration and gross movement were found to decrease as the differences in heart rate increased. This emergent response specificity has also been documented in an experiment by Miller and Banuazizi (1968) in which independent operant control of both heart rate changes and *intestinal contractions* was demonstrated. Fields (1970) subsequently demonstrated the remarkable specificity of such conditioning effects by producing instrumentally learned increases or decreases in the *P-R interval of the EKG* independently of changes in the P-P interval. The issues related to a linkage between somato-motor and cardiovascular activities in the instrumental autonomic conditioning process have not been definitely settled, however. This is seen from a recent report by Goesling and Brener (1972) which showed that two different training procedures (i.e., immobility training versus activity training), given prior to instrumental heart rate conditioning under curare, can have a greater effect upon heart rate changes in subsequently curarized rats than the reinforcement contingencies per se. Other types of training (e.g., lever pressing) given prior to the instrumental conditioning of heart rate in rats have appeared related to subsequent performance in heart rate conditioning studies (Miller & DiCara, 1967), but negative findings (i.e., no relationship between prior bar press training and subsequent heart rate conditioning) have also been reported (Slaughter, Hahn, & Rinaldi, 1970).

Response Interactions

Interaction effects involving operant heart rate conditioning and other related psychophysiological processes have been investigated in a number of animal studies. Curarized rats pretrained using operant methods to *decrease* heart rate have, for example, been shown to subsequently acquire (in the noncurarized state) shuttle-box escape-avoidance behavior more readily than rats similarly pretrained to *increase* their heart rate (DiCara & Weiss, 1969). It has also been reported (Engel & Gottlieb, 1970) that blood pressure changes were significantly positively correlated with heart rate decreases instrumentally conditioned as an avoidance response in rhesus monkeys, but such blood pressure effects were uncorrelated with instrumentally conditioned heart rate increases in these same animals. Differences in the opposite direction have been reported with respect to epinephrine and norepinephrine by DiCara and Stone (1970) who found higher endogenous cardiac and brainstem catecholamine levels in rats instrumentally trained to increase heart rate as compared to rats instrumentally conditioned to decrease heart rate. Cardiac H^3-norepinephrine retention studies by these same authors, however, suggested that rats trained to decrease heart rate under curare were subjected to greater stress than rats trained to increase heart rate. Of additional interest in this regard is the finding by DiCara, Braun, & Pappas (1970) that an intact neocortex is essential for instrumental autonomic conditioning though this appears not to be the case with respect to the classical conditioning of the same heart rate and gastrointestinal responses.

The instrumental conditioning of blood pressure in the curarized rat was convincingly demonstrated by DiCara and Miller (1968b) using a shock avoidance procedure to reinforce both increases and decreases in systolic pressure levels independently of changes in heart rate and rectal temperature. And in a subsequent study, these same investigators (1968c) using electrical brain stimulation as a reinforcer with the curarized rat dramatically confirmed the specificity of such instrumental autonomic learning by selectively conditioning vasomotor tone *increases* in one ear and vasomotor tone *decreases* in the other ear of the same animal. Significantly, these conditioned *blood flow* changes were not correlated with heart rate, rectal temperature, or vasomotor tone in the tail, suggesting a remarkable and previously unrecognized localization of sympathetic action. Following a replication of these findings, Pappas, DiCara, and Miller (1970) further demonstrated that instrumentally conditioned systolic blood pressure increases and decreases in non-curarized rats did not transfer to the curarized state, but that retraining the same animals after curarization produced even larger magnitude pressure changes than in the noncurarized state. Similar observations with respect to the specificity of instrumentally conditioned cardiovascular changes previously reported by DiCara and Miller (1968a, 1968b) received additional support from the finding of Pappas et al. (1970) that the instrumentally conditioned blood pressure effects were independent of heart rate and gross skeletal activity.

Response Magnitude and Duration

Large magnitude diastolic blood pressure elevations (50–60 mm Hg) conditioned instrumentally as a shock avoidance response in the rhesus monkey were first reported by Plumlee (1969), though the relatively short duration of the changes and the observed postural effects suggested mediation by a Valsalva maneuver (i.e., alteration of intrathoracic pressure by abdominal muscle contraction). Somewhat more modest elevations in mean arterial pressure (e.g., 25 mm Hg) were maintained in squirrel monkeys by Benson, Herd, Morse, and Kelleher (1969) for periods of 20 min or longer as a result of an operant reinforcement contingency arrangement which required the indicated pressure change as a shock avoidance response. And Harris, Findley, and Brady (1971) have also shown that substantial elevations in both systolic and diastolic blood pressure (e.g., 50–60 mm Hg) could be established and maintained in baboons by an operant conditioning procedure which provided for food delivery and shock avoidance programmed as environmental consequences contingent upon prescribed increases in diastolic pressure levels. The instrumentally conditioned blood pressure changes were sustained for intervals up to and exceeding 5 min and appeared to bear somewhat systematic but complex temporal relationships to variation in heart rate. More recently, these same authors (Harris, Gilliam, Findley, & Brady, 1973) have extended this basic instrumental autonomic conditioning procedure with the baboon to produce more sustained and clinically relevant increases (30–40 mm Hg) in both systolic and diastolic blood pressure throughout daily 12-hour experimental sessions, as illustrated in Figure 6. Significantly, the maintained instrumentally conditioned blood pressure increases can be seen to be accompanied by elevated but progressively decreasing heart rate levels.

Other Response Systems

Instrumentally conditioned *glandular response* changes have also been demonstrated in an experi-

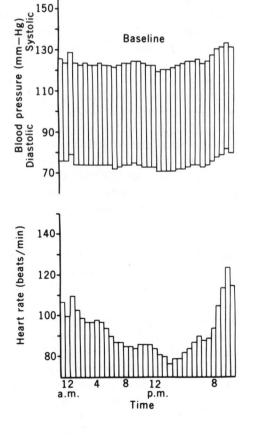
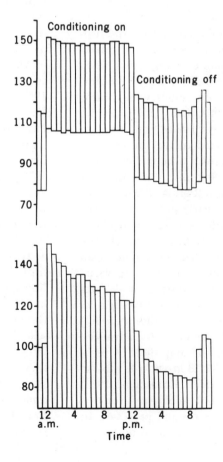

Fig. 6. Average blood pressure and heart rate values for four baboons over consecutive 40-min intervals during 16 pre-experimental baseline determinations (left panel) compared with 16 12-hour "conditioning-on", 12-hour "conditioning-off" sessions (right panel). (From Harris et al., 1973. © 1973 by the American Association for the Advancement of Science.)

ment with curarized rats rewarded by electrical brain stimulation for both increases and decreases in the rate of *urine formation* by the kidney (Miller & DiCara, 1968). Using insulin-14C and tritiated p-aminohippuric acid (PAH), it was also determined that both *glomerular filtration rate* and renal blood flow were systematically altered by the operant conditioning procedure, though heart rate, blood pressure, and peripheral blood flow were not, confirming the high degree of specificity and localization of action emphasized in previous reports (DiCara & Miller, 1968b, 1968c; Fields, 1970; Miller & Banuazizi, 1968). More recently, Banuazizi (1972) has extended the experimental analysis of selectively conditioned intestinal contractions in the curarized rat by demonstrating discriminative stimulus control of both short- and long-duration intestinal responses reinforced by shock avoidance. Significantly, the study also included a control for the unconditioned effects of the electric shock as a possible "state dependent" influence upon the contractile response, and confirmed the instrumental intestinal conditioning under even these more stringent requirements.

Feedback Factors

The role of *feedback* stimulation in the establishment and maintenance of instrumentally conditioned visceral and autonomic response changes has been emphasized in several recent studies (Harris, Findley, & Brady, 1971; Harris, Gilliam, Findley, & Brady, 1973; Hothersall & Brener, 1969; Lang, 1970) despite the somewhat equivocal status of the "interoceptive discrimination" issue as reflected in the literature of the past decade (Kadden, Snapper, Schoenfeld & Kop, 1970; Kadden, Schoenfeld, & Snapper, 1970; Mandler & Kahn, 1960; Slucki, Adam, & Porter, 1965; Slucki, McCoy, & Porter, 1969). The early and more recent studies by Miller and his students as reviewed above involved reinforcing stimulus changes (e.g., electric brain stimulation) which provided immediate feedback following visceral or autonomic response variations. As more extended duration instrumental autonomic conditioning effects have been investigated, however, exteroceptive stimuli (e.g., lights, tones) linked with the internal environment by advanced electrophysiological recording and amplification techniques (Brown & Thorne, 1964; Budzynski & Stoyva, 1969; Hefferline & Keenan, 1963; Krausman, 1972) have provided both digital and analogue presentations of critical interoceptive events and processes. In addition, such feedback stimuli serve as conditioned reinforcers bridging the temporal gap between the visceral response and its maintaining environmental consequences. Such stimulus feedback applications have been convincingly demonstrated in the instrumental heart rate conditioning studies of Hothersall and Brener (1969) with curarized rats, and the operant blood pressure conditioning experiments of Harris et al. (1971) with laboratory baboons.

Interpretive and Theoretical Issues

Despite this emergent operational orientation, *interpretive* and *theoretical* accounts of instrumental autonomic conditioning procedures and results continue to focus upon "mediational" issues as these have been reviewed and discussed at length in several recent reports (Crider, Schwartz, & Schnidman, 1969; Katkin & Murray, 1968; Katkin, Murray, & Lachman, 1969; Kimmel, 1967; Schoenfeld, 1970, 1971). The controversies surrounding experimental attempts to control such "voluntary mediators" in instrumental autonomic conditioning studies have at least emphasized the need to reexamine some basic formulations regarding conventional distinctions between the two types of learning (Schoenfeld, 1966, 1972). With respect to more focused concern involving the interrelationship between autonomic-visceral and somato-motor activity, two more or less distinguishable points of view can be identified. Miller, DiCara, and their associates (DiCara, 1970; DiCara & Miller, 1968a, 1968b, 1968c; Miller & Banuazizi, 1968; Pappas, DiCara, & Miller, 1970; Trowill, 1967) on the one hand, have appeared to take the position that evidence from their own experiments and those of others (Schwartz, Shapiro, & Tursky, 1971; Shapiro, Tursky, & Schwartz, 1970) supports the independence of somato-motor and autonomic-visceral control. Black (1967a, 1967b, 1968), Brener and Goesling (1968), and Obrist, Webb, Sutterer, and Howard (1970), on the other hand, prefer to represent autonomic-visceral and somato-motor activities as two components of a more general, centrally controlled response process. That the dividing line between the two formulations may not be too firmly drawn, however, would seem to be indicated by the fact that virtually all the adherents to the latter school of thought (Black, 1971; Goesling & Brener, 1972; Obrist et al., 1970) appear willing to concede that the postulated "normal" linkage between the two systems may be modified in a variety of ways. Indeed, a more moderate "separable but interacting" formulation (Brady, 1972) of the observed psychophysiological relationships may better serve the purposes of both clinical and experimental investigators concerned with the conditions under which dissociation or decoupling of the two systems can and do occur in the course of ongoing behavioral transactions between organism and environment.

It is probably noteworthy that amidst this flurry of interpretive and theoretical discourse, recent reports by Miller and Dworkin (1974), DiCara (1974), and others (Brener, Eissenberg, & Middaugh, 1974) have raised searching questions about the replicability of earlier findings related to instrumentally conditioned heart rate changes. Specifically, there has been a progressive decline in the magnitude of learned changes in heart rate from the first experiment conducted in 1966 through those of the 1970's (Miller & Dworkin, 1974). A number of factors are being investigated in order to provide an account of these "extraordinarily perplexing and vexing phenomena," as Miller terms it, but no proposed explanation for the discrepancy has yet been confirmed. Much of the controversy focuses upon technological and methodological details related to the proper use of curare and artificial respiration procedures. In this regard, Howard, Galosy, Gaebelein, and Obrist (1974) have enumerated several of the problems associated with curarization, including dosage, criteria for muscular blockade and artificial respiration, the side effects of ganglionic blockade, histamine release, and the alteration of sensory processes.

Controversies regarding mechanism and methodology notwithstanding, the evidence that operant conditioning procedures, whether centrally or peripherally mediated, exert orderly and specific effects upon the functional properties of physiological systems seems incontrovertible. Clearly, systematic analysis of such noninvasive, nonpharmacologic influences upon somatic processes holds considerable promise for enriching both clinical and experimental approaches to the physiopathology of health disorders. It is at least equally important that this work clearly confirms the importance of the contributions made by basic behavioral science to a comprehensive physiology of the intact, unanesthetized, conscious organism. Indeed, increasing emphasis upon the application of biotelemetric techniques (McCutcheon, 1973) in psychophysiological investigations provides tangible recognition of this developing frontier. Certainly, the identification and operational definition of such "internal state" variables and their functional interactions is of central importance in delineating a research domain which emphasizes the critical role of environmental-behavioral influences in the production of physiological alterations.

REFERENCES

ADER, ROBERT. Experimentally induced gastric lesions. *Advances in Psychosomatic Medicine*, 1971, *6*, 1–39 (Karger, Basel).

ADER, R., BEELS, C. C., & TATUM, R. Social factors affecting emotionality and resistance of disease in animals. II. Susceptibility to gastric ulceration as a function of interruptions in social interactions and the time at which they occur. *Journal of Comparative & Physiological Psychology*, 1960, *53*, 455–458.

ADER, R., TATUM, R., & BEELS, C. Social factors affecting emotionality and resistance of disease in animals. I. Age of separation from the mother and susceptibility to gastric ulcers in the rat. *Journal of Comparative & Physiological Psychology*, 1960, *53*, 446–454.

ANAND, B., & CHHINA, G. Investigations on yogis claiming to stop their heart beats. *Indian Journal of Medical Research* (Bombay) 1961, *49*, 90–94.

ANAND, B., CHHINA, G. S., & SINGH, B. Some aspects of electro-encephalographic studies of Yoga. *Electroencephalography and Clinical Neurophysiology*, 1961, *13*, 452–456.

ANDERSON, D. E., & BRADY, J. V. Pre-avoidance blood pressure elevations accompanied by heart rate decreases in the dog. *Science*, 1971, *172*, 595–597.

ANDERSON, D. E., & BRADY, J. V. Differential preparatory cardiovascular responses to aversive and appetitive behavioral conditioning. *Conditional Reflex*, 1972, *7*, (2), 82–96.

ANDERSON, D. E., & BRADY, J. V. Prolonged preavoidance effects upon blood pressure and heart rate in the dog. *Psychosomatic Medicine*, 1973, *35*, 4–12. (a)

ANDERSON, D. E., & BRADY, J. V. Effects of beta blockade on cardiovascular responses to avoidance performance in dogs. *Psychosomatic Medicine*, 1973, *35*, 84. (b)

ANDERSON, D. E., DALEY, L. A., FINDLEY, J. D., & BRADY, J. V. A restraint system for the psychophysiological study of dogs. *Behavioral Research Instrumentation and Methodology*, 1970, *2*, 191–194.

ANDERSON, D. E., & TOSHEFF, J. Cardiac output and total peripheral resistance changes during pre-avoidance periods in the dog. *Journal of Applied Physiology*, 1973, *34*, 650–654.

ANLIKER, J. Brain waves and operant behavior. *Journal of the Experimental Analysis of Behavior*, 1959, *2*, 252.

BAGCHI, B. K., & WENGER, M. A. Electrophysiological correlates of some Yoga exercises. *Electroencephalography and Clinical Neurophysiology*, 1959, Suppl. #7, 132–149.

BANKS, J. H., MILLER, R. E., & OGAWA, N. The development of discriminated autonomic and instrumental responses during avoidance conditioning in the rhesus monkey. *Journal of Genetic Psychology*, 1966, *108*, 199–211.

BANUAZIZI, A. Discriminative shock avoidance learning of an autonomic response during curare. *Journal of Comparative & Physiological Psychology*, 1972, *80*, 236–246.

BEARDSLEY, J. V. A comparison of multiple unit activity during classical, instrumental, and discrimination learning using a noxious unconditioned stimulus. *Dissertation Abstracts*, 1969, *29* (11-B), 4391–4392.

BENSON, H., HERD, J. A., MORSE, W. H., & KELLEHER, R. T. Behavioral inductions of arterial hypertension and its reversal. *American Journal of Physiology*, 1969, *217*, 30–34.

Berlanger, D., & Feldman, S. Effects of water deprivation upon heart rate and instrumental activity in the rat. *Journal of Comparative & Physiological Psychology*, 1962, *55*, 220–225.

Black, A. H. Heart rate changes during avoidance learning in dogs. *Canadian Journal of Psychology*, 1959, *13*, 229–242.

Black, A. H. Operant conditioning in curarized dogs. *Conditional Reflex*, 1967, *2* (2), 158. (a)

Black, A. H. Transfer following operant conditioning in the curarized dog. *Science*, 1967, *155*, 201–203. (b)

Black, A. H. Operant conditioning of autonomic responses. *Conditional Reflex*, 1968, *3* (2), 130.

Black, A. H. Autonomic aversive conditioning in infrahuman subjects. In F. R. Brush (Ed.), *Aversive Conditioning and Learning*. New York: Academic Press, 1971.

Black, A. H., & Dalton, A. J. The relationship between the avoidance response and subsequent changes in heart rate. *Acta Biologiae Experimentalis* (Warsaw), 1965, *25*, 107–119.

Blizard, D., & Welty, R. A technique for monitoring the heart rate of mice. *Psychophysiology*, 1970, *7*, 143–144.

Brady, J. V. Ulcers in "executive" monkeys. *Scientific American*, 1958, *199*, 95–100.

Brady, J. V. Further comments on the gastrointestinal system and avoidance behavior. *Psychological Reports*, 1963, *12*, 742.

Brady, J. V. Behavioral stress and physiological change: A comparative approach to the experimental analysis of some psychosomatic problems. *Transactions of the New York Academy of Science*, 1964, *26*, 483–496.

Brady, J. V. Experimental studies of psychophysiological responses to stressful situations. *Symposium on Medical Aspects of Stress in the Military Climate*. Walter Reed Army Insitute of Research, Government Printing Office, Washington, D.C., 1965.

Brady, J. V. Operant methodology and the production of altered physiological states. In W. Honig (Ed.), *Operant Behavior: Areas of Research and Application*. Englewood Cliffs, N.J.: Prentice-Hall, Inc., 1966.

Brady, J. V. Emotion and the sensitivity of the psychoendocrine system. In D. Glass (Ed.), *Neurophysiology and Emotion*. New York: The Rockefeller Univ. Press, 1967.

Brady, J. V. Recent developments in the measurement of stress. In B. P. Rourke (Ed.), *Explorations in the Psychology of Stress and Anxiety*. New York: Longmans, 1969.

Brady, J. V. Emotion: Some conceptual problems and psychophysiological experiments. In M. Arnold (Ed.), *Feelings and Emotions*. New York: Academic Press, 1970. (a)

Brady, J. V. Endocrine and autonomic correlates of emotional behavior. In P. Black (Ed.), *Physiological Correlates of Emotion*. New York: Academic Press, 1970. (b)

Brady, J. V. Emotion revisited. *Journal of Psychiatric Research*, 1971, *8*, 343–384.

Brady, J. V. Emotion: Some conceptual problems and psychophysiological experiments. In D. Singh & C. T. Morgan (Eds.), *Current Status of Physiologic Psychology: A Book of Readings*. Monterey, Calif.: Brooks, Cole Publishing Co., 1972.

Brady, J. V. Psychophysiological syndromes resulting from overly-rigid environmental control: Concurrent and contingent animal models. In J. H. Cullen (Ed.), *Experimental Behavior*. Dublin, Ireland: Irish Univ. Press, 1974.

Brady, J. V. Conditioning and emotion. In L. Levi (Ed.), *Emotions: Their Parameters and Measurements*. New York: Raven Press. 1975.

Brady, J. V., Anderson, D. E., Harris, A. H., & Stephens, J. H. The effects of classical and instrumental conditioning upon blood pressure and heart rate in mongrel, monkey and man. *Conditional Reflex*, 1973, *8* (3), 174–175.

Brady, J. V., Findley, J. D., & Harris, A. H. Experimental psychopathology and the psychophysiology of emotion. In H. D. Kimmel (Ed.), *Experimental Psychopathology*. New York: Academic Press, 1971.

Brady, J. V., Harris, A. H., & Anderson, D. E. Behavior and the cardiovascular system in experimental animals. In A. Zanchetti (Ed.), *Neural and Psychological Mechanisms in Cardiovascular Disease*. Milan: Casa Editrice (Il Ponte), 1972.

Brady, J. V., Kelly, D., & Plumlee, L. Autonomic and behavioral responses of the rhesus monkey to emotional conditioning. *Annals of the New York Academy of Science*, 1969, *159*, 959–975.

Brady, J. V. & Nauta, W. J. H. *Principles, Practices and Positions in Neuropsychiatric Research*. Oxford: Pergamon Press, 1972.

Brady, J. V., Porter, R., Conrad, D., & Mason, J. Avoidance behavior and the development of gastroduodenal ulcers. *Journal of the Experimental Analysis of Behavior*, 1958, *1*, 69–72.

Brady, J. V., & Polish, E. Performance changes during prolonged avoidance. *Psychological Reports*, 1960, *7*, 554.

Bremner, F. J. Hippocampal activity during avoidance behavior in the rat. *Journal of Comparative & Physiological Psychology*, 1964, *58*, 16–22.

Brener, J. M. The measurement of heart rate. In P. H. Venables & I. Martin (Eds.), *Manual of Psychophysiological Methods*. Amsterdam: North-Holland Publishing Co., 1965.

Brener, J. M., Eissenberg, E., & Middaugh, S. Respiratory and somato-motor factors associated with operant conditioning of cardiovascular responses in curarized rats. In P. A. Obrist, A. H. Black, J. Brener, & L. V. DiCara (Eds.), *Current Issues in Response Mechanisms, Biofeedback and Methodology*. Chicago: Aldine Publishing Co., 1974.

Brener, J. M., & Goesling, W. J. Heart rate and conditioned activity. Presented at *Meetings of the Society for Psychophysiological Research*. Washington, D.C., 1968.

Brown, C. C. *Methods in Psychophysiology*. Baltimore: Williams and Wilkins, 1967.

Brown, C., & Thorne, P. An instrument for signalling heart rate to unrestrained human subjects. *Psychophysiology*, 1964, *1* (2), 192–194.

Brown, G. M., Schalch, D. S., & Reichlin, S. Patterns of growth hormone and cortisol responses to psychological stress in the squirrel monkey. *Endocrinology*, 1971, *88*, 956–963.

Brush, F. R., & Levine, S. Adrenocortical activity and avoidance learning as a function of time after fear conditioning. *Physiology and Behavior*, 1966, *1*, 309–311.

Budzynski, T. H., & Stoyva, J. M. An instrument for producing deep muscle relaxation by means of analog information feedback. *Journal of Applied Behavior Analysis*, 1969, *2*, 231–237.

Campeau, E., Adey, W. R., Durham, R. M., Tolliver, J.

D., Ringler, R., & Kanner, R. M. EEG discriminators of delayed matching to sample performance in *Macaca nemestrina*. *Physiology and Behavior*, 1971, *6* (4), 413–418.

Cannon, W. B. *Bodily Changes in Pain, Hunger, Fear and Rage*. New York: Appleton, 1915.

Clark, R., & Polish, E. Avoidance conditioning and alcohol consumption in rhesus monkeys. *Science*, 1960, *132*, 223–224.

Conger, J. J., Sawrey, W. L., & Turrell, E. S. The role of social experience in the production of gastric ulcers in hooded rats placed in a conflict situation. *Journal of Comparative & Physiological Psychology*, 1958, *51*, 214–220.

Coover, G. D., Goldman, L., & Levine, S. Plasma corticosterone increases produced by extinction of operant behavior in rats. *Physiology and Behavior*, 1971, *6* (3), 261–263.

Crider, A., Schwartz, G. E., & Shnidman, S. On the criteria for instrumental autonomic conditioning: A reply to Katkin and Murray. *Psychological Bulletin*, 1969, *71*(6), 455–461.

Crider, A., Shapiro, D., & Tursky, B. Reinforcement of spontaneous electrodermal activity. *Journal of Comparative & Physiological Psychology*, 1966, *61*, 20–27.

Davis, R. C., & Berry, F. Gastrointestinal reactions during a noise avoidance task. *Psychological Reports*, 1963, *12*, 135–137.

Deguchi, T. On the biochemical theory of learning. *Japanese Psychological Review*, 1969, *12* (1), 18–29.

Delini-Stula, A. The development and the extinction of hyperthermia induced by conditioned avoidance behavior in rats. *Journal of the Experimental Analysis of Behavior*, 1970, *14* (2), 213–218.

Delse, F. C., Marsh, G. R., & Thompson, L. W. CNV correlates of task difficulty and accuracy of pitch discrimination. *Psychophysiology*, 1972, *9*, 53–62.

DeToledo, L. Changes in heart rate during conditioned suppression in rats as a function of US intensity and type of CS. *Journal of Comparative & Physiological Psychology*, 1971, *77*, 528–538.

DeToledo, L., & Black, A. H. A technique for recording heart rate in moving rats. *Journal of the Experimental Analysis of Behavior*, 1965, *8* (3), 181–182.

DeToledo, L., & Black, A. H. Heart rate: Changes during conditioned suppression in rats. *Science*, 1966, *152*, 1404–1406.

DeVietti, T. L., & Porter, P. B. Heart rate response during aversive conditioning. *Psychological Reports*, 1970, *27* (2), 651–658.

DiCara, L. V. Learning in the autonomic nervous system. *Scientific American*, 1970, *222* (1), 30–39.

DiCara, L. V. Some critical methodological variables involved in visceral learning. In P. A. Obrist, A. H. Black, J. Brener, & L. V. DiCara (Eds.), *Current Issues in Response Mechanisms, Biofeedback and Methodology*. Chicago: Aldine Publishing Company, 1974.

DiCara, L. V., Braun, J. J., & Pappas, B. A. Classical conditioning and instrumental learning of cardiac and gastrointestinal responses following removal of neocortex in the rat. *Journal of Comparative & Physiological Psychology*, 1970, *73* (2), 208–216.

DiCara, L., & Miller, N. E. Changes in heart rate instrumentally learned by curarized rats as avoidance responses. *Journal of Comparative &Physiological Psychology*, 1968, *65*, 1–7. (a)

DiCara, L. V., & Miller, N. E. Instrumental learning of systolic blood pressure responses in curarized rats: Dissociation of cardiac and vascular changes. *Psychosomatic Medicine*, 1968, *5*, 489–494. (b)

DiCara, L. V., & Miller, N. E. Instrumental learning of vasomotor responses by rats: learning to respond differentially in the two ears. *Science*, 1968, *159*, 1485–1486. (c)

DiCara, L. V., & Miller, N. E. Long-term retention of instrumentally learned heart rate changes in the curarized rat. *Communications in Behavioral Biology*, 1968, *2* (pt. A), 19–23. (d)

DiCara, L. V., & Miller, N. E. Heart rate learning in the non-curarized state, transfer to the curarized state. *Physiology and Behavior*, 1969, *4*, 621–624. (a)

DiCara, L. V., & Miller, N. E. Transfer of instrumentally learned heart rate changes from curarized to noncurarized states: Implications for a mediational hypothesis. *Journal of Comparative & Physiological Psychology*, 1969, *62* (2, pt 1), 159–162. (b)

DiCara, L., Pappas, B. A., & Pointer, F. A technique for chronic reading of systemic arterial blood pressure in the unrestrained rat. *Behavior Research Methods and Instrumentation*, 1969, *1* (6), 221–223.

DiCara, L., & Stone, E. A. Effect of instrumental rate training on rat cardiac and brain catecholamines. *Psychosomatic Medicine*, 1970, *32* (4), 359–368.

DiCara, L., & Weiss, J. M. Effect of heart rate learning under curare on subsequent non-curarized avoidance learning. *Journal of Comparative & Physiological Psychology*, 1969, *69*, 368–374.

Dixon, C., DeToledo, L., & Black, A. H. A technique for recording electromyographic activity in free-moving rats using an all-purpose slip ring commutator. *Journal of the Experimental Analysis of Behavior*, 1969, *12* (3), 507–509.

Donchin, E., Gerbrandt, L. A., Leifer, L., & Tucker, L. Is the contingent negative variation contingent on a motor response? *Psychophysiology*, 1972, *9*, 178–188.

Eldridge, L. *Respiration rate change and its relation to avoidance behavior*. Unpublished Doctoral Dissertation, Columbia University, 1954.

Engel, B. T., & Gottlieb, S. H. Differential operant conditioning of heart rate in the unrestrained monkey. *Journal of Comparative & Physiological Psychology*, 1970, *73* (2), 217–225.

Estes, W. K., & Skinner, B. F. Some quantitative properties of anxiety. *Journal of Experimental Psychology*, 1941, *29*, 390–400.

Ferraro, D. P., Silver, M. P., & Snapper, A. G. A method for cardiac recording from surface electrodes in the rat during free-operant procedures. *Journal of the Experimental Analysis of Behavior*, 1965, *8* (1), 17–18.

Fields, C. Instrumental conditioning of the rat cardiac control systems. *Proceedings of the National Academy of Science*, 1970, *65* (2), 293–299.

Figar, S. Conditioned circulatory responses in men and animals. In F. Dow (Ed.) *Handbook of Physiology* (Sec. 2, Vol. 3). Baltimore: Williams and Wilkins, 1965.

Findley, J. D., Brady, J. V., Robinson, W. W., & Gilliam, W. J. Continuous cardiovascular monitoring in the baboon during long-term behavioral performances. *Communications in Behavioral Biology*, 1971, *6*, 49–58.

FINDLEY, J. D., ROBINSON, W. W., & GILLIAM, W. J. A restraint system for chronic study of the baboon. *Journal of the Experimental Analysis of Behavior*, 1971, *15*, 69–71.

FITZGERALD, R. D., VARDARIS, R. M., & TEYLER, T. J. An on-line method for measuring heart rate in conditioning experiments. *Psychophysiology*, 1968, *4* (3), 352–353.

FOLZ, E. L., & MILLER, F. E., JR. Experimental psychosomatic disease states in monkeys. I. Peptic ulcer "executive monkeys". *Journal of Surgical Research*, 1964, *4*, 445–453.

FORSYTH, R. P. Blood pressure and avoidance conditioning. *Psychosomatic Medicine*, 1968, *30* (1), 125–135.

FORSYTH, R. P. Blood pressure responses to long-term avoidance schedules in the unrestrained rhesus monkey. *Psychosomatic Medicine*, 1969, *31*, 300–309.

FORSYTH, R. P. Regional blood-flow changes during 72-hour avoidance schedules in the monkey. *Science*, 1971, *173*, 546–548.

FORSYTH, R. P. Sympathetic nervous system control of distribution of cardiac output in unanesthetized monkeys. *Federation Proceedings*, 1972, *31* (4), 1240–1244.

FORSYTH, R. P., & HARRIS, R. E. Circulatory changes during stressful stimuli in rhesus moneys. *Circulation Research*, 1970, *27*, Suppl.: 1–13.

FORSYTH, R. P., HOFFBRAND, B. I., & MELMON, K. L. Hemodynamic effects of angiotensin in the normal and environmentally stressed monkeys. *Circulation*, 1971, *44*, 119–129.

FORSYTH, R. P., & ROSENBLUM, M. A. A restraining device and procedure for continuous blood pressure recordings in monkeys. *Journal of the Experimental Analysis of Behavior*, 1964, *7* (5), 367–368.

FOWLER, R. L., & KIMMEL, H. D. Operant conditioning of the GSR. *Journal of Experimental Psychology*, 1962, *63*, 563–567.

FRAZIER, T. W., WEIL-MELHERBE, H., & LIPSCOMB, H. S. Psychophysiology of conditioned emotional disturbances in humans. *Psychophysiology*, 1969, *5* (5), 478–503.

GANTT, W. H. Cardiovascular component of the conditional reflex to pain, food, and other stimuli. *Physiological Review*, 1960, *40*, 266–291.

GOESLING, W. J., & BRENER, J. Effects of activity and immobility conditioning upon subsequent heart rate conditioning in curarized rats. *Journal of Comparative & Physiological Psychology*, 1972, *81*, 311–317.

GRAHAM, L. A., COHEN, S. I., & SHMAVONIAN, B. M. Urinary catecholamine excretion during instrumental conditioning. *Psychosomatic Medicine*, 1967, *29* (2), 134–143.

GRANGER, L. Variation of heart rate in different types of visual attention situations. *Canadian Journal of Psychology*, 1970, *24* (5), 370–379.

HAHN, W. W., STERN, J. A., & McDONALD, D. G. Effects of water deprivation and bar pressing activity on heart rate of the male albino rat. *Journal of Comparative & Physiological Psychology*, 1962, *55*, 786–790.

HALAS, E. S., BEARDSLEY, J. V., & SANDLIE, M. E. Conditioned neuronal responses at various levels of conditioning paradigms. *Electroencephalography and Clinical Neurophysiology*, 1970, *28* (5), 468–477.

HARRIS, A. H., & BRADY, J. V. Animal learning: visceral and autonomic conditioning. *Annual Review of Psychology*, 1974, *25*, 107–133.

HARRIS, A. H., FINDLEY, J. D., & BRADY, J. V. Instrumental conditioning of blood pressure elevations in the baboon. *Conditional Reflex*, 1971, *6* (4), 215–226.

HARRIS, A. H., GILLIAM, W., FINDLEY, J. D., & BRADY, J. V. Instrumental conditioning of large-magnitude daily 12-hour blood pressure elevations in the baboon. *Science*, 1973, *182*, 175–177.

HEARST, E., BEER, B., SHEATZ, G., & GALAMBOS, R. Some electrophysiological correlates of conditioning in the monkey. *Electroencephalography and Clinical Neurophysiology*, 1960, *12*, 137–162.

HEFFERLINE, R. F. The role of proprioception in the control of behavior. *Transactions of the New York Academy of Science*, 1958, *20* (8), 739–764.

HEFFERLINE, R. F., & KEENAN, B. Amplitude-induction gradient of a small-scale (covert) operant. *Journal of the Experimental Analysis of Behavior*, 1963, *6*, 307–315.

HEFFERLINE, R. F., KEENAN, B., HARFORD, R. A., & BIRCH, J. Electronics in psychology. *Columbia Engineering Quarterly*, 1960, *13*, 10–15.

HERD, J. A., & BARGER, A. C. Simplified technique for chronic catheterization of blood vessels. *Journal of Applied Physiology*, 1964, *19*, 791.

HERD, J. A., MORSE, W. H., KELLEHER, R. T., & JONES, L. G. Arterial hypertension in the squirrel monkey during behavioral experiments. *American Journal of Physiology*, 1969, *217*, 24–29.

HIGGINS, D. J. Set and uncertainty as factors influencing anticipatory cardiovascular responding in humans. *Journal of Comparative & Physiological Psychology*, 1971, *74* (2), 272–283.

HOKANSON, J. E., DEGOOD, D. E., FORREST, M. S., & BRITTAIN, T. M. Availability of avoidance behaviors in modulating vascular-stress responses. *Journal of Personality and Social Psychology*, 1971, *19* (1), 60–68.

HOTHERSALL, D., & BRENER, J. Operant conditioning of changes in heart rate in curarized rats. *Journal of Comparative & Physiological Psychology*, 1969, *68* (3), 338–342.

HOWARD, J. L., GALOSY, R. A., GAEBELEIN, C. J., & OBRIST, P. A. Some problems in the use of neuromuscular blockade. In P. A. Obrist, A. H. Black, J. Brener, & L. V. DiCara (Eds.), *Current Issues in Response Mechanisms, Biofeedback and Methodology*. Chicago: Aldine Publishing Co., 1974.

JENNINGS, J. R., AVERILL, J. R., OPTON, E. M., & LAZARUS, R. S. Some parameters of heart rate change: Perceptual versus motor task requirements, noxiousness, and uncertainty. *Psychophysiology*, 1970, *7* (2), 194–212.

JOHN, E. R., & KILLAM, K. F. Electrophysiological correlates of avoidance conditioning in the cat. *Journal of Pharmacology and Experimental Therapeutics*, 1959, *125*, 252–274.

JOHNSON, R. J. Operant reinforcement of an autonomic response. *Dissertation Abstracts*, 1963, *24*, 1255–1256.

JOLLEY, A. Effects of food deprivation and consummatory activity on the heart rate of the rat. *Animal Behavior*, 1970, *18* (1), 92–95.

KADDEN, R. M., SCHOENFELD, W. N., & SNAPPER, A. G. Cardiac pacing in the rhesus monkey: A technique and some behavioral data. *Proceedings of 78th Annual Convention of the American Psychological Association*, 1970.

KADDEN, R. M., SNAPPER, A. G., SCHOENFELD, W. N., & KOP,

D. Intravenous intracardiac pacing in the rhesus monkey. *Communications in Behavioral Biology,* 1970, *5,* 255–258.

KATKIN, E. S., & MURRAY, E. N. Instrumental conditioning of autonomically mediated behavior: Theoretical and methodological issues. *Psychological Bulletin,* 1968, *70* (1), 52–68.

KATKIN, E. S., MURRAY, E. N., & LACHMAN, R. Concerning instrumental autonomic conditioning: a rejoinder. *Psychological Bulletin,* 1969, *71* (6), 462–466.

KELLEHER, R., MORSE, W., & HERD, J. A. Effects of propranolol, phentolamine, and methylatropine on cardiovascular function in the squirrel monkey during behavioral experiments. *Journal of Pharmacology and Experimental Therapeutics,* 1972, *182,* 204.

KIMMEL, E. & KIMMEL, H. D. Replication of operant conditioning of the GSR. *Journal of Experimental Psychology,* 1963, *65,* 212–213.

KIMMEL, H. D. Instrumental conditioning of autonomically mediated behavior, *Psychological Bulletin,* 1967, *67* (5), 337–345.

KIMMEL, H. D., & HILL, F. A. Operant conditioning of the GSR. *Psychological Reports,* 1960, *7,* 555–562.

KONORSKI, J., SANTIBANEZ-H, G., & BECK, J. Electrical hippocampal activity and heart rate in classical and instrumental conditioning. *Acta Biologiae Experimentalis* (Warsaw), 1968, *28* (3), 169–185.

KRAHENBUHL, G. S. Stress reactivity in tennis players. *Research Quarterly,* 1971, *42* (1), 42–46.

KRAUSMAN, D. Automatic on-line print-out of peak systolic and diastolic blood pressures. *Psychophysiology,* 1969, *5* (3), 337–341.

KRAUSMAN, D. Heart rate derived from blood pressure and other physiological signals. *Psychophysiology,* 1970, *7,* 503–507.

KRAUSMAN, D. A system for providing an on-line analogous display of beat-by-beat cardiac output. *Medical and Biological Engineering,* 1972, *10,* 81–88.

KRAUSMAN, D., EHRLICH, W., & BRADY, J. V. Preprocessor adapts cardiovascular signals to a minicomputer. *Psychophysiology,* 1972, *9* (5), 554–563.

LAFORGE, H. The influence of random reinforcement on heart rate during extinction. *Journal of Psychology,* 1971, *77* (1), 89–99.

LANG, P. J. Autonomic control or learning to play the internal organs. *Psychology Today,* 1970, *3.*

LAWLER, J. E., MEYERS, K. A., & OBRIST, P. A. Cardiovascular integration during performance on a Sidman avoidance schedule. Presented at *Annual Meeting of Society for Psychophysiological Research,* Boston, 1972.

LEVINE, M. D., GORDON, T. P., PETERSON, R. H., & ROSE, R. M. Urinary 17-OH-CS response of high- and low-aggressive rhesus monkeys to shock avoidance. *Physiology and Behavior,* 1970, *5* (8), 919–924.

LISINA, M: I. The role of orientation in the transformation of involuntary reactions into voluntary ones. In L. G. Voronin, A. N. Leontiev, A. R. Luris, E. N. Sokolov, & O. S. Vinogradova (Eds.), *Orienting Reflex and Exploratory Behavior.* Washington: American Institute of Biological Sciences, 1958.

LOWER, J. S. *Approach-avoidance conflict as a determinant of peptic ulceration in the rat.* Ph.D. Dissertation, Western Reserve University, 1967.

MALCUIT, G., DUCHARME, R., & BERLANGER, D. Cardiac activity in rats during bar-press avoidance and "freezing" responses. *Psychological Reports,* 1968, *23* (1), 11–18.

MALMO, R. B. Slowing of heart rate after septal self-stimulation in rats. *Science,* 1961, *133,* 1129.

MANDLER, G., & KAHN, M. Discrimination of changes in heart rate: Two unsuccessful attempts. *Journal of the Experimental Analysis of Behavior,* 1960, *3* (1), 21–26.

MARCZYNSKI, T. J., ROSEN, A. H., & HACKETT, J. T. Postreinforcement electrocortical synchronization and facilitation of cortical auditory evoked potential in appetitive instrumental conditioning. *Electroencephalography and Clinical Neurophysiology,* 1968, *24* (3), 227–241.

MARCZYNSKI, T. J., YORK, J. L., & HACKETT, J. T. Steady potential correlates of positive reinforcement: Reward contingent positive variation. *Science,* 1969, *163,* 301–304.

MASON, J. W., & BRADY, J. V. Plasma 17-hydroxycorticosteroid changes related to reserpine effects on emotional behavior. *Science,* 1956, *164,* 983–984.

MASON, J. W., BRADY, J. V., POLISH, E., BAUER, J. A., ROBINSON, J. A., ROSE, R. M., & TAYLOR, E. D. Patterns of corticosteroid and pepsinogen change related to emotional stress in the monkey. *Science,* 1961, *133,* 1596–1598.

MASON, J. W., BRADY, J. V., ROBINSON, J. A., TAYLOR, E. D., TOLSON, W. W., & MOUGEY, E. H. Patterns of thyroid, gonadal and adrenal hormone secretions related to psychological stress in the monkey. *Psychosomatic Medicine,* 1961, *23,* 446.

MASON, J. W., BRADY, J. V., & SIDMAN, M. Plasma 17-hydroxycorticosteroid levels and conditioned behavior in the rhesus monkey. *Endocrinology,* 1957, *60,* 741–752.

MASON, J. W., BRADY, J. V., TOLLIVER, G. A., TOLSON, W., GILMORE, L., MOUGEY, E. H., TAYLOR, E., ROBINSON, J., JOHNSON, T. A., KENYON, C., COLLINS, D., JONES, J., DRIVER, G., BEER, B., RICKETTS, P., WHERRY, F., PENNINGTON, L., GOODMAN, A., & WOOL, M. Organization of psychoendocrine mechanisms. *Psychosomatic Medicine,* 1968, *39,* 565–808.

MASON, J. W., BRADY, J. V., & TOLSON, W. W. Behavioral adaptations and endocrine activity. In R. Levine (Ed.), *Proceedings of the Association for Research in Nervous and Mental Diseases.* Baltimore: Williams and Wilkins, 1966.

MASON, J. W., MANGAN, G., BRADY, J. V., CONRAD, D., & RIOCH, D. Concurrent plasma epinephrine, norepinephrine, and 17-hydroxycorticosteroid levels during conditioned emotional disturbances in monkeys. *Psychosomatic Medicine,* 1961, *23,* 344–353.

MASON, J. W., NAUTA, W. J. H., BRADY, J. V., ROBINSON, J. A., & SACHAR, E. J. The role of limbic system structures in regulation of ACTH secretion. *Acta Neurovegetativa,* 1961, *23,* 4–14.

MCCUTCHEON, E. P. (Ed.), *Chronically Implanted Cardiovascular Instrumentation.* New York: Academic Press, 1973.

MILLER, N. E. Learning of visceral and glandular responses. *Science,* 1969, *163,* 434–445.

MILLER, N. E., BANKS, J. H., & CAUL, W. F. Cardiac conditioned responses in avoidance and yoked-control rats. *Psychonomic Science,* 1967, *9,* 581–582.

MILLER, N. E., & BANUAZIZI, A. Instrumental learning by

curarized rats of a specific visceral response, intestinal or cardiac. *Journal of Comparative & Physiological Psychology,* 1968, *65,* 1–7.

MILLER, N. E., & CARMONA, A. Modification of a visceral response, salivation in thirsty dogs, by instrumental training with water reward. *Journal of Comparative & Physiological Psychology,* 1967, *63,* 1–6.

MILLER, N. E., & DICARA, L. Instrumental learning of heart rate changes in curarized rats: Shaping and specificity to a discriminative stimulus. *Journal of Comparative & Physiological Psychology,* 1967, *63,* 12–19.

MILLER, N. E., & DICARA, L. Instrumental learning of urine formation by rats: changes in renal blood flow. *American Journal of Physiology,* 1968, *215,* 677–683.

MILLER, N. E., & DWORKIN, B. R. Visceral learning: Recent difficulties with curarized rats and significant problems for human research. In P. A. Obrist, A. H. Black, J. Brener, & L. V. DiCara (Eds.), *Current Issues in Response Mechanisms, Biofeedback and Methodology.* Chicago: Aldine Publishing Co., 1974.

MIYATA, Y., & SOLTYSIK, A. The relations between salivary, cardiac and motor responses during instrumental performance. *Acta Biologiae Experimentalis* (Warsaw), 1968, *28* (4), 345–361.

MOOT, S. A., CEBULLA, R. P., & CRABTREE, J. M. Instrumental control and ulceration in rats. *Journal of Comparative & Physiological Psychology,* 1970, *71* (3), 405–410.

MORSE, W. H., HERD, J. A., KELLEHER, R. T., & GROSS, S. A. Schedule-controlled modulation of arterial blood pressure in the squirrel monkey. In H. Kimmel (Ed.), *Experimental Psychopathology: Recent Research and Theory.* New York: Academic Press, 1971.

NATHAN, M. S., & SMITH, O. A. JR. Differential conditional emotional and cardiovascular responses—A training technique for monkeys. *Journal of the Experimental Analysis of Behavior,* 1968, *11* (1), 77–82.

NORTON, P. R. Differences in the electrophysiological correlates upon receipt of food reward and nonreward in the rat. *Brain Research,* 1970, *24* (1), 134–138.

OBRIST, P. A., WEBB, R. A., SUTTERER, J. R., & HOWARD, J. L. The cardiac-somatic relationship: some formulations. *Psychophysiology,* 1970, *6* (5), 569.

PAPPAS, B. A., DICARA, L. V., & MILLER, N. E. Learning of blood pressure responses in the noncurarized rat: Transfer to the curarized state. *Physiology and Behavior,* 1970, *5* (9), 1029–1032.

PARE, W. The effect of chronic environmental stress on stomach ulceration, adrenal function, and consummatory behavior in the rat. *Journal of Psychology,* 1964, *57,* 143–151.

PARE, W. Six-hour escape-avoidance work shift and production of stomach ulcers. *Journal of Comparative & Physiological Psychology,* 1971, *77* (3), 459–466.

PARE, W., ISOM, K. E., & REUS, J. F. Recording the electrocardiogram from the squirrel monkey, *Saimira sciureus. Physiology and Behavior,* 1970, *5,* 819–821.

PARRISH, J. Classical discrimination conditioning of heart rate and bar-press suppression in the rat. *Psychonomic Science,* 1967, *9,* 267–268.

PAVLOV, I. P. Uber die normalen Blutdruk-schwantugen bein hunde. *Archiv fur Gesamte Physiologie,* 1879, *20,* 215.

PEREZ-CRUET, J., BLACK, W. C., & BRADY, J. V. Heart rate: differential effects of hypothalamic and septal self-stimulation. *Science,* 1963, *140,* 1235–1236.

PEREZ-CRUET, J., PLUMLEE, L., & NEWTON, J. E. O. Chronic basal blood pressure in unanesthetized dogs using the ring-catheter technique. *Proceedings of the Symposium on Biomedical Engineering,* 1966, *1,* 383–386.

PEREZ-CRUET, J., TOLLIVER, G., DUNN, G., MARVIN, S., & BRADY, J. V. Concurrent measurement of heart rate and instrumental avoidance behavior in the rhesus monkey. *Journal of the Experimental Analysis of Behavior,* 1963, *6,* 61–64.

PETERS, J. V., KNOTT, J. K., MILLER, L. H., VANVEEN, W. J., & COHEN, S. J. Response variables and magnitude of the contingent negative variation. *Electroencephalography and Clinical Neurophysiology,* 1970, *29,* 608–611.

PHILLIPS, M. I., & OLDS, J. Unit activity: motivation-dependent responses from midbrain neurons. *Science,* 1969, *165,* 1260–1271.

PLUMLEE, L. A. Operant conditioning of increases in blood pressure. *Psychophysiology,* 1969, *6,* 283–290.

POLISH, E., BRADY, J. V., MASON, J. W., THACH, J. S., & NIEMECK, W. Gastric contents and the occurrence of duodenal lesions in the rhesus monkey during avoidance behavior. *Gastroenterology,* 1962, *43,* 193–201.

PORTER, R. W., BRADY, J. V., CONRAD, D., MASON, J. W., GALAMBOS, R., & RIOCH, D. Some experimental observations on gastrointestinal lesions in behaviorally-conditioned monkeys. *Psychosomatic Medicine,* 1958, *20,* 379–394.

PORTER, R. W., CONRAD, D. G., & BRADY, J. V. Some neural and behavioral correlates of electrical self-stimulation of the limbic system. *Journal of the Experimental Analysis of Behavior,* 1959, *2,* 43–55.

RAMSAY, D. A., POMERLEAU, O. F., & SNAPPER, A. G. Two methods of obtaining electrocardiograms of chair-restrained monkeys. *Conditional Reflex,* 1968, *3* (3), 200–204.

RASMUSSEN, A. J., MARSH, J. T., & BRILL, N. Q. Increased susceptibility to herpes simplex in mice subjected to avoidance-learning stress or restraint. *Proceedings of the Society for Experimental Biology and Medicine,* 1957, *96,* 183–189.

RAZRAN, G. The observable unconscious and the inferable conscious in current Soviety psychophysiology: Interoceptive conditioning, semantic conditioning, and the orienting reflex. *Psychological Review,* 1961, *68,* 81–147.

REBERT, C. S. The effect of reaction time feedback on reaction time and contingent negative variation. *Psychophysiology,* 1972, *9,* 334–339.

RICE, H. K. The responding-rest ratio in the production of gastric ulcers in the rat. *Psychological Reports,* 1963, *13,* 11–14.

ROSE, R. M., MASON, J. W., & BRADY, J. V. Adrenal responses to maternal separation and chair adaptation in experimentally-raised rhesus monkeys (*Macaca mulatta*). *Proceedings of Second International Congress on Primatology,* Atlanta, Ga., New York: Karger-Basel, 1969.

ROSS, G. S., HODOS, W., & BRADY, J. V. Electronencephalographic correlates of temporally spaced responding and avoidance behavior. *Journal of the Experimental Analysis of Behavior,* 1962, *5,* 467–472.

SAUNDERS, J. C. Selective facilitation and inhibition of

auditory and visual evoked responses during avoidance conditioning in cats. *Journal of Comparative & Physiological Psychology,* 1971, *76* (1), 15–25.

Sawrey, J. M., & Sawrey, W. L. Ulcer production with reserpine and conflict. *Journal of Comparative & Physiological Psychology,* 1964, *57,* 307–309.

Sawrey, J. M., & Sawrey, W. L. Age, weight, and social effects on ulceration rate in rats. *Journal of Comparative & Physiological Psychology,* 1966, *61,* 464–466.

Sawrey, W. L. Conditioned responses of fear in relationship to ulceration. *Journal of Comparative & Physiological Psychology,* 1961, *54,* 347–348.

Sawrey, W. L., Conger, J. J., & Turrell, E. S. An experimental investigation of the role of psychological factors in the production of gastric ulcers in rats. *Journal of Comparative & Physiological Psychology,* 1956, *49,* 457–461.

Sawrey, W. L., & Long, D. H. Strain and sex differences in ulceration in the rat. *Journal of Comparative & Physiological Psychology,* 1962, *55,* 603–605.

Sawrey, W. L., & Sawrey, J. M. Fear conditioning and resistance to ulceration. *Journal of Comparative & Physiological Psychology,* 1963, *57,* 150–151.

Sawrey, W. L., & Sawrey, J. M. Conditioned fear and restraint in ulceration. *Journal of Comparative & Physiological Psychology,* 1964, *56,* 821–823. (a)

Sawrey, W. L., & Weisz, J. D. An experimental method of producing gastric ulcers. *Journal of Comparative & Physiological Psychology,* 1956, *49,* 269–270.

Schoenfeld, W. N. Some old work for modern conditioning theory. *Conditional Reflex,* 1966, *1,* 219–223.

Schoenfeld, W. N. Oyepk on mediating mechanisms of the conditioned reflex. *Conditional Reflex,* 1970, *5,* 165–170.

Schoenfeld, W. N. Conditioning the whole organism. *Conditional Reflex,* 1971, *6,* 125–128.

Schoenfeld, W. N. Problems of modern behavior therapy. *Conditional Reflex,* 1972, *7,* 33–65.

Schwartz, G. E., Shapiro, D., & Tursky, B. Learned control of cardiovascular integration in man through operant conditioning. *Psychosomatic Medicine,* 1971, *33* (4), 57–62.

Shapiro, A. P., & Horn, P. W. Blood pressure, plasma pepsinogen and behavior in cats subjected to experimental production of anxiety. *Journal of Nervous and Mental Disease,* 1955, *122,* 222–231.

Shapiro, D., Crider, A. B., & Tursky, B. Differentiation of an autonomic response through operant conditioning. *Psychonomic Science,* 1964, *1,* 147–148.

Shapiro, D., Tursky, B., & Schwartz, G. E. Differentiation of heart rate and systolic blood pressure in man by operant conditioning. *Psychosomatic Medicine,* 1970, *32* (4), 417–423.

Shearn, D. W. Operant conditioning of heart rate. *Science,* 1962, *137,* 530–531.

Sidman, M. Avoidance conditioning with brief shock and no exteroceptive warning signal. *Science,* 1953, *118,* 157–158.

Sidman, M., Mason, J. W., Brady, J. V., & Thach, J. Quantitative relations between avoidance behavior and pituitary-adrenal cortical activity. *Journal of the Experimental Analysis of Behavior,* 1962, *5,* 353–362.

Simson, L. R. Some physiological correlates of psychological stress in the adrenal organs of the white mouse. *Journal of Science Laboratories, Denison University,* 1958, *44,* 135–150.

Slaughter, J., Hahn, W., & Rinaldi, P. Instrumental conditioning of heart rate in the curarized rat with varied amounts of pretraining. *Journal of Comparative & Physiological Psychology,* 1970, *72* (3), 356–369.

Slucki, H., Adam, G., & Porter, R. W. Operant discrimination of an interoceptive stimulus in rhesus monkeys. *Journal of the Experimental Analysis of Behavior,* 1965, *8* (6), 405–414.

Slucki, H., McCoy, F. B., & Porter, R. W. Interoceptive SD of the large intestine established by mechanical stimulation. *Psychological Reports,* 1969, *24* (1), 35–42.

Smith, O. A., Jr., & Nathan, M. A. The development of cardiac and blood flow conditional responses during the acquisition of a differentiated "conditioned emotional response" in monkeys. *Conditional Reflex,* 1967, *2* (2), 155–156.

Smith, O. A., Jr., & Stebbins, W. C. Conditioned blood flow and heart rate in monkeys. *Journal of Comparative & Physiological Psychology,* 1965, *59,* 432–436.

Smith, R. M., & Hain, J. D. Relationship between somatization and effects of stress on electrogastric waveforms in humans. *Psychological Reports,* 1970, *27* (3), 755–765.

Soltysik, S., & Kowalski, M. Studies on the avoidance conditioning: Relations between cardiac (Type I) and motor (Type II) effects in the avoidance reflex. *Acta Biologiae Experimentalis* (Warsaw), 1960, *22,* 157–170.

Stebbins, W. C., & Smith, O. A., Jr. Cardiovascular concomitants of the conditioned emotional response in the monkey. *Science,* 1964, *144,* 881–883.

Stern, J. A., & Word, T. J. Heart rate changes during avoidance conditioning in the male albino rat. *Journal of Psychosomatic Research,* 1962, *6,* 167–175.

Stoyva, J., Forsyth, R. P., & Kamiya, J. Blood pressure during sleep in the rhesus monkey before and after stress. *American Journal of Physiology,* 1968, *214* (5), 1122–1125.

Sutterer, J. R., Howard, J. L., Loth, E., & Obrist, P. A. Alterations of heart rate and general activity during aversive conditioning procedures. *Psychophysiology,* 1970, *6,* 635–636.

Swadlow, H. A., Hosking, K. E., & Schneiderman, N. Differential heart rate conditioning and lever lift suppression in restrained rabbits. *Physiology and Behavior,* 1971, *7* (2), 257–260.

Swinnen, M. E. T. Blood pressure digitizer. *Proceedings of the Annual Conference on Engineering in Medicine and Biology,* 1968, *10,* 18.

Tecce, J. J. Contingent negative variation. *Archives General Psychiatry,* 1972, *24,* 1–16.

Trowill, J. A. Instrumental conditioning of the heart rate in the curarized rat. *Journal of Comparative & Physiological Psychology,* 1967, *63,* 7–11.

Uphouse, L. L., MacInnes, J. W., & Schlesinger, K. Effects of conditioned avoidance training on polyribosomes of mouse brain. *Physiology and Behavior,* 1972, *8* (6), 1013–1018. (a)

Uphouse, L. L., MacInnes, J. W., & Schlesinger, K. Uridine incorporation into polyribosomes of mouse brain after escape training in an electrified T-maze. *Physiology and Behavior,* 1972, *8* (6), 1019–1023. (b)

Vanderwolf, C. H., & Vanderwart, M. L. Relations of

heart rate to motor activity and arousal in the rat. *Canadian Journal of Psychology*, 1970, *24* (6), 434–441.

WALTER, W. G. The relations between electrical signs of expectancy in the human brain and autonomic function during operant and classical conditioning. *Abhundlungen der Deutschen Akademie der Wissenschaften zu Berlin*, 1966, No. 2, pp. 47–55.

WEISS, J. M. Somatic effects of predictable and unpredictable shock. *Psychosomatic Medicine*, 1970, *32* (4), 397–408.

WEISS, J. M. Effects of coping behavior in different warning signal conditions on stress pathology in rats. *Journal of Comparative & Physiological Psychology*, 1971, *77*, 1–13. (a)

WEISS, J. M. Effects of punishing the coping response (conflict) on stress pathology in rats. *Journal of Comparative & Physiological Psychology*, 1971, *77*, 14–21 (b)

WEISS, J. M. Effects of coping behavior with and without a feedback signal on stress pathology in rats. *Journal of Comparative & Physiological Psychology*, 1971, *77*, 22–30. (c)

WEISS, J. M. Psychological factors in stress and disease. *Scientific American*, 1972, *6*, 104–113.

WEISS, J. M., STONE, E. A., & HARREL, N. Coping behavior and brain norepinephrine level in rats. *Journal of Comparative & Physiological Psychology*, 1970, *72*, 153–160.

WEISZ, J. D. The etiology of experimental gastric ulceration. *Psychosomatic Medicine*, 1957, *19*, 61–73.

WENGER, M. A., & BAGCHI, K. Studies of autonomic functions in practitioners of Yoga in India. *Behavioral Science*, 1961, *6*, 312–323.

WENGER, M. A., BAGCHI, K., & ANAND, B. K. Experiments in India on "voluntary" control of the heart and pulse. *Circulation*, 1961, *24*, 1319–1325.

WENZEL, B. M. Changes in heart rate associated with responses based on positive and negative reinforcement. *Journal of Comparative & Physiological Psychology*, 1961, *42*, 638–644.

WERDEGAR, D., JOHNSON, D. G., & MASON, J. W. A technique for continuous measurement of arterial blood pressure in unanesthetized monkeys. *Journal of Applied Physiology*, 1964, *19*, 519–521.

WILLIAMS, D. R., & TEITELBAUM, P. Control of drinking behavior by means of an operant-conditioning technique. *Science*, 1956, *124*, 1294–1296.

WILLIAMS, J. L. Response contingency and effects of punishment: changes in autonomic and skeletal responses. *Journal of Comparative & Physiological Psychology*, 1969, *68*, 118–125.

21

Procedures for the Acquisition of Syntax

George Robinson

A spoken word is a complex sound that can be produced by the vocal apparatus. As an auditory stimulus or as a piece of speech behavior, a word can be studied in the laboratory in ways that are similar to the investigation of other stimuli and behaviors. For example, reinforcing the production of a particular word in the presence of a particular stimulus object can increase the probability that the word will be produced in the presence of the same object or similar objects in the future. Employing a word as a discriminative stimulus in a particular context links it to the presence of a set of reinforcement contingencies. Skinner (1957) refers to these two situations as, respectively, "controlling" the word and "being controlled" by the word. Outside the behavior laboratory, we say that the word *means* something; the controlling stimulus or controlled behavior involves or is related to the word's *referent,* the concept it stands for. Individual words associated with "things" in the world become associated with the concepts which the things instantiate. Concepts usually are instantiated by many things that fall under them (e.g., the concept "dog"); proper names normally have only one instantiation as a concept (e.g., the concept "Victor Borge"). The term *things* is used in a general sense to include objects, abstractions, relations, attributes, events, etc. This is just another way of stating the law of generalization. When more than one organism shares the same word-concept association, a number of linguistic functions can be performed. A speaker can, by emitting the word, induce a change in the behavior of the hearer which is appropriate to the concept the word stands for. For instance, uttering the word *blimp* on a crowded streetcorner is usually followed by most hearers looking upward.

Uttering the word which stands for a particular concept can serve other functions besides alerting the hearer to the presence of an instantiation of that concept. Using the same word in the presence of different things may be used to indicate a class resemblance; i.e., the shared word facilitates generalization. Uttering the word which stands for one concept in the presence of a thing which instantiates a clearly different concept may induce the hearer to discover a connection between the concepts. Even a metaphoric connection might be communicated in which the speaker indicates that two different things are the same in some special sense. With information derived from appropriate nonlinguistic context, uttering a word can serve as a request for the thing which instantiates the word's concept or for something connected with it, as an offer to produce the thing, or as a proposal that the speaker and hearer become involved with or enact the thing.

A set of words each associated with a concept is a *lexicon*. With a lexicon, speakers can name, mention, or raise the topic of the concept(s) which each individual word stands for. The acquisition of a lexicon, the production of and response to individual words, does not seem to be an impossible extrapolation from laboratory studies of operants and discriminative stimuli. Critics (e.g., Chomsky, 1959) of the learning theorist's approach to language do not direct their main criticisms against explanations of the acquisition of a lexicon in and of itself. Nor is the learning of lexicons considered to be unique to the human species (see Segal, chapter 22 in this volume).

However, even with the varied use of contexts the uttering of and the response to an individual word associated with a concept is only a small part of linguistic behavior. The speaker of a natural language not only mentions topics but can say something about them. To say something about a concept or its instantiation usually requires more than a single word —e.g., a word for an object and a word for its attribute. Not only must the words for the object and attribute be present in an utterance, but there must also be a way to inform the hearer that the object and attribute named by the words in an utterance are related. This information about relatedness makes the difference between a grammatical string and a list of words. A grammatical string, therefore, uses two information-carrying systems:

1. *Lexical*—the individual words (more properly, *lexemes*) encode, stand for, signify the things and/or concepts the message is about; and
2. *Syntactic*—a system which encodes, maps the relationships among, the things and/or concepts as relationships among the words in the string.

In English, conceptual relationships are encoded by the order of the words in a string and the use of inflections (additions to and changes in the forms of words).

A learning theoretic account of language must show how such a system of encoding relationships is acquired. This is not a trivial problem. The difficulty can be more easily seen by comparing the real-world, natural-language situation to an artificial, very simplified world and language. Imagine a population of organisms that are rooted in place, each one in front of a narrow window. Through the window, a creature can observe a small portion of a moving conveyer belt which passes by the windows of each of them. On the belt at irregular intervals appear objects of a limited number of types. Presupposing some survival value in being able to anticipate the appearance of particular kinds of objects, imagine that the creatures have a lexicon which enables them to name each of the objects on the conveyer belt. By calling out these names, a creature can apprise her downstream neighbor of what will appear in the window and when. The only data which the language must encode are the type of each object and its temporal appearance. The temporal order and proximity of the objects are directly mapped by the temporal order and proximity of the uttered names. The relationship in time among objects on the conveyer belt is exactly the same as the relationship in time among the words which name the objects. The "syntax" of this language maps the temporal order and spacing of objects on the conveyer belt as the temporal order and spacing of the words which stand for these objects. Such a mapping is called "iconic" (Peirce, 1931). It hardly presents a problem for the learning theorist; the system requires no learning beyond the lexicon.

The difficulties arise when we leave the simple world of the conveyer belt creatures. In natural language, the word symbols of speech still appear one after the other in a linear temporal sequence, but the relationships among concepts and things communicated by natural-language speakers are much more varied and complicated. Somehow, the linear sequence must contain sufficient information to enable the hearer to determine how the individual words work together to encode the relationships among concepts and/or things. Encoding these relationships by means of a linear sequence of individual symbols requires that there be a *pattern* to the appearance of the symbols. In the pattern must be the syntactic information from which the hearer infers the way in which the concepts and/or things named by the individual words are related.

The simplest kind of syntactic information signals the hearer that a sequence of words should be treated as a linguistic *unit*. Even without any other syntactic information, this can be done by, for example, temporally grouping a sequence of words by placing a relatively long pause at its beginning and end. The information that the individual words in a sequence are to be taken as a linguistic unit is adequate for the complete understanding of many strings so long as the hearer has learned the meanings of the individual words and has adequate nonlinguistic experience. For example, no additional syntactic information is necessary to understand the string *"Pregnant deer nibble tree roots."* Even if the word order is scrambled, thereby destroying the syntactic information, knowing that the words function together as a linguistic unit is enough. There is only one state in the mundane world whose description can be derived by considering these words as a linguistic unit. In a science-fiction tale of carnivorous trees in ecological competition with *Cervidae,* two interpretations are possible.

Even without such bizarre situations, the syntactic datum that the words of a string "go together" is often, perhaps usually, inadequate by itself to understand a sentence unambiguously. More information from the pattern of the word sequence is necessary. Consider the simple sentence *"The fast girl pushes the fat boy."* Unambiguous interpretation could not be made without using the syntactic information which is derived from the order of the individual words in the sentence. If the order is scrambled, this interpretation would be lost: *"The fast boy pushes the fat girl"; "The girl pushes the fat boy fast";* etc. As we will see later, the most *essential* syntactic information is that which enables the hearer to determine which words form a subunit which in turn works together with other subunits in the string.

Skinner (1957) suggested that the language user can learn to discriminate the grammatical categories of individual words. The series of grammatical categories of the words in a sentence form a pattern which serves as a complex discriminative stimulus controlling the response to the set of words in the sentence. Skinner called these patterns of grammatical categories "autoclitics." In the presence of (i.e., appearing in the format of) a particular autoclitic, the individual words are taken to be related in a particular sort of way. For example, in *"Alice gives Susan the wrench,"* the autoclitic "proper noun–verb–proper noun–article–noun" signals that the first proper noun is the agent, the verb is the activity, etc. Along with intonation cues or punctuation, the pattern also indicates the mode of the sentence, whether declarative, interrogative, etc.

Although the parallel with laboratory paradigms is suggestive, Skinner was not clear about how the grammatical patterns and their significance could be learned. There are complicating factors which make this approach unwieldy. For example, identifying the pattern of grammatical categories of a string of words cannot be done by treating the words one at a time. The category to which a word belongs often depends on its relationship to other words in the sentence, including those which are not adjacent to the word in question. Consider the difficulty in identifying the autoclitic pattern of grammatical categories upon hearing the following sentence: *"With a beat beat the beat beat with a beet"* (Rhythmically strike the exhausted hippie with a red vegetable). Since a procedure for assigning grammatical categories to each of the words could not succeed by treating each word in isolation, the language user must consider the *relationship* each word has with other words—i.e., what it does with and to other words. That is, the language user must perform some kind of analysis on the sentence; syntactic information is not available as an autoclitic cue by taking the sentence as an unanalyzed whole.

There is another argument, based on what linguists call the *generative* property of language, that the grammatical category sequence of a sentence taken as a whole could not always be available as an autoclitic: language users can process (i.e., construct and interpret appropriately) sentences whose grammatical sequences (or similar ones) they have not been exposed to before. Considering the sequence of grammatical categories of the words of the entire sentence as an autoclitic cue, generalization from previously experienced sentences is usually inadequate to explain the processing of novel sentences. The dimensions of similarity along which generalization occurs are impossible to specify for unanalyzed whole sentences. But the capacity to process novel sentences can be explained if we assume that the language user is able to combine and permute *components* of grammatical sequences.

The advantages of a generative, combining system can be appreciated by considering the problem of training an organism to emit only a restricted subset of a set of possible sequential behavior patterns. Imagine a row of six levers each of which can be pushed up or down from the neutral position. We arrange the system so that the set of lever patterns leading to reinforcement (call it "set A") is defined, for example, as follows: the first lever must be up and somewhere in the sequence an adjacent pair of levers must be up. There are 24 different patterns in set A out of a total of 64 possible patterns altogether. To encourage the organism to learn the entire set, we arrange the reinforcement schedule so that any particular pattern is reinforced only once every 24 reinforced trials. The experiment may be terminated after 24 reinforced trials.

A subject treating the lever sequence as a set of whole patterns, even one with a perfect memory (e.g., a scratchpad), would need to produce all 64 patterns in order to be sure of having determined all the ones belonging to set A. A picture of the whole-pattern learner's information would be a list of 24 sextuples: *UUDDUD, UDDUUD, UUUDDU,* etc. If you try this experiment as a paper-and-pencil task, you will find that very few subjects require experience with all 64 patterns to be able to produce all and only those of the reinforced set. In fact, most subjects will be able to list every one of the members of set *A* before having reinforcement experience with all of them.

What the subjects learn is something *about* the way in which components of the lever position sequences go together. It is something which is not itself one of, or all of, the members of set *A*. What they learn might be pictured something like this:

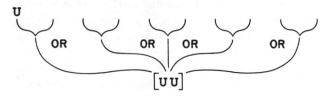

It is an *algorithm,* or generating principle, for all and only the sequences of set *A*. Not only can such an algorithm be learned without the subject having experience with every member of set *A,* but the algorithm is very much easier to remember than the list of 24 sextuples.

Of subjects who are able to produce nonrandomly the remaining members of set *A* without having prior reinforcement experience with them, we must infer that they are using a generating algorithm. Many subjects, in fact, are able to describe such an algorithm. A traditional account involving generalization from previously learned to novel lever sequences requires the dimensions of similarity between new and old sequences to be specified. A description of the similarity turns out to be a restatement of the algorithm.

The algorithm can be called an "underlying structure." Skinner and other behaviorists have been reluctant to allow explanations involving underlying structures which include more than input and output "surface" data. On the other hand, linguists and some psychologists have readily adopted underlying structures as formal description of language data while disregarding the question of how such structures, generating algorithms, might be acquired by the principles of learning. In fact, many linguists, because they believe such structures are innate and could not possibly be learned, assume that the learning theorist *should not* have an interest in underlying language structure. Lakoff (1973) critically summarizes the arguments by some of his fellow linguists (Chomsky in particular) that underlying linguistic structure should not be in the domain of the learning theorist:

There are at present no general learning theories that can account for [linguistic structure]. It is hard to imagine what any such theories could be like. Therefore, it is plausible to assume that there can be no such theories. But the argument is fallacious: Nothing follows from a lack of imagination.

The set of grammatically correct sentences of a natural language is somewhat analogous to set *A* in the lever sequence experiment. The language user must be capable of generating and recognizing sequences of words that are well-formed sentences in the language. Because the language user, analogous to the lever sequence subject, can generate and identify more sentences than have previously been experienced, some sort of underlying information structure —a generating algorithm—must be involved. As mentioned earlier, the pattern in which the words of a sentence are arranged encodes information about the ways in which the things and/or concepts indicated by the words are said to be related. This encoding system is syntax. Since language users employ the syntax encoding system to process sentences they have not previously experienced, syntax must, like generative capacity per se, involve the underlying information structure.

We can describe the lever sequence generating structure as being used by the subject to *parse* the reinforcement contingencies into those of set *A* and those not of set *A*. Natural language syntax performs an analogous task.

The following section demonstrates that the learning and use of the underlying linguistic information structure need not be considered a mysterious process. A very simple learning mechanism, controlled by linguistic input and reinforcement, shows how the underlying structure could be acquired and used. The discussion is based on the *syntax crystal* model (Block, Moulton, & Robinson, 1974, 1975; Robinson & Moulton, 1972).

The task is threefold. First, the syntactic model must show how relationships among concepts can be mapped onto relationships among words—i.e., order and inflections. Such a mapping must enable the language user to *generate* a sentence from which another language user can determine the way in which the concepts named by the words go together. How the concepts go together is what is meant by the *semantics* of the string. The model must show how and under what conditions an organism can *learn* to perform this reversible mapping operation. Finally, the psychological operations required should be plausible and clear. To the extent that these demands are satisfied, we shall have demonstrated that syntactic structure is accessible to the learning theoretic approach.

Consider the set of concepts, discussed earlier, named by the following words: *girl, boy, fast, fat, push(es)*. These concepts can combine with each other in several ontologically coherent ways. For example, if our language user observes the intramural sprint champion of Wellesley giving her overweight brother a swing ride, the concepts are connected as in Figure 1A.

To apprise another of the essentials of the scene, the language user must transmit the names of the concepts and the set of relationships portrayed by connections 1–4. This particular set of relationships is transmitted by ordering the words which name the concepts as follows: *"Fast girl push(es) fat boy."* The syntactic model must map the set of brackets into the proper sequence of words. Further, the hearer must be able to determine the correct set of conceptual relationships from the order of the words. The reversible mapping is portrayed in Figure 1B. The connections are numbered to show their correspondence to those in Figure 1A. We think of the upper diagram as an orrery (planetarium mobile), and the job of syntax is revolving the units around the swivel joints (the dots) until they are in the proper left-right relation to one another. In essence, the syntactic model must constrain the correlation of word order and conceptual relations to those of the set of well-formed English sentences.

The syntax crystal is described in terms of a two-dimensional crystal built up of rectangular units which join together under the control of "connection codes" on their edges. Two rectangles can join together, like dominoes, if their apposing edges bear the same code. The rectangular "cards" are originally blank and completely undifferentiated. Words and connection codes are entered, reinforced, and extinguished during the language-acquisition process. Upon completion, the units of the crystal are so differentiated that they can only be assembled in structures which correctly correlate the word order and conceptual relationships of well-formed English sentences. The body of any completed crystal actually takes the shape of the correlation map of the sentence (like that shown in Figure 1B).

We assume that syntax acquisition requires a linguistically competent speaker (Parent) who talks with the language learner (Child) about aspects of the world which the Child can comprehend. We further assume that the Child has learned the meanings of some individual words. To begin the process, the Parent might stride about the room and say to the Child: *"Parent walks."* All the Child need do is recognize that there is *some* relationship in the world between what it knows to be the referents of *"parent"* and *"walks."* It doesn't need to distinguish this relationship as, for instance, "actor-activity." It only needs to detect that a relationship, any relationship, *exists*. In this case, a description of the data used to detect the presence of a relationship might be that at the occurrence of the utterance *"Parent walks,"* the things named by the two words are simultaneously very salient. The Gestalt "law of common fate" could be invoked here. Whenever the Child detects that two things spoken of are related, it forms a connection between the words of the accompanying utterance which name those things. The conceptual connection, derived from the Child's observation of the environment, is combined with the order of the words derived from the utterance (see Figure 2A). The syntax crystal models this as shown in Figure 2B. The words are entered on the bottom of adjacent blank cards and the connection pathway is formed by entering the (arbitrary) codes R, R, A, A, S, S, on apposing edges of the word cards and two additional blank cards as shown. If separated, these four cards can combine with one another in only one way. Each pair of identical letters on apposing edges of two cards symbolizes a learned connection. Since the word cards are not con-

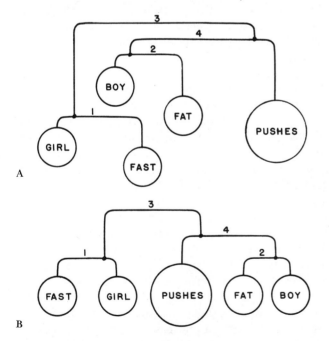

Fig. 1. Conceptual structure underlying a sentence portrayed by the orrery model. A: Unordered concepts are connected according to their scope and dependency relations. B: Using syntactic information, the same connections are rotated to yield the word order of the corresponding sentence.

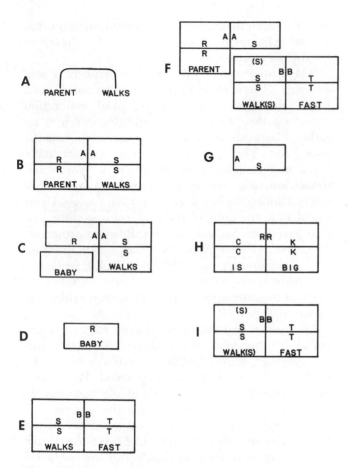

Fig. 2. The first of a set of syntax crystal cards generated according to the learning algorithm. Conceptual relations and word order determine the construction of underlying syntactic structure. See text for details.

nected directly to one another, the connection between word cards is a mediated one. The mediation is abstract and internal—the information on the two upper cards has no relationship to the linguistic or nonlinguistic input other than representing the language learner's detection of a conceptual connection between *"parent"* and *"walks."*

Now, perhaps the Parent, observing the Child walking, says: *"Baby walks."* The Child, noticing that the concepts named by the two words are related, forms a connection between *"baby"* and *"walks."* To rely as much as possible on past learning, the Child uses as many of the previously established cards as possible—namely, the three attached cards shown in Figure 2C—and adds the connection code "R" onto the *"baby"* card, as shown in Figure 2D.

For more complicated strings, *"Parent walks fast"* and *"Baby walks fast,"* the Child must realize that there is *some* connection between the concepts expressed by *"walks"* and *"fast."* It doesn't have to know that such a connection is "predicate plus qualifier." It just needs to recognize that there is *some* state of the world that obtains when *"walks"* and *"fast"* are used together which does not obtain when they are used separately. To connect the *"walks"* card to the new *"fast"* card, the Child constructs the set of cards shown in Figure 2E and joins it to the previously created structure as shown in Figure 2F. *"Parent"* is connected to the entire phrase *"walk(s) fast"* and not just to the verb *"walk(s)."*

Placing parentheses around a connection code indicates that the connection is optional. An optional code is one which may be left unconnected in a completed crystal. This permits *"Walk fast"* to be constructed using existing cards as a result of the Parent saying *"Walk fast"* to the Child.

Two or more connected words which are in turn connected to another part of the crystal structure by a single card (e.g., the card in Figure 2G) form a "constituent." (A single word may also be a constituent.) If a word or phrase can be substituted for a particular constituent and the result is a well-formed utterance, the new unit is connected by the same code as the constituent it replaces. For example, the set of cards shown in Figure 2H could be substituted for that in Figure 2I; so it, too, is given the (S) top code.

Feedback as to whether the substitution of a constituent results in a well-formed utterance comes from the response of the Parent. In most cases the response informs the Child whether its trial utterance is *acceptable*. Usually such feedback confounds syntactic, semantic, and possibly stylistic acceptability; parents tend to withhold positive responses when their children's utterances are ungrammatical, nonsensical, impolite, or any combination of these faults. In addition, criteria of acceptability vary widely across parents and the age of the child. The important point is that the linguistic knowledge symbolized by connections in the syntax crystal is shaped by parental responses: a coded connection is maintained when its use results in an acceptable utterance; a connection is eliminated when its use results in an unacceptable utterance.

This "on-or-off" connection code is not a necessary feature and is used here for simplicity. Alternatively, we can suppose that the "strength" of each code varies as a function of how frequently its use results in an acceptable utterance. Then if the use of a new code results in unacceptable utterances, extinction will lower the strength of the new code below threshold while the stronger, more frequently used codes remain active.

We can now outline in brief a "strict learning procedure" (as distinct from the "strict training procedure" of Premack, 1970) which constructs a set of syntax crystal cards representing underlying linguistic structure.

I. Basic Connection.
   A. *For a two-word string or a longer string in which the Child only knows the meanings of two words:*
      1. Place two blank cards with short edges adjacent.
      2. Enter the first word on the left card, the second word on the right card.
      3. Place two blank cards above the word cards and assign them arbitrary but distinct matching codes that connect them to one another and to the word cards.
   B. *For sentences where three or more words are known to name things which are conceptually connected:* Connect two adjacent words and then connect the block of four cards so formed to the third word and then that block to the fourth word and so on. Which two words are first connected together as a subunit is determined by the way in which the concepts named by the words are related. The most important feature of the relationship is the *scope* of each word—i.e., which other words name concepts that are operated on by the concept named by the word in question. An example shows what is involved: *"Big parent walks."* The scope of *"big"* is *"parent,"* while the scope of *"walks"* is *"big parent."* Therefore, the syntax crystal connects *"big"* to *"parent"* and then connects that pair as a unit to *"walks."* There are many details about scope which are omitted from this discussion. Well-formed sentences can still be processed by a syntax crystal without these details, but some power to unambiguously encode complex conceptual relations may be lost. The interested reader should consult the references.

II. Substitution of Constituents.
   A. If replacing a previously connected constituent by a new word or string results in an acceptable sentence, the new "candidate constituent" receives at its attachment edge the same code as the one for which it is substitutable. Existing connection codes should be tried first. If assigning existing codes results in the production of unacceptable sentences, the candidate constituent is connected with a new code. As the need for finer syntactic distinctions develops, some previously acceptable substitutions may result in the production of unacceptable utterances. In these cases, the old connection codes which are shared by other constitutions are replaced by new, unique codes, as in I above.
   B. Whenever a unique side code (on a short edge of a card) is assigned, the bottom code of that card must also be changed in order to make it unique.

III. Optionally Connectable Codes.
   Whenever an acceptable string can result from leaving a coded edge unconnected, the code is made optional by placing parentheses around it.

Here follows an illustration of these procedures to generate a syntax crystal. For heuristic purposes, the connection code letters suggest the conventional grammatical categories: N for noun, etc. Finer distinctions within a category are made by subscripting the letters N_1, N_2, etc.

Starting with the string *"Big parent,"* the learning procedure generates four cards (reading the card edges clockwise):

Card	Bottom	Left	Top	Right
1.	big	—	J_1	—
2.	J_1	—	—	J_1
3.	N_1	J_1	—	—
4.	parent	—	N_1	—

The codes on cards 1 and 4 must be different from each other by rule IIA because *"big big"* and *"parent parent"* are unacceptable strings.

A second input string, *"Parent walks,"* results in:

5.	N_1	—	—	S_1
6.	V_1	S_1	—	—
7.	walk(s)	—	V_1	—

and card 4 will have the code N added to the top as required by rule IIB:

4.	parent	—	$N_{1,2}$	—

A novel string can be produced by adding (N_2) to the top of card 3:

3.	N_1	J_1	(N_2)	—

As described earlier, the connections are made with *"big parent"* and *"walks"* as constituents which would eventually predominate over *"big"* and *"parent walks."* The string *"Walk slowly"* results in:

8.	slowly	—	B_1	—
9.	B_1	B_1	—	—
10.	V_2	—	—	B_1

and the addition of V_2 to the top of card 7:

7.	walk(s)	—	$V_{1,2}$	—

"*Parent walks slowly*" can be produced by adding (V_1) to the top of card 10:

10.	V_2	—	(V_1)	B_1

"*Parent pushes*" results in:

11.	pushes	—	$V_{1,2}$	—

after producing and receiving positive feedback for "*Parent pushes slowly.*" "*Pushes*" is at this time syntactically equivalent to "*walks.*"

This equivalence breaks down with the string "*Parent pushes baby.*" At first, "*baby*" appears to be substitutable for "*slowly*" in the previous string. But substitution for "*slowly*" in "*Parent walks slowly*" fails (assuming the less usual transitive meaning of "*walk*" has not yet been learned). Therefore, "*baby*" receives a unique top code:

12.	baby	—	N_3	—
13.	N_3	N_3	—	—

Also required is:

14.	V_3	—	V_1	N_3

and the modification of card 11:

11.	pushes	—	$V_{1,2,3}$	—

The string "*Push parent*" allows the V_1 code of card 14 to be made optional:

14.	V_3	—	(V_1)	N_3

and requires that N_3 be added to the top of card 4:

4.	parent	—	$N_{1,2,3}$	—

The string "*Walk toward baby*" results in:

15.	toward	—	P_1	—
16.	P_1	—	B_1	N_3

The string "*Parent can push*" results in:

17.	can	—	M_1	—
18.	M_1	—	V_1	M_1
19.	V_4	M_1	—	—

and card 11 will have V_4 added to its top:

11.	push(es)	—	V_{1-4}	—

Only 10 input strings were provided. With the substitution tests and modification on the basis of parental reinforcement, the following 19 cards of a syntax crystal result:

Card	Bottom	Left	Top	Right
1.	big	—	J_1	—
2.	J_1	—	—	J_1
3.	N_1	J_1	(N_2)	—
4.	parent	—	N_{1-3}	—
5.	N_2	—	—	S_1
6.	V_1	S_1	—	—
7.	walk(s)	—	$V_{1,2,4}$	—
8.	slowly	—	B_1	—
9.	B_1	B_1	—	—
10.	V_2	—	($V_{1,2,4}$)	B_1
11.	push(es)	—	V_{1-4}	—
12.	baby	—	N_{1-3}	—
13.	N_3	N_3	—	—
14.	V_3	—	($V_{1,2,4}$)	N_3
15.	toward	—	P_1	—
16.	P_1	—	B_1	N_3
17.	can	—	M_1	—
18.	M_1	—	V_1	M_1
19.	V_4	M_1	—	—

With these 8 word cards and 11 "structure" cards, over 1,000 well-formed strings of nine words or less can be generated. Examples are: "*Big parent can push slowly,*" "*Baby walks slowly toward parent.*"

Connecting word cards hierarchically through structure cards is not an arbitrary procedure. Structure cards can be considered to arise from a kind of natural selection process. Think of the word cards to be connected as surrounded by a matrix of blank cards. Initially the language learner generates a (perhaps random) variety of paired codes on surrounding cards, connecting the two word cards through a number of different pathways, direct word-word connections, and mediated hierarchical connections. Through substitutivity of words and larger constituents, the hierarchical pathways are more general and used more often compared with the direct word-word pathways which are specific to particular word sequences. Let the connections be strengthened as a function of use, perhaps supplemented by a "housecleaning" operation which weakens or eliminates the infrequent connections. This does not deny that some word-word connections remain—they are such stuff as clichés are made on.

The syntax crystal is thus a system for acquiring and using underlying linguistic information. It represents coordinately the relations among concepts and the sequence of words which encodes these relations. Linguists often test the adequacy of such representations by applying them to ambiguous sentences to determine whether the representation is able to portray the difference between the multiple meanings. A famous stumbling block is a sentence like *"Visiting professors can be dull."* It may be taken to suggest the possibility either that paying social calls on academics is dull or that academics from other universities are dull. These two interpretations can be "read off" the two different crystal structures which generate the sentence. They are shown in Figure 3 in skeleton form. The second half of the sentence, *"can be dull,"* is the same for both versions, but in the crystal in Figure 3A it is connected directly to *"visiting,"* with *"professors"* connected less directly as a qualifier. In the crystal in Figure 3B *"can be dull"* is connected directly to *"professors,"* with *"visiting"* connected less directly as a qualifier.

Given any well-formed string, the syntax crystal can be used to determine the conceptual structure(s) underlying the sentence. Building the crystal up from the words until no more coded edges remain unconnected produces a structure (like those illustrated in skeleton in Figure 3) which shows how the various constituent units go together. This information, the *parse*, enables the hearer to infer the conceptual relationships encoded by the syntax of the sentence. The reader interested in further details of the model should consult the references.

To sum up, this discussion tries to describe the underlying structure of natural-language syntax in a manner congenial to the operant approach. Structure is crucially involved in understanding and generating sentences. Many linguists and psychologists view language structure as beyond the reach of learning theory and consider language acquisition to be a species-specific, innately controlled process. This chapter uses the recently developed syntax crystal model to show that the hierarchical structure which appears to underlie language can be acquired through learning. An iterative mediated association principle, controlled by reinforcement, can produce such structure without assuming innate linguistic organization.

The model in its present stage of development constitutes a logical argument that structure *can* develop by learning principles; we have yet to demonstrate that children *do* operate this way. There is much to be done. I hope that researchers in the field of learning will be encouraged to consider the structure of language as falling within their domain.

REFERENCES

BLOCK, H. D., MOULTON, J. M., & ROBINSON, G. M. A robot to learn natural languages. In *Proceedings of the 1974 Conference on Biologically Motivated Automata Theory*. New York: Institute of Electrical and Electronic Engineers and MIT Research Corporation, 1974.

BLOCK, H. D., MOULTON, J. M., & ROBINSON, G. M. Natural language acquisition by a robot. *International Journal of Man-Machine Studies*, 1975, 7 (4),

CHOMSKY, N. Review of Skinner's *Verbal behavior*. *Language*, 1959, 35, 26–58.

LAKOFF, G. Deep language: A letter to the editors. *New York Review of Books*, 1973, 20 (1), 34.

PEIRCE, C. *The collected papers of Charles Sanders Peirce* (Vol. 1) (C. Hartshorne & P. Weiss, Eds.). Cambridge: Belknap Press of Harvard University Press, 1931.

PREMACK, D. A. A functional analysis of language. *Journal of the Experimental Analysis of Behavior*, 1970, 14, 107–125.

ROBINSON, G. M., & MOULTON, J. M. Three games for psychologists to play with. Paper presented to the Duke University Psychology Colloquium, Spring 1972.

SKINNER, B. F. *Verbal behavior*. New York: Appleton-Century-Crofts, 1957.

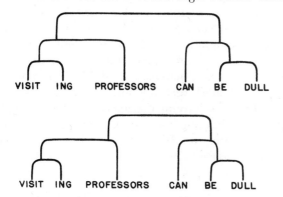

Fig. 3. Simplified skeleton crystal structures for two interpretations of an ambiguous sentence. A: The second half is connected directly to "visiting," and less directly to "Professors" to provide one meaning. B: The reverse arrangement provides a different meaning.

22

Toward a Coherent Psychology of Language*

Evalyn Segal

TOWARD A COHERENT PSYCHOLOGY
OF LANGUAGE

In the vintage year 1957 two important theoretical treatises on language appeared, Chomsky's *Syntactic Structures* and Skinner's *Verbal Behavior*. In the years since, two rival camps have grown up in psychology, one following Chomsky and the other Skinner. The rivalry seems vain, however, for grammatical theory, especially in its more recent versions, rather complements the behavioral view of language than clashes with it. The plan of this chapter is to sketch one version of generative grammatical theory, the version of Chomsky's (1965) *Aspects of the Theory of Syntax,* which is often called the "standard" generative-transformational theory of syntax. Then I will sketch Skinner's (1957) theory of verbal behavior. Then I will try to show, in a general way, how the theories complement one another.

Readers will learn little about the interesting research on language and verbal behavior that psycholinguists and some behaviorists have been doing, but perhaps they will find that a wish to learn more has been awakened and that they are open to what each group has to offer. Throughout, I shall speak interchangeably of psycholinguists, generative grammarians, and cognitive theorists, although the terms are not exactly coextensive. As I see it, the two broad divisions that cut across several disciplines are cognitive theory and functional theory. Among cognitive theorists I count generative grammarians, psycholinguists, mentalists, nativists, Gestaltists, information theorists, memory theorists, and so on. Among functional theorists I count the many varieties of behaviorists and learning theorists as well as students of verbal learning in the traditional functional camp (Hilgard & Bower, 1975).

COMPETENCE:PERFORMANCE::STRUCTURE:
FUNCTION

At places in his writings Chomsky claims to be aiming only for an economical but comprehensive formal (structural) description of the sentences a language

---

* I thank Derek Hendry, for his sympathetic criticism of an earlier version of the manuscript, and Suzette Elgin, whose expert criticism rid the manuscript of a few (surely not all) of its more glaring linguistic solecisms.

may contain. This, when reached, would be a theory of "competence." Ideally, it would be general enough to apply to all natural (human) languages, and not just to one language. At other places Chomsky suggests a special relevance of grammatical theory for psychology—that is, that grammatical theory shows the way to a theory of "performance." The least relevance a competence theory would have is that it would prescribe part of the scope that an adequate functional theory must have, the grammatical facts that psychological mechanisms must explain (Catania, 1972, 1973). Beyond this, the formal theory of generative grammar could offer more; its proposals about deep and surface structures and the formal rules that (deductively) generate each of these may (not "must") be adopted as hypotheses about psychological reality, about the psychological machinery that (functionally) generates utterances. Psycholinguists have treated grammatical theory in this second way; they have adopted one or another current version of generative theory as a theory of verbal performance (productive and receptive).

The value of the theory as a linguistic formalism (as a theory of competence) of course does not depend on its utility as a theory of verbal behavior (a theory of performance). Whether generative grammar turns out to be a useful psychological theory will be answered in the course of time. I will not evaluate that question, nor will I survey the various competing variants of generative grammar that are the daily concern of linguists. The question I address is this: *as a theory of performance*, what relation does the theory of generative grammar (as exemplified in Chomsky's 1965 theory) bear to a behavioral, functional theory (as exemplified in Skinner's 1957 theory)? The surprising conclusion I have come to is that the theories are in part complementary, in the sense that they deal with different but not conflicting problems, and in part isomorphic, in the sense that when they do address the same problems, they propose (roughly) the same answers. This broad compatibility (neglecting differences in detail) has gone unnoticed because of the different vocabularies in which the theories are couched. As it turns out, mentalists and behaviorists are talking about much the same things.

CHOMSKY'S STANDARD THEORY OF TRANSFORMATIONAL-GENERATIVE GRAMMAR

A generative grammar must be a system of rules that can iterate to generate an indefinitely large number of structures. This system of rules can be analyzed into the three major components of a generative grammar: the syntactic, phonological, and semantic components.

The syntactic component specifies an infinite set of abstract formal objects, each of which incorporates all the information relevant to a single interpretation of a particular sentence. Since I shall be concerned here only with the syntactic component, I shall use the term "sentence" to refer to strings of formatives rather than to strings of phones. . . . A string of formatives specifies a string of phones uniquely . . . but not conversely.

The phonological component . . . determines the phonetic form of a sentence generated by the syntactic rules. . . . The semantic component determines the semantic interpretation of a sentence. . . . The syntactic component of a grammar must specify, for each sentence, a *deep structure* that determines its semantic interpretation and a *surface structure* that determines its phonetic interpretation. . . .

The central idea of transformational grammar is that [deep and surface structures] are, in general, distinct and that the surface structure is determined by repeated application of certain formal operations called "grammatical transformations" to objects of a more elementary sort. . . . The syntactic component must generate deep and surface structures, for each sentence, and must interrelate them. . . .

The *base* of the syntactic component is a system of rules that generate a highly restricted (perhaps finite) set of *basic strings*, each with an associated structural description called a *base Phrase-marker*. These base Phrase-markers are the elementary units of which deep structures are constituted. . . . Underlying each sentence of the language there is a sequence of base Phrase-markers, each generated by the base of the syntactic component. I shall refer to this sequence as the *basis* of the sentence that it underlies.

In addition to its base, the syntactic component of a generative grammar contains a *transformational* subcomponent. This is concerned with generating a sentence, with its surface structure, from its basis. . . .

Since the base generates only a restricted set of base Phrase-markers, most sentences will have a sequence of such objects as an underlying basis. Among the sentences with a single base Phrase-marker as basis, we can delimit a proper subset called "kernel sentences." These are sentences of a particularly simple sort that involve a minimum of transformational apparatus in their generation. . . . One must be careful not to confuse kernel sentences with the basic strings that underlie them.

A grammar that generates simple Phrase-markers . . . may be based on a vocabulary of symbols that includes both *formatives* (*the, boy,* etc.) and *category symbols* (S, NP, V, etc.). The formatives, furthermore, can be subdivided into *lexical* items (*sincerity, boy*) and *grammatical* items (*Perfect, Possessive*, etc. ; . . .). (Chomsky, 1965, pp. 15–18, 65—italics his)

In summary, the "base" in Chomsky's theory is a set of "phrase structure" or "rewriting" rules that generate "base phrase markers." (I will give an example in a moment.) The set of all base phrase markers underlying a sentence are together called the "deep structure" of that sentence. The base phrase markers of a language are "highly restricted (perhaps finite)." However, transformational rules applied to single base phrase markers or to sets of base phrase markers allow for the generation of an infinite variety of observed surface structures in a language. This is an important point, for Chomsky has often argued (e.g., Chomsky, 1959) that a theory of verbal performance, just as a theory of verbal competence, must account for the infinite number of sentences that can occur in a language, and that associationistic stimulus-response theories, in principle, cannot do so, for they lack the requisite transformational rules that permit a speaker to generate a variety of surface sentences from a single basis. (But see Robinson, chapter 21 in this volume and later sections of this chapter.)

Deep Structures

The phrase structure rewriting rules that generate the restricted set of base phrase markers incorporate basic grammatical relations like subject-predicate, verb-object, and so on and describe the *hierarchical* arrangement of these grammatical categories. Here is an example, from Chomsky (1965, pp. 106–107), of some phrase structure rewriting rules:

In each case, the term to the left of the arrow can be rewritten as the terms to the right of the arrow. Brackets indicate that the term on the left can be rewritten as any one of the sets of terms within the brackets on the right, and parentheses indicate that the parenthetical term is optional. When these rewriting rules are interpreted graphically, the result is a "tree diagram" that shows diagramatically the hierarchical structure of a base phrase marker. For example, the rules given above would generate, among others, this tree diagram:

```
                         S
            ┌────────────┴────────────┐
           NP                  PREDICATE PHRASE
    ┌──────┼──────┐              ┌──────┴──────┐
   DET     N      S'            AUX            VP
    │      │     ╱ ╲             │          ┌───┴───┐
PRE-ART OF ART POST-ART Δ  Δ   TENSE        V    MANNER
                                │
                               PAST
```

The diagram shows that a sentence (S) is constituted of two main parts ("immediate constituents"): noun phrase (NP) and predicate phrase. These two main constituents are themselves constituted of immediate constituents: for the noun phrase, Det (determiner), N (noun), S' (embedded sentence), and for the predicate phrase, Aux (auxiliary) and VP (verb phrase). At the next level ("up" or "down" makes no difference) in the phrase structure hierarchy, the determiner is shown to consist of the immediate constituents pre-article *of*, article, and postarticle; the embedded sentence (S') is subdivided into two "dummy" parts to show that it, like all sentences, consists at the least of a noun phrase and a predicate phrase; the auxiliary in this case is rewritten as its single immediate constituent, tense; and the verb phrase is subdivided into its immediate constituents (V: verb; Manner: adverb of manner). Except for the "lexical formative" *of* and the "grammatical formatives" Past and S', the tree diagram shows no "terminal symbols" but only "pre-terminal category symbols," and it is therefore unfinished. Further rewriting rules would rewrite all the

i. S → NP Predicate phrase
ii. Predicate phrase → Aux VP (Place) (Time)
iii. VP → $\begin{Bmatrix} \text{Copula Predicate} \\ \text{V} \begin{Bmatrix} \text{(NP) (Prep-Phrase) (Prep-Phrase) (Manner)} \\ \text{S'} \\ \text{Predicate} \end{Bmatrix} \end{Bmatrix}$
iv. Predicate → $\begin{Bmatrix} \text{Adjective} \\ (like) \text{ Predicate-Nominal} \end{Bmatrix}$
vii. NP → (Det) N (S')
xvi. Aux → Tense (M) (Aspect)
xvii. Det → (pre-Article *of*) Article (post-Article)

preterminal symbols into terminal formatives, yielding such basic strings as:

1a. Many of the young chimpanzees (S') (Past) learn quickly.
1b. One of the clever chimpanzees (S') (Past) sign fluently.
1c. Several of the verbal chimpanzees (S') (Past) lie shamelessly.

Surface Structures

One must distinguish between basic strings (such as the strings of formatives 1a, 1b, 1c) and their associated structural descriptions or base phrase markers. The unfinished tree diagram given above shows part of the structural description of each of the basic strings in diagramatic form. (An alternative method of displaying these phrase markers is "labeled bracketing" of the string.) The distinction is important because transformations apply to the base phrase markers and not directly to the basic strings. The basic strings, as such, do not show the "derivational history" of the strings, but the hierarchical base phrase markers do show exactly the derivational history by which the strings were generated by phrase structure rules from the initial symbol S. This derivational history (or hierarchical structure of the string) determines the transformations that will apply to the deep structure to generate a surface structure.

The basic strings of set 1 still contain the symbol S', standing for an embedded sentence. That means that the analyses of these deep structures are still incomplete. Another base phrase marker would need to be generated by phrase structure rules to yield the structural description of each of these embedded sentences. Suppose the additional base phrase markers were associated with these basic strings of terminal formatives:

2a. (That) Rumbaugh (Past) train chimpanzees.
2b. (That) The Gardners (Past) raise chimpanzees.
2c. (That) Chimpanzees (Past) talk to Premack.

Then the two base phrase markers associated with strings 1a and 2a would together make up the deep structure of surface string 3a (see below); base phrase markers associated with strings 1b and 2b would make up the deep structure of surface string 3b; and so on.

Given the deep structures, transformational rules would now be applied to generate surface structures. Some transformational rules apply to single base phrase markers. [For example, simple transformational rules would transform "(Past) learn," "(Past) sign," "(Past) lie" and so on into "learned," "signed," "lied," and so on.] If the phrase markers associated with set 1 did not contain embedded S's, and if the phrase markers associated with set 2 did not contain symbols [such as "(That)"] marking their status as embedded, then these transformations on individual base phrase markers could complete the generation of six simple kernel sentences:

3a. Many of the young chimpanzees learned quickly.
3b. One of the clever chimpanzees signed fluently.
3c. Several of the verbal chimpanzees lied shamelessly.
3d. Rumbaugh trained chimpanzees.
3e. The Gardners raised chimpanzees.
3f. Chimpanzees talked to Premack.

(I am simplifying these examples. In standard generative theory, the adjectives in prenominal position in the basic strings of 1 might actually indicate other embedded phrase markers, associated with the basic strings:

4a. The chimpanzees were young.
4b. The chimpanzees were clever.
4c. The chimpanzees were verbal.

Then a transformation would permute the adjectives from predicate-adjective to prenominal position.)

However, the base phrase markers of set 1 do contain embedded S' symbols, so further transformational rules must be applied to the sets of base phrase markers associated with (1a, 2a), (1b, 2b) and (1c, 2c) to yield the following complex surface sentences (with associated surface structures):

5a. Many of the young chimpanzees that Rumbaugh trained learned quickly.
5b. One of the clever chimpanzees that the Gardners raised signed fluently.
5c. Several of the verbal chimpanzees who talked to Premack lied shamelessly.

All the sentences in set 1 are called "matrix" sentences, and all the sentences in set 2 are called "constituent" sentences. One of the axioms of generative theory is that any base phrase marker can contain the symbol S'. In other words, a constituent phrase marker can be at the same time a matrix phrase marker, incorporating another embedded sentence within it. Transformational-generative syntax is thus said to be "recursive," infinitely recursive, and this is one of the reasons that the grammatically acceptable sentences in any language are infinite in number and, theoretically, infinite in length as well. In performance theory, however, there is realistically a stopping point determined by the speaker's inability to generate endlessly long sentences and the listener's inability to understand them (Gleitman & Gleitman, 1970). Such items as "The rat the cat my mother bought bit died" (Roeper, 1973) occur with a saving infrequency outside linguistic discussions.[1]

Semantics and Phonology

Deep structures "determine semantic interpretation" and surface structures "determine phonetic interpretation." This seems odd at first, because if generative theory is to account for the *production* of utterances, one might have supposed that semantics (what the speaker "means to say") would determine deep structure, rather than the other way around. On the other hand, if generative theory is to account only for the *reception* (understanding) of utterances, one might have supposed that the heard utterance (the phonetic event) comes first, and then the listener infers an appropriate surface structure for what was heard, as in the traditional problem of speech perception. Fodor, Bever, & Garrett (1974, p. 389) resolve the puzzle:

> Direction of information flow makes no difference in a grammar. According to Chomsky, . . . "the standard theory generates quadruples [of phonetic representations, surface structures, deep structures, and semantic representations]. It is meaningless to ask whether it does so by 'first' generating [a deep structure then mapping it onto a semantic representation (on one side) and a phonetic representation on the other]." (material in brackets is theirs)

They go on to remark:

> In the case of performance models, however, the situation is quite different. . . . A performance model attempts to specify the actual sequence of computations which underlies the speaker-hearer's production and recognition of sentences. For such models, the direction of information flow is critical. (p. 390)

---

[1] W. K. Honig pointed out to me that such sentences are not infrequent in German. German's case inflections, very likely, help the reader to make sense of multiply embedded sentences, but English, almost devoid of case inflections, offers no such help.

In fact, any performance model that supposes that surface structures are generated by transformations from deep structures has the problem of accounting for deep structures themselves—that is, the problem of what sets the phrase structure rewriting rules into operation. In a rival theory of generative grammar called "generative semantics," "deep structures and semantic representations are identical" (Fodor et al., 1974, p. 388), but in the standard theory of transformational-generative grammar this is not so, and then performance theory requires a prior step in "the translation function from mentalese to English" that maps "from formulas in mentalese to deep structures" (Fodor et al., p. 389). We shall return to the problem of "translating from mentalese to English" at the end of the chapter.

THE PSYCHOLOGICAL REALITY OF TRANSFORMATIONAL-GENERATIVE GRAMMAR

As a general approach to formulating the problems of syntax, the division between deep structures (or their relatively unmodified manifestations as kernel sentences) and surface structures (generated by more elaborate transformations from deep structures) seems plausible. There is evidence (e.g., Brown, 1973) that children's first sentencelike utterances (i.e., utterances longer than a unit verbal response) have the simple and straightforward syntactic structure implied by the notion of kernel sentence. Only later do utterances appear that have more complex syntactic structure. The point transformational grammarians make is that these more complex utterances *could* be generated from one or more kernel sentences (with equivalent meaning) by application of transformational rules. It does not seem implausible that complex sentences *are* so generated, that kernel sentences are psychologically more fundamental, that speakers learn to generate them before they learn to transform them, and that underlying any complex utterance is one or more kernel sentences (or base phrase markers) that, in some sense, are prior to it and give rise to it. The idea is not unlike Skinner's theoretical distinction between "primary" verbal behavior and autoclitically modified verbal behavior.

These issues, however they are formulated, are within the scope of a functional analysis of verbal behavior, for which the central problem is to determine the behavioral laws that account for the performances of speakers and listeners. If, as seems possible, the formal distinction between deep structure and surface structure reflects some aspect of psychological reality, and if, as seems certain, the formal structure of utterances is hierarchical, then functional theory must deal with the questions: What are the behavioral variables that determine (or that instantiate) deep structures and surface structures? and What "meanings" are carried by the internal, hierarchical structure of utterances that are not carried by the individual response terms viewed as an unstructured string? (See Robinson, chapter 21 in this volume.) Psycholinguistics, long in the thrall of transformational-generative syntax, seems lately to be shifting to a greater concern with semantic problems (i.e., problems of stimulus control) and pragmatic problems (i.e., problems of the reinforcement contingencies that shape and maintain verbal behavior) (e.g., Brown, 1973; Carter, 1975; Farwell, 1975; McNeill, 1974; Moore, 1973; Slobin, 1975; Thompson & Chapman, 1975). This may reflect psycholinguists' despair at solving the problems of syntax set by transformational-generative grammarians, but it may alternatively reflect their growing sense that the solution to these syntactic problems will come from a fuller analysis of semantic (stimulus control) and pragmatic (reinforcement) variables.

SKINNER'S FUNCTIONAL THEORY OF VERBAL BEHAVIOR

Skinner's theory, as MacCorquodale (1969, 1970) emphasized, is a plausible extrapolation of the laws of animal operant behavior to human verbal behavior, embodying the hypothesis that the facts of verbal behavior can be accounted for by application of the familiar "three-term contingency" of operant analysis. In this case, the three-term contingency must explicate two functional relations: (1) the function between discriminative stimuli (or a motivational state) and the response they control, and (2) the function between the operant unit constituted of this antecedent variable-response relation and the reinforcing consequences shaping the operant (S–R) unit.

Skinner defined the domain of verbal behavior as operant behavior whose third term (reinforcement) is mediated by other organisms. The definition was intended to capture, in a nutshell, the communicative function of verbal behavior, the fact that it constitutes a social transaction between a speaker and a listener and that the transaction has utility for both participants. Having defined the domain, Skinner proceeded to subdivide it by classifying verbal operants in terms of their antecedent controlling variables.

Mands

A *mand* is a verbal response controlled by an antecedent motivational state. Formally, the motivational state occupies the position in the three-term contingency more commonly occupied by a discriminative stimulus. It sets the occasion for reinforcement of a specific class of response topographies. For example, food deprivation sets the occasion when the mand "Food" or the mand "Gimme eats" can be reinforced by a listener's supplying food. Because food is only a reinforcer when an organism is food-deprived, deprivation sets the occasion for reinforcement of the class of food mands. There is a peculiarly close fit between the motivational condition setting the occasion for reinforcement of a mand and the particular form of reinforcer appropriate to that mand, which Skinner summed up by saying that the mand "specifies its reinforcement." We can avoid the teleological seductions of this expression, however, by focusing on the antecedent motivational control of the mand. (Note, however, that from the listener's viewpoint the mand does "specify" very explicitly what behavior the listener should engage in.) In *Verbal Behavior,* Skinner almost invariably speaks of the antecedent conditions controlling emission of the mand as "states of deprivation or aversive stimulation," but this seems to give an unwanted drive-reduction flavor to the mand that, as MacCorquodale (1970) pointed out, was never intended. Among "states of deprivation" Skinner included such items as needing a pencil to complete a drawing, but completing a drawing is not your usual primary reinforcer, and needing a pencil is not your usual primary state of deprivation. MacCorquodale (1970) suggests that mands for such conditioned reinforcers as pencils to complete drawings are best understood as under the control of some other, more primary deprivation correlated with some other, more primary reinforcer with which pencils and completed drawings have been paired in the speaker's past history. I wonder if a simpler solution would not be to abandon the primary-conditioned reinforcer distinction, as Premack (1959) did, and simply to regard reinforcers and their correlated motivational states as in various ways situationally determined. The neo-Hullian concept of incentive motivation seems a suitable way to talk about the antecedent motivational state controlling a mand. (I shall return to this shortly.)

Echoics

An *echoic* is a verbal response controlled by an antecedent verbal stimulus where, in addition, reinforcement depends on a strict one-to-one correspondence between the sound pattern of the discriminative stimulus and the auditory product of the response. The stimulus and the auditory product of the response must match, within limits set by the reinforcing community. For example, if a parent says "Dinosaur," and a child repeats, "Dinosaur," the parent's utterance serves as a verbal stimulus for the child's echoic response. Fragmentary echoics also occur. In this case some part of the response matches the sound pattern of the prior stimulus, but the match is not complete. Alliteration is an example of fragmentary echoic verbal behavior. If someone says, "Sing," and a speaker responds, "A silly song," the repeated *s* sounds suggest fragmentary echoic control. Rhymes are other examples of fragmentary echoics. Whenever the sound match is not complete, then other variables must be supposed to have determined other aspects of the speaker's response.

Intraverbals

An *intraverbal* is a verbal response controlled by an antecedent verbal stimulus where, in addition, the sound match is lacking. It is the verbal unit par excellence of conventional paired-associates verbal learning. If a parent says, "One, two," and a child responds, "Button your shoe," the response as a whole is most likely a rote-learned intraverbal. (The sound match between the last part of "two" and the last part of "shoe" suggests fragmentary echoic control as well. In a given instance fragmentary echoic control may not occur: the child's "shoe" may simply be part of the rote-learned unit phrase "Button your shoe." Still, the historical origin of the rhyme certainly owed something to fragmentary echoic control.) More "significant" examples of intraverbals are easy to find. A lot of the educated speaker's repertoire consists of "book-learned" or otherwise rote-learned intraverbals.

Tacts

A *tact* is a verbal response controlled by a nonverbal discriminative stimulus. It is the unit most susceptible to "semantic" generalization, what Skinner and psycholinguists (e.g., Moore, 1973) have both called "extension." When a tact, initially learned to the particular package of stimulus properties making up a specific, dated environmental event, later transfers to other packages of stimulus properties making up other specific, dated environmental events, and when, in addition, the basis of transfer is exactly those stimulus properties the verbal community regards as "definitive" for that "word" (the community imposes differential reinforcement contingencies to bring this about), then, for Skinner, we have a case of *generic* extension of the tact and, for cognitive theorists, a case of *concept* learning. (See Robinson, Chapter 21 in this volume.) Despite the vocabulary difference, everyone is talking about the same phenomenon. For example, when a child who has learned to tact an activity performed by his parent as "walking" extends the response to other instances of the activity, such as his own walking or the dog's walking, the child has acquired the generic tact "walking," or alternatively, the concept of walking.

When the basis of transfer of the tact is accidental stimulus properties that just happen to be shared by two environmental events (one of them, of course, the event in whose presence the tact was originally reinforced), Skinner speaks of *metaphoric* extension of the tact, and cognitive theorists of *overextension* of a word or concept. Again, despite the vocabulary difference, everyone is talking about exactly the same phenomenon. The literature on children's language acquisition abounds with amusing examples of metaphoric extension. For example, a child who first learned to utter "moon" in the presence of the moon later extended the response to round postmarks and the letter *O*. (This is so common a metaphoric extension, apparently, that we have an expression "moon-faced," meaning round-faced.) Another child who learned the response "fly" in the presence of the appropriate little insect later extended the response to his own little toes (Clark, 1973, pp. 80–81).

Finally, when the basis of transfer of the tact is not shared properties of two environmental events, but rather some fortuitous association of events, then Skinner speaks of *metonymic extension* and everyone else speaks of plain "associative learning" or, to revive an apt phrase of Thorndike's (1911), "associative shifting." According to Ervin-Tripp (1973, p. 267), metonymic extension may be the origin of the syntax of the possessive in children's speech. It is common, for example, to find a young child saying, "Mommy," when pointing to Mommy's shoe. (Later on the child will learn to tact the shoe as a generic, tact Mommy as a metonymic, order them and affix *-'s* to the metonymic, and utter "Mommy's shoe.")

An example of metonymic extension offered by Skinner (1957) and discussed by MacCorquodale (1969) is uttering the response "orange" in the presence of a fruit bowl or a breakfast table that sometimes contains an orange but does not in this instance. The sophisticated speaker will usually qualify the response with other responses, such as "That fruit bowl makes me think of oranges," or "Strange, there's no orange on the breakfast table this morning." Only "orange" is a "tact in metonymic extension." The qualifying terms ("no," "makes me think of") are autoclitics.

Autoclitics

An *autoclitic*, finally, was defined by Skinner as a verbal response controlled by stimulation (demonstrable or merely hypothesized) arising from the speaker's immediately prior (covert, usually) verbal behavior. Autoclitics are first cousins of intraverbals, in the sense that their controlling stimuli are said to be preceding (albeit covert) verbal stimuli (*auto* = "self," *clitic* = "leaning on"). The autoclitic depends for its occurrence on a self-generated verbal stimulus or, really, some more abstract and hypothetical *preverbal* (possibly even central) event. Autoclitics can have the clear topographical dimensions of an uttered word, or they can be, so to speak, dimensionless, being detectable only by their effect of *ordering* these more familiar terms syntactically.

Some examples of autoclitics have just been mentioned. In "That fruit bowl reminds me of oranges" speakers, so to say, find themselves about to utter "oranges" but, noticing that the response is not at peak strength, or perhaps vaguely sensing that the circumstances are not quite right for saying "oranges," qualifies the response in the process of uttering it. The qualifying autoclitic, having the dimension of a "word," is "reminds." The sentence illustrates the difference between "primary" verbal responses and autoclitic responses. "Oranges" is a metonymic tact controlled by the fruit bowl as a discriminative stimulus. "Fruit bowl" is a generic tact controlled by the same discriminative stimulus. "Me" is perhaps a generic tact of a complex private event, or perhaps should be regarded as another autoclitic: a response to the speaker's privately sensed disposition to speak. The distinction between primary verbal behavior (the immediate responses to the stimulating environment) and autoclitic behavior (complex responses to the disposition to speak) is reminiscent of the distinction between deep and surface structure, but the correspondence is not exact. (More on this later.)

Skinner suggested that the syntactic structure of utterances is determined, at least in part, by *autoclitic frames*. These would correspond, roughly, to such syntactic sequences as noun phrase–predicate phrase, or determiner–noun. Thus, although "reminds" in "That fruit bowl reminds me of oranges" is an autoclitic having clear response dimensions and is triggered by the prior strengthening of "oranges," "fruit bowl," and something peculiar about the stimulating conditions evoking "oranges," the temporal arrangement of the terms into a grammatical sentence requires the notion of a (dimensionless) autoclitic frame. (The fixed-interval scallop is, in this sense, a "dimensionless frame" into which concrete responses such as bar presses or key pecks "fit." "Temporal frame" is perhaps a more apt expression.)

The difficulty with the concept of an autoclitic frame is the same difficulty posed by deep structures, or Robinson's (this volume) cards with side codes but no words written on them. Robinson's card metaphor suggests how the autoclitic frames that "mediate" the syntactic connections between words might be learned within a reinforcement theory framework, but none of the present notions (autoclitic frames, deep structures, coded cards) helps one to imagine what the physical embodiment of syntactic structure might be. All of these notions imply some mysterious preverbal processes within the organism, to which Fodor et al. (1974) give the name "mentalese." Autoclitic frames, deep structures, and coded cards equally represent abstract theories about syntactic behavior, and as theoretical concepts they can, of course, function without reference to physical events within the organism. To the extent that one takes them as references to real biological events, they must be understood as metaphors. (More on this, too, later.)

COMMENTS ON SKINNER'S FUNCTIONAL THEORY

This brief review has laid out the bare elements of Skinner's theory of verbal behavior. For fuller expositions, the interested reader should consult MacCorquodale (1969, 1970), Segal (1975a), or best of all, Skinner himself (1957). As MacCorquodale (1969) noted,

> Everything considered, the basic explanatory apparatus seems very meager, while verbal behavior is very complex. [But] the power of a single variable is seen to multiply when we take into account its multiplicity of effects. . . . First, a single variable controls many responses, giving a speaker a great deal to say even in a static environment. . . . [Second,] if several responses are concurrently strong, additional variables . . . control the order of their emission and whatever response selection, and rejection, occurs. (pp. 838–839)

Skinner's theory remains in its pristine state. It has been too little modified since its publication in 1957, first because behaviorists have apparently not been interested in subjecting it to the experimental test and revision appropriate to theories, and second, because psycholinguists, who are acquainted with real data germane to the theory, have not been at pains to improve a theory they scorn. Even so, the theory is powerful, it is in touch with much of the data that psycholinguists have uncovered, and it is available as a means of systematizing and making sense of what psycholinguists are finding out, especially now that their interests have begun to shift to "semantics" and "pragmatics." In the interests of advancing understanding as rapidly as may be, one hopes that psycholinguists will not insist on working out all over again the integrative insights into semantic and pragmatic issues that Skinner's book makes available, free for the asking.

Comments on the Mand

What is one to say about the reinforcers, and the associated controlling motivational states, for novel, generative mands? Suppose, to take an example of Skinner's (1957), a child in a toy store sees an attractive new toy whose name he doesn't know. On being told by his parents that it's a "doodler," he immediately says, "Buy me a doodler!" As Skinner notes, "He has never been reinforced for this response in the manner required to construct a mand" (1957, p. 188). If the response has never been reinforced, it could never have come under the control of the child's new motivational state. What accounts for its emission, then? Skinner suggests, "It is possible that all mands which are reinforced by the production of objects or other states of affairs may be interpreted as manding the behavior of the listener and tacting the object or state of affairs to be produced" (1957, p. 180). Let us consider this further.

The doodler is an incentive, automatically inducing a novel motivational state. Piaget (1952) gives many examples of novel objects apparently functioning automatically as incentives—automatically, that is, presupposing certain prior sensorimotor or "cognitive" learning. Novel incentives of this kind do not clearly sort out as primary or conditioned reinforcers. Perhaps they are best regarded as *induced* (Segal, 1972) incentives, their incentive value arising in some yet-to-be-explicated way from prior learning. Being incentives, they induce a correlated motivational state (incentive motivation) and so insure that any behavior that results in obtaining the incentive will be reinforced (that, as I take it, is the definition of incentive). (See Ayllon & Azrin, 1968, for a demonstration of human incentive motivation at work.)

Given a novel motivational state induced by a novel incentive and an environmental setting which, in concert with incentive motivation, has already come to control mands of the form "Buy me _____," the mand frame is emitted. The "generative" appearance of the mand frame on this novel occasion, then, is understandable *if* all induced incentive motivations, novel or not, have enough in common, and *if* all stores (places where incentives are bought) have enough in common, so that these two variables together are able to support generative appearance of the response form "Buy me _____."

The appearance of the response "a doodler" in the blank in the mand frame is still to be explained. Other things being equal, a response that tacts an attractive incentive should have a high probability of emission (as a tact, mind you, not yet as a mand). There must have been occasions in the past when the child "merely tacted" an incentive but was understood by his parents to be manding, and so (unexpectedly) the child found the incentive object handed over to him. Supposing that the incentive had aroused an incentive motivation, obtaining the incentive should have reinforced the tact response, which from then on could be evoked, as mand, by the motivational state, as well as evoked, as tact, by the object itself. After a few such experiences, all responses that were previously acquired as tacts (when the child was not motivated to have the object) might be available also as potential mands when the child was in the appropriate incentive motivational state. In short, a new set of conditional discriminations, with generative effects, would have been learned. Given an incentive, and given availability of a tact of the incentive, and given a correlated incentive motivation, the child would emit the tact. The specified reinforcement would then *follow* this emission of the tact, which would then come under independent control of the motivational state and would no longer depend, as mand, on the presence of the incentive to evoke it. (Notice one new factor here. We presuppose that, given a novel incentive motivation, the speaker can discriminate the incentive object that roused the motive and will not be likely to tact irrelevant objects.) The analysis suggests why speakers are prone to tact their motivational states by reference to expected reinforcers, giving to statements of intention their characteristically teleological flavor.

This account is given at length to suggest what

must be a common and powerful basis for generative (creative, productive) manding: tacting incentives. We shall find problems enough later on when we come to consider generative syntax, but generative echoic responding, generative tacting, and generative manding do not seem to present serious difficulties for Skinner's functional theory of verbal behavior. Working through the functional analysis in individual cases and testing it against experimental or naturalistic data are not necessarily easy, but they can be done. The general strategy for attacking the semantic and pragmatic problems of language seems clear.

The Reinforcement of Verbal Behavior

Once Skinner leaves the discussion of the mand, the third term in the three-term contingency (the reinforcing consequences of verbal responses) is taken pretty much for granted—not because reinforcement is unimportant in the acquisition and maintenance of verbal behavior, but rather because the reinforcements flow so naturally from the fact that the speaker is communicating with a responsive listener. Except for a limited class of mands that specify primary commodity reinforcers the listener is to supply, the reinforcers for verbal behavior mostly reside in the social response of the listener. Furthermore, they may be self-supplied by the speaker, in his or her role as a listener. Much of a mature speaker's verbal behavior is addressed to oneself, as self-instructions and the like. Whatever reinforcers ultimately flow from the speaker-listener's reactions to their own self-instructions provide the necessary conditions for the maintenance of self-addressed verbal behavior.

Finally, intermittent reinforcement must play at least as important a role in the acquisition and maintenance of verbal behavior as it plays in the control of other operant behavior. It would not violate the spirit of a behavioral analysis if it turned out, even, that new verbal operants (new stimulus-response units) are often learned without any evident reinforcement. (MacCorquodale, 1970, makes the same point.) A kind of secondary contiguity principle may operate, such that the direct reinforcement of some of the speaker's verbal acquisitions generates a strong and persisting tendency to acquire new verbal operants even when there is no possibility of their immediate reinforcement. Experimental analyses of generative imitation—for example, Sherman (1971)—seem to demonstrate the operation of such a secondary contiguity principle. Such a principle also seems the most parsimonious way to account for much of the paired-associates learning that goes on in the verbal learning laboratory, as well as in the natural environment. (Possibly the relatively low energy requirements involved in vocal responding make it, like perceptual responding, especially available to a simple contiguity-learning process.)

The Stimulus Control of Verbal Behavior

When we leave the mand, we leave a dominating concern with reinforcement and correlated motivational states. From here on, the focus of the analysis is on stimulus control. Echoic control leads eventually to the emergence of the "minimal (phonemic) echoic repertoire," enabling speakers to match, phoneme by phoneme, verbal stimuli they hear, even for the first time. Generative echoic responding raises no explanatory problems just because the echoic stimulus provides the speaker with such detailed and explicit instructions on what to do. Also arising out of the minimal echoic repertoire are *formal classes* of responses controlled by isolated phonetic features of verbal stimuli. In the dominant vernacular of the day, responses in the "memory store" can be addressed by such "retrieval cues" as "Give me some words that begin with *p*" or "Give me some words that rhyme with *luck*" or "Give me some words in spondaic meter."

Among the by-products of the development of intraverbals and tacts are the appearance of *thematic classes* of responses controlled by events (whence "episodic memory") and by words (whence "semantic memory"). The organization of verbal memory is currently an active topic of research. Skinner argued that all the organization to be found in the speaker's interrelated tact and intraverbal repertoires (i.e., in his or her thematic classes) were the result of sheer contiguity, but contemporary memory researchers, reviving some of the perceptual insights of Gestalt psychology, have insisted that other factors besides sheer contiguity are important. Hilgard and Bower (1975) review some of the arguments in their chapter on Gestalt psychology. To summarize their arguments, responses tacting events that occur together in the speaker's perceptual experience are much more likely to become interrelated in memory (such that the perceptual cues controlling each tact as a generic will also have a high probability of evoking the other tacts as metonymics) if the original events were so structured as to be perceived as related to one another in some intrinsic way. For example, two stimulus features structured so as to be attributes of a coherent figure are more likely to evoke one another's generic tacts as metonymics than are two stimulus features presented with identical spatial contiguity but so structured that one is perceived as a figural attribute and the other as an independent attribute of the background. (See Hilgard and Bower, 1975, Figure 8.6, p. 265, for several examples taken from experiments by Asch, 1969.) The arguments against sheer contiguity seem, on balance, to be persuasive. It seems clear now that there are much more interesting things to say, and to discover, about the organization of verbal memory than simply that it derives from contiguity of perceptual experiences.

Despite the fall of sheer contiguity as the exclusive organizing principle of thematic response classes, Skinner's insight into the organization of the verbal repertoire in terms of controlling stimuli remains valid. Some of the phenomena that memory researchers puzzle over seem not quite so puzzling, nor their contemporary explanations quite so original, viewed in this light. "Encoding specificity" (Tulving & Thomson, 1973) is the current expression for the independence of verbal operants controlled by different antecedent stimuli. Some of the phenomena of encoding specificity, such as the greater ease of "recall" over "recognition" in some circumstances (Tulving, 1974; Tulving & Thomson, 1973), or the appearance of formal ("auditory") "errors" in immediate free recall ("short-term memory"), replaced by thematic ("semantic") "errors" in delayed free recall ("long-term memory") (Kausler, 1974), could have been predicted from Skinner's analysis. It must be said, however, that they were *not* predicted. Alas, no original research on verbal memory flowed from Skinner's theory, because no one conversant with it was interested in doing the research, and so equivalent theoretical explanations have had to be reinvented without help from Skinner, and behaviorists can take no credit for the interesting results that have been emerging in research on verbal memory.

Control by Relations Between Stimuli

This is not to say there are no difficulties in Skinner's account of the stimulus control of verbal responses. There are basic problems in the definition and specification of controlling stimuli. For example, Skinner suggested that the regular past tense inflection on English verbs, -*ed,* is a tact controlled by "that subtle feature of the environment called action-in-the-past." But it is not clear that action in the past is an explicit feature of the physical environment. Other relational terms present the same problem. Is plurality, which is said to control the tact inflection -*s* on nouns, an explicit feature of the physical environment? What are the physical dimensions of the stimulating environment that control relational terms such as "familiar," "similar," "Mozart" (said of a piece of music), "Dutch" (said of a painting), and so on? Cognitive theorists (e.g., Chomsky, 1959) object to Skinner's treating the stimuli controlling such tacts as purely objective, physical events. They would argue, for example, that the relation of similarity is not in the physical stimuli, but in the way organisms (are built to) react to ("process") them. Skinner would agree. The issue, of course, is not whether organisms can respond in such a way as to exemplify the rule "Pick the comparison stimulus that is similar to the sample stimulus." The literature on matching to sample clearly demonstrates that they can. The issue is whether it is necessary to posit a "cognitive process" or a "comparator device" within the organism, over and above what is in the external physical world, to account for the organism's ability to match to sample. I think a comparator device is called for, and behavior theory will have to make room for it. In general, relations are not describable solely in physical terms. Behaviorists can, of course, give an operational definition of what it means for an organism's behavior to be controlled by relations between physical stimuli, but the fact that such operational definitions require mention of an organism's behavior makes such definitions question begging, so far as cognitive theorists are concerned.

A point that is rarely mentioned, and little understood, is that it does no violence to functional behaviorism to concede that the stimulus relations which control behavior may not literally be in the environment but in the way the organism reacts to the environment. Functional behaviorists take for granted that the organism brings something of its own to the behavior-environment interaction that defines the operant. Perhaps this should be mentioned more often. MacCorquodale (1970) spent a good deal of space on this matter, but it was almost as an aside that Skinner himself remarked, in *Verbal Behavior,* "All behavior, verbal or otherwise, is subject to Kantian a priori's in the sense that man as a behaving system has inescapable characteristics and limitations" (1957, p. 451). Among the "inescapable characteristics" that organisms bring to an operant transaction with the environment is their disposition (call it "cognitive" or not) to perceive (even impose) relations between physical events. The relations do not inhere in the physical events themselves; Skinner pointed out, for example, that it is not literally a temporal relation between earlier and later occurrences of a stimulus that marks the later-occurring stimulus as "familiar," but some change in the way the organism responds to earlier and later occurrences. Still, perceived relations among physical events are describable, even if it takes an organism (such as the experimenter) to describe them, and this is all that a functional analysis requires. Only if the experimental subject were able to perceive a relation that the experimenter could not would functional analysis be in trouble, for then the experimenter would be unable to formulate the determinants of the subject's behavior. What divides behaviorists and cognitive theorists on this issue is whether to focus on analyzing the structure of the environment or the structure of the organism. Clearly, both participate in determining the functional relations between organism and environment embodied in operant behavior. The behaviors focus on the environment, regarding the internal structure of the organism as beyond reach of current experimental technique. The cognitive psychologists focus on the organism, even if they must invent the internal structure they seek to understand.

Transfer of Verbal Responses to New Stimuli

Although the problem of similarity does raise questions about the necessity of "filtering" the description of the stimulus relations controlling the tact "similar" through another perceiving organism, this problem is not necessarily involved in generative (productive) extensions of verbal responses. Skinner's treatment of extensions of stimulus control is a "common elements theory of transfer," (Prokasy and Hall 1963). Perhaps that is why Skinner avoided the expression "stimulus generalization" in *Verbal Behavior,* an avoidance MacCorquodale (1969) found puzzling. Still, a too-casual use of the term *stimulus* causes confusion. If a tact were extended from one "stimulus" to another, nonidentical "stimulus," the extension would have to be on the basis of some troublesome "similarity." But if a tact is extended from one collection of stimulus elements or properties or features, each of which can be separately specified, to another collection of stimulus elements or properties or features, on the basis of shared, common, identical elements or properties or features, then a "comparator device" that evaluates degree of similarity is not required. For cognitive theorists the problem of "recognition" of *identical* stimuli then replaces the problem of evaluating the degree of similarity of *nonidentical* stimuli. Behaviorists can shed no light on the question of stimulus recognition. They simply take it for granted.

The Functional Approach to Syntax

The difference between functional and cognitive approaches to verbal behavior can be illustrated in the approach to problems of syntax. Schumaker and Sherman (1970) applied differential reinforcement contingencies that succeeded in getting retardates to utter the verb inflections *-ed* and *-ing* in appropriate intraverbal contexts—for example, in such sentences as "Now the man is painting. Yesterday he . . . *painted*" and "Yesterday the man painted. Now he is . . . *painting*." Echoic prompts were initially used to induce the inflectional responses on sample verb stems such as *paint,* but eventually the subjects added the inflections to novel untrained verb stems such as *skate* under appropriate intraverbal control of the phrases "Now he is . . ." or "Yesterday he . . . ." This qualifies as generative (productive) syntactic behavior because (1) from an unfamiliar stimulus word such as *skating* subjects extracted the verb stem (*skate*); (2) they added the alternate ending to yield *skated;* and (3) they uttered the two response elements in grammatically correct order (*skated,* not *edskate*).

In several experiments (Garcia, Guess, & Byrnes, 1973; Guess, 1969; Guess & Baer, 1973; Guess, Sailor, Rutherford, & Baer, 1968; Sailor, 1971), experimenters trained retardates to utter the plural noun inflection *-s* under appropriate nonverbal stimulus control—that is, to tact plurality. Again this qualifies as generative syntactic behavior because (1) subjects added *-s* to novel noun forms on which they had not had echoic training in the plural; (2) they uttered the plural forms in response to newly paired objects (familiar previously only as singletons); and (3) they uttered the response elements in grammatically correct order (e.g., *rocks,* not *srock*). Again, the experimental methods employed to bring about productive syntactive behavior involved differential reinforcement of echoically prompted responses and gradual shifting of stimulus control from echoic prompts to nonverbal stimuli (single objects or pairs of objects). Lutzker and Sherman (1974) employed comparable procedures to produce generative utterance of the verb forms *is* and *are* under appropriate nonverbal stimulus control of pictures of single or several actors engaging in some action.

Whitehurst (1971, 1972) taught 2-year-old children a miniature artificial language consisting of some nonsense syllables that functioned as color "adjectives" and some nonsense syllables that functioned as "noun" labels of geometric forms. A procedure involving differential reinforcement, echoic prompting, and shifting of control from echoic to nonverbal (color and form) stimuli created appropriate functional response classes (a class of color tacts and a class of form tacts) and appropriate syntactic ordering of response terms in two-word utterances. The prescribed order was color tact (adjective) followed by form tact (noun), as in standard (surface) English. By these procedures Whitehurst succeeded in producing generative syntactic behavior: given novel combinations of familiar color-plus-form stimuli, the children correctly tacted the two properties in the prescribed adjective-noun order.

Premack (1970) has also reported getting his chimpanzee subject, Sarah, to emit generative tact sequences in syntactically prescribed orders; Gardner and Gardner (1969, 1971, 1975) have reported generative syntactic response sequences in their chimpanzee subject, Washoe; and Rumbaugh, von Glaserfeld, Warner, Pisani, and Gill (1974) obtained generative syntactic mand sequences in their chimpanzee subject, Lana.

These are only an exemplary few of the spate of research reports in recent years dealing with a functional analysis of simple syntactic behavior. In all this work, explicit training procedures involving differential reinforcement, prompting, and stimulus fading (associative shifting) were employed to bring about the productive syntactic behavior. Premack, however, has concisely stated the demurrer that divides behavioral and cognitive theorists in dealing with problems of verbal behavior: "A strict training procedure is not an explanation of how, as a result of carrying out the prescribed steps, the organism accomplished the function in question. A recipe is a method, not a theory" (1970, p. 107). Functional behaviorists are content to devise "strict training procedures" that succeed in producing generative syntactic behavior in experimental subjects. In the course of devising effective procedures, such research unavoidably identifies critical functional variables controlling syntactic behavior, insofar as these reside in environmental contingencies among the antecedent variables, the behavior, and the reinforcing consequences. A functional analysis, however, does not attempt to specify what, apart from its ontogenetic history, the organism brings to the learning task. Premack (1970) suggested that strict training procedures do no more than teach the experimental subject to "map concepts" it already possesses—that is, to tact the environmental events and relations it already perceives. (Also see Robinson, Chapter 21 in this volume.) Premack doubted the possibility of teaching subjects to perceive relations they do not perceive spontaneously. This is an open question for the functional behaviorist. It is interesting that some psycholinguists (e.g., Brown, 1973) entertain the possibility that the environmental relations a young child tacts in his first multiunit utterances are exactly those relations he learned to respond to nonverbally in the immediately prior sensorimotor stage of development (Piaget, 1952). In any case, it is certainly true that behaviorists have shown no interest in the question of what internal cognitive machinery makes possible the perception of relations, although this kind of question is the meat-and-potatoes of cognitive theorists. Premack is correct: a functional analysis is not a cognitive theory (although Skinner's hypothesis of the autoclitic probably qualifies as a cognitive theory).

FUNCTIONALISM VS. MENTALISM

Theories

The question of whether to have or not to have theories (alternatively, what constitutes a proper explanatory theory) is at the heart of the so-called mentalist-behavioral controversy. Cognitive theorists often employ the vocabulary of mentalism, but a look at the footnotes (e.g., Chomsky, 1965, pp. 193–194) reveals that all they mean by *mind* is a theory about the internal machinery of the organism. Sometimes such theories are couched in the metaphors of neurophysiology, sometimes in the metaphors of computer and information science, sometimes in the metaphors of plant genetics (unfolding of phenotypic characters in a favorable soil, and so on). But behaviorists should take note that the temptation to theorize in metaphors appropriate to another domain is so great, up against the mysteries of syntax, that even Skinner succumbed. The concept of the autoclitic is a groping step toward a theory of syntactic behavior, and, like the theories Skinner elsewhere (1950) enjoined, the theory of the autoclitic is metaphoric. (MacCorquodale, 1969, disagrees.) It proposes that the unobserved processes that must be supposed to underlie the observed (surface) syntactic structure of verbal behavior are in some sense operant, albeit covert, even "preperipheral." It remains to be seen if Skinner's choice of metaphor for the unseen processes underlying syntax was apt. The internal parts of machines rarely resemble their external parts, and so other cognitive theorists (for in this matter Skinner himself must be classed as a cognitive theorist) have opted for other metaphors. Note that "deep structure" and "surface structure" and the whole transformational-generative apparatus make up an extended metaphor, too, insofar as they are claimed to describe psychological processes and not simply to stand as an abstract, formal analysis.

Nativism vs. Environmentalism

The so-called nativist-environmentalist controversy between behaviorists and cognitive theorists is another expression of the different emphases they give to the functional analysis of environmental contingencies of reinforcement versus the invention of models of the organism's internal machinery. The following passage briefly summarizes Chomsky's supposedly nativist view of language learning:

> Consider an acquisition model . . . that uses linguistic data to discover the grammar of the language. . . . Just how the device . . . selects a grammar will be determined by its internal structure, by the methods of analysis available to it, and by the initial constraints that it imposes on any possible grammar. If we are given information about the pairing of linguistic data and grammars, we may try to determine the nature of the device. (1972, p. 119)

This passage appears to rest all the weight of syntactic development on genetically given characteristics of the organism. Yet in a footnote, Chomsky (1965, p. 202) acknowledged that the language-acquisition device's internal structure "might possibly be developed on the basis of deeper innate structure, in ways that depend in part on primary linguistic data and the order and manner in which they are presented." This sounds like learning. Finally, Chomsky drew a distinction between "two functions of external data—the function of initiating or facilitating the operation of innate mechanisms and the function of determining in part the direction that learning will take" (1965, p. 34).

The influence of the organism's "deeper" internal structure on the grammar it "selects" is a matter of Kantian a prioris, the organism's "inescapable characteristics and limitations." Again it should be said that behaviorists (until quite recently) have been amiss in too seldom acknowledging genetic constraints and thus allowing the misconception to be broadcast that behaviorism denies their very existence. On the other hand, Chomskians have been derelict in too seldom mentioning Chomsky's admission that the language-acquisition device's internal structure and functioning might very well evolve under the influence of environmental learning contingencies.

Chomsky's distinction between two functions of external data, that of engaging internal learning and perceptual mechanisms and that of determining the behavioral direction of learning, corresponds approximately to Premack's (1970) distinction between the organism's perceiving environmental events and relations and its learning to map its perceptions verbally. The search for "linguistic universals" through comparison of culturally given "pairing[s] of linguistic data and grammars" then becomes, not a search for the unknowable noumena behind verbal behavior, but a search for functional correlations between environmental contingencies and syntactic behavior—that is, a search for the general characteristics of verbal behavior "ultimately determined by the genetic and ecological universals of a species" (Braine, 1971, p. 185). The search for linguistic universals, in short, is part of the search for general laws of behavior, and surely the physiological constitution of organisms helps to determine the form of such laws. Psycholinguistic theories of linguistic performance modeled after abstract theories of linguistic competence anticipate physiological knowledge by proposing models of neurological functioning in advance of empirical neurological findings. As Salzinger (1975) has noted, behaviorists regard such anticipatory theories as no more necessary than physiological theories of learning in general, but there is no attempt to proscribe physiologizing by those so inclined.

Lashley's Critique

Lashley's (1951) classic paper on the problem of serial order in behavior is often cited by cognitive theorists as posing an unanswerable challenge to a behavioral analysis of language, but in fact Lashley's paper (which is perhaps more widely cited than read) indicts, not behavioral analysis, but simplistic physiologizing in terms of "concepts of the reflex arc, or of associated chains of neurons" (p. 526 in the Beach et al., 1960, reprinting). Skinner has consistently refrained from such simplistic physiologizing, even in his most theoretical discussions of syntax. To quote Lashley further:

> Language presents in a most striking form the integrative functions that are characteristic of the *cerebral cortex*. . . . In spite of the ubiquity of the problem [of serial order] there have been almost no attempts to develop *physiological* theories to meet it. . . . I have chosen to discuss the problem of temporal integration here, not with the expectation of offering a satisfactory *physiological* theory to account for it, but because it seems to me to be both the most important and also the most neglected problem of

cerebral physiology. (in Beach et al., pp. 507-508; italics mine)

In the remainder of the paper Lashley proceeds to describe the problem of syntactic behavior with a perceptiveness befitting a great psychologist. So far from conflicting with Skinner's theory of autoclitic behavior, Lashley's description closely parallels it. (It is not clear which came first, inasmuch as Skinner's William James Lectures on verbal behavior were given at Harvard University in 1947 and widely circulated in mimeographed form thereafter. Questions of priority are hardly relevant in any case.) Continuing from Lashley:

> There are indications that, prior to the internal or overt enunciation of the sentence, an aggregate of word units is partially activated or readied. (p. 512)

Compare Skinner:

> The important properties of verbal behavior which remain to be studied concern special arrangements of responses. Part of the behavior of an organism becomes in turn one of the variables controlling another part. . . . The events available to him as stimuli consist of the products of his own behavior as speaker. He may hear himself or react to private stimuli associated with vocal behavior, *possibly of a covert or even incipient form.* . . . The term "autoclitic" is intended to suggest behavior which is based upon or depends upon other verbal behavior. (1957, pp. 313–315; italics mine)

Also from Skinner:

> The manipulation of verbal behavior, particularly the grouping and ordering of responses, is . . . autoclitic. Responses cannot be grouped or ordered until they have occurred or *at least are about to occur.* (p. 332; italics mine)

Once more from Skinner:

> Much of the self-stimulation required in the autoclitic description and composition of verbal behavior seems to occur *prior to even subaudible emission.* In both written and vocal behavior changes are made on the spur of the moment and so rapidly that *we cannot reasonably attribute them to an actual review of covert forms.* . . . Evidently stimulation associated with the production of verbal behavior is sufficient to enable one to reject a response before it has assumed its final form. The subject is a difficult one because it has all the disadvantages of private stimulation. (p. 371; italics mine)

Now back to Lashley:

> There are at least three sets of events to be accounted for. First, the activation of the expressive elements (the individual words . . .) which do not contain the temporal relations. Second, the determining tendency, the set, or idea. . . . Third, the syntax of the act, which can be described as an habitual order or mode of relating the expressive elements; a generalized pattern or schema of integration which may be imposed upon a wide range and a wide variety of specific acts. This is the essential problem of serial order: the existence of generalized schemata of action which determine the sequence of specific acts (p. 515).

These passages from Skinner and Lashley pose the problems of syntactic behavior almost identically, except for vocabulary differences. It is unclear, therefore, why cognitive theorists approve Lashley's formulation and reject Skinner's. Skinner carefully refrained from speculating about the internal locus and dimensions of autoclitic processes, regarding the organism's physiological machinery as outside his purview. The whole extent of his "physiologizing," if one should call it that, was to assign the status of covert "responses" and "response"-produced "stimulation" to the hypothetical controlling variables immediately responsible for the autoclitic processes that order verbal behavior into surface syntactic structures. Lashley, with his excellent physiological credentials, went much farther and translated the behavioral problems of serial order into problems and hypotheses for neurophysiology. Translations of problems from the vocabulary of one science into the vocabulary of another do not, of course, constitute explanations. So far as I know, the physiological problems Lashley set in 1951 have not yet found solutions.

THE COMPLEMENTARITY OF FUNCTIONAL AND COGNITIVE THEORY

The abiding problem *is* structure. As Lashley noted, problems of temporal structure are not confined to language, but exist everywhere in behavior. Research on operant behavior divides into two broad categories: research on the exteroceptive discriminative stimulus control of operants (which has broad though so far mostly unexploited relevance to the semantics of verbal behavior), and research on the determinants of temporal structure in schedule-generated performances. Ferster and Skinner (1957) devoted a large book to the hypothesis that the temporal structure of schedule-generated performances is at least partially to be explained in terms of stimuluslike processes generated by the organism's own behavior. As they put it, "The primary purpose of the present book is to present a series of experiments designed to evaluate the extent to which the organism's own behavior enters into the determination of its subsequent behavior" (p. 13). Although they did not say so, it seems possible that Skinner's hypothesis of autoclitic processes in syntax motivated Ferster and Skinner's choice of a guiding hypothesis for their extended experimental analyses of schedules of reinforcement.

Research on the temporal structure of operant behavior continues. Recently, Hawkes and Shimp (1975) succeeded in demonstrating that differential contingencies of reinforcement imposed directly on temporal structure were effective in generating the prescribed structure in the key pecking of pigeons. They shaped an "ideal" fixed-interval–like scallop by delivering a reinforcer at the end of a 5-sec trial only if the pattern of responding during the trial approximated constant acceleration. Research on higher-order schedules of reinforcement (e.g., Findley, 1962; Kelleher, 1966) has demonstrated that hierarchically organized behavioral structures, too, are within the operant purview. It is not too much to hope that further research on higher-order schedules will illuminate not only how the structured nonverbal performances generated by first-order schedules become organized into higher-order (hierarchical) structures, but also how the hierarchical structure of verbal behavior comes about.

The Problem of Verbal Structure Stated in Functional Terms

Let us review the problem. The string of verbal responses that makes up the surface of a kernel sentence is hierarchically structured. Kernel sentences can be parsed into two broad constituents, a "subject" and a "predicate." In the kernel sentences of English, the responses constituting the subject constituent are uttered first and responses constituting the predicate constituent second. Speakers must learn these two temporal positions within the sentence. There is evidence (Brown, 1973) that children just entering the mysteries of syntax have in fact learned them (or are in process of learning them). That is, children in "stage 1" of syntactic development, when two-word (or two-morpheme) utterances first appear, tend to utter an "uninflected" unit response interpretable as "subject" followed by an uninflected unit response interpretable as "predicate." (To be sure, the interpretations are generous, but they seem to correspond to the way parents respond to their children's utterances.)

But the subject "noun phrase" can itself be parsed into an (optional) "determiner" (*the, a,* and so on) and an (obligatory) "noun" or "pronoun." In kernel sentences of English, the responses constituting the determiner (if there is one) are uttered first within the subject phrase, and responses constituting the noun are uttered second. Speakers must learn these two temporal positions within the subject constituent; that is, they must learn the "internal structure" of the subject phrase.

The predicate "verb phrase," too, can be parsed into an "auxiliary" (at the least, a "tense marker") and a "verb." In simple kernel sentences of English, the responses constituting the verb are uttered first within the predicate phrase, and the responses constituting tense are uttered as a suffix inflection on the verb. Speakers must learn these two temporal positions within the predicate phrase; that is, they must learn the "internal structure" of the verb phrase. (In standard transformational-generative grammar, the tense marker—and auxiliaries in general—appears before the verb in deep structure. It is moved to verb suffix position in surface structure by a transformation.)

Braine's Functional Experiments on Structure: Temporal Position as a Controlling Variable

The hierarchical structure so far described can be generated by a "binary fractionation" model of phrase structure (Braine, 1963b). First, a "sentence" is divided into two "fractions," subject and predicate, and then each of these two fractions is divided into two fractions, subject becoming determiner plus noun, predicate becoming verb plus auxiliary. Braine presents some sketchy evidence suggesting that speakers may learn syntactic structure of natural languages by iterative binary fractionations rather than by fractionations into, say, thirds of a phrase. That is, his experiments (to be reviewed shortly) suggest that speakers find it easier to learn the "absolute" temporal positions of first vs. last than "relative" temporal positions such as "middle" or "after the first but before the last." Moreover, Braine suggests that the learning of temporal positions in a sentence may be a species of auditory perceptual learning, speakers learning which verbal responses "sound right" in first position and which "sound right" in second position. Having learned which responses sound right in first (subject) position and which sound right in last (predicate) position, speakers then proceed to learn which responses sound right in first vs. last position within the subject phrase and which sound right in first vs. last position within the predicate phrase. Thus the learning of hierarchical structure might unfold a binary fractionation at a time.

Braine's (1963a) ingenious experiments involved the echoic or textual teaching of miniature artificial languages (devoid of "semantic content") to children between the ages of 4 and 11 years. In Experiment I (A&P language with word constituents), the experimenter presented "sentence frames" with either the anterior (A) or posterior (P) position already filled by a nonsense-syllable word from the A-class or the P-class, respectively. The experimenter also presented two choice words, one from the A-class and one from the P-class, from which the children had to choose one word to fill in the blank position in the sentence frame. Correct completions were reinforced with poker chips backed up with candy; incorrect completions were simply corrected by the experimenter. In either case, a learning trial terminated with the subject, and then the experimenter, reading aloud the correctly completed two-word sentence. In this way, the children learned what words constituted the A-class (what words were permissible completions of a blank in first position) and what words constituted the P-class (what words were permissible completions of a blank second position). As a test of generative syntax, the experimenter then presented sentence frames in which a *novel* A- or P-word occupied first or last position, respectively, and the child had to complete the frames by choosing the correct one of two offered words, one a familiar A-word and the other a familiar P-word. Because the supplied words in the test sentences were novel, they provided no intraverbal cues to correct completions. The only available cues, then, were the *positions of the blanks* in the test sentence frames. Subjects 9 and 10 years old completed 78% of the test problems correctly, showing that they had learned the A- and P-classes on the basis of temporal position within the sentence and that temporal position was a sufficient intraverbal stimulus controlling productive choice of an A- or P-word. In a replication of the experiment adapted for 4-year-old children (Experiment V), 75% of the test sentence frames were completed correctly, showing that the intraverbal learning called for was within the reach of younger children.

In another experiment (Experiment IV), 9- and 10-year-old children learned the same artificial language in the same way, except that before making their final completion choices for each sentence frame the children were required to say aloud *both* sentence completions, the incorrect one produced by putting an A-word in a blank P-position or a P-word in a blank A-position, and the correct one produced by putting an A-word in A-position or a P-word in P-position. Then the children were permitted to make their own completion choices, and they were told whether their completions were correct or not, but they were not permitted to read their final completions aloud. By this procedure Braine attempted to equate *auditory* exposure (actually, echoic practice) with correct and incorrect sentences. This experiment did not include a test of generative syntax. Nevertheless, the results from the learning trials themselves were instructive. Whereas all children in the standard Experiments I and V learned to complete the training sentences correctly within a median of 10.5 or 13 trials, respectively, and while making a median of only 4 or 4.5 errors, respectively, some children in Experiment IV did not meet the learning criterion within the allotted number of trials (50), the median trials to criterion was 32, and the median errors to criterion was 9. Braine concluded that in Experiments I and V "the relevant cue was the temporal position in the spoken sentence, and as learning progressed words . . . came to sound familiar in the positions in which they recurred. The subjects [of Experiments I and V] were then able to respond correctly in generalization problems by picking the alternative which made the sentence [literally] 'sound right' " (1963a, p. 335).

Another experiment (Experiment II: A&P language with phrase constituents) investigated whether learning would be impaired if the response elements constituting A- and P-classes were sometimes two-word phrases instead of single words. With one group of 9- and 10-year-old children, a whole (one- or two-word) phrase was left blank in the sentence frame, and children completed the frame by choosing between a one- or two-word A-phrase and a one- or two-word P-phrase. (No cues indicated whether the frame called for a one- or two-word completion.) With a second group of subjects, only the second word of a two-word A-phrase was missing in the sentence frame, or only the first word of a two-word P-phrase was missing. Thus the completed sentences were two, three, or four words long, and the blanks were in first, second, or third position in the frame. In this group, then, temporal position controlling the formation of A-classes and P-classes and cuing correct sentence completions was not "absolute" first vs. last position (with phrase constituents), but "relative" position (a P-word was called for after an A-word or phrase and before the last word of the P-phrase, or an A-word was called for before a P-word or phrase and after the first word of the A-phrase; the missing constituents were words, not phrases). Subjects in the first group, learning whole-phrase constituents under control of absolute first or last position in the sentence, performed as well as subjects in the standard Experiments I and V, who learned single-word constituents in absolute first or last position. However, subjects in the second group, learning part-phrase (word) constituents under control of relative temporal position in the sentence, showed markedly inferior performances. The results of this experiment led Braine to conclude that absolute first vs. last position is more easily learned than relative position, and therefore that the learning of syntactic structure should proceed more easily by iterative *binary* building up of a sentence into its hierarchical structure.

In the remaining experiment of this series (Experiment III: A&PQ and AB&P languages), Braine (1963a) investigated whether comparably simple procedures would enable 9- to 11-year-old subjects to learn the "internal structure" of phrases. Half the subjects learned the A&PQ language, and half learned the AB&P language, its mirror image. Only the A&PQ language will be described. The A-class in this language consisted of one- or two-word phrases, but each phrase was invariant in composition, so that terms in the A-class had no internal structure. The PQ-class consisted of two subclasses, the p-class and the q-class. Any word from the p-class could be combined with any word from the q-class, yielding internal structure $p_i q_i$. A sentence consisted of the following sequence: (phrase from the A-class) [(word from the p-class) (word from the q-class)]. During learning, children completed sentence frames by filling in a whole A-phrase or a whole PQ-phrase (of varying internal structure). Next, a "between-phrase" generalization test was given. Sentence frames were presented containing *novel* A-phrases (with the PQ-position blank) or *novel* PQ-phrases (with the A-position blank), and children were offered a choice between a familiar A-phrase and a familiar PQ-phrase to complete the frame. Again, the novelty of the supplied A- and PQ-phrases precluded the children's completing the between-phrase generalization sentences on the basis of simple intraverbal phrase cues. Only the *position of the blank* in the sentence frame indicated which choice was correct. After the between-phrase generalization test children practiced again completing familiar sentence frames with familiar A- and PQ-phrases.

Then the children were given a "within-phrase" generalization test. Sentence frames were presented containing a familiar A-phrase and a *novel* p- or q-word. The frames thus lacked only one word (in p- or q-position). Subjects were given three, instead of two, familiar alternative words to choose from ("because there were three parts of speech"—Braine, 1963a, p. 331), a familiar A-word (or phrase), a familiar p-word, and a familiar q-word.

All subjects in Experiment III reached the initial learning criterion in a number of trials comparable to, and with fewer errors than, the subjects in Experiments I, II, and V. In the between-phrase generalization test they completed 74% of the novel test frames correctly, and in the within-phrase generalization test they completed 68% of the novel test frames correctly, percentages comparable to those obtained in the generalization tests of Experiment I. Taken together, these results showed that children learned concurrently both the A- and PQ-phrase structure of the sentences (the "higher-order" structure corresponding to subject-predicate) and the internal structure of the PQ-phrases (the "lower-order" structure corresponding to the internal structure of a verb phrase, say). Both words within phrases and phrases within sentences "tend to become associated with the sentence positions in which they recur, . . . [and] within fairly wide limits, the constitution of the elements in first and last position is not an important variable for either learning or generalization" (Braine, 1963a, p. 333).

Braine summed up the results of these five experiments as follows:

> (a) "What is learned" are the locations of expressions in utterances. (b) Units (i.e., expressions whose position is learned) can form a hierarchy in which longer units contain shorter units as parts, the location that is learned being the location of a unit within the next-larger containing unit, up to the sentence. (c) The learning is a case of perceptual learning—a process of becoming familiar with the sounds of expressions in the positions in which they recur. (1963a, p. 337)

The learning of the temporal positions of words and phrases, moreover, appears to be

> a process of auditory differentiation. . . . Perceptual learning is usually assumed to be a rather primitive process and there is therefore no reason to suppose that it demands much in the way of intellectual capacity in the learner. Learning of this sort would therefore satisfy at least one requirement of any process postulated

to be involved in first language learning, namely, that it not require intellectual capacities obviously beyond the reach of the 2-year-old. (1963a, p. 326)

"Primitive process" or not, the temporal control of behavior is familiar territory to operant behaviorists (Catania, 1970; Dews, 1970; Jenkins, 1970; Killeen, 1975; Morse, 1966; Staddon, 1972; Weiss, 1970). What is perhaps less familiar is Braine's important insight that temporal position in a sentence constitutes a strong intraverbal variable controlling syntactic word order. In a later experiment Braine (1965a) showed that *middle* temporal position in a spoken sentence string (aXb, pXq) also serves as an intraverbal variable controlling the formation of a response class (of X-words). In this case, however, temporal position was not the only controlling intraverbal stimulus, for X-words generalized to novel a__b and p__q contexts, but not (to any considerable extent) to "anomalous" a__q and p__b contexts. In other words, the intraverbally linked classes a__b and p__q combined with middle position to determine the generative appearance of X-words. This kind of combined control is what Skinner (1957) termed "multiple causation" and which is otherwise familiar to behaviorists as conditional discrimination.[2]

In still other experiments, Braine (1971) pursued

---

[2] I think all of Skinner's (1957) discussion of the multiple causation of verbal behavior can be most easily understood in terms of conditional discriminations. Conditional discriminations, reflecting the concerted influence of at least two discriminative stimuli, have the general form: Given stimulus *A*, response 1 will be reinforced conditionally on the presence of stimulus *B*, but response 2 will be reinforced conditionally on the presence of stimulus *C*. Then, knowing that stimulus *A* was present, one could predict that either response 1 or response 2 would be emitted, but not which one. Knowing, additionally, that stimulus *B* was present, one could more confidently predict response 1, while knowing that stimulus *C* was present (rather than *B*), one could more confidently predict response 2. For example, if stimulus *A* were "Give me a word beginning with *m*," then the response "Marie" would be likely in the presence of the additional instruction, "which is the first name of a scientist who received Nobel Prizes in both physics and chemistry"; but the response "mother" would be likely in the presence of the additional instruction, "which rhymes with *brother*."

The point about multiple causation is that any single controlling variable typically raises the probability of a whole class of verbal responses, as "Give me a word beginning with *m*" by itself raises the probability of "Marie," "mother," and all other verbal responses, beginning with *m*, that happen to be current in the speaker's repertoire. Lacking other information, it would be impossible to predict which response from the class a speaker would utter. But if one knew all the variables controlling each response in a speaker's verbal repertoire, it would be theoretically possible to predict exactly what the speaker would say next on any occasion, as "Give me a word beginning with *m*—and rhyming with *brother*" zeroes in on just a single item.

---

the intraverbal control of syntactic structure in more elaborate artificial languages (which were still, it should be noted, devoid of "semantic content" or, in other words, contributions from the nonverbal stimulus control that defines the tact). He instructed adult subjects to echo to spoken strings of nonsense words having the structures p(Af)(Bg) and (Bg)q(Af)r, where p marked a sentence type (analogous, say, to a declarative sentence marker), and q r marked a different sentence type (analogous, say, to an interrogative sentence marker–"Wh " words, for example). (Af) and (Bg) were sentence constituents with internal structure, f and g being fixed elements (analogous to Braine's earlier—e.g., 1963b—notion of a "pivot" class) and A and B being word classes with several members each (analogous to Braine's 1963b notion of an "open" class). In this more elaborate language, the internal structure of elements within Af and Bg phrases was presumably controlled by temporal position within the phrases, but the larger structure of constituents within the sentence was presumably controlled jointly by temporal position within the sentence and by the more familiar kind of intraverbal stimulus, the "word" elements p and q__r. (Note that q__r forms a "discontinuous" intraverbal stimulus—Braine, 1965b.)

An interesting feature of Braine's (1971) experiment with the more elaborate language is that he induced one group of subjects to echo not only "well-formed" strings but also "anomalous" strings. One type of anomalous string consisted of "first-order approximations" to the grammatical language (random orders of up to six elements, where, over the set of anomalous strings, the frequency of each element was proportional to its frequency in the well-formed corpus). A second type of anomalous string consisted of "third-order approximations" to the language (strings of 3–11 elements consisting of "running triads" from the well-formed sentences of the language). Together these two types of anomalous strings made up 7% of all the strings to which the experimental subjects were exposed (and which they were asked to echo). Control subjects were exposed to (and asked to echo) only well-formed strings. Recognition tests, sentence-completion tests, and "word-association" ("lexical class") tests (asking the subject to pick out from a written vocabulary list all the words that "went with" f and all words that "went with" g) indicated that experimental subjects had learned the syntactic structure of the language as well as had control subjects, in spite of the diversionary anomalous strings which experimentals had been required to echo. The immunity of the experimental subjects to deleterious effects of echoing a corpus that included 7% anomalous strings led Braine to suggest that the "degenerate" or ill-formed sentences and sentence fragments to which children may be exposed in the course of learning their natural languages need not be thought necessarily to interfere with the development of control over children's syntactic behavior by the regular intraverbal variables in the linguistic corpora to which they are exposed (and which they probably echo, at least in part and covertly). He suggests, quite plausibly, that the intraverbal regularities (both those of temporal position and those of intraverbal word linkages) are more than enough to override the distraction of "degenerate" speech samples.

Intraverbal Contributions to Syntax

Braine's (1971) paper is worth close study for the further plausible suggestions he makes concerning the course of development of intraverbal syntactic control, including the control of inflections. For example, he notes that some intraverbal regularities may be more frequent, more consistent, and simpler, and hence may more quickly acquire a controlling role in the child's syntactic behavior than do other intraverbal variables. If that is so, the aspects of syntactic behavior controlled by these variables should appear earlier in children's speech, resulting in what Whitehurst and Vasta (1975) have called "selective imitation." Moreover, these intraverbal variables might provide a sort of "seed" around which more complex intraverbal control could "grow," rather like a crystal (see Robinson, Chapter 21 in this volume). That is, once the children were responding reliably to the simpler intraverbal variables, they might begin to come under the control of further intraverbal regularities between them and more subtle intraverbal stimuli.

Autoclitic Contributions to Syntax

Intraverbal control cannot provide a complete account of syntactic structure, however powerful it proves to be as an explanatory principle. As Braine (1963a) noted, for example, it will not account for "contrastive" word order. For example, there is nothing in the intraverbal variables to account for the contrastive word orders of "Boy bites dog" vs. "Dog bites boy." The nonverbal variables controlling the tact are importantly involved here, and it is here that the autoclitic hypothesis becomes most useful. By autoclitic hypothesis I mean the hypothesis that external nonverbal and verbal stimuli combine with private "stimuli" generated by covert or incipient verbal responses to determine a public verbal response. (Strictly speaking, only the private variables are the autoclitic contribution to syntactic verbal behavior, but the full power of the autoclitic concept depends on multiple causation—the combined action of many determinants at once, only one of which is privately generated.)

Segal (1975b) pointed out the approximate correspondence between the grammatical account of syntax in terms of deep structure vs. surface structure and the behavioral account in terms of verbal primitives vs. autoclitics. According to transformational-generative theory, the terms in deep structure are not unordered strings but rather are structured in ways that reflect basic grammatical relations (subject-predicate and so on), basic semantic relations (actor-action and so on), and complex interrelations among these (e.g., semantic-syntactic constraints on "animate" grammatical-semantic subjects with "inanimate" grammatical-semantic objects, such as those proscribing the string "The boy may frighten sincerity"). According to autoclitic theory, also (Skinner, 1957, pp. 332–333), there is some basic order among the verbal primitives. This "primitive order" reflects variously (1) phonological processes responsible for meaningful sequences of phonemes; (2) intraverbal order ("A 'train of thought' in free association follows the order in which verbal stimuli evoke other verbal responses"—Skinner, 1957, p. 333); (3) the overall, long-standing probability of verbal responses in the speaker's repertoire (perhaps, but not necessarily, mirroring the relative frequencies of "words" in the "language"); (4) the momentary probability of responses reflecting (a) the momentary salience of particular environmental variables, (b) the temporal order of the environmental variables (what Robinson, in his chapter in this volume, calls "iconic" structure), and (c) the momentary (contingent) arrangement of environmental variables into specific combinations and relations (other than sheerly temporal arrangements).

This first-order structure, supplied by the overall organization of the speaker's verbal repertoire (items 1, 2, and 3, above) and the structure of the environment itself ("semantic" items 4a, b, and c, above), is still "agrammatical." The grammatical structuring occurs when the primitively structured responses call into play autoclitic processes. Skinner would say the verbal primitives function as verbal stimuli evoking intraverbal (autoclitic) responses. Consider "Boy bites dog":

1. A semantic relation among the events in the environment (the boy is doing something), function-

ing as a second-order tact variable, in combination with the covert availability of the verbal primitive (tact) "boy," functioning as one kind of intraverbal variable, and position within the utterance, functioning as another kind of intraverbal variable, together determine the ordering of the response "boy" in first (subject) position in "deep structure."

2. Two additional semantic relations among the events in the environment (the actor of the action is singular, the action is occurring now), function as second-order tact variables jointly evoking -s.

3. The covert availability of two verbal (tact) primitives *bite* and *-s*, functioning as intraverbal variables, in combination with the semantic relations just mentioned (the actor is singular, the action is ongoing), functioning as tact variables, determine the autoclitic ordering of the primitives as *bites*. (This step is separated from step 2 because, one must suppose, *-s* cannot be ordered until it is available. Nevertheless, the semantic relations mentioned in step 2 as controlling the availability of *-s* must be mentioned again in step 3 to account for the fact that *-s* gets suffixed to *bite* and not to *boy* or *dog*.)

4. The covert availability of the autoclitically ordered "response pair" *bites*, functioning as an intraverbal variable, in combination with the semantic relation between the boy and the biting, functioning as a second-order tact variable, and with temporal position in the utterance, functioning as another sort of intraverbal variable, together determine the ordering of the response pair *bites* in second (predicate verb) position in the utterance.

5. The semantic relation between the biting and the dog, functioning as a second-order tact variable, together with the covert availability of the tact primitive *dog*, functioning as an intraverbal variable, and temporal position within the utterance, functioning as another intraverbal variable, together determine the ordering of the response *dog* in third (predicate object) position in the utterance. The final result is "Boy bites dog." (I have not included determiners in this analysis. For a perceptive discussion of the complex combination of intraverbal and tact variables controlling the English articles *the* and *a*, see Brown, 1973).

The Isomorphism of Autoclitic and Transformational Theories

At what point does deep structure turn into surface structure? For the functional behaviorist, the answer is simply when the responses are uttered publicly. Transformational-generative grammarians cannot accept such an answer, however, because for them the terms in deep structure are not covert verbal responses. They are dummy terms representing semantic and syntactic "features." For cognitive theorists, these features are simple "ideas" in the modality (whatever it may be) of mentalese. The particular collection of features that makes up a single dummy term (or "complex symbol" in Chomsky, 1965) represents a first-order complex "idea," and the organization of dummy terms that makes up a single deep structure represents, so to say, a higher-order complex "idea." Functionally these features can be construed as the independent variables (nonverbal and verbal) that determine the tacts and intraverbals of the autoclitic analysis, and in the autoclitic analysis these variables directly determine verbal responses (although the determination is complex). But in grammatical theory, even if the uttered sentence is a kernel sentence, certain basic transformations are called for before the dummy terms (ideas) in deep structure become realized as words. The speakers must dip into their "lexicon" to find "formatives" that match exactly the particular collections of semantic and syntactic features assigned to the dummy terms in deep structure. Then the speakers must dip into their "morphophonemic rule book" to transform the formatives into their realized sound sequences, words.

Despite the different ways behaviorists and grammarians talk about these matters, it seems that they equally recognize the same complex set of variables, and equally recognize the necessity for a complex analysis of how the variables combine to determine utterances. I do not think it matters a great deal whether one employs the terms "deep structure" and "surface structure," or the terms "primitive verbal responses" and "autoclitically modified verbal responses" to describe an important distinction between controlling variables in the external environment and controlling variables generated by covert processes within the speaker. I do not think it matters a great deal whether one assigns "abstract semantic and syntactic features" to "dummy terms in deep structure" (which must then be transformed through "lexical and morphophonemic rules" into "words"), or whether one regards the "nonverbal and intraverbal variables" as determining the final, uttered string of "verbal responses" through one continuous (but complex) "autoclitic behavioral process" occurring in real time. Both the behaviorist's and the grammarian's accounts of utterances are hypothetical (and metaphoric), and yet nothing less than their intricate, *but isomorphic,* hypothetical accounts seems to account for the complexities of syntax.

MacCorquodale (1969) briefly summarized the

theoretical assumptions underlying autoclitic theory. As he put it, the plausibility of the theory

> depends upon one's being able to accept the notion that a speaker can respond discriminatively to (1) what he is *about* to say; . . . (2) *why* he is about to say it; and (3) *how strong* the [covert or incipient] operant is. (p. 840; italics his)

MacCorquodale went on to argue:

> The discriminations concern complex relations between speech and its causes, and they are very rapid. In this respect it is important not to relapse into conceiving of discrimination as a separate prebehavioral *act*. Ordering *is* discriminative behavior, not the result of it, so that the complex discriminations in autoclitic behavior need not be allotted prebehavioral time. . . . The situation that strengthens the tacts *the, boy* and *runs* also contains the relation that determines the order of their emission as *the boy runs*. If I am correct in this, autoclitic behavior is not, strictly speaking, controlled by other behavior, but by other operants. There is a difference. (p. 840; italics his)

In the second passage, as I understand it, MacCorquodale is suggesting that we regard as merely metaphoric Skinner's references to incipient *responses* and *stimulation* arising from incipient responses. These metaphors simply represent the combined effects of multiple tact and intraverbal variables controlling syntactic behavior.

"Prebehavioral time" may or may not reflect psychological reality, but it is not an issue distinguishing an autoclitic account of syntactic behavior from any other account of the complex three-term contingencies determining operant behavior. There need be no more (or less) "prebehavioral time" involved in the temporal structuring of syntactic behavior than in the temporal structuring of, say, the fixed-interval scallop. Nevertheless, in both syntax and the fixed-interval scallop, the organism's earlier behavior is said by Skinner to function as a controlling variable contributing to the determination of succeeding behavior. If intraverbal variables, and not only tact variables, control autoclitics, then, metaphoric or not, incipient verbal responses seem to play an important role in the theory of the autoclitic.

An Appraisal of the Autoclitic

The autoclitic is an orphan nobody wants. Behaviorists have not wanted to claim it because they (rightly, I think, despite MacCorquodale's disclaimer) sensed its cognitive tendencies. Cognitive theorists have not wanted to claim it because of its behavioristic parentage—and for another reason, it must be said: they have a richer, more fully developed version of the same idea in the theory of transformational-generative grammar. The autoclitic was a serious attempt to grapple with the difficult problems of syntactic structure and the evident need to distinguish between something akin to deep structure and something akin to surface structure, while remaining as close as the problem permitted to the concepts and language of behaviorism. Verbal behavior *is* operant behavior, a product of the three-term contingent relation among behavior and antecedent and consequent environmental events. It turns out, though, that a full description, functional or cognitive, of syntactic verbal behavior requires the postulation of hypothetical processes within the organism, mediating between environmental "input" and response "output." There is simply no gainsaying this.

Perhaps it is time for the hypothesis of the autoclitic to give way to more sophisticated analyses of syntactic processes. Nevertheless, its place in the history of the psychology of language is an honorable one. Its lasting contribution is the insistence that syntax is the result of a complex blend of variables, at least some of which (the variables determining tact and intraverbal responses) have familiar or conceivable dimensions. It may be that current attempts within linguistics (associated with the term *generative semantics*) to incorporate semantic variables within the determinants of deep structure may profit from a study of Skinner's perceptive theorizing in the autoclitic framework. "The speaker is the organism which engages in or executes verbal behavior. He is also a locus—a place in which a number of variables come together in a unique confluence to yield an equally unique achievement" (Skinner, 1957, p. 313).

PARAPHRASE, THE PROBLEMATIC LISTENER, AND MENTALESE

Skinner's functional account of verbal behavior was deficient in its neglect of the listener. *Verbal Behavior* contains few serious references to the problems of verbal comprehension, and what references there are are mostly unsatisfactory. To a large extent Skinner shrugged off problems of accounting for how listeners learn to understand verbal stimuli as ordinary problems of discrimination, amenable to simple operant analysis and not requiring the special treatment he devoted to the behavior of the speaker. "Much of the behavior of the listener has no resemblance to the behavior of the speaker and is not verbal according to our definition. . . . The behavior of a person as listener is not to be distinguished from other forms of his behavior" (Skinner, 1957, pp. 33–34).

If the verbal stimuli to which the listener responds are extremely simple, if their temporal arrangement is "iconic" (Robinson, chapter 21 in this volume), or if the listener's only role is as an assiduous supplier of goods and services for the speaker's pleasure (his or her role as reinforcement mediator), this account is unobjectionable. Problems arise, however, when the listener is called upon to paraphrase, to translate freely from one language into another, or to understand "a fairly difficult paper . . . in the field of scientific and philosophic discourse" (Skinner, 1957, p. 278). Here the listener becomes, for Skinner, another speaker. The listener can properly say he or she understands a difficult verbal passage, having complex syntactic structure, "only when he can emit corresponding behavior *such as might occur . . . in response to nonverbal or intraverbal stimuli*" (1957, pp. 277–278; italics mine). The problem of paraphrase is central, then. And Skinner does not handle the problem of paraphrase very satisfactorily, it seems to me. The listener can paraphrase

> only after he has *identified the variables* which were mainly effective [in evoking the original speaker's utterance]. . . .
>
> It is . . . difficult to say what happens when [a person paraphrases or] listens to a passage in one language and restates it in another. The case is often offered as showing the need for some such concept as "idea" or "proposition," since something common to two or more languages [or, in the case of paraphrase, two or more utterances in the same language] appears to account for their interchangeability. . . . To say that [the listener] emits behavior which is controlled by the *variables which he infers* to have been responsible for [the original speaker's verbal behavior] . . . is . . . elliptical. (1957, pp. 280, 78; italics mine)

It is indeed elliptical. Skinner wanted to avoid positing what Pylyshyn (1973) has called "abstract propositional knowledge" and Fodor et al. (1974) have called "formulas in mentalese." This is what "lies behind" and "motivates" deep structure in cognitive grammatical theory. Rather evasively, Skinner suggests that

> verbal behavior in one language may give rise to private events within the individual which he may then describe in another language. . . . In giving the gist of what one has read in a book or heard someone else describe, in the same or a different language, the speaker is often concerned with generating behavior having the same effect upon himself.
>
> [The listener-speaker] tries out a [paraphrase], comparing the effects of the two versions upon himself and changing the [paraphrase] until the effects are roughly the same. But this does not account for the behavior which he thus compares. (1957, pp. 198, 78).

The "behavior which he thus compares" is the listener's reaction to another's utterance and the listener's reaction to the self-generated paraphrase, but the nature of this listener reaction is never specified, beyond the suggestion that it may consist of "private events." In other words, listeners infer the speakers' "semantic intentions" or "deep structure" or the "variables controlling the speaker's utterance" by consulting their own private responses to the utterance. From these, somehow, the listener constructs a paraphrase having the same private effects on themselves. To the extent that the listeners succeed in this, they may be said, "elliptically," to have inferred the variables that controlled the speakers' utterances.

Consider a concrete example. Premack (1970) described a match-to-sample experiment with his chimpanzee, Sarah, in which she was required to give a "features analysis" of an apple. With the apple present as sample, she had to choose, between pairs of comparison stimuli, those comparison stimuli that roughly matched the visual features of the apple. The pairs of comparison stimuli were: "a red plaque *vs* a green one; a square plaque *vs* a round one; a square plaque with a stem-like protuberance *vs* a plain square one; and a square plaque with protuberance *vs* a plain round one" (p. 123). After Sarah had given her features analysis of the apple, she was required to do another features analysis, but this time with the word *apple* rather than a real apple as sample stimulus. The two features analyses were identical (Premack, 1970, Table 1, p. 124). With the word as sample stimulus, she chose between pairs of comparison stimuli those features that match the visual features of an apple, not the visual features of the piece of blue plastic that functioned in Sarah's language as the word "apple." One might say Sarah "paraphrased" the word "apple" by indicating some of the physical features of an apple.

The only account I can offer of Sarah's success at this task is to suppose that the apple and the word *apple* evoked similar private "listener reactions" in Sarah. Perhaps they both evoked a private visual image of an apple, or perhaps both activated some more "abstract propositional" form in which her "knowledge" about apples was "stored." Many cognitive theorists (e.g., Fodor et al., 1974; Pylyshyn, 1973) suggest that central "storage" of "abstract propositional knowledge"—perhaps more or less directly in a form representing a features analysis—is more plausible than to suppose that all such instances of "paraphrase" are based on perceptual imagery in some covert peripheral modality.

Experiments such as Premack's (1970) seem to offer strong justification for regarding the terms underlying deep structure as having some more abstract status than covert verbal responses. Psycholinguistic research on paraphrase and on verbal comprehension generally (e.g., Gleitman & Gleitman, 1970; Johnson-Laird, 1974) suggests that listeners understand utterances, as they appear in surface structures, by inferring their underlying deep structures or the variables underlying deep structures. These represent, equivalently, abstract propositional knowledge, semantic intentions, private listener responses, or the antecedent variables (motivational, verbal, nonverbal) controlling verbal behavior. This, in a roundabout way, seems to be what Skinner intended in his discussions of paraphrase, translation, and understanding.

MORE ON THE COMPLEMENTARITY OF FUNCTIONAL AND COGNITIVE THEORIES

We come full circle back to problems of accounting for the behavior of the speaker, problems of speech production. For both cognitive theorists and Skinner, problems of speech production and speech reception are inextricably intertwined because, in any but the most simple comprehension problems, the listener must function simultaneously as a speaker in order to function at all. The theoretical problem is to identify the determinants *behind* deep structure (behind primitive verbal behavior), for these determine both what a speaker says and how a listener understands a speaker's utterances. Here are cognitive statements of the problem:

> Common sense invites the view that what happens in speech production is this: a speaker starts with a message he wants to communicate. . . . But what sort of thing is a "message"? And are we not begging the question of how a speaker chooses to utter a linguistic form if we say that the choice is contingent upon an (unexplained) previous choice of a message to communicate? . . . Nevertheless, it seems to us that there is much to be said for the old-fashioned view that speech expresses thought. . . .
>
> It seems reasonably clear that there are cases in which . . . thinking consists in merely saying to oneself bits of natural language which one might equally well have said aloud. The rehearsal which often goes on in short-term memory tasks . . . is a persuasive example, . . . and it is not implausible that some of the thinking that goes on in problem solving might consist in saying to oneself sentences or sentence fragments in one's language. . . .
>
> But . . . it seems quite clear that underlying many mental capacities, there must be computational processes which are carried out in codes other than natural languages. The computations underlying problem solving and the integration of percepts and motor gestures in nonverbal organisms must be of this kind. . . .
>
> We are, in effect, commending a view of the cognitive organization of organisms which borrows heavily from the actual organization of multipurpose computers. Such devices typically perform their computations in an "internal" language which may be quite different from the languages in which they accept their inputs and encode their outputs. (Fodor, Bever, & Garrett, 1974, pp. 374–377)
>
> Questions about the character of mentalese, however hopelessly metaphysical they may at first appear, are not entirely beyond the reach of the combined methodologies of psychology and linguistics: we can imagine data which would bear directly on such questions. . . . (Fodor et al., 1974, p. 383)

These passages illustrate a point made earlier in this chapter, that cognitive theorists focus on the hypothetical "computing" processes that must be occurring within the organism whenever complex environmental "input" variables lead to complex response "outputs." Research on artificial intelligence and computer simulation of complex "cognitive behavior" seems to hold great promise as a means of illuminating the character of (or at least delimiting the possibilities for) such hypothetical processes. (For an excellent and persuasive argument, see Turner, 1971.) Behavior theorists interested in language and other complex behavior would profit from a greater familiarity with this information-theoretic approach.

On the other hand, cognitive theorists would profit from a greater familiarity with behavioral research on the role of complex environmental variables in operant behavior. As behaviorists have been amiss in ignoring the contributions of information theorists, so cognitive theorists have been amiss in minimizing the role of environmental factors in complex behavior. Not all the determinants of cognitive behavior are within the organism, out of direct reach of experimental analysis. Psycholinguists seem not to be aware of the rich literature on stimulus control of operant behavior and the effects of complex reinforcement contingencies, a literature which would go a long way toward explaining the origins of the semantic and pragmatic aspects of verbal behavior, and which undoubtedly has relevance as well to the syntax of verbal behavior.

Psychology seems to be maturing, at last, into a science. The balkanization of psychology into doctrinaire schools, each with its separate language spoken only by initiates, is giving way to a unified conception of problems, methods, and theories. If this chapter persuades a few cognitive theorists and behaviorists to venture out from their partisan positions and join forces in grappling with the difficult problems of language, it will have succeeded in its aim.

REFERENCES

Asch, S. E. Reformulation of the problem of association. *American Psychologist,* 1969, *24,* 92–102.

Ayllon, T., & Azrin, N. H. Reinforcer sampling: A technique for increasing the behavior of mental patients. *Journal of Applied Behavior Analysis,* 1968, *1,* 13–20.

Beach, F. A., Hebb, D. O., Morgan, C. T., & Nissen, H. W. (Eds.). *The neuropsychology of Lashley.* New York: McGraw-Hill, 1960.

Braine, M. D. S. On learning the grammatical order of words. *Psychological Review,* 1963, *70,* 323–348. (a)

Braine, M. D. S. The ontogeny of English phrase structure: The first phase. *Language,* 1963, *39,* 1–13. (b)

Braine, M. D. S. The insufficiency of a finite state model for verbal reconstructive memory. *Psychonomic Science,* 1965, *2,* 291–292. (a)

Braine, M. D. S. On the basis of phrase structure: A reply to Bever, Fodor, and Weksel. *Psychological Review,* 1965, *72,* 483–492. (b)

Braine, M. D. S. On two types of models of the internalization of grammars. In D. I. Slobin (Ed.), *The ontogenesis of grammar.* New York: Academic Press, 1971.

Brown, R. *A first language: The early stages.* Cambridge: Harvard University Press, 1973.

Carter, A. L. The transformation of sensorimotor morphemes into words: A case study of the development of "here" and "there." Paper presented at the Stanford Child Language Research Forum, April 1975.

Catania, A. C. Reinforcement schedules and psychophysical judgments: A study of some temporal properties of behavior. In W. N. Schoenfeld (Ed.), *The theory of reinforcement schedules.* Englewood Cliffs, N.J.: Prentice-Hall, Inc., 1970.

Catania, A. C. Chomsky's formal analysis of natural languages: A behavioral translation. *Behaviorism,* 1972, *1,* 1–15.

Catania, A. C. The psychologies of structure, function, and development. *American Psychologist,* 1973, *28,* 434–443.

Chomsky, N. *Syntactic structures.* The Hague: Mouton, 1957.

Chomsky, N. *Verbal behavior* by B. F. Skinner. *Language,* 1959, *35,* 26–58.

Chomsky, N. *Aspects of the theory of syntax.* Cambridge: MIT Press, 1965.

Clark, E. V. What's in a word? On the child's acquisition of semantics in his first language. In T. E. Moore (Ed.), *Cognitive development and the acquisition of language.* New York: Academic Press, 1973.

Dews, P. B. The theory of fixed-interval responding. In W. N. Schoenfeld (Ed.), *The theory of reinforcement schedules.* Englewood Cliffs, N.J.: Prentice-Hall, Inc., 1970.

Ervin-Tripp, S. Some strategies for the first two years. In T. E. Moore (Ed.), *Cognitive development and the acquisition of language.* New York: Academic Press, 1973.

Farwell, C. Aspects of early verb semantics: Precausitive development. Paper presented at the Stanford Child Language Research Forum, April 1975.

Ferster, C. B., & Skinner, B. F. *Schedules of reinforcement.* New York: Appleton-Century-Crofts, 1957.

Findley, J. D. An experimental outline for building and exploring multioperant behavior repertoires. *Journal of the Experimental Analysis of Behavior,* 1962, *5,* supplement, 113–166.

Fodor, J. A., Bever, T. G., & Garrett, M. F. *The psychology of language.* New York: McGraw-Hill, 1974.

Garcia, E., Guess, D., & Byrnes, J. Development of syntax in a retarded girl using procedures of imitation, reinforcement, and modelling. *Journal of Applied Behavior Analysis,* 1973, *6,* 299–310.

Gardner, B. T., & Gardner, R. A. Two-way communication with an infant chimpanzee. In A. Schrier (Ed.), *Behavior of non-human primates* (Vol. 4). New York: Academic Press, 1971.

Gardner, R. A., & Gardner, B. T. Teaching sign language to a chimpanzee. *Science,* 1969, *165,* 664–672.

Gardner, R. A., & Gardner, B. T. Early signs of language in child and chimpanzee. *Science,* 1975, *187,* 752–753.

Gleitman, L. R., & Gleitman, H. *Phrase and paraphrase.* New York: Norton, 1970.

Guess, D. A functional analysis of receptive language and productive speech: Acquisition of the plural morpheme. *Journal of Applied Behavior Analysis,* 1969, *2,* 55–64.

Guess, D., & Baer, D. M. An analysis of individual differences in generalization between receptive and productive language in retarded children. *Journal of Applied Behavior Analysis,* 1973, *6,* 311–329.

Guess, D., Sailor, W., Rutherford, G., & Baer, D. M. An experimental analysis of linguistic development: The productive use of the plural morpheme. *Journal of Applied Behavior Analysis,* 1968, *1,* 297–306.

HAWKES, L., & SHIMP, C. P. Reinforcement of behavioral patterns: Shaping a scallop. *Journal of the Experimental Analysis of Behavior,* 1975, *23,* 3–16.

HILGARD, E. R., & BOWER, G. H. *Theories of learning.* Englewood Cliffs, N.J.: Prentice-Hall, Inc., 1975.

JENKINS, H. M. Sequential organization in schedules of reinforcement. In W. N. Schoenfeld (Ed.), *The theory of reinforcement schedules.* Englewood Cliffs, N.J.: Prentice-Hall, Inc., 1970.

JOHNSON-LAIRD, P. Experimental psycholinguistics. *Annual Review of Psychology,* 1974, *25,* 135–160.

KAUSLER, D. H. *Psychology of verbal learning and memory.* New York: Academic Press, 1974.

KELLEHER, R. T. Chaining and conditioned reinforcement. In W. K. Honig (Ed.), *Operant behavior: Areas of research and application.* Englewood Cliffs, N.J.: Prentice-Hall, Inc., 1966.

KILLEEN, P. On the temporal control of behavior. *Psychological Review,* 1975, *82,* 89–115.

LASHLEY, K. S. The problem of serial order in behavior. In L. A. Jeffress (Ed.), *Cerebral mechanisms in behavior.* New York: Wiley, 1951. (Reprinted in Beach, Hebb, Morgan, Nissen, 1960.)

LUTZKER, J. R., & SHERMAN, J. A. Producing generative sentence usage by imitation and reinforcement procedures. *Journal of Applied Behavior Analysis,* 1974, *7,* 447–460.

MACCORQUODALE, K. B. F. Skinner's *Verbal behavior:* A retrospective appreciation. *Journal of the Experimental Analysis of Behavior,* 1969, *12,* 831–841.

MACCORQUODALE, K. On Chomsky's review of Skinner's *Verbal behavior. Journal of the Experimental Analysis of Behavior,* 1970, *13,* 83–99.

MCNEILL, D. *Semiotic extension.* Paper presented at the Loyola Symposium on Cognition, Chicago, April 1974.

MOORE, T. E. (Ed.). *Cognitive development and the acquisition of language.* New York: Academic Press, 1973.

MORSE, W. H. Intermittent reinforcement. In W. K. Honig (Ed.), *Operant behavior: Areas of research and application.* Englewood Cliffs, N.J.: Prentice-Hall, Inc., 1966.

PIAGET, J. *The origins of intelligence in children.* (2nd ed.) New York: International Universities Press, 1952. (1st ed., 1936)

PREMACK, D. Toward empirical behavior laws, I: Positive reinforcement. *Psychological Review,* 1959, *66,* 219–233.

PREMACK, D. A functional analysis of language. *Journal of the Experimental Analysis of Behavior,* 1970, *14,* 107–125.

PROKASY, W. F., & HALL, J. F. Primary stimulus generalization. *Psychological Review,* 1963, *70,* 310–322.

PYLYSHYN, Z. W. What the mind's eye tells the mind's brain: A critique of mental imagery. *Psychological Bulletin,* 1973, *80,* 1–24.

ROEPER, T. Connecting children's language and linguistic theory. In T. E. Moore (Ed.), *Cognitive development and the acquisition of language.* New York: Academic Press, 1973.

RUMBAUGH, D. M., VON GLASERSFELD, E., WARNER, H., PISANI, P., & GILL, T. V. Lana (chimpanzee) learning language: A progress report. *Brain and Language,* 1974, *1,* 205–212.

SAILOR, W. Reinforcement and generalization of productive plural allomorphs in two retarded children. *Journal of Applied Behavior Analysis,* 1971, *4,* 305–310.

SALZINGER, K. Are theories of competence necessary? *Annals of the New York Academy of Sciences,* 1975, *263,* 178–196.

SCHUMAKER, J., & SHERMAN, J. A. Training generative verb usage by imitation and reinforcement procedures. *Journal of Applied Behavior Analysis,* 1970, *3,* 273–287.

SEGAL, E. F. Induction and the provenance of operants. In R. M. Gilbert & J. R. Millenson (Eds.), *Reinforcement: Behavioral analyses.* New York: Academic Press, 1972.

SEGAL, E. F. *Language: A behavioral perspective.* San Diego: San Diego State University Press, 1975. (a)

SEGAL, E. F. Psycholinguistics discovers the operant: A review of Roger Brown's *A first language: The early stages. Journal of the Experimental Analysis of Behavior,* 1975, *23,* 149–158. (b)

SHERMAN, J. A. Imitation and language development. In *Advances in child development and behavior* (Vol. 6). New York: Academic Press, 1971.

SKINNER, B. F. Are theories of learning necessary? *Psychological Review,* 1950, *57,* 193–216.

SKINNER, B. F. *Verbal behavior.* New York: Appleton-Century-Crofts, 1957.

SLOBIN, D. The more it changes . . . : On understanding language by watching it move through time. Paper presented at the Stanford Child Language Research Forum, April 1975.

STADDON, J. E. R. Temporal control and the theory of reinforcement schedules. In R. M. Gilbert & J. R. Millenson (Eds.), *Reinforcement: Behavioral analyses.* New York: Academic Press, 1972.

THOMPSON, J., & CHAPMAN, R. S. Semantic development. Paper presented at the Stanford Child Language Research Forum, April 1975.

THORNDIKE, E. L. *Animal Intelligence.* New York: Macmillan, 1911.

TULVING, E. Cue-dependent forgetting. *American Scientist,* 1974, *62,* 74–82.

TULVING, E., & THOMSON, D. M. Encoding specificity and retrieval processes in episodic memory. *Psychological Review,* 1973, *80,* 352–373.

TURNER, M. B. *Realism and the explanation of behavior.* Englewood Cliffs, N.J.: Prentice-Hall, Inc., 1971.

WEISS, B. The fine structure of operant behavior during transition states. In W. N. Schoenfeld (Ed.), *The theory of reinforcement schedules.* Englewood Cliffs, N.J.: Prentice-Hall, Inc., 1970.

WHITEHURST, G. J. Generalized labeling on the basis of structural response classes by two young children. *Journal of Experimental Child Psychology,* 1971, *12,* 59–71.

WHITEHURST, G. J. Production of novel and grammatical utterances by young children. *Journal of Experimental Child Psychology,* 1972, *13,* 502–515.

WHITEHURST, G. J., & VASTA, R. Is language acquired through imitation? *Journal of Psycholinguistic Research,* 1975, *4,* 37–59.

Author Index

NOTE: This index provides information on the citation of names in the regular text, but not in the reference lists occurring at the end of each chapter. Each author of a chapter in this book is indicated by a reference to the inclusive page numbers of his or her chapter set in **boldface,** immediately following his or her name.

Abelson, R. M., 261, 282
Abrams, R. M., 153, 157, 158
Aceto, M. D. G., 356
Ackil, J. E., 58, 60, 81, 120
Adair, E., 40, 153, 154, 155, 164
Adams, D. W., 578
Adams, H., 65
Ader, R., 604
Adey, W. R., 605
Adler, N. T., 21, 59
Adolph, E. F., 17, 32, 33, 35, 36
Ahlskog, J. E., 85, 447, 469
Aiken, L. C., 532
Akerman, B., 139
Alferink, L. A., 211
Allaway, T. A., 57
Alleman, H. D., 224
Allen, J. D., 74, 75, 135, 138
Allison, J., 29, 106, 107
Allison, T. S., 243, 244
Amsel, A., 76, 226, 509
Anand, B., 607
Anchel, H., 407
Andelman, L., 507
Anderson, D. E., 602, 603
Anderson, R. C., 7, 57
Andersson, B., 14, 139
Andry, D. K., 489
Anger, D., 143, 223, 224, 225, 263, 264, 333, 393, 400, 426
Angyan, L., 590
Anliker, J., 597
Annau, Z., 342, 357
Anokhin, P. K., 144
Antelman, S. M., 585
Appel, J. B., 139, 214, 356, 381, 382, 554
Arazie, R., 135
Arbuthnott, G. W., 585
Armstrong, R. P., 562
Arnett, F. B., 78
Asch, S. E., 638
Askew, H. R., 85, 447, 469
Atkinson, J. W., 144, 146
Auge, R. J., 320, 322, 325
Autor, S. M., 251, 297, 313, 326, 327, 329, 330, 332, 333
Averill, J. R., 603
Avery, D. D., 168, 169
Avin, E., 524
Axelrod, S., 77, 78
Ayllon, T., 309, 384, 385, 386, 429, 636
Ayres, S. L., 126, 130, 131, 132, 133, 134, 135, 137, 139, 142, 143, 147
Azrin, N. H., 23, 89, 116, 129, 136, 139, 177, 182, 183, 184, 185, 194, 253, 309, 350, 357, 358, 359, 384, 385, 386, 394, 409, 417, 418, 420, 422, 426, 429, 468, 469, 561, 563, 636
Azzi, R., 219

Bacon, F., 13
Bacon, W. E., 589, 590
Badia, P., 397, 398, 405
Baenninger, R., 116
Baer, D. M., 639
Bagchi, B. K., 607
Baker, R. A., 32, 33
Balagura, S., 32, 33, 41
Balboni, 249
Baldock, M. D., 57, 58, 66, 78, 127
Baldwin, B. A., 153
Balliet, R. F., 519
Balster, R. L., 556
Bandler, R. J., 15
Banks, J. H., 603, 604
Banuazizi, A., 608, 610
Barash, D. P., 46
Barker, E. G., 438, 483
Barker, A. C., 606
Baron, A., 291
Baron, M. R., 482, 494
Barrera, F. J., 13, 65
Barrett, J., 357
Barry, H., 555, 561
Bauer, I. A., 597
Baum, W. M., 80, 111, 127, 128, 235, 236, 238, 239, 240, 241, 242, 243, 246, 248, 254, 264, 267, 272, 277, 297, 298, 381, 386, 387, 388, 410
Baxter, L., 586
Beach, F. A., 14, 20, 21, 642
Beach, H. D., 557
Beagley, G., 580
Beale, I. L., 435, 447, 464, 528, 589
Beard, R. R., 562
Beardsley, J. V., 605
Beck, J., 605
Becker, D. I., 554
Beckman, A. L., 168, 169
Bedarf, E. W., 516
Beels, C. C., 604
Beer, B., 178, 572, 577, 597
Beier, E. M., 258, 278
Belaiche, J., 163
Bell, R. H. V., 33, 36
Belleville, R. E., 367
Belluscio, P. R., 562
Benefield, R. L., 482, 490
Beninger, R. J., 267
Benson, H., 609
Berger, B. D., 571, 585
Berkley, M. A., 520, 575, 578
Berlanger, D., 597, 603
Berlyne, D. E., 318, 324, 326
Berman, A. J., 222
Berman, J. D., 549
Bernard, C., 10
Bernheim, H. A., 166
Bernheim, J. W., 75, 78, 85, 268, 471
Bernstein, D. J., 107, 108
Berry, F., 597
Berryman, R., 58, 128, 141, 213, 375, 525
Bersh, P. J., 381, 382, 405

Besley, S., 85, 439, 444, 446, 470, 471
Bever, T. G., 632, 651
Bigelow, G., 563
Bilbrey, J., 56, 127
Bindra, D., 62, 128, 144, 407, 582, 583
Birch, D., 144, 146
Birch, J., 606
Bishop, M. P., 589, 590
Bivens, L. W., 577
Black, A. H., 118, 119, 120, 340, 352, 393, 397, 597, 598, 603, 606, 607, 610
Black, W. C., 585, 589, 606
Blackman, D. E., **340–363**, 5, 305, 341, 345, 346, 347, 348, 350, 354, 356, 358, 359, 517
Blanchard, R., 320, 324, 326
Blandau, 21
Blaustein, J., 201
Blizard, D., 606
Block, H. D., 622
Bloom, F. E., 586, 588
Bloom, W., 136
Bloomfield, T. M., 71, 75, 76, 85, 267, 275, 318, 319, 324, 325, 326
Blough, D. S., **514–539**, 5, 144, 177, 208, 225, 238, 246, 264, 434, 435, 437, 438, 448, 449, 451, 452, 453, 463, 464, 495, 504, 521, 522, 525, 530, 535, 536, 537
Blough, P. M., **514–539**, 5, 225, 434, 517, 518, 521, 523, 524, 525, 530
Boakes, R. A., 61, 76, 77, 80, 84, 85, 87, 90, 318, 320, 325, 326, 532
Bobillier, P., 586
Bogert, C. M., 157
Boice, B., 44
Boling, J. L., 21
Bolles, R. C., 14, 33, 45, 90, 113, 116, 117, 120, 138, 165, 252, 264, 364, 372, 393, 397, 398, 406, 407, 408, 409, 410, 580
Bonbright, J. C., 384, 521
Bond, N. W., 350
Boneau, C. A., 77, 78, 445, 496, 497, 534
Booth, D. A., 32, 33, 35
Bootzin, R. R., 7
Boren, J. J., **540–569**, 5, 225, 355, 369, 372, 378, 388, 394, 395, 396, 407, 540, 544, 578, 579
Boren, M. C. P., 292, 296, 301
Boudin, H. M., 563
Bouzas, 274, 275
Bowden, D. M., 571, 585
Bowen, C., 132
Bower, G. H., 86, 261, 281, 324, 336, 628, 637, 638
Bowring, A. M., 577
Boyd, E. S., 589, 590
Brady, J. V., **596–618**, 5, 38, 89, 141, 299, 302, 308, 342, 344, 347, 349, 351, 352, 353, 354, 355, 356, 357, 359, 366, 396, 540, 556, 578, 579, 596, 597, 598, 599, 600, 601, 602, 603, 604, 609, 610
Brahlek, J. A., 89, 359
Braine, M. D. S., 641, 643, 644, 645, 646, 647
Branch, M. N., 325

Braun, J. J., 608
Breese, G. R., 168
Breland, K., 3, 7, 22, 273, 406
Breland, M., 3, 7, 22, 273, 406
Bremner, F. J., 408, 409
Brener, J. M., 606, 607, 608, 610, 611
Brengelmann, G. L., 160
Bresnahan, E. L., 501, 507
Brethower, 73, 77
Brezenoff, H. E., 168
Bridgman, P. W., 30
Briese, E., 589, 590
Brigham, T. A., 1
Brill, N. Q., 598
Brimblecombe, R. W., 168
Brimer, C. J., 116, 393
Brissey, C., 515
Brittain, R. T., 167
Brittain, T. M., 603
Brobeck, J. R., 31, 154
Brodie, D. A., 578
Brodie, J. J., 578
Brody, S., 32
Brogden, W. J., 421, 426
Brower, L. P., 484
Brown, A. C., 160
Brown, C., 610
Brown, C. C., 606
Brown, C. H., 446, 465, 467, 471, 472
Brown, G. M., 603
Brown, J. L., 590
Brown, J. S., 433
Brown, P. L., 2, 7, 54, 55, 60, 62, 119, 120, 127, 139, 252, 272, 359, 406
Brown, R., 632, 633, 640, 643, 648
Brown, R. T., 509
Brown, S., 578, 590
Brown, T. G., 139
Brown, W., 307
Browne, M., 65, 138, 314, 318, 320
Brownstein, A. J., 127, 233, 238, 242, 243, 246, 248
Bruch, H., 7
Bruinvels, J., 167, 169
Brunner, A., 589
Brush, F. R., 603
Bryant, R. C., 358
Buckley, J. P., 356, 561
Budgell, P., 153
Budnik, J. E., 455
Budzynski, T. H., 610
Burks, C. D., 130
Burr, D. E. S., 498, 501, 502
Burstein, K. R., 445
Bursten, B., 589
Butcher, L. L., 586
Butcher, R. L., 162
Byrd, L. D., 193, 295, 296, 304, 314, 429
Byrnes, J., 639

Cabanac, M., 153, 157, 158, 162, 163, 164, 165, 166
Caggiula, A. R., 579, 581
Caldwell, F. T., 153, 157, 158, 166
Callard, I. P., 162
Campbell, B. A., 35, 40, 105, 261, 263, 281, 421, 581
Campbell, H. J., 582, 589
Campbell, R. L., 183, 380
Campeau, E., 605
Cane, V., 142
Canfield, D. R., 586

655

Cannon, W. B., 31, 596
Cantor, A., 167, 168
Cantor, M. B., 578, 579
Capaldi, E. J., 509
Capehart, S., 75
Caplan, H. J., 446, 465, 467, 468, 469, 471, 472
Carlisle, H. J., 129, 138, 139, 153, 154, 164, 168, 169, 577
Carlton, P. L., 153, 344, 345, 585
Carmona, A., 607
Carroll, M. E., 14
Carter, A. L., 633
Catania, A. C., 1, 71, 73, 75, 76, 78, 79, 84, 140, 143, 176, 189, 191, 213, 214, 215, 216, 217, 218, 220, 224, 233, 234, 235, 237, 240, 241, 243, 246, 248, 249, 254, 257, 258, 259, 263, 264, 265, 266, 292, 307, 321, 328, 375, 398, 410, 435, 452, 463, 464, 557, 629, 646
Caul, W. F., 604
Cave, C., 143
Cebulla, R. P., 604
Champlin, G., 72
Chan, S. W. C., 162
Chapman, R. S., 633
Chase, S., 499, 524, 536
Cheek, M. S., 135
Cheng, M. F., 18
Cherek, D. R., 136, 139, 552, 562
Chhina, G., 607
Chipman, G. D., 157
Cho, C., 116
Chomsky, N., 5, 620, 622, 628, 629, 630, 632, 638, 640, 641, 648
Chorny, H., 426
Chorover, S. L., 14
Chow, M. I., 585
Christoph, G., 90
Chu, N. D., 586
Chung, Shin-Ho, 141, 233, 251, 252, 258, 266, 301, 304, 308, 316
Church, R. M., 165, 365, 375, 398, 400
Cioé, J., **570–595**, 5, 574
Clack, T. D., 516, 522, 523
Clark, E. V., 634
Clark, F. C., 137, 139, 143, 192, 367, 370, 371, 373, 374, 377
Clark, H. B., 307
Clark, R. L., 132, 134, 142, 597
Clark, W. G., 153, 166
Clayton, K. N., 576
Clements, R. O., 78, 127, 319, 322, 323, 324, 325
Clopton, B. M., 524
Coates, J., 73
Coger, R. W., 378, 379
Cohen, H., 22
Cohen, M., 563
Cohen, P. S., 136
Cohen, S. I., 603, 606
Cohen, S. L., 304, 305, 308, 316
Cohn, M., 462
Coker, C., 397
Cole, B. K., 201, 376
Cole, J. L., 140, 534
Coleman, W. P., 162
Collier, G., **28–51**, 4, 32, 33, 35, 36, 38, 39, 40, 129, 134, 193
Collins, D., 600, 601
Collins, J. P., 438
Conger, J. J., 597

Conner, J. D., 588
Conrad, D. G., 185, 260, 280, 358, 578, 579, 597, 604
Cook, L., 74, 143, 185, 189, 191, 212, 226, 358, 427, 540, 555, 557, 559
Coons, E. E., 14, 580, 582
Cooper, B. R., 585
Cooper, K. E., 167
Cooper, R. M., 590
Coover, G. D., 603
Coppock, H. W., 557
Corballis, M. C., 528
Corbit, J. D., 154, 158, 164
Coscina, D. V., 32, 33, 40
Costa, L. D., 532
Coulson, G., 379, 380
Coulson, V., 379
Coulter, G., 407
Cowles, R. B., 156, 157
Cox, V. C., 15, 571
Crabtree, J. M., 604
Craig, W., 58
Cranston, W. I., 167
Crawford, J. M., 588
Crawshaw, L. I., 158, 168, 169
Crespi, L. P., 86, 258, 259, 278
Crichton, M., 571, 580
Crider, A., 606, 607, 610
Crissman, J. K., 162
Crites, R. J., 437
Crossman, E. K., 211, 225
Crow, T. J., 581, 585, 586, 590
Crowder, W. F., 554
Cruce, J. A. F., 582
Cruze, W. W., 69
Culberton, J. K., 575, 578
Culler, E., 421, 426
Cumming, W. W., 208, 213, 224, 525
Cunningham, D. J., 162
Cunningham, S., 7
Curtis, D. R., 588
Curto, K., 455
Cushman, A. J., 572
Cutts, D., 234, 235, 243

Daley, L. A., 602
Dalland, J. I., 519, 520, 521, 523
Dalrymple, S. D., 428, 429
Dalton, A. J., 603
Davenport, D. G., 378, 379, 380
Davenport, J. W., 258, 278
Davidson, A. B., 74, 555
Davidson, E. H., 282
Davidson, R. S., 153
Davis, A. H., 572, 589
Davis, D. D., 154, 156
Davis, D. J., 555
Davis, E., 201, 216
Davis, H., 341, 342, 356, 360
Davis, J. M., 139, 446, 447
Davis, R. C., 597
Davison, M. C., 240, 241, 248, 252, 255, 275, 276, 277, 298, 302, 324, 332, 336, 572, 573, 589, 590
Davitt, G. A., 507
Dawes, G. S., 158
Day, R. B., 226
Deadwyler, S. A., 130
De Casper, A. J., 224, 227
Deegan, J., 559
De Good, D. E., 603
Deguchi, T., 606
Delbruck, N., 248
Delgado, J. M. R., 589
Delini-Stula, A., 606

De Lorge, J., 303, 304, 317
Delse, F. C., 606
Dement, W. C., 22
Deneau, G. A., 192
Denny, M. R., 222, 226
Denny-Brown, D., 19
De Ruiter, L., 31
Descartes, R., 8, 29
De Toledo, L. E., 352, 598, 606
Deutsch, J. A., 471, 472, 575, 576, 577, 579, 581, 584, 586, 588
De Valois, R. L., 518
De Vietti, T. L., 598
de Villiers, P. A., **233–287**, 4, 78, 86, 129, 132, 140, 244, 248, 249, 250, 253, 254, 258, 260, 261, 267, 270, 271, 348, 352, 354, 355, 371, 372, 373, 374, 375, 382, 383, 386, 387, 402
Devos, M., 32, 33, 44
De Weese, J., 294, 316
Dewey, W. L., 553
Dews, P. B., 188, 202, 208, 209, 214, 218, 219, 220, 222, 223, 228, 229, 309, 333, 348, 540, 542, 551, 552, 554, 556, 559, 560, 646
DiCara, K., 571, 575, 576
DiCara, L. V., 606, 607, 608, 609, 610, 611
Dickinson, A., 74
Dickson, J. F., 460, 462
Didamo, P., 344, 345
Dillow, P. V., 143, 296
Di Lollo, V., 258, 278
Dinsmoor, J. A., 261, 282, 296, 297, 314, 318, 319, 320, 321, 322, 324, 325, 326, 368, 384, 385, 391, 392, 398, 400, 401, 407, 408, 427
Dixon, C., 606
Dobrzecka, C., 483, 484, 485
Domino, E., 585
Donchin, E., 606
Doty, R. W., 570
Downs, D. A., 553
Drabman, R. S., 309
Dragoin, W. B., 14, 485
Dreese, A., 585
Drexler, 446
Driscoll, J., 323
Driver, G., 600, 601
Ducharme, R., 603
Duclaux, R., 153, 158, 166
Dukhayyil, A., 454
Duncan, A. R., 35
Duncan, B., 252, 298, 335
Duncan, I. H. H., 35, 535
Dunham, P. J., **98–124**, 3, 4, 65, 86, 99, 100, 104, 107, 108, 117, 129
Dunn, G., 597, 606
Durham, R. M., 605
Dworkin, B. R., 611
Dykstra, L. A., 554
Dysart, J., 249, 460, 461

Eck, K. O., 498, 501, 502
Eckerman, D. A., 322, 323
Edinger, H. M., 154
Edwards, S. B., 15, 582
Egger, M. D., 56, 57
Ehrenfreund, D., 38
Ehrlich, W., 606
Eimas, P. D., 487

Eisenberger, R., 103, 105, 106, 107, 108
Eisenman, J. S., 154
Eissenberg, E., 611
Elder, S. T., 589, 590
Eldridge, L., 597
Ellen, P., 388
Ellis, B. B., 136
Ellis, W. R., 456
Elsmore, T. F., 534, 535
Emley, G. S., 418, 420, 422, 423
Engel, B. T., 608
Engen, T., 533
Epstein, A. N., 17, 20, 153, 156
Ernits, T., 164
Ernst, A. J., 489
Ervey, D. H., 113, 116
Ervin, F. R., 484, 485
Ervin-Tripp, S., 634
Estes, R. D., 33, 47, 88
Estes, W. K., 185, 253, 341, 347, 353, 357, 393, 409, 598
Evans, G., 447
Everett, P. B., 130

Faber, B., 35
Fabricius, E., 139
Faillace, L. A., 563
Falk, J. L., 23, 32, 128, 129, 130, 132, 136, 137, 138, 577, 578
Fallon, D., 131
Fantino, E., **313–338**, 4, 61, 158, 182, 184, 237, 240, 241, 242, 244, 246, 248, 252, 277, 298, 300, 303, 305, 316, 324, 326, 327, 328, 329, 330, 331, 332, 333, 334, 335, 336, 346, 355, 397
Fantz, R. C., 69
Farmer, J., 222
Farrar, C. H., 406, 407
Farrell, L., 57, 61, 127
Farris, H. F., 59
Farthing, G. W., 85, 359, 439, 444, 446, 452, 454, 470, 471, 482, 492, 496, 499
Farwell, C., 633
Fearing, F., 29
Fekety, F. R., 166
Feldberg, W., 167, 168, 169
Feldman, R. S., 408, 409
Feldman, S. M., 573, 597
Felton, M., 209, 210, 213, 217, 346
Ferguson, J., 22
Ferrari, E. A., 120, 406, 408
Ferraro, D. P., 606
Ferster, C. B., 7, 38, 54, 140, 176, 201, 204, 206, 207, 209, 210, 212, 213, 217, 219, 222, 223, 224, 225, 228, 234, 290, 291, 293, 295, 296, 298, 345, 643
Fibiger, H. C., 585, 586
Field, G. E., 394
Fields, C., 608, 610
Figar, S., 597
Findley, J. D., 38, 78, 226, 234, 235, 249, 291, 292, 295, 299, 302, 308, 366, 396, 598, 601, 602, 603, 609, 610, 643
Fisher, A. E., 586
Fitzgerald, R. D., 606
Fitzsimons, J. T., 31, 32, 36
Flaherty, C. F., 509
Flamer, R., 563
Fleshler, M., 120, 351, 407, 426, 482, 483, 489

Author Index

Fletcher, F. G., 58
Flint, G. A., 319
Flory, R. K., 129, 130, 131, 132, 135, 136, 137, 139
Flourens, M. J. P., 8
Flynn, J. P., 14, 15, 16, 21, 582
Fodor, J. A., 632, 635, 651
Folz, E. L., 604
Fonberg, E., 20
Fontaine, O., 559
Foote, W. 582
Foree, D. D., 70, 120, 407, 408, 485, 487
Forgione, A. G., 409
Forrest, M. S., 603
Forsyth, R. P., 598, 601, 602, 603, 604, 606
Fowler, H., 261, 281, 282
Fowler, R. L., 606
Fraenkel, G. S., 158
Frank, J., 140, 141, 142, 143, 147
Frankenheim, J. M., 553
Franklin, S., 56
Frazier, T. W., 603
Freed, L. M., 138
Freedman, D. X., 554
Freeman, B. J., 74, 75, 76, 78, 82
Freeman, F., 482, 490, 498, 499
Freeman, M. E., 162
Freeman, W. J., 154, 155, 156
Freud, S., 11
Friedman, H., 438, 472
Frieman, J., 498
Fritsch, G., 570
Frommer, G. P., 58, 60, 81, 120
Fry, F. E. J., 157
Fry, W. T., 143, 212, 226, 290, 293, 295, 559
Fusco, M. M., 154
Fuxe, K., 585

Gaebelein, C. J., 611
Galambos, R., 597
Galbraith, K., 509
Gale, C. C., 153, 154, 166
Gallistel, C. R., 259, 279, 580
Galosy, R. A., 611
Gamzu, E., **53-97**, 3, 55, 56, 58, 60, 61, 62, 63, 65, 67, 68, 69, 80, 81, 85, 87, 126, 127, 128, 133, 185, 272, 273, 275, 359
Gandelman, R., 574, 576
Gantt, W. H., 596
Ganz, L., 486
Garcia, E., 639
Garcia, J., 14, 91, 113, 484, 485
Gardner, B. T., 640
Gardner D. R., 158
Gardner, E. L., 590
Gardner, L. C., 379, 590
Gardner, R. A., 640
Gardner, W. M., 58
Garrett, M. F., 632, 651
Garrick, L. D., 157, 162
Gaudilliere, J. P., 44
Geller, I., 558, 560
Gentry, W. D., 136
Gerbrandt, L. A., 606
German, D. C., 571, 585
Gerry, J. E., 486
Gibbon, J., 57, 58, 127, 128, 375, 399, 400, 401, 410
Gibson, D. A., 320, 322
Gibson, W. E., 575, 576
Gilbert, R. M., 135, 144
Gilbert, T. F., 131

Gilden, L., 532
Gill, C. A., 78, 452
Gill, T. V., 640
Gillet, A., 153, 166
Gilliam, W. J., 598, 601, 602, 609, 610
Gilmore, L., 600, 601
Githens, S. H., 130
Giulian, D., 404
Giurintano, L. P., 440
Glass, D. H., 86
Glaucheva, L., 20
Glazer, H., 141, 142, 143
Glazer, R. D., 113, 115, 116
Gleitman, H., 632, 651
Gleitman, L. R., 632, 651
Glenn, M. F., 434
Glickman, S. E., 571, 580, 581, 586, 588
Goesling, W. J., 608, 610
Goff, W. R., 523
Goldberg, A. M., 542
Goldberg, S. R., 179, 192, 193, 542, 554
Goldiamond, I., 222
Goldman, L., 603
Goldstein, M. D., 573
Goldstein, R., 573, 579
Gollub, L. R., **288-312**, 2, 137, 181, 193, 194, 226, 270, 271, 272, 302, 313, 315, 318, 322, 324, 460, 462, 540
Gonzales, F. A., 61, 72
Goodman, I. J., 590
Goodrich, K. P., 258, 278
Gordon, M. S., 162
Gordon, T. P., 603
Gormezano, I., 61
Gott, C. T., 213, 223, 302, 562
Gottlieb, S. H., 608
Gottwald, P., 357
Gourevitch, G., 519, 523
Goyette, C. H., 498
Grabowski, J., 395
Graeff, F. G., 120, 406, 408
Graham, L. A., 603
Granger, L., 603
Grant, D. A., 61
Grastyán, E., 590
Gray, V. A., 482, 501, 502, 503, 505, 508
Green, D. M., 533, 534, 537
Green, H. L., 32, 35
Green, K. F., 113
Greenberg, I., 130
Greene, D., 580
Greenway, L., 380
Greer, G. L., 158
Gregor, G. L., 408
Griffiths, R. R., 561, 563
Gross, S. A., 604
Grossen, N. E., 117, 393
Grossman, S. P., 89, 116, 162
Grove, R., 548, 549
Groves, L. C., 127
Guess, D., 639
Guilkey, M., 216, 226, 302, 308
Gunn, D. L., 158
Gustavson, C. R., 408
Guthrie, E. R., 29
Guttman, N., 45, 84, 86, 249, 259, 263, 279, 280, 434, 438, 442, 443, 445, 456, 460, 461, 472, 489, 493, 527

Haberlandt, K., 495
Hackett, E. R., 168
Hackett, J. T., 605, 606
Hagamen, W. D., 589, 590

Hager, J. L., 14, 91, 407, 436
Hagguist, W. W., 258, 278
Hahn, W. W., 597, 608
Hailman, J. P., 435
Hain, J. D., 604
Hake, D. F., 23, 89, 129, 136, 182, 183, 358, 359, 380, 384, 385, 386, 409, 417, 418, 426, 429, 468
Halas, E. S., 605
Halgren, C. R., 487
Hall, G., 503, 508
Hall, J. F., 639
Halliday, M. S., 76, 77, 87, 90
Halmi, K. A., 7
Halpern, B. P., 144, 527, 529
Hamilton, B., 87
Hamilton, C. L., 162
Hamilton, E. L., 219
Hamlin, P., 32, 33, 36, 41, 42, 47
Hamm, H. D., 307
Hammel, H. T., 153, 154, 157, 158
Hammer, C., 219
Handley, S. L., 167
Hanford, P. V., 260, 281, 307, 317
Hanford, P. W., 219
Hankins, W. G., 8
Hanna, B., 102
Hansen, M. G., 168, 169
Hanson, H. M., 249, 292, 441, 442, 443, 448, 460, 494
Hardy, J. D., 154, 158
Harlow, H., 159
Harman, J., 406
Harré, R., 276, 277
Harrel, N., 604, 605
Harris, A. H., **596-618**, 5, 597, 603, 606, 609, 610
Harris, J. D., 522, 523
Harris, L. S., 553
Harris, R. E., 609, 610
Harris, R. T., 437, 556
Harrison, H., 154
Harrison, J. M., 261, 282, 367
Harrison, R. H., 440, 441, 445, 449, 450, 483, 487, 488, 489, 491, 493, 494, 495, 528
Harsh, J., 397
Harvey, J. A., 202, 574
Harzem, P., 141, 142
Hawkes, L., 225, 256, 643
Hawkins, T. D., 130, 131, 164, 179, 181, 572, 573, 575, 576, 578
Headlee, C. P., 557
Heaps, R. S., 211
Hearst, E., 54, 55, 56, 58, 60, 62, 63, 65, 68, 69, 81, 85, 90, 120, 127, 314, 347, 361, 376, 436, 439, 444, 445, 446, 447, 449, 450, 451, 453, 454, 455, 456, 466, 470, 471, 472, 482, 487, 499, 503, 560, 597
Heath, J. E., 157, 161
Heath, R. G., 589, 590
Hebb, D. O., 571, 641, 642
Hebert, D. L., 75, 448
Hefferline, R. F., 606, 610
Heinemann, E. G., 489, 490, 524, 536
Heise, G. A., 561
Heistad, G. T., 136, 561
Heller, H., 17
Hellon, R. F., 167
Hellstrom, B., 154
Helson, H., 4

Hemmes, N. S., 80, 82, 83, 86, 90, 438
Hendersen, R. W., **153-173**, 4
Hendry, D. P., 318, 319, 323, 326, 336, 350, 352, 354
Henke, P. G., 74
Henry, P., 22, 143, 296, 324
Hensel, H., 161
Henton, W. W., 89, 360, 517
Herberg, L. J., 579, 581
Herbert, E. W., 251, 252
Herd, J. A., 598, 601, 602, 603, 604, 606, 609
Herman, P. N., 516
Herrnstein, R. J., 28, 61, 63, 78, 79, 88, 99, 133, 185, 204, 205, 206, 207, 208, 209, 210, 211, 212, 214, 233, 234, 235, 236, 240, 242, 243, 245, 246, 247, 248, 251, 252, 253, 254, 257, 258, 259, 260, 261, 262, 263, 264, 265, 266, 267, 268, 269, 270, 272, 274, 275, 277, 278, 297, 298, 306, 324, 327, 328, 329, 330, 332, 333, 334, 336, 357, 373, 374, 375, 380, 381, 382, 383, 386, 387, 397, 400, 401, 402, 407, 532, 542, 543, 559
Hess, W. R., 14, 570
Higgins, D. J., 603
Hilgard, E. R., 628, 637, 638
Hill, F. A., 607
Hill, J. H., 33, 86
Hill, R. T., 560
Hill, S. Y., 579
Hilton, A., 61
Hinde, J. S., 91, 436
Hinde, R. A., 3, 8, 90, 91, 133, 139, 142, 436
Hine, B., 577
Hineline, P. H., 13
Hineline, P. N., **364-414**, 5, 13, 260, 267, 374, 375, 380, 381, 400, 401, 402, 403, 405, 406, 409
Hirsch, E., **28-51**, 4, 32, 33, 34, 35, 36, 38, 39, 40, 48, 193
Hiss, R. H., 214, 434, 516
Hitzig, E., 570
Hochachka, P. W., 157
Hodge, H. C., 562
Hoebel, B. G., 14, 32, 571, 579, 580, 581, 583, 585
Hodos, W., 141, 521, 572, 573, 574, 597
Hofer, K. G., 14
Hoffbrand, B. I., 603
Hoffman, H. S., 120, 348, 351, 353, 357, 365, 407, 409, 426, 450, 482, 483, 489
Hoffmeister, F., 179, 192
Hogan, J. A., 59, 60, 121, 159
Hokanson, J. E., 603
Hokfelt, T., 585
Holbrook, J. W., 135
Holland, C. H., 243, 282
Holland, J. G., 236, 263
Hollard, V., 248, 252, 277, 573, 590
Hollis, J. H., 563, 564
Holloway, S. M., 135
Holly, B. L., 564
Holstein, S. B., 102
Holz, W. C., 182, 194, 253, 254, 357, 384, 385, 386, 394, 429
Honig, W. K., **1-6**, 7, 53, 318, 319, 435, 445, 447, 449, 456, 464, 486, 493, 496, 497, 498,

Honig (Cont.)
499, 500, 503, 505, 507, 508, 525, 531, 572, 573, 630
Honour, A. J., 167
Horn, P. W., 597
Horowitz, Z. P., 585
Hosking, K. E., 604
Hothersall, D., 607, 610
Hovland, C. I., 493
Howard, B., 36
Howard J. L., 168, 586, 598, 610, 611
Howard, R., 446, 467, 471, 472
Hubbard, R., 10
Howarth, C. I., 575, 576, 581, 586, 588
Huang, Y. H., 582, 590
Huey, R. B., 164
Huff, R. G., 461, 462
Hughes, B. O., 35
Hughes, J. E., 303, 305
Hughes, L. H., 261, 282, 297, 304, 318, 320
Hull, C. L., 10, 29, 30, 31, 36, 75, 99, 101, 146, 217, 218, 234, 315, 370, 371, 373, 374, 377, 448, 453, 483, 491, 494, 495, 506
Humphreys, L. G., 61
Hundt, A. G., 40, 102
Hunt, G. L., 69
Hunt, G. M., 23, 136, 561, 562, 563
Hunt, H. F., 351, 353, 354, 357
Hursh, S. R., 61, 324, 332, 336
Hurwitz, H. M. B., 248, 358, 372, 376, 377, 380
Huston, J. P., 582
Hutchison, J., 21, 129
Hutchinson, R. R., **415–431**, 4, 23, 136, 183, 409, 417, 418, 420, 421, 422, 423, 426, 468, 561
Hutt, P. J., 258, 278
Hyden, H., 606

Iglauer, C., 250, 251
Ingram, D. L., 153
Innis, N. K., 127, 136, 138, 301
Inskeep, E. K., 162
Irwin, R. J., 267, 518, 537
Isaac, D., 144
Isom, K. E., 606
Ison, J. R., 86
Iverson, L., 540
Iverson, S., 540

Jacob, J., 167
Jacobs, G. H., 518
Jacobs, H. L., 557
Jacobson, F. H., 154
Jackson, D. C., 154
Jacquet, Y. F., 132
Jaffe, M. L., 74
Jaynes, J., 29
Jeddi, E., 157, 158, 159
Jenkins, H. M., 2, 7, 23, 54, 55, 58, 59, 60, 61, 62, 63, 65, 68, 69, 81, 84, 85, 119, 120, 127, 140, 220, 221, 272, 318, 320, 325, 326, 359, 361, 398, 405, 406, 439, 440, 441, 445, 449, 450, 483, 487, 488, 489, 491, 492, 493, 494, 495, 499, 509, 528, 646
Jennings, J. R., 603
Jensen, C., 131
Johanson, C., 306
John, E. R., 597
Johnson, D. F., 499, 500

Johnson, D. G., 598
Johnson, D. M., 221, 222
Johnson, R., 470
Johnson, R. J., 607
Johnson, T. A., 600, 606
Johnson-Laird, P., 651
Johnston, J. M., 294, 316
Jolley, A., 603
Jones, L. G., 598, 601
Jones, B. E., 586, 588
Jones, H., 225, 226
Jouvet, M., 22, 586, 588
Justesen, R., 590
Jwaideh, A. R., 293, 294, 295, 296, 297, 318, 320

Kachanoff, R., 137
Kadden, R. M., 376, 377, 380, 399, 410, 610
Kahn, M., 610
Kakolewski, J. W., 15, 571
Kalat, J., 8, 14, 91, 484, 485
Kalish, H. I., 434, 442, 445, 489, 527
Kamin, L. J., 54, 342, 351, 353, 354, 357, 393, 492, 507
Kamiya, J., 604
Kanarek, R., **28–51**, 4, 33, 34, 35, 36, 38, 39, 40, 47, 193
Kanner, R. M., 606
Kaplinsky, M., 583
Karpicke, J., 90, 466, 472
Karpman, M., 103
Kasatkin, N. I., 20
Katkin, E. S., 610
Kaufman, A., 291
Kausler, D. H., 638
Kazdin, A. E., 7
Keehn, J. D., 127, 137, 368, 381, 407, 408, 409
Keenan, B., 606, 610
Keesey, R. E., 258, 259, 263, 278, 573, 575
Kelleher, R. T., **174–200**, 4, 28, 143, 178, 179, 183, 184, 185, 186, 187, 188, 189, 190, 191, 192, 193, 194, 195, 196, 197, 202, 212, 213, 222, 226, 229, 288, 289, 290, 293, 294, 295, 297, 298, 299, 300, 301, 302, 303, 304, 305, 306, 307, 309, 313, 314, 315, 318, 345, 356, 358, 366, 367, 381, 384, 385, 406, 410, 428, 429, 540, 552, 555, 556, 557, 558, 559, 598, 601, 603, 604, 609, 643
Keller, A. D., 154
Keller, F. S., 219, 303, 314, 367, 407
Keller, K., 83, 84, 86, 87, 88, 273, 274, 275, 359
Kelley, M. J., 117
Kellicut, M. H., 445
Kello, J. E., 301, 304
Kelly, D. D., 89, 252, 358, 359, 598
Kemp, F. D., 158
Kemp, J. M., 588
Kendall, S. B., 292, 296, 297, 318, 320, 322, 324, 325
Kenshalo, D. R., 135
Keys, N. W., 576
Kiess, H. O., 15
Killam, K. F., 597
Killeen, P., 79, 134, 217, 246, 265, 272, 276, 277, 292, 298, 332, 333, 334, 336, 646
Kimble, G. A., 54, 67
Kimmel, E., 606

Kimmel, H. D., 606, 610
King, J. E., 589, 590
Kinnard, W. J., 356
Kintsch, W. A., 33
Kirby, A. J., 119, 120
Kirkpatrick, M. A., 564
Kirkpatrick, W. E., 168, 169
Kissileff, H. R., 32, 35, 36, 40, 43, 131, 135
Kitzes, L. A., 522
Kleiber, M., 32
Klein, M., 407, 448, 450, 451, 453
Kleinknecht, R. A., 137
Kling, J. W., 258, 259, 278, 575, 578
Klinger, J. M., 517
Kluger, M. J., 166
Knarr, F., 35
Knott, J. K., 606
Knott, P. D., 576
Knutson, J. F., 137
Koch, D. L., 262, 282
Kodera, T., 465, 467, 473, 474
Koelle, G. B., 165
Koelling, R. A., 14, 91, 484, 485
Köhler, W., 29
Komisaruk, B. R., 21
Konorski, J., 138, 144, 483, 605
Kop, D., 610
Koresco, M., 436, 454
Koster, E. D., 261, 282
Kowalski, M., 604
Kraeling, D., 261, 263, 280, 281
Krahenbuhl, G. S., 603
Kral, P. A., 14, 485
Kramer, T. J., 85, 141, 255, 447, 466, 467, 468, 469
Kramis, R. C., 589
Krantz, J. A., 448
Krasnegor, N. A., 366, 396
Krausman, D., 606, 610
Krček, J., 17
Krečková, J., 17
Kreuter, C., 360
Krost, K., 44
Kruuk, H., 33, 47, 49
Kubena, R. K., 555, 561
Kuenen, D. J., 20
Kulli, 244, 276

LaBounty, C. E., 247, 254, 266
Lachman, R., 610
Lachter, G. D., 201
LaForge, H., 603
Lakoff, G., 622
Lambert, J. V., 381, 382, 405, 406
Lamoreaux, R. R., 369, 426
Lander, D. G., 267, 435, 447
Lang, P. J., 610
Lange, K. O., 367
Lanzetta, J. T., 323
La Rue, C. G., 35
Lashley, K. S., 222, 483, 485, 487, 488, 492, 641, 642
Lát, J., 43
Laties, V. G., 142, 143, 154, 164, 166, 167, 189, 367, 542, 555, 556, 560, 562
Lattal, K. A., 75
Lawler, J. E., 603
Lawrence, C. E., 314, 318, 320
Lawrence, D. H., 38, 487
Lazarus, R. S., 603
Lea, S. E. G., 276, 342
Leach, L. J., 562
Leaf, R. C., 370, 397
Leahy, J. P., 586

Leander, J. D., 306
Lee, J. K., 226, 302
Leeming, F. C., 262, 282
Lehrer, R., 33, 35
Leifer, L., 606
Leitenberg, H., 1
Le Magnen, J., 32, 33, 35, 36, 44
Lenzer, I. I., 574, 582
Leonard, C. M., 159
Leslie, J., 350, 355, 356
Levak, M., 14
Leveille, R., 137
Levin, R., 33, 44
Levine, M. D., 603
Levine, S., 33, 44, 603
Levitsky, D., 32, 33, 34, 35, 38, 40, 129, 134
Levy, C., 14
Lewin, L., 407
Lewis, D., 61
Lewis, P., 407
Libby, M. E., 400
Liddell, H. S., 138, 421
Lieberman, D. A., 318, 319, 320, 321, 322, 326
Liebman, J. M., 586
Liebson, I., 563
Lilie, N., 561
Lilly, J. C., 589, 590
Lindsley, O., 563
Lindy, J., 577
Linholm, E., 575
Lipman, E. A., 421, 426
Lippa, A. S., 585
Lipscombe, H. S., 603
Lipton, J. M., 153, 154, 162, 166, 167
Lisina, M. I., 606
Litner, J. S., 390, 391, 392, 393
Lloyd, K. E., 243, 244
Logan, F. A., 258, 259, 260, 262, 263, 278, 281, 495, 509
LoLordo, V. M., 70, 89, 90, 120, 272, 273, 275, 359, 392, 407, 408, 485, 487, 579
Lomax, P., 165, 168, 169
Long, D. H., 604
Longstreth, L. E., 305, 309
Looney, T. A., 136
Lorens, S. K., 574
Lorenz, K., 11, 91, 138
Loth, E., 598
Lott, D. F., 289, 551
Lotter, E. C., 129, 130, 131, 132
Lotti, V. J., 167, 168, 169
Loughead, T. E., 224
Louis-Sylvestre, J., 44
Louw, G. N., 162
Loveland, D. H., 61, 63, 245, 246, 247, 254, 257, 269, 272, 274, 306
Lovejoy, E., 492, 507
Lower, J. S., 604
Lubow, R. E., 487
Luce, R. D., 530
Luke, D., 551
Lutzker, J. R., 639
Lynch, G. S., 105
Lyon, D. O., 209, 210, 213, 217, 341, 342, 345, 346, 350, 351, 355, 357
Lyons, J. E., 439, 441, 446, 447, 454, 494, 496

Maatshe, J. L., 226
MacCorquodale, K. B. K., 633, 634, 635, 637, 638, 639, 640, 648, 649

Author Index

MacDonnell, M. F., 15, 16, 21
MacFarlane, W. V., 36
MacInnes, J. W., 606
Mackintosh, N. J., **481–513**, 5, 54, 343, 441, 482, 488, 495, 497, 498, 500, 501, 502, 503, 504, 507
MacKinnon, J. R., 509
Mach, E., 30
MacPhail, E. M., 407, 590
Magnus, R., 8
Magnuson, J. J., 157
Magoun, H. W., 154
Maier, S. F., 375
Malagodi, E. F., 294, 306, 316
Malcuit, G., 603
Malis, J. L., 578
Malmo, R. B., 597
Malone, J. C., 75, 77
Malott, M. K., 434, 486, 525, 526
Malott, R. W., 224, 434, 525, 526
Malsbury, C., 572, 585, 590
Mandell, C., 536
Mandler, G., 610
Mangan, G., 597
Manocha, S. N., 553
Mansfield, R. J. W., 532
Marczynski, T. J., 605, 606
Margules, D. L., 571, 579, 581
Mariner, A., 65
Mariner, R. W., 249, 461, 462, 487
Marler, P., 144
Marmaroff, S., 103, 105
Marowitz, L. A., 144
Marr, M. J., 201, 226, 295, 297, 305
Marsh, D. F., 548
Marsh, G., 449, 451, 453, 470
Marsh, G. R., 606
Marsh, J. T., 598
Marshall, J. F., 16, 17, 586
Martin, J. M., 201
Martin, J. R., 165
Martinez, E. S., 252
Marvin, S., 597, 606
Marwine, A. G., 33, 34, 35, 36, 40, 42
Marx, M. H., 249, 260
Marx, R. A., 153
Mason, J. W., 589, 597, 598, 599, 600, 601, 604, 606
Mason, W. A., 38
Masserman, J. H., 557
Massonet, B., 163
Mathews, M., 153, 166
Matsumiya, Y., 575
Matthews, T. J., 153, 165
Maxey, G. C., 75
Mayer, J., 32, 33, 35, 36, 153, 158
Maynard, E. A., 562
McClelland, D., 570
McConahey, O. L., 565, 566
McCoy, F. B., 610
McCracken, S. B., 57
McCutcheon, E. P., 611
McDiarmid, C. G., 222
McDonald, D. G., 597
McFarland, D. J., 139, 140, 144
McGeer, E. G., 586
McGill, W. J., 141
McGillis, D. B., 116
McGinty, D. J., 21, 156
McGowan, B. K., 113
McHugh, P. R., 589
McKearney, J. W., 185, 193, 195, 222, 345, 380, 384, 404, 429, 558
McLaughlin, R., 420
McLean, J. H., 162, 249, 324, 460
McLelland, J. P., 137
McLeod, A., 225
McMichael, J. S., 323
McMillan, D. E., 553, 558
McMillan, J. C., 89, 90, 322, 323, 324, 359
McNeill, D., 633
McSweeney, F. K., 236, 240
Meacham, J., 324
Mead, R. M., 183, 428, 429
Meehl, P. E., 100, 101
Meisch, R., 553, 554, 561
Mellgren, R. L., 487
Mello, N. K., 528, 563
Melmon, K. L., 603
Meltzer, D., 89, 359
Melvin, K. B., 113, 116
Mendelson, J. H., 14, 138, 563, 583
Mentzer, T. L., 519
Metzner, R. J., 578
Meyer, D. R., 116
Meyers, K. A., 603
Meyers, W. J., 574
Miczek, K. A., 89, 356, 357, 358
Middaugh, S., 611
Migler, B., 347, 438
Miles, C. G., 492, 495, 499
Milestone, R., 153
Mill, J. L., 5
Millar, R. D., 346
Millenson, J., 13, 132, 135, 243, 244, 248, 249, 253, 348, 350, 352, 354, 355, 356, 372, 376, 377, 438
Miller, A. M., 590
Miller, F. E., 604
Miller, J. S., 137
Miller, J. T., 457, 458
Miller, L. H., 606
Miller, N. E., 14, 56, 57, 61, 99, 112, 289, 308, 426, 571, 581, 582, 590, 603, 604, 607, 608, 609, 610, 611
Miller, R. E., 604, 606
Milligan, W. L., 523, 529
Milner, P. M., 570, 571, 572, 575, 576, 584, 586, 588
Milsum, J. H., 160
Mishkin, M., 521, 525
Miyata, Y., 604
Moffatt, G. H., 262, 282
Moffitt, M., 251, 256, 266, 275, 276
Mogenson, G. J., **570–595**, 5, 571, 573, 576, 577, 578, 579, 581, 582, 583, 584, 585, 586, 587
Mole, J. S., 77
Moody, D. B., 526, 527, 532, 534
Moody, J. E., 409
Mooney, R. D., 165
Moore, A. U., 487
Moore, B. R., 9, 23, 81, 113, 118, 119, 120, 121, 122, 123, 127, 359
Moore, J. W., 55, 58, 59, 61, 62, 67, 303, 334, 489, 493, 494
Moore, K. E., 540
Moore, R. A., 168
Moore, T. E., 633, 634
Moot, S. A., 604
Moran, G., 132
Moreno, O. M., 578
Morgan, C. T., 641, 642
Morgan, C. W., 577, 578, 583, 584
Morgan, M. J., 207, 219, 342, 435
Morin, L. P., 164
Morishima, M. S., 154
Morrison, S. D., 47, 58, 65
Morse, C. W., 134
Morse, W. H., **174–200**, 4, 28, 176, 177, 178, 179, 182, 183, 184, 185, 186, 187, 188, 189, 190, 191, 192, 193, 194, 195, 196, 197, 201, 202, 204, 205, 206, 207, 208, 209, 210, 211, 212, 217, 222, 223, 226, 228, 229, 265, 288, 305, 309, 345, 356, 366, 367, 381, 384, 385, 406, 410, 428, 429, 540, 542, 543, 544, 546, 552, 556, 557, 558, 559, 598, 601, 603, 604, 609, 646
Moskowitz, H., 522
Mougey, E. H., 597
Moulton, J. M., 622
Mount, L. E., 159
Mowrer, O. H., 225, 226, 369, 426
Mrosovsky, N., 46
Muehleisen, P., 407
Muir, D., 435, 447
Mulvaney, D. E., 297, 318, 320, 324, 326
Murgatroyd, D., 154
Murray, C. S., 59, 65
Murray, E. N., 610
Myer, J. S., 408, 409
Myers, J. L., 289, 308
Myers, R. D., 167, 169
Myhre, K., 157, 158

Nakamura, K., 168
Nathan, M. A., 598
Nathan, M. S., 598
Nauta, W. J. H., 597, 603
Navarick, D. J., 61, 324, 326, 327, 332, 336
Navarro, A. P., 544
Neffinger, G. G., 375, 398, 401
Neill, W. H., 157
Neimeck, W., 597
Nelson, J. A., 249, 460
Nelson, K., 137, 144
Neuringer, A. J., 185, 205, 207, 208, 210, 211, 252, 301, 304, 308, 316, 333, 334
Nevin, J. A., 75, 77, 78, 141, 213, 236, 242, 245, 246, 248, 255, 266, 267, 268, 269, 274, 275, 276, 315, 525, 535, 537
Newman, B. L., 573
Newman, F. L., 482, 490, 494
Newton, J. E. O., 598, 606
Nichols, J. R., 557
Nickerson, M., 165
Niemegeer, C. J., 586
Ninteman, F. W., 585
Nissen, H. W., 641, 642
Noel, R. C., 496
Norborg, J., 300, 316, 317
Norton, P. R., 605
Notterman, J. M., 494
Nowicki, L. E., 589, 590
Nunes, D. L., 211
Nunnally, J. C., 449
Nye, P. W., 520

Oatley, K., 32, 36, 45
O'Boyle, M. K., 131, 132, 135
Obrist, P. A., 598, 603, 610, 611
O'Connell, M. E., 410
Oden, D. L., 130
O'Donahue, N. F., 589
Odum, E. P., 46
Ogawa, N., 603
Ogilvie, D. M., 159
Olds, J., 570, 571, 572, 574, 575, 576, 577, 579, 581, 583, 584, 585, 589, 590, 605
Olds, M. E., 572, 576, 585, 589, 590
O'Leary, K. D., 309
Olson, K., 535
Olson, L., 585
Olson, R. D., 378
Opton, E. M., 603
Orloff, E. R., 428, 429
Orme-Johnson, D. W., 357
Ost, J. W., 487
Overmann, S. R., 222, 226
Overton, D. A., 555, 556

Pachomov, N., 154
Padilla, S. G., 69
Palmer, J. A., 456
Panksepp, J., 32, 33, 35, 44, 574, 575, 576
Paolini, R. M., 585
Pappas, B. A., 606, 608, 609, 610
Pare, W., 604, 606
Parrish, J., 598
Paul, G., 564
Pavlov, I. P., 9, 22, 29, 31, 53, 54, 55, 56, 58, 59, 60, 61, 62, 68, 70, 71, 75, 80, 81, 84, 85, 88, 89, 90, 91, 118, 119, 120, 121, 122, 127, 138, 144, 340, 341, 342, 343, 344, 347, 349, 351, 357, 358, 359, 360, 397, 400, 401, 447, 476, 483, 489, 492, 493, 496, 596
Pear, J. J., 74, 86, 409
Peck, S., 375, 380
Peden, B. F., 65
Peele, T. L., 589, 590
Peindaries, R., 167
Peirce, C., 620
Pellegrino, L. J., 572
Penn, P. E., 168, 169
Pennypacker, H. S., 445
Peretz, B., 590
Perez-Cruet, J., 597, 598, 606
Perin, C. T., 260, 281
Perkins, C. C., 82, 90, 133, 273
Perlmutter, L. C., 67
Persinger, M. A., 409
Persson, N., 589
Peters, J. V., 606
Peters, R. J., 282
Peterson, C., 248
Peterson, G. B., 56, 58, 60, 81, 90, 120
Peterson, J. L., 136
Peterson, N., 485, 486, 487
Peterson, R. H., 603
Pfaffman, C., 582, 583, 585, 586, 588
Phillips, A. G., 571, 577, 578, 582, 583, 584, 585, 586, 587, 588, 589
Phillips, M. L., 605
Piaget, J., 636, 640
Pickens, R., 543, 552, 554, 557, 558, 563
Pierce, C. H., 219, 260, 281

Pierrel-Sorrentino, R. A., 434, 515
Pike, R., 537
Pin, C., 586
Pisani, P., 640
Platt, J. R., 221, 222, 224, 226
Pliskoff, S. S., 79, 139, 164, 179, 181, 222, 237, 238, 239, 240, 241, 242, 243, 244, 246, 248, 249, 250, 252, 572, 573, 575, 576, 578
Plumlee, L., 252, 359, 598, 606, 609
Pointer, F. A., 606
Poli, M., 87, 90
Polish, E., 597
Polk, D. L., 167
Pomerleau, O. F., 358, 393, 606
Popp, R. J., 372, 397
Poppen, R., 436
Porter, J. H., 135, 138
Porter, P. B., 575, 589, 590, 597
Porter, R. W., 598, 604, 610
Poschel, B. P. H., 585
Potts, M. A., 162
Pouthas, V., 143
Powell, D. A., 529
Powell, R. W., 209, 213, 217, 375, 380, 404
Powell, T. P. S., 588
Powers, P., 7
Premack, D., 4, 28, 33, 40, 99, 101, 102, 103, 104, 105, 106, 107, 108, 109, 110, 111, 112, 113, 115, 122, 123, 180, 181, 267, 268, 276, 288, 624, 631, 633, 640, 641, 650, 651
Pribram, K. H., 517
Price, T., 495
Prokasy, W. F., 318, 340, 639
Proni, T. J., 417
Proppe, D. W., 154
Purtle, R. B., 442
Pylyshyn, Z. W., 650, 651

Rachlin, H., 13, 59, 75, 80, 86, 87, 90, 99, 127, 128, 133, 138, 141, 180, 235, 238, 239, 241, 246, 248, 253, 254, 264, 267, 272, 273, 274, 275, 276, 297, 298, 328, 333, 386, 406
Rackham, D., 59, 119
Ramer, R. G., 470
Ramsay, D. A., 606
Ramsden, M., 461, 462
Randolph, J. J., 209, 307
Ranson, S. W., 154
Rashotte, M. E., 509
Raskin, D. C., 261, 282
Raslear, T. G., 515, 524
Rasmussen, A. J., 598
Ray, B. A., 438, 504, 517, 522, 525
Ray, O. S., 356, 574, 577
Razran, G., 607
Rebert, C. S., 606
Rech, R. H., 540
Rechtschaffen, A., 162
Redford, M. E., 82, 90, 133, 273
Regal, P. J., 161, 162
Rege, V., 490
Reichlin, S., 603
Reid, L. D., 575, 589
Reiss, S., 487
Renfrew, J. W., 183, 418, 420, 422
Renner, K. E., 575
Rescorla, R. A., 54, 55, 56, 58, 61, 80, 84, 85, 88, 120, 127, 128, 315, 341, 342, 343, 344, 350, 357, 358, 390, 391, 392, 393, 397, 398, 400, 409, 445, 446, 447, 448, 451, 452, 457, 470, 487, 507, 508
Reus, J. F., 606
Revusky, S. H., 153, 484, 507
Reynierse, J. H., 131, 132
Reynolds, G. S., 2, 72, 73, 74, 76, 77, 79, 84, 88, 140, 142, 213, 214, 215, 216, 217, 218, 223, 225, 247, 254, 257, 258, 259, 263, 265, 266, 267, 268, 292, 472, 573
Reynolds, M. D., 143
Ricci, J. A., 57, 90, 127
Riccio, D. C., 367
Rice, H. K., 597
Richards, R. W., 129, 137, 447, 461, 462, 466, 469
Richardson, K., 224
Richelle, M., 559
Richter, C. P., 28, 29, 30, 31, 32, 33, 34, 35, 36, 44, 46
Ricketts, P., 600, 601
Riddle, W. C., 185, 358, 427
Riesen, A. H., 486
Riess, D. A., 404, 406, 407
Riley, A. L., 89, 90, 359, 409, 410
Riley, D. A., 447
Rilling, M., **432-480**, 5, 76, 80, 85, 129, 137, 141, 222, 255, 407, 446, 447, 450, 451, 453, 455, 465, 466, 467, 468, 469, 471, 472, 473, 474, 475, 482
Rinaldi, P., 608
Ringler, R., 606
Rioch, D., 597
Ritter, S., 585
Roberts, A. E., 358, 380
Roberts, E., 586, 588
Roberts, W. W., 14, 15, 165, 582
Robinson, A. E., 5, 35, 36
Robinson, G. M., **619-627**, 622, 627, 630, 633, 634, 635, 640, 647, 650
Robinson, J. A., 597, 600, 601
Robinson, J. E., 262, 282
Robinson, W. W., 597, 598, 601, 602
Roby, T. B., 581
Rocha e Silva, M. I., 219
Rodgers, W. L., 20
Roeper, T., 632
Roll, D. L., 14
Rolls, E. T., 580, 583
Rose, R. M., 597, 603, 604
Rosen, A. H., 605
Rosen, A. P., 456
Rosenberger, P. B., 522, 523
Rosenblith, J. Z., 135
Rosenblum, M. A., 606
Rosenquist, H., 437
Ross, G. S., 141, 597
Ross, L. E., 61
Rossi, R. R., 577
Routtenberg, A., 572, 577, 585, 589, 590
Rozin, P., 8, 14, 18, 90, 153, 157, 158, 484, 485
Rozkowska, E., 20
Rubin, H. B., 409
Rudolph, R. L., 486, 489, 490, 491, 492, 493, 494
Rumbaugh, D. M., 640
Rusiniak, K. W., 8
Russell, D. B., 492
Russo, P., 102
Rutherford, G., 639
Rutstein, J., 154, 155
Sachar, E. J., 597
Sadowsky, S., 524, 575
Sailor, W., 639
Sainsbury, R. S., 528
Sakai, M., 575
Sallery, R. D., 418
Salzinger, K., 641
Sandlie, M. E., 605
Sanger, D., 347, 349
Santibanez, H. G., 605
Saslow, C. A., 522
Satinoff, E., **153-173**, 4, 146, 154, 155, 167, 168
Saunders, J., 516, 605
Sawrey, J. M., 604
Sawrey, W. J., 597, 604
Scerni, A., 586
Schachter, S., 583
Schadler, M., 440, 454
Schaeffer, R. W., 40, 102, 136
Schalch, D. S., 603
Schaller, G. B., 33, 36, 47, 48
Schaub, R. E., 318, 319, 320, 321, 342
Schipper, L. M., 61
Schlichting, U. U., 179, 192
Schiff, B. B., 571, 580, 581, 586, 588
Schlesinger, K., 606
Schlosberg, H., 467, 493
Schmaltz, L. W., 404
Schmitt, D. R., 237, 276
Schneider, B. A., 140, 207, 208, 210, 211, 213, 216, 249, 333, 530, 531
Schneider, J. W., 265, 298, 335
Schneiderman, N., 604
Schnelle, J. F., 248
Schnitzer, S. B., 589
Schnur, P., 507
Schoener, T. W., 33, 46, 47, 49
Schoenfeld, W. N., 48, 201, 203, 208, 213, 222, 303, 314, 376, 377, 398, 409, 610
Schrier, A. M., 260, 263, 280, 487
Schroeder, S. R., 236, 242
Schrot, B., 79
Schrot, S. H., 130
Schulman, A., 578
Schuster, C. R., 540, 541, 545, 553, 554, 556, 557, 563
Schuster, R. H., 289, 299, 303, 305, 309, 317, 333, 334
Schusterman, R., 519
Schwam, E., 58, 65
Schwartz, B., **53-97**, 3, 24, 63, 64, 65, 67, 69, 75, 80, 81, 82, 83, 85, 86, 87, 88, 90, 91, 126, 127, 128, 133, 141, 143, 185, 273, 275, 329, 359, 407, 408
Schwartz, G. E., 610
Schwartzbaum, J. S., 445
Schwing, R. C., 589, 590
Scobie, S. R., 358
Scott, J. K., 562
Scott, T. R., 523, 529
Scruton, P. M., 347, 348, 350
Scucki, H., 610
Scull, J., 73
Sears, G. W., 391, 392, 398, 400, 401, 407
Seevers, M. H., 192
Segal, E. F., **628-653**, 5, 129, 130, 131, 132, 135, 137, 147, 182, 296, 620, 635, 636, 647
Segal, M., 588
Seifter, J., 558, 560
Selekman, W., 440, 455
Seligman, M. E. P., 14, 84, 91, 113, 375, 407, 436, 520
Sepinwall, J., 74
Seraganian, P., 435, 447
Setzer, J., 441
Sevenster, P., 16, 118, 120, 121, 122, 123, 137
Seward, J. P., 261, 263, 282, 575, 576
Sewell, W. R., 209, 307
Seyffarth, H., 19
Shaffer, M. M., 178
Shan, S. Y. Y., 154, 155
Shanab, M. E., 136, 139
Shannon, C. E., 322
Shapiro, A. P., 597
Shapiro, D., 606, 610
Sharp, J. C., 590
Shea, R. A., 261, 282
Shearn, D. W., 607
Sheatz, G., 597
Sheffield, F. D., 63, 581
Shepard, R. N., 530, 531
Shepp, B. E., 487
Sheriff, W., 162
Sherman, J. A., 307, 637, 639
Sherman, J. E., 462
Sherrington, C. S., 8, 9, 14, 25, 29
Sherry, G., 487
Shettleworth, S., 8, 14, 69, 75, 77, 78, 91, 113, 114, 115, 118, 123, 140, 268, 436, 483, 580
Shimp, C. P., 79, 224, 225, 245, 251, 255, 256, 263, 264, 266, 267, 269, 271, 272, 274, 275, 276, 398, 643
Shmavonian, B. M., 603
Shnidman, S. R., 378, 610
Shull, R. L., 79, 140, 141, 207, 209, 216, 226, 237, 242, 243, 244, 246, 249, 302, 308
Shumaker, J., 639
Sibly, R., 144
Sidley, N. A., 516, 519
Sidman, M., 2, 30, 58, 119, 165, 185, 201, 234, 260, 280, 289, 342, 344, 349, 357, 368, 369, 370, 371, 372, 373, 374, 375, 376, 377, 378, 380, 381, 388, 390, 393, 394, 395, 396, 400, 401, 407, 426, 427, 438, 450, 504, 517, 540, 542, 551, 578, 579, 597, 598, 599, 600, 605
Sidman, R. L., 517
Siegel, P. S., 36
Silberberg, A., 58, 65, 79, 81, 87, 237, 240, 241, 242, 244, 246
Silver, M. P., 260, 281, 606
Silverman, P. J., 304, 435, 464
Simmelhag, V., 69, 81, 91, 113, 127, 129, 130, 133, 136, 137, 139, 140, 185, 272, 273, 274, 406, 464, 580
Simmonds, M. A., 168
Simpson, C. W., 139
Simson, L. R., 598
Singh, B., 607
Singh, S. D., 141, 142, 143, 553
Siskel, M., 45
Skinner, B. F., 1, 2, 5, 7, 8, 9, 23, 24, 28, 29, 30, 31, 32, 33, 36, 38, 44, 45, 46, 48, 49, 53,

Author Index

Skinner (Cont.)
54, 63, 88, 91, 127, 128, 129, 134, 140, 143, 174, 175, 176, 177, 180, 182, 184, 185, 187, 201, 204, 205, 206, 207, 208, 209, 210, 212, 213, 216, 217, 218, 219, 222, 223, 224, 225, 227, 234, 253, 290, 291, 293, 295, 296, 298, 309, 341, 345, 347, 358, 393, 406, 409, 434, 467, 469, 504, 572, 573, 580, 598, 619, 621, 622, 628, 629, 632, 633, 634, 635, 636, 637, 638, 639, 640, 641, 642, 643, 646, 647, 648, 650, 651
Slangen, J. L., 138
Slaughter, J., 608
Sloan, M., 590
Slobin, D., 633
Smith, C. B., 188, 559, 560
Smith, G. D., 379, 380, 404, 405
Smith, J. B., 90, 134, 143, 192, 359, 417
Smith, J. C., 14
Smith, N. S., 580
Smith, O. A., 598
Smith, R. F., 319, 407, 408
Smith, R. M., 598, 604
Smith, S. G., 58
Smith, W. M., 58
Smith, W. S., 69
Snapper, A. G., 376, 377, 398, 606, 610
Snowden, C. T., 32, 33
Snyder, E., 164, 577
Solomon, R. L., 54, 61, 88, 341, 342, 358, 375, 467, 493
Soltysik, A., 604
Spanier, D., 131, 132
Sparber, S. B., 542
Spealman, R. D., 270, 271, 272
Spear, N. E., 86, 457
Spector, O. J., 378, 379
Spence, K. W., 61, 75, 218, 234, 447, 448, 449, 450, 451, 453, 456, 462, 463, 476, 483, 493
Spencer, P. S. J., 167
Sperling, H. G., 516
Spies, G., 577
Spragg, S. D. S., 557
Spyker, J. M., 542
Squier, L. H., 58
Squires, N. K., 248, 298, 300, 316, 317, 329, 332, 333, 334
Squires, R. D., 154
Staddon, J. E. R., **125-152**, **1-6**, 68, 69, 73, 75, 77, 80, 81, 89, 91, 113, 126, 127, 128, 129, 130, 131, 132, 133, 134, 135, 137, 138, 139, 140, 141, 142, 143, 147, 185, 192, 204, 217, 222, 224, 235, 255, 256, 265, 266, 272, 273, 274, 275, 276, 277, 289, 293, 300, 301, 304, 305, 359, 406, 458, 464, 580, 646
Stamm, J. S., 517
Stark, P., 589
Starr, B. C., 301, 304
Stebbins, W. C., 519, 522, 525, 526, 527, 532, 598
Stein, L., 129, 156, 342, 344, 345, 349, 350, 353, 571, 574, 576, 580, 585, 586
Steinbaum, E. A., 14
Steiner, J., 324
Steiner, S. S., 178
Stellar, E., 33
Stephens, J. H., 603

Stern, J. A., 597, 604
Stevens, S. S., 242, 262
Stevenson, J. A. F., 571, 579, 581, 582, 583
Stevenson, J. G., 443
Stevenson-Hinde, J., 3, 8, 133
Stiers, M., 58, 65, 81
Stinson, R. H., 159
Stitt, C., 353
Stoddard, L. T., 438
Stokes, L. W., 393
Stolerman, I. P., 560
St. Omer, V. V., 564
Stone, E. A., 604, 605, 608
Stoyak, M., 407
Stoyva, J. M., 604, 610
Stretch, R., 428, 429
Stricker, E. M., 586
Stromme, S. B., 158
Strong, C., 564, 565
Stubbs, D. A., 218, 237, 239, 240, 243, 244, 248, 249, 250, 252, 302, 303, 304, 305, 307, 308, 316, 435, 464
Stuckey, H. L., 36
Stunkard, A. J., 7
Sturm, T., 59
Stutz, R. M., 577
Sullivan, M. A., 524
Sulzbacher, S. I., 564, 565
Sutherland, N. S., 507, 529
Sutterer, J. R., 86, 598, 610
Svensson, L., 139
Svinicki, J. G., 482, 489, 498
Svinicki, M. D., 482, 489
Swadlow, H. A., 604
Swets, J. A., 533, 534, 537
Swinnen, M. E. T., 598, 606
Switalski, R. W., 290, 291, 439, 441, 456, 494
Symmes, D., 522
Szwejkowska, G., 483

Tallen, R. R., 296
Tallon, S., 32, 33, 44
Tapper, D. N., 527, 529
Tarpy, R. M., 261, 282
Tatum, R., 604
Taub, E., 222
Taus, S. E., 314, 472
Taylor, E. D., 597
Taylor, L. H., 590
Teague, R. S., 154
Tecce, J. J., 606
Teghtsoonian, R., 421
Teitelbaum, P., **7-27**, 3, 8, 10, 16, 17, 18, 20, 35, 40, 156, 571, 579, 581, 583, 586, 597
Temple, W., 298
Templer, D. I., 579
Templeton, J. R., 156
Ten Eyck, R. L., 298, 329
Terhune, J. G., 103, 112
Terman, J. S., 516, 518, 535, 536, 537
Terman, M., 516, 521, 524, 575
Terrace, H. S., 57, 61, 73, 75, 76, 77, 84, 85, 127, 186, 268, 270, 271, 275, 441, 446, 447, 453, 454, 456, 460, 461, 462, 465, 466, 467, 468, 469, 470, 471, 472, 473, 474, 481, 483, 486, 489, 507, 553
Tersky, B., 606, 610
Teyler, T. J., 606
Thach, J. S., 367, 597
Theios, J., 365
Thoenen, H., 168
Thomas, D. R., 249, 290, 291, 292, 294, 434, 437, 438, 439, 440, 441, 453, 455, 456, 460, 461, 462, 482, 483, 487, 488, 489, 490, 493, 494, 496, 499, 500, 501, 502, 503, 504, 505, 507, 508, 509, 526, 527
Thomas, D. W., 32, 33, 35, 36, 61
Thomas, G., 305, 307, 308
Thomas, J. R., 295, 302, 306
Thomas, P. R., 441
Thompson, D. M., 139, 355
Thompson, J., 633
Thompson, L. W., 606
Thompson, R. L., 58, 59, 375
Thompson, T. I., 5, 15, 128, 136
Thompson, T., **540-569**, 395, 540, 541, 543, 545, 548, 549, 551, 552, 553, 554, 557, 558, 559, 561, 562, 563, 565
Thomson, D. M., 638
Thone, L., 559
Thorndike, E. L., 53, 99, 100, 101, 634
Thorne, P., 610
Thorpe, S. A., 517, 522
Tinbergen, N., 14, 15, 20, 22, 23, 142
Timberlake, W., 29, 106, 107
Tobias, L. L., 564
Todorov, J. C., 79, 120, 244, 249, 253, 271, 272, 274, 382, 406, 408
Tolliver G., 139, 597, 606
Tolson, W., 597, 598, 599
Tomie, A., 507, 508
Tosheff, J., 602
Tracy, W. H., 367
Tracy, W. K., 486, 487
Trapold, M. A., 261, 281, 282
Trattner, J., 103
Travis, R. P., 589, 590
Trevitt, A. J., 240, 241, 242, 255, 266, 275, 276
Trombley, J., 551
Trowill, J. A., 574, 575, 576, 578, 607, 610
Tucker, L., 606
Tulving, E., 638
Turner, B. N., 16, 17
Turner, C., 501, 502, 503, 504, 507
Turner, M. B., 651
Turrell, E. S., 597
Tversky, A., 277
Twitchell, T. E., 19, 22

Ulrich, R. E., 394, 418, 421, 422, 428
Ungerstedt, U., 585, 586
Uphouse, L. L., 606
Uretsky, N. J., 168
Ursin, H., 589
Ursin, R., 589
Uyeda, A. A., 261, 282, 575, 576

Valenstein, E. S., 15, 571, 572, 573, 574, 577
Vanderwart, M. L., 604
Vanderwolf, C. H., 118, 604
Van Dyne, G. C., 89
Vanegas, H., 582
Van Houten, R., 490, 491, 492, 493, 494
Van Ost, S. L., 459
Van Sommers, P., 160, 532
Van Toller, C., 350, 352

VanVeen, W. J., 606
Vardaris, R. M., 606
Vasselli, J. R., 129
Vasta, R., 647
Vaughan, H. G., 532
Vaughn, L. K., 166
Verhave, T., 377, 388, 389, 390, 392, 560
Vickery, C., 201
Viemeister, N. F., 319
Villareal, J., 137, 553
Vogt, C. P., 290
Vom Saal, W., 499
Von Glasersfeld, E., 640

Waddell, T. R., 306
Wade, G. N., 162
Wade, M., 483, 485, 487, 488, 492
Wagner, A. R., 61, 344, 397, 451, 452, 457, 487, 495, 496, 498, 499, 501, 502, 507, 508
Wagner, M. J., 128, 137
Wald, G., 10, 22
Walker, E. L., 99, 101
Walker, S. F., 248
Wallace, R. F., 335
Waller, M. B., 185, 186, 358, 556
Waller, P. F., 185, 358, 544, 546, 556
Walsh, M., 409
Walter, W. G., 606
Walters, G. C., 113, 115, 116
Wampler, R. S., 156
Ward, J. S., 509
Warner, H., 640
Wasserman, E. A., 56, 57, 59, 60, 61, 65, 69, 120, 121, 160, 273, 320
Wauquier, A., 586
Wayner, M. J., 130, 139
Weaver, W., 322
Webb, R. A., 610
Webbe, F. M., 306
Webster, D. M., 572, 589, 590
Weijnen, J. A., 138
Weil-Melherbe, H., 603
Weiner, H., 140
Weiskrantz, L., 352, 353, 521, 525
Weisman, R. G., 77, 85, 102, 390, 391, 392, 393, 456, 460, 461, 462
Weiss, A. B., 153, 166
Weiss, B., 142, 153, 154, 164, 166, 167, 189, 213, 223, 302, 367, 542, 555, 556, 560, 562, 646
Weiss, J. D., 597
Weiss, J. M., 604, 605, 608
Weiss, S. J., 74, 439, 443, 444, 453, 459, 460, 461, 462, 463
Weisz, J. D., 597
Weissman, N. W., 225
Wells, J. A., 551
Welty, R., 606
Wenger, M. A., 607
Wenzel, B. M., 597
Werdegar, D., 598, 606
Werner, J. S., 138
Wertheim, G. A., 383, 562
Wesemann, A. F., 116
Wessells, M. G., 23, 61, 65, 464, 465, 470
Westbrook, R. F., 73, 82, 83, 86, 90, 275, 495
Westoby, M., 36, 47, 48
Wetzel, M. C., 572, 589, 590

Wheatley, W. L., 79, 269, 270, 271, 272, 274, 460, 461, 462
Wherry, F., 600, 601
Whishaw, I. Q., 168
White, A. J., 255, 275, 276
Whitehurst, G. J., 639, 640, 647
White, K. G., 437
Wiener, N., 322
Wiepkema, P. R., 32, 35
Wike, E. L., 289, 305
Wilcoxon, H. C., 14, 99, 485
Wilkie, D. M., 74, 86, 458, 459, 461, 462, 470
Wilkinson, H. A., 589, 590
Williams, B. A., 496, 497
Williams, D. R., 2, 3, 24, 55, 56, 62, 63, 64, 65, 66, 67, 68, 70, 75, 78, 80, 87, 88, 119, 127, 128, 141, 143, 268, 272, 597, 598
Williams, H., 2, 3, 62, 63, 64, 119, 128, 272
Williams, J. L., 598
Williams, R. J., 240, 241, 242, 255

Willis, F. N., 45
Willis, R. D., 252
Wilson, A., 388
Wilson, D. M., 142
Wilson, M., 517
Wilson, R. G., 21
Wilton, R. N., 78, 127, 319, 322, 323, 324, 325
Winokur, S., 56, 127
Winton, A. S. W., 435, 464
Wise, C. D., 571, 585, 586
Witoslawski, J. J., 292
Witty, W., 216, 226, 302, 308
Wolin, B. R., 67
Wong, I. G., 589, 590
Wood, K. A., 252, 264
Wood-Gush, D. G. M., 35
Woodruff, G., 58, 60, 62
Woods, J. H., 250, 251, 263, 553, 554
Woods, P. J., 262, 282
Woods, S. C., 129
Wool, M., 600, 601
Word, T. J., 604

Wright, A. A., 518, 530, 532, 536
Wright, B., 40
Wright, B. A., 164
Wright, J. E., 164, 576, 578
Wurtman, R. J., 168
Wüttke, W., 136, 179, 192, 356, 558
Wyckoff, L. B., 30, 313, 314, 318, 322
Wynne-Edwards, V. C., 33, 34
Wyrwicka, W., 14

Xhenseval, B., 559

Yager, D., 517, 535
Yaksh, T. L., 167, 169
Yamamoto, W. S., 31
Yanagita, T., 192
Yarczower, M., 357, 447, 455, 456, 457, 460, 461, 462
Yarensky, P., 536
Yeh, S. D. J., 154
Yehuda, S., 168
York, J. L., 606

Young, G. A., 117, 119, 120, 183, 418, 420, 522
Young, J., 153, 166
Young, P. T., 32, 582
Young, W., 21
Younger, M. S., 393
Yum, K. S., 557
Yunger, L. M., 574

Zeaman, D., 258, 278
Zeigler, H. P., 32, 35
Zeiler, M. D., **201–232**, 2, 125, 140, 176, 185, 193, 204, 207, 214, 216, 224, 227, 301, 305
Zener, K., 61, 138
Zentall, T., 482
Zeilke, S., 138
Zigmond, M. J., 586
Zimmerman, D. W., 175, 299, 304
Zimmerman, J., 219, 260, 281, 306, 307, 308, 316, 317
Zis, A. P., 586
Zolman, J. F., 153, 160
Zuriff, G. E., 143

Subject Index

Abrupt procedure, and errorless learning, 466
Absolute generalization gradient:
  description, 435
  and stimulus control, 501–502
Absolute rate of responding:
  and conditioned suppression, 345, 348–351, 354
  equations for, 257, 264–267
  and law of effect, 257–263
  and magnitude of food reinforcement, 258–259
  and power function law, 277
Absorption rate, drugs, 543, 547–548
Abstract propositional knowledge, 650–651
Abstraction ability, and animal psychophysics, 525
Abundance, food, and population, 34
Abuse, of drugs, 192–193, 542, 557–558, 563
Acceleration of pecking, and postreinforcement pause, 142–143
Acceptability, of language utterances, 624
Access, to negative reinforcement, 376–377
Acetylcholine:
  and stimulus control, 555–556
  and thermoregulation, 168–169
ACh (see Acetylcholine)
Acquired distinctiveness of cues, 487–488
Acquisition:
  autoshaping, 54–58, 62
  avoidance, and drugs, 561
  with central reinforcement, 575, 589
  on chained schedules, 290–291, 299
  and conditioned reinforcement, 305
  control by incidental stimulus, 505
  dimensional control, 454–456, 475
  drug effects on, 560–562
  errorless discrimination, 464–480
  fixed-ratio performance, 227
  key pecking, 55–57
  language, 619–627, 634
  lexicon, 620
  with negative reinforcement, 374–375, 404–409
  overshadowing during, 492–493
  speed, compared to extinction, 205
  stimulus control, 483–484
  syntax, 619–627
Activity, as class of motor patterns, 144
Activity wheel (see Running wheel)
Acuity, visual:
  pigeon, 517–518
  sea lion, 519–520
Adaptation, and rate of eating, 175
Adaptation-level theory, 4
Adaptive specialization, and stimulus control, 484–485
Added clock, 296–297 (see also Clock schedule)
Added counter, on chained schedule, 295
Added cues:
  correlated with shock, 365, 390–392
  and dimensional control, 391–392, 398–400
  in escape procedure, 383–387
  and negative reinforcement, 365, 381–398
  and Pavlovian conditioning, 393, 395
  and shock averaging, 397–398
  shock-delay procedures, 392–398
  and two-factor theory, 396–398

Additive difference model, and matching, 277
Additive summation, and stimulus generalization, 443–444, 459
Additivity theory of contrast, 80–91
Adipsia, hypothalamic, 17, 20, 156
Adjunctive behavior (see also Collateral behavior, Interim activities)
  as displacement activities, 23
  eating in doves, 139
Adjusting schedule:
  avoidance, 394
  fixed-ratio, 205, 212–213
Adrenal hormones, and avoidance, 599–601
Adrenergic blocking agent, and thermoregulation, 165
Adventitious punishment:
  and conditioned suppression, 351, 357–358, 360
  and history of animal, 184–185
Adventitious reinforcement:
  in automaintenance, 63–64, 66, 68
  in autoshaping, 119
  bursting on shock schedule, 388
  on concurrent schedules, 234–235, 243
  and history of animal, 184–185
  history of concept, 127–128
  of induced attack, 136
  and induced drinking, 130, 134
  interresponse times, 225
  and nonchaining delay, 218
  and positive conditioned suppression, 359–360
  problems with, 127–128, 132
  and running, 147
  and superstitious behavior, 127, 204
  and terminal response, 127–128
Aftereffect, motion:
  in monkeys, 523
Afterimage, colored:
  in animal psychophysics, 526
Aggressive behavior (see also Attack, Biting attack, Schedule-induced behavior):
  and aversive control, 416–430
  by-product of discrimination, 467–469
  and drugs, 552, 562
  and errorless learning, 468–469
  extinction-induced, 468–469
  pigeons, 59, 120, 136–137, 139
  schedule-induced, 129, 134–137, 139
  Siamese fighting fish, 59, 65, 116
  suppression by punishment, 115–116
Air flow, stimulus control by, 491
Air licking, rats, 138
Alcohol (see also Ethanol):
  ingestion
    Rhesus monkey, 597
  reinforcer
    rats, 553, 561
  and stimulus control, 555–556
Alcoholism, human, 563
Alert posturing, gerbil, 115–116
Algorithm, in natural language, 622
Alleyway (see Runway)
Alligator, thermoregulation, 153
Allocation of resources, in feeding patterns, 47
All-or-none law, 11
Alpha-methyl-p-tyrosine, and self-stimulation of brain, 585
Alpha waves, 606
Altered physiological states, 596–611
Alternation, on concurrent schedules, 234, 244, 276
Alternative response assumption, 99
Amitryptaline, 545
Amobarbital:
  classification, 544–545
  and punishment, 558

Amount of training, and stimulus control, 453–456, 483
Amphetamine (see also d-amphetamine):
  classification, 544–545
  and clock schedule, 555
  and conditioned suppression, 355–356
  and fixed-interval behavior, 559–560
  and fixed-ratio behavior, 562
  and locomotor activity, 554
  and punishment, 558, 560
  as reinforcer, 557
  and schedule control, 188–191, 552, 557
  self-administration, 543
  and self-stimulation of brain, 571, 585
  and stimulation-induced drinking, 581–582
  and thermoregulation, 165, 556
  tolerance for, 550
Amphibians, thermoregulation, 153, 156–158, 161–164
Amygdala:
  activation by stimulation, 583
  EEG activity, 605
  self-stimulation, 590
Amyl acetate, odor stimulus, 517
Amytal (see Amobarbital)
Anaclitic operant, 67
Anaesthetics:
  excretion of, 550
  and thermoregulation, 165
Analgesic drugs (see also Heroin, Morphine, Narcotics, Opiates):
  classification, 545
  as reinforcers, 557
Analgesic effect, electrical brain stimulation, 574
Androgen, and central reinforcement, 579
Angerthas, 101
Animal psychophysics, 515–537
Animal psychophysics:
  methodological problems, 523–525
  perception, 526–530
  scaling in, 530–532
  signal detection theory, 532–537
  stimulus presentation methods, 520–525
  threshold determination, 515–525
Animate motion, 29
Annoyer, in Law of Effect, 99, 101
Anolis cristellus (see Lizard)
Anorexia (see also Aphagia):
  and amphetamines, 190, 356
Antagonist, to drugs, 179, 553, 554, 557, 563
Antecedent variables, in psychopharmacology, 553–554
Antianxiety drugs, 545 (see also Tranquilizers)
Anticholinergic drugs, 555
Anticipation, of food needs, 33, 46
Antidepressant drugs, classification, 545
Antipsychotic drugs, classification, 545
Anxiety:
  and conditioned suppression, 353, 355–357, 360, 393
  and drugs, 355–357, 559, 562
  as hypothetical drive state, 188
Anxiolytic agents, 360
Aortic flow probe, 603
Aphagia, hypothalamic, 17, 20, 156
Aplysia, 9
Apomorphine, self-administration, 586
Apparatus:
  animal psychophysics, 524
  aversive control, 416–418
  central reinforcement, 572–574
Appetitive behavior:
  and biological constraints, 114–115
  vs. consummatory behavior, 22
  as operant, 22
  in sleep, 22
Appetitive motivation, and conditioned suppression, 358

663

Approach-avoidance conflict:
    and gastric ulcers, 597, 604
    and schedule induction, 139-140
Approach behavior, pigeons, in autoshaping, 65, 69
Arbitrary response:
    in autoshaping, 61
    in chain of reflexes, 29-30
    interchangeability of, 23
    and negative reinforcement, 402-409
    operant as, 3, 23, 29
    problems with concept, 15, 23, 29, 91, 180, 408
    prototype of behavior, 11, 54-55
Artic sculpin, thermoregulation, 158
Area shift, generalization gradient, 442, 453
Arithmetic VI schedule, 215
Arousal:
    and blood pressure, 603
    and brain damage, 586
    and conditioned suppression, 352
    and electrical brain stimulation, 583
    and motivation, 584-586
    theoretical concept, 99
    and thermoregulation, 155-156
Arsenicals, excretion of, 550
Artificial mother, and thermoregulation, 159
Ascending order of stimuli, in animal psychophysics, 521
Associability (see also Conditionability, Preparedness):
    response-reinforcer, 483-485
    stimulus-response, 520
Association:
    CS and US in autoshaping, 55, 70
    linguistic, 619
Associationistic model, language structure, 5, 628-633, 647-649
Associationists, 100
Associative competition, theory of, 507
Associative learning, and verbal behavior, 634
Associative shifting, and verbal behavior, 634, 640
Asymmetry:
    in multiple schedules, 268
    reinforcement and extinction, 205
Atropine:
    and avoidance, 542
    classification, 545
    and fixed-interval behavior, 544
    and learning, 561
    and stimulus control, 555
    and thermoregulation, 169
Attack (see also Aggressive behavior, Biting attack, Schedule-induced behavior):
    and aversive control, 416-430
    brain-stimulation-induced, 14
    in cat, 15
    drug effects, 552, 562
    electrically evoked, 14-15
    extinction-induced, 468-469
    hypothalamic lesions and, 17
    as interim activity, 135-139
    in pigeon, 136-137, 139
    in rat, 17, 136, 139
    in rhesus monkey, 380
    schedule-induced, 135-139
    shock-elicited, 183-184, 380, 409, 417-425
    in squirrel monkey, 136, 139, 183-184, 380, 409, 417-425, 428
Attention:
    in animal psychophysics, 517, 523-524, 528, 536
    concept, 5, 30

formal model, 507
selective, 507-510
and stimulus control, 481-510
Attentiveness, and discrimination training, 500-502, 505, 507-510
Auditory cortex, EEG activity, 605
Auditory intensity:
    difference limen, 524
    discrimination,
        cat, 516
        chinchilla, 515-516
        monkey, 534-535
        rat, 516
Auditory learning, language, 643-647
Auditory sensitivity:
    bats, 519, 523
    mouse, 517
    rat, 518
Auditory thresholds, monkey, 516, 519, 521
Australian lizard (see Lizard)
Autoclitic:
    as discriminative stimulus, 621
    verbal behavior, 635, 640, 642, 647-649
Autoclitic frames, 635
Automaintenance (see also Negative automaintenance):
    conditions for, 54
    and contrast, 80
    heat reinforced, 65
    negative (see Negative automaintenance)
    Pavlovian-operant interaction, 62-63, 66-71, 119
    pigeons, 62-68, 119
    rats, 65
    response-reinforcer relations, 64-69, 91
    Siamese fighting fish, 65
    sign tracking in, 69
    squirrel monkey, 65-66
    stimulus-reinforcer relations, 63-69, 91
    water reinforced, 65
Automatons, animals as, 29-30
Autonomic responses, operant conditioning, 606-611
Autoshaping, 53-91
Autoshaping:
    acquisition, 54-58
    aggressive behavior, 59, 65
    chicks, 59-60, 65, 70, 120
    and classical conditioning, 2-3, 54-55, 58, 60-61, 68, 80, 91
    contingency vs. pairing, 54-56
    and contrast, 73-91, 272-274
    control procedures, 55-56, 61
    directedness of responses, 61
    dog, 58
    electrical brain stimulation in, 60
    with electric shock, 70
    and errorless learning, 464-465, 470-471
    fish, 58
    heat reinforced, 59-60
    informativeness of stimuli in, 56-57, 80, 84
    necessary and sufficient conditions, 54-56, 61, 67
    and operant conditioning, 13, 23, 54-55, 62, 70-71, 91
    partial reinforcement in, 61
    as Pavlovian conditioning, 55, 60-63, 68-71, 80-81, 91, 119, 121-122, 127, 138
    peck duration in, 24, 67-68, 81
    pigeons, 3, 7, 13, 24, 54-62, 68-70, 81, 119
    and positive conditioned suppression, 359
    quail, 58-59
    rat, 58, 60, 65, 81
    redundant stimuli, 56-57

rhesus monkeys, 58, 60
secondary reinforcement in, 56-57
sexual behavior, 59, 119
significance, 3, 7, 13, 53-71, 91
sign tracking in, 69, 81
species differences, 58, 60, 70, 91
stimulus substitution in, 62
and temporal control, 140
theories, 68-70, 119
tone stimulus, 69, 273
topography of response, 58-60, 67, 81, 119, 121-122
trial duration, 57-58, 78, 90
types of US, 58
water reinforced, 58-60, 62, 81, 119
Availability:
    food, and eating patterns, 33, 36-43, 47-48
    water, and drinking patterns, 36, 40
Availability, Law of (see Law of availability)
Averaging:
    generalization data, 437-439
    shock, and added cues, 387, 397-398
Aversive conditioning (see Avoidance, Escape, Negative reinforcement, Electric shock)
Aversive contingencies, and matching, 243-244, 253-254
Aversive control, 415-431 (see also Avoidance, Electric shock, Negative reinforcement)
Aversive control:
    and brain biochemistry, 606
    by-products, 415-430
    and generalization gradients, 450, 455-456
    human, 417-420
    methods, 416-418
    operant baseline, 5, 415-430
    patterns of responding, 418-430
    and peptic ulcers, 597, 604-605
Aversiveness:
    assessment, 415, 422
    in behavioral contrast, 76-77, 84-86
    and biological constraints, 115
    errors in programmed learning, 467, 469-470
    forced running, 103
    heat, 165
    interim period, 139-140
    and relativity of reward, 102, 111-112
    stimuli with negative outcomes, 314, 319, 325
    taste qualities, 527
    thermal stimuli, in human, 162-164
    US, and conditioned suppression, 341
Aversive situation, as drive operation, 368, 378-380
Avoidance (see also Aversive control, Electric shock, Negative reinforcement, Shock delay, Shock deletion)
Avoidance (of shock, by rats, unless otherwise specified), 367-410
Avoidance:
    abortable sequence schedule, 366
    and alcohol ingestion, 599
    and aversive control, 425-427
    and blood pressure conditioning, 608
    by-product of escape, 364-365
    cardiovascular changes in, 599-604
    cat, 193, 605
    and conditioned reinforcement, 319
    and conditioned suppression, 358, 360
    discriminated
        and animal psychophysics, 516
        and EEG activity, 605-606
        and endocrine changes, 599
    drug effects, 555-557

Subject Index

EEG activity in, 605–606
endocrine changes in, 599–601, 604
free-operant, 5, 119, 185, 369–371, 380, 597–606 (*see also* Avoidance, Sidman; Shock delay, Shock deletion)
functional relevance and, 113–119
gastrointestinal changes in, 597, 604–605
and generalization, 450, 455–456
heat, by rats, 156
and infectious disease, 597–598
long-term effects, 380, 427, 429, 599–605
multiple-variable-interval, 267–271
operant-Pavlovian interactions, 88
and peptic ulcers, 597, 604
pigeon, 13, 120, 450–451
problems with concept, 364, 369–370
rhesus monkeys, 185, 366, 597, 599–601, 604
and response strength, 260
as shock-frequency reduction, 387
squirrel monkeys, 185, 193–196
temporal pattern of behavior, 425–427
theories, 364–365, 393, 396–398
thermal change, 165
variable-interval, 260, 267–271
Avoidance, Sidman, 119, 185, 369–371, 380, 426
and physiological changes, 597–606
and thermoregulation, 165

Baboon:
blood pressure conditioning, 609–610
escape-avoidance, 601–602
thermoregulation, 153, 166
Background stimuli (*see also* Contextual stimulus):
and stimulus control, 457–458
Backward conditioning, 55, 61
Baconian induction, 2, 12, 28
Bad news, and conditioned reinforcement, 319, 322
Barbital, 544
Barbiturates:
chemistry, 544
classification, 544–545
and conditioned suppression, 355–356
and punishment, 558
reinforcer, 557
and schedule performances, 188, 191
stimulus control by, 555
tolerance, 550
Barking, in sea lion, 519–520
Bar pressing (*see* Lever pressing)
Basal ganglia, and electrical stimulation, 585
Base phrase marker, language theory, 629–630
Baseline:
stability, and drug effects, 7, 543, 551–552
stimulus control of, and drugs, 555
Basic strings, in language, 629–630
Basking, in thermoregulation, 162, 164
Bat, auditory sensitivity, 519, 523
Batesian mimicry, 484
Beak movement, as interim activity, 128
Behavior, modification:
and brain stimulation, 580
and drugs, 565
Behavioral arrest, and aversive control, 425
Behavioral clock, and induced activities, 140–148
Behavioral contrast (*see also* Local contrast, Negative behavioral contrast, Positive behavioral contrast, Transient contrast):
and autoshaping, 73–91, 272–274
by-product of discrimination, 467
definition, 73
determinants, 267, 274
equations, 267, 270
and errorless learning, 472–474
and generalization, 442, 449, 454
Herrnstein's account, 266–268, 270–275
and induced aggression, 469
inhibition and, 75–76, 84–85
and matching, 267, 272–275
necessary and sufficient conditions, 73, 76, 78, 83–85
with negative reinforcement, 382
and Pavlovian conditioning, 84–85, 88–89
and peak shift, 442, 454
quantitative account, 267, 270
and reinforcement frequency, 76–78, 84, 86
response-independent schedules, 132–133, 273
and response suppression, 76–77, 84
as schedule interaction, 88
temporal properties, 75–78, 86
theories, 75–91, 266–275
Behavioral final common path, 144
Behavioral homeostasis, and temperature-regulation, 153
Behavioral pharmacology, 5, 153–155, 164–169, 188–193, 349–360, 540–569 (*see also* Drugs, Psychopharmacology)
basic variables, 543–551
behavioral mechanisms, 551–560, 562
principles of drug action, 543–551
Behavioral state, in sequence of activities, 144
Behavioral stream, and negative reinforcement, 409, 410
Behavioral toxicology, 562–563
Behavioral variation, 127
Behaviorism:
and language, 519–527, 633–640
Skinner's radical, 1–2
Benzadrine (*see* d-amphetamine)
Benzodiazepine, and conditioned suppression, 356
Beta adrenergic blockade, and blood pressure, 603
Betta splendens (*see* Siamese fighting fish)
Bias:
animal psychophysics, and signal detection theory, 532–533
concurrent schedules, 238–239, 247–248, 251–256
drug selection, 544
generalization gradient in extinction, 438
response, in animal psychophysics, 516, 518, 521, 524, 534
Biconditional behavior, 70
Binary fractionation model, language structure, 643–647
Biochemistry, of brain, 606
Biofeedback, 571, 580
Biological control systems, 160
Biological predispositions, 113, 122
Biological relevance, 127
Biology of association, 70
Biotransformation of drugs, 550
Birds (*see also* Chick, Pigeon, Quail):
thermoregulation, 159–160
Birth rate, and food availability, 34
Bisection, animal psychophysics, 532
Biting, rats:
in automaintenance, 65
in contrast experiments, 82
Biting attack (*see also* Aggressive behavior, Attack, Schedule-induced behavior):
apparatus, 416–418
intensity, 418
mouse, 416–417
patterns, 418–430
punishment schedule, 428
schedule-induced, 136
shock-elicited, 183–184, 380
and shock reduction, 420, 426
squirrel monkey, 136, 183–184, 417–425, 428
Blackout (*see also* Timeout):
as brief stimulus, second-order schedules, 301, 304
delay of reinforcement, and matching, 251–252
fixed-interval schedule, 207–208
fixed-ratio schedule, 210–212
intertrial interval, and stimulus control, 489–490
multiple schedule, and matching, 269
Blocking, and stimulus control, 499–500, 507
Blood flow, instrumental conditioning, 571, 608
Blood pressure:
and conditioned suppression, 352, 598
conditioning, 571
and escape-avoidance, 601–604
instrumental conditioning, 608–610
measurement and recording, 598, 606
Boa constrictor, thermoregulation, 162
Body weight:
and changeover responses, 244
and escape-avoidance, 605
and matching, 269
and polydipsia, 132
"Botanizing," 2, 12, 30, 91
Bout duration, induced activities, 141–142, 146
Bowing response, pigeon, in automaintenance, 65
Boyle's law, 276
Brachium conjunctivum, self-stimulation of, 590
Brain chemistry, 606
Brain damage:
dogs, 20
humans, 20
hypothalamus, and thermoregulation, 154–156
monkey, and spiral aftereffect, 529
physiological study, 8, 16
preoptic area, and thermoregulation, 154
rats, 16–18
and self-stimulation, 582, 586–587
stages in recovery from, 8, 17, 20
Brain stem circuits, 588
Brain temperature, and thermoregulation, 154, 158
Break and run, on FI, 140
Break point, on FI, 265
Brief stimulus:
and chained schedule, 296–297, 299
on concurrent chains, 334
and conditioned reinforcement, 316–318, 334
discriminative effects, 300–309
in extinction, 305–306
hopper presentation as, 316–317
physical properties, 304–305
and second-order schedule, 299–309, 315–316
Brightness:
discrimination,
pigeons, 521, 532
rats, 526–527

Brightness (cont.)
  stimulus control by, pigeon, 490
  stimulus generalization, rat, 493
Bristol board, 98, 114
Brook trout, thermoregulation, 158
Burst duration, in contingent-response experiments, 110–112
Bursting:
  on concurrent VI schedules, 238, 246
  on interval vs. ratio schedules, 223
  in postshock period, 388, 394
Button pressing, human, and matching, 234–235
Buzzer, stimulus control by, 484
By-products:
  aversive control, 415–430
  discrimination learning, 467, 475

CA (see Catecholamine)
Caffeine, drug classification, 545
Caloric density, 33, 35, 43
Caloric regulation, 43, 47
Cannabis (see Marijuana, Tetrahydrocannabinol)
Cannula, implanted, 60
Carbachol, and thermoregulation, 169
Carbon monoxide, behavioral effects, 563
Cardiac output, and escape-avoidance, 602–603
Cardiorespiratory system, transient changes, 597
Cardiovascular responses, operant conditioning, 606–611
Cardiovascular system, experimentally induced changes, 598, 604
Carnivores:
  caloric regulation, 47
  feeding patterns, 36, 47–49
Castration, and central reinforcement, 579
Cat:
  attack behavior, 14–15
  auditory intensity discrimination, 516
  avoidance, 193, 605
  caloric regulation, 43
  carnivorous eating pattern, 49
  color vision, 515
  EEG activity, 605–606
  electrical brain stimulation, 14–15, 589–590
  meal patterning, 35–39, 49
  meal size, 34
  patterning of drinking, 36
  psychophysics, 515, 516, 520
  rat-killing behavior, 14–15
  self-stimulation of brain, 589–590
  shock avoidance, 193, 605
  shock-delay procedure, 393–394
  thermoregulation, 153, 166–167
  visual discrimination, 520
Catch trials, in animal psychophysics, 519
Catecholamine:
  and avoidance, 600
  and heart rate conditioning, 608
  and self-stimulation of brain, 571, 585–588
Catecholamine pathways:
  inhibition, 587–588
  and self-stimulation of brain, 585–589
Catecholaminergic neurons, 571, 585–588
Category symbols, in language, 630
Catheter, intravenous, drug administration by, 555–556
Caudate nucleus, self-stimulation of, 590
Causal factors, behavioral sequences, 143–148
Cebus monkey, contingent-response experiment, 102
Ceiling effect:
  in conditioned suppression, 351, 354
  generalization gradient, 452, 482, 502
Central grey matter, self-stimulation, 590
Central limit theorem, and behavioral chaining, 142
Central motive state:
  behavioral state as, 144
  and electrical brain stimulation, 582–589
Central nervous system, behaviorally induced changes, 605–606
Central reinforcement, 570–590 (see also Electrical brain stimulation)
  acquisition with, 575
  advantages, 580
  vs. conventional reinforcement, 574–581, 589
  extinction after, 575–576
  measurement, 572–574
  methodology, 572–574
  and motivation, 570, 576, 579–580, 582–589
  persistence of behavior, 576–578
  and secondary reinforcement, 576
  species and sites used, 589–590
  theories, 581–588
Central reward pathways, 582
CER (see Conditioned emotional response, Conditioned suppression)
Cerebral cortex:
  and inhibition, 588
  integrative functions, 641–642
  stimulation of, 570
Cerebral peduncle, self-stimulation, 590
Cervidae, 621
Chain pulling:
  squirrel monkey, 420–421
  and thermoregulation, 164
Chained schedule, 289–299
  central reinforcement, 573
  and choice, 335
  complex behavior on, 292
  concurrent (see Concurrent chain schedule)
  conditioned reinforcement on, 288–316
  controlling variables, 289–290, 293
  description, 289
  discriminative stimuli, 289, 293–299
  drug effects, 555
  and electrical brain stimulation, 181
  interresponse times, 223
  interval schedules, response rate, 291–292
  maintained responding, 291–293
  order of stimuli, 295–296
  ratio schedules, response rate, 292–293
  and relativity of reinforcement, 181
  and tandem schedule, 290, 293–295, 298
  thermal reinforcement, 164
  transition performances, 290–291
Chaining:
  and external stimuli, 142
  fixed-interval schedules, 221–222
  interim activities, 142
  sequence of behaviors, 141–143
  and temporal discrimination, 141–143
Chaining delay, and gradient of reinforcement, 217–218
Chaining hypothesis, schedule control, 221–222
Changeover delay:
  animal psychophysics, 523
  concurrent schedules, 79, 242–244, 250, 276
  minimum for matching, 242–244, 249
  and observing responses, 321
  response rate during, 244
  role in matching, 242–244, 250, 276
  use, 235
Changeover key, use, 234, 237
Changeover response:
  punishment, 243–244, 253
  rate, 233, 243–244, 249–250, 254, 276
Chemical structure, drugs, 544
Chewing, schedule-induced, 128–133
Chick:
  autoshaping, 59–60, 65, 70, 120–121
  nuzzling response, 65
  omission training, 65, 120–121
  thermoregulation, 153, 159–160
  wavelength generalization, 486
Chicken:
  meal patterning, 35
  misbehavior, 13
Chick-peas, reinforcer for pigeons, 259
Chimpanzee:
  language behavior, 640, 650–651
  schedule-induced polydipsia, 129
  second-order schedule, 299, 302
  token reinforcement, 306
Chinchilla, auditory intensity discrimination, 515–516, 519
Children, relativity of reward, 102
Chloral hydrate, 545
Chlordiazepoxide:
  acquisition with, 561
  classification, 545
  and conditioned suppression, 349, 356–357
  as depressant, 555–556
  and punishment, 558
  schedule control, 189, 191, 557
  stimulus control, 555–556
Chlorpromazine:
  acquisition with, 561
  classification, 544–545
  and clock schedule, 555
  and deprivation, 553
  errorless learning, 553
  escape behavior, 384
  human retardates, 564
  negative reinforcement, 367, 384
  psychiatric use, 540, 565–566
  and punishment, 558
  schedule control, 188–189, 556–557
  shock avoidance, 556–557
  stimulus control, 555
  thermoregulation, 167, 556
Choice, 233–282, 313–337 (see also Concurrent schedules, Matching)
  absolute response rate in, 257–263
  additive difference model, 277
  central vs. conventional reinforcer, 577–578
  concurrent chains, 329–337
  concurrent schedules, 235, 239, 245–246, 253–254
  and conditioned reinforcement, 313–337
  discrete trial procedure, 236
  immediate vs. delayed reinforcement, 251, 252
  interresponse time, 255–256
  and matching law, 275–276
  measurement, 235, 239
  and negative reinforcement, 366, 374–392
  and punishment, 253–254
  qualitatively different reinforcers, 252, 262
  and required response rate, 334
Cholinergic blocking agent, 169
Cholinesterase inhibitors, and thermoregulation, 165
Cholinomimetic agents, 168–169
Cingulate gyrus, self-stimulation, 589
Circadian rhythms, and thermoregulation, 161–162
Circularity, of weak law of effect, 100
Classical conditioning, 340–361 (see also

Subject Index

Pavlovian conditioning, Respondent conditioning)
  autoshaping, 119–122
  and brain stimulation, 576
  and conditioned suppression, 342, 344, 351, 358, 360, 517
  descriptions, 9, 53, 61, 138, 340, 489
  drug effects, 553, 554
  fear, and avoidance, 393–397
  galvanic skin response, 493
  gerbils, 115–116
  human, 20, 493
  and induced behavior, 125–126
  misbehavior of organisms, 3
  necessary and sufficient conditions, 343–344
  and operant behavior, 340–361
  pigeons, auditory frequency, 489
  rabbit:
    auditory frequency, 489
    eyelid conditioning, 493–496, 498
Click rate, stimulus control by, 496
Clock schedule:
  and chain schedules, 296–297, 299
  drug effects, 555
  and gastric ulcer, 604–605
CNV (see Contingent negative variation)
CO (see Changeover)
Cocaine:
  classification, 545
  and concurrent matching, 250
  reinforcer, 192–193, 250, 557
  self-administration, 543
  and self-stimulation of brain, 585
Cochlear nucleus, EEG activity, 605
Cockroaches, meal patterning, 35
COD (see Changeover delay)
Codeine, reinforcer, 192
Coding, language, 620, 622–627
Cognitive dissonance, 9
Cognitive learning, and verbal behavior, 636, 649
Cognitive processes, and central reinforcement, 582
Cognitive theories of language, 628–633, 638, 640–642, 651–652
CO-key concurrent schedule, 234–237
Cold escape, rats, 261, 263, 282
Collateral behavior (see also Adjunctive behavior, Interim activities, Schedule-induced behavior):
  and choice on IRT schedule, 255, 266
  and conditioned suppression on DRL, 347
  and temporal discrimination, 143
College students:
  lever pressing, 103, 107
  relativity of reward, 102
  wheel cranking, 103, 107
Color circle, animal psychophysics, 530–531
Color coding, animal psychophysics, 530
Color vision:
  cat, 515
  goldfish, 517, 522
  monkey, 518
Combined cues method, generalization gradient, 446–447
Combined cues test, for inhibitory control, 470–472
Comfort activities, as facultative behavior, 135
Command neurons, 588
Common fate, law of, 623
Comparator device, 638
Compatibility, instrumental and unconditioned response, 118–122
Competence, linguistic, 628–629

Competing responses:
  choice situation, 257, 262
  and conditioned suppression, 351–353, 358–359, 360
  and delay of reinforcement, 218
  and inhibitory control, 463–464
  shock situation, 260–261, 408–410
  and stimulus generalization, 438–439
Competition:
  associative, 507
  behavioral states, 144–147
  stimuli, 496, 498, 507–508
  terminal and interim activities, 132–135, 145–146
Complex symbol, in language, 648
Compound stimulus, and stimulus generalization, 439, 443–444, 459–463
Comprehension, language, 649–651
Concept learning:
  and animal psychophysics, 525
  and verbal behavior, 634
Concepts, linguistic, 619
Conceptual nervous system, 32
Concurrent chain schedule:
  and conditioned reinforcement, 303, 315, 327–337
  description, 297, 327
  matching on, 252, 297–298, 329–333
  strengths and weaknesses, 327–329
  terminological problem, 298
Concurrent generalization test, 435
Concurrent models, altered physiological states, 596–606
Concurrent schedules, 233–282
Concurrent schedules:
  absolute response rates, 265–266
  behavioral pharmacology, 551
  brief stimulus presentation, 306–308
  central reinforcement, 572–573
  conditioned reinforcement, 326–337
  and conditioned suppression, 355
  and contrast, 78–80
  description, 233–234
  electric shock, 374–375, 386, 388–392
  and extradimensional training, 501–503
  generalization test, 435
  and inhibitory control, 463–464
  interactions, 78–80, 233–256, 265–266
  matching, 78–80, 233–256, 272–276, 329–333
  generality, 248–256, 275, 276
  and multiple schedule, 272
  and negative reinforcement, 254
  and punishment, 253–254
  reinforcement frequency, 235–244, 247, 249, 252
  reinforcement immediacy, 233, 251–252
  reinforcement magnitude, 233–234, 248–251
  negative reinforcement, 254, 374–375, 386, 388–392
  and observing responses, 321
  and peak shift, 463–464
  punishment, 253–254
  types, 234–235, 254–255
Concurrent superstitions, 234–235, 243
Conditionability, negative reinforcement, 407–408
Conditionable response unit, 222–227
Conditional discrimination, and verbal behavior, 636, 646
Conditioned aversive stimulus:
  and concurrent choice, 253
  and negative reinforcement, 393–396, 400
  and stimulus generalization, 447
Conditioned cardiac respondent, 598
Conditioned confusion, 317

Conditioned emotional response (see also Conditioned suppression):
  and conditioned suppression, 353–357, 360
  and latent inhibition, 487
  and overshadowing, 492
  partial reinforcement effect, 61
  physiological changes, 598–599
Conditioned enhancement, 88–90
Conditioned flexion response:
  dog, 483–484
  goats and sheep, 487
Conditioned inhibition:
  and contrast, 84–85
  and errorless learning, 475
  and latent inhibition, 487
  measurement, 445–447
Conditioned reflex (see Reflex)
Conditioned reinforcement, 288–309, 313–337 (see also Secondary reinforcement)
  chained schedules, 288–289, 293–299, 309, 313, 315
  choice and, 313–314, 326–337
  concepts, 180, 288–289, 309, 313–315
  concurrent chain schedules, 326–337
  conjoint schedules, 307–308
  discriminative effects, 289, 309, 314–315
  discriminative stimulus hypothesis, 181
  drug effects, 558
  hypotheses, 313–315, 325–326, 336–337
  and information, 303, 313–337
  mathematical treatment, 4
  observing responses, 313–315, 318–326, 336–337
  pairing hypothesis, 313, 315–318, 334, 336–337
  paradigm experiment, 288
  relation to primary, 289
  schedule control, 2, 288–309
  second-order schedules, 302–309, 313–316
  uncertainty reduction, 318–326, 306–337
  and verbal behavior, 633
Conditioned suppression, 340–363 (see also Conditioned emotional response, Positive conditioned suppression)
  and anxiety, 355–357, 360, 393
  and autoshaping, 90, 359
  and avoidance behavior, 358, 360
  classical conditioning, 340–361
  concurrent choice, 253
  and contrast, 88–90
  description, 341–342
  drug effects, 342, 350, 355–357, 360, 554
  Estes-Skinner procedure, 341–344
  gerbils, 115
  hypotheses, 351–358
  interference hypothesis, 351–353, 357–359
  and latent inhibition, 487
  measurement, 348–351, 360
  monkey, 89, 352, 358–360
  motivational hypotheses, 353–357, 358
  mouse, 517
  and olfactory sensitivity in pigeon, 513
  and operant parameters, 5, 344–348, 351
  as Pavlovian fear conditioning, 315
  physiological changes, 598–599
  punishment hypothesis, 357–358
  schedule effects, 345–351, 360
  shock deletion procedure, 409
  shock intensity, 342, 346
  shock probability, 343–344
  Siamese fighting fish, 116
  animal psychophysics, 516–517, 522, 525
Conditioning context, and stimulus generalization, 444

Conflict:
　approach-avoidance,
　　and gastric ulcer, 597, 604
　　and schedule induction, 139–140
　and de-encephalization, 23
Conflict procedure, and gastric ulcers, 597, 604
Conjoint schedule:
　brief stimulus presentation, 306–308
　and conditioned reinforcement, 304
Conjunctive schedule:
　and delay of reinforcement, 219
　number of responses, 206–211
Consequence variables, psychopharmacology, 556–559
Constant probability schedule, and induced drinking, 135
Constant probability VI schedule, 215
Constraints:
　biological, on learning, 3, 7, 91, 101, 111–123
　biological, on reinforcement, 112–123
　environmental, on feeding, 37, 44
　genetic, on language, 641
　on reinforcer availability, 40–41, 47
　species,
　　on autoshaped response, 61
　　and central reinforcement, 580
　　on generalization gradients, 435–436
　on stimulus control, 483–485
　systems (see Systems constraint)
Consummatory behavior (see also Drinking, Eating, Feeding behavior):
　vs. appetitive behavior, 22
　autoshaping, 62, 70
　in contrast experiments, 81–82
　monkey, 58, 65
　pigeon, in autoshaping, 58, 65, 69–70
　as reflexive, 22, 28, 49, 62
Consummatory force, 144, 146
Consummatory response:
　relation to operant behavior, 3, 20, 22, 62–68, 127
　and terminal response, 127
　and theta waves, 119
Consummatory response theory, and central reinforcement, 581
Contact comfort, and thermoregulation, 159
Context, and conditioned reinforcement, 315, 330
Contextual stimulus (see also Situational stimulus):
　and stimulus control, 444, 457–458, 488–509
Contiguity:
　and conditioned reinforcement, 314–318, 334, 336
　induced drinking and food, 132
　response-reinforcer,
　　interval and time schedules, 214, 219
　　problems with, 127–128
　　on response-dependent schedules, 204, 207, 228
　in verbal behavior, 637–638
Contingencies of reinforcement, 3, 98–124, 175–176
Contingency:
　and aversive control, 425–430
　categories, 99, 101
　negative, 63, 99
　vs. pairing
　　in autoshaping, 54–56
　reinforcement
　　in animal psychophysics, 525
　　response, and schedule induction, 125–128, 130–136, 140–141
　　among responses, 98–123
　　response-shock deletion, 398–399

　　and shock probability, 375–377, 398–399
　　shock, and extinction, 379–380
　　shock, and frequency, 398–399
　temporal, in classical conditioning, 343
Contingency models, altered physiological states, 606–611
Contingency strength:
　quantitative measure, 128
　and terminal responses, 127
Contingency table:
　reinforcement and punishment, 180
Contingent variation in EEG:
　Negative, 606
　Positive, 606
Contingent-response (Premack-type) experiments, 98–123
Continuity, behavior in time, 177–178
Continuous choice procedure (see Concurrent schedule)
Continuous reinforcement schedule, central reinforcement, 573, 577
Contrast, behavioral (see Behavioral contrast, Local contrast, Negative behavioral contrast, Positive behavioral contrast, Transient contrast)
Control (see Aversive control, Schedule control, Stimulus control)
Controlling variables, types, on schedules, 203–204, 228
Control procedures (see also Truly random control, Yoked controls):
　animal psychophysics, 515–532
　behavioral pharmacology, 551–552
　classical conditioning, 55–56, 61, 84, 120, 343
　concurrent matching experiments, 242–243
　contingent-response experiments, 106–110, 115–116
　and stimulus generalization, 435–436, 442, 445
Control systems, and thermoregulation, 160–161
Control theory, and thermoregulation, 153–154, 160–162
Coping response, and gastrointestinal changes, 604–605
Copulation, 109, 122
Correction procedure, animal psychophysics, 524, 536
Correlation-based law of effect, 111
Cortical evoked activity, 605
Cost:
　procurement vs. use, 47
　response, 239, 563
Counterexperiment, method of synthesis, 10
Counting schedule, conditioned suppression, 347
Courtship:
　lock and key sequence, 142
　pigeons
　　autoshaping, 59, 119
　　as interim activity, 137
　sticklebacks, 121–122
CR, definition, 340
CRF (see Continuous reinforcement schedule)
Criteria, reinforcement vs. punishment, 186–188
Criterion, in animal psychophysics, 521, 524
Cross tolerance, drugs, 550
CS (see also Warning stimulus):
　in autoshaping, 55–61, 69–70, 80
　and conditioned enhancement, 90
　in conditioned suppression, 89–90, 342–345, 350, 359

　in contrast, 88
　definition, 340
　fear conditioning, 315
　informativeness, 58, 80
Cue (see Stimulus)
Cued escape, 383–387
Cues, acquired distinctiveness, 487–488
Cumulation, drug effects, 550–551
Cumulative record, advantages, 11
Cumulative recorder, history, 29
Curare, and autonomic conditioning, 607–611
Curiosity, 31
Cyclicities, fixed-interval behavior, 208–209
Cylert (see Magnesium pemoline)

d', signal detection theory, 532–537
DA (see Dopamine)
d-amphetamine (see also Amphetamine):
　classification, 545
　and learning, 561
　and learning disability, 564
　and negative reinforcement, 367
　reinforcer, 192
　and schedule performance, 190–191
　and thermoregulation, 164
Dark adaptation, pigeons, 521–522
Darkness, rearing in, 486
Deafferentation, 146
Debilitation, and thermoregulation, 155
Decay, rate of contingent response, 108
Decerebrate, 8, 11
Decremental generalization gradient, definition, 445
De-encephalization, 22–23
Deep structure, of language, 629–633, 648–651
Defecation, and conditioned suppression, 351
Defensive behavior, 115–117
Deficit, sensory, and thermoregulation, 155–156
Deficit theory of motivation, 31, 49
Delayed conditioning, classical, 343
Delayed escape, 261–262, 281–282
Delay of reinforcement (see also Reinforcement, immediacy):
　delayed escape, 261
　and habit strength, 217–218
　human, 262
　and matching, 234, 251–252
　and observing responses, 320, 322, 325
　and response strength, 260–262, 266, 281
　and schedule control, 218–222
　theory, 217–220
Delay of reward procedure, 125
Delay reduction hypothesis:
　conditioned reinforcement, 313–315, 324–337
　equations, 329, 332
　quantitative analysis, 329–333
Demerol (see Meperidine)
Density:
　negative reinforcement, 369–370, 375, 399, 402
　reinforcement
　　in autoshaping, 61
　　and conditioned reinforcement, 314, 316, 325–327, 329, 332, 336–337
　　differentiation schedule, 224
　　drug effects, 552
　　and induced behavior, 140
　　in time, 214–215
Dependence:
　on drugs, 185, 192–193, 550, 553
　human, 557–558, 563
Depletion-repletion model:
　problems with, 31–32

Subject Index

in regulation of eating, 31, 45–46, 49
Depressant drugs, 544, 555–556, 561–562
Deprivation:
  autoshaping, 59
  and central reinforcement, 575–576, 579–580, 584
  and conditioned suppression, 354
  contingent-response experiments, 102–105, 115, 118, 122, 181
  effect of reinforcement, 178, 186
  and magnitude of reinforcement, 259
  operation, 30–31
  and polydipsia, 130, 132
  psychopharmacology, 553
  and rate of eating, 175
  and response-produced shock, 182
  and thirst, in induced drinking, 138–139
  as unnecessary, 36
  and verbal behavior, 633
Descending order of stimuli, in animal psychophysics, 521
Desoxyn (see Methamphetamine)
Development, gape response, in thrushes, 19
Development, stages:
  compared to recovery, 17–22
  grasp, in human, 19
  rat, 18
Diabetes, chronic, and meal frequency, 35
Diabetes mellitus, 10
Diazepam:
  classification, 545
  and punishment, 558
Diencephalon:
  stimulation, 577
  and thermoregulation, 158
Diet:
  selection (see Self-selection)
  and thermoregulation, 162
Dieter's nucleus, 606
Difference concept, in animals, 518
Differential probability rules, 102–108, 111–113, 122, 181
Differential reinforcement:
  animal psychophysics, 528–529
  definition, 433
  and generalization gradient, 439–441
  implicit, 489–491
  in shaping, 177
  and stimulus control, 432–476, 493–505
Differentiation schedule (see also DRL schedule, Interresponse time schedule):
  definitions, 203
  and IRT as conditionable unit, 224
Diffuseness, and stimulus control, 490, 508
Digestion:
  herbivores, 33–34, 47–48
  and thermoregulation, 162
Digging:
  gerbil, 115–116
  hamster, 113–118
Dimensional control:
  and early experience, 485–487
  inhibitory, 453–456
  and negative reinforcement, 391–392, 398, 400
  and stimulus generalization, 444–447
Dimension of generalization, 433
Diphenhydramine, 564
Direct variables, and schedule control, 203–206, 228
Directedness:
  autoshaped response, 60–61, 69, 81
  Pavlovian responses, 61, 81, 138
Discrete-trial procedure:
  animal psychophysics, 516
  escape as, 367–368

food and shock, 485
generalization gradient, 435
go/no-go method, 516
and immediacy of reinforcement, 260, 281
matching, 236, 244, 246
observing responses on, 320
and overshadowing, 492
shock deletion, 399
and stimulus control, 495, 505
threshold tracking, 522
Discriminability, index of, 534
Discriminated avoidance (see Avoidance, discriminated)
Discrimination:
  components of second order schedules, 316, 318
  extinction, and negative reinforcement, 378–380
  problems with concept, 433
  simultaneous vs. successive, 487
Discrimination learning:
  errorless (see Errorless discrimination learning)
  and escape from S−, 469–470
  free operant, 499–505
  patterns, by pigeons, 528
  sign tracking in, 69
  Spence's theory, 447–451, 453, 456, 462, 476
  and stimulus control, 499–505
Discrimination training:
  and attentiveness, 500–502, 505
  definition, 433
  and generalization, 439–453
  and inhibition, 432, 439–453
  schedule effects, 503–505
  and stimulus control, 493–505
  types, 439–440
Discriminative control (see also Stimulus control): and conditioned suppression, 347–348
Discriminative stimulus:
  chained schedules, 289, 293–299
  concept, 180
  concurrent chains, 336
  and conditioned reinforcement, 314–315
  drugs as, 192–193, 555–556
  negative reinforcement, 381–396, 400
  in polydipsia, 129, 131, 133
  second-order schedules, 302–309
  in verbal behavior, 633–635
Discriminative stimulus hypothesis, conditioned reinforcement, 181
Disinhibited activities, 139–140
Disinhibition:
  and conditioned suppression, 347–348
  and induced activities, 139, 143–145
  and motor control, 588
  by novel stimulus, 116
  and temporal discrimination, 143
Displacement activities, 23, 139
Distribution:
  drugs, 543, 547–550
  interresponse times, 224–225
Disulfuram, 563
Diurnal rhythm:
  drinking
    rats, 36, 44
  eating
    guinea pigs, 35
    rats, 33, 444
Dog:
  auditory stimulus control, 483–484
  autoshaping, 58
  avoidance, 406, 602–605
  brain damage, 20
  cardiovascular changes, 602–603

classical conditioning, 61, 138, 483–484, 489–492
conditioned flexion response, 483–484
drugs as discriminative stimuli, 555–556
gastric motility, 20
hippocampal activity, 605
hypothalamic syndrome, 20
meal patterning, 35
negative reinforcement
  shock-delay procedure, 390, 392–393
omission training, 63
patterning of drinking, 36
Pavlovian conditioning, 61, 138, 483–484, 489
salivation
  classical conditioning, 138, 340, 489
  instrumental conditioning, 607
self-stimulation of brain, 589–590
thermoregulation, 153, 159, 166–167
Dolphin, self-stimulation of brain, 590
Dominance, and feeding behavior, 34
Domino theory, sequence of behaviors, 141
Dopamine:
  and self-stimulation of brain, 585–586
  and thermoregulation, 168
Dopamine-β-hydroxylase, and schizophrenia, 571
Dopaminergic pathways, 585–588
Dorsal noradrenergic pathway, 586
Dose-effect relations, drugs, and schedule performance, 189, 192–193, 202
Dose-response curve, behavioral pharmacology, 541, 545–547
Dove:
  schedule-induced eating, 139
  schedule-induced polydipsia, 129, 136
  thermoregulation, 153
DRH schedule (see also Differentiation schedule):
  and choice, 334
  negative reinforcement, 391
Drinking (see also Licking, Polydipsia, Schedule-induced behavior):
  adjunctive (see also Drinking, interim; Drinking, schedule-induced; Polydipsia, Schedule-induced behavior)
  and conditioned suppression, 350
  aversive control schedule, 423–425
  contingent-response experiments, 102–109, 181
  elicited by brain stimulation, 571, 579, 581–583, 589
  instrumental, 105–106
  instrumental avoidance, 118
  interim, 128–130, 134–135, 142, 144–147
  patterning
    and FR requirement, 40, 42
    guinea pigs, 42
    rats, 36, 40, 42
  postprandial (see Postprandial drinking)
  reinforcer vs. punisher, 181
  relation to feeding, 35–36, 42–43, 131, 135, 139
  schedule induced (see also Polydipsia)
    compared to attack, 137
    development, 131–132, 138
    fixed-interval schedules, 135
    hypotheses, 130–132
    interaction with running, 146–148
    as interim activity, 128–130, 134–135, 142, 144–147
    monkey, 138
    motivation, 132, 138–139
    rat, 126, 129–137, 143
    rate, 129–135, 138
    temporal locus, 133, 135, 140
    theories, 130–132
    and thirst, 138–139

Drinking (cont.)
  squirrel monkey, and aversive control, 423–425
Drinking tube, 98, 102, 104, 107, 108, 118, 181, 417
Drinkometer, 181, 417
Drive:
  emotional, conditioned suppression, 354–355, 358
  level:
    and immediacy of reinforcement, 260, 281
    and magnitude of reinforcement, 259, 278
    and matching, 262
Drive induction:
  and central reinforcement, 581
  theory, 99
Drive operation:
  central reinforcement, 576, 581, 586
  negative reinforcement, 368, 378–380, 387–388
Drive reduction:
  and electrical brain stimulation, 571, 581–582, 584, 586, 588–589
  theory, 99
  and verbal behavior, 633
Drive state:
  and central reinforcement, 576, 579–584
  and schedule control, 188
DRL schedule (see also Differentiation schedule, Interresponse time schedule):
  and carnivorous feeding pattern, 48
  central reinforcement, 578–579
  component of chain, 293
  component of conjoint, 307
  and conditioned enhancement, 90
  conditioned suppression, 89, 347, 359
  and contrast, 73, 77
  drug effects, 552
  and generalization gradient, 436, 439
  induced attack, 137
  induced behavior, 134–135, 141–143
  induced drinking, 135
  negative reinforcement, 391
  in omission training, 66
  problems with terminology, 203
DRO schedule (see also Differentiation schedule):
  and behavioral contrast, 75, 77, 267
  component of second order, 306
Drug abuse:
  animal models, 192–193
  and behavioral pharmacology, 542, 557–558, 563
Drug effects, micro-analysis, 562
Drugs (see also Behavioral pharmacology, Psychopharmacology, specific drug):
  absorption and distribution, 543, 547–550
  and aggression, 417, 552, 562
  behavioral mechanisms, 551–560
  behavioral pharmacology, 5, 188–193, 349–360, 540–569
  and blood pressure, 603
  classification, 544–545
  clinical use, 188, 540, 542, 563–566
  and conditioned suppression, 349–350, 355–357, 360
  cumulative effects, 550–551
  dose-response curves, 189, 192–193, 202, 541, 545–547
  and electric shock, 189–191, 552, 555–560
  and electrical brain stimulation, 188, 571, 574, 585–586
  fate in body, 550
  and motivation, 188–189, 559–562
  and negative reinforcement, 367, 384
  principles of action, 543–551
  and psychotic behavior, 564–566
  psychotropic, 545
  reinforcement vs. punishment, 178, 188–193
  reinforcers, 192–193, 556–558
  and relativity of reward, 179–181, 188–193
  reversibility of effects, 551
  and schedule control, 188–193, 202, 542–543, 546, 551–552, 555–560
  self-stimulation procedure, 571, 574, 585–587
  sensation and perception, 562
  solubility, 549–550
  specificity of action, 551–552
  and thermoregulation, 153–155, 164–169, 188–189, 556
  time course of effects, 548–549
  toxic effects, 546, 562–563
  type classifications, 544–545
Dry mouth:
  and grooming in hamster, 144
  theory of polydipsia, 129
Duckling, stimulus generalization, 485–486
Duration:
  bout, of induced activity, 141–142, 146
  brief stimulus, second-order schedules, 304–305
  burst, contingent-response experiments, 110–112
  component, in multiple schedule
    and contrast, 79, 87, 90
    and matching, 269–272
    and negative reinforcement, 382–383
  CS, and conditioned suppression, 89
  as discriminative stimulus, 218–219, 534–535
  interim activities, control by food, 131
  intertrial interval, autoshaping, 57–58, 66, 78
  interval component, chained schedules, 291–292
  of peck
    autoshaping, 24, 58, 67–68, 81
    and contrast, 87–88
    on fixed-interval, 67
    on fixed-ratio, 67
    food vs. water, 58–59, 67, 81, 119
  postreinforcement pause
    on fixed-interval, 213, 216
    on fixed-ratio, 209, 213, 217, 226–228
  prefood stimulus, and positive conditioned suppression, 359
  preshock stimulus, and conditioned suppression, 344–345, 350
  of ratio run, as conditionable unit, 227
  reinforcement (see also Reinforcement, magnitude)
    and absolute response rate, 259
    and conditioned enhancement, 90
    discrimination of, 249
  responding, contingent-response experiments, 108–112
  of S−, and inhibition, 447
  stimulus, and conditioned suppression, 344–345, 350, 359
  terminal links, concurrent chains, 327–337
  trials, autoshaping, 57–58, 66, 78, 90
Dynamic effects, and schedule performance, 204–210, 228
Dynamic models, stimulus control, 451–453

Eating (see also Feeding behavior):
  curve of, in rat, 174–175
  development, in rat, 17–18
  electrically-evoked, 15
  lateral hypothalamus, 16–18
  patterns, and evolution, 33, 46
  periodicity, 28–30
  rate, and FR requirement, 41–42
  recovery, after lesions, 17, 20
  as reflex, 29–31
  relation to drinking, 35–36, 42–43, 131, 135, 139
  schedule-induced, in doves, 139
  and schedule-induced polydipsia, 129–130, 135
Eatometer, 29
Echoic, in verbal behavior, 633–634, 637, 639, 644
Echolocation, in bat, 519
Ecological niche, and feeding patterns, 33, 43, 46–49
Economics, of feeding behavior, 34, 46, 48
Ectostriatal brain stimulation, and choice, 252
Ectostriatum, self-stimulation of, 590
Ectotherm, thermoregulation in, 156–161, 166
EEG (see Electroencephalogram)
Effort, of response, and thermoregulation, 164
Egg rolling, in goose, 23
Ego, 9
EKG (see Electrocardiogram)
Elavil (see Amitryptaline)
Electrical brain stimulation (see also Central reinforcement):
  and animal psychophysics, 518
  autoshaping with, 60
  and behavior, 570–590
  cat, 14–15, 589–590
  choice, 252
  concurrent schedules, 237
  conditioned suppression, 358–359
  diencephalon, 577
  and drugs, 188, 571, 574, 585–586
  elicitor and reward, 14
  gerbil, 111–112
  hypothalamus, 14–15, 60, 111, 164, 178–181, 259, 570–589
  intrapeduncular nucleus, 585
  locus coeruleus, 585
  medial forebrain bundle, 577
  methodology, 572–574
  and motivation, 14, 570–589
  partial reinforcement, 578–579
  pigeons, 252
  postponement, 178
  rat, 14, 60, 89, 120, 164–165, 178, 180, 237, 259, 279, 518, 572–590
  reinforcement magnitude, 179, 259, 263, 279
  reinforcer vs. punisher, 178–181
  and relativity of reward, 102, 181
  reward in visceral conditioning, 607–611
  septum, 570, 575–576, 583
  species and sites used, 589–590
  substantia nigra, 585
  telencephalon, 577
  and thermoregulation, 164–165
Electric shock (see also Avoidance, Escape, Negative reinforcement, Shock delay, Shock deletion):
  in animal psychophysics, 516–517, 523
  and attack behavior, 183–184, 380, 409, 417–425
  autoshaping with, 65, 70
  in aversive control, 415–430
  avoidance (see Avoidance, Negative reinforcement, Shock delay)
  and central reinforcement, 574
  changeover response, 243–244, 253
  concurrent matching, 253–254

and conditioned reinforcement, 304–305
and conditioned suppression, 341–356
and contrast, 74–77
delay of escape, 261–262, 282
density-frequency continuum, 369–370, 375, 383
density reduction (*see* Shock density reduction)
as discriminative stimulus, and negative reinforcement, 368, 369, 377–380, 383
and drug effects, 188–191, 555–556, 558–559
escape (*see* Escape)
gerbils, 115
intensity:
    and choice, 253
    and conditioned suppression, 342, 346, 354
    and number of responses, 194
intensity reduction, negative reinforcement, 375, 380
intermittent schedules, 375–377
and latent inhibition, 487
and negative induction, 74
negative reinforcement, 364–410
postponement, 185, 194–196 (*see also* Shock delay)
reinforcer *vs.* punisher, 178–180, 183–184, 193–197
response-produced, 176–185, 190, 193–196, 380
Siamese fighting fish, 116
squirrel monkeys, 173–179, 183–185, 189–190, 193–196, 415–430
Electrocardiogram, operant conditioning of, 608
Electrode implantation, methods, 572
Electroencephalogram, and avoidance, 605–606
Electromyogram, 417–418, 606–607
Electrophysiological changes, behaviorally induced, 605–606
EMG (*see* Electromyogram)
Emitted behavior, *vs.* elicited, 174–175
Emotion (*see also* Motivation, Conditioned emotional response):
    and conditioned suppression, 353–358
Encephalization, 20–23
Encoding, in natural language, 620, 622–627
Encoding specificity, and memory, 638
Endocrinological system, durable changes, 597–604
Endotherm, thermoregulation, 156
Energy balance, regulation, 31, 33, 43, 47, 129
Enhancement:
    conditioned (*see* Conditioned enhancement)
    responding, by shock, 185
    stimulus control, 500–509
Environment:
    and feeding patterns, 33, 36, 44–50
    simplification, 11
Environmental constraints (*see* Constraints)
Environmentalism, and language, 641
Epinephrine:
    and heart rate conditioning, 608
    and stimulus control, 555–556
Episodic memory, 637
Equal-brightness contour, rat, 526–527, 532
Equal-loudness functions, animal psychophysics, 526, 532
Equalizing, *vs.* matching in concurrent schedules, 272
Equanil (*see* Meprobamate)

Equipotentiality, premise of, 91
Error:
    aversiveness:
        in programmed learning, 467, 469–470
        in discrimination learning, definition, 464–465
        in operant behavior, 22, 23
Errorless discrimination learning, 5, 76, 86, 464–476
Errorless discrimination learning:
    and agression, 468–469
    and behavioral contrast, 76, 86, 472–474
    definition, 464–465
    drug effects, 553
    inhibitory stimulus control, 470–474
    reconsideration, 432, 464–476
    resistance to reinforcement, 446
    and stimulus control, 186, 464–476
    techniques, 466
    Terrace's theory, 467–468
    as transfer of control, 465–466, 475
Error signal, in thermoregulation, 160–165
Escape (*See also* Avoidance, Negative reinforcement)
    (from electric shock, by rats, unless otherwise stated):
    added cues, 383–387
    and aversive control, 99, 416, 421, 425–427
    centrifugal force, 367
    as change of situation, 387
    cold water, by rats, 261, 282
    and conditioned reinforcement, 319
    cued, 383–387
    delayed, 261–262, 281–282
    drug effects, 557
    free operant, 368
    heat, 165, 166, 168
    intense light, 367
    noise, 282, 367
    pigeon, 254
    procedure, 367–368
    and response strength, 261, 281–282, 543
    rotation, 367
    runway, 261–262, 281–282
    squirrel monkeys, 189, 380, 557
    stability of, 543
    temperature change, 162, 367
    temporal pattern of behavior, 425–427
Escape/avoidance distinction, problems with, 368–370, 387
Estrus, rat, and thermoregulation, 162
Ethanol (*see also* Alcohol):
    reinforcer, rats, 553, 561
    and stimulus control, 555–556
Ethology, 4, 7, 11–12, 15, 19–20, 49, 91, 120, 571–572
Ethyl alcohol (*see* Ethanol, Alcohol)
Evolution, feeding patterns, 33, 46–50
Excitation:
    and dimensional control, 444–445
    by reinforcement, 264, 272–274
Excitatory stimulus, definition, 444
Excretion, drugs, 550
Expectancy, electrical signals of, 606
Expectation:
    as behavioral state, 144
    in Pavlovian conditioning, 138
Experimental analysis of behavior, 1–2
"Experiments of fruit," 12
"Experiments of light," 12
Exploratory behavior:
    and motivation, 584
    rats, 60, 120
Extended chained schedule, 291
Extension, verbal, 634

Extinction:
    brief stimulus during, 305–306
    central reinforcement, 575–576, 589
    and conditioned reinforcement, 288–289, 299
    and contrast, 71–77, 80, 82–83
    drug effects, 560–562
    after fixed-ratio, 223–226
    generalization gradient in, 435, 438, 527
    heart rate conditioning, 607
    massed, and peak shift, 456
    massed, and stimulus control, 456–457, 527
    multiple schedule, 71–77, 80–83
    after negative reinforcement, 377–380
    non-passive effects, 226
    observing response procedures, 318–326
    relation to reinforcement, 205
    resistance to (*see* Resistance to extinction)
    after shock schedules, 377–380
Extinction-induced aggression, 468–469
Extinction methods, generalization gradient, 434
Extinction schedule, relation to other schedules, 203
Extradimensional shift, 487
Extradimensional training:
    analysis, 503–505
    concurrent experiments, 501–503
    and stimulus control, 497–505
    successive stage experiments, 497–500
Extraneous cues, in animal psychophysics, 524
Extrapyramidal system, and central reinforcement, 572
Eye blink, Pavlovian conditioning, 61
Eyelid conditioning, rabbit, 493, 496, 498

Face washing, hamster, 113–115, 118
Facilitation:
    by aversive stimuli, 422, 424, 428
    induced behavior, 141, 144
Facultative behavior:
    definition, 126
    examples, 135, 140
    grooming, 135
    running, 133–137, 140
Facultative periods, on periodic schedules, 134–138
Fading procedure:
    in animal psychophysics, 520
    and errorless learning, 466
    in language learning, 640
Fading trace, negative reinforcement, 400
False alarms, animal psychophysics, 516, 521, 525, 533–534
False positive responses, animal psychophysics, 516
Fasting, operation to insure eating, 28–33
Fat solubility, drugs, 549–550
Fate, drugs in body, 550
Fatigue:
    and rate of eating, 175
    and schedule control, 23
Fear:
    as incentive, 100
    Pavlovian conditioning, 315, 393–397
"Feast or famine," in large carnivores, 47
Feature, stimulus control by, 528
Features analysis, and language, 650–651
Feedback (*see also* Positive feedback, Negative feedback):
    autonomic conditioning, 610
    in avoidance, and gastric ulcers, 604–605
    between behavior and consequences, 125, 144
    behaviors in sequence, 145–148

Feedback (cont.)
  in language learning, 624
  and schedule-induced behavior, 135, 145–146
Feedback theory of reinforcement, 4
Feeding behavior (see also Eating, Meal):
  cat, 34–35, 38–39, 49
  and dominance, 34
  elicited by brain stimulation, 571, 579, 581, 583, 589
  environmental constraints, 44, 49
  and FR requirement, 42
  pecking as, in pigeon, 69
  relation to drinking, 35–36, 42–43, 131, 135, 139
  species differences, 47, 49, 58
  topography, in monkeys, 59
Feeding pyramid, 47
Fever, 160–166
Figure-ground problem, in escape paradigm, 383
Final common path, behavioral, 144
Fibonacci VI schedule, 215
First-order deviations, fixed interval schedules, 208
Fish (see also Goldfish, Siamese fighting fish, Stickleback):
  autoshaping, 58
  failure of temporal discrimination, 140
  thermoregulation, 156–158
5HT (see Serotonin)
Fixation, in animal psychophysics, 523–524
Fixed action pattern, 15, 17, 23
Fixed constant number schedule, 226
Fixed-cycle procedure, shock deletion, 371–373, 375, 400–402, 404–405
Fixed-interval schedule:
  absolute response rate, 258, 265
  adventitious reinforcement and punishment, 185
  avoidance, 367, 377, 384, 388
  central reinforcement, 578
  in chained schedule, 289–298, 335
  chaining on, 222
  compared to fixed-ratio, 206
  compared to variable-interval, 265
  concurrent matching, 252
  conditioned suppression, 341, 346–347
  and contrast, 73
  cyclicities in responding, 208–209
  definition, 202
  delay of reinforcement, 218–219
  drug effects, 188, 192–193, 544, 555, 559, 560
  dynamic effects, 205–210
  electric shock, 178–179, 182–184, 193–196
  escape, 380
  and generalization gradient, 452–453, 458
  Herrnstein's equation, 265
  induced behavior, 125, 129–130, 133, 135–136, 138–142
  local rate of reinforcement, 216
  matching, 242, 247, 252, 254, 255, 266
  negative reinforcement, 367, 384, 388
  observing responses, 318, 320, 322, 325
  peck duration, 67
  polydipsia, 129–130, 138
  punishment, 429
  reinforcement omission, 301
  response-initiated, 301
  response-produced shock, 178–179, 182–184, 193–196
  responses per reinforcer, 205–212
  response strength, 265
  in second-order schedule, 300–305
  species differences, 12
  temporal patterning, 213–214, 216
  two-state analysis, 265
Fixed-ratio schedule:
  acquisition of performance, 227
  alcohol consumption, 563
  central reinforcement, 578
  compared to fixed-interval, 206
  component of chain, 292–295
  component of conjoint, 307
  component of second-order, 299–305
  and conditioned suppression, 346, 348–349
  in contingent-response experiments, 104
  and contrast, 74
  definition, 202
  drug effects, 188, 192, 543–544, 546, 548–549, 551, 556, 559, 562–564
  duration requirement, 227
  dynamic effects, 206, 209–210
  escape-avoidance, 601–602
  induced behavior, 136, 139
  interreinforcer time, 205, 209–210, 217
  limits on size, 38–39, 45, 206, 213
  matching, 246–247, 252, 254, 266
  and meal parameters, 44–45
  and meal patterns, 36–39
  meal reinforcement, 38–39, 45
  negative reinforcement, 367, 385–386, 390
  observing responses, 320
  and pattern of drinking, 40
  and pattern of running, 40
  pause duration, 209, 213
  peck duration, 67
  response number, 209
  response-produced shock, 182, 194–195
  responses per reinforcer, 209–210, 212
  response units, 225–227
  and schedule-induced behavior, 136, 139
  and shaping history, 177
  stereotypy of responding, 227
  strained performance, 37, 543
  temporal patterning, 213
  and thermoregulation, 164
Fixed-time schedule:
  adventitious punishment, 184–185
  adventitious reinforcement, 184–185, 204
  component of chain, 335
  and concurrent matching, 252
  definition, 202
  excitation of pecking, 272–273
  and induced behavior, 126, 128, 130, 133, 139–142
  shock avoidance, 185
  shock-elicited behavior, 183
  temporal patterning, 140–141, 214
Flavor (see Taste)
Flexion response, conditioned
  dog, 483–484
  goats and sheep, 487
Flicker-fusion frequency, monkeys, 522
Floor effect:
  on generalization gradient, 471–472, 482
  in generalization of extinction, 445
Fluphenazine, 545
Food:
  as discriminative stimulus:
    on fixed schedules, 129, 131, 133
    on variable schedules, 133
  free:
    and contrast, 87–90
    during interim period, 128, 138
  interaction with water, and matching, 252
  reinforcement, and stimulus control, 484–485
  reinforcer vs. punisher, 178, 197
  type and palatability, and induced drinking, 132–133
  as US in autoshaping, 58
Food anticipation:
  interaction with running and drinking, 146–148
  as terminal response, 127, 132–134, 141–143, 146–147
Food economy, and ecological niche, 46–49
Food expectancy, as induced state, 138
Food-gathering, gerbils, 115, 118
Food intake (see also Eating, Feeding):
  and water intake, 35
  and thermoregulation, 162
Food rate (see also Rate, reinforcement):
  and schedule-induced behavior, 129–138
Forced-choice procedure, animal psychophysics, 517–518, 524, 537
Forced contingent response, 102–103, 111, 181
Forced motor activity, and central reinforcement, 573
Forgetting:
  and stimulus control, 457–458
  and thermoregulation, 155
Formal classes, verbal responses, 637–638
Formal response unit, 222–223
Formatives, in language theory, 629, 630, 648
Fourth-order deviations, fixed-interval schedules, 208
Free feeding, patterns, 28–36
Free food schedule (see Fixed time schedule, Variable time schedule)
Free operant procedure:
  avoidance, 5, 119, 185, 369–371, 380, 597–606
  discrimination, 499–505
Freezing:
  and animal psychophysics, 517
  and conditioned suppression, 351, 353
  rat, 116–117, 407–409
Frequency, of tone, generalization, 440–441, 450, 455–456
Frequency of reinforcement (see Reinforcement, frequency)
Frog:
  food response in, 121
  psychophysics, 515
  thermoregulation, 157–158
Frontal cortex, self-stimulation, 590
Frustration, 23, 85, 468, 509
Functional relevance hypothesis, 113–118, 122–123
Functional theory, language, 628–629, 633–640, 651–652
Functionalism, and language, 640–642

Galvanic skin response, 61, 493
Gamma rays, irradiation of rats, 527
Ganglionic blockade, 611
Gape response, development, in thrushes, 19–20
Gasterosteus aculeatus (see Stickleback)
Gastric motility, dog, 20
Gastric ulcer, rat, 597, 604–605
Gastrocnemius muscle, 607
Gastrointestinal changes:
  behaviorally induced, 604–605, 608
  human, and avoidance, 597
Gaussian distribution, and generalization gradients, 449
General activity:
  and estrus in rat, 162
  and induced behavior, 134
  and thermoregulation, 161–162, 165–168
Generalization (see also Stimulus generalization):

and animal psychophysics, 526–534
of extinction, 445
language behavior, 619, 621
maintained (see Maintained generalization)
mediated, 509
problems with concept, 433
semantic, 634
Generalization gradient (see also Stimulus generalization gradient):
animal psychophysics, 526–534
and chained schedule, 290–291
and conditioned suppression, 351
inhibitory, and contrast, 82, 85
LSD effects, in rats, 554–555
maintained, 529–530
postdiscrimination, 451, 493–494
and stimulus control, 482
Generalization methods, animal psychophysics, 527–530
Generative grammar, theory, 628–633, 647–649
Generative property, natural language, 621–622, 636–637, 639–640, 644–647
Generative semantics, 649
Generic extension, in verbal behavior, 634
Generic nature, stimulus and response, 30
Genetics:
and language, 640–641
species differences in avoidance, 407–408
Geometric VI schedule, 215
Gerbil:
alert posturing, 115–116
classical conditioning, 115–116
digging, 115–116
drinking, 98, 118
eating, 98, 114
electrical brain stimulation, 111–112
meal patterning in, 35
paper shredding, 98, 110–111, 114, 118–119
punishment, 115
running, 98, 114, 118
self-stimulation of brain, 589
Gestalt:
law of common fate, 623
in verbal behavior, 637
Gill extension, Siamese fighting fish, 116
Glandular response, instrumental conditioning, 609–610
Globus pallidus, self-stimulation, 590
Glucagon, and electrical brain stimulation, 579
Glucose:
concentration, and response strength, 259–260, 263, 279–280
preference, and insulin injection, 557
"Glue," reinforcement as, 99, 101
Gnawing, elicited by brain stimulation, 581
Goal-directed behavior, disruption by lesions, 586–588
Goat:
latent inhibition, 487
self-stimulation of brain, 589
Golden hamster (see Hamster)
Goldfish:
color vision, 517, 522
peak shift, 456
self-stimulation of brain, 590
shape perception, 529
thermoregulation, 153, 158
Go/no-go method, animal psychophysics, 515–516, 524
Good news, and conditioned reinforcement, 319, 336
Goose, greylag, egg retrieval, 23
Gonadal hormones (see Sex hormones)

Gradient:
generalization (see Generalization gradient, Stimulus generalization gradient)
reinforcement, 217–219
Grammar, theory, 628–633, 647–649
Grammatical items, language theory, 630
Grasp response, human, development and recovery, 19–20
Grimacing, human retardate, 564
Grooming:
on concurrent schedules, 246
as facultative behavior, 135, 140
as interim activity, 17, 137
normal, description, 17
Growth:
and meal patterning, 38
and meal size, 35
GSR (see Galvanic skin response)
Guinea pig:
caloric regulation, 43
eating behavior, 34–35, 38, 41, 44
growth, 38, 41
as herbivore, 48–49
patterning of drinking, 36
sexual behavior, 21
stimulus generalization, 441
Gull chick, generalization gradients, 435–436
Gustatory pathways, 586

Habenular nucleus, 586
Habit, 101
Habituation:
to aversive stimulation, 422
to drugs, 550
and rate of eating, 175
Haldol (see Haloperidol)
Hallucinogens:
classification, 545
and perception, 562
as reinforcers, 557
and stimulus control, 555–556
Haloperidol:
classification, 544–545
and self-stimulation of brain, 586
Hamster:
contingent-response experiment, 113–115
digging, 113, 118
eating, 113–115
face washing, 113–115, 118
grooming, 113
rearing responses, 113, 118
scrabbling, 113–114, 118
sexual behavior, 113
thermoregulation, 159
Handedness, 606
"Hard wiring," response to stimulus, 121
Head bobbing, schedule-induced, 128
Heart rate:
and conditioned suppression, 352, 598
and escape-avoidance, 602
measurement and recording, 606
operant conditioning, 607–611
Pavlovian conditioning, 61, 89
Heat:
as aversive stimulus, 154, 157, 162, 165–169
reinforcer
and drugs, 188–189
swimming response, 261, 263, 282
autoshaping, 59, 60, 120, 121
and thermoregulation, 153–158, 161–166
Hemiplegia, 19
Herbivores:
caloric regulation, 47
feeding patterns, 36, 47–48

Heroin:
addiction, human, 563
classification, 545
Hexagonal apparatus, 126, 133, 139, 147
Hibernation, 46
Hierarchy, in language theory, 630, 633, 643–647
High carbohydrate diet, and thermoregulation, 162
High-fat diet, and thermoregulation, 162
High protein diet, and thermoregulation, 162
Higher-order schedule (see also Second-order schedule):
and behavioral structure, 643
Hippocampus:
and avoidance, 605
self-stimulation, 589
Hippocampus, dorsal:
theta waves, 119
Histamine:
and curare, 611
and taste aversion learning, 14
and thermoregulation, 168
Histofluorescence technique, and neural pathways, 585
History:
individual, as determinant of behavior, 174–175, 177–178, 184–186, 192, 196–197
organism, and psychopharmacology, 553
subject, and aversive control, 422, 427
"Hits," animal psychophysics, 516
Homeostasis:
feedback in, 31, 146
and feeding behavior, 32
in hypothalamic syndrome, 17
as motive force, 31
and temperature regulation, 153, 156, 160, 164–165
Homeotherm (see Endotherm)
Hopping, schedule-induced, in pigeons, 139
Hormones:
and avoidance, 599–601, 604–605
and central reinforcement, 579, 589
and conditioned suppression, 598–599
and depletion, 32
measurement and recording, 606
and thermoregulation, 161–162
Huddling, and thermoregulation, 154, 158
Hue, scaling of, 531–532
Human:
alcoholism, 563
artificial language learning, 639–640, 643–647
autonomic conditioning, 607
aversive control procedures, 417, 421
classical conditioning, galvanic skin response, 493
concurrent matching, 234–239, 242–243
concurrent superstition, 234–235
in controlled environment, contingent-response experiments, 107
delay of reinforcement, 262, 282
drug dependence, 557–558, 563
gastrointestinal changes, and avoidance, 597
grasp response, development, 19
incentive motivation, 636
language, 619–652
memory, 639–640
noise-induced behavior, 418–419
Pavlovian conditioning, 20
psychopharmacology, 563–566
reaction time, 532
recovery from hemiplegia, 19
retardates, 564

Human (cont.)
  self-stimulation of brain, 570, 580, 589–590
  shock-elicited behavior, 417–420
  temporal discrimination, carbon monoxide effects, 563
  thermoregulation, 158, 162–164
  verbal behavior, 628–629, 633–640
  visceral conditioning, 607
Hunger:
  and conditioned suppression, 353–354
  as hypothetical drive state, 188
  and induced attack, 137
  and induced drinking, 132–133, 137–139
  and magnitude of reinforcement, 259
  and matching, 236, 269
  Skinnerian analysis, 32
Hunting behavior:
  hyena, 49
  lion, 48
Hydralic models, 11
Hyena, hunting behavior, 49
Hyperphagia:
  hypothalamic, 162
  premigration, 46
Hyperstriatum, self-stimulation, 590
Hypertension, and avoidance, 601–604
Hyperthermia:
  avoidance-induced, 606
  human, 162–163
  rat, 162, 165–166
Hypnotic drugs:
  classification, 545
  barbiturates, 544–545
Hypothalamus:
  anterior, and thermoregulation, 154, 156, 167
  and central reinforcement, 570, 572, 575–577, 579, 582–583
  and depletion-repletion, 32, 46
  electrical stimulation, reinforcer vs. punisher, 178, 180, 181
  lateral:
    and attack behavior, 14–15, 17
    and autoshaping, 60
    electrical stimulation, 14–15, 60, 111
    feeding and drinking, 14, 16–17, 20, 32, 35, 46, 155
    lesions, 16–17, 20, 35
    and motivation, 14, 17
    self-stimulation, 585, 589
    and thermoregulation, 155–156
  posterior:
    electrical stimulation, 164, 259
    and thermoregulation, 154, 156, 164
    and thermoregulation, 154–156, 164, 167–169
  ventromedial:
    lesions, and overeating, 35
    and repletion, 32
    self-stimulation, 589
Hypothermia:
  cats, 166
  drug-induced, 166–169
  human, 163
  rats, 154, 167–169
Hysteresis effects, in concurrent matching, 242, 254

Iconic mapping, in language behavior, 620, 647, 650
ICS (see Electrical brain stimulation)
Id, 9
Ideas, and language, 648, 650
"Idols of the marketplace," 13
Iguana, thermoregulation, 157–158, 166
Imipramine:
  classification, 545
  and errorless learning, 553
  and fixed-ratio behavior, 562
  and schedule control, 189, 557
Imitation, in verbal behavior, 637, 644, 647
Immediacy:
  negative reinforcement
    human, 262
    and response strength, 261–262
  primary reinforcement, and information, 318
  reinforcement
    and matching, 233, 234, 251–252, 266
    and response strength, 260–262, 266, 281
Immobility, difficulty in shaping, 177
Incentive:
  central reinforcement, 580, 582–588
  function of reinforcement, 99–101
  induced, 636
  and peak shift, 458–463
Incentive contrast:
  and induced aggression, 469
  and stimulus control, 458
Incentive function, reinforcement, 99–101
Incentive motivation:
  central reinforcement, 582–589
  verbal behavior, 633, 636
Incentive stimulus:
  and induced behavior, 128
  Pavlovian conditioning, 62
  polydipsia, 131–132
Incidental stimulus (see Contextual stimulus)
Incremental generalization gradient, definition, 445
Indifference, on concurrent schedules, 243
Indirect variables, and schedule control, 204–209, 217, 228–229
Individual differences:
  aversive control, 422, 425
  COD in matching, 243
  peak shift, 442
  schedule control, 186–187
Individual subject:
  behavioral pharmacology, 541–542
  intensive study, 2
Indoleamine, and thermoregulation, 169
Induced behavior (see Schedule-induced behavior)
Induced states, on periodic schedules, 137–138
Induction (see also Negative induction, Positive induction):
  Baconina, 2, 12, 28
  and discrimination theory, 75
Infant, thermoregulation, 158–160
Infectious disease, and avoidance, 597–598
Inferior colliculus, EEG activity, 605
Inflection, in language, 620, 623, 632, 639, 643–647
Inflection ratio, calculation, 342
Influenza, and thermoregulation, 163
Information:
  and conditioned reinforcement, 303, 313–337
  logical problem, 323–324
  in natural language, 620–621
  negative outcomes, 318–326
Information processing, and stimulus control, 458
Information theory:
  conditioned reinforcement, 322
  language, 640
Informativeness:
  CS in Pavlovian conditioning, 343
  stimuli in automaintenance, 63
  stimuli in autoshaping, 56–57, 61, 80, 84
Infusion, intragastric:
  nutrients, 35
  water, 36
Ingestion rate (see also Eating):
  curve, 174
  polydipsia, 129–131
Inhibition:
  absolute vs. relative, 462
  in autoshaping, 61
  in behavioral contrast, 75–76, 82–85
  among behavioral states, 144–148
  by-product of discrimination, 467
  courtship behavior, 121–122
  and dimensional control, 444–447
  and induced activities, 141, 144–148
  among instrumental responses, 115
  latent, 486–487
  among motivational systems, 122
  motor systems, by brain stimulation, 587–588
  by novel stimulus, 116, 588
  by reinforcement, 264, 272–274
  and self-stimulation of brain, 587–588
  and stimulus control, 5, 432–476
    measurement, 445–447
  terminal response by interim, 142–143
  tests for, 470
Inhibitory generalization gradient, measurement, 445–447
Inhibitory stimulus, definition, 444
Inhibitory stimulus control, 432–476
Inhibitory stimulus control:
  determinants, 453–456, 476
  and errorless learning, 470–474
  and schedule variables, 458–466
Initiation:
  meals, 28–40
  ratio runs, 38
  responding, disruption by lesions, 586–588
Inner-ear defect, in mouse, 517
Insect, chained reflexes in, 142
Instinctive act, 15, 23
Instinctive drift, 3
Instinctive responses, and theta waves, 119
Instrumental behavior (see also Operant behavior):
  contingencies among, 98–106
  gerbil, 98
Instrumental conditioning (see Operant conditioning)
Instrumental environment, 98–99, 111, 112
Instrumental learning, 14, 53
Instrumental responses (see also Operant behavior):
  role as stimuli, 5
Insulin:
  and choice of sugar solution, 557
  and electrical brain stimulation, 579
Integration, learned responses, 20, 22
Integration, levels of (see Levels of integration)
Intensity:
  current, and central reinforcement, 578, 782
  shock-elicited behavior, 418, 422, 427
  stimulus
    and overshadowing, 492
    and psychophysical scaling, 532
    and reaction time, 526, 532
Intensity dynamism effect, auditory psychophysics, 524
Intention, 30
Intention movements, 139
Interaction:
  activities and states, 144–145
  behavioral states, 144–148
  classical-operant, and conditioned suppression, 341, 344, 348–352, 358–360

concurrent schedules, 70–80, 233–282 (*see also* Matching)
dimensions of stimuli, 439
eating and drinking, 35, 36, 42–43, 131, 135, 139
excitation and inhibition, 447–451
and stimulus generalization, 493–494
internal and external stimuli, and reinforcement, 582–585, 588–589
multiple schedule, 71–85 (*see also* Behavioral contrast)
  controls for, 72
  definitions, 73
  and Herrnstein's equations, 266–268
  and inhibitory control, 458–463
  theories, 75–91, 266–275
among non-contingent responses, 114–115
operant-Pavlovian
  and autoshaping, 53–91
  and conditioned suppression, 341, 344, 348–352, 358–360
psychophysiological processes, 608, 610–611
punishment paradigm, 428
among reinforcers, and matching, 252–254, 264–265
response-shock and shock-shock interval, 370–371
running and drinking, 146–148
sequential:
  behavior and environment, 177
  among induced activities, 144–146
shock-elicited behaviors, 420–426, 428
stimuli, and stimulus control, 496, 507
stimulus-reinforcer, response-reinforcer, 66–71
terminal and interim activities, 132–133, 139–140, 143
terminal and interim states, 139–140, 143
two kinds of peck, 67
Interburst interval, in contingent-response experiments, 110–112
Interchangeability, stimuli, responses and rewards, 13, 91, 112, 113, 122, 407–408
Interdimensional training:
  discrimination
    description, 439–440
    effects, 444
  and peak shift, 454–455
  and stimulus control, 494–497
Interference hypothesis, conditioned suppression, 351–353, 357–359
Interfood interval, and sequential interactions, 147
Interim activities, 125–148
Interim activities:
  competition with terminal, 132–133
  and contrast, 273–274
  control of, by food, 131–132, 140
  definition, 126
  examples, 128–129, 137
  motivation, 128, 132, 137–139
  schedule-induced, 125–148
  S^Δ periods, 135–136
  variables affecting, 128–138
Interim period:
  aversiveness, 139–140
  DRL schedules, 135, 141
  FI and VI schedules, 133, 135–138, 141
  properties, 137–139
Interim states:
  interaction with terminal, 139–140, 143
  properties, 137–139, 144–146
Interlocking schedule:
  fixed-ratio, fixed-interval, 213

and ratio responding, 212
shock postponement, 194
Intermeal intervals, 32–40
Intermittent reinforcement (*see also* Partial reinforcement):
  central reinforcement, 573–574, 578–579
  and polydipsia, 131–132, 135
  and schedule control, 201–202
  thermoregulation, 164
Intermittent shock schedules, 375–377, 384–386, 397–398
Internal clock (*see* Behavioral clock)
Internal economy, 596
Interoceptive discrimination, 610
Interocular transfer, line tilt, 528
Interpeduncular nucleus, 586
Interreinforcement time:
  concurrent choice, 327–337
  differentiation schedules, 224
  fixed-ratio schedules, 205, 209–210, 217
  interval and time schedules, 214
  and response rate, 210
  and responses per reinforcement, 210–211
  as schedule variable, 204–205, 209–211, 214, 228–229
  variable interval schedules, 214–215
Interresponse time:
  and concurrent choice, 255–256
  conditionable response unit, 224
  contingent-response experiments, 109
  drug effects, 559–560
  and generalization gradient, 437–438
  as reinforced response, 223–224
  as response unit, 223–224, 263
  role in response rate, 238, 263–265
  as schedule variable, 204, 224–225
  as stimulus, 223
  theoretical unit, 223–225
  unit of behavior, 222–225, 263
Interresponse time schedule (*see also* Differentiation schedule, DRL schedule, DRO schedule):
  concurrent, and matching, 251, 255–256
  definition, 203
  regenerating property, 212
  and response strength, 263–264
Intertrial interval:
  autoshaping, 57–58, 66, 78, 127
  escape procedure, 368
  food deliveries during, 63, 67–68
Interval schedule (*see also* Fixed-interval, Variable-interval, Random-interval):
  definition, 202
  regenerating power, 212
  and time schedule, 214
Intestinal contractions, operant conditioning, 571, 608
Intestinal load, 33
Intracranial stimulation (*see* Electrical brain stimulation)
Intradimensional shift, 487
Intradimensional training:
  description, 439–440
  and errorless learning, 466
  and peak shift, 453–454
  and stimulus control, 493–494
Intrapeduncular nucleus, stimulation, 585
Intraperitoneal route, drug administration, 545
Intraverbal, in verbal behavior, 634, 646–648
Invariance, schedule performances, 187
Inverse hypothesis, stimulus control, 507–508
IRI (*see* Interreinforcement interval)
IRT (*see* Interresponse time)

IRTs/Op, and stimulus generalization, 437
Islets of Langerhans, 10
Isobias function, animal psychophysics, 536
Isocarboxazid, 545
Isomorphism, autoclitic and transformational theories, 648–649
Isosensitivity curve, animal psychophysics, 533–534
Iteration, theory of grammar, 629
ITI (*see* Intertrial interval)

Jumping stand, 497

k:
  Herrnstein's amount of behavior constancy, 262–263
  definition, 257
  Hull's incentive, 99–100
Kantian *a prioris*, and verbal behavior, 638, 641
Kernel sentences, language theory, 629–630, 632–633, 643, 648
Key pecking (*see* Pecking, Pigeons)
Key pressing, human, and matching, 239
Kidney, excretion of drugs, 550
Kidney function, instrumental conditioning, 609–610
Kinesis, 158

Language:
  acquisition, 619–627
  artificial, 639–640, 643–647
  operant analysis, 5, 619–627, 633–640
  psychology of, 619–652
  theories, 619–652
Latency, response,
  and interreinforcer time, 211
  and stimulus intensity, 526–527, 532
Latent inhibition, 486–487
Law of availability, 47–48
Law of common fate, 623
Law of effect, 233–282
Law of effect:
  and absolute response rate, 257–263
  autoshaping, 53–54, 62–63
  correlation-based, 111
  as equilibrium principle, 141
  quantitative analysis, 4, 132, 140, 233–282
  Thorndike's statement, 99
  symmetrical, 101–102, 110
  weak, 100–101, 113, 122
Laws of behavior, self-sufficiency, 28
Laws of operant behavior, 148
Laws of reflex strength, 30
Learned releasers:
  and autoshaping, 62, 70
  and Pavlovian conditioning, 70
Learning:
  artificial language, 639–640, 643–647
  constraints on (*see* Constraints)
  drug effects, 560–562
  as modification of habitat, 49
  natural language, 619–627
  two types, 54
Learning disability, human, and drugs, 564
Learning effects, animal psychophysics, 525
Leash-pulling, squirrel monkey, 183–184
Lesions (*see* Brain damage)
Leucocytes, and pyrogens, 166
Levels of function, nervous system, 8
Levels of integration, of operant, 7–24
Lever contact response, rats, 60, 65, 81–82, 120

Lever pressing (by rats, for food, unless otherwise stated):
acquisition, 561
and aversive control, 421–425, 428
avoidance, 116–118, 185, 194–195, 260, 267–268
cebus monkey, 102
college students, 103, 107
conditioned suppression, 89, 341–356
and contrast, 73–74, 81–82, 89–91
drug effects, 561
escape, 261–262, 282, 319, 367–368, 383–387
and experience, 175, 177
in extinction, 205
hamster, 114
heat reinforced, 154, 162, 164
heat avoidance, 165, 168
and induced drinking, 132, 138
as interim activity, 133
macaque, 258
monkey, 89, 178, 185, 194–195, 352
pigeon, 73, 82, 91
postreinforcement pause, 142
and reinforcement immediacy, 260–263, 281
and reinforcement magnitude, 258–259, 278–282
rhesus monkey, 352
shaping, 177
squirrel monkey, 421–425, 428
stimulus generalization, 437
and sugar concentration, 259–260, 263, 269, 279–280
as terminal response, 133, 145–146
and thermoregulation, 164–165, 167
token reinforcement, 306
Lexeme, 620
Lexical items, 630
Lexical system, 620
Lexicon:
definition, 620
use, 648
Librium (see Chlordiazepoxide)
Licking (see also Drinking, Polydipsia, Schedule-induced behavior):
air, by rats, 138
in automaintenance, 65, 120
avoidance response, in rats, 118
contingent-response experiments, 104, 108
as interim activity, 133
rate, and polydipsia, 130–131
as terminal response, 133
Light intensity (see Brightness)
Limbic pleasure area, 582
Limbic system, and central reinforcement, 572, 585
Limited availability schedule, and induced behavior, 131–132, 135–136
Limited hold procedure, animal psychophysics, 527
Limited opportunity schedule, and negative reinforcement, 398–406
Limulus, 9
Lindsley manipulandum, 602
Linear VI schedule, 215
Line orientation:
generalization, 440, 441, 445, 454–455, 458, 482, 494, 501–502, 527
and visual vertical, 527
Linguistics, 619–627, 628–652
Lion:
feeding behavior, 47
hunting behavior, 48
Listener, and verbal behavior, 649–651
Lithium carbonate, 545
Lithium chloride, 484

Lizard, thermoregulation, 153, 157–158, 161–164
Local contrast (see also Transient contrast):
additivity theory, 86–88
definition, 77
and Herrnstein's equation, 268
necessary conditions, 78
and overall contrast, 77–78, 86–88
pigeons, 75–78, 85–88
rats, 78, 85
Localizability (see also Diffuseness):
stimulus, and contrast, 82
US in autoshaping, 60, 69
Localization, stimulus on manipulandum, 490
Local rate of reinforcement:
concurrent schedules, 246–247, 272
fixed-interval schedules, 216
and schedule control, 214–218
variable-interval schedules, 214–215
variable-ratio schedules, 217
Local rate of response:
concurrent schedules, 235, 238, 244–247, 274
multiple schedules, 272
and probability of reinforcement, 214–216
second-order schedules, 302–303
Lock and key, courtship sequences, 142
Locomotion:
amphetamine effect, 554
and aversive control, 418–426
Locus coeruleus:
and central reinforcement, 586
self-stimulation, 590
Logarithm:
drug dosage regimen, 551
in matching equation, 238–239, 243, 247–250
Long box, autoshaping with, 63
Lordosis response, rodents, 21
LSD:
classification, 545
and stimulus control, 554, 556
Luminal (see Phenobarbital)
Lysergic acid (see LSD)

Macaca nemistrina (see Macaque)
Macaque:
EEG activity, 605–606
magnitude of reinforcement, 258, 263, 278–280
thermoregulation, 153, 159
Mach bands, 452
Macrosaccadic eye movement, 237
Magnesium pemoline, 545
Magnitude of reinforcement (see Reinforcement, magnitude)
Maintained generalization procedure:
animal psychophysics, 529–530
description, 434–435
Maintenance (see Automaintenance)
Mammals, thermoregulation, 158–162, 167
Mand, 633, 636–637
Manual manipulation, and aversive control, 418–430
Marijuana:
behavioral pharmacology, 545, 552
reinforcer, 557
and stimulus control, 555
Markov process, and behavioral sequences, 142
Marplan (see Isocarboxizid)
Masking:
airflow by key stimuli, 491
line orientation by color, 482–483, 491
and overshadowing, 492–493, 500

and stimulus control, 482–483, 491–492, 500, 504, 506
tone by key stimuli, 491
Massed extinction, and peak shift, 456–457
Masseter muscle, 417–418
Matched shock, extinction procedure, 379–380
Matching:
and behavioral contrast theories, 272–275
concurrent chained schedules, 297–298, 329–333
concurrent schedules:
evidence, 239–243
generality, 243, 248–256, 275, 276–277
vs. maximizing 245–246
measurement, 235, 248
vs. multiple schedules, 272–275
necessary conditions, 234, 242–244
negative reinforcement, 254
and punishment, 253–254
and reinforcement immediacy, 251–252, 329–333
and reinforcement magnitude, 233–234, 248–251
discrete trial procedure, 237, 244–246
humans, 234–239, 242, 243
and IRT reinforcement, 225
and k-parameter, 262–263
and multiple schedules
and component duration, 269–272
conditions for, 269
and contrast, 79–80
and Herrnstein's equations, 260–270
negative reinforcement, 373–374, 382–383, 386–388
responses, concurrent schedules, 235–237, 242–244, 272–274
responses and time, 237
concurrent schedules, 238, 246–248, 250, 255
multiple schedule, 272
time:
concurrent schedules, 238–239, 246–248, 254, 272, 274
in interresponse class, 264
Matching law:
deviations from, 242–243, 256, 266, 270–272, 276–277
as empirical law, 275–276
equations, 233, 236, 238, 245, 248, 253, 255, 257, 275, 277, 329
generality, 243, 248–256, 275–277
as intuitive assumption, 275–276
linear, 233–234
proportional ratio, 238–239, 242, 247–249, 252–257, 277
as tautology, 276
as theoretical law, 276
Matching to sample:
animal psychophysics, 518, 525
and conditioned reinforcement, 307–308
pigeons:
chained schedule, 292
second order schedule, 301
and verbal behavior, 638
Mathematical analysis, Law of effect, 4, 132, 140, 233–282
Mathematical model:
avoidance, 365
generalization gradient, 449
Mathematical theory, discrimination learning, 448–451
Maximization, energy yield/time expended, 47–49
Maximization function, 47–49
Maximizing vs. matching, on concurrent schedules, 245–246, 254

Subject Index

Maze:
  central reinforcement, 572
  contrast effects, 86
  drug effects, 555
Meal:
  criterion, 36
  duration, 28, 33, 42
  frequency, 28, 33–38
  initiation, 32, 36, 38, 40
  patterning, 28–30, 32–37, 42–45
  and polydipsia, 130–132
  size, 32–35, 37–38, 130–132
  termination, 32, 36, 38, 45
  as unit of analysis, 31–32, 34, 45–46, 49
Measurement:
  central reinforcement, 572–574
  conditioned suppression, 348–351, 360
  drug effects, 189, 192–193, 202, 541, 545–547
  physiological changes, 606
  preference structure, 108–110
  sensory thresholds, 515–525
  stimulus control, 433–436, 482–483
Mechanical models, animal behavior, 29–31
Mechanism, behavioral and psychopharmacology, 551–560
Mechanism of action, psychopharmacology, 541
Medial forebrain bundle:
  central reinforcement, 577, 585, 589, 607
  and thermoregulation, 156
Medial geniculate, EEG activity, 605
Mediated generalization, 509
Mediating responses, avoidance theory, 364, 397, 400
Mediation:
  in autonomic conditioning, 607–608, 610
  in syntax learning, 624
Mellaril (see Thioridazine)
Memory:
  and stimulus control, 457–458
  and verbal behavior, 637–638
Mentalese, and verbal behavior, 635, 648–651
Mentalism, and language, 640–642
Mentalistic concepts, how avoided, 29
Meperidine, 545
Meprobamate:
  classification, 545
  and conditioned suppression, 356
  and schedule control, 189, 191, 557
Mercury vapor, behavioral effects, 562–563
Meriones unguiculates (see Gerbil)
Mescaline, 545
Mesocricetus auratus (see Hamster)
Metabolic rate, and thermoregulation, 154, 161–162, 168
Metaphoric extension, verbal behavior, 634
Metastability, response patterns, 192
Methadone:
  classification, 545
  and heroin addiction, 563
Methanol, 549
Methamphetamine:
  classification, 545
  and punishment, 560
  and schedule control, 559
  and ratio strain, 543
Methaqualone, 545
Methedrine (see Methamphetamine)
Method of constant stimuli, animal psychophysics, 521–522
Method of limits, animal psychophysics, 520–522
Method of successive approximations, in shaping behavior, 54, 62

Methodology:
  central reinforcement, 572–574, 589
  and schedule control, 204–229
Methylphenidate:
  classification, 544–545
  and learning disability, 564
Metonymic extension, verbal behavior, 634, 637
Metronome, 138, 484
Microstructure, stimulus generalization gradient, 437–439
Midbrain, and electrical stimulation, 583, 585
Milieu externe, 33
Milieu interne, 33
Milieu therapy, 565
Miltown (see Meprobamate)
Minimal unit hypothesis, 67–68
Minor tranquilizers, 545, 555
Mirror image, and interocular transfer, 528
Misbehavior of organisms, 3, 7, 13, 23
"Misses," animal psychophysics, 516
Mixed schedule:
  and chaining, 221–222
  conditioned reinforcement, 320–321, 323–324, 336
  and contrast, 74
  drug effects, 556
  observing responses, 320–321, 323, 324
Model:
  central and conventional reinforcement, 584–585
  as method of synthesis, 10
Modulation:
  behavior
    by electric shock, 180, 183, 193, 195–196
    by environment, 410
    by food presentation, 182
  response rate, chained schedules, 293, 299
Modulus, for measuring behavior, 262
Molecular weight, drugs, 549
Momentary response probability, 108–109, 112
Mongolian gerbil (see Gerbil)
Monkey (see also Squirrel monkey, Rhesus monkey, Cebus monkey, Macaque)
Monkey:
  auditory intensity discrimination ROC curves, 534–535
  auditory thresholds, 516, 519, 521
  avoidance, 366, 406
  central reinforcement, 578
  cocaine reinforcement, 250–251
  color vision, 518
  conditioned suppression, 89, 352, 358–360
  dark-reared, 486
  equal-loudness contour, 526
  flicker discrimination, 522
  matching on concurrent schedules, 250–251
  motion aftereffect, 523
  negative reinforcement, 390, 395
  observing responses, 320–321
  pica, 137
  positive conditioned suppression, 358–360
  schedule-induced drinking, 138
  second-order schedule, 302
  self-stimulation of brain, 578, 589–590
  spiral aftereffect, 529
  stimulus generalization, 490
  tactual discrimination, 517
  thermoregulation, 164, 167
  visual fixation training, 523

Monoamine oxidase inhibitors, and self-stimulation of brain, 585
Monochromatic light, rearing, and generalization, 485–486
Mood, and schedule-induced behavior, 137–138, 144
Morphine:
  classification, 545
  dependence, 179, 554, 557
  and fixed-ratio behavior, 551
  and punishment, 558
Morphonemic rule book, in language behavior, 648
Motility, gastric, dogs, 20
Motion aftereffect, monkey, 523
Motivation:
  and conditioned suppression, 353–358, 360
  drug effects, 188–189, 559–562
  and electrical brain stimulation, 570, 576, 579–580, 582–589
  feeding behavior, 49
  homeostasis as, 31
  and interim activities, 128, 132, 137–139
  and matching, 269
  as maximization function, 49
  and the operant, 12–13, 15, 19, 22–23
  problems with concept, 14–15
  and schedule-induced behavior, 128–132, 137–139, 144
  and schedule performances, 188
Motivation hypothesis:
  conditioned suppression, 351, 353–357, 358
  induced drinking, 130, 132
Motivational properties, induced states, 138–140
Motivational state, as behavioral state, 144
Motor behavior, and self-stimulation of brain, 586–588
Mouse:
  auditory sensitivity, 517
  biting attack, 416–417
  brain biochemistry, 606
  conditioned suppression, 517
  killing, by rat, 17
  meal patterning, 35
  neurological mutant, 517
  thermoregulation, 153, 159, 167
Müller-Lyer illusion, 526
Multiple causation, verbal behavior, 646–647
Multiple concurrent schedule, matching, 249
Multiple schedule:
  animal psychophysics, 515–516
  avoidance, 267–271
  behavior pharmacology, 551–552, 556–557, 559
  central reinforcement, 575
  and chained schedule, 290
  chained and tandem, 294
  component duration
    and contrast, 79, 87, 90
    and matching, 269–272
    negative reinforcement, 382–383
  and conditioned reinforcement, 317, 323–324, 336
  conditioned suppression, 345, 347
  contrast on, 75–91, 266–275
  drug effects, 188–191, 551–552, 556–557, 559
  and Herrnstein's equations, 266–268, 270–272, 373–374
  induced behavior, 132, 136–137, 138
  interactions on (see Interaction)
  matching, 269–272, 373–374
  negative reinforcement, 367, 369, 381–387

Multiple schedule (cont.)
    and peak shift, 441–443, 458–463
    relation to concurrent, 78–80, 266–270
    relative response rates, 268
    responses per reinforcer, 211–212
    response-produced shock, 195
Multiple-stimulus method, generalization gradient, 434

Nalorphine:
    and conditioned suppression, 554
    and morphine dependence, 179, 557
    reinforcer vs. punisher, 179, 192
Naloxone, 557
Narcosis, cold, 157
Narcotics (see also Opiates, Analgesics):
    classification, 545
    as reinforcers, 557
    tolerance, 550
Nardil (see Phenelzine)
Nativism, and language, 641
Naturalistic environments, behavior in, 4, 28–50
Natural selection, in language learning, 626
NE (see Norepinephrine)
Necessity, as driving force of behavior, 31
Neck stretching, as interim activity, 137, 139
Negative automaintenance, 13, 23, 63–65, 128 (see also Omission effect, Omission training)
Negative behavioral contrast, 72–75, 78, 85–86, 267–268
    additivity theory, 85–86
    definition, 73
    logical problems, 75, 86
    pigeons, 75, 78, 85–86
    and positive contrast, 75, 85–86
    rats, 78, 85–86
Negative contingencies, in omission training, 99, 128
Negative feedback:
    in homeostasis, 31
    as self-inhibition, 144–148
    in thermoregulation, 153–154
Negative induction:
    definition, 72–73
    pigeons, 82–83, 89–90
    rats, 74, 82
Negative reinforcement, 364–410 (see also Escape, Avoidance, Electric shock, Aversive control)
    access to, 376
    acquisition, 404–409
    added cues, 365, 381–396
    concurrent schedules, 254, 375, 386, 388–392
    contingency vs. frequency, 398–399
    definition, 364
    density, 369–370, 375
    discriminative stimuli, 392–396
    escape procedure, 367–368, 383–387
    extinction after, 377–380
    frequency, 260, 369–370, 398–399
    illustrative experiments, 365–367
    immediacy:
        human, 262, 282
        and response strength, 261–262, 282
    intermittent shock schedules, 375–377, 384–386
    magnitude:
        and response strength, 261, 263, 281–282
        scaling, 387–388
    and matching, 254, 269–270, 373–374, 382–383, 386–388
    noncontingent shock, 378–380
    and Pavlovian conditioning, 364–365, 390–393, 395–398, 400
    procedures, 364–406
    shock-delay procedure, 365, 370–371, 380, 383, 388–391, 400, 402, 407, 409
    shock delay vs. frequency reduction, 402–406
    shock-deletion procedure, 365, 371–373, 375, 382, 384, 386–387, 398–401, 403
    shock-density reduction, 375
    shock-frequency reduction, 365, 373–378, 380–383, 386–387, 392, 400–406
    similarity to positive, 365–368, 373, 382, 384, 386, 406
    and stimulus generalization, 450
    and supplementary positive reinforcement, 404–405
    two-factor theory, 364–365, 393, 396–398, 400
    two modes of, 387–388
Negative stimulus, and conditioned reinforcement, 318–326
Nembutal (see Pentobarbital)
Neocortex, and instrumental autonomic conditioning, 608
Neostriatum, self-stimulation, 590
Nephrectomy, bilateral, and drinking, 36
Nervous system, development, 8, 17–19
Nest building, gerbils, 115
Neural basis, reinforcement, 571, 574, 580–581, 585–589
Neural pathways, and self-stimulation, 585–588
Neurochemistry, and thermoregulation, 167–169
Neurons:
    catecholaminergic, 571, 585–588
    temperature sensitive, 154, 158, 160, 166, 169
Neuropharmacology, catecholaminergic pathways, 585–586
Neurophysiological system, transient changes, 597
Neurotransmitters:
    and drugs, 544
    and thermoregulation, 167–169
Neutral stimulus, after errorless learning, 467, 471
Neutral zones, and stimulus control, 453
Nialamide, 545
Niamid (see Nialamide)
Nigrostriatal pathway, 586–588
Noise escape, 282
Noise-induced behavior, 418–419
Nonchaining delay, and gradient of reinforcement, 217–218
Noncontingent schedule (see Time schedule)
Noncontingent shock, and negative reinforcement, 378–384
Noncontingent stimuli, 2
Nondeprived animals:
    large ratios tolerated by, 36, 38, 43
    meal patterning, 30, 34–35, 45
Nondifferential reinforcement:
    definition, 433
    and generalized gradient, 436, 439–441, 454–456
    and overshadowing, 507–508
    and stimulus control, 488–490
Non-matching to sample, 307–308
Non-reinforcement, as de-encephalization, 23
Nonsense syllables, 639–640, 643–647
Noradrenalin, and self-stimulation of brain, 571
Noradrenergic hypothesis, reward, 571
Noradrenergic neurons, and self-stimulation of brain, 585–586
Noradrenergic pathways, 571, 585–588
Norepinephrine:
    and escape-avoidance, 605
    and heart rate conditioning, 608
    and stimulus control, 555–556
    and thermoregulation, 167–169
Nose-key pressing:
    cats, 520
    monkeys, 58
    rats, 516
Not-responding, and temporal patterning, 217
Novel stimulus:
    effects on ongoing response, 116
    inhibition by, 588
Noxious stimuli (see also Electric shock, Escape, Avoidance, Aversive control, Negative reinforcement):
    and maintenance conditions, 182
Noyes pellets, 43, 45, 89
Nursing, rats, 18–19
Nutritional quality, and eating patterns, 33, 47–49
Nuzzling response, chicks, 65

Obesity:
    and electrical brain stimulation, 14, 579
    experimentally produced, 597
Object carrying, elicited by brain stimulation, 571, 582
Object substitution, Pavlovian conditioning, 62
Observation method, several responses at once, 4, 126–127, 139, 147–148
Observing responses:
    animal psychophysics, 517–519, 523
    and attention, 30
    and conditioned reinforcement, 313–315, 318–326, 332, 336–337
    in discrimination training, 508
    maintaining variables, 322
Obstruction box, and central reinforcement, 572, 574
Octopus:
    failure of temporal discrimination, 140
    shape perception, 529
Oddity problem, animal psychophysics, 518, 525
Odorant, stimulus control by, 517, 523
Olfaction:
    and central reinforcement, 582
    and lateral hypothalamus, 16
Olfactory bulb, self-stimulation, 589
Olfactory bulbectomy, and meal frequency, 35
Olfactory discrimination:
    pigeons, 517
    rats, 523
Olfactory pathways, 586
Olfactory tubercle, self-stimulation, 589
Omission, reinforcement, second-order schedule, 301
Omission effect (see also Omission training, Negative automaintenance):
    automaintenance, 63–68, 128
Omission training (see also Omission effect, Negative automaintenance):
    chicks, 65, 120–121
    dogs, 63
    pigeons, 63–68, 119
    rats, 65
    squirrel monkeys, 65
    stimulus-reinforcer relations, 63–64
Omnivores:
    caloric regulation, 47
    feeding patterns, 47
Ongoing behavior:
    and negative reinforcement, 409–410

and reinforcement *vs.* punishment, 176, 180–182, 191, 197
Ontogenic contingencies, 580
Operant (*see also* Instrumental):
  as behavioral state, 144
  concept, 3, 7–8, 11–14
  as conditionable unit, 222
  criterion of motivation, 13–14
  de-encephalization, 22–23
  definitions, 175, 186
  as emitted, 174–175
  encephalization, 20–21
  as functionally identifiable class, 175
  hierarchical structure, 22–23
  history, 8–11, 28–31, 53–54, 174–175
  and human behavior, 13
  on interresponse time schedules, 255
  levels of integration, 7–24
  physiological thinking and, 8–11
  problems with concept, 7, 13–14, 23
  relation to general psychology, 2, 4–5, 8
  self-stimulation of brain as, 580
  Skinner's justification, 11–12
  and terminal response, 127
  as unit, 2, 174–177, 222
Operant analysis, basic assumption, 29
Operant behavior:
  and chronic somatic changes, 597
  and classical conditioning, 53–91, 340–361
  and conditioned suppression, 340, 341–351
  language as, 619–627, 633–640
  laws, 148
  and Pavlovian conditioning, 53–91, 340–360
  technical advances, 186–187
  and thermoregulation, 153–169
Operant conditioning:
  autonomic responses, 606–611
  and autoshaping, 62, 66–67, 70, 120
  history, 8–11, 28–31, 53–54, 174–175
  definition, 175
  parameters, and conditioned suppression, 344–348, 351, 360
  and physiological states, 596–611
  relation to Pavlovian, 54–55, 62, 71, 88, 91, 120
  visceral responses, 606–611
Operant discrimination, and central reinforcement, 575
Operant methods:
  advantages, 2, 5, 7
  aversive control, 415–430
  animal psychophysics, 515–537
  central reinforcement, 572–580
Opiates (*see also* Heroin, Morphine, Narcotics):
  classification, 544–545
  self-administration, 545
Opportunity hypothesis, induced drinking, 130–132
Optimal-duration model, response probability, 109–113, 122–123
Optimal level theory, 99
Optimization, cost-benefit, in feeding, 46
Order effects, concurrent matching experiments, 242, 254
Oral route, drug administration, 545
Orientation response:
  animal psychophysics, 523
  in autoshaping, 65, 69
  and contrast, 89
  and hypothalamic lesions, 16–17
Orrery, language model, 623
Outcome-dependency, instincts and operants, 15
Overextension, verbal behavior, 634

Overmatching, concurrent schedules, 242, 244, 248, 254–255
Overshadowing:
  and blocking, 500
  and masking, 492–493
  necessary conditions, 507
  and stimulus control, 492–493, 496, 499–501, 503, 506
  theory, 506–508
Overtraining, 23

Paced schedule, and choice, 255–256, 266, 276–277
Paced VI schedule, and IRT reinforcement, 225
Pacing procedure, 345, 354
Pacing response, schedule-induced, 128, 137
Paired-associates learning, 637
Pairing:
  concurrent chains, and conditioned reinforcement, 333–336
  and conditioned reinforcement, 303–308
  US and CS, in autoshaping, 55–58, 127
Pairing hypothesis, conditioned reinforcement, 313, 315–318, 325, 334–336
Palatability of food:
  and diurnal eating cycle, 44
  and induced behavior, 132–133, 138
Paleostriatum, self-stimulation, 590
Pallidum, self-stimulation, 590
Pancreatectomy, 10
Panel pressing, dogs, on shock delay schedule, 390
Panting, and thermoregulation, 154, 167
Paper shredding, gerbils, 98, 110–111, 114–115, 118–119
Parallels:
  applied to operant, 11
  as method of synthesis, 10
  between recovery and development, 8, 17–22
Paraphrase, in language behavior, 649–651
Parenteral route, drug administration, 545
Parieto-occipital activity, cat, 605
Partial reinforcement (*see also* Intermittent reinforcement, Reinforcement):
  advantage of schedules, 299
  and autoshaping, 61
  brain stimulation, 576, 578–579, 589
  and persistence, 509
Partial reinforcement effect:
  in autoshaping, 61, 64, 119
  generalized, 509
  operant conditioning, 61
  Pavlovian conditioning, 61
  and resistance to extinction, 201
Path-independence, feeding behavior, 46
Pattern:
  drinking, 36, 40, 42
  meals, 28–30, 32–37, 42–45
  responding
    and matching, 255–256, 276
    in preshock stimulus, 350
    and schedule performance, 213–221, 265
Pause:
  interresponse (*see* Interresponse time)
  postreinforcement (*see* Post-reinforcement pause)
Pavlovian conditioning (*see also* Classical conditioning):
  aggressive behavior, 59
  and altered physiological states, 596
  in automaintenance, 62–63
  in autoshaping, 53–55, 58, 60–61, 80–81, 119–122
  and avoidance, 364–365, 393, 396–398, 400

  in behavior contrast, 81, 84–85, 88–89
  blood pressure, 89
  and conditioned suppression, 88–89
  description, 61–63
  dogs, 61, 138, 340, 483–484, 489, 492
  expectations in, 138
  eye blink, 61
  fear, and conditioned reinforcement, 315
  galvanic skin response, 61
  heart rate, 61, 89
  human infants, 20
  mechanisms, 61–62
  and negative reinforcement, 364–365, 390–393, 395–398, 400
  and operant behavior, 53–91
  partial reinforcement, 61
  relation to operant, 54–55, 62, 71, 88–89, 91
  salivation, 9, 53, 61, 138, 340, 489, 493
  sexual behavior, 59
  and shock-correlated stimuli, 390–391
  stimulus substitution in, 61–62
  trace, and shock-delay, 400
Pavlovian hypothesis, contingent-response experiments, 119–123
Pawing:
  in automaintenance, 65
  schedule-induced, 128, 133
PD (*see* Pseudodiscrimination)
PDG (*see* Postdiscrimination gradient)
Peak shift:
  and area shift, 442, 453
  and behavioral contrast, 442, 454
  by-product of discrimination, 467
  compounding theory, 459–463
  concurrent schedules, 463–464
  determinants, 442, 453–456, 476
  double, 442
  and errorless learning, 467, 471
  goldfish, 456
  and interdimensional training, 454–455
  and intradimensional training, 453–454
  and massed extinction, 456
  mathematical constraints, 448–449
  necessary and sufficient conditions, 456
  negative, 443
  and negative reinforcement, 451, 453
  positive, 441–443
  and schedule variables, 458–466
  Spence's theory, 448–449
  tone frequency, pigeons, 441
  wavelength, pigeons, 249, 441–442
Peck, duration:
  in autoshaping, 24, 67–68, 81
  and contrast, 87–88
  on FI and FR, 67
  food *vs.* water reinforcement, 58–59, 67, 81, 119
  in omission training, 67–68
Pecking (by pigeons, for food, unless otherwise stated):
  acquisition, 55, 57, 62–63
  aggressive, in pigeon, 59
  automaintenance, 62–68
  autoshaping, 3, 7, 13, 24, 54–62, 69–70, 81, 119
  chicks:
    autoshaping, 59, 60, 65, 120, 121
    thermoregulation, 159–160
  conditioned suppression, 345, 346, 351, 353, 357
  effect of experience, 177
  errorless learning, 464–480
  extinction, 205
  as interim response, 128, 133, 140, 144
  maintenance, and Pavlovian conditioning, 63, 81, 88, 91, 119, 120
  negative reinforcement, 406–407
  operant *vs.* reflexive, 67

Pecking (cont.)
   as Pavlovian response, 54–55, 58, 63, 69, 81, 89, 91, 119
   positive conditioned suppression, 359
   postreinforcement pause, 142–143
   as prototypic operant, 54–55, 71, 100
   rate:
      as controlling stimulus, 504
      as constant, 238–246
      and reinforcement magnitude, 259, 278
   schedule-induced, 128, 130, 140, 144
   shaping, 177
   as terminal response, 126–128, 133, 135, 140–144
   voluntary vs. reflexive, 54–55, 67
Pedal pressing, pigeon, observing responses, 318, 320
Pedal pushing, dog, avoidance, 605
Pentobarbital:
   classification, 544–545
   clock schedule, 555
   extinction effects, 561–562
   fixed-interval behavior, 559
   fixed-ratio behavior, 544, 546, 548–549, 559, 562
   and punishment, 558
   as reinforcer, 192
   schedule control, 542–543, 546, 559
   and stimulus control, 555
   and thermoregulation, 556
Peptic ulcers:
   and aversive control, 597, 604–605
   and avoidance procedure, 597, 605
   monkeys, 605
Percentage reinforcement, brief stimulus schedule, 316
Percentile schedule, and IRT reinforcement, 224
Perception:
   animals, 526–530
   and drugs, 562
Perceptual learning, and language, 643–647
Performance theory, language behavior, 629
Periodicity, responding on FI, 208–209
Periodic schedules (see also Fixed interval, Variable interval, Fixed time, Variable time):
   and induced behavior, 126–140
Peripheral resistance, and cardiac output, 602–603
Permitil (see Fluphenazine)
Perphenazine, 544–545
Persistence:
   and central reinforcement, 576–578, 589
   and partial reinforcement, 509
   running as facultative activity, 147–148
Pharmacology:
   behavioral (see also Behavioral pharmacology, Drugs, Psychopharmacology):
   behavioral, 5, 188–193, 202, 540–569
   and conditioned suppression, 349, 350, 355–357
   thermoregulation, 167–169
Phenelzine, 545
Phenobarbital, 544–545
Phenothiazine:
   classification, 544–545
   and conditioned suppression, 356
   and stimulus control, 555–556
Philanthus triangulum (see Wasp)
Phone, element of language, 629
Phonology, component of language structure, 629, 632
Phrase marker, in language theory, 629–630
Phylogenic contingencies, 29, 580

Phylogeny of aggression, 417
Physiological psychology, relation to operant, 5
Physiological states:
   altered, 596–618
   durable, 597–598
   experimental alteration, 596–611
   measurement, 606
   technological and methodological developments, 606
   transient, 597
Physiologizing, 9
Physiology vs. operant in analysis of behavior, 8–12
Pica, schedule-induced, 23, 137
Pig:
   rooting response, 13
   thermoregulation, 153, 158–159
Pigeon:
   absolute response rate, 257–258
   adventitious punishment, 184
   adventitious reinforcement, 185
   aggressive behavior, 23, 59, 120, 136–137, 139, 468–469, 552
   auditory stimulus control, 485, 487–491, 494–495
   automaintenance, 62–68
   autoshaping, 13, 23, 54–62, 68–70, 80–81, 119
   avoidance, 13, 120, 450–451
   behavioral contrast, 76–78, 84–86, 266–275, 442, 454
   blocking, 499–500
   brightness discrimination, 521, 532
   central reinforcement, 572, 589
   chained schedule, 291–298
   classical conditioning, 489
   clock schedule, 555
   COD in matching, 243
   conditioned suppression, 345–346, 351, 353, 357, 517
   concurrent chained schedule, 327–337
   concurrent schedule:
      brief stimuli, 307–308
      matching, 236–256
   concurrent superstition, 234–235
   conditioned enhancement, 89
   conditioned reinforcement, 318–337
   conjoint schedule, 307–308
   dark adaptation, 521–522
   delay of reinforcement, 219
   drug effects, 552–555, 559–560, 562–563
   electrical brain stimulation, 252
   errorless learning, 464–480
   escape, 254
   fixed-time schedule, 126–127
   FR FI performance, 187
   interocular transfer, 528
   interresponse time as basic, 263–264
   key pecking (see Pecking)
   matching:
      concurrent vs. multiple, 272
      concurrent schedules, 236–256
      multiple schedules, 269–272
      and reinforcement immediacy, 251–252, 266
   meal patterning, 35
   negative contrast, 78, 85–86
   negative induction, 82
   negative reinforcement, 386–391, 406–407
   observing responses, 318–326
   oddity problem, 518
   olfactory sensitivity, 517
   overshadowing vs. masking, 492–493
   pecking (see Pecking)
   polydipsia, 129, 136
   positive conditioned suppression, 359
   positive contrast, 73–74, 78, 81–82

   punishment, 65, 253–254
   reinforcement magnitude, 248–251, 259
   response-produced stimuli, 221–222
   schedule-induced behavior, 126–129, 136–139
   second-order schedules, 299–306
   self-stimulation of brain, 572, 589–590
   stimulus generalization, 434–443, 450, 454–456, 458, 482, 489, 490, 493–496, 501–502, 527–528, 530–532
   time discrimination, 218, 219
   treadle pressing, 82, 89–90, 236
   VI vs. VR performance, 210
   visual acuity, 517–518, 521,
   wild, 236
   wing flapping, 59
Piloerection, and conditioned suppression, 351
Pimozide, 586
Piperazine, 544
Placebo effect, 554
Plasticity principle, response units, 222
Pleasantness, thermal stimuli, 162–164
Poikilotherm (see Ectotherm)
Polydipsia (see also Drinking, Licking, Schedule-induced behavior):
   ethanol, in rats, 561
   psychogenic, 23
   schedule-induced:
      behavioral determinants, 129–131
      and body weight, 132
      chimpanzees, 129
      control by eating, 129–135, 138
      doves, 129, 136
      measurement, 129–130
      motivation hypothesis, 130, 132, 138
      pigeons, 129, 136
      and postprandial drinking, 129–131
      rats, 129–130, 132, 136
      regulatory mechanisms, 129
      squirrel monkeys, 129
      stimulus control of, 129, 131
      theories, 130–132
Polyribosomes, mouse brain, 606
Population, matched to available resources, 33
Positive behavioral contrast:
   definition, 73
   and induced drinking, 132, 138
   and matching low, 266–268, 273–274
   and negative contrast, 75, 85–86
   pigeons, 73–74, 77–78, 80–83, 266–268, 273–274
   and punishment, 77
   rats, 72–74, 78, 82–86
Positive conditioned suppression:
   and autoshaping, 359
   and Pavlovian conditioning, 88–90
   and punishment, 357–360
   schedule effects, 359
Positive feedback, in autoshaping, 70
Positive induction, 72–73
Postdiscrimination gradient, 451, 493–494
Posterior marginal gyrus, EEG activity, 606
Post food period, and polydipsia, 131
Postprandial drinking:
   and matching, 252
   and polydipsia, 129–131, 135
Postreinforcement pause:
   and acceleration of response, 142–143
   conditionable unit, 226–228
   fixed-interval schedules, 213, 216
   and polydipsia, 131
   ratio schedules, 42, 209, 213, 217, 226–228, 293, 346, 355
   and ratio size, 209, 212–213, 217
   and rate of responding, 142–143
   tandem schedule, 258

Power function:
  concurrent schedules
    generality of, 255, 256, 277
    VI vs. FI, 255
  human reaction time, 532
  and temporal differentiation, 224, 227
  visual intensity, 532
Power function matching, equations, 255, 277
Power law, sensory magnitude, 530
Prandial drinking, rats, 18
PRE (see Partial reinforcement effect)
Pre-avoidance period, cardiovascular changes, 602–603
Prebehavioral time, and language, 649
Predictability, shock, and gastric ulcer, 604
Prediction:
  as method of synthesis, 10
  outcomes of instrumental contingencies, 98–101, 115, 122
Predictiveness (see also Informativeness):
  stimulus, in autoshaping, 63, 80, 84, 127
  and terminal response, 126–128
Preening:
  as facultative behavior, 135, 140
  as interim activity, 137, 146
Preference:
  and avoidance, 366
  central vs. conventional reinforcement, 577–578
  central reinforcement sites, 572–573
  color, in pigeons, 524
  among concurrent schedules, 233, 235
  among events in world, 101–110
  FI over chained schedule, 335
  and incentive, on multiple schedules, 459
  multiple over mixed schedules, 336
  position, and animal psychophysics, 518, 524, 532
  response, in animal psychophysics, 516, 518, 521, 524
  saccharine concentration, 106
  scaling of, concurrent schedules, 298
  shorter IRTs, 256
  stimulus
    in animal psychophysics, 524
    and generalization gradients, 435–436, 440, 442
  thermal
    animals, 153, 158–159
    humans, 162–164
  VI over FI schedules, 255, 332
  wavelength, effect of rearing, 486
Preference function, and generalization gradient, 435–436
Preference procedure, central reinforcement, 574
Preference structure, measurement, 108–110
Pre-loading, and induced drinking, 138
Preoptic area, and thermoregulation, 154–156, 167–169
Preparedness:
  and animal psychophysics, 520
  and negative reinforcement, 407–408
Primates (see also Monkeys, specific primates):
  autoshaping, 58, 60
Priming, and central reinforcement, 576
Primitives, in verbal behavior, 647–648
Probabilistic schedule, shock-frequency reduction, 375
Probability:
  positive stimuli, and observing responses, 322–324
  reinforcement:
    on concurrent schedules, 234, 237, 244–245
    and conditioned reinforcement, 326–327
    and schedule control, 214–215
  responses, and reinforcement vs. punishment, 181
  shock, and shock-frequency reduction, 374–377
  of US, in classical conditioning, 315, 343–344
Probability, differential rules (see Differential probability rules)
Progesterone, and thermoregulation, 162
Programmed instruction, 7, 467
Progressive ratio schedule, and central reinforcement, 573–574
Prolixin (see Fluphenazine)
Promazine, and clock schedule, 555
Prompting, in language learning, 639–640
Proportional ratio matching, 238–239, 242, 247–249, 252–257, 277
  equations, 238, 248
Propranolol, and blood pressure, 603
Protein, component of self-selected diet, 44
Proximity:
  food and water, and induced drinking, 139
  to reinforcement in time:
    in chained schedule, 289, 293
    and conditioned reinforcement, 326–337
    and Herrnstein's equations, 265
    and induced behavior, 127, 140
    and interval relativity, 221
  stimulus to reinforcer, in autoshaping, 127
Pseudodiscrimination procedure, 495–505, 507–509
Psilocybin:
  classification, 545
  and stimulus control, 556
Psychiatry, and drugs, 540, 542, 563–566
Psychoanalysis, hydralic models, 11
Psychoendocrine studies, 597–604
Psycholinguistics, 619–627, 628–652
Psychological distance, to reinforcement, 335
Psychological independence, dimensions of discrimination, 439–440
Psychology of language, 619–652
Psychopharmacology (see also Behavioral pharmacology, Drugs):
  acquisition and extinction, 560–562
  antecedent variables, 553–554
  and behavioral mechanisms, 541, 551–560
  consequence variables, 556–559
  and drug abuse, 542, 557–558, 563
  human, 563–566
  motivation, 188–189, 559–560, 562
  and schedule control, 542–543, 546, 551–552, 555–560
  and self-stimulation of brain, 571, 580
  sensation and perception, 562
  stimulus variables, 554–556
  thermoregulation, 153–155, 164–169, 188–189, 556
Psychophysics, animal, 515–537
  methods, 515–532
  signal detection theory in, 5, 516, 532–537
Psychophysics of association, 70
Psychophysiology, classical, 596–597
Psychosomatic disorders, and central reinforcement, 571
Psychotic behavior, drug effects, 564–566
Psychotomimetics (see Hallucinogens)

Psychotropic drugs, 545
Puffer fish poison, 166
Punisher, definition, 176–177
Punishment, 174–198
  adventitious (see Adventitious punishment)
  animal psychophysics, 523–524
  and aversive control, 425, 427–430
  change over in matching, 243–244, 253
  and choice on concurrent schedules, 253–254
  and choice of reinforcer delay, 252
  and conditioned reinforcement, 320, 322, 324–325, 326
  and conditioned suppression, 357–358
  contrast experiments, 74, 76, 77
  criteria for, 186–188
  definitions, 176–177, 182, 186
  drug effects, 558–560
  functional relevance and, 113, 115, 116–117
  gerbils, 115
  instrumental behavior, 98, 101–103
  lever pressing, and pattern of behavior, 428
  in observing procedure, 320–325
  pigeons, 65, 253–254
  problems in testing for, 102
  as process, 176–177, 182, 186
  recovery from, 194
  relation to reinforcement, 175–180, 182, 197
  as reproducible process, 176–177, 182, 186
  Siamese fighting fish, 116
Pure operant, self-stimulation of brain, 580
Pure stimulus act, 30
Purposive acts, 12–13, 23
Putamen, self-stimulation, 580
Pyriform cortex, self-stimulation, 589
Pyrogens, and thermoregulation, 165–166

Quaalude (see Methaqualone)
Quail:
  autoshaping, 58–59
  sexual behavior, 59
  wavelength generalization, 486
Quantitative analysis:
  discrimination learning, 448–451
  law of effect, 4, 132, 140, 233–282
Quantitative comparison, drugs, 547
Quiet biting attack, in cat, 14
Quinine:
  excretion, 550
  and thermoregulation, 155, 167

Rabbit:
  classical conditioning, auditory frequency, 489, 494
  eyelid conditioning, 493–496
  pancreatectomized, 10
  self-stimulation of brain, 589
  thermoregulation, 159, 166–167
Raccoon, misbehavior, 13
Rage, in cat, 14
Random-interval schedule:
  conditioned suppression, 354
  definition, 202
  induced drinking, 135
  shock avoidance, 267–268
  temporal patterning, 213, 265
Random order of stimuli, animal psychophysics, 521, 524
Random-ratio schedule:
  definition, 202
  and positive conditioned suppression, 359
  temporal patterning, 213

Random schedule:
  definition, 202
  shock frequency reduction, 374–375, 380–381
Random-time schedule, definition, 202
Rat:
  absolute response rate, 258–259
  adventitious reinforcement and punishment, 184
  aggressive behavior, 136
  alcohol reinforcement, 553, 561
  animal psychophysics, 518
  automaintenance, 65
  autonomic conditioning, 607–611
  autoshaping, 58, 60, 81
  avoidance, 116–117, 165, 260, 267–271, 561
  behavioral contrast, 73–74, 78, 81–86, 267–268, 270–271
  brightness discrimination, 526–527
  caloric regulation, 43
  central reinforcement, 572–590
  COD in matching, 243
  concurrent matching, 237, 248–250, 278
  conditional enhancement, 89
  conditioned suppression, 89–90, 341–359
  contingent-response experiments, 102–109
  delay of reinforcement, 260–262, 281
  development of infant, 18
  discrimination training, 501–502
  diurnal eating and drinking patterns, 33, 36
  drug effects, 188–191, 349, 355–357, 544, 546, 548–549, 551, 554–556, 560, 561
  eating rate, 41
  electrical brain stimulation, 14, 60, 120, 178–180, 237, 259, 279, 518, 572–590
  equal-brightness contour, 526–527
  errorless learning, 467
  escape, 117, 261–263, 281–282, 319, 367–368, 383–387
  exploratory behavior, 60, 120
  extinction, 378, 380
  FR behavior, 36–38, 551
  FR FI performance, 187
  gastric ulcers, 597, 604
  grooming, 17
  heart rate in CER conditioning, 352
  heat reinforcement, 154–155, 188, 261, 263, 282
  hypothalamic syndrome, 16–17
  insulin and sugar preference, 557
  interim activities, 126–139, 143, 147
  isobias functions, 535
  killing of, by cat, 14–15
  latent inhibition, 487
  lever contact response, 65, 81, 82, 120
  lever pressing (see Lever pressing)
  matching on concurrent schedules, 237, 248–250, 278
  meal patterning, 28, 30, 34–38, 41–44
  mouse-killing, 17
  negative induction, 82
  negative reinforcement, 373–375, 378–384, 390–406
  nursing, 18–19
  obesity, 597
  olfactory discrimination, 523
  omission training, 65
  as omnivore, 47
  orientation response, 16–17
  patterning of drinking, 40
  pica, 137
  polydipsia, 129–139, 147, 561
  prandial drinking, 18, 129–131, 135, 252
  reinforcement immediacy, 260–262, 281
  reinforcement magnitude, 248–250, 258–261, 278–279
  relation of eating and drinking, 131
  relativity of reinforcement, 102–109, 181
  response-produced stimuli, 222
  running, 100, 103–107, 129–135, 175, 181–182, 258–263, 278, 281–282
  schedule-induced behavior, 126–139, 143, 147
  schedule performance, 188–191
  self-stimulation of brain, 572–590
  shape perception, 529
  shock-correlated stimuli, 390–398
  shock-frequency reduction, 373–375, 380–384, 402–406
  stimulus generalization, 439, 441, 493, 497, 554–555
  sugar concentration, 259–260, 263, 279–280, 557
  swimming response, 261, 263, 282
  taste-aversion learning, 13–14, 24, 484
  thermoregulation, 153–156, 162–168, 188–189, 556
  thigmotaxis, 117
  thyroidectomy, 18
  token reinforcement, 306
  tooth chattering, 17
  visceral conditioning, 607–611
Rate:
  changeover, and matching, 234, 243–244, 249–250, 254, 276
  eating (see Eating, rate)
  ingestion (see Eating, rate)
  local (see Local rate)
  members of reflex chain, 29
  pecking in pigeons, as constant, 238, 246
  reinforcement
    and conditioned reinforcement, 314
    and conditioned suppression, 345, 355
    local, 214–218
    and matching, 233–244, 247, 249, 252
    and schedule-induced behavior, 130
  response
    absolute, 257–263
    and central reinforcement, 572, 574, 576–578
    chained vs. tandem schedule, 293–295
    during COD, 244
    and conditioned suppression, 345, 348–351
    and FR requirement, 37
    and measure of reflex strength, 28
    property of behavior, 174–176
    and psychophysical scaling, 532
    role of interresponse time, 263–264
    schedule determinants, 228–229
    shock-delay procedures, 370–371
    shocks received, shock-delay procedure, 371, 373
Rate dependency, drug effects, 189–191, 555, 558–560
Rating method, animal psychophysics, 535
Rayleigh distribution, in animal psychophysics, 534
Ratio schedule (see also Fixed ratio, Random ratio, Variable ratio):
  components of chain, 292–293, 296
  and concurrent choice, 246–247, 254
  definition, 202
  non-regenerating property, 212
  shock delay, 377
  temporal patterning, 217, 219–220
  variable vs. fixed, responses per reinforcer, 207
Ratio strain, 37, 543
Reaction time methods, animal psychophysics, 526–527, 532
Reactive inhibition, 146
Rearing response:
  gerbil, 111
  hamster, 113, 118
  rat, 117–118
Recall, and memory, 638
Receiver operating characteristic, animal psychophysics, 533–537
Receptive field model, shape discrimination, 529
Recognition, and memory, 638
Recovery, stages of:
  compared to development, 17–22
  in hypothalamic dogs, 20
  in hypothalamic rats, 17
Red nucleus, self-stimulation, 590
Redundancy, stimuli in autoshaping, 56–57
Reference procedure, extinction, 377–380
Referent, of words, 619
Refinement experiment, 30–31
Reflex:
  and aversive control, 425
  chain, in insects, 142
  chain, within meals, 28, 45–46
  conditioned, 9
  eating as, 29–31
  functional properties, 174
  gape, in thrushes, 19–20
  grasp, in humans, 19
  laws of, 31
  and minimal unit, 67
  Sherrington's definition, 29
  sleep, 22
  as source of behavior, 67
  spinal, 8–9, 11
  strength, 29–30
  thermoregulatory (see Thermoregulation, reflex)
  as unit of analysis, 29–31, 49, 53
  as unmotivated, 9, 13, 23
  variables governing, 9
Reflex arc:
  and language, 641
  model of learning, 53
Reflex reserve, 11, 205
Refractory phase, of reflex, 29
Regenerating property, interval and time schedules, 212, 229
Regression toward the mean, responses per reinforcer, interval schedules, 212
Regulation, temperature (see Thermoregulation)
Regulatory mechanisms, in polydipsia, 129
Regulatory system:
  constraints on learning, 118–119, 122
  water, in rats, 118
Reinforcement, 98–123, 174–198 (see also Conditioned reinforcement, Central reinforcement, Negative reinforcement)
  adventitious (see Adventitious reinforcement)
  analysis and history, 98–100
  central, 570–590 (see also Electrical brain stimulation)
    similarity to conventional, 574–581, 584–585, 589
  choice, central vs. conventional, 577–578
  conditioned (see Conditioned reinforcement)
  contingency (see Contingency)
  in contingent-response experiments, 98–112
  criteria for, 186–188
  definitions, 175, 186, 202, 433, 584
  delay (see Delay of reinforcement)
  density:
    in autoshaping, 61
    and conditioned reinforcement, 314, 316, 325–327, 329, 332, 336–337

Subject Index

on differentiation schedule, 224
and drugs, 552
and induced behavior, 140
in time, 214–215
depletion-repletion model, 31–32
by drugs, 192–193, 556–558
electrical brain stimulation (*see also* Reinforcement, central; Electrical brain stimulation)
magnitude, 259
and matching, 252
as effect of operation, 202
excitatory effects, 264, 272–274
food *vs.* water, and matching, 252
free, in contrast experiments, 87–90
frequency and conditioned suppression, 345–355
and contrast, 76–78, 84, 87
and induced aggression, 469, 475
and IRT reinforcement, 225
and matching, 235–244, 247, 249, 252
and peak shift, 462
functionally defined, 4
immediacy (*see also* Delay of reinforcement)
and central reinforcement, 575
and matching, 233, 251–252
and response strength, 260–262, 266, 281
inhibitory effects, 264, 272–274
interchangeability, 13–14, 23, 112–113, 122
intermittent (*see also* Intermittent reinforcement, Partial reinforcement)
and drugs, 558
and partial reinforcement effect, 201
and thermoregulation, 164
of IRTs, and schedule performance, 223, 225
magnitude:
and absolute response rate, 257–259, 278
conditioned reinforcement, 320, 322, 326–327
and contrast, 86, 267
drugs, 192–193, 250–251, 558
electrical brain stimulation, 179, 181, 259, 279
incentive, 100
and induced behavior, 132–133
and IRT reinforcement, 225
and matching, 233–234, 248–251, 262, 278
with meal reinforcement, 45
and observing responses, 320, 322
and polydipsia, 130–132
thermal reinforcement, 157, 164
model of, central and conventional, 584–585
negative (*see* Negative reinforcement, Escape, Avoidance)
neural substrate, 571, 574, 580–581
nondifferential:
definition, 433
and generalization gradient, 436
noradrenergic hypothesis, 571
omission, as second-order schedule, 301
as operation, 176
partial (*see* Partial reinforcement, Intermittent reinforcement)
percentage, and FI schedule, 301
Premack's theory, 101–106, 108–109
as process, 176–177, 182
quality:
and absolute response rate, 259–260
and choice, 252, 262
re-evaluation of concept, 4
relation to extinction, 205
relation to punishment, 175–182, 197

relative frequency, and matching, 233–244, 247, 249, 252
as reproducible process, 176–177, 182, 186
resistance to, and stimulus generalization, 446, 450
schedules (*see* Schedules)
secondary (*see* Secondary reinforcement, Conditioned reinforcement)
shock-frequency reduction, 365, 373–378, 382, 387, 392, 400
shock delay, 402–406
strength, central reinforcement, 572–574
systems of, 580–582
of temporal pattern, 643
token, 306
traditional theory, 99
of verbal behavior, 637
Reinforcements per opportunity (*see* Probability, reinforcement)
Reinforcement theory:
and mathematical analysis, 4
Premack's, 101–109
traditional, 99–101
Reinforcer:
definitions, 2, 175–177, 202
examples, 178
temporal placement, 213–214
Reinforcibility (*see* Conditionable response unit, Conditionability, Associability)
Relations, and control of verbal behavior, 638–639
Relative generalization gradient:
description, 435
and schedule control, 436, 438
and stimulus control, 501–502
Relative proximity principle, 221
Relative proximity rule:
as equilibrium principle, 140
and induced behavior, 140–141
Relative reciprocal, and IRT reinforcement, 225
Relativity:
conditioned suppression, 348–351
inhibition, 462
reward *vs.* punishment, 101–110, 178–182
stimulus control, 496
thermal preference, 162–165
time within intervals, 220–221
Releasing stimuli:
in attack behavior, 15, 23
ethological concept, 410
learned, in autoshaping, 62, 70
REM sleep, ontogeny, 22
Repletion (*see* Depletion)
Replication, in behavioral pharmacology, 542
Reproducibility, of behavioral baseline, and pharmacology, 551
Reproducible behavioral processes, 174–176, 182, 186–188, 197
Reproductive state, and thermoregulation, 161–162
Reptiles, thermoregulation, 156–158, 161–162, 166
Reserpine:
classification, 545
and conditioned suppression, 355–356
psychiatric use, 540
and schedule performance, 189
and self-stimulation of brain, 585
Resistance to extinction:
drug reinforcement, 558
and generalization, 436, 445, 450, 483
and partial reinforcement effect, 201
Pavlovian conditioning, 61
response unit hypothesis, 225–226

and stimulus control, 436, 445, 450, 482, 509
Resistance to reinforcement, and stimulus generalization, 446, 450–451
Resistance-to-reinforcement test for inhibitory control, 470–472
Resource allocation, in feeding patterns, 47
Respondent (*see also* Classical, Pavlovian):
elicited by brain stimulation, 573, 580
Respondent behavior:
and conditioned suppression, 341, 342, 348–352
as interfering response in conditioned suppression, 351–353, 358–359, 360
Respondent conditioning, 3, 9, 53
Response:
differences, and negative reinforcement, 407–408
interchangeability, 13, 91, 112–113, 122
types, in operant conditioning, 183
Response contingency, and schedule-induced behavior, 125–128, 130–136, 140–141
Response cost:
and alcohol consumption, 563
in human matching, 239
Response dependency:
as stereotypic effect, 204
and temporal contiguity, 228
Response-dependent schedule, 204 (*see also* Specific schedule types)
Response deprivation hypothesis, 103–113, 122–123
Response enhancement, by electric shock, 185, 194–195
Response frequency, variables determining, 206–213
Response functions:
observing responses, 322–324
in polydipsia, 130
in schedule-induced behavior, 132
Response-independent food, in response-dependent schedule, 128, 138
Response-independent schedules, 126–128, 132–133, 141, 204 (*see also* Fixed time, Random time, Time schedule, Variable time)
Response-independent shock, and aversive control, 415–425
Response-initiated schedule, fixed interval, 301
Response number:
as discriminative stimulus, 222
on FI schedules, 206–208
on FR schedules, 209
Response-pacing procedure, 345, 354
Response patterning:
interval and time schedules, 214
ratio schedules, 217–220
temporal organization, 213–221
Response-produced shock (*see* Electric shock, response produced)
Response-produced stimuli:
and chaining hypothesis, 221–222
and conditioned reinforcement, 319, 322–323
Response rate (*see* Rate, response)
Response-reinforcer relation:
in automaintenance, 63–71, 91
as temporal, 204
Response-shock interval:
description, 369–370
ratio shock-delay schedule, 377
relation to shock-shock interval, 370–371, 388
shock-delay procedure, 369–371, 388
shock-deletion procedure, 372

Response-shock interval (cont.)
  in Sidman avoidance, 369, 370–371
  standardized 20 sec, 599
Responses per reinforcement:
  differentiation schedules, 224
  fixed-interval schedules, 205–213, 229
  and interreinforcer time, 211–213
  ratio schedules, 207–214
  and schedule performance, 228–229
Response strength:
  and conditioned suppression, 348–351, 360
  equations for, 257, 264–267
  and meal termination, 45
  measures, 258, 262
  and negative reinforcement, 260–262
  reinforcement parameters, 234, 239, 257–263, 278
  theories, 263–264
Response suppression:
  in behavioral contrast, 76–78, 84
  in contingent-response situation, 103, 105–107, 112
  by electric shock, 183, 185, 193, 195
  and forced running, 103
Response unit, specification of types, 222–225
Restraint:
  in animal psychophysics, 523, 527
  and aversive control, 421
  and temporal discrimination, 140–143, 147
Retardates, human:
  brain stimulation, 581
  chlorpromazine, 564
Reticular formation, EEG activity, 605
Retrieval cues, in verbal behavior, 637
Reversal, discrimination:
  and errorless learning, 470
  and stimulus control, 457, 470
Reversibility:
  drug effects, 551
  interactions in multiple schedules, 72
Reversing chains schedule, and avoidance, 366
Reward (see Reinforcement)
r_g, 99–101
Rhesus monkey:
  alcohol ingestion, 597
  autoshaping, 58
  avoidance, 185, 366, 599–601, 604
  blood pressure conditioning, 609
  conditioned suppression, 352, 598–599
  drug dependence, 179, 553
  drug-maintained responding, 192
  endocrine changes in avoidance, 599–601, 604
  epinephrine and stimulus control, 556
  hormones and avoidance, 599–601, 604
  hypertension and avoidance, 601
  morphine dependence, 179, 553
  peptic ulcers, 597, 605
  shock avoidance, 185, 366, 599–601, 609
  shock-elicited attack, 380
  shock-frequency reduction, 376–377, 380
  shock postponement, 185
  sugar concentration and response strength, 260
Rhodopsin, experimental synthesis, 10, 22
Ribonucleic acid, rat brain, 606
Ritalin (see Methylphenidate)
RNA (see Ribonucleic acid)
ROC (see Receiver operating characteristic)
Rooting response:
  pig, 13
  pigeon, 65
Rough grain, on chained schedules, 291
Routes, drug administration, 543, 545

RS interval (see Response-shock interval)
Ruminants, 33, 34, 47
Running:
  in contingent-response experiments, 101–109, 181
  as emitted, 175
  as facultative behavior, 133–137, 140, 146
  and food rate, 133–134
  forced, 102–103, 181
  interaction with induced drinking, 146–148
  pattern, effects of schedule, 182
  rat:
    fixed-time schedules, 126, 133–134, 147
    immediacy of reinforcement, 260, 281
    magnitude of reinforcement, 259, 263, 278, 280
    negative reinforcement, 407
    shock escape, 261–262, 281–282
    temporal pattern, 175, 182
  reinforcer vs. punisher, 181
  and schedule induction, 129, 133–135, 146–147
Running wheel:
  avoidance, 116–118
  gerbils, 98, 114, 115, 118
  motorized, 102, 111
  rats, 102–108, 146, 181–182
Run time distribution, fixed-ratio schedule, 228
Runway:
  central reinforcement in, 572
  contrast effects, 86
  reinforcement magnitude, 259–261, 278–282
  shock escape, 261–262, 281–282

Saccharine, in contingent-response experiments, 106, 108
Saccharine-glucose solution, preference by rats, 578
Salience, stimulus:
  and conditioned reinforcement, 317
  relation to validity, 496
  and stimulus control, 483, 492, 496, 500, 506
Salience, warning stimulus, and shock postponement, 394–395
Saline, control in psychopharmacology, 548, 554, 556
Salivary conditioning:
  classical, 9, 53, 61, 138, 340, 489, 493
  description, 340
  lesions and, 20
  operant, 607
Salivation:
  hamsters, and grooming, 114
  instrumental conditioning, 607
  and thermoregulation, 165
Sample size, behavioral pharmacology, 541–542, 551
Satiation:
  central reinforcement, 576–578, 580, 589
  thermoregulation, 164
Satisfier, in law of effect, 99, 101
Scalar property, timing on response-delay procedure, 400
Scaling, animal psychophysics, 530–532
Scallop, fixed-interval, 140, 143, 384, 458, 643
Schedule complex, and negative reinforcement, 384
Schedule control, 201–229, 288–309
  chained schedules, 289–299
  and conditioned suppression, 345–351, 360
  drug effects, 188–191, 202, 542–543, 546, 551–552, 555–560

  electric shock, 193–196
  and generalization gradient, 436, 438–439
  induced behavior, 129–138
  and inhibitory control, 458–466
  negative reinforcement, 367, 375–378, 384–386, 390, 395–398
  and positive conditioned suppression, 359
  property of operant behavior, 197
  as reproducible process, 176–177, 186, 197
Schedule-induced attack (see Attack, Aggression)
Schedule-induced behavior, 125–148 (see also Interim activities, Polydipsia, Attack, Drinking)
  definition, 126
  hypotheses, 130–132
  measurement, 129–130
  motivation, 128–132, 138–139, 144
  pigeon, 126–127
  rat, 126–127, 130
  regulatory mechanisms, 129
  and schedule variables, 129–138
  temporal and sequential structure, 135, 140–148
  types, 127
Schedule-induced drinking (see Polydipsia, Drinking)
Schedule-induced running (see Running)
Schedule performance, 125, 140, 176, 186–188, 197, 265
Schedule performance:
  chained schedules, 288–299
  direct and indirect variables, 204, 228–229
  drug effects, 188–191, 202
  and electric shock, 193–196
  interval vs. ratio, and matching, 255
  as multiply determined, 228
  and reinforced IRTs, 223–225
  second-order schedules, 299–306
  theories, 217–221
Schedules of reinforcement, 201–229 (see also Schedule control, specific schedules):
  biological significance, 48
  characteristic effects, 176–177, 181, 197, 201, 213
  and extradimensional training, 503–505
  as fundamental determinants, 201–202, 229
  history, 201–202
  types, 202–203
Schizophrenia, 571
Scopolamine:
  classification, 545
  clock schedule, 555
  and learning, 561
  and stimulus control, 555
Scrabbling response, hamster, 113–114, 118
S△:
  on chained schedule, 296
  in shock-frequency reduction, 381
S△ periods, and induced behavior, 132, 135–136, 141
Seal, animal psychophysics, 519
Sea lion, visual acuity, 519–520
Search time, 48
Secobarbital, 544–545
Seconal (see Secobarbital)
Secondary reinforcement (see also Conditioned reinforcement)
  in autoshaping, 56
  and brain stimulation, 576, 589
Second-order deviations, on fixed-interval schedules, 208–209

Subject Index

Second-order schedule:
  brief stimuli, 299–306, 313, 315–318
  description, 299
  discrimination of components, 316–318
  drug effects, 193
  electric shock effects, 193
  induced drinking, 135
  interval components, 300–301, 303, 305
  and pairing hypothesis, 315–318
  ratio components, 301–302
  and response units, 226
  and tandem schedule, 294, 300, 301
Seizure activity, and central reinforcement, 573
Selection, terminal response, 127, 133
Selective attention, 507–510
Self-administration, drugs, 192–193, 543, 556–558, 561, 563, 586
Self-regulation procedure, central reinforcement, 574
Self-selection, balanced diet, 43, 44, 47–49
Self-stimulation of brain (see Electrical brain stimulation, Central reinforcement)
Semantic, in language structure, 629, 632–633
Semantic memory, 637–638
Semantics, natural language, 622–624
Sensation, drug effects on, 562
Sensitivity index, animal psychophysics, 533
Sensory control:
  eating, 20
  transformation, 19–20
Sensory deficit, and thermoregulation, 155–156
Sensory fields, 14–16, 21
Sensory neglect, 16–17
Sensory scanning, and aversive control, 418–430
Sensory stimuli, and central reinforcement, 582–583, 586, 588–589
Sensory thresholds, measurement in animals, 515–525
Septum, stimulation, 570, 575–576, 583
Sequence:
  behavior, and shaping, 175–178, 180
  behavioral states, 144–148
  as conditionable response unit, 226–227
  induced activities, 126–127, 140–143
  response, during errorless learning, 464–465
  stimuli:
    on chained schedule, 295–296, 334–336
    and stimulus control, 456–457
  as theoretical response unit, 225–226
Sequential dependency, in animal psychophysics, 524
Sequential interaction:
  behavior and environment, 177, 180, 197
  among behaviors, 144–145
Sequential organization, responses between reinforcers, 221
Sequential relations, responding on FI, 209
Sequential structure, induced behavior, 140–146
Serial order, problem in behavior, 641–642
Serotonin, and thermoregulation, 167, 169
Set point:
  and control theory, 154, 160
  definitions, 154, 160
  in thermoregulation, 160–169
"Sets," 9
17-hydroxycorticosteroid:
  and avoidance, 599–601, 604
  and conditioned suppression, 598–599

17-OH-CS (see 17-hydroxycorticosteroid)
Sex hormones:
  and avoidance, 599–601
  and self-stimulation of brain, 579, 589
  and thermoregulation, 162
Sexual behavior:
  and electrical brain stimulation, 579, 581
  guinea pigs, 21
  pigeons:
    autoshaping, 59, 119
    as interim activity, 137
  quail, Pavlovian conditioning, 59
  rat, and thermoregulation, 162
Shape perception, animal psychophysics, 529
Shaping:
  animal psychophysics, 520
  and continuity in time, 177–178
  heart rate conditioning, 607
  in language learning, 624
  with negative reinforcement, 406–407
  by response-produced shock, 196
  by successive approximations, 23, 54, 62, 177, 182, 406
  unnecessary in nondeprived animals, 37, 43
Shaping schedule, 224
Sharpening, generalization gradient, 434, 494–495
Sheep, latent inhibition, 487
Shivering, and thermoregulation, 154–155, 164–168
Shock (see Electric shock)
Shock delay (see also Avoidance)
  as reinforcer, 402–406
  vs. shock-frequency reduction, 402–406
Shock-delay procedure:
  cues added, 392–398, 400
  description, 365, 370–371
  extinction after, 378–380
  multiple schedule, 383
  multiple response patterns, 388
  negative reinforcement, 365, 370–371, 380, 383, 388–391, 400, 402, 407, 409
  ratio schedules, 377
  response bursting, 388
  and stimulus generalization, 450
  temporal discrimination, 399–401
Shock-deletion procedure (see also Avoidance):
  description, 365, 371–372
  negative reinforcement, 369, 371–373, 375, 382, 384, 386, 387, 398–399, 400–401, 403
  temporal discrimination, 400–401
Shock-density reduction, 375
Shock-elicited behavior:
  human, 417–420
  mouse, 416
  and negative reinforcement, 380, 408–409
  squirrel monkey, 417–430
Shock-free periods, concurrent schedules, 390, 392
Shock-frequency reduction (see also Avoidance, Negative reinforcement):
  as controlling variable, 365, 373–375, 382–383, 387, 392, 400–406
  direct manipulation, 374–375, 380–381
  Herrnstein's equations, 373–374, 386–387
  vs. shock delay, 402–406
Shock-intensity reduction, 375, 380
Shock postponement (see Shock delay)
Shock-shock interval:
  description, 369–370
  fixed vs. variable, 397

relation to response-shock interval, 370–371, 388
  shock-delay procedure, 369–370, 388
  shock-deletion procedure, 372, 384–385
  Sidman avoidance, 369–370
  standardized 2 sec, 599
  typical values, 370
  variable, 372
Shuttlebox:
  central reinforcement, 572, 574, 582
  escape by pigeons, 254
  and heart rate conditioning, 608
Shuttle response:
  negative reinforcement:
    pigeons, 407
    rats, 400, 406
  shock delay, dogs, 393
Shuttling, and thermoregulation, 157–158, 164, 166
Siamese fighting fish:
  attack behavior, 15, 59, 65
  automaintenance, 65
  Pavlovian conditioning, 59, 65
  punishment, 116
Sign stimuli, 15, 23
Sign tracking:
  autoshaping and automaintenance, 69, 81, 127
  discrimination learning, 69
Signal detection theory, animal psychophysics, 516, 532–537
Signaled shock, and negative reinforcement, 397–398
Similarity:
  perceptual, in animal psychophysics, 530–532
  S+ and S−, and errorless learning, 465–466
Simultaneous discrimination, transfer to successive, 487
Simultaneous method, generalization gradient, 435
Single-process model of conditioning, 99
Single-response methods, animal psychophysics, 515–517
Single-stimulus method, generalization testing, 434
Situational stimulus (see also Contextual stimulus):
  and stimulus control, 494–500
6-hydroxydopamine (see also Dopamine):
  lesions made with, 586
  and schizophrenia, 571
Skeletal behavior, Pavlovian conditioning, 61
Skeletal system, and conditioned suppression, 598–599
Skinner box, 2, 11, 29, 572
Skin temperature, and thermoregulation, 154, 156, 163–164
Sleep:
  ontogeny, 21–22
  slow-wave, 22
  stages, 22
Smell (see Olfaction)
Smooth curves, as criterion for laws, 11–12, 29–30
Snake, thermoregulation, 162
Snuggling response, chicks, 60, 121
Social behavior, and feeding behavior, 49
Sodium chloride, excretion, 550
Sodium light, ducklings reared in, 485–486
Sodium salicylate, and thermoregulation, 167
Solubility, drugs, 549–550
Somatic effects, chronic, behaviorally-induced, 597–598
Somnolence, and hypothalamic lesions, 156

Somnos (*see* Chloral hydrate)
Sopor (*see* Methaqualone)
Spaced responding, shock-delay procedure, 400
Spaced responding schedule (*see* DRL schedule)
Species differences:
    acquisition with negative reinforcement, 406–409
    animal psychophysics, 519–520
    associability of responses and reinforcers, 484–485
    automaintenance, 65–66
    autoshaping, 58, 60, 70, 91
    COD in matching, 243
    conditioned enhancement, 90–91
    conditioned suppression, 346, 359
    contrast, 73–74, 78, 81–82, 91
    feeding patterns, 46–49, 58
    generalization gradients, 435–436
    negative reinforcement, 390
    positive conditioned suppression, 359
    schedule control, 186
    stimulus control:
        tone frequency, 441
        wavelength, 483
    thermoregulation, 153, 156, 167–169
Species-specific behavior:
    aggression in pigeon, 468
    and aversive control, 425
    central reinforcement, 580–581
    constraints on learning, 3, 112–118, 120–121
    contrast, 273, 275
    and negative reinforcement, 406–409
    and operant conditioning, 183
    pecking in pigeon, 273
Species-specific defense reaction, 116–118, 120, 165, 407
Species-typical behavior:
    and brain stimulation, 571–572
    constraints on learning, 112–118, 120–121
    and negative reinforcement, 408, 410
Specificity:
    autonomic conditioned response, 608, 610
    drug action, 551–552
Spectral sensitivity, goldfish, 517
Spindle activity, 605
Spiral aftereffect, monkey, 529
Sprawling, and thermoregulation, 154, 165
Squirrel:
    animal psychophysics, 519
    self-stimulation of brain, 589–590
Squirrel monkey:
    adjusting schedule, 212–213
    attack behavior, 23, 136, 417–430
    automaintenance, 65–66
    autoshaping, 60
    avoidance, 185, 193–196
    blood pressure conditioning, 609
    color vision, 518
    conditioned reinforcement, 304–305
    conditioned suppression, 89
    drug effects, 189–191, 557
    electric shock:
        conditioned reinforcement, 304–305
        reinforcer *vs.* punisher, 178–179, 183–185, 193–196
    environmental thermoregulation, 41
    FR FI performance, 187
    hypertension and avoidance, 601
    negative reinforcement, 367, 380, 385–386
    omission training, 65
    schedule-induced attack, 136, 417–430
    schedule-induced drinking, 129, 138
    shock-elicited responses, 183–184, 380

shock escape, 189, 380, 557
shock-induced attack, 136, 417–430
thermoregulation, 41, 153, 156
S-R relations, 11–13, 24
SS interval (*see* Shock-shock interval)
SSDR (*see* Species-specific defense reaction)
Staircase method, animal psychophysics, 521–522
Stalking:
    carnivores, as DRL schedule, 48
    cat, 15
State (*see* Behavioral state, Interim state, Terminal state)
State-space, and motivation, 144
Steady states, and schedule control, 227–228
Steepening, generalization gradient:
    and discrimination training, 439–453
    in extinction, 438, 483
Steepness, generalization gradients, and peak shift, 448–449, 454
Stelazine (*see* Trifluoperazine)
Stereotaxic procedure, implantation of electrodes, 570, 572
Stereotypic effects:
    and reinforcement, 204
    and schedule performance, 204–205, 228
Stereotypy:
    activities on fixed-time schedules, 126, 204
    collateral behavior, and conditioned suppression, 347
    fixed-ratio performance, 227
    interim activities, 137
    operant responses, 177
    superstitious behavior, 127, 204
Steroids, and avoidance, 599–601, 604
Sterols, excretion, 550
Stickleback:
    aggression, 121–122
    sexual behavior, 15–16, 121–122
Stimulants:
    classification, 545
    self-administration, 543
    and stimulus control, 555
Stimuli:
    interchangeability, 13, 23
    relations among, in control of behavior, 3, 5
Stimulus change:
    cue in escape, 386
    and maintenance of observing, 321
Stimulus compounding, and generalization, 459–463
Stimulus context, and stimulus control, 457–458
Stimulus contingencies, and terminal response, 128
Stimulus control, 432–476, 481–510
Stimulus control:
    acquired distinctiveness of cues, 487–488
    acquisition, conditions affecting, 483–486
    and acquisition speed, 454–456
    by air flow rate, 491
    and amount of training, 453–456
    attentional factors, 481–510
    auditory, 483–495, 528
    aversive baselines, 450, 455–456
    and avoidance, 366, 369
    by behavior, 221–222
    by brightness, 490
    and central reinforcement, 582–583
    as continuum, 433
    definitions, 433, 482
    dimensional, and early experience, 485–487
    drug effects, 554

    by drugs, 192–193, 555–556
    dynamic models, 451–453
    and EEG activity, 605–606
    by elapsed time, 218–219
    and errorless discrimination, 186
    examples, 481
    experimental procedures, 488–505
    heart rate conditioning, 607–608
    inhibitory, 432–476
        and amount of training, 453–456
        concurrent schedules, 463–464
        determinants, 432, 453–464, 476
        and errorless learning, 470–474
        measurement, 445–447
        on multiple schedules, 458–463
        and schedule variables, 458–466
    by interresponse time, 223
    of interresponse times, and generalization, 437–438
    and intradimensionl training, 493–494
    Lashley and Wade's theory, 483, 485–486
    by light, and early experience, 485–486
    by line orientation, 440–441, 445, 454–455, 458, 482, 494, 501–502, 527
    and masking, 482–483, 491–492, 500, 502, 506
    measurement, 433–436, 482–483
    multiple schedule, generalization, 458–463
    nature of response and reinforcer, 483–484
    and negative reinforcement, 366, 369, 381–396, 399
    by an odorant, 517
    overshadowing, 492–493, 496, 499–501, 503, 506
    and prior experience, 485–488
    resistance to extinction, 436, 445, 450, 509
    schedule-induced behavior, 129, 131, 140
    signal detection analysis, 536
    theory, 505–510
    and threshold tracking, 522
    by tone frequency, 440–441, 450, 455–456
    verbal behavior, 637–640
    by wavelength, 434–439, 441–443, 454, 485–486
    by wavelength difference, 525, 531, 534
Stimulus generalization (*see also* Generalization):
    aversive control, 450
    brightness, 490, 493
    compound stimulus, 439
    and conditioned reinforcement, 316–318
    conditioned suppression, 351
    diffuse stimuli, 490, 508
    discrimination learning, 447–451
    discrimination training, 493–505
    after errorless learning, 471–472
    extradimensional training, 497–505
    line orientation, 440–441, 445, 454–455, 458, 482, 494, 501–502, 527
    monkey, 490
    and Pavlovian conditioning, 481, 483–484, 487, 489, 492, 493
    Pavlovian theory, 483
    and shock avoidance, 395
    tone frequency, 440–441, 450, 455–456, 493
        human, 493
        rabbit, 493
    wavelength
        ducklings, 485–486
        pigeons, 434–439, 441–443, 454, 489
Stimulus generalization gradient:
    absolute *vs.* relative, 435

as artifact, 438–439
compounding theory, 459–463
as continuous, 438
definition, 433
determinants, 432, 436–439
fixed-interval schedule, 458
inhibitory, 445–447, 453–456, 459–463
interdimensional training, 494–497
maintained, 434, 435, 529–530
measurement, 433–436
microstructure, 437–439
necessary and sufficient conditions, 483
peak shift, 441–443
Spence's theory, 447–451
techniques for obtaining, 433–436
transient methods, 434
Stimulus presentation methods, animal psychophysics, 520–525
Stimulus-reduction procedure, and generalization gradient, 447
Stimulus-reinforcer relations:
in automaintenance, 63–67, 70–71
autoshaping, 54–56, 70–71, 80
behavioral contrast, 80–84, 86–88
in operant procedures, 71–75, 91
Stimulus set, and generalization, 443–444
Stimulus substitution:
autoshaping, 62, 70
Pavlovian conditioning, 61–62
Stimulus surrogation, autoshaping, 62, 70
Stimulus variables, psychopharmacology, 554–556
Stochastic process:
in behavior sequences, 142, 146
and temporal discrimination, 141–142
Stochastic transitivity, and choice, 322–333
Strain, on ratio schedules, 37, 543
Strategies, feeding behavior, 38–39, 46–49
Stress, effects of, 5, 597
Strict learning procedure, linguistic structure, 624–626
Strict training procedures, language learning, 624, 640
Stroke, recovery from, 19
Structural analysis, language, 5, 629–633, 642–651
Structure:
induced behavior, 140–146
language, 622–633, 642–651
Subduction, of behavioral state, 145
Substantia nigra:
lesions, 582
self-stimulation, 585, 590
Success, as method of synthesis, 12
Successive approximations, method of shaping, 54, 62
Successive discrimination:
multiple schedules, 71
transfer to simultaneous, 487
Successive stage experiments, extradimensional training, 497–500
Sucrose:
concentration, and response strength, 259–260, 263, 279, 280
pellets, and response strength, 278
solution, magnitude of reinforcement, 248–249, 259–260
Sugar (see Sucrose)
Summation, stimulus, 443–444, 459
Summation method, and generalization gradient, 446–447
Sunflower seed, 98, 114
Superego, 9
Superimposition procedure, errorless learning, 466
Superstitions, concurrent, 234, 235
Superstitious behavior (see also Adventitious reinforcement):
Skinner's view, 127

"Superstitious" responding, 13, 127, 132, 204, 359
Suppression:
behavior, prior to shock, 422, 425
concurrent response, by punishment, 253
conditioned (see Conditioned suppression)
interim activities, by prevention, 140–143, 147
response:
in behavioral contrast, 76
by free food, 128
by S– on chained schedule, 297
by shock, 182, 185, 193, 195
running, by terminal and interim activity, 133
terminal response by interim, 143
Suppression ratio:
calculation, 342
problems with, 342, 345, 348–351
Suppressive summation, and stimulus generalization, 443–444, 459
Supraliminal stimuli, animal psychophysics of, 525–532
Surface structure, language, 629, 631–633, 648–649
Surrogate mothers, and thermoregulation, 159
Surrogation, stimulus (see Stimulus surrogation)
Sweating, and thermoregulation, 154, 165, 167
Swimming, escape response in rats, 261, 263, 282
Switching response (see also Changeover)
Switching response, concurrent schedules, 234–235
Syndrome:
lateral hypothalamic, 16–18
morphine withdrawal, 179, 554
Syntactic behavior:
generative, 639–640
theories, 640–642
Syntactic structures, 628
Syntactic system, definition, 620
Syntax:
acquisition, 619–627, 643–647
in chimpanzee, 640
component of language structure, 629–632
functional approach, 639–640, 643–647
Syntax crystal, 622–627, 647
Synthesis, experimental methods, 10–11
Synthetic VI schedule, 263–264
Systems, reinforcement, 580–582
Systems constraint hypothesis, 118–119, 122

"Tables of discovery," 12
Tact, verbal behavior, 634–635
Tactual discrimination, monkeys, 517
Tandem schedule:
absolute response rate, 258
and chained schedule, 290, 293–295, 298
description, 290, 315
drug effects, 542–543, 555
fixed-interval and fixed-ratio, 210–211, 223
and IRT as conditionable unit, 224
and second-order schedule, 300–301, 316
Taste:
aversiveness, in rats, 527
and central reinforcement, 582
pathways, 586
Taste-aversion learning, 7, 13–14, 24, 484
Taxis, 158
Taxonomy:
behavior, 12, 24

behavioral interactions, 144–145
TD (see True discrimination)
$t^D — t^\Delta$ schedules, negative reinforcement, 376–377, 399
Tegmentum, single unit recording, 605
Telencephalon, stimulation, 577
Temperature regulation (see Thermoregulation)
Temporal contingency:
classical conditioning, 343, 349–350
and terminal responses, 127–128
Temporal control:
and conditioned reinforcement, 314, 317–318, 336–337
interval schedules, 217
language behavior, 643–647
ratio schedules, 217
Temporal discrimination:
carbon monoxide effects, 563
and conditioned suppression, 349–350, 352
and interim activities, 140, 142–143
and polydipsia, 132
restraint effects, 140, 142–143
and schedule control, 217–219
and shock-delay, 399–401
stochastic processes, 140–141
and theory of patterning, 217–220
Temporal factors, in conditioned reinforcement, 314, 317–318, 326–337
Temporal frame, in verbal behavior, 635
Temporal integration, in cerebral cortex, 641–642
Temporal location, component of chain schedule, 289, 293
Temporal pattern:
in contingent-response experiments, 107–108
escape behavior, 425–427
in preshock stimulus, 350, 352
and proximity to reinforcement, 265
punishment behavior, 427–430
reproducible behaviors, 175–176
responses:
and brief stimuli, 302, 303
chained schedules, 289–291
second-order schedules, 300–302
and schedule control, 213–215
on schedules, theories, 217–221
shock-elicited behavior, 418–425, 428
as unit of behavior, 222
Temporal placement, reinforcer, 213–218, 229
Temporal structure:
drug effects, 562
induced behavior, 140–146
verbal behavior, 643–647
Temporalis muscle, 417–418
Temporospatial factors, and central reinforcement, 575
Terminal periods, on periodic schedules, 133, 137–139
Terminal ratio, definitions, 573–574
Terminal response:
competition with interim, 132–133, 139
definition, 126
and errorless learning, 464, 475
operant view, 127
Pavlovian view, 127
relation to reinforcer, 273–274
schedule-induced, 126, 133, 139, 141
Terminal state:
interaction with interim, 139–145
properties, 137–138
Termination, meals, 28, 32, 45
Tetrahydrocannabinol (see also Marijuana):
and acquisition of avoidance, 560
classification, 545

Tetrahydrocannabinol (cont.)
  and peck rate in pigeons, 552
  and stimulus control, 555
  tolerance, 553
Tetrodotoxin, 166
Thalamus:
  EEG activity, 605
  self-stimulation, 590
THC (see Tetrahydrocannabinol)
The Behavior of Organisms, 9, 32
Thematic classes, verbal responses, 637
Theoretical response unit, 222-226
Therapeutic effects, drugs, 540, 542-545, 563-566
Thermal gradient, 157
Thermal preference, 153, 159, 162-164
Thermal reinforcement, 153
Thermally sensitive units, 154, 158, 160, 166, 169
Thermocline, 157-161
Thermodynamics, 31
Thermoregulation, 156-169
Thermoregulation:
  alligators, 153
  amphibians, 156-158
  baboons, 153, 166
  and behavioral homeostasis, 153
  birds, 159-160
  cats, 153, 166-167
  chicks, 153, 159-160
  and diet, 162
  digestion and, 162
  dogs, 153, 159, 166-167
  doves, 153
  drug effects, 153-155, 164-169, 188-189, 556
  fish, 156-158
  frogs, 157-158
  goldfish, 153, 158
  hamsters, 159
  and hormones, 161, 162
  human, 158, 162-164
  and hypothalamus, 154-156, 164, 167-169
  iguanas, 157-158, 166
  infants, 158-160
  lizards, 153, 157-158, 161-164
  macaque, 153, 159
  mammals, 158-159, 162, 167
  monkey, 164, 167
  mouse, 153, 159, 167
  negative feedback in, 153-154
  neural controls in, 153-155, 167-168
  operant, 153-161, 164-169
  pig, 153, 158-159
  and preoptic area, 154-156, 167-169
  rabbit, 159, 166-167
  rats, 153-156, 162-165, 167-168, 188-189, 556
  reflex, 153-156, 160-161, 165-168
  reptiles, 156-158, 161-162, 166
  respondent, 154-156, 160-161, 166-168
  snake, 162
  squirrel monkey, 41, 153, 156
Theta waves, 119, 605
Thigmotaxis, 117
Thiobarbiturates, 549
Thioridazine, 545
Third-order deviations, in fixed-interval schedules, 208, 213
Thirst, and induced drinking, 138-139
Thorazine (see Chlorpromazine)
Three-term contingency, and verbal behavior, 633
Threshold:
  definitions, 520-522
  sensory, in animals, 515-525
Threshold tracking, animal psychophysics, 521-523, 525

Thrush, gape response, 19-20
Thwarting, 23-24
Thyroid hormones, and avoidance, 599-600
Thyroidectomy:
  rats, 18
  and thermoregulation, 154
Tilt (see Line orientation)
Time:
  allocation, and generalization, 435
  as discriminative stimulus, 217-219
  distribution of responses in, 106-108
  as indicator of value, 101
  matching:
    on concurrent schedules, 238-239, 246-248, 254, 272, 274
    in interresponse class, 264
  as stimulus on FI, 218-219
Time course, drug effects, 548-549
Time distribution:
  among concurrent schedules, 233, 246-247, 272
  among interresponse times, 263-264
Time out:
  on electric shock schedule, 179, 194-195
  escape from S−, 469-470
  negative reinforcement schedule, 367, 385-386, 388-390, 398
  punishment in animal psychophysics, 523
  from reinforcement:
    and alcoholism, 563
    as punisher, 244, 253
  and reinforcement omission on FI, 301
  and schedule-induced behavior, 139
Time schedule (see also Fixed time, Random time, Variable time):
  definition, 202
  and interval schedules, 214
Timing, induced behavior sequences, 141-143
Titration method:
  animal psychophysics, 521
  self-stimulation of brain, 574
T-maze, drug effects, 555
Tofranil (see Imipramine)
Token economy, 7
Token reinforcement, and conditioned reinforcement, 306
Tolerance:
  drugs, 550, 553
  large fixed ratios, 36, 38-39, 45
Tone:
  as contingent stimulus, 115
  stimulus in autoshaping, 69, 273
  stimulus in conditioned suppression, 89, 341-344, 351
  stimulus in contrast, 274-275
Tone frequency, generalization:
  guinea pig, 441
  pigeons, 440-441, 450, 455-456, 495, 528
  rat, 441
Tongue flip, frogs, 121
Tooth chattering, rat, 17
Topography:
  instrumental *vs.* contingent response, 108
  lever contact response, 60, 65, 81-82, 120
  pecking, on FI and VI schedules, 141
  response:
    in autoshaping, 24, 58-60, 67, 81, 119-122
    on differentiation schedules, 203
    and matching, 262
    and negative reinforcement, 406-408
Toxic effects, drugs, 546
Toxicology, behavioral, 562-563
Tractus solitarius, 586

Traditional pairing hypothesis, conditioned reinforcement, 314, 318, 325
Tranquilizer (see also Drugs, specific drugs):
  and conditioned suppression, 349, 355-357
  punishment effects, 558-559
  and schedule control, 188
Transfer (see also Generalization, Stimulus generalization):
  in animal psychophysics, 526-530
  in behavioral sequences, 147-148
  common elements theory, 639
  simultaneous to successive discrimination, 487
  stimulus control, and errorless learning, 465-466, 475
  in verbal behavior, 634, 649
  visceral learning, 608
Transfer tests:
  conditioned reinforcement, 288-289
  induced states, 138
Transformational grammar, theory, 629-649
Transient contrast, 77, 268, 275 (see also Local contrast)
Transient generalization, methods, 434
Transition, of situation, as reinforcer, 381
Transition performance, chained schedules, 290-291
Transition states, and schedule control, 227-228
Transitivity, stochastic, and choice, 332-333
Transituational reward, 100-101, 113
Translation, language, 650
Transposition, in discrimination learning, 447, 497
Treadle pressing, pigeons:
  avoidance, 450, 455-456
  concurrent schedules, 236
  conditioned enhancement, 90
  contrast, 82, 89
  negative reinforcement, 386-387, 391, 407
  positive conditioned suppression, 359
  relation to reinforcement, 273
  stimulus control, 438, 455-456
Treadmill, 40
Trial, duration, in autoshaping, 57-58, 66, 90
Trifluoperazine:
  classification, 545
  and punishment, 558
Triflupromazine, 545
Trigeminal nerve, section of, 15
Trilafon (see Perphenazine)
True discrimination procedure, 495-505, 507-509
Truly random control procedure, 55-56, 61, 84, 120, 343, 391
$t - \tau$ schedules:
  explanation, 203
  and IRT reinforcement, 223
Turtle, animal psychophysics, 519
Twittering, chicks, 60
Two-factor theory, negative reinforcement, 364-365, 393, 396-398, 400
Two-key concurrent schedule, description, 234
Two-process model, conditioning, 99
Two-response methods, animal psychophysics, 517-519
Two-stage model, food motivation, 32
Two-state analysis, fixed-interval responding, 265

Ulcers, and aversive control, 597, 604-605

Uncertainty reduction, and conditioned reinforcement, 318–326, 336–337
Uncertainty reduction hypothesis:
 conditioned reinforcement, 313–315, 318, 322–325, 336–337
 quantitative implications, 322–325
Undermatching, concurrent schedules, 242–243, 248–255
Unit, linguistic, 620–621, 629–630
Unit, response (see Response unit)
Unit schedule:
 part of chain schedule, 289
 part of second-order schedule, 299–302
 token delivery, 306
Units of behavior, problem of specification, 29
Universals, linguistic, 641
Up-down method, animal psychophysics, 521
UR, definition, 340
Uridine, in mouse brain, 606
Urination:
 and conditioned suppression, 351
 guinea pigs, 21
US:
 autoshaping, 55, 58, 61, 69–70, 80
 conditioned suppression, 342–344
 in contrast, 81, 88
 definition, 340
 fear conditioning, 315
Utility:
 and matching, 277
 rate increase in FR, 44

Validity, stimulus, and stimulus control, 494–496, 500, 506
Valium (see Diazepam)
Valsalva maneuver, 609
Value:
 of events to organism, 101
 intervening variable, in matching experiments, 276
 scaling, concurrent schedules, 298
Variability, behavioral sequences, 142, 146
Variable cycle procedure, shock deletion, 387
Variable delay procedure, shock delay, 372–373
Variable-interval schedule:
 absolute response rates, 257–265
 and adventitious punishment, 184
 autoshaping, 127
 aversive control, 428
 avoidance, 260, 269–271
 central reinforcement, 578
 concurrent (see Concurrent schedules)
 and conditioned suppression, 89, 341–345, 356, 359, 598
 contingent-response experiments, 108–109
 and contrast, 71–85
 definition, 202
 electric shock, 178–179, 194
 electrical brain stimulation, 181, 259
 escape, 384, 386
 generalization gradient, 434, 436, 438, 440, 446, 460, 462
 induced behavior on, 132–135, 141
 induced drinking on, 129, 132, 135
 interim periods on, 133, 135
 local rate of reinforcement, 216
 matching on (see Matching, Concurrent schedules)
 negative reinforcement, 384
 observing responses, 319–320, 323–324
 paced, 225
 probability of reinforcement, 214–215
 relation to variable ratio, 210
 response strength, 257–265
 temporal patterning, 213
 types of distribution of intervals, 215
 uncorrelated shock, 350
Variable-ratio schedule:
 conditioned suppression, 346
 definition, 202
 and generalization gradient, 436, 439
 matching, 246–247, 254
 observing responses, 321
 relation to variable interval, 210
 and sexual behavior in sticklebacks, 121
 temporal patterning on, 213, 217
Variable-time schedule:
 concurrent matching, 237–238
 contrast, 76–77, 80–81, 84–85, 90
 definition, 202
 electric shock, 397–398
 induced behavior, 127, 130
Vasoconstriction, and thermoregulation, 154, 168
Vasodilation, and thermoregulation, 154, 165, 167–168
Vasomotor responses, and thermoregulation, 154, 161
Vector properties, responses, 177
Ventral noradrenergic neurons, stimulation, 585
Ventral tegmentum, self-stimulation, 590
Verbal behavior, 5, 628, 635–636, 638, 639, 642, 649
Verbal behavior, theory, 628–629, 633–640
Verbal learning, and language, 637
Vertical, perception of, in pigeons, 527
Vesprin (see Triflupromazine)
Vibratory stimulus, stimulus control by, 498
Visceral-alimentary system, durable changes, 597
Visceral learning, 607–611
Visceral responses, operant conditioning, 571, 606–611
Vision, rats, after lesions, 16
Visual acuity:
 pigeon, 517–518, 521
 sea lion, 519–520
Visual discrimination, LSD effects, 554
Visual fixation training, in monkey, 523
Visual stimulus control (see also Brightness, Line orientation, Wavelength, Stimulus control):
 pigeon, 482, 483, 485, 488–492
Vitamin A, 10, 22
Vitamin deficiency, and thermoregulation, 154
Vocalization response, animal psychophysics, 519–520
Voltage reduction, reinforcement, in rats, 261
Voluntary behavior, key pecking as, 53–55, 67
Voluntary mediators, in instrumental autonomic conditioning, 610

Walden Two, 7
Warm up effect:
 animal psychophysics, 521
 aversive control, 426
 negative reinforcement, 409
Warning signal, in avoidance:
 and endocrine changes, 599
 and gastrointestinal changes, 604
Warning stimulus (see also CS):
 aversiveness, 365
 and avoidance theory, 364–365, 393–398, 400
 central reinforcement, 579
 shock-delay procedure, 393–398
Wasp, hunting behavior, 142

Water:
 escape, by rats, 261, 263, 282
 interaction with food:
  and induced behavior, 131, 135, 139
  and matching, 252
 reinforcement, and peck duration, 58–60, 67, 81, 119
 reinforcer in automaintenance, 65, 67
 reinforcer in autoshaping, 58–60, 62, 81, 119
 reinforcer in induced drinking, 138–139
Water balance, in polydipsia, 129
Water bath, and thermal preference, 163
Water holes, patterning of visits, 36
Water intake, and food intake, 35
Water restriction, and meal patterning, 35
Wavelength:
 difference, stimulus control by, 525, 531, 534
 maintained generalization, pigeons, 530
 stimulus generalization:
  chicks, 486
  ducklings, 485–486
  Japanese quail, 486
  monkeys, 486
  pigeon, 434, 439, 441–443, 454, 489, 493–494, 501–502, 531–532
Wavelength discrimination, pigeon, 519, 534
Weak law of effect, 100–101, 113, 112
Weber fraction, time discrimination, 218
Weight loss:
 between meals, 33, 36
 and performance, 36, 45
"Well-behaved" operants, 183
Wheel cranking, college students, 103, 107
Wheel running (see Running)
Wheel turning, and negative reinforcement, 390–391
White light, and wavelength generalization, 486
Wing flapping:
 aggressive, in pigeon, 59
 schedule-induced, in pigeon, 126, 137, 139
Wistar rats, 605
Withdrawal syndrome, morphine, in monkey, 179, 554
Within-meal behavior:
 as locus of analysis, 30, 48
 rate changes, 44
Words, as discriminative stimuli, 619, 621
Worsening, conditions, and contrast, 76

X-ray, poisoning by, association with food, 13–14, 484

Yes-no procedure, animal psychophysics, 518–522, 524
Yoga, and physiological conditioning, 607
Yoked controls:
 avoidance, and peptic ulcer, 604–605
 brain biochemistry, 606
 chained schedules, 296
 conditioned reinforcement, 319
 conditioned suppression, 346, 357
 contingent-response experiments, 106–108, 111, 115
 differentiation and variable-interval, 224
 fixed-ratio vs. interval, 217
 and matching, 272
 omission training and automaintenance, 65–66, 128
 VI vs. VR in pigeons, 210
 and stimulus generalization, 436

Zona incerta, self-stimulation, 590